THE ROUTLEDGE HISTORY OF MEDIEVAL MAGIC

The Routledge History of Medieval Magic brings together the work of scholars from across Europe and North America to provide extensive insights into recent developments in the study of medieval magic between c.1100 and c.1500.

This book covers a wide range of topics, including the magical texts which circulated in medieval Europe, the attitudes of intellectuals and churchmen to magic, the ways in which magic intersected with other aspects of medieval culture, and the early witch trials of the fifteenth century. In doing so, it offers the reader a detailed look at the impact that magic had within medieval society, such as its relationship to gender roles, natural philosophy, and courtly culture. This is furthered by the book's interdisciplinary approach, containing chapters dedicated to archaeology, literature, music, and visual culture, as well as texts and manuscripts.

The Routledge History of Medieval Magic also outlines how research on this subject could develop in the future, highlighting under-explored subjects, unpublished sources, and new approaches to the topic. It is the ideal book for both established scholars and students of medieval magic.

Sophie Page is an Associate Professor in Late Medieval History at UCL. She is working on medieval magic and astrology, especially in relation to religion, natural philosophy, medicine, and cosmology.

Catherine Rider is an Associate Professor in Medieval History at the University of Exeter, UK. Her research focuses on the history of magic in the later Middle Ages, looking especially at the relationship between magic and the medieval church.

THE ROUTLEDGE HISTORIES

The Routledge Histories is a series of landmark books surveying some of the most important topics and themes in history today. Edited and written by an international team of world-renowned experts, they are the works against which all future books on their subjects will be judged.

THE ROUTLEDGE HISTORY OF THE RENAISSANCE
Edited by William Caferro

THE ROUTLEDGE HISTORY OF MADNESS AND MENTAL HEALTH
Edited by Greg Eghigian

THE ROUTLEDGE HISTORY OF DISABILITY
Edited by Roy Hanes, Ivan Brown and Nancy E. Hansen

THE ROUTLEDGE HISTORY OF NINETEENTH-CENTURY AMERICA
Edited by Jonathan Daniel Wells

THE ROUTLEDGE HISTORY OF GENDER, WAR, AND THE U.S. MILITARY
Edited by Kara Dixon Vuic

THE ROUTLEDGE HISTORY OF THE AMERICAN SOUTH
Edited by Maggi M. Morehouse

THE ROUTLEDGE HISTORY OF ITALIAN AMERICANS
Edited by William J. Connell & Stanislao Pugliese

THE ROUTLEDGE HISTORY OF LATIN AMERICAN CULTURE
Edited by Carlos Manuel Salomon

THE ROUTLEDGE HISTORY OF GLOBAL WAR AND SOCIETY
Edited by Matthew S. Muehlbauer and David J. Ulbrich

THE ROUTLEDGE HISTORY OF TWENTIETH-CENTURY UNITED STATES
Edited by Jerald R. Podair and Darren Dochuk

THE ROUTLEDGE HISTORY OF WORLD PEACE SINCE 1750
Edited by Christian Philip Peterson, William M. Knoblauch and Michael Loadenthal

THE ROUTLEDGE HISTORY OF MEDIEVAL MAGIC
Edited by Sophie Page and Catherine Rider

THE ROUTLEDGE HISTORY OF MEDIEVAL MAGIC

Edited by
Sophie Page
and Catherine Rider

Routledge
Taylor & Francis Group
LONDON AND NEW YORK

First published 2019
by Routledge
2 Park Square, Milton Park, Abingdon, Oxon OX14 4RN

and by Routledge
605 Third Avenue, New York, NY 10017

First issued in paperback 2021

Routledge is an imprint of the Taylor & Francis Group, an informa business

© 2019 selection and editorial matter, Sophie Page and Catherine Rider; individual chapters, the contributors

The right of Sophie Page and Catherine Rider to be identified as the authors of the editorial material, and of the authors for their individual chapters, has been asserted in accordance with sections 77 and 78 of the Copyright, Designs and Patents Act 1988.

All rights reserved. No part of this book may be reprinted or reproduced or utilised in any form or by any electronic, mechanical, or other means, now known or hereafter invented, including photocopying and recording, or in any information storage or retrieval system, without permission in writing from the publishers.

Trademark notice: Product or corporate names may be trademarks or registered trademarks, and are used only for identification and explanation without intent to infringe.

Publisher's Note
The publisher has gone to great lengths to ensure the quality of this reprint but points out that some imperfections in the original copies may be apparent.

British Library Cataloguing-in-Publication Data
A catalogue record for this book is available from the British Library

Library of Congress Cataloging-in-Publication Data
A catalog record has been requested for this book

ISBN 13: 978-1-03-209399-4 (pbk)
ISBN 13: 978-1-4724-4730-2 (hbk)

Typeset in Baskerville
by codeMantra

CONTENTS

List of figures ix
Acknowledgements xi
List of contributors xii

Introduction 1
SOPHIE PAGE AND CATHERINE RIDER

PART I
Conceptualizing magic 13

1 **Rethinking how to define magic** 15
   RICHARD KIECKHEFER

2 **For magic: Against method** 26
   CLAIRE FANGER

3 **A discourse historical approach towards medieval learned magic** 37
   BERND-CHRISTIAN OTTO

4 **The concept of magic** 48
   DAVID. L. D'AVRAY

5 **Responses** 57
   RICHARD KIECKHEFER, DAVID. L. D'AVRAY, BERND-CHRISTIAN OTTO, AND CLAIRE FANGER

PART II
Languages and dissemination 69

6 **Arabic magic: The impetus for translating texts and their reception** 71
   CHARLES BURNETT

v

CONTENTS

7	**The Latin encounter with Hebrew magic: Problems and approaches** KATELYN MESLER	85
8	**Magic in Romance languages** SEBASTIÀ GIRALT	99
9	**Central and Eastern Europe** BENEDEK LÁNG	112
10	**Magic in Celtic lands** MARK WILLIAMS	123
11	**Scandinavia** STEPHEN A. MITCHELL	136

PART III
Key genres and figures 151

12	**From Hermetic magic to the magic of marvels** ANTONELLA SANNINO	153
13	**The notion of properties: Tensions between *Scientia* and *Ars* in medieval natural philosophy and magic** ISABELLE DRAELANTS	169
14	**Solomonic magic** JULIEN VÉRONÈSE	187
15	**Necromancy** FRANK KLAASSEN	201
16	**John of Morigny** CLAIRE FANGER AND NICHOLAS WATSON	212
17	**Cecco d'Ascoli and Antonio da Montolmo: The building of a "nigromantical" cosmology and the birth of the author-magician** NICOLAS WEILL-PAROT	225

CONTENTS

18 Beringarius Ganellus and the *Summa sacre magice*: Magic as the promotion of God's Kingship   237
DAMARIS ASCHERA GEHR

19 Jerome Torrella and "Astrological Images"   254
NICOLAS WEILL-PAROT

20 Peter of Zealand   268
JEAN-MARC MANDOSIO

PART IV
Themes (magic and…)   285

21 Magic and natural philosophy   287
STEVEN P. MARRONE

22 Medicine and magic   299
PETER MURRAY JONES AND LEA T. OLSAN

23 Illusion   312
ROBERT GOULDING

24 Magic at court   331
JEAN-PATRICE BOUDET

25 Magic and gender   343
CATHERINE RIDER

26 Magic in literature: Romance transformations   355
CORINNE SAUNDERS

27 Music   371
JOHN HAINES

28 Magic and archaeology: Ritual residues and "odd" deposits   383
ROBERTA GILCHRIST

29 The visual culture of magic in the Middle Ages   402
ALEJANDRO GARCÍA AVILÉS

CONTENTS

30	**Medieval magical figures: Between image and text**	432
	SOPHIE PAGE	

PART V
Anti-magical discourse in the later Middle Ages 459

31	**Scholasticism and high medieval opposition to magic**	461
	DAVID J. COLLINS	
32	**Pastoral literature and preaching**	475
	KATHLEEN KAMERICK	
33	**Superstition and sorcery**	487
	MICHAEL D. BAILEY	
34	**Witchcraft**	502
	MARTINE OSTORERO	
35	**Epilogue: Cosmology and magic – The angel of Mars in the *Libro de astromagia***	523
	ALEJANDRO GARCÍA AVILÉS	

Further reading	533
Index	538

LIST OF FIGURES

2.1	Forms of superstition in the *Summa Theologiae*	30
6.1	The *figura Almandal* or Table of Solomon in Florence, Biblioteca nazionale, II. iii. 214 fol. 74v	80
6.2	The rings and sigils of the planets to be inscribed on talismans, in Florence, Biblioteca nazionale, II. iii. 214 fol 49v	81
7.1	Traditions of magic in medieval Europe	86
18.1	The *Sigillum Salomonis*, a sigil to be inscribed on parchment	242
18.2	The first and second Hebrew tables	246
27.1	"Asperges me" from the thirteenth century	373
27.2	Cryptography using neumes: "Didacus notuit"	379
28.1	Silver brooch inscribed with the Holy Name from West Hartburn	386
28.2	Sword with possible magical inscription of unknown meaning in Roman and Lombardic lettering from the River Witham	387
28.3	Deliberately damaged ampullae	391
28.4	Location of stone axes from the workshops at San Vincenzo Maggiore	393
28.5	Lead spindle-whorl cast with reversed "Rho"	394
29.1	Hostanes from the Florentine Picture Chronicle, British Museum	403
29.2	Egyptian magicians with magic staffs from a thirteenth-century Parisian *Bible moralisée*. Oxford, Bodleian Library, MS Bodley 270b, fol. 43v	405
29.3	Cyprian as a magician from Gregory Nazianzen, *Homilies*, Paris, Bibliothèque nationale de France, MS Gr. 510, fol. 332v	407
29.4	"Philosophus" and "Magus". Sculptures on Chartres Cathedral	409
29.5	"Magus". Chartres Cathedral (detail of Fig. 29.4)	410
29.6	Nigromance from Brunetto Latini, *Trésor*, London, British Library, Additional MS 30024, fol. 1v	411
29.7	Monk inside a magic circle, El Escorial, Real Biblioteca del Monasterio de San Lorenzo, MS T.I.1, fol. 177v	413
29.8	Sorcerers with a clay magic figurine and the shepherd Menalcas, Dijon, Bibliothèque municipale, MS 493 fol. 15v	415
29.9	Hermes from the *Florentine Picture Chronicle*. Engraving attributed to Baccio Baldini or Maso Finiguerra. British Museum	417
29.10	Tree with male sexual organs being harvested by women (*Wunderbaum*). Mural painting set in the wall of the Fountain of Abundance, Massa Marittima (Italy)	420

LIST OF FIGURES

30.1	A lamina for a difficult birth and an Abraham's Eye experiment, London, Wellcome MS 517, fol. 67r	434
30.2	A silver pendant with an image of Venus and the Venus magic square. British Museum	437
30.3	A silver pendant with an image of Venus and the Venus magic square (reverse)	437
30.4	A lamina for identifying a thief. Oxford, Bodleian Library, MS Rawlinson D 252, fol. 104v	438
30.5	Seven circular magical figures, Paris, Bibliothèque nationale de France, MS lat. 3269, fol. 85r	439
30.6	The figure of St Michael. Cambridge, University Library, Additional MS 3544, p. 93v	441
30.7	Matrix of a magic seal found in Devil's Dyke, Cambridgeshire. Oxford, Museum of the History of Science	445
30.8	Composite magic circle with the names and characters of each planet, London, Wellcome, MS 517, fol. 234v	447
30.9	The pilgrim and the student of necromancy from John Lydgate's *Pilgrimage of Man*. London, British Library, MS Cotton Tiberius AVII, fol. 44r	448
30.10	A magic circle from an experiment for love, Florence, Biblioteca Medicea Laurenziana, MS Plut. 18 sup. 38, fol. 286r	450
30.11	A magic circle from an experiment for love. Munich, Bayerische Staatsbibliothek, MS Clm 849, fol. 10r	451
35.1	Angels rotating the universe from a French translation of Bartholomeus Anglicus, Bibliothèque Sainte-Geneviève, Paris, MS 1029, fol. 108	526
35.2	The creation of the universe, dome of the Chigi Chapel, Santa Maria del Popolo (Rome)	527
35.3	Pietro Facchetti (after Raphael's drawings for the Chigi Capel), the angel of Mars guiding his planet. Museo Nacional del Prado	527

ACKNOWLEDGEMENTS

This book has taken several years to put together, and we would first like to thank the chapter authors for their hard work and patience. Tom Gray at Ashgate and then Morwenna Scott at Routledge offered a great deal of advice and support as the volume took shape and moved through the publication process. The anonymous reviewers gave invaluable feedback on our original proposal. We are grateful to UCL for paying for the translation of chapters by Julien Véronèse and Martine Ostorero, and we would also like to thank the translators, Alex Lee and Victoria Blud, for their hard work. Another thank you goes to Jeremy Yapp, who copy-edited several chapters. Finally, we would like to thank our families – Jeremy, Clancy and Wolfie, and Laurence and Stephanie – for their interest and encouragement.

Sophie Page and Catherine Rider
London and Exeter, July 2018

LIST OF CONTRIBUTORS

Michael D. Bailey is a Professor of History at Iowa State University. He has published widely on magic and superstition, both within the medieval period and beyond. Among his books are *Battling Demons: Witchcraft, Heresy, and Reform in the Late Middle Ages* and *Magic and Superstition in Europe: A Concise History from Antiquity to the Present*. More recently, he has published *Fearful Spirits, Reasoned Follies: The Boundaries of Superstition in Late Medieval Europe* (2013) and *Magic: The Basics* (2018).

Jean-Patrice Boudet is a Professor of Medieval History at the University of Orléans (France) and an honorary member of the Institut Universitaire de France. His book, *Entre science et nigromance. Astrologie, divination et magie dans l'Occident médiéval* (xiie-xve siècle), 2006, received the first Gobert Prize of the Académie des Inscriptions et Belles-Lettres in 2007.

Charles Burnett, MA, PhD, FBA, LGSM, is a Professor of the History of Arabic/Islamic Influences in Europe at the Warburg Institute, University of London. His research centres on the transmission of texts, techniques, and artefacts from the Arab world to the West, especially in the Middle Ages. He has documented this transmission by editing and translating several texts that were first translated from Arabic into Latin, and also by describing the historical and cultural context of these translations. Throughout his research and publications, he has aimed to document the extent to which Arabic authorities and texts translated from Arabic have shaped European learning, in the universities, in medical schools and in esoteric circles. Among his books in this subject area are *The Introduction of Arabic Learning into England* (1997), *Arabic into Latin in the Middle Ages: The Translators and Their Intellectual and Social Context* (2009) and *Numerals and Arithmetic in the Middle Ages* (2010).

David J. Collins, S.J., is an Associate Professor of History at Georgetown University in Washington, DC. He has written extensively on the medieval cult of the saints, Renaissance humanism and early modern history writing, especially in Germany. His current research focuses on scholastic attitudes towards magic, especially those inspired by the work of Albertus Magnus. He recently served as the editor of and a contributor to the *Cambridge History of Magic and Witchcraft in the West: From Antiquity to the Present* (2015).

David L. d'Avray has been at University College London since 1977 as a Lecturer, Reader and then Professor of Medieval History. He is a Fellow of the British Academy and Corresponding Fellow of the Medieval Academy of America.

LIST OF CONTRIBUTORS

Isabelle Draelants is the Director of Research at the Centre national de la recherche scientifique, in the *Institut de recherche et d'histoire des textes* in Paris. She is interested in the textual sources of medieval natural philosophy. She completed her Ph.D. in 2001 at the Université catholique de Louvain-la-Neuve and defended her habilitation thesis at Paris-Sorbonne University (Paris IV) in 2008. From 2009 to 2013, she ran a research laboratory, the *Centre de médiévistique Jean-Schneider* in Nancy, France. Since 2003, she has been responsible for the *Atelier Vincent de Beauvais*, which specializes in the study of medieval encyclopaedism; she has also led a project called *SourcEncyMe* (Sources of medieval encyclopedias), aimed at developing an annotated online corpus of medieval encyclopaedic texts. She has published several works on the transmission of knowledge, *natura rerum* and experimental science, including *Le Liber de virtutibus herbarum, lapidum et animalium (Liber aggregationis), Un texte à succès attribué à Albert le Grand* (2007) and with Th. Bénatouïl, Expertus sum. *L'expérience par les sens dans la philosophie naturelle médiévale* (2011).

Claire Fanger teaches in the Religion Department at Rice University in Houston, Texas. Her research focuses on Christian Latin writing in late medieval Europe, with special attention to magic texts, especially angel magic in a Christian context. She has edited two essay collections on this topic (*Conjuring Spirits* [1998] and *Invoking Angels* [2012]) and has a body of work on the writings of the magically literate fourteenth-century Benedictine John of Morigny, whose magnum opus, *The Flowers of Heavenly Teaching*, she edited with Nicholas Watson. She discusses the implication of John's Flowers in another book, *Rewriting Magic* (both published in 2015).

Alejandro García Avilés is a Professor of Medieval Art and Director of the Center of Visual Studies (VISUM), University of Murcia. Formerly, he was a Frances Yates Fellow (Warburg Institute), Postdoctoral Research Fellow (Getty Grant Program) and Maître de conferences associé (École des Hautes Études en Sciences Sociales). He is serving as an associate to the Board of Directors of the International Center of Medieval Art (New York). His publications in the field of the iconography of magic and astrology include articles in the *Journal of the Warburg and Courtauld Institutes, Kritische Berichte, Bulletin of Hispanic Studies*, etc., and books like *El tiempo y los astros* (2001). His forthcoming books are *Images magiques: la culture visuel de la magie au Moyen Âge* (Paris: Arkhè), *The Iconography of Alfonso X's Book of Astromagic* (Turnhout: Brepols) and *El arte de fabricar dioses* (Madrid: Akal).

Damaris Aschera Gehr studied Philosophy and Latin at the University Ca' Foscari in Venice, where she completed a dissertation on late medieval learned magic. Since 2007, she has been a Postdoctoral Researcher at the Warburg Institute and the British Library; the Swiss Institute in Rome and the Vatican Library; the Staatsbibliothek in Berlin; the Bernoulli-Euler Zentrum at Basel University and the Herzog August Bibliothek in Wolfenbüttel. Since 2017, she has been an editor at the Rudolf Steiner Archiv in Dornach, Switzerland. Her main fields of study include medieval learned magic literature, especially as transmitted in unpublished Latin and vernacular manuscripts from the thirteenth to the eighteenth centuries, and its reception in modern and contemporary esotericism, literature and art.

Roberta Gilchrist is a Professor of Archaeology and Research Dean at the University of Reading. Her research focuses on the archaeology of later medieval religion and belief and their intersection with gender, magic, and the life course. She has published pioneering works on medieval nunneries (1994), hospitals (1995), burial practices (2005), magic (2008) and the life course (2012), as well as major studies on Glastonbury Abbey (2015) and Norwich Cathedral Close (2005). She is an elected Fellow of the British Academy, a trustee of *Antiquity* and former president of the Society for Medieval Archaeology.

Sebastià Giralt is a Senior Lecturer in Classics (Latin) at the Universitat Autònoma de Barcelona. His research primarily focuses on medieval medicine, magic and astrology. He has studied and edited a number of Latin works on practical medicine and the occult arts attributed to Arnau de Vilanova. He has also studied the survival of Arnau's corpus and figure in the early Modern Age. His research has approached the scholastic reception of magic and divination, as well as some magical and astrological texts in Romance languages. In addition, he has extensive experience in digital humanities for teaching and research purposes.

Robert Goulding is an Associate Professor in the Program of Liberal Arts and the Program in History and Philosophy of Science at the University of Notre Dame. He specializes in the history of Renaissance science and the history of magic. His publications include *Defending Hypatia: Ramus, Savile, and the Renaissance Rediscovery of Mathematical History* (2010).

John Haines is a Professor of Music and Medieval Studies at the University of Toronto. He has published on medieval and Renaissance music and its modern reception in a variety of journals, both musicological, from *Early Music History* to *Popular Music*, and non-musicological, from *Romania* to *Scriptorium*. His recent books are *Music in Films on the Middle Ages: Authenticity vs. Fantasy* (2014), *The Notory Art of Shorthand: A Curious Chapter in the History of Writing in the West* (2014).

Peter Murray Jones is Fellow Librarian of King's College, Cambridge. He has published studies of medieval medicine and surgery, and also written on medieval amulets and charms (with Lea T. Olsan).

Kathleen Kamerick is a retired Lecturer in History at the Center for the Book, University of Iowa. Her research interests include late medieval piety and material culture, literacy and the history of the book and magic. She has written articles on prayer books, superstition and magic, and is the author of *Popular Piety and Art in the Late Middle Ages*. Her current research on magic and sexuality in late medieval England focuses on the life and trial of Eleanor Cobham.

Richard Kieckhefer teaches at Northwestern University (Evanston, Illinois) in the departments of Religious Studies and History. He has worked mainly on late medieval religious culture, including the history of witchcraft and magic. His books include *Magic in the Middle Ages* (1989), *Forbidden Rites: A Necromancer's Manual of the Fifteenth Century* (1998), and *Hazards of the Dark Arts: Advice for Medieval Princes on Witchcraft and Magic* (2017).

Frank Klaassen is an Associate Professor of History in the Department of History at the University of Saskatchewan. His publications include *The Transformations of Magic: Illicit Learned Magic in the Later Middle Ages and Renaissance* (2013) and *Making Magic in Elizabethan England* (forthcoming).

LIST OF CONTRIBUTORS

Benedek Láng is a Professor and Head of the Philosophy and History of Science Department at the Budapest University of Technology and Economics. He has published *Unlocked Books, Manuscripts of Learned Magic in the Medieval Libraries of Central Europe* (2008) and articles on the history of cryptography in *Cryptologia* (2010 and 2015) and *The Sixteenth Century Journal* (2014). Currently, he is working on the English edition of two of his formerly published Hungarian books: *Ciphers in Early Modern Hungary: Secrecy and the Social History of Cryptography* and *The Rohonc Code*.

Jean-Marc Mandosio is *maître de conférences* at the École Pratique des Hautes Études in Paris. He specializes in the late medieval and early modern history of science and philosophy.

Steven P. Marrone is a Professor of History at Tufts University. His latest book is *A History of Science, Magic and Belief from Medieval to Early Modern Europe*.

Katelyn Mesler is a Postdoctoral Researcher at the Westfälische Wilhelms-Universität in Münster, where she is engaged in the project "The Visual in the Medieval Jewish World." She is an editor, along with Elisheva Baumgarten and Ruth Mazo Karras, of the volume *Entangled Histories: Knowledge, Authority, and Jewish Culture in the Thirteenth Century* (2017).

Stephen A. Mitchell is a Professor of Scandinavian and Folklore at Harvard University. For his research on Scandinavian traditions of magic and witchcraft, he was awarded the Dag Strömbäck Prize from The Royal Gustav Adolf Academy (2007) and was named a Walter Channing Cabot Fellow for his monograph, *Witchcraft and Magic in the Nordic Middle Ages* (2011). He is a former fellow of the Radcliffe Institute for Advanced Study, the Swedish Collegium for Advanced Study and the Centre for Viking and Mediaeval Studies at Aarhus University.

Lea T. Olsan is a Professor Emerita of English and Foreign Languages at the University of Louisiana at Monroe. She now resides in Cambridge, UK. She has published articles on charms, amulets and rituals. Recently, she has published on the circulation of performative rituals in medieval medicine (with Peter Murray Jones), on images and texts found on medieval prayer rolls and on correspondences between artisanal and medicinal recipes.

Martine Ostorero is an Associate Professor of Medieval History at the University of Lausanne (Switzerland). Her research focuses on the history of the repression of witchcraft (Western Switzerland and the Alpine region) and demonological literature at the end of the Middle Ages. She has published in particular *Le diable au sabbat. Littérature démonologique et sorcellerie* (Florence, Micrologus 'Library, 38, 2011) and *L'énigme de la Vauderie de Lyon. Enquête sur l'essor de la chasse aux sorcières entre France et Empire (1430–1480)*, with Franck Mercier (Florence, Micrologus' Library, 72, 2015).

Bernd-Christian Otto is a Postdoctoral Researcher at the Max Weber Centre for Advanced Cultural and Social Studies at the University of Erfurt, Germany. His research focuses on the conceptual and ritual history of "magic" and on new ways to deal with the problems of that category. His book publications include *Magie. Rezeptions- und diskursgeschichtliche Analysen von der Antike bis zur Neuzeit* (Berlin 2011), and, as co-editor, *Defining Magic: A Reader*

(London 2013), and *History and Religion: Narrating a Religious Past* (Berlin 2015); his most recent book is a monograph co-authored with Daniel Bellingradt entitled *Magical Manuscripts in Early Modern Europe: The Clandestine Trade with Illegal Book Collections* (Basingstoke 2017).

Sophie Page is an Associate Professor in Medieval History at University College London, UK. Her research focuses on medieval magic and astrology, especially in relation to religion, medicine, cosmology, and the history of animals. Her publications include *Magic in the Cloister: Pious Motives, Illicit Interests, and Occult Approaches to the Medieval Universe* (2013) and an edited collection, *The Unorthodox Imagination in Late Medieval Britain* (2010).

Catherine Rider is an Associate Professor in Medieval History at the University of Exeter, UK. Her research focuses on the history of magic, and the church's attitude to magic, in the Middle Ages, and on the history of popular religion, pastoral care, as well as sex and reproduction. Her publications include *Magic and Religion in Medieval England* (London, 2012) and *Magic and Impotence in the Middle Ages* (Oxford, 2006) and she is co-editor, with Siam Bhayro, of *Demons and Illness from Antiquity to the Early Modern Period* (Leiden, 2017).

Antonella Sannino is a Professor of History of Medieval Philosophy (M-Fil/08) at the Università degli Studi di Napoli "L'Orientale" (UNO). She has been a Visiting Professor at Hill Museum Monastic Library Collegeville, Minnesota (2015) and the Frances A. Yates Fellow at the Warburg Institute, University of London. She received a postdoctoral grant from Herzog August Bibliothek in Wolfenbüttel. At present, she is a board member of Società italiana per lo Studio del pensiero medieval (SISPM) and the Société Internationale pour l'Étude de la philosophie médiévale (SIEPM). She is a Chief Editor of review "Studi Filosofici" and Director of "Bibliotheca Philosophica Virtualis" (www.bph.eu). Her research focuses on the appeal of the Hermetic and Neoplatonic tradition in the Latin Middle Ages. She has also produced critical editions of some important hermetic texts and the famous magic text *De mirabilibus mundi*.

Corinne Saunders is a Professor of English and Co-Director of the Centre for Medical Humanities at Durham University, UK. She specializes in medieval literature and the history of ideas, and is Co-Investigator on the *Hearing the Voice* project and Collaborator on the *Life of Breath* project, both funded by the Wellcome Trust. Her third monograph, *Magic and the Supernatural in Medieval English Romance*, was published in 2010. Her co-edited books include (with Jane Macnaughton and David Fuller) *The Recovery of Beauty: Arts, Culture, Medicine* (2015) and (with Carolyne Larrington and Frank Brandsma) *Emotions in Medieval Arthurian Literature: Body, Mind, Voice* (2015).

Julien Véronèse is a Senior Lecturer in Medieval History at the University of Orléans (France) and a specialist in medieval ritual magic. Within the framework of the project *Salomon Latinus* (Florence), he published various studies (with editions) on traditions of learned magic such as the *Ars notoria* (2007), the *Almandal* (2012), and the *Vinculum Salomonis* (2015). He is also interested in divinatory arts and in theological and legal discourses against magic and divination, for instance studying some important unpublished treatises by the famous Dominican inquisitor of Aragon, Nicholas Eymerich.

LIST OF CONTRIBUTORS

Nicholas Watson teaches in the Department of English and the program in Medieval Studies at Harvard University. His main areas of interest include visionary and mystical writing of the later Middle Ages and the history of medieval vernacular religious writing, especially in England and France. He is a co-editor, with Claire Fanger, of an edition and commentary of John of Morigny's *Flowers of Heavenly Teaching* (2015); co-editor with Jacqueline Jenkins of the writings of Julian of Norwich (2006); and has written or edited several other books and more than fifty articles. At present, he is finishing a monograph entitled *Balaam's Ass: Vernacular Theology Before the English Reformation*.

Nicolas Weill-Parot is a Professor at the École Pratique des Hautes Études (Section des sciences historiques et philologiques) and Chair of "History of Science in Medieval Latin West". His research deals with scientific rationality confronted with external challenges (magic, especially astral magic) and internal challenges (occult properties, magnetic attraction, abhorrence of a vacuum). He has published notably *Les "Images astrologiques" au Moyen Âge et à la Renaissance. Spéculations intellectuelles et pratiques magiques* (xiie-xve siècle) (Paris, 2002); an edition of Jérôme Torrella (Hieronymus Torrella), *Opus praeclarum de imaginibus astrologicis,* (Florence, 2008); and *Points aveugles de la nature: la rationalité scientifique médiévale face à l'occulte, l'attraction magnétique et l'horreur du vide* (xiiie-milieu du xve siècle) (Paris, 2013).

Mark Williams studied Classics and English before undertaking graduate work in Celtic Studies at Jesus College, Oxford. He is a Darby Fellow and Tutor in English at Lincoln College, Oxford, and currently works in the Department of Anglo-Saxon, Norse, and Celtic at Cambridge, where he teaches medieval Irish. He is the author of *Fiery Shapes: Celestial Portents and Astrology in Ireland and Wales, 700–1700* (2010), and *Ireland's Immortals: A History of the Gods of Irish Myth* (2016). He is currently working on a monograph on magic in medieval Irish and Welsh literature.

INTRODUCTION

Sophie Page and Catherine Rider

The study of medieval magic has seen a great deal of important work in recent decades. Since the 1990s, scholars have demonstrated that a wide range of people were engaged in magical activities from all groups in society, and that a great variety of magical texts were in circulation. In addition to this, they have continued to explore topics that have long attracted attention, such as the relationship between medieval magic and the witch trials of the early modern period. It has become clear from this recent scholarship that magic was not a marginal area of medieval culture but intersected with many larger and more conventional historical topics. Taking a lead from Richard Kieckhefer, who in an influential 1989 book described magic as a "kind of crossroads where different pathways in medieval culture converge",[1] historians have explored the ways in which magic interacted with mainstream religion, medicine and science, law, and the culture and politics of royal and aristocratic courts, to name but a few areas. The resulting publications are spread widely across academic publishers and journals – another sign that medieval magic is no longer regarded as a marginal topic – but the subject has found a place particularly in Pennsylvania State University Press's *Magic in History* series and SISMEL's *Micrologus Library* series.

This Routledge History therefore has two aims. First, it offers an overview of the work that has been done since the 1990s, exploring historiographical trends and the lively debates that now exist in many areas of medieval magic studies. Second, it aims to act as a guide for future research, setting out what still needs to be done, highlighting manuscripts and texts that would benefit from further study, and discussing topics that remain under-researched. It is not primarily intended to act as an overview of the history of medieval magic as there are other publications that offer this, some focusing purely on the Middle Ages and others covering a longer chronological span.[2] Rather, it aims to move beyond these surveys to set a research agenda.

The book looks primarily at the period from the twelfth to fifteenth centuries, which have been the focus of most of the recent work on magic by medievalists.[3] In several respects, these centuries can be seen as a distinct period in the history of magic.[4] This is not to say that the twelfth century marked a complete break from what had gone before, and important points of continuity with magic in the earlier Middle Ages are discussed in this volume. One of these was the influence of Augustine (d. 430), who laid the foundation for much of the medieval theorization and critique of magic. Another was the nature and use of texts and objects that were accessible to the illiterate.[5] These practices, which Richard Kieckhefer termed the "common tradition" of magic, saw a high degree of continuity from the early Middle Ages into the early modern period and beyond.[6]

Nevertheless, the twelfth century saw the beginning of two developments that had profound implications for the ways in which magic was understood and practised in later centuries, as well as how it was viewed by the secular and ecclesiastical authorities. The first of these was the appearance in Latin of magical texts translated mostly from Arabic but also, to a lesser extent, from Greek and Hebrew.[7] This was part of a much broader translation movement that took place in the Latin West in the central Middle Ages. Beginning in the late eleventh century and continuing into the thirteenth, numerous philosophical, scientific and medical works were translated into Latin from these languages. The translations from Arabic were made in the areas of Europe that had Muslim and Jewish populations most notably Spain, southern Italy and Sicily. Their impact has been well documented by historians of medicine, science and philosophy but they had an equally profound effect on magic, because a significant number of magical texts were translated alongside other works. Indeed, magical works were often closely related to scientific and philosophical knowledge.

Scholars such as David Pingree and Charles Burnett have outlined some of the routes by which Arabic, Greek and Hebrew magical texts entered the Latin West and were disseminated but much remains to be discovered.[8] Although these magical texts were at first only accessible to the small minority of the medieval population that was literate in Latin and able to gain access to sometimes rare manuscripts, they offered to intellectuals new techniques for doing magic such as the creation of images or talismans linked to celestial influences. They also sometimes sought to justify the place of magic in wider schemes of learning, for example by presenting it as one of the seven liberal arts.[9] By the mid-thirteenth century, however, learned magic texts were beginning to circulate in court circles and in the vernacular, reaching new audiences such as the nobility and the urban elites.[10]

The second development that shaped the history of magic after 1100 was the establishment of universities and the emergence of a class of educated clerics who studied there. Again, the development of universities, from the informal schools of early twelfth-century France to the carefully organized and powerful corporations of the thirteenth century and later, has been well studied. So too has their impact on later medieval society. However, the rise of universities had several implications for the history of magic in particular. They provided one setting in which magical texts circulated: for example William of Auvergne, Bishop of Paris (d. 1249), claimed to have read magical texts as a student. Perhaps more importantly, the university disciplines of canon law and theology shaped later medieval thought about magic by offering systematic, detailed discussions of what magic was, how it worked, and which aspects of it were, or were not, legitimate. Canonists sought to clarify which ritual practices should be categorized as magic and prohibited by the Church.[11] Theologians and natural philosophers explored the place of magic in the universe, including such issues as the role of demons in magic and their relationship with human magicians, as well as the question of why magic was wrong.[12] And sometimes why it was right. Some thinkers approved of the use of the term "natural magic" to refer to the production of marvellous but natural effects, argued that the science of images was based on natural forces and used the vocabulary of experiment or empirical knowledge to explain the effects of occult properties in the natural world that magic texts utilized.[13]

When they considered these issues, medieval canonists and theologians drew on earlier Christian writers (particularly Augustine) but from the twelfth century onwards their discussions were far more detailed and covered a wider range of practices. They also engaged with texts, such as works of astrological image magic or the *Ars Notoria*, which had not existed in Augustine's time but were circulating in later medieval universities. The legal and theological frameworks that resulted shaped educated churchmen's attitudes to magic throughout the late Middle Ages and also informed the laws that were made against it and the activities of secular and ecclesiastical courts and inquisitors.

This volume ends in the fifteenth century, which again marks a transitional period in the history of magic. It saw the beginning of two developments in particular which continued to the early modern period. The first was a growing fear of magic, and with this a growing emphasis on the relationship between demons and magical practitioners. Superstitions were being demonized more strongly than before, and clearly defined and gendered mythologies of witchcraft were emerging. This was also the period which saw the increasing numbers of trials for witchcraft.[14] This increased readiness to demonize magic and put practitioners on trial was far from universal in fifteenth-century Europe but nonetheless it marked a change from earlier centuries. For much of the Middle Ages, although churchmen had repeatedly condemned magic as demonic, trials of magic workers (or alleged magic workers) seem to have been comparatively rare.[15] During the fifteenth century, this began to change. The 1430s–1440s saw the emergence of a new mythology of diabolical witchcraft in the Alpine areas of modern Switzerland, Austria and Italy. This new mythology encompassed a cluster of characteristics. Besides being a practitioner of harmful magic, the witch came to be seen as a member of a devil-worshipping sect that engaged in a variety of antisocial activities. The nature of the witch and her (or, less often, his) practice varied according to different trials and areas, but key to the stereotype of diabolical witchcraft (at least in the Lausanne region) was that witches attended secret meetings known as "sabbaths", at which they worshipped the devil and engaged in orgies, cannibalism and child murder as well as harmful magic. According to some sources, they also flew to these sabbaths. At the same time, some regional authorities, clerics and secular elites became convinced of the existence of sects of devil worshipers and initiated trials. The number of witch trials and witchcraft treatises really only intensified after 1560 (although scholars of early modern witchcraft now emphasize that even then many suspected witches were never prosecuted and peaks in witch-hunting were often short-lived and localized)[16]; nevertheless the fifteenth century laid the conceptual and legal foundations for these later prosecutions.

However, the fifteenth century also saw a second important development: the emergence of less fearful and more confident attitudes to learned magic which continued into later centuries. Magic texts were reaching ever wider audiences through vernacular translations, with learned magic appealing to readers from the court to the cloister.[17] In fifteenth-century Italy, a new intellectual climate allowed authors of learned magic texts to underpin their writings with Neoplatonic, Hermetic and humanist currents of thought. The translation of Neoplatonic texts from Greek gave educated writers such as Marsilio Ficino (1433–1499) new ways to conceptualize magic and develop philosophical justifications for the human capacity to manipulate the forces of the universe.

Scope of this book

This companion to medieval magic's history begins by discussing the conceptual issues involved in studying medieval magic, focusing on the difficult question of definition. Scholars working on many different societies – historical and modern – have long debated how to define magic and how magic relates to religion on the one hand, and science on the other. This issue is intimately bound up with practical questions about how medievalists should approach magic: Which practices and ideas fit into a history of "magic"? What questions should scholars ask? And what methodologies should they use? The four short pieces in the first section of the book offer different approaches to this problem. Richard Kieckhefer argues that "magic" is too general and ambiguous a term to allow for rigorous analysis, and instead suggests that scholars focus on "constitutive terms", that is, subcategories such as "conjuration". These constitutive terms refer to individual elements of the broader phenomenon of magic that may, or may not, be combined and are, he argues, precise enough to allow for meaningful analysis. Claire Fanger, from a different perspective, argues that scholars should not be afraid to use the term "magic" (or other large, ambiguous terms) as the focus for analysis. Instead, she suggests that we acknowledge the term's ambiguity and view it not as a single entity but as denoting "a particular kind of problem" in medieval thought: the problem of how to deal with phenomena (positive or negative) whose causes were mysterious or opaque. Viewed in this way, medieval anti-magical and pro-magical arguments are part of the same conversation rather than simply opposing views of particular practices.

Bernd-Christian Otto agrees with Kieckhefer that a generalized or universal definition of magic is not precise enough for scholarly analysis. Focusing on learned magic in particular, he argues for the importance of understanding the "insider discourse" of magic, as articulated by its medieval practitioners. Finally, in contrast to Otto, David L. d'Avray argues that we cannot just focus on the categories used by medieval writers themselves, either the "insider" categories used by those who practised magic, or the categories of churchmen who condemned magic. He suggests that scholars need to find their own modern, scholarly terms for the phenomena they study. These will allow analyses of medieval magic which distinguish between different phenomena that medieval writers may group together, or conversely highlight the similarities between phenomena which medieval writers regarded as distinct. He goes on to suggest some possible categories that can be used to analyse different aspects of the relationship between magic and religion.

These four pieces highlight different, often contrasting, approaches to how scholars can or should define magic; whether the term "magic" is useful for scholarly analysis at all; whose definitions scholars should use (medieval or modern, insider or outsider); and the ways in which different definitions allow us to ask different questions about medieval magic or focus on different aspects of the topic. The responses – in which Kieckhefer, Fanger, Otto and d'Avray discuss aspects of each other's chapters – show just how much scope for debate there is. Taken together, this section demonstrates that there is no single "right" way to define or approach magic, in the Middle Ages or in any other period. However, it also underlines the importance of thinking carefully about the concepts and definitions one plans to use, however one plans to approach the history of a particular aspect of medieval magic. Definitions are tools that can be used to serve a variety of purposes, and the ones that scholars choose will direct them towards particular questions and problems in the history of magic.

The other sections of the book cover the major areas where research into medieval magic has occurred in the last twenty years. "Languages and Dissemination" examines the dissemination and impact of magic as it acquired distinctive identities in different parts of Europe. It focuses first on the reception into Europe and later influence of the magic texts from the Arabic and Jewish traditions, which transformed the status of late medieval learned magic from an illicit activity into a branch of knowledge. Later chapters examine the geographical spread of these works into central and Eastern Europe; their dissemination in the vernacular; and the ways in which Western European magic interacted with existing magical traditions in two areas of Europe where these are especially well documented: Scandinavia and the Celtic lands.

INTRODUCTION

"Key Genres and Figures" examines one of the most significant research areas in the recent historiography of late medieval magic: learned magic texts. These texts circulated in manuscripts, described complex rituals and often drew on the same cosmological concepts as more scientific works such as ideas about the influence of the stars on earth, or the nature and powers of spirits. More than one hundred distinct texts and several hundred surviving manuscripts with magical contents have now been identified by scholars, although many remain hardly studied and new copies of magic texts are frequently being identified. In the fourteenth and fifteenth centuries, some authors of magical texts also, for the first time, allowed their works to circulate under their own name rather than ascribing them to legendary figures such as Hermes or Solomon. Since theological condemnation made it dangerous to claim authorship of a magical text, the fact that authors were becoming confident enough to put their real names to works of magic is a striking development, and is evidence of a gradual shift towards more positive attitudes towards certain magical texts and ideas in Western Europe. The second half of this section examines the work that has been done on these important "author-magicians".

The fourth section, "Themes", looks beyond the traditions, genres and authors of medieval magic to explore the ways in which magic interacted with other aspects of medieval culture. Several of the chapters in this section highlight areas that have seen exciting scholarship in recent years such as Jean-Patrice Boudet's chapter on magic at court, or Peter Murray Jones and Lea T. Olsan's chapter on magic and medicine. Others discuss important issues that would benefit from more research, for example Robert Goulding's chapter on conjuring and illusion, and Catherine Rider's chapter on magic and gender (a topic that has received more systematic attention from early modernists than from medievalists). The final chapters in this section explore the relationship between magic and other media and disciplines: visual and material sources for magic; magic in medieval literature; and the role of music in magic rituals. These chapters are intended on the one hand to highlight sources that have been underexploited by scholars and on the other to bring expertise from other disciplines to bear on the history of magic.

The final section of the book surveys the key ways in which medieval writers – often, but not always, clergy – tried to categorize magic and discourage people from practising it. The sources left by condemnations and trials provide much of the surviving evidence for medieval magic and for ecclesiastical concerns about illicit rituals. They range from the sophisticated critiques of magic made by highly trained theologians in medieval universities, discussed by David J. Collins, to simpler works aimed at a wider audience of clergy and laity, as discussed by Kathleen Kamerick. Michael D. Bailey's chapter examines negative medieval attitudes towards popular "superstitions", exploring how by the fifteenth century churchmen were increasingly concerned with "elite" as well as common superstitions, and how they were diabolizing common practices and associating superstitious error increasingly with women. The chapter on Witchcraft by Martine Ostorero brings this section together and concludes the volume by examining the early witch trials, drawing on the large amount of important work done by Swiss scholars in recent decades which is discussed in more detail below. Finally, a short piece by Alejandro García-Aviles concludes the book by analysing the cover image in detail and the cosmological ideas that lie behind it. It is a helpful illustration of the ways in which visual and textual sources can be brought together to shed light on medieval ideas about magic and is an example of the kind of work this book hopes to stimulate, which combines the approaches of different disciplines to shed new light on medieval magic.

Recent developments in the history of medieval magic

The individual chapters in this volume discuss, and draw on, several major developments in the historiography of medieval magic that have taken place since the 1990s. The most important of these is the discovery and detailed study of surviving magical texts, which has revealed the extraordinary cosmologies of learned magic texts originating in diverse Arabic, Jewish, Greco-Roman traditions, their successive Christianization through processes of translation, adaptation and dissemination, and the richness of the imaginative worlds that their readers subsequently had access to.[18] In the exotic rituals of occult texts translated and disseminated in the twelfth and thirteenth centuries, Christian authors found Arabic and Jewish spirit hierarchies, images and characters, lists of occult properties in natural objects and correspondences between heaven and earth. Perhaps surprisingly, they interpreted these as viable instruments for achieving goals that ranged from the pious seeking of the vision of God to the transgressive pursuit of knowledge from demons.[19] Significant work in this field has investigated the hermetic roots of ritual magic, and more recent scholarship has focused on unpacking the "Solomonic" tradition and its influence.[20]

In addition to discovering and editing learned magic texts, historians in this field have begun exploring their readership and circulation among physicians and in the clerical underworld, competitive court circles and the monastic cloister.[21] Our knowledge of the routes of transmission of magic texts is still patchy, and it is hard to bring individual practitioners to rounded life based on the surviving sources, but it has become increasingly clear that manuals of ritual magic were tailored to the individual interests of their owners, whether this was talking to spirits or having success in love.[22] The circulation of ritual magic texts among physicians and in universities is less well studied, and research into the vernacularization of magic texts from the mid-thirteenth century onwards is at a very early stage.[23] In addition, few links have yet been made between this process of vernacularization and the "common tradition" of magic, although historians have long acknowledged that many collectors of learned magic texts were also interested in charms, recipes and textual amulets and that non-literate practitioners were influenced by the ritual magic tradition.[24] Whether this frequent (if not typical) combination of interests influenced the increasing condemnation of popular practices as superstitious in the fifteenth century has not yet been explored. But historians have recently revealed vibrant and inflammatory links between ritual magic and other parts of mainstream religious practice such as mystical texts and exorcism.[25]

As noted above, historians generally agree that there was a shift towards positive attitudes to learned magic in the late Middle Ages, despite increasing concerns about witchcraft.[26] This means that the strategies with which the authors of learned magic texts appealed to the intellectual curiosity and the spiritual thirst of medieval men and women were to a large extent successful and flourished even in the difficult conditions of the late Middle Ages. Historians have begun to explore one of the reasons for this success: the fact that the theology of witchcraft shifted the authorities' gaze onto female popular practitioners and away from the male practitioners of learned magic.[27] Another contributing factor to the late medieval success of ritual magic was the ways in which texts were stored, annotated and rewritten to avoid censorship and reflect the creative choices of scribes. Some strategies are well known such as the concealment of occult texts owned by the cleric, surgeon and writer Richard de Fournival (c.1201–c.1260) in a secret room to which only he had access, and the compilation of magic texts with more acceptable genres such as astronomy, medicine, devotional literature and natural philosophy. Some readers took the view that a pious vocation enabled them to safely handle suspicious texts and even draw out useful things from them, while powerful secular rulers did not necessarily need to conceal their occult interests.[28] Finally, in manuscripts themselves, tactics to evade suspicion took the form of cautionary marginalia or even notices condemning magic, which allowed the piety of the owner to be expressed while the usability of a ritual was unaffected. The general history of the censorship (and self-censorship) of magical texts, of rituals being cut out of manuscripts, names erased, magical characters being altered to turn them into crosses and books being revised and burnt has yet to be written. When it is explored more fully, it is likely that further lines of comparison and influence will be opened up with contemporary attitudes to heresy and witchcraft.

Important work has also been done on other kinds of source material. Some of this has sought to shed new light on genres of source which scholars have known about for a long time. For example, texts produced as part of the activities of the medieval church have long played a central role in the history of medieval magic. Ecclesiastical sources have been especially crucial to studies that focus on tracing the earlier medieval origins of fifteenth-century ideas about diabolical witchcraft. Since, as Norman Cohn argued in the 1970s, these ideas seem largely to have originated among the educated,[29] the writings produced by educated clergy are one obvious place to look for evidence. Cohn himself used inquisitorial manuals and theological treatises, alongside other kinds of source material, to analyse changing stereotypes of magical practitioners and the relationship of those stereotypes to early modern witchcraft.[30] A number of more recent studies have continued this line of investigation, including Michael D. Bailey's 2001 discussion of changing clerical attitudes to magic (which used the fourteenth-century inquisitorial manuals of Bernard Gui and Nicholas Eymeric) and Jean-Patrice Boudet's important book on magic and astrology in the medieval West, which included substantial discussion of ecclesiastical condemnations of magic, among many other sources.[31] New studies have also analysed individual genres of source in depth such as Patrick Hersperger's survey of magic in the commentaries on the twelfth-century canon law textbook, Gratian's *Decretum*.[32]

Even with ecclesiastical sources, however, in recent decades the focus has broadened to include a wider range of texts. For example, Alain Boureau has published and analysed a document from 1320 (first rediscovered in 1952) in which Pope John XXIII consulted a series of theologians and canon lawyers about ritual magic.[33] Another broader kind of source material that has attracted renewed attention is the literature of pastoral care, including sermons, preaching materials and treatises on confession.[34] These sources, often structured around mnemonic schemes such as the Ten Commandments or Seven Deadly Sins, were intended to help clergy in their dealings with the laity, and so often focus on the sins and problems that priests might encounter on the ground. They frequently included some discussion of magic and "superstition", although these particular sins were not the first concern of most preachers or authors of confessors' manuals. Related to these general works on pastoral care are treatises that focus on the sin of superstition. These were primarily a product of the fifteenth century and scholars such as Karin Baumann, Michael D. Bailey and Kathleen Kamerick have investigated what concerns they express about magic and why, as well as their relationship to emerging ideas about diabolical witchcraft.[35] Some of this work intersects with a wider scholarly discussion of "superstition" in other periods.[36] These genres of source were not completely neglected by earlier scholars (Cohn, for example, uses the thirteenth-century *exempla* of Caesarius of Heisterbach and a pioneering article published by G. R. Owst in 1957 considered magic in medieval English sermons)[37] but recent scholarship has investigated this material in far greater depth.

Looking across these different forms of ecclesiastical text, we now have a much more diverse view of medieval churchmen and their attitude to magic. Authors of canon law texts, pastoral care literature and treatises on superstition were always influenced by a core of authoritative texts and ideas but within these general parameters there was a considerable amount of variation. Authors differed as to which practices they discussed, with some describing activities they claimed happened in their own regions. We can also see varying levels of concern. Much of the confession and preaching literature of medieval England, for example, devoted a relatively small amount of space to magic and superstition.[38] By contrast, authors of fifteenth-century superstition treatises were clearly more concerned about these issues, but even then there were differences. Some worried about any unofficial ritual practice that might be defined as superstition or magic, while others identified genuine (if sometimes muddled) expressions of lay piety or legitimate protective practices that could be employed against maleficent witchcraft.[39]

A further important development links to the work on fifteenth-century superstition treatises. This is a renewed interest in the fifteenth-century sources that describe the new crime of diabolical witchcraft. At the heart of this is a large project centred on the University of Lausanne, which since 1989 has published and analysed many of the earliest witch trials and witchcraft treatises.[40] The many scholars involved in this project have made these previously understudied sources available in modern editions and translations (usually into French, sometimes German) as well as studying the trial procedures, defendants and evidence for witchcraft. One focus of their research has been a register of twenty-seven fifteenth- and early sixteenth-century trial records which was probably put together in the early twentieth century, but the team has also published an important anthology of the earliest treatises which described devil-worshipping witches.[41] More recently, some of the scholars involved in this project have published detailed studies that discuss demonology (Martine Ostorero) and the relationship between fifteenth-century witchcraft and heresy (Kathrin Utz Tremp).[42] Taken together, these studies have emphasized the importance of understanding the local factors and local judicial systems that lay behind individual trials. They have also underlined the continuity between earlier persecutions of heretics and fifteenth-century witchcraft trials, at least in Western Switzerland.[43] In addition, this work has given us a far more nuanced understanding of the intellectual debates surrounding the new stereotype of the witch, and has led several scholars to suggest that ideas about witchcraft were less homogeneous than earlier studies often suggested.[44]

Finally, scholars have turned to sources that did not set out to discuss magic but often mentioned it within their scope. Medical and scientific texts often include information that could be categorized as magical. Their authors discussed (sometimes in great detail) how astrological forces or powerful words could affect the human body; treatises on the properties of stones, plants and animals list the marvellous effects these objects could have; and medical texts included remedies for illness which involved the speaking of charms or the wearing of amulets.[45] The power of words – both written and spoken – has received particular attention.[46] Meanwhile, Michael McVaugh, and Lea T. Olsan and Peter Murray Jones have focused on incantations and charms, examining their relationship with other aspects of medieval medicine and the ways in which medical writers presented them, as well as how these rituals might have been performed.[47] Don C. Skemer has investigated the related area of textual amulets – powerful words and symbols that were written down and worn on the body, focusing in particular on their relationship to mainstream religion.[48] Much of this research has emphasized that many so-called "magical" cures in fact held an accepted, if marginal place in medieval culture.

Other significant sources for understanding late medieval magic are the visual and material culture of magic and literary instances of spells and enchantment. The former is very underresearched, a situation that three chapters in this book, respectively on the iconography of magic and magicians, magical diagrams and the material culture of magic, address. Visual sources in particular allow us to track transformations in the perceptions of magic and its relationship with mainstream religion and science (as García-Aviles does in his discussion of the cover image), and to note the appearance of late medieval Christian innovations such as the magic circle. The rich evidence of literary magic is explored in chapters by Mark Williams and Corinne Saunders, who ask questions that reveal fruitful contrasts to current understandings of medieval magic and complicate our view of it: "Where does magical power come from? What are the imaginative conventions which govern its representation? What are the range of attitudes to its use, and how do they differ by genre?"[49] One of the aims of this volume is to set these analyses of diverse genres side by side so that new connections can be revealed. The richly imagined vision of a pre-Christian world in medieval Irish literature, with magical immortals and fantastic sequences of enchantment, complicates the Christian understanding of the cosmos in an appealing and provocative way that is comparable to the syncretic cosmological frameworks of learned magic texts. Another example of similar connections being made in different genres is the close relationship between necromancy and natural magic, and of both to the theory and practice of medicine. This is discussed by Corinne Saunders in the context of medieval romance and by Isabelle Draelants in her chapter on natural philosophical texts. We hope that our readers will notice further connections.

Conclusion

The study of medieval magic is developing in many exciting ways. As the footnotes to this Introduction make clear, a great deal of work has been published in recent decades by scholars from many countries including the USA, Canada, France, Spain, Italy, Germany, Switzerland, Hungary and Britain. Although much remains to be done, our understanding of certain areas – in particular the contents and readers of magical texts – is now much clearer than it was three decades ago. One result of this is that the field is now so large and lively that even scholars who research medieval magic struggle to keep up with all the new work being published, in several languages. It is therefore a good moment to take stock, to summarize new developments for the benefit of scholars in the field as well as other medievalists and to consider where to go next. This Routledge History is designed to showcase the new research that has been carried out in recent years and is still ongoing, with contributions from both established scholars in the field and recent Ph.Ds. However, many sources, in a range of genres, are still unpublished and little studied. For this reason, the book sets out some of the directions that the field could take in the future. It discusses areas that would benefit from more research; questions that remain unanswered or only partially answered; and authors and texts that need more in-depth study.

The chapters in the book were chosen to reflect the vitality of medieval magic studies at this point in time. They also reflect its diversity. As editors, we gave all the authors featured here a similar remit: to outline the most important developments in their field and discuss future directions for research. They have responded admirably. Within this general framework, however, we have tried to preserve the different approaches and styles employed by scholars who work in different places, different languages and different scholarly disciplines. We hope that the results will inspire scholars in the field and in related areas, as well as students who are embarking on their studies of medieval magic.

Notes

1 Richard Kieckhefer, *Magic in the Middle Ages* (Cambridge: Cambridge University Press, 1989), 1.
2 For surveys of medieval magic, see Jean-Patrice Boudet, *Entre Science et Nigromance: Astrologie, divination et magie dans l'Occident médiéval* (Paris: Publications de la Sorbonne, 2006); Karen Jolly, Catharina Raudvere and Edward Peters, *Witchcraft and Magic in Europe: The Middle Ages* (London: Athlone, 2002); Kieckhefer, *Magic in the Middle Ages* is still a useful and accessible overview. Recent works with a longer span which cover the Middle Ages include *The Cambridge History of Magic and Witchcraft in the West*, ed. David J. Collins (Cambridge: Cambridge University Press, 2015) and *The Oxford Illustrated History of Witchcraft and Magic*, ed. Owen Davies (Oxford: Oxford University Press, 2017).
3 The most recent book to survey magic across the early medieval period remains Valerie Flint, *The Rise of Magic in Early Medieval Europe* (Oxford: Clarendon Press, 1990), although many aspects of Flint's interpretation have been debated. For a recent discussion, see Yitzak Hen, "The Early Medieval West," in *The Cambridge History of Magic*, ed. Collins, 183–206.
4 Michael D. Bailey, "The Age of Magicians: Periodization in the History of European Magic," *Magic, Ritual and Witchcraft* 3 (2008): 9–17 also views the twelfth to fifteenth centuries as distinct, although he emphasizes (p. 17) that the fifteenth century should be seen as a period of transition rather than an end point.
5 On Augustine, see especially the chapters in this volume by Claire Fanger, Robert Goulding and David J. Collins. On continuities in the use of magical and ritual elements in medicine and apotropaic objects, see the chapters by Lea Olsan and Peter Jones, and Roberta Gilchrist.
6 Kieckhefer, *Magic in the Middle Ages*, 56–94.
7 For an overview of this, see Sophie Page, "Medieval Magic," in *Oxford Illustrated History*, ed. Davies, 32–44. At least two Greek works were translated in the early Middle Ages; see Charles Burnett, "Late Antique and Medieval Latin Translations of Greek Texts on Astrology and Magic," in *The Occult Sciences in Byzantium*, ed. Maria Mavroudi and Paul Magdalino (Paris: La Pomme D'Or, 2007), 325–59. Although several magic texts claimed to have Hebrew origins, the *Book of Raziel* represents the only confirmed translation of learned magic from Hebrew into Latin during the Middle Ages; see Katelyn Mesler's chapter in this volume.
8 See Charles Burnett's chapter in this volume. See also David Pingree, "The Diffusion of Arabic Magical Texts in Western Europe," in *La diffusione delle scienze islamiche nel Medio Evo Europeo (Roma, 2–4 ottobre 1984)* (Roma: Accademia dei Lincei, 1987), 57–102; "Learned Magic in the Time of Frederick II," *Micrologus* 2 (1994): 39–56; Boudet, *Entre science et nigromance*; Charles Burnett, *Magic and Divination in the Middle Ages: Texts and Techniques in the Islamic and Christian Worlds* (Aldershot: Ashgate, 1996).
9 Charles Burnett, "Talismans: Magic as Science? Necromancy among the Seven Liberal Arts," in Burnett, *Magic and Divination*, 1–15.
10 On magic at court, see the chapter by Jean-Patrice Boudet. On vernacularization, see the chapter by Sebastià Giralt.
11 See Edward Peters's pioneering, *The Magician, the Witch and the Law* (Philadelphia: University of Pennsylvania Press, 1978), 63–108. For more recent studies of magic and canon law, see Patrick Hersperger, *Kirche, Magie und "Aberglaube". Superstitio in der Kanonistik des 12. und 13. Jahrhunderts* (Cologne: Böhlau, 2010); Catherine Rider, *Magic and Impotence in the Middle Ages* (Oxford: Oxford University Press, 2006), 113–34.
12 See David J. Collins' chapter in this volume; Alain Boureau, *Le pape et les sorciers: une consultation de Jean XXII sur la magie en 1320* (Rome: Ecole française de Rome, 2003); Alain Boureau, *Satan hérétique: Naissance de la démonologie dans l'Occident médiéval (1280–1330)* (Paris: Odile Jacob, 2004), chs. 1 and 2.

13 On the relationship between natural philosophy and magic, see the chapters in this volume by Stephen Marrone and Isabelle Draelants; see also Nicolas Weill-Parot, "Astrology, Astral Influences, and Occult Properties in the Thirteenth and Fourteenth Centuries," *Traditio* 65 (2010): 201–30.
14 See Michael D. Bailey and Martine Ostorero's chapters in this volume. For an overview of fifteenth-century witchcraft, see also Brian P. Levack, *The Witch-Hunt in Early Modern Europe*, 3rd edn (Harlow: Pearson Longman, 2006), 32–67; Richard Kieckhefer, "Mythologies of Witchcraft in the Fifteenth Century," *Magic, Ritual, and Witchcraft* 1 (2006): 79–107; Richard Kieckhefer, "The First Wave of Trials for Diabolical Witchcraft," in *The Oxford Handbook of Witchcraft in Early Modern Europe and Colonial America*, ed. Brian P. Levack (Oxford, Oxford University Press, 2013), 159–78.
15 On perhaps the most significant trial and execution of a learned magician in the Middle Ages, Cecco d'Ascoli, see Nicolas Weill-Parot's chapter in this volume.
16 See for example Robin Briggs, *The Witches of Lorraine* (Oxford: Oxford University Press, 2007), 6.
17 See the chapters by Jean-Patrice Boudet and Nicolas Weill-Parot in this volume and Sophie Page, *Magic in the Cloister: Pious Motives, Illicit Interests, and Occult Approaches to the Medieval Universe* (University Park: Pennsylvania State University Press, 2013).
18 On magic and cosmology, see Alejandro García Avilés' chapter in this volume on the iconography of the *Astromagia*. On the Christianization of learned magic see, for example, Vittoria Perrone Compagni, "Studiosus incantationibus: Adelardo di Bath, Ermete e Thabit," *Giornale critico della filosofia italiana* 80, no. 1 (2001): 36–61 for different treatments by translators of Thabit's *De imaginibus*; Nicolas Weill-Parot, *Les "images astrologiques" au Moyen Âge et à la Renaissance* (Paris: Honoré Champion); Julien Véronèse, *L'Almandal et l'Almadel latins au Moyen Âge. Introduction et éditions critiques* (Florence: Sismel Edizioni del Galluzzo, 2012).
19 See, for example, the chapters of Claire Fanger and Nicholas Watson and Frank Klaassen in this volume.
20 On "hermetic" magic, see especially *Hermetism from Late Antiquity to Humanism: La tradizione ermetica dal mondo tardo-antico all'umanesimo*, ed. Paolo Lucentini, Ilaria Parri and Vittoria Perrone Compagni (Turnhout: Brepols, 2003); Paolo Lucentini and Vittoria Perrone Compagni, *I testi e i codici di ermete nel Medioevo* (Florence: Polistampa, 2001) and Antonella Sannino's chapter in this volume. On Solomonic magic, see Jean-Patrice Boudet and Julien Véronèse. "Le secret dans la magie rituelle médiévale," *Micrologus* 14 (2006): 101–50 and Julien Véronèse's chapter in this volume.
21 On the reception of Arabic image magic by learned physicians, see Weill-Parot, *Les images astrologiques*, part 3 and his chapter on Jérôme Torrella in this volume. Richard Kieckhefer's theory of the clerical underworld is first explored in *Magic in the Middle Ages*, ch. 7. See also Boudet, *Entre science et nigromance* and Frank Klaassen, *The Transformations of Magic: Illicit Learned Magic in the Later Middle Ages and Renaissance* (University Park: Pennsylvania State University Press, 2013). For magic at court, see Jan R. Veenstra, *Magic and Divination at the Courts of Burgundy and France* (Leiden: Brill, 1997), Benedek Lang, *Unlocked Books: Manuscripts of Learned Magic in the Medieval Libraries of Central Europe* (University Park: Pennsylvania State University Press, 2008), 209–40 and Jean-Patrice Boudet's chapter in this volume. Monastic collectors of magic texts are discussed in Page, *Magic in the Cloister*, Claire Fanger, *Rewriting Magic: An Exegesis of the Visionary Autobiography of a Fourteenth-Century French Monk* (University Park: Pennsylvania State University Press, 2015) and Julien Véronèse, *L'Ars notoria au Moyen Âge. Introduction et edition critique* (Florence: Sismel Edizioni del Galluzzo, 2007).
22 For the former, see Oxford, Bodleian Library MS Rawlinson D 252 and for the latter, see Bibliothèque nationale de France, MS italiano 1524, recently edited by Florence Gal, Jean-Patrice Boudet and Laurence Moulinier-Brogi: *Vedrai mirabilia. Un libro di magia del Quattrocento* (Rome: Viella, 2017).
23 For individual physicians' interest in ritual magic, however, see *Médecine, astrologie et magie entre Moyen Âge et Renaissance: autour de Pietro d'Abano*, ed. Jean-Patrice Boudet, Franck Collard and Nicolas Weill-Parot (Florence: Sismel Edizioni del Galluzzo, 2012); Sebastià Giralt, "The Melancholy of the Necromancer in Arnau de Vilanova's Epistle against Demonic Magic," in *Demons and Illness from Antiquity to the Early-Modern Period*, ed. Siam Bhayro and Catherine Rider (Leiden: Brill, 2017), 271–90 and the chapters by Jean-Marc Mandosio on Peter of Zealand and Nicolas Weill-Parot on Jérôme Torrella in this volume.
24 On the latter, see Boudet, *Entre science et nigromance*, 431–46.
25 On mystical texts, see especially Nicolas Watson and Claire Fanger's chapter on John of Morigny. On the relationship between necromancy and exorcism, see especially Julien Véronèse and

Florence Chave-Mahir, *Rituel d'exorcisme ou manuel de magie? Le manuscrit Clm 10085 de la Bayerische Staatsbibliothek de Munich début du XVe siècle* (Florence: Sismel Edizioni del Galluzzo, 2015).

26 Many recent studies on learned magic take this position, but see, for example, Claire Fanger and Frank Klaassen, "Magic III: Middle Ages," in *Dictionary of Gnosis and Western Esotericism*, ed. Wouter J. Hanegraaff in collaboration with Antoine Faivre, Roelof van den Broek and Jean-Pierre Brach (Leiden: Brill, 2005), 724–31; Page, *Magic in the Cloister*, epilogue and chapters on author-magicians in this volume.

27 See Martine Ostorero's chapter in this volume.

28 See Page, *Magic in the Cloister* and Boudet, *Entre science et nigromance*, 357.

29 Norman Cohn, *Europe's Inner Demons: The Demonization of Christians in Medieval Christendom*, 3rd edn (London: Pimlico, 1993) (first published 1975), xi.

30 Cohn, *Europe's Inner Demons*.

31 Michael D. Bailey, "From Sorcery to Witchcraft: Clerical Conceptions of Magic in the Later Middle Ages," *Speculum* 76 (2001): 960–90; Boudet, *Entre science et nigromance*.

32 Hersperger, *Kirche, Magie und "Aberglaube"*.

33 Boureau, *Le pape et les sorciers*; Boureau, *Satan hérétique*, chs. 1 and 2.

34 Catherine Rider, *Magic and Religion in Medieval England* (London: Reaktion Books, 2012); Kathleen Kamerick, "Shaping Superstition in Late Medieval England," *Magic, Ritual and Witchcraft* 3 (2008): 29–53.

35 Karin Baumann, *Aberglaube für Laien: zur Programmatik und Überlieferung mittelalterlicher Superstitionen-kritik*, 2 vols (Würzburg: Königshausen und Neumann, 1989); Michael D. Bailey, *Fearful Spirits, Reasoned Follies: The Boundaries of Superstition in Late Medieval Europe* (Ithaca, NY: Cornell University Press, 2013); Kamerick, "Shaping Superstition."

36 For example, two articles on medieval superstition appear in *The Religion of Fools? Superstition Past and Present*, ed. S. A. Smith, *Past and Present* supplement 3 (2008); Michael D. Bailey, "Concern over Superstition in Late Medieval Europe," 115–33 and Stephen Bowd, "'Honeyed Flies' and 'Sugared Rats': Witchcraft and Superstition in the Bresciano, 1454–1535," 134–56.

37 Cohn, *Europe's Inner Demons*, 25–27; G.R. Owst, "*Sortilegium* in English Homiletic Literature of the Fourteenth Century," in *Studies Presented to Sir Hilary Jenkinson*, ed. J. Conway Davies (London: Oxford University Press, 1957), 272–303.

38 Rider, *Magic and Religion*, 177.

39 Bailey, *Fearful Spirits, Reasoned Follies*.

40 For an overview of the many publications from this project, see Kathrin Utz Tremp, "Witches' Brooms and Magic Ointments: Twenty Years of Witchcraft Research at the University of Lausanne (1989–2009)," *Magic, Ritual and Witchcraft* 5 (2010): 173–87.

41 Martine Ostorero, Agostino Paravicini Bagliani and Kathrin Utz Tremp, *L'imaginaire du Sabbat: édition critique des textes les plus anciens (1430c.–1440c.)* (Lausanne: Université de Lausanne, 1999).

42 Martine Ostorero, *Le diable au Sabbat: Littérature démonologique et sorcellerie (1440–1460)* (Florence: Sismel, 2011); Kathrin Utz Tremp, *Von der Häeresie zur Hexerei: "Wirkliche" und imaginäre Sekten im Spätmittelalter* (Hannover: Hahnsche Buchh., 2008).

43 Utz Tremp, "Witches' Brooms and Magic Ointments," 186–87.

44 Kieckhefer, "The First Wave of Trials for Diabolical Witchcraft" 159–78; see also Levack, "Introduction," *Oxford Handbook of Witchcraft*, 3.

45 See the chapters by Draelants, Sannino and Jones and Olsan in this volume.

46 Béatrice Delaurenti, *La puissance des mots: virtus verborum. Débats doctrinaux sur les incantations au Moyen Âge* (Paris: éditions du Cerf, 2007); Claire Fanger, "Things Done Wisely by a Wise Enchanter: Negotiating the Power of Words in the Thirteenth Century," *Esoterica* 1 (1999): 97–132.

47 Michael R. McVaugh, "*Incantationes* in Late Medieval Surgery," in *Ratio et Superstitio: Essays in Honor of Graziella Frederici Vescovini*, ed. Giancarlo Marchetti, Orsola Rignani and Valeria Sorge (Leuvene-la-Neuve, Belgium: Fédération Internationale des Instituts d'Etudes Médiévale, 2003), 319–46. Lea T. Olsan, "Charms and Prayers in Medieval Medical Theory and Practice," *Social History of Medicine* 16 (2003): 343–66; Peter Murray Jones and Lea T. Olsan, "Performative Rituals for Conception and Childbirth in England, 900–1600," *Bulletin of the History of Medicine* 89 (2015): 406–33.

48 Don C. Skemer, *Binding Words: Textual Amulets in the Middle Ages* (University Park: Pennsylvania State University Press, 2006).

49 See Mark Williams's chapter in this volume.

PART I

CONCEPTUALIZING MAGIC

1

RETHINKING HOW TO DEFINE MAGIC

Richard Kieckhefer

What is magic? We know perfectly well what it is if no one asks us, but when someone asks and we try to define it, we are confused. Or perhaps we give definitions adequate to some forms of magic but not others. Or we have definitions that make sense to us but not to others around us, who, when pressed, come to the table with rather different notions. We tell people, "When I speak of magic, what I mean by it is …", but then we should not be surprised if they tune out our abstractions and understand us in terms of their own vague preconceptions. Defining magic is notoriously tricky business. And one reason for that is, I wish to argue, that we try to make the word "magic" accomplish what it is ill equipped to do. It is the wrong kind of term for what we want to do with it.[1]

A comparison may help. It has long seemed to me useful to think of mysticism – another difficult concept – not as a single phenomenon but rather as a cluster of phenomena that may at times be distinct but tend to become intertwined.[2] There is mystical prayer, mystical relationship and mystical consciousness. *The Cloud of Unknowing* is a guide to contemplative prayer: fervent and intense, highly concentrated, focused prayer, cultivated within the setting of the contemplative or monastic life.[3] One might call it apophatic prayer, because it requires the simplest forms of praying and the simplest perception of the God to whom one prays. It entails disciplined attention to that God, and the realization that one's own effort of attention is ultimately not one's own effort at all, but the fruit of grace. The contemplative prayer of *The Cloud* is one classic manifestation of mysticism. Quite different is the mysticism of, say, Bernard of Clairvaux or the German sister books that are deeply steeped in "theoerotic" relationship, intensely amorous relationship with Christ.[4] They borrow the language and the narrative of the Song of Songs to tell what it is like to burn with love for the God-man. Different again are the vernacular sermons of Meister Eckhart, who wants his hearers or readers to gain a lively awareness of God's presence within herself – within her every cell, in the depths of her soul, within that mysterious inner chamber to which he gives many different names – and of her own true and eternal presence within God.[5] If *The Cloud* teaches mystical prayer, and Bernard advocates mystical relationship, Eckhart seeks to heighten mystical consciousness. Yet, we cannot really speak here of different forms or types of mysticism, because there is no reason in principle why they cannot be combined, and in writers such as Teresa of Ávila they very much are intertwined.[6] They represent distinguishable *elements* of Christian mysticism, not three different types.

The situation with magic is, I propose, similar. There are distinguishable practices that have long been called magical. If they have anything to do with each other – and they often do – it is not because they are different forms of one clearly definable thing, but for other reasons that we need to explore. Like "mysticism", so too "magic" is what I will call an *aggregating term*. The same can probably also be said for "sainthood", "authority" and numerous other terms, surely including "religion", all of which I would class as aggregating. They are difficult to define, because they encompass diverse elements that may or may not be combined with each other. The different elements may not share any common defining feature that brings them under the umbrella of the aggregating term; they are not linked by a shared essence. They may not even have shifting combinations of shared features; they are not necessarily bound by family resemblance. Mystical prayer, mystical relationship and mystical consciousness may or may not involve ecstatic experiences, and in any case it is not such experiences that qualify them as mystical. Even if they share no common features, they may be mutually supportive, and for that reason they may be cultivated jointly, which is sufficient reason to think of them as elements of something which is perhaps loosely called mysticism. But it is the type of intense prayer, or the type of fervently erotic relationship, or the depth of awareness that constitutes each of these phenomena as mystical. Mystical prayer may begin with intense focus on a single word and lead towards an experience of divinely infused prayer based on neither words nor concepts. Mystical relationship may involve a cycle of courtship, teasing withdrawal and erotic union with one's divine lover. Mystical consciousness typically involves a keen awareness of God always present within oneself, and of one's own true self as eternally present within God. It is not the aggregating category but the more specific one that constitutes them as elements of mysticism, and thus I will call these more specific forms of reference *constitutive terms*.[7]

We devote most of our energy to refining our aggregating terms, supposing that this is where our efforts are repaid by clarity and constructive value, and we often think of sub-categories as afterthoughts – but this is precisely the opposite of what we should be doing. It is the constitutive terms that are more likely to serve as useful tools for analysis and finely tuned comparison; aggregating terms are terms of convenience. While constitutive terms tend to be taken from and largely at home in specialized analytic discourse, aggregating terms tend to be widely used in general and popular discourse. Constitutive terms are relatively intolerant of ambiguity and imprecision; aggregating terms are by comparison open to ambiguous and imprecise usage. Constitutive terms are less connotative, aggregating terms more so. Constitutive terms tend to be univocal; aggregating terms are more often, in scholastic language, analogous or even equivocal.

Let me pursue a bit further my discussion of the term "mysticism". Those who rely on it as a tool for comparative study are often drawn towards something like William James's marks of mystical experience as ineffable, noetic, transient and passive.[8] On the surface, these may seem useful as common denominators of mysticism across cultures. But to take these as defining features of mysticism risks giving emphasis and importance to discrete mystical experiences even when the mystics we are reading spoke slightingly of them (Eckhart) or thought of them as belonging to earlier and lower levels of attainment (Teresa of Ávila). In any case, centring attention on such alleged common features risks turning away from what was of central importance to the mystics themselves. Bernard of Clairvaux no doubt did have experiences that were ineffable, noetic, transient and passive, but what was important to him was not these qualities of experience but rather the living and lively presence *of Christ*. If we want to do comparative study of mysticism that will combine rigour with sensitivity to the values of our subjects, the term "mysticism" may not be the most helpful tool to use. It means too many different things and is too connotative. Much more can be accomplished by more focused comparison of constitutive terms. There is theoerotic literature in many religious traditions, and comparison of the late medieval German mystic

Dorothea von Montau (who was overwhelmed with love for Christ), the Islamic mystic Rābi'a (similarly on fire with love of Allah) and the Hindu mystic and poet Mīrā Bāī (who sought only the love of Krishna) can elucidate patterns of similarity and difference that will lead to insightful understanding.[9] Most religious traditions provide disciplines of contemplation or meditation, and these too are fruitful subject matter for comparison.

What, then, are the constitutive terms that might be used to elucidate the aggregating term "magic"? This is a question that clearly calls for discussion, but provisionally I would suggest at least these three constitutive terms: conjuration, symbolic manipulation and directly efficacious volition.

By "conjuration", I mean here the ritual summoning and command of spirits. A long tradition of "skrying" claims that by gazing intently into a reflective surface and uttering incantations one can conjure angels or demons who will reveal secret and future things, perhaps telling who has stolen one's property. In the Yiddish play and film *The Dybbuk*, a young Kabbalist named Khonnon goes into the ritual bath and conjures Satan.[10] The spirits conjured may be thought of as good, evil, neutral or ambiguous; different observers may conceive them differently. In any case, the conjuration involves ritual that is in some measure complex and requires specialized skills, which helps to explain why the practitioner often belongs to some professional elite such as a priest or monk. The techniques, the assumptions and the status of the operator all show that conjuration is closely linked with religion, and may indeed be seen as part of a religious system, even if most people view it as a perversion of proper ritual. Summoning assumes that the spirits have local presence and locomotion: they are *there*, until they are called *here*. Command implies not manipulation but an exercise of authority in the face of potential resistance. Conjuring a spirit is decidedly not like activating an impersonal machine. A spirit has a will, and to be commanded must be brought into submission. The point of the ritual is precisely to effect that submission. Necromancy clearly falls under this category, but so does angel magic, and techniques of spirit magic in other cultures that in various ways resemble or relate to necromancy and angel magic. The very category "spirit" will surely require nuancing in comparative study, but taking into account different conceptions of what a spirit could be, and how a spirit relates to a ghost or an embodied being, is part of the task of comparison.

When I speak of "symbolic manipulation", I mean to include both of James G. Frazer's classic categories, sympathy and contagion, both of which involve exploitation of natural forces identified and explained in symbolic terms.[11] Assumed here is an order of nature rife with symbolic links on which magical efficacy depends. Plants, gems and artefacts are symbolically linked with the stars and planets, and can channel their power. Plants may resemble human organs and prove to benefit or harm those organs. Breaking and burying a candle symbolizes breaking and burying the power of a phallus and may cause impotence. Putting human excretions, bones from beneath a gallows, and other noxious substances in a bundle and placing it near an intended victim is no less a way of manipulating symbolic links: other objects may contaminate in more ordinary ways, but these substances are harmful because their natural decay symbolizes a deeper contamination, moral and spiritual as well as physical. Figures and images taken to resemble and channel powers from or towards what they represent are among the symbols manipulated by such magic. Names and recital of events can also hold symbolic power: the magician can invoke the force contained in the name "Jesus" or some form of "Jahweh", or in an event of sacred history. In all these cases, the symbol can be viewed as a sign in either of two ways: if it is a sign to be interpreted by a demon or other spirit, who serves as the agent effecting the magician's will, then symbolic manipulation turns into a form of conjuration; however, even within proper symbolic manipulation, the links between symbols (objects, words, ritual actions) and what they symbolized are conceived as intelligible and in that sense signifying. If a plant shaped like a liver is useful for healing the liver, it is in that sense a sign of what it is thought to affect, and the intelligible resemblance is what effects the healing. The magical power of symbolic manipulation may still not be automatic, but it is more nearly so than the power of conjuration. If conjuration is a reprobate branch of religion, symbolic manipulation claims an efficacy like that of science and will be seen by its practitioners as a type of science. The magician who manipulates symbolic links in the natural order might be thought of as tugging on invisible cords that link one level of that order with another. The symbolic links may be articulated in terms of cosmic correspondences or sympathies, at least in sources that provide theoretical grounding for magical practice. If the invisible cords are not thought of as efficacious symbolically, then the process is not magical; the user may not be told explicitly that symbolic links are entailed, and may simply be assured that the results are tried and proven, but in magical operations, the symbolic causality is at least implied by the types of word, ritual and object used.

As for "directly efficacious volition", the clearest example is cursing.[12] Threatening and cursing a neighbour may cause ill will, anxiety, high blood pressure, ill health and in the extreme case or the long run death. It counts as magical, however, only if someone – the magician, the victim, a neighbour, an inquisitor – thinks of the effect as more direct, as flowing directly from the will and its expression, without being mediated through external agencies and mechanisms.[13] This was the crux of Freud's understanding of magic as grounded in an infantile confusion of will with reality: the magician, like a child, supposes that willing something to happen can in itself make it happen, and such "magical thinking" in an adult is for a Freudian a form of neurosis.[14] Usually, the will seen as having this efficacy is one supported by vehement and even violent psychological energy. Typically, it is focused by becoming explicit, not only in the magician's mind but also in speech. Language is a vehicle of energies, positive and negative, and aggressive energy can be thought of as directly harming or coercing a victim. It may be difficult to distinguish between a curse that has inherent power and a threat that is *followed* by an act of magic. In principle, however, malediction is not just an expression but a tool of a malevolent will; whereas in conjuration the magician engages in a contest of wills with the spirit conjured, malediction is a weapon wielded by a malevolent will against an enemy.

Note, however, the asymmetry here: conjuration can be seen as either benevolent or malevolent (those who profess to conjure angels typically insist they are engaged in positive and even pious activity), and symbolic manipulation likewise can be used for health and healing as well as for affliction and coercion, but while there is no reason in principle why directly efficacious volition could be positive and still count as magical, it is malediction that is more often seen as magic. We would not usually speak of blessings or benedictions as magic, at least in traditional Western settings, perhaps mostly because Judaism and Christianity have conditioned us to think of them as mainstream ritual acts, but more deeply because wishing someone well is more of a social process typically integrated into all the expressions of sympathy and support that characterize a harmonious network of relationships.

What is it, then, that links these three phenomena? Usually, one would seek some shared feature or set of distributed characteristics as the defining factor or factors, either an essence or a family resemblance. It certainly would be possible to find characteristics typical of these three elements of magic: they are usually clandestine, worked for personal rather than public interest, and thus subject to distrust, condemnation and opposition. But much the same could be said of many other activities that would not be called magic, including political conspiracy and crime of various sorts. Nor do these characterizations point to what is most important in any of these elements of magic: the power of spirits brought into submission, the efficacy of symbolic networks within the order of nature and the role of language as a vehicle for negative energy. If conjuration, symbolic manipulation and malediction are all recognized as "magic", it is not because of shared features but for two other reasons. First, they have been thought of as activities to which the same sorts of individuals are inclined: "magic" is, in its original usage, the set of activities characteristic of "magoi" or mages, and that way of conceiving it persisted in medieval and post-medieval usage.[15] Second, they are mutually supportive and often found in combination. Symbolic associations are occult, and hidden within the order of nature, and they can be known (the argument goes) only because they have been taught by demons, with whom the magicians have at least an implicit agreement or pact. Conjuring and symbolic manipulation are connected not by shared characteristics but by the reliance of the latter on the former and vice versa. Spirits are conjured not only by verbal commands but also by symbolically effective rituals such as suffumigation with specific aromatic substances, or the sacrifice of particular animals. Symbolic actions such as breaking a candle or piercing an image can have efficacy in part because the action is accompanied by an incantation. Symbol is reinforced by malediction. And curses often draw upon symbolic associations as in the case of the blasphemous curse that invokes the pain of the Virgin in bearing Christ and projects that pain onto a victim. Conjuration, symbolic manipulation and malediction are in principle distinguishable, and none of them necessarily entails the others, but in fact they tend to be linked.

One difference between the terms "magic" and "mysticism" is that "magic" is a word used in the historic sources from antiquity onwards, used by opponents and sometimes also by practitioners, whereas "mysticism" is a seventeenth-century coinage, adapted from the adjective "mystical", and would not have been used by most of the figures recognized as mystics. The author of *The Cloud of Unknowing* would have known himself as a contemplative, not a mystic, but a thirteenth-century European could well have recognized himself as a magician practicing magic. A word invented by outsiders to the culture is not tied to the semantics of that culture, but when a word is taken from the culture being studied there is good reason to respect common usage within its original context. The anthropologist cannot tell the Polynesian how to use the term *mana*, and the historian of medieval Europe needs to know precisely how "magic" was used by medieval Europeans. Importing alien meanings alongside indigenous ones can only confuse.

But from antiquity onwards "magic" has in fact always been an aggregating term. It could refer to the various activities of the magoi, which might include star-gazing, fortune telling, healing and other activities viewed by outsiders as charlatanry. When Isidore of Seville gave his influential account of magic, he listed a long string of magical activities without ever indicating what essential feature constituted them all as magical.[16] In later medieval usage, "magic" could refer to the conjuring of demons or to the exploitation of occult powers within nature – but a third activity, the conjuring of angels, coexisted with the others, resembled demonic magic, and was conflated with the summoning of demons, but did not actually coincide with that form of magic.[17] And while "natural magic" could be defined as the exploitation of "occult" powers within nature, there was no single conception of what qualified these powers as occult: the term could mean simply little known, or known only through demonic instruction, or unknowable in terms of Aristotelian physics or unknowable from the study of the sublunary world alone. Precisely if we wish to be respectful of historical usage, it is important to recognize that "magic" has always been an aggregating rather than constitutive term, and "natural magic" has also been more an aggregating than a constitutive concept.[18]

My purpose, then, is not simply to rethink the definition of magic but to rethink *how* to define magic. We are best served, not by insisting on precise and carefully conceived definitions of magic, but by focusing our attention more on the specific definitions of those constitutive terms for which "magic" serves as an umbrella. This is not to dismiss the word "magic" as unimportant. Aggregating terms are vitally important, but as terms of convenience. They are best recognized as such, without the artificiality of precise definition that will always prove inadequate. From one culture to another and even within a culture, there will always be different constitutive terms brought together explicitly or (perhaps more often) by assumption under an aggregating term, adding to the imprecision of the term. An argument can be made for or against including astrology as a form of magic, although elements of astrology are clearly entailed in various forms of magic, most obviously the magical use of inscribed astrological images. It is harder to justify viewing alchemy as magic, but a history of magic must take it into account among the "occult sciences" imported from Arabic culture in the high medieval West.[19] As for the term "mysticism", I have given what some might see as an overly restrictive set of constitutive terms: some might wish to include certain forms of visions, even if they are not theoerotic, and some would emphasize links between paramystical phenomena such as the stigmata and what I take as the defining elements of mysticism. For comparative study as well, constitutive terms are more useful than the aggregating term "magic", even though different constitutive terms may be needed for the study of different periods and cultures. Whatever the terms required, a particular comparison will in any case be more finely tuned and useful for analysis than an inevitably commodious and imprecise catch-all category. The constitutive terms will always need to be reviewed and perhaps redefined in the light of particular circumstances, but that is a task more likely to be productive than refining the term "magic" itself.

I want here to steer between the Scylla of essential definition and the Charybdis of repudiating and avoiding broad terms. It is easy enough to show the perils of finding or inventing an "essence" of magic, religion or anything else. Persuaded by the arguments against essentialism, one may fall into the opposite trap of dismissing such terms altogether. Both extremes fail to recognize the utility of aggregating terms that do not pretend to the specificity and precision that we might more realistically expect in other forms of language. It might seem as though I am giving up on precision in defining magic, and embracing a counsel of despair. I would say that I am, rather, giving counsel of realism – that I am not giving up on the pursuit of clarity and precision, but suggesting they can be expected on the level of constitutive rather than aggregating terms.

My argument has perhaps obvious implications not only for defining but also for theorizing magic. Definitions of magic nearly always entail theories of magic: of how it works and how it relates to religion and to science.[20] Such theories, meant to apply to "magic" generally and across cultures, almost always apply better to some cultures and to some manifestations of magic than to others. A substantial part of the problem is that "magic" is too amorphous a concept to admit of rigorous theorizing. It is the constitutive terms that lend themselves to theoretical and comparative analysis. I am by no means anti-theoretical, but I maintain that theoretical work is more promising on a level that lends itself more towards specificity and rigour than on one where the fundamental terms are vague and highly connotative. Symbolic manipulation, directly efficacious volition, and perhaps also conjuration remain fruitful subjects for theoretical investigation, but attempting a theory of "magic" is a futile exercise, because the aggregating term means too much and thus too little.

One clarifying distinction must again be emphasized: the constitutive terms I am proposing refer not to distinct *types* of magic, but to individually sufficient *elements* that tend to combine. To say they are individually sufficient means that any of them by itself might be taken to qualify a practice as magical: conjuring a spirit is usually thought of as magic, even without symbolic manipulation or directly efficacious volition is involved, and so too any of the elements is recognizably magical even if it is not linked with the others. In practice, however, different elements of magic (like different elements of mysticism) do tend to become linked and mutually supportive. If it is pointless to make general statements about magic, as if they could apply to all magic, it is equally pointless to try to sort out distinct types or forms of magic, as if there were enforceable boundaries. Typologies are no more helpful than essences.

A second clarification is important. One might expect that if the constitutive terms can be given clear, precise and stable meaning, this precision would then transfer to aggregating term "magic" – that the clarity of the parts would be communicated to the whole that they constitute. The problem is that even if the constitutive terms can be given stable meaning in themselves, they are unstable in relationship to each other and to the aggregating term that encompasses them. In actual usage, historical and modern, different speakers and hearers, writers and readers, will have different sets of particulars in mind. I am proposing three constitutive terms under the category of magic, but others might offer or assume other constitutive terms alongside mine, or in place of them. Even if there were agreement about the constitutive terms, different contexts would make one or another of them salient, and they would become unpredictably conflated and confused. Furthermore, the strongly connotative character of the aggregating term, again both in historical and in modern usage, means it will tend to resist precise usage. Thus, even if precision can be sought, expected and developed on the level of constitutive terms, it cannot be expected for the aggregating term.

The resulting ambiguity is well illustrated by the complexities of astrological magic. The stars and planets could be seen as natural forces whose power is exploited in symbolic manipulation, but often they were associated or identified with spiritual beings that might be addressed in a way that shaded into conjuration. Even the planets themselves, identified with the deities for which they were named, were intelligences subject to what Nicolas Weill-Parot calls "addressative" magic.[21] Thus, the Arabic compilation taken over into Latin and known as *Picatrix* is a classic of symbolic manipulation, largely concerned with the exploitation of astral forces accessible in the sublunary realm, but in some passages these very forces are subject to conjuration. This is especially the case in Book 3, Chapter 7 of *Picatrix*, which describes the properties of the planetary deities, tells what requests can be made from each of them, then goes on to explain how each of them can be addressed, with ritual accompaniments that include animal sacrifice, personal adornment and enthronement, and especially suffumigation. The practitioner both beseeches and commands these planetary deities: the verbs are sometimes *rogo, invoco, peto* or *queso*, but most often *coniuro*. The conjuration is done by the power of the deities' names in various languages, by the names of God or of angels, by God himself or by angels assigned by God to aid these planetary beings. The requests are stated in generic form: "that you may at this very time and hour fulfill my petition," or some variant. The planetary spirits are not themselves asked to come down and make themselves present; they act at a distance, through unspecified means. In one case, however, the operator asks Mars to send a spirit to an enemy, to enter into his body and undermine all his members and powers. This chapter of *Picatrix* does not fuse symbolic manipulation with conjuration so much as it passes over from the one to the other, except that the symbolic properties of the planets are still presupposed, so that Mars and Venus, for example, serve the purposes they would tend to serve in any magic.[22]

A different form of ambiguity arises with angel magic, in which any boundaries between conjuration and prayer may become obscured. In the *Liber iuratus*, probably written in the early fourteenth century, not only evil but also good angels are straightforwardly conjured. Prayers are offered to God in a tone of humble and pious submission (as they may be even in explicitly demonic conjuration or necromancy), but the intent of those prayers is to gain power that can be used to command the spirits to come and do one's will. Certain formulas are addressed to angels of the planets, who are not equated with the planets or the deities for whom they are named, nor clearly identified as movers of celestial spheres,[23] but are associated with the planets in a manner that allows movement into the sublunary realm. They are at first humbly invoked and besought to descend and appear in benign form within the magic circles, but then immediately the magician says, "I therefore seal (*sigillo*), demand, invoke, and even conjure you, most holy angels, by the seals of God's most holy names, to obey my petitions," commanding them by the power of God. In the next formula, he says, "I humbly beseech and obediently command (*obedienter precipio*)" that they descend from their planetary spheres. Before long, he addresses these spirits and all those spirits and demons who serve them, with a string of verbs ("invoke," "call to witness," "command," "exorcize," "conjure," "constrain"), to come next to the circle, appear, respond, obey and fulfill his commands.[24] It is not only the tone of command that marks these formulas as conjurations, but also the conception of the spirits as capable of locomotion and thus subject to summons. Still, what is true of the *Liber iuratus* is not necessarily true of all angel magic, which may use some of the trappings of conjuration but still address the angels in terms of petition rather than command. One particularly fascinating example is the *Liber florum* by John of Morigny, which involves a kind of symbolic manipulation focused on a series of meditative figures, and also entails the ministration of angels – but one might say that this is a form of magic involving angels that is not in any ordinary sense angel magic.[25] The concept of conjuration remains clear, but its application to this particular practice is sometimes ambiguous – and the clarity of the concept actually highlights the ambiguity of the practice by holding up a mirror to its complexities. The situation is yet more complex in Cairo Genizah texts that identify the "holy angels" with the Hebrew letters and treat them as symbols to be used in magical operation, in which case conjuration and symbolic manipulation are so closely linked as to be virtually fused.[26]

Again a different sort of ambiguity is illustrated in fictional terms by Hans Wiers-Jenssen's play *Anne Pedersdotter*, on which Carl Dreyer's film *Day of Wrath* was based.[27] While the play and the film are loosely inspired by particular witch trials at Bergen, the psychological mechanism it depicts gives a plausible interpretation of how witch-hunting might work in any of the various cases. The title character wishes her much older husband dead, leaving her free to pursue romance with a younger man. When she gives expression to her desire, the shock in fact kills the husband. But social pressure compels her to see the efficacy of her will not in natural terms, nor even as a simple case of magical thinking, but rather as a sign that she is in league with the Devil. In the end, she confesses being a witch, but she is not shown forming a pact with the Devil, attending Sabbaths or engaging in any other activities one would expect of a witch. We are left with two possibilities: she could be invested by the Devil with the power of directly efficacious volition (presumably Anne's own interpretation), or her will could be a subtle and implicit means of conjuring a spirit who is the actual agent in the killing (the more likely view of those who see her exposed as a witch). In either case, the concepts of directly efficacious volition and conjuration remain in themselves clear, but the way they relate to each other is less so.

We have seen, then, natural magic that veers into conjuration, angel magic that takes on features sometimes of conjuration and sometimes of natural magic (if not simply of prayer) and directly efficacious volition linked with a variety of conjuration. In all these cases, it is possible to form definitions that are clear and adequate to the phenomena, but their application is sometimes straightforward and at other times more complex. There are cases of conjuration that conform to all the usual characteristics of that category without admixture of other magical elements, and likewise there are instances of symbolic manipulation and directly efficacious volition *simpliciter* – but often, perhaps more often than not, these terms provide vocabulary for analysing the different elements that go into a composite. By way of analogy, the distinct terms of a recipe in cooking are perfectly intelligible, even if some of the ingredients tend not to occur unmixed (few people would sit down to a meal consisting only of nutmeg), and so too the constitutive terms I am proposing can be defined with precision even if the phenomena they refer to often enter into combination and may at times be difficult to distinguish. This is an important part of what I am arguing about how constitutive terms work under an aggregating umbrella.

What, then, is magic? The term is difficult to define, but not because it refers to something so basic to experience we cannot back away to perceive contexts within which it might be analysed, or alternatives to which it might be compared, as is the case for a word such as "time". Rather, it is difficult mainly because we are so accustomed to thinking of it as a term different from what it usefully can be, expecting more of it than it can deliver, and forcing upon it a level of precision that belongs to a different kind of terminology.

Notes

1 I am grateful to the editors of this volume, to Barbara Newman and to Katelyn Mesler for their help in developing this article.
2 Richard Kieckhefer, "Mystical Experience and the Definition of Mysticism," in *The Comity and Grace of Method: Religious Studies for Edmund F. Perry*, ed. Thomas Ryba, George D. Bond and Herman Tull (Evanston, IL: Northwestern University Press, 2004), 198–234.
3 *The Cloud of Unknowing*, ed. James Walsh (Ramsey, NJ: Paulist Press, 1981).
4 Michael Casey, *Athirst for God: Spiritual Desire in Bernard of Clairvaux's Sermons on the Song of Songs* (Kalamazoo, MI: Cistercian Publications, 1988).
5 Bernard McGinn, *The Mystical Thought of Meister Eckhart: The Man from Whom God Hid Nothing* (New York: Crossroad, 2001).
6 St. Teresa of Avila, *The Interior Castle: Study Edition*, trans. Kieran Kavanaugh and Otilio Rodriguez (Washington, DC: ICS, 2010).
7 After writing this *article*, I realized my term "constitutive" might cause confusion, because Thomas Tweed, in *Crossing and Dwelling: A Theory of Religion* (Cambridge, MA: Harvard University Press, 2006), uses the same term in a different sense. For him, "Constitutive terms are those that constitute or mark the boundaries of a field of study" (p. 30). What I have in mind is not terms that indicate fields of inquiry but rather terms referring to usefully distinguished objects of inquiry. A scholarly discipline might well work with multiple constitutive terms, in my sense. My contention is that scholarly inquiry is properly constituted with reference to carefully framed constitutive terms,

rather than the aggregating terms that might seem to guide it. In some cases, including the study of religion, the terms used for fields of inquiry are what I would call aggregating rather than constitutive terms.
8 William James, *The Varieties of Religious Experience: A Study in Human Nature* (1902, reissued Harmondsworth: Penguin, 1982), lectures 16–17, 379–429.
9 Richard Kieckhefer, *Unquiet Souls: Fourteenth-Century Saints and Their Religious Milieu* (Chicago, IL: University of Chicago Press, 1984), 22–33; Margaret Smith, *Rāb'a the Mystic and Her Fellow Saints in Islam: Being the Life and Teachings of Rābi'a al-'Adawiyya Al-Qaysiyya of Basra Together with Some Account of the Place of the Women Saints in Islam* (Cambridge: Cambridge University Press, 1984); Robert Bly, *Mira Bai: Ecstatic Poems* (Boston, MA: Beacon, 2004).
10 S. Ansky [Solomon Rappoport], *The Dybbuk*, trans. Henry G. Alsberg and Winifred Katzin (New York: Boni & Liveright, 1926).
11 James George Frazer, *The Golden Bough: A Study in Magic and Religion* (reissued Oxford: Oxford University Press, 1997).
12 On cursing, see the classic discussion in Keith Thomas, *Religion and the Decline of Magic* (London: Weidenfeld & Nicolson, 1971), 502–12. The boundary between magical cursing and liturgical imprecation is problematized by Lester K. Little, *Benedictine Maledictions: Liturgical Cursing in Renaissance France* (Ithaca, NY: Cornell University Press, 1993).
13 The point is made in classic form by Marcel Mauss, *A General Theory of Magic*, trans. Robert Brain (London: Routledge & Kegan Paul, 1950; reissued London and New York: Routledge, 2001), 78: "Between a wish and its fulfilment there is, in magic, no gap." But of course this like most theoretical statements about magic applies to some but not all magical operations. The necromancer who conjures demons does not simply wish them present, but engages in complicated rituals presupposing an intense conflict of wills between the practitioner and the spirit, and symbolic manipulation too may entail complex mediation between the wish and its fulfilment. Note also that Mauss uses the term "element" in a sense different from mine, for aspects of magic that enter into his "general theory".
14 Ariel Glucklich, *The End of Magic* (New York: Oxford University Press, 2011), 32–33; George Serban, *The Tyranny of Magical Thinking* (New York: Dutton, 1982); Ellen Peel, "Psychoanalysis and the Uncanny," *Comparative Literature Studies*, 17 (1980): 410–17.
15 See the conception of mages discussed in Richard Kieckhefer, "Jacques Lefèvre d'Étaples and the Conception of Natural Magic," in *La magia nell'Europa moderna: tra antica sapienza e filosofia natural*, ed. Fabrizio Meroi and Elisabetta Scapparone (Florence: Olschki, 2007), 63–77.
16 For a survey of definitions, see Lynn Thorndike, "Some Medieval Conceptions of Magic," *The Monist*, 25 (1915): 107–39.
17 Richard Kieckhefer, "Angel Magic and the Cult of Angels in the Later Middle Ages," in *Contesting Orthodoxy in Medieval and Early Modern Europe: Heresy, Magic and Witchcraft*, ed. Louise Nyholm Kallestrup and Raisa Maria Toivo (London: Palgrave Macmillan, 2017), 71–110.
18 On medieval conceptions of natural magic, see now Nicolas Weill-Parot, *Points aveugles de la nature: la rationalité scientifique médiévale face à l'occulte, l'attraction magnétique et l'horreur du vide (XIIIe-milieu du XVe siècle)* (Paris: Les Belles Lettres, 2013).
19 Charles Burnett, *Magic and Divination in the Middle Ages: Texts and Techniques in the Islamic and Christian Worlds* (Aldershot: Variorum, 1996).
20 Stanley Jeyaraja Tambiah, *Magic, Science, Religion, and the Scope of Rationality* (New York: Cambridge University Press, 1990); Steven P. Marrone, *A History of Science, Magic and Belief from Medieval to Early Modern Europe* (New York: Palgrave Macmillan, 2015).
21 Nicolas Weill-Parot, "'Astrological Images' and the Concept of 'Addressative' Magic," in *The Metamorphosis of Magic from Late Antiquity to the Early Modern Period*, ed. Jan N. Bremmer and Jan R. Veenstra (Leuven: Peeters, 2002), 167–87, especially 169 ("A magical 'addressative' act can be defined as an act by means of which the magician addresses a sign to a separate intelligence (a demon, an angel or some other spirit or intelligence) in order to obtain its help to perform the magical operation") and 176 ("addressivity is the key concept for medieval theories of magic").
22 *Picatrix: The Latin Version of the Ghāyat Al-Hakīm*, ed. David Pingree (London: Warburg Institute, 1986), 112–35.
23 Joseph Bernard McAllister, *The Letter of Saint Thomas Aquinas De Occultis Operibus Naturae Ad Quemdam Militem Ultramontanum* (Washington, DC: Catholic University of America Press, 1939), 170–78.

24 *Liber iuratus Honorii: A Critical Edition of the Latin Version of the Sworn Book of Honorius*, ed. Gösta Hedegård (Stockholm: Almqvist & Wiksell, 2002), 121–39; further categories of spirit are similarly addressed on pp. 140–43. See also the angel conjuration in Robert Reynes, *The Commonplace Book of Robert Reynes of Acle: An Edition of Tanner MS 407*, ed. Cameron Louis (New York: Garland, 1980), no. 29, pp. 169–70, where the angels are commanded only after their arrival in a child's fingernail, and their summoning takes the form of a prayer addressed to Christ.

25 Claire Fanger, *Rewriting Magic: An Exegesis of the Visionary Autobiography of a Fourteenth-Century French Monk* (University Park: Pennsylvania State University Press, 2015), and John of Morigny, *Liber florum celestis doctrine, or Book of the Flowers of Heavenly Teaching: The New Compilation, with Independent Portions of the Old Compilation: An Edition and Commentary*, ed. Claire Fanger and Nicholas Watson (Toronto: Pontifical Institute of Mediaeval Studies, 2015).

26 See Elliot R. Wolfson, "Phantasmagoria: The Image of the Image in Jewish Magic from Late Antiquity to the Early Middle Ages," *Review of Rabbinic Judaism*, 4 (2001): 78–120 (here 111–12), an article rich in material that is useful for analysis in the terms I am proposing.

27 Hans Wiers-Jenssen, *Anne Pedersdotter: A Drama in Four Acts*, trans. John Masefield (Boston, MA: Little, Brown, 1917), later published as *The Witch: A Drama in Four Acts*; Carl Th. Dreyer, *Day of Wrath* (1943).

2
FOR MAGIC

Against method

Claire Fanger

In religious studies, it has become increasingly common to shy away from the use of "magic" as an analytical term in scholarly discourse. In his landmark essay, "Trading Places," Jonathan Z. Smith suggests that magic is a word without content, defined only privatively, i.e. in terms of what it is "deprived of" – what it is not. "Magic", he says, marks a "shadow reality known only by looking at the reflection of its opposite ('religion', 'science') in a distorting fun-house mirror".[1] In a similar vein, in recent studies of magic in a modern context, scholars have noted that what magic shadows is often the modern itself, so that in some writings "magic" almost becomes a shorthand for a particular *haunting* of the modern – its inverse, a marker for all that is non-modern.[2] If the word was in legitimate use in premodern cultures or modern countercultures, in contemporary academia, "magic" is treated by many as wholly off limits for use in discourses of scholarship, theory or methodology.

For medievalists, however, magic is, for various reasons, harder to see as an empty signifier, a mere shadow. While in the Middle Ages, the magic arts were denigrated as false knowledge or non-knowledge (as they still may be), or as demonic (a related accusation), at the same time *ars magica* and its analogues and subcategories (*sortilegium, nigromantia, geomantia* and the other mantic arts) are not empty of content. Nor do they line up neatly with orality or cultures (pagan or peasant) associated with orality. In fact, the *artes magicae* included specific knowledge disciplines, sometimes containing texts that were handled, copied, studied and in some cases authored by intellectuals. Magic was if anything a more intense concern in the learned environment than it was as a view of a pagan or peasant practice. If the lifeworlds of medieval people were different from ours, nevertheless their assessment of magic is very recognizable. Medievalists are thus in a privileged position to understand things about magic that modernists do not. Yet, even among medievalists, there can be observed a certain hesitation around the use of the term. An obeisance to its difficulty is often preliminary to discussions of its history, particularly for novice or student audiences (of which this forum may be seen as one example).

But surely we can make use of the medieval potential for seeing magic as something with an actual *knowledge content* to counter the increasingly prevalent idea that magic must be handled by academics only as a historical datum, something empty, dead and pinned to a card. What I would like to do here is enter a plea for learning to use the word "magic" again; I would like scholars to see the kind of distinctions the word allows as potentially useful rather than intrinsically foggy or oppressive. First, I will sketch the kinds of historical conversations I am interested in. I will then introduce selected short passages by medieval authors discussing magic and superstition and reinterpret them, with the aim of showing continuities between modern and medieval reasonings about magic, both positive and negative. In my conclusion, I will argue for a freer and easier use of the term "magic" – a use less constrained by the tired dogma of its extreme difficulty.

In studying medieval magic, I am always interested in the problem it posed (and continues to pose) for people who think about it. This has been true since long before I paid attention to Foucault, but it aligns very well with many things Foucault has written about the role of problematization in what he calls the "history of thought". "Problematization", Foucault has said, is "the set of discursive or non-discursive practices that makes something enter into the play of the true and false, and constitutes it as an object for thought (whether under the form of moral reflection, scientific knowledge, political analysis, etc.)".[3] So I am interested in magic when it becomes a topic of reflection, when it enters into the play of true and false. I am interested in how its actual practices colour the judgements that get made about it, positive and negative, and how discursive judgements get pulled back into the practices themselves. When I write about it, my concern is never exclusively the plus nor minus side of the equation, but the whole ball of wax: the theological, philosophical, liturgical, rhetorical and pragmatic elements involved in crafting the knowing of magic, constituting it as a problem for knowledge and ethics.

When writing about magic, I like to emphasize that the medieval anti-magical and pro-magical arguments are part of the same conversation: the composition and rewriting of magic texts are done in awareness of, and often in response to, engagements with the discursive formations that condemn them. All the texts routinely brought up in the histories of medieval magic, from the writings of Augustine, Thomas Aquinas and the *Speculum astronomie* on the one hand, to the *Ars notoria*, the *Sworn Book*, Montolmo's *Liber Intelligentiarum* and the *Summa sacre magice* on the other, can be seen as engagements with the problem in the sense I am indicating. Works like Roger Bacon's *Opus Maius* and John of Morigny's *Liber florum* tread a complex ground between full acceptance and full condemnation, and are also part of the conversation. I use the word "conversation" to underscore that it is not merely a set of polemics.

The other thing I like to emphasize is that these are learned engagements constituted within a single social and administrative order. For this reason, in the kinds of work I mostly look at, the notion of magic as a word used by colonializing societies to subjugate subaltern religion is out of place. It is also out of place to think in terms of class struggle. To say that magic is contested turf, ritually, ethically and epistemologically is not the same as saying its use reveals systematic subjugation. Proponents and derogators of intellectual magic texts are in the same social order, sharing and reading the same books.

I present below four brief case studies, representing a range of medieval thoughts about magic, to show how it is constituted as irrational in premodern contexts, and also to show the esoteric thought that tends to come into play when it is appropriated as a positive category. In some cases, allied or contiguous terms are present alongside or instead of the word magic, including superstition (*superstitio*), sorcery (*sortilegium*) and necromancy (*nigromantia*). Various forms of divination (*divinatio, mantike*, distinguished from prophecy) also traditionally come under the heading in medieval discourses.

Augustine: magic as a mistake in thinking (non-knowledge; wrong science)

I begin with Augustine since he is so obviously important as a touchstone for thinking about magic, sign theory and natural causality through the Middle Ages. Beyond this, Augustine's distinctions have an elegant simplicity that merit appreciation. Getting down to the basic moving parts of the Augustinian theory shows the lineaments of an idea transferable across various discursive fields and boundaries.

Augustine grounds his address to magic in a discussion of superstition. In *De doctrina Christiana*, Augustine begins with a treatment of sign theory that posits that there is no necessary connection between a sign and its meaning, and that a sign in itself cannot cause change in the world. His examples of superstitions in the *De doctrina Christiana* are very recognizable; I quote only part of the list (omitting the jokes mocking the stupidity of superstitious persons). He characterizes superstitions as "frivolous practices", including,

> to tread upon the threshold when you go out in front of the house; to go back to bed if any one should sneeze when you are putting on your slippers; to return home if you stumble when going to a place; when your clothes are eaten by mice, to be more frightened at the prospect of coming misfortune than grieved by your present loss.[4]

Superstitions, then, are random behaviours believed to promote good or ill luck, ungrounded in any theory of natural causation and unmoored from any legible system (religious, linguistic or philosophical). They point neither to exotic intrusions from persons outside the social order (like the "gods" of other cultures, things that would make sense in their own cultural domain).[5]

They do not equate to the idolatry of a pagan "other"; indeed, they are not rooted in any cultural context at all. The examples he gives of superstitions are exactly the kinds of things we would consider superstitious now, and for the same reasons.

Magical signs share with superstitions the quality of being signs that have drifted free from any mooring in human communication. However, they are more complicated than superstitions because they are not always so clearly unconnected to accepted domains of knowledge. Even so, the index of magicality, for Augustine, remains fundamentally similar to the index of superstition: it is the presence of signs that cannot possibly do what they claim to do by the powers they claim to use:

> In this class we must place also all amulets and cures which the medical art condemns, whether these consist in incantations, or in marks which they call characters, or in hanging or tying on or even dancing in a fashion certain articles, not with reference to the condition of the body, but to certain signs hidden or manifest.[6]

The signs interpreted in all forms of divination including astrology are also similarly "unmoored", though astrology requires a longer dismissal because astrological signs are embedded in a system that appeared (to many people in Augustine's intellectual milieu if not to Augustine himself) to make sense, and thus had to be unveiled as an arbitrary human construction. Following a euhemeristic theory of the pagan gods (itself a pagan invention, but one that attracted many Christian apologists), he points out that until humans ascribed them, stars and planets had no names or qualities. Their names and qualities are obviously cultural products rather than natural ones; thus, what is "read" by astrologers in their charts are all qualities of human attribution, whose institution was governed by sociopolitical processes, the desire of the powerful to enshrine themselves in the heavens. Even while the *fact* of stellar rays may be granted by Augustine, he does not grant that the *attributed names and qualities* reflect real natural powers; there can be no causal connection between the star's names and attributes and the natural events it supposedly influences. Astrology, like other divinatory sciences comprising the traditional magic arts, like all superstition, is thus rendered as a kind of fake knowledge or non-knowledge.

Picatrix: magic as higher knowledge (esotericism)

Composed in Arabic and translated into Latin in the mid-thirteenth century, an apologia for magic opens the compendium of magical writings that circulated in Latin under the title *Picatrix*, whose Arabic title, *Ghāyat al-Ḥakīm*, is usually translated *Goal of the Wise*. I bring up *Picatrix* because the positive attitude to magic expressed in it is evident in many other texts in the image magic tradition.[7] The kind of thinking represented here is almost as important as Augustine's in understanding what magic meant to Thomas Aquinas. The generic word for magic in *Picatrix* is translated from Arabic to Latin as *nigromantia* though the positive valence of the word in *Picatrix* is clear.[8] The prologue to *Picatrix* lays out the terms:

> Oh you who desire to turn your attention to philosophical types of knowledge, and to know and see into their secrets, first seek out the great marvels of art which they have put in their books; turn your attention to the marvels of the science of *nigromantia*. Moreover you should know first off that philosophers hid this knowledge and were unable to disclose it to men; nay rather they veiled it so far as they could, and with hidden words they covered up whatever they said about it with signs and resemblances as if they spoke of other kinds of knowledge .... because if this knowledge were disclosed to human beings, they would confound the universe. And so they spoke figurally about it.[9]

Here, magic is definitely a *kind of knowledge* (not a mistake in thinking, or a non-knowledge as in Augustine). It is something philosophers actually need to know. However, it is equally definitely *not normal knowledge*; it is cast as something hidden, powerfully effective, but difficult to understand and intrinsically obscure as to its causal mechanism. Later in the chapter, the use of *nigromantia* is delimited thus: "generally we use the word *nigromantia* for all things hidden from sense, and which the greater part of men do not grasp how they are done nor the causes from which they come".[10] In this mystery around the causal mechanism, we see an index of magic that actually bears a close similarity to Augustine's: the causal structure of magical effects is not only *not evident*, but it is in fact *hidden*, though this attribute is necessary as its mode of causality is too dangerous to be widely revealed.

In *Picatrix* and texts in allied traditions of image magic, we have a presentation that, while positive, gives magic a position on the very edge of the order of knowledge. To be clear, the procedures and processes it advocates have a knowable content, a learnable praxis, some of which (notably the parts connected to astrology, Augustine's bête noir) seem connected to known domains of knowledge; but the exact mechanisms by which talismans operate are concealed. Thus, one might say that in *Picatrix*, magic is recognizable by the same index of causal hiddenness evident in Augustine, but the attitude towards it has been flipped. Augustine and the compiler of *Picatrix* would have recognized one another's attitude.

Thomas Aquinas: magic as wrong religion

Thomas follows Augustine in discussing magic in the category of superstition, under the broader category of vices antithetical to the virtue of justice, but his distinctions are further refined. According to Thomas "superstition is contrary to religion by excess ... because it offers divine worship either to whom it ought not, or in a manner it ought not".[11] Thomas breaks magic down into subcategories according to how its specific practices relate to religion:

> The species of superstition are differentiated, first on the part of the mode, secondly on the part of the object. For the divine worship may be given either to whom it ought to be given, namely, to the true God, but "in an undue mode," and this is the first species of superstition; or to whom it ought not to be given, namely, to any creature whatsoever, and this is another genus of superstition .... the first species of this genus is "idolatry," which unduly gives divine honor to a creature. The second end of religion is that man may be taught by God Whom he worships; and to this must be referred "divinatory" superstition .... Thirdly, the end of divine worship is a certain direction of human acts according to the precepts of God the object of that worship: and to this must be referred the superstition of certain "observances."[12]

In essence, Thomas holds that magic is a set of forms of behaviour or devotional kinds of activity ("observances") that either fail to recognize the true God, or engage ritual acts that are misdirected or inappropriate. In Figure 2.1, I schematize some of the surrounding material that comes up near this locus in the *Summa Theologiae* to show examples of the types of magical practices Thomas is thinking of. In the third subdivision of superstitious error, he is clearly targeting the use of amulets condemned by Augustine, which ties, for him, explicitly into image magic, and another contemporary practice often condemned as magic (though it does not call itself by that name), the *Ars notoria*.

Forms of Superstition in *Summa Theologiae* (General heading: *Virtues*: Sub-heading: *Justice* Superstition opposes Justice through errors of excess)			
Error in mode or means of worship:	**Error in object or ends of worship:**		
worship of true God in undue mode; hypocrisy; to use "in the time of grace ... the rite of the old law" (unclear if he thinks here of Jews or judaizing Christians, perhaps both)	1. *worshipping* not God but creature (i.e. idolatry).	2. *seeking teaching* not from God but creature (i.e. in divination, including *sortes*, or controlled randomization, and *nigromantia*, or demon summoning)	3. *orienting behavior* not to God (in rites not properly Christian or Christian but ill thought out, including use of amulets as in image magic; the *Ars notoria*)

Figure 2.1 Forms of superstition in the *Summa Theologiae*.

It is clear from his account that Thomas is aware of various forms of divination and necromancy (item 2), and separates out from these both the *Ars notoria* and image magic texts (item 3). He devotes an article to the *Ars notoria*, and he was well aware that it does not claim to be magic, does not invoke demons and declares for itself the highest Christian goals; about image magic, he makes an explicit distinction between image magic and *nigromantia*. He is not here suggesting that the users of astrological images are deliberately trying to summon demons but understands a dividing line between types of images.[13] The benign type of images is included in the third category of superstition for a reason that has to do with the etiquette, so to speak, of the treatment of the sacred. Pairing benign image magic with the *Ars notoria*, Thomas sees both practices as involving a recognition of the true God (such practices are not idolatrous), but an error in the manner of approach. The ritual behaviour relating the human to God has something wrong with it. Expressively, these types of ritual confuse or mystify, rather than clarify, the appropriate relation between divine and human things. One might say it is their very esotericism that he reacts to as theologically pernicious.

John of Morigny's *Liber florum*: sacramental magic, or the theurgic problem

John of Morigny was a Benedictine active in the early fourteenth century whose *Flowers of Heavenly Teaching* comprises a set of prayers for obtaining knowledge, partly delivered by and partly a homage to the virgin Mary, interwoven with a compelling visionary autobiography. He never advocates magic, though he engages with it extensively. He acknowledges copying a book of necromancy, finding and engaging the *Ars notoria* in a sustained way before giving it up, practicing with known texts of necromantic magic, including one called *The Four Rings of Solomon*, and writing a "new necromancy" of his own, before giving that practice up as well.

Unlike the authors just treated, John does not explain or define what magic is nor offer a lineage for it; yet, he is deeply embedded in writings that do this, both magical and ecclesiastical. His own writings are not represented as magic, but a path away from the error it represents to a conversion of life, written for others in the process of resisting the same temptations. Like Thomas Aquinas, John sees magic as a problem of religion and knowledge and the ethics of thinking and knowing; more than this, for John, magic is a problem of self-formation. He learns to eschew what it stands for, but his path through it is by no means straight and narrow just because he condemns it. In fact, he clearly (and in the case of the *Ars notoria* explicitly) relies on texts he understands as problematically magical to construct his own antidote to it in the *Liber florum*. The ambiguity of magic as a marker of unstable knowledge is thus not diminished but enhanced by the depth of John's experience with it.

Many passages could be chosen from John's *Flowers* that highlight this, but I here quote from his first description of the book that led him astray in the beginning, the *Ars notoria*. In a nutshell, the problem with *Ars notoria* is that it claims to be – and from various angles appears to be – a path or ladder to God, something of divine institution that offers a route to the knowledge of Paradise – but in fact it is a fake. John describes a copy of the *Ars notoria*:

> Now this book, the *Ars notoria*, at first glance (that is outwardly) seems to be of all books the most beautiful and useful and even the most holy ... and through it almighty God promises to operators and bestows on them in a brief time the acquisition of all the sciences of scripture and the arts. In it are prayers holy and wondrous, and figures whose mystery, as it says therein, is rather a miracle than a normal

exemplar of eruditon. O cunning of the ancient serpent! O frenzy of the wicked lion, circling and seeking someone to devour! ... By it are all evils compounded. What more is there to say? That it is not possible without it to accomplish anything in necromancy. In fact, inasmuch as it is the more subtle, it is the more deceptive. It is composed in five tongues – Greek, Latin, Hebrew, Chaldean, and Arabic – in such a way that it cannot be understood or expounded by anyone, and the more it is studied, the more obscure it becomes.[14]

John does not call the *Ars notoria* magic, but it is clear that it is in the same family of knowledge objects by the comparison with necromancy. John makes the case against the *Ars notoria* via its dangerous ambiguity: the *Ars notoria* appears beautiful and useful, even "most holy" but this holy appearance is part of its temptation. If magic is categorized as sham knowledge by Augustine, and sham religion by Thomas Aquinas, the *Ars notoria* is the epitome of sham, not because it is obviously done by demons, but for the reverse reason: it looks and feels and smells sacred; but it is not. Yet, if we believe John's story, it has powerful effects; it *does* work to obtain visions that appear to be, and sometimes really are, shot through with divine messages. It *does* work to teach the liberal arts and to obtain other kinds of knowledge. This does not argue for its goodness; in fact, John says, it is worse than necromancy because it is more "subtle", made of good and true things interwoven with diabolic temptations. It only gets worse with expertise; "the more it is studied, the more obscure it becomes."[15] In seeing the *Ars notoria* as primarily a ritual error (not an idolatrous practice, but a ritual aimed at the correct object that errs in its protocols), John's condemnation is akin to Thomas Aquinas's.

But this condemnation is complicated. The rejection of magical knowledge that he achieves is not just the beginning of his own redemption; it is also the rescue of the sacramental promise of the *Ars notoria* as John attempts to correct the alignment by clarifying the ritual. The knowledge he finds through repentance, self-examination and consultation with the Virgin Mary takes the form of another book – his own book, the *Flowers of Heavenly Teaching* – that yields a true sacred knowledge to the initiate. In part because of the peculiarities of John's past, in part because of the intrinsic ambiguity of all things on the edge of the order of knowledge, his book may look like magic to some critics, but is cast by him as something different: a properly attuned heavenly and not worldly form of knowing.[16]

Magic, ambiguity and the history of thought

To note that John's condemnation of magic is complicated is not the same as saying his views are unclear; it is only to point out that thought is required to understand them. If we take magic as a particular kind of problem, it becomes available to thought in ways that it will always resist if it is assumed to be a narrow rigid grid ("belief in demons" versus "occult natural powers"). To sketch a few lines around the problem as I have tried to render it visible here, magic (and its related and analogous terms) indicates, among other things, a difficulty around the articulation of causality in the production of certain phenomena: whether the powers involved are seen as beneficially mystical or decried as evil or fake, they share an opacity of causal structure.[17] (This is not the only line one can draw through these materials, but I maintain it because of its utility in tying medieval rationalities to our own.)

In medieval Christian terms, divine causality (miraculous or sacramental causality) is equally opaque and therefore needs to be theologically justified and carefully delimited, confined (where possible) to one incarnation, seven sacraments and a channel of holy power stretching into the ecclesiastical hierarchy from the apostles. As soon as it starts to manifest too often, or to become too available outside the normal structures meant to contain it, it must be examined, proved or disproved, pushed back to be more clearly distinguished from the profane. In practice, though, it is hard to keep the idea of divine causality constrained within its best-case theological limits. As we see in the oeuvre of John of Morigny and other late medieval theurgic texts, it tends to keep escaping into the world, in part because the creation of the world itself is a sacramental institution that maps onto Christ's body. Where the divine escapes to manifestation, there will be a temptation for some people to see its effects as magical (whether or not its operators see it that way themselves) because of the ways its cause eludes discursive reasoning, remaining secret, unknowable, a mystery.

Demonic action, in this picture, was less a necessary presupposition for "belief" in magic, than a hypothesis concerning the obscure cause of magical action where it could not be seen as divine. In the Augustinian logic that influences later anti-magical discourse, it was a given that magical signs could not do what they claimed by the powers they claimed to use. If signs had an effect in the world, such effects suggested intentional intervention. They might be achieved by sleight of hand, or because the meaningless signs were actually meaningful to invisible demons. But since demonic action was usually hidden or invisible itself, it was also difficult to prove. If the suspect action had no harm in it, it was always possible to posit a divine or natural cause.

Many positive versions of "magic" or extraordinary sacramentality could thus make plausible claims for their own legitimacy, and positivized uses of the word "magic" as well as non-standard Christian rituals claiming divine delivery or sacramental status continued to proliferate. Through all of these conversations, in both positive and negative instances, the emergence of talk about magic and its cognate and analogue terms tends to mark a place of insecurity or instability. Magic crops up where something causes a problem with canonical knowledge patterns or content, or where a particular philosophical claim or liturgical usage seems to offend logic, theological propriety or common sense. Because the central orthodoxies of the proper order of knowledge are always shifting, the places where magical conversations emerge may be seen to resemble a water boundary, moving with the tides and rain. This feature of the conversation surrounding magic is interesting to me because it reveals certain properties – one might say the fluid nature – of knowledge itself.

In the same article by Jonathan Z. Smith that I cited in the beginning of this essay, Smith suggests that there is little merit in continuing the use of the substantive term "magic" in second-order, theoretical academic discourse, among other reasons because

> we have better and more precise scholarly taxa for each of the phenomena commonly denoted by "magic" which, among other benefits, create more useful categories for comparison. For any culture I am familiar with, we can trade places between the corpus of materials conventionally labeled "magical" and corpora designated by other generic terms (e.g. healing, divining, execrative) with no cognitive loss.[18]

But while I concede the benefits of using these taxa for comparative purposes, it seems plain to me that the excision of "magic" from our scholarly/theoretical discourse does entail a cognitive loss; for *the problem itself* is lost in any attempt to reduce magic to any specific set of instantiations, theories, practices or technologies. I find this to be a difficulty with all lines of thought, which, following Smith, suggests that "magic" can be eschewed as a scholarly category because it is ambiguous, value-laden or insufficiently neutral.[19]

The fact that magic is an inherently ambiguous and polyvalent term – even a *Kampfbegriff* – does not actually make it different from any other large abstract terms we use for carving up reality into manageable pieces in order to talk about them. It is a distorting premise to posit that scholars should only be allowed unambiguous terms, or that losing the *Kampfbegriffe* would enable a clean, neutral kind of language that would mean no further sullying ourselves by tumbling in the mud of the fields of discourse. This is a pipe dream. Indeed, if actually applied, the demand for non-ambiguous language in history would rule out nearly everything we use to talk about history with (including, but not limited to, terms like "science", "religion", "medieval", "modern", "Western", "culture" and so forth).

The idea that we need large, abstract and necessarily ambiguous terms to make reality manageable in conversation is consistent with the arguments of Paul Feyerabend, whose last (unfinished) work, *Conquest of Abundance*, offers possible ways of thinking about ambiguity as a fruitful and necessary part of the apprehension of reality (at least if the large abstractions are not reified by taking them too seriously). His argument is too complex to do justice to here; however, Chapter 1 concludes with these preliminary propositions about human knowing:

> (1) that completely closed cultures (conceptual systems) do not exist; (2) that the openness of cultures is connected with an inherent ambiguity of thought, perception, and action…; (3) that the ambiguity can be mobilized by feelings, visions, social pressures, and other nonlinguistic agencies; (4) that these agencies have structure, they can "pressure us to conform with them" …; (5) that argument has power only insofar as it conforms to nonargumentative pressures; (6) that a reality that is accessible to humans is as open and as ambiguous as the surrounding culture and becomes well defined only when the culture fossilizes….[20]

The suggestion that magic should be eschewed as an "etic" term is in a sense to demand that it only appears to us as fossilized in cultures that have already died. But it is obviously not realistic to suggest that we will understand the past better if we refuse for ourselves the terminology by which the past understood itself. Large abstract terms (like "magic" or "mysticism", "science" or "religion") can only serve us productively when they are allowed a certain natural movement. This is not to say that no one should define "magic" in a specific way to make it contextually available for a particular discussion; it is only to say that its ambiguity is a function of its broad reach, part of its life in the language. Magic is certainly not a special problem of modernity (which is far from being the only era that has ever claimed to have "real knowledge"). Surely it is arrogance to imagine that it is only in our own time that people are capable of seeing a *difficulty* when startling effects are claimed for apparently ritualistic actions worked by no known natural or divine rules.

In many respects, those who study the premodern world are best positioned to understand the potentialities inherent in the term "magic" – its distinctions, rationalizations and cues for use. But whatever the time period or geographical area we actually make the object of our study, I suggest that we cannot afford to treat "magic" as something that once had a stability that it has but lately lost. Knowledge is essentially fluid, and has always been so. I thus propose abandoning methodological reflection, defining the word as it suits us – or not – and moving on. Language is a river. It is more efficient to learn to ride the rapids than to portage round them.

Notes

1 Jonathan Z. Smith, "Trading Places," in *Relating Religion*, ed. Jonathan Z. Smith (Chicago, IL: University of Chicago Press, 2004), 218.
2 For example, *Magic and Modernity*, ed. Birgit Meyer and Peter Pels (Stanford, CA: Stanford University Press, 2003); "haunting" occurs on pp. 30, 79, 127, 203, 216. See also Randall Styers, *Making Magic* (Oxford: Oxford University Press, 2004). A push back against this tendency to isolate and stigmatize the term is evident in writing by Michael Taussig, who engages freely with all the available valences of magic in his writings; see, e.g. his essay "Viscerality, Faith, and Skepticism: Another theory of magic," in *Magic and Modernity*, ed. Meyer and Pels, 272–306. A use of "magic" at the opposite end of the spectrum, engaging it as an empty colonialist construct with no utility but subjugation, is evident in the essay by Margaret J. Weiner, "Hidden Forces: Colonialism and the Politics of Magic in the Netherlands Indies," in *Magic and Modernity*, ed. Meyer and Pels, 129–58.
3 Foucault, from interview, "The Concern for Truth," in *Michel Foucault: Politics, Philosophy, Culture*, ed. L.D. Kritzman, trans. A Sheridan (Abingdon: Routledge, 1988), 257. A cognate approach to modern esotericism is seen in Egil Asprem, *The Problem of Disenchantment* (Leiden: Brill, 2014), hiving off methodological suggestions in Kocku von Stuckrad, *Locations of Knowledge* (Leiden: Brill, 2010).
4 Augustine, *On Christian Doctrine* II.xx.30, ed. Marcus Dods, trans. J.F. Shaw, in *The Works of St. Augustine*, vol IX (Edinburgh: T & T Clark, 1873), 56–57.
5 Augustine is aware that "gods" in the Greek neoplatonic context are not equivalent to demons in their own domain, that is, he is aware that the neoplatonists regard them as he regards angels. The idea that in commerce with them demons are invoked requires a complex argument; see *City of God* 10.9. For discussion of Augustine's understanding of magic and its later influence, see Claire Fanger, "Magic," in *The Oxford Guide to the Historical Reception of Augustine*, ed. Willemien Otten, et al. (Oxford: Oxford University Press, 2013), 860–65.
6 Augustine, *On Christian Doctrine*, p. 56.
7 For an overview that usefully identifies key features of the image magic genre, see Chapter 4 in Sophie Page, *Magic in the Cloister* (University Park: Pennsylvania State University Press, 2013).
8 "Nigromantia" is called in to translate the Arabic "*siḥr*", a term condemned in Qu'ran 2:102 as a form of knowledge taught by deceptive demons. Though often condemned, *siḥr* also covered a variety of specific and defensible types of knowledge; for wider context, see Charles Burnett, "Talismans: Magic as Science? Necromancy among the Seven Liberal Arts," in Charles Burnett, *Magic and Divination in the Middle Ages* (Aldershot: Variorum, 1996). Qu'ran 2:102 becomes a focal point for distinctions about magic in later commentaries; see, e.g. al-Tabari, *Jami` al-bayan `an ta`wil ayy al-Qur'an*, vol. 1 (Beirut: Dar Ihya al-Turath al-`Arabi, n.d.), 515ff (commentary to Qur'an 2:102) and al-Baqillani, *Kitab al-bayan `an al-farq bayna al-mu`jizat wa-l-karamat wa-l-hiyal wa-l-kihana wa-l-sihr wa-l-narnajat* (Beirut: Dar al-Mashriq, 1958), 91ff. (I thank David Cook for these references.) In *Picatrix*, then, *siḥr* is being upheld as positive in a specific context; it is not a word always or necessarily positive in the Arabic culture where it is at home.
9 *Picatrix: The Latin Version of the Ghāyat al-Ḥakīm*, ed. David Pingree (London: Warburg Institute, 1986), ch. 2, p. 5; translation mine.
10 *Picatrix*, ed. Pingree, ch. 2, p. 5.
11 IIa IIae, Q 92. Art. 1, response. *The Summa Theologica of St Thomas Aquinas*, 2nd edition, 1920, trans. Fathers of the English Dominican Province, online edition 2008 by Kevin Knight, www.newadvent.org/summa/.
12 Thomas Aquinas, *Summa Theologica*, IIa IIae, Q 92, Art. 2, response.
13 "Astronomical images" he writes "differ from necromantic images in this, that the latter include certain explicit invocations and trickery, wherefore they come under the head of explicit agreements made with the demons." Thomas Aquinas, *Summa Theologica*, IIa IIae, Q 92, Art. 2, response to objection 2.
14 John of Morigny, *Flowers of Heavenly Teaching*, ed. Claire Fanger and Nicholas Watson (Toronto: Pontifical Institute of Mediaeval Studies, 2015). I.i.3.
15 John of Morigny, *Flowers of Heavenly Teaching*, I.i.3.
16 For a fuller account of John's magical journey, see Claire Fanger, *Rewriting Magic: An Exegesis of the Visionary Autobiography of a Fourteenth-Century French Monk* (Pennsylvania, PA: State University Press, 2015).

17 Cf Asprem's use of the term "capricious agency," *Problem of Disenchantment*, 551.
18 Smith, "Trading Places," 218.
19 For example, Wouter Hanegraaff writes, citing Smith among others, that the terms "superstition" and "magic" are "wholly unsuitable as neutral instruments in scholarly interpretation: they belong to the category of value judgments and political *Kampfbegriffe* (battle concepts), not of valid 'etic' terminology." Wouter Hanegraaff, *Esotericism and the Academy* (Cambridge: Cambridge University Press, 2012), 157.
20 Paul Feyerabend, *Conquest of Abundance: A Tale of Abstraction versus the Richness of Being* (Chicago, IL: University of Chicago Press, 2001), 78.

3

A DISCOURSE HISTORICAL APPROACH TOWARDS MEDIEVAL LEARNED MAGIC

Bernd-Christian Otto

This chapter proposes a discourse historical approach towards medieval learned magic and is divided into two sections. In the first section entitled "Clarifying terminology", I will introduce some technical terminology that may be helpful for understanding the approach proposed here. In the second section entitled "Magic as a discursive concept" said terminology is applied to the study of medieval learned magic. The main argument of this chapter is that it is possible and indeed helpful to investigate medieval learned magic without adopting second-order definitions of magic; in contrast, magic should be understood and used as a discursive concept in medieval studies.

Clarifying terminology

Before outlining the approach proposed in this chapter in greater detail, it may be sensible to introduce some technical terminology that will facilitate its understanding. Namely, I will discuss the distinction between first-order, second-order and third-order scholarly concepts; the so-called insider/outsider problem in the study of religion (and/or magic); and, finally, the concomitant differentiation between emic and etic scholarly analyses.

The most important theoretical distinction on which the present approach relies is the distinction between first-order, second-order and third-order concepts. The terms first-order and second-order have originally been applied in philosophical logic, where second-order logic has usually referred to an enhanced set of predicate symbols.[1] Over the course of the past decades, these terms have been taken up by scholars of religion and often employed – yet, with a somewhat translocated meaning – in the ongoing debate about the concept of religion. The sociologist of religion James A. Beckford, for example, has claimed that religion is a "second-order concept. It is an observer's construction that is supposedly based on the first-order beliefs, practices and experiences of human actors".[2] His main argument is that whereas social actors may or may not subsume their actions and beliefs under the term "religion" (which would then represent a first-order use of the term), scholars may nonetheless adopt a – supposedly more clearly defined – concept of religion while analysing these actors (this would then represent its second-order use). Accordingly, Beckford insists "on a clear conceptual distinction between first-order and second-order notions of religion".[3] The idea that social actors (that is, the objects of scholarly research) use first-order language, whereas scholars use second-order language to analyse these actors (such as comparative categories or taxonomies), has become an established pattern of argumentation in the ongoing debate on the concept of religion.[4] Some scholars have used the distinction with a different meaning which shall not interest us here[5] but Russel T. McCutcheon's addition of a third level of reflection which he calls "third-order category of redescription"[6] is nonetheless noteworthy (as it could be applied to the tendency of scholarly debates in the humanities to become increasingly abstract, up to the degree of being completely detached from any real-life "data" – this has often happened in the debate on magic).

In this chapter, I suggest that the distinction between first-order and second-order language should be implemented more systematically in the study of medieval learned magic. I will thus argue that the use of the term magic *within* medieval sources should be referred to as first-order, whereas its second-order use refers to the application of the concept of magic by modern scholars who investigate these (or other) sources. A third-order use of the concept of magic may refer to its eventual generalization and universalization, for example when scholars (such as medievalists) move beyond their particular corpus of sources and engage in interdisciplinary debates on whether magic is a human universal or not. As will be argued below in greater detail, both second-order and third-order talk on magic entail, in my view, a range of basic methodological difficulties and should be avoided on principle.

Related to the differentiation of first-order and second-order language is the so-called "insider/outsider-problem", which has been a major point of discussion in the study of religion over the past years.[7] The main argument here is that believers and/or practitioners of a particular religious tradition (who may be considered "insiders") tend to speak very differently about their tradition than adherents of other (for example "competing") religious traditions or further "outsiders" to the tradition in question.[8] Seen from this perspective, scholars of religion are necessarily "outsiders" to their objects of study, even when they have acquired substantial insider knowledge (for example by reading primary sources or conducting interviews). This may also be due to their use of second-order language which is often considerably different from the first-order language used by the "insiders" of a given tradition.

With regard to medieval learned magic, this distinction is useful as it points to the necessity of distinguishing two very different medieval discourses about magic which could be called insider and outsider discourse. The first may refer to medieval ritual texts that have been written, copied or used by practitioners (or theoreticians) of the art who have, in fact, often applied the first-order concept of magic to refer to themselves or the rituals described or theorized in these texts.[9] The second may refer to medieval sources that have spread and advocated polemics against such insider texts or against magic in general (elsewhere, I have used the analytical terms "discourse of inclusion" for insider sources, and "discourse of exclusion" for polemical outsider literature).[10] This distinction is, by now, fairly established in medieval studies (and it also underlies the rationale of the present volume) and is applied more and more frequently in other historical contexts and disciplines, too.[11] Note that both medieval insider and outsider sources are on the level of first-order language, as both make frequent use of the Latin term "magia" and/or established medieval synonyms of that term (for example "necromantia", "nigromantia").

The distinction between emic and etic approaches is directly related to the differentiation of first-order and second-order categories and the "insider/outsider-problem". In an important article published in 1967, the American linguist Kenneth L. Pike derived both terms – emic and etic – from linguistics (where they originally referred to different, namely phonemic and phonetic, conceptualizations of sounds) and suggested applying these to the study of human behaviour.[12] His main argument is that it makes a great difference whether a scholar tries to analyse human behaviour as "from inside the system"[13] – that is, from the perspective of the actors' own experiences, understanding and terminology (this would then represent an emic approach) – or whether a scholar reframes such first-order data by making use of more systematic and/or comparative second-order concepts and categories (which would then correspond to the etic approach). These second-order categories may be completely alien and incomprehensible to the social actor(s) in question but may nonetheless be useful for systematic and/or comparative purposes. The differentiation between emic and etic approaches has been particularly important in anthropology, but has also been applied more and more frequently in the study of religion and various historical sciences over the past decades. Note that, with regard to medieval learned magic, an emic approach is not to be equated with the insider perspective of medieval practitioners, nor the outsider perspective of medieval polemicists: both emic and etic standpoints are an exclusive preserve of scholarly analysis.[14]

Magic as a discursive concept

On the basis of these conceptual clarifications, I shall now move on to elucidating what I mean by a discourse historical approach towards medieval learned magic. To cut a long story short: the approach proposed here strives for an emic analysis and reconstruction of the medieval insider discourse of learned magic. The latter is here understood as a collection or "group of statements"[15] (to quote Foucault) that employ an etymological derivate, linguistic equivalent or culturally established synonym of magic as an identificatory first-order term of self-reference. The addendum "learned" is used to point out that the analytical focus lies on such medieval insider sources (which are here referred to as learned magic for various reasons – see below), while contemporaneous polemical (outsider) sources are mostly neglected. The approach is called "discourse historical" as it is essentially an application of the method of discourse analysis in a historical setting.[16] Accordingly, it is argued that magic here functions as a discursive concept, as the analytic focus lies on its first-order use within historical sources and discourses, and not as a second-order scholarly category.

Applying a discourse historical approach towards medieval leaned magic entails some important methodological implications that may or may not differ from the analytical use of magic in other medievalist works on the topic (including some chapters within this volume). Let me sketch out some of these implications in greater detail.

1. The approach proposed here refrains from any second-order or third-order notions of magic: that is magic is neither defined, nor theorized, nor generalized nor universalized in any essential manner. In line with other discursive approaches in the study of religion, the approach can be considered anti-essentialist,[17] as magic has no intrinsic meaning in itself but is "constructed and informed by the particular discourses that surround it in particular historical, social, and cultural contexts".[18] Scholars have sometimes applied the term "empty signifier" in this sense,[19] but I find it more plausible to perceive magic as a floating signifier: its semantics are obviously not empty but rather floating, in the sense of being dependent on the context of its use.[20] In contrast, second- or third-order (scholarly) concepts of magic are usually essentialist in the sense that they refer to an "essence" of magic that may be derived from substantial definitions, disciplinary habits or simply everyday language. In my view, such essentialist second-order notions of

magic are neither necessary nor helpful for understanding the insider perspective(s) of medieval authors and practitioners of learned magic.[21]

2. As already mentioned, the approach proposed here is oriented towards sources that include an etymological derivate, linguistic equivalent or culturally established synonym of magic as an identificatory first-order term of self-reference; this is in fact its main criterion for setting up a corpus of medieval learned magic.[22] I would like to stress that this criterion is neither arbitrary nor trivial: over large parts of Western history, it has obviously involved serious personal risks to consciously denote one's own ritual practices and texts as magic, when at the same time powerful elitist discourses have devalued and condemned magic or even initiated legislative action. This is even more evident with regard to late medieval author-magicians.[23] What is more, the criterion is empirically well-documented. Not all medieval texts that seem to belong to the medieval insider discourse include the Latin term "magia" or one of its synonyms (partly because their authors may have avoided the term on purpose), but many of them do, so we are indeed able to reconstruct a fairly coherent discourse of inclusion in the European Middle Ages.[24] Apart from this purely philological criterion, there appear to be numerous family resemblances and further stereotypic narrative and/or ritual patterns across the texts that justify allotting them within the same category (consider the use of common pseud-epigraphs such as Solomon, Hermes or Apollonius; the recurrent narratives of a holy art or angelic transmission; the adoption of "voces magicae", "charaktêres", talismans, sigils, ritual circles and other sophisticated ritual techniques; and so on). It may be useful to continue exemplifying and fine-tuning these family resemblances in future research as they justify the scholarly configuration and investigation of a fairly clear-cut textual corpus of medieval learned magic without the need to define magic as a second-order category.[25]

3. The analytical focus on medieval learned magic calls for a pronounced differentiation of medieval insider and outsider discourse. Of course, there has always been a dialectical interplay between these two discourses in (and beyond) the European Middle Ages.[26] We come across sceptical but curious encounters with learned magic, enthusiastic discussions – albeit without practical experience – or nuanced, ambivalent judgements that seem to represent rather intermediary positions. Medieval examples of such positions may be the discussion of the concept of "magia naturalis" by medieval theologians[27] or surveys of relevant literature by authors such as (Ps.?) Albertus Magnus (*Speculum Astronomiae*),[28] Michael Scotus (*Liber Introductorius*),[29] Berengarius Ganellus (*Summa Sacre Magice*)[30] or Johannes Trithemius (*Antipalus Maleficiorum*).[31] However, as the conceptual history of magic was – particularly in premodern times – extremely controversial, morally and religiously value-laden, full of social stereotypes and often a matter of legislation, the insider/outsider poles are fairly clearly marked, so that most medieval actors and sources will be assignable to one of either of these two poles (this does not preclude that some authors may have partaken in or adopted arguments from both discourses).

From a discourse analytical perspective, this differentiation is crucial because the first-order concept of magic is employed not only in very different ways (for example with a valorizing or polemical function) but also while referring to very different things in medieval insider and outsider sources[32] (according to Foucault, discourses are "practices that systematically form the objects of which they speak").[33] These differences call for analysing medieval insider sources as independently as possible from the misleading claims and distortive narratives that pervade medieval polemics against magic. Certainly, outsider texts can be useful, for example when they provide lists of insider texts that were circulating at a given time (for example *Speculum Astronomiae*). However, as soon as one wishes to know more about the contents of such texts, outsider sources should be read with great caution as they tend to simplify, distort or – consciously or not – misunderstand the insider tradition of medieval learned magic. A telling example is Thomas Aquinas's argument that the angels invoked during the *Ars notoria* ritual (I am now referring to the first-order terminology used within the text, that is to the apparent insiders' perspective) may really be demons (*Summa Theologiae* 2, 2, 96, 1).[34] From the viewpoint of the modern study of religion, the "demon pact" narrative – which has informed Christian polemics against magic ever since Augustine[35] – is obviously nothing more than a tool of religious "othering"[36]: it neither leads to, nor is it interested in, a proper understanding of the "other" (in this case the medieval learned magician), but rather distances the latter by projecting a stereotypic, distortive pattern of interpretation onto him. Given this basic tendency, one might generalize that outsider accounts are usually not trustworthy for reconstructing the insider perspectives of authors and practitioners of learned magic (this is the case also in other epochs).

4. The approach proposed here also adopts an anti-essentialist stance towards medieval insider sources. In fact, a comparative reading of these sources quickly reveals that medieval learned magic is not a homogenous category: there is no conceptual "core" or ritual "essence" that can be deduced from the sources apart from the fact that the first-order concept of magic usually refers to a "ritual art" (as most insider texts are ritual texts or theoretical reflections on such texts; the corresponding first-order formulation is thus "ars magica").[37] Even though medieval insider narratives tend to suggest otherwise, this art is strikingly heterogeneous, hybrid and ever-changing from an analytical perspective. It is heterogeneous, as the ritual procedures described in most medieval insider sources consist of a vast variety of different ritual (micro-) techniques and varying concepts of ritual efficacy. It is hybrid, as these techniques are usually combined in the manner of "building-blocks" in a multiplicity of ways, depending on the preferences of the respective author or copyist (this is what I refer to as "ritual hybridity" elsewhere)[38]; what is more, these techniques have often been derived from different cultural or religious contexts (this is what I refer to as "religious hybridity" elsewhere).[39] It is ever-changing, because learned magic is – within and, the more so, beyond the European Middle Ages – in permanent motion: it continuously adopts ritual patterns and techniques from older sources, it discards unnecessary or unwanted elements, it adapts to novel cultural and religious environments or practitioner milieus and it continuously invents novel modes of ritual performance or efficacy.

All three features call for non-essentialist analyses of medieval insider sources and nuanced modes of analytical description. In contrast to adopting essentialist second-order definitions of magic that may obscure or completely bypass the heterogeneity, hybridity and changeability of medieval learned magic, I suggest adopting a typological perspective, maybe inspired by the concept of "family resemblances" (as suggested above) or the recently proposed concept of "patterns of magicity".[40] The idea would be to develop open and flexible taxonomies of ritual techniques, ritual goals and concepts of ritual efficacy (and/or other features) that may be consecutively derived from medieval insider sources, but also applied to these for comparative purposes and for the reconstruction of intertextual dependencies or ritual dynamics.

5. I speak of medieval learned magic – and not of magic in general – in this chapter for two reasons. First, the addendum "learned" refers to two fairly distinctive characteristics of medieval insider sources: (i) they stem from people who were not only able to read and write (already a tiny elite in the European Middle Ages), but often quite sophisticated authors with apparent expertise in several languages and religious traditions; and (ii) the "ritual art" described in these sources tends towards complex, time- and resource-consuming ritual performances. The addendum "learned" thus operates as a marker of specificity of this particular corpus of sources and thereby helps to demarcate it from other (allegedly magical) ritual traditions that may have been transmitted only orally and whose ritual performances may have remained rather short and simplistic (consider so-called medieval folk magic traditions).[41]

    Second, the addendum "learned" points to the fact that medieval insider sources are not unique but the result of a complex interplay between intercultural transmission[42] and inner-cultural appropriation.[43] Seen from this entangled perspective, medieval learned magic is obviously part and parcel of a much larger textual–ritual tradition that is considerably older (as it goes back at least to late antiquity) and continues up to this day: "Western learned magic".[44] The historical embeddedness of medieval insider sources within the overall history of Western learned magic calls for interpreting these sources not (only) by reference to medieval polemics (that is, contemporaneous outsider sources), but (also) by reference to other – that is, preceding and/or subsequent – insider sources.

6. The last argument ties in with a recently proposed research programme on "Historicising Western learned magic" which consists of eight theoretical issues that should, in my view, be considered in the course of its historicization: continuity, changeability, hybridity, deviance, morality, complexity, efficacy and multiplicity.[45] It is, of course, impossible to go through all these issues in the final section of this chapter. Apart from word-count restrictions, such a discussion would require a coherent, diachronic and cross-cultural narrative on the history of Western learned magic at hand in order to systematically relate medieval insider sources to preceding (for example late ancient, medieval Jewish, Islamic or Byzantine) and subsequent (for example early modern, modern or even contemporary) insider sources. For the time being, such a work is still a scholarly desideratum.[46] However, even on the current state of research, the analysis of medieval insider sources from the viewpoint of the overall history of Western learned magic may reveal interesting insights and thus serve as an important complement to their (so far, prevailing) interpretation and contextualization within medieval studies.

Note that such an analysis poses different questions to medieval insider sources than medievalist in-depth studies or critical text editions. For example, it puts greater emphasis on the changeability of learned magic texts and techniques from a diachronic and cross-cultural perspective (thereby tying on novel approaches towards ritual dynamics).[47] If one combines all eight theoretical notions mentioned above – continuity, changeability, hybridity, deviance, morality, complexity, efficacy and multiplicity – and projects these onto medieval insider sources, one might even come up with a bold research hypothesis: the European Middle Ages may have operated as some sort of "bottleneck" within the overall history of Western learned magic. In fact, medieval insider sources seem to display a more or less significant *decrease* on a range of domains, compared to antecedent and subsequent insider sources: regarding (i) the quantity of circulating insider texts, (ii) their conceptual complexity (this refers to the existence of elaborate insider definitions and systematizations), (iii) their ritual complexity (this refers to the length and complexity of the "ritual art" outlined in insider sources), (iv) their social evaluation (this refers to the quantity and quality of liberal milieus where learned magic may have thrived for the time being) and (v) their position towards morality (greater restriction in this matter may lead to rejecting malevolent ritual goals, for example).[48]

For the time being, this is nothing but an ambitious hypothesis that may provide food for thought and eventually point to future avenues of research. Regarding the latter, it might call for enhanced and more systematic modes of cooperation among those historical disciplines that may be considered relevant to historicizing Western learned magic – such as classical studies, medieval studies, Arabic, Jewish and Byzantine studies, early modern history or the study of Western and contemporary esotericism. Like other contemporary approaches in historiography (consider entangled history, transcultural history or global/world history),[49] historicizing Western learned magic challenges the plausibility of investigating a limited set of insider sources within the boundaries of single historical disciplines. Instead, it calls for engaging in interdisciplinary, diachronic and cross-cultural analyses – and, eventually, large, communal research projects – that do justice to the complexity of this novel and fascinating field of research. The present volume is a laudable step in this direction.

Notes

1 See, exemplarily, Shaughan Lavine, "Second- and higher order logics," in *Routledge Encyclopaedia of Philosophy*, vol. 8, ed. Edward Craig (London: Routledge, 1998), 591–95.
2 James A. Beckford, *Social Theory and Religion* (Cambridge: Cambridge University Press, 2003), 21.
3 Beckford, *Social Theory and Religion*, 22.
4 See, exemplarily, Tim Murphy, *Representing Religion* (London: Equinox, 2007), 20; Ann Taves, *Religious Experience Reconsidered* (Princeton, NJ: Princeton University Press, 2009), 25; even philosophers of religion have adopted the distinction with this translocated meaning: see James Harris, *Analytic Philosophy of Religion* (Dordrecht: Kluwer Academic Publishing, 2002), 59, or Timothy D. Knepper, *The Ends of Philosophy of Religion* (New York: Palgrave Macmillan, 2013), for example z, 42, 58. As far as I know, Jonathan Z. Smith has been the only scholar so far to apply the distinction to the debate on magic: Smith, "Trading Places," in *Relating Religion*, ed. Jonathan Z. Smith (Chicago, IL: Chicago University Press, 2004), 219.
5 For example, in a different article, Jonathan Z. Smith – namely, in Smith, "Religion, Religions, Religious," in *Critical Terms for Religious Studies*, ed. Mark C. Taylor (Chicago, IL: Chicago University Press, 1998), 281–82 – locates first-order also on the level of academic language where it refers to the *scholar's description* of the social actors' accounts of their experiences and behaviour ("they talked about god" would thus be a first-order formulation, whereas religion would be a potential second-order category for this observation).
6 Russell T. McCutcheon, *Critics not Caretakers* (Albany: State University of New York Press, 2001), 134.
7 See Russell T. McCutcheon, *The Insider/Outsider Problem in the Study of Religion* (London: Cassel, 1999) for an introduction into the debate.
8 See further Kim Knott, "Insider/Outsider Perspectives," in *The Routledge Companion to the Study of Religion*, ed. John Hinnels (London: Routledge, 2010).
9 See below, footnote 22.
10 See Bernd-Christian Otto, "Towards Historicising Magic in Antiquity," *Numen* 60, no. 2/3 (2013): 308–47, and Bernd-Christian Otto, "A Catholic 'Magician' historicises 'Magic'," in *History and Religion: Narrating a Religious Past*, ed. Bernd-Christian Otto et al. (Berlin: De Gruyter, 2015), 419–43. In Bernd-Christian Otto, *Magie. Rezeptions- und diskursgeschichtliche Analysen von der Antike bis zur Neuzeit* (Berlin: De Gruyter, 2011), I have used the terms "selbstreferentieller" and "fremdreferentieller Magiediskurs" that are hardly translatable into English.

11 For example, an analogous focus on insider or practitioner discourses of magic can be found in recent works on contemporary esotericism; see, exemplarily, Egil Asprem, "Contemporary Ritual Magic," in *The Occult World*, ed. Christopher Partridge (London: Routledge, 2014), 382–95; Kennet Granholm, *Dark Enlightenment: The Historical, Sociological, and Discursive Contexts of Contemporary Esoteric Magic* (Leiden: Brill, 2014).
12 See Kenneth L. Pike, "Etic and Emic Standpoints for the Description of Behaviour," in *The Insider/Outsider Problem in the Study of Religion*, ed. McCutcheon, 28–36.
13 Pike, "Etic and Emic Standpoints," 28.
14 In other words, an emic approach may reconstruct and re-narrate the first-order perspective of medieval practitioners of learned magic, but medieval insider texts should not themselves be called emic. See on this important differentiation also *The Insider/Outsider Problem in the Study of Religion*, ed. McCutcheon, 17f.
15 Michel Foucault, *The Archaeology of Knowledge* (New York: Pantheon Books, 1972), 22.
16 I am thereby applying Stuckrad's idea of a "discourse-historical approach to knowledge about Religion" to the study of magic – see Kocku von Stuckrad, "Discursive Study of Religion: Approaches, Definitions, Implications," *Method & Theory in the Study of Religion* 25, no. 1 (2013): 21. From the viewpoint of Moberg's useful distinction of first-, second-, and third-level discourse analytic approaches, the approach proposed here represents a third-level approach: see Marcus Moberg, "First-, Second-, and Third-level Discourse-Analytic Approaches in the Study of Religion: Moving from Meta-theoretical Reflection to Implementation in Practice," *Religion* 43, no. 1 (2013): 19f.
17 See on "anti-essentialism" Moberg, "First-, Second-, and Third-level Discourse-analytic Approaches," 8.
18 Moberg, "First-, Second-, and Third-level Discourse-analytic Approaches," 13.
19 On the concept of "empty signifier", see Moberg, "First-, Second-, and Third-level Discourse-analytic Approaches," 13; Stuckrad, "Discursive Study of Religion," 17. The classic text is Ernesto Laclau, "Why do Empty Signifiers Matter to Politics?" in *The Lesser Evil and the Greater Good*, ed. Jeffrey Weeks (London: Rivers Oram Press, 1994), 167–78.
20 See Daniel Chandler, *Semiotics: The Basics* (London: Routledge, 2007), 78: "floating signifiers" have "a vague, highly variable, unspecifiable or non-existent signified. Such signifiers may mean different things to different people: they may stand for many or even any signifieds; they may mean whatever their interpreters want them to mean".
21 There is no room in this chapter to go into greater detail with the methodological problems that arise from adopting second-order or third-order notions of magic in scholarly research: see – to name only two major difficulties – for the "magic-science-religion-triangle" (i.e. the impossibility of defining these terms independently of one another and the related problem of defining *ex negativo*) and for the problem of ethnocentrism (i.e. magic's tendency to produce distorted perspectives and findings in comparative and cross-cultural research by highlighting alleged similarities and suppressing difference), Bernd-Christian Otto and Michael Stausberg, *Defining Magic: A Reader* (Sheffield: Equinox, 2013), 4–7.
22 From the perspective of discourse analysis, the criterion is related to Foucault's idea of the "formation of enunciative modalities": see Foucault, *The Archaeology of Knowledge*, 50:

> First question: who is speaking? Who, among the totality of speaking individuals, is accorded the right to use this sort of language (langage)? Who is qualified to do so? Who derives from it his own special quality, his prestige, and from whom, in return, does he receive if not the assurance, at least the presumption that what he says is true? What is the status of the individuals who – alone – have the right, sanctioned by law or tradition, juridically defined or spontaneously accepted, to proffer such a discourse?

23 On medieval "author-magicians", see Julien Véronèse, "La notion d'ʻauteur-magicien' à la fin du Moyen Âge: Le cas de l'ʻermite Pelagius de Majorque († v. 1480)," *Médiévales* 56 (2006): 119–38; Nicolas Weill-Parot, "Antonio Da Montolmo"s *De occultis et manifestis* or *Liber intelligentiarum*: An annotated critical edition with English translation and introduction," in *Conjuring Spirits: Texts and Traditions of Medieval Ritual Magic*, ed. Claire Fanger (Stroud: Sutton, 1998), particularly 221ff; and chapter 17 in this volume.
24 The self-designative term "magia", including synonyms (such as "necromantia", "nigromantia"; I would not count the terms "scientia"/"ars", "experimentum" or "operare" as culturally accepted synonyms, even though these frequently appear in insider sources), can be found in the

following texts: *Astromagia*, ed. Alfonso D'Agostino (Naples: Liguori, 1992), for example pp. 146, 150; *L'Almandal et l'Almadel latins au Moyen Âge*, ed. Julien Veronèse (Florence: Sismel Edizioni del Galluzzo, 2012), for example 134; *Liber Razielis* – see, exemplarily, book 7 entitled *Liber magice* (Halle MS 14 B 36, fol. 178r: "Hic incipit liber qui dicitur Flores Mercurii de Babilonia super opera artis magice…") in Ms. Biblioteca Apostolica Vaticana, Reginense MS Lat. 1300; see also *Sefer ha-Razim*, ed. Bill Rebiger and Schäfer (Tübingen: Mohr Siebek, 2009), Vol I, 28; *Picatrix: The Latin Version of the Ghāyat al-ḥakīm*, ed. David Pingree (London: Warburg Institute, 1986), 83, 87, 96 and so on; Berengarius Ganellus' *Summa Sacre Magice* (self-evident due to the title, but see also further instances in Ms. Kassel university library 4° astron. 3, for example fol. 13r); *Liber Iuratus Honorii*, ed. Gösta Hedegård (Stockholm: Almqvist & Wiksell, 2002), for example 60, 66; Ms. Munich Clm 849, ed. Richard Kieckhefer, *Forbidden Rites: A Necromancer's Manual of the Fifteenth Century* (University Park: Pennsylvania State University Press, 1998), for example pp. 211, 221; "Antonio da Montolmo's *De occultis et manifestis* or *Liber intelligentiarum*," ed. Weill-Parot, for example 258, 264, 274, 286; *De quindecim stellis, quindecim lapidibus, quindecim herbis et quindecim imaginibus*, ed. Louis Delatte, *Textes latins et vieux francais relatifs aux Cyranides* (Liège: Faculté de Philosophie et Lettres, 1942), for example 242, 275, 281, 286); *Clavicula Salomonis* (I am referring to the presumably earliest Latin witness, [former] Amsterdam BPH 114 A [now Ms. Coxe 25], f. 74–138) and most later texts belonging to the so-called "Solomonic cycle", such as the *Heptameron*, uncritic. ed. Joseph Peterson, "Peter de Abano: *Heptameron*" (online edition), based on the 1565 appendix to Agrippa of Nettesheim's *De occulta philosophia*, and the *Lemegeton*, uncritic. ed. Joseph Peterson, *The Lesser Key of Solomon* (York Beach, ME: Weiser Books, 2001). The term is not used in a self-referential and/or identificatory manner in most versions of the *Ars notoria/Ars nova*, apart from "magos" used as a *vox magica*: Julien Véronèse, *L'Ars notoria au Moyen Age* (Florence: Sismel Edizioni del Galluzzo, 2007), 84; apologetically, "ars notoria" is here even demarcated from "nigromantia" which is understood negatively: Veronèse, *L'Ars notoria*, 58/59; Jean of Morigny's, *Liber Florum Celestis Doctrine/The Flowers of Heavenly Teaching*, ed. Claire Fanger and Nicholas Watson (Toronto: Pontifical Institute of Mediaeval Studies, 2015); *Lapidario*, ed. S. Rodriguez Montalvo, *"Lapidario" segun el manuscrito escurialense H.I.15* (Madrid: Gredos, 1981); Juris Lidaka "The Book of Angels, Rings, Characters and Images of the Planets: Attributed to Osbern Bokenham," in *Conjuring Spirits*, ed. Fanger, 32–75 (Lidaka's English translation, however, includes magic numerous times, mostly referring to Latin "operare"); *Liber de essentia spirituum* (communication by Sophie Page); *Liber Runarum*, ed. Paolo Lucentini, in *Hermes Trismegisti. Astrologica et Divinatoria*, ed. Gerrit Bos et al. (Turnhout: Brepols, 2001), 401–51; *Liber Antimaquis*, ed. Charles Burnett in *Hermes Trismegisti. Astrologica et Divinatoria*, ed. Bos et al. 177–221; "Al-Kindi. De radiis," ed. Marie-Thérèse d'Alverny and Françoise Hudry, *Archives d'histoire doctrinale et litteraire du moyen age* 49 (1974): 139–260; Latin *Cyranides*, in *Textes latins et vieux francais relatifs aux Cyranides*, ed. Delatte. Note that there may be two very different reasons for omitting the term: (1) the omission may indicate that the respective author didn't perceive the contents of the text to be covered by the (first-order) concept of magic (two examples are, in my view, al-Kindī's *De radiis stellarum* or the Latin *Cyranides*; yet, as these texts have influenced later insider sources, they should be counted to the insider discourse); (2) the author would have used the (first-order) concept, but has avoided its use in order to avoid animosities in a restrictive cultural environment (technically speaking, both *Ars notoria* as well as *Liber florum celestis doctrine* belong to the outsider discourse as they engage in polemics against magic; yet, as they have adopted textual and ritual contents from insider sources – such as the *Liber Iuratus Honorii* – they should be counted to the insider discourse). This is an incomplete list that may, of course, be enhanced.

25 This involves continuous "boundary work" on alleged subgenres such as Astral magic, Solomonic magic or Hermetic magic that, from the viewpoint of the approach outlined here, are problematic for various reasons (for example, pseud-epigraphs as genre titles are inconvenient as their first-order use within the sources is not systematically related to the textual or ritual contents of these sources). The category of medieval learned magic is thus broader than these subgenres while my idea of "family resemblances" is tied to the development of more nuanced and fine-grained "typologies" – see on these further below, point (4).

26 See on this observation also Marco Pasi, "Theses de Magia," *Societas Magica Newsletter* 20 (2008): 3–5, and, in greater detail, Otto, *Magie*, ch. 12.

27 Like William of Auvergne, Albertus Magnus, Michael Scot, Roger Bacon or Pietro d'Abano – see, for an overview, Claire Fanger and Frank Klaassen, "Magic III: Middle Ages," in *Dictionary of Gnosis*

& *Western Esotericism.*, vol. 2, ed. Wouter Hanegraaff et al. (Leiden: Brill, 2005), 724–31; Frank Klaassen, *The Transformations of Magic: Illicit Learned Magic in the Later Middle Ages and Renaissance* (University Park: Pennsylvania State University Press, 2012), especially Part I; and Liana Saif, *The Arabic Influences on Early Modern Occult Philosophy* (New York: Palgrave Macmillan, 2015), especially ch. 3–4.

28 Ed. Paola Zambelli, *The Speculum Astronomiae and Its Enigma* (Dordrecht: Kluwer, 1992), 203–73.
29 See the discussion in David Pingree, "Learned Magic in the Time of Frederick II," *Micrologus* 2 (1994): 39–56.
30 See Damaris Gehr's chapter in this volume.
31 See Paola Zambelli, *White Magic, Black Magic and the European Renaissance* (Leiden: Brill, 2007), 101–12.
32 In Foucauldian terms, both the "formation of concepts" (see Foucault, *The Archaeology of Knowledge*, 56f.) as well as the "formation of objects" (48f.) are dependent on the ("insider/outsider") perspective of the respective author.
33 Foucault, *The Archaeology of Knowledge*, 49.
34 See in greater detail Claire Fanger, "Plundering the Egyptian Treasure: John the Monk's *Book of Visions* and Its Relation to the Ars Notoria of Solomon," in *Conjuring Spirits*, ed. Fanger, 222–24.
35 See Otto, *Magie*, ch. 8.
36 See recently Olav Hammer, "Othering," in *Vocabulary for the Study of Religion*, ed. Robert A. Segal and Kocku von Stuckrad (Leiden: Brill Online, 2016): http://referenceworks.brillonline.com/entries/vocabulary-for-the-study-of-religion/othering-COM_00000398 (9 February 2016).
37 This is one of the reasons why the often-used second-order notion of "ritual magic" appears to be either redundant or tautological; in my view, it cannot function as a "marker of specificity" of Western insider sources (as, from the viewpoint of the conceptual history of magic, "ritual" is simply an integral part of its semantic field).
38 On the differentiation between ritual hybridity and religious hybridity, see Bernd-Christian Otto, "Historicising 'Western Learned Magic': Preliminary Remarks," *Aries* 16 (2016): 199–203.
39 Otto, "Historicising 'Western Learned Magic'".
40 See Otto and Stausberg, *Defining Magic*, 10f.
41 See, for example, Richard Kieckhefer, *Magic in the Middle Ages* (Cambridge: Cambridge University Press, 1989), ch. 4.
42 Different overviews can be found in David Pingree, "The Diffusion of Arabic Magical Texts in Western Europe," in *La diffusione delle scienze islamiche nel medio evo europeo*, ed. Scarcia Amoretti (Rome: Accademia Nazionale dei Lincei, 1987), 58–102; Charles Burnett, "The Translating Activity in Medieval Spain," in Charles Burnett, *Magic and Divination in the Middle Ages* (Aldershot: Variorum, 1996), 1036–58; R. Lemay, "Books of Magic in Translation from the Arabic and the Birth of a Theology of the Sacraments of the Church in the Twelfth Century," in *Charmes et sortilèges: magie et magiciens*, ed. R. Gyselen et al. (Bures-sur-Yvette: Groupe pour l'Étude de la Civilisation du Moyen-Orient, 2002), 165–92; Charles Burnett, "Late Antique and Medieval Latin Translations of Greek Texts on Astrology and Magic," in *The Occult Sciences in Byzantium*, ed. Paul Magdalino and Maria Mavroudi (Geneva: La Pomme d'Or, 2006), 325–59; Julien Véronèse, "La transmission groupée des textes de magie "salomonienne" de l'Antiquité au Moyen Âge: bilan historiographique, inconnues et pistes de recherche," in *L'Antiquité tardive dans les collections médiévales: Textes et representations, VIe-XIVe siècle*, ed. Stephane Gioanni and Benoît Grevin (Rome: École Française de Rome, 2008), 193–223; Peter Forshaw, "The Occult Middle Ages," in *The Occult World*, ed. Partridge 34–48; Saif, *The Arabic Influences on Early Modern Occult Philosophy*; and the chapters in Part II of this volume.
43 The relationship between these two distinct yet related historical processes has been the focus of the recent volume *Les savoirs magiques et leur transmission de l'Antiquité à la Renaissance*, ed. Veronique Dasen and Jean-Michel Spieser (Florence: Sismel Edizioni del Galluzzo, 2014).
44 See for an overall conceptualization and theorization of this "textual-ritual tradition" Otto, "Historicising 'Western learned magic'," 161–240.
45 See Otto, "Historicising 'Western learned magic'".
46 But see Michael D. Bailey, *Magic and Superstition in Europe: A Concise History from Antiquity to the Present* (Lanham, MD: Rowman & Littlefield, 2007); Owen Davies, *Grimoires: A History of Magic Books* (Oxford: Oxford University Press, 2009), and the recent *The Cambridge History of Magic and Witchcraft*

in the West: From Antiquity to the Present, ed. David J. Collins (Cambridge: Cambridge University Press, 2015), for useful and inspiring – yet partially unsystematic and incomplete – attempts of such overviews.

47 See recently *Ritual Dynamics and the Science of Ritual*, ed. Harshav Barbara and Axel Michaels et al, 5 vols. (Wiesbaden: Harrassowitz, 2010–11); *Ritual und Ritualdynamik: Schlüsselbegriffe, Theorien, Diskussionen*, ed. Christiane Brosius et al. (Göttingen: Vandenhoeck & Ruprecht, 2013).

48 See for some further thoughts and observations concerning this hypothesis Otto, "Magie im Islam. Eine diskursgeschichtliche Perspektive," in *Die Geheimnisse der oberen und der unteren Welt: Magie im Islam zwischen Glaube und Wissenschaft*, ed. Sebastian Günther and Dorothee Pielow (Leiden: Brill 2018), 515–546.

49 See, exemplarily, *Transcultural History: Theories, Methods, Sources*, ed. Madeleine Herren-Oesch et al. (Berlin: Springer, 2012), with a particular focus on the Middle Ages; *Transkulturelle Verflechtungen im mittelalterlichen Jahrtausend: Europa, Ostasien, Afrika*, ed. Michael Borgolte and Matthias Tischler (Darmstadt: Wissenschaftliche Buchgesellschaft, 2012); *A Companion to World History*, ed. Douglas Northrop (Oxford: Wiley-Blackwell, 2012); Diego Olstein, *Thinking History Globally* (Basingstoke: Palgrave Macmillan, 2015).

4

THE CONCEPT OF MAGIC

David L. d'Avray

This paper focuses on "emic" and "etic" concepts of magic: the "emic" concepts of the medieval people we are studying, and the "etic" concepts we, the students of medieval magic, create to help us get a grip on medieval concepts and practices. The paper attempts to add something to understanding of the medieval, "emic" concepts, but I argue that "etic" concepts too are needed to clear our heads about medieval magic.

Perhaps it is good to start by studying medieval magic from the inside and in terms of the concepts of medieval people. Catherine Rider does this in her excellent *Magic and Religion in Medieval England* (London: Reaktion Books, 2012). She simply follows the contours of the categories of the pastoral manuals which she mines so successfully for data on magic. Ultimately, this is also the approach advocated with great sophistication in a classic article by Richard Kieckhefer.[1] He was engaged in a polite polemic against the view of Valerie Flint that a lot of what the medieval Church got up to could be called magic (but in a good way): in particular, pagan practices had been incorporated to ease the process of conversion. Against that, Kieckhefer put the case for taking seriously the medieval clergy's categories, and especially the idea of magic as involving demonic power.

Certainly, it is a medieval, "emic", idea that the use of the mysterious *virtutes* attributed to stones or herbs or diagrams is really a cover for demonic activity. The thirteenth-century Franciscan Eudes Rigaud, in his commentary on the *Sentences* of Peter Lombard, sets up the position he intends to destroy, grouping occult properties together with such things as snake charming. (It should be said that the *quaestio* is telegraphic and confusingly laid out, probably because oral transmission was involved.)

> Finally, it is asked whether there is any sin in exercising those magic arts. It seems not.[2] To know: this is not evil; similarly, neither is being able to do something the same as performing an evil action. Even performing the action is not evil, since the devil does it, not man. Therefore it seems that there is no sin in such things. Therefore if there is, it will be because they are forbidden. But then it is asked why they are forbidden? # Again, that person brings it about that, or makes, a serpent come out of a cave by means of an incantation: surely he does not sin? He seems not to, since the action is not evil. # Again, the words which he says are not evil, since he says: "Our Father", and other natural things which are good. # Again: whether in words, stones and herbs there are powers (*virtutes*) as people say? But to use words [and] stones for the powers for which they exist is no sin. Therefore similarly with herbs. # Again, concerning the diagrams which are made: whether there might

be sin there? It seems that there is not, since there is either some power in them, and then it does not seem to be a sin, or not, and then it seems to be useless, not sinful…[3]

The refutation is rather a mélange: stones and herbs get swallowed up in a general attack on various sorts of magic, but the implicit argument is that demons are the source of the apparent power of spells, diagrams and other things, which would include stones and herbs.[4] Occult properties are clearly being lumped together with more unambiguously magical practices.

Not everyone would have shared Eudes's ideas. The attribution of occult powers to supernatural help, i.e. to demons or the devil operating clandestinely, was not a consensus view.[5] For many entirely respectable medieval religious writers, "occult" meant no more than "not understood". Taken in this sense, occult properties are natural properties that happen not to have been elucidated by natural science. In this sense, modern science too is quite happy with the idea of occult forces, like gravity for example, which has never been actually explained. This kind of "magic" has little to do with the other medieval understanding of the term: which points to a world of demonic activity or at least to non-natural forces quite different in kind to those that science explicates, and available as a special source of power. As a category, *ars magica* includes too much to generate questions going beyond "what did they mean by *ars magica*?"

The problem might be dodged by concentrating our attention on different medieval terms: *divinatio*, *divinus* (sorcerer, magus), *divina* (sorceress, witch). A fascinating discussion of *divinatio* etc. by a northern Italian Franciscan writing circa 1300 (whose thoughts on this and many other subjects are recorded in MS Birmingham University 6/iii/19) takes us through most of the types of activity and forms of thought we associate with medieval magic; and there is the added bonus that these various practices are illustrated by vivid stories. These stories flesh out the "emic" idea of *divinatio* that we find in his work, and provide not a bad typology of medieval magic.

Real, terrifying and lethal demonic power is represented by a story about a noble young man from Prague who went to a magical specialist for help in getting a girl with whom he was obsessed. A simulacrum of the girl tempted him out of the protective magic circle which was a key part of the ritual and he was killed in a disgusting manner.[6] The Franciscan writer certainly believed in demons but he also thought that magic could be faked. He tells another story that is probably true because its source, who is also the main protagonist in the narrative, went on after a (presumably) thoroughgoing conversion to become a Franciscan himself. This time it was a peasant who wanted the girl, and he wanted to marry her. The fake magician pretended to be reluctant but gave in after the peasant had brought him money and capons. The charlatan then got together some accomplices and gave them the names of demons. The peasant was put in a magic circle but the "demons" attacked him. He cried for help and the pseudo-magician "rescued" him (but did not return the fee).[7] In a similarly sceptical vein, the anonymous Franciscan tells of a woman who boasts to her parish priest that she had saved him when she was flying at night on beasts with "the ladies". Our narrator says she was under an illusion inspired by the devil. The priest said that he had anyway been protected by a door that would have kept them out. (The conversation seems to have taken place in the church, so the door in question presumably led into his own room or house.) The woman said that locks and doors were not a problem for her. The priest said that he would like to test that so that he could thank her. Then, he locked the door of the Church and started to beat her, inviting her to escape through the locked door if she could. After that, he made her swear not to say such things again.[8]

Again, a serving maid claimed that she could use her powers to get for her mistress a rich and loving husband. Her mistress pointed out that the maid's husband was poor and had a mistress, so why didn't she do better for herself with her powers?[9] A more sinister narrative is set in a village where the plague is rampant. The villagers go to a little old lady who was thought to be a *divina*, who told them that the solution was to bury their priest alive, which they managed to do when he was conducting a burial service.[10]

The rich quasi-sermon on *divinatio* in MS Birmingham University 6/iii/19 suggests that this category might enable us to circumvent some of the problems of the phrase *ars magica*, in that *divinatio* includes so much of real or claimed counter-Christian supernatural powers, but not "natural magic". But substituting *divinatio* for *ars magica* is probably not the answer. *Divinatio* is not always used in so comprehensive a sense as with our Italian Franciscan. In the *Summa Theologica* of Thomas Aquinas (Summa Theologica, 2-2 q. 95 a.2–3) notably, its scope seems to be confined to predicting the future by magical means.

Making the concepts of the past our own analytical concepts can thus create more complication that we want, if the policy is consistently applied. Our analytical framework could end up with the complexity of the Oxford English Dictionary or the *Thesaurus Linguae Latinae*. There are also other more serious problems, whether our starting point is the term *divinatio* or the term *ars magica*.

One problem is the obverse of the awkwardness created by inclusion of "hidden forces of nature" within the *ars magica*. In the latter case, the difficulty is that the same phrase covers heterogeneous phenomena. The symmetrically opposite difficulty is that the orthodox medieval distinction between magic and religion makes it harder to articulate some significant similarities between phenomena. Kieckhefer was no doubt right to think that Valerie Flint was unduly prone to collapse the distinction between magic and religion, but her instinct, like Keith Thomas's before her, was surely correct insofar as she saw striking similarities between some aspects of medieval Christianity and practices that one can in a loose and provisional way call "magic". Keith Thomas pertinently quotes from the fifteenth-century commonplace book of Robert Reynys:

> Pope Innocent hath granted to any man that beareth the length of the three nails of Our Lord Jesus Christ upon him and worship them daily with five Paternosters and five Aves and a psalter, he shall have seven gifts granted to him. The first, he shall not be slain with sword nor knife. The second, he shall not die no sudden death. The third, his enemies shall not overcome him. The fourth, he shall have sufficient good and honest living. The fifth, that poisons nor fever nor false witness shall grieve him. The sixth, he shall not die without the sacraments of the Church. The seventh, he shall be defended from all wicked spirits, from pestilence and all evil things.[11]

Yet another problem with confining ourselves to "emic" medieval categories is that they may not be consistent across the board. Not all medieval intellectuals thought alike about the border between magic and religion: as scholars well represented in the present volume have emphasized, some people whom a Thomas Aquinas might have put on the "Magic" side of the "Religion/Magic" divide, would by no means have put up their hands to dealing with demons, rather than interesting spirits, as with the *Sworn Book* of "Honorius Son of Euclid"; as Kieckhefer puts it, the "spirits addressed are neither straightforwardly demonic nor conventionally angelic".[12] Similarly, with the people attacked by Eudes Rigaud. Or again, Eudes Rigaud might think that demons were operating undercover to make stones appear to possess unexplained powers, but the people Eudes is attacking presumably thought they genuinely possessed those powers. Or again, some thought that the

> power of a plant to cure certain ailments, or the power of a gem to ward off certain kinds of misfortune, may derive not from the internal structure of the object but from ... emanations coming from the stars and planets... The properties in question were strictly within the realm of nature.[13]

If we confine ourselves to "the concepts of the time", we enter a world of conflicting notions.

All this suggests that "emic" concepts, the concepts of the time, are necessary but far from sufficient for historical analysis. Sociocultural lexicography, as one may call the process of understanding such "emic" concepts, can take us a long way – but not all the way. Modern historians do not have to take everything medieval people say about their beliefs and practices at face value. We may need to distinguish things that medieval terminology blurs, as with *ars magica*. Conversely, a modern scholar may want to draw attention to similarities between practices that contemporaries put in quite different categories: just as we might think that torture and enhanced interrogation techniques are not so different as some in that world would have it.

Furthermore, cultural lexicography does not help us draw comparisons between societies that use different languages: for any comparative analysis, a set of common terms must be devised by the historian. This is a point to which we must return. Devising such "common terms" is what I mean by conceptual technique, a key component of Weber's "ideal-type" methodology. The purpose of conceptual technique or ideal-type methodology is to give as a slightly specialized language, not identical either with that of the people in the past whom scholars study or of the discourse of the modern world around those same scholars: a slightly special language constructed to enable us both to identify differences and point to similarities we cannot otherwise easily articulate.

We need something between the Kieckhefer conformity to medieval concepts and the tendency of a Valerie Flint brush them aside. Flint's assimilation of magic with religious practices pointed to genuine commonalities but it was too blunt a conceptual instrument. It is the same way with Keith Thomas's idea of the "magic of the medieval Church": it goes too far if only in that it would logically lead to including baptism and the Eucharist in the category of magic:[14] the fact that "the sacraments worked automatically" gave "medieval Christianity an apparently magical character" (53). It is not clear what Thomas means by the "apparently". He goes on to say that "most other ecclesiastical operations could only be accomplished by a good priest and a pious laity" (ibid) but that in practice there was not much difference from pagan magic and that the "difference between churchmen and magicians lay less in the effects they claimed to achieve than in their social position, and in the authority on which their respective claims rested" (56).

The idea that magic was what Church authorities happened not to legitimate, but which is otherwise much the same as what the Church did legitimate, runs into an immediate problem: there is no clear difference in this conceptual scheme between magic and heresy. Would one want to call the Cathar *consolamentum* a magical ritual? If so, the category of magic has become unduly indiscriminate, a baggy holdall without separate compartments for forms of thought and ritual quite distinct in many medieval minds.

So the middle way is careful conceptual technique. Where "magic" and "religion" are concerned, the historian's ideal types are concepts for understanding the concepts of those they study. Ideal types should not cut against the grain of medieval categories, but they can have a much higher degree of precision – just as they are more precise than the everyday concepts of the historian's own world, with which they should not be confused. Reality is a system of parts, complicated far beyond what the mind can master. Ordinary language is a system of parts, rather crude. It blurs the distinction between some parts of reality and stops us seeing the similarities between other parts. Academic language stays as close as it can to ordinary language but tries to line up its system of parts a little more closely with reality. It never gets that close, but can approximate to the real system of parts more and more. The process of approximation is a technical skill, a bit like representational art. One should not say: what is the difference between magic and religion? One should say: how can I put together a set of concepts that together make up a slightly less crude model of the infinite complexity of thought and practice in this area.

Conceptual engineering is part of our job. From time to time we cannot get by as historians with our day-to-day concepts or with the concepts of the people we study. Then, we need to refine our analytical concepts. Twenty-first century concepts (as one might find them defined in the Oxford English Dictionary or Webster) are no more up to the job of understanding medieval life and thought than are medieval concepts on their own. The historian's "conceptual technique" has to supply the deficiencies of both.

To avoid confusion, medievalists could do worse than use Latin or medieval vernacular words for medieval concepts: *ars magicia, divinatio, sortilegium*, etc. It would be a clear way of marking out these "emic" concepts from the "etic" concepts that the historian constructs. Evidently, the "etic" concepts created by historians should be carefully and clearly articulated, a process closer to the heart of the historians task than the phrase "defining one's terms" might suggest.

So I would suggest the following categories or ideal types:[15]

Magic = the use of non-physical (and not merely mental) forces to serve the magicians ends, whether good or bad.

Religious magic = the above, within the framework of a religious system. The passage quoted above, after Keith Thomas, from the commonplace book of Robert Reynys, is an example from within the later medieval Church. The thinking is genuinely magical as we have defined it, and theologians would probably have disapproved while dismissing it as harmless.

A *religious system* = a set of ways of giving meaning to the world and human action in which non-physical (and not merely mental) factors play a part (it is best not to mention divinity, because that would exclude the atheistic forms of Buddhism).

Non-magical religion = religious practices insofar as they are not instruments in the service of the practitioners. A really clear illustration is the *Bhagavad Gita*. Carrying out of caste duties needs to be without any desire for the fruits of so doing. Asceticism and sacrifice are useful for salvation only if one internally renounces their fruits and does them for their own sake.[16] Note however that "non-magical religion" also includes supernatural forces believed to work through human agency, but with a proviso. The condition to correspond to the "non-magical religion" ideal type is that the supernatural forces are not harnessed by the human agent. The human agent may be a vehicle for the exercise of supernatural forces by a divine agent, but those forces must not be regarded as his, the human agent's, own tool or weapon. If this condition is met, then the practices can be called "non-magical" even if they work automatically granted a given intention (i.e. not as a joke or in a play). This is important because it brings out the difference between medieval sacraments such as baptism and the Eucharist and magical practices, as Keith Thomas did not manage to do. The consecration of the host at mass could be called non-magical – even though the effects follow automatically, in a manner quite different from that of supplicatory prayer – provided that the priest seems himself as an instrument of God's power, rather than a man with a special power at his personal service. Similarly, those who receive the consecrated host believing it to be the body and blood of Christ are not thinking magically if they see the process as instrumental to God's purpose of bringing them closer to him, but it would be magical (as well as religious) if they thought it likely to save them from illness or violent death.

Superstition is a fragment separated from the religious or magical system in which it originated.[17] The following is probably a case in point. Some laypeople in thirteenth-century England believed that if they received the sacrament of extreme unction and then recovered from their illness, they had to give up sex with their wives and meat eating (also, for some reason, walking bare foot).[18] The ban on bare foot walking is beyond my powers of explanation, but the rest looks like a fragment of Cathar belief that had somehow become detached and found its way across the channel. Cathars who had received the *consolamentum* were indeed bound to give up sex and meat, because they had technically joined the ranks of the perfect.

It must be emphasized again that these are ideal types: conceptual distinctions drawn by the historian to identify forms of life and thought that are inextricably mixed up together in the actual life of the past. One can think of them as a kind of colour coding to help us identify different elements in the complex mixture that we are working on. Note too that "religion" and "magic" are not treated even conceptually as mutually exclusive categories. This enables the conceptual scheme to cope comfortably with the distinctively religious forms of magic studied, notably, by Sophie Page.

This conceptual scheme has another advantage: It avoids collapsing the categories of magic and heresy into one another, as the idea of magic as "what lacked official approval" would logically tend to do. Yet, another advantage is that these concepts are relatively free from value judgements. The "concepts of the time" are mostly "thick" with implicit value judgements. A historian may disapprove of magic and approve of heresy, or of orthodox Catholicism, but that should not affect the analysis.

Using an "etic" conceptual scheme has a further advantage already adumbrated above, viz. that it enables comparative history. Ideal types are crucial intermediaries between the categories expressed in the different languages (in the literal sense) of different cultures. Some historians have no interest in comparative history, but those who do need a neutral academic language into which the words of both cultures can be translated. Edward Evans-Pritchard wrote a classic study of *Witchcraft, Oracles, and Magic among the Azande*.[19] We cannot really know how far the word "*Boro ngua*" corresponds to "*divinus*", or "*Mangu*" to "*Maleficium*" without a vocabulary to mediate between the two. A conceptual scheme with categories capable of accommodating those of both cultures has to be the answer. The one sketched out above is not unduly elaborate but it does the job of identifying the commonalities linking Azande and medieval magic. If we went all the way with Kieckhefer's approach, it would be hard to link *Mangu* and *Maleficium*, in that demons to not seem to play a part in Azande witchcraft. A witch's power derives from witchcraft substance in their bodies, not from evil spirits. This substance can be revealed by an autopsy and it is transmittable genetically. Yet, the power is non-physical. Azande distinguish clearly between magical and physical causation: "if a man is killed by an elephant Azande say that the elephant is the first spear and that witchcraft is the second spear and that together they killed the man" (25–6). So *Mangu* is clearly different from medieval natural magic. *Mangu* is not the only kind of magic as defined above. Notably, there is *Wene ngua*, which can mean magic that is socially approved (227). Good magic is important for combatting witchcraft (199–200). It will be apparent that our definition of magic shows the commonalities between different Azande categories without blurring the boundaries between them.

Many medieval Christian religious categories could legitimately be categorized as "socially approved magic", in that they were implicitly or explicitly in the service of the practitioner's power. It depended on the attitude of mind. It can be difficult to tell exactly how persons engaged in rituals saw themselves and their rituals, but nonetheless we can put it like this: *insofar as* the persons conducting rituals saw them as their instruments, we can speak of magical religion. On the other hand, insofar as practitioners saw both themselves and the ritual as instruments of God, their activities can be detached from the category of magic. (Note well: anyone who conflates the preceding sentence with the idea that religion is supplicatory while magic is coercive has misunderstood my argument.) A priest saying mass or anyone baptizing an infant was supposed to be carrying out God's will rather than exercising personal power. But if the exercise of personal power became an element of the action, then one can indeed speak of religious magic, just as one can with prayers that were regarded as a way of obtaining advantages unavailable to the impious. Richard Kieckhefer has suggested that "intentions are so ambiguous, complex, and variable that it is unhelpful to take the intended force as the crucial and defining characteristic of magic in general".[20] This seems like a non sequitur. Historians need clear-cut concepts, ideal types, precisely in order to analyse out the elements in the messy mix of reality. One may define "altruism" as actions performed by someone who would be just as happy to someone else carry them out and get the credit, then follow on not with the question: "was this action altruistic?" but "how far was this action altruistic?" Second, there are the private intentions of those involved and the public intentions embodied in the rituals.[21] In the public context of a baptism ritual, the baptiser is an instrument of God's will to save, even if she or he may privately enjoy seeming important. Third, public intentions embodied in rituals actually manifest the type of power being invoked, so we are not so far from Kieckhefer after all: as he wrote, "That which makes an action magical is the type of power it invokes".[22] The ritual of consecration at the mass invokes divine power channelled through the priest.

The external character of a ritual often makes it clear how far it is an instrument of power at the disposal of the one who conducts the ritual. Keith Thomas and Valerie Flint were right to think that much medieval religious practice was also magical. Richard Kieckhefer was right to argue that the medieval clergy's categories must be taken seriously. The conceptual scheme proposed here is meant to be complex enough to do justice to the insights of both sides of the argument.

Notes

1 Richard Kieckhefer, "The Specific Rationality of Medieval Magic," *American Historical Review* 99 (1994): 813–36.
2 This presupposes a tentative emendation of the passage as transcribed below to "videtur quod non. Scire – hoc malum non est, neque …."
3 "Ultimo queritur utrum peccatum sit in exercendis artibus illis magicis: quod videtur scire hoc malum non est; Similiter neque posse est malum operari. Operari etiam non est malum, quia

dyabolus hoc operatur, non homo. Ergo videtur quod non sit peccatum in talibus. Si ergo est, erit quia prohibita sunt. Sed tunc queritur quare sunt prohibita. # Item iste operatur vel facit serpentem exire de caverna ad incantationem: nunquid peccat? Quod non videtur, quia actus non [*supplied in margin*] est malus. # Item verba que dicit non sunt mala, quia dicit: Pater noster, et alia naturalia que bona sunt. Item, si in verbis, lapidibus et herbis sunt virtutes, sicut consuevit dici ? - Sed uti verbis, lapidibus ad virtutes ad quas sunt nullum est peccatum. Ergo similiter herbis. # Item de figuris que fiunt: utrum sit ibi peccatum ? Videtur quod non, quia aut est virtus aliqua in eis, et tunc non videtur esse peccatum, aut non, et tunc videtur esse inutile, non peccatum…." Paris, BNF MS lat. 14910, fol. 124va.

4   Arguments from authority (the "Contra" section) are followed by a rather messy demolition of the arguments stated at the start:"Respondeo dicendum quod peccatum est sine dubio, quia prohibitum est in can[one] et adiuncta pena excommunica|tionis. [**col. b**] Ad illud quod primo obicit [*read* obicitur?] dicendum est quod prohibitum quia occasio superbiendi hiis qui faciunt, et occasio infidelitatis et ydolatrie. Superbiendi quidem quia dyabolus fingit se eis esse subiectum et cogi ad imperium eorum ut se reputent magne potentie et in hoc extollantur. Infidelitatis etiam quia demones asserunt se cogi ad eorum verba atque figuras, ut in hiis habeant fidem et credant in huiusmodi talem esse virtutem et ita a fide abducantur. Occasio ydolatriandi quia ipse dyabolus per familiare eorum contubernium [conturbernium *ms.*] ortatur eos ut sibi aliquam faciant reverentiam et aliquas immolationes et oblationes faciant, et orationes, et huiusmodi – alioquin [aliquin/aliqm *ms.*] dicunt se non venturos. Et etiam occasio omnis mali. Nam huiusmodi sunt in potestate [potestatem *ms.*] dyaboli, qui ducit eos per diversa peccata; et iterum nunquam bono fine faciunt que faciunt, quia demones semper ad malum ordinant, neque faciunt rem que valeat sed semper ludibria, ut serpentes, ranas, et huiusmodi, et hoc eis permittit ad prioris facti memoriam. # Ad aliud dicendum quod peccat quia credit illis esse virtutem, et similiter in figuris. Nulla enim in verbis illis vel figuris est virtus, sed dyabolus ad verba illa divino [dicit *ms.?*] iudicio permittente, compescit [*after* consp *expunged*] serpentem ut vir vel mulier malefica habeat in illis fidem et aberret a fide. Similiter de huiusmodi brevibus que fiunt et catareribus [? = characteribus] que fiunt. In talibus verbis, quantum ad effectum illum, nulla est virtus, sed dyabolus, sagax, ad verba illa facit ut terrorem adducat, maxime cum homo subiugavit se ipsi dyabolo, qui avidus est de animabus lucrandis." Paris, BNF MS lat. 14910, fosl. 124va-b.

5   For a rich analysis of "natural magic" in the context of one monastery and other kinds of learned magic, see Sophie Page, *Magic in the Cloister: Pious Motives, Illicit Interests, and Occult Approaches to the Medieval Universe* (University Park: Pennsylvania State University Press, 2013).

6   D. L. d'Avray, *The Preaching of the Friars: Sermons Diffused from Paris before 1300* (Oxford: Clarendon Press, 1985), 198–201.

7   "Ad idem facit quod retulit quidam frater noster qui cum esset in seculo quidam rusticus venit ad eum, rogans ut faceret suis incantationibus quod haberet quandam aliam rusticam in uxorem; qui repulit eum, dicens quod rem periculosam et difficilem postulabat. At rusticus, [*supply* credens?] quod hoc diceret quia exennia non portasset, cum sabbato venisset ad forum, et suum asinum vendidisset, portavit illam pecuniam et capones, eidem supplicans sicut prius. At ille dixit: 'Vade ad ta|lem [**col. b**] campum et ibi me expectabis.' Ivit rusticus ille, et homo ille, convocatis quibusdam discipulis suis, ait: 'Videte, quidam rusticus rogat me de tali negotio. Unde volo quod adiuveris me modo, et sic habebimus pecuniam quam portavit. Talis de vobis [duobus *ms.*] vocabitur Belzebul, talis Asmodeus, et quilibet vestrum sit transfiguratus' – et sic v nomina diversa imposuit. 'Unde quando vocabo *Veniat Belzebul*, talis veniat deferens secum baculum, ostendens quod velit ipsum percutere.' Cum igitur ad locum destinatum discipuli ivissent, venit magister illorum ubi rusticus ille erat et, facto circulo, precepit quod intraret circulum, de qua nulla ratione exiret. Intravit rusticus circulum, et magister ille cepit demones invocare, clamans altissime: 'Veniat Belzebul.' Imposuerat totus niger, portans baculum, et vibravit baculum super caput rustici. Ad quem magister: 'Precipio tibi ne ipsum percutias, sed modo veniat talis'. [**fo. xiiii**[ra]] Cum igitur venissent omnes, ceperunt per capillos rusticum, et ipsum proiecerunt ad terram, et durissime verberaverunt. Cumque rusticus timeret et dolores sentiret, clamavit ad magistrum, dicens: 'Domine, adiuva me !' At magister imperavit discipulis ut recederent, et amplius non venirent. Cumque illi recessissent: 'Domine, satis est'; et sic rusticus ille pecuniam [pecunia *ms.*] perdidit et non habuit quod optavit." Birmingham University MS 6.iii.19, fols. xiiivb-xiiiira.

8   "Legitur enim quod fuit quedam mulier que dicebat quod ibat super bestias cum dominabus, quod ideo credebat quod sic eam faciebant demones sompniare. Cum autem illa mulier in ecclesia suo

diceret sacerdoti: "Domine, hac nocte multum vobis profui, et a magnis periculis liberavi, quoniam domine, cum quibus vado in nocte, fuerunt hac nocte in camera ista, et volebant vobis multa mala facere nisi vos iuvissem." Cui sacerdos ait: "Istud est inpossibile, quoniam hostium meum fuit in nocte bene clausum." Cui vetula dixit: "Domine, nec hostium nec sera potest re|tinere [**fo. xiii^{va}**] nos. Et sacerdos: "Certe volo hoc probare, ut te valeam de tanto beneficio remunerare"; et clauso hostio ecclesie, ac, fortiter ferrato, accepit bonum baculum et cepit eam durissime [durissimam *ms.*] verberare. At illa clamabat dicens: "Domine, miserere mei." Cui sacerdos: "Modo fuge si potes, ex quo hostium non potest te retinere. Iura michi igitur quod amplius talia non loqueris." At illa ei iuravit quod de cetero non diceret talia, et sic sacerdos dimisit eam." Birmingham University MS 6.iii.19, fols. xiiirb-va; cf. London, British Library MS Add. 33956 fols. 81va-b for the same motif with different details.

9   "Sed vellem quod domine nostri temporis, que tot predicationes audiverunt, totiens figmenta falsa esse cognoverunt, responderunt talibus vetulis divinantibus sicut legitur quandam prudentem [prudrentem *ms.*] dominam cuidam vetule respondisse, que dicebat ei [eis *ms.*] quod si faceret hoc vel hoc, virum haberet divitem, qui ipsam multum amaret. "Ecce tu habes maritum pauperem et amasiam retinentem, qui te nec vult nec audire [*sic – supply say* curat]. Quomodo igitur quod tibi non potuisti facere facies michi, scilicet quod habeam [habeat *ms.*] maritum divitem ac potentem et [*between lines*] me affectuosius diligentem?" MS Birmingham University 6.iii.19, fo. xiira-b

10 "Ecce quantum mulieres credunt talibus divinationibus et fictionibus, quoniam invenitur scriptum in quodam opusculo exemplorum quod in quibusdam locis viri et mulieres, quando obviabant sacerdoti, statim se signabant, quod malum signum est obviare sacerdoti. Unde erat apud illos esset quedam mortalitas, quandam divinam vetulam consuluerunt, que dixit quod nisi sepeliatur sacerdos vivus, plaga illa ab eis cessare non poterit. Et occulte statuerunt [**fo. xii^{ra}**] in prima fossa facta sepelire [sepelierunt *ms.*] proprium sacerdotem, pro mortuo aliquo tumulando. Cum igitur mortua esset quedam vetula que longo tempore fuerat infirmata, et ad fossam populus convenisset, sacerdotem indutum sacris vestibus, qui faciebat officium, illi rustici apprehenderunt, ponentes eum in fossa, et super ipsum, licet fortiter clamaret, terram illam proiecerunt, atque tantum piaculum [praculum *ms.?*] pro divinatione unius vetule pessime conmiserunt". MS Birmingham University 6.iii.19, fol. Xivb-xiira.

11 Keith Thomas, *Religion and the Decline of Magic* (Harmondsworth: Penguin, 1971).
12 Richard Kieckhefer, *Magic in the Middle Ages* (Cambridge: Cambridge University Press, 1989), 170.
13 Kieckhefer, *Magic in the Middle Ages*, 13.
14 Title of chapter 2 of his *Religion and the Decline of Magic*, 27–57, esp. 53.
15 They are logically compatible with Kieckhefer's, *Magic in the Middle Ages*, 14, but more helpful because Kieckhefer's lump natural and demonic magic, which is justified by the common name "magic" but otherwise a distraction from more important distinctions.
16 See Max Weber, *Gesammelte Aufsätze zur Religionssoziologie* ii *Hinduismus und Buddhismus* (Tübingen: J. C. B. Mohr (Paul Siebeck), 1988), 193–4.
17 This perceptive definition comes from my colleague John North.
18 Statutes of Worcester III, 1240, in *Councils and Synods with Other Documents Relating to the English Church*, II: *A.D. 1205–1313*, ed. F.M. Powicke and C.R. Cheney, 2 vols. (Oxford: Oxford University Press, 1964), I, 305.
19 E.E. Evans-Pritchard, *Witchcraft, Oracles and Magic among the Azande* (Oxford: Clarendon Press, 1976).
20 Kieckhefer, *Magic in the Middle Ages*, 16.
21 For similar lines of thought, see M. Baxandall, *Patterns of Intention: On the Historical Explanation of Pictures* (New Haven, CT: Yale University Press, 1985), and Quentin Skinner, "Motives, Intentions and Interpretation," in *Visions of Politics*, I: *Regarding Method*. (Cambridge: Cambridge University Press, 2002), 90–102.
22 Kieckhefer, *Magic in the Middle Ages*, 14.

5

RESPONSES

*Richard Kieckhefer, David L. d'Avray,
Bernd-Christian Otto, and Claire Fanger*

Richard Kieckhefer

The essays by David L. d'Avray and Bernd-Christian Otto are stimulating, insightful, deeply engaging reflections, pointing in opposite directions: D'Avray argues for using etic alongside emic terms, giving "magic" the clarity and precision of a Weberian ideal type so that it becomes a sharp analytic tool for both European history and cross-cultural study; Otto draws back from "second-order" or "third-order" terms and urges instead a "discourse historical" analysis that tracks and analyses language within historical texts. Claire Fanger and I come from different directions but reach concordant conclusions, both advocating flexible understandings of "magic" while allowing (in Fanger's case) or urging (in mine) more technical use of alternative terms. I have questions for both d'Avray and Otto.

1. Does d'Avray's definition take into account the phenomena usually classed as natural magic? He defines magic as "the use of non-physical (and not merely mental) forces to serve the magician's ends, whether good or bad." The forces in question are the magician's "own tool or weapon." Natural magic as traditionally defined, however, does not involve "non-physical" powers but rather exploit powers inherent within nature, in plants, gems or other objects. They may be mysterious and elude understanding, but no more than gravity. They may be thought of as the effects of the "whole substance", or as coming from heavenly bodies. In any case, they are decidedly physical. Further, the powers are not in any meaningful sense the magician's own; the powers of natural magic can be shared with a client, with all the readers of a treatise, in principle even with someone who discovers them by accident. They do not require a magician with "special power at his personal service." The power resides in the physical object, not in its user.
2. Is d'Avray's definition adequate to the conjuring of demons and other spirits? He says the magician uses his powers as "tools or weapons". The conjurer uses formal commands, which the conjured spirit is likely to resist. The conjurations have their force from the sacred power of the names and events that the conjurer invokes. At times, they explicitly request divine aid. The conjurer is tapping into a source of numinous power as an aid to the exercise of his own will. No doubt the magician does have formulas or implements that can be spoken of metaphorically as his tools or weapons, but they work only within a kind of force field, a complex interplay of spiritual powers, divine and demonic, on which the conjurer relies. What makes the conjuration work, and *what makes it count as magic*, can hardly be reduced to one simple element in the complex.

3. D'Avray's definition might be revised to take answer these objections, but can it be clarified or amended to answer both objections while remaining a single and useful definition of magic? Or if it is adjusted to fit more adequately the particularities of natural magic on the one hand, and of conjuration on the other hand, is it likely to become either too vague to be useful or else closer to what I have called an aggregating definition?
4. Can we define "religious magic" more precisely? D'Avray defines it as "the above [i.e. magic according to his definition], within the framework of a religious system." The criterion is whether the forces in question are regarded as those of a divine agent, which may use a human vehicle, or those of a human agent using them as "his own tool or weapon." Clearly, there is a broad area of overlap between magic and religion – and my disagreement with Valerie Flint was never about that. A person who receives communion and then uses the host as a love amulet, or one who uses litanies and psalms in conjuring a demon, is clearly mixing magic and religion, using religious forms and objects as if they had inherent occult virtue like that of a magical gem or plant, or exploiting the power of the sacred in the exercise of overtly demonic magic. Cases of this sort abound. But what if a woman prays in her own words, asking God for health of soul and body? Calling her prayer magical as well as religious would be odd. But then at what point does a practice become "one's own" and a "tool"? D'Avray does not rely on the Frazerian distinction between supplication and coercion. What distinction does serve, then, without placing prayer generally in the same category as using the host as an amulet? Even the devotional formula for warding off harm given by Robert Reynys, which a late medieval theologian would probably refer to as superstition (*this* is how they typically used that word), is not obviously magical: the protections are "granted" to the user, presumably by God, and the devotion requires "worship" with specific prayers, which imply an appeal to God. We can say the formula is magical *to the extent that* the user sees himself as having special power, but anyone, even the priest at mass, can think in those terms. We are unlikely to have evidence for such allegedly magical thinking on the part of the priest – or of Robert Reynys and his reader. Surely there are more useful ways to think of this area of overlap.
5. Even if one grants, as I do, the utility of etic terms, is it appropriate to use *emic terms as etic*, or does this needlessly confuse? Etic vocabulary may be needed, but it does not follow that any particular etic term is useful. And distinguishing between etic "magic" and emic *magica* does not work when the subjects themselves use the vernacular.
6. Why precisely does comparison require mediating terms? Why, to compare X and Y, must they both be instances of a univocally defined Z? Someone seeking shared essences (e.g. the "mystical experience" found in all traditions) will indeed need to define those essences. But comparison can cite similarities and differences without assuming a shared essence, in which case any encompassing label will be a term of convenience, preferably one best adapted to express the similarities without exaggerating them, and without privileging the tradition from which the term derives.
7. How relevant is the discourse analysis that Otto recommends to contexts where there is no discourse, or where the discourse is not sufficiently reflective to allow sophisticated analysis of terms? If we have before us a clay image pierced with needles, a bundle of noxious substances found beneath the threshold of a house and a birthing girdle inscribed with the SATOR AREPO square, we will probably refer to all these as magical objects, and rightly so, although they are diverse in type, and they may perhaps qualify as magical in different ways. If we seek to contextualize these objects, we will find

relevant material mainly in judicial records, magical miscellanies and other texts that do not contain reflection on magic (and may well not even use that term, although its use for these practices would have been familiar from the broader culture). I would not want to relegate these objects and practices to an ambiguous category of "allegedly 'magical' ritual traditions" on the grounds that they are orally transmitted and thus likely to have been short and simple. I would not restrict the history of magic to discourse analysis, or privilege material that lends itself to such analysis.

8. I share with Claire Fanger a concern about sharp distinctions between the discourses of insiders (magical practitioners) and outsiders (including their critics). For example, is the pact narrative necessarily a tool of "othering"? Ambiguity and uncertainty about the nature of the spirits conjured can be found within the texts of angel magic. Magicians and critics alike believed in both fallen and unfallen angels, and in the capacity of both types to respond to human summons. Magicians were generally more optimistic about the possibility of conjuring unfallen or neutral spirits, but some of them did also explicitly and deliberately conjure fallen ones. Magicians and their critics both lived within a culture that saw conjuration as playing with fire. What separated them was not a clear distinction in what they believed so much as a difference in what they saw as a risk worth taking. Discerning both the agreement in belief and the difference in risk engagement is a crucial challenge for discourse analysis.

David L. d'Avray

Both Claire Fanger and Bernd-Christian Otto offer "emic" accounts of medieval magic: their interest is mainly in "first order" concepts. Both make references to Foucault, it is true, but their pieces would work just as well without him. As analyses of medieval concepts, their papers are nuanced and valuable. Fanger's idea of a "conversation", between sympathizers with and opponents of magic, is attractive. There are affinities between her ideas and the analysis of conflict by Niklas Luhmann, *Soziale Systeme* (Frankfurt, 1984), pp. 530–33.

Fanger is reacting against modern interpretations of magic which start from the idea of a *Entzauberung der Welt*: magic is what modernity got rid of. We can agree to distance ourselves from that schema, which she classifies as "etic", but we do not need to give up all attempts at a clearer etic understanding. Fanger argues that we need some shifting and ambiguous concepts. Agreed. That does not mean that we can do without at least some clear concepts.

Currently, discussions of magic and religion in the Middle Ages remind me of after dinner arguments by slightly inebriated undergraduates, each enjoyably pursuing their own train of thought, feeling that they are communicating but often at cross purposes, relishing the exchange while if anything enhancing their initial collective confusion. Richard Kieckhefer's contribution is a model of ideal-type methodology, whether or not he would put it that way. Some good scholars use it without even thinking about it. Many others think that they know what it is without really understanding it. For anyone in that case, a look at what Kieckhefer does is a good introduction to the method. A starting point is that everyday language is good for navigating the contemporary world but not designed for analysing complex problems in the past. Kieckhefer rightly says that the word "magic" as generally used is all over the place and of limited value for research, compared with what he calls "constitutive terms". These are a particular form of ideal type: concepts carefully defined for academic analytical purposes with a lot of prior familiarity with the field underpinning them. It is a helical process: familiarity with the field enables the formulation of precise concepts with the help of which the field can be better understood. In the case of magic, the concepts are "conjuration", "symbolic manipulation" and "directly efficacious volition": terms not too far from ordinary speech but used in slightly technical senses defined by the scholar. In the later part of his paper, we see a key aspect of ideal-type methodology in action: Kiechkhefer is prepared to find the reality of the past messier than the ideal types, a.k.a. constitutive concepts, but clear-cut concepts nonetheless enable one to measure the messiness and note phenomena that only partly embody the concept or where it is mixed up with other elements. That his three constitutive concepts correspond to three types of thought and practice that tend to be associated "on the ground" is a further stage of analysis. The association between these three practices is itself an illuminating ideal type. They do not have to go together, but in the Middle Ages they tended to go together. All this advances our understanding of the field by providing better conceptual tools.

"Magic" is relegated by Kieckhefer to the category of "aggregative concepts" that maps fairly well on to what I would call the concepts of ordinary language as opposed to precise idealtypes. He makes clear his view that "magic" is a lost cause if one wants precise conceptual language. So far as that is concerned, his colours are nailed so firmly to the mast that I entertain no hope of shaking his views. I would only comment that abandonment of any hope of using "magic" in a precisely defined way has some consequences. It rules out a comparative sociology of magic, though not of "directly efficacious volition", etc. It leaves an unanswered question about the medieval concept of "natural magic". Kieckhefer keeps this within his composite ideal type by saying that occult properties were taught by demons. But was that the only way to know about them? I think some medieval intellectuals thought of them as we think of gravity: forces that are natural and that we know about, though we do not understand how they work. So understood, natural magic fits less well into his interpretative scheme. Finally, his three constitutive concepts come close to including a lot of sacramental religion. Kieckhefer gives strong hints that the difference is the attitude to the practitioner's power and I suspect we could reach agreement on that point.

In an ideal world, this conversation would continue. This contributor would certainly have much to say about the responses of the other two.

Bernd-Christian Otto

In his chapter "Rethinking How to Define Magic", Richard Kieckhefer calls into question the possibility of properly defining and theorizing "magic" as it is an "aggregating term" and therefore – just like many other broad, overarching concepts (e.g. "mysticism", "religion") – only a "term of convenience" which is "open to ambiguous and imprecise usage" and "encompass[es] diverse elements that may or may not be combined with each other". As definitions of "aggregating terms" such as "magic" necessarily remain arbitrary and inadequate, Kieckhefer suggests that we should stop "expecting more of it than it can deliver", and instead focus on identifying and refining three "constitutive terms" that denote *elements* or *subcategories* of the undefinable meta-category "magic": "conjuration", "symbolic manipulation" and "directly efficacious volition".

I am very sympathetic to Kieckhefer's approach as it resembles my own suggestion to develop "open and flexible taxonomies" of narrative or ritual patterns that appear in sources of medieval "learned magic". Alluding to a formulation recently used by Egil Asprem, both

Kieckhefer and I seem to believe that a substantial "reverse-engineering"[1] of the concept of "magic" is necessary, as it allows for breaking down this "complex cultural construct" (to use Asprem's terminology) into smaller, more specific and thus easier to handle "building blocks". The same idea underlies the concept of "patterns of magicity" which I have elsewhere proposed with Michael Stausberg,[2] but which has not (yet) been adapted to medieval sources.

Even though I share Kieckhefer's desire to neglect the "aggregating term" and to focus on a more nuanced and differentiated analytical language, I believe that there are, at least from the perspective of my own "discourse historical approach", two basic problems with Kieckhefer's selection of these three "constitutive terms". One problem is rather theoretical, the other historical. The theoretical problem is that Kieckhefer does not seem to restrict his "constitutive terms" to medieval material, but seems to perceive them as systematic (i.e. ahistorical) and comparative (i.e. universal) categories. This evokes an arsenal of classical problems: I shall only point to the inevitable "magic-science-religion" triangle (for example, Kieckhefer's notion of "symbolic manipulation" could be ascribed to large parts of medieval medicine – which, I believe, is rather confusing) and the "insider-outsider" problem (referring to the above example: most medieval physicians would probably not have agreed with Kieckhefer that their practices are essentially "symbolic manipulation" and, thus, "magical"; in other words, their "first-order" terminology and interpretation contradict Kieckhefer's "second-order" categorization, which is, at least in the light of my own "discourse historical approach", unsatisfactory).

The second, historical problem can be divided into three sub-problems: (1) The three "constitutive terms" discussed by Kieckhefer may denote ritual means typically associated with "magic" in the European Middle Ages (note, however, that one rarely encounters "directly efficacious volition" in medieval "learned magic"), but they lack relevance with regard to "insider" sources from other epochs; this is problematic for two reasons: first, it undermines Kieckhefer's claim that these three terms are actually sufficient to grasp the whole of "magic"; second, Kieckhefer's selection is apparently too constrained to acknowledge one of the most striking characteristics of "learned magic": its ongoing "changeability" (in contrast, Kieckhefer seems to suggest that "magic" was and is *always* constituted by these three "constitutive terms" – and thus more or less unalterable). (2) Even with regard to medieval "insider" sources (now using my own terminology), Kieckhefer's "constitutive terms" may not be exhaustive; in other words, we may encounter textual or ritual elements in these sources that are not covered or addressed by these terms (consider the ritual goal of *visio beatifica* in the *Liber iuratus*, or the ritual technique of *contemplating upon notae* in the *Ars notoria*). Alluding to my own suggestion to develop "open and flexible taxonomies of (i) ritual (micro-) techniques, (ii) ritual goals, and (iii) concepts of ritual efficacy", I believe that Kieckhefer's "constitutive terms" are simply not fine-grained enough. (3) Finally, all three "constitutive terms" may be found in other medieval contexts and milieus, too, and these other contexts and milieus may be completely detached from medieval discourses of "magic" (consider Kieckhefer's telling reference to "blessings or benedictions" while discussing "directly efficacious volition", or the importance of "symbolic manipulation" in medieval medicine, which I have already hinted at above). In other words, "conjuration", "symbolic manipulation" and "directly efficacious volition" do not even denote *specific* elements of medieval "learned magic" (in contrast to *charaktêres* or *ring letters*, for example) and, as a consequence, cannot actually constitute any meaningful, overarching category.

In her chapter "For magic: against method", Claire Fanger makes a strong argument for continuing the use of "magic" in modern scholarship and claims that medievalists may even be in a "privileged position to understand things about magic that modernists do not", namely, "to understand the potentialities inherent in the term 'magic'". Fanger rejects the position of critical scholars – such as Jonathan Z. Smith – who have advocated the abandonment of "magic" from scholarly language. At the end of her chapter, Fanger goes as far as to suggest "abandoning methodological reflection, defining the word as it suits us – or not – and moving on".

I agree with many of Fanger's historical observations and believe that our chapters complement each other very well. Even though Fanger does not use the technical terminology which I propose in my chapter, I consider her interpretations of Augustine, the *Picatrix*, Thomas Aquinas and John of Morigny to be in line with my understanding of a "discourse historical approach". However, I believe that she overshoots the argument in the last part of her chapter. Particularly, her final suggestion to "abandon methodological reflection" is hard to digest, given that her analysis is nothing but the result of a *very sophisticated methodological reflection*. Fanger produces – in my terminology – an "emic" analysis of the "first-order" use of the concept of "magic" within selected medieval sources, and thereby outlines various distinct semantic and evaluative patterns as well as different discursive functions and motifs. Her approach is therefore – inevitably – "anti-essentialist" and it is important to note that Fanger *nowhere* applies or advocates a meaningful "second-order" notion of "magic". This absence of "second-order" notions is crucial as it stands in stark contrast to – or even contradicts – her final claim to support definitions of "magic" ("I propose [...] defining the word as it suits us"). Fanger's argument is in fact incoherent here: if she would have stipulated a definition and thereby projected a single, context-free meaning of "magic" onto her material, she would have obscured or distorted precisely those "first-order" notions of "magic" which she has so brilliantly unveiled in the historical section of her chapter.

In a similar vein, Fanger's criticism of Jonathan Z. Smith is, in my view, misleading. In her analysis, Fanger *does* – in effect – eschew "magic" as an "etic" term (!), and she *does* "trade places" in Smith's sense: instead of one monolithically defined concept of "magic", we encounter a wide range of nuanced formulations and different semantic facets in her own narrative – such as "ungrounded in any theory of natural causation and unmoored from any legible system", "devotional kinds of activity [...] that [...] fail to recognize the true God", "a ritual aimed at the correct object that errs in its protocols" and so forth. Alluding to my own chapter, I believe it is crucial to differentiate between "etic" analyses that *employ* "second-order" notions of "magic" – these are the ones criticized by Smith – and "emic" analyses that *reconstruct* "first-order" notions of "magic" – this is actually pursued by Fanger. If one does not conflate these two research agendas, it turns out that Smith's and Fanger's position do not contradict but complement each other. I am even quite sure that, if Smith ever reads the piece, he would approve Fanger's analysis and perceive it as a materialization of what he had suggested in his 1995 article.

For these reasons, I would strongly object to Fanger's endorsement of a methodological "anything goes" position in the final part of her chapter, and I also believe that Fanger would not be satisfied with the results if her wish became true. The analytical turn which is currently taking place in the academic study of "magic" – the turn *from* adopting (single) essentialist or even universalistic "second-order" definitions *to* reconstructing (diverse) "first-order" notions, functions and evaluative patterns in the research material – is a major step forward, particularly in historical research. Calling for a methodological "anything goes" position runs the risk of relapsing into arbitrary reifications, normative misinterpretations, distortive projections and interdisciplinary misunderstandings. Fanger's excellent interpretation of medieval notions of "magic" demonstrates that we are way beyond that now.

In his chapter "The concept of magic", David L. d'Avray challenges the idea that it could be sufficient or satisfactory to engage in "emic" analyses of medieval notions of "magic", and makes a strong case for developing and applying a set of "etic" terms as these may provide greater analytical precision in medieval studies (note that what d'Avray calls "emic" concepts of "magic" are, in my terminology, "first-order" concepts; the same goes for his formulation "ordinary language"; what d'Avray calls "ideal types" correspond to my idea of "second-order" notions of "magic").

From the viewpoint of my own methodological approach, there are two basic problems with d'Avray's "ideal types". The first problem relates to the plausibility and consistent applicability of the "ideal types" themselves. Is it possible to find counterexamples that contradict or undermine these notions? As with all "second-order" categories – categories that come with general or universal pretensions and therefore collapse in the light of counter-evidence – this is done quite easily. For example, d'Avray's notion of "magic" could be applied to homeopathy (and many other types of healing methods that are disputable from a strictly "physical" viewpoint, whatever that precisely is),[3] which is surely not satisfactory; in other words, the definition covers "data" which it is not intended to do, and this undermines its alleged discriminatory power. Additionally, one wonders whether "magic" in d'Avray's sense can actually be observed in the European Middle Ages at all. I find it hard to imagine medieval practices that employ "non-physical (and not merely mental) forces" and which are not simultaneously embedded in or informed by any "religious system" (e.g. Christianity). It is for precisely this reason that many sources of medieval "learned magic" (now using my own terminology) actually fall under d'Avray's category of "religious magic", and some sources might even be subsumed under his rather indigestive category "non-magical religion" (consider the pivotal ritual goal of *visio beatifica* in the *Liber iuratus* which seems to correspond to his formulation "The human agent may be a vehicle for the exercise of supernatural forces by a divine agent, but those forces must not be regarded as his own tool or weapon"). However, as d'Avray himself concedes that his "ideal types" are artificial and only serve analytical purposes in specialized scholarship, he might accept these lacunae in the light of other insights gained by the suggested "etic" apparatus.

But even if d'Avray's "ideal-types" had sufficient conceptual *validity*, it remains to be asked whether they actually have analytical *value*. If it is not for comparative purposes (as in the case of his swift comparison with Evans-Pritchard's Azande, which rather reveals that there is not much to compare, as major differences prevail), I wonder whether the stipulation of such artificial "ideal types" actually serves to clarify anything in the study of medieval "magic". When "first-order" and "second-order" notions differ in such a substantial manner and, as a consequence, scholars engage in arguments about "magic" that most medieval actors would misconceive or object, then scholarly discourse runs the risk of becoming too detached from its research material to say anything meaningful about it. What is actually gained by classifying large parts of medieval Catholicism as "magical religion" (thereby incidentally aligning Catholic to "learned magic" practice, which is precisely what d'Avray intended to avoid in the first place), or, in contrast, the "correct" performance of the Eucharist as a manifestation of "non-magical religion"? In my view, nothing is gained by such artificial classifications and scholars should not feel privileged to decide upon these – ultimately normative – matters. From the viewpoint of the "discourse historical approach" suggested in my own chapter, I find it more plausible and illuminating to observe and reconstruct the manifold and ever-shifting historical debates about these alleged boundaries.

Claire Fanger

In the course of thinking through my responses to the other contributors' work in this forum (most of whom do have some sort of loose definition of magic behind their writing, whether they make this explicit or not), it has become clearer to me that I need to acknowledge the definitional qualities of my own representation of magic, and also that I should give a nod to the necessity and utility of definitions in general.

Thus, I will admit that in my own piece, I proposed a rough and ready definition of magic as "contested ritual". I did not represent this as a definition; I only noted that my interests lay in the elements that make "magic" a contested term in the discourses linked to it. However, this might as well be treated as the nub of a definition. I want to use my responses to the other contributors' work to approach a more positive way of looking at definitions generally.

Bernd Christian Otto's approach is expressed in a theoretical terminology similar to mine. He does not define magic (though something like a definition can be extrapolated from his argument).[4] I share his concern to attend closely to the medieval pro-magical sources that are still certainly the most undertreated data in the scholarly conversation.

Yet, despite our affinities, I find his call to analyse medieval "insider" sources wholly apart from "outsider" sources problematic. Otto's premise is that the two are distinct in principle. He sees "insider" discourses as comprising ritual sources and being theological only defensively. By contrast, "outsider" discourses are represented as authoritatively theological; they are ignorant of magical practice, and propagate polemics that distort and misrepresent "insider" views. The *Ars notoria* and *Liber florum* are claimed as "insider" sources (though both engage "polemics against magic"; but, according to his note 24, this is only because they aimed "to avoid animosities in a restrictive cultural environment").

I am uneasy with the postulate that "insider" discourses of learned magic (i.e. ritual) occur in a social space segregated from the clerical disciplines in which he finds only "polemics". John of Morigny may be the best documented example to date of a learned magic user. Otto rightly notes that he was an "insider" to magical discourse; but I counter that he was equally an "insider" to the institutional traditions of theology, exegesis and canon law. And if John confesses to working magic, to writing a "new necromancy", how surprising can this be? We always knew that magic texts were clerical productions. Perhaps it was easier to ignore what this meant in the absence of John's autobiography; but his *Liber florum* provides a model case of Foucault's proposition that discourses do not just constitute objects of knowledge; they constitute subjects too. And only those first constituted as subjects within, and by, the discourses Otto calls "outsider" that are positioned to become "insiders" to the world of learned magic at all.

And if the clerical world is the *point of entry* into learned magic, how can we think of the two as mutually exclusive? Discourse analysis must surely stay open to the ways magic remained permeable to thought, embedded in the learned disciplines that birthed it.

What I most appreciate in Richard Kieckhefer's approach is his recognition of the openness of conceptual systems and his willingness to live with definitions that are not too strictly reined in. He, too, rejects the opportunity to define magic, while offering useful ways of looking at the taxonomic project. I agree on the independent utility of aggregative terms (large, loose "umbrella" terms) and constitutive terms (specific forms of reference within the broad category of the aggregative term). I remain on the same page when he suggests that the smaller "constitutive terms" are better for comparative purposes.

Nevertheless, I am uneasy around the specific "constitutive" terms he uses to refine the idea of magic (conjuration, symbolic manipulation, efficacious volition). It seems problematic that his elaboration of these terms leaves unclear how a magical conjuration (e.g.) differs from a normal liturgical one. There are, of course, many conjurations that would not have been perceived as magical by medieval observers, including those done over water, salt, liturgical implements, over a child in the context of baptism, over a body in the context of a saint's healing, and I think too of the conjuration that brings Christina Mirabilis down from the rafters, and the conjuration of the ghost of Gui of Corvo. None of these are represented as magic in the texts where we read about them. How do we tell when we are looking at a *magical* conjuration? Similar things could be said about the constitutive terms "symbolic manipulation" and "efficacious volition"; I will not cite instances here, but I could adduce them.

This brings us back to the problem of the aggregative term of which these are to be seen as subclasses – magic itself. I think we need a way of using the word "magic" to make some critical distinctions in these subcategories before we go on. In short, and reluctant as I have been to admit it, I think we need a *definition of magic* here. At least it seems to me a desideratum to find some way of distinguishing the concepts informing these constitutive terms from religious instances of the same thing.

What I admire most in David d'Avray's approach is first off that it accepts the challenge of providing a proper definition (a challenge the rest of us have mostly sought to evade), and second that it aligns magic in relation to religion, neither opposing them nor subsuming one in the other. I can imagine situations where it might be useful to think in terms of religious and non-religious forms of magic (I am hard pressed to think of medieval instances, but I can think of some in other cultural contexts).

One feature of his definition seems problematic, however: the idea that magic calls upon, as he puts it, "non-physical (and not merely mental) forces". This is the nub of his distinction, so it is important for it to be clear; but I do not always find it easy myself to tell when a force counts as physical, even in my own daily experience, but especially in historical or comparative contexts. Is the force to be seen as non-physical in the eyes of medieval magic users? Or non-physical for modern (i.e. post-Newtonian, but perhaps pre-quantum theory) readers of medieval magic texts? Or for participant observers of magic in contemporary domestic or ethnographic arenas? (I think of one anthropologist's account of a medium in a possession dance being "thrown to the ground" by a possessing spirit.) Can such forces be definitively non-physical to all observers all the time?

In medieval discussions, what is accepted as the "physical" cause of magical effects is so often itself in dispute. What disturbed both Augustine and Thomas Aquinas is that meanings are non-physical but magic words often seemed to have physical effects. William of Auvergne refined this position by noting that words do have some physical forces in sound and breath, though this force is mostly very small. For him, as for Thomas, but pace al-Kindi and Berengar Ganell, meaning is not a force. And what degree of physical work were demons capable of? In medieval investigations of magical effects, the physicality of the force is often the very thing in question.

D'Avray argues that historians need etic definitions because emic ones (i.e. here, medieval ones) are sometimes unclear (i.e. mutually contradictory, among other things). He aims to construct a definition that will be broadly applicable and clear to everyone all the time. But nearly all definitions are capable of clarifying things in some contexts while introducing obscurity in others. This is true whether they are historical or contemporary, and no matter what context they arise from. To what extent is it really possible to formulate an "etic" definition of the kind d'Avray seeks here?

Ian Hacking defines a "concept" as "a word in its sites".[5] He notes that concepts have memories: a philosophical problem can arise as a result of discrepancies between an earlier state of the concept and a later one.[6] Perhaps the problem of magic grows acute for us because we have forgotten prior arrangements of ideas that made the concept work, but I am reluctant to let things rest here, in part because of the number of sites over centuries of use in which "magic" fingers a philosophical problem about the physicality of forces and the powers or effects of ritual. To shy away from the word, to claim that it is undefinable now, or should not be defined as an "etic" term, seems like a way of asserting that we no longer have this problem. But I think we do.

Obviously, the word "magic" is still actively in use; it can be found in conversation, in the media and in scholarship whether we like it or not. The fact that no single definition of "magic" describes all its potential sites may not be a good reason to hold back from venturing definitions that attempt to be scholarly; it may only mean that our definitions need to be more site-specific (more "emic"?) than we are making them.

Looking at this another way, the functionality of concepts may depend on how many sites of operation we ourselves keep active as much as (or more than) how many sites we limit our definitions to. Indeed, the attempt to control a concept by limitation of the sites it is allowed to interact with may itself be a form of dysfunction. An ability to recognize the concept of "magic" in play across a broad range of sites is arguably useful to the historian – more useful, surely, than discounting large ranges of instances as "outsider" polemics, or alternatively as "emic" definitions rendered unclear by their multiplicity.

When Crowley calls "magick" the science and art of causing change to occur in conformity with will, I recognize what he is getting at. When Weber talks about the elimination of magic from the world as the great historic process of all religions, I recognize that too. I know what Durkheim means when he says there is no church of magic; and similarly also I recognize Michael Taussig's intent when he treats magic as the skilled revelation of skilled concealment. All these usages and definitions are both etic (in that they aim at broad applicability) and emic (in that they target an in-group, a specific readership in a particular time and place). All show expertise in the context of their specific language games, and my intellectual world would be the poorer without them.

So I suggest we own up to our definitions; indeed, let us bring on more and better ones. I thank Otto, Kieckhefer and d'Avray for giving me the benefit of this useful exercise.

Notes

1 See Egil Asprem, "Reverse-Engineering 'Esotericism': How to Prepare a Complex Cultural Concept for the Cognitive Science of Religion," *Religion* (2015). DOI: 10.1080/0048721X.2015.1072589.
2 See Bernd-Christian Otto and Michael Stausberg, *Defining Magic: A Reader* (Sheffield: Equinox, 2013), 10ff.
3 Note that the formulation "non-physical (and not merely mental) forces" – which lies at the core of d'Avray's definition of "magic" – is not self-explanatory but can be interpreted from different

angles, all of which are problematic: (1) modern, experimental physics cannot serve as a meaningful backdrop of the formulation, given its numerous ambiguities (see on this issue recently Egil Aprem, "Dis/unity of Knowledge: Models for the Study of Modern Esotericism and Science," *Numen* 62, (2015): 538–67); (2) From the viewpoint of medieval notions of physical causation (or "philosophia naturalis", "magia naturalis"), many sources of "learned magic" would not be covered by d'Avray's formulation: consider literature on the *qualitates occultae* of stones (e.g. *Lapidario*) or the fabrication of astrological talismans (e.g. *Picatrix*).

4   That is, in essence, "outsider" discourse = (orthodox) thought; "insider" discourse = (heterodox) practice.
5   Referenced frequently in the essays in Ian Hacking's *Historical Ontology* (Cambridge, MA: Harvard University Press, 2002); for his formal definition, see 35–37.
6   Hacking, *Historical Ontology*, 37.

PART II

LANGUAGES AND DISSEMINATION

6

ARABIC MAGIC

The impetus for translating texts and their reception

Charles Burnett

In a prologue accompanying the Latin translation of a classic text on magic, Thābit ibn Qurra's *On Talismans*, we are told that the translator, having thoroughly studied the courses of the planets and other parts of the science of the stars, went to search in parts of Spain inhabited by wild races (*Hispanae partes...gentes inter efferas*) for something that he felt he lacked. A "magister" had pity on him, and took down from his bookshelf a small volume written in Arabic. He told the poor man that mastery of the science of the stars was by no means adequate. The scholar who knew the whole construction of the heavens (*totius caeli machina*) was as far from true knowledge as someone who had never tasted anything of it. *His* people (the Arabs), however, had subtly considered the nature and significance of the planets, both for good and for evil, and had summarized their knowledge in a book called "On talismans". Having been assured by the master that it was legitimate to practice the art described in this book, as long as it was used for a good end, the now satisfied wandering scholar translated it into Latin.[1]

Whether this prologue is genuine or not,[2] it shows the main elements of the position of Arabic magic in the West:

1. That this kind of magic is the culmination of the study of the rest of the arts and sciences, and in particular, follows that of the astral sciences.
2. That knowledge of such magic is to be sought in Islamic realms.
3. And that this knowledge is contained in books.

In this article, I shall trace, in turn, the rise of the idea that knowledge of magic is the culmination of human endeavour, the search for Arabic texts to provide the material for this knowledge, and the transmission of this knowledge through books. The focus will be on learned magic, which is usually called *siḥr* in Arabic, and *necromantia* or *nigromantia* (later *magica*) in Latin.[3]

Magic as the culmination of human knowledge

The "culminating" aspect of magic is already present in the title of Maslama ibn Qāsim al-Qurṭubī's *Ghāyat al-Ḥakīm* – "the aim (or goal) of the wise man" – the compendium of magic written in al-Andalus in the early tenth century. Its companion volume, the *Rutbat al-Ḥakīm* ("The rank of the wise man") begins by saying that the wise man must have mastered geometry, astronomy, logic and Aristotelian natural science before he can reach the rank (*rutba*) for studying alchemy and magic.[4]

The culminating position of magic (this time embracing alchemy, *nīranjāt* and talismans) is already apparent in the *Letters* of the Ikhwān al-Ṣafā' (the Brethren of Purity), which were an important source for the *Ghāya*. These letters comprise the mathematical sciences, the natural sciences, the psychological and rational sciences, and the theological or metaphysical sciences, which are supposed to be studied in this order. The last letter (no. 52), however, is on magic.[5] In fact, its definition of magic is repeated by the *Ghāyat* – as encompassing "all words and actions that "magic" (using the verbal form of the root *s-ḥ-r*, which also gives *siḥr*) souls and bind intellects".[6]

It is evidently a similar program that underlies Adelard of Bath's translations from Arabic into Latin in the early twelfth century. For he translated from Arabic Euclid's *Elements*, al-Khwārizmī's *Astronomical Tables* (on the courses of the planets), Abū Ma'shar's *Abbreviation of the Introduction to Astrology* and the *Centiloquium* attributed to Ptolemy, but added the book of talismans of Thābit ibn Qurra and perhaps some other magical texts.[7]

In a division of science occurring in a Latin translation of an as yet unidentified Arabic text, *De ortu scientiarum* ("On the rise of the sciences"), as a part of the practical parts of physics, "necromantia" finds a place among the physical sciences:

> The parts of this science (physics) according to what the first wise men have said are eight: i.e. the science of (astrological) judgements, the science of medicine, the science of *necromantia* according to physics, the science of talismans, the science of agriculture, the science of navigation, the science of alchemy, which is the science of converting things into other species, and the science of (burning) mirrors.[8]

The common feature of all these sciences is man's manipulation of nature, and changing the natural course of things. It is difficult to draw the line between magic and other forms of human intervention in nature. But a convenient place to begin is again, the *Ghāyat al-Ḥakīm* of Maslama.

The divisions of magic

The *Ghāyat al-Ḥakīm* was translated into Castilian in 1256 and soon after, into Latin, under the title *Picatrix*.[9] It divides magic (*siḥr, nigromantia*) into three parts – talismans, *nīranjāt* and alchemy, according to the operation of spirit (*rūḥ*) and body (*jasad*): *nīranjāt* involve the operation of spirit on spirit, talismans, of spirit on body, and alchemy, of body on body. Even though the Latin translation somewhat garbles this passage, it is still useful to consider which texts might fit into these three divisions, and how a Latin scholar might have sought them out.

Alchemy is aptly described as the operation of body on body, since its materials are the whole of God's creatures within the sublunar sphere, divided into animal, vegetable and mineral. Alchemical recipes use only corporeal ingredients. No numinous influences are brought to bear in the mixing of these ingredients – whether they be the rays of the planets, or the effects of spirits. The planets feature not as spiritual influences but only as the names ennobling the metals.

In the case of talismans, the body is the material out of which the talisman is made, noble materials for good effects, base materials for bad. The spirit is brought into the body to enliven it, by means of prayer (*khiṭab, oratio*) and the burning of incense (*dakhn, suffumigatio*). The vaporous nature of the smoke encourages the ghostly nature of the spirit to enter the talisman. The very practice of the talismanic art is a continuation of the late Antique art of vivifying statues or theurgy. A Latin text called Mercury of Babylon, i.e. Hermes of Baghdad's *Flores super opera artis magice* ("An anthology on the operations of the magical art") includes a chapter on "The seven vivifications of each talisman" (*De vii vivificationibus cuiuslibet ymaginis*).[10] The talisman must be made in the appropriate shape: a serpent for binding snakes, a woman for making a woman take off her veil, etc. They can be used against stings and bites, and for medical complaints such as gallstones. But, above all, they can be used for having influence over other people, animals or objects, whether to harm them, or make them well-disposed.

Intense concentration with "correct thought" (*ḍamīr ṣaḥīḥ, intentio verax*) must be brought to bear when making the talisman. Above all, the right astrological conditions had to be observed. A strong part of the "spiritual" element of the talismanic art is the influence of the rays of the stars (described in the Ikhwān al-Ṣafā' as "the emanation of the powers of the universal soul").[11] Hence, the talismanic art is considered as being part of the astrological art of elections: the choosing of the best time astrologically for undertaking any activity – when the effluences from the stars are most supportive.[12]

Nīranj is a term taken from the Persian word for magic (*nērank*), but which was replaced by a variety of terms in Latin.[13] It is a magical practice which includes a combination of mixing and processing ingredients, reciting magical words, burning incense (suffumigation) and making figurines in order to manipulate spiritual forces. A good example of the *nīranj* being the operation of spirit on spirit is given by a short work simply called "The book on the four *nīranjāt* for capturing wild animals". This has survived in three versions: (1) an original Arabic text which is said to come from the *kitāb al-maknūn* or the "Hidden book" of Hermes[14]; (2) the quotation of this same text by the Ikhwān al-Ṣafā'; and (3) a Latin translation of the original text, under the title *Liber de quatuor confectionibus* ("The book on the four confections").

This is how the work begins:

The book of the drawing of the spirits of all brute animals, according to the words of Hermes, with the commentary of Aristotle. …

ARISTOTLE SAID: I asked the father of the wise men, Hermes, concerning the hunting of these beasts of prey, wild animals, birds and reptiles, whether there is a way to hunt and kill them and whether there is a way to arrive at this by wisdom, not like the technique of the common people.

HERMES SAID: Yes there is, O Aristotle! I have found in the Hidden Book (*kitāb al-maknūn*) on the secrets of occult sciences that Hādūs, when he taught Admānūs the science of the natures of moving animals, told him about *nīranjāt* and other remedies…, (You make a mixture). Then you say: "I have taken the spirit of this or that animal", naming the wild animal you want, whether it be a lion, an elephant, a tortoise or whatever, "by the power of the wind of these spiritual spirits and drive them towards my soul the way the north wind drives the clouds. I pray you, O spirits who lie hidden in this or that body, by virtue of these concordant spirits, answer me obediently and be driven towards me humbly".

And when you burn these incenses and speak these words, that wild animal which you want will subject itself to you, so that it will come to you obediently from wherever it comes, and when it comes to you, offer meat smeared with the prepared mixture, and it cannot refrain from pouncing on it and eating it. When it has eaten it, it will subject itself and it will become like a drunk man and its pernicious spirit will be oppressed. Then tie it with a rope and lead it anywhere you want, and, if you wish, slaughter it.[15]

What is effected here is the drawing of a spirit by a spirit – of the soul of the animal by the soul of the practitioner. *Nīranjāt* are particularly appropriate to control emotional or psychological situations: love or hatred between two people, obedience and subjection, causing impotence and release from impotence. The spirit is the means of sensation (e.g. the visual spirit allows one to see, the auditory spirit allows one to hear), and the *nīranjāt* that follow the one quoted here operate through being smelt and tasted by the victim; the wild animals have to eat the *nīranj*, the girl has to smell the *nīranj*. What *nīranjāt* do not involve is any astrological input. Spiritual forces coming from the heavens are completely lacking. The prayers are not to celestial spirits, but to the spirits of the animals, or of the woman whose love is sought. The magician's spirit has the power to draw and bind.

The characterizing of talismans as bodies into which spirits have been drawn would seem to be questionable in the light of another tradition that divides talismans into two kinds, those in which spirits are addressed, and those in which natural forces alone are utilized.[16] This division is most sharply made in the *Speculum astronomiae* of the mid-thirteenth century, in which the former are called "necromanticae", while the latter "imagines astronomicae". But it is already present in much earlier texts. Thābit ibn Qurra's *On Talismans* survives in two versions. The first, translated by Adelard of Bath, as we have seen, includes prayers to the spirits and suffumigations, and was probably already a composite text in the original Arabic. The second partially survives in a Judaeo-Arabic version, and in the Latin translation of John of Seville and Limia, and concentrates solely on the natural forces of the planets and stars that can be used to make the talisman effective. In an anonymous division of sciences known from its incipit as "Ut testatur Ergaphalau", talismanic science (*scientia ymaginaria*) is divided into *pura* and *exorcismalis*: "pure" is that which teaches talismans to be made without incantations and exorcisms, but only by inspecting the state of the heavenly bodies; "exorcismal" is that which teaches how, through exorcisms and incantations, to include spirits in working with the talismans.[17]

Petrus Alfonsi was also aware of the difference between natural and spiritual *nigromantia*; for he described *nigromantia* as being divided into nine parts of which the first four deal only with the four elements, showing how one could use them naturally, and the other five cannot be performed except with the invocation of bad spirits (*maligni spiritus*), also called "devils".[18] And this is presumably the difference implied in the divisions of practical physics described in *De ortu scientiarum*: "science of *necromantia* according to physics" and "the science of talismans". By the early thirteenth century, "*necromantia* according to physics" was interpreted as "natural magic".[19]

The division into "spiritual" and "natural" can be applied more widely. Alchemical and astrological texts (to the extent that they are classified as magic) fall under the category of "natural". But so does a whole tradition of "natural" experiments (some of which are described as *nīranjāt*) which one finds in works attributed to the alchemist Jābir ibn Ḥayyān (*c.* 721–815) – the *Kitāb al-Tajmīʿ* ("The book of assembling") and the *Flos naturarum* ("The flower of natural things") – the *Kitāb al-Sumūm* ("The book of poisons") and *Al-Filāḥa al-Nabaṭiyya* ("The Nabatean agriculture") by Ibn Waḥshiyya (fl. tenth century) and the *Kitāb al-Nawāmīs* ("The book of laws") attributed to Plato (translated into Latin as the *Liber vacce* – "The book of the cow").[20] The last-mentioned work consists of a series of experiments, such as producing bees from a cow (hence the Latin title), inducing rain and making a *homunculus*, as well as examples of causing optical illusions (such as flying through the air and walking on water). A cosmological or astronomical basis for this natural branch of magic can be found in al-Kindī's *De radiis* ("On the rays"), also called *Theorica artium magicarum* ("The theory of the magic arts"), whose Arabic original has not yet been found.[21]

The search for Arabic texts

This, then, is the kind of magic that stimulated the imagination of Western scholars. The earliest work relevant to magic arose in a medical context. Constantine the African may not have travelled to Baghdad or Cairo to learn magic, but he is likely to have been the translator in the later eleventh century of a work by the ninth-century scholar, Qusṭā ibn Lūqa, lost in Arabic, but known in Latin as *De physicis ligaturis*.[22] This short text explains how doctors use magical remedies, especially amulets suspended from the body (*ligaturae*), as a kind of placebo: if the patient trusts the doctor sufficiently, he or she will be persuaded that the remedy will be effective.[23]

It is not until the early twelfth century that we see evidence of the transmission of learned magic as an elevated body of knowledge. The first example is that of Adelard of Bath, mentioned above. His translation of Thābit ibn Qurra's *Book on Talismans* (*Liber prestigiorum Thebidis*) is a composite work (evidently reflecting the state of his original Arabic text), including prayers to the spirits of the planets, and suffumigations to activate the talismans, and quotations from Pseudo-Ptolemy's *Centiloquium* and the commentary on it by Aḥmad ibn Yūsuf (tenth-century Cairo), and references to Pseudo-Ptolemy on the talismans of the decans, and Ṭumṭum al-Hindī on those of the individual degrees.[24] The *Centiloquium* quotations include the oft-quoted *verbum* 9, that the images in this world follow those in the higher world, so that the lion and the scorpion on this earth follow the constellations of Leo and Scorpio. Adelard may also have translated two other texts on the construction of talismans according to the seven planets: the *Liber planetarum ex scientia Abel* ("The book of planets from the knowledge of Abel") and the *De imaginibus septem planetarum* ("The talismans of the seven planets") of Belenus.[25]

A more concerted attempt to translate works on magic and divination was made a little later, in Northeast Spain, where Hugo Sanctelliensis, a "magister" attested in a document from the cathedral in 1145, translated texts for bishop Michael of Tarazona (bishop from 1119–51). In this case, it is the bishop who is said by Hugo to have visited an Arabic library – that of the Banū Hūd kings of Saragossa, who had retreated to the stronghold Rueda de Jalón, some 56 miles away from Tarazona.[26] It is significant that Michael is said to have found the manuscript "in the more secret depths of the library" (*inter secretiora bibliotece penetralia*), rather than in a public area where Islamic texts are likely to have dominated. Most of the works translated by Hugo are on astronomy and astrology, but he did have a predilection for works on divination attributed to Hermes: a book on divination by sheep's shoulder blades (*Liber Amblaudii et Hermetis de spatula*, "The book of Amblaudius and Hermes on the shoulder-blade"), a book on weather forecasting (*Incipit liber imbrium ab antiquo Indorum astrologo nomine Jafar editus, deinde vero a Cillenio Mercurio abbreviatus*, "The book of rains published by the ancient astrologer of the Indians called Jafar, then abbreviated by Cillenius Mercurius")[27] and above all his translation of *On the Secrets of Nature*, attributed to Apollonius of Tyana.[28] This last work recalled how Apollonius discovered under a statue of Hermes the body of Hermes Trismegistus himself, with a book beside him, which was the *De secretis naturae* ("On the secrets of nature"), and a tablet between his hands on his chest, which was the "Emerald Tablet" (*Tabula Smaragdina*). Apollonius's work (which survives in Arabic) is probably the original context of the Emerald Tablet which later became a canonic text of the alchemists.[29] Shared by these works is the idea of secrecy, elevation of knowledge and intense concentration. The work on weather forecasting begins:

> We ought to attend with all our desire, to the unbeatable truth of the higher discipline, as the authority of the Indians warns, guard it, once gained, with the greatest zeal, and beware lest it flee from the hidden vaults (*arcana*) of our memory.[30]

The work on shoulder-blade divination explains how

> God invested a secret (*archanum*) of this discipline and an inner force in the very buds and plants of the earth, pouring down the rain as if like the manna of His own grace and wisdom, and with their traces He wonderfully inscribed the shoulder blades of the animals which enjoy such nourishment ... to instruct the ignorance of humanity.[31]

Apollonius of Tyana was renowned as a magic worker, contemporary with Jesus Christ, and several magical texts are attributed to him in Arabic (usually under the name "Balīnūs"). The *De secretis naturae* itself is not a work of practical magic, but sets out the cosmology implied in magic (including alchemy) for the elemental qualities are alternately masculine and feminine, and "marry" to produce the elements, which again are masculine and feminine, and give birth to all creation. The metals are caused by the solidification of a watery material; sulphur and mercury are their basic ingredients, and the planets determine their species. Prevailing through the whole work is the idea of the unity of nature and bonds connecting all things – the idea which reaches its culmination in the *Emerald Tablet* which completes the work:

> The higher is from the lower, and the lower from the higher.... All things take their origin from one and the same thing, and from one and the same counselling arrangement, whose father is the Sun and whose mother is the Moon.[32]

Hermann of Carinthia, the translator and author of an original cosmology called *De essentiis* ("On the essences"), written 1143, probably had access to the same kind of material as Hugo, since he was active "in the valley of the Ebro" (near which lay Tarazona). In the *De essentiis*, he shows that he knows several Arabic texts, including Hermes's *Golden Rod*,[33] the *De secretis naturae* of Apollonius and a work he calls Aristotle's *Data Neiringet* (probably *dhāt al-nīranjāt* "the essence of the *nīranjāt*"), from which he quotes a passage concerning the appearance of the spirit of Venus to the king of the Persians in a dream, telling him to sacrifice a lamb at an astrologically propitious time, and to recite some names (unfortunately not recorded by Hermann), which will bring to him servants who will do for him whatever he wants.[34] This passage can be identified in an Arabic work belonging to the talismanic Pseudo-Aristotelian Hermetica (works purporting to be the wisdom of Hermes taught by Aristotle to his royal pupil, Alexander the Great).[35] Hermann says that such a spirit is called a "privatus" (a familiar spirit) or "socrates" (since Socrates was known to have had a familiar spirit). He mentions the talisman-makers (*telesmatici*), Iorma Babilonius and Tuz Ionicus,[36] as summoning spirits by artifice or prayer, in order to bring about a certain effect, which is reminiscent of the method in Adelard's *Liber prestigiorum*.

With the focusing of the Arabic–Latin translation movement on Toledo after the middle of the twelfth century, we come to the first example of translations of texts of "natural talismans": John of Seville's translation of Thābit's *On Talismans* (whose preface was quoted at the beginning of this article) and (presumably) the same translator's book on the talismans of the thirty-six decans attributed to Ptolemy. The same two works occur together (without a prologue or any theoretical statements, as far as we can see) in a Judaeo-Arabic version.[37] But John did not eschew spiritual magic for, according to stylistic analysis, he had some involvement in the translation of *De quatuor confectionibus* ("The book on the four confections").[38] Two of the short works by Toz Grecus on the worship of Venus (*De quatuor speculis Veneris*, "On the Four Mirrors of Venus" and *De stationibus ad cultum Veneris* "The stations leading to the worship of Venus") are said to have been translated from Hebrew by "John of Seville and Limia."[39]

Spiritual forces evidently formed no part of the very wide-ranging translation enterprise of the greatest of the Toledan translators, Gerard of Cremona (1114–87) – at least not in the works officially ascribed to him. Amongst the 70 odd translations of Gerard are three works on alchemy, two on geomancy and two on lots, but nothing specifically on magic. Gerard apparently does not subscribe to the idea that magic is the culmination of an educational program – at least not publicly.[40]

The case, however, is different for Gerard's contemporary, Dominicus Gundisalvi. Here, we have a translator who also composed original works. It is quite clear from his choice of works to translate and his original works that he had a particular interest in psychology and noetics. As a person interested in the soul, it is likely that he was also interested in spirits, and in areas of science which go beyond the curriculum of the mathematical and physical and even metaphysical sciences. Gundisalvi quoted in his *De divisione philosophiae*, the eight divisions of practical physics, from what could have been his own translation of the *De ortu scientiarum*.[41] The translation of al-Kindī's *De radiis* ("On the Rays"), which survives only in a Latin translation, also shows features that suggest Gundisalvi's involvement.[42]

The last phase of the introduction of Arabic magical works occurred in the court of Alfonso X, king of Castile and León (1252–84). Here, we find both Arabic and Hebrew works on magic. It is tempting to think that Arabic works could have been discovered in Seville, which had fallen to the Christians in 1248 and where Alfonso was to set up a school for Arabic learning. But since Jews were the principal translators of these Arabic works, these works could have already belonged to the Jewish culture in Spain. The Arabic texts were translated into Castilian, and from that language into Latin. Alfonso was particularly interested in astronomy, astrology and magic, for all of which he commissioned translations and original works to form large and beautiful manuscripts. To complement his *Libro del saber de astrología* (astronomical instruments), he commissioned *Libro de las formas et las ymagenes* and *Libro de astromagía*, in which several works of spiritual and talismanic magic were collected together (unfortunately these have only survived incomplete), and the *Liber Razielis* and its appendices, for natural and Solomonic magic (first translated 1259).[43] To complement the large single-volume books on astrology by 'Alī ibn Abī-l-Rijāl (*Kitāb al-Bāri'*) and 'Alī ibn Riḍwān (his commentary on Ptolemy's *Tetrabiblos*), he commissioned the translation of Maslama ibn Qāsim al-Qurṭubī's *Ghāyat al-Ḥakīm*, which received the Latin title *Picatrix* (translated into Castilian in 1256).

Up to this point the translations from Arabic to Latin by known translators have been documented. But it must be realized that in the case of many more Latin texts on magic the translator is not mentioned.[44] Most of these, rather, place the text under the name of the ancient sage who is purported to have been the original author: Hermes, Aristotle, Solomon, Enoch, Abel, Belenus (Apollonius of Tyana), Toz Grecus or Germa Babilonicus. Some, of course, are clearly Latin compositions that just take the credit from an ascription to such an author: e.g. Hermes, *Liber de sex rerum principiis*, and *Liber viginti quatuor philosophorum*.[45]

When the work is obviously a translation, the original language is usually not mentioned, and since there was a close exchange between Arabic and Hebrew magic, it is not always evident that a text is translated from Arabic rather than Hebrew. Nevertheless, more and more Arabic originals are now being recognized, and a close stylistic analysis might allow us to assign certain texts to certain known translators, as Perrone Compagni has done for the two texts on talismans which she has now attributed to Adelard of Bath, and Dag Nikolaus Hasse has done for the texts attributed to John of Seville (*De quatuor confectionibus*) and Gundisalvi (*De radiis*).

Among these anonymous translations are the *Liber vacce*, whose Arabic sources are being successively revealed among Arabic works of natural magic and alchemy,[46] and the *Liber Antimaquis* which draws from the rich corpus of Arabic Pseudo-Aristotelian Hermetica.[47] Some of the texts on the veneration of Venus and the fabrication of her talismans have been recognized in Arabic works of magic by Fakhr al- Dīn al-Rāzī and Abū Ya'qūb al-Sakkākī.[48]

For the dates of many of these anonymous translations, one has to look at the manuscript evidence and the references to these works in other texts. Thus, we can turn to the third and last of our subjects: the place of books in the transmission of Arabic magic.

Books

Arabic learned magic was transmitted in books, and it was the translations of these books into Latin (and later into Castilian) that transmitted this magic to the West. The designation "Brethren of Purity" suggests an élite group whose canonical literature was the 52 letters written under their name. It is difficult, however, to identify groups of people who might identify themselves as a guild of magicians, or of perfect men, and to imagine a *diadokhe* of such a guild from the Islamic to the Christian world. The doctrine of the magical texts does not constitute an alternative religion, or a heresy, and the readers of such literature would claim to be good Muslims, Jews or Christians. It rather provides an education which is complementary to the education of the madrasas, yeshivas and universities, and which does not become part of the curriculum of these establishments. In the West, because such texts never became part of official education programs, they were not copied in cathedral scriptoria or by university stationers and seem to have been diffused in a clandestine way, probably from individual to individual. The result is that, for most of these texts, we have few manuscripts contemporary with or closely following on their translation, and more open and frequent copying only emerges in the Renaissance. When they are copied, they tend to be grouped together, often in large numbers, in one manuscript. Thus, we have (in approximate chronological order) the manuscripts Oxford, Corpus Christi College, 125 (fourteenth century),[49] Darmstadt, Hessische Landes- und Hochschulbibl., 1410-I, Halle, Universitäts- und Landesbibliothek Sachsen-Anhalt, 14. B. 36 (fourteenth century), Venice, Marciana lat. XIV. 174 (fourteenth century), Biblioteca Vaticana, Ms. Reg. lat. 1300 (fourteenth century), Florence, Biblioteca nazionale, II. ii. 214 (fifteenth century), Vatican, Vat. Lat. 10803 (fifteenth century), Darmstadt, Hessische Landes- und Hochschulbibl., 1410-I (sixteenth century) and British Library, Sloane 3850 (seventeenth century). Most of these collections contain anonymous translations, and few clues as to whether the Latin texts rely immediately on the Arabic.

We are, however, aware that these books were known, for Daniel of Morley already refers to "scientia de imaginibus, quam tradit liber Veneris magnus et universalis, quem edidit Thoz Grecus..." (the science of images, which the great and universal Book of Venus, published by Thoz Grecus, handed down).[50] Hermann of Carinthia, as we have seen, knows works attributed to Toz the Greek and Germa the Babilonian. William of Auvergne in his *De legibus* (1228–30) and *De universo* (1231–6) provides a substantial list of these works in the context of criticizing them.[51] About thirty years later, a fuller list is provided in the *Speculum astronomiae* (ca. 1260), which, notoriously, provides titles and incipits of all texts on the science of talismans, dividing them into necromantic (or spiritual) and "astronomical". And some ten years later, the *Errores philosophorum*, attributed to Gilles de Rome, shows the detailed knowledge of al-Kindī's *De radiis*.[52] In fact, the two texts that have a more continuous manuscript tradition are the *De radiis* (29 MSS dating between the thirteenth and eighteenth centuries) and Thābit ibn Qurra's *De imaginibus* in John of Seville's version (61 MSS dating between the thirteenth and the sixteenth centuries), with whose prologue (extant in at least three manuscripts) this chapter began.[53]

On the basis of the manuscript testimonies and the references in other authors, David Pingree traces how these texts

> spread to southern France, especially among the *médecins*, Christian and Jewish, of Montpellier, in the decades before and after 1300; and finally from Montpellier these new magical traditions spread to northern Italy, to Brabant, and especially to Canterbury during the course of the fourteenth century.[54]

This perhaps describes only one (though a very significant) path of transmission. Other paths could be identified, such as those that brought translations of Greek magical works into Europe. Others will be described elsewhere in this volume, and there is no need to trace them in detail here (Figures 6.1 and 6.2).

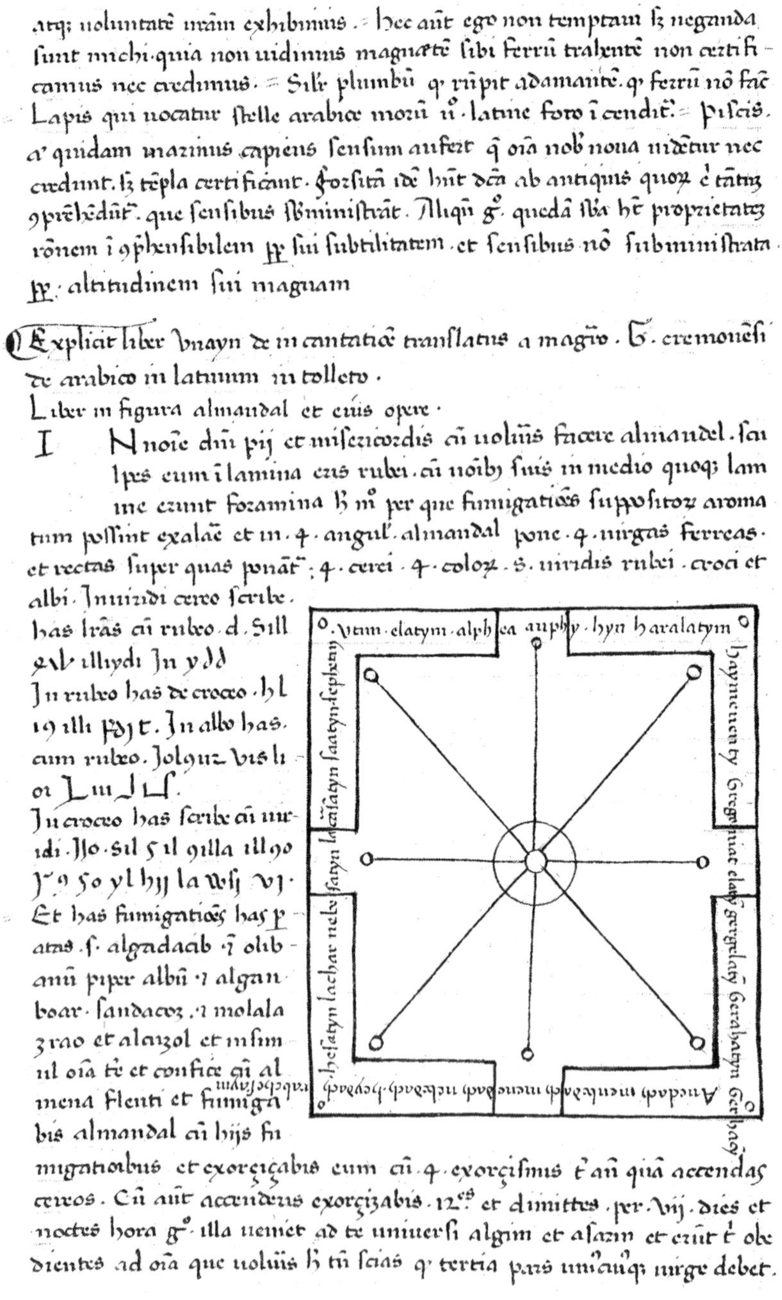

atq; uolumtatē mīam exhibimus. Hec aūt ego non temptaui s; neganda sunt mchi. quia non uidimus magnetē sibi ferrū trahente non certificamus nec credimus. Silr plumbū q' rūpit adamante. q' ferrū nō fac Lapis qui uocatur stelle arabice motu u. latine foro i cendit. Piscis. a' quidam marinus capiens sensum aufert q̄ oīa nob noua mīetur nec credunt. s; tepla certificant. forsitā ideo hūt dcā ab antiquis quoq; e tātz c̄prehēdūt. que sensibus sūministrat. Aliqũ g̃. quedā sīa hr proprietates rōnem i c̄phensibilem pp sui subtilitatem et sensibus nō subministrata pp. altitudinem sui magnam

Expliciat liber Imayn de incantatioē translatus a magro. G. cremonesi de arabico in latinum in tolleto.

Liber in figura almandal et eius opere.

IN noīe dīi pij et misericordis cū uoluis facere almandal. Sci Ipes cum ī lamina eris rubei. cū noībj suis in medio quoq; lamine erunt foramina b; nō per que fumigatiōes suppositorz aromatum possint exalāe et in. 4. angul. almandal pone. 4. uirgas ferreas. et rectas super quas ponāt; 4. cerei. 4. coloz. s. uiridis rubei. croci et albi. In uiridi cereo scribe has lrās cū rubeo. d. Sill et illi idi. In y ll. In rubeo has de croceo. h l 19 illi fo j t. In albo has. cum rubeo. Jolguz vis li oi L ui J l f.
In croceo has scribe cū ui idi. Iso sil ſ il gilla ill go y q so yl hy la wſ j vj. Et has fumigatiōes has p atas f. algadaab ī olibanū piper albū ʒ algan boar sandacoz ʒ molala 3 rao et alazol et insi mul oīa tr et confice cū almena flenti et fumiga bis almandal cū hijs fumigationibus et exorcizabis eum cū. 4. exorcismis t aū qūa accendas cereos. Cū aūt accendere exorcizabis. 12.s et dimittes per iiij. dies et noctes hora g̃. illa ueniet ad te uniuersi algim et asazin et erūt t obedientes ad oīa que uoluis s; tū scias q' tertia pars unicuiq; uirge debet.

Figure 6.1 The *figura Almandal* or Table of Solomon in Florence, Biblioteca nazionale, II. iii. 214 fol. 74v. Reproduced by permission of the Ministerio dei bene e delle attività culturali del turismo/ Biblioteca Nazionale Centrale, Firenze.

℣ Jouis
℣ Venus
℣ Mercurij.

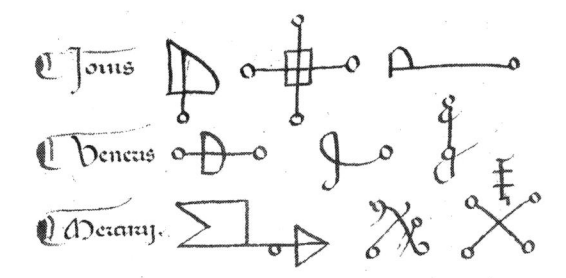

Hec sunt sigilla planetarum oibus alijs meliora.

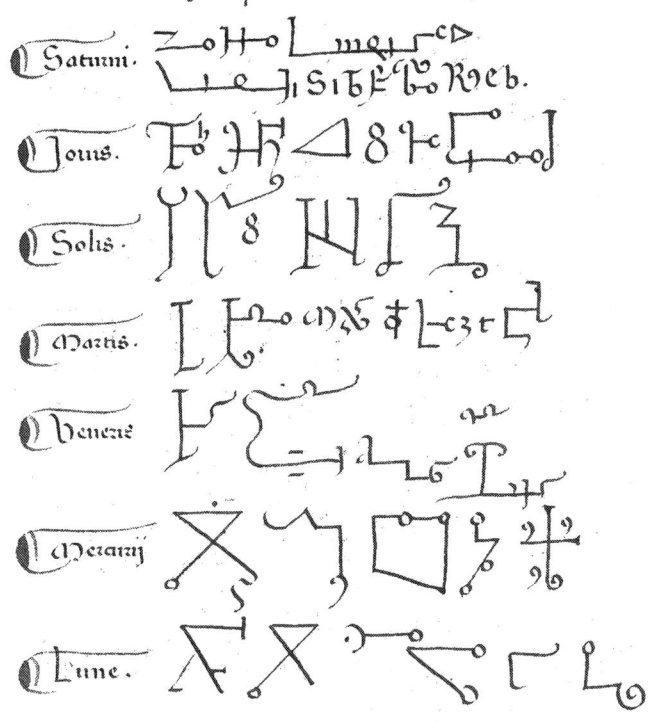

℣ Saturni.
℣ Jouis.
℣ Solis.
℣ Martis.
℣ Veneris
℣ Mercurij
℣ Lune.

Incipit liber de indicijs ptīn ptolomei et primo de parte fortūe hic accipitur in die a sole in lunam in nocte eq̃°. et prohicitur ab ascendente.

Quoniam

Figure 6.2 The rings and sigils of the planets, to be inscribed on talismans, in Florence, Biblioteca nazionale, II. iii. 214 fol 49v. Reproduced by permission of the Ministerio dei bene e delle attività culturali del turismo/Biblioteca Nazionale Centrale, Firenze.

Conclusion

A strong magical tradition, in which the study of magic, along with alchemy and astrology, was regarded as the culmination of the education of the sage, was present in al-Andalus, at least from the early tenth century onwards. Awareness of this program appears in Latin biographies of scholars and divisions of science from the early twelfth century. Translators were spurred on to seek out these texts and translated them during the course of the twelfth and thirteenth centuries. The translations were piecemeal, and there is no evidence of a consorted attempt to transmit a whole corpus of texts that could form the basis of a sect or an alternative education; the *Letters* of the Ikhwan al-Ṣafaʾ were not translated as a set. Nevertheless, the impact of the texts that were translated was considerable, as witnessed by the strong attacks against them, and their imitations in Latin. While Greek and Hebrew sources contributed to this body of literature, Arabic texts dominated the field, and determined the course of Western learned magic until the advent of the Christian kabbala in the fifteenth century.

Future directions

The authors of texts on magic tended to hide under the names of ancient sages (Hermes, Apollonius, Enoch, etc.), and the translators of the texts were also wary about revealing their identities. Studies of style and vocabulary have helped, and will continue to help reveal the hidden authors, or at least the context in which the works were written and translated. Such studies, in turn, should be based on reliable editions of the texts. The editions of the various medieval versions of Maslama's *Ghāyat al-Ḥakīm*, closely connected with the history of the Warburg Institute, should be soon completed by an edition of the Hebrew versions by Reimund Leicht. Plans are afoot for providing a critical edition of the *Liber vacce* along with its parallel texts in Arabic.[55] An increasing number of Arabic originals to Latin magical texts are being found, and would provide material for PhD theses. The wide range of works available to William of Auvergne in his criticism of magic are being explored in a current project at the Thomas Institut in Cologne. What still needs attention is the use to which magical texts were put in the Arabic and Latin world. Do they merely reflect a literary tradition, or can they be linked with actual practices, ceremonies and even cults?

Notes

1 This preface is edited and translated in Charles Burnett, "'Magister Iohannes Hispalensis et Limiensis' and Qusṭā ibn Lūqa's *De differentia spiritus et animae*: a Portuguese Contribution to the Arts Curriculum?" in *Mediaevalia. Textos e estudos*, 7–8 (Porto: Fundação Eng. António de Almeida, 1995), 221–67.
2 The prologue appears only in a few, late manuscripts.
3 Thorough and accurate accounts of this transmission can already be found in the works of David Pingree (David Pingree, "The Diffusion of Arabic Magical Texts in Western Europe," in *La diffusione delle scienze islamiche nel Medio Evo Europeo (Roma, 2-4 ottobre 1984)*, (Roma: Accademia dei Lincei, 1987), 57–102; "Learned Magic in the Time of Frederick II," *Microlgus* 2 (1994): 39–56; and Jean-Patrice Boudet, *Entre science et* nigromance *Astrologie, divination et magie dans l'Occident médiéval (XIIe-XVe siècle)* (Paris: Publications de la Sorbonne, 2006). To all of these accounts, this article is complementary.
4 Godefroid de Callataÿ and Sébastien Moureau, "Again on Maslama Ibn Qāsim al-Qurṭubī, the Ikhwān al-Ṣafāʾ and Ibn Khaldūn: New Evidence from Two Manuscripts of the *Rutbat al-ḥakīm*", *Al-Qanṭara* 37, no. 2 (2016): 339–72; Maribel Fierro, "Bāṭinism in al-Andalus. Maslama b. Qāsim al-Qurṭubī (d. 353/964), Author of the *Rutbat al-Ḥakīm* and the *Ghāyat al-Ḥakīm (Picatrix)*," *Studia Islamica* 84 (1996): 87–112; Godefroid de Callataÿ, "Magia en al-Andalus: *Rasāʾil Ijwān al-Ṣafāʾ*, *Rutbat al-Ḥakīm* y *Ghāyat al-Ḥakīm (Picatrix)*," *Al-Qanṭara* 34.2 (2013): 297–344.
5 Godefroid de Callataÿ and Bruno Halflants, *The Epistles of the Brethren of Purity, On Magic. 1. An Arabic Critical Edition and English Translation of Epistle 52A* (Oxford: Oxford University Press in association with the Institute of Ismaili Studies, 2011); see p. 9.

6 Ikhwān al-Ṣafāʾ, *Rasāʾil* (Bombay edition), IV 310, 17–19; *Picatrix. "Das Ziel des Weisen" von Pseudo-Maǧrīṭī, I. Arabischer Text*, ed. H. Ritter (Leipzig: Teubner, 1933), p. 7, lines 1–2.
7 Adelard's *Liber Prestigiorum Thebidis secundum Hermetem et Ptolemaeum* ("Book of Talismans of Thābit following Hermes and Ptolemy") is a different translation of Thābit ibn Qurra's *On Talismans* from that with whose preface this chapter opens. See below, p. 74.
8 *De ortu scientiarum*, ed. Clemens Baeumker, Beiträge zur Geschichte der Philosophie des Mittelalters, 19 (Münster-in-W.: Aschendorff, 1918), 20. According to the recent stylistic analysis by Dag Nikolaus Hasse, this work shows characteristics of Dominicus Gundisalvi: Dag Nikolaus Hasse and Andreas Büttner, "Notes on Anonymous Twelfth-Century Translations of Philosophical Texts from Arabic into Latin on the Iberian Peninsula", in *The Arabic, Hebrew and Latin Reception of Avicenna's Physics and Cosmology*, ed. Dag Nikolaus Hasse and Amos Bertolacci (Berlin: De Gruyter, 2018), 313–69.
9 *Picatrix. Das Ziel des Weisen*: Picatrix. *The Latin Version of the Ghāyat al-Ḥakīm*. ed. David Pingree (London: Warburg Institute, 1986).
10 This is the fourth Appendix to the Latin *Liber Razielis* as found in MS Halle, Universitäts- und Landesbibliothek Sachsen-Anhalt, 14. B. 36.
11 Ikhwān al-Ṣafāʾ, *Letter on Magic*, 93.
12 This is its position in the *Speculum Astronomiae*, ed. P. Zambelli, in *The Speculum astronomiae and Its Enigma: Astrology, Theology and Science in Albertus Magnus and His Contemporaries* (Dordrecht-Boston-London: Kluwer Academic Publishers, 1992), 240–41.
13 Charles Burnett, "Nīranj: a Category of Magic (Almost) Forgotten in the Latin West," in *Natura, scienze e società medievali. Studi in onore di Agostino Paravicini Bagliani* (Florence: Sismel Edizioni del Galluzzo, 2008) 37–66.
14 This is extant in the manuscript of magical texts, London, British Library, Oriental and India Office Collections, Delhi 1946, fols 22–23.
15 This translation is taken from an edition of the text in Arabic and Latin which Liana Saif and I are currently preparing. I am grateful to Liana Saif for her help.
16 This subject is fully explored in Nicolas Weill-Parot, *Les 'images astrologiques' au Moyen Âge et à la Renaissance* (Paris: Honoré Champion, 2002), who distinguishes between them using the terms "addressative magic" and "non-addressative magic": see pp. 123–38.
17 See Max Lejbowicz in *Adélard de Bath, L'Un et le divers, Questions sur la Nature (les causes des choses) avec le pseudépigraphe Comme l'atteste Erphalau*, ed. Charles Burnett, trans. and comm. Max Lejbowicz, Émilia Ndiaye and Christiane Dussourt (Paris: Les Belles Lettres, 2010), 317.
18 Petrus Alfonsi, *Diálogo contra los judíos*, ed. K.-P. Mieth, trans. E. Ducay (Huesca: Instituto de Estudios Altoaragonese), 150.
19 William of Auvergne, *De legibus*, c. 24, Paris Bibliothèque nationale de France, lat. 15755, fol. 71vb: "Et de huiusmodi operibus est magica naturalis, quam nigromanciam secundum phisicam philosophi vocant." ("And from operations like this derives natural magic, which the philosophers call 'nigromancy according to physics'"): quoted in Boudet, *Entre science et* nigromance, 128, n. 40.
20 See David Pingree, "Between the *Ghāyat* and the *Picatrix*, II: the *Flos naturarum* ascribed to Jābir," *Journal of the Warburg and Courtauld Institutes* 72 (2009): 41–80, and Liana Saif, "The Cows and the Bees," *Journal of the Warburg and Courtauld Institutes* 79 (2016): 1–47.
21 Al-Kindī, *De radiis*, ed. Marie-Thérèse d'Alverny and Francoise Hudry, *Archives d'histoire doctrinale et littéraire du moyen âge* 41 (1974):139–260.
22 Pingree, "The Diffusion of Arabic Magical Texts," 69.
23 See Judith Wilcox and John M. Riddle, "Qusṭā ibn Lūqa's Physical Ligatures and the Recognition of the Placebo Effect," *Medieval Encounters* 1 (1995): 1–50.
24 Burnett, "Ṭābit ibn Qurra the Ḥarrānian," 24–27.
25 Vittoria Perrone Compagni, "'Studiosus incantationibus'. Adelardo di Bath, Ermete e Thabit," *Giornale Critico della Filosofia Italiana* 82 (2001): 36–61.
26 See Charles H. Haskins, "Translations of Hugo Sanctallensis," in *Studies in the History of Mediaeval Science* (Cambridge, MA: Harvard University Press, 1924), 73; Charles Burnett, "The Establishment of Medieval Hermeticism," in *The Medieval World*, ed. Peter Linehan and Janet L. Nelson (London and New York: Routledge, 2001), 118–24 and Charles Burnett, "A Hidden Programme of Astrology and Divination in mid-Twelfth-Century Aragon: The Hidden Preface in the *Liber novem iudicum*," in *Magic and the Classical Tradition*, ed. Charles Burnett and William F. Ryan (London and Turin: The Warburg Institute and Nino Aragno Editore, 2006)

27 The "Mercury of Cyllene" who abbreviated the work is Hermes who, according to Greek mythology, was born in a cave on Mount Cyllene.
28 The Arabic text is edited by Ursula Weisser, *Buch über das Geheimnis der Schöpfung* (Aleppo: Institute for the History of Arabic Science, 1979). The Latin translation is edited by Françoise Hudry in *Chrysopoeia* 6 (1997–99): 1–206. See also Pinella Travaglia, *Una cosmologia ermetica: il* Kitab sirr al-halīqa = De secretis naturae (Napoli: Liguori, 2001).
29 See Julius Ruska, *Tabula Smaragdina* (Heidelberg: C. Winter's Universitätsbuchhandlung, 1926), Irene Caiazzo, "Note sulla fortuna della Tabula Smaragdina," in *Hermetism from Late Antiquity to Humanism*, ed. Paolo Lucentini, Ilaria Parri and Vittoria Perrone Compagni (Turnhout: Brepols, 2003), 697–711.
30 Charles Burnett, "Lunar Astrology. The Varieties of Texts Using Lunar Mansions, With Emphasis on *Jafar Indus*," *Micrologus* 12 (2004): 43–133; see p. 87.
31 *Liber de Spatula*, in *Hermes Trismegistus, Astrologia et divinatoria*, vol. 4, part 4, ed. Gerrit Bos et al. (Turnhout: Brepols, 2001), 205.
32 Apollonius, *De secretis naturae*, 152. The original Arabic is found in *Sirr al-khalīqa* III 20, ed. Weisser, 306–7.
33 A work with such a name is referred to in the *Fihrist* of al-Nadīm: see Manfred Ullmann, *Die Natur- und Geheimwissenschaften im Islam* (Leiden: Brill, 1972), 291.
34 Hermann of Carinthia, *De essentiis*, ed. Charles Burnett (Leiden: Brill, 1982), 182.
35 The Pseudo-Aristotelian Hermetica are most comprehensively represented in MS British Library, Delhi, 1946.
36 These two authors are mentioned together in the first folios of Manchester, John Rylands Library, MS Mingana 372 [404], the *Mushaf zuhra*: Ṭā'ūs al-Yunanī and J.r.m' al-Babilī.
37 Both works appear together also in a fragmentary Judaeo-Arabic version, which is the only manuscript of the Arabic text yet to be found: see Gideon Bohak and Charles Burnett, "A Judaeo-Arabic Version of Ṯābit ibn Qurra's *De imaginibus* and Pseudo-Ptolemy's *Opus imaginum*," in *Islamic Philosophy, Science, Culture, and Religion: Studies in Honor of Dimitri Gutas*, ed. Felicitas Opwis and David Reisman (Leiden and Boston: Brill, 2012), 179–200.
38 This is according to the research of Dag Hasse (see n. 8 above).
39 See Paolo Lucentini and Vittoria Perrone Compagni, *I testi e I codici di Ermete nel Medioevo* (Florence: Edizioni Polistampa, 2001), 84 and 89.
40 Gerard is described as lecturing on astrology by his student Daniel of Morley, although no translations of astrological works are assigned to him. Whether the attribution of the *Figura Almandel* in MS Florence MS BNC, II.III.214, fols 74v–78v to Gerard of Cremona hints at an esoteric branch to his translations is still to be proved.
41 Dominicus Gundissalinus, *De divisione philosophiae*, ed. Ludwig Baur, *Beiträge zur Geschichte der Philosophie des Mittelalters*, 4.2-3 (Münster-in-W.: Aschendorff, 1903), 20.
42 Hasse, "Twelfth-Century Latin Translations of Arabic Philosophical Texts".
43 Alejandro García Avilés, "Two Astromagical Manuscripts of Alfonso X," *Journal of the Warburg and Courtauld Institutes* 59 (1996): 14–23; Alfonso d'Agostino, *Astromagia: ms. Reg. lat. 1283a* (Naples: Liguori, 1992) and Sophie Page, "Magic and the Pursuit of Wisdom: the 'familiar' spirit in the *Liber Theysolius*," *La Corónica* 36 (2007): 13–40.
44 Among these texts are many listed in Lucentini and Perrone Compagnai, *I testi*.
45 These works are edited in *Hermes Latinus*, vol. 2 (Turnhout: Brepols, 2006) and vol. 3, part 1 (Turnhout: Brepols, 1997).
46 Saif, "The Cows and the Bees".
47 Burnett, *Liber Antimaquis* in *Hermes Trismegistus Astrologia et divinatoria*, Hermes Latinus, vol. 4, part 4, ed. Gerrit Bos et al. (Turnhout: Brepols, 2001), 195–214.
48 I owe this information to Michael Noble.
49 This collection is the subject of Sophie Page, *Magic in the Cloister, Pious Motives, Illicit Interests, and Occult Approaches to the Medieval Universe* (University Park: Pennsylvania State University Press, 2013).
50 Gregor Maurach, "Daniel de Merlai, *Philosophia*," *Mittellateinisches Jahrbuch* 14 (1979): 204–55, see 239.
51 Boudet, *Entre science et necromance*, 214–20.
52 Giles of Rome, *Errores philosophorum*, ed. Joseph Koch, trans. John O. Riedl (Milwaukee, WI: Marquette University Press, 1944), 47–58.
53 These statistics are taken from the unpublished *Latin Translations of Works on Astronomy and Astrology (c. 1110-c. 1450)*, by David Juste and Charles Burnett.
54 Pingree, "The Diffusion of Arabic Magical Texts," 56–57.
55 These were discussed in a workshop in Paris in October 2016, convened by Maaike van der Lugt.

7

THE LATIN ENCOUNTER WITH HEBREW MAGIC

Problems and approaches

Katelyn Mesler

The Jews of medieval Western Europe lived alongside their Christian neighbours. They met in the marketplace, talked in the street, disputed in court, shared public space, engaged in both friendly and sexual relationships, acted together in plays, sought each other's professional services and interacted daily in countless ways that are lost to the historical record. Notable points of contact have been discovered in areas of thought and practice, ranging from art and literature to exegesis and ritual. Magic is no exception. And yet, while there are many distinct elements of Christian magical traditions in sources produced by the Jewish minority, historians have made surprisingly little progress in identifying similar evidence in the sources of the majority Christian culture. The problem, I will argue, lies precisely in the proximity of the medieval Christian and Jewish cultures. The practices that were most often shared were those that did not differ significantly in Jewish and Christian contexts and therefore bore few traces of their origins and transmission. In order to assess Christians' debt to Jewish magic, we must first recognize certain characteristics of Jewish–Christian encounters and of the diverse contexts within which different types of magic were shared. These will suggest promising avenues of inquiry still to be explored.

In what follows, I offer an overview of some of the most important texts, themes and approaches for studying the Jewish contribution to medieval Christian magic. The analysis mainly concerns the period from roughly the twelfth through fifteenth centuries, which encompasses the proliferation of textual traditions of magic in both the Jewish and Christian cultures of Europe and ends at the point when the social and intellectual changes of the late fifteenth century fundamentally altered Jewish–Christian relations, redefined aspects of magic in both traditions and offered Christians unprecedented access to Hebrew writings.

The boundaries of the traditions themselves, however, are more difficult to define. Most magical writings and practices did not contain implicit identifiers marking them as specifically Christian or specifically Jewish, and a significant portion of magic in both traditions had shared roots in Arabic magical traditions. Although I will return to the problem of identity at the end of this essay, for practical purposes let us say that Jewish magic was that performed by self-identifying Jews or written down in Hebrew characters (whether Hebrew or vernacular languages), and Christian magic was that performed by self-identifying Christians or written down in Latin characters (whether Latin or vernacular languages). In addition, medieval Jews and Christians would not necessarily have agreed on what constituted magic. Yet, Jews shared the Romance or Germanic vernaculars whose distinction of terms

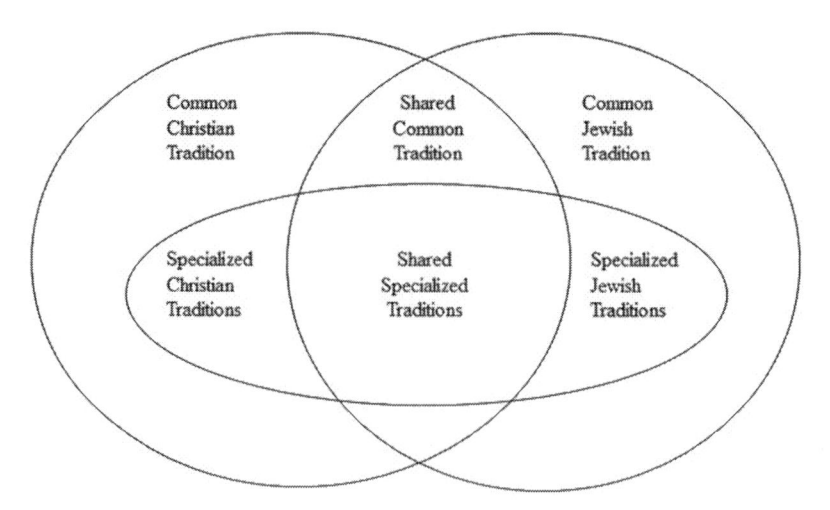

Figure 7.1 Traditions of magic in medieval Europe.

owed at least somewhat to the intellectual developments in the Latin world, so we should not posit an unbridgeable conceptual gap.[1] Since we are primarily interested here in the impact of Jewish/Hebrew magic on the Latin magical tradition, we can safely confine our scope to elements commonly considered magical in the latter.

In his work on medieval Christian magic, Richard Kieckhefer developed a distinction between the *common tradition* and *specialized traditions* of magic.[2] The latter refer to magical practices, often represented in learned treatises, that are accessible only to certain specialized groups, generally limited by education, profession or other social factors. Astral magic, for example, often required not only Latin literacy but enough training in astrology to identify the relevant astrological conditions. The common tradition, in contrast, incorporates those areas of magical practice that cannot be limited to a specific group or milieu such as the wearing of amulets. If we expand Kieckhefer's framework to encompass both Christian and Jewish traditions, we could separate out specialized traditions unique to Christians, specialized traditions unique to Jews and shared specialized traditions that are accessible to a subset of both Jews and Christians. Likewise, there are magical practices of a common tradition within each culture as well as one that is broadly shared among Jews and Christians (Figure 7.1). In the terms of this framework, we can say that the shared specialized traditions are almost exclusively of Latin or Arabic origins, whether translated from Latin to Hebrew or separately into both languages from Arabic. This contact also results in the appropriation of specialized Latin elements in original Hebrew compositions. Sharing of the common tradition, however, is more difficult to discern, both because it is often more rooted in oral than textual traditions and because the evidence usually defies simple analysis of origins, reception and identity. This framework will help guide our understanding of what kinds of magic were exchanged and how.

Magical texts and the sharing of specialized traditions

The transmission of specialized traditions from Latin to Hebrew is easier to evaluate than whatever may have been transmitted from Hebrew to Latin. Numerous learned treatises of magic and occult sciences were translated from Latin (or vernacular languages) to Hebrew during the Middle Ages, including the *Ars notoria*, the *Techel/Azareus Complex*, the lapidary of Marbode of Rennes, Odo of Meung's herbal (*Macer Floridus*), the *Key of Solomon*, the *Book of the Cow*, Ibn al-Jazzar's *On Occult Properties*, the *Picatrix*, Pseudo-Ptolemy's *Hundred Aphorisms*, the *Book of the Moon*, a work on planetary magical squares,[3] some geomantic texts and an extensive corpus of medical literature that often includes charms and other forms of healing magic. Towards the end of the fifteenth century, Yohanan Alemanno mentioned a Hebrew version of the *Almandal*, he knew Pseudo-Albertus's *On the Marvels of the World* and he understood the Hebrew translation of Raymond Lull's *Short Art* as providing instructions for magical practice.[4] Not all of these works convey material of Latin origin; some are translations of Arabic works. Nevertheless, these translations contributed to a shared repertoire of magic, as did those Arabic works that were translated independently into Latin and Hebrew such as the *Secret of Secrets* and some additional Hermetic treatises. The dominance of translations in one direction, from Latin to Hebrew, is one of the main reasons why Christian elements are more likely to be found in Hebrew texts than Jewish elements in Latin texts.

In the case of other shared texts, the relationship between the Latin and Hebrew versions has not yet been established. These include *On the Twelve Images* and the *Use of the Psalms* (though in one specific case a Christian appropriated a Hebrew psalter to produce a hybrid set of magical Psalms).[5] As for astral magic, Reimund Leicht has observed,

> By the Renaissance at the latest, various basic teachings of astrology and astral magic had become the common property of Jews and Christians so thoroughly that in most cases a direct source can be determined only with great difficulty, if at all.[6]

But there are also instances in which the texts provide their own claims of provenance. A Hermetic text known as *On the Stations for the Cult of Venus* includes the detail that it was translated from Hebrew by John of Seville, a statement that raises some doubt since the translator in question is only known to have translated works from Arabic.[7] A similar assertion of translation from Hebrew appears in Thomas of Cantimpré's version of the *Techel/Azareus Complex*, in which case it is demonstrably false.[8] Likewise, the German *Book of Abramelin*, allegedly written in the fifteenth century by a certain Abraham of Worms, is a later composition of undoubtedly Christian origin. This phenomenon is not limited to magical texts, as spurious claims of Hebrew translation appear in texts as diverse as the *Gospel of Nicodemus* and the Pseudo-Joachite *Liber Horoscopus*. Nor is this literary device more prominent with respect to Hebrew than to other languages, for Geoffrey of Monmouth's alleged vernacular source for his *History of the Kings of Britain* and Cervantes's claim that *Don Quixote* was translated from Arabic are only a few of many such examples. Such claims surely serve to add a mysterious, exotic or even authoritative element to a text, but they tell us little about transmission.

Finally, there are a few texts that derive directly or indirectly from Hebrew sources. One Latin version of the Pseudo-Aristotelian lapidary retains traces of Hebrew names for stones and bears some important similarities to two Hebrew manuscripts of the text, but the details of transmission have yet to be determined.[9] More notably, the *Book of Raziel* represents the most extensive translation of learned magic from Hebrew to Latin during the Middle Ages.[10] This work of astral and angel magic was not originally produced in Hebrew as a coherent treatise but rather as a series of magical, mystical and astrological texts – some with Arabic roots – that began to circulate together in manuscripts, forming a textual complex that included works such as the *Book of Secrets* (*Sefer ha-Razim*), the *Book of the Garment* and the

Book of the Upright. By the time the Hebrew text was printed (Amsterdam, 1701), it contained texts and textual fragments including ancient mystical cosmology, amulets and writings of the medieval German Pietists. In the thirteenth century, however, a version of the *Raziel* complex was translated into Latin under the auspices of Alfonso X of Castile. The translated work gives the impression of a coherent treatise. In addition, the translator claims to have also translated a dozen related texts. Some of these texts have been found in a single Latin manuscript of *Raziel*, while others remain to be identified. Only a few titles have thus far been matched to known Hebrew sources. Finally, in a remarkable demonstration of shared magical traditions, the Latin *Raziel* was soon translated back into Hebrew. Only in the late fifteenth century was there a concerted effort to translate Hebrew texts with magical contents. The convert Flavius Mithridates supplied Pico della Mirandola with translations of works such as Elazar of Worms's commentary on *Sefer Yetsirah*, a compilation of German Pietist magic (*Book of Man*) and the *Uses of the Torah*.[11]

If it was rare for a Hebrew text to be translated into Latin, we might still investigate whether smaller elements of Hebrew magic, such as divine and angelic names, appear in specialized Latin traditions. But here too there are difficulties. Latin Christians could learn about certain Hebrew divine names from Jerome, Isidore of Seville and other early authorities. Thus, the use of Hebrew names such as El, Eloim, Eloe, Elion, Ia, Adonai, Sabaoth, Saddai and the Tetragrammaton is not necessarily indicative of any real contact with Hebrew. The magical name AGLA, common in both medieval Latin and Hebrew magic, is often said to derive as an acronym of a phrase in the Hebrew liturgy, *Ata gibor l'olam adonai*, "You are forever mighty, Lord." This interpretation has become so standard in Jewish traditions that some modern prayer books signal the name AGLA at this place in the liturgy. After much searching, I have yet to find evidence of such an interpretation prior to the late fourteenth or fifteenth century, a couple centuries after AGLA begins appearing in magical writings. Ultimately, the origins and transmission of this divine name remain to be established. Even the Christian notion of 72 names of God may have owed no more than the number to Jewish tradition.[12] As for angels, Christians did not need access to Hebrew to recognize that Gabriel, Michael, Raphael and Uriel all end with the theophoric suffix *-el*. Christians could thus invent angelic-sounding names in a similar fashion to Jews, differing only in that the latter usually built the name from a meaningful root word. Similarities between individual Latin and Hebrew angelic names may at times be nothing more than coincidence, and so angelic names are not always a good indicator of contact. Likewise, the Hebrew alphabet and certain terms found in Latin manuscripts, such as the Hebrew names of the planets, could be inherited from earlier Latin sources rather than Hebrew ones.

Part of the problem, as I have suggested, is that elements of Jewish magic that appear in Latin texts are not likely to be marked as specifically Jewish. If a Latin incantation contains New Testament references, for example, it may still remain recognizable in Hebrew translation.[13] But a Hebrew spell translated into Latin is not likely to stand out, unless it contains extra-Biblical references, or describes the few distinctly Jewish practices such as "opening the heart," adjuring the "prince of the Torah" and "the princes of thumb and cup" or the form of teleportation known as "path jumping."[14] Most magical procedures, goals and Old Testament citations are similar enough between Jews and Christians as to make the question of origins difficult to answer. And this is why authentic traces of the Hebrew language – bearing in mind the minimal Hebrew accessible to educated Christians – remain the clearest indication of contact with Jewish magic. Indeed, for some Christians, it is the foreignness or incomprehensibility of the language itself that is the most characteristic trait of Jewish magic. Anselm of Besate describes a fictional magician who spoke "Hebrew or rather diabolical" words.[15] Similarly, in the sorcery trial of Hugues Géraud (Avignon, 1317), it is repeatedly said that a Jew taught Hugues to pronounce an incantation that was either Greek or Hebrew.[16] In a sorcery trial at Briançon in 1443, the accused, an alleged convert from Judaism, was asked to provide the (Hebrew) formula he used when renouncing God. The record preserves his response phonetically as *Adonay, ich milhema czemo*, which is recognizable as "The Lord is a man of war, [the Lord] is his name" (Ex 15:3), although the trial record insists that these words mean "I renounce God and all that believe in him."[17] Furthermore, several trials of the Spanish Inquisition point to the possession of talismans with Hebrew writing as evidence of Judaizing.

While translated elements usually provide the clearest evidence of transfer, the impact of Jewish magic can occasionally be discerned through more general, conceptual elements. Two treatises from the early fourteenth century, John of Morigny's *Book of Flowers* and the *Sworn Book of Honorius*, both present connections between magic and visionary experience that find no precedent in Latin sources but strongly resemble concepts found in contemporary Jewish sources.[18] In the case of the *Sworn Book*, the angels described in the text exhibit roles and attributes characteristic of the Arabic and Hebrew magical traditions.[19] These two texts stand out as well for their explicit repudiations of Jewish magic, suggesting a certain self-consciousness about the origins of the material.[20] Unfortunately, Latin texts rarely address their relationship with Jewish magic as explicitly as these do.

Condemnations of magic

Medieval Christians wrote more about Jewish magic in the context of condemnations than in writings of practical or theoretical magic. Yet, I have argued elsewhere that literary and polemical representations of Jewish magic tell us more about the author's conception of magic than about the alleged users.[21] There is no reason to suspect that such accounts derive from awareness of actual Jewish practices. That said, they might still contribute to Christian perceptions of Jewish magic in ways that are not easy to discern. There are, however, a few condemnations of magic that rely directly on Jewish writings.

In the wake of the Paris Talmud trial of 1240, the first formal disputation between Christians and Jews about the validity of the Talmud, a convert named Thibaut de Sézanne compiled a Latin dossier of passages from the Talmud. These passages are first grouped by the specific error that they represent (such as "blasphemy"); then, later in the manuscript, they are repeated following the order of the tractates of the Talmud. Among the categories of error, we find the rubric "On sorcery" (*De sortilegiis*).[22] The section begins with the passage, "Whoever places his bed between north and south will have male children. Rabbi Naaman says that his wife who placed her bed thus did not suffer miscarriages" (Berakhot 5b). The passages that follow include rabbinic anecdotes about the evil eye, interactions with angels and demons, healing, divination and the avoidance of various supernatural dangers. Many of these Talmudic excerpts might be more accurately categorized as superstitious beliefs rather than sorcery. These particular passages were not central to the disputation itself, but in the dossier they served as additional evidence to discredit the Talmud. But this concern with Talmudic sorcery did not last long. By the time of the next disputation, held in Barcelona in 1263, Christian polemicists were developing ways to employ their own readings of Rabbinic literature in arguing against Jews. From this new perspective, Rabbinic references to issues such as theology and messianism became central.

This change, and its implications for the discussion of magic, is reflected in the Hebrew report of a second disputation in Paris (ca. 1269–1273). When the Christian disputant cites a Rabbinic text to prove that Jesus was well versed in Rabbinic literature, his Jewish opponent comments on the change in tactic: "Up until now, you have said that all our books are magicians' books (*sifrei qosemim*)."[23] Subsequent disputations and condemnations of the Talmud found little use for accusations of sorcery.

Another event that impacted Christian discussions of magic was the translation of Maimonides's *Guide for the Perplexed*, which is worth considering here even though it was composed in Arabic. Even before the work as a whole was translated into Latin, an anonymous fragment was available in Paris. This version likely served as the basis for some of William of Auvergne's thought in his work *On the Laws* (1228–1230), where he draws on Maimonides's particular condemnation of sorcery in *Guide* 3.37. In this section of the *Guide*, Maimonides argues that many commandments that seem irrational – such as the prohibition on cross-dressing in Deut. 22:5 or the prohibition to eat a young tree's fruit in Lev. 19:23–25) – are actually safeguards that prevent people from turning to sorcery, which for Maimonides is inherently idolatrous and linked to star worship. In these two examples, he explains, cross-dressing is associating with certain practices in the cult of Venus, while the waiting period on eating fruit prevents the impatient person from being tempted to use magic in order to speed up the tree's production of first fruits. Not only does William accept Maimonides's rationale for the commandments and his direct link between idolatry and sorcery (*Laws*, chs. 1, 13, 24) but he even connects cross-dressing to sorcery and the cult of Venus in the same manner (*Laws*, ch. 13). In addition to Maimonides, William also reports traditions according to which the golden calf represented the astrological sign of Taurus (*Laws*, ch. 26). In Jewish writings, astrological interpretations of the golden calf appear most notably in Judah Halevi's *Kuzari* and Abraham Ibn Ezra's two commentaries on Exodus.[24] I know of no direct connection between William and these Jewish works, but it is noteworthy that William seems to be having conversations paralleling those in the Jewish world. Another author who drew on Maimonides was Raymond Martini in his *Pugio fidei* (after 1278), a landmark work in the polemical use of Rabbinic literature. In a discussion of the divine name, he reproduces a passage from *Guide* 1.62 that condemns the misuse of divine names for magical ends (*Pugio* III.III.iv.4). In the same work can be found Latin translations of a small number passages from rabbinic literature involving sorcery or demons. However, none of these, including the passage on divine names, serves to condemn magic per se. Rather, all of these passages are adduced in the service of other theological or polemical concerns.

In a different manner, Christians might condemn a magical practice through association with Jews. For example, Kati Ihnat and I have recently argued that medieval Christians came to associate wax figurines – including those used for sorcery – with Jews in order to help establish the boundaries between acceptable use of devotional objects (votive offerings) and misuse or abuse of such objects (effigies, sorcery).[25] In this respect, Christian perspectives on Jews and their presence in Christian society affected the way Christians understood their own magical practices. Polemical and literary accounts of Jewish magic may thus have much to reveal, even if they bear little resemblance to Jewish practice.

The role of personal contact: specialized and common traditions

Nearly all forms of Jewish–Christian exchange in question imply a degree of personal contact. For example, the translation of a text from Latin to Hebrew involved, at a bare minimum, a Jew obtaining a Latin copy of the text. Often, the process of translation was itself a collaborative activity. According to a standard technique, known as "four-handed translation," a Christian would read through the Latin (or vernacular) text, reciting it orally in the vernacular, while a Jew listened and copied it down in Hebrew. It could work in the other direction as well, but translations from Hebrew to Latin were much less common, not just for magical texts but in general. In the twelfth and thirteenth centuries especially, Arabophone Jews collaborated with Christians in translating Arabic works of science, philosophy, astrology, medicine and magic. Jewish translators were employed most notably at the court of Frederick II in Sicily and the court of Alfonso X in Castile. At Alfonso's court, Jews played an important role in translating Arabic astro-magical works such as the *Picatrix*, as well as the Hebrew the *Book of Raziel*.[26] We can only imagine what kinds of conversations may have accompanied these contacts. Other sources may offer suggestions, such as Yohanan Alemanno's descriptions of various conversations about magic that he had with Christians,[27] but we must also be cautious in overgeneralizing from his interactions.

Perhaps no specialized context entailed more personal contact between Jews and Christians than the medical profession. Jewish doctors, who were not permitted to learn at the medical faculties, came to hold Latin medicine in high esteem; there is evidence that they sometimes turned to their Christian colleagues in order to keep up to date in medical developments. Indeed, medicine is remarkable for being an area of knowledge – in contrast to philosophy and other sciences – in which Jews quickly came to rely on the Latin tradition more than the Arabic one. Collaborative translations from Latin to Hebrew are thus particularly prominent in medicine. Furthermore, there were not merely friendly contacts between Christian and Jews, but there is even evidence that they practised medicine together on occasion. Given these circumstances, medieval medicine can offer important insights into the transmission of medical and even astral magic – for a working knowledge of astrology was an essential tool for doctors. For example, Jewish and Christian doctors of Montpellier both shared an interest in the astro-medical talismans of *On the Twelve Images*.[28] In addition, two medical manuscripts of fifteenth-century Spain reveal that Jews had access to two different versions of a certain Latin incantation against epilepsy.[29] We can only speculate whether this access was oral or textual, but it surely involved some form of contact.

If we wish to form a better picture of how Christians may have come into personal contact with Jewish magical practices and ideas, sorcery trials involving Jews provide valuable evidence. If the narratives in these sources cannot always be taken at face value, in the aggregate they form a picture of what was at least seen as socially plausible. Some of these trials involve high-ranking patrons, usually at court, who employ Jewish magicians. In 1308, in Paris, Bishop Guichard of Troyes was accused of having used magic against the queen consort of France, Joan I of Navarre (d. 1305). Witnesses tell of a Jew from Troyes named Hagin, with whom Guichard frequently consulted. Among other tasks Hagin performed for Guichard, he created a wax figurine, presumably the same one that was used to bewitch Joan. Another bishop, Hugues Géraud of Cahors, was accused in 1317 of trying to kill Pope John XXII and some cardinals with that same method of sorcery. Witnesses claimed that wax figurines were provided on different occasions by a certain Jew and a certain converted Jew. According to different accounts, the Jew (named Bomacip by Hugues) was an acquaintance of either Hugues or his treasurer. Either way, it is said that he was an expert in the use of wax figurines and that he taught Hugues the method of baptism, the incantations and the techniques of pricking the figurine in order to cause someone's death.

While it is possible that the Jews described in both these trials are fictional or at least highly constructed, this is not always the case. In 1318, a Jew named Moses of Trets was brought to the papal court to testify about the astrological predictions and the astrological rings that he produced for Robert of Mauvoisin, the archbishop of Aix. Likewise, when Jaime Roig was accused of sedition in Mallorca in 1345, the charges drawn up against him noted his connections with Master Menachem the Jew, "a great experimenter and necromancer,"[30] who later came into the service of Peter IV of Aragon. Notably, Bomacip, Moses of Trets and Master Menachem are all identified as physicians. This is the case as well with a certain Master Helias, an expert in magic and necromancy who worked on behalf of the antipope Gregory XII, according to the Council of Pisa (1409).

In other cases, average Christians supposedly hired local Jews to perform magic. In 1334, Solona, a Jewish woman of Barcelona, performing a service for hire, attempted to kill a woman by pricking wax hearts and placing them in the bed of the intended victim. In contrast to the techniques attributed to Bomacip, we are not told of specialized rituals or incantations accompanying her actions. To this case, we can add that of a woman of Paris who was arrested for sorcery in 1381 because her Jewish creditor, who also provided her with medical help, had sold her an amulet to help her obtain the love of a certain man. Around the same time in the City of Valencia, a Jew named Salamies Nasci had come to the attention of King Peter IV of Aragon as a magician and invoker of demons. In 1384, we learn, a trial against Salamies concerned "invocations, thurifications, suffumigations and worship of devils, carried out by certain Christians in the home of Salamies."[31] Further details are lacking in this case, but we know much more about the 1416 trial of Samuel of Granada, a Jewish doctor – and according to some a relapsed convert – also in the City of Valencia. On behalf of his clients, Samuel allegedly used magic to discover the source of a patient's impotence, instructed a patient to drink a bowl of water in which words from the Gospel of John had been soaked and used the Psalms to discover a thief. One witness claimed that he had asked Samuel to cast a fidelity spell on his lover, but Samuel only offered relationship advice instead. Ultimately, many of the witnesses spoke highly of Samuel and seemed to respect his place in the community.[32]

There are only a few hints in trial sources about contacts that do not rely on some sort of professional–client relationship between the Jewish and Christian parties. In the inquisitorial register of Jacques Fournier, we read about Beatrice of Planissoles, who had strange ingredients in her possession at the time she was arrested for heresy. Beatrice explained that a converted Jewish woman had taught her to carry umbilical cords of male children in order to ensure victory in legal disputes, and that a girl's first menstrual blood can be added to a man's drink to make him love that girl. Other than the reference to her source, there is nothing that would identify these kinds of practices as specifically Jewish. The same could be said in the case of Jaco Abutarda of Daroca, a Jew who was arrested in 1334 for, among other things, miscegenation and punching a tax collector. The letter of remission for Jaco's case indicated that he bore "names, characters and precious stones" to protect him from the law.[33] Other than the writing itself – presumably in Hebrew, although the letter gives no such indication – there is nothing about this practice that was unique to Jews. Christians would have understood Jaco's talismans in much the same way he did, for the powers of stones and simple amulets of names and characters would have been part of the shared common traditions.

However brief, such glimpses into this particular set of Jewish–Christian contacts have much to teach us, such as the significance of the repeated references to physicians, which

I would argue is more a function of the social relations between Christians and Jewish doctors than evidence that the latter were particularly fond of magic, or the prominence of wax figurines that are much rarer in Jewish practice but, as noted above, were significant in the medieval Christian imagination. What I would like to stress here, however, is that the practices described in these records would have generally been familiar to Jews and Christians alike. From the technical procedures to the simpler ones, the stamp of Jewishness lies always in what we are told of the source, for even the incantations in Hugues's trial are ambiguously described as Hebrew or Greek. If these procedures were read out of context or compiled together into a manual of magic, on what basis would we ever suspect Jewish involvement? This is the fundamental problem of assessing the impact of Jewish magic in the Latin Middle Ages. The more that Jews and Christians came to share specialized and common traditions, the less we can assess their respective contributions.

Future directions

Although the preceding discussion has emphasized the methodological difficulties inherent in assessing the Jewish contribution to Latin Christian magic, I do not wish to suggest that it is a fruitless line of inquiry. On the contrary, an awareness of the difficulties is crucial for making progress and avoiding pitfalls in the future. Research on both the Jewish and Christian sides has and will surely continue to bring us closer to understanding the significance of contact between the Jewish and Christian magical traditions.

The comparative study of Jewish and Christian magic is hindered from the outset, because there is no adequate survey of medieval European Jewish magic. Joshua Trachtenberg's *Jewish Magic and Superstition: A Study in Folk Religion* (1939) remains the closest to such a study, and Trachtenberg even highlights points of contact between Jewish and Christian traditions, but the work presents problems for the understanding of medieval Jewish magic in several respects. To name just a few of relevance to our discussion, Trachtenberg prioritized certain evidence – and especially that of the German Pietists – over other sources, his presentation offers misleading distinctions between popular and elite traditions, he relied almost exclusively on printed materials and secondary sources and he minimized the differences between widely different contexts. This work remains an important point of reference, but there is better research that has been done and much more that remains to be done.

The contours of some of the Jewish specialized magical traditions are becoming clearer. The most well-known example is the magic of the *Hasidei Ashkenaz*, the "German Pietists" of the Rhineland, who flourished at the end of the twelfth century and the first half of the thirteenth. Their traditions serve as the foundation for much of the medieval material treated in Trachtenberg's work. Their manuscripts provide the sole extant sources for much of the ancient *Hekhalot* mystical tradition, and their elaborate angelological and demonological speculations and associated magical practices owe much to the *Hekhalot* materials. The content of *Hasidei Ashkenaz* writings has received a great deal of attention, but more knowledge of their circulation and influence is a great desideratum. Ephraim Kanarfogel has shown that the magical and mystical traditions of the *Haside Ashkenaz* were influential among the Talmudic scholars of Northern France,[34] but there is much more to learn about the dissemination of these materials in Spain, Italy and elsewhere.

Another specialized tradition that has proven fruitful is astral magic. Dov Schwartz has signalled the richness of intellectual engagement with astral and other kinds of magic in medieval Jewish thought, perhaps most notably in supercommentaries on

Abraham Ibn Ezra's biblical commentaries.[35] The significance of Ibn Ezra's other astrological works has recently been highlighted thanks to Shlomo Sela's editions and translations.[36] In addition, the broader terrain of Jewish astrology has been mapped with remarkable thoroughness by Reimund Leicht, whose *Astrologumena Judaica* (2006) identifies relevant texts and manuscripts, with notes on translation, circulation and reception. Leicht's work thus offers a solid foundation for the important textual work that remains to be done. These astro-magical writings are particularly important, because they figure prominently among the aforementioned shared texts, including the *Book of Raziel*, which we have discussed as a rare translation of Hebrew magic into Latin.

The specialized tradition that raises the most difficult questions is the Kabbalah. Scholars have represented it as everything from an intellectual tradition devoid of magic to a system of thought and practice embedded in a fundamentally magical or theurgic worldview. Furthermore, the term "Kabbalistic" has often been used as a generic designation for anything strange, obscure, magical or mystical, regardless of connections with Jewish traditions, let alone the Kabbalah. And so, there is much to disentangle when trying to assess the relationship between Kabbalah (which, it must be stressed, was never a unified tradition) and magic.[37] If we leave aside the larger theoretical issues, we can make several useful observations. First of all, medieval Kabbalistic writings are not packed full of the kinds of rituals and techniques that Christian contemporaries would generally consider magical. Inasmuch as many Kabbalistic treatises are devoted to theosophical speculation or midrashic exegesis, there is little room for instruction in practical magic. Second, Kabbalists differed widely on their attitudes towards magic. Writers such as Abraham Abulafia and Joseph Gikatilla were very critical of magic, acknowledging the possibility that aspects of Kabbalah could be misused in magical ways. Other writers like Nehemiah ben Shlomo and texts such as the *Book of the Responding Entity* offer elements that even more conservative definitions are likely to consider magical. Third, whatever we may say about the Kabbalah, it was common for magical writings to circulate alongside Kabbalistic writings in medieval manuscripts. And finally, there are very few magical practices during our period that could be considered Kabbalistic, if we limit our definition to magic that is fundamentally rooted in a Kabbalistic cosmology (for example, magic relying on the divine emanations known as the *sefirot*). In other words, the magical traditions found in and alongside Kabbalistic writings are rarely unique to the specialized tradition of Kabbalah. Even the traditions surrounding the *Book of Creation* and the Golem, which many would consider magical, did not originate within nor are they exclusive to the Kabbalah.[38]

A more self-conscious integration of magical and Kabbalah arguably begins in the late fifteenth century with Yohanan Alemanno, the teacher of Pico della Mirandola. Alemanno's work, coupled with the translations that Flavius Mithridates produced for Pico (which included Kabbalah proper as well as German Pietist writings and other materials), and the radical reinterpretation of Kabbalah by Pico himself created a much closer association between magic and Kabbalah in both the Jewish and Christians worlds, which has often been anachronistically applied to earlier traditions by both historians and by texts (such as the aforementioned *Book of Abramelin*). The context of fifteenth- and sixteenth-century Italy has been recognized as important for the study of Jewish magical traditions for reasons such as the translations of Hermetic writings and other notable magical texts, the influx of immigrants from Spain and some remarkable extant compilations of magic. As research in fifteenth- and sixteenth-century Jewish magic in Europe continues, it is important to understand both the continuities and discontinuities of Jewish magical traditions.

Much less work has been done on the common tradition among Jews than among Christians. One exception is the tradition of the *Use of the Psalms*, which circulated widely in different contexts, and was thus not limited to Kabbalists, those knowledgeable in astrology or any other specialized group. More aspects of the common tradition can be brought to light through the study of unpublished charms, recipes, marginalia and magical compilations. Of particular note are medieval prayer books, many of which were privately owned. These books frequently contain angelic invocations and apotropaic charms – not as marginalia as Eamon Duffy has highlighted in Books of Hours,[39] but rather incorporated into text. In addition, the Cairo Geniza, a storeroom for discarded texts, has preserved a treasure trove of magical writings from the medieval period, spanning the breadth of specialized and common traditions. Studies of the Geniza have revealed surprising parallels with Christian magic from Western Europe,[40] and additional work on such parallels will surely increase our understanding of the underlying contacts. If the common tradition is the point of greatest contact between Jewish and Christian magic, as I have suggested, then this kind of work may yield the most important results.

The Hebrew language can be a significant limiting factor for scholars of Christian magic. Only a few relevant Hebrew texts are available in translation, much of medieval Jewish magic remains unedited, and the existing secondary literature is insufficient for learning about the varieties of Jewish magic. Nevertheless, the scholar who wishes to identify Jewish elements in Christian magic can begin by turning to those primary sources that have been translated. Under the guidance of Peter Schäfer, several texts of mystical and magical significance have been edited and translated into German, including the major manuscripts of *Hekhalot* literature (Schäfer), *Tractate Hekhalot* (Klaus Herrmann), the *Book of the Garment* (Irina Wandrey), the *Book of the Upright* (Wandrey) and three volumes to date of magical texts from the Cairo Geniza (Schäfer and Shaul Shaked). Schäfer's team has also published the *Use of the Psalms* (Bill Rebiger) and the *Book of Secrets* (Rebiger and Schäfer).[41] The Hermes Latinus project has made the Hebrew versions of some Hermetic texts available, and a future volume is planned that will contain additional Hebrew texts. There is no translation or edition of the *Book of Raziel* as it existed in the Middle Ages, although some of its component pieces are included in the aforementioned publications, nor have the magical writings of *Hasidei Ashkenaz* been translated. An exception are those works translated by Flavius Mithridates, which are being edited and translated as part of *The Kabbalistic Library of Pico della Mirandola*. One of the most accessible texts is the *Sword of Moses*, which was edited and translated by Moses Gaster and again, more recently, by Yuval Harari.[42] Unfortunately, there is no evidence that this text was known in medieval Europe. Finally, medieval texts containing significant medical magic have been edited and translated, including *The Book of Women's Love* (Carmen Caballero-Navas) and both *The Book of Medical Experiences* and *The Book of Segulot*, that is "occult virtues" (J.O. Leibowitz and S. Marcus).

Methodologically, we are in need of innovative approaches to discern Jewish influence in Christian magical texts. As mentioned above, Kieckhefer proposed a conceptual approach, and I followed in his footsteps by drawing attention to the portrayal of angels.[43] Similar conceptual comparisons could be carried out for numerous aspects of magic such as the role of divine names, purity and impurity, rituals and invocations, relationships to source material, underlying cosmological assumptions, the development of magical diagrams, the power of the written word, the use of magical "characters" and more. Writing about Jewish magic, Elliot Wolfson has drawn attention to the central concept of images, whether material, textual and onomastic or psychic.[44] To my knowledge, no one has yet searched for traces of parallel concepts in Christian texts. In addition to conceptual approaches, there may still be great value in simple textual and philological approaches. While I suggested above that the appearance of a Hebrew divine or angelic name may not be an indication of any actual Jewish influence, the tracing of a cluster of such names might be more compelling. Both Jewish and Christian texts frequently list names in long series. If certain names appear together, we may discover unknown connections between texts. In addition, analysis of magical texts with respect to the liturgy is perhaps one of the most important desiderata for the study of magic. The late Stephen Stallcup presented an example of such scholarship that shed important new light on the *Sworn Book of Honorius*.[45] Before we go seeking external sources, it is important to understand a text's relationship to its own tradition.

Finally, we are faced with a difficult question, whose answer bears heavily on our approach to this subject: how distinct was Jewish magic in the eyes of medieval Christians? The author of the *Sworn Book of Honorius* seems to suggest both possibilities: by explicitly repudiating Jewish magic, he seems to expect that his readers will recognize Jewish influence on the text. And yet, by asserting that Jews lost the ability to use this magic with their rejection of Christ, and that it is now the inheritance of Christians, he seems to suggest that there is no meaningful difference in form between Jewish and Christian magic. Given the exoticism of claiming foreign origins of texts, did Christian authors ever try to make the context of a magical text "look Jewish"? If so, what did that entail? The evidence of sorcery trials presents Jewish magic with no distinguishing characteristics, besides the rare reference to Hebrew words. And the *Techel/Azareus Complex*, which in some manuscripts bears a preface attributing the text to an ancient Israelite, contains no obvious Jewish references, while one version does reference baptism. If we could be certain that Christians would identify specific elements as Jewish, we might be able to use those elements as a starting point for assessing the underlying contacts. If Christians saw the two traditions as fundamentally the same, what exactly should we expect Jewish influence to look like?

Notes

1 For a particularly interesting example, see Reimund Leicht, "Nahmanides on Necromancy," in *Studies in the History of Culture and Science: A Tribute to Gad Freudenthal*, ed. Resianne Fontaine, Ruth Glasner, Reimund Leicht and Giuseppe Veltri (Leiden: Brill, 2011), 251–64.
2 Richard Kieckhefer, *Magic in the Middle Ages* (Cambridge: Cambridge University Press, 1990), esp. ch. 4; Richard Kieckhefer, "The Specific Rationality of Medieval Magic," *American Historical Review* 99, no. 3 (1994): 833.
3 On this text, see Reimund Leicht, *Astrologumena Judaica: Untersuchungen zur Geschichte der astrologischen Literatur der Juden* (Tübingen: Mohr Siebeck, 2006), 329–31.
4 See, respectively, Moshe Idel, "The Study Program of R. Yoḥanan Alemanno" (Hebrew), *Tarbiz* 48, no. 3–4 (1979): 312; Moshe Idel, "The Magical and Neoplatonic Interpretations of the Kabbalah in the Renaissance," in *Jewish Thought in the Sixteenth Century*, ed. Bernard Dov Cooperman (Cambridge, MA: Harvard University Press, 1983), 195; Harvey J. Hames, "Between the March of Ancona and Florence: Jewish Magic and a Christian Text," in *Invoking Angels: Theurgic Ideas and Practices, Thirteenth to Sixteenth Centuries*, ed. Claire Fanger (University Park: Pennsylvania State University Press, 2013), 294–311.
5 Mark Zier, "The Healing Power of the Hebrew Tongue: An Example from Late Thirteenth-Century England," in *Health, Disease and Healing in Medieval Culture*, ed. Sheila Campbell, Bert Hall and David Klausner (New York: St. Martin's Press, 1992), 103–18.
6 Leicht, *Astrologumena Judaica*, 331. My translation.

7 On the Arabic translations attributed to John of Seville, see Charles Burnett, "John of Seville and John of Spain: A *mise au point*," in *Arabic into Latin in the Middle Ages: The Translators and Their Intellectual and Social Context* (Surrey: Ashgate, 2009), essay VI.
8 Katelyn Mesler, "The Medieval Lapidary of Techel/Azareus on Engraved Stones and Its Jewish Appropriations," *Aleph: Historical Studies in Science and Judaism* 14, no. 2 (2014): 88–91.
9 The Latin text is printed in Valentin Rose, "Aristoteles de lapidibus und Arnoldus Saxo," *Zeitschrift für deutsches Alterthum* 18, new ser. 6 (1875): 384–423.
10 On the complex textual history of the *Book of Raziel*, see Leicht, *Astrologumena Judaica*, 187–294, 331–41.
11 See esp. Flavia Buzzetta, "Aspetti della magia naturalis e della scientia cabalae nel pensario di Giovanni Pico della Mirandola (1486–1487)" (Ph.D. diss, Ecole pratique des hautes études, Paris / Università degli studi, Palermo, 2011); Flavia Buzzetta, "Il simbolismo della 'scrittura ad occhi' nel *Liber misteriorum venerabilium* (*Shimmushei Torah*): Aspetti di un peculiare retaggio della magia ebraica medievale," *Aries* 14 (2014): 129–64.
12 See René Nelli, "La prière aux soixante-douze noms de Dieu," *Folklore* 8, no. 4 (issue 61) (1950): 70–74, in which there is no sign of genuine Hebrew influence.
13 See Katelyn Mesler, "The Three Magi and Other Christian Motifs in Medieval Hebrew Medical Incantations: A Study in the Limits of Faithful Translation," in *Latin-into-Hebrew: Texts and Studies*, vol. 1, ed. Resianne Fontaine and Gad Freudenthal (Leiden: Brill, 2013), 161–218.
14 See Michael D. Swartz, *Scholastic Magic: Ritual and Revelation in Early Jewish Mysticism* (Princeton, NJ: Princeton University Press, 1996), 44–47 ("opening the heart"), *passim* ("prince of the Torah"); Joseph Dan, "The Princes of Thumb and Cup" (Hebrew), *Tarbiz* 32, no. 4 (1963): 359–69; Mark Verman and Shulamit H. Adler, "Path Jumping in the Jewish Magical Tradition," *Jewish Studies Quarterly* 1, no. 2 (1993/94): 131–48.
15 Karl Manitius, "Magie und Rhetorik bei Anselm von Besate," *Deutsches Archiv für Erforschung des Mittelalters* 12, no. 1 (1956): 55.
16 Rome, Archivio Segreto Vaticano, Camera Apostolica, Collectoriae 493, fols. 23v, 24r, 26v, 28r.
17 Jean Marx, *L'inquisition en Dauphiné: Etude sur le développement et la répression de l'hérésie et de la sorcellerie du XIVe siècle au début du règne de François Ier* (1914; Paris: Honoré Champion, 1978), 220.
18 Richard Kieckhefer, "The Devil's Contemplatives: The *Liber iuratus*, the *Liber visionum* and Christian Appropriation of Jewish Occultism," in *Conjuring Spirits: Texts and Traditions of Medieval Ritual Magic*, ed. Claire Fanger (University Park: Pennsylvania State University Press, 1998), 250–63.
19 Katelyn Mesler, "The *Liber iuratus Honorii* and the Christian Reception of Angel Magic," in *Invoking Angels*, ed. Fanger, 113–50.
20 See esp. Claire Fanger, "Covenant and the Divine Name: Revisiting the *Liber iuratus* and John of Morigny's *Liber florum*," in *Invoking Angels*, ed. Fanger, 192–216.
21 Katelyn Mesler, "Legends of Jewish Sorcery: Reputations and Representations in Late Antiquity and Medieval Europe" (Ph.D. diss, Northwestern University, 2012); Eadem, "Accusations of Jewish Magic and Sorcery in Premodern Latin and Greek Sources," in *A Handbook of Ancient and Medieval Jewish Magic*, ed. Ortal-Paz Saar and Siam Bhayro (Leiden: Brill, forthcoming).
22 Paris, Bibliothèque nationale de France, lat. 16558, fols. 33v–37r.
23 Joseph Shatzmiller, *La deuxième controverse de Paris: Un chapitre dans la polémique entre chrétiens et juifs au Moyen Age* (Paris: Peeters, 1994), 54 (French translation at 72).
24 On the Jewish tradition, see Dov Schwartz, *Studies on Astral Magic in Medieval Jewish Thought*, trans. David Louvish and Batya Stein (Leiden: Brill, 2005), 3–6, 16, 21–22, 97–98, 222–23.
25 Kati Ihnat and Katelyn Mesler, "From Christian Devotion to Jewish Sorcery: The Curious History of Wax Figurines in Medieval Europe," in *Entangled Histories: Knowledge, Authority, and Jewish Culture in the Thirteenth Century*, ed. Elisheva Baumgarten, Ruth Mazo Karras and Katelyn Mesler (Philadelphia: University of Pennsylvania Press, 2017), 134–58.
26 See esp. David Romano, "Le opere scientifiche di Alfonso X e l'intervento degli ebrei," in *Oriente e Occidente nel Medioevo: Filosofia e scienze* (Rome: Accdemia Nazionale dei Lincei, 1971), 677–711; Norman Roth, "Les collaborateurs juifs à l'oeuvre scientifique d'Alphonse X," in *Chrétiens, musulmans et juifs dans l'Espagne médiévale: De la convergence à l'expulsion*, ed. Ron Barkaï (Paris: Editions du Cerf, 1994), 203–25; Jean-Patrice Boudet, *Entre science et nigromance: Astrologie, divination et magie dans l'Occident médiéval (XIIe–XVe siècle)* (Paris: Publications de la Sorbonne, 2006), 187–98.

27 Idel, "Magical and Neoplatonic Interpretations," 195.
28 Joseph Shatzmiller, "In Search of the 'Book of Figures': Medicine and Astrology in Montpellier at the Turn of the Fourteenth Century," *AJS Review* 7 (1982): 383–407.
29 Mesler, "The Three Magi," 180–81.
30 Jusep Maria Quadrado, "Proceso instruido en 1345 contra el Gobernador Arnaldo de Erill, su asesor Des Torrents y el Procurador Real Bernardo Morera, acusado de favorecer a los partidarios del destronado Jaime III," *Bolletí de la Societat Arqueológica Luliana* 15, year 30, no. 406 (1914): 6.
31 Johannes Vincke, *Zur Vorgeschichte der Spanischen Inquisition: Die Inquisition in Aragon, Katalonien, Mallorca und Valencia während des 13. und 14. Jahrhunderts* (Bonn: Peter Hanstein, 1941), 123.
32 Mark D. Meyerson, "Samuel of Granada and the Dominican Inquisitor: Jewish Magic and Jewish Heresy in post-1391 Valencia," in *Friars and Jews in the Middle Ages and Renaissance*, ed. Steven J. McMichael and Susan E. Myers (Leiden: Brill, 2004), 161–89.
33 David Nirenberg, *Communities of Violence: Persecution of Minorities in the Middle Ages* (Princeton, NJ: Princeton University Press, 1998), 163.
34 Ephraim Kanarfogel, *"Peering through the Lattices": Mystical, Magical, and Pietistic Dimensions in the Tosafist Period* (Detroit, MI: Wayne State University Press, 2000).
35 Dov Schwartz, *Amulets, Properties and Rationalism in Medieval Jewish Thought* (Ramat-Gan: University of Bar-Ilan, 2004) [Hebrew]; Idem, *Astral Magic in Medieval Jewish Thought* (Ramat-Gan: University of Bar-Ilan, 1999). The latter has been partly translated as *Studies on Astral Magic*.
36 Shlomo Sela, ed. and trans., *Abraham Ibn Ezra's Astrological Writings*, 5 vols. (Leiden: Brill, 2007–17).
37 The classic discussion is Gershom Scholem, *Kabbalah* (Jerusalem: Keter, 1974), 182–89, where he uses the term "Practical Kabbalah" in a very broad sense. See also 317–19. For a range of perspectives, see esp. Moshe Idel, "On Judaism, Jewish Mysticism and Magic," in *Envisioning Magic: A Princeton Seminar and Symposium*, ed. Peter Schäfer and Hans G. Kippenberg (Leiden: Brill, 1997), 195–214; Jonathan Garb, "Mysticism and Magic: Opposition, Ambivalence, Integration," *Mahanaim* 14 (2002): 97–109 [Hebrew]; Yuval Harari, "Jewish Magic: An Annotated Overview," *El Prezente: Studies in Sephardic Culture* 5 (2011): 50*–60* [Hebrew]; Gideon Bohak, *A Fifteenth-Century Manuscript of Jewish Magic* (Los Angeles: Cherub Press, 2014), 1: 23–24 [Hebrew]; Josef H. Chajes, "Kabbale et magie juive," in *Magie: Anges et démons dans la tradition juive*, ed. Gideon Bohak and Anne Hélène Hoog (Paris: Flammarion, 2015), 105–12.
38 On these traditions, see esp. Marla Segol, *Word and Image in Medieval Kabbalah: The Texts, Commentaries, and Diagrams of the Sefer Yetirah* (New York: Palgrave, 2012); Moshe Idel, *Golem: Jewish Magical and Mystical Traditions on the Artificial Anthropoid* (Albany: State University of New York Press, 1990).
39 Eamon Duffy, *The Stripping of the Altars: Traditional Religion in England, c.1400–c.1580* (New Haven: Yale University Press, 1992), 266–87; Idem, *Marking the Hours: English People and Their Prayers, 1240–1570* (New Haven: Yale University Press, 2006), 81–96.
40 E.g., Gideon Bohak, "Catching a Thief: The Jewish Trials of a Christian Ordeal," *Jewish Studies Quarterly* 13 (2006): 344–62; Mesler, "The Three Magi," 182–84; Ortal-Paz Saar, "A Genizah Magical Fragment and Its European Parallels," *Journal of Jewish Studies* 65, no. 2 (2014): 237–62.
41 All of these works appear in the series *Texts and Studies in Ancient Judaism*, published by Mohr Siebeck. An English translation of some of the Hekhalot materials is available in James R. Davila, *Hekhalot Literature in Translation: Major Texts of Merkavah Mysticism* (Leiden: Brill, 2013).
42 See Yuval Harari, "The Sword of Moses (Ḥarba de-Moshe): A New Translation and Introduction," *Magic, Ritual, and Witchcraft* 7, no. 1 (2012): 58–98.
43 See above, nn. 18–19.
44 Elliot Wolfson, "Phantasmagoria: The Image of the Image in Jewish Magic from Late Antiquity to the Early Middle Ages," *Review of Rabbinic Judaism* 4, no. 1 (2001): 78–120.
45 Stephen Stallcup, "Alma Chorus Domini: Divine Names in Religious and Magical Contexts," paper presented at The 43rd International Congress on Medieval Studies, Kalamazoo, MI, May 9, 2008.

8

MAGIC IN ROMANCE LANGUAGES

Sebastià Giralt

During the thirteenth century, the Romance languages of Western Europe began to convey secular learned knowledge while expanding their audience to new social groups, such as the nobility or the bourgeoisie, after centuries of having been monopolized by Latin and by the clergy.[1] Magic was one of the specialized fields in which Romance texts were translated and produced earliest, as a result of rulers' and courtiers' ambition to dominate occult forces. However, although the origin of magical writings was at first related to those who held power, these writings later suffered persecution and censorship on the basis of religious orthodoxy, and this made it difficult for them to be preserved, especially in the Iberian Peninsula. This chapter will focus on astral magic, which includes ritual and image magic that observed astrological conditions, and which poses specific problems regarding its illegitimacy and circulation.

Castile: learned magic in the vernacular for a learned king

The process of vernacularization began in thirteenth-century Castile and spread from there to the rest of the Romance-speaking world. The necessary condition for Castile's precocity was the possibility of accessing the knowledge translated and produced by Islam, as a result of the Arabic manuscripts obtained in the territories taken from Muslims and of the Arabic speakers who remained there, mainly Jews; however, the impulse came from King Alfonso X of Castile (1252–84), called the Learned precisely because of his ambitious intellectual programme. His aspiration to recover the sciences from Arabic sources for Latin Christendom, where they had deeply declined, is expressed in several prologues of the Alfonsine corpus. Different models of learned kingship, such as Solomonic or Platonic, have been proposed for Alfonso's decision to resort to intellectual activity in order to gain prestige and power for the monarchy, but it is difficult to deny the influence of the Islamic model of the sovereign. Indeed, as was the case with many Muslim monarchs, one of his main interests was the "science of the stars", which included astronomy, astrology and astral magic.

Although other European monarchies also patronized the science of the stars and promoted its vernacularization, especially from the fourteenth century onwards, Alfonso's case is unusual not only because of its earliness or its use of direct sources in Arabic but also because the Alfonsine corpus brings together a diversity of magical–astrological traditions, including ritual and image magic addressed to the spirits of the stars. In addition, throughout the thirteenth century, the process of sifting out the texts translated from Arabic to Latin during the previous century, mostly in the Iberian Peninsula, took place in European universities, with the aim of rejecting those not considered compatible with the Christian faith. Whereas natural magic and astrology that was not determinist were widely accepted, ritual and astral magic addressed to angels, demons and other spirits were generally rejected as illicit by intellectual elites and categorized as necromancy.[2] We should therefore ask ourselves whether Alfonso had any scruples when it came to admitting such practices.

Alfonso's position regarding the legitimacy of magic, sorcery and divination is expressed in his legal code, the *Siete Partidas* (1254–65): Law VII, 23, 1, distinguishes between divination performed by learned experts using astrological techniques and that conducted by sorcerers and diviners employing other techniques such as hydromancy, ornithomancy or chiromancy, with the latter divination being prohibited under penalty of banishment. The following two laws forbid necromancy on pain of death, defining it as "the art of enchanting evil spirits", as well as the use of images, philtres and any witchcraft intended to bring about or break up love. In contrast, magical operations carried out with good intentions, such as protection from demons, breaking curses and avoiding storms or pests, were worthy of reward.[3]

Nevertheless, Alfonsine compilations and translations include magical operations designed to do both good and evil. Specifically, both necromantic practices and experiments to bring about or break up love are found there. Hence, the basis for judging whether the magic is acceptable or not must be other than a strictly moral one, with its learned transmission, guaranteed by the Arabic sources, being a more determining factor. Thus, Castile, and particularly Alfonso's entourage, was yet to be reached by the condemnation of necromancy expressed by European intellectual elite. It was possible to produce texts with such contents because their production was patronized by the king independently from the Church.

If we compare the Alfonsine production in the sciences with the twelfth-century Toletan versions, certain fundamental differences may be detected, especially the breadth of subjects covered and the target language of the translations. Whereas Alfonso's scriptorium focused on the science of the stars, the translations of the previous century also covered other disciplines such as philosophy, natural philosophy, medicine, alchemy or mathematics – all the branches of knowledge of Arabic origin that interested European intellectuals, both those who chose and translated the works and those who made up their readership. By contrast, the intellectual activity of the thirteenth century was promoted and directed by the king, and this is why it was mainly related to the needs of the monarchy and the court, including the science of the stars, which could help the ruler to make decisions, as well as historiography, musical compositions, chess and other board games – some of them astrological.

The choice of language can also be related to the courtly character of Alfonsine production, as well as to its independence from the Church, although other factors were involved. In twelfth-century Toledo, translation into the vernacular was used merely as a bridge between Arabic and Latin: the text was rendered orally into Castilian by an Arabic speaker while at the same time a *clericus* (Latin scholar) wrote out the text in Latin.[4] The use of the vernacular was therefore instrumental and ephemeral, even though it may have been the first time the Castilian language was employed for an intellectual purpose. By contrast, in Alfonso's scriptorium, Castilian was the final language. Alfonsine versions were also the product of teamwork: sometimes not only the presence of two translators – a Jew and a Christian – is attested but also of a corrector. There are signs of both technical and linguistic correction and successive later additions. The latter is the case of the *Lapidario*, a book on the natural magical properties imbued by the stars in stones. Texts were often not simply translated but often reworked with additions and omissions, as the *Picatrix* shows, and sometimes new treatises and compilations were created from Arabic sources.

A lengthy debate has existed among scholars as to why Alfonso promoted the writing or the translation of astronomical-astrological-magical works in Castilian rather than in Latin. This has often been attributed to the fact that such activity was carried out mainly by Jews, who did the bulk of the task because they knew Arabic and the science of the stars, but were not familiar with Latin.[5] Moreover, very few of the Iberian Christian scholars of the Alfonsine scriptorium demonstrated sufficient proficiency in Latin to write such works in this language: uniquely, Álvaro de Oviedo is known to have translated Abenragel's *Liber Conplido* into Latin, but his version was replaced some years later by a new one by Egidio de' Tebaldi and Pietro da Reggio. Alfonso resorted to his Italian chancellors, who were Ghibellines and whose Latin complied with European standards, to produce the Alfonsine Latin translations from the previous Castilian versions, which demonstrates his aim to project them into Western Europe while he was a pretender to the Holy Roman Empire (1257–75).

However, the use of Castilian as a learned language seems to be related also to the readership of the Alfonsine works. The main target audience was probably the court and the nobles of Castile rather than European scholars as in the twelfth century, and hence Castilian was the most suitable language for reaching such a public. This is also why the works written or translated in the royal scriptorium were copied in luxurious, beautifully illustrated codices.

Different production periods for the science of the stars have been distinguished during Alfonso's time. In the 1250s, particular works were translated from Arabic such as *Picatrix*. Then after a decade focused on observations and treatises about astronomical instruments, from the mid-1270s, a new encyclopaedic vision was added in the form of large compilations, including the *Libro de las formas* and *Astromagia*.

The *Ghāyat al-ḥakīm* or *Picatrix*, probably composed in al-Andalus in the tenth century, is one of the greatest manuals of talismanic magic. It was translated from Arabic to Castilian probably by Yehuda ben Moshe by order of Alfonso between 1256 and 1257, and subsequently from Castilian to Latin.[6] Only a few fragments of the Castilian version of the *Picatrix* are preserved in *Astromagia*. Picatrix (Picatriz in Castilian) is actually the author's name transmitted in the Latin (and Castilian) versions and, according to the Latin preface, the title given by the author. However, there is evidence in Romance texts that it was still known by its Arabic title – or approximate variants of this – until the fifteenth century, being indirectly cited in Enrique de Villena's *Tratado de aojamiento o fascinación* (c. 1422), under the title of *Gayad Alhaqim*,[7] and directly by the Barberini codex (c. 1430) discussed below, under the names of *Art de yayet alphaqui* and *Alfaqui gaihet*. These are the first known references to the *Picatrix* before it became one of the cornerstones of the Renaissance occultist flourishing.

One of the longest compilations produced by the royal scriptorium was the *Libro de las formas y las imágenes* [*Book of forms and images*], but the sole surviving codex of this book (MS El Escorial, Real Biblioteca, h-I-16) only transmits the preface and the table of contents with a brief description of each part.[8] It was an anthology composed between 1277 and 1279 in order to provide a comprehensive overview of astral images, using extracts taken from earlier Alfonsine treatises such as *Lapidario*, *Astromagia*, *Picatrix* and *Liber Razielis*, in addition to other texts that were prepared especially for this volume.

Another compilation of mainly astral magic, dated c. 1280 and entitled *Astromagia* by its editor, is also partially preserved in the MS Vatican, BAV, Reg. Lat. 1283a.[9] Again, it was composed by joining different parts of works which had been previously translated in Alfonso's scriptorium, and adding new texts. Some of the sources are well known – Albumasar, *Picatrix*, *Liber Razielis* – whereas others remain unidentified. Several extant fragments deal solely with purely astrological images but most of them include a number of operations addressed to angels or spirits.

Some of the texts transmitted in *Astromagia* have been identified as parts of the Castilian version of the *Liber Razielis*. This is one of the longest, most varied and most enigmatic medieval compilations on ritual and image magic, consisting of seven books, fully preserved only in its Latin version and accompanied by a series of short treatises with related contents.[10] In the prologue to the Latin version of the *Liber Razielis*, Iohannes Clericus provides a semi-legendary account of how this corpus was formed: the work was initially a gift from the angel Raziel to Adam, and subsequently compiled by Solomon. He also explains that the whole compilation was collected and translated on the initiative of Alfonso, but he does not specify the source language. Iohannes declares that his own tasks have been to select and translate the annexed treatises from Latin to Castilian. If this is true, the Castilian version of these treatises has been lost, as has almost all of the Castilian translation of the *Liber Razielis*. Above and beyond this legendary Solomonic origin, the compilation in fact brings together magical and astrological material from different origins: the largest number of works are Hermetic writings in their Latin versions, whereas the Hebrew tradition of the *Sefer Razi'el* paradoxically represents but a small part of the collection, even though it was responsible for giving it its name.

From its very prologue, the *Liber Razielis* and the treatises associated with it pose many specific problems as an Alfonsine product, and specifically regarding the role of the Castilian version in its transmission. The first question is who was Ioannes Clericus and what was his task? He was identified by D'Agostino with Juan d'Aspa, who had rendered two treatises into Castilian together with ben Moshe in 1259, although this identification is not demonstrated. Although his known translations are Arabic–Castilian, being probably in charge of improving the final Castilian text, his title of cleric makes proficiency in Latin likely. However, as seen above, when there is a double Alfonsine translation, the first version is always the Castilian one, with the Latin one coming afterwards; therefore, it is surprising that he says he has translated the treatises from Latin to Castilian, unless the Latin was not the original version. Indeed, although some scholars, such as Alfonso D'Agostino and Jean-Patrice Boudet, also consider Iohannes to be the translator of the *Liber Razielis* and while Damaris Gehr argues that Iohannes was in fact its real author, he actually only admits to having edited and translated the treatises appended to it, and in my opinion it would make no sense for him to have hidden in his prologue his main translation. Actually, we cannot know for certain what the original language of the *Liber Razielis* was and when it was compiled. Since Hebrew sources seem to be in a minority, it is unlikely that it is a translation from Hebrew as has sometimes been deduced from the mention of the Hebrew title in the prologue. Scholars also disagree on when it was compiled: Reimund Leicht thinks that it was prior to Alfonso's time, Alejandro García Avilés considers it an Alfonsine creation and Gehr defends the hypothesis that it was composed in the late fourteenth century as a forgery, although there was an earlier two-part Latin version of the *Liber Razielis* used in *Astromagia*. In any case, we should consider that in Alfonsine works, the titles given to the king are a useful indication when it comes to dating them. In the prologue to the *Liber Razielis*, the series of titles used is identical to that of the *Libro conplido*, including that of King of Badajoz, which only appears in these two books. This fact may be interpreted as a hint that the Alfonsine attribution is a forgery (Gehr), or that the book was composed or translated earlier than the date proposed by D'Agostino (c. 1259), since the *Libro conplido* was translated in 1254.

At any rate, the editing and study of the *Liber Razielis* begun by Gehr will hopefully help to throw light upon its real origin, its sources and its relationship with Alfonso's corpus, which seems to be difficult to deny. In fact, she misses the overlap, discovered by García Avilés, between the second book of the *Liber Razielis* (*Liber Alarum*) and the eighth chapter of the *Libro de las formas* concerning the properties of twenty-four gems under the attribution of Raziel.[11] Another extant book related to Alfonso whose contents coincide with the *Liber Alarum* is the *Livre des secrez de nature*, discussed below.

As with the *Picatrix*, there are a few clear witnesses to the medieval reception of the *Liber Razielis*. It was one of the main sources of the *Libre de puritats*, as we will see. In the *Tractado de la divinança* (1449–53), Lope de Barrientos attests to the wide circulation of the *Liber Razielis* in the Iberian Peninsula and critically describes the book, whose copy from Enrique de Villena's library he declares to have burned in 1434, following the orders of King Juan II, in order to purge the library of magic books.[12]

French reception of some Alfonsine works

Both *Astromagia* and the *Libro de las formas* were passed to the library of Charles V of France, as a significant example of the transmission of magic from court to court, either in their original form or in translation. By 1373, the *Libro de las formas* had been rendered into French by Pierre Lesant by order of the Duke of Berry, as shown by King Charles's inventory, since many books belonging to the Duke were transferred to the royal library of the Louvre. The same inventory also seems to indicate the presence of a copy of *Astromagia* in Charles's library.[13]

In contrast to these two lost books, the *Livre des secrez de nature sur la vertu des oyseauls et des poissons, pierres et herbes et bestes lequel le noble roy Alfonce d'Espagne fit transporter de grec en latin*, attributed to Aaron – a biblical character sometimes related to stones – is preserved in a fourteenth-century manuscript.[14] It deals with the natural magical properties of animals, herbs and stones, including images engraved in these stones. Nevertheless, a direct Alfonsine origin, separated from the *Liber Razielis*, is doubtful since it does not correspond to any independent work in Alfonso's corpus. In addition, it is impossible to believe that the Castilian king ordered it to be translated from Greek, when this language was alien to Alfonso's milieu. Finally, the vicissitudes of the book reported in its explicit are suspiciously legendary.[15]

Magic in Catalan: an almost vanished corpus

In inquisitorial records, there is evidence of the circulation of magic books in the Catalan linguistic domain, and witnesses of various and numerous vernacularized texts in Catalan on all branches of knowledge remain from the mid-thirteenth century. Therefore, the existence of a number of magic texts in this language seems probable. Unfortunately, there is apparently nothing extant. It has not been proven that the *Picatrix* is the basis for a Catalan version of *De duodecim imaginibus Hermetis*, a short writing on therapeutic astral images, contained in a manuscript from Andorra, together with other Catalan texts on medical astrology (1430–40).[16] In fact, the Latin version not only circulated as an interpolation in the *Picatrix* but also as an independent text. It was therefore most probably translated from an independent copy and not from the *Picatrix*.

An important indication of the existence of such a corpus is the set of magical books belonging to the mason Pere Marc, which were burned by the Inquisition in Barcelona in 1440, according to the inquisitorial records.[17] There were books in Latin and in Romance languages, different magical traditions and a variety of writings, namely treatises and *experimenta*, isolated or in collections. Marc's library included Catalan versions of an unknown *Key of Semiphoras* (*Clau del Semiforas*), the *Liber Semiphoras*, the *Key of Solomon* (*Clavícula de Salomó*), the *Liber orationum planetarum* (*Oracions dels set planetes*), the astrological *Liber similitudinum* (*Llibre de la semblança de tots els hòmens*) and other writings on medical magic, astral magic, the conjuring of spirits, images to find stolen objects and operations to seduce women. Other texts were in Latin and one in Castilian. Some scholars have assumed that there were also extracts from the *Liber Razielis*. In fact, only some "pieces of paper" with operations addressed to Raziel are recorded, one of them bearing Marc's name, but they do not necessarily come from the *Liber Razielis*.

Such a library, in addition to his reputation and some objects found in his house – circles, pieces of paper or parchment with characters, names and figures, pieces of glass, sulphur, wax, herbs, stones – suggests that Pere Marc had a deep dedication to magic. This is significant, since it demonstrates that in magic, as in other branches of knowledge, vernacularized texts also reached an audience other than the courtly one: practitioners, that is, secular magicians or necromancers, who had an irregular knowledge of Latin. However, any surviving texts used by magicians should be looked for in a closely related language: Occitan.

Occitan texts by and for magicians

In contrast to Catalan, some witnesses to what seems to have been a splendid Occitan magic tradition survive. Surprisingly, rather than translations, what remain are treatises and compilations on ritual and image magic directly written in Occitan. In fact, to date, it is the only Romance language in which this phenomenon has been identified.

A miscellaneous codex copied in the early fifteenth century, in Provence (MS Paris, BNF lat. 7349), contains numerous occultist and divinatory texts both in Latin and Occitan. One of them is the *Liber experimentorum* (ff. 118v-5r), a booklet dealing mainly with planetary magic.[18] Several allusions to the "masters of necromancy" – understood as both ritual and image magic – indicate that the target audience was magicians. Contrary to what the title suggests, it only gives general indications for experiments and does not describe any particular one in detail. In a fictional preface, Guillem de Perissa, who is probably the author of the work, presents himself as a simple translator from Latin to Occitan and attributes the original to Arnau de Vilanova, whom he claims to have served as a secretary. According to his account, after Arnau's death, he took refuge in the court of the Countess Sibilia de Ventamilha, and at her request, he translated the *Liber experimentorum* into Occitan so that she could read it and understand it. The core of the treatise is the indication of the days and hours that are astrologically suitable for various purposes, distributed according to the seven planets and concerning both everyday actions and actions related to different occult arts. In many cases, these experiments are explicitly referred to as necromantic or are aimed at subduing the spirits. The last part is devoted to the preparation of materials and procedures for necromantic experiments. Although the dedication to Sibilia seems to be inauthentic, it might be a hint that was probably written in the fourteenth century in a courtly entourage, which also helps one to explain the use of a Romance language. The attribution to Arnau de Vilanova, who died in 1311 and was in fact an opponent of necromancy, is due to his legend as a magician and the desire to release the work under a prestigious name.

A more outstanding testimony is the miscellaneous MS Vatican BAV, Barb. Lat. 3589, copied c. 1430. It contains many texts belonging to different traditions of magic, although the primary interest of the compiler, who should be identified with the copyist, proves to be ritual and image magic. The texts are incompletely or only partially copied, most of them in Occitan – with a strong Catalan influence – but some of them are in Latin. The use of both languages gives us the opportunity to examine the interaction of Romance languages with Latin.[19]

The most remarkable work is the anonymous *Libre de puritats* [*Book of secrets*], which occupies the first two-thirds of the codex (ff. 3r-51v). It supposedly consisted of three sections. The first section, based above all on Book VI of the *Liber Razielis* and some of the treatises associated with it, teaches how to control angels, demons and other spirits by reciting the relevant Psalms and performing rites, suffumigations and animal sacrifices in suitable astrological conditions in order to achieve the magician's aims. The second section, the only one copied by another hand, seeks to explain a treatise entitled *Art de caractas* [*Art of characters*], attributed to Theberiadi (Omar Tiberiades?) focused on characters, namely combinations of stars that correspond to beings of the universe. The core of this part are ten tables giving the value of the characters and letters. Almost all these come from another treatise appended to the *Liber Razielis* (*Liber quorundam sapientum*) but here they are accompanied by explanations and examples of the rites associated with them. Finally, the third section, completely lost, aimed to explain the *Art de ymages* [*Art of images*] attributed to Hermes.

The third and final part of the codex (ff. 52r-79r) consists of a series of anonymous or apocryphal extracts, experiments and brief treatises in Latin and Occitan. They belong to several magical traditions, but a clear predominance of interest in astral images, especially planetary ones, and a noteworthy presence of the Hermetic corpus can be observed. The longest text in this part is the Occitan *Libre de ydeis* [*Book of images*], ff. 65r-77r), which is merely a poorly assembled compilation of materials derived from a large number and a wide variety of texts, even though the majority apparently fall within the Hermetic tradition. However, it is only possible to have an approximate idea of the original collection because the compiler of the codex only copied a small part of it. A number of general rules are followed by repertoires of images and prayers: images of Saturn, images of the Moon, prayers to the seven planets and images of Venus.

Another untitled, brief and unfinished Occitan text aims to show where treasures can be found in Spain (f. 59r-v). The starting point is said to be the *Libre del rey Peyre de Aragon* [*Book of King Peter of Aragon*], translated by order of the monarch in order to show the location in the Iberian Peninsula of treasures enchanted by Saracens and Gentiles. This book may be related both to the legend of treasures hidden by Muslims in Valencia, attested by Francesc Eiximenis, and to the real activity of treasure hunting promoted by Pere the Ceremonious and other kings of Aragon.[20]

Throughout the codex, the compiler selects works and operations with the aim of completing his library, which, to judge by all the clues, specialized in ritual magic and astral, above all planetary, images: he copies the greater part of some works omitting operations that he already possesses or considers superfluous because he already has equivalent ones. In the case of other texts, he only transcribes those experiments that he needs. The number of titles that he copies or claims to possess is considerable. In some cases, he makes a written assessment of the experiments or the writings, usually comparing the text copied with others. In other marginal annotations, he corrects the organization or relates certain passages with others. Therefore, the copy clearly reflects the compiler's own interests in a subject about which he has in-depth knowledge and we catch a glimpse of what undoubtedly is the library of a real magician, where the *Picatrix* and many other titles of magical literature are found.

Occitan is widely prevalent along the codex. Nevertheless, Latin emerges sometimes in the vernacular texts, which demonstrates that the sources were in Latin. In the first section of the *Libre de puritats*, Latin appears especially in the Psalms employed in rituals, where only their first words are reproduced. In the second section, the tables and their titles are generally in Latin, while the explanations are in Occitan. In the third part of the manuscript, Latin and Occitan really alternate, which is understandable given the diversity of the collection copied. Usually, both languages are kept separate from one work to the next, but there are some exceptions. Occasionally, we find Latin in the *Libre de ydeis*: in a passage Occitan and Latin are mixed (f. 65r), and two other passages start in the vernacular and pass into Latin (f. 66v). Sometimes (e.g. f. 67v) Latin words or sentences emerge in the vernacular text, and are left untranslated. Furthermore, some prayers in Latin are included in the Occitan text or vice versa: a prayer to Saturn from the *Liber orationum planetarum* in Latin is inserted in another text in Occitan (f. 68v); but on another occasion, the explanation and the ritual of the image are translated into Occitan, while the prayer is maintained in Latin. In another collection, titled *Experimenta Salomonis*, a prayer in Occitan to the Eastern Star (f. 53v) is placed among independent operations in Latin. However, in this case, the language switch is less surprising on account of the heterogeneity of this particular collection.

In the preceding examples, the coexistence of both languages seems to be due to the source of the text or of the translation. But interestingly, Occitan and Latin also coexist in the compiler's notes on the manuscript, which give us some clues that allow us to sketch his profile and to understand the formation of the codex. First, both in the notes and in the process of copying, the compiler demonstrates only elementary proficiency in Latin, as can be deduced from his frequent grammatical errors, inconsistent spelling and Romance interference. He also shows some knowledge of Hebrew when he rectifies the outline of the letters of the Hebrew alphabet. Such linguistic skills and especially the indications revealing the compiler's possession of an extensive magical library strongly suggest that he was a professional magician.

As to the origin of the codex, it is difficult to discern whether it originated in the Occitan- or Catalan-speaking area. Logically, the language employed points to the first option. However, the Catalan imprint and the use of Iberian sources, such as the *Libre del rey Peyre de Aragon*, the *Picatrix* and the extended *Liber Razielis*, might indicate a relationship with the Iberian Peninsula or at least an origin between Occitan and Catalan areas, closely connected as they were in the Middle Ages by linguistic and cultural ties. Another indication to be considered is the use of the word *puritat*, from the Latin *puritas* "purity", to refer to secret (magical) experiments, which seems to have a Castilian origin, because in this language *poridad* meant "secret" in medieval times, as employed in Alfonsine texts, perhaps because of Arabic influence, whereas it does not occur in Occitan or in Catalan.[21]

The Barberini codex gives us an insight into two different profiles of individuals dedicated to magic: the magician-author and the magician-compiler. We find the magician-author in the *Libre de puritats*, although unfortunately his name is missing, probably because of the hazards of manuscript transmission. Despite following his sources accurately, he speaks in the first person and demonstrates his ambition to create a digest of works with a planned structure. In comparison, the also anonymous *Libre de ydeis* fails to be a well-organized compilation. On the other hand, the formation of the codex has been done by an unnamed magician-compiler, who limits himself to collecting materials for his repertoire of resources. This second procedure evidences that magical knowledge is particularly prone to circulate fragmentarily.

A courtier's manual from Milan?

Another miscellaneous codex, copied in Milan in 1446 (MS Paris, BNF, ital. 1524), contains a number of writings on astrology and magic ritual organized and rendered from Latin to Tuscan by an anonymous translator who selected them from a set of manuscripts which he had at his disposal. The part entitled *Necromantia* occupies most of the manuscript (ff. 69r-235r) and, among other texts, includes many magical operations, mostly related to love and sex, in addition to the *Clavicula di Salomone* [*Key of Solomon*][22] (179r-235r). This is the earliest witness to this work, although it is partial because the translator based it on an incomplete copy. The translator's notes allow us to gain some understanding of his editorial work and the problems which he faced, such as the damaged or missing parts detected in the original manuscripts and the difficulties of interpretation posed by certain texts. At one point (f. 80v), he apologizes for not being able to copy some passages from the original due to its poor condition and for not being able to complete the text because he has not found another copy to compare it to. He says that he only can try to correct what is wrong or supply what is missing as a grammarian but not as a necromancer. Therefore, this codex, unlike the Barberini, is not the work of an expert and practitioner of magic but someone simply commissioned to translate the texts on account of his linguistic skills. This becomes more evident when the translator distances himself from necromancy and warns that the subject of the book, which he qualifies as vile or something even more abominable, is not believable for Christians, although it may have some effect in the eyes of people who believe in it or who are victims of false diabolical visions (ff. 69r and 73r). As in the Barberini codex, Christian Psalms and prayers are left in Latin. A number of passages are crossed out, although it is not clear what criteria pursued in such censorship were. The contents and the beautiful workmanship of the book suggest that the recipient was a man of high rank interested in love affairs and social promotion, and who, according to Jean-Patrice Boudet, might have belonged to the court of the Visconti.

Circulation, persecution and survival of Romance language magic books

Most of the magic texts studied here are translations from a learned language, namely Arabic or Latin. However, at least one, the *Liber experimentorum* was written directly in a Romance language, but presented as a translation, and the identity of its real author was hidden in favour of a prestigious name. Therefore, false translation and false authorship were occasionally used as a means of dignifying texts written in a language considered inferior, and about a subject such as magic, which was often stigmatized. Nevertheless, later on, in the fifteenth century, a small number of works seem to have been circulating as original texts such as the *Libre de puritats* and the *Libre de ydeis* transmitted in the Barberini codex.

Some Castilian versions served as a means of projecting these texts into Western Europe via Latin translation. Although it is not possible to affirm this in the specific field of magic given the few extant texts, in the vernacularization process, more generally Latin was often the vehicle between a Romance language and another. However, there are exceptions, such as the French translation of the *Libro de las formas e imágenes*, and indications of a possible circulation of Castilian texts in Catalan- and Occitan-speaking areas: the use of words such as *puritats* or *calapech* (*cf.* Cast. *galápago* "tortoise") and some references to the *Picatrix* in the Barberini codex, as well as the Castilian book burned with Marc's library.

From the extant evidence analysed here, the origin of most magic texts in Romance languages seems to be the court, which used to consume such literature in luxurious codices, but later their circulation expanded into other social groups, especially practitioners of magic. Such dissemination led to poorer manuscripts and libraries containing mixed Latin and Romance texts. Therefore, their users – such as Marc or the compiler of the Barberini codex – would have some proficiency in Latin, a fact which is not surprising in a domain in which this language was so overwhelmingly present.

Different reasons can be considered for the absolute predominance of Latin and the scarcity of texts written in all Romance languages in ritual and image magic, in comparison with other branches of knowledge. As Richard Kieckhefer has stressed, most of its practitioners were in fact clergymen, in the broad medieval sense of the term, and knew Latin.[23] Furthermore, the rituals of the Christian religion must have served as a linguistic model for these other kinds of rituals. However, recognizing the prevalence of the clergy does not imply that magic did not expand its audience to lay people. The university and the court have been shown to be contexts into which it permeated. Since Latin was also the language of the university, magic's expansion to the courtly milieu is doubtless the most important factor in explaining the use of the vernacular, as we have seen in most cases. Nevertheless, Marc's case demonstrates that there were also common people involved.

Based on Marc's case, Lluís Cifuentes attributes the paucity of magic books preserved in Castilian and Catalan to a more intense persecution by defenders of the Christian faith because of the danger posed by them being available for the unlearned, an argument which is supported by two early modern testimonies.[24] However, I suspect that there was no real difference between the persecution of occultist books written in Latin and Romance languages in the Iberian Peninsula. Marc's books were all burned, without distinction of whether they were in the vernacular or not. In the fourteenth century, the inquisitor Nicolau Eimeric set many magic books on fire in Catalonia; yet, he was apparently not concerned whether they were in Latin or the vernacular. Neither do we know from Barrientos if the copy of the *Liber Razielis* that he burned was in Castilian or Latin, although he complained that the circulation of this book was more abundant in the Iberian Peninsula than elsewhere. The inquisitorial indexes of the sixteenth and seventeenth centuries prohibited all books on occult arts, except those concerned with non-determinist astrology, without any consideration of their language. Certainly, a more intense persecution in both the late medieval and early modern Iberian Peninsula than in other European areas might explain why so little of the magic written in Castilian and Catalan remains, but also why Latin manuscripts of the great magic compendia produced in the Spanish kingdoms, such as the *Picatrix* and the *Liber Razielis*, are not preserved in Spain. Actually, the remaining codices of both Castilian and Latin magic of Iberian origin have been conserved in other countries. While none of the Alfonsine compilations on image and ritual magic have been preserved in their entirety in Castilian – two of them are conserved in Latin and two in Castilian are partially lost – only two of the twenty-six Alfonsine Castilian texts on astronomy and astrology have been disappeared and are only conserved in their Latin version.

Nevertheless, although medieval manuscripts on natural astrology are preserved more frequently, there is substantial evidence that they too were often censored in the early modern Spanish kingdoms, albeit not so systematically since it depended on the personal criteria of inquisitors. (Early modern printed works on astrology also suffered censorship but as they were printed outside the Spanish kingdoms they are better preserved.) For example, a Castilian copy of Abenragel's *Libro Conplido* (MS Madrid, BNE, 3065) was mutilated by the inquisitorial expurgation, and two Latin copies of the same work were relegated to the restricted room of forbidden books in the monastery of El Escorial.[25] Such censorship can be regarded as one of the factors that caused a scarcity of astrological manuscripts in Spanish libraries.

Future directions

Although surviving astral and ritual magic writings in Romance languages are scarce, it does not mean that new texts cannot be found in libraries and catalogues. For instance, Castilian fragments of the *Liber Razielis* have been recently discovered in a fifteenth-century codex (MS Frankfurt, Stadt- und Universitätsbibliothek, Lat. Oct. 231, ff. 96r-97v)[26] and they deserve to be edited and studied. Moreover, some other Italian texts have been preserved in several Florentine manuscripts. In addition to a treatise on rings transmitted by a fifteenth – and sixteenth-century codex,[27] Frank Klaassen's catalogue of medieval magical manuscripts includes two texts conserved in two fifteenth-century manuscripts and which have not been edited or studied: one is a manual with conjurations in the vernacular, sigils and a list of spirits; the other seems to be a collection of Solomonic images translated from Latin to Tuscan.[28] Another avenue of research worth exploring is to investigate archive documents such as inventories of properties or libraries, wills, and inquisitorial and judicial records that may provide new data on the circulation and persecution of magic in Romance languages.

Many of the manuscripts or writings presented here require further research to a greater or lesser extent. One of the least studied and most promising is the Barberini codex, which deserves attention from philologists and historians of medieval magic, even though it does not provide us with an entire work but rather comprises incomplete texts or fragments. It allows us to see a magician at work and shows his access to contemporary magical literature both in Latin and in Romance languages. It gives us evidence of the circulation and use of outstanding magic books, and provides relevant testimony about them. Critical editions of at least some of these works should take this witness into consideration. A special regard should also be paid to its major work, the *Libre de puritats*, a work of very considerable length, which reflects an ability not only to rework texts with a high degree of technicality but also to combine theory with practice. It can be considered the only ambitious work on ritual and image magic so far known to have been written directly in a Romance language. Without question, this outstanding treatise requires in-depth study and a critical edition. The *Libre de ydeis* and the other minor Occitan writings are also worth studying. Linguistic analysis on Catalan influence and Occitan dialectal bias can help us to understand where, how and by whom the manuscript was composed. On the other hand, a great number of texts and sources have still not been identified in this codex, because they are incomplete or partial copies, and are not well known to scholars or for other reasons. Nor have the sources of the *Liber experimentorum* (MS Paris, BNF lat. 7349) been analysed. The sources of Alfonsine magic compilations, despite the fact that their texts have thus far been well edited and studied, especially by philologists, also remain only partially disclosed. Hopefully, as magic works in Latin and Arabic are studied and edited, it will become easier to identify the sources of the Romance writings derived from them, but, considering the amount of magic literature that has been lost, many of them will probably remain unknown.

Notes

1. On vernacularization, see Claude Thomasset, "Les traités scientifiques," in *Grundriss der romanischen Literaturen des Mittelalters*, VIII.1, ed. Hans Robert Jauss et al. (Heidelberg: Carl Winter Universitätsverlag, 1988), 306–9; William C. Crossgrove, "The Vernacularization of Science, Medicine, and Technology in Late Medieval Europe: Broadening Our Perspectives," *Early Science and Medicine* 5 (2000): 47–63; Clara Floz, *El Traductor, la Iglesia y el rey: la traducción en España en los siglos XII y XIII* (Barcelona: Gedisa, 2000); Lluís Cifuentes, *La ciència en català a l'Edat Mitjana i el Renaixement* (Barcelona – Palma: Universitat de Barcelona, 2006); Lluís Cifuentes, "La traducció i la redacció d'obres científiques i tècniques," in *Història de la literatura catalana*, ed. Àlex Broch (Barcelona: Enciclopèdia Catalana, 2014), II, 118–31. This contribution is a result of the research project funded by the Spanish Ministry of Economy and Competitiveness FFI2014-53050-C5-2-P.
2. Richard Kieckhefer, *Magic in the Middle Ages* (Cambridge: Cambridge University Press, 2000), 8–17, 151–75, 181–201; Nicolas Weill-Parot, *Les "images astrologiques" au Moyen Âge et à la Renaissance (XIIe-XVe siècle)* (Paris: Honoré Champion, 2002), 36–37; Jean-Patrice Boudet, *Entre science et nigromance: astrologie, divination et magie dans l'Occident médiéval* (Paris: Sorbonne, 2006), 205–78; Sebastià Giralt, "Magia y ciencia en la Baja Edad Media: la construcción de los límites entre la magia natural y la nigromancia (c. 1230-c. 1310)," *Clío & Crimen* 8 (2011): 15–72. On the evolution of the meaning of the word "necromancy", see Sebastià Giralt, "Estudi introductori", in Arnau de Vilanova, *Epistola de reprobacione nigromantice ficcionis*, *Arnaldi de Villanova Opera Medica Omnia (AVOMO)*, VII.1 (Barcelona: Universitat, 2005), 59–66.
3. Alfonso X, *Las siete partidas*, III (Madrid: Imprenta Real, 1807), 667–69.
4. David Romano, *La ciencia hispanojudía* (Madrid: Mapfre, 1992), 128–58; Julio Samsó, "Traducciones científicas árabo-romances en la península Ibérica," in *Actes del VII Congrés de l'Associació Hispànica de Literatura Medieval*, I, ed. Santiago Fortuño - Tomàs Martínez (Castelló: Universitat Jaume I, 1999), 199–231; Gerold Hilty, "El plurilingüismo en la corte de Alfonso X el Sabio," in *Actas del V Congreso Internacional de Historia de la Lengua Española*, I, ed. Maria Teresa Echenique and Juan Sánchez (Madrid: Gredos, 2002), 207–20; Laura Fernández, *Arte y ciencia en el* scriptorium *de Alfonso X el Sabio* (Seville: Universidad, 2013).
5. Américo Castro, *España en su historia: cristianos, moros y judíos* (Barcelona: Editorial Crítica, 1983), 454–64, in addition to Samsó and Romano's publications cited above.
6. The *Picatrix* was edited by David Pingree: Picatrix. *The Latin version of the Ghāyat al-hakīm* (London: Warburg Institute, 1986). On its Castilian fragments: David Pingree, "Between the Ghāyat and the Picatrix. I: the Spanish Version," *Journal of the Warburg and Courtauld Institutes* 44 (1981): 27–56.
7. *Tratado de aojamiento*, ed. Anna M Gallina (Bari: Adriatica, 1978), 109.
8. Edited with the *Lapidario* in Alfonso X, *Lapidario and Libro de las formas & ymagenes*, ed. Roderic C. Diman and Lynn W. Winget (Madison, WI: Hispanic Seminary of Medieval Studies, 1980), and in Alfonso X, *Lapidario, Libro de las formas y las imágenes que son en los cielos*, ed. Pedro Sánchez-Prieto (Madrid: Fundación José Antonio de Castro, 2014). See Anthony J. Cárdenas, "Alfonso X's *Libro de las formas & de las ymagenes*: Facts and Probabilities," *Romance Quarterly* 33 (1986): 269–74; Alejandro García Avilés, "Two Astromagical Manuscripts of Alfonso X," *Journal of the Warburg and Courtauld Institutes* 59 (1996): 14–23.
9. Edited in Alfonso X, *Astromagia*, ed. Alfonso D'Agostino (Naples: Liguori, 1992). See also Alejandro García Avilés, "Alfonso X y el *Liber Razielis*: imágenes de la magia astral judía en el *scriptorium* alfonsí," *Bulletin of Hispanic Studies* 74 (1997): 21–40.
10. See García Avilés, "Alfonso X"; Boudet, *Entre science*, 195–98, Reimund Leicht, *Astrologumena Judaica. Untersuchungen zur Geschichte der astrologischen Literatur der Juden* (Tübingen: Mohr Siebeck, 2006), 257–94, and Damaris Gehr, "La fittizia associazione del *Liber Razielis* in sette libri ad Alfonso X il Saggio e una nuova determinazione delle fasi redazionali del trattato, della loro datazione e dell'identità dei compilatori coinvolti," *Viator* 43 (2012): 181–210.

11 Alfonso X, *Lapidario and Libro de las formas*, 151.
12 Lope de Barrientos, *Tractado de la divinança*, ed. Paloma Cuenca (Madrid: Universidad Complutense, 1992), 197 and 200.
13 García Avilés, "Two Astromagical".
14 MS Paris, Bibliothèque de l'Arsenal, manuscrits français, 2872, ff. 38r-57v. Edited in Louis Delatte, *Textes latins et vieux français relatifs aux Cyranides* (Liège-Paris: Université de Liège, 1942), 291–352. See García Avilés, "Alfonso X".
15 "Yci fenist le livre des secrés de nature, lequel fit Aaron, et après vint a Kirem le roy de Perse, et après fu porté a Athenes et u sac de vie fu mis pour tresor, dont il vint a la notice du noble roy Alfons d'Espaigne, lequel le fit translater de grec en latin et chier le tint et garda" (f. 57v).
16 MS Andorra, Arxiu Nacional, Arxiu de les Set Claus, 1, ff. 70r-2r. See Susanna Vela, *Tencar: una miscel·lània d'astrologia del s. XV a Andorra* (Andorra: Consell General, 1996), 105–216, 201–17, where the relationship with the *Picatrix* is defended. On the original Latin text, see Weill-Parot, *Les "images astrologiques,"* 477–96.
17 Josep Hernando, "Processos inquisitorials per crim d'heretgia i una apel·lació per maltractament i parcialitat per part de l'inquisidor (1440): documents dels protocols notarials," *Estudis Històrics i Documents dels Arxius de Protocols* 23 (2005): 75–139. Also analysed in Cifuentes, *La ciència*, 224–27.
18 Edited and studied in Katy Bernard, *Compter, dire et figurer: édition et commentaire de textes divinatoires et magiques en occitan médiéval*, I (Bordeaux: Université Michel de Montaigne, 2007), 99–119; 645–59. See also Antoine Calvet, "Le *Liber experimentorum* attribué à Arnaud de Villeneuve," in *Alchimies (Occident-Orient)*, ed. Claire Kappler and Suzanne Thiolier-Méjean (Paris: Association Kubaba - L'Harmattan, 2006), 127–36, and Sebastià Giralt, "*Liber experimentorum*, un llibre de màgia en occità falsament atribuït a Arnau de Vilanova," *Medioevo romanzo* 41 (2017): 188–93.
19 See a complete description of this codex and a discussion of its composition and contents in Sebastià Giralt, "The manuscript of a medieval necromancer: magic in Occitan and Latin in MS. Vaticano, BAV, Barb. lat. 3589," *Revue d'Histoire des Textes* n. s., 9 (2014): 221–72.
20 Sebastià Giralt, "Astrology in the Service of the Crown: Bartomeu de Tresbens, Physician and Astrologer to King Pere the Ceremonious of Aragon," *Journal of Medieval History* 44 (2018): 104–29.
21 Cf. *Astromagia*, 142 and 228. The title of one of the Castilian versions of the *Secretum secretorum* was *Poridat de las poridades*. On the hypothesis of an Arabic influence, see Castro, *España*, 623–26, and Gilbert Fabre, "L'expression *en poridad*, modalité d'un 'arabe silencieux'," *Cahiers de linguistique et de civilisation hispaniques médiévales*, 27 (2004), 159–70. See other possibilities in Pseudo-Aristotle, *Secreto de los secretos, Poridat de las poridades: versiones castellanas del Pseudo-Aristóteles* Secretum secretorum, ed. Hugo O. Bizzarri (Valencia: Universitat de València, 2010), 331.
22 I have consulted the manuscript through a microfilmed copy. See Boudet, *Entre science*, 366–68. Since writing this chapter an edition has been published: *Vedrai mirabilia! Un libro di magia del Quattrocento*, ed. Florence Gal, Jean-Patrice Boudet and Laurence Moulinier-Brogi (Rome: Viella, 2017).
23 Kieckhefer, *Magic*, 153–56.
24 Cifuentes, *La ciència*, 223–27.
25 Fernández, *Arte*, 124–29.
26 José Rodríguez Guerrero, "Los manuscritos alquímicos de Juan de Selaya (fl.1450–1490): médico, astrónomo y profesor de lógica en Salamanca," *Azogue*, 9 (forthcoming).
27 Edited in Stefano Rapisarda, "Il *Trattato degli anelli* attribuito a Pietro d'Abano: volgarizzamento italiano del ms. Palatino 1022 della Biblioteca Nazionale di Firenze" in *Médecine, astrologie et magie entre Moyen Âge et Renaissance: autour de Pietro d'Abano*, ed. Jean-Patrice Boudet et al. (Florence, Sismel Edizioni del Galluzzo, 2013), 287–92.
28 MSS Firenze, Biblioteca Medicea Laurenziana, Plut. 89, Su38, ff. 35r-51r, and Plut. 89, Su36, ff. 213r-4v: Frank Klaassen, *Societas Magica Catalogue of Manuscripts and Early Printed Books* < http://homepage.usask.ca/~frk302/MSS >, 2002 [consulted on 14/9/2015].

9

CENTRAL AND EASTERN EUROPE

Benedek Láng

Introductory considerations on territorial and periodization issues

The first general statement on the dissemination of magic texts in Central and Eastern Europe was put forward by David Pingree, who claimed that copies of such texts "found an attentive audience only after about… 1400 in Central Europe."[1] As a matter of fact, scholars did find sporadic traces of learned magic from earlier periods, for example, an illustrated copy of the *Secretum secretorum* was part of the royal library of Angevin Louis the Great, King of Hungary (1342–82) and Poland (1370–82).[2] However, Pingree's claim proved to be largely true. This seemingly belated arrival of the genre of learned magic to the Central and Eastern European area relates to several factors, among which three should be emphasized here: the relatively late institutionalization of universities (the first ones funded in the mid-fourteenth century, but reorganized and stabilized only around or after 1400); the late rise of general literacy in the royal courts; and the poor survival rate of earlier medieval codices in the libraries. As a consequence of the phenomenon pointed out by Pingree, this chapter will cover by and large one single century, the period between 1400 and 1500. Nevertheless, some geographical territories will be missing almost altogether from the survey. Bulgaria, Serbia and Russia for example have become favourite fields of magic scholars; their source material, however, almost completely lacks pre-1500 texts.

By Central and Eastern Europe, we understand two large areas of Europe: the Central European countries that joined European Christianity around the year 1000, that is the Polish, the Czech and the Hungarian kingdoms (the last including Croatia in a personal union), and the Eastern European countries belonging to Orthodox Christianity (sharply differing – both politically and culturally – from the Catholic Slavs), that is Muscovite Russia, the Kievan Rus, Serbia, Bulgaria and the Moldavian and Wallachian principalities. This very large area is cut into two not only on religious grounds but also on the basis of the number of surviving sources. While 1400 can be well chosen as a starting date for the arrival of magic texts to Poland, Bohemia and Hungary, 1500 would be its equivalent for the countries east of these three kingdoms.

Highlights of the Central and Eastern European region

Various major topics related to magic have become popular research fields in the local secondary literature (by authors such as Alexandre Birkenmajer, Jerzy Zathey, Ryszard Gansziniec, Mieczysław Markowski, Krszystof Bracha and Benedek Láng). Many of these have attracted considerable interest on an international level, too (by William Eamon, William Ryan,

Jean-Patrice Boudet, Daryn Hayton). Among these "highlights", the following issues are included: the golden age of astronomy and astrology in the University of Krakow; the hermetic interest in the royal court of Matthias, King of Hungary (1458–90); and the astronomical–astrological collection in the library of King Wenceslas IV (King of Bohemia 1378–1419). To these general issues, particular authors and magician figures can be added, such as the engineer-magician Conrad Kyeser, the crystal gazer and treasure hunter Henry the Bohemian, and the Montpellier-trained medical doctor Nicolaus, who shocked his patients with his bizarre curative methods using snake and frog flesh. Besides the general issues and the magician authors, a few particular – and fairly enigmatic – texts can be listed: the prayer book of King Wladislas that served for crystal gazing and angel summoning while also incorporating long paragraphs from the *Liber visionum* of John of Morigny; the *Alchemical Mass* of Nicolaus Melchior written, again, for a king and merging two remote literary genres; the description of the alchemical transmutation and the text of the Christian Mass; and the beautifully illustrated, colourful handbook of divination and talismanic magic, the MS Biblioteca Jagiellonska 793 that preserved – among others – the first long surviving version of the *Picatrix*. Let us review briefly these highlights!

Astrology in Krakow

The University of Krakow enjoyed a real golden age in the fifteenth century. Founded in 1364, and – thanks to royal support – reorganized in 1400, its faculties (Theology, Law, Medicine and Liberal Arts) provided training for a great number of Polish, German, Bohemian, Hungarian and other students in arts, medicine, philosophy, astronomy and astrology. A specific chair had been devoted to masters pursuing mathematical and astronomical studies since the beginning of the fifteenth century, to which another – particularly astrological – chair was added in the middle of the century. The classics of astrology (Ptolemy's *Opus Quadripartitum*, *Centiloquium* and *Almagestum*; Albumasar's *De coniunctionibus maioribus*, Johannes de Sacrobosco's *De sphaera*, and the *Tabulae Alphonsi*) formed the basis of the training. The concentration of astrologers grew quickly in the city (according to some contemporaries, Krakow was "stuffed with astrologers"), many of whom peregrinated to various Central European and Italian political centres to serve as court astrologers. The intellectual heritage (activity, travels, fame and library) of the Krakow masters and students (Marcin Król de Zurawica, Johannes Glogoviensis, Wojciech de Brudzewo, Marcin Bylica de Olkusz) has become a recurrent subject in the publications of the best historians of science, including Aleksander Birkenmajer[3] and Mieczysław Markowski.[4] For any further research, particularly useful are the catalogues and reference works of the large literary production of the Krakow masters.[5]

The court of Matthias Corvinus

Just as crucial as Krakow University for late medieval Polish history is the Renaissance court of King Matthias for Hungarian culture. Considered to be the first Renaissance court north of the Alps, strongly patronizing Platonic and Hermetic philosophy, corresponding with or inviting Italian philosophers and historians such as Marsilio Ficino, Galeotto Marzio and Antonio Bonfini, and heavily interested in astrology, divination and physiognomy, the court of Matthias has enjoyed constant academic interest both inside Hungary (Jolán Balogh, Csaba Csapodi, Tibor Klaniczay)[6] and outside (Darin Hayton, Valery Rees, Jean-Patrice Boudet).[7] The appreciation of astrology and Platonism was motivated not only by the king's support, but somewhat preceding this came from his master, Johannes Vitéz, first Bishop of Várad and later Archbishop of Esztergom, and from Vitéz' nephew, Janus Pannonius, the "first Hungarian poet".[8] Another intellectual centre for a very short period (1467–72) was the university founded in Bratislava (Pozsony, Pressburg) by the king and his archbishop, where the quadrivial arts were particularly strong. Astronomers and astrologers such as Johannes Regiomontanus (1436–76), Martin Bylica de Olkusz (1433–93), Georgius Peuerbach (1423–61) and perhaps even Galeotto Marzio (1427–97) might have been among the professors – though all this is quite uncertain due to the scarcity of the sources.[9] Astrological symbolism played a central role in the decorations of both Vitéz' and Matthias' libraries, and horoscopes were used to determine the right moment for the foundation of the university, and also for certain military actions.[10] As in the case of Krakow, cataloguing the codices has been crucial for any serious scholarship: some of this kind of effort was concentrated around Johannes Vitéz' books, but most of it around the Corvinian Library – the representative book collection of the king, comprising texts by Ptolemy, Firmicus Maternus, Pseudo Dionysios Areopagita, Chalcidius, Theophrastus, Regiomontanus, Peuerbach and Ficino. Unfortunately, only one-tenth of the books have actually been identified.[11] Matthias and his court were respected highly in Hermetic intellectual circles, a sign of which appreciation is that Marsilio Ficino dedicated a copy of his Commentary to Plato's *Symposium* to Janus Pannonius[12] and Books III and IV of his collected letters,[13] and the third book of his *De vita libri tres* (*Three Books of Life*), entitled *De vita coelitus comparanda* (*On Obtaining Life from the Heavens*), to the Hungarian king.[14]

The library of King Wenceslas IV

Significantly scarcer but not less relevant is the survived source material of another representative royal book collection, that of Wenceslas IV, "King of the Romans" and King of Bohemia. As few as eight manuscripts of the library can be identified today. The content and the illuminations of these codices express the high esteem astrology was paid to in the court, and to a lesser extent they contain alchemical and magical symbolism in the illuminations, and divinatory and ritual magic texts as well. The emperor's court astrologer, Christian de Prachatitz (1368–1439), was a well-known master and Rector of the University of Prague. Various scientific practitioners of the court (Conrad de Vechta and Albicus de Uniczow, subsequent Archbishops of Prague) had certain alchemical and even necromantic fame among their contemporaries. Magic as a means of accusation appeared in high politics – at least on the level of rumours.[15]

The *Bellifortis* of Conrad Kyeser

One of the beautifully illustrated codices that certainly belonged to Wenceslas's library was the famous *Bellifortis*, a curious handbook on military technology in which magical means of aggression are frequent. Combining engineering with astrology and magic was natural rather than exceptional in the late Middle Ages; yet, the extent to which Kyeser merges these fields is noteworthy – and has always been worth of research indeed (Lynn White, William Eamon). A representative and highly illustrated handbook offering detailed descriptions of real and imaginary martial instruments and methods (siege ladders, catapults, rockets, arrows, arbalests, scissors, clasps and horseshoes), the *Bellifortis* also contains descriptions of magical objects (rings and amulets), recipes, astrological symbols and demons. Besides the genre of military handbooks, it is heavily indebted to medieval *experimenta* literature, a crucial type of natural magic text often attributed to Albert the Great. In spite of its appearance as a handbook, the literary, weird and fantastic elements (pictures of a female chastity device, a tool for castrating men, the black queen of Sheba, a goose fastened to an anchor and a few further pictures on how to prepare a bath appropriately) make historians assume that the book served representative and entertaining goals in the court rather than real military practices on the battlefield. The *Bellifortis* might have also served to construct its author's image as an experienced court magician. It sounds fairly plausible that this magician image might have been used against Kyeser as a charge when he was finally forced into exile from the court. His book, however, enjoyed considerable success. Several early illustrated copies survived from the years following 1400 from the collections of not only Wenceslas IV but also his brother, Sigismund, Holy Roman Emperor and Hungarian king, and, a few decades later, from the Corvinian library of King Matthias.[16]

Henry the Bohemian

Another "magician figure" of the area, Henricus Bohemus, was active in Krakow in the first half of the fifteenth century. From the documentation of his court case in 1429, an exciting story of ritual magic and treasure hunting emerges. As with the career of Kyeser, Henry's story is closely related to the royal court: he was a court astrologer under Wladislas Jagiello between 1423 and 1427, he was allowed to be present at the birth of the three sons of the king and he cast their nativities. Yet, he could not avoid his destiny, and was finally accused of following the ideas of Hussitism, doing demonic magic in order to find treasure in the earth, and consulting necromantic books. For various reasons, scholars agree that the charges must have been grounded in reality and in all probability Henry did indeed pursue magical practices, performed conjurations, invocations, crystallomancy and treasure hunting with three masters of the university in the royal garden in Krakow. Being a heretic and practising illicit magic, he was probably "saved" by the royal family – that is, merely imprisoned.[17]

The prayer book of King Wladislas and crystallomancy

The most enigmatic source from late medieval Poland, Wladislas's prayer book (*Modlitewnik Władysława*) is surprisingly close to the court case of Henry both thematically and temporally. In the centre of this long repetitive text, there is again a crystal, with the help of which the praying king turns to Christ, the Virgin Mary, the Holy Spirit and the angels and asks them to reveal the hidden intentions of his subjects and the past and future secrets. As philological investigations have pointed out, the prayer book incorporates text fragments from such magical genres as the *Ars notoria* and – to a larger extent – the *Liber visionum* of John of Morigny, a derivative of the *Ars notoria* tradition particularly popular in the Central European (Austrian and German) areas. Comparing the content of the prayer book and the details of Henricus Bohemus's court case, it is plausible to suppose that the Hussite magician – experienced in crystallomancy and in demonic magic – was the author of the text, though it should be emphasized that the identification of the "Wladislas" in the prayer book as the King Wladislas whose birth had been assisted by Henry is far from being certain. Other Jagiello kings called Wladislas are also possible contestants.[18]

Nicholas of Montpellier

An eccentric medical practitioner caused no little shock in southern Poland in the last decades of the thirteenth century: Nicholas of Poland (Nicolaus de Polonia) also named as

Nicholas of Montpellier recommended that patients should consume snakes, lizards and frogs in pulverized form. Two of his writings survive: a more theoretical work, the *Antipocras*, and a rather practical text, the *Experimenta*. Nicholas's main argument was that the conventional Hippocratic methods should be rejected, and alternative practices – cures usually involving snake and frog flesh – should be favoured. In spite of the shock of some people, others – including a local duke – became enthusiastic about this alternative medicine and started collecting and consuming reptiles and amphibians. Nicholas was not an untrained charlatan; he studied in the best medical school of his day, in Montpellier, and his texts demonstrate good mastery of the Latin idiom. His ideas were by no means mainstream in medieval medicine, but they were not as unrealistic as they may seem today: they are well rooted in the natural magic of the "experimenta" literature and in the medieval genre of "snake-tracts" (*Schlangentraktate*) that were popular in the medical circles at the time. This literature explained the occult virtues of animals in general and of snakes and frogs in particular.[19]

The alchemical mass

Nicolaus Melchior's early sixteenth-century alchemical text, the *Processus sub forma missae* (Process in the Form of the Mass), dedicated to Wladislas, King of Hungary and Bohemia, received particular attention in early modern and modern times, and was – among others – a favourite example of Carl Gustav Jung when elaborating on his analogy between the *lapis philosophorum* and Jesus Christ. The alchemical mass incorporates the stages and materials of the alchemical process (vitriol, saltpetre, the philosopher's stone, the sperm of philosophers and others) into the framework of the Holy Mass (*Introitus Missae, Kyrie, Graduale, Versus, Offertorium, Secretum* and so on). The text equilibrates between being a practical alchemical text and a prayer rich in alchemical symbolism. Both the circumstances of the birth of this text and the life of its author are enigmatic. Melchior has not left much further trace in historical documents. It has long been supposed that the author was an otherwise known actor of the time (perhaps Nicolaus Oláh (1493–1568), Archbishop of Esztergom, counsellor of Queen Mary of Habsburg) hidden under a pseudonym. Although not necessarily the archbishop himself, Nicolaus Melchior Cibiniensis was probably an intellectual born in Cibinium (Nagyszeben, Hermannstadt, Sibiu, today in Romania) who played some undefined role in the Hungarian royal court in the first decades of the sixteenth century.[20]

The MS BJ 793 and the *Picatrix*

The most focused handbook of talismanic magic and divination from the area is probably the beautifully illustrated manuscript once belonging to the Polish astronomer-astrologer-physician, three times rector of the University, Petrus Gaszowiec (before 1430–74): the MS Biblioteca Jagiellonska 793. Besides a representative selection of scientific (mostly astrological and medical) texts of Polish interest, it contains a richly cross-referenced and practically oriented anthology of geomantic divination (methods of answering everyday questions with the help of a partially random, partially algorithmic procedure). The number of multi-coloured full page charts, point diagrams, squares and combinatorial wheel systems helping the user follow the divinatory practices is also exceptional. Besides divination, talismanic magic is the other main focus of the handbook, including the famous talismans of the seven magic squares (also appearing in Agrippa, Cardano and even on Dürer's engraving, the

"Melancolia I"), the practices of which involved suffumigations and other ritual magic elements. Besides that, the codex comprises such "classics" as Thebit ibn Qurra's popular *De imaginibus* (On talismans), Pseudo-Ptolemy's *Opus imaginum*, similar in nature to the previous text, Pseudo-Albertus Magnus's *Secretum de sigillo Leonis*, and several shorter texts belonging to the medieval Hermetic tradition. The anthology finishes with the first survived – and only illustrated – *long* version of the Latin *Picatrix*, more precisely its first two books. From external evidence (descriptions of sixteenth-century travellers), it seems that the zoomorphic decanic and planetary illustrations of the codex were copied on the walls of the royal palace of Krakow, the Wawel – a telling sign of the direct cultural impact of the codex.

Dissemination of manuscripts

Though the evidence is both geographically and temporally scattered, the number of magic texts that survived in East and Central European libraries from the fifteenth century is not negligible. Among these libraries, university book collections dominate, but royal collections (as we have seen above) and to a smaller extent monastic libraries also played a considerable role in the survival of magic texts. As a consequence of this pattern, namely that books belonging to professorial libraries enjoyed the highest survival rate, the codicological context of the majority of the texts is scientific: astronomical–astrological or medical.

Many classic texts, widespread and popular in the region, were simple imports that were widespread and popular in the West as well. Most of these belonged to the field of natural magic – the Pseudo-Aristotelian *Secretum secretorum*, the Pseudo-Albertian *Experimenta*, the *Kyranides* and some lesser known magico-therapeutic "herbaria" and "lapidaria" that explained the occult properties and hidden virtues of animals, vegetables and other items. The textual import from the West took place almost exclusively in Latin; for the emergence of vernacular versions, we have to wait until the sixteenth century. However, interestingly, the *Secretum secretorum* had a Russian translation (from Hebrew) already in the late fifteenth or early sixteenth century.[21] Probably, as a result of the peculiarities of the politico-cultural history of Bohemia and the rise of Hussitism, vernacularization was more advanced in this region and natural magic recipes survived in Czech as well. A local peculiarity is that an interesting lapidary on the magical properties of the stones and talismans was claimed to have been composed in honour of Wenceslas II, King of Bohemia (1278–1305).[22]

Many such texts found a natural place thematically in the medical context of the codices in which they survived (texts by or attributed to Hippocrates, Galenus, Philaretus and Arnau de Villanova, as well as anonymous works on the inspection of urine, the pulse, the interpretation of dreams, human anatomy, or the therapeutic properties and astrological correspondences of specific plants). But discussions of astrology and divination were also frequently found in natural magic texts.

The latter category, that is divinatory texts, was rather widespread in medieval manuscripts throughout Western and Eastern Europe. Geomancy (telling the future on the basis of randomly marked dots in the earth) and the onomantic device, called the *Rota Pythagorae*, were probably the most widespread, and were so common (and generally so short) that manuscript catalogues rarely even mention them. The easy availability of such divinatory texts explains why theologians kept worrying about and prohibiting divination as an abuse of the divinatory privilege not shared with humankind. Chiromancy (palmistry) also appeared in the manuscripts but to a much smaller extent, while treasure hunting – the bestseller of sixteenth- and seventeenth-century magic – was rare in the fifteenth century.

Divination is the category where the Southern and Eastern Slavs proved to be the most interested. Primarily importing from Greek but also recombining and recontextualizing the translated materials, Bulgarians, Serbians and Russians took over a wide range of Byzantine methods. These included prognostications on the basis of meteorology (Gromnik, that is thunder divination), on the basis of the calendar (Koliadnik) and other methods involving geomancy (Rafli) and scapulimancy (Lopatochnik: divination from the signs on a sheep's shoulder blade), as well as astrological almanacs based on the theory of lucky and unlucky days. Particularly interesting is the early sixteenth-century Rafli attributed to the Russian Ivan Rykov (probably a cleric from the court of Ivan IV), which is a long and elaborate text on geomancy, originally Byzantine but rewritten for Russian Christians.[23]

Besides divination, the usually short talismanic magic texts were also popular in the codices of Central European university masters, court intellectuals and monks. The classics of Thebit ibn Qurra and Ptolemy (*De imaginibus* and *Opus imaginum*), the *Picatrix*, the *Seven magic squares* of the planets and some Hermetic texts have already been mentioned. The emergence of this genre seems to be almost exclusively imported from the West, with one possible exception: two of the four surviving *Libri runarum* (a particular text combining hermetic talismanic magic with Scandinavian runes) have come to us from the Krakow region. A considerable number of survived talismanic objects testify that the methods put forward in these texts were not only consulted but also followed and taken seriously.

In contrast to divination, natural magic and talismanic magic, alchemy provided a territory for the authors of the region to prove their originality. While many were copies of Western texts (theoretical works by John of Rupescissa and Arnau de Villanova as well as recipes attributed to Albert the Great, Raymund Lull, Roger Bacon and others), this is the genre in which the most numerous texts of local origin were produced. The Alchemical Mass of Nicolaus Melchior is certainly the most exceptional among them, to which one can add the first genuine alchemical tract from Bohemian territories, the *Processus de lapide philosophorum* (*On the Philosopher's Stone*) and the *Aenigma de lapide* (*Enigma on the Stone*) both written by a monk named Johannes Ticinensis (Jan Těšínský),[24] and another treatise written in the vernacular in 1457, entitled *Cesta spravedlivá* (*The Rightful Way*) attributed later to a certain Bohemian alchemist, Johannes Lasnioro (John of Laz). These sources show that interest in alchemy exceeded the circle of those who were able to read Latin. Archaeological evidence, for instance the retorts, vessels, trays, alembics, phials, and other glass, wooden and metal objects excavated from the alchemical-metallurgical laboratory of Oberstockstall (forty miles north-west from Vienna, not far from the Bohemian lands), testifies that this interest was not only theoretical.[25] It is hard to tell how many laboratories functioned in monasteries and aristocratic courts in the fifteenth century. Oberstockstall was active in the mid-sixteenth century and the real boom in such practices took place around the end of the sixteenth century in the region, related to the court of Rudolf II. Nevertheless, one can plausibly suppose that they were not born out of nothing. The southern frontier of the Central European region, the town of Pula gave birth to the famous alchemical text, the *Pretiosa margarita novella* by Petrus Bonus, a native of Ferrara.[26]

The situation is not much different with ritual magic: besides a few – not too numerous – textual borrowings from the West (mainly shorter *Ars notoria* texts), a few original recontextualizations of classic ritual magic texts took place in the region (the author's familiarity with the *Ars notoria* is obvious in the *Bellifortis*, and the *Liber visionum* is extensively used in the prayer book of King Wladislas).

Future directions

Exploration and analysis of the Eastern and Central European magical source material have just begun in the past decades, and more research will probably follow in the coming decades. One starting point for any further investigation is certainly a more accurate cataloguing of the sources. The catalogue series of the *Biblioteca Jagiellonska* is exemplary; it should be a model for other libraries. Those manuscripts that fall into the scope of this series are adequately described, including a summary of their contents, owner, provenance and so on.[27] Several indices have been edited to help historians of science, astrology and magic[28] and many smaller ecclesiastical libraries also possess sufficiently reliable catalogues, but a few larger libraries, however rich their collections, obtained their last descriptions a century ago.[29] The longer texts contained in the codices are more or less identified, but many shorter pieces will be explored in the future when professional interest turns to these manuscripts. A particularly useful – but very slow – process is the cataloguing of manuscript fragments. In Hungary, for example, the major part of the written source material has perished, but small fragments survive in manuscript bindings. Taking them from their preserving books and identifying their contents and origin will add a lot to our understanding of the history of the region.[30]

On the basis of the appropriately identified and described source material, three fields seem to me to deserve particular attention in the future – all three are connected in one way or another to the issue of knowledge transfer. One is the relationship of "learned", or textual, magic to "popular" magic and folk practices. Learned magic survived in the libraries in the manuscripts once copied by university *magistri*. Folk practices, in contrast, are often reconstructed indirectly, on the basis of the usually condemnatory and only partially reliable sermons of preachers, episcopal visitation documentations, confessors' manuals and tracts of theologians (for example the theologian Stanislas de Skarbimierz in Poland, the preacher Jan Milicz in Bohemia and the confessor Rudolf in thirteenth-century Silesia). These texts often describe "popular superstitions and divinations", the practices of the *vetulae* and *incantatrices*, folk curing habits and inscriptions, and the "pagan rites" of the peasants.[31] Mapping the mutual influences these fields exercised on each other – or the lack of such influences – is one of the areas where scholarship can offer new perspectives.

The second knowledge transfer issue concerns the direction of the importation of learned magic. Scholars have a relatively rich picture of the reception of Western Latin magical manuscripts in Central and Eastern Europe. Somewhat less rich, but still detailed, is the picture of the reception of non-literary Greek texts among the Eastern Slavs, including the translation activity in Bulgaria (tenth century) or Serbia (fourteenth and fifteenth centuries). Studies have been written on how until the sixteenth century the influence of Byzantium on the Orthodox Slavs was stronger than the influence of Islam or Western Christianity, but the relative scarcity of Slavonic translations in the field of scientific, technical, philosophical and magical texts in this knowledge transfer channel has also been pointed out.[32] Much less is known about the importation and source of Jewish and Turkish magic texts, even though in the fifteenth century Eastern and Central Europe was already a frontier zone between the Latin and Ottoman cultures, where large Jewish populations were intellectually active. While it is possible that there was neither need nor room in the sharp military situation for an appropriation of Arabic–Turkish magic, it is much harder to imagine that Jewish magic played only a minor role in the region. This question deserves further research.[33]

Finally, I would see as particularly fruitful any systematic analysis of how science and magic interacted. A lot has been written on the relationship between late medieval astrology, astronomy and philosophy.[34] To a smaller extent, the scientific embeddedness of learned magic has also been explored.[35] However, this is a vast field and much remains to clarify. As was emphasized above, the primary context of fifteenth-century magic – at least as far as we can reconstruct it on the basis of the surviving sources – was the university. The codicological context of magic texts consisted of astrology, astronomy, medicine and other fields of science, while philosophy was rare and theology even rarer. It is reasonable to suppose – and easy to confirm – that medicine had a profound impact on natural magic and that astronomy and astrology influenced talismanic magic, but little is known about the opposite direction: whether the frequently copied, read and to a certain extent practised magic texts exercised any influence on science in the region and in the century so close to Copernicus. How exactly talismans, geomantic divination and charms found their place on the scientific bookshelves and in the minds of the university masters is a question that requires careful and complex analysis.

Notes

1 David Pingree, "The Diffusion of Arabic Magical Texts in Western Europe," in *La diffusione delle scienze Islamiche nel Medio Evo Europeo*, ed. B. Scarcia Amoretti (Rome: Accademia Nazionale dei Lincei, 1987), especially 79 and 59.
2 Oxford, Bodleian Library, MS Hertford College 2 (E.N. 2.), Pseudo Aristoteles *Secretum secretorum* (1371–82), 66 fols.
3 Aleksander Birkenmajer, *Études d"histoire des sciences en Pologne* (Wrocław: Zakład Narodowy im. Ossolińskich, 1972).
4 Mieczysław Markowski, "Die Mathematischen und Naturwissenschaften an der Krakauer Universität im XV. Jahrhundert," *Mediaevalia Philosophica Polonorum* 18 (1973): 121–31; Mieczysław Markowski, "Die Astrologie an der Krakauer Universität in den Jahren 1450–1550," in *Magia, astrologia e religione nel Rinascimento: convegno polacco-italiano, Varsavia, 25–27 settembre 1972*, ed. Instytut Filozofii i Socjologii (Polska Akademia Nauk) (Wrocław: Zakład Narodowy im. Ossolinskich, 1974), 83–89.
5 Mieczysław Markowski, *Astronomica et astrologica Cracoviensia ante annum 1550* (Florence: L.S. Olschki, 1990); Grazyna Rosińska, ed. *Scientific Writings and Astronomical Tables in Cracow: A Census of Manuscript Sources (XIVth-XVIth Centuries)* (Wrocław: Zakład Narodowy im. Ossolińskich, 1984); Zofia Włodek, Jerzy Zathey and Marian Zwiercan, ed. *Catalogus codicum manuscriptorum Medii Aevi Latinorum qui in Bibliotheca Jagellonica Cracoviae asservantur*, 10 vols. (Wrocław: Zakład Narodowy im. Ossolińskich, 1980–2012).
6 Jolán Balogh, *Mátyás király és a művészet* (King Matthias and the Arts) (Budapest: Magvető, 1985); László Szathmáry, "Az asztrológia, alkémia és misztika Mátyás király udvarában" (Astrology, alchemy and misticism in King Matthias" court), in *Mátyás király emlékkönyv* (Memorial book of King Matthias), ed. Imre Lukinich (Budapest: Franklin, 1940), 415–51; Tibor Klaniczay, and József Jankovics, ed. *Matthias Corvinus and the Humanism in Central Europe* (Budapest: Balassi, 1994).
7 Valery Rees, "Ad vitam felicitatemque: Marsilio Ficino to His Friends in Hungary," *Budapest Review of Books* 8 (1998): 57–63; and Marsilio Ficino, *The Letters of Marsilio Ficino* (London: Shepheard-Walwyn, 1975); Jean-Patrice Boudet, Darin Hayton, "Matthias Corvin, János Vitéz et l"horoscope de foundation de l'université de Pozsony en 1467," in *Actes du colloque "Mathias Corvin, les bibliothèques princières et la genèse de l'Etat moderne"* (Budapest: Országos Széchényi Könyvtár, 2009), 205–13; Darin Hayton, "Martin Bylica at the Court of Mathias Corvinus: Astrology and Politics in Renaissance Hungary," *Centaurus* 49 (2007): 185–98.
8 Zoltán Nagy, "Ricerche cosmologiche nella corte umanistica di Giovanni Vitéz," in *Rapporti veneto-ungheresi al'epoca del Rinascimento*, ed. Tibor Klaniczay (Budapest: Akadémiai Kiadó, 1975),

65–93; Tibor Klaniczay, "Das Contubernium des Johannes Vitéz: Die erste ungarische Academie," in *Forschungen über Siebenbürgen und seine Nachbarn: Festschrift für Attila T. Szabó und Zsigmond Jakó*, ed. Kálmán Benda (Munich: Trofenik, 1988), 241–55.

9 Leslie S. Domonkos, "The Origins of the University of Pozsony," *The New Review: A Journal of East-European History* 9 (1969): 270–89; Asztrik Gabriel, *The Medieval Universities of Pécs and Pozsony: Commemoration of the 500th and 600th Anniversary of Their Foundation, 1367-1467-1967* (Frankfurt am Main: University of Notre Dame, 1969); Tibor Klaniczay, "Egyetem Magyarországon Mátyás korában" (University in Hungary in the age of Matthias), *Irodalomtörténeti Közlemények* 94 (1990): 575–612.

10 Boudet, Hayton, "Matthias Corvin;" András Végh," Egy Reneszánsz felirat töredékei és a budai királyi palota csillagképei," (Fragments of a Renaisssance inscription and the celestial signs of the Buda Palace) *Művészettörténeti értesítő*, (2010): 211–32.

11 Csaba Csapodi and Klára Csapodiné Gárdonyi, ed. *Bibliotheca Corviniana: The Library of King Matthias Corvinus of Hungary* (Budapest: Helikon, 1990); Klára Csapodiné Gárdonyi, *Die Bibliothek des Johannes Vitéz* (Budapest: Akadémiai Kiadó, 1984); Katalin Barlai and Boronkai Ágnes, "Astronomical codices in the Corvinia Library," *Mem. Soc. Astron. Ital.* 65 (1994): 533–46.

12 MS Vienna, ÖNB, Cod. 2472, M. C. 38.

13 MS Wolfenbüttel, Cod. Guelf. 12, Aug. 4°.

14 MS Florence, Bibliotheca Medicea Laurenziana, Plut. 73. Cod. 39.

15 Krása, *Die Handschriften*, Milena Bartlová, "The Magic of Image: Astrological, Alchemical and Magical Symbolism at the Court of Wenceslas IV," in *The Role of Magic in the Past: Learned and Popular Magic, Popular Beliefs and Diversity of Attitudes*, ed. Blanka Szeghyová (Bratislava: Pro Historia, 2005), 19–28. Among the eight extant codices written in the last years of the fourteenth century for the emperor, three are devoted specifically to astrology: MS ÖNB cod. 2271; MS ÖNB 2352; MS Munich, CLM 826. Divinatory and ritual magic texts can be found in Vienna, ÖNB 2352.

16 Conrad Kyeser, *Bellifortis*, 2 vols., ed. Götz Quarg (Düsseldorf: Verlag des Vereins Deutscher Ingenieurie, 1967); William Eamon, *Science and the Secrets of Nature: Books of Secrets in Medieval and Early Modern Culture* (Princeton, NJ: Princeton University Press, 1996), 68–71; Lynn White, "Kyeser's 'Bellifortis': The First Technological Treatise of the Fifteenth Century," *Technology and Culture* 10 (1969): 436–41; Lynn White, "Medical Astrologers and Late Medieval Technology" *Viator: Medieval and Renaissance Studies* 6 (1975): 295–307; Rainer Leng, *Ars belli: Deutsche taktische und kriegstechnische Bilderhandschriften und Traktate im 15. und 16. Jahrhundert* (Wiesbaden: Reichert Verlag, 2002), 19–21 and 109–49.

17 Aleksander Birkenmajer, "Sprawa Magistra Henryka Czecha" (The Case of Master Henry the Bohemian), *Collectanea Theologica* 17 (1936): 207–24; Aleksander Birkenmajer, "Henryk le Bohemien," in Aleksander Birkenmajer *Études d'histoire des sciences en Pologne* (Wrocław: Zakład Narodowy im. Ossolińskich, 1972), 497–98. Stanisław Wielgus, "*Consilia* de Stanislas de Scarbimiria contre l"astrologue Henri Bohemus," *Studia Mediewistyczne* 25 (1988): 145–72; Benedek Láng, "Angels around the Crystal: the Prayer Book of King Wladislas and the Treasure Hunts of Henry the Czech," *Aries: Journal for the Study of Western Esotericism* 5 (2005): 1–32.

18 Oxford, Bodleian Library, MS Rawlinson liturg. d. 6. Ryszard Ganszyniec and Ludwik Bernacki, ed. *Modlitewnik Władysława Warneńczyka w zbiorach Bibljoteki Bodlejańskiej* (Wladislaw Warnenczyk"s Prayer Book Kept in the Bodleian Library) (Krakow: Anczyc i Spółka, 1928); see also Ryszard Ganszyniec, "Krystalomancja" (Crystallomancy). *Lud* 41 (1954): 256–339.

19 Ryszard Ganszyniec, *Brata Mikołaja z Polski pisma lekarskie* (The Medical Writings of Brother Nicholas of Poland), (Poznań: Czcionkami Drukarni Zjednoczenia, 1920); William Eamon and Gundolf Keil, "*Plebs amat empirica*: Nicholas of Poland and His Critique of the Medieval Medical Establishment," *Sudhoffs Archiv* 71 (1987): 180–96; Eamon, *Science and the Secrets of Nature*, 76–79.

20 "Processus Sub Forma Missae a Nicolao Melchiori Cibinensi Transiluano, ad Ladislaum Ungariae et Bohemiae Regem olim missum," *Theatrum Chemicum*, vol. III (Ursel: Lazarus Zetzner, 1602), 758–61; Carl Gustav Jung, *Psychology and Alchemy* (London: Routledge, 1968), 397; Gábor Farkas Kiss, Benedek Láng and Cosmin Popa-Gorjanu, "The Alchemical Mass of Nicolaus Melchior Cibinensis: Text, Identity and Speculations," *Ambix* 53 (2006): 143–59.

21 William Francis Ryan, "Magic and Divination: Old Russian Sources," in *The Occult in Russian and Soviet Culture*, ed. Bernice Glatzer Rosenthal (Ithaca and London: Cornell University Press, 1997), 35–58.

22 MS BJ 778, f. 200r-209r. Maria Kowalczyk, "Wróżby, czary i zabobony w średniowiecznych rękopisach Biblioteki Jagiellońskiej" (Divinations, Superstitions and Sortileges in the Medieval Manuscripts in the Jagiellonian Library), *Biuletyn Biblioteki Jagiellońskiej* 29 (1979): 5–18, especially 16–17.
23 William Francis Ryan, *The Bathhouse at Midnight: An Historical Survey of Magic and Divination in Russia* (Stroud: Sutton, 1999), Ryan, "Magic and Divination: Old Russian Sources;" Ihor Ševčenko, "Remarks on the Diffusion of Byzantine Scientific and Pseudo-Scientific Literature among the Orthodox Slavs," *Slavonic and East European Review* 59 (1981): 321–45; Mirko Dražen Grmek, *Les sciences dans les manuscripts slaves orientaux du Moyen Âge* (Paris: Université de Paris, 1959); Robert Mathiesen, "Magic in Slavia Orthodoxa: The Written Tradition", *Byzantine Magic*, ed. Henry Maguire (Washington, DC: Dumbarton Oaks, 1955), 155–77.
24 These two texts have not survived in their original copies, nor in their sixteenth-century Czech translation; they have come to us in a seventeenth-century German version. *Drei vortreffliche chymische Bücher des Johann Ticinensis, eines böhmischen Priesters* (Hamburg, 1670).
25 Sigrid von Osten, *Das Alchemistenlaboratorium Oberstockstall: Ein Fundkomplex des 16. Jahrhunderts aus Niederösterreich* (Innsbruck: Universtitätsverlag Wagner, 1998); Rudolf Werner Soukup and Helmut Mayer, *Alchemistisches Gold – Paracelsistische Pharmaka: Laboratoriumstechnik im 16. Jahrhundert* (Vienna-Köln-Weimar: Böhlau, 1997).
26 Chiara Crisciani, "The Conception of Alchemy as Expressed in the *Pretiosa Margarita Novella* of Petrus Bonus of Ferrara," *Ambix* 20 (1973): 165–81.
27 Włodek, Zathey and Zwiercan, ed. Catalogus codicum, 10 vols.
28 Markowski, *Astronomica et astrologica*; Rosińska, *Scientific Writings*.
29 Josef Truhlář, ed. *Catalogus codicum manu scriptorum latinorum, qui in c. r. bibliotheca publica atque universitatis Pragensis asservantur*, 2 vols. (Prague: Regia Societas Scientiarum, 1905–1906); Antonín Podlaha, ed. *Soupis rukopisů knihovny metropolitní kapituly pražské* (Catalogue of Manuscripts of the Metropolitan Chapter Library of Prague) (Prague: Česká akademie věd, 1922).
30 See Edit Madas, ed. *Fragmenta et codices in bibliothecis Hungariae* series (Wiesbaden: Otto Harrassowitz, 1983–).
31 Stanisław Bylina, "La Prédication, les croyances et les pratiques traditionelles en Pologne au Bas Moyen Age," in *L'Église et le peuple Chrétien dans les pays de l'Europe du Centre-Est et du Nord (XIVe-XVe siècles)* (Rome: École Française de Rome, 1990), 301–13; Stanisław Bylina, "Magie, sorcellerie et culture populaire en Pologne aux XVe et XVIe siècles," *Acta Ethnographica, A periodical of the Hungarian Academy of Sciences* 37 (1991): 173–90; Beata Wojciechowska, "Magic in Annual Rites in Late Medieval Poland," in *Religion und Magie in Ostmitteleuropa (Spielräume theologischer Normierungsprozesse in Spätmittelalter und Frühe Neuzeit)*, ed. Thomas Wünsch (Berlin: LIT Verlag, 2006), 225–38; Ryan, *The Bathhouse at Midnight*, Chaps. 2 and 4; Kowalczykówna, "Wróżby, czary i zabobony"; Krszystof Bracha, "Magic und Aberglaubenskritik in den Predigten des Spätmittelalters in Polen," in *Religion und Magie in Ostmitteleuropa*, ed. Wünsch, 197–215; *idem*, "Katalog magii Rudolfa" in *Cystersi w społeczeństwie Europy Środkowej*. (Poznan: Wydawnictwo Poznańskie, 2000), 806–20; Krszystof Bracha, *Teolog, diabeł i zabobony: świadectwo traktatu Mikołaja Magni z Jawora De superstitionibus* (The Theologian, the Devil and the Superstitions: The Testimony of the Treatise of Nicolaus Jawor, *De superstitionibus*) (Warsaw: Instytut Historii PAN, 1999).
32 Ševčenko, "Remarks on the Diffusion."
33 František Šmahel, "Stärker als der Glaube: Magie, Aberglaube und Zauber in der Epoche des Hussitismus," *Bohemia: Zeitschrift für Geschichte und Kultur der böhmischen Länder* 32 (1991): 316–37; Ryan "Magic and Divination: Old Russian Sources," 57; Ryan, *The Bathhouse at Midnight*, 16 and 394.
34 Mieczysław Markowski. "Astronomie und der Krakauer Universität im XV. Jahrhundert," in *Les universités à la fin du Moyen Age, Actes du congrès international du Louvain (26–30 mai, 1975)*, ed. Jozef Ijswijn and Jacques Paquet (Leuven: Leuven University Press, 1978), 256–75; Markowski, "Die Astrologie an der Krakauer Universität in den Jahren 1450–1550," 83–89.
35 Benedek Láng, *Unlocked Books, Manuscripts of Learned Magic in the Medieval Libraries of Central Europe*, (University Park: Pennsylvania State University Press, 2008).

10

MAGIC IN CELTIC LANDS

Mark Williams

Research into literary and historical magic in the Celtic countries is at an early stage, so much so that even the scale and parameters of the problem remain unclear. This state of affairs is a legacy of the early days of Celtic Studies, in which Victorian critics took the view that the fantastic and supernatural were defining characteristics of the literatures of medieval Wales and Ireland, and that the "Celtic race" (so called) possessed an essential kinship with the irrational.[1] In counter-reaction to excitable notions of this kind, Celtic scholarship has traditionally focused on empirical linguistic, historical and textual issues. The production of literary criticism *per se* has been spasmodic, and as a result the analysis of the Celtic supernatural – potentially spectacularly rich – is one area among many that have lain in neglect.

It is necessary to begin with some problems of definition and evidence. "Celtic" is a difficult term, precise only when deployed in a linguistic context: it is used in a parallel manner to "Romance" and "Germanic" to denote a major branch of the Indo-European language family. Thus, while popular usage allows Scotland, for instance, to be referred to as one of the "Celtic lands", scholarship reserves the term only for material produced in one of the Celtic vernaculars: Irish, Scottish Gaelic and Manx (which together form one linguistic subgroup), and Welsh, Cornish and Breton (which form another). Such is the scale of the material to be covered, however, that only Ireland and Wales – the regions with the richest surviving bodies of medieval literature – can be considered in this chapter.

It should also be stressed here that many scholars no longer share previous generations' confidence that Irish and Welsh literature can be lumped together under the "Celtic" heading; it is increasingly acknowledged that similarities between the two countries' literary traditions – formerly taken as evidence for a shared cultural inheritance – may in fact be medieval borrowings or independent innovations.[2] Still less clear is the relationship between magical traditions represented in the Celtic vernaculars and those current in medieval Europe more generally, especially as regards the question of the interplay between ancient, native elements on the one hand and classical and biblical models on the other hand. The question of what medieval Irish literature in particular owes to the Bible and to the wider European world was a controversial area of critical debate for much of the second half of the last century, and the examination of magic is likely to constellate the issue once again in significant ways.

The field of Irish and Welsh magic is therefore excitingly wide open, and a reconsideration of all the surviving records and representations of magical practices is badly needed. (That two recent symposia on Irish magic have been held at the National University of Ireland, Maynooth, is highly encouraging). This is as true of the early Middle Ages as it is of the half-millennium under consideration in this volume, which brings me to a final point before we turn to the material itself: though this is a companion to *late* medieval magic, "early" and "late" are not particularly useful descriptors when dealing with the Celtic material. For the Irish language, for example, there was no decisive morphological transformation of the sort that English underwent; the language of *Beowulf* would have been incomprehensible to Chaucer, but Irish scribes of the later Middle Ages were able to read and transmit texts composed seven centuries before. It is likely in many cases that we possess the literary monuments of the early Middle Ages thanks to the tastes of the copyists and compilers of the twelfth to fifteenth centuries.

In contrast, no body of sagas has been preserved from early medieval Wales; the first depiction of a magic-worker in the literature probably dates from the mid-eleventh century. The greatest literary depictions of enchantment – the prose *Four Branches of the Mabinogi* and the "legendary poems" in the voice of the über-bard Taliesin – probably date to the period between 1100 and 1225. Once again these have come down to us in later manuscripts, the most important of which date to the fourteenth century. In the case of both Wales and Ireland, therefore, any discussion of "late medieval magic" must really turn on the manner in which earlier – sometimes much earlier – material was received, remembered and revised.

Historical magical practices in Wales and Ireland

My focus below is on magic in literary narrative, but first something must be said about our knowledge of historical magic in the regions under discussion. Richard Kieckhefer has emphasized that medieval magic is a "crossing-point" between fiction and reality, and cautions against artificially separating the magic of literature from the magical activities that medieval people actually undertook.[3]

But for Ireland and Wales, there does seem to have been a genuine gulf between the two, in so far as the evidence allows us to tell. Certainly, the literary magic of medieval Irish saga bears scant relation to the information we possess about practice. From the early Middle Ages, our data for the latter – elliptical as it is – derives mainly from legal texts.[4] This is one area in which excellent work has already been done.[5] As elsewhere in medieval Europe, the evil eye was feared, and taken seriously at law; Jacqueline Borsje has been the key voice here, producing a full-length study of the motif.[6] The early Hiberno-Latin penitentials condemn both *ars diabolica* and *maleficia*, meaning the laying of curses and other attempts to cause harm by magical means. There is some evidence that these powers were thought to belong especially to women, but also to smiths and those who clung to pagan beliefs during the conversion period: an early prayer for protection placed in the mouth of St Patrick asks for protection from "the spells of women and smiths and druids", though we have no clear sense of what kind of magical techniques might be implied by this phrase.[7] An early ecclesiastical text known as "The Synod of Patrick" notes the presence in Irish society a kind of woman it calls a *lamia* or *striga*, and clearly meaning workers of negative magic. My suspicion is that the Latin terms correspond to the native words *túaithech* or *bantúathaid*, "sorcerer, witch", but not enough work has been done as yet to determine the semantic ranges of the various descriptors.[8]

Less sinisterly, the perennial human endeavour of love magic has recently been examined. Once again there is clear evidence from the early penitentials; we also have charms against impotence.[9] Finally, charms – a notoriously difficult category of text, both semantically and sociologically – have begun to receive major attention.[10] Many of them are for healing or protection, and though they postdate the island's conversion, some interestingly mention Irish pagan deities in the same breath as Christian powers, in ways that have not as yet been sufficiently theorized or explained. Recent work on them provides a model for how the responsible investigation of "Celtic magic" might be undertaken, and once again Jacqueline Borsje has led the way. Her work is characterized by a sophisticated grappling with the meaning of the Old Irish texts and a wide comparative knowledge of the charm tradition as a major European magical genre, not least in Old English.

We also have evidence for the existence of forms of divination, likely of pre-Christian origins, into early Christian Ireland. Visiting an augur is condemned in early law tracts, and this was undoubtedly a historical phenomenon. Elsewhere, we hear of forms of prophecy proper to professional poets (*fili*, pl. *filid*) some of which were supposedly adjudged licit by Patrick, while one was forbidden, because it involved chewing on the flesh of a cat or dog, which was too reminiscent of pagan animal sacrifice. How literally these accounts should be taken is a matter of dispute. There is evidence that in the ninth and tenth centuries some professional poets were keen to emphasize the archaic mystique of their profession, and this may have led them to play up their supposed connections with a lost paganism.[11] There needs to be a reassessment of the whole issue of the magic powers associated with learned poets in Irish tradition – including the ability to unman individuals or even raise blisters upon the face with a kind of extempore satire known as *glám dicend*.

All this evidence for historical magic is essentially early, mainly from before the year 1000. For the later Middle Ages, the data is thin. There is, as far as I know, no manuscript evidence for learned ritual magic of the high medieval grimoire tradition; among the occult sciences, astrology was certainly known in Ireland from the very late Middle Ages, largely and perhaps exclusively in the context of medicine.[12] Mention should be made here of medieval Ireland's earliest and most famous witchcraft trial, that of Dame Alice Kyteler, in 1324. The case is telling, precisely because its background was conspicuously European and not Irish: the trial was in response to papal concerns about heresy, and the wealthy and well-connected Kyteler was accused of consorting with demons in the classic late medieval and early modern conception of witchcraft. This had little to do with Gaelic folk custom, still less with the representation of female magic-workers in Irish vernacular literature: the Kyteler trial shows that the extension of Anglo-Norman power to Ireland eventually brought with it a new and international set of medieval conceptions about magical practice, which were to become very common in the later European witch craze of the sixteenth and seventeenth centuries.[13]

So much for Ireland. In Wales, the popular and enduring imaginative link between the country and magic has a long history. It was crystallized in the early modern period: one thinks not only of John Dee, astrologer to Elizabeth I, who made much of his Welsh connections, but also of Shakespeare's Glendower (Owain Glyndŵr), who like any Renaissance magus boasts of his ability to "call spirits from the vasty deep".[14] Very little of this stereotypical association had older roots. From the late twelfth century, we have Gerald of Wales's story of a Welsh magician (*maleficius*) whose spirit continued to work evil magic beyond the grave, until destroyed by an English knight. Much more famously, the figure of Myrddin – a crazed poet-prophet in Welsh tradition – entered the European mainstream thanks to Geoffrey of Monmouth's twelfth-century *Historia regum Britannie*; he became the basis for most subsequent literary representations of male enchanters.[15] Accordingly, it would be desirable to have a cultural history of the stereotype.

The study of magical materials from medieval Wales is at an early stage, partly because there seems not to be very much to examine. There is evidence from the late twelfth century for a kind of prophecy by ecstatic trance, performed by persons termed *awenyddion* in Welsh, "those inspired". It is striking that Gerald of Wales, the Cambro-Norman cleric who describes the *awenyddion*'s obscure utterances, is prepared (after some debate) to assign their gifts to divine grace.[16] In contrast, a fourteenth-century Latin tract condemning divination refers – as an example of the illicit petitioning of evil spirits – to Welsh soothsayers who invoke Gwynn ap Nudd, king of the fairies, with the formula: "Gwynn ap Nudd, you who are yonder in the woodland, for the love of your bedmate, allow us to come into the house!"[17] The words were used before entering the home of a sick person – perhaps in an effort to keep malevolent spirits away and thus help the person's recovery. In the folklore of the Middle Ages, Gwynn is a supernatural hunter and fairy king, but he has long been thought to be the afterimage of a Celtic god: this passage may therefore represent one of the most persuasive pieces of evidence for the survival of a pagan deity into medieval folk magic in the whole of the British Isles. That it is not well known among folklore specialists is down in large part to it having only been edited and discussed in Welsh.

In general, the best that can be said is that the social background to late medieval magic in Wales is currently unclear. Thanks to Richard Suggett, we have a secure sense of the terminology and evidence for magical practices in Wales in the early modern period: in particular his analysis of the 1595 anti-witchcraft tract *Dau Gymro yn Taring* ("Two Welshmen Tarrying") reveals a rich landscape of enchanters and folk magicians with various different names and specialities. Suggett points out that the advent of transparent English borrowings such as *wits* ("witch") suggests a degree of transformation among the ranks of Welsh magical practitioners in the period, on the principle that a word is likely to be borrowed for a concept for which native terminology is not sufficient. Hence, the extent to which these early modern attitudes and their associated terminology represented continuations from the late Middle Ages is an open question.[18]

Literary magic in medieval Irish literature

Why is there such a gulf between sparsely attested historical magic and richly evidenced literary magic? (By "literary magic", I mean explicit instances of spells and enchantment, not a non-specific atmosphere of the marvellous, miraculous or supernatural.) The crucial factor is that literary magic in the Celtic world is usually set in the past, never in the contemporary medieval world. We might contrast Middle English romance: *Havelok the Dane*, for example, was written *c*.1290 and is set in the Anglo-Danish world of three hundred or so years before. In Irish terms, this would be a very piddling time-depth, for by the turn of the twelfth century, the island's men of learning had woven an intricate web of story which detailed the native past all the way back to the time of Noah. Magic – meaning transformations of shape, deceptive illusions, distortion of the elements and the conjuring of beings or objects out of nothing – was used to round out a richly imagined vision of a pre-Christian world. That world might in some sense be thought to have been both unclean and inadequate, but it could nonetheless be used to emblematize the triumphant progression of the medieval Irish towards a Christian present.

Setting stories in the island's ancient past brought with it certain complications, and for our purposes the major one concerns the ontology of magical personnel. According to the national backstory described above, the island had once been ruled by the *Túatha Dé*, the "god-peoples", also known (though more rarely) as the *áes síde*, "the people of the hollow hills", for which "fairies" is the conventional but not very satisfactory English term. In origin, at least some of the Túatha Dé were former Celtic gods, and there was never full agreement on how they should be fitted into a Christian cosmos: serious suggestions referred to them as angels, devils, "half-fallen" angels, human beings who were invisible and immortal because they had somehow avoided original sin, and (last but not least) an entire race of pagan magicians who had augmented their powers through occult knowledge.[19] It will be clear that the Irish material has a way of complicating categories that are much clearer in other medieval literatures. To take a familiar example, the lack of ontological clarity characteristic of Morgan la Fay (a goddess, learned enchantress, or fairy?) is shared by a vast number of magic-users in Irish medieval literature, enveloping them in an atmosphere of luxuriant ambiguity. This very ambiguity had high aesthetic value to Irish saga authors, and they were perfectly able to choose whatever explanation of the god-people's nature best suited their literary purposes at the time.

This means that it is often difficult to draw a hard and fast distinction between ontologically magical immortals – otherworld beings for whom magic is an intrinsic part of their being – and mortal practitioners of the magical arts, especially as the social arrangements of the god-peoples were often imagined to mirror those of humans: in many texts, the societies of both the god-peoples and ordinary mortals are described as having professional classes of spellcasters. Without a full survey of the material, it is hard to say whether the literary magic of humans and that of otherworld beings differs in scope and technique: a subjective assessment suggests that shape-shifting is a particular specialty of the *áes síde*.

The literary druid

With this background in mind, it will be apparent that a raft of basic questions about magic in Irish literature remains. Where does magical power come from? What are the imaginative conventions that govern its representation? What are the range of attitudes to its use, and how do they differ by genre? Some sense of the complexity of the material can be gained if we focus in on a crucial class of magic-worker, embodying all the various tensions – historical versus literary, human versus supernatural – identified above. I refer of course to the figure of the druid (Old Irish *druí*, later *draoi*, Hiberno-Latin *magus*).

We know that historical druids existed; they acted as the magico-religious specialists of at least some Celtic speaking peoples in the centuries either side of the birth of Christ. It is not clear, however, whether either the Graeco-Roman descriptions of Gaulish and British druids (which may be very unreliable) or the fictional depictions of druids in Irish saga and hagiography in fact tell us anything about what the druids of pre- and partially Christian Ireland actually got up to. For the druids of history, we have only very limited pointers from early Irish legal texts, which tells us that they were originally of high status but lost that status with the conversion; that they may have witnessed oaths and acted as soothsayers; and that they ceased to be a going concern in Irish society during the early 700s. An eighth-century law tract on church–community relations lumps them, with distaste, together with "satirists and inferior poets and farters and clowns and bandits and pagans and whores and other bad people".[20]

Ronald Hutton has pointed out that Ireland is the only region of Europe in which druids continued to be an object of interest during the Middle Ages, and this underscores how badly we need a full investigation of the Irish literary druid.[21] It is entirely possible that many images of druids in the literature are textual stereotypes constructed centuries after actual druids faded from the historical record, perhaps using non-native models. In

Muirchú's late seventh-century *Life of St Patrick*, for example, the druids are clearly modelled on the frenzied priests of Ba'al in 1 Kings 18. Biblical prototypes were also at work in more positive ways too: *magus* was the normal Hiberno-Latin term for druid, and there is some evidence that the *magi* of the Bible influenced early Irish depictions of druids as wise foretellers of Christianity, illuminated by a certain measure of natural grace.

Certainly, the medieval Irish never forgot that their pre-Christian ancestors had had druids as an essential part of their society. As a result, any narrative set in the ancient past was liable to feature them, including stories set in the ancient days when the "god-peoples" were supposed to have ruled over Ireland. Such a scenario was only possible because the Irish essentially cut out the priestly function of the druids. Graeco-Roman sources make plain that continental druids were involved in the worship of the gods, but this is something we almost never see in Ireland, where there was a strong taboo against depicting pre-Christian cult in saga, even in the depiction of an otherwise gorgeously imagined pagan past. (On this point, Irish tales contrast sharply with the literature of medieval Iceland, in which we see inside pagan temples and meet individuals devoted to particular deities.) Instead *magic* was what was stressed: the druid was primarily a magician. Hutton has argued that the term "druid" became generalized in Irish, so that anyone who happened to be doing magic at a given time could be referred to as a *druí* while they did so.[22] My own sense is that this has not yet been conclusively demonstrated; certainly, the abstract noun *druídecht* ("druidism") became the standard Irish term for magic, but the related agent noun *druí* seems to have retained a more precise sense, at least in the early period. The evolution of the terminology – and its symbiosis with the Hiberno-Latin term *magus* – encapsulates the gap between historical and literary with which we are dealing.

Nonetheless, druids are depicted in the sagas in a considerable variety of ways. Almost always they are men; they have pupils and (like any other early Irish person of substance) they foster the children of nobles. They have their place in an imagined version of ancient Irish society, and can be envisaged as good, evil, skilled or foolish as anyone else. One saga, *Mesca Ulad*, "The Drunkenness of the Ulstermen", written *c*.1100, makes them comic: it features a pair of bickering druids who are so frightened by an approaching army that they faint in terror and fall off a wall.[23]

Broadly, it can be said that across both secular and religious narratives, druids seem to have two main functions: clairvoyance or the power of prophesy on the one hand, and the ability to induce or control natural phenomena on the other hand, especially the weather. On the whole, the former talent seems to be regarded as essentially allowable, and those who exercise it are viewed in a positive or at least neutral light. This mode of representation was enabled not only by the Magi of the New Testament but also by the Old Testament tradition of the gentile prophet, directly inspired by God though not himself of the people of Israel, of which Balaam in Numbers 22 is the major example. Thomas Charles-Edwards has drawn attention to the fact that the native and probably pre-Christian form of clairvoyance known as *imbas forosnai* ("the encircling knowledge which sheds light") is depicted as essentially identical to the miraculous insight born of grace which Christian holy persons might enjoy, though this interestingly cuts across the hints in the literature that in the case of pagan persons this capacity for vision was thought of as a technique that had to be formally acquired as a professional skill.[24] The classic instance is in the saga *Aided Conchobuir* ("The Violent Death of Conchobor") in which the druids of a legendary king of Ulster are able to perceive and explain Christ's crucifixion in "real time", thanks to their capacity for magical seership: the result is that king Conchobor becomes a kind of proto-convert to Christianity, moments before he himself dies. An ambiguous case is provided by the druid foster father of Saint Brigit in the *Vita Prima Brigitae* – he is able to recognize the infant's sanctity with his prophetic powers but she is unable to keep down his food, implying that he and his household are in some sense unclean.[25] Elsewhere in the literature, we find druids determining days of good and ill omen, and conducting a plausibly pre-Christian prophetic ritual called the *tarbfheis* ("bull-sleep") which involves a dreamer going to sleep wrapped in the hide of a sacrificed bull.[26] (It is clearly this visionary and prophetic capacity of the literary druid that forms the object of parody in *Mesca Ulad*, in which the two bickering druids cannot see what is in front of their faces until it is too late.)

Negative or illicit druids are also widely attested in both hagiography and saga, and – as the prime symbols of opposition to Christianity – their associations are essentially demonic. In a range of early texts, druids cause magical snowstorms and fogs; they also invoke demons, whom we are clearly supposed to understand as the source of their power. The manipulation of natural phenomena, as noted, is key: they have the power to dry up lakes and rivers. They also curse or damage others magically, often using tools, sometimes including magic wands made of yew or rowan. The wand is of course the standard accessory of the classical magician, first attested in the *Odyssey*, where the enchantress Circe uses one to transform Odysseus's men into pigs, but whether the Irish wand goes back to historical druidism or is a medieval literary imitation of the classics is at present an open question.

I would like to suggest here that this polarization of role stands personified in the two most celebrated druids of Irish tradition, Cathbad and Mog Ruith, who – inexplicably – have never been properly compared. Cathbad is the chief druid of the Ulstermen and father of their king, Conchobor mac Nessa; he is a kind of recurring special guest star in the Ulster Cycle, a collection of sagas set around the time of the birth of Christ. Mog Ruith's skills, in contrast, are pressed into service by Fiacha Muilleathan, a legendary king of the south-western province of Munster, in order to oppose the military ambitions of Cormac mac Airt, a likewise legendary overking of Ireland, who was supposed to have lived in the fourth century AD. Mog Ruith stars in a single saga telling the story of the clash between Fiacha and Cormac, *Forbuis Dromma Damghaire*, "The Siege of Knocklong", which survives in two manuscripts, the Book of Lismore and the Yellow Book of Lecan, both compiled between 1400 and 1420. But the tale itself is clearly older, and existed in some form in the twelfth century, as surviving Irish tale lists show.[27] The tale is grouped into the so-called "Cycle of the Kings", another of the major subdivisions into which modern scholarship divides Irish vernacular literature.

These two great druids of literary tradition, Cathbad and Mog Ruith, are therefore supposed to have flourished some centuries apart, in opposite ends of Ireland, and the literary cycles in which they appear were also basically Old Irish and basically Middle Irish. A comparison between the two would therefore be an excellent device for examining how the Irish literary druid changed between the eighth century and the early fifteenth. Cathbad is largely an exemplary and admirable figure: as father of Conchobor he is both, so to speak, a patriarch and prophet. In one of the most wrenching of all medieval Irish literary works, *Longes mac n-Uislenn*, "The Exile of the Sons of Uisliu", he is described as a *fissid*, a "sage" or "seer", literally, "one who knows".[28] The knowledge referred to is the clairvoyance identified above, for he is able to place his hand on a pregnant woman's belly and foretell in verse the catastrophic future appearance, name and career of the unborn heroine Derdriu. He therefore acts as the mouthpiece of fate, and his oracular utterance sets up the narrative.

Mog Ruith, in contrast, is a more morally ambiguous figure. In *Forbuis Dromma Damghaire*, he is Fiachu's major secret weapon against the forces of Cormac (though Cormac has his own team of druids too), being a miracle-worker possessed of a spectacular repertoire. He can alter his size at will, set things on fire with his breath, cause rains of blood, send people to sleep for long periods and create magical animals which go after enemy champions, all of which he does despite being blind. At one point, he puts on a cloak and "bird-headdress" and ascends into the air. The saga emerges as one of the most intense (and entertaining) attempts by a medieval Irish author to imagine the pagan magic of Ireland's ancient past. Notably, it is nearly the only place in Irish saga in which we see a non-Christian, though tactfully unnamed, deity invoked, for Mog Ruith calls upon his "god above all other gods". A medieval audience might well have taken to be a depraved reference to the devil. It is similar in this regard to other distinctively high medieval Irish productions, not least the complex prose-and-verse pseudo-history *Lebor Gabála Érenn*, "The Book of the Taking of Ireland" (late eleventh and twelfth century), which contains episodes in which warriors are created out of grass and an army summoned up by infusing demonic spirits into corpses.[29] In other words, Ireland seems to have shared the characteristically high and late medieval interest in working fantastical and alarming sequences of enchantment into vernacular narrative. In the case of Mog Ruith, there seems likely to have been influence from pious legend as well; he is persistently associated in Irish tradition with the biblical figure of Simon Magus – known in Irish as *Símón druí*, "Simon the druid" – who fed into the circulating medieval legend of Antichrist. I have argued elsewhere that many of the traits associated with Mog Ruith's druidic magic can be traced to the "anti-hagiography" which developed around Antichrist just before the turn of the first millennium.[30]

Divine magic

I want to leave druids behind at this point and turn to an example of the problems around magic which are yet to be explored by critics of medieval Irish saga. One of the most spectacular instances of these is a fourteenth-century saga known as *Altrom tigi dá medar*, "The Fosterage of the House of Two Vessels", which amounts to a poignant mixture of theological speculation and domestic drama.[31]

The story begins in the deep past of Ireland, when the island was ruled by the Túatha Dé Danann – as seen these were clearly in some sense after-images of Ireland's pre-Christian divinities, but here they are imagined as a race of pagan magicians. They live within hollow *síd*-mounds –the hills and Neolithic tumuli which dot the Irish landscape –envisaged as splendid royal dwellings whose inhabitants enjoy a life of blissful ease. The core of the story involves Eithne, a woman of the Túatha Dé Danann, who experiences a mysterious interior access of grace which allows her to separate from her pagan kin and become a saintly convert to the Christian religion.

It is in the earlier part of the saga, however, that we find our intriguing example of magic. Aengus (usually known as the *Mac Óc*, the "Young Son") desires the house of his foster father Elcmar to be his own. Manannán, the overking of the Túatha Dé, urges him to violate all ties of loyalty to Elcmar and simply to eject him using a *sén* – a "spell", ultimately from Latin *signum* – which cannot be withstood; this Aengus duly does.

What is alarming is the origin of this spell, for Manannán explains that it was the incantation which God himself used to eject Lucifer and his angels for heaven. We have a situation, therefore, in which the overking of a race of magically augmented pagans is in possession of the irresistibly powerful word of God. The unknown author of the saga increases the sense of unease by showing Manannán, and later his protégé Aengus too, as beings who possess genuine theological knowledge but are nonetheless unmoved by it. Manannán knows not only about Lucifer's fall but also about the Trinity; and yet such intellectual knowledge is not enough. It is, in fact, a kind of theological knowledge proper to demons – as which the Túatha Dé Danann were sometimes identified – for as James 2.19 tells us, "the devils believe, and tremble": they know the theological facts intellectually, but are nonetheless damned.

What I would suggest is that the knowledge of God's "spell" in this story can be seen in the context of medieval learned magic. Power resides in the word of God itself – and that power is recognized by pagan magicians, even if they do not fully understand the implications of their knowledge. The saga suggests a view of magic as inappropriate knowledge of secrets of God, and as the use of God's word for base purposes of self-aggrandizement. Manannán's theological knowledge and yet absence of belief contrasts with the spiritual trajectory of the woman Eithne, who knows nothing of Christianity to begin with but is transformed by interior grace; the tale emerges as a subtle theological parallel in which magic is envisioned as a force ultimately deriving its power from God, but inevitably perverting and perverse when used by lesser beings.

Magic in medieval Welsh literature

In Wales too, literary magic was a phenomenon imagined to have belonged to the past. Certainly it plays a part in the Arthurian milieu of *Culhwch ac Olwen* – the earliest Arthurian tale to survive in any language – but the most spectacular instances of enchantment in the tradition are set even earlier, in the pre-Saxon, indeed pre-Roman world of the *Pedeir Keinc y Mabinogi*, "The Four Branches of the Mabinogi", probably written around the year 1100.[32]

Elsewhere, I have argued that the author of the Four Branches – who has struck many critics as bringing a striking mixture of compassion and sober thoughtfulness to bear upon his often fantastical material – has a more coherent "theory of magic" than has been realized.[33] The Four Branches are filled with magical events, which include an appearing and disappearing castle, a cauldron that functions as a "resurrection device" – bringing slain men back to life but depriving them of the power of speech – and the reduction of Dyfed in south-west Wales to an empty wilderness. Most memorable, however, is the astonishingly rich and sometimes perverse collection of transformations in the four tales. Humans take on the appearances of other humans; humans are changed into animals; animals are changed into humans; plant matter is refashioned into shields and ships, and even – more alarmingly – into a woman, who later is turned into a bird.

My own view is that the unknown author of the Four Branches, writing somewhere in Wales – we do not know where – at the turn of the twelfth century, managed to anticipate some of the complex debates about shape-shifting that were to become part of the intellectual currency of European learning in the century or so after he wrote. He may well have been the earliest European writer to be troubled by issues surrounding what Caroline Walker Bynum has called (in a now classic study) "metamorphosis and identity", a wave of intellectual anxiety in the wake of the twelfth-century rediscovery of Ovid's *Metamorphoses*.[34] To take only one example, he seems prepared to ascribe to Math son of Mathonwy and his nephew Gwydion son of Dôn – his prime pre-Christian enchanters – the power to create human souls from nothing. At one point in the Fourth Branch, Math uses his magic wand to transform a wolf cub, a fawn and a wild piglet into three boys, to whom he gives names that memorialize their animal origins. Though they are the offspring of human beings – a pair of brothers, no less – who have been transformed into pairs of male and female animals, these three have never been human themselves, and in terms of non-magical, natural biology, their conception would have been an impossibility. And yet they seem to be as fully human and fully ensouled as any other characters in the stories: this represents an alarming degree of power to place at the disposal of a wizard.

I think the author of the Four Branches meant us to notice and be inwardly troubled by this usurpation of divine power, for he returns to the same theme later in the same story, when Math and Gwydion create a woman, Blodeuwedd, out of "the flowers of the oak and the flowers of the broom and the flowers of the meadowsweet" to be a wife for the hero Lleu. Though exquisitely beautiful, the resultant woman, Delilah-like, soon betrays and attempts to murder her husband, and a medieval audience would very likely have assumed a direct connection between her unorthodox mode of coming into being and her infidelity. Once again, on the face of it, wizardry appears to have created a human soul (this time with disastrous consequences), but I suspect that the incident is intended to leave open the possibility that Blodeuwedd is an evil spirit animating a temporary body. Her adultery and attempt on her husband's life would have aligned her with *succubi*, demonic spirits taking the form of women and a demonstrable focus of concern at the time of the Four Branches' composition.[35]

Future directions

As will be clear by now, magic in the Celtic lands is an area of research with great potential but one currently dogged by a lack of conceptual precision, so that there is much ground clearing to be done. The following strike me as the most obvious priorities.

First, we urgently need a full and theoretically sophisticated survey of historical magical practice in medieval Ireland and Wales, correlated and compared with that of related and parallel cultures (most obviously Anglo-Saxon and later medieval England). This is already being done for charms and in relation to legal texts.

Second, the literary magic of both countries needs to be surveyed and investigated methodically, in the manner that has been done for (say) kingship or landscape. This is a vast task, problematized by issues of definition – take, for instance, the question of the difference between magic and miracle – but it would certainly be useful to have a database of every example of the use of enchantment from both Irish and Welsh vernacular narratives and hagiography. This would enable article-length overviews of particular areas of magical technique. A simple example: universally in ancient and medieval Europe, the left side is associated with ill-luck and malediction; but in Ireland, we find this taken further in that a well-attested kind of cursing involves standing on one's left leg, with one's left hand out, and one's right eye closed, the native name for which was *corrguinecht*. Still later, we find that the Fomorians – a malevolent race of beings in Irish mythology – are supposed to be one-legged, one-armed and one-eyed. This is presumably to underscore their blighting power, but the relationship between their corporeal semiology and *corrguinecht* is just one area among many that have not been sufficiently explored.

Third, such surveys would allow for fruitful comparisons between magic in Irish, Welsh and other medieval literatures – and I emphasize that I think scholars should feel free to undertake such comparisons without feeling it necessary to justify them with reference to a supposed shared Celtic inheritance. There is the potential for a new comparitivism between literatures in the Celtic languages which would focus on how things work in their synchronic literary context. In some cases, there can be remarkably close resemblances between situations and characters when the possibility of one text having influenced another is remote. To give a simple example, the character of Brian son of Tuireann in the fourteenth-century Irish saga *Oidheadh Chloinne Tuireann*, "The Tragic Deaths of the Children of Tuireann", bears some striking similarities to one of the great enchanters of Welsh literature, namely Gwydion son of Dôn. Both disguise themselves as poets in order to obtain supernatural pigs; both are accompanied by a clearly junior brother (or brothers, in the case of Brian); both are magicians; both are conspicuously skilled as poet-storytellers. At present, the similarities between the characters are unexplained, and my suspicion is that "asking the right questions" would involve thinking about what cultural forces might lead such ambivalent figures – for Brian and Gwydion are both heroic and anti-heroic simultaneously – to be depicted as magicians; after all, magic is a signally flexible symbol for the double-edged nature of power and self-will.

In terms of areas of research which are small enough for doctoral dissertations, one especially rich subject to look at would be the relationship between magic and animals, in both Ireland and Wales. We need a more synoptic understanding of the Irish literary druid, as indicated above; a gendered analysis of magic in both countries would also be desirable. (Does women's magic differ from that of men in the Celtic literatures, and, if so, how? So far, the question has not even been asked.) Finally, the whole sphere of magical technology – the wand, for instance, or the plethora of "treasures" and magical objects in both Irish and Welsh tradition – should be surveyed, and this would be particularly useful if done in collaboration with an expert on the wider medieval romance tradition, so that such objects could be seen in a European literary context.

Finally, I would hope that the research directions suggested above might have a considerable secondary benefit, allowing medievalists from outside Celtic Studies to use Celtic evidence in building up wider arguments about medieval magic, rather than regarding Irish and Welsh vernacular literature as obscure backwaters filled with treacherously unpronounceable names. (An early modern example of how well this can work is the historian Ronald Hutton's recent demonstration that the witch craze was demonstrably less prominent in traditionally Gaelic-speaking areas, because in the folklore of such regions, the malevolent activities ascribed elsewhere to witches were deemed to be the work of fairies, and therefore scapegoating was not extended to the same degree to human beings.)[36] Medieval scholarship – both in Celtic Studies and in the wider field – would be immeasurably enriched.

There is, it must be said, a long way to go. The reader would be justified in asking why these Celtic texts – if they are truly so compelling – have been neglected to the extent that they have in mainstream medieval studies. The answer lies in the difficulty of the languages: while medieval Welsh is easier than medieval Irish, the latter is among the most difficult languages of Europe: far harder than Latin, Old High German, Old English or Old French. Apprenticeships in the discipline are therefore long, and this fact – coupled with the limited number of institutions in the world in which the languages are taught – means that progress on editing, translating and assessing a vast body of material has been slow. It would be highly desirable for Celticists to write not only for peers in their field but also for scholars of other medieval literatures; the study of magic and enchantment offers an ideal area in which such an outward-looking approach could be tested out.

Notes

1 Chief among them Matthew Arnold, on whose views see Rachel Bromwich, *Matthew Arnold and Celtic Literature: A Retrospect, 1865–1965* (Oxford: Oxford University Press, 1965), and W.E. Buckler, "On the Study of *Celtic Literature*: A Critical Reconsideration," *Victorian Poetry* 27.1 (Spring, 1989): 61–76. Also useful is Patrick Sims-Williams, "The Visionary Celt: The Construction of an 'Ethnic Preconception'," *Cambridge Medieval Celtic Studies* 11 (1986): 71–96.
2 See especially Patrick Sims-Williams, *Irish Influence on Medieval Welsh Literature* (Oxford: Oxford University Press, 2011).
3 Richard Kieckhefer, *Magic in the Middle Ages* (Cambridge: Cambridge University Press, 1989), 1–2.
4 John Carey, "Téacsanna draíochta in Éirinn sa mheánaois luath" ["Magical texts in early medieval Ireland"], *Léachtaí Cholm Cille* 30 (2000): 98–117.
5 See Fergus Kelly, *A Guide to Early Irish Law* (Dublin: Dublin Institute for Advanced Studies, 1997), 174–75.
6 Jacqueline Borsje and Fergus Kelly, *The Celtic Evil Eye and Related Mythological Motifs in Medieval Ireland* (Leuven: Peeters, 2003).
7 The term used for "spell" –*bricht* in Irish – has a long history: an earlier form of the word (*brictom*) seems to be attested in a Gaulish lead-tablet inscription from Larzac which appears to describe the casting of spells, again by women. The word's root seems to have meant "glitter" or "shine", though it has undergone considerable semantic change. See Pierre-Yves Lambert, *Recueil des inscriptions gauloises: II.2 Textes gallo-latins sur instrumentum* (Paris: Éditions du C.N.R.S, 2002), L-98, 251–66.
8 The source for points on legal material and penitentials in this paragraph is Ludwig Bieler, *The Irish Penitentials* (Dublin: Dublin Institute for Advanced Study, 1963), 56–57.
9 See Jacqueline Borsje, "Love Magic in Medieval Irish Penitentials, Law and Literature: A Dynamic Perspective," *Studia Neophilologica* 84, Supplement 1 (2012): 6–23, and her "Rules & Legislation on Love Charms in Early Medieval Ireland," *Peritia* 21 (2010 [2011]): 172–190.
10 A limited selection, the references of which lead to further discussion, includes: Ilona Tuomi, "Parchment, Praxis and Performance of Charms in Early Medieval Ireland," *Incantatio: An International Journal on Charms, Charmers and Charming* 3 (2013): 60–85; David Stifter, "A Charm for Staunching Blood," *Celtica* 25 (2007): 258–61; Jacqueline Borsje, "Druids, Deer and "Words of Power": Coming to Terms with Evil in Medieval Ireland," in *Approaches to Religion and Mythology in Celtic Studies*, ed. Katja Ritari and Alexandra Bergholm (Cambridge: Cambridge Scholars Publishing, 2008), 122–49.
11 See John Carey, "The Three Things Required of a Poet," *Ériu* 48 (1997): 41–58.
12 The best example known to me is Corpus Christi College, Oxford, MS 129, which dates from the early sixteenth century; it contains a number of medieval texts in Irish and Latin, and a spectacular pair of *volvellae* – rotating circles of parchment pinned into the manuscript – one of which was used to work out the zodiacal sign of the moon, which determined the advisability of blood-letting. Images reproduced in colour in the frontispieces to Brian Ó Cuív, *Catalogue of Irish Language Manuscripts in the Bodleian Library at Oxford and Oxford College Libraries*, 2 vols. (Dublin: Dublin Institute for Advanced Studies, 2001–3), i., with the text discussed at 281–96.
13 Bernadette Williams, "'She was usually placed with the great men and leaders of the land in the public assemblies': Alice Kyteler: a woman of considerable power," in *Women in Renaissance and Early Modern Europe*, ed. Christine Meek (Dublin: Four Courts Press, 2000), 67–83.
14 *1 Henry IV*, III.i, 52.
15 See Stephen Knight, *Merlin: Knowledge and Power through the Ages* (Ithaca, NY: Cornell University Press, 2009).
16 See Marged Haycock, "Literary Criticism in Welsh before *c*. 1300," in *The Cambridge History of Literary Criticism: Volume 2: The Middle Ages*, ed. Alistair Minnis and Ian Johnson (Cambridge: Cambridge University Press, 2005), 336–37.
17 In the original, *Gwynn ap Nwdd* [sic] *qui es ultra in silvis pro amore concubine tue permitte nos venire domum*. See Brynley F. Roberts, "Gwynn ap Nudd," *Llên Cymru* 13 (1980–81): 288.
18 Richard Suggett, *A History of Magic and Witchcraft in Wales* (Stroud: History Press, 2008).
19 See Mark Williams, *Ireland's Immortals: A History of the Gods of Irish Myth* (Princeton: Princeton University Press, 2016), especially Chapters three and four.
20 *Córus Béscnai*, in *Corpus Iuris Hibernici*, 6 vols., ed. Daniel. A. Binchy (Dublin: Dublin Institute for Advanced Study, 1978), ii., 526, ll.15-9.

21 R. Hutton, *Blood and Mistletoe: The History of the Druids in Britain* (London and New Haven, CT: Yale University Press, 2009), 32–33.
22 Hutton, *Blood and Mistletoe*, 32–33.
23 Discussion in Ralph O'Connor, *The Destruction of Da Derga's Hostel: Kingship and Narrative Artistry in a Mediaeval Saga* (Oxford: Oxford University Press, 2013), 163–64.
24 In *Táin Bó Cuailnge*, the great Irish epic, the female poet Fedelm remarks to Queen Medb of Connacht that she has come "after learning the art of poetry in Britain"; Medb immediately asks her if she possesses *imbas forosnai*, implying that this part of the repertoire which someone trained in such a curriculum might command. See *Táin Bó Cuailnge: Recension I*, ed. and trans. Cecile O'Rahilly (Dublin: Dublin Institute for Advanced Studies, 1976), 2 (trans. 126).
25 See Thomas Charles-Edwards, *Early Christian Ireland* (Cambridge: Cambridge University Press, 2000), 198.
26 See O'Connor, *The Destruction of Da Derga's Hostel*, 8, 62, 104–5, 285–86.
27 The only edition is "Forbuis Droma Damhghaire," ed. and French trans. Marie-Louise Sjoestedt, *Le siège de Druim Damhghaire*, *Revue celtique* 43 (1926): 1–123.
28 *Longes mac n-Uislenn: The Exile of the Sons of Uisliu*, ed. and trans. Vernam Hull (New York: Modern Language Association of America, 1949), 43, l.20.
29 Best introductions both by John Carey: *The Irish National Origin-Legend: Synthetic Pseudohistory* (Cambridge: Quiggin Pamphlets on the Sources of Mediaeval Gaelic History 1, 1994), and "*Lebor Gabála* and the legendary history of Ireland," in *Medieval Celtic Literature and Society*, ed. Helen Fulton (Dublin: Four Courts Press, 2005), 32–48. The (very problematic) edition is *Lebor Gabála Érenn*, 5 vols., ed. and trans. Robert A.S. Macalister (London: Irish Texts Society, 1938–56, repr. 1993).
30 Mark Williams, *Fiery Shapes: Celestial Portraits and Astrology in Ireland and Wales, 700-1700* (Oxford: Oxford University Press, 2010).
31 *Altrom tigi dá medar*, ed. and trans. Margaret. C. Dobbs, "Altromh tighi da medar," *Zeitschrift für Celtische Philologie* 18 (1930): 189–230, and ed. and trans. Lilian Duncan, "Altram Tige Dá Medar," *Ériu* 11 (1932): 184–225. The major study so far is Cathinka Dahl Hambro, "Waiting for Christian Fish and Milk from India: A Textual and Contextual Analysis of *Altram Tige Dá Medar* ('The Nourishment of the House of Two Milk Vessels')," unpublished Ph.D. dissertation, University of Oslo, 2013.
32 Standard edition remains *Pedeir Keinc y Mabinogi: allan o Lyfr Gwyn Rhydderch*, ed. Ifor Williams (Cardiff: University of Wales Press, 1930); see too *The Mabinogion*, trans. Sioned Davies (Oxford: Oxford University Press, 2007).
33 Mark Williams, "Marvels and Magic in Medieval Wales," in *The Cambridge History of Welsh Literature*, ed. Geraint Evans and Helen Fulton (Cambridge: Cambridge University Press, forthcoming 2019).
34 Caroline Walker Bynum, *Metamorphosis and Identity* (New York: Zone Books, 2001).
35 See Corinne Saunders, *Magic and the Supernatural in Medieval English Romance* (Cambridge: D.S. Brewer, 2010), 115, 156.
36 Ronald Hutton, "Witch-Hunting in Celtic Societies," *Past and Present* 212 (August, 2011): 43–71.

11

SCANDINAVIA

Stephen A. Mitchell

Medieval Scandinavia comprised a vast geographic region, anchored culturally in modern Norway, Sweden, Denmark and Iceland, and with important outposts in the Faroes and other North Sea islands (i.e. Shetland and the Orkneys); southern Greenland; the Isle of Man, the Hebrides, and other portions of Scotland; and areas within modern Germany, Finland and the Baltic states. Thus, although principally associated with North Germanic-speaking peoples, Scandinavia of the Viking and Middle Ages was historically highly diverse as regards populations and cultures (e.g. the indigenous Sámi), meaning that Nordic practices of magic had over the centuries been shaped in contact with cultural traditions of many different sorts, including, after Christianization, Church thinking about magic.[1] The Conversion process played out over some three centuries but is generally held to have had been accomplished, at least with regard to politically powerful segments of Norwegian, Danish and Icelandic society, by the millennium, whereas Sweden is considered to have been similarly converted by c. 1060.

What we today label "magic" – especially when looking back at the pre-Christian era, whose practices necessarily form the backdrop for this discussion – is in the words of one anthropologist, "not an entity distinct from religion but a form of ritual behaviour and thus an element of religion".[2] Establishing the contours of the earlier pre-Christian beliefs is of critical importance in discussing Scandinavian magic in the period 1000–1500, as this heritage forms the bedrock on which the later Christian construction of magic in Scandinavia was largely erected.[3] Direct witness to such magico-religious practices in the pre-Conversion period is sparse, consisting mainly of commentary related to the missionary efforts, often given at second- and third-hand; the archaeological record; and, not least, much later written sources drawing on dynamic native cultural traditions.[4]

One of the most significant, and enigmatic, aspects of these earlier traditions is the practice of *seiðr*, a form of divination with frequently noted multicultural connections.[5] The role of Sámi shamanism, *noaidevuohta*,[6] or other *techniques archaïques de l'extase* "archaic techniques of ecstasy", in Mircea Eliade's famous formulation,[7] in the development of pre-Christian Nordic religious and magical traditions has been the subject of much scrutiny, with some scholars favouring of its significance,[8] and others viewing the relationship between the two traditions more sceptically.[9] Among scholars focused on the medieval literary evidence,[10] Dag Strömbäck's 1935 classic, *Sejd*, merits special consideration for its early and comprehensive source-critical review of the data and for the book's methodology combining the fields of folklore and philology in its conclusion in favour of the Sámi connection. Just as pre-Christian Nordic magic should be considered in the context of neighbouring Finnic peoples, Scandinavian practices also need to be viewed within the broader historical, and presumably inherited, Germanic context as well, especially as these magical traditions have been explored in Anglo-Saxon England and among continental Germanic peoples.[11]

Although the *seiðr* issue has dominated scholarship on pagan Nordic magic, lively debates abound about other aspects, and understandings, of pre-Christian magical practices in the North.[12] One approach interprets pre-Christian Nordic magic as a worldview and an alternative perception of reality: Regis Boyer, for example, accepts Norse magic as a refracted version of Norse religion, *le monde du double*, of his study's title.[13] Catherine Raudvere's excellent considerations of medieval Scandinavian magic also highlight perception, occult knowledge and insight, noting that divination rituals and other magical performances "were expressions of ways of finding the keys to hidden parts of reality and measuring what was given".[14]

Sociological interpretations of magic in the pre-Christian Nordic world, for example, within the context of cultic practices,[15] represent another important line of inquiry. François-Xavier Dillmann's remarkably detailed *Les magiciens dans l'Islande ancienne. Études sur la représentation de la magie islandaise et de ses agents dans les sources littéraires norroises* provides the most comprehensive investigation to date of the surviving Icelandic texts, suggesting that from them, it is possible to develop an accurate image of Icelandic practitioners of magic (i.e. their social standing, origins, gender, occupations), and of the prevailing attitudes towards these people and the forms of power they are represented as controlling.[16] A further key concern about the socio-historical outlines of pre-Christian Nordic magic has been the role of gender in the practice and representation of Norse magic.[17] Although the number of magical actors in surviving saga literature is roughly equal as regards gender, some scholars argue that the situation might in reality have been quite different in earlier times. One noted historian, for example, concludes, "women were the original and remained the most powerful magicians, whereas men gained access only later and never attained parity with women, either in numbers or power".[18]

These areas of investigation represent only a few of the most significant issues in an increasingly robust research field focused on the complex systems of religious belief of pagan Scandinavia. It is important to recognize, of course, that given a region stretching from Greenland to Finland, in societies with diverse demographic compositions, a cultural realm lacking anything like a central controlling religious hierarchy, there would never have existed anything like a uniform understanding of that part of religious and social life believed to allow those with special knowledge to communicate with, and acquire the supernatural assistance of, otherworldly powers, i.e. "magic". That pre-Christian Scandinavian religions inherited, borrowed and developed techniques that were understood to allow particularly active tradition bearers and other specialists to look into the future, protect, charm, heal, employ supernatural aggression and so on, that is, to make manifest the practitioner's volition on the environment and on others, can be and has been adduced from the surviving material and textual cultural monuments, bolstered by cultural analogies.

"Magic" in Medieval Christian Scandinavia

It is on this variegated pre-Christian magico-religious situation that the Catholic church began to impose its own complex and evolving positions about "magic" following the Christianization of the Nordic region. As detailed elsewhere in this volume, the Church had by the millennium formulated the view that the user of magic commanded dark, powerful forces, with the corollary that since God and the angels cannot be compelled to do a ritual actor's bidding, magic must therefore derive from diabolical forces. In time, this view led to the concept of the Satanic pact (*pactum cum diabolo*), views which inevitably flavoured how the traditions of pagan Scandinavia, both those bygone and those still living, were received and interpreted by authorities in the Christian Middle Ages. A later development in elite circles was an interest in so-called "natural magic", a branch of science looking for "occult virtues" or hidden powers within nature. What the authorities viewed, by contrast, as so-called "demonic magic" was not really distinct from religion, "but rather a perversion of religion. It was religion that turned away from God and toward demons for their help in human affairs".[19]

A modern typology of magic in the Nordic Middle Ages thus suggests a division between the traditions practiced by non-elites and the "natural magic" of elites – on the one hand, there were various forms of charm magic and witchcraft-related activities; on the other hand, there existed a growing interest in, for example, alchemy and what might be termed Christian "magic", that is, practices that operationally resemble charm magic but which were carried out with the tacit, sometimes explicit approval of Church authorities.[20]

Magic is categorized differently in the medieval Nordic sources themselves, however, a bifurcation that mainly concerns itself with the effects of such practices. Here, working within the world of living traditions of charms and other practical applications of inherited and borrowed magic, medieval Scandinavian ecclesiastical and secular authorities periodically established carefully wrought typologies of magic. Thus, for example, the medieval Icelandic laws known collectively as *Grágás* begin one section by condemning the veneration of "heathen beings" (*heiþnar vættir*), and go on to prohibit the use of spells, witchcraft and lesser forms of magic (*galldra eþa gørningar. eþa fiolkyngi*). The law then notes what constitutes this sort of magic, for which the penalty is lesser outlawry (*fiorbavgs Garþ*): "he uses magic if he utters or teaches someone else or gets someone else to utter words of magic over himself or his property" (*þa ferr hann með fiolkyngi ef hann queðr þat eþa kennir. eþa lætr queða. at ser eþa at fe sinv*). The law then details the contrasting, darker kind of magic, that is, words or magic that lead to the sickness or death of men or cattle (*þat ero fordæs skapir. ef maþr gérir i orðvm sinvm. eþa fiolkyngi sott eþa bana. fe eþa mavnnvm*). This more serious form of magic is punishable by banishment (*þat varþar scogGang*).[21] Among the observations to be made about this and similar documents are: the association authorities were keen to make between magic and the pagan past and its heathen deities; the distinction the laws imply between general and specialist users of magic; and their acceptance of the reality of magic.

The sources for researching magic – whether theoretical, fanciful or real – in medieval Scandinavia are mainly *textual* (e.g. runic inscriptions, chronicles, synodal statutes, letters, skaldic poems, episcopal edicts, sermons) and, to a lesser degree, *material* (e.g. amulets, house deposits). All of them contribute importantly to our understanding but every source must be examined for its so-called "truth value", a point of special significance when dealing with the Icelandic sagas and eddas, given their alluringly realistic presentations of magic, especially when dealing with much older traditions. Some of their reports may fairly represent empirical reality; others, mere borrowing from foreign models; still others, fantasies cut from whole cloth. The principal sources of information about magic in the medieval North are here for ease of presentation divided into the following categories: *normative texts*; *narratives*; *vocabulary*; *charms*, including *runic inscriptions*; and *material culture*.

The common thread among *normative texts*, such as the Nordic law codes, synodal statutes, homilies, penitentials and so on, is that they all reflect the authorities' overtly negative assessments of magical behaviours and frequently detail appropriate sanctions against practitioners. Another commonly shared feature is that they often refer only in passing, sometimes even obscurely, to the practices they condemn; in some instances, this tendency may be supposed to depend on the fact that these phenomena were widely known and required no explanation or detailed description, but in other instances, perhaps such treatment should be understood to suggest that novel concepts are being introduced.

So, for example, the Norwegian law codes periodically condemn and prohibit the practice of "sitting out" (*utiseta, sitja úti*): the *Older Law of Gulaþing* sanctions capital punishment "for [deeds of] murder or for [the practice of] witchcraft or for going abroad at night [lit., sitting out] to call forth evil spirits and to promote heathendom thereby" (*oc sva firi morð oc fordæðo skape. oc utisetu at vekia troll upp. at fremia heiðrni með því*).[22] Set against the various surviving references to this practice, "sitting out" appears to be a divinatory custom whereby the practitioner "sits out" on a grave mound, where the reference points to an old custom often mentioned, but, so far as we know, never fully described, in surviving texts. On the other hand, something novel, and apparently eminently traceable, occurs when there are reports of magical flights: "'evening-riders' or 'shape-shifters' believe themselves to travel with Diana the goddess and Herodias quickly over great oceans, riding whales or seals, birds or wild animals, or over great lands" (*kveldriður eða hamleypur þykkiaz með Diana gyðiu oc Herodiade a litilli stundu fara yfir stor hóf riðandi hvolum eða selum, fuglum eða dyrum, eða yfir stor lond*).[23] The context and references make it clear that this saint's legend has been written under the influence of the materials also reported in the *Canon episcopi*; yet, this image also dovetails with traditional Nordic perspectives on magical abilities of this sort.[24]

Other instances related to magical transvection can be considerably more opaque, as when the thirteenth-century Swedish *Older Law of Västergötland* (*Äldre Västgötalagen*) states that among the felonious, actionable insults about a woman is to say, "I saw that you rode on the pen-gate, with your hair loose, and in a witch's shape, when all was equal between night and day" (*Iak sa at þu reet a quiggrindu lösharæp. ok i trols ham þa alt var iamrift nat ok daghér*).[25] Yet, this case too can be placed within known belief systems;[26] much more perplexing are references to charm magic such as the following from *Ældre Borgarthings Christenret*, a Norwegian law code, "But if a woman bites off a finger or toe from her child and does that [in order to secure] long life, she is fined three marks" (*En ef kona bitr fingr af barne sinu eda to ok gerer þat til langlifis hon er sæck.iij. morkum*).[27]

One early Norwegian church law declares simply that people should "not pay heed to soothsaying, incantation, or wicked sorcery" [*eigi lyða spám ne golldrum ne gerningum illum*] and details the penalties for such acts (loss of property and outlawry), as well as the procedures for defence against the charge.[28] Taken as a group, the medieval Nordic laws treat magic and those who practice it in ways that appear to reflect changes in perspectives over time. In the case just cited for the laws of Gulaþing, these statutes are located amid the law sections treating religious and moral topics, such as heathenism, incest and bestiality: (28) *Um spár oc um galldra* [Concerning Sorcery and Soothsaying]; (29) *Um blot* [Concerning heathen sacrifice]; (30) *Um udaða menn* [Concerning evildoers].[29] The earliest Old Swedish provincial laws (e.g. *Äldre Västgötalagen, Upplandslagen*), by contrast, tend to situate magical practices and their practitioners in the narrowly relevant parts of the code; thus, statutes about superstition find a home among the Church Laws, those about poisoning – widely believed to be a witchcraft-related crime – among the criminal statutes and so on. Over time, however, these offences are increasingly situated amid high crimes threatening social order such as perjury and treason. By Magnus Eriksson's mid-fourteenth-century codification of the Swedish laws (*Magnus Erikssons Landslag*), witchcraft is placed in the following series: different forms of murder (of spouses, children and so on); murder through *trulldom* "witchcraft";

the death of stepchildren; traitors who would raise an army against the king; those who would bring a foreign army against their homeland and rightful lord; the murder by servants of their masters; arson; rape; and poisoning (again, usually understood as a witchcraft statute).[30] That the use of *trulldom* should now be placed together with topics concerned with the preservation of the state, such as treason and armed rebellion, as well as with important civil crimes that also threaten social order, like murder and rape, represents, one suspects, more than simple reorganization of the codes, and something more like a re-evaluation about just what the entire magical arena was understood to be.

The rich stock of native and imported Nordic medieval *narratives* too often offer detailed and valuable opportunities to get a purchase on the evolving character of magic – presumably also both native and imported – in the Scandinavian Middle Ages. Among the most well-regarded traditional sources are the *skaldic and eddaic* poems that were preserved in the Icelandic Middle Ages, many of which presumably hark back to the era before the Conversion and the use of the Latin alphabet in Scandinavia. The surviving texts include numerous, albeit often obscure, suggestions about the range of pagan Nordic magic. The master of magic within the pre-Christian Nordic Pantheon, Óðinn, claims in *Hávamál* st. 146-st. 163, for example, to know many different charms – although he makes this claim without revealing their secrets. The character says that he know, for example, charms against sorrows; medical charms; charms to dull an enemy's weapons; charms to escape from fetters; spells to stop arrows; magic that allows him to turn charms of hatred back against their conjurer; incantations against fire; charms to still hostility; spells to calm a wild sea; magic against witches; spells to protect others in battle; necromantic charms; spells for victory in battle; incantations that allow him to know supernatural details; charms that give strength, success and wisdom; charms that give him the pleasures of a woman; and spells for love, as well as a mysterious eighteenth charm.[31]

Detailed in its presentation of magical practices is the eddaic poem *Skírnismál*, which provides a comprehensive image of a charm being worked. In the frame story, Skírnir, the servant of the god Freyr, travels to the giantess Gerðr in order to acquire her for his master. After various bribes and threats fail, Skírnir wins her hand for Freyr by engaging in a magical performance, a performance marked by Skírnir's frequent references to a wand (called a *tamsvǫndr* and *gambanteinn* in the poem); that this is a special part of the text is further marked by the fact that the meter of the poem goes over to *galdralag* ("incantation meter", in which the final line echoes the penultimate line), and by the content and wording of the poem, a portion of which reflects charm magic known from runic inscriptions.[32] In *Bósa saga*, the witch Busla similarly wields a versified charm against King Hringr, a further detailed, if incomplete, example of an incantation being performed.[33]

Given its functions, generally to offer praise and commemoration, skaldic poetry does not usually provide these sorts of detailed views of magic, although there are exceptions. In a section of Snorri Sturluson's thirteenth-century *Heimskringla* called *Ynglinga saga*, and building on a skaldic poem known as *Ynglingatal*, believed to have been composed by Þjóðólfr úr Hvinir ca. 900, a "witch" carries out an act of supernatural aggression that causes King Vanlandi to be killed by a "trollwoman", who rides him to death (*Ynglinga saga*, ch. 13).[34]

Among the most intriguing presentations of traditional Nordic magic are such scenes in the Icelandic sagas as the enumeration of the magical abilities of the pagan deity, Óðinn, in *Ynglinga saga* (*Ynglinga saga*, ch. 6–7; pp. 10–11); Þorbjǫrg *lítilvǫlva* "little seeress" (also referred to as *vísendakona* "wise woman" and as *spákona* "prophetess") performing a *seiðr* ceremony in *Eiríks saga rauða* (ch. 4; pp. 81–83); Egill's performance of a curse to drive King Eiríkr and Queen Gunnhildr from Norway through the use of a *níðstǫng* "scorn pole" and a verbal charm in *Egils saga Skalla-Grímssonar* (ch. 57; pp. 148–49); the so-called *Bulsubæn* "Busla's prayer" and *Syrpuvers* "Syrpa Verses" of *Bósa saga* (ch. 5; pp. 204–08); Gunnlaugr's attempt to learn witchcraft in *Eyrbyggja saga* (ch. 16; pp. 59–60); and Þuríðr's charm magic against Grettir Ásmundarson (*Grettis saga Ásmundarsonar*, ch. 78; pp. 161–62).[35] The Icelandic sagas, as even this brief list makes clear, provide a treasure trove of materials, one carefully investigated over the decades for evidence of magical practices,[36] although with as yet still much debated results. Recent research has tended to underscore the tendentious character of how magic is presented in these texts, which are literary productions of the thirteenth and fourteenth centuries, often treating topics from earlier eras.[37]

Vernacular Icelandic sagas and poetry, albeit by far the most renowned texts from the Scandinavian Middle Ages, are by no means the only textual sources at our disposal as regards the question of magic in the medieval North – translations into the Nordic languages of foreign materials and Latin treatments of native traditions also provide important windows. Thus, the process of turning large numbers of foreign texts, such as *Legenda aurea*, *Seelentrost*, and *Historia de preliis Alexandri Magni*, into various Nordic vernaculars, such as the Old Swedish *Ett Forn-Svenskt Legendarium*, *Siælinna thrøst* and *Konung Alexander*, often introduced alternative and evolving continental views of magic into Scandinavia.[38] And local traditions are frequently noted in Latin texts. So, for example, the history of Norwegian monarchs from the ninth to twelfth centuries (*Historia de antiquitate regum Norwagiensium*) of Theodoricus monachus speaks of idols and prophecies uttered by demons in connection with ritual specialists of both genders who are called *seithmen* (i.e. *seiðmenn*) "sorcerers, witches" in the vernacular.[39] The king has eighty of these *seiðmenn* brought into a building and burned, a story also found in other texts.[40]

Given the often tendentious character of these sources, researchers are always at pains to examine the texts' comments and contexts with care, a fact that complicates, but does not necessarily prevent, analysis. The same source-critical problem applies, for example, to the presentation of magic and magicians in relation to the old heathen religion and godhead in the *Gesta Danorum* of Saxo Grammaticus:

> At one time certain individuals, initiated into the magic arts, namely Thor, Odin and a number of others who were skilled at conjuring up marvellous illusions, clouded the minds of simple men and began to appropriate the exalted rank of godhead. Norway, Sweden and Denmark were ensnared in a groundless conviction, urged to a devoted worship of these frauds and infected by their gross imposture.[41]

Generally, statements of this sort reinforce the association also found in the laws, namely, of magic being understood to be pagan holdovers from before the Conversion. This view of magic and superstition as "survivals" is, of course, a perspective made famous by Edward B. Tylor, who describes superstitious beliefs as "fragments of a dead lower culture embedded in a living higher one".[42] Hardly a modern invention, the idea that magic represents the persistence of paganism and pagan beliefs is routinely woven into the medieval laws and sagas.

The *vocabulary* employed to describe the magical world, its possibilities, activities and practitioners, offers a rich opportunity for exploring what magic was thought to be in the Nordic Middle Ages, although it must be borne in mind that Latin terms (e.g. *maleficium* "witchcraft", *maleficare* "to bewitch", *incantatio* "spell", *sortilegium* "fortune-telling") are usually used in legal and ecclesiastical documents. Nevertheless, there exists a very large inventory of native terms from which it is possible to tease out what magic was thought to be in the North. Naturally, this magical vocabulary often derives from usages the Scandinavian languages share with other Indo-European languages, making it important to review the Nordic terms against this key linguistic backdrop.[43] A significantly richer stock of vocabulary items exists from medieval Icelandic texts than from the other Nordic traditions, but whether this is due to the fact that there exist more, and more varied, surviving medieval Icelandic texts, or from the possibility that Iceland had a differing view of magic, is unclear.

The very large Nordic inventory of words for magical acts and actors principally builds on such concepts as: prophecy (e.g. *spákona, vǫlva*); wisdom (e.g. *fjǫlkyngi, vísdómsmeistari*); deeds (e.g. *fordæðuskap, firigæra*); performance (e.g. *seiða seið, gala galdr, útiseta*); transformations and transvection (e.g. *renna gǫndum, hamfarir*); the paraphernalia of magic (e.g. *seiðhjallr, gambanteinn*); charms (e.g. *álag, atkvæði*); and the heathen past (e.g. *fornfróðr, fornspjǫll*), as well as the abundant lexis connected to *trolldómr* "witchcraft", terms derived from *troll*, a monstrous being.[44]

There exists an impressive, and to a great extent as yet underexplored, body of Nordic *charm magic* from, or with roots in, the Middle Ages. Some of these are to be found in medical treatises and other so-called leechbooks, some in the form of *runic inscriptions*. An early tendency to over-interpret the connection between magic and runes led to the view that runes are something other, or more, than an epigraphic system[45]; at the same time, of course, it must be borne in mind that runes are as capable of reflecting magic as any other writing system.[46] And naturally among the particularly important aspects of these records are the facts that they do not hazard being copies in the same way manuscripts often are and that knowledge of them does not require the agency of, for example, a church school. Thus, we presumably have here opportunities to hear more directly the *vox populi*.

The early eleventh-century Kvinneby amulet from Swedish Öland (Öl 52) offers an intriguing example of heathen apotropaic magic in the context of a runic amulet.[47] It was produced from sheet copper, bears the image of a fish and bears a hole that is interpreted as indicating that it was worn as a periapt. There is little modern scholarship agrees on with respect to the amulet apart from those details, *and* the text's use of a *historiola*, that is, a reference to a mythic narrative embedded in a magic formula, namely, the myth of Þórr's fishing for the World Serpent and the appearance in it of his hammer, Mjǫllnir. That central section of the text reads, "…hold all evil away from Bófi. May Þórr protect him with that hammer which came from out of the sea" (*En bra haldi illu fran Bofa. Þorr gæti hans með þæim hamri sem uR §B hafi kom*).

Where the Kvinneby amulet is heathen in its character, an example of a mixed heathen-Christian charm in runes, comes from medieval Norway (N B241). The charm invokes not Christian powers in the first instance, but the pagan god, Óðinn (*ek særi þik, Óðinn*).[48] On the other hand, the charm's broader Christian framework can be seen when the text calls the old god "the greatest among devils" (*mestr fjánda*) and invokes Christianity as part of the charm as well (*fyr kristni*). The full text is understood to read,

> I invoke you, Óðinn, with (heathenism), the greatest among devils. Agree to it. Tell me the name of the man who stole. For Christianity. Tell me now (your) evil deed. One I scorn, (the second) I scorn. Tell me, Óðinn. Now (multitudes of devils?) are called forth with all (heathenism). You shall now acquire/raise for me the name of the one who stole. (Amen).[49]

An early fifteenth-century Danish medical treatise, AM 187, 8°,[50] contains some obviously magical and divinatory charms, when, for example, it offers methods to prognosticate death (*Probacio galieni*), determine the gender of an unborn child (*Om thu wildæ widæ*) and protect "Against devil's arrows" (*Contra sagittas dyaboli*). A Norwegian anthology of religious and other materials, *Vinjeboka*, written serially between ca. 1480 and the 1530s, contains a variety of magical formulas, cures and remedies for men and animals, occasional verses in Latin, a Marian legend and nearly a dozen hymns to the Virgin by various hands. The text's editor estimates that roughly thirty per cent of the recipes in *Vinjeboka* contain powerful charms and symbolic materials, e.g. "To blunt an enemy's sword", "To gain power over a woman", "To win the love of a young woman", "To expose a thief".[51] As is often the case, it is generally *how* the remedies are thought to work, rather than the problem they are thought to work on, that matters. For example, as a recipe, "To improve soil in fallow land" may sound like a simple matter of mucking the field or other practical bit of farming tradition, but instead this recommendation depends entirely on ritual and spiritual matters:

> For fallow land: Make the sign of the cross over the fallow land with your foot and say thus, May the five holy wounds [of Jesus] heal this wounded [land] in the name of the Father, the Son and the Holy Spirit.

Finally, we have an important opportunity to recover medieval Nordic magical practices and beliefs from *material culture*. Naturally, there can be no absolute divisions among the sources: runic inscriptions and other written sources, for example, are in one sense, of course, forms of textual evidence that require philological expertise; at the same time, they are also preserved as, or on, physical objects – runestones, talismans, manuscripts and so on – and thus the end products of procedures executed by human hands (i.e. manufactured in an etymological sense), where the kinds of information archaeological methods can glean are also fruitful. A prime example would be the large number of amulets that come from medieval Scandinavia.[52] Some of these amulets bear inscriptions, some not, but their interpretations, both in the narrow and broad senses, will in almost all cases be improved from knowledge of their physical composition, their manufacture, the circumstances of their discovery and other empirical facts relating to their production and provenance.

Another kind of situation can also happen, that is, cases where we have only the material evidence and no surviving texts. Thus, for example, a series of studies, concerned with house floor assemblages and other ritual depositions in Scandinavia, variously referred to as "house deposits", "foundation sacrifices" and so on, show both the critical importance of material data, as well as some of the problems that occur where there is no corresponding written information. Defining what such evidence represents – are they accidental deposits or intentional ones? are these depositions to be connected with magical, ritual and ceremonial purposes or are they items hidden below ground in order to guarantee their security? – let alone the specific spiritual purpose, if any, is not easy to know, all the more so given the complete absence of any contemporary commentary about the practice. In this regard, these physical echoes of bygone practices are of special interest since they provide evidence of traditional behaviours otherwise completely unnoticed and uncommented on by medieval legal, literary and historical writers.[53] The work of Ann-Britt Falk,[54] for example, demonstrates the dynamic continuity of such a tradition as part of south Scandinavian social life into the Middle Ages. Falk traces the continuity of these and related practices throughout the Middle Ages, with animal bones, especially skulls, and ceramics being common offerings. In the absence of evidence from such routine medieval sources as the laws and the Icelandic sagas, we would, without the archaeological record (and much later traditions observed by folklorists), simply have no knowledge of these practices or their longevity.

Future directions

Researchers have through many decades of scrutiny been able to reveal much about Nordic magic both in the period before 1000 and the era after 1500 but the period in-between the Conversion and the Reformation has generally been subject to less analysis, although there have been a number of recent advances. There remain, however, *desiderata*. Thus, despite the exhaustive attention given to the Icelandic family sagas, other literary resources, such as the Icelandic *rímur*, have been but little exploited and such "new", that is, underexplored, resources may, with more thorough examination, yield novel information about the nature of, and thinking about, magic in the medieval North. Similarly, the substantial work that earlier generations invested into assembling and publishing the various national traditions of charm magic (e.g. *Danmarks Trylleformler; Íslenzkar þjóðsögur og ævintýri; Norske Hexeformularer;* and *Signelser och besvärjelser*) has largely remained underexploited.[55] Here is an area where there exist particularly exciting opportunities for new discoveries, work that can develop in tandem with evolving methodological insights, as discussed below.

In addition to more thoroughly investigating the full range of medieval sources themselves, there are some topics, such as "natural magic", towards which it seems far too little attention has been paid with regard to the medieval Scandinavian situation, a bias that derives in part, one suspects, from the tendency of scholars to shy away from the East Norse sources, that is, the Old Danish and Old Swedish materials, whose philological traditions tend to leave the texts less accessible than are the West Norse, that is, Old Norwegian and Old Icelandic materials. Furthermore, expanding our understanding of "natural magic" may require a broader reach in other ways as well, such as a higher degree of cross-disciplinary work from such fields as the history of science and the history of ideas, than has thus far been the case. Certainly, the extent to which we understand an area like alchemy will prove central to providing a clearer image of the degree to which elite concepts of magic from the Continent penetrated medieval Scandinavia.

This issue points to a further sphere where one senses more research could profitably be invested, namely, Scandinavia's contacts with non-Scandinavian cultural traditions. Thus, the relationships of Nordic magical traditions to those of their Baltic neighbours, and colonial possessions, are of great interest, and although important work has been done with respect to the Sámi and adjacent Finnic peoples,[56] there is undoubtedly more to be accomplished in investigating, for example, the degree to which the traditions of the various Balto-Slavic peoples with whom Scandinavians had routine contact before, during and after the Age of the Vikings may have provided models and influenced the character of Nordic magic in the medieval period.

Along similar lines, and perhaps of equal significance for our understanding of the development of Nordic magic, are the various lines of communication that ran between specific monasteries and seats of learning on the Continent such as the universities in Paris, Orléans and Bologna, and the ecclesiastical centres in Scandinavia (e.g. Niðarós, Ribe, Lund, Skara, Vadstena). Numerous multinational connections between and among the various European religious houses once existed,[57] and investigating these pathways would substantially further our understanding of the medieval situation. Jan Wall, for example,[58] makes a credible case for British influence from the *Handlyng Synne* of Robert of Brunnes, or one of its models, on the Nordic tradition of the milk-stealing witch, arguing that the idea may have been introduced through the *Homo conditus* (1330–50) of Magister Mathias, a Swedish theologian, who might have learned of it during his time in Paris. Likewise, the well-established connections between Norway, Niðarós in particular, and the Abbey of St. Victor in Paris, where instruction in Hebrew was possible, might, for example, explain the strain of Jewish magical traditions known to have existed in medieval Scandinavia.[59] In a similar fashion, the medical traditions of Salerno (Schola Medica Salernitana) are prominent in the works of Henrik Harpestreng, the most famous of medieval Nordic medical figures, whose works in turn feed into late medieval Nordic charm traditions.[60]

As a disciplinary matter, it is almost certain that what some have termed "an archaeology of magic" holds out tremendous promise for new information, a potential as yet largely unfulfilled, with some notable exceptions;[61] whereas it is unlikely that large numbers of new manuscripts relating to medieval magic will be discovered in Scandinavia, it is virtually certain that over time researchers will discover, and recognize, new objects relevant to our understanding of medieval magic in the North. At the same time, new methodologies are allowing us to understand our copious written sources in new ways, theories concerned with recontextualizing magical practices and understanding how such activities were actually performed.[62] Another, and related, approach that has come to prominence in recent years is so-called "memory studies", a field which has already begun to show promise with respect to the use and recollection of charms in other tradition areas.[63]

As has been noted in a context parallel to the present essay's concern with magic in the Nordic Middle Ages,

> …the situation in medieval Scandinavia, due to the unusual nature and richness of its textual and other sources of information, its geographical location and its connections to adjacent cultures, represents a unique case, a tradition-rich area that may hold unparalleled promise for future interdisciplinary efforts.[64]

Scholarship has come a long way towards fulfilling this promise; yet, despite significant advances in recent years, there remains much to be done if we are to understand fully medieval Nordic magic.

Notes

1 See Thomas A. DuBois, *Nordic Religions in the Viking Age* (Philadelphia: University of Pennsylvania Press, 1999); Stephen A. Mitchell, *Witchcraft and Magic in the Nordic Middle Ages* (Philadelphia: University of Pennsylvania Press, 2011).
2 Dorothy Hammond, "Magic: A Problem in Semantics," *American Anthropologist* 72, no. 6 (1970): 1355.
3 With respect to magical practices in these earlier periods, cf. the reviews in, e.g. Peter Buchholz, "Schamanistische Züge in der altisländischen Überlieferung," Inaugural-Dissertation zur Erlangung des Doktorsgrades, Westfälischen Wilhelms-Universität Münster (Bamberg, 1968); DuBois, *Nordic Religions*; Neil S. Price, *The Viking Way: Religion and War in Late Iron Age Scandinavia*, vol. 31, Aun (Uppsala: Institutionen för arkeologi och antik historia, Uppsala universitet, 2002); Catharina Raudvere, "*Trolldómr* in Early Medieval Scandinavia," in *Witchcraft and Magic in Europe: The Middle Ages*, ed. Bengt Ankarloo and Stuart Clark (Philadelphia: University of Pennsylvania Press, 2001), 73–171; Catharina Raudvere, *Kunskap och insikt i norrön tradition: Mytologi, ritualer och trolldomsanklagelser*

(Lund: Nordic Academic Press, 2003); François-Xavier Dillmann, *Les magiciens dans l'Islande ancienne. Études sur la représentation de la magie islandaise et de ses agents dans les sources littéraires norroises*, vol. 92, Acta Academiae Regiae Gustavi Adolphi (Uppsala: Kungl. Gustav Adolfs Akademien för svensk folkkultur, 2006); Clive Tolley, *Shamanism in Norse Myth and Magic*, vols. 296, 297, Folklore Fellows Communications (Helsinki: Suomalainen Tiedakatemia. Akademia Scientarum Fennica, 2009); Mitchell, *Witchcraft and Magic*; and Stephen A. Mitchell, "Magic and Religion," in *Pre-Christian Religions of the North. Histories and Structures*, ed. Anders Andrén, John Lindow and Jens Peter Schjødt (Turnhout: Brepols, forthcoming).

4 Concerning survivals, continuity and Nordic pre-Christian beliefs, see Andreas Nordberg, *Fornnordisk religionsforskning mellan teori och empiri: Kulten av anfäder, solen och vegetationsandar i idéhistorisk belysning*, vol. 126, Acta Academiae Regiae Gustavi Adolphi (Uppsala: Kungl. Gustav Adolfs Akademien för svensk folkkultur, 2013), as well as Stephen A. Mitchell, "Continuity: Folklore's Problem Child?" in *Folklore in Old Norse – Old Norse in Folklore*, vol. 20, ed. Daniel Sävborg and Karen Bek-Pedersen, Nordistica Tartuensis (Tartu: Tartu University Press, 2014), 34–51.

5 Early works in this area include Johan Fritzner, "Lappernes Hedenskab og Trolddomskunst sammen holdt med andre Folks, især Nordmændenes, Tro og Overtro," *Norsk Historisk Tidsskrift* 4 (1877): 136–217; Dag Strömbäck, *Sejd. Textstudier i nordisk religionshistoria*, vol. 5, Nordiska Texter och Undersökningar (Stockholm: Hugo Gebers förlag, 1935); Walter Jaide, *Das Wesen des Zaubers in den primitiven Kulturen und in den Islandssagas* (Leipzig: Noske, 1937); and Åke Ohlmarks, "Arktischer Schamanismus und altnordischer *seiðr*," *Archiv für Religionswissenschaft* 36 (1939): 171–80.

6 DuBois, *Nordic Religions in the Viking Age*, 122–38; Price, *The Viking Way*, 233–78; Tolley, *Shamanism in Norse Myth and Magic*, I:75–8 et passim.

7 Mircea Eliade, *Le chamanisme et les techniques archaïques de l'extase* (Paris: Payot, 1951), 15.

8 DuBois, *Nordic Religions in the Viking Age*; Price, *The Viking Way*; Neil S. Price, "The Archaeology of Seiðr: Circumpolar Traditions in Viking Pre-Christian Religion," *Brathair* 4, no. 2 (2004): 109–26.

9 Dillmann, *Les magiciens dans l'Islande ancienne*, 269–308; Tolley, *Shamanism in Norse Myth and Magic*.

10 E.g. Buchholz, "Schamanistische Züge"; Hermann Pálsson, *Úr landnorðri: Samar og ystu rætur íslenskrar menningar*, vol. 54, Studia Islandica (Reykjavík: Bókmenntafræðistofnun Háskóla Íslands, 1997).

11 E.g. Godfrid Storms, *Anglo-Saxon Magic* (The Hague: Nijhoff, 1948); Audrey L. Meaney, *Anglo-Saxon Amulets and Curing Stones* (Oxford: British Archaeological Reports, 1981); Karen Louise Jolly, *Popular Religion in Late Saxon England: Elf Charms in Context* (Chapel Hill: University of North Carolina Press, 1996); Alaric Hall, *Elves in Anglo-Saxon England: Matters of Belief, Health, Gender and Identity* (Woodbridge: Boydell Press, 2007); Karl A. Wipf, "Die Zaubersprüche im Althochdeutschen," *Numen* 22 (1975): 42–69; and Verena Holzmann, *"Ich beswer dich wurm vnd wyrmin--": Formen und Typen altdeutscher Zaubersprüche und Segen*, vol. 36, Wiener Arbeiten zur germanischen Altertumskunde und Philologie (Bern & New York: P. Lang, 2001).

12 Reviewed in, for example, Price, *The Viking Way*, 76–89; Dillmann, *Les magiciens dans l'Islande ancienne*, 6–9; Mitchell, *Witchcraft and Magic*, 1–15.

13 Regis Boyer, *Le monde du double: la magie chez les anciens Scandinaves* (Paris: Berg international, 1986).

14 Raudvere, "*Trolldómr*," 96; Raudvere, *Kunskap och insikt*.

15 E.g. Walter Baetke, *Die Religion der Germanen in Quellenzeugnissen* (Frankfurt am Main: M. Diesterweg, 1937); Åke Ohlmarks, *Studien zum Problem des Schamanismus* (Lund: C. W. K. Gleerup, 1939).

16 Dillmann, *Les magiciens dans l'Islande ancienne*.

17 Morris, *Sorceress or Witch?*; Britt-Mari Näsström, *Freyja – The Great Goddess of the North*, vol. 5, Lund Studies in [the] History of Religion (Lund: Department of History of Religions, 1995); Jenny Jochens, *Old Norse Images of Women* (Philadelphia: University of Pennsylvania Press, 1996); Brit Solli, *Seid. Myter, sjamanisme og kjønn i vikingenes tid* (Oslo: Pax Forlag A/S, 2002); Helga Kress, "'Óparfar unnustur áttu': Um samband fjölkyngi, kvennfars og karlmennsku í Íslendingasögum," in *Galdramenn. Galdrar og samfélag á miðöldum*, ed. Torfi H. Tulinius (Reykjavík: Hugvísindastofnun Háskóla Íslands, 2008), 21–49; Jóhanna Katrín Friðriksdóttir, "Women's Weapons. A Re-Evaluation of Magic in the *Íslendingasögur*," *Scandinavian Studies* 81, no. 4 (2009): 409–36; Mitchell, *Witchcraft and Magic*, 175–200 et passim.

18 Jochens, *Old Norse Images of Women*, 130–31.

19 Richard Kieckhefer, *Magic in the Middle Ages* (Cambridge: Cambridge University Press, 1989), 9; Richard Kieckhefer, "The Specific Rationality of Medieval Magic," *American Historical Review* 99 (1994): 813–36; Michael D. Bailey, *Magic and Superstition in Europe: A Concise History from Antiquity to the Present* (Lanham, MD: Rowman & Littlefield, 2007).

20 Cf. Stephen A. Mitchell, "Spirituality and Alchemy in *Den vises sten* (1379)," in *Lärdomber oc skämptan: Medieval Swedish Literature Reconsidered*, ed. Massimiliano Bampi and Fulvio Ferrari, vol. 5, Svenska Fornskrift-Sällskapets Samlingar. Serie 3, Smärre texter och undersökningar (Uppsala: Svenska Fornskrift-Sällskapet, 2008), 97–108; Stephen A. Mitchell, "Leechbooks, Manuals, and Grimoires. On the Early History of Magical Texts in Scandinavia," *Arv. Nordic Yearbook of Folklore* 70 (2014): 57–74.

21 *Grágás. Konungsbók*, ed. Vilhjálmur Finsen (1852; Rpt. Odense: Universitetsforlag, 1974), 22–23; *Laws of Early Iceland: Grágás. I. The Codex Regius of Grágás, with Material from Other Manuscripts*, ed. and trans. Andrew Dennis, Peter Foote and Richard Perkins (Winnipeg: University of Manitoba Press, 1980), 39. The translators' use of the terms "black sorcery" and "black magic" is not literal but is intended to sharpen the difference between *galldra eþa gørningar. eþa fiolkýngi* "spells or witchcraft or magic" for which lesser outlawry is appropriate and the more sinister form of magic, *fordæðuskapr*, for which full outlawry is required.

22 *The Earliest Norwegian Laws, being the Gulathing Law and the Frostathing Law*, trans. Laurence Marcellus Larson, vol. 20, Records of Civilization, Sources and Studies (New York: Columbia University Press, 1935), 58; *Norges gamle Love indtil 1387*, ed. R. Keyser and P. A. Munch (Christiania: Chr. Gröndahl, 1846–95), I:19.

23 Tolley, *Shamanism in Norse Myth and Magic*, 131–32; *Postola sögur. Legendariske fortællinger om apostlernes liv, deres kamp for kristendommens udbredelse, samt deres martyrdød*, ed. C. R. Unger (Christiania: B.M. Bentzen, 1874), 914.

24 Cf. Mitchell, *Witchcraft and Magic*, 131–36; and Stephen A. Mitchell, "*Ketils saga hængs, Friðþjófs saga frækna*, and the Reception of the *Canon Episcopi* in Medieval Iceland," in *Skemmtiligastar Lygisögur: Studies in Honour of Galina Glazyrina*, ed. Tatjana N. Jackson and Elena A. Melnikova (Moscow: Russian Academy of Sciences. Dmitry Pozharskiy University, 2012), 138–47.

25 *Samling af Sweriges Gamla Lagar. Corpus iuris Sueco-Gotorum antiqui*, ed. D. C. J. Schlyter [vols. 1–2 ed. with D. H. S. Colin] (vols. 1–3, Stockholm; vols. 4–13, Lund: vol. 1, Z. Haeggström; vols. 2–3, Norstedt & Söner; vols. 4–13, Gleerups, 1822–77), I: 38. Important early discussions of this curious passage include Evald Lidén, "Ett par fornsvenska bidrag," in *Svenska studier tillägnade Gustaf Cederschiöld den 25 juni 1914* (Lund: C.W.K. Gleerup, 1914), 413–18; Hugo Pipping, "Fornsvenskt lagspråk. V. Studier över *Äldre Västgötalagen*," *Studier i nordisk filologi* 7, no. 1 (1915): 68–71; Emanuel Linderholm, "Nordisk magi. Studier i nordisk religions- och kyrkohistoria," *Svenska landsmål och svenskt folkliv* B.20 (1918): 141–42; *Svenska landskapslagar*. ed. and trans. Åke Holmbäck and Elias Wessén, 2nd unrev. edn. (1933–46; Rpt., Stockholm: AWE/Geber, 1979), V:xi-xxxvii.

26 Mitchell, *Witchcraft and Magic*, 150–52.

27 *Norges gamle Love indtil 1387*, I:362.

28 *Norges gamle Love indtil 1387*, I:17; *The earliest Norwegian Laws*, 56–57.

29 *Norges gamle Love indtil 1387*, I:17–18; *The earliest Norwegian Laws*, 56–57.

30 *Samling af Sweriges Gamla Lagar*, X:273–82.

31 *Edda. Die Lieder des Codex Regius nebst verwandten Denkmälern. I. Text*, 5th rev. edn., ed. Gustav Neckel and Hans Kuhn (Heidelberg: Carl Winter. Universitätsverlag, 1983); *The Poetic Edda*, trans. Carolyne Larrington (Oxford: Oxford University Press, 1999); John McKinnell, "Wisdom from the Dead: The *Ljóðatal* section of *Hávamál*," *Medium Aevum* 76, no. 1 (2007): 85–115.

32 On this aspect of the poem, see Konstantin Reichardt, "Die Liebesbeschwörung in *Fǫr Scírnis*," *Journal of English and Germanic Philology* 38 (1939): 481–95; Stephen A. Mitchell, "Anaphrodisiac Charms in the Nordic Middle Ages: Impotence, Infertility, and Magic," *Norveg* 38 (1998): 19–42; Stephen A. Mitchell, "*Skírnismál* and Nordic Charm Magic," in *Reflections on Old Norse Myths*, ed. Pernille Hermann, Jens Peter Schjødt and Rasmus Tranum Kristense, (Turnhout: Brepols, 2007), 75–94.

33 Cf. *Fornaldar Sögur Nordrlanda, eptir gömlum handritum*, ed. Carl C. Rafn, (Copenhagen: n.p., 1829–30); *Seven Viking Romances*, trans. Hermann Pálsson and Paul Edwards (Harmondsworth, England & New York: Penguin Books, 1985); Claiborne W. Thompson, "The Runes in *Bósa saga ok Herrauðs*," *Scandinavian Studies* 50, no. 1 (1978): 50–6; Mitchell, *Witchcraft and Magic*, 190.

34 *Snorri Sturluson. Heimskringla I*, ed. Bjarni Aðalbjarnarson, vol. 26, Íslenzk fornrit (1941; Rpt., Reykjavík: Hið íslenzka fornritafélag, 1962); *Heimskringla. History of the Kings of Norway by Snorri Sturluson*, trans. Lee M. Hollander (1964; Rpt., Austin: University of Texas Press for the American-Scandinavian Foundation, 2005).

35 *Snorri Sturluson, Heimskringla; Heimskringla; Eyrbyggia saga. Brands þáttr ǫrva. Eiríks saga rauða. Grænlendinga saga. Grænlendinga þáttr*, vol. 4, ed. Einar Ól. Sveinsson and Matthías Þórðarson, Íslenzk fornrit (1935; Rpt., Reykjavík: Hið íslenzka fornritafélag, 1957); *The Vinland Sagas. The Norse Discovery of America. Grænlendinga Saga and Eirik's Saga*. trans. Magnus Magnusson and Hermann Pálsson (Hammondsworth: Penguin, 1965); *Egils saga Skalla-Grímssonar*, Sigurður Nordal, vol. 2, Íslenzk fornrit (1933; Rpt., Reykjavík: Hið íslenzka fornritafélag, 1979); *Egil's Saga*, trans. Hermann Pálsson and Paul Edwards (Harmondsworth: Penguin, 1980); *Fornaldar Sögur Nordrlanda; Seven Viking Romances*, trans. Hermann Pálsson and Edwards; *Grettis saga Ásmundarsonar. Bandmanna saga. Odds þáttr Ófeigssonar*, ed. Guðni Jónsson, vol. 7, Íslenzk fornrit (1936; Rpt., Reykjavík: Hið íslenzka fornritafélag, 1964); *Grettir's saga*, trans. Denton Fox and Hermann Pálsson (Toronto: University of Toronto Press, 1985).
36 E.g. Strömbäck, *Sejd*; Dillmann, *Les magiciens dans l'Islande ancienne*; Tolley, *Shamanism*; Mitchell, *Witchcraft and Magic*.
37 E.g. Jochens, *Old Norse Images*; Friðriksdóttir, Women's Weapons, 409–36; Mitchell, *Witchcraft and Magic*.
38 *Ett Forn-Svenskt Legendarium, innehållande Medeltids Kloster-Sagor om Helgon, Påfvar och Kejsare ifrån det 1:sta till det XIII:de Århundradet*, vol. 7, Svenska Fornskrift-Sällskapets Samlingar, ed. George Stephens and F. A. Dahlgren (Stockholm: P. A. Norstedt och Söner, 1847–74); *Siælinna thrøst*, ed. Samuel Henning, vol. 59, Svenska Fornskrift-Sällskapets Samlingar (Uppsala: Almqvist & Wiksells Boktryckeri AB, 1954); *Konung Alexander. En medeltids dikt från latinet vänd i svenska rim omkring år 1380 på föranstaltande af riksdrotset Bo Jonsson Grip efter den enda kända handskriften*, vol. 12, Svenska Fornskrift-Sällskapets Samlingar, ed. Gustaf E. Klemming (Stockholm: P. A. Norstedt och Söner, 1862).
39 *Theodorici Monachi Historia de antiquitate regum Norwagiensium*. In *Monumenta Historica Norvegiae. Latinske Kildeskrifter til Norges Historie i Middelalderen*, ed. Gustav Storm (Christiania: A. W. Brøgger, 1880), 18–19; *Theodoricus Monachus. An Account of the Ancient History of the Norwegian Kings*, vol. 11, Viking Society for Northern Research Text Series, ed. and trans. David McDougall and Ian McDougall (London: Viking Society for Northern Research, 1998), 15.
40 Cf. Mitchell, *Witchcraft and Magic*, 33–34.
41 "Olim enim quidam magicę artis imbuti, Thor uidelicet et Othinus aliique complures miranda prestigiorum machinatione callentes, obtentis simplicium animis diuinitatis sibi fastigium arrogare coeperunt. Quippe Noruagiam, Suetiam ac Daniam uanissimę credulitatis laqueis circumuentas ad cultus sibi pendendi studium concitantes precipuo ludificationis suę contagio resperserunt." *Saxo Grammaticus. Gesta Danorum. Danmarkshistorien*, ed. Karsten Friis-Jensen and trans. (into Danish) Peter Zeeberg (Copenhagen: Det Danske Sprog- og Litteraturselskab / Gads forlag, 2005), 6.5.3; *Saxo Grammaticus. The History of the Danes. I. Text*, ed. H. R. Ellis Davidson and trans. Peter Fisher (Cambridge: D. S. Brewer, 1979), 170. Cf. the essays in Karsten Friis-Jensen, ed. *Saxo Grammaticus: A Medieval Author between Norse and Latin Culture*, vol. 2, Danish Medieval History & Saxo Grammaticus: A Symposium Held in Celebration of the 500th Anniversary of the University of Copenhagen (Copenhagen: Museum Tusculanum Press. 1981).
42 Edward B. Tylor, *Primitive Culture: Researches into the Development of Mythology, Philosophy, Religion, Art, and Custom* (London: J. Murray, 1871).
43 Carl Darling Buck, *A Dictionary of Selected Synonyms in the Principal Indo-European Languages: A Contribution to the History of Ideas* (Chicago: University of Chicago Press, 1949); Jan de Vries. *Altnordisches etymologisches Wörterbuch*, 2nd rev. edn. (Leiden: Brill, 1962).
44 Cf. the analyses in, e.g. Jochens, *Old Norse Images of Women*; Dillmann, *Les magiciens dans l'Islande ancienne*; and Mitchell, *Witchcraft and Magic*.
45 Cf. the overviews and discussions in, e.g. Anders Bæksted, *Målruner og Troldruner: Runmagiske Studier* (Copenhagen: Gyldendal, 1952) and Stephen E. Flowers, *Runes and Magic. Magical Formulaic Elements in the Older Runic Tradition*, vol. 53, American University Studies (New York: Peter Lang, 1986).
46 Two anthologies of runic inscriptions relating to magic, *Runes, Magic and Religion: A Sourcebook*, vol. 10, Studia medievalia Septentrionalia, ed. John McKinnell, Rudolf Simek and Klaus Düwel (Vienna: Fassbaender, 2004) and *Runic Amulets and Magic Objects*, ed. Mindy MacLeod, and Bernard Mees (Woodbridge, UK and Rochester, NY: Boydell & Brewer, 2006), have in recent years supplemented the excellent electronic file of transcriptions, transliterations and translations available through Lennart Elmevik, Lena Peterson and Henrik Williams. *Samnordisk Runtextdatabas* (Uppsala: Institutionen för nordiska språk, Uppsala universitet, 1993–). Available at www.runforum.nordiska.uu.se/samnord/.

47 *Runes, Magic and Religion*, 65–66; *Runic Amulets*, 27–29.
48 This and other uses of the pagan gods in runic inscriptions from Bergen are addressed in James E. Knirk, "Tor og Odin i runer på Bryggen i Bergen," *Arkeo* 1 (1995): 27–30.
49 This reading follows the interpretation suggested by Jonna Louis-Jensen and James Knirk.
50 *Det arnamagnæanske Håndskrift Nr. 187 i oktav, indholdende en dansk Lægebog*, ed. Viggo Såby (Copenhagen: Thieles Bogtrykkeri for Universitets-Jubilæets danske Samfund, 1886).
51 *Vinjeboka. Den eldste svartebok fra norsk middelalder*, ed. Oskar Garstein (Oslo: Solum, 1993), 26; nos. 7, 12, 13 and 18.
52 Cf. Erik Moltke, "Medieval Rune-Amulets in Denmark," *Acta Etnologica* 3 (1938): 116–47; Signe Horn Fuglesang, "Viking and Medieval Amulets in Scandinavia," *Fornvännen* 84 (1989): 15–25; *Runic Amulets*.
53 Cf. Anne Carlie, *Forntida byggnadskult. Tradition och regionalitet i södra Skandinavien*, vol. 57 Riksantikvarieämbetet Arkeologiska undersökningar, skrifter (Stockholm: Riksantikvarieämbetets förlag, 2004).
54 Ann-Britt Falk, "My Home is My Castle. Protection against Evil in Medieval Times," in *Old Norse Religion in Long-term Perspectives: Origins, Changes, and Interactions*, ed. Anders Andrén, Kristina Jennbert and Catharina Raudvere (Lund: Nordic Academic Press, 2006), 200–05; Ann-Britt Falk, *En grundläggande handling: Byggnadsoffer och dagligt liv i medeltid* (Lund: Nordic Academic Press, 2008).
55 Major anthologies of Nordic charms, arranged by national tradition, include *Danmarks Trylleformler*, vol. 3, Folklore Fellows Publications. Northern ser., ed. Ferdinand Ohrt (Copenhagen & Christiania: Gyldendal and Nordisk Forlag, 1917–21); Jón Árnason, ed. *Íslenzkar þjóðsögur og æventýri*, 2nd edn., rev. Árni Böðvarsson and Bjarni Vilhjálmsson (Reykjavík: Bókaútgáfan þjóðsaga, 1954–61); *Norske Hexeformularer og Magiske Opskrifter*, vol. 1, Videnskabsselskabets Skrifter. II. Historisk-filos. Klasse, ed. A. Chr. Bang (Christiania: Jacob Dybwad, 1901); *Signelser ock besvärjelser från medeltid ock nytid*, vol. 41, Svenska landsmål och svenskt folkliv. B, ed. Emanuel Linderholm (Stockholm: Norstedt, 1917–40).
56 E.g. DuBois, *Nordic Religions*, Price, *The Viking Way*.
57 Cf. Sten Lindroth, *Svensk lärdomshistoria. Medeltiden, reformationstiden* (1975; Rpt. n.p.: Norstedt, 1989).
58 Jan Wall, *Tjuvmjölkande väsen*, vols. 3, 5, Acta universitatis Upsaliensis. Studia ethnologia Upsaliensis (Stockholm: Almqvist & Wiksell, 1977–78), I: 75–86.
59 On these traditions, see Dror Segev, *Medieval Magic and Magicians – in Norway and Elsewhere: Based upon 12th-15th centuries Manuscript and Runic Evidence*, vol 2, Senter for studier i vikingtid og nordisk middelalder. Skriftserie (Oslo: Senter for studier i vikingtid og nordisk middelalder, 2001), and on the Victorine connections, see David Brégaint, *Vox regis: Royal Communication in High Medieval Norway*, vol. 74, The Northern World: North Europe and the Baltic c. 400–1700 AD. Peoples, Economics and Cultures (Leiden: Brill, 2015), 94–5; and especially, Richard Cole, "The Jew Who Wasn't There: Studies on Jews and Their Absence in Old Norse Literature", (Ph.D. Dissertation, Harvard University, 2015), 75–95.
60 Cf. Mitchell, "Leechbooks, Manuals, and Grimoires," 57–74; and Sigvard Skov, "Henrik Harpestreng og middelalderens medicin," *Danske Studier* 45 (1945): 125–39.
61 E.g. Falk, *En grundläggande handling*; Price, "The Archaeology of *Seiðr*," 109–26; Leszek Gardeła, "The Dangerous Dead? Rethinking Viking-Age Deviant Burials," in *Conversions: Looking for Ideological Change in the Early Middle Ages*, vol. 23, Studia Medievalia Septentrionalia, ed. L. Słupecki and R. Simek (Vienna: Fassbaender, 2013), 99–136.
62 Mitchell, "*Skírnismál* and Nordic Charm Magic"; Terry Gunnell, "'Magical Mooning' and the 'Goatskin Twirl': 'Other' Kinds of Female Magical Practices in Early Iceland," in *Nordic Mythologies: Interpretations, Intersections, and Institutions*, ed. Timothy J. Tangherlini (Berkeley and Los Angeles: North Pinehurst Press, 2014), 133–53. Here one should also acknowledge those modern heathens who strive to develop performance practices appropriate to these older materials, whether one agrees with their results or not. Cf. Michael Strmiska, "Ásatrú in Iceland: The Rebirth of Nordic Paganism?" *Nova Religio: The Journal of Alternative and Emergent Religions* 4, no. 1 (2000): 106–32.
63 Lea T. Olsan, "Charms in Medieval Memory," in *Charms and Charming in Europe*, ed. Jonathan Roper (London: Palgrave Macmillan, 2004), 59–88.
64 Stephen Mitchell, Neil Price, et al., "Witchcraft and Deep Time – A Debate at Harvard," *Antiquity* 84 (2010): 2.

PART III

KEY GENRES AND FIGURES

12

FROM HERMETIC MAGIC TO THE MAGIC OF MARVELS

Antonella Sannino

Hermetic magic and the magic of marvels are two of the most characteristic features of medieval and early modern magic. They did not form a single coherent genre, but rather were two different sources of astrological techniques that were categorized frequently under the natural sciences and empirical and experimental approaches to nature. The magical texts associated with the names Hermes, Belenus and Toz Graecus, which form the basis of Hermetic magic, have been identified by modern scholars as a distinctive group, with a common origin.[1] The most significant magic text to treat marvels, the *Book of the Marvels of the World (De mirabilibus mundi)*, has recently received detailed attention from scholars who have examined its sources. This paper will focus on the relationships between these two different genres of magic. Both are centred on how magic operates to create artificial life. The Hermetic image magic texts deal with instructions for the drawing down of spiritual power or celestial virtue into objects, in order to transform them into instruments of magical action,[2] whilst the magic of marvels represents an attempt to situate magical practices within a broader natural philosophical framework.

David Pingree, in his essay *From Hermes to Jabir*, has shown that three cultural traditions – symbolically represented in the legend of the "three Hermes" (Egyptian, Harranian and Mesopotamian) – contributed to the variety of Hermetic techniques for creating artificial life. Here, we will deal with the first and second.[3] The first cultural tradition contributing to Hermetic magic has roots in the Egyptian art of vivifying statues, Proclus's telestic art and the rituals of the Sabians. Magical texts in this tradition describe how to induce planetary spirits to enter talismans made of metal, stone or wood at astrologically appropriate times. The second tradition of Hermetic magic is based on Plato, Aristotle and Galen and includes works such as the pseudo-Platonic *Liber vaccae (Book of the Cow)*. This tradition describes the artificial generation of animals using semen, wombs and magical substances.[4] Conversely, the *Book of the Marvels of the World* operates only with hidden forces in nature, which are its "images" and "forms". Its talismanic magic in this tradition uses planetary forces channelled through amulets and talismans, reflecting the principles of the Universe.

Many scholars have stated that a large number of the recipes present in the *Book of the Marvels* have been taken from the *Liber vaccae* or the *Liber Aneguemis minor*, a Latin translation of the *Kitâb al-Nâwamîs*. David Pingree has also suggested that the connection between the *De proprietatibus*, a twelfth-century Latin translation of Ibn-al Jazzar's work *Kitâb Al-Khawass*, and the *Book of the Marvels of the World* needs further investigation:

> Some of the magical practices described in the *De proprietatibus* are attributed to numerous Greek and Arab authorities. These are found also in Qustâ ibn Lûqâ's

De phisicis ligatures and in *De mirabilibus mundi* which is attributed to Albertus Magnus. The interrelation of these and other texts on amulets remains to be investigated.[5]

Maaike van der Lugt has analysed the *Liber vaccae*'s manuscripts, examining the strong links between the *Liber vaccae* and the *De proprietatibus*, as well as the influence of these two works on the Latin treatise, the *Book of the Marvels of the World*.[6] The critical edition of the *Book of the Marvels of the World* and the study of its sources and concepts have shown that the anonymous author of this text borrowed extensively from *De proprietatibus* and the *Liber vaccae* but also from other sources, such as the *Picatrix*, the Latin translation of the *Ghāyat al-hakīm*, which draws on rituals originating in the practices of the Sabians of Harran; the *De radiis* of Al-Kindi, translated from Arabic before 1259; the *Liber ignium* of Marcus Graecus that mentions Hermes as an authority; and a Hermetic text, the *Kyranides*, which describes the magical and therapeutic properties of birds, fishes, plants and stones.

The *Book of the Marvels of the World* and the Latin Hermetic magic texts

My discussion of the relationship between the magic of marvels and the Latin Hermetic texts is centred on two points: a) formal aspects; b) content aspects.

The Latin Hermetic texts deal with sympathetic, amuletic and talismanic magic, so Hermetic magic can be divided into natural magic (for example, the *Kyranides* and the *Liber de quattuor confectionibus ad omnia genera animalium capienda*, discussed below) and ceremonial magic. Almost all the Hermetic texts on ceremonial magic are as yet unpublished and they can be classified according to the manuscripts' attributions to Hermes, Belenus, Toz Graecus and Toz Graecus – Germa Babilonensis.[7] A study of the sources of the *Book of the Marvels of the World* showed the links in terms of content between this work and the sympathetic magic of the *Kyranides* and the *Liber de quattuor confectionibus*. In particular, the manuscript Montpellier, École de médecine, MS H 277 is very useful for understanding the precise links between the different magical traditions that are found in the *Book of the Marvels of the World*.[8]

In contrast, we know less about the links within the Hermetic ceremonial magic *corpus*. All of these writings were translated from Arabic to Latin over a century between the first half of the 1100s and the first decades of the 1200s, continuing to c. 1260. According to David Pingree and Vittoria Perrone Compagni, most of these texts reached the West from the Muslim world between the end of the eleventh century and the first half of the twelfth. These ceremonial writings present

> themselves in the form of mere collections of precepts [...]; like all learned magic, Hermetic magic has its institutional basis in astrology. The direct relationship between the motion of the stars and sublunary events, the existence of a specific influence of each celestial body on given aspects of worldly life and hence the possibility of establishing causal links by calculable laws [...]; the texts include operative rituals such as prayers, suffumigations, and pronunciations and writing of mysterious names.[9]

Talismanic magic uses planetary forces channelled through amulets and talismans, according to the principles of the universe. In the *Picatrix*, for example, planetary forces are used to perform spells, and to prepare poisons or medicines, with the aim (for example) of helping someone gain their beloved or have revenge on their enemy.[10] The talisman acts as the connection between heavenly virtues and earthly virtues. One who wants to learn the system of making talismans has to know in depth the science of correspondences between the planets, and of constellations and conjunctions relating to movements in the heavens.[11] He must ensure that the Moon is in a favourable position. To harness the best of the talisman's power, the enchanter should use a material which is suitable to receive the strength of the heavenly bodies, and wait for the right time and place. These two factors and the movements of the planets are crucial to the success of the spell. It is also essential that the enchanter has confidence in himself. Then, he can add words and prayers. A good example is found in *Picatrix*, book III chapters six and seven,[12] but we can also find these concepts in the Hermetic *Liber orationum planetarum septem*, which survives in three manuscripts and was edited by Perrone Compagni in 2001.[13] The theoretical basis of these concepts lies in the art of animating statues or rather the art of creating artificial life, as it is described in *Asclepius*.[14] William of Auvergne in the thirteenth century was aware of these works and he made a classification of them that constitutes a very important source.[15]

Hermetic ceremonial magic involves invoking intelligent spiritual essences (*spiritus*) linked to the planets. These essences differ from Christian angels and they are invoked through an *imago*, in order to focus the action on the world, and to force, bend and dominate nature. The Hermetic *spiritus* represents an ordering principle, a quickening of reality and the merging of an astrological conception of the world with a spiritual one. In this way, the kind of *vivificatio* found in these operational texts is not the sort that invokes the soul of a demon to settle in the talisman. The idea of *spiritus* can be identified with *virtus* or "virtue.": As a result of the encounter between correctly disposed matter and the *spiritus* of a particular celestial body, the talisman receives its power. From Hermetic magical texts therefore, there emerges a conception of magic that engages with practical aspects of knowledge of the world, based on the principle of experience. Similarly, in the *Book of the Marvels of the World*, magic is based on two principles: experience and authority. The enchanter must have a good moral disposition, and follow the correct diet and an appropriate lifestyle. In the *Asclepius*, for example, it is written that meat is prohibited.[16]

Vittoria Perrone Compagni has shown how two translators of Hermetic texts, Adelard of Bath and Herman of Carinthia, strove to present magic as a useful and powerful art in the scientific *curriculum*. They strove to legitimize it as the *operating side of astrology*. "Adelard renders the *Liber planetarum ex Scientia Abel* into Latin,[17] Herman refers to Iorma the Babylonian and Toz the Ionian as 'operators of talismans', *thelesmatici*".[18] Other translators such as John of Seville and Daniel of Morley concurred, affirming talismanic magic as a science. The problem with this approach to talismans was an ethical one, which put good Christians in a difficult position. Ultimately, magic was excluded from the philosophical curriculum not for its content, because this was recognized to be ultimately founded on astrology, but for its potential to be used for evil; indeed, it was described as the *magistra omnis iniquitatis* (the mistress of every iniquity). In Michael Scot, for example, the attitude to magic was suspended between scientific recognition and religious condemnation.[19] This ambivalent position makes clear how difficult it was to integrate this new material within traditional culture. This situation continued into the fifteenth century, as can be seen by the *Recommendatio astronomiae*, an anonymous tract defending astrology and magic in which Hermetic texts are related to the works of the accepted authority Claudius Ptolemaeus in an attempt to bring talismanic images back into the framework of science.[20]

The Hermeticism of the Latin Middle Ages represented Hermes Trismegistus as the mythical custodian of an ancient wisdom, a kind of prophet, but also as a philosopher in whose writings Arabic, Latin and Hebrew thinkers had sought answers to questions relating to theology, cosmology, ethics and the natural and occult sciences (in particular, medicine, astral magic and alchemy).[21] Recent scholarship on medieval Hermeticism, and on the magical, astrological, medical and alchemical texts that were translated from Arabic and attributed to Toz and Germa Babiloniensis, has expanded our view of Hermes Trismegistus and his image during the Middle Ages. Furthermore, scholars have recently argued that the old distinction between philosophical Hermeticism and occult Hermeticism is no longer sustainable.

Hermetic magic texts

David Pingree has suggested that the ceremonial magical literature of Arabic origin can be classified by distinguishing texts on the basis of the means used to achieve their effect: amulets or talismans. In this reading, an amulet is a stone, usually a gem, naturally endowed with occult virtues, whilst talisman is an image moulded or carved in metal, or in rare cases modelled in wax or clay. Vittoria Perrone Compagni has also introduced a distinction within Hermetic ceremonial texts according to their attribution to Hermes, Belenus and Toz Graecus.[22] I will therefore deal with ceremonial magic texts according to this useful distinction, beginning first with the group of texts attributed to Hermes, and proceeding second to those attributed to Belenus and third to those attributed to Toz Graecus.

First, I turn to an example from the group of texts attributed to Hermes, that is the *De imaginibus sive annulis septem planetarum*, which describes the manufacture of seven planetary rings. The enchanter sculpts the image of the planet on the appropriate gem, then embeds the gemstone in a ring, which belongs to the appropriate planetary rulership. The ring will exert its influence only if the enchanter complies with precise sexual and dietary prohibitions and with certain rules of conduct. For example, the Venus Ring in this text is used to arouse love, but it requires that the enchanter wears women's clothes and adorns his head "ut mulier".[23] Another text in this group, the *Liber Saturni*, part of the *Liber planetarum*, describes the creation of ten rings of Saturn. The "excavator" paints an image of Saturn on the gem, encasing it in a ring of iron while his assistants, dressed in gowns of black, begin to sing a kind of dirge (*lugubrus*), wailing and shedding tears. Magical rites with smoke, exorcisms, prayers, animal sacrifices and the lighting of candles are then performed.[24] Another of the books of the planets, the *Liber Mercurii*, describes how the craftsman should fabricate two rings in order to obtain scientific knowledge, memory and eloquence. As part of the ritual, he must ride a white mule (the sacred animal of Mercury) with a book in his hand and a crown on his head; he then recites a long prayer while an assistant performs a magic rite with smoke and the burning of incense.[25] My final example from this group of Hermetic magic texts, the *De imaginibus et horis*, describes the talismans to be fabricated at different times of the day, every day of the week.[26]

My second group of Hermetic magic texts on talismans are those attributed to Belenus, among which the most popular and well known was the *Liber imaginum Lunae*. This work lists the talismans to be created when the moon is in each of its twenty-eight mansions. The mansions refer to a star or a group of stars in which the moon appears or rests every night during its monthly orbit.[27] This composite text includes the *De viginti quattuor horis*, which lists the names of each of the twenty-four hours, specifies the classes of bodies that, in every single hour, direct their prayers to God, and for each hour indicates the projects that can be brought to completion.[28] The *De imaginibus diei et noctis* is an amplification of the original Arabic version of *De viginti quattour horis* and indicates the rules and precepts for fabricating the talismans in a twenty-four hour period.[29] Paolo Lucentini has transcribed the *Liber imaginum lunae* and the *De viginiti quattuor horis* from the copy of the *Liber introductorius* in Munich, Bayerische Staatsbibliothek, MS CLM 10268.[30] My final example from this group is the *De imaginibus septem planetarum* which describes the fabrication of planetary talismans made from the metal appropriate to each planet, and at an appropriate day and time. The talisman must then be filled with spices, burned to create a mystical smoke, folded up in a cloth upon which a seal of the planet has been painted, and buried.[31]

In my third category, the amuletic writings attributed to Toz, the *De lapidibus veneris* lists ten stones belonging to the dominion of Venus. The occult properties described in this text are medical and there are no ritual elements. For this reason, the level of magic present in the text can be categorized as natural.[32] A further text in this group, the *De stationibus ad cultum Veneris*, according to the title which William of Auvergne cites, has many ties to the *Liber Veneris* (that is the text on this planet that forms part of the *Liber Planetarum*) and therefore is probably the same text. The version of this text in Marciana National Library of Venice, MS lat. XIV was translated by John of Seville.[33] This *Liber Veneris* is attributed to Toz Graecus and/or Germa Babilonensis, the "second Hermes" who lived after the flooding of Babylon, and (in contrast to the *De lapidibus veneris*) presents a form of talismanic magic with highly pronounced ceremonial components.[34]

Turning now to the Hermetic texts belonging to the category of natural magic, the *Kyranides*, referenced as an authority by the *Book of the Marvels of the World*, describes in alphabetical order the magical healing powers of plants, animals and stones, and their secret relationships.[35] Also entitled *The Book of Physical Virtues, Diseases and Treatments or Liber Medicinalis*, this work is made up of two sections, the *Kyranis* attributed to the Persian king Kyranus, and the *Liber Therapeutikos* by Harpokration of Alexandria. It was compiled by a Byzantine author between the fifth and eighth centuries and was probably translated into Latin by the cleric Paschalis Romanus in 1169 at Constantinople. The first *Kyranis*, said to have been carved in Syriac characters on an iron pillar, was given by Hermes Trismegistus to men so that they could be educated about the virtues of plants, fish, birds and twenty-four stones, alphabetically ordered according to the Greek alphabet. The treatise has three bestiaries in Greek alphabetical order, and instructions for preparing potions and talismans with medicinal and magical properties.[36]

A second significant work of natural magic attributed to Hermes is the *Liber de quattuor confectionibus ad omnia genera animalium capienda*, the Latin translation of an Arabic treatise in the form of a dialogue. Preserved in a single manuscript, the text is mentioned by the author of the *Speculum astronomiae* and by William of Auvergne in his *De universo*. The dialogue between Hermes and Aristoas (Aristotle) in this text describes four confections for catching wolves, wild beasts, birds and reptiles. *Suffumigationes* and prayers to the *spiritus animalium* to obtain their obedience follow recipes using animal and plant substances. The *secreta* of the confections was revealed by Arod, namely the archangel Gabriel, to Ismenus, that is Adam. This kind of magic is very different from Hermetic ceremonial magic, and is much more similar to the magical procedures in the *Book of the Marvels of the World*.[37] The recipes are limited to using the occult properties of physical things, by means of a simple practical application of the knowledge of the relationships between the stars and the events of the sublunary world; therefore, it is a type of talismanic magic that includes only three elements: astrological knowledge, the figure to be engraved and the material used.

Platonic magic

The *Liber Aneguemis* (or *Nemith* or *Neumich*) also known as the *Liber vaccae* (from the first version) is the Latin translation, made in Spain in the thirteenth century, of an apocryphal Arabic text from the ninth century. The Arabic version, the *Kitāb 'an-nawāmīs*, today remains only in small fragments, preserved in a manuscript at the Bibliothèque National in Paris. This text, attributed to Abu Zayd Hunanyn ibn Ishāq Sulaymān ibn Ayyūb 'al-'Ibādī, appears to be a translation from the Greek of a work by Galen in which he comments on *The Laws of Plato*. The *Liber vaccae* has been considered "the dark side of *Picatrix*": if the *Ghāyat al-Hakīm* is concerned with the use and manipulation of celestial forces with the help of talismans in order to govern the world, the *Liber vaccae* contains recipes to create animals with the ability to reason, as well as recipes that enable the operator to speak with demons, become invisible and perform many other occult acts. It is a Hermetic text of natural magic that can also be linked to alchemy. One indication of Hermetic origins is noted by David Pingree who, in "From Hermes to Jābir and the *Book of the Cow*", hypothesized that the word *nawāmīs*, transcribed *namusa*, and meaning "secrets", is not in fact the Greek *nomos*, meaning law. Thus, the term *tegumentum*, which is found in the Latin prologue and which means the hiding or keeping of secrets, can be explained. The original Syriac version would be the work of Thabit ibn Qurra, and the *Kitāb 'an-nawāmīs* attributable to the prophet Hermes.[38]

The *Liber vaccae* is divided into two books, the *Aneguemis maior*, with forty-six experiments and the *Aneguemis minor* with forty-one, introduced with a commentary by pseudo-Hunayn. The contents of these two books are set out in the prologue. This refers to the preparation and preliminary study of the plants, stones, animals and tools required for the magical operation:

> Ignorance is not an excuse not to learn about this topic, neither for those who read it, nor for someone who already knows or meditates. It means that the lack of knowledge of the tool to be used in an operation, or the name of a species, mineral, vegetable, animal or some wonder results in failure. I have already spoken about it: that first the operators should strive to identify the ingredients they do not know, identifying them by their reputation, and only then [should they] begin to work. This knowledge is what we can get from this work: so, you learn.[39]

In the recipes, the virtues of plants and stones, and the power of organs and parts of animals are used as tools that enable the operator to walk all over the globe, speak with demons, create rational animals or change the appearance of himself or the objects of his operations. The first four operations are aimed at generating a rational animal, bees and oxen without mating, using in the first case an animal as artificial incubator.

The *Book of the Marvels of the World*

The *Book of the Marvels of the World* is an anonymous work, wrongly attributed to Albertus Magnus, and probably written between 1223 and 1273 in Paris. The work fits into the medieval discussion on *Quid sit magia*. Focusing on its contents, the *Book of the Marvels of the World* is a collection of extravagant prescriptions, framed within two discussions of philosophical and scientific theories. It can be subdivided into: a) Prologue; b) *Experimenta* and c) Epilogue. The prologue has a theoretical–philosophical emphasis and is the most original section of the work. The *Experimenta* are precepts, formulas and mixtures. This is the prescriptive part of the text where the theory is put into practice. Here, the theoretical and speculative level of the previous pages is debased to the level of recipe and ritual, more typical of other hermetic magic texts. In this middle section, the prescriptions for lamps and the fire derived from the work of Marcus Graecus, and experiments from the *Aneguemis minor* and the *De proprietatibus* come together. On the one hand, our author seems to deliberately ignore the *Aneguemis maior*, recognizing, in a sort of self-censorship, the danger of mixtures between humans and animals. On the other hand, the debt of the *De mirabilibus* towards the *Aneguemis minor* or *Liber vaccae* is great, as has already been shown.[40] In fact, the philosophical momentum of the first and third parts includes a not insignificant percentage of originality. In the *Epilogue*, the reflection returns to a "learned" mode. The conclusion is almost symmetrical, even stylistically, to the *Prologue*.

The magic in the *Book of the Marvels of the World* can be located particularly:

a. In the form of organic magic that originates in the *Liber Aneguemis minor*;
b. In the form of magic that works through the senses to bind men. The incantations, orations and spoken formulas work through the sense of hearing. Characters that are figuratively inscribed work through the sense of seeing. *Veneficia*, which can refer to poisons or potions, works through the sense of taste.

These different registers do not result in a stylistically crude attempt to hand down *experimenta*, derived from works that are part of the Hermetic and pseudo-Platonic traditions. Rather, they reveal a conscious decision, a choice to highlight the non-abominable nature, *praeter naturam*, of mixtures of human and animal. These qualities had become more credible during the thirteenth century because of the *Liber vaccae*, but were often viewed as abominable. By contrast, the author of the *Book of the Marvels of the World* decided to hand down ancient teachings that revealed the extraordinary phenomena of nature, the secrets it hides and that scholars in turn concealed in order to excite the wonder of the common people. The task of the wise man is presented in a clear and incisive way: to unpack and reveal the things that seem extraordinary to man, discovering the causes within an *ordo rerum* regulated by sympathetic principles. The author speaks in the first person and makes reference to the common people, and writes in a long-winded and formulaic style. The secrets or *experimenta* are usually introduced by the formula: "Si vis igitur experimentari". The epistemological criteria identified by the author fall in two main areas: experience and tradition; in this way, the text has a double perspective, that of practice and that of theory.

A significant example of this double perspective is the author's reference to the authority of Avicenna when he explains how ligatures work. Ligatures can be done:

a. When the human soul is affected by a great passion, whether this is love or hate. This passion can convert desire into action. For Avicenna, passion lies in the transitive and creative imagination, and only the Prophet can convert this into action. In the *Book of the Marvels of the World* by contrast, it is extended to all kinds of souls.
b. When the operator is able to use a sympathetic correspondence between things. This kind of ligature is based on the idea that one can influence something based on its relationship or resemblance to another thing.

This emphasis on a great emotional feeling or desire of the soul is a marker of the influence of Al-Kindi. The power of the imagination described by Avicenna is connected to the idea of desire as a force in the operation discussed by Al-Kindi.[41] The author of the *Book of the Marvels of the World* does not worry about the free will of the recipient of the ligature, nor does he manifest concerns of a theological type; what matters is the strong imaginative determination of the operator. The recipient, who is naturally inclined or endowed with determination and passions just as the enchanter is, can, however, break the ligature, if he or she has the strength to do so.

In the *Book of the Marvels of the World*, some actions appear to be secret and mysterious because their causes are unknown. But these causes can be found in a doctrine of similarity and universal sympathy, which this text explains with reference to the authority of philosophers, doctors, alchemists and astrologers. All things attract things with like qualities, and they repel things with opposite qualities. It is not secret – we read in the *Book of the Marvels of the World* – and hidden from the people that every like thing suffers with the things it is like, or loves, moves and embraces them.

Every living thing has a natural inclination towards its own species, and has active and rational virtues that lead them to others like themselves. This virtue is a force that drives and infects things, depending on their species, but also depending on the individual. It is interesting to note the use of two words in this magic text, "publicum" (in the sense of known) and "verificatum" (verified and understood by all men), terms close to scientific language, that are used to attest the veracity of an action that seems far removed from modern standards of science. The ligature is also mysterious (secret) and can be explained by experience rather than science. Thus, this phenomenon still remains suspended between scientific language and mystery, even though the text does not refer to either scientific demonstration or magic-philosophical revelation.

The *similitudo* between primary and secondary properties, innate and accidental properties, and the related antagonism between species demonstrates a cosmological conception that revolves around the doctrine of specific form, "virtus activa rationabilis" and that of natural images. According to this doctrine, every living thing has its own virtue that derives from the planets and is in accord with its own celestial image. This correspondence of images between a created entity and an astrological figuration illustrates a sort of astrological determinism.[42]

The Book of the Marvels of the World therefore outlines a sympathetic Cosmos, in which every living thing consists of different proportions of the elements, and where each species is endowed with an obscure *virtus rationabilis* determined by and dependent on the planets, in a world centred on correspondences between heaven and earth. Man is the final cause of the Universe. He is the end of natural things, and all natural things are for him.[43] These philosophical echoes of the anthropology of the *Picatrix*[44] and of some passages in *Asclepius* VI,[45] relating to man as *minor mundi*, contribute to the presentation of man as a great wonder in the *Book of the Marvels of the World*.[46] No theological problems emerge: there is never a reference to nature as created and man and his knowledge lose the sacral aura which they possess in the *Picatrix*. The wise man is not a priest and the pursuit of knowledge and understanding does not have a soteriological and eschatological function here. In fact, the magician-philosopher has a rather social role: he is a communicator of scientific knowledge, although at times he rises to the tone of a prophet, who appears to reveal secrets.

As in the Hermetic texts, here magic emerges as knowledge that gives power. Secrets and wonders, however, require a specific course of study that the author claims to have learned from Plato's *Liber Regimentis*, that is, the *Liber vaccae*. In the *Book of the Marvels of the World*, the *curriculum studiorum* for students includes dialectic, natural philosophy, astrology and necromancy.[47] Man can achieve a deep knowledge of *mirabilia*, availing himself of an art of the *trivium*, dialectic, a discipline of the *quadrivium*, astrology and necromancy, which is here understood as the knowledge of hidden things (*scientia de rebus absconditis*). However, in the *Book of the Marvels of the World*, the garb of the necromancer is not that of the makers of talismans portrayed in the *Picatrix* but rather the dress of the natural philosopher, who reveals through experience the causes of phenomena that only appear to be secret. In the *Picatrix*, necromancy is a science and an art, the knowledge and practice of "any fact concealed to the senses"[48] which involves operations drawing on intelligent spiritual essences linked to the planets. But in the *Book of the Marvels of the World*, there are no prayers, suffumigations or the pronunciation and writing of mysterious names, such as we find in the *Picatrix*, and also in Hermetic image magic texts.

The *Book of the Marvels of the World* also has some continuities with the traditions represented by the Hermetic *Kyranides* and the *Liber de quattuor confectionibus*. The *vademecum* of the natural philosopher includes knowledge of the primary qualities, heat and cold, and of natural properties. So if you want to excite cool passions, heat can help. If you want to instill courage in someone, you should advise them to carry a lion's organ, since the lion is brave as a species, or they should wear the shirt of a courtesan, who is brave as an individual (*singulariter*). Likewise, if you want to excite love, you should look for an animal that has a loving nature such as the swallow or the dove. Continuing in the field of organic magic, if you want to make someone talkative, simply bring near them the tongue of a dog or a bird. Similarly, any living being has one natural property in excess, which could be used to stimulate the same virtues in another living being, as it is proven that "every virtue moves toward what is similar".[49] This knowledge is based on experience, and that which has no visibly explicit cause is classified as a secret or a marvel.

The *Epilogue* of the *Book of the Marvels of the World* presents the following classification of marvels:

1. A rare and unusual phenomenon whose cause is unknown. This is an extraordinary manifestation of the highest grade;
2. A phenomenon that is not new or uncommon, but whose cause is unknown. The extraordinary nature of this phenomenon is of medium grade;
3. A phenomenon that is not uncommon, but whose identified cause is not in itself sufficient to provide a complete explanation for it. This phenomenon is exceptional but not in a significant way.

All these phenomena, and the actions, agents and subjects they encompass, eventually come to an end, meaning that they are brought back within the natural order.

In the final section of my discussion of the *Book of the Marvels of the World*, I discuss the origin and classification of the c. 167 recipes it contains that take up the largest portion of the text.

Thirty recipes were excerpted from the *Liber vaccae* (or *Aneguemis minor*), and others derive from Jabir's *De proprietatibus*, fPliny's *Naturalis Historia*, Albertus Magnus's *De animalibus*, the *Epistula de secretis operibus artis et naturae* attributed to Roger Bacon, and Marcus Graecus's *Liber ignium*.

The recipes can be classified with respect to their purpose, ingredients and method.

Sympathetic magic in its simplest form is the basis of many recipes that are founded on the natural qualities of stones, plants and animals. In the *Book of the Marvels of the World*, there are many recipes designed to cause birds, animals or fishes to congregate. These have a natural, magical character such as we can also find in the Hermetic *Liber de quattuor confectionibus* and in the *Kyranides*. The precepts in these three texts are greatly simplified and do not involve any of the ritualistic complications associated with Hermetic talismanic magic. Other recipes in the *Book of the Marvels of the World* deal with medicinal magic to heal men and stimulate the fertility of women, as well as early methods of Viagra; others deal with magic candles and lamps. Some of the first group of recipes are for familiar purposes: to catch birds in the hand, to ward off dogs and snakes, to catch a mole, to break charms and loose bonds, to see the future in one's sleep, to make a chicken or other animal dance in a dish and so on.

These recipes operate with regard to the following principles: an affinity or attraction between things with similar qualities or virtues; the association of second and third qualities with first quality; a distinction between qualities innate to a whole kind (species) or to individual things and antagonism between things with opposite qualities. All these principles are listed in many popular recipes, collected from philosophers and ancient authors. For example, the lion's virtue gives boldness and magnanimity; the dove, swallow and sparrow's virtue gives love; the magnet's virtue is attraction and so on. With regard to the recipes collected from the *De proprietatibus*, many authorities are cited such as Mesue, Aristotle, Galen, Avicenna, Cleopatra and Tabariensis. As Sophie Page has shown: "they seem to relate to the extraction of groups of recipes from a number of different sources which have been compiled together".[50] The references to Aristotle come from the Arabic version of Aristotle's *On Animals*. Other recipes cite only "Philosophers." According to my research, these are not only Aristotle and Pliny but also William of Auvergne, Albertus Magnus and Roger Bacon.[51] A particularly clear example of these precepts is one which takes a part of the mule or of the hare to incite carnal appetites. Other recipes are gathered from Archigenus's *Liber de aegritudibus cronicis*, and Qusta ibn Luqa, who prescribes several medical remedies using animal parts for conception, contraception, the acquisition of valuable qualities and playing tricks.

The recipes of the *Book of the Marvels of the World*, like their sources (not only the *De proprietatibus*), use the principles of sympathy and antipathy to create relationships between the animal world and the human one.[52] For example, animal parts and substances are used to effect a change in four of the human senses (touch, taste, hearing and sight); on the other hand, herbs, stones or even parts of the human body are used to affect animals. Touch and taste are stimulated by proximity and contiguity. For example, touch is stimulated by contact with an object: if a woman is anointed with the urine of a wolf, she will not conceive; if you grease the tongues of oxen with fat, they will starve. Other examples concern natural medicine: the dress of a pregnant woman can cure someone suffering from quartan fever, if he wears it; the left canine tooth of a child, placed on the skin, acts as a contraceptive. Taste implies that someone drinks or eats something; for example, in the *Book of Cleopatra*, when the woman collects two samples of mule urine each month, and drinks them, she will not conceive, and Galen says that when you eat sorrel leaves or drink its seeds mixed in a potion, this regularizes the bowels.[53] Sight and hearing imply action at distance. A good example comes from the *De Theriaca* of Galen: the Serpent which is called *Regulus* in Latin is somewhat white, and upon its head there are three hairs. When any man sees them, he will die soon.[54]

Animal substances and parts are used in the magical recipes: the ankle of a hare is said to cure colic, while sitting on the skin of lion cures haemorrhoids, etc.[55] Women are the protagonists in the precepts linked to sexuality: she gives life and she is a loving woman.

FROM HERMETIC MAGIC TO THE MAGIC OF MARVELS

Many recipes are aimed at the acquisition of love, conception, increased fertility, birth and contraception. The large numbers of precepts relating to female contraception using animal parts, as well as recipes aimed to induce women to fall in love or reveal secrets, reveal a medieval point of view: woman is more imperfect than man, she is closer to animals and for this reason is more affected by them. There are no recipes according to a female point of view: a woman cannot avoid the adultery of her husband nor increase his love.[56]

Some recipes make references to Hermetic texts; the precepts describe how to transform water into wine, and how a wet cloth placed in mercury will not burn in a fire so that the operator's hands will not burn when he touches it. This precept is ascribed to Belbinus, who is Belenus or Apollonius of Tyana (a Hermetic author), but it is not found in the *De secretis naturae* nor in the *De viginti quattuor horis* or *De imaginibus diei et noctis*.[57] In the *Book of the Marvels of the World*, Belbinus suggests taking the white of an egg and mercury and spraying a cloth with it, and washing it off with sea water. When it is dry, the operator is instructed to throw it into the fire, and it will not burn.[58] Another recipe says: when red arsenic and mercury are taken, and broken and confected with the juice of the herb *sempervivum* and the gall of a Bull, and a man sprays his hands with it, he will not be burned. Another recipe prescribes the use of the herb "portaluca" against visions.[59] There are forms of sympathetic magic like those found in the *Kyranides*.

The recipes that come from the *Liber Aneguemis minor* belong to a kind of magic totally different from natural magic and the magical pharmacopeia of the texts that we have so far considered. This kind of magic appears to be more closely related to the alchemical theories of transformation and illusion. It includes recipes for changing the shape of a man into that of an elephant or horse by means of lamps; producing the illusions of specific shapes; getting visions during sleep; making men invisible; inducing flooding in the house; and so on.[60]

The recipes at the end of the *Book of the Marvels of the World* are very similar to those in the *Liber ignium* of Marcus Graecus. They deal with magic candles and lamps, which make the house green and full of snakes, and men appear headless or with three heads, or black, or with animals' or angels' faces. There are recipes for making lamps to see something wonderful. The lamps are made from the skin of a snake, from the bile of a tortoise, from glow-worms, from the putrefied brain of a dead man, from yellow sulphur and so on. Some others are pyrotechnic; for example, one recipe allows a man to carry fire in his hand and the fire will not hurt him.[61] At the end, recipes for alcohol and gunpowder (*aqua ardens, ignis graecus, ignis volans*) are given.[62]

Most of these precepts use the principle of affinity and the only "images" are the shadows on the walls. Only in two recipes are there references to the construction or fabrication of images.

The first deals with producing the appearance of horrible men to scare away demons; the second deals with an image of a man or any other thing which, when it is put in water, becomes inflamed.[63] The absence of the operative rituals, typically associated with Hermetic magic, assured the appeal of the *Book of the Marvels of the World* from the Middle Ages into the modern age.

Future directions

A new research project, addressing the interrelations of the manuscript traditions of the following texts: *Book of the Marvels of the World*, the *Liber vaccae* and the *De proprietatibus*, could provide some interesting results. We also trust that the appeal of the Hermetic talismanic magic texts and *Book of the Marvels of the World* in the Renaissance, for example in the works of Giovanni Battista Della Porta, Cornelius Agrippa of Nettesheim and John Dee will promote a fruitful interchange between scholars of medieval and Renaissance magic.

New research could also highlight how the magic of marvels employs alchemy and herbal medicine. Finally, a comprehensive historical census of the vernacular translations of *the Book of the Marvels of the World*, with particular attention on the sources and their arrangement, could help scholars to realize the potential of these projects.[64]

Notes

1 P. Lucentini and V. Perrone Compagni, *I testi e i codici di Ermete nel Medioevo* (with appendix by Paolo Lucentini and Antonella Sannino, *Le stampe ermetiche*) (Florence: Polistampa, 2001), 59–93; V. Perrone Compagni, "I testi magici di Ermete," in *Hermetism from Late Antiquity to Humanism. La tradizione ermetica dal mondo tardo antico all'Umanesimo, Atti del Convegno Internazionale di Studi Napoli, 20-24 novembre 2001*, ed. P. Lucentini, I. Parri and V. Perrone Compagni (Turnhout: Brepols, 2004), 505–33. P. Lucentini, "L'ermetismo magico nel secolo XIII," in *Platonismo, ermetismo, eresia, nel Medioevo* (Louvain-La-Neuve: F.I.D.E.M., 2007), 264–310; P. Lucentini and V. Perrone Compagni, "Hermetic Literature II. Latin Middle Ages," in *Dictionary of Gnosis and Western Esotericism*, ed. W.J. Hanegraaff, A. Faivre, R. Van den Broek and J.-P. Brach (Leiden: Brill, 2005), 499b–529a, in particular 517a–26b for Vittoria Perrone Compagni's contribution on Hermetic magic. Translated into English with the help of Marianna Zuppieri, revision by Sophie Page. Thanks to them.

2 S. Page, "Image-Magic texts and a Platonic Cosmology at St. Augustine's Canterbury in the Late Middle Ages," in *Magic and the Classical Tradition*, ed. C. Burnett and W.F. Ryan (London: Warburg Institute, 2006) 70.

3 The final tradition is the Mesopotamian ritual known as "The Washing of the Mouth", that according to Pingree influenced the practices of the Sabians of Harran.

4 D. Pingree, "From Hermes to Jābir and the Book of the Cow," in *Magic and the Classical Tradition*, ed. Burnett and Ryan, 19–28.

5 D. Pingree, "The Diffusion of Arabic Magical Texts in Western Europe," in *La Diffusione delle scienze islamiche nel Medio evo europeo*, ed. B. Scarcia Amoretti (Roma: Accademia Nazionale dei Linceii, 1987), 71; D. Pingree, "Plato's Hermetic Book of the Cow," in *Il Neoplatonismo nel Rinascimento*, ed. P. Prini (Roma: Istituto dell'Enciclopedia Italiana Treccani, 1993), 144: "Much of the second book was incorporated into the *De mirabilibus mundi*, falsely ascribed to Albertus Magnus". J.P. Boudet, *Entre science et nigromance. Astrologie, divination et magie dans l'Occident médiéval (XIIe-XVe siècle)* (Paris: Publications de la Sorbonne, 2006), 409–17; L. Thorndike, *A History of Magic and Experimental Science*, vol. 1 (New York and London: Columbia University Press, 1923), 734: "*De mirabilibus mundi* seems to have copied from it, especially as its citations of Plato in *libro Tegimenti* (or *Regiminis*)."

6 M. Van der Lugt, "'Abominable mixtures': The *Liber vaccae* in the Medieval West, or the Dangers and Attractions of Natural Magic', *Traditio* 64 (2009): 249–51; *Liber Aneguemis. Un antico testo ermetico tra alchimia pratica, esoterismo e magia nera*, ed. P. Scopelliti and A. Chaouech (Milan: Mimesis Edizioni, 2006), 46.

7 Lucentini and Perrone Compagni, *I testi e i codici di Ermete nel Medioevo*, 59–93.

8 A. Sannino, "Altri due testimoni manoscritti del *De mirabilibus mundi*," *Bruniana & Campanelliana* 18 (2012): 693–98.

9 Lucentini and Perrone Compagni, "Hermetic Literature II. Latin Middle Ages," 517b.

10 See, for example, "Capitulum decimum. De demonstracione confectionum spirituum planetarum et retrahendi damnamenta operum et effectuum, miraculorum nigromancie et cibariorum, suffumigacionum, unguentorum, odorum quibus uti debet operator spirituum planetarum; et effectus planetarum proprios et opera que nisi visu operantur," *Picatrix: the Latin Version of the Ghāyat al-ḥakīm*, Book III, c. 10, ed. D. Pingree (London: Warburg Institute: 1986), 146.

11 *Picatrix*, ed. Pingree, c. 6, 51–57:

> De virtutibus ymaginum, et cuius maneriei possunt haberi, et quomodo ymagines possunt recipere vim planetarum, et quomodo opera fiunt per ymagines; et hec est radix scienciarum nigromancie et ymaginum. Et scias quod istud quod dicitur virtus est id quod natura et experimento comprobatur. Si illud agens quod in ipsa virtute agit habuerit naturam in illo opere manifestam. et maxime ut talis operacio sit virtutem habens in ipsis rebus. non natura manifesta quam habeat in eis, tunc opus illud erit forcius et magis apparens. et quod ex eo effectualiter apparebit veracius et magis cognitum.

12 *Picatrix*, ed. Pingree, c. 7–8, 112–66.
13 V. Perrone Compagni, "Una fonte ermetica: il Liber orationum planetarum," *Bruniana & Campanelliana* 7 (2001): 189–97, edition of the manuscript Darmstadt 1410.
14 *Asclepius* 24, in Hermès Trismégiste, *Corpus Hermeticum*, ed. A.D. Nock and A.-J. Festugière, Paris: Les Belles Lettres, 1960), 326, 11: "statuas animatas sensu et spiritu plenas tantaque facientes et talia, statuas futurorum praescias eaque sorte, uate, somniis multisque aliis rebus praedicentes, inbecillitates hominibus facientes easque curantes, tristitiam laetitiamque pro meritis"; *Asclepius* 38, 348, 21–349, 2: "Constat, o Asclepi, de herbis, de lapidibus et de aromatibus diuinitatis naturalem uim in se habentibus"; *Asclepius* 38, 349, 2–5: "Et propter hanc causam sacrificiis frequentibus oblectantur, hymnis et laudibus et dulcissimis sonis in modum caelestis harmoniae concinentibus". Cf. I. Parri, *La via filosofica di Ermete. Studio sull'Asclepius* (Florence: Polistampa, 2005), 180–81.
15 P. Lucentini, "L'ermetismo magico nel secolo XIII," 274–81; A. Sannino, "Ermete mago e alchimista nelle biblioteche di Guglielmo d'Alvernia e Ruggero Bacone", *Studi Medievali* 41 (2000): 151–209; D. Porreca, "Hermes Trismegistos: William of Auvergne's Mythical Authority", *Archives d'Histoire Doctrinale et Littéraire du Moyen Âge* 67 (2000): 143–58.
16 *Asclepius* 41, 355, 13–14: "Haec optantes convertimus nos ad puram et sine animalibus cenam".
17 On Adelardus Bathensis, see Perrone Compagni, "Hermetic Literature II: Latin Middle Ages," 521:

> A fascination with knowledge, which is also power is evident throughout Adelard of Bath's career as a translator. In his *Quaestiones naturales* Adelard (ca. 1080–1155) unhesitatingly acknowledges his interest in magic and tells us how he took lessons from an aged expert in magical operations. He is a true pioneer in exploring works on magic, and has the deliberate cultural objective of introducing this "useful" and "puissant" art into the scientific curriculum and legitimizing it as the operative branch of astrology.

18 Hermannus de Carinthia, *De essentiis* II, 72vF, ed. Charles Burnett (Leiden: Brill, 1982), 182: "thelesmatici Iorma Babilonius et Tuz Ionicus".
19 Michael Scotus, *Liber Introductorius*, Prooem., ms. München, Bayerische Staatsbibliothek, Clm 10268, fol. 1vb, quoted in Lucentini, "Ermetismo magico":

> scientia secretorum que exaltat hominem inter magnates et facit, eius quantum ad corpus, quasi habere iam principium paradisi'; *Introduct.*, dist. II, Clm 10268, fol. 116va: "Licet autem hec et alia sint contradicta et vetita, possibilia tamen sunt, sed scientia talium sive actus perturbat fidem catholicam, que est mater nostra, et sic maculat puritatem anime hominum.

20 P. Lucentini and A. Sannino, "Recommendatio astronomiae: un anonimo trattato del secolo XV in difesa dell'astrologia e della magia," in *Magic and the Classical Tradition*, ed. Burnett and Ryan, 190, "Super quod verbum fundantur multa secreta sapientum celantium artem de talis ymaginibus per multos libros qui ad nos non pervenerunt, et per ignaros et socios phylosophantium, qui tardi fuerunt ad perscrutandum secreta nature, attribuuntur nigromancie".
21 A. Sannino, "I ritratti leggendari di Ermete Trismegisto," *Micrologus* 21 (2013): 173–89.
22 Lucentini and Perrone Compagni, *I testi e i codici di Ermete nel Medioevo*, 59–93.
23 Ibid., 59–61.
24 Ibid., 61–63.
25 Ibid., 63–64.
26 Ibid., 64–65.
27 Ibid., 70–73.
28 Ibid., 73–76.
29 Ibid., 76–78.
30 Lucentini, "L'ermetismo magico nel secolo XIII," 311–24.

31 Lucentini and Perrone Compagni, *I testi e i codici di Ermete nel Medioevo*, 80–83.
32 Ibid., 83–84.
33 Ibid., 84–86.
34 Ibid., 86–89.
35 Lucentini, "L'ermetismo magico nel secolo XIII," 268–69.
36 Ibid., 34–37.
37 Lucentini, "L'ermetismo magico nel secolo XIII," 49–50; A. Sannino, "Oro te, o spiritus qui lates in illo corpore: Guglielmo d'Alvernia e il *Liber de quattuor confectionibus*," in *Labor Limae. Atti in onore di Carmela Baffioni, Studi Maghrebini* XII, I (2014), but 2017, pp. 475–91.
38 Pingree, "From Hermes to Jābir," 22–23.
39 *Liber aneguemis*, ed. Scopelliti and Chaouech, 145.
40 Van der Lugt, "Abominable mixtures," 249–51; Sannino, Il *De mirabilibus mundi*.
41 Al-Kindi, *De radiis*, ed. M.T.D'Alverny and F. Hudry, *Archives d'histoire doctrinale et littéraire du Moyen Âge* 41 (1975): 139–260; *De mirabilibus*, ed. Sannino, 85–86: "Et cum diu sollicitaverimus animum super hoc, invenimus sermonem probabilem Avicennae sexto Naturalium quod hominum animae inesset quaedam virtus immutandi res, et quod res aliae essent oboedientes ei, quando ipsa fertur in magnum excessum amoris aut odii aut alicuius talium. Cum igitur anima alicuius fertur in grandem excessum alicuius passionis, invenitur, experimento manifesto, quod ipsa ligat res et alterat ad idem, quod desiderat'; Avicenna, *Liber de anima seu Sextus de Naturalibus*, ed. S. Van Riet (Leuven: Peeters, 1968), IV c. 4, pp. 65, 45–66, 58: "Non est mirum si anima nobilis et fortissima transcendat operationem suam in corpore proprio ut, cum non fuerit demersa in affectum illius corporis vehementer et praeter hoc fuerit naturae praevalentis constantis in habitu suo, sanet infirmos et debilitet pravos et contingat privari natures et permutari sibi elementa, ita ut quod non est ignis fiat ei ignis, et quod non est terra fiat ei terra, et pro voluntate eius contingent pluviae et fertilitas … et hoc totum secundum necessitatem intelligibilem … materia etenim omnino est oboediens animae et multo amplius oboedit animae quam contrariis agentibus in se.
42 *De mirabilibus mundi*, ed. Sannino, 96: "Et qui credit quod mirabilitas rerum sit in stellis et aspectibus, in quibus contrahunt res proprietates mirabiles et occultas, scire potest quod omnis res habet propriam figuram coelestem sibi convenientem, ex qua etiam provenit ei mirabilitas in operando. Nam omne quod incipit sub determinato ascendente et influentia coelestis incipit et contrahit numquam propriam efficaciam.
43 *De mirabilibus mundi*, ed. Sannino, 95: "Et est apertum omnibus, quod homo est finis omnium naturalium, et quod omnia naturalia sunt per ipsum, et ipse vincit omnia naturalia et omnia naturalia habent insitam naturalem oboedientiam ad ipsum hominem, et quod homo est plenus omni mirabilitate, eo quod in ipso sunt omnes conditiones, et distemperata in caliditate et frigiditate, temperata in omni eo quod vis, et in eo sunt omnes virtutes rerum, et ad humanam naturam favent et oboediunt daemones, et ipso humano corpore operantur omnes secretae artes, et omne mirabile exit ex ipso.
44 *Picatrix*, ed. Pingree, I. 2, p. 5:

> Scias quod ista sciencia nominatur nigromancia. Nigromanciam appellamus omnia que homo operatur et ex quibus sensus et spiritus sequuntur illo opere per omnes partes et pro rebus mirabilibus quibus operantur quod sensus sequatur ea admeditando vel admirando. Et ista sunt difficilia intellectui racione sensus et visui latent suis similitudinibus. Et hoc est propter quod sunt potencie divine pro antepositis rebus pro accedendo ad predicta; et hec sciencia nimis est profunda et fortis intellectui. Et pars istius sciencie est in practica propter quod sua opera sunt de spiritu in spiritum, et hoc est in faciendo res similes que non sunt essencia. Et ymaginum composicio est spiritus in corpore, et composicio alchimie est corpus in corpore. Et generaliter nigromanciam dicimus pro omnibus rebus absconditis a sensu et quas maior pars hominum non apprehendit quomodo fiant nec quibus de causis veniant.

45 *Asclepius* 6, pp. 301, 18–302, 19: "Propter haec, o Asclepi, magnum miraculum est homo, animal adorandum atque honorandum. hoc enim in naturam dei transit, quasi ipse sit deus, hoc daemonum genus novit, utpote qui cum isdem se ortum esse cognoscat, hoc humanae naturae partem in se ipse despicit, alterius partis divinitate confisus. o hominum quanto est natura temperata felicius! diis cognata divinitate coniunctus est; partem sui, qua terrenus est, intra se despicit; cetera omnia, quibus se necessarium esse caelesti dispositione cognoscit, nexu secum caritatis

adstringit; suspicit caelum. sic ergo feliciore loco medietatis est positus, ut, quae infra se sunt, diligat, ipse a se superioribus diligatur. colit terram, elementis velocitate miscetur, acumine mentis maris profunda descendit. omnia illi licent, non caelum videtur altissimum; quasi e proximo enim animi sagacitate metitur. intentionem animi eius nulla aeris caligo confundit, non densitas terrae operam eius impedit, non aquae altitudo profunda despectum eius obtundit. omnia idem est et ubique idem est.

46 *De mirabilibus mundi*, ed. Sannino, 95: 'sed non habet homo omnia secundum idem tempus, sed in diversis temporibus et in diversis individuis, et in eo invenitur efficacia omnium rerum hypocritorum verborum vegetabilium'.

47 *De mirabilibus mundi*, ed. Sannino, 97–98: 'Plato vero dixit in *Libro Tegimenti*, quod qui non fuerit opifex dialecticae ex qua fit pronus et elevatus intellectus agilis et expeditus, et qui non est eruditus in scientia naturali in qua declarantur mirabilia calidi et frigidi et in qua aperientur proprietates cuiuslibet entis in se, et qui non fuerit doctus in scientia astrologiae et in aspectibus et figuris stellarum ex quibus est unicuique eorum quae sunt sublimia virtus et proprietas, et qui non fuerit doctus in scientia nigromantiae in qua manifestantur substantiae immortales, quae dispensant et administrant omne, quod est in rebus ex bono et malo, non poterit intelligere nec verificare omnia quae philosophi scripserunt, nec poterit certificare omnia quae apparebunt sensibus hominum, et invadet eum tristitia animi, quoniam in illis rebus est mirabilitas omnium quae videntur'; pp. 99–100: 'Merito ergo *Plato* dixit, quod qui non fuerit valde solers in dialectica et doctus in virtutibus rerum naturalium, similiter in signis stellarum et nigromanticarum virtutum, non videbit rationabilitatem mirabilium, nec ipse sciet ea, et non communicabit thesaurum philosophorum';

48 See n. 44.

49 *De mirabilibus mundi*, ed. Sannino, 93: 'Non est secretum neque occultum gentibus, quoniam omne simile adiuvet et confirmet suum simile et diligat et moveat, et amplectatur illud'.

50 S. Page, "Magic at St. Augustine's, Canterbury, in the late Middle Ages," Unpublished Ph.D. Thesis, Warburg Institute, London 2000, 57.

51 *De mirabilibus mundi*, ed. Sannino, 46–50; 86, 91, 93, 95, 97, 102, 105, 108, 112, 120, 123, 124, 127, 131 134, 147, 150.

52 Page, "Magic at St. Augustine's," 59.

53 *De mirabilibus mundi*, ed. Sannino, 110: "Et in *libro Cleopatrae*: quando mulier accipit omni mense de urina mulae pondera duo, et bibit ipsam, non concipit"; 111: "Et dixit Galienus, quod quando folia acetosae comeduntur, solvunt ventrem, et quando bibitur semen eius, solvunt ventrem".

54 *De mirabilibus mundi*, ed. Sannino, 108: "Et in *libro de theriaca Galieni* dicitur, quod serpens, qui dicitur regulus, est subalbidus, supra cuius caput sunt tres pili, et quando videt eum aliquis, moritur statim, et quando audit sibilum eius aliquis vel aliquid moritur, et omnis bestia quae comedit ex eo mortuo etiam moritur.

55 *De mirabilibus mundi*, ed. Sannino, 112: "Et dixit Aristoteles: qui sedet super pellem leonis, recedunt ab eo haemorrhoidae."

56 *De mirabilibus mundi*, ed. Sannino, 114: "Si vis ut mulier non corrumpatur nec quaerat viros, accipe priapum lupi, et pilos palpebrarum eius, et pilos qui sunt sub barba eius, et combure illud totum, et da ei in in potu ipsa nesciente et nullum alium volet. Et dixerunt: quando mulier non vult virum suum, tunc accipiat vir eius aliquid de sepo hyrcorum mediorum inter parvos et magnos, et liniat cum eo priapum suum, et coeat, ipsa enim amabit eum, et non coibit postea cum aliquibus.

57 *De mirabilibus mundi*, ed. Sannino, 118: "Et dicitur in *libro Hermetis*: quando proiicitur semen porri super acetum, recedit acetositas eius."

58 *De mirabilibus mundi*, ed. Sannino, "Et dixit Belbinus: quando accipis albumen ovi et alumen, et lenis cum eo pannum et ipsum abluis cum aqua salis, sicca eum, prohibet ignem comburere."

59 Ibid.: 'Et dixit alius, quando accipitur arsenicum rubrum et alumen et teruntur et conficiuntur cum succo sempervivae et felle tauri, et linit cum eo homo manus suas, deinde accipit ferrum ignitum, non comburit ipsum."

60 *De mirabilibus mundi*, ed. Sannino, 130: Ut homines videantur habere quorumlibet animalium capita, accipe sulphur vivum et lythargirium, et istis simul pulverizatis sparge in lampade oleo plena, habeantque candelam de cera virginea, quae permixta sit cum felle illius animalis, cuius caput vis ut videatur habere tenens candelam accensam de lampadis igne; 139–40: Licinium aliud, quod cum accenditur, omnia videntur alba et argentea: accipe lacertam unam nigram et abscinde caudam eius, et accipe quod exit, quia est simile argenti vivi. Deinde accipe licinium,

et madefac cum oleo, et pone ipsum in lampade nova, et accende, domus eius videbitur splendida et alba velut argentata; 143: Si vis facere contrarium, scilicet imaginem aliquam hominis aut alterius, et quando ponitur in aqua, accenditur, et si extraxeris eam, extinguitur, accipe calcem non extinctam, et permisce eam cum aliquantulo cerae, et oleo sesami et naphta, id est terra alba, et sulphure, et fac ex illo imaginem: nam quando tu roborabis aquam, accendetur ignis; 144: Si vis facere, ut quando aperis manus tuas super lampadem, extinguatur lumen, et quando claudis eas super eam, accenditur, et non cessat illud facere, accipe speciem quae dicitur spuma India et tere eam, deinde confice eam cum aqua camphorae et line cum ea manus tuas, deinde aperi eas in facie lampadis, delebitur lumen eius, et claude eas et reaccendetur."

61 *De mirabilibus mundi*, ed. Sannino, 145–46: Si vis portare in manu tua ignem, ut non offendat, accipe calcem dissolutam cum aqua fabarum calida et aliquantulum magranculis et aliquantululm malvaevisci et permisce illud cum eo bene, deinde line cum eo palmam tuam, et fac siccari, et pone in ea ignem et non offendat et non nocebit; 149–50: Experimentum mirabile, quod facit homines ire in ignem sine laesione vel portare ignem vel ferrum ignitum in manu. Recipe succum bismalvae et albumen ovi et semen psilii et calcem, et pulveriza et confice; cum illo albumine ovi succi raphani commisce. Ex hac confectione illinias corpus tuum vel manum, et dimitte siccari, et postea iterum illinias, et post hoc poteris audactersustinere ignem sine nocumento. Si autem velis ut videatur ardere, illud linitum asperge de sulphure vivo bene pulverizato, et videbitur comburi, cum accendetur sulphur, et nihil ei nocebit: si in flammam candelae, quam quis tenet in manu, colophoniam vel picem graecam insufflaveris subtilissime tritam, mirabiliter auget ignem, et usque ad domum porrigit flammam. Ut ignem illaesus portare possis, cum aqua fabarum calida calx dissolvatur, et modicum terrae rubeae de Messina, postea parum malvavisci adiicias, quibus in simul coniunctis vel commixtis palmam illinias et desiccari permittas, sic eum ignem quolibet illaesus portare poteris.

62 *De mirabilibus mundi*, ed. Sannino, 150–51:

> Aquam ardentem sic facies: recipe vinum nigrum spissum potens et vetus, et in una quarta ipsius distimperabis, sulphuris vivi subtilissime pulverizati, tartarum de bono vino et salis communis albi grossi, postea pone in cucurbita bene plumbeata et desuper posito alambico distillabis aquam ardentem, quam servare debes in vase vitreo. Ignem Graecum sic facies: recipe sulphurem vivum, tartarum, sarcocollam, picollam, sal coctum, petroleum et oleum commune, omnia fac bullire invicem bene, et si quid imponitur in eo, accendetur, sive lignum sive ferrum, et non extinguitur nisi urina, aceto vel arena.

63 J. Riddick Partington, *A History of Greek Fire and Gunpowder*, intr. B.S. Hall (Baltimore, MD and London: Johns Hopkins University Press, 1999), 85.

64 On the Italian translations of the *Book of the Marvels*, see R. Tarantino, "*Le traduzioni italiane del De mirabilibus mundi: il caso di due redazioni singolari*," *Studi filosofici* 35 (2012): 51–73.

13

THE NOTION OF PROPERTIES

Tensions between *Scientia* and *Ars* in medieval natural philosophy and magic

Isabelle Draelants

This chapter looks at a central notion used in medieval natural philosophy and magic: the properties of creatures and substances, called *proprietas, vis, virtus* (or *virtus specifica*), *qualitas* or even *natura*. The importance of this concept comes from its use both in traditional Western thought, in order to define the nature of a thing or physical action, and in Arabic medicine, as an essential concept to explain a transformation or an effect. The first half of the thirteenth century was the time when these disciplines came together most intensely, because it was the period when we see the assimilation of Aristotle's natural philosophy and its commentators, and of the works of Arab physicians and philosophers which had been translated into Latin during the last hundred and fifty years. We also see in thirteenth-century scholasticism a growing curiosity about nature and about the science of the soul's faculties ("psychology", coming from the *De anima* of Aristotle), and a growing importance given to causation, all of which enhanced considerably theories of knowledge and the study of perceptions and sensations. In this period, the comprehensive notion of *natural property* served equally to describe and define nature for educational purposes, and to explain natural or magical properties for therapeutic or prophylactic purposes. Therefore, it helps us to address the intellectual context of the birth of natural magic in medieval Europe as a peripheral branch of natural philosophy.

The concepts of *proprietas* and *virtus* were the basis of the traditional study of *De rerum natura* (The Nature of Things) in the West. Medieval scholars read and interpreted the natural features of a body or a creature in terms of properties that allowed them to define it unequivocally. In the early thirteenth century, various explanatory traditions relating to physical dynamics in the world were connected under a common term, "property": 1. The concept of the "property and nature of things" that underlay the traditional description of the universe, 2. The description of a sensible effect (i.e. one that could be seen or felt) of a transformation in the physical world, following Aristotelian physics. 3. A therapeutic operation, according to Arabic medicine, 4. The virtue of magical action. The notion of natural *proprietas/virtus* was particularly convenient for learned medieval thought, which was increasingly interested in causality and sensation, and it seemed, therefore, that it would play a central role in medieval physics. However, in its relationship with magic, the notion of properties did not have the expected epistemological success, for reasons that are partly due to competition between classifications coming from the various inherited sciences. Indeed, the various traditions (Latin, Greek, Arabic) for classifying knowledge did not find a durable way to coexist in the West, at this time. First, medicine was attempting to gain a more important place as an intermediary between art and science, and second, the theoretical branches of natural philosophy were coming to be defined according to the Aristotelian books on nature.

Amid these epistemological developments, "natural magic" was a paradox that struggled to find its place in the West: in both a theoretical and practical sense, it also sought to marry the natural and the extraordinary, while at the same time avoiding the trap of superstition. Over the following centuries, as religious orthodoxy became increasingly defined, and scholarly disciplines increasingly professionalized, the "naturalistic bet" of natural magic was not won, although there were still numerous attempts to legitimize it during the Renaissance.

This chapter seeks to clarify the meaning of "natural magic" by focusing on the notion of the natural property in the thirteenth century, and examining the significant intellectual traditions and textual sources at this crucial moment in medieval thought. The chapter is divided into five parts: the first part examines the areas where the concept of *property* was applied; the second recalls the legacies and origins of this concept; the third is about the diverse vocabulary of medieval magic; the fourth argues that *nigromancy* was accepted as the *science of properties* and the final part examines attempts to theorize this science. The chapter concludes with some new research directions that could fruitfully develop from the current state of research.

Proprietas, vis/virtus, natura: the ubiquity of the notion of property in medieval *natura rerum* literature

Traditionally, the term "nature", for a thing, covers its essence, that is the set of constant and universal characteristics that distinguishes it from other things and enables it to be defined. Philosophically, the form of a living being becomes approximately identified with its nature (*physis*) in its etiological and essential characterization. As for the *properties* of a living thing, they represent its internal and external characteristics that allow us to describe it as belonging to a given species, but also to explain how it can be the origin of a transformation, called *operatio* in medieval treatises.

In the Middle Ages, the quest for the nature of things and the conception of their properties was rooted in the long literary tradition of the Latin *Natura rerum* literature (for example, Varro, first century AD), and more distantly in the collections of *physika* and *paradoxa* in Hellenistic literature. In the twelfth century, the exegetical, tropological tradition, which was based on seeing the constant correspondences between things in the lower world as a reflection of the divine one, greatly influenced by Augustine of Hippo, was merged with a new philosophical conception influenced by Aristotelianism and the humoural theory of Galenic medicine. *Physis* then came to be seen as a reality apprehensible by the senses (*a sensu*), and physical transformations were explained by the four fundamental elements (earth, water, fire and air). Indeed, the craze for texts on *natura rerum* increased at the beginning of the thirteenth century, under the influence of two related factors: a new interest in nature for its own sake, and an explosion of the former *quadrivium*, now widened to "natural philosophy", thanks to the translations of philosophical and medical texts from Arabic and Greek made during the twelfth century.

In the thirteenth century, the literature on nature and on the properties of things provided an encyclopaedic description of the world, using the new concepts of *materia* and *forma*, and organizing reality according to the four sublunary elements. This approach competed with the previous naturalistic discourse that was built according to the sequence of the *Hexaemeron* and described biblical realities.[1] An excellent example of this new literature is the prologue of the *De proprietatibus rerum* (1230–40) of the Franciscan Bartholomeus Anglicus.[2] All these medieval works on nature divided up reality into short descriptive notes that tried to understand the essence of every thing according to a number of properties or, ideally, a unique, symbolic property. This univocity is more convenient for allegorical thought, as every thing could play the role of a symbol, following the example of the *Physiologus*' animal sections.

At the same time, in the natural philosophy of the thirteenth century, in Latin and in Hebrew,[3] every compound sublunary body, whether it is mineral, vegetal or animal, was constituted of elements and primary qualities which together made up its *complexion*. This concept of *complexion* was well understood only after the translation from Arabic, in *c*. 1230, of the Aristotelian work *De generatione et corruptione*.[4] As a consequence, whether in the field of physics, medicine, physiology, zoology or alchemy, the cause of a transformation was explained by the effect resulting from the property of the body at the origin of this action.

The lapidaries are another rich scholarly literature describing natural properties. Often incorporated into natural history, *summae*, or *pharmacopoeias*, some "scientific" or "philosophical" lapidaries aimed at describing and classifying the mineral realm and at explaining its chemical transformations and therapeutic applications. Most often, they took their main inspiration from the fifth book of the Greek herbal of Dioscorides (which had undergone several revisions in Greek, and then in Latin, before the twelfth century), and from Book 16 of Isidore of Seville's *Etymologiae*, which classifies stones by colours and has as its main source Book 37 of Pliny's *Naturalis historia*. Another ancient source was the syncretic Greek–Latin Damigeron-Evax lapidary. We tend to think that all these sources were gathered together in the environment of Montecassino *c*. 1100, along with some of the first Arabic contributions that emphasized celestial influences such as the *Liber de gradibus*, the *Practica Pantegni* of Constantine the African and the *De physicis ligaturis* of Qustā ibn Luqā.[5] Written at the end of the eleventh century, the poem *Liber lapidum* by the bishop of Rennes, Marbode, remained the most significant testimony of this kind of *philosophical* lapidary until the remarkable rise of encyclopaedic lapidaries between 1220 and 1260. The *De mineralibus* (1250–63) of the Dominican Albertus Magnus offers, in this regard, a textbook example, accumulating all previous knowledge on the subject.[6] Like the encyclopaedic lapidary of Arnoldus Saxo (*c*. 1230–45), which is the main source of the second and third *tractatus* of Albertus's Book 2, it also integrates lapidaries that deal with astrological seals, and these show clear antique and Eastern influence. The most famous of these astrological lapidaries is the work of the Jew Zael, known under the name of Thetel's *De sigillis* in the versions transmitted by Arnoldus Saxo and by Thomas of Cantimpré's *De natura rerum* (and consequently by Konrad von Megenberg and Camille Leonardi). In these astrological lapidaries, the physical, medicinal and magical virtues of the stones are connected to a "seal" which is engraved, and which is supposed to strengthen the stone's basic virtue by making a connection to the celestial power (*virtus celestis*). To this category of astrological lapidaries, we can add "magical" lapidaries, where stones are treated as talismans that should be worn in order to benefit from their powers, and sometimes consecrated with incantations as well. The mineral section of the *Kyranides* collection,[7] first written in Greek in the Alexandrine period and attributed to Hermes-Harpocration, and then translated into Latin *c*. 1168–69, is an example with which we may compare the later pseudo-Albertinian *De virtutibus herbarum, plantarum et animalium*, probably compiled *c*. 1240. The latter constituted the first part of the so-called *Liber aggregationis*, an extremely famous collection of texts of natural magic, which was printed more than 300 times during the next two centuries, despite the fact that only a few manuscript copies are preserved.[8]

In the middle of the thirteenth century, the border was thin and sometimes invisible, between the diverse types of literature on the properties of stones. They merge together in Book 3 of Albertus Magnus' *De mineralibus*, as is shown by the following excerpt, which emphasizes the value of nigromancy as the science of natural, astrological and magical properties. This passage appears in the book dedicated to astrological seals that are supposed to strengthen the intrinsic virtue of the stone:

> After that, it is necessary to speak about lapidary images and seals: although this section is a part of *nigromancy*, according to this sort of *nigromancy* which is subordinated to astronomy, and that we say concerns images and seals. However, because of the quality of this knowledge, and because our companions wish to learn it from us, reckoning as completely unfulfilled and false whatever we can find written about that by numerous [authors], we shall say something about it here. Because few know the writing of the ancient wise men concerning lapidary seals, and it cannot be known, unless one knows at the same time, astronomy, and magic things, and the *necromantic* sciences. […].[9]

Apart from the *De virtutibus lapidum* and the *De virtute universali* of Arnoldus Saxo, there is no doubt that one source in particular influenced Albert in his conception of how the lapidary virtue was connected with the celestial virtue: the letter *De physicis ligaturis* or *Epistola de incantationibus* of the Arabic mathematician and astronomer Qûstâ ibn Luqâ (830–910),[10] an author that Albertus confuses with Constantine the African,[11] as does Roger Bacon. This treatise is dedicated to talismans and ligatures, i.e. amulets made from natural substances, which are to be carried in order to achieve a therapeutic effect. Qûstâ ibn Luqâ, who used a Syriac or Arabic version of the pseudo-Aristotelian lapidary, considers that stones and animal substances worn as amulets act by means of an *occult property* that he does not want to conflate with their nature: "Ego quoque in multis antiquorum libris legi, suspensa collo suffragari *occulta proprietate*, non sua natura".[12] Certain causes of physical movement, or actions (*operationes*) or properties generated by certain bodies have effects that can be observed by experience, that is to say, by perception using the five senses. This effect is expressed in Qûstâ ibn Luqâ's final words, after mentioning magnetic attraction and the inflammability of saltpetre:

> All of which things, if not seen, we do not believe, yet if they are tested [*tentata*], they are confirmed [*certificantur*]; and perhaps the sayings of the Ancients are to be considered the same way. The action of these things is therefore of the order of properties and not of reasoning [enim *actio ex proprietate* est non *rationibus*]: this is why it cannot be understood by this pathway. Indeed, reasoning leads to understanding only of what is accessible to the senses. Certain substances therefore sometimes have a property that cannot be understood by reason because of its subtlety, providing nothing to the senses because of its great elevation.[13]

The physician Arnau of Villanova would later attach great importance to this opuscule in his own treatise against nigromancy, *Epistola de reprobacione nigromantice fictionis*.[14]

The concept of natural properties: legacies from Hellenistic, Hermetic and Arabic thought

In naturalistic, medical and more particularly pharmacological Arabic literature relating to properties, the notion of *khawāṣṣ* (Pl. of *khāṣṣa*, خاصّة) dominates. This notion continues the Hellenistic neo-Pythagorean tradition of the Φυσικα developed in Egypt and Syria. It expresses the specific quality that characterises a compound natural body, that is to say a specific property (*mujarrabāt*) that allows the physical transformation defined by the medieval word *operatio*. This quality is expressed by its effect, often without the cause being detectable or demonstrable by the usual laws of natural science. In the collections of properties rooted in the Greek tradition, such as the *Kyranides*,[15] the components of the mixed bodies that demonstrate these qualities are often introduced as pairs or triplets of associated qualities, linked by correspondences or mysterious sympathies. A Latin version of Ibn al-Jazzār's (d. 1004) *Kitāb al-Khawāṣṣ*, entitled the *De proprietatibus*, also survives, and this text became the main source of *The Book of the Marvels of the World* (*De mirabilibus mundi*), a work claiming to pertain to natural magic which was sometimes attributed to Albertus Magnus.[16] Abû l-'Alā' Zuhr ibn 'Abd al-Malik (d. 1131), a Cordovan physician, wrote another book on occult sympathies, classifying numerous qualities in alphabetical order, illustrated with quotations from Hermes, Razi, Aristotle, Pythagoras, Serapio, Johannes Mesue, Galen, Diascorides and other Persian and Roman authors; there is some evidence to suggest that the contents of this book were also transmitted in Latin.

The basis of a substance's *khawāṣṣ* is the mixture of the primary qualities of the four elements (air, fire, water, earth) in proportions which are determined during the composition of a natural body. This corresponds with the teaching of Galenic medicine, in which the proper complexion of every body is determined by medical tradition, but the way in which the primary qualities are compounded is nevertheless not enough to explain the operations that result from the constitutions of certain compound bodies, which are owed to their *specific form*. The specific form constitutes the fourth and last kind of quality that Arabic physicians employed to characterize a medicinal action. The action (*operatio*) of the specific form is an "added value" that can only be determined by experience. Avicenna, in his *Canon*, delivered the most precise definition of the specific virtue emanating from a substance taken in its entirety (i.e. linked to the substantial form), in order to complement Galenic complexion theory.

In formulating a theory of compound medicines, Avicenna established the essential meaning of *forma specifica* as "that by which a thing is what it is [for] when simple elements mix with one another and an individual thing is generated from them, preparation is thus made for the reception of a species and a form is added to what its simple elements possess. A specific form therefore imbued the substance with particular occult powers. This form is "not from primary qualities ... nor from the complexion generated from them, but is perfected more than acquired following the aptitude that [the form] acquired from [the matter's] complexion, as in the attractive force of a magnet."[17]

This Avicennian quotation appeared for the first time in Latin *c.* 1235, in the preface of Part 4 of Arnoldus Saxo's natural encyclopaedia, a work dedicated to the properties of the so-called "universal virtue",[18] and whose matter was afterwards reused in Book 2 of Albertus Magnus' *De mineralibus*. In these works and in most others, the emblematic example of a specific virtue is the magnet's attraction to iron.[19] At the end of the thirteenth century, the *virtus specifica*, connected with *tota substantia*, supported by the assimilation of

Avicenna's *Canon*, had become a causal commonplace in medicine. It was used in particular to explain the so-called "occult" action of poisons, which had been proved by experience, for example by Jean of Saint-Amand (d. 1303) in Paris; by Arnau of Villanova (d. 1311) in Montpellier; by Pietro d'Abano (d. 1316) in his *De venenis*; and also by Bernard of Gordon (d. 1320) in his *Lilium medicinae*.[20]

In natural magic, as in other works which discussed nature, the properties called "occult", because their causes are invisible, are always considered in relationship with their actions (*operationes*). In fact, the word *occult* is related both to the nature of the object being studied and to the methods of investigation used in medieval natural science.[21] Thomas Aquinas (c. 1225–74) traced the origin of occult properties to the heavens,[22] while others attributed them to the "substantial form" of the matter itself. The latter is defined as follows by Saint Bonaventure: "The substantial form of every thing, considered in itself, is called *essence* and, is considered with regard to the operation, its *nature*."[23]

In natural philosophy, the notion of the "specific property" was spread from the beginning of the thirteenth century in the West because it was a useful concept for causal explanation. It was part of a typically medieval desire to explain everything in a rational way in order to reach the universal truth and extend the boundaries of the known. It seems that the specific virtue, which was known to Arabic physicians as the "fourth virtue", was not really identified as such in the West, but it penetrated into the compilations of natural properties that linked the fields of natural philosophy and medicine to magic.[24] Between the Middle Ages and the Renaissance, this virtue passed from being seen as natural to supernatural. Largely illustrated by the *Speculum astronomiae*'s listing of astrological and Hermetic works (see below), the concept of *nigromancia* lays on the borders of natural philosophy; its magical part could also be considered as natural, if it did not use incantations and malefic powers. But little by little, the part of *nigromantia* which came to be defined as not natural became part of illicit occultism.

The medieval understanding and vocabulary of natural magic

The difficulty of defining "natural magic" lies especially in the evolution of intellectual categories between the Middle Ages and the present day, because the limits of and relations between science, magic and religion have changed so much that neither the retrospective vision of the *progress* of the sciences away from superstition (which is often employed in an anachronistic way by historians) nor anthropological distinctions between science and magic as formulated by modern structuralists as Marcel Mauss or Claude Levy-Strauss are useful.

The claim of medieval magic to be considered as a natural discipline, that is one in accord with nature, also renders inadequate the current definitions of medieval magic that emphasize the use of tricks and rites to provoke extraordinary effects.[25] Only a precise investigation of this transitional stage in intellectual history, which seeks to define the contents and the characteristics of a *natural* discipline that acts as an intermediary between science and art(ifice) in the classification of natural philosophy, seems able to answer the following questions: Did the theoretical and philosophical texts, which some scholastic authors used to explain magical operations, give magic, in any sense, the status of a learned discipline? And for how long was it able to maintain this learned status? The discipline that scholars of the thirteenth century called the *science of properties* (see below) seems to be a valid candidate for the scholarly natural discipline that was defined as the "natural" part of nigromancy. In the thirteenth century, this discipline, which was both theoretical and practical at the same time, not only distinguished itself from ancient necromancy (defined as divination using corpses, according to the definition infinitely repeated since Isidore of Seville)[26] but it also extended beyond the territory of natural magic into the pure study of nature.

In the history of scholarship on magic, Lynn Thorndike was the first, in 1923, to find an adequate way of conceptualizing the domain of natural medieval magic as *Experimental Science*, that is to say a branch of knowledge that concerned the *testing* of certain effects by the *senses*,[27] whose repercussions would eventually develop into modern experimentation. A discipline that focused on effective, *natural* magic was an *objective* magic, that is to say that it was intended to have an effect on objects or people other than the operator. It is also worth highlighting that the works that transmit natural magic or claim to belong to it are testimonies to a *learned discipline*, not a *popular practice*, and argued from the basis of rationality, an important justification for medieval scholars. Two central medieval criteria that define natural magic are, on the one hand, natural causality, and on the other hand, the exclusion of rites, invocations or charms aimed at devils or spiritual entities, purely deceptive illusions, and "characters". These criteria allow us to exclude from the field of natural magic the following arts: ritual magic, the so-called "solomonic" magic, which seeks to subdue demons; "theurgic" or angelic magic, which uses sacraments to let the operator contact God through angels – like the *Ars notoria*, which aimed at mastering universal knowledge – and also the forms of magic, which seek to increase the natural, physical efficiency of an action by using talismans (astral magic) or incantations (demonic magic). As regards textual sources, natural magic has a more "native" heritage in the Latin world than Solomonic magic, which has distant Jewish roots, or than Hermetic magic. In *c.* 1255, these demarcations clearly appear the first time in an essential repertory for the knowledge of works focusing on astral sciences: the *Speculum astronomiae* (see below).

To avoid anachronism, it is important to build on key medieval concepts and terminology. Generally speaking, when talking about magic, medieval Latin authors do not use the noun *magia*, which appears only in the fifteenth century at the time of Marsilio Ficino, but rather adjectives *magica* (feminine singular or neutral, plural) or *magicalis*. Particularly in the canonical literature or the penitentials, references are made to words such as *ars magica/artes magicae* that emphasize processes, tricks, fabrication, and demonic intervention, which are all considered to be superstitious practices. For instance, the words of Augustine in *De doctrina christiana*, taken up by Gratian's *Decretum*, speak of *artes magicae*[28] and, among the works translated from Arabic, the *De radiis* attributed to Al-Kindî – which tries to offer a universal theory of the celestial influence on *naturalia* – bears in manuscript copies the name of *Theorica artium magicarum* (the "theory of the arts of magic").[29] But it was in *c.* 1230 that the bishop of Paris, William of Auvergne, first used the term *ars magica naturalis* (considered below) to refer to the knowledge of surprising natural phenomena that we can experience.

The word *prestigia*, or rather the expression *in prestigiis*, appears also to underline the prodigious illusions worked by the *magus*. It is used, for instance, in Isidore's *Etymologiae*,[30] and in the prologue of Ps.-Appolonius of Tyana's *De secretis creaturae*, which begins: *in prestigiis et prodigiorum novitate anmirandus*.[31] It is also found in the mineralogical notes of the naturalistic compendia, which list, among others, the following property for *iscustos* in unnatural circumstances: *et prestigiis valet contra dolorem oculorum* (Arnoldus Saxo);[32] or describe how it acts as a natural protection against magical illusions: *veneficiis resistit omnibus et precipue magorum prestigiis* (Thomas of Cantimpré, *Liber de naturis rerum*, 14. 40).[33]

It is significant that in some theoretical and practical contexts, however, natural magic is related to *nigromancia*. This is the case, for example, in the important work of spiritual astral magic entitled the *Picatrix*, which has roots in Harranian doctrines and dedicates a whole chapter to the question *quid sit nigromancia*.[34] This last term is frequently used in the thirteenth century, in the context of both natural magic and astral divination, and it is often associated with a Toledan origin,[35] reflecting both the origin of the translations that introduced it and the reputation of this Spanish city in the teaching of magic. Astrology and other divinatory or magical sciences may well have been the prime driving forces for the translating activity in Spain, as Charles Burnett has argued.[36] In this context, it is likely that the term *nigromantia* was used to describe magic in a broad sense, from the beginning of the twelfth century, by translators and scholars in touch with Arab culture, such as the Spanish Jew Petrus Alfonsi, who converted to Christianity at the very beginning of the twelfth century and lived in al-Andalus before spending some years in England as a *magister* of Arts. These translators began to use the term *nigromantia* to translate the Arabic word *sihr*, which has no real Latin equivalent. A crucial question is why this term prevailed over *prestigium* or *magica*, which were also recorded in the Latin tradition. Once again, the answer lies most likely in the fame of the Isidorian words ("νεκρόν means dead and μαντεία divination") that were constantly reiterated. The transmission of this quotation led to a confusion between *necros* and *nigrum* to identify a sort of ancient divination through the animation of the dead or the use of the blood of dead bodies that was no longer a well-known practice at the time of Arabic–Latin translations.[37] The Isidorian distinction provided the word *necromancy*, inherited from the semantic field of the demonic, as the correct designation for a new multifaceted science, and was used to cover the recently translated works that did not qualify for other categories of knowledge.

Experimenta and the birth of *nigromancy* as the "Science of Properties" at the beginning of the thirteenth century

In his *Disciplina clericalis* on the training of clerks, Petrus Alfonsi lists the six main liberal arts as follows: (1) dialectic (standing in for the rest of the *trivium*), and then (2) arithmetic, (3) geometry, (4) medicine (i.e. *phisica*), (5) music and (6) astronomy. But he said the following about the seventh art: "The philosophers who are adept at prophecies say that the seventh art is *nigromancia*; some of those who do not, say it is philosophy ... and those who do not study philosophy say that it is grammar."[38] It can therefore be inferred that for Petrus Alfonsi philosophy stemmed from an extended *quadrivium* and that *nigromancia* became the science that headed all the subdivisions of philosophy. Petrus Alfonsi was more precise about the "art" of *nigromancia* in his *Dialogus contra Judeos*, which subdivided this science into nine sections. The first four concern the study of the four elements, characterizing the content of what became "natural magic" in the West during the thirteenth century. According to Alfonsi, the other five sections of *nigromancia* operated by means of the invocation of evil spirits. As has been shown by Charles Burnett, the division in the *Speculum astronomiae* of *nigromancia* into three disciplines – two unlawful and one permitted, "depending on whether they operate naturally" or not, was thus prefigured by Petrus Alfonsi.[39]

In Toledo in the mid-twelfth century, Dominicus Gundisalvi, a Spanish translator of treatises on natural philosophy, adapted the classification of sciences set out by Alfarabi (d. 950). In his *De divisione philosophiae*, Gundisalvi separated *humana scientia*, or what he called "universal natural science" (*scientia naturalis universalis*) into eight parts: (1) medicine, (2) (astrological) judgements, (3) necromancy (*nigromancia*), specifying *secundum physicam* – which recalls the interpretation given by Petrus Alfonsi, (4) the science of images, that is to say talismans or astral magic in a more general sense, (5) agriculture, (6) navigation, (7) the science of mirrors (catoptrics) and (8) alchemy.[40] Charles Burnett has shown that Gundisalvi's division was taken from the *De ortu scientiarum*, a work on the division of sciences that was adapted from an anonymous Arabic work.[41] This text probably also influenced Daniel of Morley, an Englishman who said that he went to Toledo at the end of the twelfth century to observe the dynamism of the new Arabic sciences. In his *Liber de naturis inferiorum et superiorum* (between 1175 and 1187), he mentioned "those who calumniate astrology" (*astronomia*).[42] He classifies *nigromancia* among the eight sciences that derived from astrology and benefited from it. For Daniel of Morley, in comparison with the writings of Gundisalvi, the *scientia de prestigiis* replaced navigation, and astrology took the predominant place in a universal natural science divided into the following hierarchy: (1) *scientia de iudiciis* (astrological judgements), (2) *de medicina*, (3) *de nigromancia "secundum physicam"*, (4) *de agricultura*, (5) *de prestigiis* (illusionism),[43] (6) *de alchimia*, (7) *de ymaginibus* (astrological images) "which the great and universal book of Venus published by Thoz Grecus transmitted," and finally (8) *de speculis*, catoptrics.

In the same vein, the translator Michael Scot uses the term *scientia de proprietatibus* as an equivalent of *nigromancia*. Both a translator of Arabic to Latin and an original author, he worked as an astrologer in Toledo and then in Sicily at the Court of Emperor Frederick II Hohenstaufen. These three features make him a close witness to the establishment of new notions coming from Arabic science. Before 1237 (the presumed year of his death), he offered a division of the sciences that only Vincent of Beauvais passed on.[44] There, he placed *nigromancia* within practical philosophy, which was not the usual position of the *quadrivium* in the tree of sciences:

> Also the practical (part of) philosophy is divided into three parts, of which the first is that which was invented on the model of natural things and pertains to natural things [*ad similitudinem naturalium et quae pertinet ad naturalia*], such as medicine, agriculture, alchemy, and also the science which is concerned with the properties of things [*scientia quoque de proprietatibus rerum*], which is called *nigromancia*; but also the science concerning the significations of things, which is called the science of judgements; moreover, the sciences of optics, navigation and many other sciences which have a relation to that part of theory which is called natural [*partem Theoricae* quae dicitur *naturalis*], belong to it as if to its practical (part).[45]

This division agreed fundamentally with what we have read in the works of Dominicus Gundisalvi and Daniel of Morley. However, it stresses three linked aspects that enrich the definition of *nigromantia*. First, the fact that all these disciplines are practical; this option for the new sciences at a time when the *quadrivium* had changed was probably influenced by the last part of the *Didascalicon* (bef. 1137) of Hugh of St. Victor, where the passage involving divination (ch. 15) makes astrology a part of the mechanical sciences, said to be *adulterine*, that copy natural reality by art or artifice.[46] Second, the fact that the disciplines formed part of *philosophia naturalis* insofar as they involved resemblances to the products of nature, *naturalia* (referred to as mixed bodies, as seen above). In the third place, the fact that as a result, *nigromancia* is par excellence the science of the properties of natural things (resulting from occult causes), referring presumably to the word *khāṣṣa*, pl. *khawāṣṣ* in Arabic. Therefore, the works compiling and listing the properties of stones, plants and animals in order to form collections of *experimenta* are part of natural science.

The Parisian bishop William of Auvergne seems to have been the first person in the West to talk of "natural magic" in the form of *ars magica naturalis*, in which he sees the *nigromancia secundum physicam* found in the writings of Gundisalvi and Daniel of Morley as part of natural science or astrology.[47] However, he says that it is wrong to describe it in this way: "the science of this kind of operation [wonders that have natural causes but that are considered by ignorant people to be the work of demons] is natural magic, that philosophers call '*nigromanciam* according to physics', but in a very inappropriate manner, and that is the eleventh part of natural science."[48] From the context, we can understand that William includes in natural philosophy magic, alchemy and the knowledge collected in the books of *experimenta*, all of which are acceptable to the Creator as they are all natural things coming from his beneficence, and because their operations have natural sources. He says something similar in his impressive *De universo* (written *c.* 1220, with additions until 1240), where he draws a parallel between the knowledge of how human and animal organs can be linked with "spiritual substances," and seemingly used as amulets or talismans, and "*magica naturalis* as a part of natural science."[49] Like Michael Scot, he associates "magic works" (*opera magica*) with "necromantic" works in his chapter devoted to the arts of illusion (*ludificationes – praestigium*) in the introduction to the third part of the second volume of *De universo*, but the part of necromancy that is related to apparitions and the summoning of demons is not considered to be natural and tends towards idolatry.[50] It should be stressed that in the same part of *De universo*, in a passage concerning *libri experimentorum* in the chapter *De tribus generibus magicorum operum, et de mirificis virtutibus quarundam rerum*, William links the notion of the art of natural magic (*ars magica naturalis*) with the natural properties of the plants listed in these books. He underlines that this art of natural magic is much practised "among the Indians," who were to the Arabs what the Arabs were to the Europeans,[51] and that the *libri naturalium narrationum* aim at explaining the causes of wonderful phenomena. In these so-called books, we may see works on *de natura rerum* and compilations *de proprietatibus*:

> From all that and from similar things which can be read in the books of *experimenta*, and in many books on nature, you could in one way or another know the cause and the reasons for certain magical acts which are proper to natural magic (*ex arte magica naturali*).[52]

Again in 2, pars 3, c. 25, 1 (col. 1060aG-H), William gives examples of natural virtues arising from the properties of natural (animal and vegetal) bodies. It therefore seems that William of Auvergne did not always draw a clear distinction between the marvellous effects of natural substances that have natural and knowable causes, and the wonders that result from vivification caused in nature by the action of a demon. He keeps the former within natural science and condemns the latter but he seems to consider that the term *nigromancia* applies to both practices.

Magic was a particularly rich discipline in the Iberian Peninsula, especially under King Alfonso X, who encouraged, from 1250 to 1260 onwards, the translation of Arabic works into the vernacular, and sometimes into Latin afterwards. Among other works, he ordered in 1256 the Castilian translation of the *Ghāyāt al-hakîm*, a work written in Arabic probably in the eleventh century, whose Latin version, retranslated from Castilian, was titled *Picatrix*. This work transmitted the idea that *nigromancia* was a science, and attributed to Thābit ibn Qurra, a Sabean of the eleventh century, the idea that "the most noble part of astrology is the science of (astrological) images".[53] The "natural" part of *nigromancia* dealing with natural properties seems then to have disappeared, in favour of the science of talismans and *prestigia*.[54] Consequently, in the *Book of Seven Parts* that bears the name of Alfonso X, there is in the seventh part a chapter devoted to the "nigromancers" (VII, title 24, law 2 and 3), giving the following definition: "*Nigromancia dicen en latin a un saber estraño que es para escantar los espiritus malos.*"[55] This knowledge became the prerogative of a few, which somehow manifests how it had failed to be recognized as an "honest" and useful science.

Towards a Western "Natural" magic: philosophical theorization and problems of orthodoxy

The thirteenth century was a period of dynamic assimilation of new knowledge coming from competing and complementary traditions that saw important strides in the classification and subdivision of the sciences. Medieval authors working at the crossroads of Jewish, Arabic and Latin influences extended the scope of nature, out of a desire to explain the transformations of the world in a rational way, and the need to make a distinction between what was lawful and what was forbidden, in order to build religious orthodoxy and draw the boundaries of superstition.[56] In the medieval debate about the interrelations of religion, science, magic and superstition, the scholastics revised the definition of superstition to include incorrect or improper Christian practice, usually on the basis of Gratian's *Decretum*. The final result was that in the late Middle Ages, Christian thinkers endorsed the thoughtful deployment of natural and divinely aided magic.

The *Speculum astronomie* attributed to Albertus Magnus illustrates plainly the rational preoccupation to list works covering "astral science" and to identify the works that were suspected of employing demonic intervention.[57] The author justifies the "naturalness" of talismans by arguing that the power that acts through them is a *natural virtue* used by man. He succeeds in rendering the science of talismans compatible with Aristotelian science and Christian rational theology, by referring to the theory of the hierarchy of causes and subtracting phenomena from the devil, while preserving free will.[58]

The animation of mixed bodies must be limited to recognizing or stimulating in them the action of their specific virtue, as in encyclopaedic pharmacopoeias or lapidaries, and not, in addition, employing the calling up of demons by invocations and inscriptions. Within the broad field of scholastic natural philosophy, this limit marks the boundary of the study of *naturalia* in the "books of experiments" mentioned several times by William of Auvergne;[59] but natural properties are also described in the lists of stones, plants and animals in thirteenth-century encyclopaedias. However, this did not make them worthy of being called nigromantic works. The sources they use gather together various classical and patristic Latin authors of compilations about nature, such as Pliny the Elder, Ambrose of Milan, Isidore of Seville, but also authorities coming from late Hellenistic Antiquity, such as Hermes, Evax and Aaron, Belbetus-Bālinus (Apollonius of Tyana), Ps-Aesculapius and Thetel the Jew, all these last close enough to the ancient tradition of *physika*.

With Marsilio Ficino's translation of the *Corpus hermeticum* at the end of the fourteenth century grows a learned magic increasingly ruled by platonism and hermetism; the principle of universal animation spreads and magic is addressed as an anti-religion heresy, causing a clearer and different split from the thirteenth century.[60]

Future directions

David Pingree traced the routes of the spreading of magic as an independent art, surveying the movement and transmission of magical texts.[61] This initial mapping of the dissemination of magic (dealt with in more detail elsewhere in the volume) deserves to be put to the test and qualified, by an investigation dealing with the regional assimilation of the distinctive doctrinal concepts of medieval physics such as specific "force", "property" and "form", and "occult virtue". Among the concepts that deserve to be explored more deeply, it seems that the shared territory and the slight differences between "universal virtue", *virtus celestis*, and the platonic and neo-platonic doctrines of *anima mundi* should be further investigated to establish new definitions, bearing in mind both the importance of textual source transmission (Greek, Jewish and Arabic hermeticism) and all the areas in which these concepts were applied: medicine, astrology, sciences of the properties, mineralogy and talismans. It would also be useful to further explore the doctrinal connections with the theory of rays that is found in the works of Ps.-Al-Kindi, Roger Bacon or later Agrippa von Nettesheim.

Furthermore, the importance of Toledo in the philosophical Arabic–Latin translations has been thoroughly studied for the twelfth century, to the extent of being overestimated at the expense of other regions, but the map of the dissemination of knowledge through medieval translations has been extended and become far more diversified. Very recently, the scholarly gaze, criticized for being too Eurocentric, is starting to look not only at the original productions in Greek, Syriac, Arabic and Hebrew but also towards the intellectual context of the areas in which these texts were produced, and to retrieve them and assess their sources. This trend must continue and should perhaps revisit nineteenth-century orientalism, which had the advantage of considering various textual contents, without drawing an unnatural border between the various civilizations and languages that produced or received them.

To give an example that probably led to the legend of the Faustian pact, it would be worth examining in greater depth and on a comparative basis the recurring theme of the magus' initiation, crystallized in some medieval Western tales in the form of the meeting between a member of a religious order and a Toledan necromancer which results, sometimes briefly, in an agreement giving privileged knowledge of magic. The pattern can already be identified in Syriac literature but also in the pseudo-Clementinian tradition in Ethiopian, Latin and Spanish, in the form of the teaching of magic to Îdhāshîr or Ardeshir (in the Syriac *Cave of Treasures*)[62] or to 'Esdzir (in the Ethiopic "Qalementos", the seven-book Revelation of Peter to Clement).[63] It may be compared with the episode featuring the future pope Gerbert of Aurillac[64] (e.g. in William of Malmesbury's *Gesta regum Anglorum*, in the *Chronicle of Pseudo-Turpin* or in Michael Scot's *Liber introductorius*) and all its later variations (such as Salimbene de Adam's Chronicle).

In medieval scholasticism, a particular science is defined by its interest in the *nature* of a being and its *properties*. The concept of property and virtue, on which we have particularly focused in this chapter, needs to be explored further as it became integrated into various philosophical disciplines in the period by focusing on a single author, and on a comparative basis by focusing on various medieval authors and various languages. In this way, the definition of property in Albertinian works on natural philosophy, such as the *De mineralibus, De animalibus* and *De vegetabilibus et plantis*, should be investigated in comparison with the term's meanings in his *Logic*, a work which was strongly influenced by the grammatical legacy of Avicenna, Al-Ghazzāli and Al-Fārābî. This is shown for instance in this section of Albert's commentary on Porphyrian *Isagogè*, dealing with the unequivocal property of "biting":

The various names of various things are equivocal, owing to the fact that the one who imposes [these names] was influenced in instituting them, by the various *properties* of various things, like "horse" and "donkey". [Names] are equivocal when a name was imposed on various things, but according to a diversity of definitions, owing to the fact that some unique property found in these various things, influences the ones who name them; however, this property cannot be found in them according to a single definition. For instance, "dog": this name was imposed on [the animal] able to bark, on a celestial star, and on a sea fish because of a single property found in them, which is that all these things can bite, although they do so not according to a single definition.'[65]

This chronological horizontal approach will also provide a better and more detailed appreciation of the difference of the treatment of the physical concept in pseudepigraphic works attributed to a key author such as Albert us Magnus. But the concept should also be better studied in Jewish works written in the West in a key period such as these of Abraham ibn Ezra in the twelfth century:

This resemblance between living creatures is called sympathy since this matter is not more precisely understood. So things which act by their whole essence are called *segula* (propriety) by agreement, in other words this is the uniqueness of sympathy. (...) It does not matter if you call it force or propriety or similarity, since all of these refer to the notion of propriety alone. This is the view of Hippocrates and Plato and their precursors on the axiomatic statement which has no proof.[66]

In the literature dealing with magic and the so-called occult sciences which derived from them in the Renaissance, emphasis has been placed chronologically on the end of Middle Ages and on humanists such as Agrippa von Nettesheim, Giordano Bruno and Marsilio Ficino. More recently, attention has focused on older authors like Arnau de Villanova, Pietro d'Abano, and Hieronymus Torrella. The defining moment of the attempt of magic to assert itself between 1230 and 1260, and the importance of the testimonies of William of Auvergne and of the *Speculum astronomiae* for the definition of it are now recognized because of the decisive works of David Pingree, Charles Burnett, Paola Zambelli, Paolo Lucentini and Vittoria Perrone-Compagni. Recent historiography has investigated further, examining accurately some short works translated between 1130 and 1230, following up and correcting some cases of attribution and authentication at the border of naturalistic knowledge,[67] examining further angelology and demonology, and developing titles and classifications suitable for medieval magic such as the concept of "addressativity" formulated by N. Weill-Parot. The remarkable progress of the *Micrologus* journal and series in dealing with natural medieval philosophy testifies to a keen interest in these fields of study. It remains, however, to explore certain aspects or authors whom the attentive interest of scholars has maybe not considered enough.

Notes

1 On the definition of medieval encyclopaedia, see Isabelle Draelants, "Le 'siècle de l'encyclopédisme': conditions et critères de définition d'un genre," in *Encyclopédire: Formes de l'ambition encyclopédique dans l'Antiquité et au Moyen Âge*, ed. Arnaud Zucker (Turnhout: Brepols, 2013), 81–106.

2 Bartholomaeus Anglicus, *De proprietatibus rerum*, vol. I, *Prohemium*, ed. H. Meyer; *Libri I-IV*, ed. M.W. Twomey (book 1); B. Roling (book 2); R.J. Long (books 3–4) De diversis artibus 78 (Turnhout: Brepols, 2007).
3 The notion of *segulah* [property/virtue] is significant for the study of late medical Hebrew works, as noted by the way M. Steinschneider, giving the example of Meir Aldabi in 1360: Mauritz Steinschneider, *Zur pseudo-epigraphischen Literatur, insbesondere ueber die geheimen Wissenschaften des Mittelalters aus hebraeischen und arabischen Quellen* (Berlin: 1862), 41.
4 Giovanna R. Giardina, *La Chimica Fisica di Aristotele. Teoria degli elementi e delle loro proprietà. Analisi critica del De generatione et corruptione* (Roma: Aracne editrice, 2008).
5 The works of Qustā and Constantine were probably transmitted together when an alphabetical version of the mineralogical Book 5 of Dioscorides' lapidary was made. An alphabetical version of Dioscorides' lapidary is attributed to Constantine the African in Bamberg, Staatsbibliothek, MS Med. 6, fol. 28v–29r: *Incipit prologus sequentis libri per alfabetum transpositi secundum Constantinum*. Ed. Colle, 1478 (based on Ms. Paris, B.n.F. lat. 6820), also with Pietro d'Abano's glosses, and Lyons, 1512.
6 Isabelle Draelants, "La science encyclopédique des pierres au 13ᵉ siècle: l'apogée d'une veine minéralogique," in *Aux origines de la géologie de l'Antiquité au Moyen Âge. Actes du colloque international 10–12 mars 2005, Paris Sorbonne (Paris IV)*, ed. C. Thomasset, J. Ducos, and J.-P. Chambon (Paris: Champion, 2010), 91–139.
7 Louis Delatte, *Textes latins et vieux français relatifs aux Cyranides* (Liège-Paris: Droz, 1942).
8 Ed. and study of the sources: Isabelle Draelants, Le Liber de virtutibus herbarum, lapidum et animalium (Liber aggregationis), *Un texte à succès attribué à Albert le Grand* (Florence: Sismel –Edizioni del Galluzzo, 2007).
9 Albertus Magnus, *De mineralibus* II, tr. 3, c. 1, ed. A. Borgnet, *Opera omnia*, V, 1895, 48b–49a.

> De imaginibus autem lapidum et sigillis post haec dicendum est: licet enim pars ista sit pars *necromantiae* [mss: *nigromancia*] secundum illam speciem *necromantiae* quae astronomiae subalternatur, et quae de imaginibus et *sigillis* vocatur: tamen propter bonitatem doctrinae, et quia illud cupiunt a nobis scire nostri socii, aliquid de hoc hic dicemus, omnino imperfecta et falsa reputantes quidquid de his a multis scriptum inuenitur. Antiquorum enim sapientium scripturam de sigillis lapidum pauci sciunt, nec sciri potest nisi simul et *astronomia* et *magica* et *necromantiae scientiae* sciantur. […] Volo autem primo narrare quae vidi, et expertus sum ego ipse, et postea ostendere causam. […]

10 Judith Wilcox and John M. Riddle, eds., "Qustā ibn Lûqā's Physical ligatures and the Recognition of the Placebo Effect," *Medieval Encounters* 1, no. 1 (1994): 1–50; Roberto Casazza, "El De physicis ligaturis de Costa ben Luca: Un tratado poco conocido sobre el uso de encantamientos y amuletos con fines terapéuticos," *Patristica et Mediaevalia* 27 (2006): 87–113.
11 "Costabulence" (cf. Albertus Magnus, *De mineralibus*, II, tr. 3, c. 6, *De ligaturis et suspensionibus lapidum*, in Borgnet, *Opera Omnia*, 55 and 56, where Qûstâ is mentioned with Hermes and Zeno from a quotation found in Arnoldus Saxo's *De virtute universali*). Cf. Isabelle Draelants, "Expérience et autorités dans la philosophie naturelle d'Albert le Grand," in Expertus sum. *L'expérience par les sens en philosophie naturelle médiévale. Actes du colloque international de Pont-à-Mousson, 5-7 février 2009*, ed. Th. Bénatouïl and I. Draelants (Florence: Sismel – Edizioni del Galluzzo, 2011) 89–122, see 97.
12 Wilcox and Riddle, "Qustā ibn Lûqā's Physical ligatures," 34.
13 Wilcox and Riddle, "Qustā ibn Lûqā's Physical ligatures," 37–38.
14 *Arnaldi de Villanova opera medica omnia*, VII.1, *Epistola de rebrobacione ficcionis (De improbatione maleficiorum)*, ed. Sebastià Giralt (Barcelona, 2006). See in particular the Commentary on occult property, 153–59.
15 Cf. Julius Röhr, *Der okkulte Kraftbegriff im Altertum*, Philologus, Supplementband 17,1 (Leipzig: Dieterich, 1923), 96–133, about ancient conceptions of *dynamis, energeia, praxis*, and *potentia, potestas, efficacia, virtus*.
16 I.e. the second part of the *Liber aggregationis*. ed. Antonella Sannino, *Il De mirabilibus mundi tra tradizione magica e filosofia naturale* (Florence: Sismel – Edizioni del Galluzzo, 2011), where the following manuscripts are not mentioned: Montpellier, École de médecine, H. 277, and Milano, Bibl. Ambrosiana, G. 89 sup.
17 See Avicenna, *Liber canonis*, I, fen 2, doct.2, Sun.1, cap. 15, éd. Lyon, 1522, f. 29v–30r. On the connections between specific qualities and the *tota substantia* made by Galen and his successors,

see Brian P. Copenhaver, "The Occultist Tradition and its Critics," in *The Cambridge History of Seventeenth-Century Philosophy*, vol. I, ed. Daniel Garber and Michael Ayers (Cambridge: Cambridge University Press, 1998), 454–512, esp. 459.

18 Isabelle Draelants, "La *virtus universalis*: un concept d'origine hermétique? Les sources d'une notion de philosophie naturelle apparentée à la forme spécifique," in *Hermetism from Late Antiquity to Humanism. La Tradizione Ermetica dal Mondo Tardo Antico all'Umanesimo, Atti del Convegno Internazionale di Studi* (Napoli, 20–24 novembre 2001), ed. Paolo Lucentini, Ilana Parri and Vittoria Perrone Compagni (Turnhout: Brepols, 2003), 157–88.

19 The *virtus occulta* is already used to mean the natural but extraordinary attractive power of a fish capable of delaying a boat in Alexander Neckam's *De naturis rerum* (c. 1200), I, c. 43, ed. Thomas Wright (London: Longman, 1863), 156.

20 For these examples, see Frederick W. Gibbs, "Specific Form and Poisonous Properties: Understanding Poison in the Fifteenth Century," *Preternature: Critical and Historical Studies on the Preternatural* 2, no. 1 (2013): 19–46, esp. 24 and *Le poison et ses usages au Moyen Âge, Cahiers de Recherches Médiévales* 17 (2009), ed. Frank Collard, in particular the article by Joël Chandelier, 23–38.

21 N. Weill-Parot has recently published on the concept of the "occult" in the Middle Ages and Renaissance. See especially, *Points aveugles de la nature. L'occulte, l'attraction magnétique et l'horreur du vide (XIIIe-milieu du XVe siècle)*, (Paris: Les Belles Lettres, 2013), 57, about the meaning of the "specific form" and its confusion with the "substantial form": 64 ff., "le terme *occultus* et ses emplois," and 164 ff., "Nature et origine de la vertu magnétique."

22 On the discussion of the substantial form by Thomas Aquinas, see Paul Richard Blum, "*Qualitates occultae*: Zur philosophischen Vorgeschichte eines Schlüsselbegriffs zwischen Okkultismus und Wissenschaft," in *Die okkulten Wissenschaften in der Renaissance*, ed. August Buck (Wiesbaden: Harrassowitz, 1992), 45–64, esp. 50–51 and Sancti Thomae de Aquino, *De operationibus occultis naturae ad quendam militem ultramontanum*, in *Opera omnia iussu Leonis XIII P. M. edita*, vol. 43: *Opuscula IV*, ed. H.F. Dondaine (Rome: Editori di San Tommaso, 1976), 159–86.

23 Bonaventura, *Commentaria in quattuor libros Sententiarum Magistri Petri Lombardi*, I, dist. xxxi, pars 2, dub. 5, in *Opera omnia*, ed. studio et cura PP. Collegii a S. Bonaventura, vol. 1, 2 (Ad Claras Aquas, Quaracchi: ex typographia Collegii S. Bonaventurae, 1883), 551.

24 There is a large scholarship on this. See, for example, Albert Heinekamp and Dieter Mettler, eds., *Magia naturalis und die Entstehung der modernen Naturwissenschaften, Studia Leibnitiana* 7, (Wiesbaden, 1978); Brian P. Copenhaver, "Scholastic Philosophy and Renaissance Magic in the *De vita* of Marsilio Ficino," *Renaissance Quarterly* 37, no. 4 (1984): 523–54; John Henry, "Occult Qualities and the Experimental Philosophy: Active Principles in Pre-Newtonian Matter Theory," *History of Science* 24 (1986): 335–81; Brian P. Copenhaver, "A Tale of Two Fishes: Magical Objects in Natural History from Antiquity through the Scientific Revolution," *Journal of the History of Ideas* 52 (1991): 373–98; Lorraine Daston and Katherine Park, *Wonders and the Order of Nature* (New York: Zone Books, 1998); Brian P. Copenhaver, "Natural Magic, Hermeticism, and Occultism in Early Modern Science," in *Reappraisals of the Scientific Revolution*, ed. David Lindberg and Robert Westman (Cambridge: Cambridge University Press, 1990), 261–301; Keith Hutchison, "Dormitive Virtues, Scholastic Qualities, and the New Philosophies," *History of Science* 29 (1991): 245–78; Gundolf Keil, "*Virtus occulta*: Der Begriff des *empiricum* bei Nikolaus von Polen," in *Die okkulten Wissenschaften in der Renaissance*, ed. August Buck (Wiesbaden: Otto Harrassowitz, 1992) 159–96; Graziella Federici Vescovini, "La concezione della *virtus occulta* nella dottrina medica di Arnaldo di Villanova e di Pietro d'Abano," in *Ecriture et réécriture des textes philosophiques médiévaux*, ed. Jacqueline Hamesse and Olga Weijers (Turnhout: Brepols, 2006), 107–35; Sebastià Giralt, "*Proprietas*: las propriedades ocultas según Arnau de Vilanova," *Traditio* 63 (2008): 327–60; N. Weill-Parot, "Astrology, Astral Influences and Occult Properties in the Thirteenth and Fourteenth Centuries," *Traditio* 65 (2010): 201–30.

25 Jean-Patrice Boudet, "Magie," in *Dictionnaire du Moyen Âge*, ed. Claude Gauvard, Alain De Libera and Michel Zinck (Paris: Quadrige/PUF, 2002), 863–64.

26 Isidorus Hispalensis, *Etymologiae* 8, c. 9, 2–3 and 10–11, ed. Wallace M. Lindsay (Oxford, 1911; 2nd ed., 1957). The text is almost literally the same in Isidore's *De natura rerum*, 15, c. 4, *De magis*. On the sustained influence of this Isidorian definition, see Isabelle Draelants, "*Magica vero sub philosophia non continetur*: Statut des arts magiques et divinatoires dans les encyclopédies et leurs *auctoritates*, c. 1225–1260," in *Geomancy and Other Forms of Divination*, Micrologus' Library 87, ed. Irene Zavaterro and Alessandro Palazzo (Florence: Sismel – Edizioni del Galluzzo, 2017), 463–518.

27 Lynn Thorndike, *A History of Magic and Experimental Science*, vol. 2 (New York: Columbia University Press, 1923).
28 Gratianus, *Decretum*, Pars 1, causa 26, qu. 2, in *Corpus Iuris Canonici*, vol. 1, ed. E. Friedberg (Leipzig, 1879, repr. Graz, 1959).
29 Al-kindi, *De radiis*, ed. Marie-Thérèse d'Alverny and Françoise Hudry, *Archives d'histoire doctrinale et littéraire du Moyen Age* 41 (1974): 139–260; Pina Travaglia, *Magic, Causality and Intentionality. The Doctrine of Rays in al-Kindî*, (Florence: Sismel – Edizioni del Galluzzo, 1999). Transl. (French) *Al-Kindî, De radiis*, traduction, commentaire et notes par Didier Ottaviani (Paris: Allia, 2003).
30 Isidore, *Etymologiae* 8. 9, § 3 (borrowed as well by *Decretum*, Pars 1, causa 26):

> Apud Assyrios autem *magicae artes* copiosae sunt testante Lucano: Quis noscere fibra facta queat, quis prodat aves, quis fulgura caeli servet, et Assyria scrutetur sidera cura? Itaque haec vanitas *magicarum artium* ex traditione angelorum malorum in toto terrarum orbe plurimis saeculis valuit. Per quandam scientiam futurorum et infernorum et vocationes eorum inventa sunt aruspicia, augurationes, et ipsa quae dicuntur oracula et *necromantia*. Nec mirum de *magorum praestigiis*, quorum in tantum prodiere *maleficiorum artes* ut etiam Moysi simillimis signis resisterent, vertentes virgas in dracones, aquas in sanguinem.

31 Ed. Françoise Hudry, "Le *De secretis nature* du pseudo-Apollonius de Tyane, traduction latine par Hugues de Santalla du *Kitâb sirr al-halîqa* de Balinus," *Chrysopoeia* 6 (1997–1999): 1–153.
32 Arnoldus Saxo, *De virtutibus lapidum*, in an enlarged manuscript copy of Ms. Heidelberg, Pal. germ. 263, fol. 165r.
33 Thomas Cantimpratensis, *Liber de natura rerum, Teil I: Texte*, ed. Helmut Boese (Berlin and New York: De Gruyter, 1973), 363.
34 *Picatrix. The Latin Version of the Ghâyat Al-Hakîm. Text, Introduction, Appendices, Indices*, ed. David Pingree (London: Warburg Institute, 1986). See also Vittoria Perrone Compagni, "*Picatrix latinus*. Concezioni filosofico-religiose e prassi magica," *Medioevo* 1 (1975): 237–70; *Images et magie: Picatrix entre Orient et Occident*, ed. Jean-Patrice Boudet, A. Caiozzo, Nicolas Weill-Parot in *Sciences, Techniques et Civilisations du Moyen Âge à l'aube des Lumières*, ed. D. Jacquart and Cl. Thomasset (Paris: Champion, 2011).
35 E.g. in the works of Anglo-Norman Benedictine William of Malmesbury *c.* 1120, *Gesta rerum Anglorum*, vol. 1, II, 168, 3, ed. and trans. R.A.B. Mynors (Oxford: Clarendon Press, 1969), 284, and N. Bubnov, *Gerberti Opera mathematica (972–1003)*, (Berlin, 1899), 386–88); by Henry of Andeli, before 1229, in the satirical work *Bataille des sept ars*, ed. Alain Corbellari, *Les Dits d'Henri d'Andeli*, Les classiques français du Moyen Âge 146, (Paris: Champion, 2004).
36 Charles Burnett, "Astrology, Astronomy and Magic as the Motivation for the Scientific Renaissance of the Twelfth Century," in *The Imaginal Cosmos: Astrology, Divination, and the Sacred*, ed. Angela Voss and Jean Hinson Lall (Canterbury: University of Kent Press, 2007), 55–61.
37 E.g. Thomas Aquinas, *Summa theologiae* 2–2, qu. 95, art. 3, corpus. Literally translated by the Fathers of the English Dominican Province (London, 2nd and revised ed., 1920):

> When demons are expressly invoked, they are wont to foretell the future in many ways. Sometimes they offer themselves to human sight and hearing by mock apparitions in order to foretell the future: and this species is called 'prestigiation' because man's eyes are blindfolded [*praestringuntur*]. Sometimes they make use of dreams, and this is called 'divination by dreams': sometimes they employ apparitions or utterances of the dead, and this species is called 'necromancy,' [*nigromancia*] for as Isidore [*Isidorus ... in libro etymol.*] observes in Greek, νεκρόν [*nigrum*] "means dead and μαντεία divination, because after certain incantations [*praecantationibus*] and the sprinkling of blood, the dead seem to come to life, to divine and to answer questions. Sometimes they foretell the future through living men, as in the case of those who are possessed: ... Sometimes they foretell the future by means of shapes or signs which appear in inanimate beings.

38 Petrus Alfonsi, *Disciplina clericalis*, ed. Alfons Hilka and Werner Söderhjelm, I, *Lateinischer Text*, Acta societatis scientiarum Fennicae 38.4, (Helsinki, 1911), 10; on Petrus Alfonsi and *necromancy*, see Burnett, "Talismans: Magic as Science? Necromancy among the Seven Liberal Arts," art. I in in Charles Burnett, *Magic and Divination in the Middle Ages* (Aldershot: Ashgate, 1996).
39 Burnett, "Talismans: Magic as Science," 4–5.

40 Dominicus Gundissalinus, *De divisione philosophiae*, ed. Ludwig Baur, Beiträge zur Geschichte der Philosophie des Mittelalters 4, 2–3 (Münster i. W.: Aschendorff, 1903), 20.
41 Burnett, "Talismans: Magic as Science," 2. On the influence of the eight species of natural science in *De ortu scientiarum* on the thought of Gundisalvi: "Two Approaches to Natural Science in Toledo in the Twelfth Century," in *Christlicher Norden – Muslimischer Süden. Ansprüche und Wirklichkeiten von Christen, Juden und Muslimen auf der Iberischen Halbinsel im Hoch- und Spätmittelalter*, ed. Matthias M. Tischler and Alexander Fidora (Münster i. W.: Aschendorff, 2011), 69–80.
42 Gregor Maurach, "Daniel von Morley *Philosophia*," *Mittellateinisches Jahrbuch* 14 (1974): 204–55, esp. 239.
43 On the science *de prestigiis* and the science of images, and on the influence of Adelard of Bath on Daniel of Morley in this respect, see Charles Burnett, "Thābit ibn Qurra the Harrānian on Talismans and the Spirits of the Planets," *La Corónica* 36 (2007): 13–40, esp. 19–20.
44 This was shown by Charles Burnett, "Vincent of Beauvais, Michael Scot and the 'New Aristotle'," in *Lector et compilator. Vincent de Beauvais, frère prêcheur. Un intellectuel et son milieu au XIIIe siècle*, ed. Serge Lusignan and Monique Paulmier-Foucart, Rencontres à Royaumont (Grâne: Créaphis, 1997), 189–213.
45 *Speculum naturale* 1, c. 16, ed. Burnett, "Vincent of Beauvais, Michael Scot," 200–201.
46 Hugo de Sancto Victore, *Didascalicon*, II, ed. C. Buttimer, Studies in Medieval and Renaissance Latin 10 (Washington: The Catholic University Press, 1939), 1639: Also in *Epitome Dindimi in philosophiam*, ed. Buttimer, 197.
47 On this claim of "naturality" for magic, see Thorndike, *History of Magic*, II, 81 and 346–63, and Richard Kieckhefer, "The Specific Rationality of Medieval Magic," *American Historical Review* 99 no. 3 (1994): 813–36, esp. 819.
48 I thank Jean-Patrice Boudet for showing me an alternative manuscript reading of this passage after my lecture on "*Nigromancy*" held at Louvain-la-Neuve (Belgium) on 7 February 2007. "Et de huiusmodi operibus est *magica naturalis*, quam *nigromanciam secundum phisicam* philosophi vocant, licet multum improprie, et est *totius scientie naturalis pars undecima*": William of Auvergne, *De legibus*, c. 24, Paris, BnF. MS lat. 15755, fol. 71vb, quoted by Jean-Patrice Boudet, *Entre science et 'nigromance'. Astrologie, divination et magie dans l'Occident médiéval (XIIe-XVe siècles)*, (Paris: Publications de la Sorbonne, 2006), 128, rather than the incomprehensible reading of the edition of Hotot, *Guilielmus Alverniensis Episcopus Parisiensis, Opera omnia*, I, (Orléans-Paris, 1674) (repr. Frankfurt-am-Main, 1963), 1, 69CDb.
49 William of Auvergne, *De universo* 1, pars 1, end of c. 43, ed. *Guilielmus Alverniensis Opera Omnia* I, col. 648Ga
50 William of Auvergne, *De universo* 2, pars 3, Preface, ed. col. 1015Cb See also *De Legibus* 24, 1, col. 67aB, about the fifth type of idolatry).
51 These treatises may cover hermetic astral magic, which was studied by Pingree, "Indian Planetary Images and the Tradition of Astral Magic," *Journal of the Warburg and Courtauld Institutes* 52 (1989): 1–13 and Charles Burnett, "Arabic, Greek, and Latin Works on Astrological Magic attributed to Aristotle," in *Pseudo-Aristotle in the Middle Ages*, (London: Warburg Institute, 1986), 84–96.
52 William of Auvergne, *De universo* 2, pars 3, c. 22, ed. col. 1060 Fb, and again col. 1065Aa (on the subject of Indian *experimentatores* and illusionists). In *De universo* 1, *pars* 1, c. 43 is another mention of *libri naturales narrationum*. On the identity of works in this category, see Steven P. Marrone, "William of Auvergne on Magic in Natural Philosophy and Theology," in '*Was ist Philosophie im Mittelalter', Akten des X. Internationalen Kongresses für mittelalterliche Philosophie der Société Internationale pour l'Étude de la Philosophie Médiévale, 25. bis 30. August 1997 in Erfurt*, ed. J. Aersten and Andreas Speer (Berlin, New York: 1998), 741–48.
53 *Picatrix*, I, V, 36, ed. Pingree, 23.
54 The affirmation in the *Picatrix* is confirmed by the fact that the *scientia de prestigiis* came to the West via the early twelfth-century translation by the Englishman Adelard of Bath of a work of Thābit ibn Qurrā named *Liber prestigiorum Thebidis secundum Ptolomeum et Hermetem*. According to David Pingree, this was an early translation of *De imaginibus*, which was then translated again in the second quarter of the twelfth century by John of Seville and Limia. David Pingree, "The Diffusion of Arabic Magical Texts in Western Europe," in *La diffusione delle scienze islamiche nel medio evo europeo, Convegno internazionale (Roma, 2–4 ottobre 1984)*, ed. Bianca Scarcia Amoretti (Roma, 1987), 74–75.
55 *Las siete partidas del rey Don Alfonso el Sabio, cotejadas con varios codices antiguos por la Real Academia de la Historia*, part. 7, tit. 24, leg. 2 (vol. 3, 1807, repr. 1972), 668.

56 Michael D. Bailey, *Fearful Spirits, Reasoned Follies: The Boundaries of Superstition in Late Medieval Europe*, (Ithaca, NY: Cornell University Press, 2013).
57 The *Speculum astronomiae* and related bibliography are dealt with in more detail in the chapters by Marrone and Collins in this volume. See the theoretical and epistemological light shed by Paola Zambelli, *L'ambigua natura della magia. Filosofi, streghe, riti nel Rinascimento*, 2nd ed. (Venice: Marsilio, 1996), and Nicolas Weill-Parot, "Science et magie au Moyen Âge," in *Bilan et perspectives des études médiévales (1993–1998). Euroconférence (Barcelona 8–12 June 1999). Actes du IIe congrès Européen d'Etudes Médiévales*, ed. Jacqueline Hamesse, (Turnhout: Brepols, 2004), 540–42. Also Nicolas Weill-Parot, "Astral Magic and Intellectual Changes (Twelfth-Fifteenth Centuries). 'Astrological Images' and the Concept of 'Addressative' Magic," in *The Metamorphosis of Magic from Late Antiquity to the Early Modern Period*, ed. J.N. Bremmer and J.R. Veenstra (Leuven-Paris: Peeters, 2002), 167–87.
58 *Speculum astronomiae* 3, ed. Zambelli, *The* Speculum Astronomiae *and Its Enigma. Astrology, Theology and Science in Albertus Magnus and His Contemporaries*, Boston Studies in the Philosophy of Science 135, (Dordrecht, Boston, and London: Kluwer Academic, 1992), 218–20, explained by Lucentini, "L'ermetismo magico nel secolo XIII," in *Sic itur ad astra. studien zur Geschichte der Mathematik und Naturwissenschaften. Festschrift für den Arabisten Paul Kunitzsch zum 70. Geburtstag*, ed. M. Folkerts and R. Lorch, (Wiesbaden: Harrassowitz, 2000), 409–50: 426–28.
59 See e.g. Richard Lemay, "*Libri naturales* et sciences de la nature dans la scolastique latine du XIIIe siècle," in *XIVth International Congress of the History of Science* (Proceedings 2), (Tokyo-Kyoto, 1974), 61–64.
60 See Graziella Federici Vescovini, *Le Moyen Age magique* (Paris: Vrin, 2011), chap. 1, about relations between magic and science.
61 Pingree, "The Diffusion of Arabic Magical Texts," 57–58.
62 *The Book of the Cave of Treasures. A History of the Patriarchs and the Kings Their Successors from the Creation to the Crucifixion of Christ*, Transl. from the Syriac Text of the British Museum Ms. Add. 25875, by Sir E.A. Wallis Budge, (London, Manchester, Madrid, Lisbon, and Budapest: Religious Tract Society, 1927), 142–44.
63 French transl. from Ethiopian by Sylvain Grébaut, "*Littérature pseudo-clémentine*," III, "*Traduction du Qalémentos (suite)*," *Revue de l'Orient Chrétien* 17 (1912): 16–31.
64 On Toledo as a centre for necromancy (particularly on Gerbert of Aurillac as a necromancer), see Jaime Ferreiro Alemparte, "La escuela de nigromancia de Toledo," *Anuario de estudios medievales* 13 (1983): 206–7.
65 Albertus Magnus, *Super Porphyrium De V universalibus*, tr. 1, *De antecedentibus ad logicam*, ed. Manuel Santos Noya, in Albertus Magnus, *Opera omnia*, I, pars 1A, (Monasterii Westfalorum: In aedibus Aschendorff, 2004) 10.
66 J.O. Leibowitz and S. Marcus, eds, transl. and comm., *Sefer Hanisyonot. The Book of Medical Experiences Attributed to Abraham ibn Ezra. Medical Theory, Rational and Magical Therapy. A Study in Medievalism* (Jerusalem: Magnes Press, Hebrew University, 1984), f. 133v, l. 5–6, 9–10.
67 See the studies carried on magic and alchemical texts attributed to Aristotle in Arab–Latin tradition (e.g. the last book of the *Meteora* studied by Jean-Marc Mandosio) or to Albertus Magnus, after the works of Pearl Kibre (e.g. Draelants, *Le De virtutibus*; and Paravicini-Bagliani 2001 and others on the *Speculum astronomiae*), or on alchemical works that circulated in the West under various names (e.g. *De anima in arte alchemiae* attributed to Avicenna, recently studied by Sébastien Moureau, 2016).

14

SOLOMONIC MAGIC

Julien Véronèse

The problems of defining a corpus of Solomonic ritual magic

While the origins of "Solomonic" magic may be found in the twelfth century, it is not until the thirteenth century that the dissemination of a certain number of texts or experiments on magic attributed to King Solomon is attested in the Latin West, in an essentially indirect fashion to begin with. The anonymous author of the *Speculum astronomiae* (c. 1260), long thought to be Albertus Magnus, is a privileged witness to the reception of these traditions that were distinct from the "common tradition" of Western magic.[1] By mentioning a series of *libri Salomonis*, for which he provides, with notable precision, titles and incipits, the author of the *Speculum* was effectively the first to define the boundaries of what we might consider a corpus of "Solomonic" texts. For the purposes of defending natural "astrological images" whose use could not, in his estimation, be outlawed in Christendom, he classed them (along with some others attributed to Mohammed) in that category of texts that featured "detestable images", taking care to distinguish them – in a somewhat artificial manner – from those whose efficacy was based on "abominable images", in other words on the principles of astral magic (perhaps based in astrolatry), attributed to Hermes, and which were still more dangerous in his view.[2] The author of the *Speculum* thus makes an inventory of five books of Solomon "which proceed with exorcism by the inscription of characters and through certain names": the *De quatuor annulis*, attributed to four of the king's disciples; the *De novem candariis*; the *De tribus figuris spirituum*; the *De figura Almandal*; and one final "little" book entitled *De sigillis ad demoniacos*.[3] He also mentions a "great book by Raziel which we call *Liber institutionis*",[4] by which he is referring to the Hebraic tradition of the *Liber Razielis*, whose Solomonic attribution is attested both in its late antique template, the *Liber Samayn*, and in Latin manuscripts of the fourteenth and fifteenth centuries. While he says nothing about the origin of these texts, nor about the ways in which they circulated in his time, his inventory remains a precious resource in more ways than one.

To begin with, other indirect contemporary references to these texts, which also bear witness to the dissemination of *artes magice* or of new *libri*, are somewhat more laconic. Around 1267–70, the Franciscan scholar Roger Bacon, for example, mentions in the *Tractatus brevis*, which serves as an introduction to the glosses on the pseudo-Aristotelian *Secretum secretorum*, the existence of *libri Salomonis* that "false astrologers" use to obtain the aid of demons; however, he does not provide further details about them and at the same time mentions books attributed to other figures such as Adam, Moses, Aristotle and Hermes.[5] He is more precise in the *Opus tertium* (c. 1267), in which he enumerates, in order to condemn them anew, a number of *libri magici* founded on the invocation of demons and not on the command of the forces of nature that alone rendered a category of magic acceptable. He cites the *De morte anime* (also documented in the *Speculum astronomiae*), the *Liber fantasmatum*, the *De officiis et potestatibus spirituum* and the "books of the *Ars notoria*", but the attribution to Solomon here only explicitly concerns "the books" entitled *De sigillis Salomonis*,[6] even though the *Ars notoria*, for example, also claims Solomon as an authority, as the manuscripts of the thirteenth century attest.[7] With regard to this last work, Bacon is more verbose in a correspondence that has recently been attributed to him (c. 1257–63); he writes of a "liber Salomonis qui dicitur *Ars notoria*" alongside a Hebrew book by Solomon known as the *Liber Semamphoras*, which refers to Jewish tradition concerning speculations on the unspeakable name of God that would be destined for dissemination in the West, notably as part of the *Liber Razielis* tradition.[8] But these longer treatises alone do not constitute a precise bibliography of "Solomonic" magic.

The survey in the *Speculum astronomiae* also enables us to better appreciate older attributions of certain works to Solomon, for example those found in the prologue of the *Liber introductorius* by the translator and astronomer Michael Scot († c. 1236), where an *Ydea Salomonis*, which alludes, perhaps, to the version of *De quattuor annulis* mentioned in the *Speculum astronomiae*, is cited without further details among the arts that "destroy faith in divine law",[9] or in the *De legibus* of William of Auvergne, bishop of Paris (c. 1180–1249), who mentions – similarly for the purposes of condemnation – diverse signs, figures or images ascribed to Solomon. These include the "pentagon", the "Mandal", the four "rings", the "seal", the "nine *candarie*" or simply, as in Michael Scot, the *Ydea Salomonis*, which leads its user straight to idolatry or even to demonolatry. While not presenting clearly identified "books", they seem to refer, at least in essence, to the *libri Salomonis* inventoried several decades later by the *Magister Speculi*.[10] William also reports on the belief that Solomon was capable of enclosing demons in artefacts such as glass vials, in order to better denounce those who believe they can achieve this power themselves.[11] This ancient belief is indeed commonly enlisted in the texts of ritual magic at the end of the Middle Ages and the "Solomonic" signs mentioned earlier played an essential role in this regard.[12]

Finally, the *Speculum astronomiae* gives an insight into the state of play for the form of the Latin Solomonic tradition in a period in which no manuscripts are preserved (except in the particular case of the *Ars notoria*, which is not mentioned by this author). Furthermore, it allows us to gauge, up to a point, the subsequent evolutions of the "corpus" that can be found in other, later, inventories, this time together with rare preserved manuscripts. To illustrate the first case, we can turn to the inventory of *libri magici* made in 1508 by the abbot of Sponheim, Johannes Trithemius, in his *Antipalus maleficiorum*. A quick comparison shows that the number of texts attributed to Solomon rose during the latter centuries of the Middle Ages. Trithemius thus refers, with explicit reference to the Hebrew king, to nine out of the forty-three texts whose usage every Christian should condemn. Certain notes echo the *Speculum astronomiae*: this is the case with regard to the *Liber Almadal*, the *Liber quattuor annulorum*, the *De novem candariis*, the *De tribus figuris spirituum*, even the *Sepher Razielis* in seven books, even if, in view of the incipits given by Trithemius, he does not seem to be consistently referring to the same versions.[13] On the other hand, the same is not true of the *Clavicula Salomonis*, placed first, the *Liber Lamene*, the *De officiis spirituum* and the *Liber pentaculorum*.[14] Trithemius additionally claims to have passed over certain elements concerning this type of books in silence.[15] It must finally be taken into account that he makes his inventory without putting forward a Solomonic attribution for a text such as the *Vinculum spirituum*, even though we know that Solomon is well and truly established as the "author" in certain manuscripts.[16]

Manuscripts from the end of the Middle Ages or the beginning of the modern era, though not numerous, also illustrate this quantitative growth. Some combine several Solomonic texts, in diverse proportions, alongside other traditions, notably astral magic.[17] Others, more rarely, maintain a clear or even an overwhelming majority of Solomonic texts and in this way take on the appearance of collections, even if they are never exhaustive. The finest example up to this point is, without doubt, the manuscript Coxe 25 (preserved in a private French collection), which is of Germanic provenance and datable to the end of the fifteenth century. Its contents (the work of a single hand) indicate that certain late medieval scribes might have been tempted to create a true Solomonic corpus, even if the general title given to the book, *Liber Hermetis sive de rebus occultis*, appears from this perspective quite paradoxical and shows the limits of the exercise well, unless it is a camouflage strategy.[18] Notably, this manuscript includes two versions of the *De quattuor annulis*, of which one, ascribed to four of Solomon's disciples, Fortunatus, Eleazar, Macarius and Toz (those to whom the *Speculum astronomiae* alludes), mentions the *Ydea Salomonis*, two versions of the *Vinculum spirituum* (also known by the title *Vinculum Salomonis*),[19] the *Clavicula Salomonis* (the only known medieval Latin witness to this work), the *Liber Samayn* (here *Liber sextus*) from the *Liber Razielis* in seven books, the *De officiis spirituum*, the *Liber consecrationum* linked to Solomonic catalogues of demons, the *Liber Almadel*, as well as a *Liber angelicus* that is attributed first to Hermes and secondarily to Solomon. The latter purports to be a compendium of astral and ritual magic mainly based on the *De quattuor annulis*, the *Clavicula*, and the *Liber Almandal*. One might speculate that it was a manuscript of this type that Johannes Trithemius relied on to devise his inventory, even if, in view of the order in which his notes occur, he did not isolate a specifically Solomonic corpus within it. At any rate, according to the description and the incipits of the texts he consulted, the points of contact are numerous; these relate notably to the *Clavicula*, the *Liber angelicus*, the *Liber Almadel*, the *De quattuor annulis*, the *De officiis spirituum* and the *Vinculum spirituum*, a majority being texts not mentioned by the author of the *Speculum astronomiae* in his day. If we have privileged texts in Latin here, we should also not forget that translations and adaptations in vernacular languages appeared from the late medieval period, and remain important sources for modern scholars.[20]

This quick survey of the situation invites caution from the outset when dealing with Solomonic magic in the Latin West in the late Middle Ages and the beginning of the early modern period. Evidently, postulating the existence of a corpus that was well defined from its inception is impossible. On the contrary, it seems to evolve extensively between the thirteenth and fifteenth centuries, and to bring together, under a single authority, texts with sometimes markedly different origins, histories and contents.[21] If certain texts, like those mentioned by the author of *Speculum astronomiae*, perhaps circulated side by side in manuscripts from the thirteenth century, this does not mean that they had a common origin: the case of the *Liber Almandal*, whose Arabic provenance can scarcely be in doubt, is in this regard appreciably different from that of the *De quattuor annulis*, known in different versions and whose origin remains to be determined. A Solomonic tradition like the *Ars notoria*, not mentioned by William of Auvergne and the author of the *Speculum astronomiae*, has for its part a history that is well attested by manuscripts from the first part of the thirteenth century, evidently distinct from that of known Solomonic texts from this period, which have not been preserved. Revisions and rewrites of these texts should also be taken into account. They meant that the same tradition, even when it was well structured on a formal level, may over time have altered due to its pseudo-epigraphic attribution, the sometimes decidedly degraded material condition in which it circulated, its original lack of Christian associations, or even, though this list is not exhaustive, due to the interests of the specific scribe or *magister*.

Because the corpus of texts explicitly ascribed to Solomon evolved over time and was gradually enriched by new strata, with different origins and sometimes with no link between them in the first instance, as the case may be, an attribution to Solomon should not be made into a criterion that is too absolute or too necessary to the identification of a particular type of magic, for a number of reasons.

First, the pseudo-epigraphic attribution, which is linked in a general fashion to the ambivalent image of Solomon – at once a wise and inspired scholar, an authority on the natural world, an exorcist and, by extension, a master of spirits or magician in the Judeo-Christian and Islamic tradition – reflects a common narrative strategy that does not determine in itself either the content or the origin of the implicated texts,[22] even if, as the *Magister Speculi* senses, it conveys an "ambience" that is quite clearly distinct in the genre of magic texts.[23] For example, between the *Liber Almandal*, from the Arab-Muslim world, which aims to compel, for various purposes, the *jinn* and the *shayātīn* of Islamic tradition (classed in a Christian context as demons), and the *Ars notoria* of Western origin, the intention of which is to establish a privileged relation with the angels and whose end goal is the revelation of wisdom, there are scarcely any immediate connections other than their attribution to Solomon and the pretensions to the domestication of certain types of spirits through the ritual use of powerful signs revealed in ancient times.[24] It is all the more true, in this particular case, that the *Ars notoria* seems to have been first of all attributed to Virgil, towards the end of the twelfth century, when he was considered a philosopher and teacher without peer, before, in a second stage of its history which takes into account manuscripts from the 1220s, coming under the authority of Solomon, a figure who was a better fit, in a Christian context, to be the founder of a supposedly divine art.[25] This is how the anonymous *magister artium* of the *Ars notoria* garnishes his text of exemplary stories of the wise king and of the quotations attributed to him, and refers again, without much consistency with the rest of the narrative scheme, to a number of Solomonic books that are evidently fictional, with the aim of creating the feeling that one is dealing with a more venerable text, part of a larger tradition.[26] The *Ars notoria* does not appear to be isolated in this regard, since the *Clavicula*, another high art revealed to the wise king, but much more subversive than the former text, also refers, for example, to ancient books of Solomon to back up its authority.[27]

Second, it is possible that some texts that are not explicitly attributed to Solomon in twelfth and thirteenth-century sources were in fact attributed to him in other manuscripts of this period, which have unfortunately been lost. We might think, for example, of the *Liber sacratus* mentioned by William of Auvergne along with explicitly Solomonic treatises with which he seems closely acquainted.[28] Even when texts of this type were not directly attributed to Solomon, they were certainly recorded among others that were in a common category, that of texts of ritual magic.[29] This category, even if there might be points of contact and significant amounts of interpolation and contamination in the course of copying and revising,[30] was quite clearly distinct from astral or talismanic magic. The liturgical, paraliturgical, indeed literally spiritual and devotional dimension, always predominates, allowing the magician to enter (without danger) into contact with demons, spirits or angels, who are generally recalcitrant but who finally submit to the power that God grants the magician, sometimes described as an "exorcist"; knowledge linked to planets or stars is here secondary, if it exists at all.[31] Whether or not the traditions relating to this methodology that rests primarily on the power of naming are attributed to Solomon is thus, to a certain extent, of little importance, as is also shown by the remainder of the manuscripts themselves, which in certain cases mentions a connection to Solomon and in others ignores it or passes over it in silence.[32]

Third, without going so far as to postulate a general equivalence between Solomonic magic and ritual magic, in order to accurately measure the true scope of Latin Solomonic magic, we also need to consider the strong influence exerted by certain traditions belonging to Solomonic magic on the renewal of ritual magic more broadly, especially in the fourteenth and fifteenth centuries. This concerns other pseudo-epigraphic texts as well as the productions of the first "author-magicians" of the late Middle Ages. In the former case, one could give the example of the *Liber sacratus sive juratus* attributed to Honorius of Thebes, notably in the version recently edited, datable to the 1330s.[33] This vast compilation, which explicitly claims to curate the *opera Salomonis*, reuses the glossed version of the *Ars notoria* on a massive scale. "Honorius" (who probably drew on an older version of the *Liber Sacratus*, perhaps the one mentioned by William of Auvergne a century earlier) made heavy use of the *verba mystica* and Latin prayers found in this version of the *Ars notoria* which was elaborated at the turn of the fourteenth century[34] He may also have used, with regard to certain aspects of the *modus operandi*, other Solomonic texts such as the *Clavicula*.[35] In the field of the exploitation of Solomonic sources, the "author-magicians" of the late Middle Ages were not insignificant. Thus, at the very start of the fourteenth century, the Benedictine monk John of Morigny embarked on a complete, progressive and very personal revision of the *Ars notoria* in his *Liber florum celestis doctrine*.[36] The *Summa sacre magice* (1346) of the Catalan "philosopher" Bérenger Ganell, a vast compilation of ritual magic in five books known in its Latin form through an incomplete manuscript, draws part of its substance from two distinct versions of the *Liber juratus* of Honorius.[37] But in order to better establish its claim to offer "a [magic] science that consists of compelling good and bad spirits", Bérenger's work draws on numerous Solomonic traditions including the *Ydea Salomonis*, the *De officiis spirituum*, the *De quattuor annulis*, the *De novem candariis*, the *Vinculum Salomonis*, the *Almandal* and perhaps also the *Clavicula*. Bérenger even refers several times, mentioning seven books divided into different "titles", to a source he calls the *Biblia* or *Magica Salomonis*, perhaps a collection (which would be the only one of its kind) that he might have had at his disposal and of which we have no trace.[38] But the question remains as to how much credit should be accorded to his remarks, since the existence of a compilation organized in the manner of a university text prompts scepticism *a priori* in view of the general state of the conservation of Solomonic texts (and more broadly of ritual magic texts), and what this teaches us about their mode of circulation and their form, including the more complete collections.

Finally, to the traditions that are explicitly attributed to Solomon and to the texts which are not but which have recourse, in varying degrees, to what we might call the *materia magica salomonica*, it is appropriate to add a number of *experimenta*, in other words recipes stripped of all narrative devices, which to a greater or lesser extent profess Solomonic associations. These often circulated alongside Solomonic texts in manuscripts, or ultimately fall within the remit of a kind of magic founded on the same principles. This is the case, for example, in MS Munich Clm 849 which, besides two versions of the *Liber consecrationum* (no. 31) and a version of the *Vinculum Salomonis* incorporated into an *experimentum* on catoptromancy (no. 33), preserves numerous *experimenta* referring to Solomon and to his seals, his rings and other characters capable of "binding" spirits.[39] An *experimentum* for love involving the conjuration of demons even specifies, by playing implicitly and somewhat ironically on the theme of Solomon's eventual downfall (III Kings 11: 1–13), that it was thanks to this that the king obtained all the women he desired.[40] Other manuscripts of the fifteenth century, such as MS Oxford Rawlinson D.252, are no less stingy with such references in their ritual magic *experimenta*.[41] MS Coxe 25 (cited above) puts forward, among other things, a magnificent *Experimentum verissimum Salomonis* for oneiromancy, as well as an *experimentum* for crystallomancy that aims to cause "King Solomon" to appear in person in order to acquire revelations about the future.[42]

Western "Solomonic magic" of the Middle Ages, mostly in Latin, is thus an extensive category whose coherence should not be overstated and which remains "difficult to determine".[43] On a historical level, it is the result of a process of accumulation of texts that are, on the one hand, influenced by each other (as the case may be) in the course of their often collective manuscript dissemination, but also have, on the other hand, distinct histories, whose tangled threads historiography has barely begun to untangle. Aside from the *Ars notoria*, which possesses a solid independent manuscript tradition from early on, the fact that we only have later witnesses that are, moreover, not numerous hardly facilitates the task of the historian who hopes to determine the origin and original form of these frequently short texts, which much of the time are derived from translations. Nevertheless, the specialist finds himself in a situation that is a little more comfortable than that of his counterparts studying the Greek Solomonic traditions, in as much as these, created in late antiquity, are for the most part known via the intermediary of manuscripts dating from the fifteenth century at best.[44]

Principal historiographical advances and future fields of research

The heuristic foundations of a study of Solomonic magic are thus far from obvious. On a historiographical level, in addition to the seminal studies by Lynn Thorndike[45] and David Pingree,[46] in-depth historical study of Solomonic magic has coincided with a renewed interest on the part of historians since the 1990s in ritual magic as a whole, following the lead of Richard Kieckhefer,[47] and especially an interest in its primary sources, hitherto little studied. Based on a more systematic survey of manuscripts – which remains an ongoing project – and a more accurate identification of the texts, some studies have been carried out or are currently in progress as part of the international *Salomon Latinus* project, which aims to put all the Latin texts attributed to Solomon, in their different versions, at the disposal of the scholarly community.[48] This editorial programme does not exhaust the subject, as numerous other texts or *experimenta* of ritual magic are related in one way or another to Solomonic magic and as such can hardly be dissociated from it.

In this way, certain Solomonic traditions have emerged from the shadows. This is the case with the *Ars notoria*, preserved in 38 medieval manuscripts and therefore widely distributed,[49] the *Almandal/Almadel*[50] and the *Vinculum Salomonis*,[51] two texts preserved, in different versions, in several manuscripts of the fourteenth and especially the fifteenth centuries. Others are the subject of preliminary studies. Although they do not resolve all the difficulties, these works permit us to draw some general conclusions concerning Solomonic magic in itself, and more broadly concerning Western ritual magic.

First, although numerous grey areas still remain, it appears that the Latin texts on ritual magic that have been attributed to Solomon do not possess a single common origin, which is one of the factors that ultimately explain the difficulty of establishing a coherent "corpus". Most of the time they are imported, via a Latin translation, from Jewish, Arab-Muslim or even Greek culture. The *Liber Almandal* thus stems, in view of a version close to the thirteenth-century witnesses, from an Arabic prototype of which nothing is known.[52] The *Ars notoria* itself has a home-grown tradition in the Western world, its Eastern inflections notwithstanding: in its *notae*, it exhibits, among other things, a number of references to the Vulgate and to iconographic tradition partly based on older mnemonic and didactic diagrams, reflecting the ambition of establishing the ultimate means of privileged access to wisdom and of being the quintessence of scholarly magic.[53] The *Liber Razielis*, which circulated in two or in seven books (the version attributed to Alphonse X of Castile) from at least the mid-thirteenth century, took as its model the *Sefer ha-Razim* from late antique Jewish tradition, which inspired the *Liber Samayn*, the first or sixth book, respectively, of the two Latin versions of the *Raziel*.[54] The *Clavicula Salomonis*, which appears for the first time in 1310, maintains links with the Greek tradition of the *Hygromantia Salomonis* whose true nature has yet to be determined.[55] This diversity, which applies equally to the more and the less subversive texts and to their *modus operandi*, may explain the specific modes of circulation in the manuscripts and their differing fortunes, even if, owing to the state of the documentation, our understanding remains very fragmentary. The *Ars notoria* thus circulated from the first half of the thirteenth century in manuscripts that were specifically devoted to it, unlike, it would seem, other contemporary Solomonic texts, a situation that largely continued in subsequent centuries, even if we find it later in certain compilations alongside other texts of ritual magic.[56]

Additionally, these texts were sometimes subject to significant revision processes, which exceed the inevitable variants that can be found in any single manuscript copy. This is owing to the fact that these pseudo-epigraphic texts remain fundamentally "open" texts, even when they are given well-established structures and they purport to contain ancient wisdom whose performance depends, in principle, on the preservation of the original language and signs that they reveal to the user. The modalities of magic writing can take different directions, which can combine with each other. This might concern the creation of different versions, sometimes by successive shifts in order to simplify a potential application. This case is well illustrated by the *Ars notoria*, for which the oldest preserved version (version A, *c.* 1220) is already an amalgamation of an early and little used stratum, the *Flores aurei*, and an *Ars nova*, shorter and simpler, intended to short-circuit the former. But from the mid-thirteenth century, a supplementary version appeared, also simplified: the *Opus operum*, which, with version A, would aid the progressive elaboration of the glossed version at the start of the fourteenth century, whose principal function was to better order and codify the ritual.[57] Version A itself shows awareness of specific evolutions, with the appearance of a version known as A2, which is characterized by, among other things, the addition of a new prologue celebrating the wisdom of Solomon. It can also concern the amplification of the material endowed with performative power (*nomina*, *verba*, *figurae*, etc.), without this necessarily being inconsistent with the desire to make the implementation of the ritual easier. The glosses of version B, for example, explain in very practical terms when and in what order the Latin prayers and lists of *verba* and *nomina* that will eventually enable an acquisition of the understanding of the arts of the university curriculum should be recited; equally, they provide very precise instructions concerning the critical phase of the consultation of the *notae* dedicated to the arts in question.[58] But this formatting and clarification of the *modus operandi* goes hand in hand with a base text which, for its part, sees the Latin prayers and *verba* to be recited multiply, as well as the number of *notae* to examine. This accumulation is designed to increase the text's efficacy, according to a tendency we find elsewhere. In other cases, the revisions, which are often profound, may proceed from a wish to Christianize or at least to appear less heterodox, notably when the tradition was the object of recurring censure. Without even going so far as to mention the connections between John of Morigny and the *Ars notoria*,[59] we might mention, as examples that have remained under the guise of pseudo-epigraphy, a supplementary version of the *Ars notoria* that appeared in the fourteenth century, the *Ars brevis*, which resorts to a liturgy based on the mass and expurgates the majority of the text of its mysterious *verba* and *nomina*. Another example is an art datable to the fifteenth century which is also derived from it, the *Ars Paulina* – attributed, as its name suggests, to Paul the Apostle – which dedicates Latin prayers and figures to the Trinity, to the different divine persons, to angels or simply to the Virgin.[60] We can also observe this in more complex cases, such as in the manuscript tradition, tenuous though it may be, of the *Liber Almandal*. From a version that is even more marked by its Arabic heritage, based on the fabrication of a *figura mandal* and the recitation of exorcisms capable of binding *jinn*/demons for various purposes (to spark love or hate, to cure or cause disease, etc.), we arrive at the development, certainly by the fourteenth century, of a profoundly changed art which, while preserving the use of a *figura* that was now akin to a portable shrine, consists of soliciting angels and their messengers from the celestial plane for the purposes of, among other things, acquiring knowledge. From a form of necromancy that was still deeply Arabic, we arrive at a model of theurgy based on the *Ars notoria* and perhaps on a text related to the *Liber Razielis*; beyond its immediate effects, the ritual now aims to bring the human being towards salvation, by nevertheless keeping only to the margins of Christian affiliation. Ultimately, it would be necessary to wait for a gloss on this latest version, conveniently attributed to St Jerome, for the Christianizing process to become more marked (which obviously does not imply orthodoxy); in the same period, the *modus operandi* that mobilizes Christian liturgy became subject to a more workable format.[61] These few examples, in addition to what has already been said on the subject of "author-magicians", demonstrate that revision also sometimes signals the use of other texts, notably Solomonic texts; the interpolative and intertextual phenomena are thus numerous. To the extent that we only have later versions at our disposal, these games, which may be more or less direct or successful, obscure our knowledge of the form these texts may have taken on their introduction into the West; the quest for origins, which are doubtless illusions in part, is only made more difficult.

Finally, it appears that (and this applies to ritual magic more generally) these texts and "books" possess diverse natures. Though all are conceived as divine secrets, and all possess a virtue that rests on the use of signs revealed in ancient times that, subject to certain conditions – notably ritual purity – may summon the infinite power of God,[62] some aim primarily to bind demons or turbulent spirits, which can be made to conform for many purposes, whereas others aspire to establish a less strained relationship with the angelic world, most often for the purposes of obtaining understanding or revelations, or even, finally, salvation. The first type, such as the *Clavicula Salomonis*, the *Liber consecrationum* and the catalogues of demons that accompany them, belongs, strictly speaking, to necromancy[63]; they are based on the conjuration of demons, related when necessary to liturgical exorcism, which aims to "bind" the demons to the will of the *exorcista/exorcizator* or the *magister* – the *Vinculum spirituum* (also known as the *Vinculum Salomonis*) is a good example.[64] The second type, such as the *Ars notoria* and its derivatives, draws above all on prayers addressed to the angels, and indeed to God and to Christ; to a certain point, they represent the expression of a form of individual piety, more or less within the framework of Christian liturgy.[65] The former are, on the whole, more likely to transgress from the religious norm (the *Clavicula*, for example, demands that one make sacrifices to the spirits), while the latter integrate it to a greater degree – although, by definition, never completely – which eventually renders them more pernicious in the eyes of some theologians. This line of schematic demarcation between necromancy and theurgy (incidentally a category that the Latin West scarcely knows) can nevertheless be faint, even ineffective, as several specific cases show. The same tradition can shift over time from one category to the other and circulate in parallel in its different forms, as in the case of the *Almandal/Almadel*.[66] Some *experimenta* founded on conjurations or exorcisms can be destined for angels, which are constrained by them, like demons are in the books of necromancy.[67] The use of elements of the Christian liturgy, in a Western culture that was increasingly receptive to the cult of angels, and especially of the guardian angel, is by no means the prerogative only of theurgy; a text like the *Clavicula Salomonis*, which enables the user to conjure demons and spirits for potentially malevolent ends, involves, among other things, a priest, the sacraments of baptism and confession, and the liturgy of the mass. Finally, if the rituals addressed to angels were generally aimed less at producing bad effects, it was nevertheless true that this matter was not confined to demons,[68] who incidentally, in the manner of the *daïmones* of antiquity, were not always considered as bad in this context.[69] The power of God being by its very nature ambivalent (in the sense that it can encompass both good and evil) and without limits, it could subsume, once delegated to the *magister*, the categories of spirits who, good or bad, did not always conform to the Christian *doxa*.[70] If we add to this the occasional intertextual links with astral magic, we note that complexity and fluidity are *de rigueur* within these traditions, and that there is little sense of a system.

On these foundations, future research must, on the one hand, continue to produce monographic studies based around editions of texts. A number of works are, moreover, underway. Jean-Patrice Boudet is preparing an edition of the catalogues of demons, often attributed to Solomon or which make mention at least of the wise king's ability to bind spirits.[71] These circulated from perhaps the twelfth century, but only the later versions are preserved, in Latin and sometimes in the vernacular; some, which are related, are also attributed to the authority of St Cyprian, a converted magician.[72] Beyond the teeming demoniacal imaginary they conjure up, they all present a demonology that is partly an alternative to that defined by the Church. I am even planning an edition of the *Clavicula Salomonis*, that long, meticulously organized treatise on the conjuration of demons that was first attested in the West at the start of the fourteenth century and was disseminated in Italy, Spain and Germany in the late Middle Ages. At the time of writing, it is preserved in Latin, in an almost complete form, in a unique medieval manuscript, MS Coxe 25. Thus far for the Middle Ages, we know of a table of contents for the Latin version (MS Paris, BnF, lat. 7162), some modified extracts (for example in Florence, BML, Plut. 89, sup. 38) and principally an Italian version that is incomplete but close to the Latin version (MS Paris, BnF, it. 1524) dated to 1446 and linked to the court at Milan.[73] On the other hand, the manuscripts are much more numerous when it comes to the modern era. The edition of the Latin text must therefore take into account certain versions from the sixteenth and seventeenth centuries that are close to the medieval version.[74] With regard to this topic, Odile Dapsens, under the direction of Jean-Patrice Boudet and Paul Bertrand, is undertaking a doctorate devoted to the *Liber Razielis*, particularly the version in two books preserved in MS Paris, BnF, lat.

3666, whose importance has been well noted by Sophie Page[75]; this study is expected to be part of a research project built around the *Liber Razielis* and its appendices which, in view of its difficulty and scale, could only be a collective endeavour, bringing together specialists in Latin and Jewish magical traditions.

If editions of texts continue to be indispensable, their drawback is that they does not provide an overall picture of Solomonic magic and ritual magic in general. They can even deliver results that do not make the most of the best examples from the materials being studied and lack perspective: for example, the 2002 edition of the *Liber juratus sive sacratus* of Honorius of Thebes, in order to be more useful to specialists, does not clearly inscribe this tradition within the related history of the *Ars notoria*, of which certain versions, themselves the results of a long evolution, served nonetheless as sources for its "author". Ultimately, such an approach, though necessary for a primary stage of research, leads to an incomplete reconstruction, to say the least, of the history of the text and the modalities of its writing. Additionally, it now appears necessary to register, as far as possible, the work of editing and studying texts on ritual magic within a more overarching, heuristic approach, on a scale that is both collective and also complements the text's "genre", balancing the general and the particular. The objective in the long term is to work out the most comprehensive picture possible of the dissemination of the totality of these traditions in the Latin medieval West (without breaking at the Renaissance), and above all to contribute to the creation of a precise "cartography" of the intertextual links that are the lifeblood of the Solomonic "corpus", which only a large-scale approach can capture in all their complexity. In other words, the time for an initial synthesis is near, once a number of milestones have been reached.

Finally, there are sources that may turn out to be rich seams for those who are interested in this area and which have scarcely been considered. These are the rituals of exorcism in the late Middle Ages, for which the liturgy enables us to measure in unexpected ways the relationship cultivated between ritual magic and the norms of Christianity. We know that Solomonic magic, especially necromancy, comes within the framework of a liturgy that, sometimes in parodic mode, borrows from canonical practice (masses, benedictions, consecrations, use of the sacraments, etc.). Specialists have also noted that the formulas for conjuring demons maintain a formal kinship with the canonical formulas of exorcism.[76] This last point has never been studied in any depth; yet, this is fertile ground for discovery. Not only do certain "magic" conjurations borrow from the exorcisms of the Church, particularly the tradition in the *Romano-Germanic Pontifical* (this topic alone would merit a systematic examination), but it equally appears that "magic" formulas were used in their turn – sometimes on a massive scale – to develop new rituals of exorcism, which flourished from the beginning of the fifteenth century, especially in the Germanic regions, which are the best documented. The review of the first known ritual, preserved in MS Munich, BSB, Clm 10085 (*c.* 1400), illustrates this well: in addition to maintaining intertextual links with the content of the now celebrated manuscript Clm 849, remarkably, we also find here the *Vinculum Salomonis*, for the purposes of expelling demons from someone who is possessed![77] Thus, at the moment when, in a society troubled by the invasion of the demoniacal, a liturgical norm for exorcism is composed, founded in part on ancient formulas, the permeability between "magical" practices and canonical exorcisms appears very powerful. It therefore remains to assess, over the fifteenth and sixteenth centuries, the scale and the forms of these crossovers for which, ultimately, the ambivalent figure of Solomon, both exorcist and magician, is a magnificent emblem.

Notes

1 On this "tradition" that predates the large shifts in translation in the twelfth century and which still survives, see Richard Kieckhefer, *Magic in the Middle Ages* (Cambridge: Cambridge University Press, 1989), 56–94; Jean-Patrice Boudet, *Entre science et* nigromance. *Astrologie, divination et magie dans l'Occident médiéval (XIIe-XVe siècle)* (Paris: Publications de la Sorbonne, 2006), 120–22.
2 See Antonella Sannino's contribution in this volume.
3 P. Zambelli (ed.), *The* Speculum astronomiae *and Its Enigma. Astrology, Theology and Science in Albertus Magnus and His Contemporaries* (Dordrecht: Kluwer Academic, 1992), ch. 11, 244.
4 Zambelli, *The* Speculum astronomiae, 246.
5 *Secretum secretorum cum glossis et notulis. Tractatus brevis et utilis ad declarandum quaedam obscure dicta*, ed. R. Steele, in Fr. Roger Bacon, *Opera quædam hactenus inedita*, V (Oxford: Clarendon Press, 1920), 6.
6 *Part of the Opus Tertium of Roger Bacon including a fragment now printed for the first time*, ed. A.G. Little (Aberdeen, 1912), 333.
7 See below.
8 É. Anheim, B. Grévin and M. Morard, "Exégèse judéo-chrétienne, magie et linguistique: un recueil de *Notes* inédites attribuées à Roger Bacon," *Archives d'Histoire Doctrinale et Littéraire du Moyen Âge*, 68 (2001): 120–21, note 61; MS Toulouse, BM, 402, fol. 273rb, reprinted in S. Berger, *Quam notitiam linguæ hebraicæ habuerint Christiani medii ævi temporibus in Gallia* (Nancy, 1893), 41–42.
9 Paris, BnF, MS nouv. acq. lat. 1401 (short version, late thirteenth century), fol. 12v: "[…] quod vero non est experimentatus Librum ymaginum Lune, Pietatis Aristotelis, Consolationis medicine, Lucidarium in natura, Lucidarium in divinitate, Septuaginta, Alchiranum simplicem et compositum, Notoriam, Alpharay, Adam, Ydeam, Floronem, Petrum Abaleardum, et quosdam alios nomina quorum hic nolumus pandere"; Munich, BSB, Clm 10268 (long version, c. 1340), fol. 1va: "[…] quod vero non est experimentatus Librum ymaginum Lune, Pietatis Aristotilis, Consolationis medicine, Lucidarium in natura, Lucidarium in divinitate, Septuaginta, Alchiranum simplicem et compositum, Artem notoriam, Alpharay, Adam, Ydeam, Floronem, Petrum Abalehardum, et quosdam alios nomina quorum hic nolumus pandere."; fol. 17vb: "Et est sciendum quod spiritum quidam, quandoque intravit in corpora mortuorum, imprime et per illa sonant responsa dare sapiens convocator, ut probatur in arte Alphyrei, Florieth, Ydee Salomonis, etc.".
10 William of Auvergne, *De legibus*, in *Opera omnia* (Paris: apud L. Billaine, 1674), I, ch. 26, 84b.
11 William of Auvergne, *De legibus*, 84.
12 See, for example, Richard Kieckhefer, *Forbidden Rites. A Necromancer's Manual of the Fifteenth Century* (Stroud: Sutton, 1997), 246.
13 Boudet, *Entre science et* nigromance, 539–48, here 542, note 15; 543, note 18; 546, notes 39 and 40; 540, note 5.
14 Boudet *Entre science et* nigromance, 539, note 1; 545, note 29; note 33; 546, note 35.
15 Boudet *Entre science et* nigromance, 547.
16 Boudet *Entre science et* nigromance, 545–46, note 34; 547.
17 See, for example, the notes of the MSS Florence, BNC, II.iii.214 (c. 15), and BML, Plut. 89 sup. 38, dated from 1494, in J. Véronèse, *L'Almandal et l'Almadel latins au Moyen Âge. Introduction et éditions critiques* (Florence: Sismel Edizioni del Galluzzo, 2012), 69–72 and 94–99.
18 This manuscript is the former MS 114 of the Bibliotheca Philosophica Hermetica in Amsterdam. See the note in Véronèse, *L'Almandal et l'Almadel latins*, 119–21. One could also cite MS Halle, ULSA, 14.B.36 (late c.15): cf. Véronèse, *L'Almandal et l'Almadel latins*, 122–25.
19 See, for example, a collection of *experimenta* from the fifteenth-century Suppr. 15, MS Oxford, Bodleian Library, Rawlinson D.252, fol. 87v–89v.
20 See, for example, for the Italian region, MS Paris, BnF, ital. 1524, dated 1446, which notably preserves an Italian version of the *Clavicula Salomonis*: cf. F. Gal, J.-P. Boudet and L. Moulinier-Brogi, *Vedrai mirabilia. Un libro di magia del Quattrocento* (Rome: Viella, 2017); and for the Occitan region, MS Vatican, BAV, Barb. Lat. 3589 (c. 15): cf. S. Giralt, "The Manuscript of a Medieval Necromancer: Magic in Occitan and Latin in MS Vatican BAV, Barb. Lat. 3589," *Revue d'histoire des textes*, 9 (2014): 221–72.
21 See below.
22 For an analysis of certain prologues, ideal places for Solomonic attribution and creation of narrative, cf. J.-P. Boudet and J. Véronèse, "Le secret dans la magie rituelle médiévale," in *Il Segreto, Micrologus. Natura, Scienze e Società Medievali*, 14 (2006): 101–50.

23 N. Weill-Parot, *Les "images astrologiques" au Moyen Âge et à la Renaissance. Spéculations intellectuelles et pratiques magiques (XIIe-XVe siècle)* (Paris: Honoré Champion, 2002), 59.
24 See below.
25 J. Véronèse, "Virgile et la naissance de l'*Ars notoria*," in *Micrologus* 21 (2013) (*The Medieval Legends of Philosophers and Scholars*): 219–42.
26 J. Véronèse, *L'*Ars notoria *au Moyen Âge. Introduction et édition critique* (Florence, 2007), version A (c. 13), for example § 8, 36; § 19, § 20b; § 74, 60; § 111, 74; § 134, 89.
27 *Clavicula Salomonis* II, 1, MS Coxe 25 (private collection; ex MS Amsterdam, BPH, 114), 113:

> Unde isti et primi [spiritus] demonstrant se pulcherrimi et per consequens omnes generationes alias que specificuntur per Salomonem in *Libro Dogmaton* et in *Libro decorarum* habent summe substanciam in vestibus preornatis gaudentes in pulchretudine mundana et habuerunt a Deo peticionem hanc.

28 See above, note 10.
29 E. Butler, *Ritual Magic* (Stroud: Sutton, 1998, 1st edn., 1949); Claire Fanger, "Medieval Ritual Magic: What It Is and Why We Need to Know More about It," in *Conjuring Spirits: Texts and Traditions of Medieval Ritual Magic*, ed. Claire Fanger (Stroud: Sutton, 1998), vii–xviii.
30 We might cite as an example of the mixing of genres the *Liber angelicus* (cf. *supra*).
31 This refers, more or less, to the definition of Solomonic magic provided by D. Pingree, "Learned Magic in the Time of Frederick II," *Micrologus* 2 (1994) (*Federico II e le scienze della natura*): 43.
32 See, for example, *supra* regarding *Vinculum spirituum* or *Vinculum Salomonis*.
33 G. Hedegård (ed.), *"Liber iuratus Honorii": A Critical Edition of the Latin Version of the Sworn Book of Honorius* (Stockholm, 2002); J.-P. Boudet, "Magie théurgique, angélologie et vision béatifique dans le *Liber sacratus* attribué à Honorius de Thèbes," in *Les anges et la magie au Moyen Âge*, J.-P. Boudet, H. Bresc and B. Grévin (dir.), "Actes de la table ronde de Nanterre (8 and 9 December 2000)," *Mélanges de l'École française de Rome. Moyen Âge*, 114, no. 2 (2002): 851–90; J.R. Veenstra, "Honorius and the Sigil of God: The *Liber juratus* in Berengario Ganell's *Summa sacre magice*," in *Invoking Angels: Theurgic Ideas and Practices, Thirteenth to Sixteenth Centuries*, ed. Claire Fanger (University Park: Pennsylvania State University Press, 2012), 151–91, has recently shown that the *Summa sacre magice* (1346) by Bérenger Ganell drew on an older version of *Liber juratus* besides the version edited by Hedegård.
34 J. Véronèse, "The *Ars notoria* in the Middle Ages and Modern Times: Diffusion and Influence(s)," in *Dialogues among Books in Medieval Western Magic and Divination*, ed. S. Rapisarda et E. Niblaeus (Florence: Sismel Edizioni del Galluzzo, 2014), 166–67.
35 J. Véronèse, "Pietro d'Abano magicien à la Renaissance: le cas de l'*Elucidarius magice* (ou *Lucidarium artis nigromantice*)," in *Médicine, astrologie et magie entre Moyen Âge et Renaissance: autour de Pietro d'Abano*, ed. J.-P. Boudet, F. Collard et N. Weill-Parot (Florence: Sismel Edizioni del Galluzzo, 2012), 314–15.
36 Claire Fanger, *Rewriting Magic: An Exegesis of the Visionary Autobiography of a Fourteenth-Century French Monk* (University Park: Pennsylvania State University Press, 2015); *John of Morigny, "Liber florum celestis doctrine", or "Book of the Flowers of Heavenly Teaching": The New Compilation, with Independent Portions of the Old Compilation. An Edition and Commentary*, ed. Claire Fanger and Nicholas Watson (Toronto: Pontifical Institute of Mediaeval Studies, 2015). See the two editors' chapter in this volume.
37 Veenstra, "Honorius and the Sigil of God". See also Damaris Gehr's contribution in this volume.
38 MS Kassel, Landesbibliothek und Murhardsche Bibliothek der Stadt Kassel, 4° astron. 3, lib. 2, cap. 3 "De vestibus", fol. 2: "Item utile ad invocandum spiritus est habere vestes tales quales decet artem. De quibus ait Salomon in 7° suo biblo quod sint nigre vel albe."; fol. 3: "Item dicit [Salomon] in principio tituli sexti 5^i bibli quod tue vestes sint [...]"; lib. 2, cap. 4 "De corolla", fol. 7: "Quia in universali forte esset necesse tibi habere coronam magnam Salomonis quam mandat facere dificiliter in 5° suo biblo."; lib. 2, cap. 7 "De Semenphoras", fol. 21: "Ita dicit Salomon in principio *Magice*.", etc.
39 Kieckhefer, *Forbidden Rites*, for example, 243, 246, 250, 333.
40 Kieckhefer, *Forbidden Rites*, 203.
41 MS Oxford, Bodleian Library, Rawlinson D.252 (15th century), for example, fol. 5v, 9r, 11v–12r, 23v, 27v, 28v–29r, 48v, 55r, 59r, 100v, 102v, 111v–12v, 119v, 146v.
42 J. Véronèse, "La magie divinatoire à la fin du Moyen Âge: autour de quelques *experimenta* inédits," *Cahiers de Recherches Médiévales et Humanistes*, 21 (2011): 311–41, notably texts 2B and 3 edited in the appendix.
43 Weill-Parot, *Les "images astrologiques"*, 59.

44 P.A. Torijano, *Solomon, The Esoteric King: From King to Magus, Development of a Tradition* (Leiden: Brill, 2002); J. Véronèse, "La transmission groupée des textes de magie 'salomonienne' de l'Antiquité au Moyen Âge. Bilan historiographique, inconnues et pistes de recherche," in *L'Antiquité tardive dans les collections médiévales: textes et représentations, VIe-XIVe siècle*, ed. S. Gioanni et B. Grévin (Rome: École française de Rome, 2008), 193–223.
45 L. Thorndike, *History of Magic and Experimental Science*, vol. II (New York: Colombia University Press, 1923), 279–89.
46 Pingree, "Learned Magic", 39–56.
47 Kieckhefer, *Forbidden Rites*.
48 This programme, supported by SISMEL, is published in a sub-series of the *Micrologus Library*, under the scholarly authority of Jean-Patrice Boudet.
49 Véronèse, *L'Ars notoria au Moyen Âge*; Véronèse, "The *Ars notoria* in the Middle Ages and Modern Times". To the list of manuscripts presented in this article can be added: MS Düsseldorf, Universitäts- und Landesbibliothek, K07: 073 (c. 15), which was identified by László Sándor Chardonnens (we are very grateful to him for sharing his discovery with us) and which presents, in an incomplete form of the text and with no figures, the glossed version (B) and a secondary branch of the *Ars notoria*, the *Opus operum*; and MS Paris, BnF, N.A. lat. 1565 (c. 14), a glossed version (B) with figures.
50 J. Véronèse, *L'Almandal et l'Almadel latins*.
51 F. Chave-Mahir et J. Véronèse, *Rituel d'exorcisme ou manuel de magie? Le manuscrit Clm 10085 de la Bayerische Staatsbibliothek de Munich (début du XVe siècle)* (Florence: Sismel Edizioni del Galluzzo, 2015).
52 Véronèse, *L'Almandal et l'Almadel latins*, 15–30 and 75–92.
53 Véronèse, *L'Ars notoria au Moyen Âge*, 25–27.
54 B. Rebiger and P. Schäfer, *Sefer ha-Razim I und II. Das Buch der Geheimnisse I und II* (Tübingen, 2009), vol. 1, 28 and 31–52; vol. 2, 82–85. On the different versions of the Latin *Raziel*, see S. Page, "Uplifting Souls: the *Liber de essentia spirituum* and the *Liber Razielis*", in *Invoking Angels*, ed. Fanger, 79–112, especially 94–105; J.-P. Boudet, "Adam, premier savant, premier magicien," in *Adam, le premier homme*, ed. A. Paravicini Bagliani (Florence: Sismel Edizioni del Galluzzo, 2012), 277–96, especially 286–91.
55 Boudet and Véronèse, "Le secret dans la magie rituelle médiévale", 105–6.
56 For example, in MS Halle, ULSA, 14.B.36.
57 For details on these evolutions, we refer for the moment to our doctoral thesis, partially available online: *L'Ars notoria au Moyen Âge et à l'époque moderne. Étude d'une tradition de magie théurgique (XIIe-XVIIe siècle)*, vol. I, dir. C. Beaune (Université Paris X-Nanterre, 2004), 49–301.
58 Véronèse, *L'Ars notoria au Moyen Âge*, especially 217–31.
59 See above.
60 Véronèse, *L'Ars notoria au Moyen Âge et à l'époque moderne*: for the *Ars brevis*, vol. I, 303–17 and vol. II, transcription, 967–984; for the *Ars Paulina*, vol. I, 331–39.
61 Véronèse, *L'Almandal et l'Almadel latins*, 15–51. See also the recent discovery of a De consecratione lapidum by Vajra Redan, certainly from the second part of the thirteenth century, which borrows several topics to the "arabic" version of the Liber Almandal: "The De consecratione lapidum: A Previously Unknown Thirteenth-Century Version of the Liber Almandal Salomonis, Newly Introduced with Critical Edition and Translation," The Journal of Medieval Latin, 28 (2018), 277–333.
62 Especially the divine names: cf. J. Véronèse, "God's Names and Their Uses in the Books of Magic Attributed to King Solomon," *Magic, Ritual, and Witchcraft*, 5, no. 1 (2010): 30–50.
63 Cf. Frank Klaassen's contribution in this volume.
64 J.-P. Boudet and J. Véronèse, "Lier et délier: de Dieu à la sorcière," in *La légitimité implicite. Actes des conférences organisées à Rome en 2010 et en 2011 par SAS en collaboration avec l'École française de Rome*, vol. I, ed. J.-Ph. Genet (Paris and Rome: Publications de la Sorbonne, 2015), 87–119.
65 See, for example, the theurgy of Pelagius of Majorca, implicitly based on the tradition of the *Ars notoria*: cf. J. Véronèse, "La notion d'"auteur magicien' à la fin du Moyen Âge: le cas de l'ermite Pelagius de Majorque († v. 1480)," *Médiévales* 51 (2006): 119–38.
66 See above.
67 Véronèse, "La magie divinatoire à la fin du Moyen Âge".
68 See, for example, in the *Liber Samayn* of the *Liber Razielis*, in which the aims are far from being exclusively oriented towards the good, since the angels can bring about sickness or death: cf. Rediger and Schäfer, *Sefer ha-Razim I und II*, vol. I, especially § 42–45, 34–35.

69 J.-P. Boudet, "Les *who's who* démonologiques de la Renaissance et leurs ancêtres médiévaux," *Médiévales* 44 (2003): 117–39.
70 Boudet and Véronèse, "Lier et délier", especially 105–10 on the *Liber Razielis*.
71 *De officiis spirituum*, MS Coxe 25, 173–87, especially 173: "De maliciis demonum. Vidit ergo Deus quod cuncta malicia demonum erat in terra cujusdam filio regis David, scilicet Salomoni, universam tradidit scientiam vel sapientiam […]"; 178: "[…] deinde sapientissimum Salomonem credunt [demones sive spiritus] ad invenisse et tamen cum aliter prudens fuerit [instructor hujus artis] poterit spiritum vel spiritus, reges vel principes cogere […] usque in abyssum proicere", etc.; Boudet, "Les *who's who* démonologiques".
72 J.-P. Boudet is working on the copies of *Secreta Cipriani* preserved in MSS Cambridge, University Lib., Dd. 4.35, fol. 27r–40v (*c.* 1415) and Oxford, Bodleian Lib., Digby 30, fol. 1r–28v.
73 Gal, Boudet and Moulinier-Brogi, *Vedrai mirabilia*.
74 Boudet and Véronèse, "Le secret dans la magie rituelle médiévale".
75 Page, "Uplifting Souls".
76 Kieckhefer, *Forbidden Rites*, 144–49.
77 Chave-Mahir and Véronèse, *Rituel d'exorcisme ou manuel de magie?*

15

NECROMANCY

Frank Klaassen

The intentional or unintentional conjuring of demons was the great spectre medieval anti-magic literature, something to which practitioners and non-practitioners alike reduced almost all forms of magic at one time or another in order to reject them. John of Morigny constructed and supported his revision of the *Ars notoria* in opposition to the threat of demons it provoked.[1] Renaissance authors such as Marsilio Ficino and Henry Cornelius Agrippa constructed their positive views of magic in conscious opposition to necromancy.[2] Later, necromancy and magic in general were used in the rhetoric of the reformation to attack not only Catholicism but also sectarians and atheists.[3] This rhetorical habit even continued with modern authors. Lynn Thorndike, Frances Yates and a host of others have used it to designate the sort of magic that was decidedly unlike science: the magic of the Renaissance, natural or spiritual magic, astral magic or whatever sort of magic they championed. This concern also had institutional expressions. To at least the mid-fifteenth century, the learned necromantic practitioner was the principal focus of law and legal procedures against magic. The middlebrow nature of much necromantic literature and its generally self-serving goals make it an easy target for this sort of thing, but given how large its spectre looms in writing on medieval magic and the Middle Ages in general, and its consistent presence in modern commentaries about premodern magic, it is curious that so little is really known about it.

During the past two decades, this situation has improved a great deal, but, with a few significant exceptions, explorations of necromancy in its own right remain rare. As a result, significant areas for future study remain almost entirely unexplored.

Definitions

Necromancy is a category of ritual magic that concerns itself principally with conjuring demons, though sometimes also angels, terrene spirits such as fairies, and very rarely spirits of the dead. It employs repurposed liturgical fragments and structures, a variety of consecrated objects and lengthy ritual invocations reflecting the standard rhetoric of prayer and exorcism. It observes liturgical and astrological calendars for its operations, as well as atmospheric conditions. The operations generally require the creation or use of specific ritual spaces, such as conjuring circles, specially prepared rooms, or altars, and the interactions with the conjured spirits occur through various media, including scrying stones, mirrors, crystals, child mediums, dreams or waking visions.

Necromantic practitioners were generally members of what Richard Kieckhefer has called the "clerical underground."[4] This is to say, they were sometimes monks and sometimes held secular church offices, but also sometimes belonged to the clerical world only insofar as they had attended university. Some were decidedly on the fringes of this group but identified with it, having had enough education through grammar school and personal study to have functional Latinity. The content of the surviving texts certainly suggests lowly status and modest learning. As the most worldly of the learned magicians, the goals of their rituals include sex or love, treasure hunting, gaining status, secret knowledge, invisibility or the creation of wonders. Reflecting this focus on worldly results, they make few claims that their practices are spiritually or intellectually enriching.

Contemporaries typically referred to the genre as *necromantia* or *nigromantia*, but neither are entirely satisfying terms for the purposes of modern classification. The former was used to describe bad magic, which is to say demonic magic, sometimes including forms in which demons were not explicitly conjured; the latter had a positive valence but was also used to refer to a wide and nebulous range of magic practices from demonic conjuring to purely astrological magic. By a narrow margin, *necromantia* more accurately reflects a genre that did involve demon conjuring. Although necromancy is the closest thing to "black magic" we find in the medieval period, the simplistic division of white and black magic misrepresents the realities. Medieval necromancy is fundamentally Christian in conception, and the operators positioned themselves as virtuous Christians, working entirely through the power of God. In fact, the author of the *Speculum astronomiae* regarded this kind of literature as *less* abominable than astral magic or Hermetic magic, which had all the trappings of a non-Christian religion. The term "demonic magic" also misrepresents the realities, as medieval necromantic practice sometimes included other sorts of spirits.

Among the most important identifiable texts are the *Thesaurus spirituum*, the closely related *Practica nigromancie*, the *De officiis spirituum* and the *Liber consecrationum*. The library of necromancy also included a good deal of literature from the Solomonic tradition in addition to other texts. The *Clavicula Salomonis*, for example, was a standard work, as were a range of short texts attributed to Solomon such as the *Vinculum Salomonis*, an intensified conjuration to bring a spirit to heel. In addition to these, necromantic collections also commonly included many anonymous operations and scattered materials useful to the operator such as prayers, biblical passages or tables identifying associations between a variety of things such as angels, demons, sigils, suffumigations, astrological conditions, days of the week or hours of the day. Since Solomonic magic is being treated as a separate category in this volume, this discussion will focus primarily on the non-Solomonic and anonymous materials where possible.

Historical outlines

As this rough description suggests, the origins of necromancy are multiple. Literary representations connect it with Toledo, which is unsurprising as it drew heavily upon Arabic and Jewish sources.[5] The conjuring practices in the latter portions of the London version of the *Liber iuratus Honorii* which derived from the Iberian Peninsula have a good deal in common with the later traditions. While Jewish demon magic has some very suggestive commonalities with necromancy, much of this remains conjectural at this point and it is often difficult to assess whether Jewish manuscripts (seemingly attesting to earlier Judaic practices) may actually have derived from Christian or Arabic sources.[6] Certainly, the long list of "less detestable" magic texts given in the *Speculum astronomiae* suggests that, whatever its origin, there was a lively literature in circulation in the thirteenth century employing "exorcisms" or conjurations and configured in Christian form.[7]

Most of the witnesses to medieval necromantic practice are early modern and most of the medieval witnesses are late medieval. A few fifteenth-century collections survive such as the Rawlinson and Munich Manuals.[8] These contain either fragmentary or full copies of earlier texts such as the *Liber consecrationum* and *Thesaurus spirituum*. The latter survives, in varying but apparently complete sixteenth-century versions. The classic Solomonic text of necromancy, the *Clavicula Salomonis*, survives in one fifteenth-century copy but is mostly witnessed in later manuscripts.[9] Although medieval witnesses are very rare in comparison to other works, explicitly necromantic works make up a substantial proportion of sixteenth- and seventeenth-century manuscripts. Whether this is due to a relatively high attrition rate in the medieval period or a sudden growth in interest after 1500 remains unclear.[10] Certainly, together with medieval references to circulating conjuring works, it suggests that medieval versions were considerably more numerous than the surviving witnesses suggest.

These texts have a relatively high level of textual variance that was at least in part the result of the intellectual culture that surrounded them, including a kind of "mix-and-match" approach to operations. Ritual magic texts in general tended to promote a view of the magician as a kind of divinely guided editor who discovered the ancient truths hidden in magic texts through long practice and could be expected to create a new book of magic at the end of the process. Certainly, such mythology would have helped to justify the creation of new texts when a user only had fragmentary sources or when the available texts did not agree. Surviving fifteenth-century manuals also suggest that practitioners collected a variety of texts often from disconnected or even incompatible traditions. They also employed these texts interchangeably as circumstances demanded or in an effort to create something that worked.[11] These habits are visible in the marginalia of necromantic manuals and in cross-references in the texts themselves. So, for example, a conjuration might refer the operator to a particular prayer or a text such as the *Vinculum Salomonis* that might or might not be included elsewhere in the volume. Fragmentary texts or opuscula were thus not considered problematic but potentially useful or even necessary.

Certainly, a good deal of the necromantic literature was created in a process of pillaging and raw invention. Well-known works such as the *Ars notoria* and *Liber iuratus* served as sourcebooks for creating new operations, and the Munich Manual contains a demonic variation on the *Ars notoria*.[12] Necromantic practitioners also commonly drew upon the liturgy rather than simply employing the liturgical fragments already incorporated in pre-existing magic texts. Even as late as the early sixteenth century, magicians with access to reasonable collections of classic magic texts also used liturgical books to construct magic operations.[13] Similarly, many of the apparently anonymous sections in medieval necromantic handbooks were derived from standard texts such as the *Thesaurus spirituum* without their sources being identified.[14] Local traditions were also incorporated into the operations. The *Thesaurus spirituum*, for example, contains a ritual for conjuring spirits that are clearly fairies and that corresponds to the traditions represented in medieval fairy literature.[15] Finally, as this material spread into vernacular languages starting in the fifteenth century, the texts also changed under the influence of its new middlebrow transmitters. As a result, the history of the texts is difficult to trace, and this process is made more difficult by the fact that most of the surviving manuscripts post-date 1500, when major shifts in social, intellectual, and religious conditions were underway.

Necromantic texts travelled in a relatively stable social context through the medieval period, although that began to break down in the fifteenth century. The clerical underworld described above had ragged edges and included educated courtiers, grammar school teachers and itinerant clerics who had deserted their posts or had never held an ecclesiastical income. The texts demanded at least a close association with the clerical world because they required functional Latinity, some knowledge of the liturgy and often the services of an ordained priest. However, as the literature slowly filtered into vernacular versions and as the learned world itself became less overtly clerical, the social coherence of this group began to break down and a growing group of lay and non-Latinate practitioners took it up. This in part explains why the vernacular texts evince significant transformations. This process began in the fifteenth century, but became significant only in the early modern period.

Although necromancy was condemned repeatedly and with increasing sophistication, and despite being in some ways the least defensible form of learned magic, there was little institutional will to seek out and prosecute practitioners. Necromantic practitioners were unquestionably aware of each other, sought books through informal networks and frequently performed necromantic magic in groups (something that the texts often require). In short, not only did they evince many of the mythological trappings of heresy and witchcraft, but it also would have been possible for dedicated investigators to seek out these wider communities and eradicate them. However, such far-reaching investigations were very rare indeed. Instead, church courts tended to deal with individual cases when they appeared in Episcopal visitations or were otherwise unavoidable due to public scandal, and even in the later Middle Ages confined themselves to a strategy of correction through confession, penance and the destruction of the offending books and equipment rather than execution. Secular courts certainly had a growing concern with this sort of magic towards the end of the Middle Ages, but similarly tended to deal with them on a case-by-case basis and only inflicted capital punishment when the offending party had committed or attempted to commit a felony such as murder or sedition.[16]

State of the field

The scholarly study of necromantic magic began among practitioners and anti-magic writers soon after its appearance. The book collections of people like John Erghome, the analysis of texts in the *Speculum astronomiae*, the bibliographic work of Trithemius and the broad humanistic research of Henry Cornelius Agrippa are but a few examples of early explorations that ultimately became fundamental tools for the historical bibliography of magic.[17] Although scholarship motivated by anti-magic sentiments dropped off after 1600, nineteenth-century occultists like Eliphas Levi, Arthur Edward Waite and Gregory Mathers continued in many respects to approach the material as scholars. Their activities include both extending the bibliographic research of the earlier authors and some basic editing of early magic texts, although naturally their primary goals were practical rather than scholarly. Along with other occultists, they also formed an important bridge between the premodern and modern, making this literature relevant in new ways to modern readers. Lay researchers continue to make valuable contributions to the field to the present day.[18]

In a strict sense, the scholarly study of necromantic texts began in the twentieth century with writers like Lynn Thorndike and Elizabeth Butler. Like many others after him, Thorndike's documenting of necromantic literature was grudging, since it generally did not confirm his preconceptions of the close relationship between magic and science and the decline of "use of superstitious ceremonial and magical rite, of incantation, word and number" in the early modern period.[19] Nonetheless, his dedication to manuscripts and his extensive documenting of manuscript sources remains profoundly valuable. Elizabeth Butler's contribution was almost the opposite. Her interest in tracing the backdrop for the Faust legends led her to an unapologetic focus upon demon conjuring in its various forms, particularly in the early modern period. However, her explorations of the literature were limited to printed sources, so the picture she paints of medieval magic was somewhat anachronistic.

D. P. Walker, Frances Yates and others inspired a new generation of scholars to examine premodern magic, but they had little time for medieval necromantic magic, which (together with most medieval ritual magic) Yates referred to as "the old dirty magic."[20] In fact, the old traditions served as a useful foil to emphasize the distinctive nature of Renaissance high magic and its connections to Arabic, Neoplatonic and Hermetic sources, a habit of mind found also among historians of science who have regarded works on natural magic as centrally important due to their integration with sixteenth-century science. The few medievalists who worked directly on learned magic also tended to focus more on Arabic texts or astrological magic. David Pingree's attention rarely shifted from texts like the *Picatrix*, and Charles Burnett has similarly been preoccupied with texts of Arabic origin and other sorts of magic. Vittoria Perone Comangni has worked to catalogue medieval astrological magic and Paola Zambelli's attention has focused principally on questions surrounding natural magic.[21]

Although explored briefly in his *Magic in the Middle Ages* and a number of articles, it was not until Richard Kieckhefer published *Forbidden Rites* that any scholar gave close attention to a manuscript collection of medieval necromantic texts for its own sake.[22] This was a crucial step since so little was known about such works, much less at the level of detail a textual edition can facilitate. Previously, even occultists had preferred to examine single works of explicitly Solomonic magic rather than the disordered collections of anonymous and ragged material that are typical of surviving medieval handbooks. Kieckhefer's work broke new ground by attempting to understand necromantic texts not as isolated travellers but as elements in a larger collection purposefully assembled by a particular user. He also made the first attempt to treat the practice on its own terms and to develop ways of thinking about it. He categorized the constituent operations and sought to connect the collection to the intellectual, religious and social environment of fifteenth-century Germany. This remains the single most important publication on the topic. Perhaps the most interesting and valuable feature of his work is his grappling with how to understand the relationship of this literature to religious practice.

Since that time a number of scholars have taken up the study of texts and manuscripts. While it does not add to our understanding of medieval material, Davies's book *Grimoires* provides a remarkably broad survey of the magic books in general to the present day and provides a valuable overview of these book in both Europe and its colonies.[23] Other surveys of medieval manuscript material by Jean-Patrice Boudet, Nicolas Weill-Parot, Julien Veronese and myself, however, have opened up areas almost invisible in Thorndike's work, providing a more nuanced picture of the library of medieval learned magic.[24] Perhaps more significantly, editions of texts that are important to necromantic practice, including the *Liber iuratus Honorii*, *Almandal* and Montolmo's *De occultis et manifestis*, have helped to provide an expanded sense of the practice of spirit conjuring.[25] Scholars have also conducted focused studies on particular manuscripts such as the Rawlinson Manual, Society of Antiquaries 39 and a manuscript of the *De oficiis spirituum*.[26] Studies of sixteenth-century manuscripts based upon medieval texts will also expand our understanding of both medieval necromancy and the ways it changed in the early modern period.[27]

Most of the analyses of texts relating to demon conjuring concern the relationship of the practice to the intellectual world of the Middle Ages. Kieckhefer has explored in particular the relationship to the mental world of late medieval piety and has considered the ways in which necromancy may or may not be considered as part of the medieval religious landscape.[28] Scholars have also considered the various ways in which conjuring literature has framed itself, in particular, the ways in which the mythology of secrecy should be understood, the development of the "author-magician" of the late Middle Ages and the way in which magicians understood their relationship to received texts.[29] The close relationship of the conjuring literature to medieval scientific thinking has also been explored in various ways.[30] Finally, knowledge of medieval literature, significantly necromantic literature, has led to calls for a reassessment of the place of this material in the Renaissance and in sixteenth-century science.[31]

In part following Kieckhefer's lead, scholars have explored various aspects of the social world surrounding necromantic magic or learned magic in general. Having proposed that ritual magic, and necromantic magic in particular, was generated by, transmitted in and employed by members of a "clerical underworld", Kieckhefer explored this further in *Forbidden Rites*, where he described figures such as Johannes Hartlieb as the sorts of persons who might have authored CLM 849.[32] Some scholars have explored the question of how necromancy and ritual magic may be seen as products of the homosocial world in which they were created and transmitted and in the ideals of learned masculinity that they espoused.[33] Indirectly, Kieckhefer has touched on similar questions in his discussion of erotic magic, some forms of which were necromantic.[34] Jean-Patrice Boudet and others have explored the relationship of magic to the social contexts in which it was transmitted, particularly the courts and the world of learning, and the ways in which these contexts supported and shaped it.[35] This positive relationship was, however, accompanied by opposite and negative impacts.

Much of the history of necromantic magic in its relation to the courts was conducted as part of an attempt to explain the rise of the witch trials. Edward Peters, Cohn and others after them have demonstrated that from the thirteenth to the fifteenth centuries, medieval authorities were far more concerned with the learned male practitioner of necromancy than the common female practitioners who increasingly occupied their attentions after 1550.[36] Similarly, extensive documentation of trials of necromantic practice may be found in the works of George Lyman Kittredge and Keith Thomas, neither of whom was primarily interested in necromantic magic as an intellectual tradition in its own right, and later by Richard Kieckhefer whose initial work on magic concerned the history of witchcraft.[37]

Eventually, however, more historians of learned magic took up this work. Boudet and Veenstra, for example, have demonstrated the growing sophistication of the anti-magic writers in their knowledge of ritual magic literature.[38] In particular, anti-magic writers evince an awareness of how necromantic texts positioned their practices as holy (that is as operating through the power of Christian rituals, the piety of the operator and his Christian status) and how they more than often did not require any explicit pact, sacrifice, act of obeisance to the devil. As a result of such knowledge, condemnations became more sophisticated. More recent work on cunning folk and trial records of practitioners after 1500 may shed further light on late medieval practices and practitioners, particularly in areas like England, where the crucial conceptual shift to concern with witchcraft did not take place until the latter part of the sixteenth century.[39]

Opportunities for future work

The historical focus by scholars on witchcraft on the one hand and high magic (medieval or Renaissance) on the other hand has tended to leave necromantic magic largely unconsidered, even though it was a principal concern for late medieval voices of authority to the end of the Middle Ages and its users constitute the largest group of those brought up on legal charges for magic practice. In fact, most of the studies cited here touch on necromantic practice only under the broader rubric of ritual magic. Although this situation may in part be explained by the dearth of surviving medieval manuscripts, the genre is represented by a host of sixteenth-century witnesses, all of which attest to late medieval practice. Court records of late medieval prosecutions for necromantic practice also merit investigation in their own right rather than under the rubric of witchcraft.[40] As a result, there remains a good deal of scope for further study.

The surviving manuscripts betray origin or circulation in various literate environments. Studies drawing on such evidence could help to situate necromantic practice more fully in particular settings, monastic, clerical, university or bourgeois. This is especially the case where it is possible to supplement this with evidence from court cases involving necromantic magic. Looking at such locations is important for another reason. Studies of ritual magic often give the impression that necromantic magic was the product and practice of single isolated users and have often been treated that way rather than as the products of communities, despite the fact that many necromantic rituals explicitly involve several people performing a variety of roles. Studies of this kind would thus not only help us to better understand how necromancy related to particular social settings but also how necromantic rituals were developed, conceived and performed by groups of people.

Trial records and literary representations also offer other opportunities for broad surveys. Although the relationship of magic and heresy has been sketched out to some extent, no broad study has been conducted that compares court cases for conjuring with those for other forms of magic such as witchcraft or those for heresy, which is often assumed to share a similar conceptual space. Similarly, examinations of magic literature have contextualized particular literary representations of magic by referring to necromantic manuscripts, but these studies have remained focused only on isolated examples.[41] Tremendous opportunities thus exist for broad comparative studies of literary representations that would seek to understand their relationship to, and continuities or discontinuities with, the textual traditions of medieval magic. In fact, since studies concerned with literature tend to have been written as ways of explicating particular literary texts, no comprehensive survey of European literary representations of necromancy has yet been written.

The growing body of scholarly editions provides concrete evidence for the ways in which this literature was transmitted, but there remains a good deal more to do. We have no edition of the most important works of necromantic magic, such as the *Thesaurus spirituum*, and although we have single-witness editions of texts like the *Liber consecrationum*, the lack of critical editions makes it more difficult to assess how the text was compiled and transmitted. The medieval library of necromancy also included an assemblage of a variety of small texts used for specific purposes. More manageable projects (particularly for graduate students) would be to provide editions and studies of these smaller texts such as the *Vinculum Salomonis*. At this point, it is not even clear whether these texts have a real textual tradition or whether there are numerous texts circulating under their names, the writing of which was prompted by the fact that another text cited them. Undoubtedly, there are also other texts yet to be identified among the great variety of anonymous and untitled material.

As a literature characterized by regular textual pillaging, transformation, and reinvention, a good deal can be gleaned about the intellectual culture of magic from the ways in which necromancy changed over time. Such studies will be increasingly possible as more of this literature is published in scholarly editions. In addition to examining the ways in which the texts themselves were transformed, such studies can look at three issues: relations with Jewish and Arabic sources, medieval cross-pollination and vernacularization. The growing body of research on Jewish and Arabic magic will no doubt reveal further ways in which magic traditions were appropriated from these sources but also fed back into Jewish traditions. Interrelations between texts and common traditions such as fairy lore tell us a good deal not only about magic but also about the relationship between learned and popular culture (assuming such a division is valid). More crucially, dedicated study of the relationship between necromantic magic and the liturgy could provide a variety of valuable insights into the religious sensibilities of the authors. For example, it would be interesting to know the extent to which necromantic scribes and authors drew ritual forms from contemporary and local liturgical traditions as they created their texts, as opposed to drawing this sort of material from other magic texts serving as a kind of independent liturgical tradition.

Dramatic opportunities may also be found in examining the fortunes of magic at the very end of the Middle Ages, in the sixteenth century, and beyond. The foundations of much of modern magic are medieval and this is particularly the case with the conjuring literature. The transmission of the originally Latin necromantic material into the vernacular began in earnest in the fifteenth century and this was by no means a neutral process. In fact, vernacular translations seem to have been common locations for the dramatic revision of the original texts, while Latin texts more often preserved the original forms.[42] Studies of vernacular versions of medieval literature will provide interesting perspectives on the ways in which magic transformed as it shifted to a more popular and secular environment.

In a similar way, the changes associated with the Renaissance deserve closer examination. The conventional narrative of Renaissance magic suggests a dramatic break with the medieval past in the 1480s. However, the greatest proportion of sixteenth-century magic manuscripts contains medieval ritual magic, and most of these are necromantic. Without an understanding of medieval traditions of magic, it remains easy to misconstrue the significance of Renaissance or early modern magic or to misunderstand it entirely. Further study of Renaissance manuscripts will help us better understand the transitions that took place among common practitioners. In addition, the development of modern conjuring magic from its medieval sources remains almost entirely unexplored.

It is fitting to close by returning to the work of Richard Kieckhefer, particularly the ways in which his work pointed outward towards etic considerations. Necromantic literature involves a fascinating combination of seemingly contrary elements which he has referred to as "flamboyantly transgressive": a conservative dedication to liturgical form within wildly inappropriate appropriations, an insistence on being in a state of grace in order to perform magic to appease greed or lust and a fascination with the numinous that seems analogous to, but different from, the desire of the mystic for God. Certainly, the lines between this form of magic and conventional religious practice are complex and far from clear, and Kieckhefer has tried in various emic ways to articulate the complexities of the boundaries, but these explorations prompt some interesting etic questions. How does the impulse to work with demons in a Christian context compare with traditions that are explicitly demonic and operative, such as Taoist incantation texts, or those engaging in spiritual ways with malefic forces such as we find in Tibetan tantric necromancy? To what extent are our definitions of religion prefabricated to exclude such practices in ways that prevent us from engaging in a sympathetic treatment of medieval necromancy? From the perspective of world religions, is necromancy (and by implication all conventionally defined medieval magic) better understood simply as a part of the spectrum of medieval Christian religion?

Notes

1 The prologue to the *Liber florum celestis doctrine* (previously called the *Liber visionis*) details at great length the terrifying demonic visions prompted by the *Ars notoria*. It also concludes with a discussion of how to distinguish demonic visions from divine visions. John of Morigny, "Prologue to *Liber Visionum* [C. 1304–1318]," translated, edited and introduced by Claire Fanger and Nicholas Watson, *Esoterica* III (2001): 108–217.
2 Ficino's *Apology* for the *De vita coelitus comparanda* divides his good magic from bad magic on these grounds. Marsilio Ficino, *Apologia*, ed. Carol V. Kaske and John R. Clark, trans. Carol V. Kaske and John R. Clark, *Three Books on Life* (Binghamton, NY: Medieval & Renaissance Texts & Studies in conjunction with the Renaissance Society of America, 1989), 398–99. See also Heinrich Cornelius Agrippa von Nettesheim, *De Incertitudine & Vanitate Omnium Scientiarum & Artium Liber* (Hagae-Comitvm: Ex Typographia Adriani Vlacq, 1662), ch. 45, 151–56.
3 G. J. R. Parry, "Occult Philosophy and Politics: Why John Dee Wrote His Compendious Rehearsal in November 1592," *Studies in History and Philosophy of Science* 43 (2012): 480–88; Gary K. Waite, *Heresy, Magic, and Witchcraft in Early Modern Europe* (Basingstoke and New York: Palgrave Macmillan, 2003), 102, 75–76, and 229–34.
4 Richard Kieckhefer, *Magic in the Middle Ages* (Cambridge: Cambridge University Press, 1989), 153–56; Richard Kieckhefer, *Forbidden Rites: A Necromancer's Manual of the Fifteenth Century* (Stroud: Sutton, 1997), 4.
5 Richard Kieckhefer, "The Devil's Contemplatives: The Liber Iuratus, the Liber Visionum, and Christian Appropriation of Jewish Occultism," in *Conjuring Spirits: Texts and Traditions of Medieval Ritual Magic*, ed. Claire Fanger (University Park: Pennsylvania State University Press, 1998), 250–65; Katelyn Mesler, "The Liber Iuratus Honorii and the Christian Reception of Angel Magic," in *Invoking Angels: Theurgic Ideas and Practices, Thirteenth to Sixteenth Centuries*, ed. Claire Fanger (University Park: Pennsylvania State University Press, 2011), 113–50.
6 Kieckhefer, *Forbidden Rites*, 33–39 and 115–16; Katelyn Mesler, "The Three Magi and Other Christian Motifs in Medieval Hebrew Medical Incantations: A Study in the Limits of Faithful Translation," in *Latin into Hebrew: Texts and Studies. Volume I: Studies*, ed. Resianne Fontaine and Gad Freudenthal (Leiden: Brill, 2013), 164–66.
7 "Speculum Astronomiae," in *The Speculum Astronomiae and Its Enigma: Astrology, Theology, and Science in Albertus Magnus and His Contemporaries*, ed. Paola Zambelli (Dordrecht: Kluwer Academic, 1992), ch. 11.
8 For a discussion of the Munich Manual (CLM 849), see Kieckhefer, *Magic in the Middle Ages*; *Forbidden Rites*. For the Rawlinson Manual (Rawlinson D. 252), see Frank Klaassen, *The Transformations of Magic: Illicit Learned Magic in the Later Middle Ages and Renaissance* (University Park: Pennsylvania State University Press, 2012), 134–55.
9 For the most recent discussion of manuscripts of this work, see Jean-Patrice Boudet and Julien Véronèse, "Le Secret Dans La Magie Rituelle Médiévale," *Micrologus* 14 (2006): 101–50.
10 Frank Klaassen, "Medieval Ritual Magic in the Renaissance," *Aries* 3, no. 2 (2003): 166–199.
11 Klaassen, *Transformations of Magic*, 115–55; Kieckhefer, *Forbidden Rites*, 34–39.
12 Kieckhefer, *Forbidden Rites*, 193–96.
13 York, Borthwick, Abp Reg 26 fol. 68r–72v. For a fuller discussion of this case, see Frank Klaassen and Sharon Wright, *The Magic of Rogues* (forthcoming).
14 Materials in the Rawlinson Handbook, for example, were derived from the *Thesaurus spirituum*.
15 See for example London, British Library, Sloane MS 3853, ff. 36r–38r. For sixteenth-century copies of this ritual, see Frank Klaassen and Katrina Bens, "Achieving Invisibility and Having Sex with Spirits: Six Operations from an English Magic Collection Ca. 1600," *Opuscula: Short Texts of the Middle Ages and Renaissance* 3, no. 1 (2013): 1–14.
16 For a rehearsal of this curious situation, see Frank Klaassen, "The Middleness of Ritual Magic," in *The Unorthodox Imagination in Medieval Britain*, ed. Sophie Page (Manchester: Manchester University Press, 2011), 131–65.

17 On John Erghome, see Klaassen, *Transformations of Magic*, 57–80. On Trithemius's bibliography for necromancers, Paola Zambelli, *White Magic, Black Magic in the European Renaissance: From Ficino, Pico, Della Porta to Trithemius, Agrippa, Bruno* (Leiden: Brill, 2007), 73–112. Although it certainly seeks to put forward a particular cosmological perspective on magic, Henry Cornelius Agrippa von Nettesheim's *De occulta philosophia* (1533) was in functional terms an encyclopaedia of magic with materials drawn from a vast array of sources.

18 Perhaps most significant is Joseph Peterson whose contributions as a layperson, particularly his vast online collection of transcribed texts, have been substantial and valuable. See http://esoteric archives.org.

19 Lynn Thorndike, *A History of Magic and Experimental Science* (New York: Macmillan, 1923), VI: 591.

20 Frances Yates, *Giordano Bruno and the Hermetic Tradition* (Chicago, IL: University of Chicago Press, 1964), 80–81.

21 Pingree's most important work was "Picatrix," in *Picatrix: The Latin Version of the Ghayat Al-Hakim*, ed. David Pingree (London: Warburg Institute, 1986). Charles Burnett's voluminous production cannot be adequately summarized. For a representative set of materials, see Charles Burnett, *Magic and Divination in the Middle Ages: Texts and Techniques in the Islamic and Christian Worlds* (Aldershot, UK: Variorum, 1996). For a representative collection of Paola Zambelli's works, see Paola Zambelli, *White Magic, Black Magic in the European Renaissance*. Paolo Lucentini and V. Perrone Compagni, *I Testi E I Codici Di Ermete Nel Medioevo*, Hermetica Mediaevalia, vol. 1 (Firenze: Polistampa, 2001).

22 Kieckhefer, *Magic in the Middle Ages*; *Forbidden Rites*.

23 Owen Davies, *Grimoires: A History of Magic Books* (Oxford: Oxford University Press, 2009).

24 While neither Weill-Parot or Boudet concerns themselves directly with necromantic texts, their works provide a broad framework in which this material can be situated. My work explicitly deals with situating necromantic material in this larger frame. Klaassen, *Transformations of Magic*; Jean-Patrice Boudet, *Entre Science et Nigromance: Astrologie, Divination et Magie dans l'Occident Médiéval, XIIe-XVe Siècle* (Paris: Publications de la Sorbonne, 2006); Nicolas Weill-Parot, *Les 'Images Astrologiques' Au Moyen Age Et a La Renaissance* (Paris: Honore Champion, 2002).

25 Nicolas Weill-Parot, "Antonio Da Montolmo's *De Occultis Et Manifestis* or *Liber Intelligentiarum*: An Annotated Critical Edition with English Translation and Introduction, " in *Invoking Angels*, ed. Fanger, 219–93. Jan R. Veenstra, "The Holy Almandal," in *The Metamorphosis of Magic*, ed. Jan N. Bremmer and Jan R. Veenstra (Leuven: 2006). Gösta Hedegård, ed. *Liber Iuratus Honorii – A Critical Edition of the Latin Version of the Sworn Book of Honorius* (Stockholm: Almovist & Wiksell International, 2002), 189–229.

26 Jean-Patrice Boudet, "Les Who's Who Démonologiques De La Renaissance Et Leurs Ancêtres Médiévaux," *Médiévales* 44, no. printemps (2003): 117–39; Klaassen, *Transformations of Magic*, 115–55.

27 See for example *The Cambridge Book of Magic: A Tudor Necromancer's Manual*, ed. Francis Young, trans. Francis Young (Cambridge: Texts in Early Modern Magic, 2015). For sixteenth-century texts based in significant measure on medieval sources, see also V. Perrone Compagni, "Liber Orationum Planetarum Septem." In "Una Fonte Ermetica: Il Liber Orationem Planetarum," in *Bruniana & campanelliana*; Lucentini and Compagni, *I Testi E I Codici Di Ermete Nel Medioevo*.

28 Kieckhefer, *Magic in the Middle Ages*; Richard Kieckhefer, "The Holy and the Unholy: Sainthood, Witchcraft, and Magic in Late Medieval Europe," *Journal of Medieval and Renaissance Studies* 23 (1994); Kieckhefer, "Devil's Contemplatives"; Kieckhefer, *Forbidden Rites*.

29 Jean-Patrice Boudet and Julien Véronèse, "Le secret dans la magie rituelle médiévale"; Julien Véronèse, "La notion d' 'auteur-magicien' à la fin du moyen âge: le cas de l'ermite Pelagius de Majorque," *Médiévales* 51 (2006). On the construction of the magician as a divinely guided editor and the intellectual culture that encouraged creative reinvention, see Frank Klaassen, "Religion, Science, and the Transformations of Magic: Manuscripts of Magic 1300–1600" (Ph.D. Thesis, Univesity of Toronto, 1999); Klaassen, *Transformations of Magic*, 119–22.

30 Richard Kieckhefer, "The Specific Rationality of Medieval Magic," *American Historical Review* 99 (1994); Weill-Parot, "Antonio Da Montolmo's *De Occultis Et Manifestis* or *Liber Intelligentiarum*." For the relationship to engineering and technology, see William Eamon, "Technology as Magic in the Late Middle Ages and the Renaissance," *Janus* 70 (1983). For an examination of the relationship of science and necromancy in the sixteenth century, see Frank Klaassen, "Ritual Invocation and Early Modern Science: The Skrying Experiments of Humphrey Gilbert," in *Invoking Angels*, ed. Fanger, 341–66.

31 Stephen Clucas, "'Non Est Legendum Sed Inspicendum Solum': Inspectival Knowledge and the Visual Logic of John Dee's *Liber Mysteriorum*," in *Emblems and Alchemy*, ed. Alison Adams and Stanton J. Linden, Glasgow Emblem Studies, V. 3 (Glasgow: Glasgow Emblem Studies, 1998), 109–32; "*Regimen Animarum Et Corporum:* The Body and Spacial Practice in Medieval and Renaissance Magic," in *The Body in Late Medieval and Early Modern Culture*, ed. Darryll Grandley and Nina Taunton (Aldershot: Ashgate, 1999), 113–29; Klaassen, "Middleness of Ritual Magic"; Klaassen, "Ritual Invocation and Early Modern Science: The Skrying Experiments of Humphrey Gilbert."

32 Kieckhefer, *Forbidden Rites*, 30–34.

33 Frank Klaassen, "Learning and Masculinity in Manuscripts of Ritual Magic of the Later Middle Ages and Renaissance," *Sixteenth Century Journal* 38, no. 1 (2007). For a study of early modern ritual magic and masculinity, see Frances Timbers, *Magic and Masculinity: Ritual Magic and Gender in the Early Modern Era* (London: Taurus, 2014).

34 Richard Kieckhefer, "Erotic Magic in Medieval Europe," in *Sex in the Middle Ages: A Book of Essays*, ed. Joyce E. Salisbury (New York: Garland Pub., 1991).

35 Boudet, *Entre Science et Nigromance*; Klaassen, "Middleness of Ritual Magic."

36 *The Cambridge Book of Magic: A Tudor Necromancer's Manual*; Norman Rufus Colin Cohn, *Europe's Inner Demons: An Enquiry Inspired by the Great Witch-Hunt* (New York: Basic Books, 1975); Edward Peters, *The Magician, the Witch, and the Law*, Middle Ages Series (Philadelphia: University of Pennsylvania Press, 1978).

37 George Lyman Kittredge, *Witchcraft in Old and New England* (New York: Russell & Russell, 1956); Keith Vivian Thomas, *Religion and the Decline of Magic* (New York: Scribner, 1971). Richard Kieckhefer, *European Witch Trials: Their Foundations in Popular and Learned Culture, 1300–1500* (Berkeley: University of California Press, 1976).

38 Jean-Patrice Boudet, "Les Condemnations De La Magie À Paris En 1398," *Revue Mabillon* nouv. série 12, no. 73 (2001); Jan R. Veenstra, *Magic and Divination at the Courts of Burgundy and France: Text and Context of Laurens Pignon's Contre Les Devineurs (1411)* (Leiden and New York: Brill, 1998), 343–55.

39 Owen Davies (as a part of his examination of cunning folk) and Ruth Martin (under the larger rubric of witchcraft) have documented cases of necromancers in the courts. Owen Davies, *Cunning-Folk: Popular Magic in English History* (London: Hambledon and London, 2003); Ruth Martin, *Witchcraft and the Inquisition in Venice, 1550–1650* (Oxford: Blackwell, 1989). Klaassen and Wright, *The Magic of Rogues* (forthcoming).

40 Kieckhefer included the confession of Jubertus of Bavaria in his introduction to Forbidden Rites, and cited a number of other instances, but did not explore them in any detail. Kieckhefer, *Forbidden Rites*, 30–32.

41 For example, Barbara A. Mowat, "Prospero's Book," *Shakespeare Quarterly* 52, no. 1 (2001): 1–33.

42 Sebastià Giralt, "The Manuscript of a Medieval Necromancer: Magic in Occitan and Latin in Ms. Vaticano, Bav, Barb. Lat. 3589," in *Revue d'Histoire des Textes* (Turnhout: Brepols, 2014), 221–72.

16

JOHN OF MORIGNY

Claire Fanger and Nicholas Watson

John of Morigny (fl. c. 1301–15) is important both for what his writing reveals about the culture of learned magic at the turn of the fourteenth century and for his own contribution to that culture, the *Liber florum celestis doctrine*. The *Liber florum* is an unusual work, some 55,000 words in its most commonly circulated form, comprising a devotional autobiography with visions (the Book of Visions), a long liturgy for knowledge acquisition (the Book of Prayers) and a work of meditative figures (the Book of Figures). Unknown between the mid-sixteenth and late twentieth centuries, copies of the book began to be noticed in the late 1980s. The majority of its more than twenty currently known manuscripts have been found over the last fifteen years. It survives in two authorial versions, the Old Compilation (OC) (1311) and the New Compilation (NC) (1315), and two versions of a later redaction.[1]

The book draws on many sources, including works of theology and liturgy that may be linked to John's Benedictinism, and works classified as magical that may be linked to his years at university. Notable in the latter category is the *Ars notoria*, a book of rituals involving prayers and figures attributed to Solomon, the main purpose of which is to transmit the liberal arts, philosophy and theology into the mind of the operator by divine infusion with the assistance of the angels.[2] John discovered the *Ars notoria* to be demonically corrupt and evil in operation, although he clearly saw it as holy in its original conception. Although the *Liber florum* also took on other agendas, it began as his attempt to provide a new ritual that could achieve the same goals as the *Ars notoria* in a spiritually secure fashion.

The prayers of the *Ars notoria* are idiosyncratic in that they feature invocations in what is said to be a mix of "Greek, Latin, Hebrew, Chaldean, and Arabic" written in such a way that they "cannot be understood or expounded by anyone".[3] Its figures are characterized by the same constructed illegibility. Although they often borrow from the *Ars notoria*, the prayers of the *Liber florum* are written in Latin and its figures are differently conceived. In the OC version of the Book of Figures, John drew in part on the astrological image tradition, carefully reinterpreted to represent it in an orthodox Christian light.[4] In the NC version, written in response to criticism of the earlier figures, he constructed new figures around images of the Virgin, a logical culmination of a major theme in the *Liber florum* as a whole. John understood the work to have been written under the patronage of the Virgin and it is suffused with the language of Marian devotion.

Despite the revisions he had undertaken, the *Liber florum* was burned in 1323 by unknown parties at the University of Paris, according to the *Grandes Chroniques de France*, which explicitly identifies the work as a revival of the heretical *Ars notoria*. Nonetheless, the work was actively transmitted for two centuries, surviving in copies widespread across Europe, most of which appear to understand it as orthodox, indeed holy.

John and the composition of the *Liber florum*

The sole source for John's biography is the *Liber florum* itself, a work produced in installments, begun in 1301 and rewritten and expanded over the next fifteen years.[5] The work contains many traces of its accretive process. It is clear, for example, from the epistolary openings of prologues to certain sections of the text, as well as the note reproduced in many manuscripts, "This page should go in the beginning of the book before the incipit *No one lights a candle*,"[6] that John sent out new sections to his readers with instructions about where they should be placed in the copies his followers already had. The epistolary prologues offer a guide to his process, sometimes including dates and other information about composition. Most of the liturgical sections[7] were explicitly written in response to Marian visions, at least some of the time deliberately cultivated for the purpose of asking questions. At a fairly late stage of the project, he also decided to record the visions themselves, to a total of more than fifty. Visionary evidence must always be assessed with caution. However, many of John's visions are closely linked to occasion, place and the stages of the writing and can thus be pieced together with surrounding materials to produce a conjectural account of his life.[8]

John was born in the late 1270s and grew up in Autruy, a village forty-five kilometres north of Orléans. We hear of his sister Bridget, his mother, perhaps the family head; and John le Boeuf, perhaps the priest of the parish church of St. Peter's. At age thirteen, John was at Chartres, where he had his first vision. Like its successors, this took the form of a dream. While living inside the close, probably as a choirboy, John is woken from sleep by the "enemy of the human race",[9] who chases him until he flees into the cathedral through the door of the liberal arts in the west front, to be rescued by an image of the Virgin beckoning him to safety. In *Liber florum*, the struggle between Satan and the Virgin for John's soul depicted in this vision allows it to function as a thematic key to the book.[10] Five years later, he entered the Benedictine Abbey of Morigny, a few kilometers from Étampes (south of Paris) and thirty north of Autruy. Within four years of his entry into the order, probably in 1300 or 1301, he was sent to Orléans, where he eventually took a degree in canon law.[11]

Soon after arriving at Orléans, John encountered two books: first a ritual compilation "in which there were contained many nefarious things of the necromantic art", which he borrowed from "a certain cleric", copied in part, then had to return; and the *Ars notoria*, a glossed manuscript of which he found in the library after being directed there by Jacob, a "medical expert" from Bologna, with the assurance that he would find in it the means to master not only necromancy but also "all forms of knowledge".[12] The twin desires for dangerous knowledge and for comprehensive knowledge and the relationship between these desires are a major theme of the *Liber florum*. John next seeks to quench his thirst for knowledge through the *Ars notoria*, and we learn, through an account of eleven visions spanning three years, how John undertook the ritual it describes; how he used it to learn all the "arts and sciences", including necromancy and other magical arts; and how he was led to repudiate it, along with other ritual practices, and to do penance for his sin.

Most of the visions John solicited and received using the *Ars notoria* prayers are depicted as confusing mixtures of diabolical and divine influence. Visions of a looming diabolical figure who takes on the appearance of a holy man in a black diadem, of three persons purporting to be the Trinity, of a sinister figure who demands homage and of an avenging cherub who throws him to his enemy, slowly reveal to him that the *Ars notoria* is perverted.

However, two penitential visions bring about his renunciation of the *Ars notoria*, one before the Virgin and the apostle John, the other before Christ himself. Swearing off the *Ars notoria* for good, John descends briefly into necromancy, before a final penitential vision, in which he is beaten in the presence of Christ, terminates his relationship to the magic arts entirely. His reformation prepares the way for a second series of holy visions which show him that he is now on the right path.[13]

During the years in which he operated the *Ars notoria* then gave it up, John also worked on a set of prayers to the Virgin and John the Evangelist. These he gathered into a small book, the Grace of Christ, the earliest portion of *Liber florum* published,[14] later prefacing it with a prayer to Christ from this period to form the Seven Prayers, the first part of the Book of Prayers. Narratively, the Grace of Christ commemorates the visions by which the Virgin rescued John. Practically, it forms a ritual that *petitions* for visions. This was the ritual John used, probably in August of 1304, six months after renouncing all condemned practices, to obtain the Virgin's licence to write "a book of only thirty simple prayers" that would allow users to gain the knowledge of the "arts and sciences" and thus supplant the *Ars notoria*.[15] The Thirty Prayers that John wrote in the three years that followed, along with an instruction manual called the First Procedure, became the second and third parts of the Book of Prayers.

During the time he was operating the *Ars notoria*, John's colleagues and students in this art included another monk named John, from the Cistercian abbey of Fontainejean, whom he likely met at Orléans. After learning and being dissuaded from the *Ars notoria*, John of Fontainejean helped our John with the composition of portions of *Liber florum*. Less expectedly, John's students also included his younger sister, Bridget, who at the age of fifteen persuaded him to teach her to read, a project for which he engaged the *Ars notoria* to good effect before diabolical apparitions forced her also to set it aside. After doing so, Bridget began to have her own visions of God and the Virgin, first making a private profession of virginity then determining to become a nun at the convent of Rozay, west of Sens, under their influence.[16] She also helped with John's book, undertaking its rituals and contributing at least one of her own.

The Thirty Prayers were finished in Orléans in 1307. However, by the time John published them as the centrepiece of the Book of Prayers, he was back at Morigny. John dates his return to late summer 1308, when he was summoned to vote in the abbatial election of William of Ransignan, who appointed him to the office of *praepositus*, in charge of lands and rents under the prior.[17] It was William who persuaded him into the chapterhouse pulpit to preach his visions.[18] Sometime during this period, John received a new insight, mentioned several times in later parts of the work, that during the previous decade he had not merely been the recipient of divine visions but had received the spirit of prophecy.[19] Preacher, prophet and theologian (all by licence of the Virgin), John evidently enjoyed high status at Morigny between 1308 and at least 1311.

From other standpoints, these began as difficult years. Before he finished the First Procedure late in 1308, John had already decided that his ritual demanded a Second Procedure, in which meditative figures were added to the prayers.[20] But as he recounts in the OC Book of Figures, his attempts to persuade the Virgin to license or endorse the project failed. Taking her refusal as a sign of the need to seek her patronage more ardently, he was obliged in the meantime to work without her approval, receiving her verdict as to its excellence only after the ninety or so figures were finished early in 1310.[21] His visionary licence to preach came after a period of more than three months, late in 1309, when he lost his visionary gift and had to write new prayers to beg the Virgin to restore it.[22] Things settled later in 1310 as John completed the design of the *Liber florum*, writing the Book of Visions as a prologue to the entire work probably in the autumn of that year, then returned to finish the Book of Figures, finally publishing this new mass of material in two instalments at the end of 1311.[23]

Of the years from 1312 to 1315, we know little. During the early part of that time, he was working on a Book of Particular Experiments, which may be lost, but is mentioned as existing in the year 1314.[24] At some point, perhaps in 1313, he produced a revised collected edition of *Liber florum* for those who had not copied it piecemeal as he worked on it.[25] This edition, which forms the basis of all presently known NC copies, suggests that his readership was growing beyond the original circle, perhaps mainly of Orléans alumni and Morigny monks, who were his first audience.[26]

Late in 1315, however, he returned to the *Liber florum* a final time and over three months wholly recast its Second Procedure, cancelling the old figures and the rituals associated with them and devising a set of seven new figures as a substitute. He also made changes to the Particular Experiments, folding a set of cautions about it into the new Book of Figures while adding a single new experiment which his sister Bridget had apparently received licence to perform.[27] He further reports gaining the Virgin's permission to make an engraved ring in her honour to wear in the daytime while reciting the prayers and at night when expecting a vision.[28] John is scrupulous about making clear that every detail of the new figures and the ring has been approved by God and the Virgin in a set of carefully dated visions.

Some of these new additions (notably the visions connected to the ring) were already in process before 1315, but John is explicit that the cause of most of his revisions to the Book of Figures was scandal arising from criticism by "barking dogs", who argued that the old figures had a necromantic cast.[29] They also questioned his spiritual discernment in believing and following the directives of his visionary dreams, suggesting they were mere phantasms. Several chapters of the NC Book of Figures are given over to closely argued scholarly defences of dreams as a medium of divine communication.[30] Bridget's continuing importance to *Liber florum* in this period is reinforced by John's successful visionary struggle to be allowed to include her name with his in the circumference of the new figures, allowing both to use them for ritual purposes.[31]

However, most of the circumstances surrounding this crisis are unknown; we do not know the names of the barking dogs, nor whom they represented, nor what incidents may have sparked the critical reading of his book. It is also unknown whether there was any connection between these events of late 1315 and the burning of the *Liber florum* eight years later. Neither in the *Grandes Chroniques* nor in the Cartulary of the University of Paris is any mention made of the presence of the "monk of Morigny" who wrote the book at its incineration, nor is his name used. The Cartulary makes no mention of a legal process of any kind. The *Grandes Chroniques* account mentions some fairly specific sounding imputations of heresy, but does not detail a legal process nor mention the parties who levelled the charges, if any were officially laid.[32] Perhaps John was dead by this time, although he would only have been in his late forties. Perhaps the burning was symbolic, unconnected to any previous heresy process, indicating a merely local alarm at the spread of the *Liber florum* among students at the University of Paris.

After the end of 1315, we lose all trace of John and Bridget; though now that John's book has resurfaced in multiple manuscripts, it seems possible that more information is out there. In the meantime, the versions of the *Liber florum* already in our hands are compelling.

The shape of the *Liber florum* and how it worked

Despite the winding process of its composition, the *Liber florum* is a work of careful artistry. The narrative in the Book of Visions works in the manner of a *confessio* to encourage the many sinners mired (as John was) in the opaque and bewildering prayers of the *Ars notoria* to give them up in favour of the transparently sacred alternative that is the *Liber florum*. Likening himself to the apostle Paul and the penitent Theophilus,[33] John casts the *Liber florum* as the instrument of a covenant between God and modern Christians, made at the Virgin's behest to provide grace and knowledge to all sinners, perhaps especially those dedicated to the intellectual vices of magic.

While it is woven through with interpretative commentary, most of the rest of the *Liber florum* is a script for a ritual performance: a specialized version of the private liturgical scripts that are Books of Hours. The Book of Prayers is divided into two rituals, a vision ritual (constituted in the initial work of Seven Prayers) and a knowledge ritual (constituted in the Thirty Prayers licensed by the Virgin). Drawing on the *Ars notoria* but also the Book of Revelation, the Song of Songs, hymns both standard and recondite, sequences by Adam of St Victor, poetry from Alan of Lille and much more, the Book of Prayers tracks a spiritual progress from confusion and darkness to full enjoyment of God. In the prayers and visualizations (*ymaginaciones*), John weaves elements of his own visionary experiences, sometimes as visualizations, sometimes as lines or verses, in a large movement that conveys for the operator the impression of a journey following John from earth to the court of heaven with the angels as companions. The Book of Prayers is followed by a set of instructions for operation that John calls the First Procedure, which includes additional ancillary prayers and an office of angels.

Following the Book of Prayers in both OC and NC versions, we have a Book of Figures, meant to be used with the Book of Prayers and sometimes referred as a Second Procedure. In both forms, we are missing substantial portions of the instructions for use, though what remains is tantalizing. We cannot judge the full extent of the artistry of the OC figures, since only two examples survive, but these offer remarkable evidence for the complexity of conception of the whole.[34] These two figures clearly travelled with the text in graphic form rather than being reconstructed from John's descriptions. By contrast, the two renditions of the NC figures were apparently constructed from different elements of John's instructions: depictions of the Virgin cradling the infant Jesus, accompanied by plants and birds dictated in the text, with Christ's nails in the corners and a square or circular surround.[35] John was concerned to avoid elaboration or fetishizing of the power of the figures or their specific forms. In an undated Chartres vision, the Virgin, plainly dressed as in a nativity scene, declares "I do not want prayers nor figures … without your heart".[36] But beauty is as intrinsic to the work as it is to the *Ars notoria*: "colored in diverse colours", John says, so that it seems "of all books the most beautiful and useful and even the most holy".[37]

In the normative form of the First and Second Procedures, these two rituals are conjoined parts of a nine-week sequence, which is said twice, once without, once with the aid of figures. In the first week, the "operator" (*operans* or *opifex*) asks the Virgin for leave to proceed in the work, using a version of the same Grace of Christ prayers through which John gained permission to compose the Thirty Prayers. He recites the prayers for each day morning, noon and night – a pattern followed throughout.[38] After receiving permission in a visionary dream, ideally at the end of the first week, he spends a second week praying his way up to the court of heaven, through each of the nine orders of angels and the souls who dwell with them to the queen of the angels, asking for gifts identified with each order: memory, eloquence, understanding, perseverance and more (Prayers 1–12). These gifts are identical to those petitioned for in a work related to the *Ars notoria*, the *Opus operum*, which John knew and used; yet, the mise en scène for these prayers resembles visionary texts like *The Ascent of Isaiah*. John's narrative strategy thus provides an ascent structure for the action that is absent from the *Ars notoria*. During the next two weeks, with prayer and fasting, the operator asks the court of heaven for the purification of his senses and the illumination of his mind necessary for what follows (Prayers 13–20). Thus end the "general" prayers that make up the first half of the knowledge ritual.

There follow four weeks of "special" prayers for each of the disciplines of knowledge: the seven liberal arts, philosophy, theology and knowledge as a whole (Prayers 21–30A). In each case, the operator addresses Christ, asking him to direct the appropriate angelic order to confer the branches of the discipline in question – the Angels in the case of grammar, the Archangels in that of dialectic, the Thrones in that of rhetoric – before turning to the angels and an order of the blessed to petition directly for the infusion of the knowledge sought. Each liberal art is allotted a day; philosophy, theology and the arts and sciences as a whole, these last bestowed by Christ himself, are given a week each. The arts prayers can be adapted for law, medicine and other disciplines. In the revision of 1313, John added brief further references to the mechanical and magical or "exceptive" arts (Prayer 28). Finally, in the last week, the operator praises and offers thanks to the Virgin for all that has taken place, completing the ritual.

Throughout the Thirty Prayers, an underlay of *Ars notoria* and *Opus operum* prayers would have been obvious to any operator who knew these works. However, John's prayers differ not only in their narrative structure and systematic use of the angelic orders but also in their updated account of the academic disciplines themselves. John's prayers draw on a thirteenth-century genre of didascalic works associated with the Paris Faculty of Philosophy that divides the seven liberal arts according to Aristotelian categories as follows: grammar, dialectic and rhetoric become divisions of Rational Philosophy; arithmetic, music, geometry and astronomy those of Natural Philosophy. At a higher level, Philosophy is divided into Metaphysics (allied with Natural Philosophy) and Moral Philosophy (with its Monastic, Economic and Political branches). Theology is Contemplative Philosophy; its branches include the four senses of Scripture: historical, tropological, allegorical and anagogical.[39]

Although the Book of Prayers includes both, the vision and knowledge rituals differ in kind. The success or failure of the vision ritual is relatively clear: either visions occur or they do not. By contrast, the success of the knowledge ritual is admitted to be a matter of degree. In order to say the prayers, the operator, like John, must know "a little about the arts".[40] The first repetition of the ritual, with prayers only, is merely introductory, and it remains uncertain how the infusion of knowledge it promises is meant to work. Only once the figures are brought into play do we get a sense of how the ritual might be felt to succeed. On their second repetition, the prayers have become preliminary to the inspection of a relevant figure. According to the more discursive OC Book of Figures, these are visualized so that their form and lettering become imprinted on the mind of the operator, who is spiritually rapt into heaven as he silently utters brief requests for the relevant branches of knowledge ("May I know and understand perfectly the whole art of grammar, pure, preceptive, prohibitive; and orthography, prosody, etymology and syntax", etc.).[41]

The form of this ritual seems to imply that the figures are points of access and that some part of the efficacy is instant. In the tradition of astrological image magic on which John drew, an image acts as a focal point of heavenly influence. Ritually constructed on days and times associated with the planets, and using images, words and symbols identified with specific heavenly bodies, the image is imbued with powers that associate the object with certain clusters of qualities. Like these images, John's figures were initially intended to be constructed at specific days and times and contained words and letters in a variety of alphabets as well as certain non-alphabetic symbols. Some of the figures depict the twelve houses of the zodiac and the seven planets. Yet, the figures are not exactly like astrological images either, for all of them have a visual and diagrammatic structure that is thoroughly Christian and in this respect ally more closely with the visualizations from the Bible and the life of Christ often used in monastic and lay devotions.[42] The question of the efficacy of the figures is complicated by John's insistence that his figures have no power of themselves. Rather, the ritual is an act of petitionary worship, its meaning allegorical, its efficacy a matter of grace.[43] There is thus a certain tension between the form of John's OC figures and their meaning that may be connected to the difficulties he had in producing them. Perhaps this also helps to explain his readiness to give figures and ritual the devotional form they take in the NC Book of Figures, once the criticism of the "barking dogs" had reopened the text to revision.

Tension between the desire to affirm ritual efficacy, not least in comparison to *Ars notoria*, and the doctrinal need to respect God's freedom and mystery is a general feature of the *Liber florum*. In the preliminary rituals laid out in the OC and presented in simpler form in the NC, the operator devotes elaborate attention to writing and drawing the book at proper times, personalizing its prayers and figures with his own name, as though only thus will the ritual work.[44] He also makes a profession to the Virgin, adapted from the Benedictine profession rite, and seeks visionary confirmation of his finished book, entering a personal covenant with her.[45] This is then confirmed by other visions he experiences as he goes forward and by his undertaking a lifelong commitment to repeat the prayers in a ritual called the Voluntary Work on a regular basis, as well as to say weekly Offices of the Virgin and the Angels.[46]

Having been accepted by the Virgin, the operator who does not go astray gains a potentially regular and habitual access to visions. The injunction to "believe not every spirit" (1 John 4:1) common in visionary writings is also iterated in *Liber florum*. But John then adds quite specific instructions for recognizing when the devil might be appearing to the visionary in the guise of the Virgin – as when she contradicts herself or tempts the visionary to wanton behaviour.[47] Even if the visions do become habitual, the action of grace is never automatic, depending both on the Virgin's will and the condition of the operator's soul. As John's accounts of his relationship with the Virgin show, the benefits the Virgin bestows and the times and places in which she appears to bestow them are as unpredictable as dreams and as grace themselves. Because of this, John builds into the *Liber florum* variable modes of access to the visionary work, the adaptability of the text reflecting the divergent needs, aptitudes and moral state of those who are to operate it.

When John published the OC of figures, he offered a ritual specific to the recovery of visions lost through bad behaviour, to be done after appropriate penance. In the same part of the text, he anticipates that there may be some operators who might wish to forego extensive work on the knowledge ritual and just perform the vision ritual. If this was the case, operators were released from copying those parts of the *Liber florum* that are not relevant for having visions.[48] His work on "particular experiments" in the years that followed was based on the assumption that the Virgin would empower each operator to develop different experiments – usually if not always in visionary form – and that these might not be replicable by others.[49] In writing the NC Book of Figures, John affirmed his belief in the value of the knowledge ritual. But he also brought it closer to the vision ritual, sometimes appearing to treat it as almost as a mode of preparation for the successful operation of the vision ritual, rather than (as in the Book of Prayers) the other way around. Despite the considerable knowledge benefits bestowed by the Thirty Prayers, John ultimately appears to have understood the relationship with the Virgin enjoyed through visionary dreams as the most important benefit of operating the *Liber florum* – a benefit that evidently kept operators copying it for more than two hundred years.

Reception and use of the *Liber florum*

The importance of John's book, as attested by the actual count, distribution and style of the manuscripts in which it is contained, is radically out of proportion to the negligible place in history that seems to be suggested by the record of his condemnation. If the condemnation in the *Grandes Chroniques de France* aligns the work with an idea of frivolous and derivative magic, dismissing it as a vain route to rapid learning, the transmission history by contrast shows that it was seen by the operators who copied it as a serious devotional text. Since it was not copied for any other reason than use, it is entirely due to the ritual seriousness of its operators, their sharing of the book, their sense of its efficacy, that the book survived at all.

We are currently aware of twenty-four manuscripts containing versions or recognizable portions or adaptations of John's book, from Austria, England, Germany, Italy, Poland and Spain, including more than one deluxe copy.[50] The tracing of manuscripts is still very much a work in progress and discoveries are ongoing (indeed, the most recent one turned up while we were writing this article),[51] and all generalizations about reception will be subject to change based on future discoveries. Nevertheless, certain patterns are evident from the manuscripts we have in hand. The earliest copies known to us are dated to 1374 and 1377, a scant half century after the burning, and the latest to 1519 and 1522.[52] We know dates of inscription from colophons where individual copies are often signed by the scribe or operator.

However, the personalization of manuscripts goes well beyond the colophon. John's book instructs that all the images in the text should be inscribed with the name of the person by whom it is intended to be used; operators were to petition the Virgin for visionary licence to carry forward with the work and to consecrate the book once licence was granted. In practice, operators put names in the prayers as well. Consistent with a tradition of transmission by operators, the majority of manuscripts contain names in the prayers. So far all of these are men's names: Albert, Andreas, Bernard, Erasmus, Geoffrey, Jacob, Peter, Rupert, and Ulric. Some copies that do not contain personal names are exemplars, in at least two cases originating from religious houses, presumably made for monks to copy and personalize for themselves.[53] Two manuscripts contain erasures in the places where the names go, showing that they were personalized once, in one case the erasures having clearly been done by a second operator in order to reuse the text.[54] Strikingly, even the (so far) unique OC manuscript in Oxford, Bodleian Library Liturg. 160, is personalized for the use of one "frater Galfridus", showing that it too derives from an operator tradition, albeit a minority tradition that has left fewer traces than the new.

Further evidence that copies of *Liber florum* were made for use comes from the redaction we are calling the "Third Compilation", which exists in two versions and is contained in six manuscripts identified so far. The cleanest manuscript of the type is Manchester, Chetham's Library A.4.108, hereafter "Manchester", dated 1522 by its operator, one Jacob Smith.[55] In essence, the third compilation text is a pragmatic redaction of John's prayers designed to make the liturgy easier to use. To this end, all autobiographical materials – the complex visionary episodes contained in the *Liber visionum* and interwoven with subsequent prayers – have been stripped away. Instead of visions, the book opens with a set of instructions that provide an orderly overview of how to initiate the ritual system, including the copying of the book, the rite of profession and the visionary experiment. The nine opera of the First Procedure are briefly detailed, followed by a discussion of confirmation of the book and ring and subsequent vow to perform a special service for Mary and the angels lifelong. All these instructions are adapted and simplified from the complicated and sometimes conflicting directions that John scatters through later parts of the "original" book, some in the First Procedure and others in the NC Book of Figures.

Pragmatically, also, the book opens not with the first prayer actually found in the book (Prayer *1, O Rex regum) but with a lengthy and complicated set of prayers listed by John in the First Procedure, chapter 1.3, starting with the Pater noster, Creed and Ave Maria, meant to be said prior to starting each opus of the work. Since the user cannot proceed even into the initiatory level of the work without them, the presence of these prayers at the beginning would have been useful to anyone serious about undertaking the work methodically in the prescribed fashion.

That this redaction was made by a third party and not by John himself becomes clear from the prologue, which references John in the third person:

> This book was composed against the *Ars notoria* by brother John, monk of the order of Saint Benedict at Morigny, by the will and teaching of the blessed virgin Mary, because she saw that many had been undone by that same *Ars notoria*, which is diabolical and full of necromantic experiments. And because the aforesaid John also labored through the *Ars notoria* and through diabolical deceptions, for that reason, moved by mercy, the Mother of Mercy marvellously revealed it to him, as is shown in the original <book> by John himself, which is the exemplar of all the others.[56]

The writer was obviously familiar with the narrative that guides the Book of Visions, though the description of the Notory art as being "full of necromantic experiments" makes clear that the author is less than intimately familiar with the *Ars notoria* itself (a work that never admits a relation to necromancy, and which John himself handles as part of a different category).[57] While we do not know the exact date of this redaction, all known copies are fifteenth- or early sixteenth-century productions.[58]

Only one known manuscript of the *Liber florum* preserves any memory of the condemnation of 1323. This is a fifteenth-century manuscript composed mainly of Dominican materials, now housed in Halle, Universitäts- und Landesbibliothek, Stolb.-Wernig. Za 74. The *Liber florum* is discontinuous with the surrounding materials and was clearly at one time an operator copy: there are gaps in the prayers where the names should be, but the gaps show marks of erasure, so the book was once personalized. The manuscript shows many signs of care, including coloured initials, marginal decorations and some glosses from a secondary copy of the text. On the folio where the work begins is a cautionary note in another hand, describing it in a language that echoes the account of the condemnation in the *Grandes Chroniques*:

> This is a book which is called the *Flower of Heavenly Teaching*, and it is a book wholly crammed with superstition, whose author, though he feigns that he wanted to avoid the pernicious *Ars notoria*, nevertheless in a deceptive and hidden way appears rather to have handed it on to cheat the simple with the devil's tutoring, since he administers its deadly venom using the sweetest prayers like a kind of honey.

Yet, even as this note recalls the 1323 chronicle account with its accusation that John only "feigned" to dismiss the *Ars notoria*, it reflects a milieu in which John's prayer practice is evidently in active use, its accessibility in multiple copies witnessed by the operator's glosses. The *Liber florum* was very much alive and well in fifteenth-century Germany.

We have found no evidence that John's book ever appeared in print before our 2015 edition (outside the unattributed prayers in the Polish crystallomancy text edited by Ganszyniec and our own earlier partial edition in 2001).[59] Yet, a market for printed editions is perhaps not to be expected for a book whose copying was always part of the operator's relation to the text, preliminary to a process of visionary approval and consecration. Indeed, if the link between use and transmission was too close to make any sort of mass production viable, the broad reach and persistence of the text across Europe through the early sixteenth century become rather more remarkable. It is evident even from the brief sketch of transmission patterns here that we must regard the *Liber florum* as a successful attempt at reworking the *Ars notoria* into a workable Catholic paraliturgy.

Future directions for research

From the perspective of the history of magic, there are several areas on which we may expect John's work to have an increased impact as it becomes better known. The most obvious of these, perhaps, is in the prehistory of the great Renaissance author-magicians like Ficino, Pico and Agrippa. If the *Liber florum* claimed its work for the Christian religion, not magic,[60] John's work did not completely exclude an idea of magic either. In the Book of Prayers, John eventually allows the seven "exceptive" or magic arts into the domain of knowledge that is governed by the Cherubim, the rank of angels associated with philosophy, second only to the Seraphim.[61] Though he does not advocate practice of these arts – and he allows the operator to use his own judgement about taking them theoretically – nevertheless in principle magic can be seen to inhabit the order of knowledge at a very high level. Here and elsewhere, John's work demonstrates a complex, religiously attentive engagement with magic that foreshadows many impulses evident among author-magicians over the next two centuries.

Like other author-magicians, indeed perhaps more like Ficino and Pico than like those nearer his own day, John's aim is always divine knowledge. His engagement with both secular learning and magic is always in service of an essentially Christian goal, a set of illuminations that will help to prepare him, and help him to prepare others, for the heavenly life. John shares this religious impulse with later author-magicians, and shares with them, too, a Platonic outlook, an interest in astrological images, a semi-sacral view of the science of astronomy and an attraction to Judaica – specifically an interest in finding ways of combining the ancient mysteries of Judaism with Christian goals.[62] Thus, if the *Liber florum* was read as a manual for operation of a Catholic and devotional kind, it can nevertheless also be seen as part of the ongoing conversation about magic in that it positivized some of its uses. Much remains to be explored about the background of John's knowledge, particularly its small but interesting suggestions of Jewish–Christian exchange, but in general his work demands that we see how magic texts, despite their controversial nature, might be counted as one source among many in the building up of knowledge and disciplinary models in the later Middle Ages. Set apart in principle, the magic arts were affiliated and integrated in practice with both religious and secular kinds of knowledge and discursive practices.

Beyond the history of magic, the *Liber florum* can also be expected to impact the larger historical picture of medieval life and institutions in many ways. The book as a whole is a significant addition to the array of late medieval works of visionary theology, not less important because it evidences a masculine engagement with a genre whose most notable exponents are female (exemplified in the work of Angela of Foligno, Bridget of Sweden or Julian of Norwich). The Book of Prayers is remarkable for its innovative and expert liturgy, which shows one manner of movement from monastic *libelli precum* to lay books of hours. The Book of Visions and autobiographical portions of the Book of Figures together witness the increasing value placed on university learning and the opportunities for social mobility that might be offered to an ambitious monk. They also yield valuable information about John's sister, Bridget, providing a unique window into the life of a teenage girl as she struggles to make a transition between the lay and monastic life. The *Liber florum* thus impacts the study of theology, liturgy, monasticism, the arts and sciences in general, visionary literature, mysticism and other allied discourses. Ultimately, future work on John of Morigny is not separable from the wider discipline of medieval historical research.

Notes

1 John of Morigny, *Liber Florum Celestis Doctrine*, ed. Claire Fanger and Nicholas Watson (Toronto: Pontifical Institute of Mediaeval Studies, 2015); henceforth *Liber florum*.
2 Julien Véronèse, *L'Ars notoria au Moyen Age* (Florence: Sismel Edizioni del Galluzzo, 2007). All references to the *Ars notoria* are to this edition.
3 "Est in quinque linguis compositus, videlicet Grece, Latine, Ebraice, Caldayce, Arabice, ita quod ab aliquo non potest intelligi nec exponi." *Liber Florum* I.i.3, drawing on *Ars notoria* §8.
4 See chapter 5 of Claire Fanger, *Rewriting Magic* (University Park: Pennsylvania State University Press, 2015).
5 Evidence for dating is complex; see *Liber florum* Introduction A, I.1, by Nicholas Watson; Introduction B, III.3, by Claire Fanger; and Table 14.
6 *Liber Florum* II.Rit Prol, rubric.
7 The book of prayers uses many liturgical forms, not only prose prayers but poetic sequences, hymns, antiphons and even entire offices. A Christmas Day mass (in a standard form) is a major part of Prayer 3, and an office of Angels (composed by John) is given in chapter 3 of the First Procedure. John wrote as a fluent and expert liturgist, sometimes drawing on old liturgical forms, sometimes creating new ones, sometimes interweaving his own writing with that of others.
8 The account that follows in this and the next section is based on *Liber florum* Introduction A, which contains a summary in Table 2.
9 "inimicus humani generis." I. Prol.
10 I. Prol.
11 I.i.2, NC III.i.1.b and *Liber florum* Introduction A, I.1 and Table 2.
12 I.i.2.
13 I.4-13, I.ii.
14 I.ii, Prayers *2–*7.
15 I.ii.5.

16 I.iii; NC III.ii.4.
17 I.i.
18 OC III.6.a, 25.b.
19 OC III.21c; OC III. 25.a–d; NC III.i.14.b–c
20 OC III.3.
21 OC III.3–8.
22 OC III.22–23, 25.b.
23 NC III.i.14.e.
24 NC III.iii.3.a
25 Introduction A, III.1.
26 NC III.i.12.e also suggests this first audience included some secular priests and laypeople.
27 NC III.ii.4
28 NC III.iii.27–28.
29 NC III.i.1.b.
30 NC III.i.5, iii.3, 5–6.
31 NC III.iii.4.b, 7.a.
32 For translation of the 1323 *Grandes Chroniques de France* entry, see Nicholas Watson, "John of Morigny's *Book of Visions*," in *Conjuring Spirits: Texts and Traditions of Medieval Ritual Magic*, ed. Claire Fanger (University Park: Pennsylvania State University Press, 1998), 164; see also *Chartularium Universitatis Parisiensis*, vol. 2, ed. H. Denifle and E. Chatelain (Paris: Delalain, 1897), item 827, p. 274.
33 I.Gen Prol.c; see also Prayer *2.1.
34 See Fanger, *Rewriting Magic*, ch. 4.
35 See *Liber florum*, Plates 7 and 9: New Compilation figures from Salzburg, Studienbibliothek Salzburg Cod. M I 24, fol.77v and Bologna, Biblioteca Comunale dell'Archiginnasio MS A. 165, fols. 68v, 69r. Salzburg's figures are based on the instructions given in NC III.iii.23.a; figures in the Bologna manuscript are based on the earlier account in III.i.2.c and III.iii.7.b.
36 "nolo oraciones neque figuras … nisi cor." *Liber florum* I.iii.2.c.
37 "diuersis coloribus colorate …omnium librorum pulcherrimus et vtilissimus et eciam sanctissimus." I.i.3.
38 II.iii.caps 1–2.
39 Rubrics to II.ii, Prayers 21–30.
40 OC III.8.
41 "Vellem scire et intelligere perfecte omnem artem gramaticam: permissiuam, preceptiuam, prohibitiuam; et ortographiam, prosodiam, ethimologiam et diasenticam." OC III.18.b.i.
42 See Fanger, *Rewriting Magic*, ch. 5.
43 OC I.iv.10.b; III.12.
44 OC I.iv.6.
45 OC I.iv.5; NC III.i.12; I.iii.cap 4.
46 OC I.iv.11–12, III.16–17.
47 OC I.iv.10.d-h, NC I.iv.4. See also NC III.iii.11.
48 OC III.24; see also NC III.iii.35.a–b.
49 NC III.ii.
50 All manuscripts show care in production, but the two copies including full sets of executed figures are of especially remarkable quality; these are Salzburg, Studienbibliothek Cod M I 24 and Bologna, Biblioteca Comunale dell' Archiginnasio MS A. 165 (16. b. III. 5). The sketch of use and transmission here and following is based on *Liber florum* Introduction B, by Claire Fanger.
51 As of 3 January 2015.
52 1374 and 1377 are, respectively associated with London, British Library, Additional MS 18027 and Vienna, Schottenkloster, MS 140 (61); 1519 and 1522 are, respectively, associated with Munich, Bayerische Staatsbibliothek Clm 28864, and Manchester, Chetham's Library MS A.4.108. For manuscripts overview as of 2015, see Table 13 in *Liber florum* Introduction B.
53 Klagenfurt, Universitätsbibliothek, Cart. 1 (originally from the Benedictine monastery of St. Paul, Kärnten, Austria) and Klosterneuburg, Augustiner-Chorherrenstift Cod. 950. Other manuscripts with no personalization include Milano, Biblioteca Ambrosiana MS Z.412 sup and Torino, Biblioteca Nazionale MS G. II. 25, likely made as exemplars also, though they cannot be traced to particular religious houses.

54 The manuscript where names were erased for reuse is Salzburg, Studienbibliothek Salzburg Cod M I 24, and Halle, Universitäts- und Landesbibliothek, MS Stolb.-Wernig. Za 74.
55 For a fuller account, see *Liber florum* Introduction B, IV.2; see Table 13 for other manuscripts.
56 "Qui liber est contra Artem notoriam compositus a Fratre Johanne, monacho ordinis sancti Benedicti de Moriginaco ex voluntate et informatione beate virginis Marie. Quia ipsa vidit quod multi perierunt per eandem artem notoriam que est diabolica et plena nigromanticis experimentis. Et quia dictus Johannes etiam per notoriam laborauit et per deceptiones diabolicas, ideo misericordia mota ipsa Mater Misericordie sibi eum mirabiliter reuelauit ut patet in originali ipsius Johannis qui est exemplar omnium aliorum." Manchester, Chetham's Library MS A.4.108, p 2.
57 For overview of John's distinctions, see Fanger, *Rewriting Magic*, ch. 5.
58 The earliest dated copy is Hamilton, McMaster University Library MS 107, inscribed in 1461.
59 The crystallomancy is in Bernacki, Ludwik and Ryszard Ganszyniec, ed. *Modlitewnik Władysława Warneńczyka: w zbiorach Bibljoteki Bodlejańskiej* (Krakow: Anczyc i Spólka, 1928). Our partial edition was published in *Esoterica* 3 (2001): 108–217; www.esoteric.msu.edu/VolumeIII/Morigny.html.
60 In fact, the consecrated book is said to be effective at driving out demons that *ars magica* has imprisoned in objects; see the operation for consecration of the book, II.iii.cap 4.1.d.
61 See Prayer 28.7.a
62 See Claire Fanger, "Covenant and the Divine Name," in *Invoking Angels: Theurgic Ideas and Practices, Thirteenth to Sixteenth Centuries,* ed. Fanger (University Park: Pennsylvania State University Press, 2012), 192–216.

17

CECCO D'ASCOLI AND ANTONIO DA MONTOLMO

The building of a "nigromantical" cosmology
and the birth of the author-magician

Nicolas Weill-Parot

Cecco d'Ascoli (†1327) and Antonio da Montolmo (fl. 1360– after 1394) can be put side by side in many ways, despite the chronological gap between them. Apart from the fact that they were acting in the same area, Northern and Central Italy, and in the same academic milieu, and that the same manuscript (Paris, Bibliothèque nationale de France, lat. 7337) keeps some of their magical works together, they display a very similar kind of magic, based on an astrological–demonic cosmology. Their diverging destinies – Cecco d'Ascoli was burnt by the Inquisition in 1327, whereas Antonio da Montolmo, as far as we know, carried on teaching at university – are an interesting clue for grasping the main intellectual and cultural change that was going on at the end of fourteenth century and at the beginning of the fifteenth century, at least in the Northern and Central Italy: a kind of "release of the magical discourse" as well as the birth of the "author-magician".[1] Previously, magical texts were ascribed to legendary authorities, whether ancient such as Hermes or Solomon or more recent such as Albert the Great or Arnald of Villanova, and thus promoted these figures as magicians after their death.

Cecco d'Ascoli, the demonic sphere and astrological nigromancy

Francesco Stabili, also known as Cecco d'Ascoli, taught the "science of stars" at the University of Bologna from 1322. There he wrote a commentary on the *Sphaera* ("Sphere") by Johannes de Sacrobosco, a widespread handbook on cosmology written in the first half of the thirteenth century, and in around 1323–24 he did the same for the *De principiis astrologie* ("The principles of astrology") by the tenth-century Arabic astrologer Alcabitius (al-Qabîsî), one of the most famous handbooks on astrology. During this time, he appeared before the Inquisitor Lamberto da Cingoli, but it seems he was easily released without charge and went on teaching astrology. At the same time, he was asked by the urban authorities to give astrological forecasts. In 1326, he became the personal astrologer of Charles, Duke of Calabria and lord of Florence. But in July the following year, he had very serious trouble with the Inquisition. He was jailed and sentenced on 15 September by the Inquisitor of Toscana and was burnt at the stake the next day. Besides the two aforementioned commentaries, an astronomical treatise *De excentricis et epicyclis* ("On eccentrics and epicycles") and his Italian poem *L'Acerba* are also extant.[2]

Both commentaries left by Cecco are permeated with nigromantical elements. Thorndike had defined Cecco's magic as an "astrological necromancy"; it can rather be qualified as an "astrological nigromancy" (since *nigromancia* usually means magic with the assistance of demons, whereas *necromancia* generally means divination through the invocation of the dead).[3] This is worthy of note since neither the *Sphaera* of Sacrobosco or "the Alcabitius" contains any magical component. The first deals with pure cosmology, the second with astrology. Only a few of the commentators of the *Sphaera*, such as Robertus Anglicus,[4] dealt with magic. Thus, both commentaries of Cecco are like palimpsests: under an apparently academic cosmological or astrological commentary, another, hidden, text in small brush strokes can be discovered.[5] Cecco reveals a special demonology that is related to specific places according to the cosmic sphere.

In his commentary on the *Sphaera*, one of Cecco's favourite processes involves giving two meanings to technical terms such as *colurus*, *zenith*, *arcus*, *clima*, *oppositio*, etc. Besides their cosmological, astronomical or astrological meaning, Cecco introduces a nigromantical meaning for these words. The colures (*colurus*) are the two great circles that intersect at the poles of the celestial sphere at right angles and that cross the ecliptic at the equinoxes and the solstices, respectively. But the nigromantical meaning of "colure", writes Cecco, derives from the etymology – *colon* means "member", and *urere* means "to burn": Incubi and succubi, superior demons whose place was under the solstitial colure, would burn the genital organs of men and women while they slept. When there is a conjunction between the three superior planets (Saturn, Jupiter and Mars) in one of the two solstitial signs (Cancer and Capricorn), the incubi carry the sperm of a man into a woman's womb in order to produce men who seem to be divine but are actually demoniac, such as Merlin or the coming Antichrist. The succubi take the aerial shape of a woman in order to seduce men.[6]

Demons located under the equinoctial colure, precisely under the equinoctial points, are called *marmores* and *asmitus*. When addressing the demons from the four angular signs, Cecco gives new clues for their places. Thus, it seems the incubi are located under the sign of Cancer, the succubi under Capricorn, the *asmitus* under Aries and the *marmores* under Libra.[7] In *L'Acerba*, Cecco also mentions the "Mormores" summoned by the *piromanti*, that is diviners through fire.[8]

The "opposition" (*oppositio*) has also two meanings, says Cecco: astrological and nigromantical. First, according to astrology, it is an (evil) aspect of 180 degrees. Second, according to "Hipparchus" (actually a pseudo-Hipparchus), there is an *oppositio crucialis* (a cross-shaped opposition). Legions of elementary spirits are located under the cardinal points, and are thus possibly the legions depending from the spirits of the cardinal signs or climes (see below). Those elementary spirits have functions according to their proper element: the spirits of fire make columns of fire moving up to the heavens when troops are about to attack; the demons of the air produce clouds having shapes of snakes, dragons and other animals; they also cause swirls of powder. The demons of earth sow discord amongst people: for this purpose, they take shapes of poor people, pilgrims or fairies; at night, they make people hear awful shouts.[9]

The "zenith" has two meanings too. Besides its obvious astrological meaning, in its nigromantical meaning (given by "Hipparchus"), a zenith is a higher hierarchy of demons.[10]

The "poles" have a well-known astronomical signification but also a nigromantical one: they refer to "the powers" of the Arctic or Antarctic spirits or *manes*. Solomon teaches how to pray to these Intelligences, who are outside the order of grace. Each category of these evil Intelligences gives answer through idols made of a specific matter: gold, silver, tin and so on.[11]

The "arcus" has three different significations. In astronomy, this word refers to an arc of a circle, for instance the different arcs of the ecliptic through which the Sun goes during a year. In chiromancy, it means the lines of the hand; in nigromancy, the "arci" are noble demons from the North who know the secrets of the worldly elements and give answers and produce wonders "when God wants them to". They willingly stay in houses of noble families, to talk to them and help them. Sometimes, in the "houses of usurers and base people, they throw stones and excrement", and they "upturn dishes and the sheets of beds". They utter terrible shouts at night.[12]

The "climes" are understood again in two ways: astronomically they are seven areas, parallel to the equator, into which the habitable part of the world is divided; according to nigromancy, as Zoroaster told, this name is given to certain very powerful spirits, since "clime" means raising (*elevatio*) and these spirits overhang all the others. They rule over cross-shaped places such as the West, East, South and North; their names are, respectively, Oriens, Amaymon, Paymon and Egim. Each has twenty-five legions of spirits under his command. They demand sacrifices of men or cats. Invoking them is a danger for the Christian faith.[13]

The word "tropic", Cecco explains, comes from the Greek *tropos;* in Latin, it is *conversio*, i.e. revolution, because "the sun begins to go in the inferior hemisphere and to move away from us". In addition to their astronomical meaning ("circles described by the Sun"), the "tropics" are spirits belonging to a specific hierarchy. They are so named *Tropici*, because they are turned (*conversivi*) by their prince called Tropos.[14]

Thus, every kind of demon has a specific place according to significant cosmological-astronomical points in the *Sphere*. Cecco sometimes gives his reader scattered clues that allow him to deduce the exact position of a particular demon. This occurs especially with the demon Floron. Before the fall of the evil angels, Floron was part of the Cherubins, a very high level within the Dionysian hierarchy. Men invoke and compel this demon using a steel mirror. But whereas Floron knows many secrets of nature, he always tries to deceive men, as when he promised victory to King Manfred of Sicily – Cecco is probably alluding to the defeat of Manfred and to his death at the Benevento battle in 1266. Floron also promised a man that he would find treasure and keep it until his death: this man actually found it in a cavern that collapsed over him and killed him. Floron is called "the shadow of the Moon"; during a full moon, his shadow can be seen entirely and spirits – probably including Floron – give true answers and not lies, through the process of catoptromancy, which is divination through polished bodies such as a mirror, a crystal, a sword or a fingernail, using a young virgin boy as a medium. Because Floron has a very noble nature, he foretold the coming of Christ, just like the Sibyl. Concerning the place where Floron stays, Cecco gives, as it seems, some half-hidden hints. In the *Sphaera*, Sacrobosco had written that

> the part of the colure, which is located between the first point of Cancer and the arctic circle is almost twice as long as the maximum declination of the Sun or than the arc of the same colure which is included between the arctic circle and the arctic pole of the world – [this arc] being equal to the maximum declination of the Sun.

As Sacrobosco writes, a quarter of a colure – a colure being a complete circle – represents 90 degrees. The maximum declination of the Sun is the arc delineated between the equator and the tropic of Cancer (that is, where the ecliptic intersects with the tropic of Cancer). According to Ptolemy, the maximum declination of the Sun is 23°51′ and the arc between the arctic circle and the arctic pole is the same; thus, the addition of these two arcs gives almost 48°. The arc between the arctic pole and the equator being 90°, if we subtract 48° from 90°, it remains 42°; hence, the arc of the colure between "the first point of Cancer and the arctic circle" is 42°, i.e. almost 23°51′ multiplied by 2.[15] Now Cecco relates that Solomon explains: "just like the distance of the tropic of the constellation of the Moon", that is Cancer in which the Moon has its domicile, "and the arctic pole is said to be twice longer than this distance, i.e. between the tropic of Cancer and the arctic circle is said to be twice longer that the maximum declination of the life of the heaven", which is the Sun, "so the distance in power between Floron and Asmitus". Now we know that Asmitus is located in the equinoctial colure, hence in the equator; since it seems likely that the distance between the circles and the distance between the powers are more than a mere analogy, Floron is located in the arctic circle. It is probably one of the aforesaid *manes arctici*.[16]

The tragic death of Cecco d'Ascoli and its possible reasons

The reason why Cecco d'Ascoli was burnt at stake has been a long-debated issue.[17] The archive sources are partial or not reliable. Some information is given by two chronicles: the *Cronaca fiorentina* written until 1386 by Marchionne di Coppo Stefani and, especially, the earlier *Nuova Cronaca* (1322–48) by Giovanni Villani – a witness of the events.

Some explanations given seem to be more signs of an unfavourable context than actual causes for his condemnation: according to Villani, the physician Dino del Garbo was jealous. The inquisitor of Tuscany was Accursio Bonfantini, a commentator of Dante, but Cecco in the *Acerba* had accused the famous poet of supporting astrological fatalism;[18] Cecco had foretold that the newborn daughter of the Duke would become a lustful woman.

But the actual causes are more likely to be found in Cecco's unorthodox thoughts and writings. Villani tells that, despite his first trouble with the Inquisition of Bologna and the promises he had made to the inquisitor, Cecco carried on referring to his commentary on the *Sphaera* of Sacrobosco. He could have been sentenced by the inquisition for three statements contained in this work. First, because he wrote that "in the superior spheres there were generations of evil spirits, which could be compelled through incantations under appropriate constellations to do many wonders", i.e. astrological nigromancy. Second, because there he had supported astrological fatalism ("moreover, in this treatise he put necessity in the influence of the celestial course"). Third, because he wrote notably that "Christ came on earth according to God's will with the necessity of the astrological course, and because of his horoscope of birth he had to be and to live with his followers as a vagabond and to die in the way he died" and also that "the Antichrist would come, according to the course of planets, wearing the clothes of rich and powerful men". This statement seemed to apply astrological determinism to sacred events, which is an idea contrary to divine omnipotence.[19]

As far as the extant versions of Cecco's commentary on the *Sphere* are reliable, the accusations dealing with astrology seem somehow unjustified. For instance, he asserts that the eclipse that occurred during the Passion of Christ was miraculous and not natural. He refers to the doctrine of Zoroaster according to which, when the eighth sphere achieves one quarter of a revolution, men endowed with divinity are born by the power of the incubi and succubi; but he calls Zoroaster a "beast", because he explained the birth of Christ in this way. Cecco adds that "writing such words seem horrible to him"; definitely, Christ was not "one of these gods" generated thus, but "the Son of the true living God".[20]

Concerning astrological nigromancy, the accusation reported by Villani seems more well founded. As we have seen, the commentary on the *Sphere* is actually a treatise of nigromantical astrology. But the inquisitor made a mistake when he alluded to evil spirits generated "in the superior spheres", since Cecco d'Ascoli specifies in his commentary that they are actually *under* the lunar orb, in the sublunary region, in accordance with the theological model of the cosmos. The superlunary region had been entirely filled with divine grace and perfection, with only the good angels allowed to stay there; demons, that is evil angels, since their fall, had been thrown down to the sublunary region.

In 1320, Pope John XXII had summoned an expert committee in order to decide if several magical practices were heretical; since the answers were generally affirmative, he ordered some prosecutions against practitioners of magic. In 1326/1327, the bull *Super illius specula* (whose authenticity is not certain) was directed against ritual magic.[21] In such a context, the condemnation of the reckless Cecco d'Ascoli should not be surprising.

Antonio da Montolmo, one of the first "author-magicians"

Compared to Cecco d'Ascoli, Antonio da Montolmo (Antonius de Monte Ulmi) is a much less well-known author. Lynn Thorndike was the first to devote a chapter to him, in his *History of Magic and Experimental Science*.[22] Recent research has undertaken a systematic analysis and edition of his works.[23] Antonio seems to have been the pupil of the physician and astrologer Tommaso da Pizzano, the father of the famous writer Christine de Pizan. He appears in 1360 as a lecturer on grammar at the University of Bologna. There he taught medicine and astrology from 1387 to 1392. Later, in 1393, he taught philosophy and medicine in Padua and in 1394, he was teaching in Mantua. Among his writings, the astrological work *De iudiciis nativitatum liber praeclarissimus* ("Illustrious Book on the Judgments of Nativities"), completed in Mantua, is the only one that was later printed by Regiomontanus, in 1540. Two works on magic are kept in late medieval manuscripts: a short *Glosa super ymagines duodecim signorum Hermetis* ("Gloss on the images of the twelve signs of Hermes") and a longer treatise *De occultis et manifestis* ("On Occult and Manifest Things"). Both of them are extant in an Italian codex from the fifteenth century: ms. Paris, Bibliothèque nationale de France, latinus 7337; the *Glosa* is also contained, anonymously, in a manuscript of the Bibliotheca Apostolica Vaticana, latinus 4085. Both texts have been recently edited. Three "experimenta" or tales about talismanic experiences, found in both manuscripts, can also be ascribed to him.[24]

Besides the obvious reasons of theological censorship and legal risks, as shown by the tragic example of Cecco's death, it was also a theoretical impossibility to assume the authorship of a magical text. Generally, a magical text contained specific recipes, rituals, invocations and other signs, which were thought to be effective on the implicit or explicit grounds that they had been revealed by a very ancient and sacred tradition. Indeed, no rational rules could account for the choice of such and such strange word or name used in the magical operation, and hence no human being could pretend to deduce them from his own mind. Therefore, those texts were ascribed either to such ancient legendary authorities as Hermes, Solomon, Apollonius or Abel, or to medieval authors who had acquired, shortly after their death, a similar legendary aura, like Albertus Magnus or Arnald of Villanova. The underlying idea was that the magical rituals had been transmitted through many generations and that they originated from a very ancient revelation. This process is obvious in the *Liber lunae*: the prologue tells how Abel and other ancient authorities decided to engrave all the knowledge in the marble; after the Flood, Hermes Trismegistus found these engraved books in Hebron. The magic here described is viewed as revealed directly by God himself.

Then how to become an author-magician? How to assume the authorship of a writing displaying such powerful secrets? The author can become an author in three ways: as a compiler, as a commentator or as an author of a theoretical treatise that makes use of some magical material drawn from the extant traditions. Cecco d'Ascoli cannot be considered as openly an author-magician, since his magic is hidden under a commentary on non-magic books, handbooks of cosmology and astrology. Nevertheless, this hide-and-seek game did not spare him trouble with the Inquisition. Hence, by contrast, the obvious assumption of magical authorship by Antonio da Montolmo gives clear evidence of a fundamental change of context that was going on at this time in the northern part of Italy.[25]

In the *Glosa super ymagines duodecim signorum Hermetis*, Antonio acquires the status of author as a "glossator". Furthermore, his additions to this traditional magical hermetic text are daring enough to reveal the new intellectual framework of magic. The *Ymagines duodecim signorum Hermetis*, also known as *Liber formarum duodecim signorum* or *Liber electionum secretorum superiorum*, is a talismanic text that is extant in several manuscripts and also in a section of the Latin version of *Picatrix* (*Ghayât al-hakîm*). Amongst them, the above-mentioned ms. Bibliotheca Apostolica Vaticana, latinus 4085 contains this opuscule, and the name of Antonio da Montolmo is mentioned within the section devoted to the sign of Lion.[26] This talismanic text describes how to make astrological seals for each of the twelve zodiacal signs. The figures that are to be engraved into the metal are not always the traditional figures of the zodiacal signs, and the aim of each seal does not really square with the usual zodiacal melothesia (that is, the influence of each zodiacal sign on a specific part of the human body). Anyway, one of the main distinctive features of this short work is the complete lack of any "addressative" practices: there are no prayers, invocations, inscriptions or other signs *addressed* to an Intelligence (angels, demons, other spirits). This is a very exceptional situation in a talismanic text. Hence, the efficacy of talismans is seemingly supposed to derive only from the natural power of the constellations under which they are built. If we refer to the typology invented by the Magister Speculi, the anonymous author of *Speculum astronomiae* (by the middle of the thirteenth century), these astrological seals could be called purely "astrological images". But, in a very surprising way, instead of ridding the traditional texts of any "addressative" practices like any previous medieval author eager to promote the "theologically correct" notion of "astrological image" would have done, Antonio da Montolmo, on the contrary, introduces several "addressative" elements in his *Glosa*! Later, he gives advice to act in this way with other texts, like the *De imaginibus* of Thebit (another talismanic text, deprived from "addressative" practices, which was the main reference for building up the concept of the "astrological image" in the *Speculum astronomiae*).

Indeed, at the beginning, Antonio says that he wants to "make this work more perfect". The practitioner has to be previously purified: clean, sober and chaste. He must write the names and *characters* of the angels that are associated with the zodiacal sign and with the Lord of this sign in a virgin leaf of paper. He must utter these names three times and make some good smelling fumigations. He also has to perform some exorcisms. He has to say a specific prayer to the angel of the sign, the planet and the hour. To tell the truth, Antonio gives a theological justification for these "addressative" practices in order to reassure the faithful Christian reader: the angels that are invoked in these operations are not the evil "spirits of the air", but the good angels belonging to the order of the Powers (according to the *Celestial Hierarchy* by Pseudo-Dionysius). Note that even such a theologian as Thomas Aquinas had suggested that the Intelligences moving the celestial spheres were angels, precisely the Powers.[27] A priest is required to consecrate the talismanic image. The magician himself must say some specific psalms and prayers addressed to God himself and the angels. However, this argument would not have convinced a standard theologian, since, for instance, Thomas Aquinas had excluded any possibility for theurgy or angelic magic: in his view, the magician believed he was calling on angels but actually invoked evil spirits (demons). In any case, Antonio dared to write himself performed such operations: "In Bologna as well as in Mantua, I tried out these images, whose effects were wonderful".[28]

In the *Glosa*, Antonio refers to his other work *De occultis et manifestis*. In this work, he can also be called an author-magician insofar as he writes a theoretical treatise on magic that includes "addressative" elements borrowed from previous traditional magical works. In the introduction, Antonio explains the title of his work, since it deals with "occult" as well as "manifest" operations of the Intelligences – an alternative title is *Liber intelligentiarum* ("Book of Intelligences").[29] In the first chapter, Antonio explicitly refers to evil Intelligences. There are four parts in the heavens, he writes, each one belonging to one of the four cardinal signs: Aries, Libra, Capricorn and Cancer, and accordingly there are four orders of Intelligences. This is the reason why the magician must perform the required exorcisms at a crossroad of four roads. Antonio asks four scholastic questions, which he then answers: Why are these Intelligences established under their own cardinal signs? Because they make use of the influences of these zodiacal signs. Why are some people able to see them, whereas others are not? Because the Intelligences are able to produce images playing with rules of optics, so these images are seen or not by people according to their nature or abilities. Why do these Intelligences appear to virgins and unpolluted people? Because the nature of the evil angels is pure or because sexual intercourse causes the human soul to be endowed with a dignity that makes the Intelligences jealous. Why do they prefer to come into sight in transparent bodies such as water or crystals? Because they give a more perfect reflection to the image of these Intelligences.

Chapter 2 tells the moment when the invocations must be performed. In Chapter 3, Antonio writes about the Altitudes, or the Intelligences standing under the twelve zodiacal signs. Each order of *Altitudines* reacts to the others according to the astrological aspect between their respective zodiacal signs. Every human being, he adds, receives when he is born his own evil angel belonging to this order of Intelligences.[30] In Chapter 4, Antonio makes a threefold distinction: images, rings and phylacteries are either astrological, magical or both astrological and magical. This distinction, probably inspired by that in the *Speculum astronomiae* but quite different from it, is very similar to ideas of such authors like Giorgio Anselmi da Parma (before 1386– after 1449) or Jerome Torrella (1456– after 1500)[31] The first category defines a purely astral (and natural) magic, just like the *Magister Speculi*'s "astrological images". This kind of magic is epitomized by an image made by a servant who wishes to incline a prelate to give him a better position. Thus, three questions are asked and answered. First, how is a heavenly quality able to incline someone to do something? The astral quality is infused in the limbs of every living being as it is born. Just like a traveller puts good smelling substances in his new wooden bottle so that the liquid will smell good, so does the heavens give such a quality to a newly made image. Second, why must the material of the image (wax) be virgin and clean? The reason is that the wax has to be deprived of any previous and inconsonant qualities. Third, how to explain that the influence affects precisely the aforesaid prelate and not another human being? Because the image is put close to the prelate and because the operator through his will orientates the influence towards this man. This is why it is better when the operator makes the image himself, since his own confidence is instilled within the material of the image. Antonio here combines the two available doctrines of natural magic: occult properties deriving from astrological influence, and the power of imagination. This, for example, justifies the popular belief that meeting an unfortunate man in the morning is nasty.

The second category of images, rings and phylacteries is "magical": they are occult insofar as they are "rather remote from" our "sensory faculties". The process includes rituals such as incantations, exorcisms and suffumigations. As it seems, Antonio suggests two different ways: either compelling the Intelligences – probably through the divine power – or praying to the Intelligence and showing reverence to them. Old women are particularly effective in these magical operations, because their will is especially strong.

The third kind of magical objects is based on a combination of the first two categories, the astrological and magical. Antonio writes that this procedure is regarded as the most powerful. Indeed, the action of the Intelligences is added to the effect of astral influences. The Intelligences make use of the astral influences in order to perform the operation.

Chapter 5 addresses the functions of the Intelligence of the planets and the places where they remain. The Saturnine Intelligence, for instance, is able to produce melancholic diseases, treacheries and other misfortunes. These kinds of Intelligences are outside the divine grace, Antonio says; they must be clearly distinguished from the Intelligence that moves the planetary orbs. In Antonio's view, ancient pagan religion is a cult to these evil Intelligences living under specific planets. But besides this obviously nigromantical magic, Antonio seems to allude to another kind of magic or another interpretation of these practices: according to "someone", the angels to which Solomon's *Almadel* refers belong to the Dionysian order of Powers, these would be the zodiacal Altitudes and, therefore, good angels. (This "someone" is likely to be Cecco d'Ascoli, who also refers to Powers). Hence, Antonio seems to suggest two categories of magic: astrological nigromancy or astrological theurgy. The weather for such operations must be clear and quiet, because in such conditions, the Intelligences can produce apparent shapes more easily. Again, he puts forward his own experience: when it was raining, he succeeded in making the intelligences appear, but their shapes were less easily produced. Antonio also explains the requirement – often reminded in magical treatises – that the place must be secret: first, the (evil) Intelligences do not like to show themselves as compelled to by the divine power; and second, when we are isolated, our senses are more susceptible to the actions of these Intelligences.

In the last chapter, Antonio recalls the usual requirements that can be found in nigromantical treatises (especially those belonging to the so-called Solomonic tradition). The operator has to be born under a specific constellation so that he shares common propriety with the spirits. Some qualities are also needed: sagacity and learning (so that he will be able to grasp the secrets of the spirits), courage (so that he will not fear them), eloquence (in order to say perfectly and with strength the words addressed to the spirits, making them tremble). He has to be skilled in astrology in order to know the moments for operating. He must also have a firm confidence in the performance of the magical operation. He has to be a Catholic and must be clean and free of any vice so that he bears likeness with the spirits. A bath and suffumigation are also required.

Antonio gives rational explanation for the drawing of circles in these magical operations that are intended to protect the operator from the spirits he has called upon. He answers two questions. First: Why is it a circular figure? Because a circle has neither beginning nor end, a property that it shares with the Prime Mover. God put the circle which was in His mind into the world. The circle is the most capacious figure. Second: Why does this figure have the operative power? Because this circular figure is called "word of God". Antonio explains that the operator makes the circle blessed through various rituals and inscriptions of characters. He also mentions pentacles and the way for preparing these arts of protection.

In both manuscripts (BnF lat. 7337 and Vat. lat. 4085), three "experiments" are presented anonymously.[32] Some clues, including a comparison with Antonio's genuine texts, lead to the possible conclusion that Antonio da Montolmo is the actual author. These experiments are ascribed to three individuals. The first is Tommaso da Pizzano (Thomas de Pisan) (died between 1385 and 1389), the famous astrologer who became a physician of Charles V, King of France. The narrator, probably Antonio da Montolmo, writes that Tommaso da Pizzano himself told him this experience when he was in Paris when he was in favour with him. Thomas would have made an astrological talisman according to the image in order to remove scorpions from a place, which is the first of Thebit's *De imaginibus*. The purpose of this talisman was to drive the Englishmen away from the Kingdom of France. The Kingdom of France was divided "by imagination" into four parts. Five metallic figurines were made under a specific astrological chart (when Scorpio was ascendant, and other requirements). The names of the English king and his main captain were written on the figurines. One of the four figurines was buried in the centre of the kingdom, the four others in the middle of each side of the tetragon. Words explaining that this was the grave of these enemies were uttered. Names for expulsion were also written on the images: Baliatot, Hariaraiel and others, which were probably names of spirits.

The second experiment is ascribed to a certain master Bartholomeo di Sangibene, a Venetian follower of Duke Leopold (of Austria?) (*Venetorum fidelis ducis Leopoldi*), who operated several times in Germany. He made five figurines, the stomachs of which were deep; there he put some soil gathered from the five parts of the area concerned.

The narrator, Antonio himself, tells the last experiment: he observed three times that when Mars is in the sign of Gemini, and especially when it is retrograde and when Scorpio is ascendant and when the moon is in the latter sign, an image can be made in front of which the name of the enemy is written; in the same hour, the image has to be buried upside down, uttering Tommaso da Pizzano's words, in the place where the enemy is about to cross.

The other magical texts by Antonio give several evidences in favour of his identification with the narrator. First, in *De occultis et manifestis*, he mentions the experience made for "King Charles" (Charles V) "against his enemies": this obviously refers to Tommaso da Pizzano's *experimentum*. Second, Antonio's tale in the *Glosa* that he himself made talismanic images at Bologna and Padua – he also alludes to his own practice in *De occultis et manifestis* – is consonant with the third experiment made by the narrator himself.

The sources and the meaning of Cecco d'Ascoli and Antonio da Montolmo's magic

Cecco d'Ascoli and Antonio da Montolmo make use of common sources belonging to the form of ritual magic also called nigromancy, very often ascribed to such legendary authorities as Solomon (hence the name sometimes given to it is Solomonic magic). In Cecco's commentaries, the sources are usually hidden under otherwise unknown titles ascribed to such authorities as Apollonius (*De arte magica, De hyle*…), Astaphon (*De mineralibus constellatis*),

Hipparcus (*De rebus*, *De hierarchiis spirituum*, *de ordine intelligentiarum*, *De vinculo spiritus*...) or Zoroastes (for example *De dominio quartarum octave spere*). They are not always fake references invented by Cecco; some of them are likely to be real apocryphal texts disguised by Cecco under fake titles and authorities.

For example, Cecco refers several times in both commentaries to a book ascribed to the ancient magician Apollonius (of Tyana): *De angelica factura* or *De angelica factione*, notably when dealing with the *tropici*. Antonio da Montolmo quotes a *De angelica fictione* attributed to Solomon when he addresses the *Altitudines*; these "angels" are mentioned in the *Almadel* or *Liber intelligentiarum* of Solomon, a deeply modified Christian-Latin version of the previous *Almandal* (from an Arabic origin).[33] It seems possible that Cecco had these texts in mind but chose to cover them with fictitious titles and names, maybe in order to confuse the issue.

Both authors refer to the spirits of the cardinal points; Antonio gives the name of Oriens, Cecco also gives the three other names: Amaymon, Paymon and Egim. Those names are actually mentioned in Solomonic sources: *The Four Rings* (*De quatuor anulis*) also called *Idea of Solomon* (*Idea Salomonis*) or the *Key of Solomon* (*Clavicula Salomonis*). The reason here could be the condemnation of the nigromantical books by the author of the *Speculum astronomiae* (by the middle of the thirteenth century). The quotations made by Cecco do not correspond exactly, as far as it can be known, to any sections of those "Solomonic" books mentioned by the Magister Speculi, the anonymous author of this normative bibliography. By contrast, Cecco mentions Thebit's *De imaginibus*, almost the only talismanic text that the Magister Speculi evaluates as licit, because the talismanic images described are made according to pure astrology – these are "astrological images".[34] Another reason could be Cecco's willingness to build up a consistent theory of demonic places in the Sphere by referring to sections of the book that are half-real, half-invented.

Scholarly sources on philosophy (such as Aristotle's *Ethics* and *On the soul*) and astrology (Ptolemy's *Quadripartitum*, Alcabitius' *De principiis astrologiae*) are found in Antonio's works (scholarly texts could also be found in Cecco's commentaries). But Antonio da Montolmo quotes several magic sources: not only the widespread *De quindecim stellis* (a Hermetic text whose commentary was ascribed to the astrologer Messahalla), Thebit's *De imaginibus*, or Hermes's *Liber formarum*, but also more dubious works of ritual magic ascribed to Solomon: *Almadel*, *Clavicula Salomonis*, the aforementioned *De angelica fictione* and a *Magica* allegedly written by Aristotle himself – an *Ars magica* was attributed by Cecco to Apollonius. Antonio also refers to such great "magical" authorities as Moses or Virgil.

It is clear from his *De occultis et manifestis* that Antonio knew Cecco's commentary on the *Sphere*. He alludes to the "author" who wrote the chapter "chronic rising and setting": this is Sacrobosco, who wrote in the *Sphere* that the rising is called "chronic" or "temporal" because "it is the moment of the astrologers (*mathematicorum*)". But Antonio suggests an emendation: the moment of the magicians (*magicorum*). This is typically the kind of nigromantical shift produced by Cecco. Cecco's distinction between the three meanings of *arcus* (astrological, nigromantical and chiromantical) is the obvious source for Antonio's distinction between the two meanings of "horoscope", that is astrological (horoscope means "ascendant") and chiromantical (a "certain sign" in the hand). Thus, when Antonio in the same chapter alludes to "the magicians" practising magic under the sign of Cancer, "heart of Septentrion" and other required conditions, he probably alludes to Cecco d'Ascoli or, at least, to that specific section of his *Commentary* on the Sphere where Cecco writes, "if you want to make an image in which you want an answer from some spirit, the heart of Septentrion, i.e. Cancer, which is the ascendant of nigromancers, must be ascendant."[35]

Despite their boldness in supporting an astrological nigromancy – Antonio claims that he himself practised this kind of magic – both Cecco and Antonio take particular care to respect the Christian cosmological frame: good angels in the superlunary region, demons exclusively in the sublunary world. Both of them refer to specific circles and points of the Sphere, but the places where the evil demons stay are always projections of these circles and points in the sublunary region.[36] This makes sense, since in order to catch and control the powers of demons, Cecco and Antonio, both Christian magicians, needed to share a common worldview with their contemporaries.

Future directions

Cecco d'Ascoli and Antonio da Montolmo's cases give some clues for the study of the development of a Latin astral nigromancy based on an intricate demonic cosmology, that is a specific demonology linked to specific parts of the sphere. The history of the surfacing of such cosmological demonologies should be written. The rise of the "author-magician" in late fourteenth-century Italy is another path for further studies.

Notes

1 On these phenomena: Nicolas Weill-Parot, *Les 'Images astrologiques' au Moyen Âge et à la Renaissance. Spéculations intellectuelles et pratiques magiques (XIIe-XVe siècle)* (Paris: Honoré Champion, 2002), 492–95 and 591–638.
2 Lynn Thorndike, *A History of Magic and Experimental Science*, 8 vols. (New York: Columbia University Press, 1923–58), 2: 948–68; Nicolas Weill-Parot, "Cecco d'Ascoli," in *Dizionario storico dell'Inquisizione*, ed. Adriano Prosperi, collab. Vincenzo Lavenia and John Tedeschi, 2 vols. (Pisa: Scuola normale superiore, 2010), 1: 316–17. For detailed studies: *Cecco d'Ascoli: cultura, scienza e politica nell'Italia del Trecento*, ed. Antonio Rigon (Roma: Istituto Storico Italiano per il Medio Evo, 2007). Commentary on the *Sphere*: Lynn Thorndike ed., *The Sphere of Sacrobosco and Its Commentators* (Chicago, IL: University of Chicago Press, 1949), 343–411; edition of the commentary on "Alcabitius": Giuseppe Boffito, *Il Commento inedito di Cecco d'Ascoli all'Alcabizzo* (Vaticano: Leo S. Olschki, 1905).
3 On the general distinction between nigromancy and necromancy: Jean-Patrice Boudet, *Entre science et nigromance. Astrologie, divination et magie dans l'Occident médiéval (XIIe-XVe siècle)* (Paris: Publications de la Sorbonne, 2006), 92–94.
4 Thorndike, *The Sphere of Sacrobosco*, 55.
5 Nicolas Weill-Parot, "I demoni della Sfera. La 'nigromanzia' cosmologico-astrologica di Cecco d'Ascoli," in *Cecco d'Ascoli: cultura, scienza e politica*, ed. Rigon, 103–31.
6 Cecco d'Ascoli, *In Spheram*, ed. Thorndike: ch. 2, 387–88.
7 Ibid., 388 and 398–99.
8 Cecco d'Ascoli, *L'Acerba*, ed. Marco Albertazzi (Lavis: La Finestra, 2002): Bk 4 ch. 3 verse 9 ("Anch'io te voglio dir como nel fuocho/ fanno venir figure i piromanti/ chiamando 'Scarbo', 'Mormores' e 'Smocho'.")
9 Cecco d'Ascoli, *In Spheram*: ch. 3, 403.
10 Ibid., ed. Thorndike, ch. 3, 403–4.
11 Ibid., ch. 2, 397.
12 Ibid., ch. 4, 406.
13 Ibid., ch. 3, 404.
14 Ibid., ch. 2, 395.
15 John of Sacrobosco, *De Sphera*, ed. Thorndike, *The Sphere of Sacrobosco*, 93.
16 On Floron: Cecco d'Ascoli, *In Spheram*, ch. 2, 398–99 and ch. 4, 408–9.

17 Since Giuseppe Boffito, "Perché fu condannato al fuoco l'astrologo Cecco d'Ascoli ?," *Studi e documenti di Storia e diritto* 20 (1899), 357–82, many studies could be mentioned, amongst them: Lynn Thorndike, "Relations of the Inquisition to Peter of Abano and Cecco d'Ascoli," *Speculum* 1 (1926): 338–43; Lynn Thorndike, "More Light on Cecco d'Ascoli," *Romanic Review* 37 (1946): 296–306; G. A. Gentili, "Un esemplare bolognese della sentenza capitale contro Cecco d'Ascoli Maestro d'Errori," *Rivista di storia delle scienze mediche e naturali* 44 (1953): 172–87; Massimo Giansante, "Cecco d'Ascoli. Il destino dell'astrologo," *Giornale di astronomia* 23, no. 2 (1997): 9–16; Massimo Giansante, "La condanna di Cecco d'Ascoli fra astrologia e pauperismo," in *Cecco d'Ascoli: cultura, scienza e politica*, ed. Rigon, 183–99; Graziella Federici Vescovini, *Medioevo magico. La magia tra religione e scienza nei secoli xiii e xiv (Torino: UTET, 2000)*, 277–311; Emanuele Coccia et Sylvain Piron, "Cecco d'Ascoli à la croisée des savoirs," *Bolletino di italianistica* 1 (2011): 27–37.
18 Cecco d'Ascoli, *L'Acerba*, Bk II ch. 1 v. 19–24 and ch. 12, v. 31 sqq.
19 Giovanni Villani, *Nuova cronica*, ed. Giuseppe Porta (s.l. – Pavia: Fondazione Pietro Bombo - Guanda, 1990–91), vol. 2: XI. 41, 570–71.
20 Cecco d'Ascoli, *In Spheram*, ch. 4, 408.
21 On these condemnations, see now Alain Boureau, *Satan hérétique. Histoire de la démonologie (1280–1330)* (Paris: Odile Jacob, 2004). On the bull Super illius specula, see now Martine Ostorero, "Les papes et les sorcières: la postérité de *Super illius specula*," in *L'Historien et les fantômes. Lectures (autour) de l'oeuvre d'Alain Boureau*, ed. Béatrice Delaurenti, Blaise Dufal and Piroska Nagy (Paris: Les Belles Lettres, 2017), 101–16.
22 Thorndike, *A History of Magic*: 3, 602–10; Vittorio De Donato, "Antonio da Montolmo," in *Dizionario biografico degli Italiani* (Roma: Istituto della Enciclopedia italiana, vol. III, 1961), 559–60.
23 See notably Nicolas Weill-Parot [with collab. Julien Véronèse], "Antonio da Montolmo's *De occultis et manifestis* or *Liber Intelligiarum*. An Annotated Critical Edition with English Translation and Introduction," in *Invoking Angels: Theurgic Ideas and Practices from the Thirteenth to the Sixteenth Century*, ed. Claire Fanger (University Park: Pennsylvania State University Press, 2012), 219–93; Nicolas Weill-Parot, "Antonio da Montolmo et la magie hermétique," in *Hermetism from Late Antiquity to Humanism*, ed. Paolo Lucentini, Ilaria Parri and Vittoria Perrone Compagni (Turnhout: Brepols, 2003), 545–68.
24 Weill-Parot, *Les "Images astrologiques"*, 605–22.
25 Ibid., 492–95 and 602ff. A previous example of an author magician could be found: Berengario Ganell and his *Summa sacre magice* (1347). See in addition to Damaris Gehr's chapter in this volume, Boudet, *Entre science et nigromance*, 398 and Carlos Gilly, "Tra Paracelso, Pelagio e Ganello: L'ermetismo di John Dee," in *Magia, alchimia, scienza dal '400 al '700: L'influsso di Ermete Trismegisto*, ed. Carlos Gilly and Cis van Heertum, 2 vols. (Florence: Centro Di, 2002), 1, 275–85.
26 Nicolas Weill-Parot, "Astrologie, médecine et art talismanique à Montpellier: les sceaux astrologiques pseudo-arnaldiens," in *L'Université de Médecine de Montpellier et son rayonnement (XIIIe-XVe siècles)*, ed. Daniel Le Blévec, with collab. Thomas Granier (Turnhout: Brepols, 2004), 157–74.
27 On the angels moving the celestial spheres: Tiziana Suarez-Nani, *Les Anges et la Philosophie. Subjectivité et fonction cosmologique des substances séparées à la fin du XIIIe siècle* (Paris: Vrin 2002).
28 Critical edition of the *Glosa*: Weill-Parot, "Antonio da Montolmo et la magie hermétique," 560–66.
29 Critical edition of this text with an English translation: Weill-Parot, "Antonio da Montolmo's *De occultis et manifestis*," 238–93.
30 On the belief in personal good and evil angels: *De Socrate à Tintin. Anges gardiens et démons familiers de l'Antiquité à nos jours*, ed. Jean-Patrice Boudet, Philippe Faure and Christian Renoux (Rennes: Presses universitaires de Rennes 2011).
31 See the chapter on Torrella in this volume.
32 Critical edition: Weill-Parot, *Les "Images astrologiques"*, 897–900.
33 On the Almadel and Almandal: Julien Véronèse, *L'Almandal et l'Almadel latins au Moyen Âge. Introduction et éditions critiques* (Firenze: Sismel Edizioni del Galluzzo, 2012).
34 See Weill-Parot, *Les "Images astrologiques"*, 25–219.
35 (2.2, 258–59) cf. Cecco, ch. 3, 402 (*ascendens necromanticorum*, ed. Thorndike; *ascendens nigromanticorum*, ms. Paris, BnF, lat. 7337, p. 36).
36 Nicolas Weill-Parot, "Dans le ciel ou sous le ciel? Les anges dans la magie astrale, XIIe-XIVe siècle," *Mélanges de l'Ecole Française de Rome. Moyen Âge* 114, no. 2 (2002): 753–71 [=*Les Anges et la Magie au Moyen Âge*, ed. Jean-Patrice Boudet, Henri Bresc et Benoît Grévin].

18

BERINGARIUS GANELLUS AND THE *SUMMA SACRE MAGICE*

Magic as the promotion of God's Kingship

Damaris Aschera Gehr

Around 1346, the Catalan magician Beringarius Ganellus completed the *Summa sacre magice* or *Compendium of sacred magic* in five books. Due to its complexity and its length of over 200,000 words, this work stands out as the most thorough overview of Latin medieval magic transmitted to our day.

In modern scholarship, the *Summa* was first signalled in the 1960s by Paul Oskar Kristeller, who discovered its text in a fourteenth-century manuscript in Kassel.[1] Some twenty years later, Carlos Gilly studied that manuscript more closely and detected a sixteenth-century German translation in a codex kept in the Staatsbibliothek in Berlin, where it is concealed under the frontispiece of the ארבעתאל *Arbatel De magia veterum*, a Paracelsistic treatise first published in Basel in 1575.[2] In 2009, I identified consistent sections of the original version of the *Summa* in an early sixteenth-century manuscript kept in Halle, where they come as an addition to the appendix of the *Liber Razielis*.[3] These are the documents that can be related at present to Ganellus with certainty.[4] Yet it may be that other texts of his are preserved. For instance he could be the author of the anonymous tract on Christian magic entitled *Magisterium eumantice artis*, partially preserved in a late fifteenth-century manuscript copied in Rome.[5] Only a few studies have been devoted to Ganellus and his oeuvre so far.[6] In this chapter an outline is given in anticipation of closer treatment in my forthcoming edition of the *Summa*.

Biographical information on Ganellus

Unlike many late medieval magical authors, who attribute their work to an authority of the past following the pseudepigraphic convention, Ganellus introduces himself by his real name. On the other hand, he provides no dedication or biographical account, but just minimal hints about his life and activity. Towards the end of the *Summa*, when describing a ritual in which the angels associated with the current date are to be mentioned, he indicates Monday, 10 July 1346.[7] This tells us that he had probably completed the treatise by that year. Elsewhere he writes that the rituals of the spirit invocations must be explained in detail since the young have a poor education.[8] At the time of writing this, he had probably reached middle age, so he must have been born between the last decades of the thirteenth and the beginning of the fourteenth century. In a passage expounding the use of the quadrant, Ganellus reveals that his current residence is Perpignan.[9] This matches the Catalan influences perceptible in his Latin, already underscored by Gilly.[10] The author offers another clue when he compares the hooded coat (*capa*) used by magicians with the coat of the licentiates in Paris.[11] Before writing the *Summa*, he had thus probably been in northern France and visited the Sorbonne, where he may have acquired the title of "magister philosophus" mentioned in the incipit and the explicit of the *Summa*.[12]

The life of Ganellus during and shortly after the composition of the *Summa* is further documented in the acts of a trial that took place during the last months of 1347 at Mende, a town in today's French region Languedoc-Roussillon which belonged at the time to the Crown of Aragon.[13] In the acts, the defrocked friar Stephanus Pipini, charged for having made a defixional wax figure of a bishop, recounts having made a long journey through Spain in search of the *Liber iuratus* by Honorius. Towards the end of 1343 he met in Mende Guarinus de Castronovo, the chamberlain of James III of Mallorca. On his advice, he consulted the "magister in artibus" Ganellus in Perpignan in the castle of Trassor, at the time an estate of James III.[14] Ganellus showed him his own copy of the *Liber iuratus* and hosted him for several months as his assistant.[15] A direct connection between Ganellus and James III is not mentioned in the acts, but is in principle not to be ruled out. At that time, the king was waging war against his cousin Peter IV of Aragon and may have hoped to find a remedy in the occult arts. Pipini indeed recounts having been generously rewarded for teaching James III the science of the philosopher's stone, a thing which Ganellus, who was no alchemist, could not do.[16]

Ganellus's subsequent reputation

The earliest reference to Ganellus's reputation of which we have knowledge is contained in the acts of the Mende trial mentioned above. There Ganellus appears as a well-known among the learned circles in the surroundings of Perpignan already in 1343.[17] His experience with magic prior to the composition of the *Summa* seems to be confirmed by the *Magisterium eumantice artis*, a learned text based on citations from the Scriptures and from magical literature that, if it is by him, must have been written before the *Summa*.[18]

But Ganellus was well known also in a wider area and his reputation endured until the sixteenth century. This is attested by the manuscript tradition, which up to the early modern period reached from Spain to France, Germany and possibly to Italy,[19] and by authors active outside the magical tradition who knew his work directly or through references by others. The oldest reference is given by Johannes Trithemius in the *Antipalus maleficiorum* (1508). There the *Summa* turns up in a bibliography of the most important magical books in the chapter *De tertio genere maleficarum cuius professores commercium habent cum daemonibus manifestum*, dealing with the magical practices involving the cooperation of demons. Trithemius depicts the *Summa* as a collection of "fatuous, superstitious and frivolous" doctrines and Ganellus (distortedly, as we shall see) as "a soldier of the demons rather than of God".[20] I have been able to ascertain that the abbot owned his own specimen of the *Summa*, possibly the surviving Kassel manuscript, and that he lent it to his friend, the physician and astrologer Johannes Virdung von Hassfurt (ca. 1463–1538) so that he could copy it. The book exchange is recalled in Trithemius's letter of the 20 August 1507, best known for containing the first mention of the historical Faust.[21] The Kassel manuscript later accompanied John Dee on his European tour of 1583–89 and passed in 1586 or 1589 to either the Landgrave Wilhelm or the learned Moritz of Hessen in Kassel.[22]

In *Le triumphe des vertuz*, the *miroir des princes* from 1508 to 1517 commissioned by Louise de Savoie for the education of the future king François d'Angoulême, Jean Thenaud recounts that, during a trip to hell, Albert the Great introduced him to Raziel (author of the *Liber Razielis*), Sumach (author of a book on talismans mentioned in the *Summa*), Sul (possibly Solomon), Vaxinius (author of the *Liber vaccae*), Abolard (Peter Abelard), Pradellus (author of the prologue of the *Liber iuratus* by Honorius),[23] "Berengarius, Ganellus", Roger Bacon, the four kings of Toledo (including Alfonso X), Michael Scot, Honorius, Picatrix, Thebit, Hermes and the Sibyl. A similar list of magicians appears in Thenaud's *Cabale metrifiée* from 1519, where Ganellus's surname and last name are again separated by a comma and thus treated as the names of two separate authors.[24] The latter detail seems to suggest that Thenaud did not know Ganellus directly and quoted the list from an earlier source. Ganellus stands out as the youngest figure in the account, so that source was probably written back in the fourteenth century.

The translator and copyist of the German version of the *Summa* transmitted in the Berlin manuscript, probably active in the last quarter of the sixteenth century in eastern Saxony, introduces Ganellus as a "highly popular and experienced master of philosophy".[25]

A reference to our author might be found also in the *Recommendatio astronomiae*. This anonymous, supposedly late medieval tract in defence of magic and astrology praises one "Burgarius", author of a chapter *De diffinicione mulierum et virorum* or *On the definition of women and men* revealing "the most important secrets of the philosophers, similarly to well-known books as the *Liber Ptholomei*, the *Liber Lune Hermetis*, the *Liber runarum*, the *Liber Hermetis de caracteribus et sigillis* and the *Liber Balemi*". Scholars have considered *De diffinicione* to be a chapter of the *Summa* and identified "Burgarius" with our Beringarius.[26] The *Summa*, yet, does not contain or mention the writing *De diffinicione*, which is probably lost, so this identification is uncertain.

Ganellus's definition and treatment of magic

The *Summa* opens with an introduction defining magic and explaining its status:[27]

> Magic is the science of binding evil and good spirits by the use of the name of God, His names and the names of the things of the world. Hence it follows that magic is a science of words, because each noun is a word, since a word is each thing which is uttered by the tongue on condition that it can be written with letters. But there are many sciences of the word such as grammar, logic, rhetoric and magic [...] magic is about the word which serves to coerce the spiritual substance. Some words are indeed infused with a wonderful power created by the only Maker who is the almighty God and cause of all causes, as you can well see of herbs and gems, but in a more excellent way, almost endlessly and beyond compare. And the inexperienced can ponder this through their religion. For in the Scriptures it is stated that [...] God created the skies and the angels with words. [...] And it is also stated that whatever one may ask by the use of the word, if one believes with faith and without hesitation, it will happen. [...] Magic thus deals with wonder-working words swarming out of faith or proceeding from firm belief, so that one believes in the true God and the art and one's teacher and the religion to which one is devoted. But it is better if one believes in the Christian faith since, as my experience in magical matters teaches, the faith of any other religion is worthless straw.[28]

By using the term *scientia* rather than *ars* or *sapientia*, Ganellus classifies his subject in the domain of the sciences. Magic, he explains, deals with words and stands as such alongside grammar, logic and rhetoric, the disciplines of the *trivium*. The specific difference distinguishing magic from those sciences is its object: the wonder-working word.[29] The introduction says nothing more on the epistemological status of magic, but the reason why magic can be considered a science is dealt with more closely throughout the treatise. Ganellus uses the term "science" with the meaning that it gained through the epistemological shift that invested the concept of knowledge in the twelfth century under the influence of the Aristotelian corpus. In the *Summa*, magical science is in effect described as a system each component of which – be it the theoretical background of magic, the manifold rituals, the material and verbal instruments used in them or the deontology of the magician – is regarded and justified in its relation to the whole. Ganellus exposes the principles upon which this system rests by use of the Aristotelian doctrine of the four causes. He writes that God and the magician are the first and second *causae efficientes*, that is the efficient causes enacting the magical process; the word and the material instruments are the first and second *causae materiales*, that is the material elements necessary for the execution of the rituals;[30] the cause in itself on the one hand and the contents of the magical teaching and the way in which magic is taught on the other hand are the first and second *causae formales*, that is the accounts of the what-it-is-to-be of magic; the worship of God, support for the poor and the fight against the unfaithful on one side and the magical invocation and consecration (the two main aspects of the ritual action) on the other are the first and second *causae finales* or ends for the sake of which magic is practised.[31] This determination of the final cause, which channels the magical practice towards a typology of ends that are equally central in the scriptural teaching, is directly linked with the most pregnant definition of magic given by Ganellus. There one reads that *theologia* or theology is divided into a theoretical part, consisting in the divine laws exposed in the Scriptures, and a practical part, consisting of the factual application of those laws by the use of magical science. As the "practical part of all divine laws", magic stands as the "second and noblest part of spiritual wisdom", that is, of theology.[32] By formulating the connection between magic and theology in these terms, our author possibly follows the Aristotelian doctrine, where practical philosophy is presented in its dependence from metaphysics.

Ganellus holds that since magic is a science, it must be treated through the method fit for a science. In particular, he opts for instruments, approaches and structures recurrent in the scholastic tradition. In a methodological chapter, he explains that magic is best treated through the definition of its concepts and components (*definitio*), its division into parts (*divisio*), its theoretical justification (*probatio*) and the indication of the reasons why its components and principles are so and not otherwise (*positio*).[33] As one can already see in the brief introductory passage quoted above, Ganellus effectively applies these means in his work. The scholastic approach is also mirrored by the choice of the genre of the *summa*, a choice which is unique in the magical tradition. Admittedly, Ganellus's *summa* is not typical in all regards. Among other things, it contains very few *quaestiones*.[34] Even so, it follows the scholastic model in several respects. The text aims to give a comprehensive and systematic exposition of a field of knowledge and for this purpose it cites ample source material. The reference to elder authorities is a common trait of both the scholastic and the magical traditions. The approach to sources nevertheless differs markedly from one to the other. One main difference is that the magicians, in line with magic's claim of divine and ancient origins and of the immutability of its doctrine, tend to present a static image of its literature. Usually, they compose their writings through the revision of elder sources but do conceal their personal method and contributions. Their work lacks a metadiscursive framework and a declared and thus clearly recognizable historical dimension, an aspect which is enhanced by the recurrent use of the pseudepigraphic style. Ganellus's attitude instead rather reminds that of the scholastic authors. Even though he does not question the divine origins attributed to the magical literature and thus the authority of the texts, he is interested in presenting the magical tradition in its historical development that hosts phases, changes and a plurality of currents and theories. In line with this approach, he openly takes positions in the first person when treating his subject (however, it needs to be said that since at least the thirteenth century other Latin magicians seem to have followed a similar line).[35] He often signals whether a passage is his own or a quotation and indicates the author or the title and the section of his source. When arranging, again in a typically scholastic fashion, the many sources in a unitary system through textual hinges and cross references, paraphrases, conceptual hierarchies and clarifications of controversial questions, he mostly allows the reader to identify his contributions. Moreover, he strives towards rigorousness on a philological level. Some passages of the *Summa* reveal that he does not use all the sources that he owns or knows, but carefully tests the quality of the texts and selects those which, in his opinion, allow the most reliable exposition of the subject.[36]

On the whole, Ganellus is not interested in presenting an encrypted doctrine, but in making magic accessible to a possibly large number of persons.[37] Throughout his work, he conveys the idea that if magic is difficult to understand, this is due, not to its remote origins or obscurity, but to its complexity and connection to other sciences. He underscores that, in addition to being a part of theology and to its affinity with the sciences of the *trivium*, magic is significantly related to *astrologia*, the liberal art combining astronomy and astrology. The magician therefore needs to master this art and should ideally study it at a school before dealing with magic.[38] As shall be seen below, moreover, besides a good familiarity with Latin, the magical practice demands an acquaintance with Hebrew, Greek and Arabic, which are called, together with Latin, the "four languages of the world".[39] The magician is thus depicted in the *Summa* as someone who, rather than executing ready-made ritual sequences, actively moulds the ritual according to his[40] purpose by applying his knowledge of the theoretical background of magic, which is composed of astronomical/astrological, theological, philosophical, cosmological and linguistic notions. In the *Summa*, thus, the active approach of the magician to his science parallels Ganellus's approach to his subject as an author.

The magical rituals, their ends and their relation to religious worship

The *Summa* is entirely devoted to techniques for invoking evil spirits, demons, winds and angels, that is the branch of magic currently classified as "ritual" in both its demonic and angelic forms. "Natural" means such as talismanic garments and instruments drawing their power exclusively from God and from the planets do occur, but they are employed in rituals involving intermediary spiritual substances.[41] The rituals described in the treatise are considerably complex and can take over a year. For their execution, a wide range of instruments both verbal, such as prayers, name lists, invocations and written or uttered seals, and material, such as garments, accessories, talismans and altars, is used (Figure 18.1).

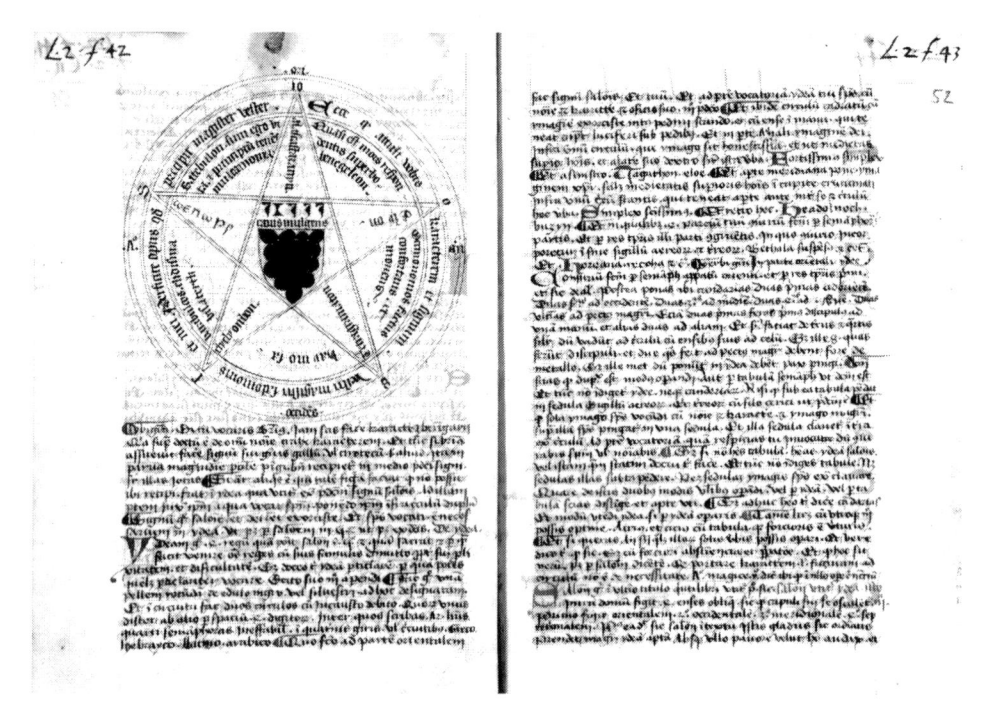

Figure 18.1 The *Sigillum Salomonis*, a sigil inscribed on parchment, is one of the instruments employed to constrain the evil spirits (Ganellus, *Summa*, ms. *Ka*, fols. 42v–43r).

The ritual practices mainly fall into two models according to whether spirits, winds or demons, who are evil by nature and dwell in the sublunar world, or angels, who are by nature good and reside in the heavens, are addressed. Each model in turn unfolds specifically depending on the number of spiritual entities invoked, the ends pursued and the means available to the magician. Notwithstanding this variety, all ritual options can be schematically divided into five phases. The magician purifies his body and soul through ascetic and devotional practices. In a second phase, he prepares the material instruments to be used in the ritual and the site of the practice. In these phases he performs several consecrations. Thereafter he expresses his devotion to God through orations and prayers, pleads to God for support in the magical practice and invokes one or several spirits or angels in His name. At this point the spirits or angels appear visibly or invisibly and perform their services for the magician (in the case that evil spirits are invoked, the spirits first test the religious faith of the magician through temptation; in the case that his faith should prove steadfast, they fulfil his wishes; otherwise, they drive him to hell for eternal punishment). In the last phase of the ritual (occurring only in the event that the magician should prove pious), the magician discharges the invoked entities.

Through these rituals, goals traditional to learned magic are pursued: all forms of knowledge including the arts taught at university, magic, prophecy and the knowledge of occult and divine truths; the overcoming of material, spatial and temporal limitations; the transformation of things and the modification of nature; military success through illusions or actual destruction and killing; and the acquisition or loss of material goods, of a social status or love. According to Ganellus and his sources, these wonders are brought about for humans by the spirits and angels, who are versed in the most disparate domains of knowledge and action. The magician can identify the suitable addressee for his invocation by means of lists indicating the names and the services of the spirits or find out the spirits' function by ascertaining the wonder-working virtue of their name's letters.[42]

Most interestingly though, when exposing the primary and secondary ends of magic (*causa finalis prima* and *secunda*), Ganellus does not mention the wonders carried out for man by the spirits and angels. As has already been noted above, he identifies magic's primary ends as the worship of God, the support of the poor and the fight against the unfaithful, and its secondary ends as the consecration and invocation (the two main ritual actions previous to the apparition of the spirits or angels). According to Ganellus, before seeking the service of spirits or angels, the magician must pursue these supreme ends. As has also been mentioned, these ends coincide with those prescribed in scriptural teaching; this is clear not only as to the primary, but also as to the secondary ends, since they always imply that the magician praises God.[43] So here the duties of the Christian come to include the magical practice itself, which – rather than being a means through which humans can attain benefits – is first of all conceived as a form of religious worship. Ganellus explains that only subsequent to the pursuit of the supreme ends can the magician's particular purposes be fulfilled. This happens through the mediation of the spirits and angels, who are appointed to serve man by God. In sum, the accomplishment of the particular goals of the magician is here defined as a divine reward in exchange for the execution of the primary ends. This also explains the reason why according to Ganellus only Christians can be safe and fulfilled magicians. Tying in with the introductory section of the *Liber iuratus*, he specifies that the magician must not only be a faithful believer, but precisely a follower of Christ. Since they worship false gods, the magicians of other religions act instead beyond divine grace.[44]

The clause according to which a set of primary ends have to be pursued prior to the particular ones is unique among the medieval magical texts preserved today; yet it cannot be considered an absolute innovation. On the one hand, in most[45] texts the ends of magic are identified with the particular purposes put into execution by the spirits and angels, and not with religious worship or the promotion of God's Kingship. On the other hand, nevertheless, the rituals through which the spirits and angels are invoked generally comprise formulas in which the magician worships God and proclaims his opposition to evil, which is embodied by the devil and evil spirits. Already the traditional ritual is thus essentially founded on a devotional component. With his clause, rather than being an absolute innovator, Ganellus appears to further highlight the relationship that ties magic to religion in the tradition which he is promoting.

The link between magic and religion is rooted in the very origins and nature of magic. Again in continuity with tradition, Ganellus explains that magic is a science devised by God and modelled, more precisely, on the divine act of Creation. Already in the introduction he states that the principal instruments of magic are words that are "infused with a wonderful power created by the only Maker". Further on he clarifies the terms according to which the transfer of the divine power to humans actually unfolds. The intrinsic divine nature of magic implies that the person who makes use of the magical words is a "god similar to God". But he also specifies that the divinity of the magician is not absolute, since God is divine by nature and the magician is divine only by participation.[46] This statement reflects the way in which the magician is depicted both by Ganellus and his sources. In the tradition summarized by Ganellus, man's intrinsic magical resource is generally declared to be religious faith. But this faith, which is by itself already an expression of man's dependency, serves merely as a starting point for a process that is ultimately executed by God, since it is He who, in response to the magician's faith, permits the magical invocations to be successful (here, again, is expressed the view that the primary end of magic is piety).[47] A similar status of dependency characterizes the angels and the evil spirits. The angels are depicted in the texts as functionaries instructed by God to fulfil the pious magicians. The evil spirits, similar to the devil in the Gospels, are in addition instructed by God to prove man's faith. According to whether that faith is steadfast or not, they are ordered to fulfil or punish him.[48] The subject compelling the spirits in occasion of each ritual appears therefore to be God rather than the magician. The angels, the magician and the evil spirits, who are the main actors of magic besides God, ultimately possess no magical power on their own. In line with the Scriptures, according to which God is the only possible source of miracles, the ultimate actor of magic is thus declared to be God alone. The magical system bears here a circular structure beginning and ending in God, who is its principle and its final end.

The clarification of both the status of the magician and the evil spirits in the dynamics of magic is crucial to Ganellus, not least because the involvement of spirits (and of man who, due to his free will, is a potential sinner oscillating between the good and the evil) is a structural and irrenounceable ingredient of the magical tradition that he follows, but in the meantime one major argument by which the contemporary opponents of magic reinforce their identification of magic with idolatry.[49] On a similar note, by further highlighting the relationship which ties magic to religion through the treatment of the teleology of magic, Ganellus intends to refute the widespread argument that magic contrasts with the true Christian faith because of its pursuit of earthly or evil-minded ends.[50] The definitions and explanations found in the *Summa* are still useful today since they permit us to reach a clearer understanding of what late medieval theorists and magicians generally understood by magic. Among other things, they serve to clarify that although learned magic introduces new ideas and practices in the context of Christian belief, even in its demonic form it intends to strictly maintain, indeed to endorse, the absolute supremacy of the one God.

The sources of the *Summa*

The five books of the *Summa*, divided into eighty-six chapters, are composed for the most part of quotations from older sources. These are all Latin and mainly consist of more or less substantially revised translations of Hebrew and Arabic texts. Some are quoted in full, while others occur in the form of extracts, abridgements, short references or paraphrases. Through his sources, Ganellus intends to represent two traditions: the *ars vetus* or ancient magic, founded on the Old Testament and open to Jews, Arabs, Pagans and Christians, and the *ars nova* or modern magic, centred on the New Testament and reserved to Christians. Ganellus incorporates both traditions in his work, since the second substantially stems from the first through the reuse of its concepts and texts. But in line with his view that only the Christian law is perfect and thus the true foundation for successful magical practice, he labels the Old Testament-based *ars vetus* as imperfect and invites its user to complement it with the teachings of the *ars nova*.[51]

Quantitatively speaking, the main source of the *Summa* and the main exponent of the *ars vetus* is a pseudo-Solomonic treatise called *Magica*. The *Magica* is now lost, but many insights into its contents are possible precisely through an investigation of the *Summa*. Devoted to techniques for summoning spirits and angels, its seven books were redacted through the amalgamation of Hebrew and Arabic sources, probably in the twelfth century, by Christians located in Spain or France.[52] The *Magica* was one of the most thorough Latin pseudo-Solomonic texts circulating in the West between the twelfth and the fourteenth centuries. Its relevance is reflected by recurrent mentions both within and outside the magical tradition, such as for example that by Nicolas Eymerich, who records in the *Directorium Inquisitorum* having publicly condemned and burned in Spain, during the pontificate of Innocent VI, a *Liber Salomonis* in seven parts treating the invocations of demons.[53]

The author of the *Magica* defined magic – in terms very similar to Ganellus in his introduction – as "a holy knowledge dealing with holy names of the Maker and of the stars, angels, spirits and winds".[54] Thus he dealt with a word-centred magic relying mainly on the power of two sets of instruments: the names of God and the names of some elements of Creation. He called the names of God with the term *semamphoras* (*shem ha-mephorash* is in Hebrew the secret, unpronounceable name of God) or *semiphoras*. This he defined as "the name whose miraculous virtue can be accomplished by means of fasting and prayer, faith and humility, purity and love, patience and firmness, mercy and truth".[55] Ganellus in turn defines it as the "name of God which can fiercely coerce the angels, winds, demons, spirits and souls, the stars and the other creatures so that they are obedient to humans".[56]

The *semamphoras* stands at the centre of a specific magical tradition that originated in connection with Jewish circles and developed, probably in southern Spain, more than a century before Ganellus wrote his *Summa*. One important source of that tradition used in the *Magica* is the *Liber semamphoras*, also called *Liber vite*.[57] The *Liber semamphoras* has not yet been traced, but some revisions of its text are preserved. Among these, the closest to the *Liber semamphoras* are likely to be the still unpublished *Rationes Libri semiphoras*. In the anonymous *Rationes* one reads that Solomon, encouraged by an old sage called Zebraymayl, opened the Ark of the Covenant and found several media inscribed with names called "semiphoras". Together with objects such as the rod of Moses, the tablets of the Ten Commandments and twenty-four magical rings, the Ark is said to have contained a "book called Razyel" (one text of the *Liber Razielis* corpus) and, what mostly interests us here, a tripartite "book Semiphoras" that Moses received from God on Mount Sinai. The *Rationes* expose several *semiphoras* that derive from the latter book and that are said to have been pronounced by Adam, Noah, Moses, Aaron and Joshua when performing their miracles mentioned in the Scriptures.[58]

The *Magica* and the *Rationes* shared the idea that the *semamphoras* have been revealed to man by God and that they can be used, in combination with the names of planetary angels, to perform wonders and to invoke spirits. Common to both treatises was also the idea that magic makes use of names containing letters of the Jewish, Arabic, Greek and Latin alphabets.[59] Yet the *Magica* also included material related to the theoretical background of the *Rationes*, but not contained in them. For example, it exposed a peculiar theory on the astral origins of the four alphabets that can be classified as part of the Hermetic tradition. According to Solomon, writes Ganellus, "the wise men have drawn the letters of the alphabet from the stars" by connecting with lines clusters of stars internal to the classical forty-eight constellations. As a result, when words are uttered, the underlying stars are named.[60] Probably the lines used by the wise men can be interpreted as stellar rays and a link to the theories summarized by al-Kindî in *De radiis* can be individuated.[61] The core of the astro-magical tradition transmitted in the *Magica* has though most likely Jewish rather than Arab origins.[62] Unsurprisingly, Cornelius Agrippa von Nettesheim, who shows knowledge of the tradition transmitted in the *Magica*, ascribes the invention of the astral alphabet, which he calls *scriptura coelestis*, to the Jews.[63]

From the *semamphoras* tradition, the *Magica* also took over the technique of the so-called magical tables (*tabule magicales*). These tables were formed with the letters of the Hebrew, Arabic, Greek and Latin alphabets disposed like the numbers of the Pythagorean table, but with the letters proceeding from right to left (Figure 18.2).

In the *Magica*, as in the case of the astral alphabets, the Hebrew table was declared to be more original than the others. From the tables, the magicians would extract (*extrahere*) magical names or *semamphoras*. Each letter bore a numerical value and the extraction was carried out through combinatory procedures based on mathematical principles. This technique was central in the *Magica*, but Ganellus also quotes other versions of the same theory attributed to Toz Grecus and minor authors not mentioned by name. He writes that the tables lay at the core of magical science and that the advanced magician can reduce his entire practice to their use, since from them can be extracted not only the *semamphoras* but every type of word.[64] The theory of the tables is directly linked to the Jewish prophetic kabbalah. One table similar to those in the *Magica* can be found for example in the *Sefer ha-tseruf* or *Book of the combinations of letters* attributed to the thirteenth-century Spanish kabbalist Abraham Abulafia.[65] Tables such as those provided by Ganellus, notwithstanding their clear importance in the magical theory of the time, appear in no other transmitted text of the Latin Middle Ages. However, similar ones are featured in a work inspired by medieval magic, Cornelius Agrippa's *De occulta philosophia*, where the term *tabula commutationum* is used.[66]

The theory of the alphabets and tables documented by Ganellus is a rare instance of a thorough theoretical foundation of word magic and of magic's link with astrology in medieval times. Al-Kindî for example, who also treats word magic in great detail, observes that words harmonize with and draw their power from heavenly figures, but he does not

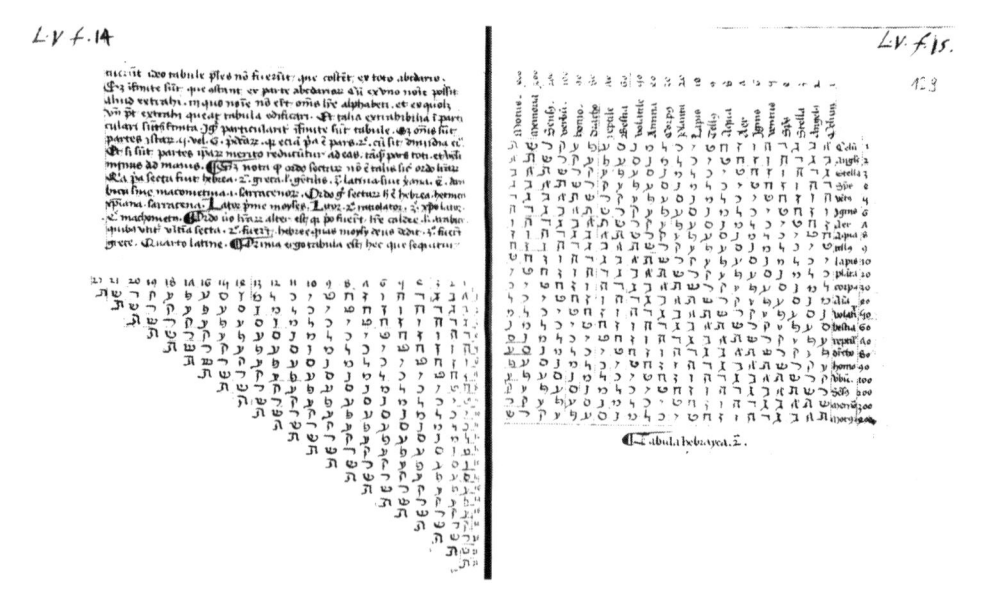

Figure 18.2 The first and second Hebrew tables, through which the magicians used to generate wonder-working words (Ganellus, *Summa*, ms. *Ka*, fols. 128v–129r).

treat the more basic level of the alphabets.[67] Elements of the tradition treated in the *Summa* re-emerge only later, in the work of an early modern author such as Agrippa. The *Summa* and the *Magica* which is recorded in it are thus seminal indicators of the strong astral basis of medieval pseudo-Solomonic magic, a basis no less developed than that of the magic classified as Hermetic.

Let us come to the other carriers of magical power in the *Magica*, the names of the elements of Creation. Here we enter the domain of planetary magic. Regarding this aspect, the *Magica* again stood in continuity with the *Liber semamphoras* and its tradition. Both the *Magica* and the *Rationes Libri semiphoras* combined the use of the *semamphoras* with the invocation of planetary spirits. Yet, whereas in the *Rationes* only the angels of the seven skies were invoked,[68] in the *Magica* the names of the planetary angels were more numerous and differentiated and were pronounced in the rituals together with the names of many other concrete or abstract entities such as the hours, days, weeks, seasons, winds, elements, planets and signs of the zodiac. The latter names mostly corresponded to those listed in the fourth book of the *Liber Razielis*, called *Liber temporum*. A close relationship thus linked the *Magica* to the literary tradition from which also stems the *Liber Razielis*, a text that in turn unsurprisingly highlights the importance of the *semamphoras* in the magical practice.[69]

In the rituals of the *Magica*, these sets of verbal instruments were used in written or spoken form, mostly embedded in magic formulae, in combination with a panoply of material instruments. Of the ritual objects, the treatise indicated the features, the specific materials and the methods of preparation and utilization. Their power was deemed to spring from their material, which was considered to stand in relation to the planets, from the inscriptions which they bore, from their consecration and not least from an act of divine concession.[70]

Besides the *Magica* and the *Liber semamphoras*, Ganellus refers to several other texts of the *ars vetus*. One *Magica* attributed to Toz Grecus, not recovered so far, shared some contents, such as spirits' lists and ritual practices, with the homonymous writing by Solomon. The *Orationes artis veteris*, a set of twenty-one orations, as well as the *Orationes testimoniales*, four long orations corresponding to the seasons, both quoted in full in the *Summa*, were either contained or mentioned in Solomon's *Magica*.[71] A selection of rituals is cited from the *Liber Razielis*, of which Ganellus had the short version consisting in the translation of the Hebrew *Sefer ha-Razim*.[72] To the *ars vetus* also belongs a group of writings currently classified as Hermetic such as the *Prestigia* by Toz Grecus, the *Liber Saturni*, the *Liber Lune*, the *Liber Veneris*, the *Liber de capite Saturni* and the *Liber Antimaquis*, all devoted to planetary magic, and some texts considered by Ganellus to be less reputable such as the *Liber vacce* and the *Liber karacterum* by Sumach.

Less space but not less importance is given in the *Summa* to the sources of the *ars nova*. The main texts of this group are Honorius's *Liber iuratus* from which are cited rituals of angel invocation, an anonymous collection of prayers called *Liber trium animarum*, freely inspired by the Psalms and written in the West probably in the first half of the fourteenth century, and an equally anonymous litany in which the names of the Christian saints are followed by a long list of spirit and angel names recurrent in the magical tradition.[73] To the *ars nova* also belong the chapters genuinely composed by Ganellus, including the sketch of a frugal and simplified ritual affordable to the poorest Christians,[74] as well as sections, which I have partly discussed in this chapter, on the division of magic into parts, on the methodology through which it is best studied and taught, and on its relation to religion.

The aims of the author

Summing up, it appears that Ganellus pursues several goals. First of all he intends to promote and divulge magic. In an epoch in which magical books are difficult to trace and owning them is incriminating, he collects in a unique volume those which are, in his eyes, the pivotal doctrines on the subject. In parallel, through his systematic and clear explanations, he aims to expound the meaning of the science of magic. Among other things, he shows that, when accessed through the sources written by the magicians, this science appears radically different from the way in which it is represented and interpreted by contemporary critics, who are usually outsiders not involved in magic. Ganellus furthermore intends to cast off magic's traditional trait of secrecy. In contrast, for example, with his nearly contemporary Pradellus, who establishes that each specimen of the *Liber iuratus* can be copied only three times, thus restricting dramatically the text's circulation,[75] he is interested in spreading magic to a possibly large number of persons, virtually to every pious Christian. For his purpose he chooses the genre of the *summa*; in view of a public propagation, he underscores magic's affinity to the sciences taught at university. Another obstacle that he tries to overcome is magic's economic and social exclusiveness. According to tradition and in particular to the pseudo-Solomon, magic necessarily implied the use of lavish instruments and was reserved as such to wealthy practitioners. In Ganellus's view, instead, the only essential prerequisite in every form of magical practice is the genuine religious (Christian) faith of the operator. In order to break down the social boundaries of magic, he drafts ritual procedures that are economically and intellectually accessible to the middle and lower class.[76] These choices respond to the aim of divulging magic. Divulgation, though, is not Ganellus's only purpose. As seen above, he believes that through magic it is possible to put into practice religious commandments. In this respect, he even writes that in the case of extreme necessity the resort to magic is not a mere possibility, but a proper duty of the Christian.[77] By divulging magic, Ganellus thus ultimately intends to deliver to Christianity an instrument through which it can, and must, promote God's Kingship. Evidently, he envisages his own magical practice and authorship as his personal fulfilment of that duty.

The interest of the *Summa* for research

Through the *Summa*, our knowledge of late medieval magic and its literature is fruitfully enriched. The writing transmits ample textual material that played a central role in the magical discourse of the Latin Middle Ages but has otherwise become lost and includes still unknown versions of a number of surviving texts.[78] Second, it was composed through ample use of Latin translations of Arabic, Hebrew and Greek magical literature, a source base that (with a fate similar to that of other Latin texts on magic, the best-known of which is *De radiis*, the translation of al-Kindī's Arabic work) has not yet been recovered and is probably lost. The *Summa* offers therefore precious insights not only for medieval Latin studies but also for Oriental, Jewish and generally Classical studies.

The value of the *Summa* for research is also due to the high theoretical level of its discourse. Not only in the Arab and Jewish traditions (as testified by texts as *De Radiis*, the *Picatrix* or the corpus of the *Liber semiphoras*), but also in the Latin West the rituals of medieval learned magic were rooted in a complex theoretical ground. Even so, most magical texts of the Latin late Middle Ages preserved today present the practical aspects of magic bereft of theoretical foundations, or touch upon the theory that underlies the rituals only implicitly. Thanks to the focus set by its author, the *Summa* instead combines the description of rituals with theoretical sections illustrating the principles and ideas underlying magical science. These sections, which are often quoted from major older sources that are now lost (such as the *Magica* by Solomon and that by Toz Grecus), shed light on the deeper meaning that the rituals and their manifold components assumed in the magical system by locating them in a cosmological, theological and philosophical framework. To this framework belong for example the above-mentioned concept of the magic of the four alphabets, the astral genealogy of the alphabets or the doctrine of the tables, as well as the cosmic hierarchy and the position occupied in it by the magician.

Thanks to the style tailored on the scholastic model, the contents of the *Summa* appear in great clarity and detail. Particularly useful for the medieval but also for the contemporary reader are the many definitions of seminal terms of the science of magic that are scattered throughout the work. In this chapter, I have looked amongst others at the definition of magic in terms of the practical part of theology. That definition, which underlines the affinity between magic and religion rather than generically identifying the two terms, enriches significantly the debate on the definition of magic, a debate which still stands at the centre of scholarly research.

On the whole, Ganellus demonstrates that Latin learned magic in its original form, when it was still close to the non-Latin sources from which it derived, was a remarkably refined doctrine. As has been seen above, it was for example essentially rooted in the science of *astrologia*. The comparative study of the *Summa* alongside other late medieval texts (such as the pseudo-Solomonic *Clavicula Salomonis*, *Tractatus discipulorum Salomonis*, *De novem candariis* and *Almandal*) suggests that the minor complexity of the latter is the result of a simplification process intrinsic to the transmission of ideas and texts over time.[79]

The *Summa* is also a central resource for the study of magical literature from a philological and historical perspective. Its precise dating, which is a feature uncommon in magical literature, offers a reliable *terminus ad quem* for its contents. This implies that other texts can be classified in relation to those contained in the *Summa* and the still fragmentary history of medieval magic and its literature can be further assessed and reconstructed.

In addition to discussing traditional doctrines and sources, the origins of which can be partly traced back to the twelfth century, Ganellus offers self-authored sections and treats the trends and debates of his time. The *Summa* is therefore an important document for the magical theory and literature of the mid-fourteenth century as well. The conciliation of magic with Christianity is seminal to the entire work, and the treatise contains the most explicit confrontations of a fourteenth-century magician with the papal condemnation of magic of which we have knowledge today. In the footsteps of the *Liber iuratus*, in an audacious passage probably referring to the policy of Pope John XII, Ganellus replies to the interdiction of the teaching of magic and of the production of magical literature. In his view, the relationship between the magician and God skips any mediating instance, since the bonds set by God with his believers can be broken by God alone.[80] Even so, Ganellus maintains some original views. Notably, in spite of his Christianizing programme, he remains true to the markedly demonic nature of magic. Unlike Honorius, his near contemporary and the founder of the *ars nova*, who classifies the invocation of evil spirits as a form of idolatry practised by the pagans, and who sets a fundamental trend for his contemporaries and followers by reducing licit Christian magic to the invocation of angels, Ganellus maintains the involvement of evil spirits as an essential element that not only does not stand in contradiction with the religious character of magic, but even plays a vital role in the definition of the relationship between magic and religion.[81]

For these many reasons, the *Summa* of Ganellus is a fundamental reference point for achieving a more accomplished and documented panorama of late medieval magic. The text is a premise for new research on the genesis, the history and the meaning of the magical literature of the twelfth to fourteenth centuries and encourages us to revisit several aspects central to that tradition from a new angle.

Notes

1 Paul Oskar Kristeller, *Iter italicum* (London: Warburg Institute, 1963–1997), vol. 3, entry nr. 585: Kassel, Murhardsche- und Landesbibliothek, ms. Astron. 4° 3, fols. 2r–149r (hereafter *Ka*).
2 Berlin, Staatsbibliothek, Preussischer Kulturbesitz, ms. Germ. Fol. 903, fols. 3r–806v (hereafter *Be*). See Carlos Gilly, *Spanien und der Basler Buchdruck bis 1600. Ein Querschnitt durch die spanische Geistesgeschichte aus der Sicht einer europäischen Buchdruckerstadt* (Basel and Frankfurt am Main: Helbing und Lichtenhahn, 1985), 276–78; Sebastiano Gentile and Carlos Gilly, *Marsilio Ficino and the Return of Hermes Trismegistus* (Florence: Centro Di, 1999–2000), 276–78; Carlos Gilly and Cis Van Heertum, *Magic, Alchemy and Science Fifteenth-Eighteenth Centuries, The Influence of Hermes Trismegistus*, vol. 1 (Florence: Centro Di, 2002), 286–94. On the *Arbatel* see Damaris Aschera Gehr, *Magie und Alchemie in der paracelsistischen Schrift* ארבעתאל *Arbatel De magia veterum (Basel, 1575)*, in: Petra Feuerstein-Herz and Ute Frietsch (eds.): *Alchemie – Genealogie und Terminologie, Bilder, Techniken und Artefakte. Forschungen aus der Herzog August Bibliothek*, Wiesbaden 2019, forthcoming.
3 Halle, Universitäts- und Landesbibliothek, ms. 14 B 36, several sections from fol. 185r onwards (hereafter *Ha*).
4 The Latin manuscripts are both fragmentary: four quires are missing in *Ka*, and *Ha* offers of the *Summa* only a selection of chapters. The gaps in the Latin manuscript tradition can be filled by recourse to the German translation (with exception for the final part of chapter 20 and the entire chapter 21, which are missing also in the ms. *Be*; in addition, some passages in the German version are misleading).
5 This text, preserved in the ms. Florence, Biblioteca Medicea Laurenziana, Plut. 89 Sup. 38, fols. 377r–79r, is edited and commented in Damaris Gehr, "'Spiritus et angeli sunt a Deo submissi sapienti et puro': il frammento del *Magisterium eumantice artis sive scienciae magicalis*. Edizione e attribuzione a Berengario Ganello," *Aries: Journal for the Study of Western Esotericism* 11, no. 2 (2011): 189–217.
6 Substantial contributions can be found in: Gilly, *Spanien und der Basler Buchdruck*, 276–78; Gentile and Gilly, *Marsilio Ficino*, 276–78; Gilly and Van Heertum, *Magic, Alchemy and Science*, vol. 1, 286–94; Jan R. Veenstra, "Honorius and the Sigil of God: The *Liber iuratus* in Berengario Ganell's *Summa sacre magice*," in *Invoking Angels: Theurgic Ideas and Practices, Thirteenth to Sixteenth Centuries*, ed. Claire Fanger (University Park: Pennsylvania State University Press, 2012), 151–91; Gehr, "Spiritus et angeli", 189–217; Damaris Gehr, "La fittizia associazione del *Liber Razielis* in sette libri ad Alfonso X il Saggio e una nuova determinazione delle fasi redazionali del trattato, della loro datazione e dell'identità dei compilatori coinvolti," *Viator. Mediaeval and Renaissance Studies* 43 Multilingual (2012): 181–210; Damaris Gehr, "'Gaudent brevitatem moderni': Rielaborazioni della teoria magica nel tardo Medioevo sull'esempio dell'*Almandal* di Salomone," *Società e storia* 139 (2013): 1–36. The *Summa* was the subject of my doctoral dissertation "La *Summa sacre magice* di Berengario Ganello" (Venezia: Università Ca' Foscari, 2007).
7 Ganellus, *Summa*, ms. *Ha*, fol. 194v.
8 Ganellus, *Summa*, ms. *Ka*, fol. 84v.
9 Ganellus, *Summa*, ms. *Ka*, fol. 126r.
10 Gilly, *Magic, Alchemy and Science*, 290.
11 Ganellus, *Summa*, ms. *Ha*, fol. 193v.
12 Ganellus, *Summa*, ms. *Ka*, fol. 3r and fol. 149r.
13 Mende, Archives ecclésiastiques de la Lozère, ms. Série G n. 936, fols. 1r–27r; a somewhat inaccurate transcription is found in Edmond Falgairolle, *Un envoûtement en Gévaudan en l'année 1347* (Nîmes: Librairie-Editeur Catélan, 1892).

14 Mende, Archives ecclésiastiques de la Lozère, ms. Série G n. 936, fols. 6v–8r.
15 Ibid., fols. 6v–7r.
16 Ibid., fol. 3v.
17 Ibid., fol. 17r.
18 The dating of the *Magisterium* in respect to the *Summa* is discussed in Gehr, "Spiritus et angeli," 189–217.
19 The manuscript *Ka* was copied in France, *Ha* in Spain, *Be* in Germany and that transmitting the *Magisterium eumantice artis* in Rome.
20 Johannes Trithemius, "Antipalus maleficiorum," in *Paralipomena opusculorum Petri Blesensis et Joannis Trithemii aliorumque*, ed. Ianus Busaeus (Mainz: Balthasar Lippius, 1605), 297–98.
21 Johannes Trithemius, *De septem Secundeis* [...] *Adiectae sunt aliquot epistolae* [...] (Coloniae: Ioannes Birckmannus, 1567), 140–44, letter "Ioannes Tritemius Abbas Monasterij S. Iacobi suburbio ciuitatis Herbipolensis Ioanni Virdungo de Hasfurt Mathematico doctissimo salutem."
22 Gilly, *Magic, Alchemy and Science*, 290.
23 This information on the elsewise unknown Pradellus is found in the acts of the Mende trial of 1347; see Mende, Archives ecclésiastiques de la Lozère, ms. Série G n. 936, fol. 4v.
24 Jean Thenaud, *Le triumphe des vertuz. Premier traité, Le triumphe de prudence*, ed. Titia J. Schuurs-Janssen (Genève: Droz, 1997), 108; on the passage of the *Cabale metrifiée*, see 312, footnote 273.
25 Ganellus, *Summa*, ms. *Be*, fol. 7r. Place and date of translation are suggested by the watermarks found in the manuscript *Be*.
26 Paolo Lucentini and Antonella Sannino, "*Recommendatio astronomiae*: un anonimo trattato del XV secolo in difesa dell'astrologia e della magia," in *Magic and the Classical Tradition*, ed. Charles Burnett and W. F. Ryan (London: Warburg Institute, 2006), 177–98. The *Recommendatio* is here dated on the grounds of its alleged connection to the *Summa*; since no such connection exists, for the dating, a different criterion must be found.
27 This and the following translations from the Latin are mine.
28 Ganellus, *Summa*, ms. *Ka*, fol. 3r: "Magica est sciencia artandi spiritus malignos et benignos per nomen Dei et per nomina sua ac per nomina seculi rerum. Unde sequitur quod magica est sciencia verborum, quia omne nomen est verbum, cum verbum sit omnis res que lingua profertur si literis scribi possit. Multe autem sciencie sunt verborum ut gramatica, logica, recthorica, magica [...] magica est de verbo quo ad spiritualem substanciam coartandam. Est enim in quibusdam verbis virtus mira concreata a creatore solo qui Deus est omnipotens et causa omnium causarum, recte ut tu vides de herbis et gemmis, nisi quod excellenciori modo, quasi in infinitum sine comparatione. Et potest hoc perpendi apud inexpertos per legem suam. Quia lex ait quod [...] cum verbis creavit Deus celos et angelos. [...] Item dicit quod quicquid verbo petetur fide credendo et non hezitando, quod fiet. [...] Magica ergo est de verbis miris ex fide pullulativis aut ex firma credulitate processivis, ita ut credat Deo vero et arti et magistro suo ac legi cui habet devotionem. Sed melius est sibi quod credat christiane, que est stipula utralibet aliarum frivola ut docet magice met experiencia".
29 With different arguments, magic was already classified among the liberal arts in earlier medieval writings. See Charles Burnett, *Magic and Divination in the Middle Ages* (Aldershot: Variorum, 1996), 1–15.
30 The classification of the words among the *material* instruments of magic is to be understood in connection with the kabbalistic foundation of the doctrine promoted by Ganellus, according to which the words used in magic share the nature of the word used by God in Creation and bear as such a strong ontological status. The kabbalistic background is announced already in the introduction now cited, where the word is defined as each thing which is uttered "on condition that it can be written with letters".
31 Ganellus, *Summa*, ms. *Be*, fols. 447v–50v.
32 Ganellus, *Summa*, ms. *Ka*, fol. 60v: "Quia hec ars nulli profuit nisi sapientibus valde ultra omnes, non sapiencia mundana, que est stulticia apud Deum, sed sapiencia spirituali, cuius est ipsa secunda pars nobilior eius, cum sit pars practica theologie omnium legum divinarum in quibus fundatur".
33 Ganellus, *Summa*, ms. *Be*, fols. 450v–451r.
34 The argumentative structure of the *quaestio* is applied substantially only in the passages ms. *Ka*, fols. 60v–61r, where the argument according to which the magicians test the power of God's name when using it for the conjuration of spirits is pondered, and ms. *Ka*, fols. 87v–88r, where some debated aspects of the ritual of spirit invocation are discussed.

35 A brief treatment of the divine revelation of magic can be found for example in Ganellus, *Summa*, ms. *Be*, fol. 447v. The existence of other magical authors making no use of the pseudepigraphic style is attested, among others, by the same Ganellus, who mentions on several occasions the work of "magistri" or "doctores minores".
36 See for instance ibid., ms. *Ka*, fol. 40v and fol. 145r, where it is noted that the lists of angel names contained in the *Liber Razielis* are more corrupted than those in Solomon's *Magica*.
37 With the only restriction that they be pious Christians. See the next paragraph.
38 In the *Summa*, *astrologia* stands, after "theoretical theology" or the divine laws contained in the Scriptures, as the science most close to magic. For the case that the magician should be impeded to study *astrologia* at a school, Ganellus provides a specific chapter with "rudiments" taken from Ptolemy's *Tetrabiblos*, the *Liber introductorius* by Alcabitius and the *Liber antimaquis* (a Hermetic treatise otherwise preserved in an only manuscript, see Aristoteles/Hermes, "Liber Antimaquis," in *Hermetis Trismegisti Astrologica et Divinatoria*, ed. Charles Burnett (Turnhout: Brepols, 2001), 177–221). See Ganellus, *Summa*, ms. *Ka*, fols. 122r–27r.
39 The learned character of magic, however, does not conflict with Ganellus's plan of making magic accessible to large numbers of believers, since he also provides a version of the magical ritual for the poor and thus, we may assume, for the untaught. See the paragraph "The aims of the author".
40 In line with Western late medieval magical literature, Ganellus holds that, similarly to priesthood, the magical knowledge and practice are male prerogatives.
41 Those of "ritual" and "natural" magic are central categories used in the current scholarly classifications of learned magic, but it must be kept in mind that they do not occur in the *Summa* and in its sources.
42 The main lists of this kind are contained in chapters 48 dedicated to demons, 59 on the planetary angels and 77 exposing the virtues of a particular group of spirits. The meaning of the letters is explained in chapters 70 and 86.
43 Ganellus, *Summa*, ms. *Be*, fol. 450r–v.
44 Honorius, *Liber iuratus*, ed. Gösta Hedegård (Stockholm: Almqvist & Wiksell, 2002), III, 16–26.
45 I could find an approach similar to that of the *Summa* in the long version of the *Liber Razielis*, where one reads that "magic is a fine and spiritual science which is formed in the skies and in man. [...] And its first end is above in the skies and in the stars. And its second end resides in man, in order that he may be able to operate. And the common end is the approved operation, which happens through the judgement and the knowledge of the things of the sublunar world" (ms. Città del Vaticano, Biblioteca Apostolica Vaticana, Reg. Lat. 1300, fols. 139v–140r: "magica est sciencia subtilis et spiritualis formata in celis et in homine. [...] Et primus finis eius est sursum in celis et in stellis. Et secundus finis est in homine quod sit aptus ad operandum. Et finis omnium est opus cum probatione, et hoc cum intellectu et noticia rerum inferiorum"). Notwithstanding the similarity of the two definitions, the classification of the final ends of magic given by Ganellus remains unique, since it classifies both the primary and the secondary end of magic within the divine sphere.
46 Ganellus, *Summa*, ms. *Ha*, fol. 196r–v.
47 See Damaris Gehr, "The Use and Meaning of Material Instruments in Medieval Magic. A Case Study on the Sacred Book (*liber sacer* and *liber consecrationis*)," in *The Material Culture of Magic*, ed. Leo Ruickbie et al. (Brill), forthcoming.
48 See Damaris Gehr, "Towards a Definition of Medieval Magic. The Function of the Evil Spirits in pseudo-Solomonic Texts", forthcoming, based on the paper which I gave in November 2012 in Orléans at the conference *Démonologues et démonologies (XIIIe-XVIIe siècles)*.
49 Around 1326, with John XXII's bull *Super illius specula*, magical practices involving the summoning of spirits were declared to be founded on a "base servitude" to evil and on a "pact with hell", and were classified as a form of heresy. See Joseph Hansen, *Quellen und Untersuchungen zur Geschichte des Hexenwahns und der Hexenverfolgung im Mittelalter* (Bonn: Carl Georgi, 1901), 5–6.
50 The pursuit of evil-minded ends and the legitimation of violence that goes with it is a central and debated aspect of late medieval magic that deserves further study. Generally, I believe that the argument according to which certain strands of medieval magic contrast with the Christian doctrine because of their pursuit of evil ends is founded on an idealized interpretation of Christianity that is not sustainable in the context of scientific studies. The example of Ganellus, who justifies the use of violence for the prosecution of the unfaithful, shows that in this tradition the discourse is nuanced and that evil-ended goals, in case they should serve to promote God's Kingdom,

are admitted. On a more general level, according to all late medieval magical texts including the *Summa*, no single magical operation can be successful without God's punctual approval, whereas God is said to approve only those actions that are not conflicting with His own will or law. Outside the context of magical studies, this theme has been devoted several publications in the field of religious studies, see for instance *Coping with Violence in the New Testament*, ed. Pieter G. R. de Villiers et al. (Leiden: Brill, 2012).
51 Ganellus, *Summa*, ms. *Ka*, fols. 117v–118r.
52 So far, Solomon's *Magica* has been discussed in my publications alone, see footnote 6. I infer the text structure from the circumstance that Ganellus cites from seven books.
53 Nicolas Eymerich, *Directorium Inquisitorum*, vol. 2, Quaestio XXVIII (Romae: in aedibus Populi Romani, 1585), 336B. This passage has late been interpreted as a reference to the *Liber Razielis*; the reasons why more probably the *Magica* is meant are adduced in Gehr, "La fittizia associazione," 204–5.
54 Ganellus, *Summa*, ms. *Ka*, fol. 37v.
55 Ibid., fol. 43r.
56 Ibid., fol. 43v.
57 Ibid.
58 *Rationes Libri semiphoras*, ms. *Ha*, fols. 244r–248v.
59 Ibid., fol. 248v.
60 Ganellus, *Summa*, ms. *Ka*, fol. 144v and ms. *Be*, fol. 765v.
61 Al-Kindî, *De radiis*, ed. Marie-Thérèse d'Alverny et al., in *Archives d'histoire doctrinale et littéraire du Moyen Âge* 41 (1974).
62 In chapter 70 of the *Summa*, exposing the magical properties of the four alphabets, the Arabic, Greek and Latin sections appear to have been modelled on the Hebrew section.
63 Cornelius Agrippa, *De occulta philosophia libri tres*, ed. Vittoria Perrone Compagni (Leiden, New York and Köln: Brill, 1992), 491–92.
64 Ganellus, *Summa*, ms. *Be*, fol. 600r.
65 Abraham Abulafia, *Sefer ha-tseruf*, vol. 13, ed. Amnon Gros (Yerushalayim, 2003), 48.
66 Cornelius Agrippa, *De occulta philosophia libri tres*, 475.
67 Al-Kindî, *De radiis*, 234.
68 *Rationes Libri semiphoras*, ms. *Ha*, fols. 245v–246r.
69 *Liber Razielis*, Città del Vaticano, Biblioteca Apostolica Vaticana, ms. Reg. Lat. 1300, see for instance at the fol. 11v.
70 Ganellus cites the sections on the instruments mainly in book II. On the material instruments, see Gehr, "Luxus und Luxusdiskurse".
71 Ganellus, *Summa*, ms. *Ha*, fols. 265r–66r/ms. Ka, fols. 97r–100r, and ms. *Ka*, fols. 9v–28r.
72 Gehr, "La fittizia associazione", 203.
73 Ganellus, *Summa*, ms. *Ka*, fols. 111v–117r, and ms. *Ha*, fols. 209r–212v/ms. *Ka*, fol. 145r.
74 Ibid., fols. 192r–93r.
75 Pradellus, prologue to *Liber iuratus* by Honorius, I 21.
76 Gehr, "Luxus und Luxusdiskurse".
77 Ganellus, *Summa*, ms. *Ha*, fol. 192r.
78 Only very short text rations of the sources contained in the *Summa* are today preserved in other writings, be it in unpublished manuscript texts, or in texts of which an edition exists already. To these text rations count some extracts from the *Liber iuratus* by Honorius, from the *Liber introductorius* by Alcabitius, from Ptolemy's *Tetrabiblos* and from the *Liber Antimaquis*, as well as an explanation of the meaning of the letters of the Jewish alphabet which I could also find in the *Liber ale*, the second book of the *Liber Razielis*.
79 Two case studies of this simplification are Gehr, "Spiritus et angeli", and Gehr, "Gaudent brevitatem moderni".
80 Pradellus, prologue to *Liber iuratus* by Honorius, I 1–11; Ganellus, *Summa*, ms. *Be*, fols. 606v–7v.
81 The fundamental role of the evil spirits is that of tempting the magician in order to test his faith. On the function of temptation in the self-definition of magic, see the paragraph "The magical rituals, their ends and relation to religious worship".

19

JEROME TORRELLA AND "ASTROLOGICAL IMAGES"

Nicolas Weill-Parot

The concept of the "astrological image" is fundamental to understanding the endeavours of some medieval thinkers to build a theory able to justify a natural astral magic. The *Opus praeclarum de imaginibus astrologicis* ("Remarkable work on astrological images"), written in 1496, is the most comprehensive contribution to the debate about the so-called "astrological images", a concept defining a certain kind of talisman that could be traced back to the mid-thirteenth century. Its author, Hieronymus Torrella (Jeroni Torrell, Jerónimo Torrella, Jerome Torrella), was born in Valencia in 1456. His father, Ferrer Torrella, a master of arts and medicine, had studied at the University of Montpellier, whose school of medicine was celebrated; Jerome called him a "very famous physician and expert in the science of the stars". Jerome's brothers, Gaspar Torrella and one whose name could be Ausía, were also physicians. Gaspar was a well-known physician of Pope Alexander VI who wrote several treatises notably on syphilis; the other probably worked in Cagliari (Sardinia). Jerome, along with his brother Gaspar, studied at the universities of Siena (1474) and of Pisa, where he graduated as a doctor of medicine in 1477. He was the student of the renowned physicians Alessandro Sermoneta and Pier Leoni da Spoleto. Later, he became the physician of Queen Joan of Naples, wife of King Ferrante the First and sister of King Fernándo of Castile and León – a queen who played an important political role since she was the regent from 1494 to 1496. Torrella went back to Valencia, the place where he completed his *Opus praeclarum de imaginibus astrologicis* in 1496 (published around 1500). He is next mentioned in 1502 as "examiner" (*examinador*) of arts and medicine. Nothing sure is known about his later life.[1]

"Astrological images": a history of a concept

The "astrological images" to which Torrella's work is devoted was a name given to a certain category of talismans.[2] The general term "talisman" can be applied to every artificial object (hence bearing a certain form or figure such as a seal or a figurine) endowed with a magical power. Within this comprehensive definition, a subcategory has to be singled out: the "astrological talisman", namely a talisman in the making of which astrology plays a certain role; its figure represents a star or a constellation or it was made at a certain astrological moment. Two different kinds of astrological talisman should be distinguished: on the one hand, a "source-figured talisman", whose figure represents the alleged main source of its power, that is a planet, a star or a constellation (for example, a seal of Leo represents the zodiacal sign of Leo); on the other hand, a "target-figured talisman", whose figure represents the goal of the talisman (for example, a talisman for love shows two people embracing).[3] Within the category of "astrological talismans", there is another subcategory of talismans, namely "astrological images" (although *imago* is no more than the most common translation of the Arabic word *tilsam* [talisman], which itself derives from the Greek τέλεσμα).

The concept of an "astrological image" was coined in a theological and philosophical context, in the mid-thirteenth-century work *Speculum astronomiae* ("Mirror of the science of stars"), an anonymous book sometimes wrongly ascribed to Albert the Great. The book proposed a normative bibliography for each part of astronomy and astrology. After addressing astrological "elections" – the part of astrology devoted to finding the right astrological moment for undertaking such or such action – the anonymous author writes that, in the classification of the parts of astrology, under the elections is put the "science of images", that is the art of making magical figures and talismans, though not every kind of image, but only the "astrological images". To catch the real meaning of this notion, we must briefly look back to the history of astrological talismans in the Latin Middle Ages.

Astrological talismans had been introduced to the Christian West in translations of scientific texts from Greek and Arabic to Latin in the twelfth and early thirteenth centuries. These translations brought not only astrology but also astral magic, a magic which partly originated in the oriental part of the Islamic lands. David Pingree and other scholars have proposed that this magic was mostly derived from the Sabeans of Harrân, a polytheistic sect whose religion would have been based on a cult given to the stars, but others do not agree with this hypothesis.[4]

Thus, several oriental astral-talismanic texts, often attributed to Hermes or to one of his disciples, were translated into Latin. But besides the importance given to astrology, these works displayed many rituals, invocations and prayers addressed to the planets or astral spirits. This is the reason why the "Magister Speculi", the author of the *Speculum astronomiae*, calls them "abominable" and firmly rejects them as evil and demonic. He also banned another kind of image, "less prejudicial" but nevertheless "detestable", the figures from Solomonic ritual magic that make use of characters and unknown languages. This magic, a main component of so-called European nigromancy, had various origins: Christian, Jewish and (more rarely) Muslim.

The Magister Speculi distinguishes these two condemned kinds of images from the category of the "astrological image". An "astrological image" is defined as a talisman whose power comes *only* from the natural powers of the stars. In its making, there are no prayers, no invocations, no inscriptions of any characters and no other sign addressed to a superior Intelligence. We can call a magical practice that contains these signs "addressative", because they are directed to an addressee, an Intelligence able to understand them; thus, the "astrological image" is a "non-addressative", or naturalistic, astrological talisman. The Magister Speculi created the category of "astrological images" in order to fulfil the requirements of both science and theology; he calls himself a man "zealous for faith and philosophy, each one in its own order" (*zelator fidei et philosophiae utriusque scilicet in ordine suo*). He lists only two works that seem to exhibit these pure "astrological images": the *De imaginibus* ("On images") ascribed to the ninth-century Sabean astronomer Thebit (Thâbit ibn Qûrra) and the *Opus imaginum* wrongly attributed to the Greek ancient astronomer and astrologer Ptolemy – he feels less sure about the orthodoxy of this latter text.

Once created, this concept was a matter of debate from the mid-thirteenth century onwards. Jerome Torrella gathered together almost all medieval contributions to this issue and added testimonies and ideas from his own time. In his argumentation, he rightly opposes Albert the Great's and Thomas Aquinas's positions on this issue.

The *Speculum astronomiae* actually defined the concept of the "astrological image", but gave no argumentation for their scientific foundation. This task was completed by Albert the Great in his treatise *De mineralibus* ("On minerals"). The starting point of his reasoning is the purely natural imprints or seals found in gems: the stars are the cause of these figures and also of the wonderful powers that they acquire. This kind of seal is easy to explain since the same cause, the stars, is responsible for both the figure imprinted in the seal and its power. But the question becomes more intricate when tackling the artificial astrological seal, since in this case man gives the figure to the seal whereas the stars give it their power. The gap between art and nature is therefore the main problem that Albert the Great must overcome: man has not the demiurgic power to create new substantial forms. The answer consists in putting the action of the craftsman within the causal connection between the stars and the seal. By choosing the appropriate astrological moment when such required influence is given by the stars, the craftsman makes himself an instrument of the stars and nature. Hence, the gap between art and nature is filled.[5]

On the opposite side, Thomas Aquinas, in several works, firmly rejects the concept of the "astrological image". In his view, every kind of talisman derives its efficacy from demons. All talismans are "addressative", including the "so-called astrological images": the only difference between these latter and the other nigromantical images is that their "addressativity" is implicit whereas that of nigromantical images is explicit. Thomas Aquinas's position is unambiguous: his rejection of the category "astrological images" is complete. Nevertheless, a small section at the end of the chapter 105 of the third book of his *Contra Gentiles* gave rise to a debate in the fifteenth century. In these final lines, he writes that because figures are "like specific forms", we cannot totally discard the possibility that the artefact hence created by this figure can receive an astral power. This does not mean at all that Thomas thought that such a possibility could occur; it was no more than a methodological stage without any belief in such a naturalistic talisman. But several supporters of the *Quattrocento*, such as Marsilio Ficino and Torrella, took these lines as an opportunity to credit the great Dominican friar with a more friendly attitude towards "astrological images".

The concept of "astrological images" was fundamental to medieval reflection on natural magic amongst theologians, philosophers and physicians. The physicians Arnald of Villanova (†1311) and Pietro d'Abano (†1316) introduced this notion into medicine. The type of image that they mentioned was a source-figured seal. The most famous astrological seal was of Leo, which was used against kidney pains and kidney stones. Arnald made several mentions of this seal, which he found in a hermetic text possibly originating in the Jewish milieu of Montpellier, and he is known to have used it to cure Pope Boniface VIII in 1301. Other seals were also mentioned such as the seal of Pisces against gout or the seal of Serpentarius ("serpent-bearer" or Ophiucus) against poisons.[6]

The use of these seals was justified by the concept of "specific form", a concept defined by Avicenna. In his *Canon medicine* ("Canon of medicine"), Avicenna, borrowing a neighbouring idea from Galen, had written that besides drugs that operate through primary qualities (hot, cold, moist, dry) or their mixing or complexion (*complexio*), there are drugs that operate through their whole substance (*tota substantia*) or specific form (*forma specifica*), like the scammony that attracts the bile or, outside the field of pharmacy, the magnet that attracts iron. Thus, "specific form" accounts for "occult properties" – qualities that cannot be reduced to primary qualities or to the qualities directly stemming from them and perceptible by the senses. The "specific form" of the physicians was the same concept as the "substantial form" (the form of the thing as substance) of the philosophers.

The concept of an "occult property" stemming from a specific/substantial form is the keystone of the discussion of "astrological images".

In order to justify this concept from a scientific standpoint, its supporters such as Albert the Great, Arnald of Villanova and Pietro d'Abano assume that there are two different kinds of occult properties. On the one hand, there are specific occult properties stemming from the specific/substantial form: every individual of a species has the same specific occult property, for example every lodestone has the power to attract iron. On the other hand, there are individual occult properties stemming from a particular accidental cause, namely a specific astrological chart, hence with a particular astrological influence. The new property comes from this new accidental form given by the stars. This second assumption is necessary to provide scientific foundations to the concept of the "astrological image". Whereas Thomas Aquinas agrees with these three supporters as far as specific occult properties are concerned, he strongly rejects the possibility of individual occult properties, because this would actually lead to "astrological images".

From 1348, the plague was a challenge for learned physicians. Generally, analysis of the disease was kept within the rational frame of scholastic medicine. The treatises dealing with the plague do not make much room for magical processes and those few magical means that are mentioned are always contained within a rational framework. The seal of Serpentarius is mentioned against the corrupted air, since it was previously thought as useful against poison.[7]

The real turning point in the history of "astrological images" took place at the end of the fourteenth and beginning of the fifteenth century in Northern Italy. In the context of the release of the magical discourse and the rise of the author-magician,[8] some "new magicians" such as Antonio da Montolmo and Giorgio Anselmi da Parma elaborated on "astrological images", but actually betrayed and perverted the original meaning that the Magister Speculi had given to this concept. Although they pretended to deal with "astrological images", many "addressative" means were used in their making (invocations of spirits, inscriptions of characters and so on). Therefore, the Renaissance spread of "astrological images" was window dressing: behind the orthodox name, the criterion of "non-addressativity" on which the concept had been originally built became blurred. The new philosophical trends (Neoplatonism, hermeticism) contributed to make this criterion fuzzy. Marsilio Ficino, in the third book of his *De vita* ("On Life") (1489) entitled *De vita coelitus comparanda* ("On obtaining Life from the Heavens"), gives a comprehensive and renewed theory for "astrological images". But in his view, Nature, that is the whole of natural phenomena and causes, is extended far beyond the natural world of medieval peripateticism; hence, even such processes as the uttering of words, invocations and other "addressative" operations are included in this larger nature – a nature that itself becomes a "magician".[9] But since Ficino was aware of Pico della Mirandola's trouble with the Church, he concealed somehow his true thoughts. Indeed, several *Conclusiones sive Theses DCCCC*, published in 1497 by Giovanni Pico della Mirandola, were condemned as heretical, among them a "magical" one. After publishing an *Apologia* (1487), Pico was prosecuted by Pope Innocent VIII. The theologian Pedro Garsia in the *Determinationes magistrales*, written against Pico's *Conclusiones* and *Apologia*, had argued lengthily against "astrological images".[10] Therefore, Ficino's reasoning is cautious and contorted. Ficino suggested four different explanations. The first follows the path of the scholastic explanation stemming notably from the *Speculum astronomiae* or the alleged "concession" of Thomas Aquinas's *Contra Gentiles*, though he introduces some "Neoplatonizing" patterns. The second explanation, ascribed to astrologers and the Platonists, is more fully Neoplatonic and is based on the power of the figure (*figura*). The third, attributed to the Arabs, puts forward the *spiritus* both as an impersonal *pneuma*, intermediary between soul and body, and possibly as a demonic personal spirit. One of his sources is the *Picatrix*, a magic book translated before 1256 in Spain, at the court of King Alfonso X of Castile, and which disappeared soon afterwards; Ficino is the first known user of this book. A fourth explanation is set out, but its actual purpose hides Ficino's real opinion; it is an explanation that reduces the cause to matter (*ratione materiae*). The figure would play a role only insofar as its making implies hammering and heating, which makes the matter able to receive the astral influence. As a consequence, Ficino pretends that he uses compound medicine made under the appropriate horoscope rather than "astrological images". It is of course impossible to believe this statement, which contradicts Ficino's long, detailed analysis and his whole theory of talismanic images. The final explanation, *ratione materiae*, would lead to a whole rejection of the usefulness of figure, whereas the talismans are the main topic of the third book of Ficino's *De vita*. Thus, it is an apologetic argument aimed at avoiding trouble with the Church. On the contrary, Ficino's real position is a new framework for astral magic in which the old concept of "astrological images" is subverted, since the criterion of "addressativity" has been dissolved within a Neoplatonic scheme made of consonances, harmony and connections.[11]

Torrella's *Opus praeclarum de imaginibus astrologicis*

The *Opus praeclarum de imaginibus astrologicis* is the only surviving work by Jerome Torrella – he alludes to other works but they seem to be definitely lost. The *Opus* is only extant in an edition printed around 1500 by Alfonso de Orta.[12] It is dedicated to Fernándo the Catholic, king of Castile and León; the treatise appears, in several places, as a fictitious dialogue between Torrella and the king. Torrella tells that he wrote this book at the instigation of Juán Escriva de Romaní i Ram (†1515), a nobleman from Valencia, "maestro racional" (royal agent with special financial functions) who had been sent on missions several times to the Kingdom of Naples. Juán Escriva had seen in Italy several golden images that had been made at a specified astrological moment and that were efficient against kidney, colon or foot aches, but he could not find any treatise specifically dealing with this topic. Another reason for the treatise seems to lie in the fact that King Fernándo was suffering from a kidney stone; one of the most famous "astrological images", the seal of Leo, was thought to be effective against this illness. Thus, as the political situation in Naples was becoming critical, it is likely that Torrella, after his coming back to Valencia, wrote this treatise dealing with this sickness because he was eager to become a physician of King Fernándo. He probably had to face another specific problem: maybe the Torrellas were a family of *conversos* from a Jewish origin;[13] if so, the king's protection would have been even more useful.

Torrella's treatise is a unique work specifically devoted to "astrological images". Its aim is clearly displayed in the prologue:

> We have to make a decision on two issues. The first is: if there can be some power caused by a celestial influence to heal the illness of the human body in such images made by the best astrologer. The second is: if there is anything superstitious in the making of this kind of purely astrological images, and if it is licit for us, who have a right opinion about the entirely redeeming Christian law, to make them and take them with us.[14]

Torrella rightly points out the two sides of the problem: are "astrological images" scientifically possible, that is explainable by natural causes? and are they licit from a normative and theological point of view? The two sides are linked: if the answer to the first question is positive, so is the answer to the second one. Science and faith go together.

The treatise is built according to a scholastic scheme. The first part gathers together many testimonies to the efficacy and lawfulness of "astrological images". The second part shows forty-nine arguments against this claim. Two different kinds of arguments are set out. First, several arguments aim to destroy the foundations of "astrological images" by undermining astrology itself – one of these arguments is drawn from Pico della Mirandola's *Disputationes adversus astrologiam divinatricem*, a work against which Torrella says that he was about to complete a specific book. Second, the other arguments attack "astrological images" directly. Most of these later arguments stem from Thomas Aquinas's *Summa contra Gentiles*. An artificial figure cannot change a body substantially and make it able to acquire a new power, because the craftsman, that is a human being, cannot produce anything but imperfect imitations of nature. Therefore, if the figure is effective, it is because it acts not as a cause but as a sign addressed to a demon who is the real effective agent. Some other arguments are put forward with specific aims, such as the fact that, according to the melothesia – that is the influence of specific stars or constellations on specific parts of the human body – Leo does not rule kidneys, but another part of the human body. The third part gives a deep analysis of the issue, and actually gives philosophical and scientific foundations for this notion. And the fourth part is presented as a reply by the supporters of "astrological images" to each of the forty-nine arguments contained in the second part. Then Torrella ends with a long and cautious conclusion.

The most obvious sources quoted are medieval. Torrella says that his work is a compilation and, indeed, he carefully collected most of the medieval texts dealing with astrological talismans: not only the most famous (Albert the Great, Thomas Aquinas, the ninth *verbum* of Pseudo-Ptolemy's *Centiloquium* with Hali's commentary, Thebit, Petrus Comestor, Roger Bacon, Arnald of Villanova, Pietro d'Abano, Guy de Chauliac, Jean Gerson) but also more refined sources (the astrologer John of Eschenden, the physicians Ugo Benzi and Velasco de Tharanta, the theologian Bernardo Basin). Nevertheless, his work tackles many other topics that are more or less consistent with his general argumentation: philosophy, medicine, canon law, theology, magic and especially astrology (since the science of images implies astrology), and within these different fields he refers to such ancient or recent authorities as Augustine, Isidore of Seville, Albumasar, Gratianus, Guido Bonatti, Nicolas of Lyra, Duns Scotus, Pierre d'Ailly, John Ganivet and Michael Savonarola.

Lynn Thorndike, in his great *History of Magic and Experimental Science*, was the first modern scholar to study Torrella's *Opus*. He wrote that it put "a cap and climax" to "the many discussions of astrological images during the Middle Ages".[15] As noted later by Vittoria Perrone Compagni, Torrella also used a hidden source emblematic of the *Quattrocento* renewal: Marsilio Ficino's *De vita*. Although Torrella never mentions Ficino's name, he copies *verbatim* long sections of the *De vita coelitus comparanda*.[16] Three reasons can explain why he disguised those borrowings. First, it was possibly dangerous to quote such a book in Spain, where Neoplatonic-magical ideas were not as widespread as in Renaissance Italy (Torrella can actually be seen as the first – though hidden – introducer of Ficino's ideas into Spain). Second, Torrella was eager to set out his book as the first entirely devoted to "astrological images", while the *De vita coelitus comparanda* actually contains many long chapters dealing with this topic (at the end of his *Opus*, Torrella tells that some people told him that there was another work dealing with this topic written by the Catalan physician Felipe de Soldevila, but he asserts that he could not find any copy of it).[17] Third, the habit of making mention only of texts written by dead authors (he also alludes to the fifteenth-century Italian astrologer Giovan Battista Abioso without giving his name). Nevertheless, Torrella does not borrow the more innovative parts of *De vita coelitus comparanda*, where Ficino elaborates his theory on images with Neoplatonic and "spiritual" concepts; he copies those sections that fit within the peripatetic–scholastic framework.

Interestingly enough, Torrella generally refers to several contemporaries not as writers but as witnesses of magical operations who give their opinions orally. They are usually located in Italy: Giovanni Marliani, Girolamo Manfredi, Giovanni and Alessandro Sermoneta, Pier Leoni da Spoleto, Filippo Barbieri or the Valencian Bartolomeo Gerp. Some of them, such as Lluís Mercader i Escolano or the physician Juan de Bonia, were living in Spain.[18] Alessandro Sermoneta had told that he had cured his father Giovanni from strong kidney and colon aches with a seal of Leo. Pier Leoni da Spoleto also witnessed such cures several times. A Venetian physician related how the astrologer and physician Giovanni Marliani was released from his fear for thunder by using a seal of Leo (Ficino had told the same story in his *De vita*). Bartholomaeo Gerp was said to have been cured of gout in Rome in 1474 thanks to a seal of Pisces and he himself also told how he made use of this seal in order to cure one of his friends. Torrella also mentions the Spaniard Alfonso Ivarrondo, one of those close to Queen Joan of Naples, who told how he had seen, near Naples, astrological figures whose noses were bleeding and in the royal palace of Valencia other figures able to cure some diseases.

The two main authorities to whom Torrella refers are Albert the Great and Thomas Aquinas. The opposition between "Thomists", or "those who follow Thomas Aquinas's opinion", and "Albertists", or those who follow Albert the Great and the astrologers, is the structuring line of the whole treatise (this opposition can also be found in Ficino's *De vita coelitus comparanda*). "Thomists" is the name given to the opponents, since, as Torrella points out in the *Prohemium*, Thomas "asserts that there are no healing powers in these images, and that they are nothing but superstitions". On the other hand, "Albertists" support the "astrological images" as licit.

Torrella is sometimes unsure of Thomas Aquinas's position. The first reason is Thomas's alleged "concession" in the final lines of chapter 105 of the third book of *Summa contra gentiles*. The second reason lies in the fact that Torrella, just like Ficino, believed that *De fato* – a book in which there is a positive allusion to "astrological images" – was written by Thomas, whereas we know now that it has to be attributed to Albert the Great. The third and last reason is another spurious work, *De esse et essentiis tum realibus tum intentionalibus*, wrongly ascribed to Thomas Aquinas, in which the author approves the images described in the book of Abel, by which he successfully operated: he used a talisman against the passage of horses that used to awake him every morning. Nevertheless, Torrella does not finally think that Thomas Aquinas is the real author of such a book, but ascribes it to another "Thomas".

And lastly, Torrella is able to set out an exact summary of Doctor Angelicus's position:

> There is, indeed, the opinion of Thomas Aquinas according to which in the images artificially and astrologically made, there cannot be any power caused by the celestial influence and able to cure the diseases or prevent them. On the contrary, the efficacy of such images has to be reduced to some evil spirit who interferes in the making of images of this kind. This is the reason why he asserts that carrying and making such images is superstitious. He actually does not believe that the figure of a

lion made on gold could be, owing to the likeness with the celestial Leo, a cause for the introduction of the celestial quality by the celestial Leo. In such a case, indeed, the celestial Leo, owing to this likeness, would choose to introduce the aforesaid quality into the artificial lion, and hence he would operate through a choice, and thus it would seem to act by itself; and this is a great difficulty. A figure cannot be the principle for any purely corporeal action either, and consequently it cannot arrange (*disponere*) gold in such a way that it can receive such a quality, since arranging is acting. Although, according to the opinion of several experienced men, a figure seems to have an active power with regard to intellect and senses, it has none with regard to gold, since such an action with regard to gold is purely material and corporeal, and figure cannot carry out such an action.[19]

In other words, as Torrella correctly states, in Thomas Aquinas's view, if an artificial "astrological image" acquires some power, this comes from an "addressative" process that implies the actions of demons.

The Albertist position is based on the *Speculum astronomiae*, which is attributed by Torrella to Albert the Great, and also on other authentic works by him. The analysis is intricate, but finally Torrella succeeds in defining the frame for this orthodox pro-talismanic position:

Some people who follow the opinion of the astrologers thought that by reasoning, the opinion of Albert the Great and the astrologers could be supported with the following change: in the images made in a purely astrological way, there can be a power curative or preservative from diseases, a power given to them by a celestial constellation [...]. It should also be pointed out that the aforesaid image has been made by none of the illicit means described above, such as observations of the twenty-eight lunar mansions, lights, sacrifices, fumigations, worship, supplications, invocations, characters or nigromantical figures, but that it has been made at the hour when the Sun was in Leo and at Midheaven and so on, as set out above. Thus, Albert believes that such an object made according to a certain figure acquires the power to cure a disease or to prevent from it, thanks to a defined figure of the heavens or constellation, and that there is no explicit or implicit pact in the making of a purely "astrological image". On the other hand, in the other images Albert would grant that there is a tacit or implicit pact with the evil spirit, because of the characters and other processes mentioned earlier. Therefore Albert would think that a Christian must avoid this kind of image – those who have been made with such observations and characters – and not the purely "astrological images". And those who followed Albert's opinion, when I was living in Italy, thought that if someone asserts that there is an implicit pact with the evil spirit in such a purely "astrological image", as some professors who contemplate the sacred theology think, this stems rather from their free opinion and from their zealous faith than from the authorities in Sacred Scriptures themselves.[20]

Thus, the "Albertist" position can be defined as supporting a purely "astrological image", that (as the Magister Speculi had it) is a non-addressative talisman whose power comes only from the natural power of the stars and not from a pseudo-divine or a demonic cause. But moreover another restrictive condition is added: these talismans or seals have only a corporeal power (they cannot act upon the soul even through indirect means, by a corporeal "inclination"). Furthermore, their effect does not exceed what Nature itself can achieve. Finally, the only licit "astrological images" are those whose power are therapeutic (curative and preventive).

Torrella himself never says explicitly that he agrees with the "Albertist" position, but repeatedly writes that the issue must be decided by the theologians. This very careful attitude stems clearly from his fear of trouble with the Church, since, as he writes, Albert's position is not completely sure "because it comes close to" nigromancy. Ficino in his *De vita coelitus comparanda* had claimed that he did not approve but was rather only relating ("non tam probo quam narrow"), and he had finally asserted that he would rather use astrological medicine, for example a compound made under a specified astrological chart, than "astrological images" – a very hypocritical assertion. Torrella follows Ficino's path, and he repeats this remark whose purpose is to protect him against trouble with the Church. The Spain ruled by the Catholic Monarchs was certainly even more circumspect towards magical doctrines than Italy. Nevertheless, Torrella's position is obviously an "Albertist" one, as testified by the structure of his treatise: a third part devoted to a deep analysis of doctrines in favour of "astrological images" and the fourth part which is an answer to the objections of the second part. Two opposing requirements tore Torrella in half. On the one hand, he wanted his treatise to seem useful to King Fernándo, who was suffering from the kidney stone – the *Opus* deals especially with the astrological seal of Leo, which was known as efficient against kidney aches; Torrella's main purpose was probably to seek a position as a royal physician. But on the other hand, he had to be cautious of the Church authorities and thus could not appear too openly as a supporter of such images.

Facing some difficult issues

It is impossible to run through all the topics and speculations contained in this very dense and rich treatise. Although Torrella assumes that his *Opus* is a compilation, some arguments seem quite original, at least in their elaboration. We can put forward a few examples.

Torrella goes into the "Albertist" explanation in depth and gives a very detailed account of a model which, at the same time, aims at removing every trace of "addressativity" in the figure, and intends to preserve a real function for the figure. As Ficino had suggested, Torrella elaborates from the pseudo-concession of the *Summa contra Gentiles*. The figure is not useful as a figure, but insofar as it implies a peculiar arrangement of matter so that it will receive a peculiar influence from the stars. Torrella makes great use of the logical tools of scholasticism:

> Therefore the healing does not stem from the figure as a figure, but from the gold which has received the accidental specific form of Lion as a principle *quo* [an instrumental principle, a principle by which the agent acts], and from the substantial form of gold not absolutely but shaped by this figure under a certain constellation of the orbs as principle *per quod* [a principle through which the agent acts], and from the figure, not as a figure, but insofar as it is as such and has been made in such a way, as a principle *sine quo non* [necessary principle], and from the quality of a peculiar property newly introduced by the heavens, as an instrumental principle or principle *quo*, while the action and passion of the parts of gold are cooperating in the moment when this gold is melted down and cast into a figure put in a mould by the goldsmith, so that such a figure may be received in the cast gold.[21]

In his investigation of the naturalistic explanation for "astrological images", Torrella comes very close to a pattern elaborated by the philosopher Galeotto Marzio da Narni, although he probably did not read him. In *De doctrina promiscua* (1489–90), Marzio gave the most achieved naturalistic explanation of the "astrological image" within a peripatetic framework. His pattern was able to fulfil both aforesaid requirements: saving the usefulness of a peculiar figure and putting forward a "non-addressative" explanation at the same time. The figure loses any "addressative" sign, since it is reduced to an arrangement of quantities: density of matter and spatial distribution of volumes. It is analogous to a three-dimensional barcode that is automatically detected by a barcode reader. Natural agents (without any sense or Intelligence) are able to detect the difference in matter implied by such or such figure. The peculiarity of the figure is saved: a figure of a dog and a figure of a lion cause two different arrangements of the matter (a lion has a mane, whereas a dog has not; hence, there will be a hole in matter around the lion's head and such a hole will not appear around the dog's head).[22]

Moreover, taking his inspiration from discussions about the Eucharist and also from a section of William of Auvergne's *De legibus*, Torrella dedicates a long section to the question concerning the presence of the quality in the seal of Leo. He faces three questions dealing with this intricate issue.

> Argument 35 – We have to determine if this quality extant in the figure of the lion is produced by the Sun and Leo and other stars in a divisible way according to different parts (*divisibiliter et partibiliter*) or entirely at the same time (*tota insimul*). Moreover, we must observe if this quality is divisible according to the division of the lion or if it is entirely in the whole lion and not this part [of the quality] in this part [of the lion].
>
> Argument 36 – One has also to consider if, once a degree of the aforesaid celestial quality has been destroyed, the whole celestial quality ceases in the whole lion or in a part of the whole lion, or if it is not entirely annihilated.
>
> Argument 37 – It is asked if, once some part of the lion has been destroyed, the whole power which was extant in the whole lion is entirely destroyed or if a part of it remains.[23]

The analysis of these problems leads to a very long and complex examination of two different models. The argumentation is complicated especially as Torrella brings together and superimposes two different logical distinctions, the first between *categorematice* (the word "totum", whole, is understood as such, and not as a logical function) and *syncategorematice* (by which the word "totum" means nothing by itself but acquires a logical function when it is joined with other words) and the second between *totum integrale* (for example, "underpinning" plus "walls" plus "roof" are equal to the *totum* "house") and *totum universale* (for example, "man", "horse", "cat" and so on are in the *totum* "animal"). Torrella probably wrote this long and sophisticated section in order to impress his royal reader.

Torrella also confronts its model with risky logical and philosophical challenges. Thus, he asks if an "astrological image" can bring good fortune. As Duns Scot put it, good fortune is "some quality caused by a constellation of celestial bodies in the sensitive appetite, that moves it to do something from which some good thing follows, while it knows neither the aim nor the reason of such a movement".[24] This doctrine is framed by the theory of free will: this quality obviously has the power of inclining a man to choose this or that, not the power of constraining him from such a choice. However, if we admit that an "astrological image" can receive a quality from astral influence, are we not compelled to concede that an "astrological image" can be endowed with the quality or power to incline somebody to make good choices, hence the quality of bringing fortune? Torrella writes that this was the opinion of his revered master Pier Leoni da Spoleto, but he feels actually discomforted by such a hypothesis, since he wants to constrain the field of "astrological images" only to medical and corporeal goals. Therefore, he writes cautiously:

> Some people would admit that good fortune is a quality caused into us by the powers of the superior celestial bodies and so on, but that a quality imprinted in gold by the celestial bodies is a cause for good fortune, I doubt.[25]

The development of "astrological images"

Though it was not very well known, the work of Torrella is of great importance in the history of the notion of "astrological images". But many mentions and uses of "astrological images" and even intellectual elaboration about them can be found in the sixteenth century. Even such a philosopher as Pietro Pomponazzi elaborates a neo-Aristotelian and astrological explanation of such a concept. Montaigne alludes to a small golden coin in which some celestial figures were engraved against sunburn and headache (probably a seal of Aries); he explains this efficacy by the power of imagination. Astrological medals made according to the pattern of pseudo-Arnald of Villanova's *De sigillis* are still extant – they bear characters and inscriptions that do not fit with the original definition by the Magister Speculi. The magician-philosopher Agrippa of Nettesheim writes about different kinds of astrological talismans, but with an approach that subverted the criterion of "addressativity". Lapidaries such as those of Camillo Leonardi (1502), Petrus Constantius Albinius de Villanova or Franciscus Rueus also make room for astrological seals and display a knowledge of the Magister Speculi's concept of "astrological images". Giambattista Della Porta in the first edition of *De magia naturali* (1558) also deals with astrological engravings of stones. Modern scholars still do not agree about the interpretation of the frescoes of the so-called "Salone dei Mesi" of the Palazzo Schifanoia in Florence (1469–70): are they a painted talisman just like the "figura universi" described later in Ficino's *De vita coelitus comparanda*? On the other hand, Tommaso Campanella, following Ficino's direction, was also a supporter of "astrological images".[26]

Torrella's *Opus* gives fundamental evidence of the medieval and early Renaissance debates around astrological talismans or astral magic and sheds light on the status of natural magic in a new context in which persistent scholastic thought was faced with new trends such as Neoplatonism. It therefore offers important clues for further research concerning the inheritance and metamorphosis of the concept of "astrological images" in late Renaissance times and modern esotericism, but also concerning the connection between learned medicine and magical *empirica* (empirical processes). Moreover, Torrella's testimony, as one of the first introducers of Ficino's thought in Spain (although clandestinely), invites new inquiries concerning the influence of the philosophical theory of magic of Renaissance Italy on Spain ruled by the most Catholic Kings.

Notes

1 Lynn Thorndike, *A History of Magic and Experimental Science*, 8 vols. (New York: Columbia Press, 1923–58): 574–85; Vittoria Perrone Compagni, "Le immagini del medico Gerolama Torrella," *Annali dell'Instituto di Filosofia dell'Università di Firenze, Facoltà di Lettere e Filosofia* 1 (1979): 17–45; Jon Arrizabalaga, "Medicina universitaria y *morbus gallicus* en la Italiade finales del siglo XV: El arquiatra pontificio Gapar Torrella (c. 1452–c. 1520)," *Asclepio*, 40 (1988): 3–38; Jon Arrizabalaga, Luis García Ballester and Fernando Salmón, "A propósito de las relaciones intelectuales entre la Corona

de Aragón e Italia (1470–1520): los estudiantes de medicina valencianos en los etudios generales de Siena, Pisa, Ferrara y Padua," *Dynamis* 9 (1989): 117–47.
2. On "astrological images": Nicolas Weill-Parot, *Les "Images astrologiques" au Moyen Âge et à la Renaissance. Spéculations intellectuelles et pratiques magiques, XIIe-XVe siècle* (Paris: Honoré Champion, 2002); the following sections stem from this book. See also Frank Klaassen, *The Transformations of Magic: Illicit Learned Magic in the Later Middle Ages and Renaissance* (University Park: Pennsylvania State University Press, 2012), 33ff.
3. On this distinction: Nicolas Weill-Parot, "Les images corporéiformes du *Picatrix* et la magie astrale occidentale," in *Images et Magie. Picatrix entre Orient et Occident*, ed. Anna Caiozzo, Jean-Patrice Boudet and Nicolas Weill-Parot (Paris: Honoré Champion, 2011), 117–36.
4. See notably: David Pingree, "The Sābians of Harrān and the Classical Tradition," *International Journal of the Classical Tradition* 9 (2002/2003): 8–35. This thesis was recently criticized, for example Kevin Van Bladel, *The Arabic Hermes: From Pagan Sage to Prophet of Science* (Oxford: Oxford University Press, 2009), 64–114, but other scholars still support this view, for example Anna Caiozzo, *Images du ciel d'Orient au Moyen Âge. Une histoire du zodiaque et de ses représentations dans les manuscrits du Proche-Orient musulman* (Paris: PUPS, 2003).
5. Nicolas Weill-Parot, "Causalité astrale et 'science des images' au Moyen Âge. Eléments de réflexion," *Revue d'histoire des sciences* 52, no. 2 (1999): 207–40.
6. On Arnald of Villanova and the seals: Nicolas Weill-Parot, "Astrologie, médecine et art talismanique à Montpellier: les sceaux astrologiques pseudo-arnaldiens," in *L'Université de Médecine de Montpellier et son rayonnement (XIIIe-XVe siècles)*, ed. Daniel Le Blévec, collab. Thomas Granier (Turnhout: Brepols, 2004), 157–74; Sebastià Giralt, "Medicina i astrologia en el corpus arnaldià," *Dynamis* 26 (2006): 15–38.
7. Nicolas Weill-Parot, "La rationalité médicale à l'épreuve de la peste: médecine, astrologie et magie (1348–1500)," *Médiévales* 46 (2004): 73–88.
8. See my chapter on Cecco d'Ascoli and Antonio da Montolmo in this volume.
9. Vittoria Perrone Compagni, "Natura maga. Il concetto di natura nella discussione rinascimentale sulla magia," in *Natura. XII Colloquio internazionale del Lessico intellettuale europeo*, ed. Delfina Giovannozzi and Marco Veneziani (Florence: Olschki, 2008), 243–67.
10. See Jérôme Rousse-Lacordaire, *Une controverse sur la magie et la kabbale à la Renaissance* (Genève: Droz, 2010).
11. On Ficino and "astrological images", see notably Brian P. Copenhaver, "Scholastic Philosophy and Renaissance Magic in the *De vita* of Marsilio Ficino," *Renaissance Quarterly* 37 (1984): 523–54; Nicolas Weill-Parot, "Pénombre ficinienne: le renouveau de la théorie de la magie talismanique et ses ambiguïtés," in *Marsile Ficin ou les mystères platoniciens*, ed. Stéphane Toussaint (Paris: Les Belles Lettres, 2002), 71–90 (collection: *Les Cahiers de l'humanisme*, 2); Darrell H. Rutkin, "The Physics and Metaphysics of Talismans (Imagines Astronomicae) in Marsilio Ficino's *De vita libri tres*. A Case Study in (Neo)Platonism, Aristotelianism and the Esoteric," in *Platonismus und Esoterik in byzantinischem Mittelalter und italienischer Renaissance*, ed. Helmut Seng (Heidelberg: Universitätsverl. Winter, 2013), 149–74 (Bibliotheca Chaldaica, 3).
12. Critical edition with presentation and notes: Jérôme Torrella (Hieronymus Torrella), *Opus praeclarum de imaginibus astrologicis*, ed. Nicolas Weill-Parot (Florence: Sismel Edizioni del Galluzzo, 2008).
13. Jon Arrizabalaga, Luis García-Ballester and José Luis Gil-Aristu, "Del manuscrito al primitivo impreso: La labor editora de Francesc Argilagues (fl. ca. 1470–1508) en el Renacimiento italiano," *Asclepio* 1 (1991): 6. J. Arrizabalaga noticed that several members with the family name "Torrella" were condemned as "judaizantes" as shown in the register of the Inquisition of Valencia, published by Ricardo García Cárcel, *Orígenes de la Inquisición española. El tribunal de Valencia, 1478-1530* (Barcelona: Península, 1976), 233–37.
14. "Duo autem querit iuditio nostro. Primum est si talibus imaginibus per optimum astrologum fabricatis inesse possit aliquae virtus curatiua morborum corporis humani, a caelorum influxu causata. Secundum est an sit in huiusmodi imaginum pure astrologicarum fabricatione aliquid superstitionis, liceatque nobis, bene de lege saluberrima christiana sentientibus, eas facere atque deferre". Torrella, *Opus praeclarum*, 77.
15. Thorndike, *History of Magic*, IV:574.
16. Perrone Compagni, "Le immagini". See also Maike Rotzoll, "Osservazioni sul De jmaginibus astrologicis di Geronimo Torrella," *Rinascimento*, 2^d ser., 31 (1991): 219–37.

17 The name of this author appears in Symphorien Champier's De medicine claris scriptoribus (Lyons: Janot de Camps, ca. 1506), f. 38r; cf. Weill-Parot, Les *"images astrologiques,"* 787–89.
18 Nicolas Weill-Parot, "¿La hispanidad de la magia astral? El contra-ejemplo de Jerónimo Torrella," *La Corónica* 36, no. 1 (2007) (*Critical Cluster: Magic in Medieval Spain*, ed. A. García Avilés): 145–72.
19 "Est quippe Aquinatis Thome sententia quod imaginibus artificialiter et astrologice fabricatis minime potest inesse aliqua vis morborum curatiua aut preseruatiua a caelorum influxu causata, imo reducendus est effectus a talibus imaginibus causatus in spiritum malignum qui facture huiusmodi imaginum se inmiscet. Propter quod superstitiosum esse profitetur huiusmodi imagines afferre atque facere. Non enim credit figuram leonis in auro fabricatam propter similitudinem cum Leone caelesti esse causam inductionis caelestis qualitatis a Leone caelesti. Sic enim Leo caelestis propter similitudinem eligeret qualitatem praefatam in leonem artificiatum inducere, et sic per electionem operaretur, et sic ratione vteretur ex se, quod non paruum esse videtur inconueniens. Figura etiam nullius actionis pure corporalis potest esse principium et per consequens neque disponere aurum ad huiusmodi qualitatis receptionem, quum disponere sit agere. Demum tametsi figura secundum nonnullorum peritorum virorum sententiam habere videatur vim actiuam respectu intellectus aut sensus, non tamen respectu auri, quum talis actio respectu auri sit mere materialis atque corporalis; quam actionem minime potest atingere." Torrella, *Opus praeclarum*, Concl., 244.
20 "[…] arbitrati sunt aliqui sententiam astrologorum sequentes disertionis causa defendi posse cum sequenti modificatione Alberti Magni et astrologorum sententiam quod imaginibus pure astrologice fabricatis inesse potest vis morborum curatiua aut praeseruatiua a caelorum constellatione in eis causata […]. Dictam etiam imaginem sciendo non esse factam modo aliquo illicito superius descripto, videlicet obseruando XXVIII Lune mansiones cum luminibus et sacrificiis, fumigationibus, adorationibus, supplicationibus, inuocationibus, caracteribus aut figuris nicromanticis, sed in hora qua Sol existit in Leone et medio caeli etc., vt superius narratum est, sic enim credit Albertus tale figuratum aliquam vim morbi alicuius curatiuam aut preseruatiuam acquirere a caelorum determinato situ determinataque constellatione, neque esse pactum expressum aut subauditum in editione huiusmodi imaginis pure astrologice. In aliis vero aut tacitum aut subintellectum cum maligno spiritu concederet Albertus propter caracteres et alia paulo ante commemorata. Quare huiusmodi imagines cum talibus obseruantiis aut caracteribus factas a christiano quocumque fugiendas Albertus consuleret, et non tamen imagines pure astrologicas. Quod si quis dicat in tali imagine pure astrologica esse pactum subauditum cum spiritu maligno, vt aliqui contemplatiui sacre theologie professores existimant, hoc potius voluntarie ac zelo fidei quam ex autoritatibus Sacre Scripture dictum esse putabant quidam Alberti opinionem sequentes, dum apud Italiam vitam degeremus." Torrella, *Opus praeclarum*, 236–37.
21 "Egritudinis ergo renum curatio non a figura inquantum est figura procedit, sed ab auro sub tali specifica forma accidentali leonis existente tanquam principio quo, et a forma substantiali auri non absolute sed vt induta tali figura in determinata orbium constellatione tanquam principio per quod, et figura non vt figura sed inquantum est talis taliterque fabricata tanquam principio sine quo non, et a qualitate certe proprietatis a caelo nouiter influxa tanquam principio instrumentali seu principio quo, concurrente actione et passione partium auri tempore fusionis eius ab igne et effusionis ipsius auri in figuram in sipia repositam ab aurifabro, vt talis figura in auro effuso recipiatur." Torrella, *Opus praeclarum*, III, 157.
22 N. Weill-Parot, "L'irréductible 'destinativité' des images: les voies de l'explication naturaliste des talismans dans la seconde moitié du xve siècle," in *L'Art de la Renaissance entre science et magie*, ed. Philippe Morel (Rome and Paris: Académie de France à Rome-Somogy, 2006), 469–81.
23 "Ratio 35 – Item talis qualitas in figurato leone existens est videndum an producatur a Sole et Leone et aliis diuisibiliter seu partibiliter, an tota simul. Praeterea est contemplandum an talis qualitas sit diuisibilis ad diuisionem leonis, vel sit tota in toto leone et non pars in parte. Ratio 36 – Etiam oportet considerare an, destructo vno grado dicte qualitatis caelestis, in toto leone aut in parte aliqua totius leonis desinat tota qualitas caelestis vel non tota adnihiletur. Ratio 37 – Demum quaeritur si, destructa parte aliqua leonis, destruatur tota virtus in toto leone existens, an remaneat aliqua pars eius." Torrella, *Opus praeclarum*, II, 111.
24 "Nam quum bona fortuna, secundum Scotum, sit quedam qualitas a corporum caelestium contellatione causata in apetitu sensitiuo mouens ipsum ad aliquid faciendum, ex quo bonum aliquod sequitur, nesciendo finem neque talis motus rationem." Torrella, *Opus praeclarum*, III, 140. On the concept of 'bona fortuna' and on the importance of the *Liber de bona fortuna* in the Middle Ages,

see Valérie Cordonier, "Noblesse et bon naturel chez les lecteurs du *Liber de bona fortuna* de Thomas d'Aquin à Duns Scot: histoire d'un rapprochement," in *La nobiltà nel pensiero medievale*, ed. A. Palazzo, F. Bonini and A. Colli (Fribourg: Academic Press, 2016), 99–134.

25 "Aliqui vero, bonam fortunam esse qualitatem per vires superiorum corporum caelestium in nobis causatam etc., bene concederent; sed quod qualitas in auro a caelestibus corporibus impressa sit bonae fortunae causa, nos dubitamus." Torrella, *Opus praeclarum*, III, 140.

26 See notably Nicolas Weill-Parot, "Le 'immagini astrologiche'," in *Il linguaggio dei cieli. Astri e simboli nel Rinascimento*, ed. Germana Ernst and Guido Giglioni (Rome: Carocci, 2012), 241–54; Donato Verardi, "Giovan Battista Della Porta e le immagini astrologiche," *Bruniana & Campanelliana* 21, no. 1 (2015): 143–54.

20

PETER OF ZEALAND

Jean-Marc Mandosio

Peter of Zealand is a newcomer in the history of late medieval magic.[1] No one seems to have ever read his *magnum opus*, the "Elucidation of Marvelous Things" (*Lucidarius de rebus mirabilibus*), or even noticed its existence, before the twenty-first century. Written in the 1490s, the work is preserved in a single manuscript copied around 1500, which entered at some point the library of the Dukes of Burgundy, now Royal Library of Belgium.[2] It was catalogued as a miscellany on medicine and magic by several authors (including Peter of Zealand), though all the texts it contains were actually parts of a comprehensive work, the *Lucidarius*, whose title escaped the attention of the librarians because it is buried in the prologue to the first section. Ironically, while the *Lucidarius* lay undiscovered for five centuries, another of Peter's works, a short untitled treatise on alchemy, circulated rather widely in manuscript form, and was even printed in the seventeenth century in one of the most famous collections of alchemical texts, the *Theatrum chemicum* – but the name "Petrus de Zelandia" or "de Zelante" was misspelled beyond recognition as "Petrus de Silento".[3] A third work is mentioned in the *Lucidarius* itself: Peter refers to a pamphlet he wrote "On the Prolongation of Life and Retardation of Death" (*libellus de prolongatione vitæ et retardatione mortis*),[4] as yet unfound.

The sparse autobiographical data contained in the *Lucidarius* allows us to reconstruct the main stages of the author's life. Petrus Francho[5] was born around 1430 in Zealand (West Netherlands). This date can be inferred from the fact that he became master of arts in 1450 at the University of Cologne. He visited France, Italy and Germany. He probably passed a doctorate in medicine – even though he is simply called *magister* in the manuscript (114r) – for he made his career as a physician in connection with the court of Burgundy. He retired, probably around 1490, to the Franciscan monastery of Brill, in South Holland.[6] There he composed his *Lucidarius*, between 1491 and 1494. He did not live in seclusion, for in 1494 he was in Lons-le-Saulnier (Burgundy). He died around 1500, while he was collecting fresh documentation on natural magic to complement the *Lucidarius*. After his passing, someone gathered his papers and had a copy made of them, which is all we have now.

Since it had no impact whatsoever, the historical significance of Peter's work lies in the project itself. He explains in the prologue that his intent is to elucidate "the marvelous and extremely strange things (*de rebus mirabilibus et permultum extraneis*) which appear clearly before the senses of almost every man", such as "the binding of men" through "incantations, words and fascinations, gestures and ways various and nearly innumerable, images and characters, writings, forms and figures", all of which, "to the intelligence of the common people, seem impossible and deprived of a sufficient cause".[7] This is borrowed, with slight adaptations, from the opening sentence of *De mirabilibus mundi*, a thirteenth-century anonymous work falsely ascribed to Albert the Great.[8] The "elucidation" taken on by Peter pursues a twofold objective: "to make sure that, for the sake of health and the prolongation of life, anyone be able to know how he should govern himself, and also how to obviate in no small part the evil arts".[9]

These two goals are linked by the assumption that, to be able to resist spells, one has to master the features of human physiology, in order to "govern himself" in the most effective way. Given his medical training, Peter is prone to consider that a healthy soul in a healthy body is the best defense against any attempt by a wizard or spirit to manipulate a person's will. Accordingly, the *Lucidarius* begins with a "Summary on the Properties of the Heart",[10] to which is appended a catalogue of the different types of "cordial and cheering medicines",[11] both loosely based upon Avicenna's *De viribus cordis et medicinis cordialibus*, translated by Arnold of Villanova in 1306.[12] Peter expounds the standard pneumatic theory, according to which the passions of the soul are largely shaped by the "spirits" generated in the heart and carried by blood throughout the body. In the brain, the "vital spirits" are transformed into "animal spirits" that are, as it were, the fuel of the imaginative faculty; as "imaginative spirits" (*spiritus imaginarii*), they translate the perceptions, internal condition and "accidents" of the body into feelings – joy, sadness, anger and the like. The more these spirits, which produce representations in the mind, are weakened or altered, the more a person is suggestible and may be easily manipulated. Hence, the "cordial medicines" enumerated by Peter are designed to strengthen the heart and, consequently, the spirits. Those medicines are divided into ten types, of which nine are "material" whereas the tenth, of a "celestial" nature, is the alchemical quintessence, whose wondrous effect is to prevent major diseases and prolong life (15v–16v, 89r–v).

The introductory chapters on physiology are followed by a lengthy "Summary on Rays".[13] This reproduces in full the Latin translation of al-Kindî's *De radiis*.[14] The combination is clever. In al-Kindî's system, the rays emanating from the "celestial harmony" impregnate sublunar bodies and determine their properties; the sublunar bodies become in turn capable of emitting rays, whose power depends on the strength of the constellations and planets that radiated upon them at the time of their birth. In the case of humans, this explains why some are more persuasive and more able than others to change external reality according to their will. In addition to this native power, imagination and desire are essential ingredients of success, and the capacity of strong-minded persons to concentrate on their goal is directly linked with the strengthening of "animal spirits", dealt with in the *Compendium de viribus cordis*.

Peter accepts without reticence "the opinion of al-Kindî, a most excellent man in everything marvelous".[15] He is aware, of course, that *De radiis* has been condemned, notably in the *De erroribus philosophorum* ascribed to Giles of Rome, as an abominable work teaching astral determinism and promoting pagan sacrifices.[16] He counter-attacks by adding to al-Kindî's text several glosses meant to demonstrate that the theory it expounds is in accordance with "the opinions of the learned and the authorities of the saints".[17] To do so, he draws upon the Book of Genesis, Proverbs and Jerome's "preface to the Bible".[18] These references deal for the most part with the "hidden power" of words, one of the salient topics in *De radiis*. Peter also adduces (40v) the story of Jacob's sheep told in Genesis 30, in order to confirm al-Kindî's statement about the power of artificial figures to radiate upon things and people and transform them. Another reference to Jerome corroborates it: in his commentary on this biblical episode,[19] the Father of the Church mentioned the anecdote of the white woman who gave birth to a black son because she had stared at the picture of an Ethiopian while the child was being conceived; according to Peter, this demonstrates that, when Jacob produced "cattle ringstraked, speckled and spotted" by making "the flock conceive before the rods" prepared to this effect (Genesis 30: 37–39), his "skill and ingenuity" made "the nature of the sky work together with art".[20] In other words, the artificial image (the striped rods) was displayed by Jacob at a favourable time, according to the horoscope of the conception of the sheep, so as to imprint the form of the rods on them – a feat of natural magic that would have been impossible without a perfect knowledge of astrology. Thus, the story recounted in Holy Scripture is fully explained by al-Kindî's theory of the emanations of the "celestial harmony". I know of no other medieval author who not only approved *De radiis* openly but also reproduced it in its entirety and even tried to persuade his readers that the orthodoxy of the work was guaranteed by sacred authorities.

Peter also draws an interesting parallel between *De radiis* and *Picatrix*. Al-Kindî's treatise, just like the *Lucidarius* itself that incorporates it, deals only with the theoretical foundations of magic – hence its alternate title, *Theorica artium magicarum*. Thus, neither al-Kindî's nor Peter's works may be used to learn how to perform this art. Now, according to Peter, *Picatrix* is based on the same conceptions as *De radiis* (47r), but it is half-theoretical and half-practical: as a handbook, it gives detailed descriptions of magical recipes, incantations and ceremonies, which would make it very dangerous if it came to the knowledge of people "urged by the spirit of vengeance and the desire to harm"; therefore, "the Church did well when it forbade" the secrets it contains "to be read publicly at the University", keeping "the rich and magnates, kings and princes" from "destroying one another" by putting them into practice; and in so doing, it followed the advice of *Picatrix* itself, which "casts a spell" against the revelation of its contents "to those unworthy of knowing" such things.[21] To sum up, Peter's position concerning forbidden books is nuanced: he disapproves of the theologians who dismiss them from a theoretical viewpoint, but he approves of the Church that prohibits their use for practical ends. Moreover, he agrees with the *Speculum astronomiæ*, which says that these books should not be destroyed but kept, "for perhaps the time is already at hand when, for certain reasons about which I am now silent, it will be useful on occasion to have inspected them"[22] – these mysteriously unspecified reasons being, in all likelihood, the coming of the Antichrist.

The *Compendium de radiis* gives way to a series of *quæstiones* focused on the imagination, either as a point of entry for a "spirit" – i.e. an angel or demon – wanting to change one's will,[23] or as a means to produce visions and apparitions,[24] and also as a great help for recovering health, granted that the sick person trusts the physician.[25] These *quæstiones*, and especially the last, serve as an introduction to Peter's paraphrase of Pietro d'Abano's *quæstio* on the curative power of incantations,[26] in which imagination once again plays a key role. In these chapters, he uses a variety of explicit and implicit sources, from Avicenna's *De anima* to Thomas Aquinas's *Summa theologiæ*.

He does not refrain from addressing risky issues. For instance, he builds on Pietro d'Abano's relatively discreet adduction of the Eucharist as a prime example of the actual power of incantations,[27] and connects it to al-Kindî's thesis, according to which "required conditions and circumstances contribute greatly to the achievement of the effect" of an incantation or any other magical feat.[28] The power of the ritual formula "This is my body" lies not in the words themselves, but in the occult virtue transferred upon them by their originator (Jesus), which the priest reactivates when he replays the Last Supper in the celebration of the Mass. "And therefore, if the priest utters these words without [concentrating upon] the intention or the memory of their originator, I, Peter of Zealand, declare that the transformation of bread into the sacrament does not happen."[29] However orthodox such a statement may be in itself, its insertion into the theoretical frame of al-Kindî's theory of magical "radiation" gives it an altogether different meaning.

On the disputed issue of witchcraft, Peter asserts that "it is commonly held that old and simple-minded women, haunted by evil spirits, eat and drink with spirits and with their friends and neighbours, in woods and orchards or similar places, and that they ride on a cat or a wolf and fly through the air, pass through glass, and do an infinity of impossible things"; the so-called witches are firmly persuaded that all of this really happens, but "they are deluded, for the evil spirit, by disturbing through a disorderly motion their humours and spirits, their species and fantasies, raised inside [their minds] things which do not exist in the outside world".[30] It is thus clear that for Peter the Witches' Sabbath is a fiction, a mere persuasion produced by "the evil spirit". As an imaginary action, the Sabbath is similar to the visions that appear in slumbers or when people are feverish or otherwise troubled, like for instance when they see "armies riding in the skies" with "the cross of Saint Andrew", or "a crucifix", or "Our Lady appearing in the sky with Saint John, and an infinity of fantasies depending on the diversity of their imaginative spirits and their species and fantasies,"[31] that is, according to their temperament and health. All this, says Peter, "is common knowledge among physicians".[32]

After the paraphrase of Pietro d'Abano comes a summary of the "Secrets of Albert the Great",[33] i.e. *De mirabilibus mundi*. Like his contemporaries, Peter believes that this book preserves the secret teachings of Albert the Great. True to his focus on theory, he borrows exclusively from the first part of the work, in which the author expounds the general conception of sympathies and antipathies as the foundation of natural magic,[34] while the part that enumerates magical "experiments" is left aside.

One of the aspects of *De mirabilibus mundi* highlighted by Peter is the importance of Plato as a primary source. He quotes at length the passages from "Plato" cited by "Albert". They are actually derived from the Arabic Pseudo-Platonic *Kitâb al-Nawâmîs* ("Book of Laws"), known in Latin under different titles such as *Liber aneguemis* (translitteration of the Arabic title), *Liber regimentis* ("Book of the Government") or *Liber vaccæ* ("Book of the Cow", because the first "experiment" described is the artificial production of a cow),[35] and quoted here as *Liber tegumenti* ("Book of the Covering"). This variant reading of the title fits well with Peter's conception of Plato as a philosopher who concealed elevated truths so as to keep them out of the ignorant's reach: "And therefore occultation should be used as much as possible, for he who reveals secret mysteries lessens the divinity, as Plato said".[36] The two parts of this Pseudo-Platonic work were mentioned in *Picatrix* as "the Greater and the Lesser Books of Plato",[37] and it certainly guaranteed their authenticity in Peter's eyes, together with the fact that "Albert the Great" used them as one of his main sources in *De mirabilibus mundi*. The passages quoted by Peter, who adapts them freely to his purpose, deal with the arts the magus should know in order to understand how the secret sciences work.[38]

Once again, Peter uses a work commonly deemed abominable – the *De mirabilibus mundi* was one of the few medieval works that mentioned the *Liber aneguemis* favourably[39] – as if it were a genuine doctrinal authority. He plays a dangerous game by putting forth such works as *De radiis*, *Picatrix* or *Liber aneguemis* and mixing them with legitimate and even sacred authorities. He has no problem either with Pietro d'Abano, who was not an undiscussed figure. In addition, the title of Peter's *Lucidarius* is reminiscent of the *Elucidarius magicæ* or *Lucidarium artis nigromanticæ*, forged in the second half of the fifteenth century under Pietro d'Abano's name,[40] even though, as to the contents, the two works have nothing in common.

The real Pietro d'Abano wrote a *Lucidator dubitabilium astronomiæ*, which Peter could also have had in mind when he chose a title for his own work.

Peter makes his point about the matter of authority in the chapter that follows the "Secrets of Albert", titled "Against Those Who Oppose the Secrets of the Philosophers".[41] He explains that many "theologians and lawyers" stubbornly outlaw these "secrets" out of sheer ignorance.[42] Now, there are three ways by which truth may be grasped: experience, reason, authority. As *De mirabilibus mundi* makes abundantly clear, "the major secret arts", being occult (*coopertæ*), "are not demonstrated by reason but by experience".[43] The causes that make them true and effective are mostly inaccessible to reason, for "the effects of many marvelous works are so hidden (*latentes*) that the human intellect is incapable of comprehending them", and therefore "one has to rely on experiments".[44] These *experimenta* are the data and recipes collected by ancient philosophers such as Plato, based upon the powers of man, in whom lies "the efficacy of all things, be they mineral, vegetal, animal or sensible beings, and the power of images, words and sentences".[45] Because of the lack of rational demonstrations, though, "those who oppose the secrets of the philosophers" deny their validity, and see magical "experiments" as devilish tricks or outright lies. The recourse to authority is thus mandatory for whoever wishes to convince them, because "against deniers there is not much to dispute about": the only way to silence them is "to defeat them with truthful autorities".[46] Their eagerness to dismiss as well any textual reference that does not disapprove of magic makes it necessary to bring forth the strongest possible authorities that no theologian or lawyer could deny. Just as Peter adduced Jerome's authority in support of al-Kindî, he now calls three theologically legitimate witnesses in defense of the "secrets of the philosophers".

The first one is Thomas Aquinas, whose *De esse et essentiis* contains a very positive assessment of astrological images (76v–78r).[47] It is an apocryphal work, written in the fourteenth century. Peter is well aware that its authenticity was not generally accepted by the scholars of his time. The main argument against it is that it contradicts Thomas's conclusion against astrological images in the *Summa theologiæ*.[48] Peter's reply is that the *Summa* reflects an earlier stage of Thomas's philosophy, whereas *De esse et essentiis*, written in the last period of his life, stands as his philosophical testament, recording his progression from denial to assent concerning magic and alchemy.[49] Peter recounts a personal memory in support of this opinion: the first time he was told of it was in 1450 at the University of Cologne, during the lunch which followed his promotion as master of arts, "when some doctor in theology recited the image experimented by Saint Thomas".[50] The theologian thus acknowledged Thomas as the author of the work, referring to the astrological image described therein, borrowed from "a very ancient book written by Abel, son of Adam": the *Liber Abelis de virtutibus planetarum et omnibus rerum mundanarum virtutibus*. This image was designed to prevent horses from crossing a stream. "It was the only image I put to the test", says the Pseudo-Thomas, "and since this experiment succeeded I learned that images are true and can be made."[51] After the Cologne encounter, Peter continues, the authenticity of *De esse et essentiis* was confirmed to him "by learned men in France, Italy and Flanders".[52]

The second witness is Albert the Great. Peter feels that some readers might be sceptical about the *De mirabilibus mundi*'s authorship, due to its outspoken endorsement of magic; he thus turns to the *Speculum astronomiæ* as an unquestionably authentic work – according to what was then a commonly held belief – "on lawful and unlawful arts".[53] He enlists, rather forcedly, Albert among those who "defend the art of magic, and especially the sort of astrology which is called natural",[54] because the penultimate chapter of the *Speculum*[55] "tacitly responds to the arguments of detractors" by stating that every astrological image should not necessarily be considered "an exorcism or invocation".[56] And he recalls, as we saw above, that according to Albert "nigromantic books" should be preserved for a possible future use. All this, Peter concludes, was written by Albert "in recommendation of astronomy and the sciences of the secret workings".[57]

The third witness is the strongest authority of all, for it is none other than "the friend of God named Moses", "an expert of the stars, who was a great magus".[58] Peter takes up the story, narrated by Petrus Comestor in his *Historia scholastica*, of the magical ring wrought by Moses to make sure that his Ethiopian wife would forget he ever married her (80v–81r).[59] This is his major asset, since the story comes from the respected twelfth-century handbook through which theology students all across Europe were initiated into biblical history. He says triumphantly:

> Let the enemies of the secret workings answer me upon that. It reduced to silence every theologian I met, and I never found one who knew what to respond about this last reference, even though, by cavillation, they may invent something in regard to some of the others I mentioned before.[60]

In stark contrast to the unshakable diffidence of many educated men, Peter praises the spontaneous wisdom of common people, who make earthen images "in order to acquire the health of the whole body or of one of its parts" and dedicate them "to Saint Anthony or to another saint"; they are led to do so "by a heavenly instinct" that "inclines their imaginative spirit and the force of their imagination to such sacrifices".[61] To Peter, these votive offerings are nothing but a variant form of the sacrifices dealt with by al-Kindî: though the crowds believe that saints or angels intercede to fulfil their wishes, what actually makes these ex-votos work is the "celestial harmony", whose rays are focused on the prospected outcome by the people's desire and their "imaginative spirits".[62] Popular ingenuousness is opposed by Peter to the hypocrisy of friars (he mentions the Franciscan "observants"), who anathematize astral magic as a pagan cult while they tolerate that such offerings "be brought into their churches": why, he asks, do they tacitly encourage practices they do not approve of, "if not for the sake of money"?[63]

Having concluded that "science has no enemy apart from the ignorant",[64] Peter delves deeper into the causes of ignorance with an essay "On the Hunting of Truth",[65] in which he enumerates the conditions that may help or impede the human intellect "to discern the truth" and understand "the secrets of Nature, which are astonishing and unknown to most people", although they were "perceived and known by many of the philosophers who came before us".[66] To grasp this sort of truth, rational learning, as we saw, is not sufficient. Nevertheless, as "Plato" wrote,[67] a thorough knowledge of dialectics, physics, astrology and nigromancy is required, for without these sciences one "cannot understand and verify the things which the philosophers wrote down, nor certify the things which appear before the senses of men". Astrology in particular, which teaches "the aspects and figures of the stars, whence come the powers and heavenly properties of each [sublunar] thing", and nigromancy, "by which are manifested the immaterial substances [i.e. spirits] which distribute and govern all that is good and bad in [sublunar] things", are essential to the point.[68] But imagination remains the key for whoever wants to understand, practise or resist magical operations.

A healthy balance of the imaginative faculty depends upon six factors (84v–88v): the quality of air; food and drink; exercise and quiet; sleep and waking; abstinence and repletion;

and the accidents of the soul. These are, with only slight differences, the six "non-natural things" (*res non naturales*) established by a medical tradition going back to Galen. So called because they affect the human body externally and do not proceed "from its own nature and internal composition",[69] they became the central topic of the widespread literature on "regimens of health" (*regimina sanitatis*), which was at its peak in Peter's time. He stresses how the non-natural things, when distempered, impede both "bodily health and the good disposition to understand and perform the works" of natural magic. To meet these conditions, which "anyone who wishes to have an adequate knowledge of the secrets of Nature" should possess,[70] "cordial and cheering medicines", together with "medicines which comfort the brain", are of great help.[71]

Peter also recommends leading a decorous and chaste life, wearing precious stones and "staying away from the incantations of old women or from the company of abusive people, for they are secretly harmful".[72] The seeker of truth must dedicate himself to "elevated, subtle, rare and pleasant matters, through which the senses and the intellect are disposed to the comprehension of secret and occult things".[73] Conversely, "mechanical labour, trade, litigations, and worldly matters in general are to be avoided".[74] This caveat against worldly or secular occupations is a recurring theme in the *Lucidarius*.

A list of "elevated, subtle and rare" questions on "secret and occult things" is appended (90r–92r). From then on, the work becomes for the most part a blueprint of sorts for potential elaboration, as only a few of these typically scholastic *quæstiones* are formally answered, the rest being merely enumerated. One which is fully treated is: "Whether it is lawful to acquire knowledge through fasting, abstinence, the scrutiny of figures, the psalmody of mysterious names, reading, meditating and perceiving characters, figures and sundry forms."[75] Peter's answer is that it is lawful. He seizes the opportunity to point out that

> the process of the notory art helps sedate the movement and flow of the vital, natural and animal spirits, notably those of the brain, by which the soul is sedated and [a man] is made prudent, wise, and capable of prophecy.[76]

One of the unworked questions is thus implicitly answered: "Whether the notory art may be practised lawfully".[77]

Systematic exposition returns with the "Summary on the Office of Spirits",[78] in which angelic hierarchies are described after the Pseudo-Dionysian fashion (92v–97r). This again gives way to a series of *quæstiones* concerning the attitude of angels in regard to mankind (97r–101v), mostly focused on the knowledge that they may have of human thoughts and desires and whether they can interfere with them, and on the possibility that humans may influence "celestial spirits such as the intelligences which move the heavens".[79] Peter's answer to this last question is yes, since "it is proved by experience and by the authority of the Holy Scripture".[80]

After the exposé on angels comes a summary "On Evil Spirits".[81] There Peter eventually defines what he means by "nigromancy":

> Generally speaking, we may call "nigromancy" any art which makes one capable of summoning evil spirits, so that they manifest themselves in order to do whatever the invocator wants, whether the invocation pursues good or bad goals.[82]

Once more, a series of *quæstiones* follows, but this time all of them are formally answered: "Whether some people are naturally more apt than others to be nigromancers or to dominate evil spirits" – the answer is yes[83]; "Whether divination by invocation of demons is lawful" – the answer is no[84]; "Whether someone may lawfully invoke the devil to perform a task" – the answer is yes[85]; "Whether heavenly bodies may terrify demons and imprint something upon them" – yes again.[86] The last questions deal with exorcisms (107r–13r).

The final sentence of the chapter on evil spirits serves as a conclusion to the *Lucidarius*:

> From what has been elucidated above, one can plainly see how marvelous and explainable is the virtue implanted in [natural] things, whence proceed works also made by men, so wonderful and astonishing to the crowd that they are deemed incredible. In many cases though, the wise shall be inclined to believe that such events are similar to things manifest to the senses and proven by experience.[87]

In other words, the knowledge of occult causes makes wonderment cease, and this is what ultimately distinguishes the wise from the ignorant, as stated in *De mirabilibus mundi*: "The duty of the wise man is to put an end to marvels".[88] This is followed by a conventional closing formula, with a praise of God and an "Amen", which does not imply that Peter's work was really finished, nor that he stopped writing on similar topics after that. The loose structure of the last chapters, with their series of answered and unanswered *quæstiones*, makes clear that the work was still in progress, and that Peter could consider going back to them afterwards. As a matter of fact, the manuscript does not end here.

Another *quæstio* appears after the conclusion: "Whether those who are in Purgatory may be absolved of their sins by the prayers of men on earth".[89] The incomplete answer consists only of a "third hypothesis" (*tertia suppositio*), which states that "the Pope can bind infernal spirits so as to restrain them from causing harm to the souls dwelling in Purgatory".[90] Thus, Peter grants the Pope a power which is akin to nigromancy, with the difference that, according to the definition quoted above, a nigromancer "summons evil spirits", while the Pope may bind them but not make them appear. Peter denies him, though, the power to grant indulgences to a living man, that is, the remission of his sins, for "neither the Pope nor a Franciscan"[91] has the authority to perform an action that only "an agent of infinite power", i.e. God, can do.[92] This thesis is similar to that of John Wyclif (d. 1389),[93] condemned at the Council of Constance (1414–18).

Then, there is an essay "On the Wars and Future Acts of Men, and on their Present and Future Mores",[94] again in the form of a *quæstio*: "Whether times to come shall be worse than times past."[95] A cryptic astrological argumentation is displayed. It suggests that, in order to guess whether the misfortunes of the King of France – Charles VIII, who had just lost Burgundy and Artois and was starting his Italian War – would continue or not, one has to know whether his nativity is in accordance with "the figure of the sky at the time of the beginning of his reign": for without such conditions, "no person of royal descent may maintain his kingdom or keep it in peace for a long time".[96] Even though this *quæstio prima* is not followed by any *quæstio secunda*, the essay appears to be complete, for it ends with an "Amen" and a formal explicit, bearing the date – the evening of 3 July 1494 – of its expedition from Lons-le-Saulnier to Peter's "forever true friend", a physician at the court of Maximilian I, "King of the Romans", named "Master Wolf".[97]

After these *quæstiones*, an intriguing document is preserved (118r–119v): a series of theses (*propositiones*) against "some Franciscan" (*quidam cordiger*), who claimed that astrology is not a true science and that Augustine rightly condemned it. Peter's response is double. First, it is "notorious" that "Augustine is deficient on many matters, as he himself acknowledged before his death, when he retracted several things he had written previously" (an allusion to Augustine's *Retractationes*). Second, "many opinions are known to be heretical today, which in earlier times were piously believed to be true by men of knowledge".[98] If the contents of heresy are mutable through history, then some opinions considered heretical today might be accepted in the future. This implicit statement justifies Peter's endorsement of condemned works and doctrines such as Wyclif's position on indulgences. And thus, contrary to what the leading theologians of his time may say, he asserts that "the highest point of astronomy is magic, or the science of images".[99] Peter also declares that "the astrologer-physician" (*medicus astrologus*) has the capacity, granted "by the powers and constellations of the stars", to make wise men out of fools and to bring back lunatics to mental health.[100] Peter then warns the Franciscan that he intends to dispute against him "next Sunday", i.e. in church.[101] The letter containing the theses "was sent to the Franciscan, who fled and never showed up"[102] – fortunately for Peter, who certainly would have had a difficult time, had he expounded his views so openly in public. Whether the anecdote of the fleeing monk is true or made up, it is a witness of the tensions surrounding astrology and astral magic at the end of the fifteenth century, and of the naiveté of Peter of Zealand, who was convinced that he had arguments up his sleeve so solid as to silence any opposer.

This first series of additional texts is followed by a proper documentary appendix.[103] The manuscript, in its truncated state, ends with the reproduction of two contemporary works: Pico della Mirandola's Magical, Orphic and Cabalistic theses (199v–135v), excerpted from his nine hundred *Conclusiones*,[104] published in 1486 and banned by the Church the following year; and the first pages of Jacques Lefèvre d'Étaples's *De magia naturali*, Book I (136r–139v), written in the 1490s. They are listed (114r–v) with three other works that are not present in the manuscript: a treatise "on precious stones, on seals, and on the figures of the planets, following the method of Arnold of Villanova"; "some excerpts from *Picatrix*, useful to this noble art", i.e. natural magic; and "some other theoretical considerations" by Johannes Trithemius, which may refer either to his April 1499 letter to Arnold Bostius or to the *Steganographia*, completed during the same or the following year.[105] Thus, the *Lucidarius* was to be followed by six works pertaining to its subject matter, some of them extremely recent and even written after its completion. Most surprising is the presence of *De magia naturali*, a work kept hidden by its author,[106] which was impossible to find at such an early stage unless Peter or a close friend of his had direct acquaintance with Lefèvre or his dedicatee, Germain de Ganay, a powerful royal counsellor and Parisian cleric (d. 1520). This, together with the wealth of works on astrology and magic quoted or mentioned by Peter, demonstrates that he was not an isolated amateur but was connected to an active underground milieu, in which forbidden texts were searched for, read and passed on. As Sophie Page and Frank Klaassen have shown, monasteries could be a hotbed for such activities.[107]

The presence of Pico's *Conclusiones* is also puzzling because the *Lucidarius* in itself is devoid of any humanistic influence whatsoever. It relies exclusively on medieval and scholastic sources – a fact that may be easily explained if we consider that Peter "compiled" his work in his old age, and that the modular structure of the *Lucidarius*, made of *compendia* and *quæstiones* on medical or "occult" matters, facilitated the recycling of earlier collections of notes. Then, he began to gather new works in order to keep himself up to date with the latest developments in magical theory. Book I of Lefèvre's treatise is akin to Peter's *Lucidarius*, in that it expounds medicinal and astral magic in a manner that bears some resemblance to *De mirabilibus mundi*; the influences from Pico and Ficino it contains are not overwhelming, nor is it written in humanist style, whereas the following parts of the work are distinctly

Neo-Platonic and full of classical references.[108] Pico's *Conclusiones* are another matter entirely, especially regarding their most enigmatic cabalistic side, and their main relation with Peter's project is that they confirmed that magic was an ancient wisdom, grounded in biblical secret truths.

The great absence is Marsilio Ficino. Roughly the same age as Peter (he was born in 1433), he often used the same sources – as far as magic, astrology and medicine were concerned – and dealt with the same matters, notably in Book III of his *De vita*, published in 1489. Peter seems unaware of Ficino's works and translations, since he knows only the medieval Plato. It is very strange that, accessible as they were, they could escape his attention while he eagerly collected other hard-to-find works.

It would be too long to enumerate all the books or authors mentioned by Peter. We have already seen what use he made of theological sources. On medicine, Avicenna stands out as his main authority. On astrology, Ptolemy is cited several times, together with Alî ibn Ridwân's commentary on the *Centiloquium*. On medicinal alchemy, John of Rupescissa and Pseudo-Arnaldian works are placed in the foreground. And on magic, the core sources are *De radiis*, *Picatrix*, *De mirabilibus mundi* and Pietro d'Abano, around which Peter built his *Lucidarius*, in close connection with Avicenna's *De anima*. Solomonic magic is cursorily mentioned several times,[109] and there is hardly any reference to Hermes.[110]

All those sources and disciplines are glued together by the focus on imagination that characterizes Peter's conception. The core topic of the whole *Lucidarius* is to establish how imagination and the "imaginative spirits" that serve it may be strengthened, protected from accidents or intrusions, modified and directed. This way, the two explicit goals of the *Lucidarius* are carried out, namely the preservation or restoration of health, and "how to obviate the evil arts".[111] On the last point, however, Peter's stance is ambiguous, to say the least. He promotes astral magic, which to him is not an "evil art" at all, but he also advocates the notory art and (with the support of "Plato") nigromancy.[112] Whether Peter's involvement in nigromancy went further than a mere generic praise is impossible to ascertain. In contrast to his discretion on that matter, the profusion of astrological technicalities he displays shows that he duly practised astrology, for medicinal as well as divinatory and apotropaic ends (through *judicia* and *electiones*).

The "Elucidation of Marvelous Things" is by no means a magical handbook. It is a work on magical theory, which investigates in much more detail the occult natural principles upon which magic is grounded than the workings of magic itself. In regard to recent discussions about the concept of "author-magician", I would definitely say that Peter of Zealand does not enter this category. He is not a magician but, as it were, a metamagician, who does not teach magic but expounds its philosophical foundations – just as metamathematics deals with the philosophical foundations of mathematics. Furthermore, he does not introduce himself as an author in the full sense of the word, but as a compiler: he states in the prologue that he "decided to compile an elucidation" (*lucidarium quemquam compilaturus*).[113] It is not an affectation of modesty, since the derivative nature of his work is apparent from the onset. It can be described as a summary of summaries, which paraphrases and digests works already aimed at theoretical synthesis such as Avicenna's *De viribus cordis et medicinis cordialibus*, al-Kindî's *De radiis*, and the *De mirabilibus mundi*.

Very little, if anything, of what Peter says is original, but that is not the point. He did not mean to collect his personal views but those of the physicians and the "secret philosophers" – who are to him, in typically medieval fashion, the real "authors", i.e. authorities – against the theologians and lawyers who refuse to acknowledge them. Therefore, his singularity lies more in the way he puts together the authoritative bricks of his intellectual construction, and in the candor of his statements, often verging on heresy, than in some unheard of conception. Showing off originality would have been at odds with his focus on demonstrating the consensus of the wise men of the past, be they natural philosophers or holy men: a consensus so strong as to overwhelm the arguments of "those who oppose the secrets of the philosophers" – the paradox being that this consensus is in effect so weak that it needs to be supported by an array of apocryphal works to appear more legitimate. The focus on consensus and the compositional unity of Peter's *Lucidarius* are exemplified by the way he rephrases his sources so as to make them echo Avicenna's or al-Kindî's conceptions.[114] Peter is expert at eliciting implicit affinities in the different works he stitches together, and it makes their combination very coherent.

Despite the fact that this work remained unread, the *Lucidarius* was not a notebook compiled for Peter's private use. He wanted to persuade, using the standard scholastic disputational methods in defense of the "secret sciences", not only through the form of *quæstiones* or sets of *propositiones*, but also *suppositiones*, literally "hypotheses", into which several chapters are divided. The latter formal choice may be a precaution, aimed at pretending that Peter's assertions were mere exploratory views. This cosmetic "hypothetical" stance is at odds with his tendency to state his positions rather boldly, with recurring phrases such as "I, Peter of Zealand" (*ego Petrus de Zelandia*),[115] and to go straightforwardly against what he perceives as common and unfounded prejudices.

Why did he fail to publish a work that was obviously his life task? The easy answer is that he never really completed it; but this may have been the consequence of a semi-conscious fear that its release could put him in very deep trouble, just as it happened to Pico in 1487 and to Trithemius in 1499.

Notes

1 See Jean-Marc Mandosio, "Latin technique du xiie au xviiie siècle," *Annuaire de l'École pratique des hautes études: Section des sciences historiques et philologiques* <http://ashp.revues.org/249>, 141 (2008–09), 143 (2010–11), 144 (2011–12), 145 (2012–13), 146 (2013–14), 147 (2014–15), 148 (2015–16); Jean-Marc Mandosio, "The Use of al-Kindî's Treatise *On Rays* in Peter of Zealand's *Elucidation of Marvelous Things* (End of the 15th Century)," *Micrologus* 24 (2016): 425–56.
2 Brussels, Bibliothèque Royale de Belgique, MS Latin 10870-75 (one or more quires are missing at the end). I am preparing the edition of Peter's *Lucidarius*. All subsequent references to Peter's works are to this manuscript.
3 *Opus Petri de Silento*, in *Theatrum chemicum*, vol. 4 (Strasbourg: Lazarus Zetzner, 1659), 985–97.
4 See below, note 71.
5 He calls himself "Petrus Francho" (or "Franconis") "de Zelandia". His name would be in French "Pierre Franchon" or "Françon", and in Dutch "Pieter Francken" or "Vranckx".
6 Hence his other name: "Petrus de Brielis" or "Brielis frater".
7 "De rebus mirabilibus et permultum extraneis apparentibus clare ante sensus hominum fere omnium, est ligatio hominum, et virtutum naturalium, vitalium, animalium et motivarum, breviter omnium virtutum, per incantationes, per verba et fascinationes, et gestus et modos varios et fere innumerabiles, et per imagines et caracteres, scripturas, formas et figuras, et per multa valde diversa quæ apud intellectum communis populi videntur impossibilia nec causam sufficientem habentia," f. 3r.
8 *De mirabilibus mundi*, ed. Antonella Sannino, *Il "De mirabilibus mundi" tra tradizione magica e filosofia naturale* (Florence: Sismel Edizioni del Galluzzo, 2011), 85. The work was first printed as *Opus Alberti Magni de mirabilibus mundi* (Cologne: Johann Koelhoff the Elder, ca. 1473).
9 "Lucidarium quemdam compilaturus, dignum duxi primum de viribus humani cordis compendiose aliqua præmittere, ut reliqua clarius intelligibilia fiant, et pro sanitate et vitæ etiam

prolongatione quisque scire valeat qualiter se gubernare debeat, et malis etiam artibus obviare in parte non modica," f. 3r.
10 *Compendium de viribus cordis*, ff. 3r–12r.
11 *De cordialibus et lætificantibus multipliciter dictis*, ff. 12r–16v.
12 This work was appended to Avicenna's *Canon medicinæ* in late medieval and Renaissance editions. A critical edition by Michael McVaugh is in progress.
13 *Compendium de radiis*, ff. 16v–47v.
14 Al-Kindî, *De radiis*, ed. Marie-Thérèse d'Alverny and Françoise Hudry, *Archives d'histoire doctrinale et littéraire du Moyen Âge* 41 (1974): 139–260. For the sake of convenience, I assume that al-Kindî is the author of the work, even though this issue is debated.
15 "[…] secundum sententiam Alchindi, viri excellentissimi in omnibus mirabilibus," f. 22v.
16 See d'Alverny and Hudry's introduction, 139–41.
17 "[…] adducendo sententias quorundam aliorum doctorum et auctoritates sanctorum quantum potero," f. 22v. For a complete survey of Peter's glosses, see Mandosio, "The Use of al-Kindî's Treatise," 440–55.
18 Letter 53 (to Paulinus of Nola) in modern editions of Jerome's correspondence.
19 *Saint Jerome's Hebrew Questions on Genesis*, transl. C. T. R. Hayward (Oxford: Clarendon Press, 1995), 67.
20 "[…] ad instar virgarum arte et ingenio Jacob sic formatarum. Quare vides clare quod forma et figura etiam artificialis inducit effectum et variat effectum etiam naturalem. Ita imago Æthiopis depicta et concepta in imaginativa mulieris hora casus seminis in matrice potest esse causa ut filius nascatur niger ut Æthiopus extra tamen Ethiopiam, […] cæli tamen natura cum arte ad hoc operante," f. 41r.
21 "Et bene fecit ecclesia prohibendo ne publice in universitate hæc legantur, ne animo vindicandi et appetitu nocendi, divites seu magnates, reges et principes saperent et per se hæc vel per alios in effectu deducerent, et ipsi seipsos invicem destruerent. Quare Picatrix libro primo incantat illos ad quos scientia horum poterit pervenire, ne pandatur indoctis et indignis sapere, sed solum personis secretis et sapidis, sub pœna anathematis," f. 63v. Cf. *Picatrix: The Latin Version of the "Ghâyat al-Hakîm"*, ed. David Pingree (London: Warburg Institute, 1986), 6 (Prologue, 4), 15 (Book I, 4, 33).
22 "De libris vero nigromanticis, sine præjudicio melioris sententiæ, videtur quod magis debeant reservari quam destrui et comburi. Tempus enim jam prope est, quod propter quasdam causas quas modo taceo, quo saltem occasionaliter proderit inspexisse illos," f. 80r. Cf. *Speculum astronomiæ*, 17, ed. and transl. Paola Zambelli et al., *The "Speculum astronomiæ" and Its Enigma: Astrology, Theology and Science in Albertus Magnus and His Contemporaries* (Dordrecht: Kluwer, 1992), 270–71.
23 *An spiritus potest immutare voluntatem hominis et per quem modum*, ff. 47v–50r.
24 *De visionibus et apparitionibus*, ff. 50r–51r.
25 *Utrum confidentia infirmi de medico conferat ad ejus sanitatem habendam*, ff. 51r–56r.
26 *Utrum incantatio conferat in curatione ægritudinum* (*Ex conciliatore in medicinis dictus Petrus de Albano Paduanus doctor famosus*, ff. 56r–64r). This chapter of the *Lucidarius* was most inaccurately edited by Béatrice Delaurenti, "Variations sur le pouvoir des incantations: le traité *Ex Conciliatore in medicinis dictus Petrus de Albano* de Pierre Franchon de Zélande," *Archives d'histoire doctrinale et littéraire du Moyen Âge* 74 (2007): 173–235. She has also edited Pietro d'Abano's original *quæstio*: Delaurenti, "Pietro d'Abano et les incantations: présentation, édition et traduction de la *differentia 156* du *Conciliator*," in *Médecine, astrologie et magie entre Moyen Âge et Renaissance*, ed. Jean-Patrice Boudet et al. (Florence: Sismel Edizioni del Galluzzo, 2012), 39–105.
27 "[…] experientia potest monstrari et demum ratione persuaderi præcantationem conferre […], ut aperte illud summum sacramentum cum aliis multis ostendit eucharistiæ." Pietro d'Abano, *Conciliator, differentia 156*, ed. Delaurenti, 77; see also her comments in "Variations sur le pouvoir des incantations," 192–93.
28 "Quare patet quod conditiones et circumstantiæ requisitæ multum operantur ad executionem effectus," f. 58v. Cf. *Compendium de radiis*, ff. 36v, 37v, 40v; al-Kindî, *De radiis*, 244, 245, 251.
29 "Et ideo si sacerdos dicat verba illa absque intentione instituentis vel memoria, dico ego Petrus de Zelandia quod non fit translatio panis in sacramentum," f. 58v.
30 "Quare dicunt communiter vetulæ et simplices in quibus maligni spiritus agunt, quod comedunt et bibunt cum spiritibus et cum amicis et vicinis in silvis et in viridario vel in consimili loco, et equitant super cattum vel lupum et volitant per aerem, transiunt per vitrum, et infinita impossibilia.

Sed hæc omnia vere judicantur: referendo ad apparitiones imaginarias, vere dicunt se vidisse et hæc fecisse secundum proxima instrumenta per quæ fiunt eorum judicia. Quia secundum visa illorum fantasmata intelligunt, judicant et eligunt, agunt et voluntas eorum immutatur, sed decipiuntur. Quia malignus spiritus, disturbando motu inordinato humores et spiritus et species ac fantasmata, fecit apparere interius quæ exterius non sunt in rerum natura," f. 48v–49r.

31 "Ita sunt consimili modo quidam asserentes se videre gentes armorum equitare in aere versus occidens vel oriens aut septentrionem, et antecedere crucem sancti Andreæ; alii crucifixum; alii nostram dominam apparere in aere cum sancto Johanne; atque infinita fantasmata talia diversa, secundum diversitatem spiritus imaginarii et specierum seu fantasmatum," f. 51r.

32 "Et hoc est quotidianum apud medicos et bene cognitum," f. 51r.

33 *Ex secretis Alberti Magni*, f. 64r–76r.

34 *De mirabilibus mundi*, ed. Sannino, 85–107.

35 Pseudo-Plato, *Liber aneguemis*, ed. Paolo Scopelliti and Abdessattar Chaouech (Milan: Mimesis, 2006).

36 "Et ideo quantum fuerit possibile occultatione utendum est, quia deitatem minuit qui secreta mysteria divulgat, ut dicit Plato," f. 56v. Here, Peter follows Pietro d'Abano (*Conciliator, differentia 156*, ed. Delaurenti, 71), but the sentence quoted came not from Plato but from Marbode's Lapidary: "Nam majestatem minuit qui mystica vulgat," Marbode of Rennes, *Liber lapidum*, v. 8, ed. Maria Esther Herrera (Paris: Les Belles Lettres, 2005), 7. Peter ascribes it to Plato, probably under the influence of Macrobius, *In somnium Scipionis*, I, 2, 17–21, ed. Mireille Armisen-Marchetti (Paris: Les Belles Lettres, 2001), 8–9, who explained at length that this opinion was typical of the Platonists.

37 *Picatrix*, ed. Pingree, II, 12, 59 (88).

38 An example is given below, note 68.

39 See Dag Nikolaus Hasse, "*Plato Arabico-Latinus*: Philosophy, Wisdom Literature, Occult Sciences," in *The Platonic Tradition in the Middle Ages: A Doxographic Approach*, ed. Stephen Gersh and Maarten J. F. M. Hoenen (Berlin: Walter De Gruyter, 2002), 56.

40 See Julien Véronèse, "Pietro d'Abano magicien à la Renaissance: le cas de l'*Elucidarius magice* (ou *Lucidarium artis nigromantice*)," in *Médecine, astrologie et magie entre Moyen Âge et Renaissance*, ed. Boudet et al., 295–330.

41 *Contra adversantes secreta philosophorum*, ff. 76r–81v.

42 "Sunt in hoc mundo plures viri litterati, ut theologi et juristæ, qui ut plurimum adversantur et secreta philosophorum condemnant ex ignorantia quam de eis habent," f. 76r.

43 "[…] omnes artes secretæ majores […], quia sunt coopertæ, non declarantur ratione sed experientia," f. 74r.

44 "Quia multorum mirabilium operum sunt tam latentes effectus quod humanus intellectus nequit eos comprehendere […], quare standum est experimento," f. 75r–v.

45 "Et in ipso [homine] invenitur efficaciam omnium rerum et mineralium et vegetabilium et animatorum et sensitivorum et imaginum et verborum virtus ac sermonum," f. 74r.

46 "Et quia contra negantes non est multum pro nunc disputandum, sed eos auctoritate veridica devincere ut deinceps sileant […]," f. 76r.

47 *Opusculum præclarum beati Thomæ Aquinatis quod de esse et essentiis tum realibus tum intentionalibus inscribitur*, ed. Ludovicus Rigius (Venice: Santriter & De Sanctis, 1488), I, 4, 2 (*Utrum forma corporum supercælestium sit esse…*).

48 "Et si dicat quis quod sanctus Thomas in secunda secundæ quæstione 95 [sic] reprobavit imagines astrologicas, igitur vel hic liber non est ejus vel contradicit sibi ipsi […]," f. 78r–v. Cf. Thomas Aquinas, *Summa theologiæ*, IIa IIæ, 96, 2.

49 "[…] dico quod hic bene fatetur quia diu non credidit talia in diebus suis prioribus, et quod liber hic ab eo editus est posterioriter scripto suo in secunda secundæ. Quia in isto dicit infra de mineralibus quod diu non credidit alchimiam esse veram scientiam […]. Tamen dicit quod tandem devenit per rationem naturalem et per experientiam ad verum effectum, et narrat ibidem quamplurima per eum experta in alchimia," f. 78v.

50 "Et quod hic liber de essentiis realibus ejus sit, habui primo in anno jubilæi 1450 in universitate Coloniensi, hora prandi promotionis meæ in artibus, ubi quidam doctor theologiæ recitavit jam dictam imaginem expertam sancti Thomæ," f. 78v.

51 "Non tamen has imagines probavi omnes sed unam. […] Propter quod experimento didici veras esse imagines et fieri posse," f. 77v. Cf. Pseudo-Thomas, *De esse et essentiis*, I, 4, 2.

52 "Et de post in Francia et Italia et in Flandria a doctis idem teneri, scilicet quod sit ejus liber præfatus de essentiis realibus ad regem Siciliæ," f. 78v–79r.
53 "Insuper auctoritas Alberti Magni est ad idem in libro suo de artibus licitis et illicitis […]," f. 79r.
54 "[…] ubi defendit magicam artem, et maxime astrologicam quæ dicitur naturalis," f. 79r.
55 *Speculum astronomiæ*, 16, ed. Zambelli et al., 270–71.
56 "Et idem Albertus infra circa finem libri respondet tacite ad argumenta contradicentium, dicens quod […] hoc non videtur esse exorcismus vel invocatio […]," f. 79v.
57 "Hæc ille Albertus in speculo, in recommendationem astronomiæ et secretorum operum scientiarum," f. 80v.
58 "Adhuc restat adducere contra adversantes testimonium magnum, ut ipsius amici Dei qui dicitur Moyses, vir astrorum peritus," f. 80v. "[…] Moyses, vir astrorum peritus qui magnus fuit magus," f. 76r–v.
59 Petrus Comestor, *Historia scholastica*, II (*Liber Exodi*), 6 (*De uxore Moysi Æthiopissa*), ed. Emanuel Navarro (Madrid: Antonio Gonzalez de Reyes, 1699), in *Patrologia Latina*, vol. 198 (Paris: Migne, 1855), 1144.
60 "Respondeant mihi ad hæc adversarii secretorum operum. Obmutescunt enim hic omnes theologi quos vidi, nec vidi unum nec inveni qui sciat respondere ad istud ultimo inductum, licet cavillando aliquid fabulantur super quibusdam aliis præallegatis," f. 81r.
61 "Confirmat prædicta ipsum vulgus quod ducitur instinctu naturæ cælestis. Nam imagines varias componit terreas integras et partiales, ut imagines capitis aut pectoris, brachiorum et manuum, alii pedum et tibiarum, cum confidentia magna et ferventi desiderio, causa adipiscendi sanitatem vel totius corporis aut alicujus partis, offerentes talia sancto Anthonio aut alteri sancto, juxta diversos vulgi instinctus inclinantes spiritum eorum imaginarium et virtutem eorum imaginativam ad talia sacrificia," f. 81v.
62 "Cum ergo obsecrationes ad deum ab hominibus devotæ mentis desiderio et cum debita solemnitate fiunt pro aliquo motu inducendo in subjecta materia, sequitur optatus effectus, harmonia cælesti in omnibus primo loco cooperante. Ad deum non solum diriguntur obsecrationes, sed etiam ad spiritus. […] Cum autem motus et imagines fiunt in aere vel in alio elemento vel elementato […], non est ex operatione spirituum sed tantum ex conditione cælestis harmoniæ, materiam aptante ad tales nutus et talium imaginum receptionem […]," *Compendium de radiis*, f. 38v. Cf. al-Kindî, *De radiis*, ed. d'Alverny and Hudry, 247–48.
63 "Et cur tunc observantes et alii requisitas imagines arte factas sufferunt apportari ad eorum templa nescio, si sileant et proculcant hoc potius, nisi propter eorum emolumenta," f. 81v.
64 "Concludamus igitur quod scientia non habet inimicum nisi ignorantem," f. 81r.
65 *De veritatis venatione*, ff. 81v–92v.
66 "Primum quidem perquærendo quæ permultum impediunt intellectum nostrum discernere verum ad ejus perfectum, et secretorum naturæ opera quæ admiranda sunt et a multis ignota. […] quæ tamen a nostris prædecessoribus philosophorum plurimis fuerunt percepta et cognita," f. 82r.
67 Cf. Pseudo-Plato, *Liber aneguemis*, freely quoted in *De mirabilibus mundi*, ed. Sannino, 97: "Plato vero dixit…"
68 "Plato vero dicit in libro tegumenti: Qui non fuerit artifex dialecticæ […], et qui non fuerit eruditus in scientia naturali […], et qui non fuerit doctus in astronomia et in aspectibus et figuris stellarum, ex quibus est virtus et proprietas sublimis uniuscujusque rerum, et quarto qui non fuerit doctus in nigromantia, qua manifestantur substantiæ immateriales quæ dispensant et administrant omne quod est in rebus ex bono et malo, non poterit intelligere et verificare omnia quæ philosophi scripserunt, et certificare omnia quæ apparebunt apud sensus hominum, et evadet cum tristitia animi," f. 70r.
69 "Quæ sex res non naturales dicuntur sic respectu nostri corporis, quia sunt ei extrinsecæ, et non de sua natura et compositione intrinseca," f. 84v.
70 "Quare si corpori occurrant etiam absque temperamento, idest modo distemperato, ipsum ducendo extra temperamentum, tunc impediunt corporis sanitatem et bonam intelligendi dispositionem et exercendi opera, ut convenit bene sapienti secreta naturæ rimari volenti ac sapere," f. 84v.
71 "Secundum adjutorium est uti cordialibus, uti lætificantibus, uti cerebrum confortantibus, de quibus latius in libello nostro de prolongatione vitæ et retardatione mortis mentionem fecimus," f. 89r. See also the section of the *Lucidarius* dedicated to "cordial and cheering medicines" (above, note 11).
72 "Tertium adjutorium est portare se honeste et caste, lapides pretiosos penes se habere […]. Quartum est se cavere ab incantationibus vetularum aut abusorum conversationibus, ne impedimenta secrete inferant," f. 85v.

73 "Quintum est occupari circa altissimas, subtiles et raras ac placentes materias, cum per ipsas disponitur sensus et intellectus ad secreta occultaque intelligendum," f. 89v.
74 "Secundum quod nocet sunt opera mechanica, mercationes et emptiones ac venditiones, placitationes, et omnes occupationes circa temporalia," f. 88r.
75 "Utrum sit licitum acquirere scientiam per jejunia, abstinentias, figurarum inspexiones, et per ignota nomina psallendo, legendo et meditando intuendoque caracteres et figuras ac formas diversas," f. 91v.
76 "Secundo, dico quod ille processus artis notoriæ confert ad sedandum motus et inundatione spirituum vitalium, naturalium et spirituum animalium, ut cerebri, quibus sedatur anima, et fit prudens et sapiens ac ad prophetiam aptus," f. 91v.
77 "Utrum ars notoria possit licite exerceri," f. 91r.
78 *Compendium de spirituum officiis*, ff. 92v–101v.
79 "An spiritus hominis potest immutare spiritus cælestes ut intelligentias cæli motrices," f. 99v.
80 "Dicendum est igitur ad quæsitum quod sic. Probatur experimento et auctoritate sacræ scripturæ [...]," f. 100v.
81 *De malignis spiritibus*, ff. 101v–113r.
82 "Et sic generaliter potest dici nigromantia omnis ars, omne magisterium convocandi malignos spiritus ut appareant ad aliquid faciendum quod invocator intendit, sive ad bonum sive ad malum fuerit talis invocatio [...]," f. 102r. See also above, note 68.
83 "Movetur hic quæstio, utrum scilicet aliqui sunt naturaliter plus habiles et apti ad esse nigromantici, aut ad habendum dominium super spiritus malignos. Dicendum quod sic [...]," f. 102r.
84 "Alia etiam movetur quæstio, utrum divinatio per invocationem dæmonum sit licita. Dicendum quod non [...]," f. 103r.
85 "Quæritur insuper, an quis possit invocare diabolum licite ad aliquod opus perficiendum. Dicitur quod sic [...]," f. 104v.
86 "Item quæritur, utrum corpora cælestia possunt terrere dæmones et aliquid imprimere in ipsos. Dicendum quod sic [...]," f. 104v.
87 "Ex jam sursum delucidatis patet quatinus mirabilis et denarrabilis virtus sit indita rebus, unde tam admiranda procedunt per hominum etiam opera populoque stupenda tanquam incredibilia. In pluribus tamen ad sensum evidentia et experimentis approbata inclinabuntur sapientes ad credendum consimilia," f. 113r.
88 "Opus sapientis est facere cessare mirabilia rerum," *De mirabilibus mundi*, ed. Sannino, 85.
89 "Utrum illi qui sunt in purgatorio possunt absolvi a peccatis per orationes hominum in terris," f. 113v.
90 "Quare papa potest ligare spiritus infernales ne vexent animas in purgatorio existentes," f. 114r.
91 This is clearly ironic, for Peter himself, being at Brill, was probably a Franciscan of the third order. He attacks Franciscans on two other occasions for their greediness and their misunderstanding of astral magic (see above, note 63, and his controversy with a friar recounted below).
92 "Propositio: Indulgere pœnam et culpam seu offensionem requirit agens infinitæ potentiæ, qualis non est papa nec cordiger," f. 119r.
93 See Robert N. Swanson, *Indulgences in Late Medieval England: Passports to Paradise* (Cambridge: Cambridge University Press, 2007), 297: "For Wyclif [...] God alone grants indulgence for sins."
94 *Super guerris et futuris hominum actibus et moribus præsentibus et futuris*, ff. 114v–118r.
95 "Quæstio prima: Utrum tempora ventura pejora prioribus instant," f. 114v.
96 "Non potest aliquis ex regali progenie regnum ipsum obtinere aut pacifice in ipso diu perseverare, nisi fuerit ejus nativitas conveniens figuræ cæli hora inceptionis regni," f. 117v.
97 "Expletum per Petrum Franchonis de Zelandia, Brielis frater, tamquam verum semper amicum, ex Ludone Salnerii in comitatu pro nunc Burgundiæ commorantem, die 13 Julii hora vesperarum, ad magistrum Lupum medicum in curia regis Romanorum, anno Christi 1494, transmissum," f. 118r.
98 "Propositio notoria: Augustinus in multis deficit, ut ante mortem cognovit et plura retractando reprobavit plura prius per ipsum conscripta. Multa nunc sunt cognita hæretica, prius a scientificis viris pie credita esse vera," f. 119r.
99 "Sublimitas astronomiæ est magica, seu imaginum scientia," f. 119r.
100 "Medicus astrologus per fatuos facere sapientes et restituere per virtutes et constellationes astrorum insanos ad usum rationis et rectæ voluntatis," f. 119v.

101 "Hæc die dominica proxima sustinere intendo contra vos," f. 119v.
102 "Ad cordigerum missa fuit hæc littera, qui postea fugiens non comparuit," f. 119v.
103 For full details, see Mandosio, "The Use of al-Kindî's Treatise", 435–38. The Brussels volume also contains (1v–2r) an anonymous classification of magic (*inc.*: "Magia est multiplex et partitio est triplex"), copied by another hand on a separate leaf, and bound together with the original manuscript.
104 Giovanni Pico della Mirandola, *Conclusiones DCCCC*, ed. Stephen A. Farmer, *Syncretism in the West: Pico's 900 Theses* (Tempe: Medieval and Renaissance Texts and Studies, 1998).
105 "Hic debent sequi [...] liber de lapidibus pretiosis et de sigillis et figuris planetarum secundum modum Arnoldi de Villanova, et postea [...] conclusiones comitis de Mirandula de magia naturali, et etiam conclusiones magistri Jacobi Fabri in magia sua naturali, et etiam aliqua excerpta ex Picatrici huic nobili arti servientia, cum quibusdam aliis theoreticis ex abbati Spahensis," ff. 114r–v.
106 It was never published, is preserved in very few manuscripts (of which only one contains the complete text), and its existence was only discovered in the beginning of the twentieth century. See Jacques Lefèvre d'Étaples, *La Magie naturelle/De magia naturali*, vol. 1: *L'Influence des astres*, ed. Jean-Marc Mandosio (Paris: Les Belles Lettres, 2018).
107 Sophie Page, *Magic in the Cloister: Pious Motives, Illicit Interests, and Occult Approaches to the Medieval Universe* (University Park: Pennsylvania State University Press, 2013); Frank Klaassen, *The Transformations of Magic: Illicit Learned Magic in the Later Middle Ages and Renaissance* (University Park: Pennsylvania State University Press, 2012).
108 See Mandosio, "Le *De magia naturali* de Jacques Lefèvre d'Étaples: magie, alchimie et cabale," in *Les Muses secrètes: kabbale, alchimie et littérature à la Renaissance*, ed. Rosanna Gorris Camos (Geneva: Droz, 2013), 39–79.
109 *Clavicula Salomonis*, f. 63v; Solomon as author of the *Ars notoria*, ff. 88r, 91v; the "pentacles of Solomon," ff. 102, 103r.
110 He appears only once as "Hermogenes", author of the *Liber septem planetarum ex scientia Abel*, f. 77r.
111 See above, note 9.
112 See above, note 68.
113 See above, note 9.
114 See above, notes 27–28, an example regarding Pietro d'Abano.
115 See above, note 29.

PART IV

THEMES (MAGIC AND...)

21

MAGIC AND NATURAL PHILOSOPHY

Steven P. Marrone

The story of the relation between magic and natural philosophy in the Middle Ages begins in the twelfth century. Before then, the issue was hardly relevant. Not that there were no fields of magical learning or practice in those early centuries that we might want to link to natural philosophy – or, to use a modern term, natural science. Valerie Flint's work on magic in the early Middle Ages reminds us that at no time was astrology entirely absent from the cultural world of medieval elites.[1] And as we shall soon see, astrology was one of the areas often thought of as part of magic that could plausibly vie for a place among the sciences of nature in the high and later Middle Ages. But the problem is that there existed, before the twelfth century, virtually no conception of a realm of knowledge formally distinct from all other learning and characterized as being "scientific". Thus, there was even for educated minds before the twelfth century nothing that could be designated in the language of the time as natural philosophy – or again as we might prefer, nothing specifically identified as natural science. Hence, for those early medieval centuries, there was nothing natural philosophical to which magic could be said to relate.

All this changed around the turn of the eleventh century to the twelfth. It was then that in the cultural circles of a literate, Latinate learned sort there began to emerge the notion of natural philosophy. The idea was dependent on the even more basic conviction that a part of knowledge could be separated from all the rest, characterized formally as of special certainty and associated with careful analysis and logical rigour. Even if we have to wait until the thirteenth century for this special body of knowledge to be designated by the explicit word "science" (*scientia*), in practical terms already in the twelfth century, most of the conditions for calling a portion of what was known "scientific" had begun to be met. Among the causes for this development must be included from the late eleventh century on a greater awareness in the Latin West of traditions of learning in Islamic, Hebrew and Greek cultures that had maintained a place for science, ultimately harking back to Aristotelian foundations. On the back of this awareness arose an enterprise of translation, initiated in the 1100s but continuing through the Renaissance, by means of which was made available a massive amount of knowledge that was self-consciously scientific. A good part of this knowledge concerned itself with the natural world.

The sciences of magic

The rediscovery of the "scientific" provided the minimum necessary to pose the question of how magic related to natural philosophy. But the borrowing of a treasury of scientific learning from Greek, Hebrew and especially Arabic writings had still further effect, for the natural scientific disciplines introduced into the West through translations carried much material that was, also in quite self-conscious terms, magical. There existed therefore from the twelfth century in the West much more in the way of magic to be related to and compared with the newly emergent science of nature. This novel reality made itself apparent already by the middle of the century. We see it first of all in an awareness of fields of learning that long tradition had associated with magic, and interestingly enough mention of these fields crops up in overviews of what constituted the new natural philosophy or natural science. Dominicus Gundissalinus was a cleric active in Toledo, early in the second half of the twelfth century. In his work, *On the Division of Philosophy*, he reached back to the tenth-century Arab scholar Al-Farabi to produce a list of what he said were the eight particular sciences falling under the rubric of natural science. They were in the order in which Farabi had presented them: the science of judgements, the science of medicine, the science of necromancy according to physics (*nigromantia secundum physicam*), the science of images, the science of agriculture, the science of navigation, the science of alchemy and the science of mirrors.[2]

The science of judgements consisted in the art of making prognostications by looking to the positions of the planets and stars. Though the distinction between the terms "astronomy" and "astrology" was never firm in the twelfth or the thirteenth centuries, we can draw on our own usage to say that this judgemental science corresponded to the field of astrology. The science of medicine needs no explanation, but the science of necromancy according to physics proves difficult to pin down. Just the use of the word "necromancy" makes us aware that some sort of magic was at play here. Yet, it is not clear what kind of magic that was. Most scholars are inclined to think of it as at least closely related to what soon would be designated by some medieval thinkers as "natural magic," an area of speculation and practice that will be dealt with later in this chapter. The science of images presents another art that will be touched upon later. Here, it suffices to say that it involved astrology and the fabrication of magical images or devices with which to accomplish marvellous acts. The science of agriculture would again appear to need no comment, although it must be noted that there were texts transmitted through the Arabic making available a sort of magic of wondrous combinations to be applied in the growing and use of plants and animals. As for the science of navigation, it too speaks for itself, while the science of alchemy is likewise self-explanatory but this time indicative of a field long associated with magic. Bringing up the rear is the science of mirrors, part of a much wider arena of speculation called optics but here perhaps linked as well to a practical art of producing wonders.

Gundissalinus's list is reproduced by another twelfth-century inquirer about natural science, the English scholar Daniel of Morley, and was apparently widely familiar as late as the thirteenth century.[3] Important for us is that it confirms how much of magic was brought into the Latin West in the train of the new science imported largely from the Arabic world. Equally significant is that, with the exception of astrology, these areas of magical learning were, from what we can tell, entirely unavailable in the West before this twelfth-century borrowing. They were therefore new fields in the fullest sense of the term. For much of the twelfth century, they remain more rubrics for exotic areas of knowledge than substantive fields, the particulars of which were available to and understood by the scholars who made mention of them. At least, the path lay open for eventual acceptance of them when pertinent translations were made and scholars began to delve into them to become familiar with the actual theory and practice of the art. That stage was reached by the early thirteenth century. And it is over the course of the thirteenth century that we see the magical arts or sciences – including all of those in Gundissalinus's list – go from being mere names to bodies of knowledge both comprehended and often put into practice.

Astrology

Let us therefore look at the fields of magic that have the closest link to the natural sciences. Here, modern scholarship has concerned itself both with the substance of what was involved, in theory as well as in practice, and with the exact nature of the relationship to science. We shall want to do the same thing in summary form here. To begin, we turn to astrology. This is a magical art – although many medievals would have been reluctant to associate it with magic – whose potential position among the natural sciences was more firmly grounded than for any other sort of magic. In fact, it was commonplace to set astrology, the judgemental science of the stars and planets, under the rubric of astronomy, one of the four traditional members of the quadrivial arts and a science long venerated for its ability to explain features of the natural universe. *The Mirror of Astronomy* (*Speculum astronomiae*), a late thirteenth-century composition written primarily to defend the science of images mentioned before, followed the usual paradigm by dividing astronomy into two parts, which we can call the theoretical and the practical.[4] Theoretical astronomy laid down the mathematical rules for the motions of the heavens and then determined the place of all the heavenly bodies at any specified time. Practical astronomy, on the other hand, put forth what the *Mirror* designated as the science of astral judgements, which employed the data produced in theoretical astronomy to make predictions of the future and to gauge the disposition of things here below, including crucially human beings, depending on the moment of their appearance in the sublunar world. This latter science was, of course, what we call astrology. According to the *Mirror*, it represented a most valuable part of the natural sciences.

Many thinkers of the high Middle Ages would have emphatically agreed with the *Mirror*'s estimation. No aristocratic or royal court of the period could be without its astrologer to calculate the most advantageous time to undertake any endeavour, and no university-educated physician would apply medicine without taking the counsel of astrology into consideration. Even those who were wary of astrology in general had to admit that there must be a grain of truth in some of the claims astrologers made for their prognostications and maybe all of their analyses of the dispositions of things. It was a principal of Aristotelian natural science, after all, that the motion of the heavens exercised a preponderant influence on the generation of things in the earthly realm. So the question was not whether some of astrology was valid but rather how much. By the late thirteenth century, it had practically been established that the process upon which astrology depended and by which the stars and planets influenced things below was dependent on light rays emitted by bodies in the heavens, the science of whose action had been charted most exactly by the great Arab thinker and mathematician Al-Kindi. By this measure, astrology drew upon principles of operation as concrete and as open to description, thus not occult, as any other act of nature.

Despite its apparent naturalness, however, astrology still drew from some quarters fiery words of denunciation. William of Auvergne and Robert Grosseteste were not the only theologians to say that it must be combated with fire and sword. Curiously enough, Grosseteste's attack on its validity did nothing to undermine its claim to being reliant on natural processes. One of the two arguments Grosseteste used against astrology focused instead on the ability of human beings to put it into practice.[5] No one, he said, was capable of registering with sufficient precision the time and place of a person's birth so as to be able to differentiate that person's horoscope from that of someone else – say, a twin – born under nearly the same stars. But if astrology was to work, such differentiation had to be possible. The theory behind astrology might then have been correct, but still one would have to deny it a place among the sciences available to mankind. As for Grosseteste's second argument, it totally ignored either natural mechanisms or their suitability for being measured. Instead, it laid against astrology the complaint that if it worked as claimed, then its prognostications put at risk the freedom of the human will. This was a common charge, and one that astrologers continually attempted to evade by saying that they predicted only conditions within which the will had to act while exercising its still unfettered freedom of choice. Again, no assault on astrology's natural pretensions but rather a moral challenge to those who put it into practice.

Alchemy

Perhaps second only to astrology with a claim to being one of the natural sciences was alchemy. Its association with magic probably had as much to do with its opposition to Aristotle's explanation of natural action according to the elemental properties of mixed bodies – all real objects in the sublunar world – as with its penchant for hiddenness and with the fact that in addition to seeking to change base metals to precious ones it also was engaged in the search for the elixir of life. For modern scholars, one important question has been how to characterize this science or art. On the one hand, alchemical texts speak with a highly metaphorical language, itself quite difficult to decipher, and purport to deal with the matter of the ultimate goal of human life and offer what seem to amount to prophecies of the future. There are those who would argue that such concerns constituted the primary aim of alchemy and that its talk about the transmutation of metals was largely metaphorical garb. Yet, there remains the fact that changing metals from one kind to another, and especially transforming base metals into gold, occupy the bulk of alchemical writings. Efforts in the past two decades by William Newman and Lawrence Principe to understand these writings in concrete terms that can be translated into the discourse of modern chemistry and even to try out some of its assaying recipes have given substance to the counterclaim that here is where the focus and goal of alchemy lay, with the moralizing overtones representing mere ephemera.[6] Of course, it is possible that both aims are what medieval alchemists had in mind, but it will take many more attempts to delve into the alchemical literature for the precise proportion between the two aims to be decided. Maybe the answer will vary widely from work to work.

Suffice it to say that for our present concerns, the aspect of alchemy tending towards the analysis of what we would recognize as chemical compounds and ultimately geared to the transformation of one substance into another bears the closest resemblance to natural science. And again the results of recent research have not only confirmed the seriousness with which alchemists pursued their transmutational goals but also revealed how important the efforts of the alchemists were in leading to the emergence of modern chemistry. It was the alchemists, with their vision of the combination and recombination of more fundamental substrates, and not the university-educated scholastics, dependent on an Aristotelianizing notion of irreversible mixture of the four elements, that led the way to modern chemistry's concept of compounds capable of being broken down into their elemental components, which could then be compounded anew in different ways. Moreover, the actual assaying of substances that alchemists practised in their endeavours to find the way to gold nurtured habits of proceeding that underlay the quantitative analyses of seventeenth-century "chymists", in turn the forerunners of modern-day chemists with their experimental methods of both investigating phenomena and validating hypotheses.[7] From the perspective of either of these general assertions about the relation between medieval and modern ways of approaching what we think of as chemical reality, it should come as no surprise that Isaac Newton was an enthusiastic alchemist all his adult life.

Natural magic

Of course, if we are thinking about magic's relation to natural science, we cannot overlook the one area of the medieval magical art that advertised its relation to the processes of nature – that is, natural magic. The descriptor "natural magic" actually appears first in the Latin West among the works of William of Auvergne in the second quarter of the thirteenth century. Whether or not he invented the term, it is clear that the substance of what he was describing with it had been circulating in learned circles since the influx of so much of Arabic magic into the West from the beginning of the twelfth century. As William saw it, and as those who would call themselves natural magicians would continue to assert for several centuries, the subject of natural magic had to do with the production of wondrous works. Wonders, of course, had long been associated with magic, and in William's day, the literature that bore most directly on the production of such marvellous results consisted of what were known in Latin as "libri naturalium narrationum", or what we might call books of natural philosophy. The same tradition carried through into early modern times, and current scholarship has begun to plumb the depths of this major current in the literary world of magical texts. From the work of Lorraine Daston and Katharine Park to that of William Eamon, a foundation now exists for the further study of this material in both its medieval and its early modern instantiations.[8]

William of Auvergne located natural magic as the eleventh part of natural science, and its naturalness was evident even in its name. What made it magical was that it had to do with the workings of occult powers (*virtutes occultae*), labelled as occult or hidden either because the ways of their operation were not understood or because their existence was not apparent to the majority of humankind.[9] A common example would have been the arranging for the production of things, such as frogs, lice and worms, whose generation in the natural world seemed to occur spontaneously and not by generation from parents. In such a case, the emergence of the living beings was to be traced back to seeds buried deeply in certain natural substances such as decaying flesh. By manipulating such substances, the natural magician could gather together the appropriate seeds and force a spontaneous generation that would astound onlookers. Again, William of Auvergne commented that by the adroit combination of just the right matter containing just the right seeds, it should be possible to produce species of animals never before seen. In other words, natural magic promised to extend the boundaries of nature, and enthusiasts like Roger Bacon, whose category of "experimental science" included what normally passed as "natural magic," held out hope that through its use untold marvels would result.

Of course, the magical side of such strange works led some in educated circles to denounce natural magic as an evil art. Indeed, its promoters, from early thinkers like William of Auvergne to the famous sixteenth-century natural magician Giambattista Della Porta, thought it wise to admit that in the wrong hands it could be put to nefarious use, insisting all the while that in itself it was neither immoral nor worthy of anything but praise. In fact, as suggested before, the rubric "necromancy according to physics," which appeared in those twelfth-century lists of the sciences traceable to Al-Farabi, probably denoted what would a century later be called natural magic, so that even by their words some of the early defenders of the art or science invited criticism and condemnation. But everyone in the scholarly world, even a theologian like Thomas Aquinas, had to recognize that some of the workings of occult powers in nature were fully innocent, sometimes beneficial. If they hesitated to use the terminology "natural magic", they were referring all the same to phenomena that many of their contemporaries described as magical. One recurrent example of such an occult operation in nature was iron's attraction to a magnet. And no one would have claimed that the magnet's powers, for all their wondrousness, should be regarded as suspect or shunned by inquiring minds. The basilisk, whose power to kill if it was engaged in sight was also accepted across the board, constituted another instance of natural magic mentioned frequently in medieval texts. There were moreover the special and occult properties of precious metals and gemstones. As with the sapphire's reputed power to stanch the flow of blood, many of these latter powers were of particular utility in medicine.

Discussion of how these occult virtues actually worked reverted to explanations that had been advanced in antiquity. It was clear that the normal view of the natural agency of material substances would not apply, for the action was often exercised at a distance and in any case it could not be accounted for by ascribing it to the elemental qualities of a mixture: hot, cold, dry and wet. Galen had suggested with regard to medicines that where occult powers were at work they had to be traced back to the whole substance, whose total operation could supersede that of the elemental components, and medieval thinkers readily adapted the account to their own needs. One version of the borrowing was to claim that in such instances the active substance or object worked "according to its whole nature". By the middle of the thirteenth century, it had become common to associate the process with the specific form of the agent. In that case, the operation could be said to arise "from the whole species" (*a tota specie*), which again short-circuited action by elemental properties.[10] By the terms of either explanation, the normal laws of generation or material action were bypassed, but by a form of causality that remained resistant to further explanation and hence, even for those describing it, largely hidden and wondrous. In other words, the occult quality of the forces upon which the actions of natural magic depended did not entirely disappear even in the face of claims that they were fully natural.

Medicine

As has already been suggested, many phenomena associated with natural magic found their application in medicine. Medical science thus constitutes another area where modern scholars should expect to find an overlap between magic and natural philosophy. Of course, the use of astrology to determine the critical time to apply medicine or to undertake a medical operation represented a further link between magic and medical learning. Since medicine's relationship to magic is the subject of another chapter of the present volume, there is no reason to investigate the issue further here. The interested reader should turn to the appropriate chapter.

The science of images

Yet, there remains one more area of magic important for its relation to natural science. And here the matter was fraught with greater controversy than for any of the other areas examined so far. The magical art in this instance was the science of images, mentioned in those twelfth-century lists borrowed from Al-Farabi but for practical purposes available to scholars in the West only from the thirteenth century. It was an art that relied upon the power of the stars to bring to an image object fabricated at just the right moment special powers to intervene in the operations of the natural world. Sometimes associated with the casting or fabrication of the image was the recital of particular words or incantations, intended again to focus certain powers on the images. The art had begun among the ancient Sābians of Harrān, from which it migrated into the Arabic world, where it emerged in several texts important for the art's transmission to the Latin West. Among these are two translated already before the end of the thirteenth century. The court of King Alfonso X of Castile was known for the vigour of its scholarly life, and it was at the behest of Alfonso that was translated there – first into Castilian and later into Latin – in the second half of the thirteenth century a work of Spanish origin, probably from the eleventh century, the *Aim of the Sage* (*Ghayāt al-hakīm*). This is the genesis of the famous *Picatrix*, named after the presumed author of the text and redolent of Sābian magical practice. A second work, translated surely by the same time, was the *Book of Images* attributed in the Middle Ages to Thābit ibn Qurra. It, too, takes its roots from the tradition of the Harrānian Sābians.

It is easy to imagine how such magical lore would attract the ire of theologians, already by the thirteenth century alarmed by the proliferation in Latin of works of magic providing sufficient details for actual practice. Bad enough that the practitioners of the science of images turned to the stars to bring down special powers into engraved or cast image objects. But, as noted, the image-makers also frequently uttered combinations of words or incantations to strengthen the forces drawn from the heavens. Thomas Aquinas spoke for many in the schools of theology when he argued that the very use of words was sign of an intention to convey a message and when he concluded that the subjects who would receive such communications must be demons. It was no surprise to those of Thomas's ilk that works like *Picatrix* would choose to call their art a kind of necromancy. Yet, among the science's defenders were many who claimed that nothing more was at work in the crafting of images that could produce wonderful effects than manipulation of the powers of nature. For its defenders, therefore, the science of images fell completely under the rubric of natural science.

Thomas's contemporary Roger Bacon was one of those who undertook an explanation of how the science of images could be not a call to demons but rather an appeal to the natural world. In his *Opus maius*, a work of visionary claims for the sciences addressed directly to the pope, Bacon contended that the work of the stars on the confected images had to be traced back to his theory of natural action by means of the multiplication of species, forms emanating in all directions from agents in the natural world. A similar argument, he added, could be made about the potency of words. In fact, since the rational soul possessed greater dignity than the stars, its ability to project species endowed with power should be even greater than that of the heavens. Words were, he implied, connected to such soul-induced species, perhaps even identical with them. In short, when a skilful operator cast an image at a suitably chosen moment under the stars, reciting at the same time the proper incantation, a work would result "of wondrous power to alter the things of this world."[11] And all this would be entirely natural, in the end no different, we might think, from producing a material tool to accomplish a material task, like cutting wood. A similar chain of reasoning held sway among proponents of the science of images up through the Renaissance. From this perspective, this science was plainly natural.

A much studied text from the later thirteenth century, long attributed to Albert the Great but more likely from the pen of a learned supporter of astrology, Campanus of Novara, took a different tack. Instead of arguing positively for the naturalness of the science of images, the *Mirror of Astronomy* – already introduced earlier – attempted to distinguish the science from its more nefarious imitators, which deserved the legitimate condemnation of theological critics.[12] The first of these was an art that was outright "abominable" and that depended on the actions of fumigation and invocation. Second came an art only slightly less evil, rightfully designated as "detestable", which relied upon the inscription of characters and exorcism, the latter word often used as a synonym for invocation. As should be clear from the activities involved in them, these two magical arts engaged themselves in calling upon spirits or higher beings to accomplish the wonders they produced. Of course, those spirits or beings had to be demonic, and so the arts had to be avoided as demoniacal, implicating the perpetrator in grievous sin. In contrast, the authentic science of images shunned evil spirits and made use solely of natural powers of the world, much of the sort described by Roger Bacon, to bring the marvellous forces of the heavens down to earth. It was in effect a practical art, calling upon astrology in the fabrication of image objects here below, infused with wondrous powers of action.[13] Yet, the author of the *Mirror* was able to name only one work in Latin satisfactorily representative of this art, and that was the *Book of Images* attributed to Thābit ibn Qurra and mentioned before. In point of fact, moreover, the *Book of Images* was not free of the invocations and exorcisms the *Mirror* claimed had to be avoided. Nicolas Weill-Parot has even argued that all the way up to early modern times, no one succeeded in devising a science of images to meet the specifications of the *Mirror*.[14] Perhaps it was an impossible goal.

Experiment

In addition to these fields of magic that were well developed by the high Middle Ages and have attracted the attention of scholars working on the medieval period, there are also a few themes of research that need to be mentioned if we are to understand the relation between medieval magic and natural science. First, there is the matter of experiment or empirical knowledge. Standard accounts of the history of science associate the Middle Ages with a deductive paradigm for scientific cognition, where statements worthy of such designation are drawn by demonstrative argument from presumably unassailable principles. It is only with early modernity, so the same account goes, that scholars began to turn their attention to the principles themselves, seeking not only grounds for the epistemic confidence in those principles already recognized but also new principles altogether, and in areas of the natural world hitherto unexplored. Here, the role of experiment came to be regarded as crucial, employed as a method of establishing the truth of universal statements and as a source for further principles open to fresh investigation. It is then of more than passing interest that a major body of magical literature in the Middle Ages consisted of what were called "books of experiments" (*libri experimentorum*).[15]

In many cases, the books of experiments offered directions for acts of necromancy or conjuring, presented one after another in long lists of singular experiences that one might have with such acts of magic. But sometimes a book of experiments would be a list of recipes for what might be considered examples of the art of natural magic. What was important in both cases was the expectation that an actual experience was foundational for whatever knowledge one would draw from the actions involved. There is therefore already in the thirteenth century a growing awareness among university scholars, and sometimes enterprising thinkers outside the university walls, that experience or what we might even call "experiment" had an epistemic role to play, one beyond the Aristotelian acceptance that in the end almost all human knowledge derived from information gathered by the senses. Roger Bacon was one of those scholastics who most loudly trumpeted this science-certifying role of experiential cognition. Though he advanced such claims throughout his work, he was most emphatic on this score when speaking of his "experimental science". It was noted earlier that much of what Bacon meant by experimental science fell under the rubric of natural magic, productive of various wonders. Now it must be added that even – or perhaps especially – in natural magic, Bacon held that the marvellous experience – or experiment – guaranteed a scientific commitment of certitude about the results.[16] At least in this magical guise, experimental science constituted the ultimate arbiter of most of the other sciences.

To make this observation does not amount to going back fully to Alistair Crombie's contention from the early 1950s that the tradition of scholasticism represented by those like Robert Grosseteste and Bacon foreshadowed the notion of experiment's scientific role as put forth in the Scientific Revolution of the seventeenth century.[17] As the case of Bacon plainly shows, the medieval emphasis on experiment was often tied to the experience provided by performing an act of magic and not to the verifying role of controlled experiment. But that should not prevent us from recognizing medieval magic's hand in drawing thinkers' attentions to the particularities of experience as serving an epistemic function. Out of this awareness surely arose some of the cognitive habits that would, by the seventeenth century, underwrite the turn to an empirical science in a more modern sense of the term. Here, too, we should remember the observation noted before that alchemy, another magical science, generated much of the foundation for what we think of as modern chemistry. And in this latter case, we witness already in the thirteenth century the emergence of techniques that will be adopted by early modern chemists. Newman and Principe have begun to show us how much the careful assaying of late medieval alchemists fed directly into the quantitative methods of early modern chymists and thence into the cognitive world of early modern science.

A limiting case for natural causation

Second among the special themes we need to look at if we are to appreciate the importance of medieval magic for the concerns of historians of natural science is one that has to do with the limiting role played by the notion of magical causation. Magic, and especially natural magic, pointed to places in the natural world where, as indicated before, the normal processes of causation were superseded by the workings of a cause that, because it was not open to further investigation as, for example, causation by the elemental properties, had to be labelled "occult". This meant that in debating whether a specific natural phenomenon was occult or not, scholastic thinkers were led to examine the question of the boundaries of natural causation. In my own work, I have suggested therefore that magic provides a significant locus for our own investigation of medieval ideas of causality in the natural world.[18] For me, the issue has been one of determining when in the Middle Ages we begin to see scholastics turn towards the expectation that causes in nature will have to work by contiguity – that is, the abandonment of the notion of natural causation at a distance. I have proposed that we look into the disputational literature of the high and later Middle Ages for moments when the subject of magic arises, expecting that the discussion of magic will force our scholastics to set the limit of the means of operation of a natural cause. But the same holds true for medieval debate over the line between natural operations and phenomena that have to rely on the intervention of demons. In this case, even a discipline like the science of images might hold clues for where medieval thinkers thought the reach of the normal processes of nature ended, so that recourse to the power of spirits and demons had to begin.

Conversely, the debate over workings of causality in the natural world exercised an effect on magic, or at least on what was considered to be magical in the eyes of theologians and inquisitors. Thomas Aquinas rejected, for example, the notion that words possessed a natural power of their own whereby they could influence events at a distance. Therefore, wherever incantations or any spoken formulas were involved in a magical operation, he denied that any natural process was at work. Instead, the words had to be informative, spoken as in common human discourse but this time intended for an invisible audience, demonic spirits. Magical arts like the science of images, insofar as it involved recitation of chains of words or names, thus had to be demonic. In cases like this, examination of the parameters of scholastic understanding of action and change in nature can prepare us for understanding how magic was thought to occur. The demonization of magic that several scholars, Alain Boureau chief among them, have located in the late thirteenth and early fourteenth centuries can by this reading be traced back at least in part to changes in the conception of nature.[19]

The *ars notoria*

Finally, a last theme to consider, though in this instance we are dealing less with the substance of natural science and more with knowledge of it. One of the most widespread sorts of magic among university scholars in the high and late Middle Ages was what was called the *ars notoria*, or the notorial art.[20] It prescribed a strict regimen of ablution and moral purity, accompanied by at least a month-long observance of rituals demanding the speaking of complicated verbal formulas while looking at sometimes elaborate images, all with the intention of gaining knowledge of specific arts or scientific disciplines. The aim was to bypass the long years of study in the classroom in order to be endowed with a cognitive treasury by dint of ritual alone. Among the arts for which precise rituals had been devised were the four members of the quadrivium. In addition to the mathematical arts of arithmetic and geometry, they included the natural science of astronomy (the other is music). It is hardly surprising that such a programme would be attractive to many students at the universities. Perhaps more perplexing is that its notoriety lasted so long, given what must have been countless instances of disappointed expectations.

Future directions

Since the study of learned magic in the Middle Ages is, with the exception of the work of Lynn Thorndike, a relatively recent phenomenon, all of the subjects dealt with so far in this chapter stand in need of further development. They all, therefore, offer appropriate avenues for future research. But a few areas of interest, some of which have barely been investigated by scholars of medieval magic, demand our special attention. They are, one might say, subjects where the profits from an investment of scholarly capital promise to be especially great. We can begin with the field of natural magic. Interest in William of Auvergne, who was fascinated with natural magic and may have coined the phrase by which it came to be known, has begun to pick up of late. But there are centuries between William's time and the period of the great natural magicians of the Renaissance – the sixteenth-century Della Porta mentioned before being perhaps the most renowned – where the trail of natural magic has been allowed to grow quite cold. We need to know much more about what natural magic consisted in during the intervening three hundred years. Who was interested in it? What works of natural magic were composed, or what translations made, and exactly what sort of material did they contribute to the tradition? What relation did medieval natural magic bear to that of the Renaissance, and was the development from the former to the latter continuous, or was it marked by a dramatic shift?

Sometimes related to natural magic were the books of experiments (*libri experimentorum*). Though some of the experiments collected in handbooks in the Middle Ages offered recipes for works of necromancy, many promised to give their practitioners experience in the wonders of the natural world. It was noted before how such wonders were most often linked causally to occult forces. And investigation of how such occult causality was conceived, especially again in the long stretch of years between the thirteenth century and the Italian Renaissance, is worthy of special attention. But here, where the connection to natural science is particularly close, there are two paths of research that demand much greater attention in the decades to come. First of all, we need to delve into the work of the "experimenters" in the medieval world of learning – figures like the Peter of Maricourt so effusively praised by Roger Bacon – so as to understand how their efforts – in the case of Peter, exploration of the phenomenon of the magnet – fed into magic or how magical traditions influenced what they did.[21] We need to know much more about these people and to have greater familiarity with their work, neither of which is very likely without considerable searching out in medieval manuscript collections. Second, much remains to be done in understanding how medieval "experiments" relate to the experimental current of the Scientific Revolution of the seventeenth century. Not that the medieval figures were experimenters in the modern sense of the word. Yet, the enthusiasm for experience as an avenue towards knowledge and a certifier of truth certainly fed into a similar excitement felt by seventeenth-century empiricists like Francis Bacon. We need to know much more about this process.

Not too far afield is an area of magic modern scholarly knowledge that is just in its infancy. The *Nabataean Agriculture* is a work of early magic available in Arabic before the high Middle Ages and translated into Latin by the thirteenth century.[22] It represents a type of medieval magic concerned primarily with plant lore and detailing the way the extraordinary, even magical properties of herbs and occasionally other substances could be turned to medical use. A similar text was the work *On the Wonders of the World*, recently edited by Antonella Sannino.[23] Here is a strain of magic about which little is known but which probably figured quite large in Latin learned circles in the Middle Ages. Like the books of experiments, these works of medico-magical wisdom are probably best seen as belonging at least in part to medieval natural science, especially if we approach them from the perspective of those who promoted and drew from them. Locating such works in medieval manuscripts, editing them and then studying what they had to say are projects deserving of scholarly attention.

Finally, I return to the science of images and to alchemy. Little connects these two in the realm of magic, but both are important for our understanding of the ties between medieval magic and natural science. In each case, moreover, it is how they were used and practised that is of just as much interest as how they were expounded in the literature surrounding them. For alchemy, a major start in this direction is found in the work of Newman and Principe commented on before. For the science of images, there is actually very little that has so far been done. Either could be the basis for an excellent programme of future work. The payoff for our appreciation of medieval magic and natural science is likely to be great.

Notes

1 Consult Valerie I.J. Flint, *The Rise of Magic in Early Medieval Europe* (Princeton, NJ: Princeton University Press, 1991).
2 Dominicus Gundissalinus, *De divisione philosophiae/Uber die Einteillung der Philosophie*, ed. and trans. Alexander Fidora and Dorothée Werner (Freiburg-im-Breisgau: Herder, 2007), 76.
3 See Daniel of Morley, "Philosophia" X, 158, ed. Gregor Maurach, *Mittellateinisches Jahrbuch* 14 (1979): 239.
4 *Speculum astronomiae* 1 and 3, ed. Stefano Caroti, Michela Pereira and Stefano Zamponi, under the direction of Paola Zambelli (Pisa: Domus Galilaeana, 1977), 6–8 and 13–14.
5 For Grosseteste's arguments, see his *Hexaëmeron* V, ix, 1, and V, x, 1. ed. Richard C. Dales and Servus Gieben (London: Oxford University Press, 1982), 165–67.
6 See, for example, William R. Newman and Lawrence M. Principe, *Alchemy Tried in the Fire. Starkey, Boyle and the Fate of Helmontian Chemistry* (Chicago, IL: University of Chicago Press, 2002); Lawrence M. Principe, *The Secrets of Alchemy* (Chicago, IL: University of Chicago Press, 2013).
7 For both claims, see William R. Newman, *Atoms and Alchemy. Chymistry and the Experimental Origins of the Scientific Revolution* (Chicago, IL: University of Chicago Press, 2006).
8 Lorraine Daston and Katharine Park, *Wonders and the Order of Nature, 1150–1750* (New York: Zone Books, 1998); William Eamon, *Science and the Secrets of Nature. Books of Secrets in Medieval and Early Modern Culture* (Princeton, NJ: Princeton University Press, 1991).
9 On such occult powers or qualities, see especially Nicolas Weill-Parot, "Astrology, Astral Influences, and Occult Properties in the Thirteenth and Fourteenth Centuries," *Traditio* 65 (2010): 201–30.
10 See Brian P. Copenhaver, "Scholastic Philosophy and Renaissance Magic in the *De vita* of Marsilio Ficino," *Renaissance Quarterly* 37 (1984): 523–54; "Natural Magic, Hermetism and Early Modern Science,' in *Reappraisals of the Scientific Revolution*, ed. David C. Lindberg and Robert S. Westman, 261–301 (Cambridge: Cambridge University Press, 1990).
11 For all this on species, see Roger Bacon, *Opus maius* IV, 2, cc. 1–3, and IV, treatise on astrology, in *The "Opus maius" of Roger Bacon*, 2 vol., ed. John Henry Bridges, and supplement (Oxford: Clarendon Press, 1897, and London: Williams and Norgate, 1900), vol. 1, 109–19 and 395–99.
12 See the convincing arguments about authorship advanced by Agostino Paravicini Bagliani in *Le Speculum Astronomiae, une énigme? Enquête sur les manuscrits* (Florence: Edizioni del Galluzzo, 2001).
13 *Speculum astronomiae* 11, ed. Caroti et al., 27–33.
14 Nicolas Weill-Parot, *Les "images astrologiques" au moyen âge et à la Renaissance* (Paris: Honoré Champion, 2002), 84–85.
15 On medieval "experiment", see especially *Expertus sum. L'expérience par les sens dans la philosophie naturelle médiévale, Actes du colloque international de Pont-à-Mousson, 5–7 février 2009*, ed. Thomas Bénatouïl and Isabelle Draelants (Florence: Sismel Edizioni del Galluzzo, 2011).
16 Bacon, *Opus maius* VI, c. 2 and unnumbered, ed. Bridges, vol. 2, 172–73, 202 and 215–19.
17 Alistair C. Crombie, *Robert Grosseteste and the Origins of Experimental Science 1100-1700* (Oxford: Oxford University Press, 1953).
18 Steven P. Marrone, "Magic and the Physical World in Thirteenth-Century Scholasticism," *Early Science and Medicine* 14 (2009): 158–85.
19 See Alain Boureau, *Satan the Heretic*, trans. Teresa L. Fagan (Chicago, IL: Chicago University Press, 2006).
20 Consult the new edition by Julien Véronèse, *L'Ars notoria au Moyen Age. Introduction et édition critique* (Florence: Sismel Edizioni del Galluzzo, 2007).
21 On Peter, begin with Petrus Peregrinus de Maricourt, *Opera*. ed. Loris Sturlese and Ron B. Thomson (Pisa: Scuola Normale Superiore, 1995).
22 So far, only its Arabic version has been edited: Ibn Wahshīyah, *Kitāb al-Filāhah al-Nabatīyah. L'Agriculture nabatéenne*. 3 vol. ed. Tawfīq Fahd (Damascus: Al-Ma'had al-'Ilmī al-Faransī, 1993–98).
23 Antonella Sannino, *Il De mirabilibus mundi tra tradizione magica e filosofia naturale*, (Florence: Sismel Edizioni del Galluzzo, 2011).

22

MEDICINE AND MAGIC

Peter Murray Jones and Lea T. Olsan

Introduction, concepts and terminology

Pioneering early eighteenth-century histories of medicine by Daniel Le Clerc and John Freind regarded their new subject as a history of the doctrines of the great doctors from Hippocrates onwards. When they came across anything in their physician authors that smacked of magic or charms they were scornful and dismissive, referring to "superstitious receipts". The eclipse of humoral theories and the emergence of laboratory-based medicine at the end of the eighteenth century only served to reinforce this negative attitude amongst historians of medicine. But history itself changed as a discipline. With a new value attached, from the mid-nineteenth century onwards, to examining the manuscript records of medieval medicine by German scholars like Julius Pagel and Karl Sudhoff, and French scholars like Charles Daremberg, magical healing began to seem a subject worthy of serious study. From another direction, national movements to collect and study folk traditions (in time to become the discipline of "Folkloristik") were beginning to build national corpora of charms and rituals whose development was understood as a continuous process from an era before the beginning of written records. The publications resulting from this scholarly mining of original sources for medicine and magic were impressive in their size and scope, and modern historical scholarship has still only partially digested these findings.[1]

There has been a strong temptation in twentieth-century scholarship on medicine and magic in the Middle Ages to try to separate healing into categories defined as rational (usually scholastic medicine), religious (employing prayer, and the intercessory power attributed to the Virgin Mary and the saints) and magical (amulets, spells, charms). As pointed out by Peregrine Horden in "What's Wrong with Early Medieval Medicine?", this has often resulted in a dismissal of early medieval medicine as a deplorable mixing up of these categories, whereas later medieval medicine is congratulated for having sorted them out. The categories themselves are derived from twentieth-century paradigms that have little real usefulness as analytic tools for historians. Instead, Horden argues for an approach recognizing that early (and late) medieval scribes and readers had no problem themselves in juxtaposing and combining prognostications and remedies various in origin into textual miscellanies whose character was essentially pragmatic – whatever worked in healing justified itself.[2]

For the purposes of this chapter, magic serves as an umbrella term for a variety of specific healing and medical practices that elsewhere we have termed "performative rituals."[3] The foundation of such practices is twofold: first, such rituals are intrinsically repeatable, and, indeed, their value depends in part on their being known to have been previously iterated. In other words, they have acquired a certain traditionality within the communities in which they are used. Second, such performative rituals manifest in a number of different forms, for example, wearing or carrying amulets,[4] including textual ones,[5] reciting or writing charms and prayers,[6] and carrying out procedures thought to work on the basis of past trials or experience (*experimenta*).[7] A convenience of this approach is that it does not require decisions about the religious status of healing practices. This is useful since some practices that were acceptable and orthodox at one point in time or in one community of Christians, for example the use of saints' names or the names of God, were rejected as being demonic or idolatrous at another. The people who practised magic in this sense of performative rituals might be priests or doctors, wise women or cunning men in local communities, householders or sick people.

Magic in Anglo-Saxon medicine

Anglo-Saxon medicine deserves separate consideration in this essay partly because Anglo-Saxons were writing and translating books of medicine in the vernacular before 1100 in England, earlier than anybody else in Europe. Most of Anglo-Saxon medicine is consolidated in four Old English books compiled between the ninth and the eleventh centuries, derived from a variety of sources: late antique Latin medicine, monastic medicine with Byzantine connections, Scandinavian runes, Irish medicine and local vernacular traditions. Its magical cures consist of verbal incantations, written or herbal amulets, and ritual action.[8]

Incantations to the earth (*Precatio terrae*), mother of all medically beneficial plants and food crops, were recorded for those who collected herbs as well as a long ritual to restore the land and the fertility to fields and animals damaged by sorcery or poisoning.[9] It incorporated the veneration of the earth as mother of the crops, consigning the fertility to the protection of the cross and the church. Anglo-Saxons might follow a simple Roman form, as in *Bald's Leechbook*: "I pick you, artemisia, that I may not be weary on the road." More elaborate rituals appear, especially for disturbances attributed to spiritual or demonic causes.[10] In *Leechbook III*, one requires that the plant collector approach reverently at a specific time (Thursday evening) and recite the words from Christian liturgy, the Benedicite, a Pater Noster and a litany, before sticking a knife in it and departing to return the following dawn. Then, he goes to church silently to recite the same prayers, collects the plant and lays it with the knife on the altar in the church. The healer prepares a drink by adding the plant called bishopswort, and lichen taken from a stone cross and boiled milk. Afterwards, he recites more liturgical rites and makes the sign of the cross in four directions with a sword before administering it to the sick for an illness called in Anglo-Saxon "elf-adle", that is, a sickness attributed at some point in the past to elves.[11] We do not know exactly what elf-adle was, but judging from the three remedies for it in Leechbook III, it was a serious systemic ailment that might last nine days. The most intriguing collection of medical remedies from the perspective of magic and ritual cures is British Library MS Harley 585, a manuscript written before 1025. The first part of the manuscript (folios 1–129) contains the expanded *Old English Herbarium*. The second part of the manuscript (the lacnunga folios 130r–93r) repeatedly incorporates rituals into its herbal prescriptions, as when the person who is treated for erysipelas must stay awake all night before the summer solstice and drink at cockcrow, dawn and sunrise. Masses are sung over plants for a salve to cure the "flying venom". Incantations readily incorporate Christian exorcism rites, invoking the evangelists with the sign of the cross. The compiler, clearly a Christian and probably a monk, invested liturgical, scriptural, doctrinal singing with healing powers, as seen in his recipe for a holy salve against poisonous bites. The cure is called a salve, but is actually a potion to be drunk by the healer on behalf of those under threat. An anatomically detailed account of the human body constitutes a Lorica, a metrical Christian prayer, in which the verbal recitation of body parts from "skull, head with hair, and eyes" to "spleen with winding intestines" will be preserved from pestilence, weakness and pain. Greek letters written along the arms relieve fever especially with invocations of saints. Or sacramental wafers may be inscribed with the names of the seven sleepers to cure fever accompanying an Old English metrical charm that rids the sick person of her harm.[12]

Despite the distinctive character of some of the magical and ritual elements in Anglo-Saxon medicine, there are continuities with aspects of later medieval healing, for example, the use of written amulets, incantations of herbs, formulae like *sator arepo* (the magic square), Christian legends such as the seven sleepers and the Veronica legend, the tradition of the heavenly letter and the intense use of liturgical materials and devotions to the cross for protection against demons. Some practices like writing and tying on amulets and incanting herbs are continued from Roman practices, while other rituals are derived from Christian legends and liturgy through monastic sources. Early sources for magical and ritual healing among the Anglo-Saxons multiply and ramify during the late Middle Ages, and although new magical techniques such as alchemy and astrology develop, the sick and fearful still had recourse to therapeutic practices in the later Middle Ages that existed during the Anglo-Saxon period.

Materiality and orality

Both materiality and orality contribute to a thicker, better contextualized understanding of performances intended to cure illnesses, or prevent harms, because in contrasting ways they emphasize aspects of medical magic often overlooked by textual studies. Material substances and spoken language are essential aspects of magical remedies. Each of these warrants our attention. Moreover, the combination of a numinous object or substance and a voiced ritual constitutes a familiar type of cure, where making something and saying something have magical consequences.

A commonplace medieval assumption was that every part of creation could be used for healing since God intended that creation to be for human use. Things endowed with magical healing properties were identified in long-established Latin textual genres like herbals, lapidaries and bestiaries. Extracts from these found their way in turn into short vernacular texts on *materia medica*. Francis Brévart provides an excellent survey of those in German, giving specific examples of wonder plants (vervain), minerals (the Aries seal designed by Arnau of Villanova) and animal parts (from the vulture).[13] By and large when these things were used for healing, they were perishable and no longer survive as material evidence or only in tiny numbers. But there are important archaeological remains of manufactured magical objects used in healing. These range from Muslim healing bowls to cramp rings, personal jewels, brooches and pilgrim badges. Many of these objects are inscribed or are decorated with images, as means of promoting their apotropaic and healing purposes. The more precious the object, the more likely it is to have survived, so we have to be careful not to give undue significance to those affordable only to the aristocracy.[14]

Spoken formulas necessarily employ attributes of breathed language, from meaningless sounds to the symbolic. Such features include meter, rhyme, repetition, the prevalence of nonsense syllables, *magicae voces*, and the like, being among the most common. Meaningless, magical words are a familiar register in the language of magical healing.[15] Of outstanding importance is the most obvious characteristic of orality – that spoken and sung remedies assume the presence of the healer in the same space as the patient. The presence of an authoritative and trusted speaker and a human voice, whether or not the patient or those standing around understand the words, changes the psychological circumstances of the sick, answering the complaint not only with an implied confrontation to rid the sick of it, but the reinforcement of hope for relief. More often than not, incanted remedies are accompanied by physical medicines, prayers and ritual gestures, all of which contribute to the effect of a verbal remedy. The circumstances and actions in which healer, patient, and observers are joint participants and the sufferer is the focal point of multiple healing strategies belong to the oral–aural world, in our era as well as in the past, in which presence in time and space, as well as concrete objects, is a key factor.

Most of what we know about magical and ritual practices in medical contexts comes through written sources.[16] We have no direct access to oral traditional practices with regard to the magical therapies of amulets and ligatures or incantations, charms and spells during the medieval period. This period was defined by the eruption of writing on the new medium of skins and the popularization of the book format. Medieval medical rituals are first recorded in manuscripts written within religious foundations sometimes associated with elite households. From such sources, they circulated in less literate communities and became accessible to people whose healing traditions depended on what they had learned in face-to-face encounters with older healers or family members or practising medicine. Conversely, charms and rituals that were widely known and accepted in a common tradition, to use Richard Kieckhefer's useful term, were passed around both by word of mouth and in writing on fly-leaves or blank pages of manuscripts. They became incorporated into medical recipe collections as prescriptions or as practical prayers in Books of Hours and into household miscellanies and personal commonplace books. Medical amulets made of animal and plant substances had a long history from Pliny through late antiquity, and such amulets combined easily with medical recipes and spoken incantations. Spoken incantations or charms differ little from written amulets, especially when the written amulets contain the same words, or a charm to be spoken is also to be written and attached to the patient. In the Middle Ages, the words were themselves often borrowed from written sources. Characters, symbols or anagrams were written on amulets, on the body or on consumable substances or other objects, so that the technology of writing was deeply integrated into traditional healing.[17] The efficaciousness of oral performances and ritual objects, while doubted or rejected as demonic in some religious and medical circles, was accepted on traditional grounds as inherited medical or religious practice, or it was justified by various theories regarding natural and supernatural powers.

Early theories and scholastic debates

Amulets and incantations for medical purposes were matters worth serious theoretical discussion in the twelfth century. Translations from Arabic texts enabled this new theoretical turn in medicine and in magic. Qusta ibn Luqa (or Costa ben Luca), a Greek-speaking Christian physician and scientist born in Baalbek (now Lebanon), wrote an essay in Arabic during the ninth century that was translated into Latin in Italy probably by Constantine the African (who was also responsible for translating key medical texts used in the school of Salerno).[18] The original has not survived, but the Latin treatise, *On Incantations, Adjurations, and Suspensions around the Neck* (or *On Physical Ligatures*) circulated widely throughout the Middle Ages variously associated with Constantine, Arnau of Villanova, Galen and Henry Cornelius Agrippa.[19] Qusta's short epistle is grounded in Greek medical ideas that the motions of the mind (soul) affect the humours of the body and the reverse. For example, a choleric person, one whose body is dominated by choleric humour, has a tendency to feel anger in the soul; by the same token, someone prone mentally to anger increases choler in the body with consequences to physical health. Second, if the mind believes something strongly, the body will respond. Qusta reports having healed a noble who complained of not being able to have sex because of being "tied" by a spell. Qusta was unsuccessful in changing his mind until he hit on the clever device of reading him a passage from *The Book of Cleopatra* in which a spellbound man was cured by coating himself in raven's gall and sesame oil. After hearing the passage, the patient was convinced, carried out the prescription, and being cured, could have sex again. Like an incantation, the story strengthened the man's confidence so that he acted and found relief. According to Qusta, the complexion of the soul is helped by an incantation, adjuration or suspension around the neck, but if a medicine is joined with it, health will come more quickly, since the soul is aided by an incantation and the body by medicine; in the conjunction of the two, the health of each one necessarily follows speedily.[20]

Maaike van der Lugt has carefully studied Urso of Salerno's *Aphorisms* and his *Commentary* on incantations.[21] According to Urso's natural philosophy, expounded in his Gloss to aphorism 39,[22] the air around the physician is purified through his respiration and then drawn in by the patient. Through this exchange, the patient's spirit is changed or replaced with a purer spirit diffused through his bodily humours and members resulting in a cure. There is a downside. A bad physician can corrupt the air around him via his breath or his speech, so that when the patient draws in this impure air, he suffers corruption in body and soul and he is weakened and becomes subject to disease. Finally, Urso's Gloss also extends the effect of a physician to the manner in which the physician speaks to his patient. The physician "by promising health firmly with soothing speech and pleasant promises," eases the patient's mind, increases his confidence in recovery, and cheers him up. The heart, previously constricted by the intensity of his illness and fear of death, is dilated, takes in air and spirit and boosts the power that governs the body enough to bring on a "perfect crisis". Pain itself is relieved by focusing the mind on recovery, so that the patient's spirit withdrawing from the part of his body in pain towards his brain no longer feels it.

These arguments clearly work on the borderline of theology and natural philosophy as van der Lugt has shown in the case of Urso. The concept of healing action through the use of words in charms and prayers was a subject that became the focus of intense scholastic debate in the medieval university. It was a matter of common agreement that verbal formulas did possess this power, the *virtus verborum* – the question was how they achieved this effectiveness. The theologian William of Auvergne had suggested in the 1230s that this effectiveness had nothing to do with the meaning of the words, even though music and sound do have certain natural effects on man. The suspicion was that demons must be involved in incantation. Roger Bacon (1266–68), however, argues that three natural phenomena combine to create the power of words.[23] One is the power of the stars, which emit rays that infuse all things on earth and are emitted by all earthly objects containing elements. From Al-Kindi's *De radiis stellarum*, he takes the idea that sounds (speech sounds) contain two kinds of power, one the force from the stars and another from the soul projected by human speech. Sounds, whether heard or not, propagate a celestial force, which is strongest when used at the moment when planet or constellation most closely related to the objects has most influence on them and on the souls of the participants. But Bacon stresses the intentionality in those involved, for "the power of the human soul" (*anima rationalis*) is essential to the successful conveyance of the power of words. To project its *species*, a soul uses words.

The physician Pietro d'Abano (1250 or 1257–1315 or 1316) agreed that the meaning of words could not explain the power of healing charms and prayers but argued that this power was derived from the soul of the speaker and that of the listener so that one had persuasive power over the other built on a relationship of trust. The sources of d'Abano's argument go back to the *De physicis ligaturis* of Qusta ibn Luca. Later in the fourteenth century, Nicole Oresme argued instead that the particular configuration of sounds is the source of the power of words. A particular state or defect of the imagination on the part of the listener is required to make incantation effective. Both d'Abano and Oresme accept a naturalistic frame of explanation of the *virtus verborum*, rejecting the role of demons.[24]

Medical conditions and complaints

From the perspective of people with certain common or chronic medical problems, a ritual, amuletic or verbal remedy provided accessible therapy.[25] Doctors were not necessarily the first people approached for cures, especially when the sufferer lived in the countryside, lacked the money to pay a doctor or the complaint was minor. Magical remedies, including amulets, charms and ritual cures, might be offered by anyone who possessed the knowledge to relieve the specific complaint or who could offer some preventative magic for recurrent symptoms. In the case of medical problems caused by *maleficium* or sorcery, the evil magic had to be removed by magical means.[26] Individuals who came to be called "cunning men" or "cunning women" in Britain made healing and divination their particular concern.[27] On the other hand, a civic-minded villager like Robert Reynes, the fifteenth-century reeve of Acle, included charms that could be used as amulets for fevers, the falling evil and toothache in his commonplace book; he was not a healer. Such ritual remedies cost the healers who administered them little more than personal time with a client.[28] But such therapies and protections of health could be painted or written by cloistered religious, as Friedman has shown.[29]

Not all symptoms were equally amenable to ritual or magical therapies. W.L. Braekman lists twenty-nine human ills for which magical therapies were prescribed in the Netherlands, most of which can be found elsewhere in Europe.[30] German charms for healing recorded before 1200 include many to staunch bleeding and treat fevers, wounds, blindness, worms, falling sickness, sore throat, ganglion cists and catarrh or head cold.[31] From the thirteenth century, charms, amulets and personal rituals were available to stop bleeding, induce sleep, ease childbirth and relieve fevers, stomach problems, diarrhoea, wounds and sores, gout and worms. Perennial complaints that come and go like headaches, toothaches, nosebleeds and some eye complaints could be helped by charms, sometimes combined with a medicinal remedy. Mental disturbances and epilepsy were often managed with ritual or amuletic treatments. Among acute conditions, bleeding was one of the most common complaints for which rituals were available. From cuts to nosebleeds to serious wounds threatening to bring on shock, to excessive menstruation and flux, or bloody diarrhoea, healing rituals were available to stem the flow.

Old wounds and sores including painful felons and fistulas, gout, superficial cankers, mouth cankers and cancers of the womb belonged to a group of related maladies. Effective medicinal cures consisted of plasters and unguents; but fistulas, felons and worms were amenable to charms alluding to Job's suffering or to counting-down formulae. Fresh wounds were treatable by an encounter charm *Tres boni fratres*, in which Christ instructs the three good brothers to give up looking for herbs and use oil and wool and a charm to stop bleeding and prevent infection instead.[32] Wounds caused by arrows or bolts might require the ritual use of molded wax to remove the foreign object. Metal plates with crosses inscribed on them, accompanied by voiced devotions to the five wounds of Christ, were applied like bandages to wounds. Verbal devotions to each of Christ's wounds, known as the charm of Saint Susanna, reputedly delivered in a letter from heaven by the Angel Gabriel, could be recited over a wound so that like Christ's wounds it would not be painful or the flesh become corrupted.[33]

Fevers were diagnosed according to their intensity and recurrence. Those lasting more than one day could be treated with ritual administrations of holy words to be consumed on leaves or apples or communion hosts over three days.[34] Sleep could be induced in a sick person through writing the name Ishmael on a leaf and laying it under the restless person's head. Childbirth was an ever-present condition fraught with the possibility of suddenly going wrong at any time with life-threatening consequences to the child and the mother. An Anglo-Saxon woman concerned about bringing her child to term might have warded off miscarriage by stepping over a grave while repeating verses in Old English and strengthen hope of a good pregnancy by similarly stepping over her sleeping husband. A wealthy fifteenth-century lady during her "lying-in" period might borrow a long prayer roll for contemplation and perhaps to be wrapped about her waist by her helpers to prevent sudden death of her child or herself. Amulets were tied to the thigh or carried on the body and recited over the heads of women going into labour. Some birth amulets had to be removed quickly after the birth lest the woman be put in danger.[35]

Some diseases were attributed to demons and evil spirits and could be exorcised through verbal charms or prevented with amulets. Epilepsy, called the falling sickness or falling evil in the vernaculars, was treatable at the time of an attack by a word such as *ananizapta* or the names of the Three Kings spoken in the victim's ear. A demon was one cause sometimes suggested for it. Constantine the African recommended accompanying the patient to church for masses over several days. A later medical ritual, recommended by John Arderne, required writing an amulet containing the names of the Three Kings, Jasper, Melchior and Balthazar, with blood taken from the little finger of the patient, then enclosing within it gold, frankincense and myrrh.[36]

There is striking continuity in the medical conditions treated with rituals and charms extending into the late Middle Ages. From around the middle of the thirteenth century, there was a revival of the genre of *Practica*, treatises written by learned university doctors on the practice of medicine organized in head to toe order of ailments.[37] *Practica* included knowledge relating to both the preservation of health and the treatment of disease with diet, medication and surgery. These writings were systematic in terms of their presentation of the definition, causes, signs, prognosis, regimen and therapeutics for each medical condition. But, though the main thrust of the *Practica* was to consider each condition in terms of its pathology of qualities and humours, as university teaching of medicine required, and to recommend regimen and treatment by contraries to restore the balance or temperament appropriate to each individual patient, the prognostics and recipes included in these *Practica* treatises did not always conform to this rational model. In an important article, Danielle Jacquart drew attention to the willingness of the authors of the *Practica*, particularly after the Black Death in 1347–50, to include in their recommendations occult practices whose justification was their experiential success rather than their rationality.[38] Apart from astrology and alchemy, these practices included those that we may label as magical – rituals, amulets, charms and treatments dependent on the occult virtues of animals, minerals and plants. No argument is usually advanced to justify the inclusion of these practices in the

Practica, and often they appear to be included as remedies of last resort. The same observation can be applied to contemporary treatises in the tradition of learned or rational surgery described by Michael McVaugh.[39]

Practica texts were sources for physician's handbooks and recipe collections but they themselves also absorbed charms and rituals circulating in recipe form.[40] In an English context, Lea Olsan has searched systematically for charms and prayers in four medical authors, two of whom wrote *Practica* texts, the *Compendium* of Gilbertus Anglicus and the *Rosa Anglica* of John Gaddesden. The other authors included were the fourteenth-century surgeon John Arderne and the fifteenth-century compiler of both medical and surgery texts, Thomas Fayreford.[41] Almost all the texts listed for these four authors concern remedies for particular complaints, though there are also three prayers to be recited before gathering herbs and one charm to free a prisoner (out of eighty-one texts in total). The most popular use of charms is to stop bleeding, but there are also many charms for toothache, for fevers, for epilepsy and for "spasm". Conception and childbirth are a focus for charms and rituals too. Charms for these complaints and others, with the exception of "spasm", also appear in late medieval medical commonplace books and remedy books. These were compiled for institutions, households and individuals not as academic texts like the *Practica* but as reservoirs of practical remedies and recipes. In the area of veterinary medicine, rituals and charms are also found in remedy books or added to texts in just the same way as with human medicine.[42] The official attitude of the medieval church to these healing rituals varied at different times and places, but there are plenty of examples copied into the margins of private prayer books and books of hours.[43]

Magic and impotence: causes and cures

Magic may be the cause of health problems as well as a means of treating them. Certain conditions could be considered as having been the result of malevolent human use of magical power. One condition more than others seems to have been the focus of medieval attention – that of impotence. Catherine Rider has made impotence the focus of a study that brings together the medieval discourses of canon law, theology, medicine, as well as the literature of chronicle and hagiography. Around 1150, impotence caused by *maleficium* was mentioned in the *Decretum* of Gratian, a work that became a canon law textbook, and in the *Sentences* of Peter Lombard, a work that became the set text for teaching theology in medieval universities. This form of hostile magic was of great dynastic as well as religious importance because it provided a uniquely acceptable reason in the eyes of the Church for the annulment of a marriage. The treatment of cases of magically caused impotence was first discussed in detail in the *Pantegni* of Constantine the African, a treatise translated from the Arabic in the late eleventh century. Rider's book offers in Appendix 1 an edition and translation of this influential Latin text, and the shorter text derived from it entitled "Remedies against Magic".[44]

In all these learned Latin texts, practices that might cause or remedy impotence are mentioned as objects of scholastic analysis. But as Rider shows narrative works such as histories and saints' lives contain incidental information about actual cases of impotence magic, and there were court cases arising in the late Middle Ages where accusations were made. For priests and friars confronting potential examples of *maleficium*, there were pastoral manuals like the *Summa confessorum* of Thomas of Chobham, which contained advice on grounds for annulment. Thomas argued that magic was never a valid reason, and recommended that the victim should fast and pray to God to be absolved from the magical spell. Most of what we know of *maleficium* and how to deal with it in legal and pastoral contexts is derived from these authoritative texts and Rider sees them as part of "a process of negotiation between popular and learned culture".[45] On the medical front, writings in the *Practica* tradition like the *Compendium* of Gilbertus Anglicus presented remedies for impotence caused by *maleficium* in the form of diet, potions made of herbs, ointment and plasters to be worn over the kidneys. For the same medical problem, he also includes a theriac, usually a medicine for poisons, and a plaster of St John's wort, supposed to be effective against demons. But if even these fail, there is a ritual remedy, an *empiricum*.[46]

Future directions

One of the themes of this chapter has been the way that magical healing as performative ritual is to be found in a wide variety of written sources – not just in books containing medical texts but in religious books and in practical books written for the use of communities and householders. Often rituals are unique items added by owners to their personal books, in the margins or between texts, as well as being found as elements within a text that may have been widely transmitted. What is more the history of medieval magical healing has to encompass significant geographical and temporal variety. The emergence of distinct vernacular traditions within Europe from the Anglo-Saxons onwards means that the shared heritage of Latinate culture cannot simply be assessed as a uniform development, much the same in one part of the continent as another. Though a lot of performative rituals can be shown to have had a long history, demonstrating impressive continuity over a millennium, these rituals were nevertheless also subject to variation depending on the contexts in which they were performed. A formula invoking the help of the holy mothers (of the Virgin, of Christ, of St John the Baptist) in childbirth may be written as an amulet or recited by a priest or used as a recipe by a medical practitioner, at different times or places. It follows from this that researchers interested in understanding the contingencies of magical healing in the Middle Ages must be prepared to look far afield. This is daunting but also spells opportunity for the enterprising. There is a wealth of discoveries to be made by the personal examination of manuscripts, for in most cases magical healing is not something of which the cataloguers of manuscripts can give notice. So the most urgent task for the historian of magical healing is a kind of fieldwork, collecting specimens, analyzing them in the light of other specimens already known and understanding the manuscript contexts and social circumstances in which they are found.[47]

Fieldwork of another kind has been taking place in the modern disciplines of ethnography and folklore studies – not so well established in the UK but flourishing elsewhere. Within university departments in these disciplines, there are systematic surveys of the use of incantation and ritual in modern cultures, most often conceived of in terms of folk narrative research. An impressive quantity of material recorded in many different vernacular languages has been collected, and those researching magical healing in the Middle Ages could profitably engage with the many publications that draw on these surveys. Many of the charms and rituals recorded in the nineteenth and twentieth centuries are remarkably similar in terms of their motifs and applications to healing to those found in medieval manuscripts.[48] Of course, it would be a mistake to assume that a ritual involving the writings of names on an amulet that can be found in a fourteenth-century manuscript is effectively the same ritual as that recorded by folklorists in a twentieth-century village – but the similarity should provoke serious thinking about the continuity and changes involved. Up until now, medieval historians have been slow to take up the challenge this material represents. But the sequence of conferences held over the last decade under the auspices of the Committee on Charms, Charmers and Charming of the International Society for Folk Narrative Research has given medievalists and folklorists the chance to engage with each other to their mutual profit.[49]

Early modern source material for magical healing also exists in considerable abundance.[50] Paradoxically much of this comes from those most hostile to magical healing. Those who compiled handbooks of charms and rituals to be condemned not only preserved them for others to read, but sometimes actively encouraged by their publications the very practices they wished to eradicate. This was evidently the case with the *Discoverie of Witchcraft* by Reginald Scot, which listed practices unable to stand up to the scrutiny of rationality and true religion.[51]

In terms of thematic approaches to medieval magical healing, there are significant gaps (or opportunities) when it comes to the investigation of particular medical complaints or conditions. Catherine Rider's work on impotence magic (see above) is a good example of the kind of case study that can be carried out. By bringing together medical, religious and legal sources, multiple perspectives open up, though this will not apply to every complaint. Conception and childbirth is another area recently studied.[52] But that leaves many other conditions indicated under "Medical conditions" above still to research. By concentrating on those specific parts of *Practica* literature, practitioner's notebooks, recipe collections and remedy books that deal with a particular condition, it is possible to pick out the incantations or rituals included and look at them as part of the spectrum of remedies on offer for that condition. Magical techniques for medical prognostications to determine whether a patient will live or die or the sex of a child also deserve more study as do the ritual aspects of veterinary medicine.[53]

Notes

1 In medicine, see, for example, the publications of Karl Sudhoff (1853–1938) and the journal *Sudhoffs Archiv*; for folklore, Ferdinand Ohrt, *Danmarks Trylleformler* (Copenhagen: Nordisk Forlag, 1917–21).
2 Peregrine Horden, "What's Wrong with Early Medieval Medicine?" *Social History of Medicine* 24 (2011): 5–25.
3 Peter Murray Jones and Lea T. Olsan, "Performative Rituals for Conception and Childbirth in England, 900–1500," *Bulletin of the History of Medicine* 89 (2015): 406–33.
4 Liselotte Hansmann and Lenz Kriss-Rettenbeck, *Amulett und Talisman: Erscheinungsform und Geschichte* (Munich: Callwey, 1966) is the most wide-ranging survey of amulets.
5 Don C. Skemer, *Binding Words: Textual Amulets in the Middle Ages* (University Park: Pennsylvania State University Press, 2006).
6 Edina Bozoky, *Charmes et prières apotropaïques*. Typologie des sources du Moyen Âge occidental 86 (Turnhout: Brepols, 2003).
7 Chiara Crisciani and Jole Agrimi, "Per una ricerca su '*experimentum/experimenta*': riflessione epistemologica e tradizione medica (secoli XIII–XV)," in *Presenza del lessico greco e latino nelle lingue contemporanee*, ed. Pietro Janni and Innocenzo Mazzini (Macerata: Università di Macerata, 1990), 9–49.
8 M.L. Cameron, *Anglo-Saxon Medicine* (Cambridge: Cambridge University Press, 1993), 130–58; Audrey Meaney, "Extra-medical Elements in Anglo-Saxon Medicine," *Social History of Medicine* 24 (2011): 41–56.
9 On this Anglo-Saxon Field Remedy, Debby Banham, "The Staff of Life: Cross and Blessings in Anglo-Saxon Cereal Production," in *Cross and Cruciform in the Anglo-Saxon World: Studies to Honor the Memory of Timothy Reuter*, ed. S.L. Keefer, K.L. Jolly and C.E. Karkov (Morgantown: West Virginia University Press, 2010), 279–318; Ciaran Arthur, "Ploughing through Cotton Caligula A.VII: Reading the Sacred Words of the Heliand and the Aecerbot," *Review of English Studies*, New series, 65 (2013): 1–17.

10 Karen Louise Jolly, *Popular Religion in Late Saxon England: Elf Charms in Context* (Chapel Hill: University of North Carolina Press, 1996).
11 Alaric Hall, *Elves in Anglo-Saxon England: Matters of Belief, Health, Gender, and Identity* (Woodbridge: Boydell, 2007), 104–8; Jolly, *Popular Religion*, 160–62.
12 *Anglo-Saxon Remedies, Charms, and Prayers from British Library MS Harley 585: The Lacnunga*, 2 vols., ed. and transl. Edward Pettit (Lewiston, NY: E. Mellen Press, 2001), nos. xvii, xviii, xxv, lxiii, lxv, lxxxi.
13 Francis B. Brévart, "Between Medicine, Magic, and Religion: Wonder Drugs in German Medico-Pharmaceutical Treatises of the Thirteenth to the Sixteenth Centuries," *Speculum* 83 (2008): 1–57.
14 Emilie Savage-Smith, "Islamic Magic Texts vs Magical Artefacts," *Societas Magica Newsletter* 11 (2003): 1–6; on cramp rings, see the London Science Museum site at: www.sciencemuseum.org.uk/broughttolife/objects/display.aspx?id=92460; Peter Murray Jones and Lea T. Olsan, "Middleham Jewel: Ritual, Power and Devotion," *Viator* 31 (2000): 249–90; R.W. Lightbown, *Mediaeval European Jewellery* (London: Victoria & Albert Museum, 1992), nos. 1–31; Geoff Egan and Frances Pritchard, *Dress Accessories c.1150–1450* (London: HMSO, 1991), nos. 1308, 1309, 1313, 1336, 1337, 1360–63, 1618; Brian Spencer, *Pilgrim Souvenirs and Secular Badges. Medieval Finds from Excavations in London*, 7 (Woodbridge: Boydell, 2010).
15 Haralampos Passalis, "From the Power of Words to the Power of Rhetoric: Nonsense Pseudo-Nonsense Words, and Artificially Constructed Compounds in Greek Oral Charms," *Incantatio: An International Journal on Charms, Charmers and Charming* 2 (2012): 6–22.
16 Peter Murray Jones, "Amulets: Prescriptions and Surviving Objects from Late Medieval England," in *Beyond Pilgrim Souvenirs and Secular Badges: Essays in Honour of Brian Spencer*, ed. Sarah Blick (Oxford: Oxbow Books, 2007), 92–107.
17 In Don Skemer's definition, "Textual amulets ... were generally brief apotropaic texts, handwritten or mechanically printed on separate sheets, rolls, and scraps of parchment, paper, or other flexible writing supports of varying dimensions." Skemer, *Binding Words*, 1. See also W.L. Braekman, *Middeleeuwe witte en zwarte magie in het Nederlands taalgebied. Gecommentarieerd compendium van incantamenta tot einde 16de eeuw* (Gent: Koninklijke Academie voor Nederlandse Taal- en Letterkunde, Reeks 6, 1997); Dick E.H. de Boer, "Protego-proterreo. Making an Amulet by Mutilating a Manuscript," *Quaerendo* 41 (2011): 112–25.
18 Judith Wilcox and John M. Riddle, "Qusta ibn Luqa's *Physical Ligatures* and the Recognition of the Placebo Effect," *Medieval Encounters: Jewish, Christian and Muslim Culture in Confluence and Dialogue* 1 (1995): 1–48 (esp. 33, lines 58–64, line 73, trans. p. 42).
19 Wilcox and Riddle, "*Physical Ligatures*," 22.
20 Ibid., 33.
21 Maaike Van der Lugt, "The Learned Physician as a Charismatic Healer: Urso of Salerno (Flourished End of Twelfth Century) on Incantations in Medicine, Magic, and Religion," *Bulletin of the History of Medicine* 87 (2013): 307–46, Appendix 2 (335–46).
22 In what follows, we have relied on van de Lugt's Appendix both for the Latin and the translations.
23 Roger Bacon, *Opus maius*, IV, p. 395, as cited by Béatrice Delaurenti, *La puissance des mots, virtus verborum: débats doctrinaux sur le pouvoir des incantations au Moyen Âge* (Paris: Cerf, 2007), 159.
24 Delaurenti, *La puissance des mots*; Béatrice Delaurenti, "Acting Through Words in the Middle Ages: Communication and Action in the Debates on the Power of Incantations," www.cairn-int.info/article-E_ASSR_158_0053--acting-through-words-in-the-middle-ages.htm [accessed 9 September 2015]; *Médecine, astrologie et magie entre Moyen Âge et Renaissance: autour de Pietro d'Abano*, ed. Jean-Patrice Boudet, Franck Collard and Nicolas Weill-Parot (Florence: Sismel Edizioni del Galluzzo, 2013).
25 For general surveys of conditions for which magical remedies existed, see *Handwörterbuch des Deutschen Aberglaubens*, 10 vols., ed. Hanns Bächtold-Staubli and E. Hoffmann-Krayer (Berlin: Walter de Gruyter, 1927–42).
26 See below, pp. 306–7.
27 Owen Davies, *Popular Magic: Cunning Folk in English History* (London: Hambledon Continuum, 2007); Willem De Blécourt, "Witch Doctors, Soothsayers and Priests. On Cunning Folk in European Historiography and Tradition," *Social History* 19 (1994): 285–303.
28 Though of course these services were not cheap for the consumer necessarily: see Davies, *Popular Magic*, 86–89.

29 John B. Friedman, *Northern English Books, Owners, and Makers in the Late Middle Ages* (Syracuse, NY: Syracuse University Press, 1995), 167–70.
30 Translated from the Dutch: haemorrhoids, bloodstilling, fiery skin, burns, diarrhoea, corns, epilepsy, abscess, birth and afterbirth, child's failure to thrive, headache, uvula swelling, canker, fever, cramp, sore breasts, spleen, skin diseases, eye complaints, plague, fingertip infections?, rabies, sleep, stone, toothache, foreign object in the body, wounds, worms, and others [cured by saints]. Braekman, *Middeleeuwe witte en zwarte magie*, VII–VIII, 48–203.
31 *Handwörterbuch des Deutschen Aberglaubens*, entries "Segen," and "Longinussegen", "Jordansegen", etc. for specific types of verbal cures; Eleonora Cianci, *Incantesimi e benedizioni nessa letteratura tedesca medievale (IX–XIII sec.)*, Göppinger Arbeiten zur Germanistik 717 (Göppingen: Kümmerle Verlag, 2004).
32 Eleonora Cianci, *The German Tradition of the Three Good Brothers Charm* (Göppingen: Kümmerle Verlag, 2013); Lea T. Olsan, "The Three Good Brothers Charm: Some Historical Points," *Incantatio* 1 (2011): 48–78.
33 Lea Olsan, "The Corpus of charms in the Middle English Leechcraft Remedy Books," in *Charms, Charmers and Charming: International Research on Verbal Magic*, ed. Jonathan Roper (London: Palgrave Macmillan, 2009), 222–23.
34 Alessandra Foscati, *Ignis sacer: una storia culturale del "fuoco sacro" dall'antichità al Settecento* (Florence: Sismel Edizioni del Galluzzo, 2013); Lea T. Olsan, "The Language of Charms in a Middle English Recipe Collection, *ANQ* 18 (2005): 29–35.
35 Jones and Olsan, "Performative Rituals"; Don C. Skemer, "Amulet Rolls and Female Devotion in the Late Middle Ages," *Scriptorium* 55 (2001): 197–227.
36 Lea T. Olsan, "Charms and Prayers in Medieval Medical Theory and Practice," *Social History of Medicine* 16 (2003).
37 Luke Demaitre, "Theory and Practice in Medical Education at the University of Montpellier in the Thirteenth and Fourteenth Centuries," *Journal of the History of Medicine and Allied Sciences* 30 (1975): 103–23; Luke Demaitre, "Scholasticism in Compendia of Practical Medicine, 1250–1450," *Manuscripta* 20 (1976): 81–95; Luke Demaitre, *Medieval Medicine: The Art of Healing, from Head to Toe* (Santa Barbara, CA: Praeger, 2013).
38 Danielle Jacquart, "Theory, Everyday Practice, and Three Fifteenth-Century Physicians," *Osiris* 6 (1990): 140–60.
39 Michael McVaugh, *The Rational Surgery of the Middle Ages* (Firenze: Sismel Edizioni del Galluzzo, 2006); Michael McVaugh, "*Incantationes* in Late Medieval Surgery," in *Ratio et Superstitio: Essays in honor of Graziella Federici Vescovini*, ed. Giancarlo Marchetti, Orsola Rignani and Valeria Sorge (Louvain-La-Neuve: Fédération internationale des instituts d'études médiévales, 2003), 321–29.
40 For definitions and discussion of remedy books, see Tony Hunt, *Popular Medicine in Thirteenth-Century England: Introduction and Texts* (Cambridge, MA: D.S. Brewer, 1990), and Linda Ehrsam Voigts, "Scientific and Medical Books," in *Book Production and Publishing in Britain, 1375–1475*, ed. Jeremy Griffiths and Derek Pearsall (Cambridge: Cambridge University Press, 1989), 345–402.
41 Olsan, "Charms and Prayers," 343–66.
42 See for example Bernard Ribemont, "Science et magie: la thérapie magique dans l'hippiatrie médiévale," in *Zauberer und Hexen in der Kultur des Mittelalters*, ed. Danielle Buschinger and Wolfgang Spiewok (Greifswald: Reineke-Verlag, 1994), 181.
43 Catherine Rider, "Medical Magic and the Church in Thirteenth-Century England," *Social History of Medicine* 24 (2011): 92–107; Catherine Rider, *Magic and Religion in Medieval England* (London: Reaktion Books, 2012), 55–69; Eamon Duffy, *Marking the Hours: English People and Their Prayers, 1240–1570* (New Haven, CT: Yale University Press, 2006), ch. 5.
44 Re-edited by Enrique Montero Cartelle as "Remedia contra maleficia: Origen y formacíon," *Revista de Estudios Latinos* 10 (2010): 131–58.
45 Catherine Rider, *Magic and Impotence in the Middle Ages* (Oxford: Oxford University Press, 2006), 214.
46 Rider, *Magic and Impotence*, 163–65; Jones and Olsan, "Performative Rituals," 412–14.
47 Laura Mitchell, "Cultural Uses of Magic in the Fifteenth Century," Ph.D. thesis, University of Toronto, 2011; László Sándor Chardonnens and Rosanne Hebing, "Two Charms in a Late Medieval English Manuscript at Nijmegen University Library," *Review of English Studies*, 62 (2010): 181–92, New Series; Rebecca M.C. Fisher, "The Anglo-Saxon Charms: Texts in Context," *RMN Newsletter* 4 (May 2012): 108–26.

48 See, for example, Patricia Ann Clark, *A Cretan Healer's Handbook in the Byzantine Tradition, Text, Translation and Commentary* (Farnham: Ashgate, 2011) and James Kapaló, *Text, Context and Performance: Gagauz Folk Religion in Discourse and Practice* (Leiden and Boston: Brill, 2011).

49 See www.isfnr.org/files/committeecharms.html for an overview of this activity. A number of the conferences have given risen to monographs noticed there.

50 For a valuable recent example from Eastern Europe, see Emanuela Timotin, *Paroles protectrices, paroles guérisseuses. La tradition manuscrite des charmes roumains (XVIIe-XIXe siècles)*, (Paris: Presses de l'Université Paris-Sorbonne, 2015). For English material, see above all, Jonathan Roper, *English Verbal Charms* (Helsinki: Suomalainen Tiedeakatemia, 2005).

51 Frank Klaassen and Christopher Phillips, "The Return of Stolen Goods: Reginald Scot, Religious Controversy, and Magic in Bodleian Library, Additional B. 1," *Magic, Ritual and Witchcraft* 1 (2006): 135–76.

52 Jones and Olsan, "Performative Rituals".

53 Matthew Milner, "The Physics of Holy Oats: Vernacular Knowledge, Qualities and Remedy in Fifteenth-Century England," *Journal of Medieval Early Modern Studies* 43 (2013): 219–45; Joanne Edge, "Licit Medicine or 'Pythagorean necromancy'? The 'Sphere of Life and Death' in Late Medieval England," *Historical Research* 87 (2014): 611–32.

23

ILLUSION

Robert Goulding

In 1829, Eusèbe Salverte published an essay on magic, in which he attempted to find a universal explanation for all supposed magical acts.[1] Writing in an age in which technology was just beginning to transform human life, Salverte looked to science as a key to understanding magic. The marvels attributed to magicians, he argued, were nothing other than the exploits of scientists, misunderstood by an ignorant populace. And where such an explanation did not seem plausible, Salverte suggested that ancient "magicians" had learned to harness the powers of lenses and mirrors in order deliberately to mislead the gullible. Sir Walter Scott, in his *Letters on Demonology and Witchcraft* the following year, proposed similar arguments, though with less of a technological bent; and, in 1832, David Brewster wrote in response to Scott a series of *Letters on Natural Magic*, in which he introduced English readers to the details of Salverte's arguments. All three works enjoyed great popularity into the early twentieth century. Their influence can be seen not only in contemporary accounts of magic but also in Victorian publications on stage magic and "phantasmagoria," which presupposed a continuity between ancient and medieval magic, and nineteenth-century special visual effects.[2]

Magic, in other words, was some type of illusion, either deliberately inflicted by magicians (using quite marvellous technology), or the product of ignorance in the face of science. This naively "scientific" theory was quite ahistorical: to begin with, the technology of illusion these authors presupposed simply did not exist in antiquity or the Middle Ages. And in the light of modern anthropological and historical theories of magic, the nineteenth-century illusion theory seems like a quaint oddity. Perhaps because this was the background against which our modern notions of magic developed, the very category of "illusion" has almost entirely disappeared from the historiography of magic.[3] Yet, it is mistake to dismiss illusion from the scholarly discourse on magic. First, because there are many ancient and medieval magical *experimenta* whose only purpose seemed to be to produce illusory appearances. And second, and most importantly, because illusion was in fact one of the most important explanatory tools for medieval philosophers and theologians: magic, for the most part, *was* an illusion. In this essay, I will limit myself to the role that illusion played in the medieval understanding of magic; at the end, I will suggest some directions for future research, including on illusory experiments.

Augustine on magic and illusion

In the midst of his long battle with pagan authorities over the nature of their gods, Augustine engaged with a story recorded by Varro,[4] that the great Greek warrior Diomedes, after his return from Troy, was constantly accompanied by birds: his former companions and comrades in arms, magically transformed. Varro reported that the apotheosized Diomedes was worshipped to his own day on the island of Diomedea, and his temple was thronged with birds – the descendants of the very same birds that had once been his companions in Troy. Augustine was, of course, sceptical of this story. For one thing, if Diomedes was really a god, why could he not change the birds back into men? But more importantly, he seized on something that Varro himself seemed to have some doubts about: the very fact of the men being transformed into birds. Varro tried to make this aspect of the story more plausible by citing other cases of animal transformation: Circe's turning of Odysseus's men into beasts, for example. And Augustine himself had heard stories of Italian landladies who transformed young men into beasts of burden by feeding them magically tainted cheese; they retained their human, rational minds, even as they were put to work in the farmyard, until they were finally restored to human shape, with full memory of all that had befallen them. Augustine's own countryman, Apuleius, had recorded a very similar incident a couple of centuries earlier, in his *Golden Ass* (a work that Augustine was unsure whether to classify as autobiography or fiction).

But how did these transformations come about? Could men really be turned into animals – and even have animal descendants centuries later? Of course, Augustine allowed, God can do anything he wants, and might well punish or favour someone with such a transformation. But none of these cases seemed to be the work of God. Augustine implied that they must instead have been the work of demons, acting (as they must always act) with the permission of God. Demons, however, are incapable of any real creation, but can only alter appearances. Moreover, it is impossible to imagine that the human form (still less the human mind), both fashioned by God, could be changed in substance by demons. So, in cases where people have experienced such a transformation, they have really only been made to experience a *phantasticum hominis*, a phantasm or illusion of a man, by which Augustine appears to mean the shape that a man can take in his dreams or wanderings of his imagination. Whoever was seen to be transformed in fact lay asleep somewhere, while his *phantasticum* was presented to the senses of the witnesses; indeed, the victim himself might be made to experience the *phantasticum* rather than his own form and senses.

The transformation of Odysseus's men must thus have been an illusion: no one was really changed; but to both Odysseus and his men themselves, they seemed to be changed into brute beasts. The story of Diomedes was a little more difficult to explain by means of illusion: these were real birds that had reproduced after their kind for centuries. Augustine suggested that, in this case, the demons used a sleight of hand to substitute real birds for Diomedes's companions: "Conjuring tricks (*praestigiae*) of this sort cannot be difficult for demons (provided God's judgement permit)."[5]

In Augustine's attack on Varro's story of Diomedes, we can discern a theory of magic – a theory that was to be enormously influential on subsequent Christian authors. Magical effects were brought about by demons (with God's permission), but their power did not extend to actually changing substances, and especially not the human body and mind. Instead, they were permitted only to create *phantasmata*, or illusions. These illusions were like dreams, but were much more vivid – indistinguishable, in fact, from reality.

In a very few cases, real alterations seemed to have taken place. One troubling example concerned the competition between Moses and Aaron, and Pharaoh's magicians, where the magicians turned their staffs into snakes, having seen Aaron do the same thing at the direction of God (Exodus 7:10–13). Had Aaron performed magic? What distinguished his feat from that of the Egyptian magicians? Augustine believed, uncontroversially, that Aaron's miracle had been performed directly by God. But in one discussion of this episode,

Augustine wrote that Pharaoh's magicians also really (not just apparently) turned their staffs into snakes, by magical incantations and the intervention of demons, who had been granted this extraordinary right to change the substance of something in order to bring about Pharaoh's downfall.[6] This curious biblical incident would continue to test theories of magic through the medieval period.

Augustine's theory of magic was not original with him. Rather, he was hewing quite closely to an understanding of magic that had been worked out by earlier Christian authors. In the writings of Irenaeus, Hippolytus, Lactantius and many others, magic was taken to be a kind of *fraus* (deception), *elusio* (delusion or illusion) or phantasm. It might be effected by a deception or sleight of hand that was within the skill of any trained human, or by means of a sleight of hand so difficult that only a demon could do it. Even in the latter case, however, it was *still* an illusion, insofar as it made that which was not present, appear to be present. Cases in which magic brought about real changes in the world were the rarest of exceptions, and were treated as extraordinary events that fell outside of the explanatory scope of the theory.[7]

Medieval theories of illusion

Two important elements of the ancient theory – illusion or imagination (*phantasia* and its cognates), and trickery (*praestigia* or *praestigium*) – were shared by the scholastic theorists of magic, despite the variety among the principal authors. There was a consensus that magic was either natural, or illusory, or a mixture of both. They agreed, in other words, that even though magic seemed miraculous and entirely outside the normal order of nature, this was only an appearance. Where scholastic authors differed was in how they divided up the labour, as it were. Were the deceptive appearances the work of the magician? Or were they the work of demons? And, in each case, were they brought about by the methods of conjurors and jugglers, or did the agent, human or demonic act directly on the imagination or senses of the observers? Finally, having determined where the causation lay, was anyone criminally culpable for these illusions?

William of Auvergne

One of the earliest and most important medieval theorists of magic was William of Auvergne (c. 1180–c. 1249), who was the bishop of Paris from 1228 until his death. As a recent study of his work has argued, William's work represents an early attempt to engage with the newly available Aristotelian texts – not in order to develop an Aristotelian natural philosophy or metaphysics for its own sake, but in order to sustain a fundamentally Augustinian theology, picking up bits and pieces from Aristotle, the commentary tradition, as well as scientific and magical texts.[8] Unsystematic though he may have been, there emerges from his writing a clear desire, inspired by Aristotle, to explain the world naturalistically, even mechanistically, and to attempt to discover the modes of causation (perhaps unseen) between substances that produce marvellous effects.[9] In the course of sifting through the various phenomena that might be taken to be inexplicable in these terms (particularly *magical* effects), William developed the notion of "natural magic," a term that first appears in his work.[10] He certainly abhorred genuine demonic magic, which he insisted should be eradicated (to use one of his favourite phrases) "by fire and sword." However, such truly diabolical magic formed a rather small part of those actions that were popularly believed to be magical. In other words, under the guise of attacking magic, William set out a robust defence of *natural* magic, saving many marvellous and (to that point) inexplicable actions from the suspicion of demonic collusion. His work is of relevance to us here because (as one might expect from this Augustinian thinker) illusion plays a very central role in his explanation of magical effects. And the importance of his work cannot be overstated: the categories he sets out will be invoked both by inquisitors and witch-hunters, and by pious natural magicians well into the seventeenth century.

The passage that is most often cited from William's work occurs towards the end of his vast treatise *De universo*, in a chapter entitled "On the three types of magical actions, and on the marvellous virtues of certain things."[11] At the very beginning of the chapter, William set out two principal divisions in apparently magical acts, both of them illusory, but in different ways. The first involves the quickness of hands "such as the placing and moving of certain things, which are commonly called manipulations or shufflings, and these are great marvels to men, until they know how they are done."[12] In other words, these are the kinds of illusions that are done by jugglers and other entertainers; they do not play a large role in William's theory, but later readers of his work will make more use of this category. The second type of magic will occupy most of William's attention: phenomena that "have no reality at all outside of appearance, which are brought about by the addition or removal of certain things."[13]

William began his examination of this second genus of magic with an illusion with certain types of lamps that produce misleading visions.[14] His first example is a lamp made of wax and "sulphurated" snake skin. This lamp is lit in a place where there are no other lamps, and where the floor is strewn with straw and chaff: then, he said, the individual pieces of straw would seem to be snakes slithering through the house. The colours in the snake skin impart a similar greenness to the pieces of straw, while the motion of the flame makes them appear to move. It was, then, a familiar trick of the light: he compared the illusion to mistaking a leaf for a frog by night, or a stick to a snake. So too did piles of rotting vegetation, fish scales and "the back-ends of certain insects" seem to be fires. William was in fact rationalizing an experiment that, in its original form, simply stated that lighting such a lamp would conjure up the appearance of countless snakes; William added all of the details about the straw on the floor, the flickering, green light and so on, in order to bring the effect claimed of the lamp into the realm of naturally explicable causation.[15]

He did something similar with a lamp that is one of the very oldest illusions of this type. The original recipe (attributed to Anaxilaus) called for the tears or semen of an ass to be mixed with the oil in a lamp. When the lamp was lit, all of those in the room would appear to have the head of an ass. William talked instead of a candle, the wax of which is blended with ass's semen or tears. Aside from some quite reasonable doubts whether you *could* mix wax with these substances – and whether such a candle would actually light – William had no difficulty believing that semen, at least, could bring about so wonderful an effect, and quite naturally reproduce its own image.

The justification for William's argument is found in the previous chapter, which is ostensibly concerned with the power of music, but which actually ranges over a wide variety of phenomena that affect the soul, apparently invisibly. Behind many such phenomena, William argued, is the inner *vis imaginationis*, a powerful faculty of visualization which, for most human beings, lies obscured by the vices of the soul and the disturbances of the senses, but can be released by various artificial means: gazing at a shiny object as a means of divination, or in certain magical mirrors.[16] But, William emphasized, nature will always outstrip art and the power even of the imagination; even alchemy cannot bring about the kinds of transmutations that nature can. From sheep, we get milk; we can turn it into butter, cheese and whey, but nature, far more marvellously, will transform it into the blood, flesh and bone of growing lambs. There are the examples of miraculous stones generated in the foreheads of reptiles and amphibians. And finally, and most importantly, semen, which can bring about the generation of all kinds of animals, in all their parts – and within its marvellous generative power, there is a divine art, which could be taught by God to humans.[17] Semen thus has a "magical," but entirely natural virtue – to generate and reproduce after its kind, and was for William a paradigm for a certain type of marvellous object and magical operation:

> There are also other things that are brought about by the mixing together and blending of natures, many of which are known, but many more of which are as yet hidden away. He who knows the hidden powers and possibilities of these natures, does many marvellous things, and would be able to do things that were even more marvellous, if there were the possibility of using plenty of these things, and if there were sufficient knowledge of them; for this reason, men of this sort have been called "magi," meaning "men who do great things (*magna*)," although the word has also been interpreted to mean that they are evil men (*mali*), who do evil things. But those who do these things through the ministry of demons truly should be called and considered evil men, doing evil.[18]

To return to William's candle, it is now clear how it might fit into his general scheme of causation. The effects of the candle, whether "real" or not, are entirely explicable given the marvellous powers found in semen; moreover, the manipulation of these powers, even to the ridiculous end of placing an ass's head on peoples' heads, is quite blameless, and nothing more than a kind of expertise in the natural powers of substance. At the same time, the effects of this lamp cannot but recall Augustine's unfortunate young men who were apparently transformed into asses. Semen may have the ability to generate real things, but (if we take Augustine seriously) if men appear to be asses, it can *only* be an appearance. William is entirely in agreement with Augustine. He noted, in this context, that it is very easy to make illusions (*apparentia*) of this kind, bringing about a great effect with very slender cause, for, among all the senses, vision (and its internal counterpart, the *vis imaginationis*) is the easiest to deceive.[19] By just a small *infectio* (by which William could mean either a disease or a manipulation), it can seem that everything is black, or pointed, or shaking or receding – and countless other deceptions. And then there is the *praestigium*, whereby someone thinks his hand is the hoof of an ass and is embarrassed to take it out of his lap, "which perhaps you've read in this sort of experiment books, if you recall."[20] So long as we can be sure that demons were not involved, this illusion too must have been performed in a similar way: by lighting a specially prepared candle, or anointing the hand itself, in order to affect the outward or inward senses.

But how can we be certain that an illusion is natural, and not the work of evil spirits? William considered, in contrast, a *praestigium* he found in an experiment book, which would make water appear where there is no water. The illusion was effected by firing an arrow made of a certain kind of wood, from a bow made of yet another kind of wood, strung with a certain kind of cord. Unlike the candle illusions, in this illusion, none of these substances had the natural power of generating water (whether in reality or as an appearance). So the effect must actually have been brought about by demons, attracted by the fact that the materials are not used in any way (*utique*). For the books say that one must collect such and such wood, or stone, or liquid or whatever else at a particular day and hour – and that, said William, is worship (*oblatio*): service and worship of demons.[21] Of course (he added), the writers of the experiment books did not actually mention worship; if they did, no one would ever try the experiment. And this is precisely the sign of diabolical fraud in these sorts of experiments: that materials are brought together that, in themselves, have no power to do what they promise; unknown to the practitioner, they are in fact used to worship the demons, and to ensnare the unwitting experimenter into collusion with diabolical powers.

As William went on to say, he permitted only experiments where the materials had been collected "anyhow" (*utique*), not at special times, or while making certain incantations. In articulating this difference, he may have been echoing Pliny's similar distinction between medicine, and the confection of medicine, astrology and religion that he considered to be magic.[22] The ingredients in Pliny's own recipes are often indistinguishable from those of the "Magi," except that his recipes never call for the materials to be gathered at an astrologically propitious time, while saying certain words, and so forth – elements that Pliny considers too superstitious.[23] In this same chapter, William actually went on to consider a marvel reported by Pliny: the power of the mineral heliotrope to cause invisibility.[24] But whereas Pliny rejected this power out of hand, because, according to the Magi, it only manifested itself after certain incantations had been made, William is willing to consider that it has this effect, so long as there are no such superstitious accompaniments and the power arises purely through the natural virtues of the stone. Having made this distinction, William went on robustly to defend the existence of myriad *virtutes occultae* in things, which demonstrate God's power, and which could, with the right intentions, be used blamelessly by the faithful.

This, then, is one important part of William's account of illusion: on the one hand, certain substances can give rise to extraordinary illusions, simply through their own natural properties; but, on the other hand, *some* illusions are actually brought about by demons, and one must use great care to distinguish these cases. In order to understand *how* these illusions take place, we need to pay some closer attention to William's theory of the imagination.

The fullest account of the imagination is found in an earlier chapter of this part of the *De universo*.[25] Here, he considered the inner light, or *vis imaginationis*, a source of knowledge (after a fashion)[26] that is occluded by the senses and the faults of the soul. This imaginative force is able to explain many odd phenomena. Blind men, for instance, are able to survive in the world because their inner imagination is magnified by the loss of sight. One blind man William knew devoted himself to fighting all his life, and was an excellent fighter, because of the strength of the *vis imaginationis*; late in life, he reformed his ways and devoted himself to religion – and that same, magnified inner light allowed him to make great progress towards holiness in a short time.[27] Similarly, dogs are able to seek out hidden thieves – and that is not because they have sharp senses of smell (after all, as William points out, a thief has no particular scent!), but because they are endowed by nature by a strong *vis imaginationis*, which allows them to perceive the thief *inwardly*.[28]

As we have seen above, William explained divination in shiny objects in terms of the *vis imaginationis*: the dazzling and temporary blinding of the external sense allowed the images in the internal sense to be recognized by the intellect. And magic lamps, or illusory candles, were to be explained in similar ways: the generative power of the ingredients in the illumination (semen, for example) overwhelmed the senses, both internal and external. William gave his fullest account of how precisely this might happen when he turned his attention to certain suffumigations that were said to be able to bring about dreams that were not only vivid but also actually contained illuminations from God.

> You should know that the eye of an Indian turtle, and the heart of a hoopoe, and everything else of this type have the power of attracting vapors that deepen sleep, and generate visions in dream, and because of this, by their powers they may free the soul from its heaviness, and make it ready, ... and in this way prepare it for receiving illuminations.[29]

William could not leave the matter here; it would be theologically difficult (to say the least) to maintain that by burning such bizarre substances, one could more or less compel God to deliver illuminating dreams. The solution, William explained, could be found in substances that were known to have *virtutes horrificae*, such as one reads about in "books of tricks" (*in libris praestigiorum*).[30] There one learns that if something inimical to human nature (such as the liver of a crow) is buried secretly, anyone visiting that place will feel inexplicably terrified. Now, fear and horror are emotions that can drive the soul inward, shaking it from its close connection with the body, and hence making it more susceptible to illuminations.[31] It would not be unusual, then, concluded William, if the turtle's eye or hoopoe's heart had the same power to terrify (and thus, *indirectly*, made illuminations possible).[32]

Such, then, is William's theory of illusions, as they may be brought about by natural substances. It remains to consider the illusions that demons create, which is the subject of an entire chapter of the *De universo*.[33] He begins with the example of coins that keep returning to their sender.[34] Just as a bow and arrow that causes the illusion of a flood must be the result of demonic activity, so too a repeatedly returning coin must be the work of demons, since gold and silver can have no *virtus gressibilis aut volatilis*. Demons can easily create appearances of coins when there are none there. Saints' lives record that demons often take on the form of beautiful women or serpents; it would be even easier for them to transform themselves into coins.

As he did with the other, natural illusions, William thought through the mechanics by which the demons could change their form, and came to much the same conclusion: that the transformation was only apparent, and took place in the *vis imaginationis*. His argument proceeds, essentially, by eliminating any alternatives. Many have thought that demons forms were in the air, but that is impossible: air cannot retain forms. William was very likely thinking of the optical transmission of visual *species* through the air: although the apparent forms of things move from the visible object to the eye, the air never "holds on" to those appearances in mid-flight, as it were. Thus, demons too would be unable to fashion appearance in the air. The optical interpretation of this passage is supported by William's subsequent statement that no transparent object could hold their forms, for, after all, one can only make a mirror (which does hold images) by obstructing a transparent glass with opaque lead. Nor could such illusions be effected by altering the form of a solid, material body. Demons (or their assumed appearances) are able to disappear in a moment; but when forms are imposed on physical objects (as in painting or sculpture), they can only be removed with effort. "And so all that remains is that a form of this type is only in the soul of the person who is being deceived by it."[35] Demons can (always provided God permits) create illusions very easily by "painting" (*depingere*) in the imagination; and these are not merely untrue thoughts, but will be sensual experiences, indistinguishable in their perceived reality from the genuine contents of the senses – much like the illusory appearances we experience in dreams.[36]

William went on to examine some difficult cases that might seem to involve actual physical transformation; and, in each case, he showed that the transformations were illusory, in the sense that the only real change was in the imaginations of the observers. For example, some report that demons transform a reed into a horse; but this cannot actually be the case. Either the imagination is fooled so that it perceives the reed as a horse, or (which is probably more likely) there never was a reed in the first place, only a horse that had been made to appear to be a reed! He concluded with a very vivid illusion which, he said, was often reported by the people of Brittany. According to their accounts, this would happen to a lone traveller on the road. He would suddenly find himself in a fabulous castle, where he saw a very beautiful woman dressed as a queen; then he would enjoy a sumptuous feast with her before, inevitably, a night of exquisite lovemaking.[37] But then the entire scene suddenly would disappear, the traveller discovering that he has spent the night lying in the filthy mud, between the thigh bones of a cow,[38] and his horse has been tied to a tree all night and has eaten nothing (thereby thwarting his next day of travel). "And I remember that I could have seen a man to whom this illusion occurred, but I didn't go to see him, by my own negligence and laziness," William added.

This account corroborated much of his theory of illusion. The reality was that one had been lying in the mud all night, relieving oneself between the thigh bones of a cow – and that sorry situation would be abundantly clear the moment one awoke. The castle, and the queen, had no reality except in the *vis imaginationis* where (as in other cases of illusion) they were experienced not as thoughts, but as things actually present and happening. They were in a sense a dream, but a dream imposed from outside. And, as the bishop bluffly puts it, when it came to being in a beautiful castle and making love to a beautiful woman, "what man hasn't had a dream like that?"[39] The purpose of the illusion, so far as one can tell, seemed to be to humiliate the traveller and delay his journey. Even though demons cannot change the appearances or forms of anything (in reality), they can, like any other agent, move things with which they are in contact. So it is the demon who pushes the traveller into the stinking mud, between the thighs of a dead cow, and it is also the demon who ties up his horse for the night.

William seems more to pity the recipients of illusions, than to blame them, except when the deceived are women. For example, peasant women believe that a *Domina abundia* rides with her fellow witches, from house to house, bringing prosperity (and illusory banquets) wherever she enters. So welcome are her visits that women leave out food and drink at night to attract these visitors.[40] Such appearances are, of course, merely the manipulation of the imagination by demons; but the women's response is idolatry, and must be "rooted out with fire and sword" (*igneque et gladio exterminanda*). And, in a very troubling passage, William describes the belief that *stryges* and *lamiae* come into houses at night, seize children and then are seen to butcher, roast and eat them. All of this is mere illusion: demons do not have bodies, and do not eat. But, he adds, God does sometimes permit them really to kill babies, in order to punish parents who love their children more than they love God. The butchering, cooking and eating are just typically grotesque demonic play with the imagination; but the murder of the children "is an expedient, and healthy way to deal with these parents, because the cause of offense to the creator is removed."[41]

William's theory of illusion, and the limits he put on the real versus the illusory action of demons, formed the basis of subsequent medieval theories of magic and illusion. In what follows, I will consider, more briefly, several medieval authors who respond, each in their own way, to William's theory. First, the arguments of pseudo-Albertus Magnus and Thomas

Aquinas; then, the more sceptical and naturalistic thought of Nicole Oresme; and finally, the inquisitors' handbook *Malleus maleficarum*, in which William's theory (and its later developments) was used to identify those who are culpable for consorting with demons.

Ps.-Albertus Magnus and Thomas Aquinas

One of the major sources of illusionistic experiments in the Middle Ages and Renaissance was the *De mirabilibus mundi*, part of the enormously popular *Liber aggregationis* attributed to Albertus Magnus. This treatise was prefaced with a defence of magic on natural grounds; while philosophically unsophisticated, its ubiquity meant that its arguments had considerable influence on later theories of magic.[42]

According to this theory, magical effects were brought about by the soul, which had the capacity to make substantial changes in the world when in a state of extreme emotional excitement. The rituals and incantations of magic served only to bring the soul into that pitch of emotion, such that its natural powers can be exercised – the author cited Avicenna for this notion.[43] In the case of natural magic, some substances caused marvellous effects because they drew together things that were in sympathy with them, or repelled those that were antagonistic. Alternatively, just as in medicine, hot substances cure cold conditions, and *vice versa*, so too the marvellous effects of natural substances may work by an application of actives to passives (to use a phrase coined later by Aquinas, to express the same concept).

The similarities with William's theory are evident. But the author of this preface differed from William in his conviction that all magic was blameless, because demons were never involved. Even ritual magic, he insisted, brought about its effects by *natural* means, not demonic. What is more, in the cases of both ritual and natural magic, the alterations made were *real*, not illusory. In fact, this preface to the largest and popular medieval collection of illusions has absolutely nothing to say about illusion at all! One consequence, for later readers of this text such as Cornelius Agrippa and Athanasius Kircher, is that illusion would come to be treated as just another natural change, an application of actives to passives. Moreover, the distinct purpose that it had in William of Auvergne of *deception* would be eroded; in both Agrippa and Kircher, the element of the marvellous becomes much more important.

Aquinas's theory of magic, in contrast to that of pseudo-Albertus, restored the roles both of demons and illusion. The groundwork for his theory is laid in the *Summa contra gentiles*, in a chapter that states "that spiritual substances bring about certain marvels, but these are not really miracles."[44] Like the author of the *De mirabilibus mundi*, Thomas opened his discussion of magic by engaging with Avicenna. Marvellous events, from extraordinary cures to bewitchments, might seem to us to be outside the order of nature, but only because we had a view of the world that was limited to physical causation. As Thomas explained, Avicenna believed that spiritual substances, whether planetary intelligences or human souls, were able to take direct action in the world, a corollary to Avicenna's (Neoplatonic) conviction that the spiritual entities moving the planets emanated all of the substantial forms of things in our world, and thus brought about, by spiritual intervention, the natural but occult effects that proceed merely from a substance being what it is. The power of the human soul to affect things at a distance was a consequence of its origin from higher spiritual substances; so too, for that matter, was the power of a magnet to draw iron from afar.

Thomas himself, however, rejected Avicenna's theory that substantial forms emanated from celestial movers, and thus also its corollary on marvellous effects. On the one hand, he followed Aristotle rather than Avicenna in insisting that all material forms (which include substantial forms) must always derive from material forms in other material objects. On the other, he insisted that the effects these forms have in the world must be through contact and local motion (here agreeing with William of Auvergne that the Aristotelian model of causation through contact must apply to even the most marvellous effects). As for inexplicable cures and bewitchments, Aquinas thought there could be only one explanation: angels or demons brought about these effects by manipulating material objects. The effects only seemed miraculous because we could not see the agent, nor could we have the same, full knowledge of natural actions that angels and demons enjoyed. The effects of ritual magic (he went on to explain) could not be attributed to celestial influences,[45] but were also brought about by demons using natural means to produce astounding effects. William of Auvergne had argued that, where simple natural explanations failed, the effects must be attributed to the natural action of demons, who accepted the actions of the magician as a kind of *oblatio*. Aquinas, however, insisted that the sigils and magical words must *mean* something (at least to the demon), and communicated the magicians' wishes.

As for the mechanics of illusion, Aquinas had considered this subject in his *Sentences* commentary, where he raised the question whether demons can make real changes in the material world – a question which he answered in the affirmative.[46] The changes were of course natural: demons could only act by joining active qualities with corresponding passive ones,[47] so that the effect followed from natural causes, *sed praeter consuetum cursum naturae*. They might, for example, bring together actives and passives that were not usually found conjoined in nature, or bring them together with greater force, or in greater magnitude. These effects were not unnatural, but at the same time were not found in the ordinary course of nature; they were preternatural.[48] As a consequence, demons could not bring about anything that was not already lying passive in nature. They could not, for example, revive the dead; or at least, "they cannot do it in reality, but only by illusions (*in praestigiis*), as will be explained later."[49] Where such explanations were insufficient, Aquinas relied on a theory of deception that was clearly indebted to William: either the demons directly affected the *imaginatio* to bring about effects indistinguishable from real sense experience, or they offered puzzling appearances to the senses, akin to the lamps that filled the house with snakes. Both types of deception were beyond ordinary human capacity, but were nevertheless entirely physical and within the bounds of natural action.[50] As he argued in the *Summa theologiae*, demonic alteration of the imagination, and physical cloaking of material objects could be so powerful that multitudes of people could be deceived at once – a possibility that William of Auvergne was much less willing to entertain.[51]

Nicole Oresme

In the fourteenth century, Nicole Oresme offered a strong naturalistic resistance to Aquinas (and William), while at the same time developing William's theory of imagination much further.[52] Oresme devoted the first chapter of his *De causis mirabilium* to marvels involving vision, an account that was clearly influenced by his reading of the thirteenth-century optician and demon-sceptic, Witelo. Oresme, like Witelo, thought that some illusions came about through tricks of the light; the real wonders, however, involved the imagination, a faculty which operated according to physical laws analogous to those that governed vision. In a theorem on the rainbow, Witelo had cited a passage from Aristotle's *Meteora* recounting the story of a man whose sight was so weak that

> he always saw an image in front of him and facing him as he walked. This was because his sight was reflected back to him. Its morbid condition made it so weak and delicate that the air close by acted as a mirror, just as distant and condensed air normally does, and his sight could not push it back.[53]

If the visual sense could create an illusory mirror image, perhaps, with the help of the imagination, it might conjure up other images as well. If "Sortes" saw his dead father in his own room, it may be because he already had the *species* of his dead father in his internal imaginative faculty and, while thinking intently about him, refashioned an imperfectly perceived stick or shadow in his room into an image of his father. In the same way, someone can withdraw within himself and then appear to see "Peter or a fortress."[54] Similarly, a fearful man, thinking about someone dead, will also mistake a shadow for that man, just as he will think that a mouse or a creaking door at night is a thief. Under the spell on the one hand, of powerful emotion, which abstracts the mind from the external world, and, on the other, of a vivid interior *species*, all kinds of illusions are possible.

The similarities to William's theory of illusion are obvious. Oresme also believed that those with disordered humours had a less secure attachment between the inner and outer world, and so were more susceptible to such illusions.[55] And there is no end to the kinds of illusions that are possible. A fearful man might see a wolf in the field, or a cat in his room, and judge it to be an enemy or a devil; a pious man, on the other hand, deep in prayer, would judge that it is an angel. It is in these last examples that we see Oresme's most radical departure from William of Auvergne. William did not doubt that demons were responsible for some *praestigia*, even if they brought them about naturally. Supernatural agency is completely missing from Oresme's account, and even the appearances of angels or demons are explicable in entirely natural terms.

Oresme explored in more detail the connections between illusion, magic and sleight of hand in his treatise on the configurations of qualities and motions – a work much better known for its important place in the history of physics. His treatment of magic began by acknowledging that *some* magic may involve demons – in particular, that sort of magic in which the magician orders demons to do certain favours for him (for which he reserves the name "necromancy"). But these demons could only act with God's permission to carry out God's will, and hence they only pretended to obey the necromancer; in reality, they were assisting God in bringing about the magician's ruin. The kind of magic that involves demons, then, was really about the action of God in the world. That is a matter for theologians, so Oresme puts it to one side. The rest of magic (almost all magic, as it turns out) will be amenable to rational explanation, without recourse to the supernatural.[56]

Excluding demonic necromancy, the magical art that remains has three "roots": false persuasion, the application of things and the power of words.[57] The first is essentially the power of suggestion. Both the observer *and* the magician may be convinced of the power of celestial bodies, or that certain words or prayers can conjure demons. Simple minds are shaken by terror, and *per fortem ymaginationem* the man leaves his senses, and begins to see and hear things that are not there. And, *pace* Aquinas, Oresme insisted that the spells and conjurations had no meaning.[58] Different cultures used different spells and addressed different beings: ancient magic addressed the ancient gods, while the contemporary *ars notoria* is Christian, invoking saints and angels. If there were something objectively powerful in the spells, both would not be efficacious. When they worked, it was through a combination of autosuggestion and a heightened expectation of success. Divination by gazing into shiny objects he explained much as William of Auvergne had done, as a kind of amplification of the internal imaginative sense. He may even have tried it out himself, to go by his vivid description of the arrival of a vision: the shiny object, he wrote, will appear to grow vastly in size, even as large as the heavens.[59]

The second root concerns "illusion," in the sense of some kind of trickery or deception by the magician, and is divided into three parts: changing the senses, truly altering things (about which he says very little) and mathematical illusion (*mathematica illusio*).[60] The senses can be changed by various substances, many of which are familiar enough from William of Auvergne's work: plants, stones, sperm and other materials. Among his examples, Oresme cited Augustine's story of the man who ate poison hidden in a cheese, and was apparently transformed into a packhorse. But for Oresme, the man in Augustine's story was overcome entirely by the natural effects of the poison; demons were not involved at all. Nevertheless, he was wary of people experimenting with semen, or other "abominable mixtures" (*mixtiones abhominandae*) found in texts like the *Liber vacce*; they do not involve demons, but nevertheless are not *bona experimenta*, and are rightly prohibited because they appeal to a kind of culpable curiosity, by trying "to violate the secrets of their chaste mother Nature."[61] "Mathematical" illusions, on the other hand, rely on the skill of the practitioner, rather than the properties of nature. As Oresme put it, the magician deludes (*illudit*) those who are present

> by means of that part of mathematics which is called perspective, or by any other applicable means, such as mirrors, quickness of motion, sleights of hands, and much else; and this is the sort of thing that jugglers usually do.[62]

Generally, these illusions were harmless, and similar optical illusions took place at night without any intention from anyone to deceive.[63]

The third and final root concerned the use of sounds and incantations, in the context of ritual magic. If, as he had said before, their power did not reside in any meaning, how did they bring about their effects? They were, he argued, yet another example of the magician's singular skill of holding up a mirror to the soul of the person deceived, as he argued in a concluding chapter "on the way the soul is deceived by the magical art." Recalling the theory, derived from Aristotle's *Meteora*, that he had propounded in *De causis mirabilium*, he wrote that all of the magical roots – suggestion, poisons, suffumigation, words and rituals – created a kind of dissociation in the mind, so that it reflected back the imagination into the sense.[64]

The *Malleus maleficarum*

From this survey of medieval theories of illusion, it is evident that illusion (*praestigium, delusio, apparentia*) was central to premodern theories of magic, and could refer to a wide variety of phenomena, from conjuring tricks, to demonic apparitions, and an equally wide range of *causes*, from human skill, to natural influences, to demonic interference. Thus, the medieval understanding of illusion is not at all the same as the modern psychological or philosophical notion of illusion as a false belief about the world[65] – not least because medieval notions of illusion usually involve an agent imposing the illusion on the unwitting subject. And although the term was intended to explain magic and bring it within the grasp of reason, as a category it was at least as contested as magic itself.

It was the participation of other parties in the creation of illusion that particularly interested inquisitors and witch-hunters. The most notorious work on the judicial treatment of witches – the *Malleus maleficarum*, first published in 1487 under the authorship of Heinrich Kramer and Jacob Sprenger – took a professional interest in illusion, and the involvement of demons in the production of illusions, especially in a chapter with the self-explanatory title, "Whether witches may work some prestidigitatory illusion so that the male organ appears to be completely removed from the body."[66] In this much ridiculed part of the text,[67] the authors soberly considered the apparently widespread belief that witches were not only the cause of male impotence, but could even steal the penis altogether; in the course of their discussion, they provided a careful, scholastic analysis of illusion itself.

In the first place, they agreed that something was certainly happening to men's penises: male genitals were under attack, because God allowed them to be, a consequence of their being organs of sinfulness. But were witches really absconding with them? This question went to the heart of the issue of whether demons are able to effect real, substantial change in the world, or only to conjur illusions. As the authors note (and as we have seen), the tradition is ambiguous on this point. In the most famous proof passage,[68] we recall that Augustine had insisted that any change wrought by demons to living things (such as turning men into donkeys) was merely an illusion; on the other hand, he seemed to suggest that Pharaoh's magicians could actually turn their staffs into snakes.[69] And men themselves could remove other men's genitals (by castration) – so, on the principle that demons act by natural means, surely they could do the same? The *Malleus* concluded that the member can be removed *both* in reality *and* by *praestigiosa operatione*; but when witches (or their demons) did it, it is always through illusion.[70] This last conclusion seemed to be based on empirical observation: just as it was well known that men did in fact have their penises stolen, so too (as the authors would verify by several anecdotes) they just as often had them eventually restored – something that would presumably be difficult if they had really been severed.

So, the disappearance of the penis must be merely illusory. But that does not mean that it is harmless or innocent. In order to show that the witch must be condemned even for this illusory theft, the *Malleus* was able to draw on the long tradition of medieval thought on illusion. And first, they clarified what they meant by illusion:

> But that illusion does not take place in the imagination of the sufferer, because his imagination can truly and really estimate that some thing is not present, since through no operation of the external sense (sight, or touch) does he perceive it to be present. And so it can be called a true theft of the member, on the part of the imagination of the victim, but not on the part of the thing itself. How this can be, some further things need to be noted.[71]

In their typical, poorly worded style, the authors were trying to make the point that the theft was not "imaginary" in the sense I might imagine that I am a boiled egg, or have no head – delusions that would be just errors of the imagination, which could be corrected by the external senses. In the case of penis theft, the imagination seems to be *correct* in judging that the member is missing, because all of the external senses will corroborate the impression of absence in the imagination. This is a powerful kind of illusion, and the tradition from William of Auvergne onwards had prepared them to make sense of it.

The *Malleus* divided illusions into two main categories: the first, in which the outer senses or inner imagination were directly altered; and the second, in which they were indirectly deluded, by some kind of trick.[72] The first kind of illusion *always* involved demonic action, and so was always culpable; the second kind might be demonic, or human, and was accordingly culpable or innocuous.

Direct illusions, the first class, could themselves be divided into three types. The first and the third will be familiar to us already from William of Auvergne and other theorists of illusion. The senses themselves of the victim can be altered, "so that what is visible becomes invisible to him, what is tangible, intangible," and so on.[73] This was a natural (though difficult) operation, and so was within the powers of a demon. Or, (the third mode), this sort of *illusio praestigiosa* could be effected by directly altering the imagination and phantasy, so that one imagined something as if it had been presented to the external senses. Again, this was natural and within the power of the devil and his minions, because (just as William of Auvergne had argued) this sort of thing happens all the time in dreams, when the imagination provides images just as if they were really in the senses. To these two types of direct, clearly diabolical illusions, the *Malleus* added one more (the second, in their division). Rather than changing the victim's perceptions via the senses or imagination, the devil could take a less subtle route: by placing a piece of flesh-coloured material over the victim's penis, the devil could obscure the member from both touch and sight. This final, bizarre explanation was added no doubt to explain the circumstance in which several witnesses, including the parish priest, confirmed the victim's perception that his penis had been stolen. The sharing of an illusion by many people had always been the most difficult part of any theory of illusion, from William of Auvergne to Oresme; this sort of protoplasmic sheath solved the problem.

To the second class of illusion – indirect delusions or tricks – they gave the general name *praestigia*, which the authors glossed with Isidore of Seville's definition: "a tricking (*delusio*) of the senses, and especially of the eyes."[74] Again, this class was divided into three types, of which two do *not* involve the intervention of demons. First were the tricks done by wandering entertainers, better called *delusio* (with the etymological emphasis on playfulness) than *praestigium*, "since it is artificially done by the agility of men who show things and conceal them, as in the case of the tricks of jugglers and mimes." The second embraced all those feats of natural magic that could give false appearances to things: the *Malleus* repeats, from Thomas and other authors (most likely William of Auvergne), the *experimentum* involving a lamp that, with its flickering light, could make surrounding objects appear to be writhing snakes.

These two types of "indirect" illusion were, therefore, definitely harmless and permitted. The third type occupied more ambiguous ground since it comprised actions apparently performed by a witch or magician, in which the real agent was actually a demon, acting with the permission of God and within nature. This final type was itself divided into five subtypes, the first of which will immediately show how problematic this division might be. It included anything done by an artful trick (*artificiali traiectione*) that surpassed human skill. Demons, it need hardly be said, excelled at stage magic, "because whatever a man knows how to do, [the devil] knows how to do it better by art."[75] It therefore became a matter of judgement whether a particular trick explicable through sleight of hand was harmless entertainment, or had been done so well that the devil must have been involved.[76]

Future directions

The central place of illusion in medieval theories of magic is evident. At the same time, even in this rapid survey, one can see that medieval authors had a different understanding of the extent of the purely illusory. Consider, for example, the lamp that would change the appearance of bystanders into asses, or would make a room fill up with snakes – only two of dozens of similar effects recorded in experimental literature. William of Auvergne, and many who read his work, had no difficulty believing that such lamps were possible, and that they brought about their effects by the natural effects of substances within them. Yet, a modern reader, with equal conviction, knows that the lamps *cannot* bring about such an effect – and if such an effect was experienced, it must have some origin other than the natural substances infused into the oil, and probably unrelated to the lamp.[77] We have also seen that medieval theorists saw a continuity between "juggling" and genuine magic, in that marvellous effects that could not be explained as deceptions of the senses might be attributed to demons performing tricks with more skill than humans could ever master.

Two directions for future research suggest themselves. First, a systematic study of purely illusory magical experiments is very much needed. My own preliminary investigations suggest that at least three different types of material cohabited quite comfortably in medieval texts. First, there are *experimenta* that are easily reproducible illusions. Among these are descriptions of conjurors' sleights of hand, and the ubiquitous practical jokes found in such collections, to make cooked meat appear to be raw or writhing with worms.[78] In a second class are those that purport to bring about an illusion by directly calling upon a demon or other power. A third class are the puzzling cases, as already mentioned, of magic that does not work, to borrow a term from an important study of magic in literature.[79] In these cases, the text instructed the reader to follow certain non-magical steps to bring about an effect. Their form is precisely like those of the first class; but the effect they promise to produce is not reproducible. What is the scholar to make of such recipes? Did medieval authors themselves think of them any differently from other types of recipes? Did they try them? Some of these questions may be difficult to answer. What seems to be clear, however, is that the recipes in the third class (magic that does not work) have more longevity than the descriptions of real, reproducible tricks. They appear in more contexts, and over a larger extent of time, than the rarer material that actually reveals the actual practices of street performers and jugglers.

And that brings us to a second area for further research: the world of magic as an entertainment. This, again, is an area on which surprisingly little has been written.[80] One open question is whether there is continuity between ancient itinerant performers and the jugglers of the medieval period. Some of the tricks attributed to each, in the limited texts that have been studied, seem similar, but need to be studied more fully. There is some very interesting material that has been compiled by modern stage magicians, in the professional magazines of their guilds, but these specialist studies have been entirely neglected by modern historians of magic. The question is an important one. The patristic and medieval authors who developed the illusionistic theory of magic most likely confronted illusion directly in the performances of entertainers, which helped to set for them the bounds of what they thought illusion could accomplish. Modern historians of magic have tended to ignore entirely the kind of performance that we call "magic" today, in favour of demonic or ritual magic. But it may be that we cannot entirely comprehend even the latter, without knowing more about the illusions that entertained spectators at court and at the fair.

Notes

1 "Des sciences occultes ou Essai sur la Magie, les prodiges et les miracles."
2 Terry Castle, "Phantasmagoria: Spectral Technology and the Metaphorics of Modern Reverie," *Critical Inquiry* 15 (1988): 26–61.
3 There is very little on illusion in Richard Kieckhefer, *Magic in the Middle Ages* (Cambridge: Cambridge University Press, 1989). Two recent surveys of the history of magic barely mention illusion at all: *The Cambridge History of Magic and Witchcraft in the West: From Antiquity to the Present*, ed. David

J. Collins (Cambridge: Cambridge University Press, 2015); Brian Copenhaver, *The Book of Magic: From Antiquity to the Enlightenment* (London: Penguin, 2016).

4 Also in the *Aeneid* 11.246–7.
5 *De civitate dei* 18. 18.
6 *De civitate dei* 10. 8.
7 The most comprehensive survey of early Christian theories of magic is Francis C.R. Thee, *Julius Africanus and the Early Christian View of Magic* (Tübingen: J.C.B. Mohr/Paul Siebeck, 1984).
8 Thomas B. de Mayo, *The Demonology of William of Auvergne: By Fire and Sword* (Lewiston, NY: Edwin Mellen Press, 2007), 47.
9 This point is made most forcefully in recent work by Steven Marrone, who places William at the beginning of a "protomechanistic" movement in scholastic philosophy. See, for example, Steven P. Marrone, "Magic and the Physical World in Thirteenth-Century Scholasticism," *Early Science and Medicine* 14, no. 1–3 (2009): 170. William (at *De universo* II.2.76) reduces causation to contrariety (an agent erases a contrary quality in a patient), and assimilation (when the agent impresses its own similitude on a patient). He gives the examples of something cold becoming hot by the action of the actually hot, or a place becoming illuminated by the presence of a lamp. These modes of causation apply both to common experiences and (almost always) to the uncanny effects of magic. We can see here the germ of the standard trope that magic comes about through the application of actives to passives.
10 On William's use, for the first time, of the term *magia naturalis*, see Marrone, "Magic and the Physical World in Thirteenth-Century Scholasticism", 173, n. 24.
11 *De universo* II, pars III, cap. 22. The text used here is William of Auvergne, *Opera omnia, quae hactenus reperiri potuerunt* (Paris, 1674) 1:1059–61. All subsequent references to page numbers (and columns and sections within those pages) will be to this edition.
12 *De universo* 1059aA.
13 *De universo* 1059aA. William does not say what his *third* type magic is. Marrone assumes, plausibly, that the third type must be (by elimination) magic in which demons really *are* involved: Marrone, "Magic and the Physical World in Thirteenth-Century Scholasticism," 168. It may also be possible that the third class are the *praestigia*, or *opera ludificatoria* – marvellous things that these men do, for which we cannot find a cause – to which William turns his attention towards the end of the chapter (1061aB); these may or may not involve demonic action.
14 These lamps have a long and complicated history in natural magic, from at least the fifth century BC to the seventeenth century. For a sketch of this history, see R.D. Goulding, "Real, Apparent and Illusory Necromancy: Lamp Experiments and Historical Perceptions of Experimental Knowledge," *Societas Magica Newsletter* (2006): 1–7.
15 The version recorded in the roughly contemporary *Liber aggregationis* attributed to Albertus Magnus reads:

> A beautiful lamp, to make the house seem to be completely full of snakes and images, as long as the lamp is lit. Take the fat of a black snake and the skin of a black snake, and a funeral shroud. Make a wick from the shroud, then smear it with the fat, and put the snake skin inside it; then light it with elder oil in a green or black lamp.

See *Liber aggregationis, seu liber secretorum Alberti Magni de virtutibus herbarum, lapidum et animalium quorundam* (London, 1483), sig. e3v–e4r.
16 *De universo* 1057bC. William refers to the *ars triblia vel syntriblia* attributed to Artesius, that is, the *ars sintrilla* of Artephius, for which see Nicholas H. Clulee, "At the Crossroads of Magic and Science: John Dee's Archemastrie," in *Occult and Scientific Mentalities in the Renaissance*, ed. Brian Vickers (Cambridge: Cambridge University Press, 1984), 57–71. At 1058aH, he describes the visions obtained by gazing into the *speculum Apollinis*, by which he most likely means the mirror of *Apollonius*, which was reputed to be able to reveal things happening in other places. See Eileen Reeves, *Galileo's Glassworks: The Telescope and the Mirror* (Cambridge, MA: Harvard University Press, 2008), ch. 1.
17 *De universo* 1058bG-H. To complete the analogy to milk, and to alchemical processes, William elsewhere argues that semen itself is concocted out of blood; when demons impregnate women, they must be using human semen – but semen they have made themselves out of human blood. See Mayo, *The Demonology of William of Auvergne: By Fire and Sword*, 172.
18 *De universo* 1058bH.

19 *De universo* 1059aD.
20 *De universo* 1059aD. I have not found this experiment in any medieval collection.
21 *De universo* 1059bA.
22 *NH* 30.2.
23 See Naomi Janowitz, *Magic in the Roman World: Pagans, Jews and Christians* (London: Routledge, 2002), 13.
24 *NH* 37.165. Heliotrope is bloodstone, or chalcedony.
25 *De universo* II, pars III, cap. 20: "On the various radiations coming from God into human souls, and concerning the obstacles to their reception."
26 Although there is clear kinship between William's "illuminative" metaphors of knowledge and the Platonism of Augustine, William in fact rejects Platonism quite vehemently, and any suggestion that knowledge occurs by means of pre-existing truths or recollection. In a more Aristotelian way, he believes that the soul has certain capacities for knowledge, which may then be fulfilled by the illumination of knowledge, especially from God or angels (these capacities having perhaps been *stimulated* into activity by the senses, which he does not seem to consider sources of knowledge *per se*). It must be said that William's epistemology is neither entirely clear nor particularly consistent. See Lewis, "William of Auvergne," sec. 7.7.2.
27 *De universo* 1053aD.
28 *De universo* 1053bA-B.
29 *De universo* 1057bD.
30 *De universo* 1058aE.
31 William argues at length (1053bC) that the fearful, mad, ill, angry and others in extreme passion are more susceptible to illuminations, for that very reason: that their soul becomes disconnected from the body.
32 It should be noted that William's explanation for the inclusion of such substances, while ingenious, is probably not correct. The eyes of animals are frequently listed among the ingredients in lamps and fumigations that cause illusions, and there can be little doubt that this is a kind of sympathetic magic: to alter the sight, use eyes. Moreover, other parts of the turtle (especially its bile) were considered particularly efficacious for vision; see Pliny, *NH* 32.37–38: "the bile of turtles clarifies the sight," and "turtle bile mixed with honey remedies all faults of vision." The magical *Liber vacce* uses this ingredient several times, including in a suffumigation that, when used during the day, will "darken the world and you will see all the stars and the moon, until the world is afraid of it" (MS Cambridge, Corpus Christi, fol. 148v: "quando tu suffumigabis cum ea in die, manifeste obtenebratur mundus et videbis stellas omnes et lunam, donec timeat mundus ex illo"); this recipe calls for turtle bile mixed with a paste of black henna (if that is the meaning of "adipem qui dicitur alcatak," or *alcatam* in some other manuscripts: "katam" is black henna). The mixture of a black dye with a substance that sharpens the vision is quite appropriate for darkening the world and making the stars visible in daytime.
33 *De universo* II, pars III, cap. 23: "On the trickeries of demons, whereby they make some things appear that do not exist, and by what power spiritual substances can move bodies."
34 Such a feat was attributed in antiquity to a certain Pases, who was frequently mentioned (as Pases or Pasetes) in early modern writings on magic. Cornelius Agrippa, for example, mentions him in his chapter on *praestigia*, *De incertitudine et vanitate scientiarum* (Cologne, 1531), sig. i1v. So too does Robert Burton in the *Anatomy of Melancholy*; see Philip Butterworth, *Magic on the Early English Stage* (Cambridge: Cambridge University Press, 2005), 18–19. The ultimate source for these writers seems to be *Suidas*, s.v. Πάσης. According to *Suidas*, Pases was a magician who was able to make banquets and waiters appear by means of his spells, and then to vanish again. He also had a half-obol coin that, if he spent it, would come back to him – and hence his name had become proverbial as "Pases' half-obol" (perhaps in the same sense as the English "bad penny"). William may have met this story, or proverb, in some patristic source.
35 *De universo* 1061bB-D.
36 *De universo* 1062aE.
37 The illusion William described reminds one of an elaborate illusion described in a much later necromantic manual; see Richard Kieckhefer, *Forbidden Rites: A Necromancer's Manual of the Fifteenth Century* (Stroud: Sutton, 1997), 50–53.
38 *De universo* 1065aB. "inter ossa crurium vaccae unius" – this is probably meant to be the sensory foundation on which the demons build the illusion of sexual intercourse with the queen.
39 Ibid. 1065aD.

40 Ibid. 1066aH-bF. The same figure as "Dame Habonde," appears in the *Roman de la Rose*. See John M. Steadman, "Eve's Dream and the Conventions of Witchcraft," *Journal of the History of Ideas* 26, no. 4 (1965): 571.
41 *De universo* 1066bG.
42 An edition of the Latin text of the magical theory (which was excised from some translations), together with a brief commentary, may be found in Antonella Sannino, "'Facere cessare mirabilia rerum': magia e scienza nel 'De mirabilibus mundi.'" *Studi filosofici* 30 (2007): 1000–16.
43 Sannino identifies the source as Avicenna's commentary on *De anima*; Ibid., 50. There is clearly some similarity here to William of Auvergne's theory of the *vis imaginationis* (perhaps because Avicenna was a common source); though it should be noted, for William, the effects of the imagination are *illusory*, while for ps.-Albertus they are *real*.
44 Thomas Aquinas, *Summa contra gentiles* (Turin and Rome: Editio Leonina, 1946), III.103. I am indebted to the analysis of this chapter and the next, in Marrone, "Magic and the Physical World in Thirteenth-Century Scholasticism," 174–80.
45 *Summa contra gentiles* III.104. The attribution of *particular* effects to heavenly action goes beyond Avicenna's Neoplatonic theory of general celestial causation. The editor of the Leonine edition of Aquinas's works suggests that he had in mind *De civitate dei* X.11, where Augustine quotes with apparent approval a passage from Porphyry's *Letter to Anebo*, in which the Platonic philosopher argues that the banal, or immoral, effects of magical rituals cannot be imputed to the celestial gods, but are the work of demons.
46 Thomas Aquinas, *Scriptum super libros sententiarum magistri Petri Lombardi Episcopi Parisiensis*. 4 vols., ed. Pierre Mandonnet and Marie Fabien Moos (Paris: P. Lethielleux, 1929–47), book II, dist. 7, q. 3, art. 1.
47 *Scriptum super libros sententiarum*, II. dist. 7 q. 3 art. 1. "Daemones ad determinata passiva possunt conjungere activa." This seems to be the first use of this phrase – conjoining or applying actives to passives – which will become part of the standard vocabulary thenceforth for understanding preternatural effects. For its use, for instance, by Pietro Pomponazzi in the sixteenth century, see Anthony Ossa-Richardson, "Pietro Pomponazzi and the Rôle of Nature in Oracular Divination," *Intellectual History Review* 20, no. 4 (2010): 441–42.
48 The classic text on this important medieval and Renaissance category is Lorraine Daston and Katharine Park, *Wonders and the Order of Nature, 1150-1750* (New York: Zone Books, 1998).
49 *Scriptum super libros sententiarum*, II. dist. 7 q. 3 art. 1.
50 Ibid. dist. 8 q. 1 art. 5.
51 Thomas Aquinas, *Summa Theologica*, 6 vols. (Turin, 1891), I. q. 114 art. 4.
52 For Oresme's dependence in this and other works on William of Auvergne's *De universo*, see Bert Hansen, *Nicole Oresme and the Marvels of Nature: A Study of his De causis mirabilium with Critical Edition, Translation, and Commentary* (Toronto: Pontifical Institute of Mediaeval Studies, 1995), 57. All future page references to Oresme's *De causis mirabilium* will be to this edition. On the *fortuna* of Oresme's work in the history of scepticism, see Stuart Clark, *Thinking with Demons: The Idea of Witchcraft in Early Modern Europe* (Oxford: Clarendon Press, 1997), 265–66.
53 *Meteora* III.4 (373b1).
54 *De causis mirabilium* ch. 1, l. 120 (p. 156). There is perhaps an echo here of the castle illusion described by William of Auvergne.
55 *De causis mirabilium* ch. 1, ll. 177–8 (pp. 160–61).
56 *De configurationibus* 2. 25. 35; Marshall Clagett, *Nicole Oresme and the Medieval Geometry of Qualities and Motions: A Treatise on the Uniformity and Difformity of Intensities known as Tractatus de configurationibus qualitatum et motuum* (Madison: University of Wisconsin Press, 1968), 336. All future page references will be to this edition.
57 *De configurationibus*, 2. 26.
58 Ibid., 2. 27.
59 Ibid., 2. 29.
60 Ibid., 2. 31.
61 Ibid., 2.32 (pp. 360–61).
62 Ibid., 2. 31 (pp. 358–59).
63 Oresme referred the reader to Witelo's uncompromisingly naturalistic and anti-demonic *De natura demonum*; Witelo considered illusions of supernatural beings that can accidentally seem to arise in dim light. This text is edited in Jerzy Burchardt, *List Witelona do Ludwika we Lwówku Śląskim: Problematyka*

teoriopoznawcza, kosmologiczna i medyczna (Wroclaw: Ossolineum, 1979). Renata Mikolajczyk, "Non sunt nisi phantasiae et imaginationes: A Medieval Attempt at Explaining Demons," in *Communicating with the Spirits*, ed. Gábor Klaniczay, Eva Pocs and Eszter Csonka-Takacs (Budapest: Central European University Press, 2005), 40–52 provides a useful summary and analysis of the treatise.

64 *De configurationibus*, 2. 33.
65 This point is well made by Simon During, *Modern Enchantments: The Cultural Power of Secular Magic* (Cambridge, MA: Harvard University Press, 2002), 32.
66 Jakob Sprenger and Heinrich Institoris, *Malleus Maleficarum* (Cologne, 1520), ch. 9 (sig. G3r).
67 For an account both of the contemporary and modern scholarly reaction to this part of the *Malleus*, and its sources in folkloric accounts, see Moira Smith, "The Flying Phallus and the Laughing Inquisitor: Penis Theft in the 'Malleus Maleficarum,'" *Journal of Folklore Research* 39 (2002): 85–117. Penis theft is still blamed on witches in parts of the world. See http://www.reuters.com/article/us-witchcraft-idUSN2319603620080423.
68 *De civitate dei*, 18. 18.
69 Ibid., 10. 8.
70 Sprenger and Institoris, *Malleus Maleficarum*, sig. G3v.
71 Ibid., sig. G4r.
72 See also During, *Modern Enchantments: The Cultural Power of Secular Magic*, 33.
73 Sprenger and Institoris, *Malleus Maleficarum*, sig. G4r.
74 Ibid., sig. G4v.
75 Ibid., sig. G5r.
76 During argues, more strongly, that the ambiguity of the distinctions in the *Malleus* is inevitable, because of the authors' conceptions of reality and unreality, as expressions of God's will. Human illusion, or magic as entertainment is, in his reading of this passage, deliberately placed under suspicion (despite its apparent exemption), because its means, and the kind of reality it produces, are identical to the works of the devil. See *Modern Enchantments: The Cultural Power of Secular Magic*, 33.
77 The first sign of this sceptical attitude towards these experiments seems to be in the seventeenth century, in the work of Athanasius Kircher.
78 On this sort of material, see Bruno Roy, "The Household Encyclopedia as Magic Kit: Medieval Popular Interest in Pranks and Illusions," *Journal of Popular Culture* 14 (1980): 60–69; Melitta Weiss Adamson, "The Games Cooks Play: Non-Sense Recipes and Practical Jokes in Medieval Literature," in *Food in the Middle Ages: A Book of Essays*, ed. Melitta Weiss Adamson (New York: Garland Pub., 1995), 177–96.
79 See Helen Cooper, "Magic That Does Not Work," *Medievalia et Humanistica* 7 (1976): 131–46. Cooper's interest is different from ours; she points out that, because of its ease in resolving plot difficulties, magic came to be seen as banal and uninteresting in medieval literature. Far more exciting was magic that failed, or magical objects that were never used.
80 Matthew Dickie has a little on ancient performers in *Magic and Magicians in the Greco-Roman World* (London: Routledge, 2001). On medieval jugglers, see Laura H. Loomis, "Secular Dramatics in the Royal Palace, Paris, 1378, 1389, and Chaucer's 'Tregetoures,'" *Speculum* 33, no. 2 (1958): 242–55.

24

MAGIC AT COURT

Jean-Patrice Boudet

In the societies of the late Middle Ages, courts – those of sovereigns and those of secular and ecclesiastical princes – are privileged domestic spaces for the political elites, places of power representation and centres of rivalries of all kinds, involving often illicit practices. The use of magic and repression of it should be considered in this highly competitive sociopolitical context, where individual strategies seem to oppose the norms imposed by the Church and the secular powers. But recent research focused on some particularly revealing periods of crisis suggests that the sovereign powers – those of the Pope, kings and territorial princes – have not built themselves up only in opposition to magicians, sorcerers and witches, but also, to some extent, with their help.

Courtly magic

Magic is an essential component of courtly romances and court culture from the Central Middle Ages to the Renaissance. It appears particularly in the Arthurian literature and the "antique romances" of 1150–70, especially in the *Roman d'Alexandre* and in Benoît de Sainte-Maure's *Roman de Troie*. Benoît, a tourangeau cleric who was probably in the service of King Henry II and Eleanor of Aquitaine, defines himself in his *Roman* as *devin* (diviner, soothsayer). Although it applies to the field of romantic fiction, this identification encourages David Rollo to speak of a *translatio nigromantiae* parallel to the *translatio studii* and contemporary with the construction of the myth of Toledo as a capital of magic.[1] Indeed, the affirmation of courtly magic corresponds to an imaginary appropriation process that forms the basis of the superiority of the clerical *litterati*, that is mastery of the Latin language and its grammar. It is testified by the promotion of a new meaning of "gramaire" in Old French: when Ulysses and Diomedes came to Troy, the first wonderful thing they saw was a "a pine tree, with branches of refined gold cast through magic, nigromancy and grimoire" ("Devant la sale aveit un pin/ Dont les branches furent d'or fin/ Tresgetees par artimaire,/ Par nigromance e par gramaire," *Roman de Troie*, vv. 6265–68). The rhyme "artimaire/ gramaire" also appears in the *Roman de Thebes* and its association with "nigromance" gives a double meaning to the word "gramaire", grammar and grimoire, the second one refering to a book of conjuration whose magical properties allow one to do many things, including raise a person from the dead.[2]

Perhaps, like the invasion of magical themes in Arthurian literature, this transfer from the area of clerical magic and miracle to the fictional universe in the vernacular aims "to challenge the clerics' monopoly of the sacred and to affirm the legitimacy of the supernatural domination claimed by the aristocracy".[3] But it is more generally a phenomenon of acculturation between "clergy" and "chivalry" that is taking place here, a phenomenon better observable in the court societies of the three last centuries of the Middle Ages.[4] In any case, the fact that the character of the court magician is often more positive than negative in the vernacular literature confirms the importance of social demand in this area. In German romance, for example, "magicians were not just fringe figures, representatives of superstition and low culture, but elegant, learned and powerful courtiers, whose services were valued in the center of power."[5] Courtly literature has probably done more to inspire the attitude of governments on this than the warnings pronounced by court clerks like John of Salisbury in his *Policraticus* (1159).

Magic at court in the thirteenth century

Significantly, it is at the court of two princes who claim their universal sovereignty through the title of emperor and who are in close contact with Arab–Muslim culture, Frederick II Hohenstaufen and Alfonso X of Castile, that magic was promoted in the thirteenth century as a way to strengthen their power.

In fact, it is as *astrologus imperatoris Romanorum et semper augusti* at the southern Italian court of Frederick II that Michael Scot († 1235 or 1236) seems to have composed the *Liber introductorius*, an extensive astrological and cosmological compilation in three books. This text poses many problems of manuscript tradition, which explains why it is still not entirely published: we have two versions of it, short and long, neither being complete. It is unlikely that either is a true copy of the original. The long version was preserved notably in a manuscript copied in northern Italy sometime between 1320 and 1340 for Hugh IV of Lusignan, King of Cyprus; it is full of contradictions, perhaps in part because it was unfinished. Perhaps Michael Scot did not have the material resources to harmonize all the work. Moreover, this long version was interpolated around 1287 by Bartholomew of Parma.[6]

One of the most remarkable aspects of the *Liber introductorius* lies in the contradiction between the prologue's global condemnation of magic as an enemy of the Christian faith, and an obvious fascination not only for magical angelology, integrated into a comprehensive view of the cosmos, but also for the most explicitly demonic practices. These were deemed effective even though they were not authorized by the Church. So magic is defined as "an art that destroys the religious link with the divine law and converts to the cult of the devil,"[7] while a little later the prologue describes a ritual of hydromancy or cristallomancy, in which a girl aged five to seven years is called to repeat word for word, after the magister, a conjuration of the spirit Floriget to know the truth about a thief. Michael Scot (or whoever pretends to be him) even mentions, in the chapter *De noticia artis nigromancie pertinentis ad ymagines* of the long version, two magical treatises that smell of sulphur: first, a kind of demonological *Who's Who* entitled *Liber perditionis animae et corporis*,

> which deals in the order of all functions of the demons and their names, parts of the world where they remain until they can be diverted from their pain and where they stand to be called to serve [men], and what orders [of angels] they fell;

and second a *Liber consecrationis* composed by him to be a *modus operandi* of the aforementioned demons' catalogue.[8] Moreover, Scot admits he practised astral magic and used his expertise in this area to the advantage of his contemporaries, friends, relatives, servants and the beneficiaries of his "domestic love" (*amore domestico*). This seems to indicate an internal use in the Sicilian court of Frederick II.

The long version of *Liber introductorius* is valuable in that it illuminates the judgement of Dante Alighieri on Michael Scot, "who knew very well all the games of magical tricks" (*Inferno*, XX, vv. 115–17). However, one may question the authenticity of this version, well fitted to discredit Frederick II through his astrologer, while the short version, deprived of most of the deviant passages, seems more "politically correct" but may be the result of an equally fictitious construction. The legend of Michael Scot is inevitably linked to that of Frederick II.

King of Castile and León (1252–84), cousin of Frederick II and son of Ferdinand III and Beatrice of Swabia, Alfonso X was chosen as king of the Romans in 1257 and renounced the imperial throne in 1275. The cultural model he wants to follow, which contributes to the attribution of the nickname *el Sabio* (the Wise or the Savant), is Solomon's: like Solomon, the king must participate in the divine wisdom, which gives him the power to govern and to be a "lord of justice, connoisseur of good and prudence". Hence the importance he attaches to his legal work; but that wisdom is supposed also to animate his quest for "philosophy and all other sciences", to give him the ability to know nature and its secrets, to understand the past and try to predict the future, like the famous king of Israel, who was understood since Antiquity to have been a kind of exorcist, magician and astrologer. Alfonso's policy of patronage for the translation and composition of scientific and magical books must be understood in this context. Moreover, Alfonso X is a direct heir of Arabic science as well as a dreamer searching for universal knowledge. It is in this spirit that in 1254 he states that he wishes to establish, in Seville, in his privileged place of residence, *estudios e escuelas generales de latín e arábico*. There is a direct link between that decision and the patronage of scientific translations by the Wise King. His policy in this regard is remarkably coherent: it transfers, mainly in the Castilian language, the Arabic science of the stars and Arabic and Jewish magic. His activity in this last field appears in the following table.

Magical works translated or written under the patronage of Alfonso X[9]

Date	Title	Authors	Translators	Translations' Characteristics
completed in 1250, revised ca. 1275	Lapidario	"Abolays" and others	Yehuda ben Moshe and Garci Pérez	Compendium of four lapidaries translated from Arabic to Castilian
1256–58	Picatrix	Maslama al-Qurṭubī	Yehuda ben Moshe and Aegidius de Thebaldis?	Magical compendium translated from Arabic to Castilian and from Castilian to Latin
1276–79	Libro de las formas e ymagenes	?	?	An astral magic compendium translated from Arabic to Castilian
ca. 1280–84	Libro de astromagia	?	?	An astral magic compendium translated from Arabic to Castilian
?	Liber Razielis in seven books	?	Iohannes clericus (Juan d'Aspa?)	A compilation of magic translated in part from Hebrew to Latin and then to Castilian, as suggested by the prologue, or a Latin compilation based in part on a older version in two books and perhaps falsely attributed to Alfonso X in the fourteenth century

The *Lapidario* was completed in 1250, two years before the accession of Alfonso to the throne of Castile, and was revised in around 1275. It is kept in an original manuscript of the Escorial. It is actually four separate lapidaries; the first and most important is attributed to an "Abolays" of whom nothing is known. The whole was translated into Castilian by the principal Jewish translator of the entourage of Alfonso, Yehuda ben Moshe ha-Kohen, helped by Garci Pérez, cleric of the King. The first three lapidaries are astrological. In Abolays' lapidary, 301 stones are classified according to the twelve signs of the zodiac. In the second lapidary, the stones are classified according to the thirty-six decans; in the third according to the seven planets, and in the fourth in the order of the Arabic alphabet.

In addition to the *Lapidario*, which may be considered a work of natural magic, Alfonso X commissioned the translation and composition of several treatises on astral and ritual magic, and was the only European sovereign of the Middle Ages to have done so. Two astral magic compilations in Castilian date from the last eight years of his reign: the *Libro de las formas e ymagenes*, now lost but of which remains a very detailed table of contents,[10] and the *Libro de astromagia*, of which remains the original manuscript, a superb illuminated codex of the Vatican Library where we find ten texts and forty remarkable miniatures representing the degrees of the zodiac signs, the decans, the mansions of the Moon, the talismans of the planets and signs, the planetary angels, sacrifices to the spirits of the planets and the accompanying suffumigations.[11] But above all, the Castilian king left his mark in the history of magic by the translation of two famous works, the *Picatrix* and the *Liber Razielis*.

The *Picatrix* is a Latin translation of the *Ghāyat al-Ḥakīm* (The Aim of the Wise), a compendium written in al-Andalus in the middle of the tenth century by Maslama al-Qurṭubī.[12] It was made from a Castilian version (of which only fragments remain) written in 1256 at the request of Alfonso X, but the prologue does not reveal the identity of the translators; perhaps Yehuda ben Moshe for the Castilian version and Aegidius of Thebaldis for the Latin. Aegidius translated for Alfonso two major astrological works from Castilian, the *Liber de iudiciis astrorum* of Hali Abenragel and Hali Abenrudian's commentary on Ptolemy's *Quadripartitum*. Allegedly inspired by more than 200 treatises, among which are different astral magic works, the encyclopeadia of the Brethren of Purity and the *Book of Nabatean agriculture*, the *Picatrix* gives great prominence to the magical and astrological talismans, prayers, sacrifices and *suffumigationes stellarum* intended to influence the planetary spirits. It has been partly written and translated from the perspective of its potential political and military use, even if that purpose is unequally manifested among its four books and their chapters. This is particularly the case in chapter 5 of Book I, where politics is one of the main goals (ten of thirty-three), almost equal with love–unlove affairs (eleven) and with prosperity or physical destruction (nine).[13] There are thus talismans "to be loved by *reges* and *magnates*", "for the master [of a country] to be loved by his people who will always obey him", "to get a dignity from the master", "to increase the power of cities that will continue to be prosperous", "to destroy an enemy", "to destroy a city", "to prevent buildings from being built", "that the king's wrath fall on someone" and so on. But it is in chapter 7 of Book III that we found this beautiful ritual inspired directly by Eastern astrolatry:

> If you want to pray to the Sun and ask him something, for example to ask for the grace of a king, for love of lords and the benefits generated by this, you will make the Sun favorable by placing it in the ascendant, and in his own day [Sunday] and hour. Put on a king's clothing, silky, yellow and mixed with gold; place on your head

a golden crown and on your finger a gold ring, and you will take the appearance of the most eminent Chaldean [Persian] men, as the Sun was the master of their ascendant. Enter into a remote house reserved for the operation; put your right hand on the left and look at the Sun with caution and humility [...] Then take a golden censer and a beautiful rooster with a beautiful neck [*sic:* a beautiful crest in Arabic]. Above his neck, put a small lighted candle wax that is located at the far end of a stick [of aloe in Arabic] to the length of one palm; in the heat of the censer put the suffumigation described below. As the Sun rises, turn the rooster up to it and, while the smoke of the incense rises continuously, say:

You who are the root of heaven, who are greater than all the stars and all the planets, you who are holy and honored, I ask you to grant my prayer, to give me the grace and love of such a king and all other kings. I implore you, for He who gives you life and light. You are the light of the world. I invoke you with all your names: Yazemiz [*sic:* for Šams] in Arabic, Sol in Latin, Maher in Chaldean, Lehuz in Roman [Byzantine Greek; Lehuz is a transliteration of Helios], Araz in Indian. You are the light of the world and its brightness; you stand in the middle of the planets. It is you who, by your virtue and your heat, produce generation in the world [...] I ask you, by your height and your will, to deign to help me that such a king and all other kings on earth put me in an elevated and sublime position, and that I will have domination and height as you who are the master of the planets and stars, from which they receive light and radiance. I ask you, you who are the root of all the firmament, to have mercy on me and be attentive to the prayers and requests that I have made.[14]

Perhaps this operation was never put into practice in late medieval Europe: it is in complete contradiction with the Christian faith; we find no trace of the *Picatrix* in European libraries before 1425, and among the twenty manuscripts preserved of this famous treatise, none dates from before the mid-fifteenth century. Nonetheless, this kind of text reveals the expansion of the potential scope of magic allowed by the Arab–Latin translations of the twelfth and thirteenth centuries.

As for the *Liber Razielis*, inspired by the *Sefer Raziel ha-Malach* (the Book of the Angel Raziel), it is preserved in two main versions: a version in two books, translated from Hebrew, seems the oldest but is only preserved in a manuscript of the mid-fifteenth century (Paris, BNF, MS lat. 3666); and a version in seven books placed under the patronage of Alfonso X and whose translation seems to have been done by a cleric of his entourage called in the prologue "Iohannes clericus" and identified by Alfonso d'Agostino as Juan d'Aspa. The version in seven books is preserved in two main manuscripts: in the oldest, an Italian codex of the second half of the fourteenth century, the *Liber Razielis* is isolated, while in the second one, which dates from around 1500, the treatise is accompanied by ten appendices, whose translation seems to have also been commissioned by Alfonso X.[15] According to Alfonso D'Agostino, this version of the *Liber Razielis* was established from a Castilian translation made around 1259[16]; according to Damaris Gehr, the attribution of this version to the patronage of Alfonso is a fiction that does not predate the fourteenth or fifteenth centuries.[17] In fact, we are probably dealing not with a translation from Hebrew into Latin through the Castilian, but with a Latin compilation of which the Castilian version is lost, coming perhaps partly from Hebrew via the version in two books.

Anyway, the basic theme that unites the pieces of this puzzle is the secret initiation, essential to the exercise of power. Raziel ("secret of God" in Hebrew) is an angel who appeared to Adam three days after his expulsion from Paradise and who gave him a magic book revealing the mysteries of creation. Two annexes to the *Liber Razielis* are devoted to the *Semaphoras*: a knowledge of this hidden and omnipotent God's name, found by Solomon, is likely to give to the magician king, a new Moses, a quasi-divine power over the elements and men, a power that could allow him to know the secrets of his people and defeat his enemies.

One can see here the phantasmagoric aspect of the motivations of Alfonso X's patronage, especially at the end of his reign, when he was in a particularly delicate political position. The long version of the *Liber Razielis* nevertheless circulated in Spain and, from the fourteenth century, in France and Italy. Two of these volumes were recorded in the library of Charles V and Charles VI of France, the latter having also recovered the original manuscript of the Alfonsine *Astromagia* and a French translation of the *Libro de las formas e ymagenes*, commissioned by his uncle, John, Duke of Berry.[18]

Magic and political affairs in the late middle ages

It is clear enough that the proliferation of texts and magical manuscripts that can be observed in Europe from the fourteenth century and even more in the fifteenth century may be explained by a sociocultural demand concerning first some members of court society and their vicinity. This is particularly evident for magical tricks and illusionist performances as part of court entertainment, of which we can see some remarkable examples in manuscripts coming from fifteenth-century military engineers, such as those of Conrad Kyeser's *Bellifortis*, of which the most beautiful specimen was sent in 1405 to Rupert, King of the Romans, or Giovanni Fontana's *Bellicorum instrumentorum liber*.[19] But it is also the case for ritual magic treatises requiring the participation of clerics such as the *Clavicula Salomonis* (Key of Solomon), reported for the first time by Pietro d'Abano in 1310, where three chapters of Book I are devoted to experiments of grace and favour, of hatred and destruction and of mockery and deception.[20] Even if we take the example of necromancy (more exactly "nigromancy", that is demonic magic and divination), we can see, reading the mid-fifteenth-century manual published by Richard Kieckhefer, that aims of the same type are almost predominant: in this manual, fourteen *experimenta* of forty-two, that is a third, can be qualified as illusions; four are for the acquisition of a horse or a spirit with its appearance, two are to obtain a boat or a flying throne, two others are expected to lead to the emergence of a banquet and a castle with its defenders and an innumerable army and, finally, three rituals are intended to achieve invisibility.[21] And if we accept Kieckhefer's idea that this kind of magic was particularly suited to a "clerical underworld",[22] we must clarify that we do not see it as an underworld mainly composed of disaffected clerics, but rather as an underground and informal network, whose real or supposed influence may ascend to the top of both secular and ecclesiastical society.

The place occupied by the charges relating to magic in the great wave of political trials of the early fourteenth century, orchestrated by the lawyers of the entourage of the King of France Philip the Fair and their allies against Pope Boniface VIII, the Bishop of Troyes Guichard and the Templars, can be better explained in this context.[23] Magical practices, real or imagined, have become power issues of great importance between the kings of France and England, the papacy, the cardinals and prelates, their advisors and other members of their courts. The policy of repression of magic and divination performed by Pope John XXII (1316–34) against great prelates like Bishop of Cahors Hugues Géraud, the Archbishop of Aix Robert de Mauvoisin, the Visconti of Milan and other more modest individuals (mostly members, like him, of the clergy in southwestern France) may be seen in a similar perspective, although John XXII, after asking in 1320 a panel of experts whether the ritual magic practices could be considered as a *factum hereticale*, finally move back on that point, for fear of being overwhelmed by the Inquisition.[24] Hence, perhaps, the unofficial publication in 1326 or 1327 of the bull *Super illius specula*, which remained apparently in draft form in the archives of the Avignon papacy until the revelation of its existence by Nicolas Eymerich in his *Directorium Inquisitorum* (1373), and the impunity that seems to have benefited some high-flying magicians such as the Catalan cleric Beranger Ganell, a member of the entourage of King Jacques III of Mallorca and author of the *Summa sacrae magicae*, a major treatise probably started at the royal court in Perpignan but completed in 1346, while Jacques and Beranger were in exile in Montpellier.[25]

Astral magic seems even to have been used at the court of France, during the reign of Charles V (1364–80), for a military issue. If one believes the Italian astrologer Antonio da Montolmo, known as author of a *De occultis and manifestis*, "Master Thomas de Pizan of Bologna, then physician to the King of France [Charles V], expelled the English companies from the Kingdom", adapting against the English soldiers the first *experimentum* of Thabit ibn Qurra's *De imaginibus* (translated into Latin from Arabic in the twelfth century), designed to drive scorpions away from any place:

> Having shared in imagination the whole territory of the kingdom of France into four parts, he took a certain amount of land in the middle of the territory, as well as a certain amount of land in the middle of each of the said four parts. [...] While the ascendant was in Scorpio, the Moon was in the same sign and Mars was retrograde in Gemini, five images [*talismans*] were made [...] representing a naked man, images which were immediately filled and consolidated, and on the front of each image was marked the name of the King of England or the master of the said companies. [...] Then, on time and under the aforesaid constellation, the said images were buried by several people, toward the middle of the territory, and each of the other four to the middle of the fourth part of that territory, reciting these words:
>
> This is the perpetual burial and total destruction and annihilation of N. — that is to say the captain or king — and all his office and his supporters. This is their perpetual expulsion from the kingdom [...] so that neither he nor any of his officers or any of his followers can in any way remain in this realm, but be forever expelled and put to flight irreversibly as this work will continue, with God's permission. Amen.
>
> And the images were buried upside down with hands or arms behind their backs. And in no time, that is to say in a few months, all the above companies fled the kingdom without a fight. [...] The names of the expulsion that were written on the back of each of the five images were these: "Baliatot, Hariaraiel, Kafieil, Abrail, Afal, Haidaienil, Maimeil, Kafieul, Gemeo, Helin, Varchalin, Arsal, disturb you, grab you and run away from this kingdom, you and all your supporters!"

The twelve names cited here are names of angels and demons of the planets, so we may note the illusory nature of the concept of *imago astronomica* being purely natural, formulated in the middle of the thirteenth century by the author of *Speculum astronomiae*, when one seeks to put it into practice. Furthermore, the only possible date corresponding to the rare astronomical event described in this text – a retrogradation of Mars in Gemini, with the Moon in the ascendant in Scorpio – which could coincide with the presence of Thomas de Pizan at the court of France (1365–87) is 25 October 1375 at seven o'clock in the morning. Dawn would probably be a good time for a magic ritual, but France and England are in a truce period (since 1 July 1375) and the English do not need to be driven out of the heart of the kingdom, since they have already left ... so we have here an *exemplum* which poses as an *experimentum*.[26]

Apart from this fictional exploit, magic and magicians appear to have played only a minor role in the course of the Hundred Years' War. But at a time when almost everyone believes in the reality of their power to spread the good and the bad, "nigromancers" represent important psychological weapons that alter the balance of power and a potential danger that must be taken into account, used or destroyed. This is particularly the case, it seems, at times of crisis or apparent weakness of royal or papal power, such as during the madness of Charles VI (1392–1422). Charles was the subject of a half-dozen magical attempts intended to deliver him from his evil. Other examples include the madness of Henry VI, the end of the Great Schism and the end of the reign of Charles VII, when Otto Castellani was accused of having used the services of the magician Pierre Mignon to replace Jacques Coeur as treasurer of the king.[27] The court of the Duke of Burgundy, at the end of the principality of Philip the Good, seems also to have been a laboratory in this matter, as is shown by the extraordinary trial of which John of Burgundy, Count of Etampes, was the object in 1463.[28] He was accused of having sponsored and participated in, using the services of two doctors and an apothecary from Brussels, an attempt at the hatred bewitchment of Count Charles de Charolais (the future Charles the Bold) and love bewitchments of Philip the Good and the King of France, Louis XI. This double attempt was considered by one of the witnesses at the trial, also a physician of Brussels, as intended to put "in the court of Monseigneur [Philip the Good] the most serious trouble which was in the court of a prince for a hundred years". It provoked the vengeance of Charles the Bold, who shortly after his accession as Duke of Burgundy in 1468 expelled John of Burgundy, meanwhile become Count of Nevers, from the Order of the Golden Fleece.

The political use of sorcery and English kings' fear of it have been well studied since the 1970s.[29] But it is only recently that the role of magic affairs in court societies has been studied without a positivistic point of view that sees in these affairs nothing more than phenomena of political manipulation. If we examine more closely the example of Charles VI's reign, we see that between 1390 (two years before his first attack of madness) and 1410, at the courts of the King of France and of the Pope and in princely circles, a series of about twenty magic cases. They seem to become epidemic, despite their diversity, because they primarily affect the curial circles. Combining the approach of magical practices and the political aspects, we find here that magic does not play only an instrumental role but may be considered as a central function in the exercise of power. The magicians claim "to bind and unbind",[30] thus usurping the power of the clergy, the official Church and emerging States, and becoming guilty of a crime against divine and human majesty. That is why the question of omnipotence, which is at the heart of magical practices, also explains at key moments how magic may become a kind of State heresy, articulating the power of the prince and the omnipotence of God. This is vividly illustrated by Jean Petit's justification of tyrannicide (1408), which for the first time in Europe fully detailed the different degrees of majesty affected by these criminal practices in order to exalt a defence of majesty itself.[31] So the famous affair involving Jean de Bar, magician of the Duke of Burgundy Philip the Bold, and the condemnations of magic by the Parisian Faculty of Theology in 1398 are not at all isolated, as the persecution of magic is the counterpart of magic's success and of the danger it poses for holders of political power.[32]

According to William R. Jones, " the English 'witch-plots' of the fifteenth century were promoted by the same conditions a century before in France — fierce partisanship on the highest levels of society, dynastic uncertainty and a politics of crime and scandal"[33] – but the situation is not the same in Italy, where learned magic seems to have been more tolerated.

It is no coincidence that a large proportion of late medieval magical manuscripts preserved now are of Italian origin.[34] The better conservation of astral magic *codices* in Italy than elsewhere in Europe may probably be explained by the sociocultural advancement of astrology in universities and the Italian city states during the Renaissance. Conversely, Solomonic magic manuscripts were more likely to be preserved in England and Germany, in connection with the development of the first books of exorcism in Germany around 1400 and in reaction against the Roman papacy during the Reformation. A review of a manuscript such as Paris, BNF, Italian 1524, copied in 1446 for a member of the court of the Duke of Milan Filippo Maria Visconti, differentiates between the spheres of public and private in the upper classes of the city states of the peninsula in a manner that is more pronounced than usual elsewherein Europe. This manuscript includes an anonymous *Necromantia* containing nearly 250 *experimenti*, and an Italian translation of the *Clavicula Salomonis* taken very probably from a copy of the Latin text that was in the library of the Duke Filippo Maria in Pavia in 1426. An original thematic feature of this codex, probably related to its being in Italian and to the fact that the recipient was a lay member of the ducal court, lies in the balance of love and sex magic. This is especially so in the *Necromantia*, of which two-thirds of the *experimenti* concern secret love and sexuality.

The position of learned magic in the East-Central European royal courts is more uncertain.[35] Wenceslas IV, Holy Roman Emperor and King of Bohemia (1361–1419), possessed some books of divination and ritual magic in his library and had a copy of Kyeser's *Bellifortis*. Another copy of it can be identified in the book collection of Wenceslas's brother, the next Emperor and Hungarian king Sigismund of Luxembourg. Kyeser spent some time in several courts, the most important of which was that of Wenceslas. He may have played the role of a court magician and may have also been involved in the political conflicts of the court of the two brothers. A few decades later, Henry the Bohemian, probable author of the *Prayer Book of King Wladislas* – a rare example of treasure hunting, combining a series of prayers and incorporating parts of the *Ars notoria*, the *Liber visionum* of John of Morigny and methods of crystallomancy – found himself in a delicate situation in the Polish court. In 1429, he was accused of conjuration of demons and propagation of Hussite ideas, and he was almost executed as *relapsus*, like Jean de Bar thirty years before. But unlike Jean de Bar, royal support saved his life and he was only imprisoned. Benedek Láng concludes that

> while the magician's political influence in the royal court made the case of Jean de Bar more serious, and led ultimately to his execution, in the East-Central European area, monarchs stood on the other side, usually trying to defend the magician under trial.

Future directions

"Magic at court is thus a complex and shifting issue, for a long time visible more in fears and accusations than in actual evidence."[36] This judgement is all the more true for those parts of Europe where first-hand documentation is almost totally lost and we know about magical practices in a way even less fully and directly than elsewhere. Such is the case of the Iberian Peninsula in the fourteenth and fifteenth centuries, where magical manuscripts appear to have been systematically destroyed, probably due to the effectiveness of the Spanish Inquisition, and the magicians' activities are known almost solely through external sources such as prosecutions and treatises against magic arts. In fact, we have proof that manuscripts of this kind were still circulating at the court of Castile in the fifteenth century: Enrique, Marquis of Villena, in his *Tratado de aojamiento* (Treatise on the Evil Eye), composed around 1425, refers to the *Picatrix*, to the *Kyranides*, to the Hebrew Kabbalah, to Costa ben Luca's *De physicis ligaturis* and to the *Liber aggregationis* ascribed to Albertus Magnus.[37] The literary fame of Enrique de Villena, the obvious passion he shows for magic, divination and astrology in several of his works, and the fact that part of his library was burned after his death in 1434 by the Bishop of Segovia Lope de Barrientos helped to make a kind of Spanish foreshadowing of the Faust myth.[38] But we cannot see the wood for the trees and there is still certainly much work to do on magic in Spain and Portugal in the late Middle Ages.

Another field of research related to the study of curial circles which remains largely unexplored is that of magical recipes and books of secrets in vernacular languages other than English or French, less marked than treatises in Latin, and sleeping especially in Italian libraries.[39]

Finally, it is necessary to undertake a systematic study of the social status of magic actors – professional magician did not really exist except as a romance character or a stereotype – as well as of the distribution of tasks between men and women in magic affairs that affected the courts and their periphery. Some great ladies, who were accused of magic, such as Countess Mahaut of Artois (in 1316), Eleanor Cobham, Duke Humphrey's second wife (in 1441) or Jacquetta of Luxembourg, King Edward IV's mother-in-law and dowager duchess of Bedford (in 1469), may have sponsored some political spells, but witches seem most of the time to have played a secondary role in curial magic affairs. However, courts, cities and rural societies located close to each other were porous environments that communicated freely, and where practices and rituals circulated unchecked by any barrier between literate and illiterate people.

Notes

1 D. Rollo, *Glamorous Sorcery. Magic and Literacy in the High Middle Ages* (Minneapolis and London: University of Minnesota Press, 2000), ch. 3, "Benoît de Sainte-Maure. Magic and Vernacular Fiction," 57–96 (especially 71 and 74).
2 Rollo, *Glamorous Sorcery*, 121; T.B.W. Reid, "Grammar, Grimoire, Glamour, Gomerel," in *Studies in French Language, Literature and History Presented to R. L. Græme Ritchie* (Cambridge: Cambridge University Press, 1949), 181–88; *Dictionnaire étymologique de l'ancien français*, vol. G, ed. K. Baldinger (Tübingen: M. Niemeyer, 1995), col. 1202–3.
3 A. Guerreau-Jalabert, "Fées et chevalerie. Observations sur le sens social d'un thème dit merveilleux," in *Miracles, prodiges et merveilles au Moyen Âge. XXVe Congrès de la Société des Historiens Médiévistes de l'Enseignement Supérieur Public (Orléans, 1994)* (Paris: Publications de la Sorbonne, 1995), 145.
4 See for example the French versions of the myth of the *translatio studii et imperii* in the XIIIth and XIVth centuries: *L'Image du monde de Gossuin de Metz*, ed. O.H. Prior (Lausanne: Payet, 1913) 77–80; *Les Grandes Chroniques de France*, vol. VII, ed. J. Viard (Paris: Champion, 1932), 61; S. Lusignan, *Parler vulgairement. Les intellectuels et la langue française aux XIIIe et XIVe siècles* (Paris and Montréal: Librairie philosophique, 1987); J.-P. Boudet, "Le modèle du roi sage aux XIIIe et XIVe siècles: Salomon, Alphonse X et Charles V," *Revue historique* 310, no. 3 (2008): 545–66.
5 S. Maksymiuk, *The Court Magician in Medieval German Romance* (Frankfurt and Berlin: P. Lang, 1996), 178.
6 Cf. C. Burnett, "Michael Scot and the Transmission of Scientific Culture from Toledo to Bologna via the Court of Frederick II Hohenstaufen," *Micrologus* 2 (1994): 101–26.
7 Munich, BSB, MS Clm 10268, fol. 17va; Paris, BnF, MS nouv. acq. lat. 1401, fol. 36rb: "Magica quidem ars destruit religionem divine legis et culturam demonum persuadet."
8 Munich, BSB, MS Clm 10268, fol. 114ra-va.

9. Cf. J.-P. Boudet, *Entre science et "nigromance". Astrologie, divination et magie dans l'Occident médiéval (XIIe-XVe siècle)* (Paris: Publications de la Sorbonne, 2006), 189–90; L. Fernández Fernández, *Arte e Ciencia en el scriptorium de Alfonso X el Sabio* (El Puerto de Santa María: Cátedra Alfonso X el Sabio, 2013).
10. See the recent edition of Alfonso el Sabio, *Lapidario, Libro de las formas e imágenes que son en los cielos*, ed. P. Sánchez-Prieto Borja (Madrid: Fundación José Antonio de Castro, 2014), 327–92.
11. Alfonso X el Sabio, *Astromagia (Ms. Reg. lat. 1283a)*, ed. A.D'Agostino (Naples: Liguori, 1992); *"Tratado de astrología y magia" de Alfonso X el Sabio*, facsimile, 2 vol. (Valencia: Grial, 2000).
12. See C. Burnett, "Magic in the Court of Alfonso el Sabio: The Latin Translation of the *Ghāyat al-Ḥakīm*," in *De Frédéric II à Rodolphe II. Astrologie, divination et magie dans les cours (XIIIe-XVIIe siècles)*, ed. J.-P. Boudet, M. Ostorero and A. Paravicini Bagliani (Florence: Sismel Edizioni del Galluzzo, 2017), 37–52.
13. *Picatrix. The Latin Version of the Ghāyat Al-Ḥakīm*, ed. D. Pingree (London: Warburg Institute, 1986), 15–25.
14. *Picatrix*, ed. Pingree, 128. See more generally J. Véronèse, "Les recettes magiques pour s'attirer les faveurs des grands," in *La Cour du Prince, Cour de France, cours d'Europe, XIIe-XVe siècle*, ed. M. Gaude-Ferragu, Br. Laurioux and J. Paviot (Paris: Champion, 2011), 321–38.
15. MSS Vatican, Reg. lat. 1300, fol. 1–202v (second half of the XIVth century) and Halle, Universitäts- und Landesbibliothek Sachsen-Anhalt, 14.B.36 (ca. 1500).
16. Alfonso X el Sabio, *Astromagia*, 39–45.
17. Cf. D. Gehr, "La fittizia associazione del *Liber Razielis* in sette libri ad Alfonso X il Saggio e una nuova determinazione delle fazi redazionali del trattato, della loro datazione e dell' identità dei compilatori coinvolti," *Viator Multilingual* 43 (2012): 181–210.
18. See L. Delisle, *Recherches sur la librairie de Charles V*, vol. II (Paris: Champion, 1907), 103, 115 and 117, nos 616, 699, 700, 714. Cf. also A. García Avilés, "Two Astromagical Manuscripts of Alfonso X," *Journal of the Warburg and Courtauld Institutes* 59 (1996): 14–23. Charles VI also possessed a *Semiphoras* and the pseudo-platonic *Liber vaccae* (Delisle, nos 715 and 677).
19. Conrad Kyeser aus Eichstätt, *Bellifortis*, vol. I, ed. G. Quarg (Düsseldorf: VDI-Verlag, 1967), 15–16, 56–67 and 78–89; vol. II, fol. 11v–12, 90v–99, 106; *Le macchine cifrate di Giovanni Fontana*, ed. E. Battisti and G.S. Battisti (Milan: Arcadia, 1984), 88, 94–97, 99–100, 131, 134–35, 137 and 140. In the *Bellifortis*, Kyeser depicted himself summoning demons.
20. MS Coxe 25 (Latin codex of the end of the XVth century, formerly preserved in Amsterdam, Bibliotheca Philosophica Hermetica 114), 106–9; Paris, BnF, MS ital. 1524 (Italian translation copied in 1446), fol. 214–15v and 216v–17v.
21. R. Kieckhefer, *Forbidden Rites. A Necromancer's Manual of the Fifteenth Century* (Stroud: Sutton, 1997), 42–68 (commentary), 208–26, 231–36, 240 and 344–45 (texts).
22. R. Kieckhefer, *Magic in the Middle Ages* (Cambridge: Cambridge University Press, 1989), ch. 7, 151–75.
23. See notably *Boniface VIII en procès. Articles d'accusation et dépositions des témoins (1303–1311). Édition critique, introductions et notes*, ed. J. Coste (Rome: L'Erma di Bretschneider, 1995); Boudet, *Entre science et "nigromance"*, 469–72; A. Provost, *Domus Diaboli. Un évêque en procès au temps de Philippe le Bel* (Paris: Belin, 2010); J. Théry, "A Heresy of State. Philip the Fair, the Trial of the 'Perfidious Templars', and the Pontificalization of the French Monarchy," *Journal of Medieval Religious Cultures* 39, no. 2 (2013): 117–48.
24. A. Boureau, *Le pape et les sorciers. Une consultation de Jean XXII sur la magie en 1320* (Rome: Ecole française de Rome, 2004); A. Boureau, *Satan the Heretic. The Birth of Demonology in the Medieval West*, trans. Teresa Lavendar Fagan (Chicago, IL: University of Chicago Press, 2006).
25. See S. Baron, "Un procès de magie en Gévaudan et ses enjeux politiques (1347)," *Cahiers de Recherches Médiévales et Humanistes*, 33 (2017), 385–417.
26. Cf. N. Weill-Parot, *Les "images astrologiques" au Moyen Âge et à la Renaissance. Spéculations intellectuelles et pratiques magiques* (Paris: Champion, 2002), 605–11 and 897–900 (edition of the Latin text); Boudet, *Entre science et "nigromance"*, 403–8.
27. P. Braun, "Maître Pierre Mignon, sorcier et falsificateur du grand sceau de France," in *La faute, la répression et le pardon. Actes du 107e Congrès national des sociétés savantes (Brest, 1982). Section de philologie et d'histoire jusqu'à 1610*, vol. I, Paris, 1984, 241–60, repr. in P. Braun, *Droits en devenir* (Limoges: Presses universitaires de Limoges, 1998), 221–42.
28. See A. Berlin, *Magie am Hof der Herzöge von Burgund. Aufstieg und Fall des Grafen von Étampes* (Munich: UVK Verlagsgesellschaft Konstanz, 2016).

29 W.R. Jones, "Political Uses of Sorcery in Medieval Europe," *The Historian* 34 (1972): 670–87; H.A. Kelly, "English Kings and the Fear of Sorcery," *Mediaeval Studies* 39 (1977): 206–38, repr. in H.A. Kelly, *Inquisitions and Other Trial Procedures in the Medieval West* (Aldershot: Ashgate, 2001), text VII.
30 J.-P. Boudet and J. Véronèse, "Lier et délier: de Dieu à la sorcière," in *La légitimité implicite*, vol. I, ed. J.-Ph. Genet (Paris and Rome: Publications de la Sorbonne, 2015), 87–119.
31 See J.-P. Boudet and J. Chiffoleau, "Magie et construction de la souveraineté sour le règne de Charles VI," in *De Frédéric II à Rodolphe II. Astrologie, divination et magie dans les cours (XIIIe-XVIIe siècle)*, ed. Boudet et al., (Florence: Sismel Edizioni del Galluzzo, 2014), 157–239.
32 J.R. Veenstra, *Magic and Divination at the Courts of Burgundy and France. Text and Context of Laurens Pignon's* Contre les devineurs *(1411)* (Leiden: Brill, 1997); J.-P. Boudet, "Les condamnations de la magie à Paris en 1398," *Revue Mabillon* 12 (2001): 121–57, n.s.
33 Jones, "Political Uses of Sorcery," 673.
34 J.-P. Boudet, "Des savoirs occultes et illicites? Les textes et manuscrits de magie en Italie (XIVe – début du XVIe siècle)," in *Frontières des savoirs en Italie à l'époque des premières universités (XIIIe-XVe siècle)*, ed. J. Chandelier and Aurélien Robert (Rome: École française de Rome, 2015), 509–39.
35 B. Láng, "Were East-Central European Royal Courts More Tolerant *vis a vis* Astrology and Magic in the 15th century?" in *De Frédéric II à Rodolphe II. Astrologie, divination et magie dans les cours (XIIIe-XVIIe siècle)*, ed. Boudet et al., 255–69.
36 A. Lawrence-Mathers and C. Escobar-Vargas, *Magic and Medieval Society (*Abingdon: Routledge, 2014), 12.
37 Enrique de Villena, *Tratado de aojamiento*, ed. A.M. Gallina (Bari: Adriatica Editrice, 1978), 109–14, 116. Besides the *Picatrix*, Enrique de Villena seems to have read and probably owned several other Alfonsine books of magic, especially the *Liber Razielis* and the *Libro de las formas e ymagenes*.
38 Cf. notably A. Torres-Alcalá, *Don Enrique de Villena: un mago al dintel del Renacimiento* (Madrid: J. Porrúa Turanzas, 1983); Á. Martínez Quasado, *Lope de Barrientos, un intelectual de la corte de Juan II* (Salamanca: San Esteban, 1994); F. Álvarez Lopez, *Arte mágica e hechiceria medieval. Tres tratados de magia en la corte de Juan II* (Valladolid: Editora Provincial, 2000).
39 See for example W. Brackman, *Middeleeuwse witte en zwarte magie in het Nederlands taalgebied. Gecommentarieerd compendium van incantamenta tot einde 16de eeuw* (Gent: Koninklijke academie voor Nederlandse taal- en letterkunde, 1997) and S. Giralt, "The manuscript of a medieval necromancer: Magic in Occitan and Latin in ms. Vaticano BAV, Barb. lat. 3589," *Revue d'histoire des textes* IX (2014): 221–72, n.s.; J.-P. Boudet, Fl. Gal and Laurence Moulinier-Brogi, *Vedrai mirabilia! Un libro de magia dell' Quattrocento* (Rome: Viella, 2017).

25

MAGIC AND GENDER

Catherine Rider

The relationship between magic and gender has received substantial attention since the 1980s when, in response to the rise of women's history and gender history, scholars of early modern witchcraft began to examine why women were disproportionately likely to be put on trial as witches in many parts of Europe. Work on this issue has since taken a wide variety of approaches, from early analyses that focused on misogyny as the motivating factor for witch trials, to more sophisticated discussions that set witchcraft in the context of wider attitudes to the body, sexuality and gender roles in early modern society.[1] More recently, attention has also turned to the men who were accused of witchcraft, and the relationship between witchcraft and masculinity.[2]

Magic and gender, then, is a well-established topic for research but much of this work has concentrated on the witch trials of the late fifteenth to seventeenth centuries rather than on the Middle Ages. In contrast, as the chapters in this volume show, the research field of medieval magic has developed in other directions, with much research into magical texts, ecclesiastical discourses about magic and the records of fifteenth-century trials, to name a few key areas. Many studies of these topics mention gender but it has rarely been their major focus. For example, a 2001 article by Michael Bailey suggested that the emphasis on women in fifteenth-century writing about witchcraft marks an important departure from earlier ecclesiastical condemnations that focused largely on learned, demonic magic practised by men, but this is one part of a broader argument about changing conceptions of magic in the later Middle Ages.[3] Similarly, Jean-Patrice Boudet's 2006 survey of medieval magic notes (following earlier work on late medieval witchcraft trials) that in the fifteenth century, documented accusations against women began to outnumber those against men for the first time. Like Bailey, Boudet links this development to a change in the kinds of magic that concerned the ecclesiastical and secular authorities: before the early fifteenth century, the authorities focused primarily on ritual magic, which was almost exclusively a male activity, whereas after this time, new concerns about popular magic and the growing association between magic and devil worship made it easier to imagine women gaining access to magical power. However, this is a small part of a large volume, much of which focuses on learned forms of magic and their social contexts.[4] Several scholars based at the University of Lausanne, who have done important work on fifteenth-century witchcraft trials in the Alps, have also raised issues of gender (notably Martine Ostorero and Catherine Chène), and this work will be discussed in more detail below.[5] Nevertheless, the majority of the Lausanne studies focus on other issues such as the development of the image of the witches' sabbath, trial procedures and the range of factors that caused certain individuals to be brought to trial.

Thus, although there have been important insights, comparatively little work has discussed magic and gender in depth for the Middle Ages, or has ranged across different kinds of source material to explore broader patterns. This chapter will survey what has been done so far and suggest some future directions. It will start by highlighting the questions that have been studied most often, which focus on the relationship between magic and women. To what extent was magic especially associated with women in the Middle Ages? If magic was strongly associated with women, why was this and how might it be connected to the development of the stereotype of the female, devil-worshipping witch in the fifteenth century? From there, the chapter will move on to look at two smaller bodies of research that have discussed gender: studies that examine how far individual magical practices were regarded as male or female activities, and work on one of the major source bases that has been used in recent years to assess how far learned stereotypes about magic – including gender stereotypes – may have reflected the situation in practice: trial records.

A female activity? Stereotypes and the origins of the female witch

The idea that women were especially likely to do magic appears in some very well-known medieval sources. One of the most notorious and most often quoted is the *Malleus Maleficarum*, written in 1486 by two inquisitors, Heinrich Kramer (also known as Institoris) and Jakob Sprenger, to describe the comparatively new crime of diabolical witchcraft:

> Everything is governed by carnal lusting, which is insatiable in them [women] … and for this reason they even cavort with demons to satisfy their lust. More evidence could be cited here, but for intelligent men it appears to be reasonably unsurprising that more women than men are found to be tainted with the Heresy of Sorceresses … Blessed be the Highest One, Who has, down to the present day, preserved the male kind from such disgraceful behaviour.[6]

According to Kramer and Sprenger, this connection between magic and lust made women more likely than men to do all kinds of magic, but it also made them especially likely to do magic in order to control love and sex – arousing love, causing impotence or infertility, or even stealing men's penises. The *Malleus* discussed these subjects in detail, and modern scholars have also done so, with the unusual stories of penis theft attracting particular attention.[7]

A reading of the *Malleus* can therefore give the impression that medieval clergy viewed magic as a female activity, at least in part because of misogynistic anxieties about women's sexuality and fears about the power magic might give women over men. This idea contains some truth but in the last twenty years, scholars have explored the *Malleus* and other ecclesiastical texts that talk about women and magic in more depth, seeking to add complexity and nuance to this general picture. Hans-Peter Broedel's 2003 study of the *Malleus* emphasized that Kramer and Sprenger's views did not come out of nowhere; rather, they drew on older misogynistic stereotypes and took material from a range of earlier texts which stated that women were more prone than men to commit the sins of magic and "superstition". Where Kramer and Sprenger departed from these stereotypes was in their assertion that witchcraft was almost always done by women, which was a more radical position than the one taken by their sources.[8] Other scholars have sought to put the *Malleus* into its fifteenth-century context by arguing that its emphasis on women was part of a wider change taking place in attitudes to magic. In particular, Bailey, Boudet, Ostorero and Chène have highlighted that many fifteenth-century clerics placed a greater emphasis on women's magic than could be seen in earlier texts: like Broedel, they argue that Kramer and Sprenger adopted a position that was radical but comprehensible in the light of what other writers were saying.[9] Around the same time, another scholar took a different approach to the *Malleus*'s misogyny. Walter Stephens's 2002 study of demonology and sex highlighted that only a small part of the *Malleus* discusses women's propensity for witchcraft. For Stephens, modern historians focus too much on misogyny and ignore other important aspects of this complex text.[10] Despite their different approaches and conclusions, these studies have all underlined the importance of placing the *Malleus*'s comments on women in a broader intellectual context instead of discussing them in isolation and allowing this one text to dominate discussions of medieval magic and gender.

While the studies cited above have focused on changing attitudes to women and magic in the fifteenth century, other scholars have turned instead to the period before 1400. The impulse behind this work has often been to trace the origins of the fifteenth-century stereotype of the female witch. Therefore, several studies have focused on identifying earlier sources that depict women engaging in magical practices similar to those described in fifteenth-century witchcraft literature such as flying or love- and sex-related magic.[11]

Many of the texts used for this enterprise have been works of canon law, theology or pastoral care and a number of these did indeed associate women with certain kinds of magic in ways that resemble the later stereotype of the witch. The most influential and most discussed of these texts is a piece of canon law first recorded by Regino, abbot of Prüm in around 906 and known from its opening word as the Canon *Episcopi*.[12] In this canon, Regino criticized women who believed they flew with the goddess Diana at night. He argued that these women could not really fly but were instead deceived by the devil, who made them mistake dreams of flying for reality. In the mid-twelfth century, the Canon was copied into Gratian's *Decretum*, which became one of the main canon law textbooks used in medieval universities, and from there its ideas were transmitted to many later writers, including eventually fifteenth-century treatises on witchcraft.[13] Later, witchcraft writers took a very different view of these night flights from Regino: unlike him, they often saw the women's flights as a real, physical phenomenon rather than a dream. But however the women's flight was interpreted, this much quoted and authoritative passage singled out women as the believers in one form of magic that later became a key part of the witchcraft stereotype and so has attracted scholars' attention.

One of the major challenges for medievalists when they study comments on women and magic such as those found in the *Malleus Maleficarum* or the Canon *Episcopi* is that most of those comments were written by educated clergy. Our view of whether magic was, or was not, seen as a female activity in the Middle Ages is therefore dominated by the views of one social group, men who were on the whole expected to be celibate and (if they were university scholars, friars or monks) spent much of their time in all-male environments. Arguably, these men may have been especially likely to regard magic as a female sin or to repeat misogynistic stereotypes about "superstitious" women who were lustful and easily deceived by the devil. Sources produced by and for other sectors of society do exist: as other chapters in this volume make clear romance literature, medical and scientific texts and archaeology allow us to explore other, less ecclesiastical perspectives. Nevertheless, when we study stereotypes relating to magic and gender, it is often difficult to move beyond ecclesiastical depictions of magical practitioners such as Regino's or Kramer and Sprenger's and hear other voices.

This does not mean that any discussion of medieval women and magic tells us about little except general clerical misogyny, however, and detailed studies have offered a range of more nuanced interpretations. One approach has been to explore the diversity of views among the educated clergy who wrote the majority of our sources. This approach has stressed that medieval "ecclesiastical" writing on magic was not monolithic and instead encompassed a wide range of authors and genres. "Ecclesiastical" texts ranged from detailed, scholastic treatises like the *Malleus Maleficarum* or one of its key sources, Thomas Aquinas's *Summa Theologiae*, to the simpler sermons and treatises on sin and confession which were designed to educate the clergy and laity and which are discussed in detail in Kathleen Kamerick's chapter in this volume. This large body of texts, written across Europe, over several centuries, and across many genres, did not offer a single view of magic and its practitioners. There were some common themes: for example, drawing on St Augustine, most clergy associated magic with demons and condemned it. Nevertheless, they varied in their details and emphases. Work by Michael Bailey, Kathleen Kamerick and Alain Boureau, as well as my own work, has therefore sought to explore the range of clerical views of magic and the debates that took place among learned writers.[14] These scholars have shown that although some authors stated, or implied, that women were especially prone to magic and the related sin of "superstition", others described both male and female magical practitioners. For example, *exempla* (short moral stories collected for use in sermons) told stories of male magicians who invoked demons as well as describing "superstitious" women.[15] There were also ecclesiastical writers who did not say much at all about the gender of magical practitioners and preferred to focus on different issues, such as the exact nature of the relationship between magicians and demons, or the question of whether or not certain unofficial ritual practices were legitimate or superstitious.[16]

More work could be done to explore both the diversity of clerical views and the long-term continuities. Looking at the differences between genres of ecclesiastical writing is one possible approach: did certain genres, such as canon law or *exempla*, lend themselves to discussing gender in particular ways? Variations over time and space are also a fruitful area for study. As noted above, several scholars have argued that women became increasingly associated with magic in the fifteenth century but what, if any, changes took place in earlier centuries and how regionally specific were they? To what extent do we see a Europe-wide clerical attitude to magic, fuelled by the use of a common language, Latin, and by international organizations like the universities or the orders of friars that spread texts and ideas across a wide geographical area? Alternatively, do we see significant regional variations as we do in the fifteenth century when the stereotype of the devil-worshipping witch appeared earlier in some areas than others?

Although much of the work on whether or not women were seen as more likely to do magic has focused on ecclesiastical sources, it is worth noting that in recent years another genre of writing has also attracted attention: works of literature. Corinne Saunders's chapter in this volume outlines the developments that have taken place in literary scholarship so they will not be discussed in detail here, but these developments include discussions of gender. In her 2010 survey of magic in medieval English romances, Saunders identified a variety of images of magical practitioners of both sexes, including the male physician who practises natural magic; the woman healer; the (usually) female practitioner of harmful magic; the clerical "nigromancer"; and the fairy mistress.[17] Beyond this, she also argues that women have a particular association with the supernatural in many romances.[18] As with work on ecclesiastical sources, women's magic has attracted more attention than men's. For example, Laine E. Doggett's study of Old French romances takes women as its focus, looking at their roles as healers and practitioners of love magic in these texts.[19] Heidi Breuer's study of magic and gender in medieval and early modern English literature discusses both male and female magicians, but the primary focus is on the development of the stereotype of the female, wicked witch.[20] Individual medieval works depicting women magical practitioners have also attracted attention. A striking example is Fernando de Rojas's *Celestina*, a

Spanish work first published in 1499, which depicts an elderly procuress invoking the devil and engaging in love magic on behalf of a male client. Among the many studies of this complex text are several that have sought to relate de Rojas's powerful depiction of a female magical practitioner to contemporary stereotypes of the female witch.[21] There is more that can be done, however. As with ecclesiastical writing, male magical practitioners deserve more attention, and so, too, do the differences between different texts, places and periods. The ways in which these literary images of magicians – male and female – interacted with stereotypes found in other sources, such as ecclesiastical texts, also deserve further study.

The gendering of magical practices

In addition to discussions of whether medieval magic was generally associated with women, scholars have also asked whether certain types of magic were especially likely to be associated with either women or men. Recent scholars have varied in the extent to which they have seen medieval magical practices as linked particularly to one gender, or to any other identifiable social group. Richard Kieckhefer, for example, has formulated the concept of a "common tradition" of medieval magic, arguing that many magical practices were widely shared across society. They were done by clergy and laity, men and women.[22] By contrast, other scholars have identified certain forms of magic as more likely to be associated with women, or with men. Female forms of magic have often received more attention than male ones, but men have not been ignored. This section will look at two examples that have received recent discussion: magic connected with love and sex, which is often linked to women, and ritual magic, which is often viewed as a male activity.

Magic relating to love, sex and fertility is probably the form of magic most often cited by modern scholars as a female activity. Individual medieval writers, such as the authors of the *Malleus*, who as we have seen linked love magic to women have attracted attention, and Richard Kieckhefer has also pointed out that women were more likely than men to be accused of doing love magic in trial records.[23] Scholars have varied in how they interpret this information. On the one hand, Kieckhefer emphasizes that although women were more likely than men to be accused, this does not mean they were necessarily more likely to do love magic in practice: rather, men may have found it more convenient than women to blame their sexual transgressions on magic, and they may also have been more able to make the authorities take their allegations seriously.[24] On the other hand, some scholars have suggested that women may really have been more likely than men to use forms of magic relating to sex and reproduction. Textual amulets to help women in childbirth were, unsurprisingly, intended to be used to benefit women, although since they were written documents, they were probably produced by men and men are often expected to play leading roles in performing the rituals involved.[25] To take another example, the association between women and magic to cause impotence is so persistent in case records and in ecclesiastical condemnations that it may reflect a real tendency for women to use this form of magic on men in particular situations, although even here accusations may reflect male insecurities and fears of what an angry former girlfriend might do to them rather than the realities of practice.[26] However, as these examples show, it is extremely difficult to write about certain forms of magic as women's magic because most of the surviving sources were written by men rather than by the women themselves. It is therefore almost impossible to know how far they reflect a genuine difference in practice and how far they draw on the kinds of stereotypes about women, sex and magic discussed in the previous section.

By contrast, it is much easier to identify one form of magic as a largely male activity: the use of learned ritual and image magic texts. Medieval sources such as *exempla* often depict male, learned magicians, often clerics, invoking demons with books and magic circles. In this case, it is possible to compare the stereotype with evidence of practice, thanks to the survival of a large number of manuscripts of medieval magical texts. These manuscripts demonstrate how socially restricted an activity learned magic must have been. Reading a magical text or carrying out one of the operations described in them required literacy in Latin, access to books and sometimes knowledge of the liturgy. These skills and opportunities were gendered and men were far more likely to possess them than women. Moreover, only certain men had these skills: clergy and others with some education. In 1997, an early, influential study of ritual magic by Richard Kieckhefer suggested that magical texts were owned and read by a particular social group, a "clerical underworld" consisting of men such as university students in minor orders, priests who did not have a regular, full-time position in a parish church, monks and friars. These men all had some education and knowledge of the liturgy, as well as the spare time to experiment with magical texts.[27] Since 1997, more detailed studies of the ownership of magical manuscripts have tended to confirm this impression and have identified many owners of magical texts as monks, university masters or students.[28] They have also noted the importance of physicians as owners of manuscripts containing image magic texts.[29] Women were not completely excluded from this world: Claire Fanger and Nicholas Watson's chapter in this volume describes the involvement of John of Morigny's sister, Bridget, in learned magic, and other female readers may yet be identified in what is still a developing field of scholarship. Nevertheless, learned magic seems overwhelmingly to have been practised by men.

The relationship between this largely male readership and the contents of magical texts has also attracted some attention. The most detailed interpretation has been offered by Frank Klaassen, who argues that ritual magic texts reflect the fears and desires of the clerics and scholars who read them, and so are gendered in their goals and aspirations. The large number of rituals to gain knowledge or intellectual skills therefore reflects the value placed on these things by clergy and university scholars. Rituals to gain wealth, acquire status symbols such as horses or win the favour of a powerful person may reflect the wishes of scholars or clerics who desired social status and needed to win the support of their superiors in order to build their careers. Even rituals to gain the love or sexual favours of women may reveal specifically male anxieties on that score, despite the fact that celibacy was officially the norm in universities and other clerical environments. Meanwhile, alongside these rituals, some texts contain stories that sound like wish fulfilment, presenting their authors as "a 'man's man', intelligent, materially successful, controlled, and bold".[30] These goals and stories may seem to contradict the high-minded prologues of many magical texts that stress the importance of secrecy, chastity and asceticism but Klaassen sees these two strands as complementary: it is this very asceticism that gives the readers of magical texts the power to achieve their goals, and this again reflects the value placed on self-discipline and learning in clerical culture.[31]

An article on secrecy in ritual magic by Jean-Patrice Boudet and Julien Véronèse also sheds light on the gendered nature of magical texts, although this is not its main focus. In particular, Boudet and Véronèse discuss how the prologues of some ritual magic texts emphasized that magic was an activity only suitable for a chosen few because it allowed the operator to do bad things as well as good ones. This elitism had a gendered aspect but gender was bound up with other factors such as age and intellectual and moral qualities: one text, the *Liber Razielis*, warned the reader: "You should not reveal your secrets to a woman, nor a child, nor an idiot, nor a drunk."[32] So far these explorations of magic and masculinity have focused primarily on ritual magic. It will be interesting to see how this area develops in the future and whether similar features appear in other genres of magical texts.

The gendering of other forms of magic has received less attention. It is not clear, for example, to what extent healing or divination was gendered or whether there were gender differences between different forms of healing and divination. In part, this is due to the difficulties posed by the sources that often do not present healing or divination as particularly male or female activities (in contrast to their depictions of women doing love magic or men calling up demons) but more could be done to unpick the stereotypes and accusations that we do see in, for example, *exempla* featuring healers and diviners. Another potential line of enquiry is to investigate whether the same kinds of healing, divination or other forms of magic were viewed differently when done by men and when done by women. Here, differences of emphasis and language in our sources may be important, as well as radical disparities in what men and women were believed to do. For example, several studies of fifteenth-century witch trials have suggested that although judges asked men and women similar questions about the witches' sabbath, they asked women for much more detail about the sabbath's sexual aspects, which may mean they viewed men's and women's participation in the same activity differently.[33] The reasons why certain forms of magic might, or might not, be gendered are also worth exploring further. In the case of learned magic, the gender of the practitioners reflects the skills and education needed, but this may not have been equally true for other forms of magic that did not rely so heavily on literacy and access to books.

The ways in which gender interacted with other factors are also important. When it came to defending oneself against accusations, a person's gender is likely to have interacted with their social position, occupation and reputation in determining how their activities were regarded and how suspicions were dealt with. Historians of witchcraft from the fifteenth century onwards have emphasized the importance of rumour and reputation in determining who might be accused of magic in court, and what the result might be.[34] Early modernists have gone further than medievalists in teasing out these connections between reputation, social status, gender and magic. In this, they are aided by the more extensive sources surviving from the sixteenth and seventeenth centuries such as inquisition records that contain very detailed descriptions of the people accused of magic, their reputations and their alleged activities. Using these sources, several scholars have suggested that prostitutes were often seen as specialists in love magic, rather along the lines depicted in the fictional *Celestina*. They have offered different views of why this might be. It may be that prostitutes really did do love magic more often than other women, because their livelihood depended on inducing passion in clients and subsequently keeping their love. On the other hand, prostitutes may simply have been more likely than women with better reputations to end up on trial.[35] Medievalists may not be able to explore these issues in so much detail but they can ask similar questions.

Accusations and trials

By the later fourteenth and fifteenth centuries, we have a body of source material that allows us to go beyond norms and stereotypes and begin to ask: How many women and men were accused of magic? What kinds of magic were they accused of and did this vary along gendered lines? Trials for magic survive in steadily increasing numbers from around 1375 onwards and especially after 1435.[36] Although these records come with their own challenges, they allow us to approach the gendering of magic in a different way from studies based on ecclesiastical or literary sources and to identify broad patterns as well as focusing on individual cases.

In a study of late medieval witch trials published in 1976, Richard Kieckhefer noted that around two-thirds of the accused were women, and that the proportion of women accused, compared to men, rose during the fifteenth century.[37] More recent work on fifteenth-century Swiss trial records has sought to bring greater nuance to this picture and has stressed that although a general "feminization" of witchcraft did take place in this period, the numbers of men and women brought to trial varied considerably between regions. In some areas, men continued to outnumber women even at the end of the fifteenth century.[38] These studies have also shown the extent to which the gendering of trials depended on whether the witches were tried by a secular or ecclesiastical tribunal, though the impact of this also varied. Susanna Burghartz's comparison of trials in Lausanne and Lucerne has found that, contrary to what we might assume about clerical misogyny, the proportion of women in witchcraft trials conducted by the secular authorities in Lucerne was far higher than in trials conducted by the inquisitors in Lausanne.[39] This was not always the case, however, and Kathrin Utz Tremp found the opposite pattern in late fourteenth- and early fifteenth-century Freiburg: in towns and before inquisitors, women appeared in greater numbers, whereas in the countryside and before secular tribunals, men outnumbered women.[40] The picture is one of local diversity within a general trend towards "feminization".

There has, therefore, been important work on Switzerland but records from other parts of Europe deserve further study. Areas such as England that did not see large numbers of trials for magic have, not surprisingly, attracted comparatively little attention but it is still possible to draw some conclusions. In a study of fifteenth- and sixteenth-century church court records from the diocese of Canterbury Karen Jones and Michael Zell have suggested that, although the number of magic cases brought before the church courts was low, there were some differences in the kinds of magic men and women were accused of. Women were more likely than men to be accused of harmful magic while men were more likely to be accused of magical treasure hunting. Conversely, other forms of magic, such as healing or finding stolen goods, were linked to men and women in roughly equal numbers.[41] More can be done in local archives across Europe to explore whether these or other patterns are found more generally.

Another tribunal that has been comparatively understudied by historians of magic is the medieval inquisition. In part, this is probably because inquisition records from before the fifteenth century yield less information about magic than we might expect. Medieval inquisitors, unlike early modern ones, focused narrowly on heresy rather than on other sins against the faith. Nevertheless, occasional accusations of magic do appear such as the case of Raymond of Pouts, a diviner, in the Toulouse records of 1277.[42] Emmanuel Le Roy Ladurie's well-known study of early fourteenth-century Montaillou also identified a handful of references to magic, when individuals who were called before the inquisition for heresy mentioned that they had consulted diviners or noted omens.[43] It is not yet clear how much can be learned about gender from these scattered examples but there may be more information to be uncovered here.

A final and perhaps more fruitful line of enquiry would be to investigate the gendering of trials and accusations at royal and aristocratic courts such as those that occurred in early fourteenth-century France or in England during the Wars of the Roses. These courtly accusations of magic have received considerable attention, as Jean-Patrice Boudet shows in his chapter in this volume, but this has often focused on the political aspects of these cases rather than on the gender of the accused. There do seem to be some gendered patterns at work, however. It seems that women may have been more likely than men to be accused of love magic at court as they were in other contexts. In England, there are the examples of

Alice Perrers, mistress of Edward III, who was accused by her enemies of gaining the king's affections by magic; and Eleanor Cobham, duchess of Gloucester, and Elizabeth Woodville, wife of Edward IV, who were both accused of using magic to induce their royal husbands to marry them. Anna Brzezinska has discussed similar cases from sixteenth-century Poland of royal wives and mistresses accused of love magic and argues that, as in non-courtly love magic cases, these accusations were a convenient way to shift the blame for men's unacceptable behaviour to their wives or mistresses. In a royal context, it allowed courtiers to avoid blaming the king directly for his misconduct or for the amount of attention he gave to certain women.[44] However, other courtly accusations of magic seem less obviously gendered: both men and women were accused of using magic to cause harm or death to their enemies, for example. Further research is needed to confirm or qualify these impressions.

Future directions

There has, therefore, been important work on medieval magic and gender, ranging across a wide variety of periods and kinds of source material. Nevertheless, there is scope for more and each section of this chapter has suggested questions and areas that scholars could explore in greater detail. Scholarship on several relevant genres of source is developing rapidly, including literature, magical texts and the archaeology of magic and there is scope for more work focused on gender here. Many of the other kinds of source discussed above also deserve further exploration by historians interested in gender, including sermons and confession treatises, canon law and trial records. Much remains unpublished in all these genres, and detailed work in local archives as well as larger libraries may reveal interesting texts or comparatively understudied sets of records. Scholars doing this work will need to keep an open mind about their exact focus because it may be that there is not always a vast amount of material on magic, let alone the gendering of magic, to be found in these sources: the medieval English church courts, for example, devoted far more time to other offences. In these cases, magic, or gender, may be best treated as one aspect of a broader study. Thus, Karen Jones discusses magic as part of a book-length study of crime in late medieval and early modern Kent as well as co-writing an article on witchcraft in the church courts.[45] Conversely, the works of Bailey and Boudet cited at the beginning of this chapter discuss gender as one aspect of changing attitudes to magic. There is therefore an element of luck in finding substantial amounts of relevant material but as Jones and Zell's study shows, even a comparatively small source base can suggest interesting patterns.

In addition to studies that focus on particular texts or kinds of text, work is also needed to explore the links between different kinds of evidence: for example, looking at the ways in which ideas disseminated through sermons or pastoral literature may have influenced the accusations made in trials, or at the links between literature written for a courtly audience and the accusations made in royal and aristocratic courts. For example, Franco Mormando has argued that the preaching of Bernardino of Siena may have played a part in provoking the trial of an Italian healer and love magic practitioner, Matteuccia di Francesco, in 1428, as well as in shaping the accusations against her.[46] A chapter on gender in Stephen Mitchell's *Witchcraft and Magic in the Nordic Middle Ages*, which brings in a range of evidence including literature, art and trial records to examine the gendering of magic in one geographical area, is another notable example of this approach and identifies both similarities and differences between different genres of source in terms of how they presented the gender of magical practitioners.[47]

Both in-depth studies of individual sources and studies that join together different kinds of evidence will be useful in order to interrogate some of the broad patterns that have been identified in general studies of medieval magic: that clergy tended to associate magic with women, for example, or that magic became increasingly associated with women in the fifteenth century. A careful analysis of the sources will allow us to see how universal these trends were and to see what other patterns, regional variations or chronological shifts emerge. The relationship between women and magical practice, and the development of stereotypes of female magical practitioners, are therefore important and have not been exhausted, but there are other possible directions too. Stereotypes relating to male magical practitioners and the relationship between magic and masculinity would benefit from more study, especially because the form of magic that we can most securely identify with one gender was learned magic performed by men.

Finally, there are also broader and more fundamental questions to be asked about the relationship between magic and gender. How much did gender matter when medieval people thought about magic, and under what circumstances did it become important? Were many, or most, practices widely shared across society as Kieckhefer's model of the "common tradition" suggests, rather than being heavily gendered? There is also the question of how easy it was to gain access to forms of magic that were restricted by gender or by other factors such as education. There are examples of people hiring a specialist to perform gendered forms of magic for them. Thus, Alice Perrers was said to have hired a male magician to perform learned magic (a stereotypically male form of magic) to help her with the stereotypically female goal of securing Edward III's love. Conversely, Matteuccia di Francesco was accused of performing love and healing magic for many clients, including at least one man.[48] If there were many similar specialists whose services were for hire, the gendering of love magic or ritual magic may not necessarily have been crucial in practice, because if someone did not have the skills to do a particular form of magic themselves, they could hire someone who did. As noted earlier, the intersection between gender and age, reputation or occupation in how magic and magical practitioners were regarded also merits further attention. Research into all these questions is likely to complicate our existing view of medieval magic and gender by uncovering variations over time, between regions and between different kinds of source material, but the answers will add an extra dimension to the work on individual sources and contexts discussed elsewhere in this book.

Notes

1 For overviews, see Katharine Hodgkin, "Gender, Mind and Body: Feminism and Psychoanalysis," in *Palgrave Advances in Witchcraft Historiography*, ed. Jonathan Barry and Owen Davies (Basingstoke: Palgrave Macmillan, 2007), 182–202; Alison Rowlands, "Witchcraft and Gender in Early Modern Europe," in *The Oxford Handbook of Witchcraft in Early Modern Europe and Colonial America*, ed. Brian P. Levack (Oxford: Oxford University Press, 2013), 449–66.
2 Hodgkin, "Gender, Mind and Body", 196–98; Rowlands, "Witchcraft and Gender", 464–65.
3 Michael D. Bailey, "From Sorcery to Witchcraft: Clerical Conceptions of Magic in the Later Middle Ages," *Speculum* 76 (2001), 985–88; see also Michael D. Bailey, "The Feminization of Magic and the Emerging Idea of the Female Witch in the Late Middle Ages," *Essays in Medieval Studies* 19 (2002), 120–34.
4 Jean-Patrice Boudet, *Entre Science et Nigromance: Astrologie, Divination et Magie dans l'Occident Médiéval (XIIe-XVe siècle)* (Paris: Publications de la Sorbonne, 2006), 484–93.
5 Catherine Chène and Martine Ostorero, "Démonologie et misogynie: L'émergence d'un discours spécifique sur la femme dans l'élaboration doctrinale du sabbat au XVe siècle," in *Les femmes dans*

la société européenne/Die Frauen in der europäischen Gesellschaft, ed. Anne-Lise Head-König and Liliane Mottu-Weber (Geneva: Société d'Histoire et d'Archéologie de Genève, 2000), 171–96. See also below, n. 33.
6 Christopher S. Mackay, trans., *The Hammer of Witches: A Complete Translation of the Malleus Maleficarum* (Cambridge: Cambridge University Press, 2009), 170 (part 1, qu. 6).
7 Walter Stephens, *Demon Lovers: Witchcraft, Sex and the Crisis of Belief* (Chicago, IL and London: University of Chicago Press), 300–21; Moira Smith, "The Flying Phallus and the Laughing Inquisitor: Penis Theft in the *Malleus Maleficarum*," *Journal of Folklore Research* 39 (2002): 85–117.
8 Hans Peter Broedel, *The Malleus Maleficarum and the Construction of Witchcraft: Theology and Popular Belief* (Manchester: Manchester University Press, 2003), 170, 175–76.
9 See above, notes 3–5.
10 Stephens, *Demon Lovers*, 33–34.
11 For example, Norman Cohn, *Europe's Inner Demons: the Demonization of Christians in Medieval Christendom*, 3rd edn (London: Pimlico Press, 1993), 165–75; Broedel, *The Malleus Maleficarum*, 101–15.
12 The most comprehensive discussion of this text and its later reception is Werner Tschacher, "Der Flug durch die Luft zwischen Illusionstheorie und Realitätsbeweis: Studien zum sog. Kanon Episcopi und zum Hexenflug," *Zeitschrift der Savigny-Stiftung für Rechtsgeschichte, Kan. Abt.* 85 (1999): 225–76.
13 Tschacher, "Flug durch die Luft," 268–75.
14 Michael D. Bailey, *Fearful Spirits, Reasoned Follies: The Boundaries of Superstition in Late Medieval Europe* (Ithaca, NY and London: Cornell University Press, 2013); Kathleen Kamerick, "Shaping Superstition in Late Medieval England," *Magic, Ritual and Witchcraft* 3 (2008): 29–53; Alain Boureau, *Satan Hérétique: Naissance de la démonologie dans l'Occident médiéval* (Paris: Odile Jacob, 2004), chs. 1–3; Catherine Rider, *Magic and Religion in Medieval England* (London: Reaktion Books, 2012).
15 Rider, *Magic and Religion*, 121–26.
16 On magicians and demons, see Boureau, *Satan hérétique*; on debates over practices, see Bailey, *Fearful Spirits* and Kamerick, "Shaping Superstition".
17 Corinne Saunders, *Magic and the Supernatural in Medieval English Romance* (Woodbridge: Boydell and Brewer, 2010), chs. 3–5.
18 Saunders, *Magic*, 185.
19 Laine E. Doggett, *Love Cures: Healing and Magic in Old French Romance* (University Park: Pennsylvania State University Press, 2009).
20 Heidi Breuer, *Crafting the Witch: Gendering Magic in Medieval and Early Modern England* (New York and London: Routledge, 2009).
21 Olga Lucía Valbuena, "Sorceresses, Love Magic, and the Inquisition of Linguistic Sorcery in *Celestina*," *PMLA* 109 (1994): 207–24; Dorothy Sherman Severin, *Witchcraft in Celestina* (London: Department of Hispanic Studies, Queen Mary and Westfield College, 1995); Paloma Moral de Calatrava, "Magic or Science? What "Old Women Lapidaries" Knew in the Age of Celestina," *La corónica: A Journal of Medieval Hispanic Languages, Literatures, and Cultures* 36 (2007): 203–35.
22 Richard Kieckhefer, *Magic in the Middle Ages* (Cambridge: Cambridge University Press, 1989), 56–57.
23 Catherine Rider, "Women, Men and Love Magic in Late Medieval English Pastoral Manuals," *Magic, Ritual and Witchcraft* 7 (2012): 190–91; Richard Kieckhefer, "Erotic Magic in Medieval Europe," in *Sex in the Middle Ages: A Book of Essays*, ed. Joyce E. Salisbury (New York: Garland Publishing, 1991), 30.
24 Kieckhefer, "Erotic Magic," 30–31; Rider, "Women", 210.
25 Don C. Skemer, *Binding Words: Textual Amulets in the Middle Ages* (University Park: Pennsylvania State University Press, 2006), ch. 5; Peter Murray Jones and Lea T. Olsan, "Performative Rituals for Conception and Childbirth in England, 900–1500," *Bulletin of the History of Medicine* 89, no. 3: (2015), 423.
26 Catherine Rider, *Magic and Impotence in the Middle Ages* (Oxford: Oxford University Press, 2006), 144–45.
27 Kieckhefer, *Magic*, 151–56.
28 Frank Klaassen, *The Transformations of Magic: Illicit Learned Magic in the Later Middle Ages and Renaissance* (University Park: Pennsylvania State University Press, 2013), 47–56, 94–102; Sophie Page, *Magic in the Cloister: Pious Motives, Illicit Interests and Occult Approaches to the Medieval Universe* (University Park:

Pennsylvania State University Press, 2013); Benedek Láng, *Unlocked Books: Manuscripts of Learned Magic in the Medieval Libraries of Central Europe* (University Park: Pennsylvania State University Press, 2008), 204, 250–55.
29 Klaassen, *Transformations of Magic*, 47–51.
30 Frank Klaassen, "Learning and Masculinity in Manuscripts of Ritual Magic of the Later Middle Ages and Renaissance," *Sixteenth-Century Journal* 38 (2007): 49–76; quote from p. 65.
31 Klaassen, "Learning and Masculinity," 73–74; see also Jean-Patrice Boudet and Julien Véronèse, "Le secret dans la magie rituelle médiévale," *Micrologus* 14 (2006): 138–39.
32 Boudet and Véronèse, "Le secret," 122–25; "Non reveles secreta tua mulieri, nec puero, nec stulto, nec ebrio," 132. See also Klaassen, "Learning and Masculinity," 71–72.
33 Martine Ostorero, *"Folâtrer avec les démons": Sabbat et chasse aux sorciers à Vevey (1448)* (Lausanne: Université de Lausanne, 1995), 111; Laurence Pfister, *L'enfer sur terre: Sorcellerie à Dommartin (1498)* (Lausanne: Université de Lausanne, 1997), 166–67; Georg Modestin, *Le diable chez l'évêque: Chasse aux sorciers dans le diocèse de Lausanne (vers 1460)* (Lausanne: Université de Lausanne, 1999), 121–22.
34 Alexandra Pittet, "Derrière le masque du sorcier: Une enquête sociologique à partir des procès de sorcellerie du registre Ac 29 (Pays de Vaud, 1438–1528)," in *Chasses aux sorcières et démonologie: Entre discours et pratiques (XIVe-XVIIe siècles)*, ed. Martine Ostorero, Georg Modestin and Kathrin Utz Tremp (Florence: Sismel Edizioni del Galluzzo, 2010), 215–18.
35 Mary O'Neil, "Magical Healing, Love Magic and the Inquisition in Late Sixteenth-Century Modena," in *Inquisition and Society in Early Modern Europe*, ed. S. Haliczer (London: Barnes and Noble, 1987), 101; Guido Ruggiero, *Binding Passions: Tales of Magic, Marriage, and Power at the End of the Renaissance* (New York: Oxford University Press, 1993), 44–45.
36 Richard Kieckhefer, *European Witch Trials: Their Foundations in Popular and Learned Culture, 1300–1500* (London: Routledge and Kegan Paul, 1976), 18–23.
37 Kieckhefer, *European Witch Trials*, 96.
38 Summarized in Chène and Ostorero, "Démonologie et misogynie", 172–74.
39 Susanna Burghartz, "The Equation of Women and Witches: A Case Study of Witchcraft Trials in Lucerne and Lausanne in the Fifteenth and Sixteenth Centuries," in *The German Underworld: Deviants and Outcasts in German History*, ed. Richard J. Evans (London: Routledge, 1988), 64–65.
40 Kathrin Utz Tremp, "Ist Glaubenssache Frauensache? Zu den Anfängen der Hexenverfolgung in Freiburg (um 1440)," *Freiburger Geschichtsblätter* 72 (1995): 47–48.
41 Karen Jones and Michael Zell, "'The divels speciall instruments': Women and Witchcraft before the 'Great Witch Hunt'," *Social History* 30 (2005): 53.
42 Peter Biller, Caterina Bruschi and Shelagh Sneddon, ed. and trans., *Inquisitors and Heretics in Thirteenth-Century Languedoc: Edition and Translation of Toulouse Inquisition Depositions, 1273–1282* (Leiden: Brill, 2011), 728–31.
43 Emmanuel Le Roy Ladurie, *Montaillou: Cathars and Catholics in a French Village 1294–1324*, trans. Barbara Bray (Harmondsworth: Penguin Books, 1978), 289–90.
44 Henry Kelly, "English Kings and the Fear of Sorcery," *Mediaeval Studies* 39 (1977): 215, 219–20, 233; Anna Brzezińska, "Accusations of Love Magic in the Renaissance Courtly Culture of the Polish-Lithuanian Commonwealth," *East Central Europe* 20 (1993): 117–40.
45 Karen Jones, *Gender and Petty Crime in Late Medieval England: The Local Courts in Kent, 1460–1560* (Woodbridge: Boydell and Brewer, 2006), 173–79.
46 Franco Mormando, *The Preacher's Demons: Bernardino of Siena and the Social Underworld of Early Renaissance Italy* (Chicago, IL: University of Chicago Press, 1999), 72–77.
47 Stephen Mitchell, *Witchcraft and Magic in the Nordic Middle Ages* (Philadelphia: University of Pennsylvania Press, 2011), 175–200.
48 Domenico Mammoli, "The Record of the Trial and Condemnation of a Witch, Matteuccia di Francesco, at Todi, 20 March 1428," *Res Tudertinae* 14 (1972): 33.

26

MAGIC IN LITERATURE

Romance transformations

Corinne Saunders

Introduction: from fantasy to intellectual history

An enduring cultural fascination with magic is reflected in its prominence in literature from the classical period onwards. Magic, often within the broader context of the supernatural, provides crucial plot mechanisms and defines legendary characters. Magical abilities offer agency and empowerment – and they present extraordinary challenges to power. While magic figures across a range of literary forms, it is most prominent in the genre of romance. Magic occurs in the earliest instances of the genre – the romances or novels of antiquity – and retains a strong hold on it, as is evinced by the Harry Potter and *Lord of the Rings* fever that has swept the world. Merlin, Morgan le Fay, the Lady of the Lake, Prospero: such figures, with their special powers, hold an enduring fascination. It is easy to dismiss magic as escapist, attractive in its exoticism, sometimes fearful, perhaps expressive of unspoken desires and fears. I have argued for a more realist approach to medieval writing, for looking beyond escapism and exoticism to the intellectual contexts of magic, and to the seriousness with which supernatural possibilities were taken in this period.[1]

From the later twentieth century onwards, scholars have traced a rich cultural history of magic for the Middle Ages, building on the groundbreaking research of historians such as Valerie Flint on pagan and Christian beliefs and rituals, Richard Kieckhefer on magic in relation to religion, science and the arts, and Edward Peters on the legal history of prohibitions against magical practice.[2] This book attests to the richness of subsequent scholarship, which has explored both popular and elite traditions across Europe, with particular attention to the ways that folk and clerical, licit and illicit beliefs intersected, as well as to the crucial connection between magic and learning.[3] Yet, even with such an embarrassment of riches in cultural studies of magic and related topics – ritual, witchcraft, the supernatural – connections have not always been drawn between different disciplines or different periods and places, as Michael D. Bailey argues in his introduction to the inaugural issue of *Magic, Ritual, and Witchcraft*.[4]

This lack of connections has, on the whole, been true of literary studies. Critics have explored aspects of magic in a variety of imaginative texts, identifying its prominent role within the romance genre and exploring its literary function, most often in relation to ideas of the marvellous, the supernatural or "fairy", and the motifs of quest and adventure. Michelle Sweeney's *Magic in Medieval Romance from Chrétien de Troyes to Chaucer* discusses magic as a literary topic that illuminates social and spiritual situations and character motivations, often in relation to testing morality and probing ambiguity. While Sweeney draws attention to the cultural importance of magic in the medieval period, her study is largely devoted to close readings of a limited number of texts, with a particular emphasis on the different treatments of magic in French and English romance.[5] Postcolonial theory has offered an alternative lens through which to consider magic. Geraldine Heng's wide-ranging *Empire of Magic* explores the political and imperialist project of romance, drawing on feminist, gender and cultural theory.[6] For Heng, romance offers an escapist response to the cultural trauma of the Crusades: she argues that Arthurian legend, in particular, arises from the encounter of East and West, and that the fantasy elements of romance allow for a licit exploration of issues of race, nation and sexuality. Her focus, despite the book's title, is not on magic *per se*, but rather on fantasy: how narratives of wonder illuminate fraught cultural topics while being profoundly shaped by Western ideologies. Neither of these studies explores in any sustained way the practice of magic: rather, the term is used loosely to signify the marvellous, magical or supernatural. Heidi Breuer's *Crafting the Witch* takes a different approach to gender in her focus on the figure of the witch and its relation to concepts of good and evil, female empowerment and gender-blending in medieval and early modern romance. Her study focuses particularly on "the villainization of feminine magic" in Arthurian literature during the period following the twelfth century.[7] Whereas the witch is a nurturing, healing figure in the works of Chrétien de Troyes and Marie de France, in later works from the Gawain romances to those of Malory and Spenser, witches figure as wicked stepmothers, loathly ladies, temptresses and hags.

By contrast to previous literary studies, my aim in *Magic and the Supernatural in Medieval English Romance* was to connect romance writing with the rich and complex cultural history of magic and ideas of the supernatural. Magic may be seen as a powerful "romance meme" of the kind identified by Helen Cooper in *The English Romance in Time*, a motif that recurs across the Middle Ages and Renaissance, treated with cultural specificity and in variously original ways, but also dependent for effect on its familiarity to audiences and on its generic and literary associations.[8] Magic is, however, much more than fantasy: it interweaves with medicine and ideas of natural philosophy, and with a sense of the marvellous that is not just fairytale but intimately connected with the Christian worldview. The romance text becomes a place where ideas, beliefs, wishes, fears and imaginings intersect, a site of cultural exploration and innovation. Magic in medieval romance is most of all associated with bodies: with physical influences that heal or harm, shift shape or place. Yet, for all its bodiliness, the affective power of magic also opens onto the mind and questions of sin and virtue, intention and identity.

Healing and harmful knowledge

Medieval literature must be placed in the context of the thought world of the later Middle Ages, with its complex blend of ideas stretching back through classical and Judaeo-Christian as well as Germanic and Celtic belief and ritual. The long history of magic, its place in natural philosophy and medicine, its use of the cosmic powers contained in plants and stones and its connections with demons and the natural world were all fundamental to medieval understanding.[9] Medieval literary texts take up the idea of a mixed tradition of what may broadly be termed white and black magic: both concerned with influencing the body, the former often connected with the desire to heal, the latter with the desire to harm.

Writers such as Chaucer (writing in the later fourteenth century) were certainly aware of the history of magic.[10] Chaucer's works, as Alexander Gabrovsky has recently shown, were shaped by his sophisticated knowledge of scientific theory.[11] A familiarity with alchemy, physics, astronomy and medicine, the interconnected disciplines central to learned understandings of magic, is evident across Chaucer's writings. His depiction in the *General Prologue* to *The Canterbury Tales* of the "Doctour of Phisik", a pilgrim perhaps more interested in gold than God, is characteristic in its representation of the physician as a practitioner of natural philosophy: medicine is "magyk natureel", requiring the knowledge of anatomy, humours and diseases, medicines, especially herbal remedies, and astrology.[12] The final book of Chaucer's *House of Fame*, a dream-vision poem poking fun at a naïve "Geffrey" (II, 729), unwilling to learn the mysteries of the cosmos from the eagle who sweeps him up to the heavens, is comically dedicated to Apollo, "God of science [knowledge]" (I, 1091). Here, the narrator finds himself in the legendary house of Fame, where he sees the practitioners of magic: magicians, "tregetours" (illusionists, III, 1260), old witches and sorceresses, and "clerkes eke, which konne wel / Al this magik naturel …" (III, 1265–66). They include celebrated magicians and enchantresses from different traditions – from classical legend, Medea, Calypso and Circe; from natural philosophy, Hermes Ballenus, disciple of the founder of magic, Hermes Trismegistus; from Biblical tradition, Simon Magus. They also include what seems to be a reference to an English magician, "Colle tregetour" (1277), apparently one "Colin T.", mentioned in a French conversation manual (c.1396) and said to have practised in Orléans, "an Englishman who was a powerful necromancer … who knew how to create many marvels by means of necromancy".[13] Chaucer's description, however, portrays him as more of an entertainer than a necromancer, producing a windmill from under a walnut shell. Magicians accompany musicians in the house of Fame, their arts of illusion sharing the power to entertain. This perception is sustained in Chaucer's *Franklin's Tale*. The lovesick knight Aurelius's brother has the idea of consulting a learned magician to help Aurelius win his beloved Dorigen, the wife of another man. The magician's knowledge of "sciences" allows him to "make diverse apparences / Swiche as thise subtile tregetoures pleye" (1140–41). They include illusions of hunting, jousting and dancing, but also the more sinister effect of causing the black rocks on which Dorigen swears her oath of faithfulness to disappear. The brother envisages this "tregetour" or illusionist as a magician who uses "thise moones mansions … / Or oother magyk natureel above" (1154–55) to harness astrological or natural powers. Learning is essential: Aurelius's brother remembers the book he saw on his fellow's desk, which speaks much of the "operaciouns" of the moon (1129) – perhaps an occult work from the Arabic tradition such as those attributed to Hermes Trismegistus. In the tale, the clerk's arts remain those of illusion, though they are illusions with the power to affect and harm the lives of the characters.

Chaucer also suggests a more threatening aspect of such clerical magic. In the *House of Fame*, clerks are depicted as practising image magic, drawing on sidereal powers not just to create illusions but "To make a man ben hool or syk" (1270). Chaucer's list includes witches, sorceresses and Phitonesses, practitioners who explicitly employ enchantments and spells, and who summon spirits. The final work in the *Canterbury Tales*, the *Parson's Tale*, is a prose treatise on the seven deadly sins and their remedies, which rehearses prohibitions of magic found in handbooks of penance.[14] The Parson places magic as a form of swearing and an aspect of anger:

> But lat us go now to thilke horrible sweryng of adjuracioun and conjuracioun, as doon thise false enchantours or nigromanciens [necromancers] in bacyns ful of water, or in a bright swerd, in a cercle, or in a fir, or in a shulderboon of a sheep. / I kan nat seye but that they doon cursedly and dampnably agayns Crist and al the feith of hooly chirche.
>
> (603–4)

The terms "adjuracioun and conjuracioun" imply the forbidden practices of exorcism and summoning up spirits or demons. The Parson refers too to the use of ligatures or amulets, remedies and "Charmes for woundes or maladie of men or of beestes" (607), so that the tale seems tantalizingly to suggest enduring practices of both popular and learned kinds.

Chaucer's learning is not typical of medieval romance writing, which does not generally engage with the minutiae of philosophy and theology, or display detailed knowledge of magical practice. Romance does, however, engage with similar cultural attitudes, ideas and beliefs concerning healing and harmful magic, weaving fictions around them. In many ways, the classical distinction between *mageia*, which can be positive, and *goeteia*, which cannot, is retained in the later Middle Ages, in the distinction between natural and illicit magic, and this is carried over into literature. Yet romance almost never depicts explicitly demonic magic; rather, it is profoundly concerned with the physical possibilities of magic –affecting the body through knowledge of the occult arts. Such arts span both natural magic, which most often heals and protects, and "nigromancy", which tends to involve more destructive shape-shifting, divination and illusion. The crucial difference lies in the motivation of those employing the arts of transformation. Both natural magic and nigromancy are depicted as within the realms of human possibility, their use illuminating their users and those they affect, but also suggesting the fearful and desirable possibilities of medicine and natural philosophy. Ultimately, transformation of the body can shape the mind and soul of the victim. Such transformation also, however, reveals the state of the practitioner's soul.

Romance, medicine and natural magic

In the course of the fourteenth century, English writers made the romance genre their own, drawing on Latin, French, Anglo-Norman and English material and on the well-established conventions of the genre, including a recurrent emphasis on the motifs of magic, the marvellous and the supernatural. The English romances *Ywain and Gawain* and *Beves of Hampton*, both written in the late fourteenth century, offer compelling examples of the seriousness with which romance treats magic and of its close connections with medicine and with women. A century later, Malory's *Le Morte Darthur* suggests a more dubious aspect of "magyk naturel" in its depiction of love magic. These works play on the enduring association of women with the practice of medicine and healing, as well as with magic. In a world where military strength is critical and the chivalric code depends on individual victory over the body in combat, women gain agency through their ability to wield powers that offer them remarkable control over the body and further, the possibility of shaping thought and emotion.

Ywain and Gawain and its source, the twelfth-century French writer Chrétien de Troyes' *Le Chevalier au Lion* (*Yvain*), trace the quest of the knight Yvain/Ywain to regain his lady Laudine/Alundyne's love and atone for the excessive devotion to deeds of arms that causes him to forget her. His journey leads from madness and despair to a new self-knowledge, partly reflected in his companionship with and care for the noble lion he rescues. A strong emphasis on healing magic is combined with an interest in contemporary medical ideas, and the woman is figured as healer, an image with some mimetic force in a world where physicians were rare and medicine was practised by those possessing folk and herbal knowledge, especially monks and wise women.[15] The account of the cure of Ywain's madness through the use of a magical ointment is finely balanced between marvel and realism, and the episode signals and explores the intimate connection between mind and body.

A maiden recognizes the sleeping Ywain through a scar, and diagnoses his mental state: "Sorow will meng [disturb] a mans blode / And make him forto wax wode [mad]".[16] Her mistress is persuaded to send a precious box of ointment given her by "Morgan the wise" (Morgan le Fay, 1753), with the power to return the wits of the man who is "braynwode" (1756). Morgan, rather than figuring as witch or enchantress, is placed by the epithet "the wise" as a practitioner of positive natural magic. The maiden is strictly instructed to be sparing with the ointment, but empties the entire box in anointing Ywain's head and body. In Chrétien's text, the narrator's comment on her folly employs careful medical realism: he explains that it is only necessary to anoint the temples and forehead, because Yvain only suffers in his brain.[17] Cure is attributed to warmth and to massaging the head. The maiden's action of anointing body and head may, however, be seen as signalling the continuum between mind and body in a period when the humours were seen as shaping both. Chrétien and his English adapter engage in strikingly precise detail with the ways that such a medicinal–magical ointment might work on body and brain.

The romance of *Beves of Hampton* (c.1300, based on an Anglo-Norman source) plays extensively with the motif of the woman healer in its extended narrative of the adventures of Beves, whose exile from his English lands and title leads him to the East, where he makes his name as chivalric knight, woos – and converts – the heathen princess Josian, and eventually, returns to England to regain his rightful inheritance. Josian is strikingly learned, with sophisticated knowledge of medicine and natural magic:

> While 3he was in Ermonie,
> Boþe fysik and sirgirie
> 3he hadde lerned of meisters grete
> Of Boloyne þe gras and of Tulete,
> Þat 3e knew erbes mani & fale,
> To make boþe boute & bale*.[18]   *healing and harm

Records survive of female medical practitioners; Hildegard of Bingen offers a celebrated example. The earliest medical faculty, established at Salerno in the mid-900s, was associated with women through the legendary female healer Trotula, said to have practised there in the twelfth century. Marie de France's *Les Deux Amants* (written in Anglo-Norman in the second half of the twelfth century) takes up this association in its depiction of how the protagonist obtains from his beloved's aunt in Salerno a marvellous potion that will give him superhuman strength, allowing him to carry her to the top of a mountain in order to win her hand in marriage. Josian's masters are from "Bologna la grassa", Italy's great centre of medical learning from the early thirteenth century, and from "Tulete" (Toledo), a centre of Arabic learning, which flourished in Spain during the period of Muslim rule. Josian herself is identified as from the Eastern, Saracen country of "Ermonie" (Armenia), rather than Egypt as in the Anglo-Norman version: she is given an exotic origin, but one that is nearer than Egypt to Spain and Italy, so that she can readily be imagined as having access to their ancient, especially Arabic, traditions of learned medicine.

Her agency in orchestrating the process of her love for and marriage to the Christian knight Beves is remarkable. She heals him through marvellous remedies, "an oyniment" to make him "boþe hol & fere" (716–17) and "riche baþes" (732) that render him "boþe hol and sonde" (734). Later, she delivers her own twins, having sent her husband and his companion out hunting to avoid her "paines" (3636). The realism of Josian's medical practice lends credibility to her more extraordinary skills in natural magic. Her herbal knowledge produces transformative effects, most strikingly when she is captured by the giant Ascopard:

> On 3he tok vp of þe grounde,
> Þat was an erbe of meche mounde*,   *power
> To make a man in semlaunt* þere,   *semblance
> A foule mesel* alse 3if a were. (3677–80)   *leper

This is medical magic of an extreme kind: the herb transforms Josian's appearance to that of a leper and causes the Muslim king Yvor to reject her, preserving her chastity. Her herbal skills allow her to play with the appearance of an illness that is most often depicted in literary texts as fearfully evocative of God's powers to test and punish. When she is rescued, Josian immediately applies "an oiniment" that returns her clear bright colour (3891–92) – perhaps evoking a herb such as henbane or verveine, supposed to cure boils. The effect is marvellous yet not so very different in kind from that of the earlier healing ointment; this too transforms the body, and despite its dramatic impact, it remains within the bounds of imaginable possibility. Like that in *Ywain and Gawain*, the scene also works to signal the profound link between body, mind and affect: physical transformation evokes revulsion and radically alters the king's intention to ravish Josian.

The marvellous ointment that can cure all ills finds a counterpart in the idea of the marvellous gem. Although the wearing of amulets or ligatures was condemned by the Church, the marvellous stone, like the healing plant, could be seen as a material sign of God's grace, a token of the beneficent forces of the universe with a power something akin to that of holy relics. As Isabelle Draelants demonstrates in this volume, stones, seen as imbued with celestial powers, played an important part in ancient notions of natural magic, and such ideas were widely circulated in the Middle Ages, including through the *Liber aggregationis* or *Book of Secrets* attributed to Albertus Magnus and current from the late thirteenth to the seventeenth century. While marvellous stones are extensively treated in learned writing, they also readily found their way into the popular imagination and particularly into the many protective magical rings of romance. Such objects are especially appealing, for their use is open to all who are fortunate enough to obtain them; no skill is needed.

Romances repeatedly depict rings containing gems "of swich vertu" that they give marvellous protection, usually from wounds and other kinds of harm, although they may have other powers too such as that of bestowing invisibility. The formulaic phrase, "a stone of swich vertu", is significant, for it indicates that the ring is not just vaguely magical but that its power is contained in the particular stone. The term "vertu" also carries something of its modern meaning. Thus, in *Ywain and Gawain*, Ywain's lady lends him a ring whose "vertu" (1532) will prevent prison or sickness so that he can return to her within a year. The poet of *Ywain*, however, unlike Chrétien, develops the motif to render the power of the ring actively moral, dependent upon thinking of the lady and truth in love. Thus, the ring serves a double function: it proves Alundyne's "grete luf" (1543) by protecting and distinguishing Ywain from harm, and allows her to test Ywain's love; if he does not return, it is because he does not choose to, rather than because he is prevented. When the ring is taken from Ywain's finger, once he has failed in his promise, he immediately falls sick, succumbing to madness. The coincidence of illness with removal of the ring seems to prove its protective quality, though this is not the dramatic or narrative focus. Rather, the scene is focused on Ywain's state of mind, as revealed by the ring and written on his body.

In *Beves*, Josian's skill in natural magic includes possession of a marvellous ring containing a stone "of swiche vertu" that it preserves her chastity (1469–72). The learning of a physician such as Josian would indeed have included knowledge of the virtues of both plants and stones. The virtue of her stone echoes that attributed in Pseudo-Albertus' *Liber aggregationis* to chalcedony pierced with emery: "it is good against all fantastical illusions, and it maketh to overcome all causes, or matters in suit, and keepeth the body against … adversaries".[19] The Anglo-Norman source for *Beves* and a later English version closer to the Anglo-Norman (Manchester, Chetham's Library 8009, c.1480) describe not a ring but a magical girdle: the change to a ring by the redactor of the Auchinleck manuscript or his direct source may suggest the association of the girdle with the ligatures and binding or weaving magic explicitly forbidden by the Church. This writer was apparently anxious to present Josian as not an enchantress but a wise woman with acceptable knowledge of natural magic, in particular the medical arts of the East. She can draw on the occult powers of nature to transform as well as to heal, but her powers remain within the bounds of the licit.

Perhaps the most problematic use of "magyk natureel" is to cause love: this is repeatedly forbidden in early laws, penitentials and treatises, and was taken seriously by the Church. The most celebrated romance treatment of love magic is found in the *Tristan* legend, which in all its forms attributes the adulterous love of Tristan and Yseut/Isolde to the potion prepared by Yseut's mother in order to cement her daughter's marriage to King Mark of Cornwall. The story exploits and proves the dangerous power repeatedly recognized in laws and canons concerning love magic. Malory's great Arthurian history, *Le Morte Darthur* (1469–70), which translates and adapts French thirteenth-century prose romances while drawing on the fourteenth-century English alliterative and stanzaic *Morte Arthur* poems, offers the most extended engagement with the Tristan story in English romance. Here, La Beale Isode and her mother are powerful practitioners of natural, healing magic: Isode, "a noble surgeon", a phrase not connected with her in the French, heals Tristram from his poisoned wound, and her mother's medicinal skill provides the potion, the positive intention of which is made clear.[20] The drink is treated with naturalism: "hit semed by the coloure and the taste that hit was noble wyne" (VIII.24, 327), and the effect is physical and immediate: when Tristram and Isode taste it, "they thought never drynke that ever they dranke so swete nother so good to them. But by that drynke was in their bodyes they loved aythir other so well that never hir love departed, for well nother for woo" (VIII.24, 327–28). Malory lessens the role of this binding love magic, however, by portraying the love between Tristram and Isode as arising naturally ("the joy that La Beale Isode made of sir Trystrames there myght no tunge telle, for of all men erthely she loved hym moste", VIII.24, 326, Malory's addition). The potion is reduced to a form of apparently natural magic that, although potentially harmful in its misuse, ultimately affirms what has already been decided by destiny. Malory depicts the love of Tristram and Isode as natural, authorized and in its own terms virtuous – though it leads, ultimately, to tragedy. The physical manifestation of magic is deeply connected to its effects on the mind, its shaping of affective being in the world and of individual destiny. Yet, there is also a sense of the limits beyond which natural magic should not go.

The dark arts of "nigromancy"

Plants, stones, the occult forces of stars and planets all have the power to transform bodies and influence minds. Yet, the magic that employs these is far from the work of demons, remaining within the sphere of medicine and natural magic. Romance writers are also careful to signal when magic transgresses the bounds of acceptability: the term "nigromancy" is repeatedly employed to suggest illicit magical arts. The word is understood to find its origins in Latin *niger*, black (rather than Greek, *nekros*, corpse), and is invariably spelled to indicate this, rather than to denote demonic arts. Romances employ the term "nigromancy" to depict rituals that are not wholly different in kind from natural magic, but that enter further into the conscious practice of magic and are more dangerous, manipulating thoughts and emotions as well as bodies. "Nigromancy", "sorcery" and "witchcraft" are treated as near-similes, and the connotation of black or dark arts is pervasive. "Nigromancy" can imply the use of illusions, and may signal human practitioners whose arts are extreme, dubious and sometimes villainous. It may include the power of invisibility, metamorphosis or shape-shifting, manipulation of mind or body for the purpose of love or power. Schooling in the occult sciences may include study of "nigromancy", which is often represented in material terms closely linked to those of natural magic, sometimes supplemented by books that may afford the means to summon demons, though this is not made explicit.

Beves makes clear that the difference between the arts of natural magic and "nigromancy" is not one of kind so much as of extent and use, and especially, of the motivation of the practitioner. Josian is left in the charge of an old king, Garcy, who "muche can of Nygremancy" (2298): he possesses a gold ring that allows him to see "What any man dooth in alle þing" (2300). His power is opposed by the natural magic of a soporific herb placed in his wine by Beves's companion, and he wakes to see in his ring that the queen has fled with Beves. Whereas Josian's protective ring is never characterized as "nigromancy", Garcy's use of a magic ring equates to divination, a practice repeatedly instanced in prohibitions. *Beves* suggests that certain kinds of intervention are acceptable, especially the use of plants or stones to protect, heal, put to sleep or even transform, whereas Garcy's magical ring is a feature of the exotic, imprisoning Eastern world from which Beves must rescue Josian, a world associated with darkness and divination. The art of "nigromancy" is set against the skill in natural magic that Josian has also gained from the East, but employs to further the beneficent plan of providence.

The roughly contemporaneous *William of Palerne* (c.1355), like *Beves*, traces the movement from exile to return, from dispossession to marriage and kingship, this time of two princes, Alphonse of Spain and William of Palerne. The narrative evokes in striking and unusual detail the rituals of "nigromancy" in its depiction of the evil arts of Alphonse's stepmother, who transforms him into a werewolf. The story opens as the werewolf intervenes to rescue William from poisoning by his evil uncle. Here, physical transformation is set against the essential nature of the self, which remains noble despite the shifting of external shape. The stepmother, Braunde, possesses forbidden learning:

> But lelliche* þat ladi in 3ouþe hadde lerned miche schame,   *truly
> for al þe werk of wicchecraft wel ynou3 che cou3þe;
> nede nadde 3he* namore of nigramauncy to lere.   *she had no need
> Of coninge* of wicchecraft wel ynou3 3he cou3de....[21]   *knowledge

There is no reference, however, to the summoning of demons, and Braunde may be seen as misusing natural magic. She transforms the child into a wolf through the use of a magical ointment:

> A noynement anon sche made of so gret strengþe
> bi enchaunmens of charmes ...

>   ...
>   ones wel anointed, þe child wel al abowte,
>   he wex to a werwolf wi3tly* þerafter,   *quickly
>   al þe making of man so mysse* hadde 3he schaped.   *deformed
>
> (136–41)

This vividly realized magic is also tantalizingly vague: the learned concoction of an ointment may employ manuals of natural magic or more dubious books of necromancy that combine physical and astrological rituals with conjuring demons. Ointments, as in *Beves* and *Yvain*, are repeatedly associated with transformation, but here the power of transformation is abused. Not demons but human sinfulness is the subject.

At the end of the work, Braunde is threatened with death by burning, perhaps reflecting the poet's knowledge of Continental or early English laws against witchcraft, or of the classification of magic practised against a member of the royal family as treason, punishable by death. Under duress, she agrees to come to "hele" the werewolf with her "queynt werkes" (4254). The stone is bound about the wolf's neck, a carefully constructed ligature; a spell is read from a precious book kept safely in a casket. Again the nature of book is unspecified: does it contain instructions for the practice of natural magic, or is it a more sinister collection of recipes that conjure demons? There is no suggestion of the latter: rather the practice of magic here is made up of a strangely prosaic set of rituals. Yet, the effects of this practical "nigromancy" are extreme, transforming man to beast and back again. Braunde's plea for forgiveness and mercy recognizes the failure of magic in the face of divine providence, "ich forschop [transformed] þe þanne / in þise wise to a werwolf and wend þe to spille [destroy]; / but God wold nou3t þat þou were lorne [lost]" (4394–96). Her intervention is, finally, limited. The virtue of William is retained throughout and ultimately triumphs over physical transformation; even Braunde is redeemed, as the conjuror of demons might not be.

While Braunde fits the familiar paradigm of the enchantress, practitioner of "nigromancy", *William of Palerne* is highly unusual in its description of the accoutrements of magic. More typical is the nebulous association of such women with the other world. Most celebrated among such enchantresses is Morgan le Fay, drawn into Arthurian legend as Arthur's half-sister but with a history that extends back into Welsh myth, signalled in *Sir Gawain and the Green Knight* by a reference to her as "Morgne þe goddes".[22] Here, a seemingly otherworldly Green Knight challenges Sir Gawain to a beheading contest that leads him on a winter journey through the wilds of Britain to a mysterious castle, Hautdesert, where the beautiful wife of his host, Sir Bertilak, attempts to seduce him. Eventually, the Green Knight is revealed to be Sir Bertilak, and the ancient loathly lady of Hautdesert Morgan le Fay, whose shape-shifting magic has been intended to frighten Arthur's court, cause Guinevere's death and test the renown of the Round Table. The magic that Gawain suspects to be demonic turns out to be effected by Arthur's half-sister, his own aunt. Morgan, we are told, has been taught her magic arts by Merlin, "þat conable [excellent] klerk" (2450), whose mistress the poet claims she is. If she is "Morgne the goddes", she is also a practitioner of human arts, involving "koyntyse of clergye", skill in (clerical) learning and "craftes wel lerned" (2447).[23] They can be firmly placed as "nigromancy", their transformations undertaken for dark, malevolent purposes: it is not coincidental that the demonic is a recurrent motif in the poem. While Morgan le Fay is typically depicted as beautiful and seductive, here Sir Bertilak's wife functions as the youthful, desirable face of the enchantress, while Morgan is her opposite, the monstrous old hag. In part, the poem engages with the two faces of the fascinating but fearful other. But as in *William of Palerne*, the emphasis is most of all on the effect of Morgan's shape-shifting, the testing of Gawain through Bertilak and his wife, and hence, the probing of his virtue. It is Gawain's integrity of mind and body, his power to resist sexual desire and his human wish to preserve his life that are the poem's real subject. Magic is the means to the illumination of sin and virtue, and it affords the exploration of human being in the world.

Morgan le Fay is also the central practitioner of magic in Malory's *Morte Darthur*. Whereas Merlin disappears early from the text, her role spans the entire work. In Morgan, "the falsist sorseres and wycche moste that is now lyvyng" (VIII.34, 344), Malory repeatedly links magic, sexual desire and force in negative ways until the end of the book, when she figures as one of the four weeping, black-hooded queens who carry the wounded Arthur to Avalon. With her own rival court, she is established as Arthur's great opponent, using magic where a male rival would use military force. Rather than emphasizing Morgan's innate supernatural quality as "le Fay", Malory relates how she "was put to scole in a nonnery, and ther she lerned so moche that she was a grete clerke of nygromancye" (I.2, 4). Like Braunde's, Morgan's arts are both human and connected explicitly with the dark, potentially demonic side of magic, "nygromancye". She possesses the arts of illusion and shape-shifting typical of the magician, changing herself into the shape of great stones when pursued, and creating the false sword and scabbard and the destructive gifts that she sends to the court. Her enchantments are violent and treacherous, causing the death of her lover Accolon, and repeatedly ensnaring the knights of the Round Table, including Arthur and Launcelot, who is also the object of her desire. Enchantment in the *Morte* is explicitly linked to the possession of male bodies and to predatory sexual desire: thus, Morgan le Fay and three queens abduct the sleeping Launcelot to a "chambir colde", and require his love: "Now chose one of us, whyche that thou wolte have to thy paramour, other ellys to dye in this preson" (VI.3, 193–94). Later, her apparently medicinal attentions place the wounded knight Alexander firmly in her control:

> Than Quene Morgan le Fay serched his woundis and gaff hym suche an oynement that he sholde have dyed. And so on the morne when she cam to hym agayne, he complayned hym sore. And than she put another oynemente uppon hym, and than he was oute of his payne.
>
> (X.37, 509)

Only on promising not to depart for a year is Alexander healed, to discover that he is kept by Morgan as prisoner "for none other entente but for to do hir plesure whan hit lykyth hir" (X.38, 510). Bodies are her focus; yet always, possession of the body represents possession of power and subjugation of the other's mind.

Malory creates the impression of a network of female practitioners who possess such arts – the damsel of the Lake, Nenyve or Vivien, who turns Merlin's magic back on him when she imprisons him within the wondrous cave that he himself shows to her; "Hallewes the Sorseres, lady of the Castell Nygurmous" (VI.15, 216), who aims to ensnare Launcelot so that she may keep his body dead if she cannot enjoy it alive:

> Than wolde I have bawmed hit and sered [embalmed and wrapped in waxed cloth] hit, and so to have kepte hit my lyve dayes; and dayly I sholde have clypped [embraced] the and kyssed the, dispyte of Quene Gwenyvere.
>
> (VI.15, 216)

The reference to embalming also returns us to the motifs of medicine and skill. "Nigromancy" never strays far away from natural magic, and the powers of its practitioners remain limited. Virtue can overcome malignant magic: Braunde is redeemed, Hallewes dies from unrequited love and Morgan returns to carry the wounded Arthur to Avalon. Yet, such "nigromancy" remains threatening and extreme, in part because its powers can be learned. Magic may be used to destroy as well as to heal – to put to sleep, to imprison, to make ill, to embalm, even to transform into a beast. "Nigromancy" and natural magic are two sides of a coin in romance, and they relate in fundamental ways to notions, both hopeful and fearful, of the practice of medicine. The practitioners of magic are ambiguous, threatening but also fascinating, their powers transformative in positive and negative ways. Magic in romance opens the way for experiences that push at, and cross, in believable ways, a boundary of actuality, expanding what is humanly possible, transgressing limits in its transformations of minds and bodies and its remarkable affective power.

Future directions: new interdisciplinary approaches

Romance is just a beginning. There is much other medieval literature to be explored across many languages. Scholars are not likely to find detailed accounts of magical practice in other literary genres, for such accounts would have been highly risky. They will, however, find the recurrence of magic, interwoven with the supernatural and configured in different ways across different kinds of texts. As my work on hagiographical and penitential romances has suggested, religious texts often oppose the true and enduring power of God to the flawed human practice of magic – and sometimes align that practice with the demonic. Saints' lives and other religious works offer a fertile ground for literary exploration within the cultural contexts so richly described by recent scholarship. So too do the genres of history and chronicle. The exploration of lesser known works will allow further research into the connections of magic with popular story, superstition, learning, moral teaching, politics, science and belief. Also waiting to be explored are later, especially prose romances: some of these, such as *Valentine and Orson*, edge much nearer to explicit engagement with magic as summoning demons, and this subject is taken up in the transition from medieval to early modern, most famously in Shakespeare's depiction of Prospero. The Renaissance reworks the magician as the mage, and Renaissance magic plays a powerful role in reshaping literary emphases, as ideas of both science and witchcraft gain force.

Does contemporary interdisciplinary scholarship offer new approaches to reading medieval texts? The rich possibilities are signalled in Lyndal Roper's *The Witch in the Western Imagination*, a "psychoanalytically informed cultural history", which explicitly aims "to bring the investigation of subjectivity into history, that is, to explore how individuals experience social processes", by drawing on the evidence of material culture: books, paintings, artefacts, clothing.[24] The collection of essays edited by Sophie Page, *The Unorthodox Imagination in Medieval Britain*, demonstrates the fruitfulness of illuminating through different disciplinary lenses the "various social sites of the medieval imagination", the complex intersection of doubt and belief, attempts at and failures of containment, and the role of the unorthodox in making sense of experience.[25] Lea Olsan's essay on medieval literature, for example, draws interesting connections between enchantment, delusion and necromancy, comparing literary representations of enchantment with those in magical handbooks.

The subject of magic in medieval literature and culture, with its deep connections to medicine, body, mind and emotions speaks in particular to the growing interdisciplinary field of the medical humanities, which brings medicine into dialogue with the humanities, with a view both to enriching the humanities and extending biomedical approaches. As researchers at the Institute for Medical Humanities at Durham University have argued, a properly critical medical humanities is also a historically grounded medical humanities: literary texts provide crucial insights into cultural and intellectual attitudes, human experience and creativity.[26] Reading from a medical humanities perspective means putting past and present into conversation, to discover continuities and contrasts with later literature and thought. Laine Doggett's study of love magic argues for an approach that brings together history of medicine with medieval literary studies, women's studies and a broad range of humanities studies. Doggett suggests that Old French literary texts reflected but also influenced practice and perception by their positive presentation of women healers; at the same time, she reclaims these figures from traditional associations with charlatanism. My recent work has explored the ways mind, body and affect are constructed and intersect in medieval thought and literature, with a particular focus on how supernatural, particularly visionary, experience is portrayed and understood.[27] Pre-Cartesian perspectives chime surprisingly closely with current approaches, illuminate the complex interrelations of mind and body, and probe the power of affect in resonant and suggestive ways. They also open onto ways of understanding that are less accessible in the secularized, progressive world of the twenty-first century. The experiences discussed in Tanya Luhrmann's anthropological study of magic and witchcraft in the present, for example, seem considerably less bizarre when placed in dialogue with medieval writing, where magic and the supernatural are familiar topics, and there is scope for a wide range of possible beliefs and imaginings.[28] Luhrmann's study explores how the practice of magic can lead to changes in observation, psychology and emotional experience, shaping intellectual strategies akin to those of religious belief. While her work is valuably contextualized by medieval studies, these in turn are illuminated by her richly textured account of how magic can be made to mean, and of its imaginative power: despite the shifts in understanding from the Middle Ages to the twenty-first century, the continuities in hermeneutics – as well as in the practices themselves – are striking. Luhrmann's exploration of the mind – its complex blend of rational and irrational, and the force of the imagination – offers a persuasive context for approaching medieval literature.

Over the past decade, medievalists have taken up some of these possibilities, turning to cognitive science to illuminate their work. Edward Bever's thought-provoking study, *The Realities of Witchcraft and Popular Magic in Early Modern Europe*, explores some of the questions addressed by Luhrmann in relation to the medieval period.[29] Bever, however, aims to go a step further than previous scholars in providing explanations rooted in cognitive science not only for belief in magic but also for magical experience itself. Thus, whereas Jesper Sørenson's *A Cognitive Theory of Magic* explores the mental processes that render individuals receptive to magical beliefs, Bever aims "to go beyond cognitive theory to cognitive neuroscience", to show how ritual magical practice (like the practices of shamanism) can effect changes in consciousness, "'tuning' and 'fine-tuning' the nervous system".[30] While Bever's analyses of individual cases from witchcraft trials are controversial, his argument for the psychosomatic effects of magic is less so. Frank Klaassen has persuasively drawn on and developed many of these ideas, alongside those adumbrated by Luhrmann's work, in relation to medieval ritual magic. Klaassen shows how demanding and extensive the operations of ritual magic were, comparing them fruitfully to monastic practice, and hence, how likely they were to have "transformed an initiate's subjective experience", to effect "a shift to associative thinking confirmed by powerful experiences resulting from this approach, a shift to new and dedicated systems of interpretation, and an actual reorientation of the nervous system".[31] Klaassen emphasizes the extraordinary discipline of such practice and its close relationship to prayer, contemplation and religious practice, which might also "bring about different neurological states".[32] Putting medieval religious and magical practices and texts into conversation may well prove suggestive. While the imaginative literature of the medieval period does not often represent the detailed operations of magic, studies such as that of Klaassen provide a valuable context for Chaucer's learned magician in the *Franklin's Tale* or for the practices of William of Palerne's stepmother, removing them from the bounds of exotic fantasy.

The Wellcome Trust-funded project "Hearing the Voice" (based at Durham University) provides a complementary example of how interdisciplinary thinking may illuminate magic and related topics. The project brings together researchers in psychology, psychiatry, neuroscience and a range of humanities disciplines, healthcare professionals and voice hearers to explore the phenomenon of hearing voices without external stimuli, now most often understood as a symptom of severe mental disorders such as schizophrenia, but also an important aspect of many people's everyday lives, which may not be satisfactorily addressed by medical diagnosis and treatment.[33] The accounts of voice hearers today can resonate very powerfully with some of the experiences recounted in medieval records – for example, the summoning of angelic or demonic spirits – and with the doubts of those who experience them concerning their beneficent or maleficent nature.[34] Just as magical ritual practice can shape subjective experience, so delusive thought systems can construct alternative explanations, and so also can shared cultural experience. Such interdisciplinary research offers insights into the complex and hidden ways in which the mind works – the interactions between affect and cognition, individual and social, inner and external experience. Interdisciplinary studies of magical belief and subjective experience that foreground cognitive processes illuminate the seriousness with which medieval literature treats magic – even when its otherworldly practitioners can effect its transformations without enacting its demanding operations, or when these are left to the reader's imagination. At the same time, it is important to recognize the limits of neuroscientific explanations; more valuable may be the doors opened onto the complexity of constructing realities by anthropological and cultural studies. As Stuart Clark writes in his powerful refutation of Bever's work, "In the full flow of social life, amid all its complexities and nuances, it is what people *perceive* reality to be that enables them, so to speak, to take the next step, to know how to go on."[35] Medieval writing opens onto those perceptions of reality, but also onto creative play with them.

Conversations need to be dynamic, for medieval thought and writing can also change understandings of contemporary experience – by detaching it from pathology, by attending to the nature of experience in ways that illuminate rather than diagnose and by exploring its creative possibilities. Unusual experience is validated in a context where magic and the supernatural are accepted, and where such experience is not placed within a biomedical framework. Yet medieval models of psychology also chime well with contemporary notions of how cognitive processes work, the interdependence of thinking and feeling, mind and body. Probing the parallels and contrasts between premodern and contemporary experience, then, both brings new insights to medieval literature and recontextualizes contemporary experience. Many medieval discourses are suggestive – history, medicine, philosophy, theology – but perhaps none more than literature itself, for it is here – and particularly in romance – that human experience is most of all probed: through narrative, but also through the textures of the imaginative worlds of literature that create character, motivation, ethos and voice – all shaping representations of mind, body and affect that open onto medieval attitudes but also play creatively with possibilities for understanding the human condition. There is much scope for further interdisciplinary research, in which past and present speak to each other. The subject of magic, with its long cultural and intellectual history, its connections both with the supernatural and with the deepest human desires and fears, undoubtedly has a role to play.

Notes

1 *Magic and the Supernatural in Medieval English Romance*, Studies in Medieval Romance (Cambridge: D. S. Brewer, 2010).
2 See Valerie I.J. Flint, *The Rise of Magic in Early Medieval Europe* (Oxford: Clarendon, 1991), which takes up the model of Keith Thomas, *Religion and the Decline of Magic: Studies in Popular Beliefs in Sixteenth and Seventeenth Century England*, 2nd ed. (London: Weidenfeld and Nicolson, 1977); Richard Kieckhefer, *Magic in the Middle Ages* (Cambridge: Cambridge University Press, 1989, Canto ed., 2000); and Edward Peters, *The Magician, the Witch and the Law*, The Middle Ages Series (Philadelphia: University of Pennsylvania Press, 1978).
3 The series Witchcraft and Magic in Europe includes many other important works. See especially Karen Jolly, Catharina Raudvere and Edward Peters, *Witchcraft and Magic in Europe: The Middle Ages* (2001; Philadelphia: University of Pennsylvania Press, 2002). On Anglo-Saxon England, see Karen Jolly, *Popular Religion in Late Saxon England: Elf Charms in Context* (Chapel Hill: University of North Carolina Press, 1996) and Alaric Hall, *Elves in Anglo-Saxon England: Matters of Belief, Health, Gender and Identity* (Woodbridge: Boydell Press, 1997); on the twelfth century, see C.S. Watkins, *History and the Supernatural in Medieval England* (Cambridge: Cambridge University Press, 2007); on later medieval England, see Catherine Rider, *Magic and Religion in Medieval England* (London: Reaktion, 2012); on magic, learning and late medieval politics, see David Rollo, *Glamorous Sorcery: Magic and Literacy in the High Middle Ages* (Minneapolis: University of Minnesota Press, 2000). Steven P. Marrone's *A History of Science, Magic and Belief: From Medieval to Early Modern Europe* (London: Palgrave, 2015) explores these interconnected themes in terms of the shift to new paradigms of knowledge, society and government, while Euan Cameron's *Enchanted Europe: Superstition, Reason, and Religion, 1250–1750* (Oxford: Oxford University Press, 2010) traces the dialogue and debate around "superstition" in relation to ideas of invisible forces, demonology, the rise of Protestantism and theories of the cosmos.
4 Michael D. Bailey, "The Meanings of Magic," *Magic, Ritual, and Witchcraft* 1, no. 1 (2006): 1.
5 Michelle Sweeney, *Magic in Medieval Romance from Chrétien de Troyes to Geoffrey Chaucer* (Dublin: Four Courts, 2000).
6 Geraldine Heng, *Empire of Magic: Medieval Romance and the Politics of Cultural Fantasy* (New York: Columbia University Press, 2003).
7 Heidi Breuer, *Crafting the Witch: Gendering Magic in Medieval and Early Modern England*, Studies in Medieval History and Culture (New York: Routledge, 2009), 10.
8 Helen Cooper, *The English Romance in Time: Transforming Motifs from Geoffrey of Monmouth to the Death of Shakespeare* (Oxford: Oxford University Press, 2004).
9 On the boundaries between natural and supernatural, the range of beliefs available, connections with magic and the complex relationship between imagination and reality, see Robert Bartlett's study, *The Natural and the Supernatural in the Middle Ages: The Wiles Lectures given at the Queen's University of Belfast, 2006* (Cambridge: Cambridge University Press, 2008). On astrology and magic, see Paola Zambelli's collection of essays, *Astrology and Magic from the Medieval Latin and Islamic World to Renaissance Europe: Theories and Approaches*, Variorum Collected Studies Series (Farnham: Ashgate, 2012).
10 The works discussed here are normally dated as follows: *The Book of the Duchess* 1368–72, *The House of Fame* 1378–80, *The Canterbury Tales* 1388–1400.
11 Alexander N. Gabrovsky, *Chaucer the Alchemist: Physics, Mutability, and the Medieval Imagination* (Basingstoke: Palgrave Macmillan, 2015).
12 Geoffrey Chaucer, *The Riverside Chaucer*, 3rd ed., ed. Larry D. Benson (Oxford: Oxford University Press, 1987), l. 416. All subsequent references to Chaucer are to this edition, cited by line number.

13 For these details, see the notes to line 1277 in the *Riverside Chaucer*, 987.
14 The tale translates parts of three of the most widely circulated *summae*, Raymond of Peñafort's *Summa de Poenitentia*, William Peraldus' *Summa Virtutum ac Vitiorum*, and its sequel, the *Summa Virtutum de Remediis Anime* (known from its opening words as *Postquam*).
15 On this role of women, see Laine E. Doggett, *Love Cures: Healing and Love Magic in Old French Romance* (University Park: The Pennsylvania State University Press, 2009): Doggett notes Chrétien's humorous treatment of the motif, 4–5.
16 *Ywain and Gawain*, in *Ywain and Gawain, Sir Percyvell of Gales, The Anturs of Arther*, ed. Maldwyn Mills, Everyman's Library (London: Dent, 1992), 1–102: ll. 1739–40. Subsequent references to *Ywain and Gawain* are to this edition, cited by line number. The work exists in a single fifteenth-century manuscript, and translates the French romance of Chrétien de Troyes, *Le Chevalier au Lion*, written c.1170.
17 See Chrétien de Troyes, *Le Chevalier au Lion (Ywain)*, ed. Mario Roques, *Les Romans de Chrétien de Troyes* IV, Les Classiques français du Moyen Age (Paris: Honoré Champion, 1982), ll. 2949, 2998–3003; *The Knight with the Lion*, in *Arthurian Romances*, trans. William W. Kibler and Carleton W. Carroll (Harmondsworth: Penguin, 1991), 295–380, 332–33.
18 *The Romance of Sir Beues of Hamtoun*, ed. Eugen Kölbing, Early English Text Society, E.S. 46, 48, 65 (London: K. Paul, Trench, Trübner, 1885, 1886, 1894), ll. 3671–76. Subsequent references to *Beves of Hampton* are to this edition, cited by line number. The work exists in seven manuscripts (including the Auchinleck manuscript, written in the 1330s and containing many celebrated romances) in two different versions, and is based on the thirteenth-century Anglo-Norman *Boeve de Hamton*.
19 Michael R. Best, and Frank H. Brightman, ed., *The Book of Secrets of Albertus Magnus: Of the Virtues of Herbs, Stones and Certain Beasts: Also a Book of the Marvels of the World* (Oxford: Clarendon Press, 1973), 37.
20 Sir Thomas Malory, *Le Morte Darthur*, 2 vols, Arthurian Studies 80, ed. P.J.C. Field (Cambridge: D. S. Brewer, 2013), vol. 1, VIII.9, 302. All subsequent references to *Le Morte Darthur* are to this edition, vol. 1, cited by the book and section numbers used in Caxton's print (1485), and by page numbers. On healing and love magic in the French *Tristan* romances, see Doggett, *Love Cures*, 134–77.
21 *William of Palerne: An Alliterative Romance*, ed. G.H.V. Bunt, Medievalia Groningana 6 (Groningen: Bouma's Boekhuis, 1985), ll. 117–20. All subsequent references to *William of Palerne* are to this edition, cited by line number. The work exists in a single manuscript and is based on an early thirteenth-century French romance.
22 *Sir Gawain and the Green Knight*, in *The Poems of the Pearl Manuscript: "Pearl", "Cleanness", "Patience", "Sir Gawain and the Green Knight"*, 5th ed., Exeter Medieval English Texts and Studies, ed. Malcolm Andrew and Ronald Waldron (Exeter: Exeter University Press, 2007), ll. 2452. Subsequent references to *Sir Gawain and the Green Knight* are to this edition, cited by line number. The poem dates to the second half of the fourteenth century and exists in only one manuscript; it has no direct source but draws on both French and English Arthurian romances.
23 See further Laurence Harf-Lancner, *Les Fées au Moyen Age: Morgan et Melusine* (Paris: Champion, 1984) and Carolyne Larrington, *King Arthur's Enchantresses: Morgan and Her Sisters in Arthurian Tradition* (London: I. B. Tauris, 2006).
24 Lyndal Roper, *The Witch in the Western Imagination: Richard Lectures for 1998* (Charlottesville: University of Virginia Press, 2012), 2.
25 *The Unorthodox Imagination in Late Medieval Britain*, ed. Sophie Page (Manchester: Manchester University Press, 2010). Lea T. Olsan's "Enchantment in Medieval Literature," 166–92, is the only essay in the volume focused on literary texts.
26 See further Corinne Saunders, "Voices and Visions: Mind, Body and Affect in Medieval Writing," in *The Edinburgh Companion to the Critical Medical Humanities*, ed. Anne Whitehead, Angela Woods, Sarah Atkinson, Jane Macnaughton and Jennifer Richards (Edinburgh: Edinburgh University Press, 2016), 411–27, and further on the field of medical humanities, the introduction to this volume.
27 See especially Doggett's introduction and conclusion, *Love's Cures*, 1–14 and 262–67.
28 T.M. Luhrmann, *Persuasions of the Witch's Craft: Ritual Magic in Contemporary England* (Oxford: Blackwell, 1989).
29 Edward Bever, *The Realities of Witchcraft and Popular Magic in Early Modern Europe: Culture, Cognition, and Everyday Life* (Basingstoke: Palgrave Macmillan, 2008), and "Current Trends in the Application of Cognitive Science to Magic," *Magic, Ritual, and Witchcraft* 7, no. 1 (2012): 3–18. See also

the range of responses to Bever's work in the forum "Contending Realities: Reactions to Edward Bever," *Magic, Ritual, and Witchcraft* 5, no. 1 (2010).
30 Bever, "Current Trends", 13, 18.
31 Frank Klaassen, "Subjective Experience and the Practice of Medieval Ritual Magic," *Magic, Ritual, and Witchcraft* 7, no. 1 (2012): 19–51.
32 Klaassen, "Subjective Experience and the Practice of Medieval Ritual Magic," 50.
33 "Hearing the Voice" (http://hearingthevoice.org) is funded by a Wellcome Trust Strategic Award (WT098455MA). I am grateful to the Trust for supporting the research in this paper, and to the "Hearing the Voice" team for their insights.
34 See the range of examples cited Katherine Kamerick, "Shaping Superstition in Late Medieval England," *Magic, Ritual, and Witchcraft* 3, no. 1 (2008): 29–53.
35 Stuart Clark, "One-Tier History," *Magic, Ritual, and Witchcraft* 5, no. 1 (2010): 90.

27

MUSIC

John Haines

Except for a dozen pages in Jules Combarieu's outdated *La musique et la magie* (1909), the study of music and magic in the Middle Ages is virtually non-existent.[1] Of all the relevant fields to magic surveyed in this volume, then, music has the dubious claim of being the one least studied. Yet, music was an indispensable ingredient in the everyday performance of magic during the thousand-year period we name Middle Ages, in practical contexts ranging from medicinal to necromantic. As made clear in other essays in this volume (notably the chapters on medicine, gender, popular culture and pastoral literature), the majority of magic practised in the Middle Ages had a performative component. Thus, it included music of some kind, music ranging from elaborate polyphonic songs to recitations similar to the spoken word. Unfortunately, the majority of these rituals were neither described nor even recorded in writing. For this reason, modern research on medieval magic has gravitated, not surprisingly, towards the erudite works of the late Middle Ages, given the impressive surviving evidence ranging from Solomonic literature to the works of Cecco d'Ascoli, both featured in the present volume. Yet, even these learned magic works involved music of some kind, since a great deal of music verges on spoken speech. As explained in a foundational medieval music treatise, Boethius's *De musica*, sung music ranged widely from melodic song (*cantilena*) to the prose (*prosa*) recitation of an epic poem (*heroum poema*). In between these two, writes Boethius, lies a giant middle ground he calls "middle voices" (*medias voces*), somewhere between speech and song.[2] Although this chapter will give equal weight to the interaction of music and magic in both learned and popular circles, it should be borne in mind that the former was the province of the medieval one per cent and the latter that of the ninety-nine per cent, to borrow a phrase from our own culture. If the aim of modern history – musical or otherwise – is to tell, to the best of our ability, the story of the majority of those living in the Middle Ages, and not just the learned few, then the history of music and magic cannot neglect, in addition to the written witnesses of famous and learned men, those sources that tell us about the anonymous majority and their musico-magical experiences.

The most frequently heard musical sound in medieval magic ritual was the human voice. It was the actual sound of the voice, "the sound of medieval song," to cite the title of Timothy McGee's important recent book, that constituted the main audible part of magic ritual. McGee has attempted to answer a question rarely addressed in musicology, namely, what did the medieval singing voice sound like?[3] This is a difficult but vital question, one on which there will likely never be a scholarly consensus, given the frequently strongly held ideals about medieval chant with relation to present-day Catholic practices. Still, although more historical research remains to be done, there can be no question that the general sound of medieval song differed substantially from that of modern times, in ways that we cannot imagine. As McGee reminds us, despite some similarities in singing "between the modern and the medieval eras, their [sounds] are quite different from one another."[4]

Thus, along with gesture and movement, the music of the human voice is the most ephemeral element of magic rituals. The texts of some charms and prayers from the late Middle Ages, for example, have survived in writing (see Peter Murray Jones and Lea Olsan's chapter in this volume). But their song or recitation has the musical notes have not. All the more reason to be mindful of their aural or performative aspect. As an example, the words of the famous Longinus charm – "Longinus miles latus domini nostri Jesu Christi lancea perforavit et continuo exivit sanguis et aqua in redemptionem nostram" ("The soldier Longinus pierced the side of our Lord Jesus Christ and immediately there gushed forth blood and water for our redemption") – have both a lyric and liturgical feel.[5] To my knowledge, no late medieval Longinus charm has survived with musical notation. Yet, it is hard to believe that such popular formulas as this one were not chanted or recited on occasion. Indeed, perhaps there was a melody or two performed often enough with this charm that it was known as the "Longinus tune." This is a common phenomenon of orality that is underestimated from our excessively written perspective.

Music of some sort, then, must have sounded often in charms. When it did, this sound of medieval song in magic rituals apparently often resembled the sounds of the Christian liturgy, as the one surviving charm with music, "Quisquis erit," makes clear.[6] The instructions for the just cited Longinus charm end with the admonition to "say" ("dica") three times both the Pater noster and the Ave Maria – here likely in the broad sense of the verb *dicere*, which would encompass both of Boethius's musical poles, *cantilena* and *prosa*, as well as his "middle voices."[7] Two of the chants most frequently mentioned by ecclesiastical writers as permissible in non-liturgical rituals are the Credo and the Pater noster. Thomas Aquinas, for example, forbids the use of any kind of "unknown names" ("ignota nomina") in connection with suspensions or amulets hung from the neck, allowing only the "Divine symbol and the Dominical prayer," that is, the Credo and the Pater noster, following Gratian.[8] The mixed status of these two chants, used in the liturgy but also in activities considered dubious by churchmen, is attested in the manuscript containing the famous Psalter of Eadwin (Cambridge, Trinity Library, R.17.1), on the folio (284v) just before the treatise that Charles Burnett famously identified as the earliest chiromancy treaty in the Latin West (fol. 285r).[9] Here, we find a page with an annotated Credo and Pater noster; the rubric for the former states that with this prayer Christ revealed to his disciples "his impenetrable science" ("inpenetrabili sapientia sua").[10] It almost goes without saying that these two chants were regularly sung at mass and office throughout the Middle Ages. Beyond these two, other liturgical chants are attested as having been sung in popular rituals, notably the Kyrie, the Sanctus, the Ave Maria, the seven penitential psalms and the "Asperges me" (Psalm 50:9).[11] The melodies of all these chants were well known to both celebrants and congregations throughout Europe, and would have been permanently attached in many minds to their texts, much in the same way certain melodies – unfortunately not written down – would have been linked to famous charms like the aforementioned Longinus, as I suggested above. As a way of reimagining the lost music of charms, then, a good starting point is the corpus of surviving chant melodies. The following "Asperges me" from the thirteenth century is representative of the chants sung at mass.

In the medieval liturgy, the "Asperges" was sung after the celebrants' entrance at mass, during the sprinkling of holy water over altars and people using a special sprinkler called the *aspergillum*. The melody of the thirteenth-century "Asperges me" shown here has an almost speech-like or recitative quality, moving mostly stepwise within the confines of a

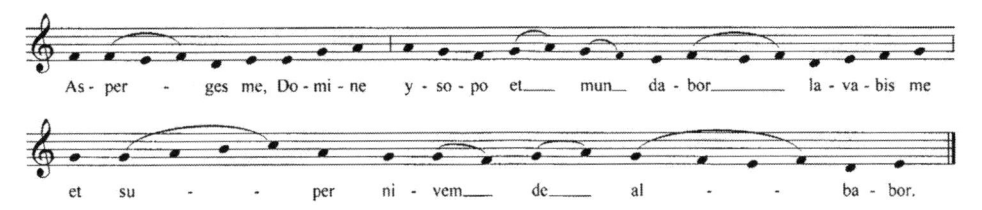

Figure 27.1 "Asperges me" from the thirteenth century.

standard E mode (Figure 27.1).[12] It includes occasional melismatic flashes, syllables sung over more than one note. This melody is only slightly more ornate than the majority of the music sung at mass and office, the recitation of psalms. The one hundred and fifty psalms sung daily in religious communities throughout Europe made use of even more straightforward melodies than this one, tunes that consisted of little more than one pitch, repeated rapidly in order to get through a maximum of text as quickly as possible. Possibly the use of water in this context made it especially relevant to unorthodox rituals not performed in church where the sprinkling of water regularly occurred. In fact, the source of this particular "Asperges me," the satirical romance *Renart le nouvel* starring the devilish Renart and the ass-priest Timer, hints at the many non-liturgical uses to which this and other chants were put. The melody occurs at the point in the romance when Renart briefly repents of his wily ways in order to avoid dying in a storm at sea. Chanting the "Asperges," a priest sprinkles the ship, the storm passes, and Renart returns to his sly self.[13] With this musical example, we find ourselves in territory that is not only liturgical, then, but clearly related to popular magical practices.

In learned medieval Latin lexicography, the porous border between magical and liturgical song can be seen in the small difference – two letters – between the two verbs *canere* and *cantare*. On the one hand, the two are generally differentiated by the texts in which they occur. The verb *canere* is generally found in texts describing or related to the official Christian liturgy; the derived nouns *precentor* and *cantor* refer to the singer of Christian chants. *Cantare* seems to have been reserved by churchmen for illicit or magical contexts, with the related noun *incantator* denoting the nemesis of the liturgical *cantor*.[14] On the other hand, the two verbs *canere* and *cantare* are not so different. Fundamentally, they both refer to the same activity: "to sing." Furthermore, both *canere* and *cantare* refer to similar types of singing, similar enough to be confused. The overlap between these songs, between liturgical and magical song, between the licit *cantus* (from *canere*) and the illicit *cantatio* (from *cantare*) or *carmen*, was enough of an issue for the famous encyclopaedist Isidore of Seville to raise it in his *Differentiae*. "*Cantare*," he writes, "means to resound with voices or with a clamor, whereas *canere* can sometimes mean 'to sing sweetly,' at other times to predict, that is, to foretell the future" ("Inter cantare et canere: cantare tantum vocibus vel clamore insonare est, canere autem interdum modulari, interdum vaticinari, id est, futura praedicere").[15] In the end, *canere* and *cantare* were not so different after all, despite the attempts of certain churchmen – notably the authors of the penitentials discussed below – to distinguish the two. As Isidore implies, singing was as important an activity to divination (one of the most common forms of magic) as it was to the observance of the Christian liturgy.

Most importantly, both *canere* and *cantare* carry the connotation of singing as a powerful, even life-altering phenomenon. They are ultimately rooted in the same historical – pre-medieval or ancient – phenomenon, namely the use of song to enhance the power of words, *verba*. The basic musicality of medieval charms is evident in the Latin word *carmen*, meaning both a song and a charm.[16] *Carmina* were *verba*, but not just *verba* in our musically deprived modern sense. The special force of these medieval *verba*, whether in liturgy or magic, came from the fact that they were sung. Because this medieval notion of singing as a powerful force is so foreign to modern notions of song, it cannot be stressed enough that singing, in the medieval view, was a spiritual phenomenon as much as it was a natural one. Song was indispensable to the human interaction with the angelic and demonic supernatural beings whose existence few questioned in the Middle Ages. Song's supernatural power was needed not only in magic rituals but also at the heart of the liturgy. In the second book of the most famous liturgical treatise from the Middle Ages, the monumental *Rationale divinorum officiorum*, William Durandus warns the celebrant at mass to be constantly on guard against the devil and his demons. Of all the liturgical celebrants, it is the cantor, Durandus notes, who, holding his priestly staff (crosier) like Moses his rod, is best able to repulse demons thanks to his powerful song.[17] The medieval theme of song as a powerful force occurs in a remarkable passage from William of Auvergne's treatise *On Faith and Laws*, in his discussion of popular incantations.

> The sound or sonority [of an incantation] would not be able to harm its hearers were it not for its loudness and volume, on account of which this song is like the breaking of thunder and the roaring of a lion; those who hear it, whether humans or animals, are deathly afraid and can even die.

William goes on to link the power of this song to affect many human emotions, from extreme joy to great sadness.[18]

In what follows, I briefly consider the relationship of music and magic in two separate spheres.[19] I begin with popular magic, that is magic practised by the majority of people in the Middle Ages. The second section looks at the musical aspects of magic practised by the learned few whose writings are well attested. I have used the labels "musica practica" and "musica speculativa" common in medieval music theory, to distinguish these two areas of musico-magical study. The medieval learned speculative tradition in music was famously formulated by Boethius in the twenty-third chapter of his famous treatise, the chapter devoted to "what a musician should be" ("Quid sit musicus"), as its title states. The true musician (*vero musicus*), as Boethius saw it, was not a practitioner of music nor of the "science of singing" (*canendi scientiam*), but rather the one who submitted the practice of music to the "empire of reflection" (*imperio speculationis adsumpsit*).[20] For Boethius, this meant following the Greek tradition of breaking down the modes and intervals of music into numbers, an activity that takes up the better part of the six books of *De musica*.

Musica practica

If the study of medieval magic today is missing the perspective of music, as mentioned above, the general historiography of medieval music is equally in need of the perspective of magic. For most of us today, the idea of music of the Middle Ages is one of "centuries of monkish dullness," to cite Henry Fielding.[21] From current historiography, one still gets the impression that the vast majority of musical sounds made in the Middle Ages occurred under the official supervision of the Church, from the pilgrimage chorus to the great responsory sung before the reading of the Gospel at mass.[22] This modern assumption of a medieval musical sound world dominated by Latin chant owes in part to the fact that the vast majority of extant sources with music notation were copied by churchmen for use in church.[23] But if we wish to study the whole of medieval music making rather than just the Latin liturgy, we must take into account a host of workaday music such as dance songs, even though no notated specimens of these survive. This change of perspective from select masterworks of church and court to music in cultural contexts for both work (*labor*) and entertainment or edification (*aedificatio*) has direct implications for the study of magic, for it opens the door to an entirely new cast of performers and repertoires neglected until now.[24]

The key question is where to find information on this lost music, especially since the official documents of the Christian church from the Carolingians onwards have become the main pillars of music history since the nineteenth century. As I discussed a few years ago, the mythography of what Anna Maria Busse Berger has called the "dead white male composer" has followed a predictable narrative for medieval music: first and mostly chant (starting with Pope Gregory), then vernacular song (starting with Guilhem of Aquitaine and the troubadours) followed by a sprinkling of instrumental music (parenthetical since it is anonymous), the entire narrative culminating in the perfection of polyphony (starting with Leonin and Perotin) that leads directly to cherished modern masterworks by the likes of Bach and Beethoven.[25] If we are to move beyond this wearisome narrative and arrive at some approximation of the bigger picture for medieval music, at a more ethnographic perspective of medieval musical sound, then we must begin with a host of thinly documented individuals whose music was never considered great enough to be written down by medieval codifiers. Here, Richard Kieckhefer's notion of a "clerical underworld," well known to historians of magic, may serve as a useful starting point. In the now classic passage from his *Magic in the Middle Ages* (1989), Kieckhefer argued that many who practised necromancy in the Middle Ages were clerics — both monks and priests, both those lapsed and those active in the Church. The proofs for this, Kieckhefer argued, are found in the surviving evidence for medieval necromancy, from the *clericus* routinely condemned in canon law for necromancy to the paraphrases of Christian prayers found in late medieval necromantic adjurations.[26]

Where to obtain information on the music of this clerical underworld, not to mention the many non-clerical individuals, women especially, who performed magic rituals of one kind or another throughout the Middle Ages? The study of magic in the last half-century has pointed musicology in the right direction, for this work has concerned itself with neglected sources. Special credit for inaugurating this approach should be given to Dieter Harmening and his landmark 1979 book *Superstitio*. In an attempt to assemble a corpus of medieval "superstitious literature" (*Aberglaubensliteratur*) and related practices, Harmening drew widely on a heterogeneous and still little-studied literature consisting mainly of homilies, canon law collections and penitentials.[27] Throughout *Superstitio*, the musical implications of Harmening's precious spadework are clear, notably in the recurring nouns *incantator* and *præcantator* used in these sources to describe individuals whose activities ranged from healing to necromancy, as well as the nouns *incantatio* and *præcantatatio*, the songs these individuals performed. Harmening singled out the *incantatio* as the canonical "magical song" (*Zauberlied*) and surmises that their musical and recitative qualities resembled liturgical song.[28]

For the future study of the "musica practica" or everyday music of magic, the sources first consulted by Harmening will prove indispensable. They range from chronicles to penitentials, the latter a vast but nearly untapped source by music historians. As initially explored in my 2010 book *Medieval Song in Romance Languages*, the penitential literature especially shows great potential to be mined for musical information on a range of popular practices deemed superstitious by the Church. As discussed in the present volume's chapter by Kathleen Kamerick, there are numerous problems with the evidence of and the related canon law collections, especially the question of whether or not an earlier condemnation literally cited by a later source refers to rituals still being practised.[29] Equally problematic for music, as I first pointed out in *Medieval Song in Romance Languages*, is the highly negative language of medieval condemnations that unfortunately convey our only portrait of a host of quotidian practices and rituals. To avoid falling into the same thinking on these practices as the acerbic medieval churchmen that harangued them, it is important to mentally convert their negative wording into a more positive one, a wording more representative of the views of these rituals' participants. To reiterate this point here, I will briefly repeat a simple exercise of "converting" a condemnation used in my earlier book. Here is the original condemnation from the Council of Arles (524), subsequently repeated by Regino of Prüm and Burchard of Worms.[30]

> Laypersons who observe funeral vigils should do so with reverence, fear and trembling. Those attending should not allow themselves to sing diabolical songs, nor to perform games or dances that the pagans devised through the teaching of the devil.
> (Laici qui excubias funeris observant, cum timore et tremore et reverentia hoc faciant. Nullus ibi prasumat diabolica carmina cantare, non joca et saltationes facere, quae pagani diabolo docente adinvenerunt.)

The terminology here is significant: *diabolica carmina*, a standard expression in penitentials, to describe popular songs or charms of different kinds, and the verb *cantare* specifying these charms or songs as a musical activity that was furthermore accompanied by energetic dancing (*joca et saltationes*). If we rephrase the entire decree using a more neutral language, the same event can be seen and heard quite differently:

> Laypersons who observe funeral vigils should do so with openness, anticipation and joy. Those attending should sing spirited songs and perform traditional games or dances.

In this new phrasing, trembling and reverence become anticipation and joy, and diabolical songs become spirited songs. Certainly, this is a hypothetical and possibly dubious reimagining of the sixth-century decree. Nevertheless, the exercise is worthwhile, since it allows us to briefly see, not only how dramatically a few small changes can change our own view of the same medieval event, but also, in looking back at the original condemnation, how easy it is to adopt, even subliminally, the negative view found in the endless tirades of churchmen whose ecclesiastical condemnations are unfortunately the only surviving witnesses to these musical practices.

Given the near complete musicological neglect of such sources as penitentials, their study until now as focused on the magical use of "words" (*verba*) as literary things, or words on a page. Again, the musical aspect of the powerful enunciation of these *verba* cannot be stressed enough. Credit should be given to a few historians, such as Edina Bozoky and Béatrice Delaurenti, who have mentioned the "sonorous effects" of charms and the "importance of the musical element" to the incantation.[31] In her 2007 published doctoral dissertation, Delaurenti singled out an important passage from Nicole Oresme's treatise on geometry where the learned man describes the performance sound of incantations. Oresme not only relates the histrionics of the performance (the performer appearing as if he is "disturbed mentally") but also vocal techniques, such as how singers "murmur some sounds that are distorted with some strange unaccustomed deformity … dissimilar to the ordinary human voice."[32] This is unfortunately a late and single witness to the performance of incantations.

Still, it allows us to begin hearing (as a sight-centred academic, I was about to say "seeing" or "envisioning") the musical performance of medieval incantations which must have been impressive and sometimes even spectacular.

From the literature of penitentials and other relevant sources ranging from chronicles to sermons, some contexts emerge for everyday musico-magical activities in the Middle Ages that are in need of deeper study with respect to their sounds: necromancy, healing, non-necromantic means of divination and weather altering ceremonies. The one most often condemned by churchmen is necromancy, whose primary tool, following the famous definition by Isidore of Seville, was song: the *præcantatio* ("Necromantici sunt quorum præcantationibus videntur resuscitati mortui divinare et ad interrogata respondere").[33] Concerning the power of song to heal, Roger Bacon cites the words of Avicenna:

> Of all health exercises, singing is the best, for not only does it rejoice the soul but it comforts the entire body by relieving the spirit ... [it] distends all of the nerves and veins in the body, and in this way malicious vapors are exhaled and subtle inspirations of air are restored.[34]

The "power of song" (*cantus vigor*), as Avicenna calls it, is also obtained for a variety of divination rituals regularly practised by medieval people. The close relation between divination and song noted earlier in Isidore's double definition of *canere* and *cantare* is emphasized by John of Salisbury in the first book of his *Policraticus* devoted to music and magic, two fields he sees as being closely related. The incomparable force (*vis*) of song, writes John, comes from its possessing "something at once human, divine and prophetic (*phitonicus*)."[35] As for specialists of weather-altering magic, their singing art is well attested, as in one condemnation by Burchard of Worms, who writes that the special type of weather-changing *incantator*, called *immissor*, can move storms with his incantations.[36]

In conclusion to this section, the literature of penitentials makes clear that music did not necessarily always accompany these various rituals, but that when it did, it conferred special force to them. Penitentials sometimes distinguish between a ritual performed with an incantation (*cum incantatione*) – in other words a ritual where singing (*cantare*) occurs – and one without singing (*sine incantatione*). In the Penitential of Silos, for example, we read that if a sick man bathes under a mill with an incantation, he must do penitence for a year; but if he does so without incanting, he will suffer a penitence of only forty days.[37] This is phrased negatively, as we have come to expect from the haughty ecclesiastical perspective, but the implication behind these words for those women and men who performed such rituals on a daily basis and often in desperate, life-or-death conditions, is that the music of a healing ritual was indispensable to this ritual's efficacy.

Musica speculativa

As with practical music, the study of medieval magic in the realm of "speculative music" has so far been hampered by a problem of perspective, namely, two tenacious modern assumptions about medieval magic. The first assumption is that there was little or no scholarly interest in music and magic in the Middle Ages and that this was only revived in the Renaissance.[38] The second assumption is that learned writers on music did not really believe in a literal sounding of the music of the spheres.[39] The main modern writer who has attempted to correct this view, Joscelyn Godwin, has unfortunately not been given due recognition; in fact, quite the opposite. Certain writers have gone so far as to consider Godwin's work "useless" and "New Age," labelling Godwin himself an "occultist" on an unscholarly quest for "intrinsic truth."[40] This is unfortunate, since for the future study of music and magic in the speculative tradition, Godwin's books remain an important chronological starting point as well as essential reading, especially as they are so far the only scholarly volumes on the subject.[41]

As Godwin pointed out three decades ago, several medieval music writers showed a deep interest in magic. One does not have to wait for the musings of Marsilio Ficino in the late fifteenth century to find an intense scholarly interest in magic, and specifically in the supernatural power of song.[42] In his indispensable *Music, Mysticism and Magic: A Sourcebook* (1987), Godwin cites and discusses medieval writers from Martianus Capella to Henry Suso.[43] The idea, prevalent from Frances Yates onwards and evident for music in the work of D.P. Walker and Gary Tomlinson, that learned writing on magic had to be revived in the Renaissance is no longer credible half a century after the publication of Walker's first book.[44] A florescence of scholarly work on magic since that time has made clear that magic was alive and well in the Middle Ages and that furthermore, as Frank Klaassen has recently emphasized, Renaissance writers were continuing a well-established conversation on magic rather than starting it up again after a medieval hiatus.[45] If Ficino discussed magical song, then, it was because there already existed a substantial medieval tradition on it. Beyond the medieval writers discussed by Godwin, one can cite, to name three of the most prominent ones, John of Salisbury, who moves seamlessly from a multi-chapter discussion on the power of song and its connection to celestial music, to a survey of magicians beginning with the *incantator*; Adelard of Bath, who in his *Conversations with His Nephew* details the power of song and Roger Bacon, who in his *Opus Tertium*, describes the marvellous physical effects of music and song to heal and alter the behaviour of humans and animals, a power (*virtus*) that Roger attributes to the music of the spheres and to music's deep antiquity (*scientia arcana*).[46] The thinking of these writers as well as others in the Middle Ages on the question of magic and its relation to music has yet to be studied in a satisfactory way.

From Boethius onwards, most learned men writing on music in the Middle Ages – and the occasional learned woman such as Hildegard of Bingen – take as axiomatic that song's power derives from the music of the spheres, the *musica mundana*. Here again, it bears repeating that there is no basis for the still commonly held assumption that the idea of a literal music of the spheres had fallen out of favour by the late Middle Ages. Rather, it was alive and well for most learned medieval writers, including all of those cited in the previous paragraph, Aristotle's scepticism notwithstanding.[47] The reason for the importance of a literal belief in the *musica mundana* doctrine is that learned medieval writers viewed this as the practical basis for most of their speculation. The few writers who openly contradict Boethius's assertion that the spheres make musical harmony are forced to deny it quite vehemently, Johannes de Grocheio in the late thirteenth century being a case in point. In a lengthy disputation-style format, Grocheio destroys Boethius's literal doctrine so that he can declare his allegiance to Aristotle by embracing the Philosopher's denial of a literal celestial music.[48] Yet, even Grocheio concedes that some heavenly music resounds, that of the angels and archangels.[49] Other Aristotle-loving writers such as Roger Bacon tactfully effect a compromise, so vital was the idea of a literal spherical melos to them. Like the majority of medieval writers, Bacon believes in the literal music of the spheres but explains it in naturalistic terms. The *musica mundana* sounds, Bacon maintains, on account of the friction between planets (*duri cum duro*) rather than because of their movements, which was the orthodox, Boethian explanation.[50]

For the future study of music and magic in the realm of "musica speculativa," it will be useful to look at other theoretical concepts beyond the just discussed harmony of the spheres. One of these is the doctrine of *proprietas*. On the heels of the New Aristotle and the scholarly habit of cataloguing the properties of all things, music writers in the thirteenth century take up the project of explaining the new graphic note shapes of measured notation in a novel terminology that synthesizes pseudo-Aristotelian with theological concepts. Thus, in the late 1200s, musical notes and ligatures are parsed according to their varying degrees of property (*proprietas*) and perfection (*perfectio*). As I pointed out a few years ago, the concept of *proprietas* in these writings seems to pay a nod not only to Aristotle but also, more importantly, to a time-honoured connection between the amulets (*ligaturae*) well known to medieval people, which objects' "properties" (*proprietates*) were indispensable to their efficacy. Equally indispensable to the working of ligatures was, as noted above in the section on "musica practica," song, and specifically the music of incantations.[51]

Another useful approach to getting at the broader perspective of medieval music writers is via the codicological context of their texts. The texts that medieval editors of manuscript anthologies chose to bring together can tell us something about how they viewed individual works such as Anonymous IV's famous treatise or individual authorities such as Boethius. This may help move us away from an older formalist view of works and authors to a broader view of these men and their works as the sum total of their medieval readers' interpretations. In an essay published a few years ago, I looked at a few manuscripts with this in mind.[52] One, a collection used at the abbey of Saint Martial (Paris, Bibliothèque nationale de France, fonds latin 3713), makes clear that monastic activities ranged widely, from esoteric writing and superstitious rituals to the music of the monochord found in Pseudo-Odo's *Dialogue on Music*. Another, compiled for the monks at Bury St. Edmunds (London, British Library, Royal 12 C VI), contains various works on writing, including a quirky offshoot of the *Ars notoria* and the musical treatise by Anonymous IV.[53] Such an approach, centred on the transmission of texts, can be useful for the further study of music and magic in the Middle Ages.

To conclude this section on "musica speculativa," I should mention a phenomenon related to the speculative tradition of music, music writing, since writing was the province of the medieval "one percent." The *notae* of music need not always be approached in a modern literalist fashion. *Notae* were also, as medieval music writers regularly remind us, temporal *figurae* of things eternal. This seems to have played out in a variety of ways. As I have suggested in an essay devoted to late medieval ligatures as esoteric writing, the basic shapes and even names of musical notes carried an important symbolism, beginning with the basic "neume" or *pneuma* (Spirit) which was drawn as a *punctus*, the point being a universal symbol for the Divine Being.[54] In certain Spanish documents from the tenth to the twelfth centuries, musical *notae* were also used as cryptography. The example shown here, spelling out "Didacus notuit" ("Didacus wrote this"), combines neumes resembling letters with less obvious shapes. Here again, as with most of the areas covered in this chapter, the surviving documentation has received precious little study (Figure 27.2).[55]

Figure 27.2 Cryptography using neumes: "Didacus notuit".

Notes

1 Jules Combarieu, *La musique et la magie: Étude sur les origines populaires de l'art musical, son influence, et sa fonction dans les sociétés* (Paris: Alphonse Picard), 108–13, 244–45, 304–10 and 336–37. However, over the last few years, I have published on the subject a few essays that are cited in the footnotes of the present chapter.
2 *Anicii Manlii Torquati Severini Boetii De institutione arithmetica libri duo, De institutione musica libri quinque*, ed. Gottfried Friedlein (Leipzig: Teubner, 1867), 199, lines 13–18.
3 Timothy McGee, *The Sound of Medieval Song* (Oxford: Clarendon, 1998).
4 McGee, *Sound of Medieval Song*, 42.
5 Text from Lea Olsan, "The Corpus of Charms in the Middle English Leechcraft Remedy Books," in *Charms, Charmers and Charming: International Research on Verbal Magic*, ed. Jonathan Roper (New York: Palgrave, 2009), 218.
6 Wolfgang Irtenkauf, "Der Computus Ecclesiasticus in der Einstimmigkeit des Mittelalters," *Archiv für Musikwissenschaft* 14 (1957): 1–15.
7 Olsan, "Corpus of Charms," 219.
8 Thomas Aquinas, *Summa theologica*, vol. 3, ed. Jean Nicolas (Parma: Petrus Fiaccadorus, 1853), 354: "Similiter etiam videtur esse cavendum, si contineat ignota nomina, ne sub illis aliquid illicitum lateat … *nisi tantum cum symbolo divino, aut Dominica oratione*," here citing Gratian's decrees.
9 Charles Burnett, "The Earliest Chiromancy in the West," in *Magic and Divination in the Middle Ages*, X, ed. Burnett (London: Variorum, 1996), 189–97.
10 M.R. James, *Western Manuscripts in the Library of Trinity College, Cambridge: A Descriptive Catalogue*, vol. 1 (Cambridge: Cambridge University Press, 1901), 406.
11 John Haines, "Le praecantator et l'art du verbe," in *Les noces de philologie et musicologie : Textes et musique du Moyen Âge*, ed. Christelle Cazaux-Kowalski, Christelle Chaillou-Amadieu, Anne-Zoé Rillon-Marne and Fabio Zinelli (Paris: École Pratique des Hautes Études, 2018), 448–464.
12 This same melody is given without commentary in John Haines, "Why Music and Magic in the Middle Ages?" in *Magic, Ritual and Witchcraft* 5 (2010), 168. It is taken from Haines, *Satire in the Songs of Renart le nouvel*, Publications romanes et françaises 247 (Geneva: Droz, 2010), 266.
13 Haines, *Satire in the Songs*, 47.
14 On the medieval cantor, see Margot Fassler, "The Office of the Cantor in Early Western Monastic Rules and Customaries: A Preliminary Investigation," *Early Music History* 5 (1985), 29–51. On the *incantator*, see below.
15 Isidore cited in Wilibald Gurlitt, "Zur Bedeutungsgeschichte von *musicus* und *cantor* bei Isidor von Sevilla," *Akademie der Wissenschaften und der Literatur. Abhandlungen der geistes- und sozialwissenschaftlichen Klasse*, 7 (1950): 554.
16 This point made in Edina Bozoky, *Charmes et prières apotropaïques*, Typologie des Sources du Moyen Âge Occidental 86 (Turnhout: Brepols, 2003), 34–36, among other places.
17 William Durandus, "*Guillelmi Duranti Rationale divinorum officiorum I-IV*," ed. A. Davril et T.M. Thibodeau, Corpus Christianorum Continuatio Medievalis 140 (Turnhout: Brepols, 1995), 147: "cantores tenent baculos […] significantes qui quod […] indigent contra demones."
18 William of Auvergne, *De fide et legibus* in *Opera omnia*, vol. 1 (1674; Frankfort: Minerva, 1963), 90:

> Sonus enim, sive sonatio non potest nocere audientibus, nisi per vehementiam acuminis sui, aut per magnitudinem suam, per quam est interdum terrificus, sicut fragor tonitrui, sicut rigitus leonis; unde etiam per terrorem seu timorem possibile est mori audientes, vel homines vel alia animalia. Manifestum est passiones animarum vehementia sua mortem posse inferre patienti, et hoc apud vulgus famosum est, videlicet nimio ardore, et odio nimio, dolore, et gaudio, nimia ira, nimiaque tristitia interdum moti homines, et etiam canes nimia tristitia de morte dominorum suorum multotiens mortuos esse audire potuisti; nimio vero acumine vocis, vel soni potest mors accidere, ex vehementi enim concussione, sive percussione ossis petrosi, in quod fit auditus, potest tanta perturbatio fieri in interioribus capitis, ut mortem inducat.

19 I used a similar division in Haines, "Why Music and Magic," 149–72 and again in John Haines, "La sapience secrète et le rêve révélateur dans le traité *Desiderio tuo, fili karissime*," in *Musique et littérature au Moyen Âge*, Cahiers de recherches médiévales et humanistes 26, ed. John Haines (Paris: Garnier, 2014), 91–107.

20 *Anicii Manlii Torquati Severini Boetii*, ed. Friedlein, 224, lines 18–20.
21 Henry Fielding, *Tom Jones* (Oxford: Oxford University Press, 1996), 67.
22 E.g. Margot Fassler, *Music in the Medieval West: Western Music in Context* (New York: W.W. Norton, 2014). Other examples are not hard to find; see Haines, "Why Music and Magic," 152–53.
23 This point made in John Haines, *Medieval Song in Romance Languages* (Cambridge: Cambridge University Press, 2010), 12–20.
24 On this nomenclature, see John Haines, "Performance Before c. 1430: An Overview" in *The Cambridge History of Musical Performance*, ed. Colin Lawson and Robin Stowell (Cambridge: Cambridge University Press, 2012), 231–47.
25 Haines, *Medieval Song*, 146–52.
26 Richard Kieckhefer, *Magic in the Middle Ages* (Cambridge: Cambridge University Press, 2003), 153–56.
27 Dieter Harmening, *Superstitio. Überlieferungs- und theoriegeschichtliche Unersuchungen zur kirchlich-theologischen Aberglaubensliteratur des Mittelalters* (Berlin: Erich Schmidt, 1979).
28 Harmening, *Superstitio*, 221–22.
29 Haines, *Medieval Song*, 5 and 55–57. Generally on pentientials, see Cyrille Vogel, *Les Libri paenitentiales*, Typologie des Sources du Moyen Âge Occidental 27 (Turnhout: Brepols, 1978) and the chapter in the present volume.
30 Taken from Haines, *Medieval Song*, 38–39. The original sixth-century decree is printed in Domenico G. Mansi, *Sacrorum conciliorum nova et amplissima collectio*, vol. 8 (Florence: Antonius Zatta, 1762), 630. Regino of Prüm's *Disciplina ecclesiastica* in *Patrologia latina*, vol. 132, col. 266A; Burchard of Worms' *Decretum* in Hartmut Hoffmann and Rudolf Pokorny, *Das Dekret des Bischofs Burchard von Worms: Textstufen – Frühe Verbreitung – Vorlagen* (Munich: Monumenta Germaniae Historica, 1991), 217.
31 Edina Bozoky, *Charmes et prières apotropaïques*, Turnhout, 2003 (Typologie des Sources du Moyen Âge Occidental 86), 44 and Béatrice Delaurenti, *La puissance des mots. « Virtus verborum »*. *Débats doctrinaux sur le pouvoir des incantations au Moyen Âge* (Paris: Editions du Cerf, 2007), 99.
32 Delaurenti, *La puissance des mots*, 412–13 and 419; an English translation of this passage is found in John Haines, "Case Study: Guillaume de Machaut: Ballade 34" in *The Cambridge History of Musical Performance*, ed. Colin Lawson and Robin Stowell (Cambridge: Cambridge University Press, 2012), 284.
33 Isidore of Seville, *Isidori Hispalensis episcopi Etymologiarum sive Originum libri XX*, vol. 1, ed. W.M. Lindsay (Oxford: Clarendon, 1988), 324, lines 24–26.
34 Roger Bacon, *Opus Tertium* in *Fr. Rogeri Bacon Opera quaedam hactenus inedita*, vol. 1, ed. J.S. Brewer (Berlin: Kraus, 1965), 299:

> Et Avicenna primo Artis Medicinae docet quod, inter omnia exercitia sanitatis, cantare melius est; quia non solum animus hilarescit, ut totum corpus confortetur per mentis solatium, sed cantus vigor omnes nervos et venas totius corporis distendit, ut vapores corrupti exhalentur, et subtiles aeris inspirationes restaurentur.

35 John of Salisbury, *Policraticus I-IV*, Corpus Christianorum Continuatio Mediaevalis 118 (Turnhout: Brepols, 1993), 46–47: "et vi sua corporum integram penetrat densitatem et quasi tactu quodam movet animum … et nunc quidem humanum, nunc divinum, nunc et phitonicum gerit."
36 H.J. Schmitz, *Die Bussbücher und die Bussdisciplin der Kirche*, vol. 2 (Mainz: Franz Kirchheim, 1883–98), 425, no. 68: "incantatores … qui se dicunt tempestatum immissores esse, possent per incantationem daemonum aut tempestates commovere."
37 L. Körntgen and F. Bezler, *Paenitentialia Hispaniae*, Corpus Christianorum Series Latina 156A (Brepols: Turnhout, 1998), 36: "Si pro infirmitate sub moline balneaberit, cum incantatione I annum peniteat; sin autem XL dies peniteat." Cf. English translation in John McNeill and Helena Gamer, *Medieval Handbooks of Penance* (New York: Columbia University Press, 1938), 289.
38 Discussed in Haines, "Music and Magic," 151–52.
39 Discussed in Haines, "La sapience secrète," 91–93.
40 Here citing Laurence Wuidar, *Musique et astrologie après le Concile de Trente* (Brussels: Belgisch Historisch Instituut te Rome, 2008), 23, note 44 and Gary Tomlinson, *Music in Renaissance Magic: Towards a Historiography of Others* (Chicago, IL: University of Chicago Press, 1993), 14–15.
41 Most useful is Joscelyn Godwin, *Music, Mysticism and Magic: A Sourcebook* (London: Routledge and Kegan Paul, 1987). See also Godwin's *Harmonies of Heaven and Earth: The Spiritual Dimensions of Music from Antiquity to the Avant-Garde* (Rochester, NY: Inner Traditions International, 1987).

42 Pace Tomlinson, *Music in Renaissance Magic*, 101–44.
43 Godwin, *Music, Mysticism and Magic*, 34–113.
44 D.P. Walker, *Spiritual and Demonic Magic from Ficino to Campanella* (London: Warburg Institute, 1958).
45 Frank Klaassen, *The Transformations of Magic: Illicit Learned Magic in the Later Middle Ages and Renaissance* (University Park: The Pennsylvania State University Press, 2013).
46 John of Salisbury, *Policraticus*, book 1, chs. 6–12, Charles Burnett on Adelard of Bath cited in Haines, "Music and Magic," 155–56 and Bacon, *Opus Tertium*, 295–301, citation at p. 298.
47 For a survey of the scholarly literature on the *musica mundana* and of medieval writers on the same topic, see Haines, "La sapience secrète," 93–98.
48 John Haines and Patricia DeWitt, "Johannes de Grocheio and Aristotelian Zoology" in *Early Music History* 27 (2008), 64–67.
49 Grocheio cited in Haines, *Medieval Song in Romance Languages*, 118.
50 Bacon's *Opus Tertium* cited in Haines, "La sapience secrète," 96.
51 "On *Ligaturæ* and Their Properties: Medieval Music Notation as Esoteric Writing" in *The Calligraphy of Medieval Music*, ed. Haines (Turnhout: Brepols, 2011), 203–22.
52 Haines, "Why Music and Magic," 159–64.
53 I since edited the *Ars notoria* branch: Haines, *The Notory Art of Shorthand (Ars notoria notarie): A Curious Chapter in the History of Writing in the West*, Dallas Medieval Texts and Translations 20 (Louvain: Peeters, 2014).
54 Haines, "On *Ligaturae*," 204. On the symbolism of square notes, see John Haines, "Perspectives multiples sur la note carrée," *Pecia* 14 (2011), 19–35.
55 See Haines, "On *Ligaturae*," 205, with note 17 citing Bernhard Bischoff's still helpful study.

28

MAGIC AND ARCHAEOLOGY

Ritual residues and "odd" deposits

Roberta Gilchrist

The use of archaeology as source material for medieval magic raises a number of methodological and theoretical issues. Many of the rituals of common magic revealed by archaeology were never (or rarely) documented in medieval texts. The lack of correlation between texts and material culture has been regarded as a methodological problem for historians[1]; to the contrary, these complementary sources permit access to social contexts and agents that are under-represented in texts, particularly women and other practitioners who operated in domestic and rural environments. It offers the potential to interrogate the distinction between "theory and practice" in medieval magic and opens up new opportunities to directly access "the mental world of the non-literate".[2] Archaeology renders a wider range of practices visible, but the absence of textual commentary makes it difficult to gauge whether these activities were sanctioned by the church or regarded as illicit magic.

Archaeological evidence prompts reconsideration of definitions of medieval magic and attention to the permeable borderlines between magic, religion, medicine and heresy. The messiness of these categories is highlighted by evidence for material practices such as "odd deposits": the burial, discard or concealment of objects that seems to defy any rational explanation. Such deposits are recorded in domestic and ecclesiastical contexts and across the social spectrum, suggesting both lay and clerical participation. Distinguishing between magic and religion was challenging for medieval people, even educated clerics, and remains an area of contention among medieval historians.[3] Archaeology adds a new perspective to these debates, illuminating the murky space between documented practice and what people were actually doing.

Archaeological sources reach a broader range of social and spatial contexts than texts usually permit, for example, magic practised within the homes, churches and churchyards of medieval England. The archaeology of magic has potential to reveal intimate rites that were never documented in clerical texts, and to explore the close relationship between magic, gender and the body, for example through burial evidence.[4] However, material sources do not provide immediate access to the thoughts and motivations of medieval people. Did they regard their actions as "magic" and why did they perceive certain acts as efficacious? Attention to *spatial context* provides some basis for considering the social identity of the practitioner – for example, whether a priest, craftsman, pilgrim or housewife – and grounds to consider the possible motivations and perceived causation behind the magic ritual. Spatial context may also provide insight into whether a rite was public or private and whether it was regarded as licit or illicit magic. Archaeological interest in *agency* overlaps with the focus on *causation* in the study of medieval magic; in other words, the conceptual frameworks that allowed medieval people to rationally attribute the cause of marvels to the intercession of saints, the occult power of nature or the intervention of demons.[5] Similarly, archaeology's concern with materiality has close affinities with themes addressed in the study of natural magic.

Archaeologists consider the material traces of magic within a "deep-time" perspective. We work at larger chronological scales and resolutions to most historians, taking a "stratigraphic" approach that relates medieval evidence to that which comes before and after it. This extended timescale highlights continuities in ritual practice and in the selection and treatment of materials that extended over hundreds of years, across the watersheds of the Christian conversion and the Reformation. Archaeology reveals an enduring repertoire of common ritual actions that may be regarded as traditional or even indigenous to northern Europe; these practices may have been influenced by ideas derived from learned magic texts of Greco-Roman, Arabic or Jewish origin, to forge new beliefs and localized meanings. This process of hybridity can be glimpsed especially in the late Saxon charms: these monastic records of popular belief may provide a bridge for understanding later medieval practice in relation to earlier rites.[6]

Magic and archaeology: text and object

The first major archaeological treatment of magic was Ralph Merrifield's *The Archaeology of Ritual and Magic* (1987), which presented an accessible overview of material evidence for ritual practices extending from the prehistoric to modern periods in Britain. Merrifield laid the methodological groundwork for an archaeology of magic, stressing the importance of establishing rigorous chronological and spatial contexts for magical practices and "odd" or "placed" deposits, such as prehistoric axe-heads discovered in medieval contexts.[7]

Another pioneering contribution to the archaeology of magic was Audrey Meaney's research on amulets in Anglo-Saxon burials. She used the evidence of grave goods to identify the burials of cunning women or seers, based on the presence of objects that were deemed magical by virtue of their substance. She focused on amulets of animal, vegetable and mineral materials, or those which were noteworthy for their exceptional age. Roman or prehistoric artefacts in graves dating from the sixth to ninth centuries were interpreted as *objets trouvé*, "found objects" that were credited with the power to bring luck or avert evil. Meaney set out two methodological premises that have been followed by much of the subsequent archaeological scholarship on medieval magic: first, the relationship between an object or material and its magical powers should be *documented* in medieval sources; and second, a *direct physical relationship* should be demonstrated between the object and the body in the grave.[8] Her work was pivotal in recognizing the agency of women in the practice of magic, through the identification of objects in Anglo-Saxon women's graves including crystal balls worn suspended from the waist, bronze relic boxes that contained scraps of thread and cloth, and bags containing collections of odd objects. Meaney interpreted these assemblages as women's toolkits for healing or divination, suggesting a significant ritual role for some Anglo-Saxon women as community healers or seers.[9]

I have drawn on Meaney's work to identify the use of magic in later medieval burial rites in Britain (eleventh to fifteenth centuries) and to demonstrate long-term continuities in the placement of apotropaic objects and natural materials with the dead.[10] This recognition of hybrid practices formed by the conversion to Christianity has prompted new study of transitional burial rites and heightened archaeological attention to magic.[11] The "deep-time" perspective of archaeology provides new insight into the changing practices and meanings of medieval magic: many rituals of common magic had their roots in pre-Christian practices, while medieval rites influenced the practice of early modern magic to protect against witchcraft.[12] Archaeologists often adopt a long-term perspective in which to evaluate magic, particularly in Scandinavia and the Baltic, where eighteenth- and nineteenth-century folklore informs the understanding of material practices that were prevalent from prehistory to the modern era.[13] Important regional distinctions arise from the nature and timing of conversion to Christianity; for example in the eastern Baltic, material practices associated with the treatment of the dead are often regarded as "syncretic" or "pagan" survivals, rather than as part of a medieval tradition of magic.[14]

Ritual deposition

Over the past thirty years, archaeologists have explored the idea that the "deposition" of materials, such as the burial of selected objects in a pit, may have constituted meaningful social practice. It has been argued that "odd", "special" or "placed" deposits were created as part of ritual practice that was integrated with aspects of everyday life in the past. Such deposits take the form of deliberately made features that seem to defy any rational explanation such as whole pots or animals buried in ditches and pits, or objects placed at critical points in settlements such as at boundaries, entrances or the corners of houses.[15] Placed deposits were first discussed in relation to Neolithic and Bronze Age settlements but are now recognized to have occurred in later prehistoric and classical contexts across Europe. It is only very recently that archaeologists have identified the occurrence of such deposits in early and later medieval contexts, with similarities in the types of objects and materials selected for use across Europe, from pagan to Christian eras.[16]

Placed deposits in pagan Anglo-Saxon houses and settlements took the form of human and animal remains buried in buildings and at boundaries and entrances, although other objects were also employed, including pottery vessels, brooches, beads, spindle whorls and loom weights. Close parallels have been drawn with earlier Iron Age and Roman practices, particularly in the deposition of human and animal remains in pits. It has also been acknowledged that these practices extended beyond the pagan period and can be detected in later Saxon (Christian) urban and rural contexts.[17] Placed deposits dating to the Anglo-Saxon period were initially categorized as "votive", but more recent discussions have evaluated this form of ritual practice within the framework of everyday life. Just as Richard Kieckhefer argued that magic should be perceived as "an alternative form of rationality" that was consistent with medieval views of the universe, archaeologists contend that these deposits were rationally conceived according to past world views, directed towards specific practical purposes such as agriculture and technology.[18]

Merrifield noted that animal skulls, pottery vessels, clothing and shoes were frequently found in extant buildings of later medieval and early modern date, usually placed in the foundations, walls or chimneys.[19] Similar practices have since been detected in excavated structures dating to the medieval period across Europe, and spanning domestic and ecclesiastical contexts. In medieval Sweden, for example, concealed deposits comprise animal remains, tools and utensils, pottery vessels, coins, personal items, prehistoric lithics and fossils; deposits of coins are particularly common finds in parish churches.[20] Placed deposits identified in medieval English churches include paternoster beads of bone and amber, silver spoons, pottery vessels, pilgrim badges and disused baptismal fonts.[21]

In medieval English houses, pottery vessels have been found buried near hearths and objects have been recovered from post-holes, including special materials such as fragments of glass and quartz crystal. There are possible cases of gaming boards deliberately buried as placed deposits: three limestone slabs with marks for "nine men's morris" were excavated from a single tenement at the hamlet of West Cotton (Northants), dating from the thirteenth to fourteenth century. Excavations at Nevern Castle (Pembrokeshire) revealed the special treatment of a late twelfth-century entrance to the castle: the threshold was formed by inverted slates with inscriptions on one or both faces. Amongst the symbols inscribed on the slates were warriors, crosses, a pentagram and three boards for "nine men's morris". It has been suggested that the grid pattern of the game may have been intended to trap or detain malevolent spirits.[22]

Eleanor Standley has drawn attention to the use of personal objects of medieval dress such as buckles and brooches as deliberate deposits. She argues that items were specially selected for their apotropaic value: for example, at the village of West Hartburn (co. Durham), a silver brooch inscribed with the Holy Name (IESUS NAZARET/IHUS REX IUDEO) was recovered near a circular hearth within a structure (Figure 28.1). The context was dated to around the fourteenth century and Standley proposes that the deposit may have been made in response to the fourteenth-century crises of famine and plague.[23]

Ritual deposition in medieval England was not confined to domestic and religious buildings, but extended to the deliberate discard of certain types of object in the landscape. Pilgrims' badges have been found in large quantities in rivers in England, France and the Netherlands, with particular concentrations recovered at the locations of bridges and river crossings.[24] Pilgrim badges were selected for deposition as special objects because of their apotropaic value to the owner. Pilgrim signs were blessed at saints' shrines like a relic; they acquired the status of quasi-relics or consecrated objects and were worn as amulets on the body, or alternatively, fixed to bedposts or fastened to textual amulets and books of hours.[25] A large number of these mass-produced, tin-alloy badges were deposited in watery places, possibly as part of the performance of a charm to mark the completion of a vow of pilgrimage, or as a thanks offering to a saint for a cure or miracle. The act of depositing a pilgrim badge in water was perhaps a common practice but not one that was documented in medieval texts.

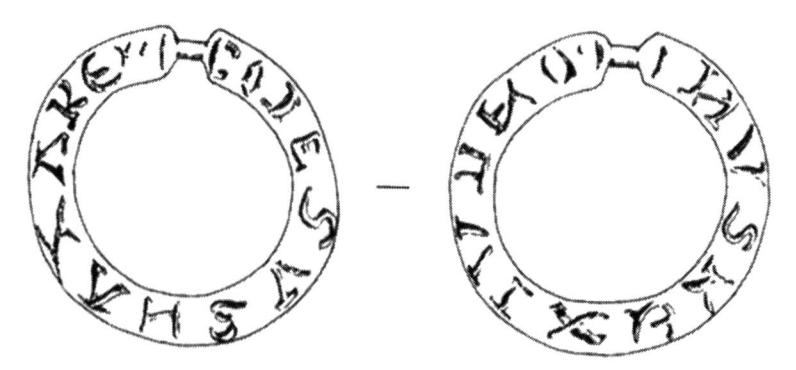

Figure 28.1 Silver brooch inscribed with the Holy Name from West Hartburn, diameter 30 mm.
Source: Reproduced with permission of Eleanor Standley (2013).

Medieval swords and daggers were occasionally deposited in rivers and bogs, extending an ancient prehistoric practice into Christian times. Merrifield argued that the medieval deposition of swords was not votive but instead part of the transition to Christian funerary rites.[26] Because the burial of weapons was not allowed in the consecrated ground of churchyards, their disposal in water provided an alternative mode of disposal. Medieval weapons have been found in the Witham Valley (Lincolnshire), which was densely settled by monasteries that were linked by ten causeways across the fenland. Artefacts recovered from the causeways confirm that the deposition of weapons had continued in the region from the Bronze Age right up to the later medieval period. A total of thirty-two medieval weapons were found, including ten swords, five daggers/long knives, six axe-heads and six spearheads. The weapons were found near causeways associated with monasteries, possibly indicating that religious houses may have controlled the ritual disposal of weapons as part of their provision of funerary rites. David Stocker and Paul Everson surmise that this practice ceased in the late fourteenth century, when it became acceptable to display military equipment around the tomb in the church.[27]

The archaeological recording of placed deposits in medieval houses, churches and monasteries confirms that the act of ritual deposition was widely practised in both lay and religious contexts, and likely executed by both lay and religious practitioners. Paradoxically, the burial or concealment of objects and clothing, or their disposal in rivers or bogs, was rarely documented in medieval texts. Such practices operated outside the highly prescriptive categories of medieval writing: they were invisible to financial records, chronicles and hagiography. The motive behind these deposits has been interpreted as broadly apotropaic or protective; however, the act of burial was more frequently documented in relation to illicit rites of harmful magic. Burial of special creatures or objects was sometimes documented in relation to malignant sorcery: for example, a lizard buried under the threshold stone of a house was intended to harm the fertility of householders and their animals.[28] The interment of animal parts in wall foundations or at boundaries is also documented in

Figure 28.2 Sword with possible magical inscription of unknown meaning in Roman and Lombardic lettering from the River Witham, dated c.1250–1330.

Source: © The Trustees of the British Museum.

the practice of natural magic and medieval recipes record the use of buried earthenware pots for distilling or fermenting ingredients to be employed in medical preparations.[29] The ubiquity of placed deposits is in stark contrast to the rarity with which the practice was documented. This dichotomy challenges previous archaeological methodologies for medieval magic that begin with *documented* associations between objects or materials and their magical powers.[30] The archaeological elucidation of magic also requires a parallel approach that takes *archaeological context and pattern* as its starting point (Figure 28.2).

Magic and materiality

The archaeological study of magic frequently focuses on the use of natural materials that were considered to possess occult properties, or objects that were perceived to hold sacred power acquired through a process of ritual consecration or physical proximity to relics. The scholastic concept of natural magic emerged in the thirteenth century as an explanation for materials and objects that possessed extraordinary properties (such as magnetism). These were regarded as natural marvels within God's universe, in contrast with magic conjured through the power of demons.[31] The boundary between natural and sacred magic was not distinct within later medieval terms of reference: objects such as pilgrim signs were treated similarly to objects made of occult materials and "found objects" such as prehistoric lithics. Even mundane objects and personal garments could acquire sacred power for use as quasi-relics. Sarah Randles discusses the widespread practice of concealing shoes and garments in the fabric of medieval domestic and religious buildings in these terms, proposing that concealment was part of a broader range of magic practices linked with cloth and clothing. She argues that the permeable quality of a garment offered "the ability to absorb virtue from its location, which it can then retain and pass on to the wearer". She quotes a fifteenth-century French vernacular literary text, *The Distaff Gospels*, in which women are encouraged to secretly place their husbands' shirts under the altar stone when the priest is celebrating mass. A husband wearing a garment treated in this way will be easy for a wife to rule over and he will never beat her.[32] It is very likely that local priests would have regarded as illicit any acts that utilized the holy spaces in which the mass was performed or the consecrated materials of the Eucharist.

The most powerful objects combined both natural and sacred properties, for example paternoster beads made from amber or jet and blessed by the priest for use in personal devotion.[33] Jet and amber share inherent physical properties that may have been perceived as evidence of occult power: when rubbed, both substances develop a static charge and emit a smell. These characteristics were stressed in medieval lapidaries, alongside the powers of many minerals and gemstones including coral, rock crystal and sapphire, which were incorporated into jewellery for wearing as amulets or used to embellish reliquaries and other religious material culture.[34] The most influential medieval lapidary was the late eleventh-century *Book of Stones* (*De Lapidis*) written by Bishop Marbode of Rennes, which formed the basis for many later texts. The particular materials revered by medieval people for their occult properties had been prized traditionally for millennia: archaeological evidence confirms the enduring significance of materials including jet, amber, quartz and rock crystal as well as animal materials such as antler and boar tusk.[35]

Jet was one of the most extensively employed occult materials, a fossilized coniferous wood, deep black in colour and easily carved. According to Marbode, jet was efficacious if worn on the body, consumed as a powder, ingested through water in which the material had been steeped or burnt to release beneficial fumes. The healing and anaesthetic properties of jet were recommended for easing conditions ranging from childbirth to toothache, and it was believed to possess powerful apotropaic value to protect from demons and malignant magic.[36] Jet occurs principally in two locations – near Whitby in North Yorkshire and in Galicia in northern Spain – and in both regions it was used to manufacture holy objects and pilgrim signs. It has been suggested that small, jet crucifix pendants were produced in workshops at Whitby Abbey: a distinctive corpus of twenty-two crucifix pendants with ring and dot motif can be dated stylistically to the twelfth century, including four recovered from graves. Damaged pendants and raw materials have been excavated from Whitby Abbey, indicating a possible source of production in monastic workshops.[37] Jet and amber were luxury commodities and it is possible that monasteries actively controlled both access to raw materials and the production of amulets in occult materials.

Jet was used to manufacture a wide range of medieval objects including beads, pendants, rings, brooches, pins, chess pieces, dice, dagger handles and bowls for possible magico-medical use.[38] This distinctive material may have been used for other types of magic such as divination. Bowls, dice and knife handles are noteworthy in this respect as objects used in divination rituals by medieval necromancers, who called upon spirits to guide them in forecasting or decision-making.[39] The archaeological distribution of jet dice and knives in England is biased towards ecclesiastical sites, including the cathedrals and vicars chorals at Winchester, Beverley and York. Divination was often associated with the clergy and this archaeological distribution may indicate the use of objects made from occult natural materials for practising clerical magic.[40]

Animal parts were also used in natural magic, with archaeological evidence for the use of boar tusks and antler tines possibly as fertility amulets: animal *materia medica* was documented especially for use in relation to sex, conception, contraception and birth.[41] Both animal and human bodies were materials for magic, with documented practices including divination from the shoulder blades of animals, human corpses and the clothing of the dead.[42] Infant corpses were evidently regarded as an especially powerful substance, possibly used in rites of sympathetic magic to prevent infant death, or as an occult material in witchcraft. Kieckhefer has suggested that outside learned circles, substances regarded as repugnant or taboo are likely to have been perceived as having occult power. He has noted evidence that midwives and other women accused of witchcraft used infant body parts, either buried as part of a charm or used as an ingredient.[43] However, it is not clear whether such practices actually occurred or whether these stories were intended to fuel the fifteenth-century witchcraft stereotype.

Archaeological evidence reveals that infant corpses were sometimes buried outside consecrated ground, interred in medieval English rural and urban houses dating from the twelfth to the sixteenth centuries. These infant burials were located in spaces that were in daily use as domestic or associated working areas; the burials were usually dug against the exterior walls of the main living rooms and sealed by later floor deposits, indicating that the buildings were still occupied when the interments took place. In some cases, the infant remains were judged to represent stillborns, but others were weeks or months old at the time of death; these infants would surely have been baptized and carried the right to burial in consecrated ground. The infant domestic burials were carefully laid out and some were accompanied by grave goods: animal parts were placed with an infant at Tattenhoe (Bucks) and a spindle whorl and an exotic shell were deposited with an infant at Upton (Gloucesters). I have suggested that the interment of infant corpses in the house may have been linked to rites of fertility, drawing on the evidence of charms for safe childbirth that were recorded in the eleventh-century *Lacnunga*. These charms involved the recitation of words and the performance of actions such as jumping over a grave or collecting grave soil from an infant who had been stillborn.[44] Did the infants buried in medieval houses serve as materials for rites of sympathetic magic, rituals that were intended to protect future births?

Magic and performance

The burial of "odd" deposits can be likened to a charm, a ritual performance that combined words and actions and sometimes involved the use of supporting herbs and objects. The efficacy of the charm was strengthened by performances of the body; for example, apotropaic formulae were written on the body and on substances such as wax to be consumed orally. Portability was also important to facilitate close contact with the body, with textual amulets enclosed in capsules, sacks and purses to be worn on the body.[45] A comparison can be made with devotional jewellery such as reliquary rings and pendants that were relatively common in the fourteenth and fifteenth centuries.[46] Charms were worn on the body by people at all social levels: devotional words were inscribed on brooches, buckles, buttons, girdles, pendants, pouches and rings, as well as on objects carried on the body such as knives, spoons, seals and mirror cases.[47] The most common devotional inscriptions invoked the name of Christ, either in the abbreviations IHS or IHC or INRI (*Jesus Nazarenus Rex Judaeorum*). Euan Cameron observed that such invocation of the names of God "wanders into the realm of the occultist grimoire or spell-book of the intellectual magician".[48] But material culture demonstrates that words and letters held an integral mystique for the non-literate: "mock inscriptions" or false lettering were also common on items such as brooches. These were made and purchased by those who believed in the power of words, but could not read or write them.[49]

The performance of magic also involved the modification or deliberate mutilation of objects, for example the bending of coins and pilgrim badges. This practice can be likened to the folding of charms written on parchment, lead or communion wafers: the act of folding increased the efficacy of the charm by preserving its secrecy and containing its magic.[50] The folding or bending of pilgrim signs can also be compared with the deliberate destruction of magico-medical amulets such as fever amulets thrown into the fire after the afflicted person had recovered.[51] The destruction of the amulet guaranteed that it was specific to the individual and could not be reused, but the act of folding or mutilation was also part of the ritual performance of magic. This premise is documented in relation to the practice of bending coins: miracles recorded at saints' shrines refer to the custom of bending the coin in the name of the saint invoked to heal the sick person.[52] Richard Kelleher notes the frequent mutilation of medieval English coins through bending, piercing and cutting, citing 130 examples of folded coins.[53]

There is growing archaeological evidence that folk magic was performed in rural communities as part of agricultural practices linked to the fertility of fields. Later medieval practices extended traditions recorded in the *aecerbot* charm, dating to the late tenth or early eleventh century, in which land believed to have been cursed by a sorcerer was cleansed through an elaborate ceremony involving the blessing of turves.[54] Recent archaeological study of metal-detected objects in England has identified a pattern in which ampullae were deliberately damaged before being discarded in cultivated fields.[55] Ampullae were pilgrim signs in the form of miniature vessels used to contain water, oil or dust collected from saints' shrines and holy wells. While pilgrim badges are more typically recovered from excavated, urban contexts (including the watery contexts discussed above), ampullae are more typically recovered from rural contexts and particularly from cultivated fields. They were deliberately damaged by crimping or even biting, presumably to open the seal in order to pour the contents on the fields before discarding the vessel. Folded coins are also

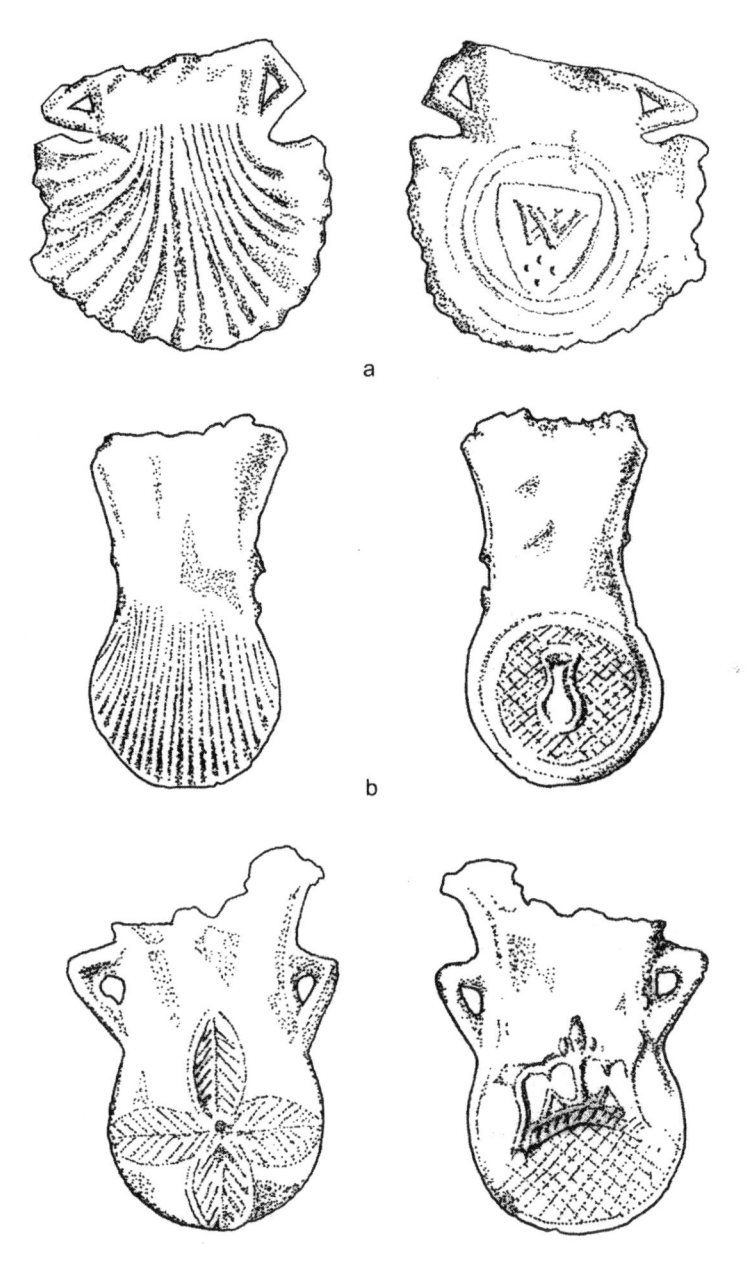

Figure 28.3 Deliberately damaged ampullae; from top to bottom PAS nos IOW-ED2A21, NCL-44A762 and LVPL-50FD62.

Source: Reproduced with permission of the Portable Antiquities Scheme.

found especially in plough-soil, suggesting the possibility of a deliberate act of discard as an offering to protect or enhance the fertility of fields.[56] Ceremonies for blessing the fields are recorded in which the parish priest sprinkled holy water and recited the biblical passage of Genesis 1: 28.[57]

> And God blessed them. And God said to them, "Be fruitful and multiply and fill the earth and subdue it, and have dominion over the fish of the sea and over the birds of the heavens and over every living thing that moves on the earth."

The archaeological evidence of discarded coins and ampullae suggests that such liturgies in the field were complemented by the performance of ritual deposition (Figure 28.3).

Magic, craft and technology

A connection between magic and technology can be demonstrated particularly in medieval monastic contexts. For example, the monks of St Augustine, Canterbury, collected medical, alchemical, craft and technical recipes and had access to facilities for making magical objects: they kept equipment and utensils in the infirmary, used the plumber's workshop and commissioned work from metal craftsmen in the town.[58] Archaeological evidence for such activities includes specialist vessels of glass and pottery. At Glastonbury Abbey, for example, two perforated pottery jars, four distilling bases and two crucibles were linked with specialist scientific and technical activities.[59] It has been suggested that the perforated pottery jars would have been used for the production of white lead and for a variety of distillation and fermentation processes, while the distilling bases may have been used in the production of medicines or in alchemical practices.

It has recently been demonstrated that monasteries drew from more popular traditions of magic to aid technical production. The workshops at the monastery of San Vincenzo Maggiore (Isernia, Italy) have produced over one hundred prehistoric stone tools, many in structural contexts including floor surfaces, post-holes and furnace linings.[60] The tradition of collecting prehistoric lithics was prevalent across medieval Europe. These objects were not recognized as ancient artefacts by medieval people; instead, stone axes were regarded as the physical residue of thunder and flint arrowheads were considered to be "elf-shot" or fairy weapons. They were believed to provide protection against lightning strikes and were employed as placed deposits in medieval domestic and ecclesiastical contexts.[61]

The prehistoric stone tools at San Vincenzo Maggiore were deposited with workshop demolition and occupation deposits dating to the eighth and ninth centuries and including semi-precious gemstones and craft residues.[62] They seem to have been employed in the production of high-status craft objects and possibly in the protection of the workshops against fire. It is suggested that a miniature greenstone axe may have been used in a manner described in a craft-working treatise dated to the twelfth to thirteenth century and attributed to Eraclius, in which green glass, burnt copper and "burnt thunder-bolts" are mixed with ground clear glass to create a green glaze for pottery vessels.[63] A large igneous axe dated to the Copper Age was discovered beneath a collapsed roof-tile deposit in a granary. The excavators suggest that this may have been suspended from the roof as a thunderbolt amulet, in the manner described by Bishop Marbode. The majority of prehistoric stone tools from San Vincenzo Maggiore were recovered from areas that were at high risk from fire such as the glass foundry, metalworking workshops and bell-casting pit (Figure 28.4). The

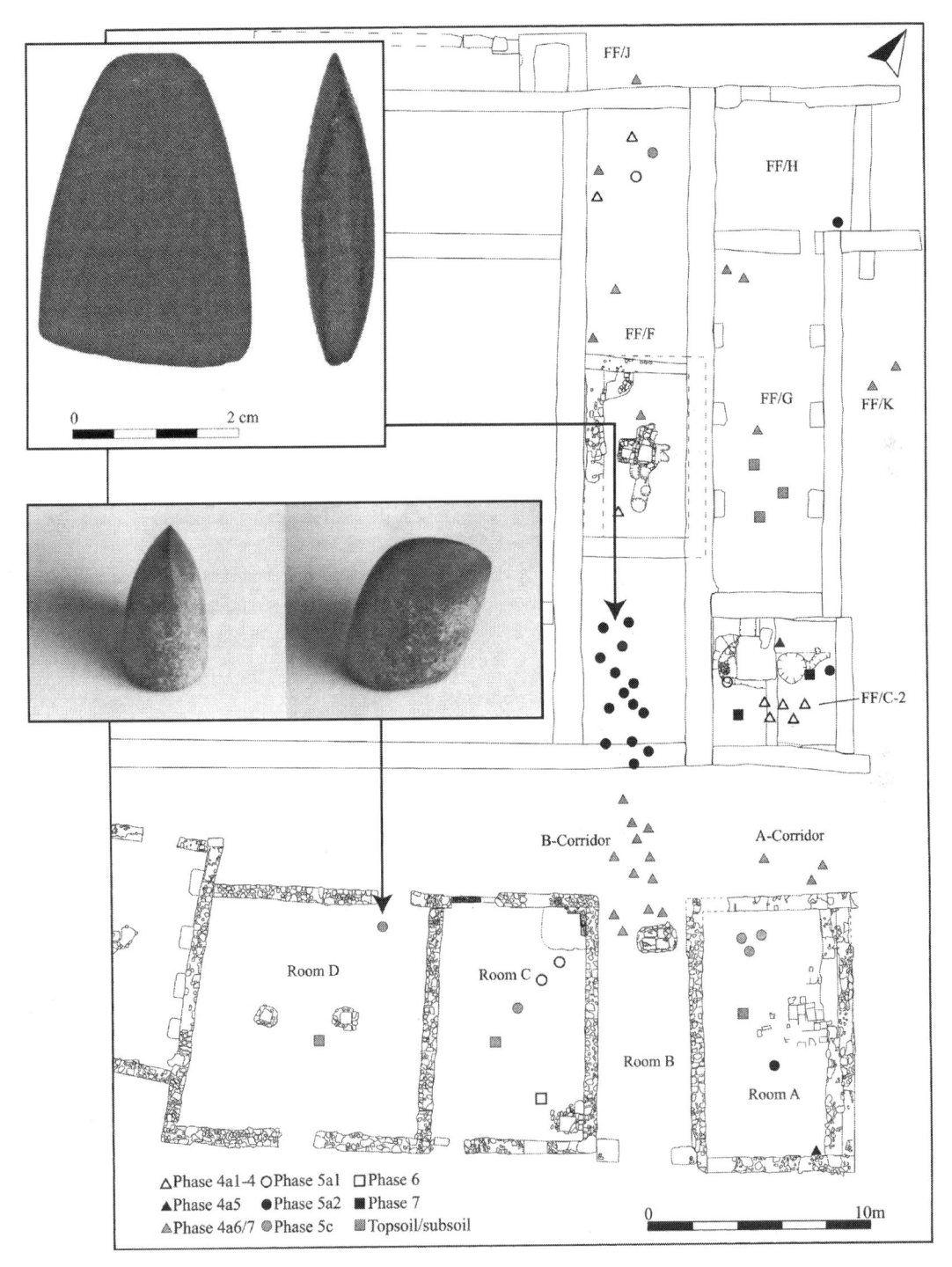

Figure 28.4 Location of stone axes from the workshops at San Vincenzo Maggiore.

Source: Reproduced with permission of Richard Hodges and John Mitchell (2011).

excavators suggest that the prehistoric lithics at San Vincenzo may have been employed as sympathetic magic – on the basis that objects believed to protect against lightning may also have been used to guard against fire.[64] The evidence from San Vincenzo indicates the use of prehistoric lithics as magic objects both for specialist technical production and for apotropaic use.

The compelling evidence from San Vincenzo demonstrates the potential for future investigation of magic in the practice of medieval technology and broader craft production. Tools in more common use were sometimes associated with magic, especially those linked with the transformation of materials. Whetstones are a good example: these utilitarian objects were used to sharpen iron tools in the home and workshop; they were also favoured objects for concealing as placed deposits in buildings in Finland and Sweden.[65] Whetstones were noted as magical objects by Pliny the Elder in his *Natural History*, and they occur in Old English and Old Norse literature as symbols of authority. The connection between power and the act of sharpening may have derived from the ritual significance of the ironsmith: the act of transforming metal was regarded as magical in many societies, for example in the British Iron Age.[66] The smith's craft was also associated with ritual deposition: a cache of smith's tools was excavated from a late Saxon building at Bishopstone (E. Sussex), interpreted as an act of ritual closure when the building was abandoned.[67]

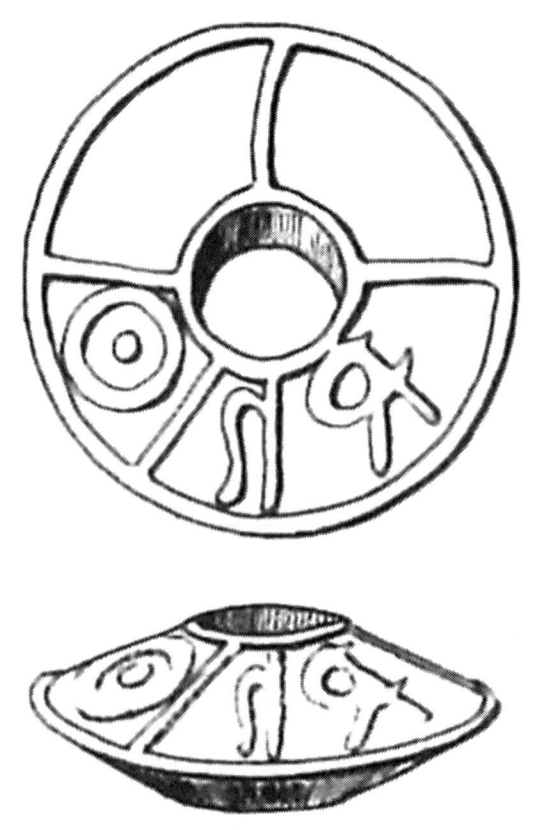

Figure 28.5 Lead spindle-whorl cast with reversed "Rho" from West Hartburn, diameter 25 mm.
Source: Reproduced with permission of Eleanor Standley (2013).

A comparison can be made with the female domestic craft of textile production, culturally associated with magic and the spinning of spells.[68] Spindle whorls seem to have been particularly significant among weaving tools, used with a drop spindle for spinning flax and wool; these common domestic objects were occasionally placed in later medieval coffins and graves, including a domestic infant burial at Upton.[69] Utilitarian objects of stone, pottery, wood, bone or lead were sometimes transformed by magic words: a lead spindle whorl excavated from the village of West Hartburn (co. Durham) was cast with the reversed letters "Rho", referring to the Christian symbol *Chi-Rho*, the monogram for *Christos* (Figure 28.5). Standley notes a corpus of at least thirty lead spindle whorls from medieval England that were marked with lettering.[70]

Magic and the dead

Material evidence for magic in Anglo-Saxon graves has been used to identify the individual burials of female *practitioners* of magic (discussed above); in contrast, material evidence in later medieval graves has been used to identify the *recipients* of magic, and from this to infer possible motivations and agents.[71] The vast majority of later medieval Christians were wrapped in a shroud and buried in a simple earth-cut grave. But a small minority of burials included special materials in the preparation of the grave lining, placed within the grave or coffin, or within the shroud. Archaeological analysis of excavated burials from medieval England suggests that around two to three per cent had objects placed in close contact with the corpse.[72] The true figure is likely to have been much greater: a high proportion of these items were organic materials – including textiles, bone, wood and even beeswax – and most would have perished in the ground. Mortuary practices were highly localized, with significant variations observed between monastic and lay cemeteries, and customs varying chronologically and regionally.

Despite these caveats, distinctive patterns can be detected in the selection of grave goods placed with the dead in later medieval England. These included personal objects (dress accessories and grooming tools), domestic and devotional items, and natural materials and antique objects (or *objets trouvé*). Some of these objects were associated with magic in domestic contexts, such as spindle whorls, or connected with pilgrimage and rites in the fields (pilgrim signs and folded coins). Occult materials are relatively rare, but jet pendant crosses have been recovered from graves in monastic cemeteries.[73] A striking number of these objects may be regarded as "traditional" grave goods, continuing practices prevalent in prehistoric, Roman and pagan Anglo-Saxon burials such as the deposition of beads, coins, fossils, animal teeth and quartz pebbles with the dead. The number of "found objects" is striking: tiles, pottery, coins and bracelets of Roman date were buried with the medieval dead. The placement of such grave goods was targeted at certain social groups, in particular children in both monastic and lay cemeteries.[74]

Potential evidence for the use of childbirth amulets has also been detected in the graves of women who may have died in childbirth: a folded lead parcel was founded near the abdomen of a female skeleton at the Benedictine monastery of St James in Bristol, which contained granular material likely to be parchment; a female burial at the hospital of St Mary Spital, London, had a textile bundle placed between her legs, also thought to contain parchment.[75] It has been suggested that the material residues of charms may have been deposited in graves in the form of wooden wands or rods. Willow, hazel or poplar wands or rods were placed in graves in England and Scandinavia, dating from the eleventh century right up to the fourteenth or fifteenth centuries, and found with men, women and children. These have been interpreted as objects connected with journeying or healing charms, for example, as indicated in an Old English metrical charm recorded in an eleventh-century manuscript given to Exeter Cathedral by Leofric (d. 1072). This invokes protection by means of a staff: "I chant a victory charm; I carry a victory staff; victory by means of words, and victory by means of an object".[76]

I have argued that traces of magic in later medieval graves were intended primarily to support the vulnerable dead on their journey through purgatory, and to protect or heal the corpse in the grave, perhaps to assist with its reanimation on judgement day. It may be suggested that magic for the dead was practised by women in the care of their families, based on evidence from visual sources that it was women who stripped and washed corpses and wrapped them in the shroud for burial. But there are also indications that magic may have been used to protect the living from the restless dead – to guard against revenants. Stephen Gordon has argued that the act of lining graves with burnt materials may have been a strategy targeted at corpses that appeared unusual and were therefore feared. He cites the use of burnt materials in *Bald's Leechbook*, dating to the ninth century, as a remedy against swelling. He extends this argument to the inclusion of burnt materials in graves, suggesting that the rite was reserved for cadavers that exhibited bloating and swelling, and which were therefore regarded as candidates for revenants.[77]

Future directions

Archaeological discussion has focused on the intersection of magic with religious devotion and the use of special materials for healing and protection. Archaeological evidence reveals a range of rites that were not documented in medieval texts, including the placement of objects with the dead, the burial or concealment of efficacious objects in houses and churches, and the deliberate discard of weapons, pilgrim signs and coins in water or on cultivated land. How should we classify these practices according to definitions of medieval magic? For example, can we regard "odd" deposits as the material residues of charms? It is likely that these rituals appealed to Christian agents and the occult power of nature and therefore would have been regarded as acceptable magic. Indeed, it is therefore debateable whether they should be regarded as magic or instead as "unofficial" Christian rituals.[78] The practice of burying infants in the home is an important exception – it seems inconceivable that medieval clergy would have sanctioned such rites. Should we regard infant burials in medieval homes as evidence for illicit magic?

Magic presents a conceptual and methodological challenge for archaeology due to the inherent difficulty in identifying material evidence as the residue of magical intent. Historians grapple with ambiguities in the definition of medieval magic but their starting point can be found in normative categories of magic as defined by the authors and critics of magic texts. The starting point for archaeologists is in the material record, which has no direct voice; the subtleties of meaning, intention and agency can only be unlocked by developing theoretical frameworks for interpreting archaeological evidence.[79] Magic as ritual practice lacks "visibility" in the archaeological record, in the same way that social categories such as gender, age and disability were seemingly invisible in material evidence until appropriate frameworks for investigation were developed. A further barrier is that the prevailing method of archaeology is to identify and interpret *normative* patterns in material evidence. This presents a paradox for the archaeology of medieval magic, where some of the most fruitful avenues of research have developed from reflection on "odd" deposits and statistically insignificant patterns, for example in relation to objects and materials placed in a small minority of medieval graves or found occasionally as concealed deposits in surviving buildings. Archaeologists may find it productive to consider magic as ritual practice that is by definition exceptional and alternative to normative categories and dominant patterns.[80] To render magic "visible" in the archaeological record, we must be alert to the *anomalous, unusual and odd*.[81] The archaeology of magic is found in practices that are detected in the archaeological record relatively rarely such as placed or "odd" deposits that may be hidden or involve the use of special materials, mysterious words or symbols.

Archaeology reveals the ritual significance over the *longue durée* of the use of certain natural materials and old or "found objects" (*objets trouvé*). Such objects were employed in medieval magic, deliberately buried in sacred and domestic contexts, placed with the dead or employed in performances linked to healing, protection, fertility and technology. How should we interpret evidence for apparent continuities in ritual practice over hundreds or thousands of years? We must be sceptical in interpreting material evidence as proof that ancient belief systems survived or that pagan practices persisted.[82] However, it is clear that some material practices continued after the conversion to Christianity such as the apotropaic use of found objects and natural materials and the creation of concealed or placed deposits. Such similarities of practice do not necessarily constitute evidence for the direct *continuity* of beliefs across time, but they perhaps indicate a long-standing, common repertoire of *ritual actions*. Future research on the archaeology of magic should focus closer attention on the *local experience* of the conversion process: how ritual actions took on new meanings in Christian contexts, how they may have been communicated between generations and how they were transformed over time.

The archaeological documentation of medieval magic is just beginning. It is not yet clear whether material practices were consistent across all social levels: for example, what is the archaeological evidence for the practice of magic in castles and other elite settlements?[83] What is the evidence for "crisis magic": did social crises such as the Black Death lead to an increase in folk magic within local communities? There is also scope to consider love magic in relation to material culture worn or carried on the body.[84] Comparative studies are needed between categories of medieval settlement, and within and between regions, to chart the incidence of particular rites, their chronological currency and the relative influence of literate magic *versus* traditional practices. For instance, is there broader evidence for monasteries controlling the production of amulets in occult materials or the disposal of weapons in water (as indicated at Whitby and in the Witham Valley)? Can we chart additional patterns in the deliberate discard of metal artefacts and whether these practices focused on particular points in the landscape? Study of magic in the landscape has been accelerated by new sources of evidence, in particular the study of metal small finds that have been reported by metal detectorists under the terms of the UK Portable Antiquities Scheme (from 1997).[85] These data have illuminated patterns in the use of material culture in the medieval countryside, balancing the increase in urban evidence that has resulted from the growing number of archaeological excavations linked to commercial developments.

There is rich potential for the archaeological examination of literate magic, particularly in the elite context of castles and monasteries. Does archaeological evidence survive for image magic, divination and necromancy? How does the archaeological study of monastic medicine and industry illuminate clerical attitudes at the intersection of religion, science and magic? Can we detect a broader connection between magic, technology and craft-working (as evidenced at San Vincenzo Maggiore)? The foundations for the archaeology of magic have been established by working from documented associations between objects and materials and their magic powers. A more contextual approach is now needed, a framework that takes archaeological context and pattern as its starting point, working from the "odd", unusual and exceptional to probe the boundaries and definitions of medieval belief.

Notes

1 Sarah Randles, "Material Magic: The Deliberate Concealment of Footwear and Other Clothing," *Parergon* 30, no. 2 (2013): 109–28; Richard Kieckhefer, *Magic in the Middle Ages* (Cambridge: Cambridge University Press, 2000), 47.
2 Euan Cameron, *Enchanted Europe. Superstition, Reason and Religion 1250–1750* (Oxford: Oxford University Press, 2010), 6; Richard Kieckhefer, "The Specific Rationality of Medieval Magic," *American Historical Review* 99 (1994): 833.
3 Catherine Rider, *Magic and Religion in Medieval England* (London: Reaktion Books, 2012), 8–15.
4 Roberta Gilchrist, "Magic for the Dead? The Archaeology of Magic in Later Medieval Burials," *Medieval Archaeology* 52 (2008): 119–59.
5 Robert Bartlett, *The Natural and the Supernatural in the Middle Ages* (Cambridge: Cambridge University Press, 2008); Kieckhefer, "Specific Rationality of Medieval Magic," 821–24; Roberta Gilchrist, *Medieval Life: Archaeology and the Life Course* (Woodbridge: Boydell and Brewer, 2012), 216–52.
6 Karen Jolly, *Popular Religion in Late Saxon England. Elf Charms in Context* (Chapel Hill: University of North Carolina, 1996); Karen Jolly, "Medieval Magic: Definitions, Beliefs, Practices," in *Witchcraft and Magic in Europe: The Middle Ages*, ed. Karen Jolly, Catharina Raudvere and Edward Peters (London: Athlone, 2002), 1–71.
7 Ralph Merrifield, *The Archaeology of Ritual and Magic* (London: Batsford, 1987), 6, 18.
8 Audrey L. Meaney, *Anglo-Saxon Amulets and Curing Stones* (Oxford: British Archaeology Report 96, 1981), 24–27.
9 Audrey L. Meaney, "Women, Witchcraft and Magic in Anglo-Saxon England," in *Superstition and Popular Medicine in Anglo-Saxon England*, ed. D.G. Scragg (Manchester: Manchester Centre for Anglo-Saxon Studies, 1989).
10 Gilchrist, "Magic for the Dead?"
11 Dawn M. Hadley, "Burial, Belief and Identity in Later Anglo-Saxon England," in *Reflections: 50 Years of Medieval Archaeology*, ed. Roberta Gilchrist and Andrew Reynolds (Leeds: Maney, 2009); Eleanor R. Standley, *Trinkets and Charms. The Use, Meaning and Significance of Dress Accessories 1300–1700* (Oxford: Institute of Archaeology, University of Oxford, 2013); Chris Caple, "The Apotropaic Symbolled Threshold to Nevern Castle – Castle Nanhyfer," *The Archaeological Journal* 169 (2012): 422–52; Sonja Hukantaival, "Finding Folk Religion: An Archaeology of 'Strange' Behaviour," *Folklore: Electronic Journal of Folklore* 55 (2013): 99–124; Stephen Gordon, "Disease, Sin and the Walking Dead in Medieval England, 1100–1350. A Note on the Documentary and Archaeological Evidence," in *Medicine, Healing and Performance* ed. Effie Gemi-Iordanou et al. (Oxford: Oxbow, 2014), 55–70.
12 Brian Hoggard, "The Archaeology of Counter-Witchcraft and Popular Magic," in *Beyond the Witch Trials: Witchcraft and Magic in Enlightenment Europe* (Manchester: Manchester University Press, 2004), 167–86.
13 Ann-Britt Falk, *En Grundläggande Handling. Byggnadsoffer Och Dagligt Liv i Medeltid* (Lund: Nordic Academic Press, 2008); Hukantaival, "Finding Folk Religion." For the folklore approach in British archaeology, see also Amy Gavin-Schwarz, "Archaeology and Folklore of Material Culture, Ritual and Everyday Life," *International Journal of Historical Archaeology* 5, no. 4 (2001): 263–80.
14 Leszek Gordela and P. Duma, "Untimely Death: Atypical Burials of Children in Early and Late Medieval Poland," *World Archaeology* 45, no. 2 (2013): 314–32.
15 Joanna Brück, "Ritual and Rationality: Some Problems of Interpretation in European Archaeology," *European Journal of Archaeology* 2, no. 3 (1999): 313–44. For a critical review of the two distinct concepts of "structured deposition" and "odd deposits" in archaeology, see Duncan Garrow, "Odd

Deposits and Average Practice. A Critical History of the Concept of Structured Deposition," *Archaeological Dialogues* 19, no. 2 (2012): 85–115.

16 Helena Hamerow, "'Special Deposits' in Anglo-Saxon Settlements," *Medieval Archaeology* 50 (2006): 1–30; Gilchrist, *Medieval Life*.

17 Hamerow, "Special Deposits"; Michael Fulford, "Links with the Past: Persuasive 'Ritual' Behaviour in Roman Britain," *Britannia* 32 (2001); James Morris and Ben Jervis, "What's so Special? A Reinterpretation of Anglo-Saxon 'Special Deposits'," *Medieval Archaeology* 55 (2011): 66–81.

18 Kieckhefer, "Special Rationality of Medieval Magic"; Brück, "Ritual and Rationality."

19 Merrifield, *Archaeology of Ritual and Magic*.

20 Falk, *En Grundläggande Handling*, 207–8.

21 Gilchrist, *Medieval Life*, 230–36; Brian Spencer, *Pilgrim Souvenirs and Secular Badges: Medieval Finds from Excavations in London* (London: HMSO, 1998), 20.

22 Andrew Chapman, *West Cotton, Raunds. A Study of Medieval Settlement Dynamics AD 450–1450. Excavation of a Deserted Medieval Hamlet in Northamptonshire* 1985–89 (Oxford: Oxbow, 2010), 157–61; Caple, "The Apotropaic Symbolled Threshold," 446–47.

23 Standley, *Trinkets and Charms*, 83.

24 Spencer, *Pilgrim Souvenirs and Secular Badges*; Merrifield, *Archaeology of Ritual and Magic*, 109.

25 Don C. Skemer, *Binding Words. Textual Amulets in the Middle Ages* (University Park: University of Pennsylvania Press, 2006), 68.

26 Richard Bradley, *The Passage of Arms: An Archaeological Analysis of Prehistoric Hoards and Votive Deposits* (Cambridge: Cambridge University Press, 1990); Merrifield, *Archaeology of Ritual and Magic*.

27 David Stocker and Paul Everson, "The Straight and Narrow Way: Fenland Causeways and the Conversion of the Landscape in the Witham Valley, Lincolnshire," in *The Cross Goes North: Processes of Conversion in Northern Europe, AD 300–1300*, ed. Martin Carver (Woodbridge: Boydell and Brewer/York Medieval Press, 2003).

28 Michael D. Bailey, "From Sorcery to Witchcraft: Clerical Conception of Magic in the Later Middle Ages," *Speculum* 76, no. 4 (2001): 981.

29 Sophie Page, *Magic in the Cloister. Pious Motives, Illicit Interests and Occult Approaches to the Medieval Universe* (University Park: University of Pennsylvania Press, 2013), 47; Stephen Moorhouse, "Documentary Evidence for the Uses of Medieval Pottery: An Interim Statement," *Medieval Ceramics* 2 (1978): 10.

30 Meaney, *Anglo-Saxon Amulets and Curing Stones*.

31 Page, *Magic in the Cloister*, 31.

32 Randles, "Material Magic," 119.

33 Standley, *Trinkets and Charms*, 67; Gilchrist, *Medieval Life*, 235.

34 Joan Evans, *Magical Jewels of the Middle Ages and Renaissance* (London: Constable, 1922); Standley, *Trinkets and Charms*, 86–88; Gilchrist, *Medieval Life*, 157–58.

35 Chantal Conneller, *An Archaeology of Materials* (London: Routledge, 2011); Andrew M. Jones, *Prehistoric Materialities: Becoming Material in Prehistoric Britain and Ireland* (Oxford: Oxford University Press, 2011).

36 Evans, *Magical Jewels*.

37 Elizabeth Pierce, "Jet Cross Pendants from the British Isles and Beyond: Forms, Distribution and Use," *Medieval Archaeology* 57 (2013): 198–211.

38 Gilchrist, *Medieval Life*, 267–71.

39 Richard Kieckhefer, *Forbidden Rites: A Necromancer's Manual of the Fifteenth Century* (Stroud: Sutton, 1997), 97.

40 Gilchrist, *Medieval Life*, 167.

41 Gilchrist, *Medieval Life*, 240–41; Page, *Magic in the Cloister*, 40–41.

42 Kieckhefer, *Forbidden Rites*, 113; Sophie Page, *Magic in Medieval Manuscripts* (London: The British Library, 2004), 56.

43 Kieckhefer, "Specific Rationality of Medieval Magic," 834; Kieckhefer, *Magic in the Middle Ages*, 59, 62.

44 Gilchrist, *Medieval Life*, 219–23, 284–85.

45 Skemer, *Binding Words*, 1–2.

46 David Hinton, *Gold and Gilt, Pots and Pins* (Oxford: Oxford University Press, 2005), 245.

47 Gilchrist, *Medieval Life*, 272–74.

48 Cameron, *Enchanted Europe*, 53.

49. Gilchrist, *Medieval Life*, 162–64.
50. Lea T. Olsan, "Charms and Prayers in Medieval Medical Theory and Practice," *Social Theory of Medicine* 16 (2003): 362.
51. Skemer, *Binding Words*, 188.
52. Merrifield, *Archaeology of Ritual and Magic*, 91; Ronald C. Finucane, *Miracles and Pilgrims: Popular Beliefs in Medieval England* (London: Dent, 1977), 94–96.
53. Richard Kelleher, "The Re-Use of Coins in Medieval England and Wales *c*. 1050–1550: An Introductory Survey," *Yorkshire Numismatist* 4 (2012): 130.
54. Jolly, *Popular Religion in Late Saxon England*, 6–12.
55. William Anderson, "Blessing the Fields? A Study of Late-Medieval Ampullae from England and Wales," *Medieval Archaeology* 54 (2010): 182–203.
56. Kelleher, "The Re-Use of Coins," 195.
57. Kieckhefer, *Magic in the Middle Ages*, 58.
58. Page, *Magic in the Cloister*, 8.
59. Stephen Moorhouse, "Medieval Distilling Apparatus of Glass and Pottery," *Medieval Archaeology* 16 (1972): 3–21; Oliver Kent, "Wares Associated with Specialist Scientific and Technical Activities," in *Glastonbury Abbey: Archaeological Investigations 1904–1979*, Roberta Gilchrist and Cheryl Green (London: Society of Antiquaries Monograph, 2015): 276–8.
60. Karen Francis and Mother Philip Kline, "Prehistoric Stone Tools in Medieval Contexts," In *San Vincenzo Maggiore and its Workshops*. Archaeological Monographs of the British School at Rome 17, ed. Richard Hodges et al. (London: The British Academy, 2011).
61. Merrifield, *Archaeology of Ritual and Magic*, 10–16; Peter Carelli, "Thunder and Lightning, Magical Miracles. On the Popular Myth of Thunderbolts and the Presence of Stone-Age Artefacts in Medieval Deposits," in *Visions of the Past: Trends and Traditions in Swedish Medieval Archaeology*, ed. Hans Anderson et al. (Stockholm: Central Board of National Antiquities, 1997); Gilchrist, *Medieval Life*, 247.
62. Francis and Kline, "Prehistoric Stone Tools in Medieval Contexts."
63. Eraclius, *De Coloribus et Artibus Romanorum* III.1; Mary P. Merrifield, *Original Treatises on the Arts of Painting* (New York: Dover Publications, 1967), 204–5.
64. Francis and Kline, "Prehistoric Stone Tools in Medieval Contexts," 398.
65. Stephen A. Mitchell, "The Whetstone as Symbol of Authority in Old English and Old Norse," *Scandinavian Studies* 57 (1985): 1–31; Hukantaival, "Finding Folk Religion," 111–12.
66. Melanie Giles, "Making Metal and Forging Relations: Ironworking in the British Iron Age," *Oxford Journal of Archaeology* 26, no. 4 (2007): 395–413.
67. Gabor Thomas, "The Symbolic Lives of Late Anglo-Saxon Settlements: A Timber Structure and Iron Hoard from Bishopstone, East Sussex," *The Archaeological Journal* 165 (2008): 334–98.
68. Meaney, *Anglo-Saxon Amulets and Curing Stones*, 185; Randles, "Material Magic," 122; Gilchrist, "Magic for the Dead?" 132–33.
69. Roberta Gilchrist and Barney Sloane, *Requiem: The Medieval Monastic Cemetery in Britain* (London: Museum of London Archaeology Service, 2005), 102–3.
70. Standley, *Trinkets and Charms*, 84.
71. Meaney, *Anglo-Saxon Amulets and Curing Stones*; Gilchrist, "Magic for the Dead?"
72. Gilchrist and Sloane, *Requiem*; Gilchrist, *Medieval Life*, 200–15.
73. Pierce, "Jet Cross Pendants"; Standley, *Trinkets and Charms*.
74. Gilchrist and Sloane, *Requiem*; Gilchrist, "Magic for the Dead?" Gilchrist, *Medieval Life*, 277–83.
75. Reg Jackson, *Excavations at St James's Priory, Bristol* (Oxford: Oxbow Books, 2006), 141; Gilchrist and Sloane, *Requiem*, 200.
76. Gilchrist and Sloane, *Requiem*, 126, 171–74; Gilchrist, "Magic for the Dead?" 128; Felix Grendon, "The Anglo-Saxon Charms," *The Journal of American Folklore* 22 (1909): 176–79.
77. Gordon, "Disease, Sin and the Walking Dead," 64–65.
78. Rider, *Magic and Religion*, 11; Kieckhefer, "Specific Rationality of Medieval Magic," 833.
79. Aleksandra McClain, "Theory, Disciplinary Perspectives and the Archaeology of Later Medieval England," *Medieval Archaeology* 56 (2010): 131–70.
80. Jolly, "Medieval Magic," 1.
81. Jones, *Prehistoric Materialities*, 2; Brück, "Ritual and Rationality"; Garrow, "Odd Deposits and Average Practice".

82 Stephen Mitchell et al., "Witchcraft and Deep Time – a Debate at Harvard," *Antiquity* 84 (2010): 864–79.
83 Candidates for odd deposits have been suggested at Barnard Castle, Co Durham, and Nevern Castle: Caple, "The Apotropaic Symbolled Threshold"; Standley, *Trinkets and Charms*. An important magic object recently identified at the Dutch castle of Doornenburg – a late medieval *Sigillum Dei* – is likely to have originated in an urban context and to have been reused as building material in the reconstruction of the castle after its destruction in 1945: László Sándor Chardonnens and Jan R Veenstra, "Carved in Lead and Concealed in Stone: a Late Medieval *Sigillum Dei* at Doornenburg Castle," *Magic, Ritual and Witchcraft* 9, no. 2 (2014): 123.
84 There is a growing literature on the material culture of love but little explicit discussion of love magic. See Standley, *Trinkets and Charms*, Gilchrist, *Medieval Life*; Malcolm Jones, *The Secret Middle Ages. Discovering the Real Medieval World* (Stroud: Sutton, 2002); Gemma Watson, "Medieval Mentalities and Material Culture: The Archaeology of Courtly Love, Gender and Sexuality in London, *c.* 1100–1500" (MA dissertation, University of Reading, 2007).
85 http://finds.org.uk/.

29

THE VISUAL CULTURE OF MAGIC IN THE MIDDLE AGES

Alejandro García Avilés

Magicians as wise men

When in the 1470s the artist of the *Florentine Picture Chronicle* depicted the sorcerer Hostanes – a follower of Zoroaster – (see Figure 29.1), he had no doubts that the magician should appear in the guise of an oriental wise man inside a magic circle with several burning censers, invoking demons, book in hand, with some of the demons and evil creatures around also holding books and rolls.[1]

Some years later, in 1511, a woodcut by Hans Schäufelein conflated ritual magic, in the figure of a male magician, with different forms of sorcery and *maleficium* as practised by witches. In the centre of the scene, a male magician is dressed in ritual garb in the middle of a magic circle with a book and sword in his hands, symbolizing the knowledge needed to perform ritual magic and the power it confers. Around Schäufelein's magician, there are different forms of sorcery and magic carried out by old women, two among them riding goats and another having sexual intercourse with a devil. Below is the final outcome of all these activities, eternal punishment in the fires of hell. We find in these pictures an iconography of the witch finding its way, as well as an already established figure of the magician as a wise man who stands inside a magic circle for the sake of protecting himself from the evil action of the demons he invokes. A magician appears inside a magical circle reading a book at least as early as the thirteenth-century *Cantigas* by Alfonso X (Cantiga 125, El Escorial, MS T.I.1, fol. 177v; ca. 1270–84), and probably in the 1307–8 paintings in the Palazzo della Ragione, which we know were repainted after a fire in 1420.[2] Magical circles are a fixed value in the late medieval imaginary of magic: Odo of Cheriton, Caesarius of Heisterbach and William of Auvergne allude to them as early as the thirteenth century,[3] and precise instructions for their fabrication can be found in Honorius's *Liber iuratus*.[4]

While early modern representations of witchcraft and witches have been the subject of intense study in recent years,[5] images of medieval magic and magicians have barely aroused the curiosity of art historians, and scarcely that of medievalists in general,[6] despite the fact that these images can help to chart the shifts in attitudes towards magic in the Middle Ages. My focus will be here on the iconography of magic and magicians in the Middle Ages, privileging learned magic over the many visual forms of "superstition" and "popular magic". A full chapter on the visual culture of magic in the Middle Ages should also consider issues such as the material culture of magic and the use of diagrams in medieval magic, but these

Figure 29.1 Hostanes from the Florentine Picture Chronicle, British Museum.

are the subjects of other chapters in this book. Last, not only images of magic but also the magic of images in the Middle Ages should be dealt with, and at the end of this chapter I will briefly comment on them as an additional direction for future research.

The discovery of natural magic in the thirteenth century and the gradual process of its adoption among certain ecclesiastical élites resulted in a new understanding of magic,[7] which can be also discerned in the iconography of the period. As I will show here, while in the early Middle Ages the word "magic" is always a wholly negative term associated with idolatry and paganism, the thirteenth century witnessed a partial change in attitude, and the study of magic even came to be depicted as a discipline in the quest for learning alongside the traditional hierarchy of the Seven Liberal Arts. However, as it was still considered a dangerous discipline, its exercise was strictly confined to the hands of men who were considered wise and morally upright.

The term *magoi* was used by the Ancient Greeks to refer to Persian astrologer-priests such as those who, according to Herodotus, accompanied Xerxes on his visit to Greece.[8] The Ancient Greek word for sorcery, *goeteia*, was joined by *mageia*, a word that described activities, usually of a ritual nature and alien to the official religion, that were designed to confer powers or benefits upon the magician or his client. Most medieval representations of magicians allude to the Persian origins of the word *magus*. In these images, magicians are simply identified as Persian priests, distinguished only by their readily identifiable Phrygian cap, as for example on a twelfth-century capital from Nazareth or in the mosaics of St Mark's, Venice of ca. 1200.[9] These images of magicians therefore lack any peculiar features that would reveal a particular attitude towards magic. In some other representations, the magicians are depicted with no identifying attributes other than being shown to be engaged in the practice of magic itself. So, for example, their privileged relationship to Hell acts as an identifier. In an eleventh-century miniature, the magician Jannes can use magic to go to Hell to rescue his brother Jambres, and it is the scene of Hell, not Jannes's personal appearance, that reveals his profession.[10] Jannes and Jambres were the names of the magicians who lost their battle against Moses and Aaron in the episode of the staff mutated into a serpent. The text illustrated in this miniature is that of the *Apocriphon of Jannes and Jambres*, which reads: "Jambres opened the magical books of his brother Jannes and performed necromancy and brought up from the netherworld the shade [literally "idol"] of his brother".[11] Another eleventh-century manuscript (this a Greek one from Constantinople) shows a scene of necromancy, where two magicians are extracting the entrails of a human corpse. Again, it is their nefarious activity plundering a corpse to use his remains for the sake of necromancy that identifies them, rather than the attributes of their clothing or their appearance.[12] In other instances, the scene illustrated is clear and the magicians do not need further attributes to be recognized, as is the case in the Old English illustrated Hexateuch, which twice depicts Jannes and Jambres together with Moses and Aaron in the presence of Pharaoh.[13]

Jesus the magician?

Only in the legal language of Late Antiquity was a concrete name, *maleficus*, used to specify the difference with the more common term "magus", which would be used throughout the Middle Ages.[14] The most famous Persian magicians in the Christian West are the Wise Men who came to pay tribute to the newly born Christ Child. The story is familiar, and is frequently represented in Christian art as an illustration of the superiority of Christ's power over that of pagan priests. The earliest Christian writers had emphasized the role as magicians of the Persian priests who adored Christ child. Later interpretations of the story, however, stressed Jesus's status as King of the Jews, and so the representations of the Persian magicians depict them as Persian kings. Jesus's miracles would be more spectacular than those of the three Eastern sages, and their visit came to be seen as acknowledgement by the Persian magicians of Christ's superior powers.

Pagans acknowledged the extraordinary importance of Jesus's miracles. The main difference between "miracle" and "magic" lies in whether or not God is understood to be behind the acts performed by the "wonder-worker". In the second century, scholars such as Justin and Origen were forced to defend Jesus from accusations made by Jews and Pagans that he was just another magician who deceived his followers with tricks.[15] Origen responded not by claiming that Jesus's magic alone was effective but by arguing that the source of his powers was divine. In the same way, other popular narratives associated with magic in medieval art, such as the account of the argument between Saint Peter and Simon Magus, are concerned with comparing the power of miracles and magic.[16] These representations emphasize the divine origins of Christian miracle over the demonic foundations of pagan magic. It is a distinction often shown in medieval representations of the Fall of Simon Magus, where devils fail to support him as he falls through the air, as shown in famous examples such as St Lazare, Autun, Vézelay or the mosaics of Norman Sicily such as those in the cathedrals of Monreale or Cefalú.[17] In Romanesque Art, in the context of Gregorian Reform, Simon the Magician represents the sin of Simony as opposed to the figure of Saint Peter:[18] a well-known example is that of the *Porte Miègeville* in Saint-Sernin of Toulouse,

Figure 29.2 Egyptian magicians with magic staffs from a thirteenth-century Parisian *Bible moralisée*. Oxford, Bodleian Library, MS Bodley 270b, fol. 43v.

where Simon is identified as *"Magus"* by an inscription, while another inscription below his feet reads: "Arte furens magica Simon in sua occidit arma" (Misled by his magical art, Simon succumbs to its own weapons).

It was suggested by Thomas Matthews that Jesus was characterized as a magician by his use of a wand or staff, an attribute he is frequently assigned in early Christian art and which is also said to identify pagan magicians.[19] Magic was a concept that Christians associated with their religious enemies, so it is unlikely they would have imagined the son of God as a magician who competed with pagan ones. Rather, they would see him as a worker of wonders, of miracles, who outdid all pagan magic in the name of the Holy Father.[20] The staff does eventually become an element in the visual representation of practitioners of magic and divination. This is an attribute of the magician and the sorcerer that appears relatively late in the history of the iconography,[21] but we can still find it in the late Middle Ages.[22] An exceptional early example is the depiction of the sorceress Circe (Kirke) transforming one of Odysseus's sailors into a pig, painted on a Greek amphora now in Berlin.[23] On other occasions, such as on a fifth-century BCE *lekythos*, the staff, which has been interpreted as a magic wand, is more likely to be simply an instrument for the magician to prepare potions. The sorcerer who holds a staff in the scene in the House of the Dioscuri in Pompei, where she is giving a potion to a young man, has it as her attribute as magician, as well as a pointed hat.[24] Diviners and soothsayers are frequently shown using a staff to read the future in water or other liquids, as for example in a fresco that depicts a scene of lecanomancy from the House of Livia on the Palatine Hill in Rome.[25] In the Middle Ages, the divining staff seems not to be mentioned until late (not before 1400),[26] but the attribute of the staff was already present in the medieval imaginary of magic, as can be seen in a Parisian *Bible moralisée* of the first half of the thirteenth century, where the Egyptian magicians (*malefici*) are depicted with their staffs (see Figure 29.2).[27]

In any case, Jesus's staff identifies him as a wonder- or miracle-worker who surpasses pagan magic and who stands as the typological successor of Moses. This typology was also associated with the figure of Saint Peter striking the rock with a rod, which often appears on Christian sarcophagi.[28]

Magic and idolatry

Early Christian literary representations do not usually attribute magic to women but rather to men.[29] In the early Middle Ages, the *magus* figure became definitively synonymous with ideas of superstition, paganism and idolatry. In his *De doctrina christiana*, Saint Augustine consolidated his attack on magic as the supreme manifestation of paganism and idolatry, and in his *De civitate Dei* he condemned it by linking it to devil worship. It was Augustine's view of magic that would prevail throughout the early Middle Ages.[30] Accounts of religious conversion emphasize Christian superiority over pagan magic. Hagiographies are full of examples of men and women who turn to Christianity after witnessing the superiority of Christian power over magic. The conversion scene in a ninth-century Byzantine manuscript illustrates in a single image how the early Middle Ages linked magic, idolatry and paganism.[31] The textual account is taken from Gregory Nazianzenus's *Homilies*, and it concerns the life of Cyprian the magician. The text, concerned with Cyprian's sainthood, says little about his interest in the sciences of the occult. The scene in Figure 29.3 shows Cyprian as a magician in his early life, and is of great interest because the artist has added details to supplement the

Figure 29.3 Cyprian as a magician from Gregory Nazianzen, *Homilies*, Paris, Bibliothèque nationale de France, MS Gr. 510, fol. 332v.

text. The depiction of Cyprian here reveals the artist's idea of the contrast between magic and the true cult, that is Christian religion.

The story is as follows: Cyprian was a magician who fell in love with a young maiden called Justina, and summoned the services of a demon to seduce her. The demon appeared to Justina, who appealed to the Virgin Mary for protection and thereby drove the demon back. In the illustration, the Byzantine artist has divided the space available into two distinct sections. One depicts pagan activities, the other Christian ones. Thus, a pagan scene of idolatry is countered by a Christian altar stripped of devotional image. Cyprian the magician is an astrologer, an occupation symbolized by the celestial globe in the background, and he has invoked the devil using two idols placed on in a base.[32] In medieval illustrations, we often find hydromancy depicted in relation to the story of Nectanebo.[33] The end of lecanomantic (or hydromantic) rituals was that the gods (or demons) were seen in the water as in a picture.[34] Augustine, quoting Varro, says of Numa that he "… was forced to perform hydromancy, so that he saw images of gods, or better mockeries of the demons (*ludificationes daemonum*)".[35] In this same sense, the Byzantine artist has interpreted the scene as a three-dimensional appearance of the idols of the god emerging from water and liberating not the god but the demon dwelling inside the idols. The demon is shown in this very much damaged miniature as coming back unsuccessful from his mission to attract Justine to Cyprian.

Cyprian's use of idols to conjure the devil is of interest to modern art historians because it reflects Christian ideas about images employed in pagan cults.[36] Pagans believed that spirits of their gods inhabited their images, which in turn gave the images the power to work miracles or to utter prophesies. Christians, on the other hand, believed that these so-called "miracles" were illusions produced by devils around or even inside the pagan statues.[37] This belief, outlined by Athanasius and Origen among others, was well established in Christian thought, as illustrated by the miniature in the Stuttgart Psalter that shows devils swarming around a pagan statue,[38] or Saint Bartholomew's exorcism of a statue as shown in the Anjou Hungarian Legendary.[39]

The choice of a magus's attributes, then, is a window onto how the early medieval artistic imagination understood the conflict between magic and religion. As we have just seen in the extraordinary image from the life of Saint Cyprian, magic, idolatry and paganism were intimately connected in early medieval visual culture. Evil and demons are of course the roots of magic, and for instance in a late Byzantine manuscript, a magician, Theodas, is shown sending demons against his enemy, Josaphat (BnF Grec 1128, fol. 151).

Magic and the Liberal Arts

Magic also represented knowledge that was illicit and forbidden. An image in the now lost copy of the *Hortus deliciarum* revealed how Augustine's condemnation of magic continued to be influential as late as the second half of the twelfth century. The schematic representation of the Liberal Arts in the *Hortus* arranges the personifications of the seven arts around the central figure of Philosophy, flanked by Plato and Socrates.[40] The idea that pagan learning could contribute to the learning of the Christian faithful was one that had already been expounded by the Church Fathers, but they were careful to add that not all pagan knowledge was permissible. In the *Hortus* diagram, a group of figures is excluded from the circle of learning. These figures write at a bookstand, and birds hover by their ears. An inscription identifies them as "poets and magicians", shut out from the circle of knowledge because they are inspired by unclean spirits. A common image in medieval art is the dove of the Holy Spirit, symbolic of divine inspiration, which hovers above well-known figures ranging from King David to Saint Augustine, and is even shown inspiring contemporary medieval authors such as Peter Lombard.[41] This traditional image of the writer inspired by the Holy Spirit was widely popularized by images of Gregory the Great.[42] But the illustration of the *Artes liberales* in the *Hortus deliciarum* inverts this traditional Christian symbol of divine inspiration, and the birds hovering beside the ears of the poets and magicians are birds of ill-omen that provide demonic inspiration instead. The importance of hearing as a means of transmitting devilish thoughts appears in earlier depictions as well. For example, a devil whispers into the ear of the heretic Jovinian in a tenth-century manuscript miniature.[43]

Although Augustine's condemnation of magic was to remain in force throughout the Middle Ages, magic gradually came to be thought of as a "discipline" or "art" in some court and ecclesiastical circles. In his *Disciplina clericalis*, for example, Petrus Alfonsi lists the Seven Liberal Arts and observes that "Philosophers who do not follow the prophets say that the seventh [Liberal Art] is necromancy".[44] Some reference to magic as a branch of the mechanical arts had been made since the twelfth century. However, Petrus Alfonsi's description of magic and philosophy as two names for the same liberal art would appear to represent a new departure in the literature of the period. Although a debate was beginning about the place of magic among the arts, condemnation of it was still rife. In the thirteenth century, for example, John of Dacia contrasted magic, which he considered useless and forbidden, with the liberal and mechanical arts, which he pronounced both useful and necessary.[45] Yet other, influential, early thirteenth-century figures disagreed. William of Auvergne, Bishop of Paris during the second quarter of the thirteenth century, and in his youth an avid student of Arabic astral magic, observed that while natural magic was sometimes labelled necromancy according to philosophy, this was incorrect because in fact it represented the eleventh part of the science of nature.[46] In his scholastic *summa*, the *Magisterium divinale et sapientiale*, William set magic firmly within the Aristotelian natural universe, which conceived of the world as one that operated according to natural laws initially established by God. In the universe seen through Aristotelian eyes, most natural operations are apparent, while some of them are occult, and so those who observe nature and know how to manipulate it are therefore able to perform what is essentially natural magic. Sometimes humans take the observation of nature a step further and try to constrain its forces using demonic powers but, William argued, this is an illusion of the senses caused by the tricks of demons, since only God himself can miraculously supersede natural laws.[47]

It was after the Aristotelian *Libri naturales* were definitely introduced into the syllabus of the Parisian arts faculty in the 1250s, that two figures labelled "Philosophus" and "Magus" were added to the north transept foreportal in Chartres Cathedral (see Figure 29.4).[48]

Figure 29.4 "Philosophus" and "Magus". Sculptures on Chartres Cathedral. Photo: Alejandro García Avilés.

Their beards and long hair are both standard attributes of age and therefore wisdom, and can hardly be said to identify their professions. However, they are depicted with other attributes that do distinguish them. The philosopher holds a stone which he scrutinizes intently. The stone is the symbol par excellence of man's interest in the natural world, and medieval natural philosophers were drawn to explore its hidden properties.[49] Already in an eleventh-century illustration of Hraban Maur's *De rerum naturis* a man holds a stone receiving the powers of the heavenly rays, some decades before Al-Kindi's *De radiis* was known to Western Europe.[50] In a miniature of ca. 1300, a wise man intently scrutinizing a stone appears as representing the observation of nature in a manuscript of *De proprietatibus rerum*, by Bartholomeus Anglicus.[51] At the beginning of the thirteenth century, Gervase of Tilbury speaks of the *virtus intrinseca* of stones, that is their apparent and hidden properties, coupled with a *virtus extrinseca*, which can be conferred on them by rituals of consecration or exorcism. The enchantment of words empower the stones, reinforcing their natural virtues.[52] For his part, the magician (see Figure 29.5) is holding a scroll, and under his feet there is a dragon or a basilisk representing the evil forces he constrains to obey him.[53]

These are substantially the same elements we find in the illustration of "necromancy" in a manuscript of ca. 1270 of Brunetto Latini's *Trésor* (see Figure 29.6).[54]

One of the many activities linked to the Liberal Arts on the sides of a Boethian ladder to reaching knowledge (*Philosophia*) was, in this exceptional image, the practice of necromancy. In the *Trésor* manuscript, the necromancer is represented as a man consulting a book on a

Figure 29.5 "Magus". Chartres Cathedral (detail of Fig. 29.4).

Figure 29.6 Nigromance from Brunetto Latini, *Trésor*, London, British Library, Additional MS 30024, 1v.

lectern, with a demon before him, summoned by the prayers uttered by the magician from the magic book. The image encapsulates the magician's belief in his power to constrain the will of demons for his own benefit.

The magician who invoked devils and who pretended to control nature with illusions and trickery crossed the fine line between passive observation and man's desire to manipulate physical reality. The philosopher, on the other hand, tried simply to understand how nature worked. The philosopher on Chartres Cathedral studies nature so as to better understand it. His counterpart the magus (see Figure 29.5), meanwhile, holds a scroll, symbolic of the ancient spells from arcane texts that he learns to try and harness the forces of evil for his own benefit. Here, these evil forces are represented by the dragon or basilisk that he crushes beneath his feet. These sculptures of the philosopher and the magus would appear to sum up the two sides of this renewed, thirteenth-century interest in nature, namely the desire to observe the natural world and the desire to constrain its hidden forces. The potential effects of magic, as Christian writers saw it, are no more than illusions conjured up by demons. Thus, a magician may believe he commands the forces of evil to perform his bidding, but in fact he is no more than an instrument in the hands of malignant powers. The dragon under the feet of the magician depicted on Chartres Cathedral is just such an evil force, which the magus wrongly believes he controls.

Magic and the demonic

An essential element in magic rituals is the invocation by the magician of demonic forces to compel them to perform his will. As I have said above, the *Liber iuratus* by Honorius of Thebes includes detailed instructions on how to draw a magic circle to protect the magus from evil powers. During the thirteenth century, this key element of the invocation ritual starts to appear in illustrations of magicians' activities as well. The tale of a priest, who lusts after a maiden and who invokes devils to cast a spell on her so his desire is reciprocated, is illustrated in the *Cantigas de Santa Maria* by Alfonso X of Castile (1252–84) (see Figure 29.7).[55]

The text of the story is careful to describe how the priest threatens to shut the demons away in a bottle if they fail to carry out his orders, but it makes no mention of the magic circle that he draws to protect himself from evil spirits. The fact the artist includes this detail when it is not mentioned in the text suggests that by this date the magic circle had come to play an important role in magic rituals. By the late thirteenth century, then, this diagram boundary between two worlds, which protected the magician from the demonic underworld, had become a standard feature of magic rituals.

The crucial aspect of this most despised form of magic, necromancy, was its ability to harness the power of devils. Necromancy involved rituals to attract occult forces, rituals which churchmen interpreted as demonically inspired illusions. The invocation of devils was, without question, contrary to the Christian religion, but on the other hand it was permissible to invoke cosmic forces using spirits that were part of the Christian tradition. These spirits were angels. As David Pingree observed, Alfonso X of Castile had learned from Arabic astral magic that "all magic acts, no matter how loathsome their performance or the baseness of their purpose, are permissible and even carried out by God's power, transmitted through his angels".[56] Alfonso saw the exercise of astral magic as legitimate, although he also recognized that knowledge of it was potentially harmful and so should not be made available to the ignorant. This conclusion was based on the assumption that the power of the stars comes ultimately from God and that this power is transmitted to earth by celestial messengers, among which the most important are angels. Alfonso saw no inconsistency

THE VISUAL CULTURE OF MAGIC

Figure 29.7 Monk inside a magic circle, El Escorial, Real Biblioteca del Monasterio de San Lorenzo, MS T.I.1, fol. 177v.

between his patronage of compilations about astral magic, such as the *Lapidario* or the *Libro de astromagia*, and his statements against magic and magicians in his legal texts, or his condemnation of magic ceremonies in the *Cantigas*. The fundamentally divine origins of the forces of magic meant it was a legitimate branch of learning. Alfonso frequently referred to these origins, and it is therefore significant that for him the supernatural mediators are angels, God's messengers, and not demons.

King Alfonso's attitude towards magic is revealed in works such as his *Book of Stones* (*Lapidario*). The first treatise in the compilation describes the first stage in the process of making talismans. The text lists stones endowed with particular supernatural properties, and gives the optimum moment in the astrological calendar to gather these stones when their latent powers are at their peak. The hidden properties of these stones represent what Gervase of Tilbury called their "virtus intrínseca", or inherent mineral virtues. Alfonso's first Lapidario explains that the culmination of the powers of these stones is the result of the influence of the stars upon them during the course of the year, the year's 360 days being equivalent to the 360 degrees of the heavenly sphere. The only manuscript of this *Book of Stones* has a series of miniatures to accompany the sections on each zodiac sign. The miniatures stress that the powers of the stones derive from God's intermediaries, angels, and in so doing legitimize the knowledge contained in the text.

Alfonso, however, was not content just to investigate the *virtus intrinseca* of stones. Towards the end of his life, he also examined their *virtus extrinseca*, exploring the way in which their natural powers could be realized by means of rituals and magic ceremonies. To this end, he compiled a series of diagrams of talismanic images, such as, for example, those associated with the moon, that could be engraved on stones and which would imbue them with supernatural forces. These diagrams and images appear in his *Libro de astromagia*, where Alfonso eventually strayed into the dangerous world of magic. An image depicting the magic ceremonies needed to capture the forces of the stars shows how he slipped from legitimate to heretical learning. Although in the *Libro de astromagia* Alfonso is careful to stress that angels, not devils, relay the planetary forces to earth, so many different magic rituals are depicted which show that his claims of religious orthodoxy are seriously undermined.

The magic of images

While artists in the early Middle Ages had linked depictions of magic with paganism and idolatry, by the thirteenth century ideas about natural magic seemed to have led to a kind of gradual acceptance of magic as a legitimate subject of study.[57] However, the magic of images was considered the worst kind of idolatry (*idololatria pessima*), mostly when it was accompanied by invocations to the devil.[58] In the fourteenth-century handbook for preachers known as *Fasciculus morum*, it is said that the main activity of necromancers is to "raise devils in their circles that are expected to answer their questions", and second only to that they "make figures of people in wax or some other soft material in order to kill them".[59] In Alfonso X's *Book of Astromagic*, we can see how a magician is enchanting a wax figure in the presence of angels and the familiar spirit who has brought the figure.[60]

In his legislative work, Alfonso had explicitly forbidden "anyone to dare to make images of wax or metal or any other figures to cause men to fall in love with women, or to put an end to the affection which persons entertain toward another".[61] In the twelfth century, John of Salisbury called *vultivuli* those persons practising enchantments by means of figures made of wax or other soft materials like clay.[62] The art of *envoutement* was so widespread by the beginning of the fourteenth century that Pope John XXII consulted his advisers about it; the result of this consultation had important consequences for the consideration of sorcery as a kind of heresy.[63] In 1323, the notorious inquisitor Bernard Gui, at the behest of John XXII, flatly condemned "the practice which involves making images of lead, or wax, or any other substance in order to achieve ends which are unlawful or harmful".[64] The use of wax or clay figures in the practice of sympathetic magic – especially love magic – is well documented in Antiquity,[65] and it was often the realm of female magicians, as Virgil narrates in his eighth

Eclogue.[66] But as late as the thirteenth century, visual representations of sorceresses still lack distinctive attributes, and when the illustrator of a manuscript of William of Tyre's *History of the Crusades* had to depict the Muslim sorceresses falling from the wall, he gave them no characteristic feature as magicians.[67] As in the case of male magicians, it is their action, their place in the story board, which identifies them. But in the fourteenth century, Roger Bacon's *vetula medica* would become Gerson's *vetula sortilega*, so that a devil appears when they are preparing some herbs.[68] The story of the sorceress in the eighth *Eclogue* is illustrated in a fifteenth-century miniature (see Figure 29.8), visually attesting to the moment when one of the sorceresses use a clay figure to retrieve the other woman's lost love.[69]

Figure 29.8 Sorcerers with a clay magic figurine and the shepherd Menalcas, Dijon, Bibliothèque municipale, MS 493 fol. 15v.

In his *Chronicon*, the monk Adémar de Chabannes had reported how towards 1027–28 a sorceress (*malefica mulier*) and her accomplices seemed to have used clay images against Count William of Angoulême.[70] We find the illustration of a magician in a magic rectangle enchanting a wax figure in Alfonso X's *Book of Astromagic*, where he ordered the reader to gather several Arabic texts of astral magic mainly devoted to giving detailed instructions for the construction of talismans through prayers and suffumigations, pouring the spirits of the celestial bodies into stones inscribed with images and characters. In these magically vivified sculptures and talismans, we find a mixture of the ancient "art of fabricating gods" – attributed to the Egyptians in the ancient world – and Arabic astral magic, whose origins were in the Ancient Near East. In both the case of the vivification of statues and that of the creation of talismans, this art of imbuing spirits in images to imprint them with life was attributed in the Middle Ages to Hermes Trismegistus. Since in his *City of God* Augustine quoted the words in the hermetic Asclepius about the "art of fabricating gods", Trismegistus was considered the champion of idolatry, and in a fifteenth-century illustration of the French version of Augustine's work, Hermes appears weeping for the fall of idols.[71] Trismegistus was also the prophet of the Harranian Sabeans,[72] the people from whom Arabic texts of astral magic spread, and in an Arabic miniature of 1399, he is shown fabricating a talisman in his temple in Harran, under an arch with representations of animals of the Chinese zodiac.[73] In the first half of the thirteenth century, William of Auvergne equates Arabic talismans made with the "false statues (*erroneas statuas*) made by man's hands" described in the *Asclepius* as full of life, "ensouled and conscious" (*sensu et spiritu plenas*),[74] and in so doing he brought together the terminology from the Latin and the Arabic traditions. Image magic texts detail rituals to be performed over an image to imbue in it the powers of spirits or heavenly bodies, or to say it with the words of William of Auvergne, they purport to fabricate images "in which a kind of splendour of divinity and power of spirit (*numen*) was poured in".[75] This mixture of two different "hermetic" traditions, the ancient "Egyptian" one and the Arabic astral magic rooted in the Ancient Near East – to which it contributed the translation of the Arabic word for talisman as "image" (*imago*)[76] – often derived in confusion between both traditions. In his *De vita coelitus comparanda*, Marsilio Ficino discusses the use of talismans in medicine, and again he relates Arabic astral magic to the hermetic tradition:[77]

> Yet the Arabs and the Egyptians ascribe so much power to statues and images fashioned by astronomical and magical art that they believe the spirits of the stars are enclosed in them. Now some regard the spirits of the stars as wonderful celestial forces, while others regard them as daemons attendant upon this or that star. They think the spirits of the stars – whatever they may be – are introduced into statues and talismans in the same way that daemons customarily use on the occasions when they take possession of human bodies and speak, move themselves or other things, and work wonders through them. They think the spirits of the stars do similar things through talismans (*imagines*). Similarly they think that through rays caught at the right time and through fumigations, lights and loud tones, the spirits of the stars can be introduced into the compatible materials of images and can work wonders on the wearer or bystander. This could indeed be done, I believe, by daemons, but not so much because they have been constrained by a particular material as because they enjoy being worshipped. <*De vita*, III, 20>

Ptolemy says in the *Centiloquium* that images (*effigies*) of things here below are subject to the celestial images (*vultus*); and that the ancient wise men used to manufacture certain talismans (*imagines*) when the planets were entering similar faces (*facies*) of the heavens, the faces being as it were exemplars of things below (...) Besides, Haly tells of a wise man who in a similar endeavor made images which moved. ... [and] Trismegistus says the Egyptians also used to make such images of specific cosmic materials and used to insert into them at the right time the souls of daemons ...<*De vita*, III, 13>

Hermes Trismegistus was considered the champion of idolatry throughout the medieval period, and by the end of the Middle Ages, this image coexisted with that of him as a precursor of Christ which we find in the famous image in Siena Cathedral. The latter image was a prophetic fashion indebted to ideas current in fifteenth-century Italy about an ancient theology (*prisca theologia*) preceding Christian truth. But when the author of the *Florentine Picture Chronicle* wished to show a gallery of the most famous magicians in history and chose Trismegistus as one of them, he had no doubts about his attributes (see Figure 29.9).[78] He would illustrate

Figure 29.9 Hermes from the *Florentine Picture Chronicle*. Engraving attributed to Baccio Baldini or Maso Finiguerra. British Museum.

him holding a gesticulating little man in his hands. Beyond doubt, this *homunculus* represents but one of these *"erroneas statuas" "sensu et spiritu plenas"* referred to in the hermetic *Asclepius*, that Trismegistus was believed to be able to vivify, and which would grant him fame as magician in the Middle Ages.

Future directions: the agency of images and the efficacy of objects

If we take into consideration the persistence of the medieval imagery of magic in contemporary culture (Disney's *Fantasia* or the *Harry Potter* films are two outstanding examples), it is astonishing to realize the scarce attention paid to the medieval iconography of magic itself. Apart from the representations of magic and magician in medieval visual cultures, future directions of research should engage the magical powers of images, considering the relationships between magic and religion as well as the efficacy of objects imbued with talismanic power and their representations in works of art. Among other possible topics, the medieval origins of the iconography of the witch also need further research. Diagrams and the material culture of magic are also outstanding aspects of our subject, but other chapters in this book deal with them.

Any work on the problem of the magic of images in the Middle Ages should point out the relationship between magical images (talismans, wax images, etc.) and holy, miraculous images in the medieval period.[79] Scholarly attention to the visual culture of magic has traditionally concentrated on apotropaic images and objects, as well as late medieval and early modern representations of witchcraft. But even these well-studied fields of study have recently been the subject of some interesting research that demonstrates there are diverse venues still to be explored further.

Regarding apotropaic objects and the magic of images, art historians have often been interested in the relationships between superstition, folk beliefs and social life involved in the apotropaic uses of sacred and profane objects.[80] Often, the absence of specific, contextual documentation for presumably apotropaic objects and sculptures has conditioned the historiography of the subject. A few sources can be quoted, for example, regarding sculptures in corbels and gargoyles decorated with animals displaying their powerful ferocity as apotropaic presences in liminal spaces of the church.[81] From Late Antiquity onwards, Church fathers prevented the use of amulets as a habit to be avoided:[82] for example, Jerome condemns the use of phylacteries as a Jewish habit in his comment to the Gospel of Matthew.[83] However, the recourse to amuletic protective devices is common from Late Antiquity to the late Middle Ages, and they can often be found depicted in works of art, from some late-antique Fayum portraits showing the prophylactic objects the dead used to carry on their necks in their daily lives to late medieval paintings – including portraits of the child Jesus.[84]

Amulets (*philacteria, ligamenta*[85]) and talismans (*imagines, praestigia*[86]) are usually used as working terms for more or less sophisticated objects hung or worn to expel evil influences. Although of course many amulets acquire their powers during the process of their preparation, a working distinction between both terms is plausible, taking into account the words by Gervasius of Tilbury quoted above: amulets would be natural objects with a *virtus intrinseca*, while talismans acquire a *virtus extrinseca* as they are inscribed with figures or characters and often consecrated with some kind of ritual. These rituals led late medieval theologians to consider talismans the worst kind of idolatry (*idololatria pessima*).[87] Also the use of ancient gems as apotropaic objects should be considered:[88] as the meaning of their iconography was lost, they were considered protective devices, so that they can be found displaying their beauty and prestige decorating even sacred objects and reliquaries,[89] as in the cases of the early medieval Asturian "cross of the angels" in Oviedo[90] or the thirteenth-century Box of the Three Wise Kings in Cologne,[91] among many others. Of course, there are also relics[92] as well as other religious objects such as pilgrim badges – all of them imbued with the sacrality of the saints' burials –that are used as common prophylactic devices: a lot of them have reached to us,[93] and also they often appear in late medieval iconography.[94] At present, medieval art historians are less concerned about formal classification or the differentiation between sacred or profane than about the agency of these objects in their cultural context. New historiographical streams are now focusing on the power of images and the efficacy of apotropaic objects,[95] agency being the fashionable term after the late anthropologist Alfred Gell.[96] Also, sophisticated uses of art as an apotropaic device and the notion of art itself as prophylaxis have recently been the subject of scholarly attention.[97]

Amulets and talismans were not only hung or worn on hats and dresses to invoke power for healing from sickness, protection against harm, malediction of adversaries and success in a variety of affairs, but were also placed on walls and close to doors to keep demons away.[98] With a similar prophylactic intention, the liminal spaces of Romanesque churches are decorated with a myriad of apotropaic figures, where Christian images coexist with others of presumably pagan origin, as it is the case of sculptures of women exposing her genitals in Romanesque churches, known in Ireland as "Sheela-na-gigs".[99] The interpretation of these marginal figures is still controversial, but there is a basic agreement that their situation in liminal spaces is for expelling evil influences under the principle *similia similibus curantur*: like attracts like, and hence also repels like by capturing its attention and so keeping it out of the sacred space.

Sexual corbels make up only one of the chapters of the long book of the obscene in medieval visual culture. Among many examples, in a fourteenth-century manuscript of the *Roman de la Rose*,[100] a nun appears picking male sexual organs as if they were fruits from a tree. In this case, the marginal location of the scene can lead to a humorous interpretation: in the text, the Old Woman wishes she could have had as many lovers as possible. In the fifteenth century, similar trees with penises as fruits or birds, alluding to fertility in an obscene way, would become popular.[101] To finish this chapter, I will deal with a related tree containing penises as birds in a thirteenth-century mural in Massa Marittima (Italy), which reveals that the story of the origins of the iconography of witchcraft has some *lacunae* still to be filled.

Decorating the town fountain in Massa Marittima, as can be seen in Figure 29.10, this mural represents eight women underneath a tree with *phalli* hanging from its branches instead of fruits, probably the first example of this kind of *Wunderbaum*, which we find in several paintings and objects after 1400. The common names for the penis in several languages refer to birds or cocks, and the phallus bird is an apotropaic symbol known from Greek art.[102] But here the phalluses in their nests acquire new connotations, opposing the fertility represented by the fountain against the threat to fertility. This activity was associated with a certain type of woman would use the source, as is made clear by a much later text from the *Malleus Maleficarum* that fits so well as a description of the Massa Marittima mural that it is easy to deduce it comes from a much earlier oral tradition:

> As for what pronouncement should be made about those sorceresses who sometimes keep large numbers of these members (twenty or thirty at once) in a bird's nest or in some cabinet, where the members move as if alive or eat a stalk or fodder,

Figure 29.10 Tree with male sexual organs being harvested by women (*Wunderbaum*). Mural painting set in the wall of the Fountain of Abundance, Massa Marittima (Italy). Bridgeman Images.

as many have seen and the general report relates, it should be said that these things are all carried out through the Devil's working and illusion. In this case, an illusion is played on the viewers' senses of perception in the ways discussed above. A certain man reported that when he had lost his member and gone to a certain sorceress to regain his well-being, she told the sick man that he should climb a certain tree and granted that he could take whichever one he wanted from the nest, in which there were very many members. When he tried to take a particular large one, the sorceress said, "You shouldn't take that one," adding that it belonged to one of the parish priests.[103]

The late medieval process of appropriation of women's knowledge of men's bodies resulted in a kind of fear that the same women who knew how to cure male impotence could become – in men's eyes – responsible for causing it by means of their bad arts.[104] The *vetula medica*, as Roger Bacon calls the wise old woman who knows all kinds of remedies against illness, became a *vetula malefica*, in the words of Jean Gerson.[105] This led to a gradual characterization of women as witches: perhaps under the influence of the text of the *Canon episcopi* – well known through the *Decretum Gratiani*[106] – women riding broomsticks appear at least by 1200.[107] Women riding a ram are often representations of lust and evil, and by the late Middle Ages it was a common belief that found its way into the iconography of witchcraft that witches rode backwards to their sabbats on rams or goats.[108] But the representation of witches would not be settled until the beginning of the sixteenth century, and the story of the formation of the iconography of the witch before the fifteenth century still has some chapters to be written.[109]

Notes

1 Charles Zika, "Medieval Magicians as People of the Book," in *Imagination, Books and Community in Medieval Europe*, ed. G. Kratzman, (Melbourne: State Library of Victoria, 2009), 246–54. About the iconography of the magicians in the *Florentine Picture Chronicle*, see I. Olah, "Demons and Mages in Renaissance Florence: Ficinian Neoplatonic Magic and Lorenzo de' Medici," *Studies in Medieval and Renaissance History*, Ser. 3, vol. 10 (2013): 149–81.

2 Giampiero Bozzolato et al., *Il Palazzo della Ragione a Padova* (2 vols), I: *Dalle pitture di Giotto agli affreschi del '400; II: Gli afreschi*, vol. II (Roma: Istituto Poligrafico e Zecca dello Stato, 1992), pl. 127; see also Alejandro García Avilés, "La cultura visual de la magia en la época de Alfonso X," *Alcanate: Revista de estudios alfonsíes* 5 (2006–2007): 49–87.

3 Jaime Ferreiro Alemparte, "La escuela de nigromancia de Toledo," *Anuario de estudios medievales* 13 (1983): 205–68; on the reference by William, see Lynn Thorndike, *History of Magic and Experimental Science*, vol. 2 (New York: Columbia University Press, 1923), 345–47. See also Richard Kieckhefer *Forbidden Rites: A Necromancer's Manual of the Fifteenth Century* (University Park: Pennsylvania State University Press, 1998), 170ff.;

4 *Liber iuratus Honorii: A Critical Edition of the Latin Version of the Sworn Book of Honorius*, ed. Gösta Hedegard (Stockholm: Almqvist and Wiksell, 2002), 67ff. See Richard Kieckhefer, "The Devil's Contemplatives: The *Liber iuratus*, the *Liber visionum* and the Christian Appropriation of Jewish Occultism," in *Conjuring Spirits: Texts and Traditions of Medieval Ritual Magic*, ed. Claire Fanger (University Park: Pennsylvania State University Press, 1998), 250–65; Jean-Patrice Boudet, "Magie théurgique, angélologie et vision béatifique dans le *Liber sacratus* attribué à Honorius de Thèbes," *Mélanges de l'École française de Rome: Moyen Âge* 114 (2002): 851–90; Katelyn Mesler, "The *Liber iuratus Honorii* and the Christian Reception of Angel Magic," in *Invoking Angels: Theurgic Ideas and Practices, Thirteenth to Sixteenth Centuries*, ed. Claire Fanger (University Park: Pennsylvania State University Press, 2012), 113–50; Jan R. Veenstra, "Honorius and the Sigil of God: The *Liber iuratus* in Berengario Ganell's *Summa sacre magice*" in *Invoking Angels*, ed. Fanger 151–91 (with new insights on the origins of the *Liber iuratus*).

5 See Sigrid Schade, *Schadenzauber und die Magie des Körpers: Hexenbilder der frühen Neuzeit* (Worms: Werner'sche Verlagsgesellschaft, 1983); Wolfgang Schild, "Hexen-Bilder," in *Methoden und Konzepte der historischen Hexenforschung*, ed. Gunther Franz et al. (Trier: Paulinus, 1998), 329–413; Linda Hults, *The Witch as Muse: Art, Gender and Power in Early Modern Europe* (Philadelphia: University of Pennsylvania Press, 2005); Charles Zika, *Exorcising our Demons: Magic, Witchcraft and Visual Culture in Early Modern Europe* (Leiden: Brill, 2003); Charles Zika, *The Appearance of Witchcraft: Print and Visual Culture in Sixteenth-Century Europe* (London: Routledge, 2007); Charles Zika, "Images of Witchcraft in Early Modern Europe," in *The Oxford Handbook of Witchcraft in Early Modern Europe and Colonial America*, ed. B.P. Levack, (Oxford: Oxford University Press 2013); Charles Zika, "Images and Witchcraft Studies: A Short History," in *Writing Witch-Hunt Histories*, ed. Marko Nenonen and Raisa M. Toivo (Leiden: Brill, 2014), 41–85; Charles Zika "The Witch and Magician in European Art," in *The Oxford Illustrated History of Witchcraft and Magic*, ed. Owen Davies (Oxford: Oxford University Press, 2017), 134–66. I am grateful to Professor Zika for sending me a copy of this recent chapter before publication.

6 One exception is Sophie Page, *Magic in Medieval Manuscripts* (London: British Library 2004), focused on late medieval manuscripts in the British Library.

7 See Richard Kieckhefer, *Magic in the Middle Ages* (Cambridge: Cambridge University Press, 1989); Steven P. Marrone, "William of Auvergne on Magic in Natural Philosophy and Theology," in *Was ist Philosophie im Mittelalter*, ed. Jan A. Aertsen and Andreas Speer (Berlin: Walter de Gruyter, 1998), 741–48; Steven P. Marrone, "Magic and the Physical World in Thirteenth-Century Scholasticism," *Early Science and Medicine* 14 (2009): 158–85; Jean-Patrice Boudet, *Entre science et nigromance. Astrologie, divination et magie dans l'Occident médiéval (XIIe-Xve siècle)* (Paris: Publications de la Sorbonne, 2006) 205–78; Graziella Federici Vescovini, *Medioevo magico: la magia tra religione e scienza nei secoli XIII e XIV* (Torino: UTET, 2008), xxi–xxxi, 35–46 and 171–204; Benedek Láng, *Unlocked Books: Manuscripts of Learned Magic in the Medieval Libraries of Central Europe* (University Park: Pennsylvania State University Press, 2008), 17–47; Frank Klaassen, *The Transformations of Magic: Illicit Learned Magic in the Later Middle Ages and the Renaissance* (University Park: Pennsylvania State University Press, 2013), 17ff.; Sebastià Giralt, "Magia y ciencia en la Baja Edad Media: la construcción de los límites entre la magia natural y la nigromancia, c. 1230 - c. 1310," *Clio & crimen* 8 (2011): 14–72.

8 Albert de Jong, *Traditions of the Magi: Zoroastrianism in Greek and Latin Literature* (Leiden: Brill, 1997); Jan N. Bremmer, "Persian *Magoi* and the Birth of the Term Magic," in Jan N. Bremmer, *Greek Religion and Culture, the Bible, and the Ancient Near East* (Leiden: Brill, 2008), 235–47. On the uses of the term *magos* in Graeco-Roman texts, see also Stephen Haar, *Simon Magus: The First Gnostic?* (Berlin: De Gruyter, 2003), 35–71.

9 Jaroslav Folda, *The Nazareth Capitals and the Crusader Shrine of the Annunciation*, (University Park: Pennsylvania State University Press, 1986), 41–42; Otto Demus, *The Mosaics of San Marco in Venice*, vol. I.1, (Chicago, IL: University of Chicago Press, 1984), 225.

10 London, British Library MS Cotton Tiberius B V, Part I, f. 87v. See Page, *Magic in Medieval Manuscripts*; M.R. James, "A Fragment of the 'Penitence of Jannes and Jambres'," *Journal of Theological Studies* 2 (1901): 572–77, esp. 573; Patrick McGurk et al., ed., *An Eleventh-Century Anglo-Saxon Illustrated Miscellany: British Library Cotton Tiberius B.V. Part I. Together with Leaves from British Library Cotton Nero D. II*, (Copenhagen: Rosenkilde and Bagger, 1983). See also its twelfth-century copy: Oxford, Bodleian Library MS Bodley 614, f. 48r.

11 Ed. and trans. Albert Pietersma, *The Apocryphon of Jannes and Jambres the Magicians* (Leiden: Brill, 1997), 218: "Aperuit Mambres libros magicos fratris sui Iamnis et fecit necromantiam et eduxit ab inferis idolum fratris sui".

12 Paris, Bibliothèque Nationale de France, Coislin Gr. 239, fol. 122r (Gregory Nazianzenus, *Oratio* 39, 5). Henri Omont, *Miniatures des plus anciennes manuscrits grecs de la Bibliothèque Nationale du VIe au XIVe siècle*, (Paris: Honoré Champion, 1929), pl. cxviii, n. 22; Franz Cumont, "Un rescrit imperial sur la violation de sepulture," *Revue historique* 163 (1930): 241–66, here 249, n. 1.

13 British Library, Cotton Claudius B. IV, fol. 8v (on the sign of the rods; Ex 7: 12) and 83r (on the plague of the lice; Ex 8:18). See *The Old English Illustrated Hexateuch: British Museum Cotton Claudius B. IV*, ed. C.R. Dodwell and Peter Clemoes (Copenhagen: Rosenkilde and Bagger, 1974) [facsimile]; Benjamin C. Withers, *The Illustrated Old English Hexateuch, Cotton Claudius B.iv: The Frontier of Seeing and Reading in Anglo-Saxon England* (London: British Library, 2007).

14 Edward Peters, *The Magician, the Witch, and the Law* (Philadelphia: University of Pennsylvania Press, 1978); José Domingo Rodríguez Martín, "El término *maleficus* en derecho romano postclásico," in *Edición de textos mágicos de la Antigüedad y de la Edad Media*, ed. Juan Antonio Álvarez-Pedrosa Núñez and Sofía Torallas Tovar (Madrid: CSIC, 2010), 145–71; James B. Rives, "*Magus* and Its Cognates in Classical Latin," in *Magical Practices in the Latin West*, ed. Richard Gordon and Francisco Marco Simón, (Leiden: Brill, 2010), 53–77.

15 Anitra B. Kolenkow, "A Problem of Power: How Miracle Doers Counter Charges of Magic in the Hellenistic World," in *Society of Biblical Literature. Seminar Papers* (Missoula, MT: Scholars Press, 1976), 105–10. The classic – but still controversial – study is that by Morton Smith, *Jesus the Magician: Charlatan or Son of God?* (New York: Harper & Row, 1978). See the recent assessments by David Aune, "Magic in Early Christianity and Its Ancient Mediterranean Context: A Survey of Some Recent Scholarship," *Annali di storia dell'esegesi*, 24, no. 2 (2007): 229–94, esp. 274–81; Bernd Kollmann, "Jesus and Magic: the Question of Miracles," in *Handbook for the Study of the Historical Jesus* (Leiden: Brill, 2011), 3057–86; Richard A. Horsley, *Jesus and Magic: Freeing the Gospel Series from Modern Misconceptions* (Eugene, OR: Cascade, 2014). See also H.S. Versnel, "Some Reflections on the Relationship Magic-Religion," *Numen* 38 (1991): 177–97.

16 Jan N. Bremmer, "La confrontation entre l'apôtre Pierre et Simon le Magicien," in *La Magie*, vol. 1 (Montpellier: Université Montpellier III, 2000), 219–31; Florent Heintz, *Simon "le Magicien". Actes 8, 5–25 et l'accusation de magie contre les prophetes thaumaturges dans l'Antiquité* (Paris: Gabalda, 1997); Dominique Côté, *Le theme de l'opposition entre Pierre et Simon dans les Pseudo-Clémentines*, (Paris: Institut d'Études Augustiniennes, 2001); Alberto Ferreiro, *Simon Magus in Patristic, Medieval and Early Modern Traditions* (Leiden: Brill, 2005).

17 Alberto Ferreiro, "Artistic representations of Simon Magus and Simon Peter in the Princeton Index of Christian Art: with Up-to-Date Inventory and Bibliography," in *Simon Magus*, ed. Ferreiro 307–35; Kirk Ambrose, "The Fall of Simon Magus on a Capital at Vézelay," *Gazette des Beaux-Arts*, series 6, 137 (2001): 151–66.

18 Gerard Luttikhuizen, "Simon Magus as a Narrative Figure in the Acts of Peter," in *The Apocryphal Acts of Peter: Magic, Miracles and Gnosticism*, ed. Jan N. Bremmer (Louvain: Peeters, 1998), 39–51; Tamás Adamik, "The Image of Simon Magus in the Christian Tradition," in *Apocryphal Acts of Peter*, ed. Bremmer, 52–64; Ferreiro, *Simon Magus*.

19 Thomas Matthews, *The Clash of Gods. A Reinterpretation of Early Christian Art*, 2nd rev. edn. (Princeton: Princeton University Press, 1999), 54–91. A repertory of images of Jesus with the staff can be found in William Storage and Laura Maish, "Christ the Magician: A Survey of Ancient Christian Sarcophagus Imagery" www.rome101.com/Christian/Magician/; David Knipp, *"Christus Medicus" in der frühchristlichen Sarkophagskulptur: ikonographische Studien zur Sepulkralkunst des späten vierten Jahrhunderts* (Leiden: Brill, 1998). See also Martine Dulaey, "Le symbole de la baguette dans l'art paléochrétien," *Revue des études augustiniennes* 19 (1973): 3–38; Martine Dulaey, "*Virga virtutis tuae, virga oris tui*. Le bâton du Christ dans le christianisme ancien" in "Quaeritur inventus colitur": *miscellanea in onore di padre Umberto Maria Fasola*, ed. Philippe Pergola (Vatican City: Pontificio Istituto di archeologia cristiana 1989), 237–45; Robin M. Jensen, *Understanding Early Christian Art* (London and New York: Routledge, 2000), 120ff.; Lee M. Jefferson, "The Staff of Jesus in Early Christian Art," *Religion and the Arts* 14 (2010): 221–51; Lee M. Jefferson, "Superstition and the Significance of the Image of Christ Performing Miracles in Early Christian Art" *Studia Patristica* 27 (2010): 15–20; Lee M. Jefferson, *Christ the Miracle Worker in Early Christian Art* (Minneapolis, MN: Fortress Press, 2014). For different interpretations, see György Heidl, "Early Christian Imagery of the "*virga virtutis*" and Ambrose's Theology of Sacraments," in *Early Christian Iconographies*, ed. A. Brent and M. Vinzent, *Studia Patristica*, LIX, vol. 7 (Louvain: Peeters, 2013), 69–75; Jean-Michel Spieser, *Images du Christ: des catacombes aux lendemans de l'iconoclasme* (Geneva: Droz, 2015) 165–31.

20 Among the huge bibliography about the topic, I should point out Howard Clark Kee, *Miracle in the Early Christian World: A Study in Sociohistorical Method* (New Haven, CT: Yale University Press, 1983); Howard Clark Kee, *Medicine, Miracle and Magic in New Testament Times* (Cambridge: Cambridge University Press, 1986); Graham H. Twelftree, *Jesus the Exorcist: A Contribution to the Study of the Historical Jesus* (Tübingen: Mohr, 1993); Graham H. Twelftree, *Jesus the Miracle Worker: A Historical and Theological Study* (Downers Grove, IL: InterVarsity, 1999); Martine Dulaey, "Le Christ médecin et thaumaturge," in Martine Dulaey, *Symboles des Évangiles* (Paris, Le livre de poche, 2007); Paul J. Achtemeier, *Jesus and the Miracle Tradition* (Eugene, OR: Cascade, 2008); Eric Eve, *The Healer from Nazareth: Jesus' Miracles in Historical Context* (London: SPCK, 2009).

21 See Ferdinand J.M. de Waele, *The Magic Staff or Rod in Greco-Italian Antiquity* (Ghent: Erasmus, 1927).

22 For example, in the scene of Circe practising magic in BnF, Français 606, fol. 19v (Christine de Pizan, *Épître d'Othéa*, France, ca. 1407–9). On this manuscript, see Sandra Hindman, *Christine de Pizan's Epistre Othea: Painting and Politics at the Court of Charles VI* (Toronto: PIMS 1986).

23 Fulvio Canciani, "Circe e Odisseo," in *Tainia. Festschrift für Roland Hampe*, ed. E.H. Cahn and E. Simon (Mainz: Zabern, 1980), 117–20; Fulvio Canciani, "Kirke," in *Lexikon Iconographicum Mythologiae Classicae* 6, no. 1 (Zürich: Artemis, 1992) 48–59; Luca Giuliani, "Odysseus and Kirke, Iconography in a Pre-Literate Culture," in *Greek Vases: Images, Contexts, and Controversies*, ed. Clemente Marconi (Leiden: Brill, 2004), 85–96; Maurizio Bettini and Cristiana Franco, *Il mito di Circe. Immagini e racconti dalla Grecia a oggi* (Torino: Einaudi, 2010); Chiara Pilo, "La rhabdos di Circe. Esegesi di un oggetto magico tra mito e immagine", *Gaia: revue interdisciplinaire sur la Grèce Archaïque* 17 (2014): 209–26.; Elisa Guevara Macías, "Posibles versiones literarias e iconográficas de la escena del enfrentamiento de Odiseo y Circe," *Káñina* 39 (2015): 151–70; Alessandra Romeo, *Kirke. Il mito di Circe nella traduzione letteraria e nell'immaginario iconografico attico* (Siracusa: Morrone 2016).

24 See a drawing of this scene in H. Hubert, s.v. "Magia," in Charles Daremberg and Edmund Saglio, *Dictionnaire des antiquités grecques et romaines*, vol. III.2 (Paris: Hachette, 1877–1919), 1494–1521, here at 1500.

25 Auguste Bouche-Leclercq, s.v. "Divinatio," in Daremberg and Saglio, *Dictionnaire*, vol. II.1, 300–1, fig. 2478. A figure in an early Christian silver vase found at Berthouville and now in the French National Library, formerly identified as a magician, is now considered to be a poet. See *The Berthouville Silver Treasure and Roman Luxury*, ed. Kenneth Lapatin (Los Angeles, CA: Getty Museum, 2014), fig. 88b and 143–44. Matz identified as a scene of lecanomancy one picture in Pompei's Villa dei Misteri, but this interpretation remains controversial (Friedrich Matz, *Dionysiake Telete. Archäologische Untersuchungen zum Dionysoskult in hellenistischer und romischer Zeit*, (Wiesbaden: Steiner 1963), 30–36.

26 Johannes Dillinger, "The Divining Rod: Origins, Explanations and Uses in the Thirteenth to Eighteenth Centuries," in *Contesting Orthodoxy in Medieval and Early Modern Europe: Heresy, Magic and Witchcraft*, ed. Louise N. Kallestrup and Raisa M. Toivo (New York: Palgrave, 2017), 127–43.

27 Oxford, Bodleian Library, MS Bodley 270b, fol. 43v; Alexandre de Laborde, *La Bible moralisée illustrée conservée à Oxford, Paris, et Londres*, 4 vols (Paris: Société française de reproductions de manuscrits à peintures, 1911–27); John Lowden, *The Making of the Bibles moralisées, I. The Manuscripts* (University Park: Pennsylvania State University Press, 2000). I am grateful to Antonia Martínez Ruipérez for pointing this image out to me.
28 Robin M. Jensen, "Moses Imagery in Jewish and Christian Art: Problems of Continuity and Particularity" in *Society of Biblical Literature Seminar Papers* (Missoula, MT: Scholars Press, 1992), 389–418; Manuel Sotomayor Muro, *San Pedro en la iconografía paleocristiana. Testimonios de la tradición cristiana en los monumentos iconográficos anteriores al siglo VI* (Granada: Facultad de Teología, 1962); Paul van Moorsel, "Il miracolo della roccia nella letteratura e nell'arte paleocristiana," *Rivista di archeologia cristiana* 40 (1964): 221–51.
29 Kimberly B. Stratton, "Male Magicians and Female Victims: Understanding a Pattern of Magic Representation in Early Christian Literature," *Lectio difficilior* 2 (2004) www.lectio.unibe.ch/04_2/HTML/stratton.htm#_edn7. Accessed 21 August 2016; Kimberly B. Stratton, *Naming the Witch. Magic, Ideology, and Stereotype in the Ancient World* (New York: Columbia University Press, 2007); Martha Rampton, *The Gender of Magic in the Early Middle Ages*, unpublished Ph.D. dissertation, University of Virginia, 1998; Heide Dienst, "Zur Rolle von Frauen in magischen Vorstellungen und Praktiken—nach ausgewählten mittelalterlichen Quellen," in *Frauen in Spätantike und Frühmittelalter: Legensbedingungen-Lebensnormen-Lebensformen*, ed. Werner Affeldt (Sigmarigen: Jan Thorbecke, 1990), 173–94, esp. 185–88; Michael D. Bailey, "The Feminization of Magic and the Emerging Idea of the Female Witch," *Essays in Medieval Studies*, 19 (2002): 120–34. See also the chapter in this book on "Magic and Gender," by Catherine Rider.
30 Valerie I.J. Flint, "The Demonisation of Magic and Sorcery in Late Antiquity: Christian Redefinitions of Pagan Religions," in *Witchcraft and Magic in Europe: Ancient Greece and Rome*, ed. Bengt Ankarloo and Stuart Clark (Philadelphia: University of Pennsylvania Press, 1999), 277–348; Fritz Graf, "Augustine and Magic," in *The Metamorphosis of Magic from Late Antiquity to the Early Modern Period*, ed. Jan N. Bremmer and Jan R. Veenstra (Louvain: Peeters, 2002), 87–103. See also Kyle A. Fraser, "The Contested Boundaries of "Magic" and "Religion" in Late Pagan Monotheism," *Magic, Ritual, and Witchcraft* 4 (2009): 131–51.
31 Sirarpie Der Nersessian, "The Illustrations of the Homilies of Gregory of Nazianzus: Paris Gr. 510. A Study of the Connections between Text and Images," *Dumbarton Oaks Papers*, 16 (1962): 195–228. George Galavaris, *The Illustrations of the Liturgical Homilies of Gregory Nazianzenus*, (Princeton: Princeton University, 1969), 103 and ill. 459; Leslie Brubaker, "Politics, Patronage, and Art in Ninth-Century Byzantium: The Homilies of Gregory of Nazianzus in Paris (B.N. GR. 510)," *Dumbarton Oaks Papers*, 39 (1985): 1–13; Leslie Brubaker, *Vision and Meaning in Ninth-Century Byzantium: Image as Exegesis in the Homilies of Gregory of Nazianzus* (Cambridge: Cambridge University Press 1999), 141–44. On the iconography of the magician in this image, see Alejandro García Avilés, "The Philosopher and the Magician: On Some Medieval Allegories of Magic," in *L'allegorie dans l'art du moyen age*, ed. Christian Heck, (Turnhout: Brepols, 2011), 241–52; Stéphanie Vlavianos, *La figure du mage à Byzance de Jean Damascène à Michel Psellos (VIIIe-fin XIe siècle)* (Paris: De Boccard 2013), 123–25; Henry Maguire, "Magic and Sorcery in Ninth-Century Manuscript Illumination," in *Les savoirs magiques et leur transmission de l'Antiquité à la Renaissance*, ed. Véronique Dasen and Jean-Michel Spieser (Florence: Sismel Edizioni del Galluzzo, 2014), 397–408.
32 On lecanomancy, see Pablo A. Torijano, *Solomon the Esoteric King: From King to Magus, Development of a Tradition* (Leiden: Brill, 2002), 153, 219–20.
33 See Hans U. Schmelter, *Alexander der Große in der Dichtung und bildenden Kunst des Mittelalters. Die Nektanebos-Sage: eine Untersuchung über die Wechselbeziehungen zwischen mittelalterlicher Dichtung und Bildkunst* (Bonn: Rheinische Friedrich-Wilhelms-Universität, 1977); Maud Pérez-Simon, *Mise en roman et mise en image: les manuscrits du Roman d'Alexandre en prose* (Paris: Honoré Champion, 2015), 186–92. On the legend of Nectanebo and the practice of lecanomancy, see Philippe Matthey, *Pharaon, magicien et filou: Nectanébo II entre l'histoire et la légende*, unpublished Ph.D. dissertation, University of Geneva, 2012, 194–231.
34 Armand Delatte, *Anecdota Atheniensia, I: Textes grecs inedits relatifs a l'histoire des religions* (Liege-Paris: H. Vaillant-Carmanne and Édouard Champion, 1927), 469–596; Richard H. Greenfield, *Traditions of Belief in Late Byzantine Demonology* (Amsterdam: Adolf M. Hakkert, 1988), 295. In the Madrid Skylitzes (XII–XIIIth centuries?), John the Grammarian appears as a lecanomancer pointing to

the skies (Madrid, Biblioteca nacional de España, Vitr. 26–2, f. 58r); see André Grabar and Manolis Manoussakas, *L'illustration du manuscrit de Skylitzès de la bibliotheque nationale de Madrid*, (Venice: Istituto Ellenico Di Studi Bizantini e Postbizantini, 1979); Vasiliki Tsamakda, *The Illustrated Chronicle of Ioannes Skylitzes in Madrid* (Leiden: Alexandros, 2002); Elena N. Boeck, *The Art of Being Byzantine: History, Structure, and Visual Narrative in the Madrid Skylitzes Manuscript*, unpublished Ph. D. dissertation, Yale University, 2003. See also the lecanomantic scene in Bologna, University Library, 3632, fol. 350v (Delatte, *Anecdota Atheniensia*, I, 595). On this manuscript and its illustrations, see *In BUB: Ricerche e cataloghi sui fondi della Biblioteca Universitaria di Bologna*, vol. 2, ed. Biancastella Antonino (Bologna: Minerva, 2010), 7–76.

35 Augustine, *Civ. Dei* 7: 35, quoting Varro *Ant.* I *fr.* IV (Burkhart Cardauns, *Varros Logistoricus über die Götterverehrung* (Curio de cultu deorum): *Ausgabe und Erklärung der Fragmente* (Würzburg: Konrad Triltsch, 1960), 28–33.

36 Alejandro García Avilés, "Imagen y ritual. Alfonso X y la creación de imágenes en la Edad Media," *Anales de Historia del Arte*, número extraordinario (2010): 11–29.

37 Paul C. Finney, *The Invisible God. The Earliest Christians on Art*, (Oxford: Oxford University Press, 1994), 54–56.

38 Beate Fricke, "Fallen Idols and Risen Saints: Western Attitudes towards the Worship of Images and the *"cultura veterum deorum"*," in *Negating the Image: Case Studies in Iconoclasm*, ed. A. McClanan and J. Johnson (Aldershot: Ashgate, 2005), 67–89; see now Beate Fricke, *Fallen Idols, Risen Saints. Sainte Foy of Conques and the Revival of Monumental Sculpture in Medieval Art* (Turnhout: Brepols, 2015).

39 On images possessed by devils, see Alejandro García Avilés, "Estatuas poseídas: ídolos demoniacos en el arte de la Edad Media," *Codex Aquilarensis: Revista de arte medieval* 28 (2012): 231–54.

40 Michael Evans, "Philosophy, the Liberal Arts and the Poets," in *The Hortus Deliciarum of Herrad of Hohenbourg*, 2 vol., vol. 1, ed. Rosalie Green et al. (London: Warburg Institute, 1979), 104–6.

41 Hugo Steger, *David Rex et Propheta. König David als vorbildliche Verkörperung des Herrschers und Dichters im Mittelalter*, Nüremberg, 1961; Jacqueline P. Turcheck, "A Neglected Manuscript of Peter Lombard's "Liber Sententiarum" and Parisian Illumination of the Late Twelfth Ventury," *Journal of the Walters Art Gallery*, 44 (1986): 48–69.

42 Jonathan K. Eberlein, *Miniatur und Arbeit: Das Medium Buchmalerei* (Frankfurt-am-Main: Suhrkamp, 1995).

43 Einsiedeln, Stiftsbibliothek, ms. 135, f. 2r.; Alessia Trivellone, *L'hérétique imaginé. Hétérodoxie et iconographie dans l'Occident médiéval, de l'époque carolingienne à l'Inquisition* (Turnhout: Brepols 2009), 236–42.

44 Petrus Alfonsi, *Disciplina clericalis*, Zaragoza: Guera, 1980, 117; see Charles Burnett, "Talismans: Magic as Science? Necromancy among the Seven Liberal Arts," in Charles Burnett, *Magic and Divination in the Middle Ages: Texts and Techniques in the Islamic and Christian Worlds* (Aldershot: Variorum, 1996), art. 1.

45 John of Dacia, *Divisio scientiae*, in *Johannis Daci Opera*, ed. A. Ott (Copenhaguen: Danske Sprog- og Litteraturselskab, 1955), 2–3.

46 William of Auvergne, *De universo*, 1, 43, in id., *Opera omnia*, I, ed. Blaise Le Ferron, Paris 1674 (rep. Frankfurt am Main: Minerva, 1963), 468; id., *De fide et legibus*, 14 y 24, in *Opera omnia*, I, 45 and 69. See also Boudet, *Entre science et nigromance*, 128.

47 Francesco Santi, "Guglielmo d'Auvergne e l'ordine dei domenicani tra filosofia naturale e tradizione magica," in *Autour de Guillaume d'Auvergne (+1249)*, ed. Franco Morenzoni and Jean-Yves Tilliette (Turnhout: Brepols, 2005), 137–53; Thomas B. De Mayo, *The Demonology of William of Auvergne: By Fire and Sword*, (Lewiston (New York): Edwin Mellen, 2007). See also the excellent recent surveys by Nicolas Weill-Parot, *Les "images astrologiques" au Moyen Age et à la Renaissance. Spéculations intellectuelles et pratiques magiques, XIIe–XVe siècle* (Paris: Champion, 2002); Boudet, *Entre science et nigromance*; Federici-Vescovini, *Medioevo magico*.

48 See Charles H. Lohr, "The New Aristotle and 'science' in the Paris arts faculty (1255)" in *L'enseignement des disciplines à la Faculté des arts (Paris et Oxford, XIIIe-XVe siècles)*, ed. Olga Weijers and Louis Holtz (Turnhout: Brepols, 1997) 251–69. The traditional stylistic datation for these figures is ca. 1120–1230 (see the bibliography in Sarah A. Levine, *The Northern Foreportal Column Figures of Chartres Cathedral* (Frankfurt-am-Main: Peter Lang, 1984). I have followed this datation in Alejandro García Avilés, "La magie astrale comme art visuel au XIIIe siècle," in *Images et magie. Picatrix entre Orient et Occident*, ed. Jean-Patrice Boudet, Anna Caiozzo and Nicholas Weill-Parot (Paris: Honoré

Champion, 2011), 95–113, but for iconographic reasons now I prefer a date after the 1250s. A date after the reconstruction of the portal by 1316 is also plausible: see Levine, *Northern Foreportal Column Figures*, and Michael Camille, "Visual Art in Two Manuscripts of the Ars Notoria," in Fanger, *Conjuring Spirits*, 110–43.

49 See Nicholas Weill-Parot, *Points aveugles de la nature: La rationalité scientifique médiévale face à l'occulte, l'attraction magnétique et l'horreur du vide (XIIIe-milieu du XVe siècle)* (Paris: Les Belles Lettres, 2013).

50 Montecassino, Archivio dell'Abbazia, Casin. 132, fol. 418B; see García Avilés, "La magie astrale," 112–13.

51 Page, *Magic in Medieval Manuscripts*, 21. See also Giuseppa Z. Zanichelli, "Tradurre le immagini: le scelte illustrative della traduzione in volgare mantovano di Bartolomeo Anglico," in *Lo scaffale della Biblioteca scientifica in volgare (secoli XIII-XVI)*, ed. Rita Librandi and Rosa Piro (Florence: Sismel Edizioni del Galluzzo, 2006) 141–57.

52 Gervase of Tilbury, *Otia imperialia*, III, 28, ed. S.E. Banks and J.W. Binns (Oxford: Oxford University Press 2002), 614. On the power of words in the Middle Ages, see Claire Fanger, "Things Done Wisely by a Wise Enchanter: Negotiating the Power of Words in the Thirteenth Century," *Esoterica* 1 (1999): 97–132; Irene Rosier-Catach, *La parole efficace. Signe, rituel, sacré* (Paris, 2004); Charles Burnett, "The Theory and Practice of Powerful Words in Medieval Magical Texts," in *The Word in Medieval Logic, Theology, and Psychology*, ed. Tetsuro Shimizu and Charles Burnett (Turnhout: Brepols, 2009), 215–31; *The Power of Words: Studies on Charms and Charming in Europe*, ed. James Kapaló, Éva Pócs and William Ryan (Budapest: Central European University Press, 2013); *Le pouvoir des mots au Moyen Âge*, ed. Nicole Bériou, Jean-Patrice Boudet and Irene Rosier-Catach (Turnhout: Brepols, 2014).

53 On the meaning of the basilisk in different contexts, see Marianne Sammer, *Der Basilisk. Zur Natur- und Bedeutungsgeschichte eines Fabeltieres im Abendland*, (Munich: Institut für Bayerische Literaturgeschichte, 1998).

54 British Library, Add. 30024, fol. Iv.; see Page, *Magic in Medieval Manuscripts*. On the manuscript, see Alison Stones, *Gothic Manuscripts 1260–1320*, II (London-Turnhout: Harvey Miller-Brepols, 2014), 185–87, pl. 355–58, color pl. 71–72. On this illustration, see Michael Evans, "Allegorical Women and Practical Men: The Iconography of the Artes Reconsidered," in *Medieval Women*, ed. Derek Baker (Oxford: Blackwell 1978), 305–30. On the iconography of Brunetto Latini's *Trésor*, see Brigitte Roux, *Mondes en miniatures: l'iconographie du* Livre du trésor *de Brunetto Latini* (Geneva: Droz, 2009).

55 José Escobar, "The Practice of Necromancy as Depicted in CSM 125 (Cantigas de Santa María, 125)," *Bulletin of the Cantigueiros de Santa María* 2 (1992): 33–43; García Avilés, "La cultura visual de la magia".

56 David Pingree, "Some of the Sources of the Ghāyat al-hakīm," *Journal of the Warburg and Courtauld Institutes*, 43 (1980): 1–15, here at 4.

57 See Sophie Page, *Magic in the Cloister: Pious Motives, Illicit Interests, and Occult Approaches to the Medieval Universe* (University Park: Pennsylvania State University Press, 2013).

58 *Speculum astronomiae*, trans. Paola Zambelli, *The Speculum astronomiae and Its Enigma: Astrology, Theology, Science in Albertus Magnus and His Contemporaries* (Dordrecht: Kluwer, 1992), 240.

59 *Fasciculus morum: A Fourteenth-Century Preacher's Handbook* (University Park: Pennsylvania State University Press, 1989), 578–79; see Kieckhefer, *Forbidden Rites*, 170. On wax figurines, see now Kati Ihnat and Katelyn Mesler, "From Christian Devotion to Jewish Sorcery: The Curious History of Wax Figurines in Medieval Europe," in *Entangled Histories: Knowledge, Authority and Jewish Culture in the Thirteenth Century*, ed. Elisheva Baumgarten et al. (Philadelphia: University of Pennsylvania Press, 2017), 134–58 and 303–9 (I am indebted to Sophie Page for pointing me out this recent paper).

60 Vatican Library, Reg. lat. 1283, f. 36 r. A digitized reproduction of this can (at date of writing) be found on the Vatican Library's website in their digitized collections. On familiar spirits, see *De Socrate a Tintin: Anges gardiens et démons familiers de l'Antiquité à nos jours*, ed. Jean-Patrice Boudet et al. (Rennes: Presses Universitaires de Rennes, 2011).

61 Alfonso X, *Las siete Partidas* <The Seven Parts>, Part VII, Title xxiii, Law 2; trans. Samuel P. Scott, ed. Robert I. Burns, *Las Siete Partidas*, vol. 5: *Underworlds: The Dead the Criminal and the Marginalized (Partidas VI and VII)* (Philadelphia: University of Pennsylvania Press, 2001), 1431. On magic in the *Partidas*, see Daniel Gregorio, *Alphonse X et la magie*, (Valenciennes: Presses Universitaires de Valenciennes, 2012), 128–54.

62 John of Salisbury, *Policraticus*, vol. I, ed. Clement C.J. Webb (Oxford: Clarendon Press, 1909), 51–52. A general survey in Michael Martin, "L'envoûtement de l'Antiquité à la Renaissance: une transmission entre continuités et innovations," in *Les savoirs magiques et leur transmission*, 5–24.

63 Anneliese Maier, "Eine Verfügung Johanns XXII. über die Zuständigkeit der Inquisition für Zaubereiprozesse," *Archivum Fratrum Praedicatorum* 22 (1952): 226–46 (reprinted in Anneliese Maier, *Ausgehendes Mittelalter. Gesammelte Aufsätze zur Geistesgeschichte des 14. Jahrhunderts*, 3 vols. (Rome: Storia e letteratura 1964–77), vol. 2, 59–80; Alain Boureau, *Le pape et les sorciers: Une consultation de Jean XXII sur la magie en 1320 (Manuscrit B.A.V. Borghese 348)* (Rome: École française de Rome, 2004); Alain Boureau, *Satan the Heretic* (Chicago, IL: Chicago University Press, 2006) (French version Paris 2004); Isabel Iribarren, "From Black Magic to Heresy: a Doctrinal Leap in the Pontificate of John XXII," *Church History* 76 (2007): 32–60. See also Alain Provost, *Domus diaboli, un évêque en procès au temps de Philippe le Bel* (Paris: Belin, 2010); Frans van Liere, "Witchcraft as Political Tool? John XXII, Hughes Geraud, and Matteo Visconti," *Medieval Perspectives*, 16 (2001), 165–73; Veronica J. Groom, *The Trial of Hugues Geraud: City, Church and Papacy at the Turn of the Fourteenth Century*, unpublished Ph.D. thesis, University of Exeter, 2001.

64 *Manuel de l'Inquisiteur*, vol. 2, ed. Guillaume Mollat, (Paris: Les Belles Lettres, 1926), 53.

65 Christopher A. Faraone, *Ancient Greek Love Magic* (Cambridge, MA: Harvard University Press, 1999); Radcliffe G. Edmonds III, "Bewitched, Bothered, and Bewildered: Erotic Magic in the Greco-Roman World," in *A Companion to Greek and Roman Sexualities*, ed. Thomas K. Hubbard (Oxford: Blackwell, 2013), 282–96 with previous bibliography. For the Middle Ages, see Richard Kieckhefer, "Erotic Magic in Medieval Europe," in *Sex in the Middle Ages: A Book of Essays*, ed. Joyce E. Salisbury (New York: Garland, 1995), 30–55; Boudet, *Entre science et nigromance*, 362–68; Jean-Patrice Boudet, "L'amour et les rituels à images d'envoûtement dans le Picatrix latin" in *Images et magie*, ed. Boudet, Caiozzo and Weill-Parot, 149–62; Catherine Rider, "Women, Men, and Love Magic in Late Medieval English Pastoral Manuals," *Magic, Ritual, and Witchcraft* 7 (2012): 190–211; Paloma Moral de Calatrava, "Frígidos y maleficiados: las mujeres y los remedios contra la impotencia en la Edad Media," *Asclepio*, 64 (2012): 353–72; Liliana Leopardi, "Erotic Magic: Rings, Engraved Precious Gems and Masculine Anxiety," in *Eroticism in the Middle Ages and the Renaissance: Magic, Marriage, and Midwifery*, ed. Ian Moulton (Turnhout: Brepols, 2016), 99–130.

66 *Vergil's Eclogues*, ed. Katharina Volk (Oxford: Oxford University Press, 2008). See Christopher A. Faraone, "Clay Hardens and Wax Melts: Magical Role-Reversal in Vergil's Eighth Eclogue," *Classical Philology* 84 (1989): 294–300; Joshua T. Katz and Katharina Volk, "Erotic Hardening and Softening in Vergil's Eighth Eclogue," *Classical Quarterly*, NS 56 (2006): 169–74.

67 BnF, Français 9081, fol. 77; see Jaroslav Folda, *The Illustrations in Manuscripts of the History of Outremer by William of Tyre*, vol. 2, unpublished Ph.D. dissertation, Johns Hopkins University, 1968, 17; Jaroslav Folda, *Crusader Art in the Holy Land, From the Third Crusade to the Fall of Acre, 1187–1191* (Cambridge: Cambridge University Press, 2005), 235–36. The text illustrated is that by William of Tyre, *Historia*, 15, English trans.: *A History of Deeds Done Beyond the Sea*, trans. Emily A. Babcock and A.C. Krey (New York: Columbia University Press, 1943), 365–66: When the infidels perceived that no skill of theirs could prevail against this, they brought two sorceresses to bewitch it and by their magic incantations render it powerless. These women were engaged in their magic rites and divinations on the wall when suddenly a huge millstone from that very engine struck them. They, together with three girls who attended them, were crushed to death and their lifeless bodies dashed from the wall. At this sight great applause rose from the ranks of the Christian army and exultation filled the hearts of all in our camp. On the other hand, deep sorrow fell upon the people of Jerusalem because of that disaster.

68 Cotton Tiberius A.vii, fol. 70r; Page, *Magic in medieval manuscripts*.

69 Dijon, Bibliothèque municipale, ms. 493, f. 15v.

70 *Chronicon*, 3.66, ed. Pascale Bourgain et al. (Turnhout: Brepols, 1999), 186.

71 Augustine, *La Cité de Dieu*, trans. Raoul de Presles, The Hague, MMV, 10 A 11, fol. 392r (Paris ca. 1475–80) illustrating *Civ. Dei*, 8, 24. See François Avril and Nicole Reynaud, *Les manuscrits à peintures en France 1440–1520* (Paris: Bibliothèque nationale de France, 1993), 52; Sharon Dunlap Smith, "New themes for the 'City of God' around 1400: the illustrations of Raoul de Presles' translation," *Scriptorium* 36 (1982): 68–82.

72 Francis E. Peters, "Hermes and Harran: The Roots of Arabic-Islamic Occultism," in *Intellectual Studies on Islam: Essays Written in Honor of Martin B. Dickson*, ed. Michel M. Mazzaoui & Vera B.

Moreen (Salt Lake City: University of Utah Press, 1990), 185–215, rep. in *Magic and Divination in Early Islam*, ed. Emilie Savage-Smith (Aldershot: Ashgate, 2004), 55–85. On Arabic astral magic, see especially the works by David Pingree and Charles Burnett, and now the useful summary by Liana Saif, *The Arabic Influences on Early Modern Occult Philosophy* (Basingtoke: Palgrave Macmillan, 2015), with previous bibliography.

73 Oxford, Bodleian Library, Oriental 133, fol. 29r; on this manuscript, see Stefano Carboni, *Il Kitab al-bulhan di Oxford* (Turin: Tirrenia, 1988). See also A. Caiozzo, "Éléments de rituels imagés dans les manuscrits de l'Orient médiéval," in *Images et magie.* ed. Boudet et al., 57–75, esp. 67–78.

74 *Hermetica: The Greek Corpus Hermeticum and the Latin Asclepius*, trans. Brian P. Copenhaver (Cambridge: Cambridge University Press 1995), 37.

75 William of Auvergne, *De legibus*, 23, in id., *Opera omnia*, 66–67, trans. Charles Burnett, "The Establishment of Medieval Hermeticism," in *The Medieval World*, ed. Peter Linehan and Janet L. Nelson (London: Routledge, 2001). See also Alejandro García Avilés, "'Falsas estatuas': ídolos mágicos y dioses artificiales en el siglo XIII," *La Corónica*, 36 (2007) (special issue on *Magic in Medieval Spain*, ed. A. García Avilés), 71–96.

76 Burnett, "Talismans"; García Avilés, "Falsas estatuas". See also *The Talisman*, ed. Benjamin Anderson and Yael Rice (Oxford: Oxford University Press, forthcoming).

77 *De vita*, III, 20 and 13; Marsilio Ficino, *Three Books on Life*, ed. and trans. Carol V. Caske and J.R. Clark, (Binghamton: State University of New York, 1989; rep. Tempe: State University of Arizona Press, 1998), 351 and 305–6. I have adapted the translation by Caske and Clark, and in some cases I have preferred to translate "*imagines*" as "talismans" instead of "images" as they do. See Brian P. Copenhaver, "Scholastic Philosophy and Renaissance Magic in the *De vita* of Marsilio Ficino," *Renaissance Quarterly*, 37 (1984), 523–54; Brian P. Copenhaver, *Magic in Western Culture from Antiquity to the Enlightenment* (Cambridge: Cambridge University Press, 2015), 102–26; Tanja Klemm, "Life from Within: Physiology and Talismanic Efficacy in Marsilio Ficino's De vita (1498)," *Representations*, 133 (2016) (*Images at Work*, ed. Ittai Weinryb, Hannah Baader and Gerhard Wolf): 110–29.

78 Olah, "Demons and Mages in Renaissance Florence," 172–80.

79 García Avilés, "Imagen y ritual"; and my forthcoming book *El arte de fabricar dioses: imagen y ritual en la Edad Media* (Madrid: Akal). The magical and miraculous powers of images are among the main topics of two classic books with different approaches, mostly anthropological and psychological the first one and historical the second one: David Freedberg, *The Power of Images: Studies in the History and Theory of Response* (Chicago, IL: Chicago University Press, 1989) and Hans Belting, *Bild und Kult: Eine Geschichte des Bildes vor dem Zeitalter der Kunst*, Munich: C.H. Beck, 1990 (English translation: *Likeness and Presence: History of the Image Before the Era of Art* (Chicago, IL: Chicago University Press, 1997). Recently see Horst Bredekamp, *Theorie des Bildakts* (Frankfurt am Main: Suhrkamp, 2010).

80 Claude Gaignebet and Jean-Dominique Lajoux, *Art profane et religion populaire au Moyen Âge* (Paris: PUF, 1985): a good repertory but their interpretations should be taken cautiously; Ruth Mellinkoff, *Averting Demons: The Protective Power of Medieval Visual Motifs and Themes*, 2 vols. (Los Angeles: Ruth Mellinkoff Publications, 2004). An overview in Gerado Boto Varela, "Representaciones románicas de monstruos y seres imaginarios. Pluralidad de atribuciones funcionales," in *El mensaje simbólico del imaginario románico* (Aguilar de Campoo: Fundación Santa María la Real, 2007), 78–115. See also Fulvio Cervini, "Pietre portentose, ovvero come i medievali vedevano le sculture apotropaiche," in *Metodo della ricerca e ricerca del metodo: storia, arte, musica a confronto*, ed. Benedetto Vetere (Galatina: Congedo, 2009) 129–50; Alessia Trivellone, "Images, rites et magie aux marges des églises dans l'Occident médiéval," *Revue de l'histoire des religions*, 231 (2014), 775–96; Nathalie Le Luel, "Des images "parlantes" pour les laïcs: l'utilisation de la culture populaire sur les portails des églises romanes," *Cahiers d'Art sacré*, 27 (2010): 18–31; Nathalie Le Luel, "Images profanes et culture folklorique," in *Les images dans l'Occident médiéval*, ed. Jérôme Baschet and Pierre-Olivier Dittmar (Turnhout, Brepols, 2015), 433–44; Nathalie Le Luel, "La voz de las imágenes románicas: iconografía profana y recepción," *Románico* 20 (2015): 186–93.

81 For example, Stephen of Bourbon, *Tractatus de diversis materiis predicabilibus*, ed. Jacques Berlioz et Jean-Luc Eichenlaub (Turnhout: Brepols, 2002), 280; Pierre-Olivier Dittmar and Jean-Pierre Ravaux, "Signification et valeur d'usage des gargouilles: le cas de Notre-Dame de l'Epine," in *Notre-dame de l'Epine, 1406–2006*, ed. Jean-Batiste Renault (Châlons-en-Champagne: S.A.C.S.A.M., 2008),

38–80, here at 42. See also Fulvio Cervini, "Talismani di pietra: sculture apotropaiche nelle fonti medievali," *Lares*, 67 (2001): 165–88; Ruth Bartal, "La coexistencia de los signos apotropaicos cristianos y paganos en las entradas dee las iglesias románicas," *Archivo español de arte*, 66 (2001): 113–24.

82 Josef Engemann, "Zur Verbreitung magischer Übelabwehr in der nichtchristlichen und christlichen Spätantike," *Jahrbuch für Antike und Christentum* 18 (1975): 22–48; Dietrich Harmening, *Superstitio: Überlieferungs- und theoriegeschichtliche Unte;rsuchungen zur kirchlich-theologischen Aberglaubensliteratur des Mittelalters* (Berlin: Erich Schmidt, 1979), 235–47; H.F. Stander, "Amulets and the Church Fathers," *Ekklesiastikos Pharos* 75 (1993): 55–66; Matthew W. Dickie, "The Fathers of the Church and Evil Eye," in *Byzantine Magic*, ed. Henry Maguire (Washington, DC: Dumbarton Oaks, 1995), 9–34.

83 Saint Jerome, *Commentary on Matthew*, IV. 23, ed. T.P. Scheck (Washington, DC: Catholic University of America, 2008) 259–60 <*PL* 26, 175; *CCSL*, 77, 211–21.

84 *Ancient Faces: Mummy Portraits from Roman Egypt*, ed. Susan Walker (London: British Museum, 1997) 101–2 and 113–14; Joaquín Yarza, "Fascinum: reflets de la croyance au mauvais oeil dans l'art médiéval hispanique," *Razo* 8 (1988): 11–37; S.A. Callisen, "The Evil Eye in Italian Art," *Art Bulletin*, 19 (1937): 450–62.

85 G.J.M. Bartelink, "Phylacterium," in *Mélanges Christine Mohrmann. Nouveau recueil offert par ses anciens élèves* (Utrecht and Antwerp: Spectrum, 1973), 25–60.

86 Burnett, "Talismans: Magic as Science?"; Weill-Parot, *Les "images astrologiques"*; García Avilés, "Falsas estatuas"; Brian P. Copenhaver, *Magic in Western Culture. From Antiquity to the Enlightenment* (Cambridge: Cambridge University Press, 2015).

87 The expression "idololatria pessima" in Pseudo-Albertus Magnus, *Speculum astronomiae*, 11, ed. Zambelli, *The Speculum Astronomiae and Its Enigma*, 240.

88 *Gemme dalla corte imperiale alla corte celeste*, ed. Gemma Sena Chiesa (Milan: Hoepli, 2002); Erika Zwierlein-Diehl, *Antike Gemmen und ihr Nachleben* (Berlin: Walter de Gruyter, 2007); Erika Zwierlein-Diehl, "Magical Gems in the Medieval and Early-Modern Periods: Tradition, Transformation, Innovation," in *Les savoirs magiques et leur transmission de l'Antiquité à la Renaissance*, ed. Véronique Dasen and Jean-Michel Spieser (Florence: Sismel Edizioni del Galluzzo, 2014), 87–130; Eleutheria Avgoloupi, *Simbologia delle gemme imperiali bizantine nella tradizione simbolica mediterranea delle pietre preziose* (Spoleto: CISAM, 2014). On the meaning of biblical gems in medieval art, see Christel Meier, *Gemma spiritalis: Methode und Gebrauch der Edelsteinallegoresse vom frühen Christentum bis ins 18. Jarhundert*, vol. 1 (Munich: Wilhelm Fink, 1977); Gerda Friess, *Edelsteine im Mittelalter. Wandel und Kontinuität in ihrer Bedeutung durch zwölf Jahrhunderte (in Aberglauben, Medizin, Theologie und Goldschmiedekunst)* (Hildesheim: Gestenberg, 1980); Ulrich Henze, "Edelsteinallegorese im Lichte mittelalterlicher Bild- und Reliquienverehrung," *Zeitschrift für Kunstgeschichte*, 54 (1991): 428–51. See also Herbert L. Kessler, ""They preach not by speaking out loud but by signifying": Vitreous Arts as Typology," *Gesta*, 51 (2012): 55–70.

89 Elena Poletti Ecclesia, "L'incanto delle pietre multicolori: gemme antiche sui reliquiari altomedievali," in *Gemme dalla corte imperiale alla corte Celeste*, ed. Gemma Sena Chiesa et al. (Milan: Hoepli, 2002), 55–74; Gia Toussaint, "Heiliges Gebein und edler Stein. Der Edelsteinschmuck von Reliquiaren im Spiegel mittelalterlicher Wahrnehmung," *Das Mittelalter* 8 (2003): 41–66. On the process of Christian appropriation of ancient gems, see Simone Michel, *Die Magischen Gemmen. Zu Bildern und Zauberformeln auf geschnittenen Steinen der Antike und Neuzeit* (Berlin: Akademie, 2004), 113ff.

90 Sabino Perea Yébenes, "Demonios en una cruz cristiana. Gemas mitológicas y gnósticas sobre la Cruz de los Ángeles (Oviedo)," in *Officium magicum. Estudios de magia, teúrgia, necromancia, supersticiones, milagros y demonología en el mundo greco-romano* (Madrid and Salamanca: Signifer, 2014), 367–87. See also Theo Jülich, "Gemmenkreuze. Die Farbigkeit ihres Edelsteinbesatzes bis zum 12. Jahrhundert," *Aachener Kunstblätter*, 54–55 (1986–87), 99–258; and *Gemme dalla corte imperiale alla corte celeste*.

91 Erika Zwierlein-Diehl, "*Interpretatio christiana*: Gems on the 'Shrine of the Three Kings' in Cologne," *Studies in the History of Art* 54 (1997) 62–83; Philippe Cordez, "La châsse des rois mages à Cologne et la christianisation des pierres magiques aux XIIe et XIIIe siècles," in *Le trésor au Moyen Âge: Discours, pratiques et objets*, ed. Lucas Burkart et al. (Florence: Sismel Edizioni del Galluzzo, 2010), 315–32.

92 Edina Bozóky, "From Matter of Devotion to Amulets," *Medieval Folklore*, 3 (1994): 91–107; Edina Bozóky, "Les moyens de la protection privée," *Cahiers de recherches médiévales*, 8 (2001): 175–92; James Robinson, "From Altar to Amulet: Relics, Portability, and Devotion," in *Treasures of Heaven*.

Saints, Relics, and Devotion in Medieval Europe, ed. Martina Bagnoli et al. (Baltimore, MD: Walters Art Museum, 2010), 111–16; John R. Decker, "'Practical devotion': Apotropaism and the Protection of the Soul," in *The Authority of the Word: Reflecting on Image and Text in Northern Europe, 1400–1700*, ed. Celeste Brusati et al. (Leiden: Brill, 2012) 357–83; and the forthcoming book by Ginevra Kornbluth, *Amulets, Power, and Identity in Early Medieval Europe*, (Oxford: Oxford University Press).

93 Jos Koldewej, "The Wearing of Significative Badges, Religious and Secular: The Social Meaning of a Behavioural Pattern," in *Showing Status: Representation of Social Positions in the Late Middle Ages*, ed. W. Blockmans and A. Janse (Turnhout: Brepols, 1999), 307–28; Thomas A. Bredehoft, "Literacy without Letters: Pilgrim Badges and Late-Medieval Literate Ideology," *Viator* 37 (2006): 433–45; Jean-Claude Schmitt, "Das Mark des Mittelalters," in *Jungfrauen, Engel, Phallustiere. Die Sammlung mittelalterlicher französischer Pilgerzeichen des Kunstgewerbemuseums in Prag und des Nationalsmuseums* (Berlin: Lukas, 2012), 9–14.

94 Adrianus M. Koldeweij, "Pilgrim Badges Painted in Manuscripts: A North Netherlandish Example," in *Masters and Miniatures* (Doornspijk: Davaco, 1991), 211–18; Hanneke van Asperen, "Pèlerinage et dévotions- les insignes dans les manuscrits du bas Moyen Age," in *Foi et bonne fortune: parure et devotion en Flandre médiévale*, ed. Jos Koldewej (Arnhem: Terra Lannoo, 2006), 234–45; Hanneke van Asperen, *Pelgrimstekens op perkament: Originele en nageschilderde bedevaartssouvenirs in religieuze boeken (ca. 1450–ca. 1530)* (Nijmegen: NKS 2009); Megan H. Foster-Campbell, "Pilgrimage through the Pages: Pilgrims' Badges in Late Medieval Devotional Manuscripts," in *Push Me, Pull You: Imaginative, Emotional, Physical, and Spatial Interaction in Late Medieval and Renaissance*, vol. 1, ed. Sarah Blick and Laura D. Gelfand (Leiden: Brill, 2011), 227–74.

95 See Hanna Baader and Ittai Weinryb, "Images at Work: On Efficacy and Historical Interpretation," *Representations*, 113 (2016) (*Images at Work*, ed. Ittai Weinryb, Hannah Baader, and Gerhard Wolf): 1–19; Thomas Golsenne, "Les images qui marchent: performance et anthropologie des objets figuratifs," in *Les images dans l'Occident médiéval*, 179–92; Ittai Weinryb, *The Bronze Object in the Middle Ages* (Cambridge: Cambridge University Press, 2016), 108ff.

96 Alfred Gell, *Art and Agency: An Anthropological Theory* (Oxford: Oxford University Press, 1998); see also *Art's Agency and Art History*, ed. Robin Osborne and Jeremy Tanner (Oxford: Blackwell, 2007); Horst Bredekamp, *Theorie des Bildakts* (Frankfurt: Suhrkamp, 2010); Caroline van Eck, *Art, Agency and Living Presence: From the Animated Image to the Excessive Object* (Munich and Leiden: Walter De Gruyter/Leiden University Press, 2015).

97 From different points of view: Kathleen M. Openshaw, "The Battle between Christ and Satan in the Tiberius Psalter," *Journal of the Warburg and Courtauld Institutes*, 52 (1989), 14–33; Openshaw, "Weapons in the Daily Battle: Images of the Conquest of Evil in the Early Medieval Psalter," *Art Bulletin* (1993), 17–38; Elizabeth Valdez del Álamo, "The Saint's Capital, Talisman in the Cloister," in *Decorations for the Holy Dead: Visual Embellishments on Tombs and Shrines of Saints*, ed. Stephen Lamia and Elizabeth Valdez del Álamo (Turnhout, 2002), 111–28; Herbert L. Kessler, "Evil Eye(ing): Romanesque Art as a Shield of Faith," in *Romanesque: Art and Thought in the Twelfth Century: Essays in Honor of Walter Cahn*, ed. C. Hourihane (Princeton: Index of Christian Art, 2008), 107–35; Herbert L. Kessler, "Christ the Magic Dragon," *Gesta* 48 (2009): 119–34; Herbert L. Kessler, "A Sanctifying Serpent: Crucifix as Cure," in *Studies on Medieval Empathies*, ed. Karl F. Morrison and R.M. Bell (Turnhout: Brepols, 2013), 161–85.

98 Eunice Dauterman Maguire, Henry Maguire and Maggie J. Duncan-Flowers, *Art and Holy Powers in the Early Christian House* (Urbana and Chicago, IL: Kranner Art Museum, 1989); John Mitchell, "Keeping the Demons Out of the House: The Archaeology of Apotropaic Strategy and Practice in Late Antique Butrint and Antigoneia," *Objects in Context, Objects in Use: Material Spatiality in Late Antiquity*, ed. Luke Lavan et al. (Leiden: Brill, 2007), 273–310;

99 Marian Bleeke, "Sheelas, Sex, and Significance in Romanesque Sculpture: The Kilpeck Corbel Series" *Studies in Iconography*, 26 (2005): 1–26; Barbara Freitag, *Sheela-na-gigs: Unravelling an enigma* (Abingdon: Routledge, 2004); Theresa C. Oakley, *Lifting the Veil: A New Study of the Sheela-Na-Gigs of Britain and Ireland* (Oxford: Archaeopress, 2009).

100 Michael Camille, *Images on the Edge: The Margins of Medieval Art* (London: Reaktion Books, 1992), 147–49; A.M. Koldeweij, "A Barefaced Roman de la Rose (Paris, B.N., ms. fr. 25526) and Some Late Medieval Mass-Produced Badges of a Sexual Nature," in *Flanders in a European Perspective: Manuscript Illumination around 1400 in Flanders and Abroad*, ed. Maurit Smeyers and Bert Cardon (Louvain: Peeters, 1995), 499–516.

101 Adrianus M. Koldeweij, ""Shameless and Naked Images": Obscene Badges as Parodies of Popular Devotion," in *Art and Architecture of Late Medieval Pilgrimage in Northern Europe and the British Isles*, ed. Sarah Blick and Rita Tekippe (Leiden: Brill, 2004), 493–510; Ben Reiss, "Pious Phalluses and Holy Vulvas: The Religious Importance of Some Sexual Body-Part Badges in Late-Medieval Europe (1200–1550)," *Peregrinations: Journal of Medieval Art and Architecture*, 6 (2017): 151–76.

102 John Boardman, "The Phallos-Bird in Archaic and Classical Greek Art," *Revue Archéologique*, n. s., 2 (1992): 227–42.

103 Heinrich Kramer and Jacobus Sprenger, *Malleus Maleficarum*, trans. Christopher S. Mackay (Cambridge: Cambridge University Press, 2006), 328. On the sources of the *Malleus*, see Hans Peter Broedel, *The Malleus Maleficarum and the Construction of Witchcraft: Theology and Popular Belief* (Manchester: Manchester University Press, 2003). On the text quoted here, see Walter Stephens, "Witches Who Steal Penises: Impotence and Illusion in "Malleus Maleficarum," *Journal of Medieval and Early Modern Studies* 28 (1998): 495–529; Stephens, *Demon Lovers: Witchcraft, Sex and the Crisis of Belief* (Chicago, IL: University of Chicago Press 2002), 300–21; Moira Smith, "The Flying Phallus and the Laughing Inquisitor: Penis Theft in the *Malleus Maleficarum*," *Journal of Folklore Research* 39 (2002): 85–117. On the Massa Marittima mural, see George Ferzoco, *Il murale di Massa Maritima/The Massa Marittima Mural* (Florence: Consiglio Regionale della Toscana, 2004) and Erica M. Longenbach, *A Fountain Bewitched: Gender, Sin, and Propaganda in the Massa Marittima Mural*, unpublished M.A. dissertation, University of North Carolina at Chapel Hill, 2008; cfr. for a different interpretation, Adrian S. Hoch, "Duecento Fertility Imagery for Females at Massa Marittima's Public Fountain," *Zeitschrift für Kunstgeschichte*, 69 (2006): 471–88.

104 Catherine Rider, *Magic and Impotence in the Middle Ages* (Oxford: Oxford University Press 2006).

105 Jole Agrimi and Chiara Crisciani, "Savoir médical et anthropologie religieuse. Les représentations et les fonctions de la vetula (XIIIe-XVe siècle)," *Annales: Économies, Sociétés, Civilisations* 48 (1993) 1281–1308; Béatrice Delaurenti, "La sorcière en son milieu naturel: démon et *vetula* dans les écrits sur le pouvoir des incantations," in *Chasses aux sorcières et démonologie. Entre discours et pratiques (XIVe-XVIIe siècles)*, ed. Martine Ostorero et al. (Florence: Sismel Edizioni del Galluzzo, 2010), 367–88; Béatrice Delaurenti, "Femmes enchanteresses. Figures féminines dans le discours savant sur les pratiques incantatoires au Moyen Âge," in *Femmes mediatrices et ambivalentes: mythes et imaginaires*, ed. Anna Caiozzo and Nathalie Ernoult (Paris: Armand Colin, 2012), 215–26; Jean-Patrice Boudet, "Femmes ambivalentes et savoir magique: retour sur les *vetule*," in *Femmes mediatrices et ambivalentes*, ed. Caiozzo and Ernoult, 203–14.

106 Werner Tschacher, "Der Flug durch die Luft zwischen Illusionstheorie und Realitätsbeweis: Studien zum sogennante Kanon Episcopi und zum Hexenflug," *Zeitschrift der Savigny-Stiftung für Rechtsgeschichte, Kanonistische Abteilung* 85 (1999): 225–76; Zika, *Exorcising Our Demons*, 237–67; Zika, *The Appearance of Witchcraft*, 99–124; "How (and Why) Do Witches Fly?" special issue of *Magic, Ritual, and Witchcraft* 11, no. 1 (2016), ed. Michael Ostling. On the representations of flying witches, see Lisa Dawn St. Clare, *As the Crone flies. The Imagery of Women as Flying Witches in Early Modern Europe*, unpublished Ph.D. dissertation, University of Oklahoma, 2016; Judith Venjakob, *Der Hexenflug in der frühneuzeitlichen Druckgrafik: Entstehung, Rezeption und Symbolik eines Bildtypus* (Petersberg: Michael Imhof, 2016).

107 Georg Troescher, "Keltisch-germanische Götterbilder an romanischen Kirchen?" *Zeitschrift für Kunstgeschichte*, 16 (1953): 1–42. On a well-known mid-fifteenth-century image of witches as female waldensians riding bloomsticks (Bnf, fr. 12476, f. 105r), see Venjakob, *Der Hexenflug*, 50ff., and Pascale Charron, *L'iconographie du* Champion des dames *de Martin Le Franc* (Turnhout: Brepols, 2016).

108 Richard Haman, "The Girl and the Ram," *Burlington Magazine* 60 (1932): 91–97; Ruth Mellinkoff, "Riding Backwards: Theme of Humiliation and Symbol of Evil," *Viator* 4 (1973): 153–76.

109 On the medieval iconography of witchcraft, see Jacqueline Kadaner-Leclercq, "Typologie des scènes de sorcellerie au Moyen Age et à la Renaissance," in *Magie, sorcellerie, parapsychologie*, ed. Hervé Hasquin (Brussels: Université de Bruxelles, 1984), 39–59; Fabio Troncarelli, "Immagini di streghe nei manoscritti medievali," in *Imaging humanity/Immagini dell'umanitá*, ed. John Casey et al. (West Lafayette, IN: Bordighera, 2000), 79–92.

30

MEDIEVAL MAGICAL FIGURES

Between image and text

Sophie Page

Medieval magical figures are a type of diagram: a simplified figure, mainly consisting of lines, that conveys the meaning of the appearance, structure or workings of something and the relationship between its parts. Magical figures acted as instruments to activate celestial and spiritual powers, and as visual devices to organize ritual elements considered powerful in their own right. They were part of the ritual toolkit with which practitioners attempted to manipulate the cosmos and very common in texts and manuscripts of learned magic. In the late Middle Ages, they were circulated both as integral parts of magic experiments and texts and independently, and they could involve an array of different shapes, images, words, letters, symbols, modes of construction and ritual uses. Although they have been little studied, magical figures are useful for exploring the relationship between image and text in learned magic and for explaining why critics identified some texts as deviant.[1] This chapter sets out several common types of figures including the "Eye of Abraham" charm, the square figures called laminas, circular apotropaic amulets, figures to aid visualization in ritual magic and magic circles to be drawn on the ground. I compare their uses, transmission histories and evidence of creativity in their production.

Magical figures have some typical features of diagrams in the modern sense: they can possess "elegance, clarity, ease, pattern, simplicity, and validity."[2] They are also "meditational artefacts" in the medieval sense, requiring the reader to pause and fill in missing or abstract connections in order to retrieve information, and offering "an invitation to elaborate and recompose, not a prescriptive, 'objective' schematic."[3] The medieval universe was teeming with vast numbers of invisible and mostly unknowable spirits. Manoeuvring abstract cosmological ideas in their minds, the users of figures had to trust that a certain character belonged to Saturn or that an unfamiliar name referred to an entity inhabiting the cosmos. The meanings of some elements in figures may have been more obvious to their designers than users, but magical figures could still be effective: human brains are naturally inclined to make connections that generate meaning even when the visual information supplied is simplified, abstract or obscure.[4]

The place of figures within the magician's ritual toolkit was set out in one of the most sophisticated theoretical works on magic circulating in medieval Europe, the *De radiis* or *Theorica artium magicarum*, a Latin translation of a ninth-century Arabic text attributed to Al-Kindī.[5] According to the *De radiis*, the ritual actions that the magical practitioner performed in order to change the matter of the world belonged either to "the speaking of the mouth" (*oris locutio*) or "the operation of the hand" (*manus operatio*). Inscribing shapes (*figurae*) was one of the four main actions of the operation of the hand; the others were inscribing characters, sculpting images and sacrificing animals. The *De radiis* instructed the practitioner to make a talisman by inscribing magical figures into the elemental matter with due solemnity (*debita sollempnitate*) and at the correct time and place in order to activate the cosmic rays.

Christian thinkers were fascinated by the idea that the power of the stars could be drawn down into objects that had been inscribed at astrologically appropriate times, and that these objects could be used to change the matter of the world.[6] The Arabic magic texts that introduced astrological talismans to the Latin West in the twelfth and thirteenth centuries disseminated many influential magical terms and ritual instruments, especially the names, seals and characters of the celestial spirits.[7] However, it was the authors of Christian magic texts who drove the creative expansion of geometric figures to enclose powerful names and graphic motifs, under the influence of ancient *lamellae*, circular apotropaic amulets, Solomonic seals and cosmological diagrams. The dual role of Christian magical figures as pictures and linguistic devices was recognized by Roger Bacon. His *Opus maius* of 1266–7 compared the way in which the makers of magical figures (*figurae*) placed magical characters together in one visual device, to the way in which the people of Cathay (China) – using the same brush they painted with – brought into one shape (*figura*) the letters that formed a single word.[8]

The graphic motifs of astral and Solomonic magic were not assimilated unproblematically, but attracted criticism on two grounds: that they were signs of communication to demons and that they were the objects of idolatrous worship. The former was an understandable response, since most diagrams are intended to communicate something. In the mid thirteenth-century, the Bishop of Paris, William of Auvergne, condemned those who used Solomonic seals and pentacles as idolaters.[9] Both critical perspectives continued to be influential throughout the Middle Ages, from the *Speculum astronomiae*'s critique of "Hermetic" idolatry and "Solomonic" *figurae* to Thomas Aquinas's harsh response to the figures in the *Ars notoria*.[10] These condemnations and the figures' associations with demonic signs and idolatry hampered efforts by some authors to establish the orthodoxy of their texts. Nevertheless, they became significant ritual instruments, in part because of already existing traditions of amulets with visual motifs. Simpler kinds of instrumental figures such as the "Abraham's Eye" charm, laminas to heal wounds or aid with conception, and small circular apotropaic figures copied onto folded parchments preceded and influenced the traditions of learned magic, but were, in turn, transformed by them.

Magical figures of all types were drawn by scribes rather than specialized illustrators. They are rarely coloured or pictorially elaborate, although some were drawn neatly with a compass, square and ruler while others were sketched in the margins. Many figures were intended to be exemplars for the production of multiple portable copies, or for creating more complex images to be drawn in blood, inscribed in metal, suffumigated, consecrated or otherwise ritually prepared. In this chapter, I have used the term "figure" to refer to a range of types of magical diagrams because the latin *figura* is the primary term used by medieval sources to denote large two-dimensional geometric diagrams that were assigned an instrumental power. Medieval sources distinguished these *figurae* from other common graphic motifs in magic texts, notably, characters and seals. The term character (*c(h)aracter*) usually refers to mysterious graphic signs, with no verbal or typographical equivalents, that are equivalent in size to normal script.[11] Seals (*sigilla*) and signs (*signa*) denote graphic elements that tend to be larger than characters, more likely to travel singly or in small groups and are often attached to a particular planetary spirit or reputed magician like Solomon or Virgil.[12]

Abraham's Eye experiments

The experiment to catch a thief by painting a representation of an eye on a wall was known in later sources as "Abraham's Eye" but circulated in the Middle Ages under the title "experiment for theft" or "the experiment of the eye" (*experimentum de oculo*). The idea of a painted eye that exposed thieves can be traced back as early as a fourth-century Greek papyrus.[13] Medieval examples range from a simply drawn eye to complex figures in which the eye is placed in a geometric enclosure inscribed with obscure names, letters and symbols (Figure 30.1).[14] In the medieval versions of this experiment, which are usually found in collections of medical recipes, charms and short occult experiments, the operator paints the eye onto a wall using a mixture of egg white, quicksilver and warm wine in a place where many people could see it. He then gathers his suspects to stand or sit around looking at the eye and activates it by

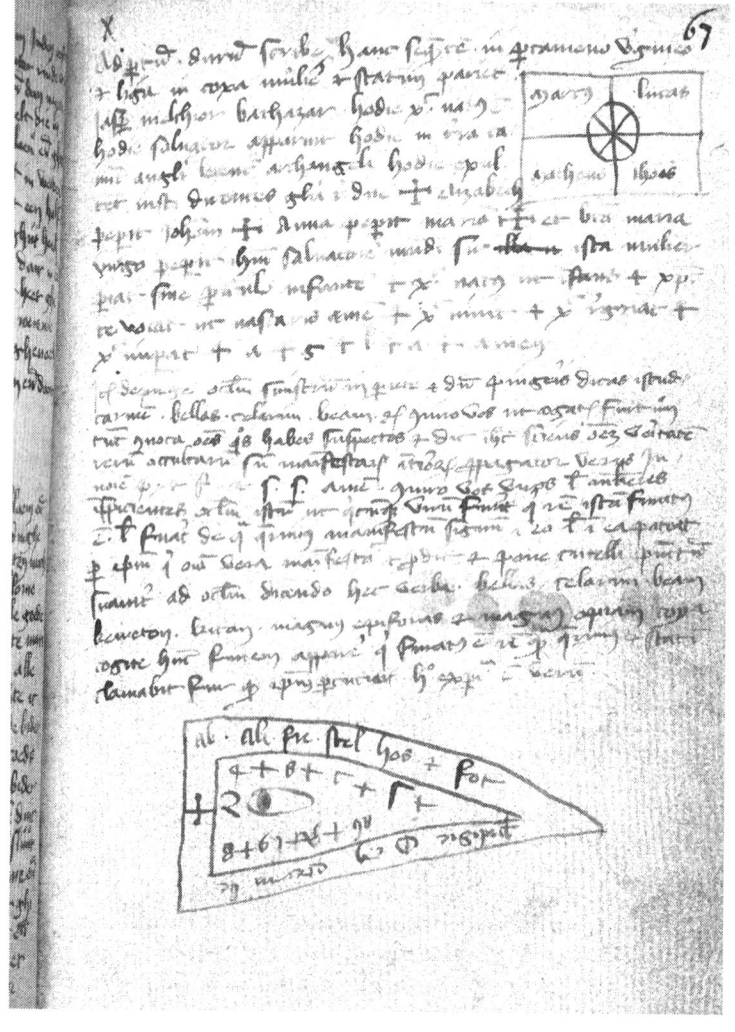

Figure 30.1 A lamina for a difficult birth and an Abraham's Eye experiment, London, Wellcome Library, MS 517, fol.67r.

reciting a charm (*carmen*), invocation to spirits or a prayer (*oratio*) calling on God, who knows the truth of all hidden things. When the eye is struck by the operator with a key, nail, hammer or knife, the thief will weep from his eye and cry out in pain and can thus be identified. If the accused refuses to confess, the operator is told to keep stabbing the eye with different implements until the initial tears of the thief turn into a raging pain. The eye is all seeing and can even find the thief in his own home.[15]

Medieval scribes adapted the *experimentum de oculo* to suit their purpose, sometimes making its figure and rituals more orthodox, at other times more magical. A fifteenth-century priest from the Netherlands copied three different "Eye of Abraham" experiments into his compilation of diverse practical and occult items.[16] The longest and most complex of these experiments includes a *historiola* based on the story of the discovery and punishment of the thief Achar from Flavius Josephus's *The Antiquities of the Jews* that bolstered the orthodoxy of the experiment and made it appear more like other charms.[17] Other "Eye of Abraham" experiments placed a band around the eye in order to add further ritual elements: magical names and letters and symbols of the cross (see Figure 30.1). The enclosing band, which became a typical feature of late medieval magical figures, also clarified the relationship between the text and visual device, making sure the reader would not simply skip over latter.

Laminas

Laminas are small square magical figures that were inscribed on thin pieces of metal or other materials and then worn or carried on the body or put in the place where they were intended to have an effect. They appear in diverse contexts, from simple charm collections to necromantic manuals. This flexibility was no accident; most late medieval Christian laminas had their origins in ancient *lamellae*, amulets made from thin sheets of metal and inscribed with magical and orthodox words and invocations, which were folded, rolled up in tubes, or even buried with the dead.[18] The two most common types of lamina experiment in charm and recipe collections were intended for treating wounds and infertility, though other uses for this magical figure included attracting or repelling animals, healing equine diseases and provoking fear in enemies.[19] These lamina experiments were closely related to the charm tradition; the inscription and recitation of sacred symbols, names and formulae were part of the process of making these objects and the source of their power. The wound lamina was made from a lead plate with an inscribed central cross and four crosses in each corner. Its dimensions were supposed to replicate those of the wound, an instruction that underlines the sympathetic relationship of affliction and cure. When the lamina was being inscribed with crosses, the operator recited a prayer and, when it was placed over the wound, a song to the Virgin Mary.[20] In the lamina figures in manuscripts, the crosses are sometimes drawn with thick strokes and additional colours to give them visual prominence.[21]

Laminas for conception and childbirth, like charms for the same purpose, were usually accompanied by petitions to the well-known biblical mothers Elizabeth, Anne and Mary, a common ritual motif known as the "sequence of holy mothers" or the *peperit* charm.[22] One of the earliest examples of the conception lamina (called, unusually, a *lamella*), from a manuscript of ca. 1200, is made of tin and inscribed with magical characters. It is accompanied by the common instruction that it can be hung on a barren fruit tree to see if it works.[23] Later examples for fertility and childbirth are made from different materials, accommodating a range of users and what they afford. The experiment for conception in Additional MS 15236 instructs the user to engrave a lead lamina with a series of mostly uninterpretable letters ending in "amen".[24] It is wrapped in leather or silk and, until she gets pregnant, worn around the neck of a woman who is trying to conceive. A less costly version of a lamina to protect in childbirth is found in Wellcome MS 517 (see above, Figure 30.1). In this experiment, a simple paper lamina for a difficult birth that should be tied onto a woman's hip has the names of the Four Evangelists written on it, while an accompanying prayer invokes Elizabeth, Anne and Mary and requests that the mother is kept safe from harm.[25]

Lamina making traditions entered the Latin West in Arabic astral magic texts as well as via early Christian adaptations of ancient *lamellae*. The metal laminas of astral magic were a subcategory of astrological images. They were made at astrologically suitable times, drew their power from celestial influences and were inscribed with names, magical characters or images relating to the goal of the operation.[26] The *Picatrix*, an eleventh-century Arabic compendium of astral magic that was translated into Castilian and Latin in the mid-thirteenth century, describes two types of metal laminas: those inscribed with representational images and others inscribed with magical characters.[27] The characters take the form of a series of small circles linked by strokes that are said to represent the figures of the stars (*figurae stellarum*).[28] Two lamina experiments with magical characters of this type – a copper lamina for repelling mice and a tin lamina for repelling flies – are part of a short excerpt from the *Picatrix* that was translated into Middle Dutch and compiled in Wellcome MS 517, a manuscript that also contains several Christian charm laminas.[29] This fifteenth-century manuscript has an eclectic range of occult items, from those addressing common household needs and problems to rituals for conjuring spirits, provoking love and becoming invisible.

The square metal shape of the lamina made it a particularly suitable vehicle for astrological "magic squares" (a set of numbers arranged in a square which give the same total when added in a straight line in any direction), a type of magic figure that is found in Arabic, Jewish and Latin traditions of magic.[30] The *Liber de septem figuris septem planetarum* (*The Book of the Seven Figures of the Seven Planets*) described seven magic squares to be inscribed onto laminas linked to each of the planets and made from metal appropriate to them. In addition, the magic squares could be inscribed onto many other objects, such as a piece of cloth, a ring, a dish, a knife, a bowl or a mirror to turn them into magical instruments. Each figure was activated differently: for example, to be healed from paralysis, you stared into the mirror inscribed with the figure of Mercury, but to have a revelatory dream you inscribed the same figure on a cloth and placed it under your head before going to sleep. A post-medieval silver pendant at the British Museum made with the correct magic square and metal for Venus represents the goddess with bird feet, an iconographical motif drawn from the *Picatrix* (Figures 30.2 and 30.3).[31] The inscription on this pendant invokes God to help its bearer conceive a boy, just as he helped Rachel (the wife of Jacob), which suggests that the lamina maker was aware of both the medical and astral traditions of this magical object.[32]

Finally, laminas were used in ritual magic experiments to protect the operator from malign spirits. These lamina figures were usually inscribed on square metal or wax plates, but could also be carved onto the white-handled knives used to draw a protective magic circle.[33] Laminas are particularly common in the fifteenth-century necromantic manual Oxford, Bodleian, MS Rawlinson D 252, which describes a variety of parchment seals, magic circles to be drawn on the ground, and square and circular figures to be inscribed on metal, glass and wax.[34] Laminas are common in the rituals to compel a spirit to appear in a pleasing form, do no harm to the practitioner and depart peacefully when he wills.[35] Spirits are required to appear on or above the lamina, suggesting that it was used as an alternative to the magic circle to trap or bind them.[36] Other laminas act as instruments to draw down

Figure 30.2 A silver pendant with an image of Venus and the Venus magic square. British Museum inventory number OA.1361.b.

Figure 30.3 A silver pendant with an image of Venus and the Venus magic square (reverse). British Museum inventory number OA.1361.b.

Figure 30.4 A lamina for identifying a thief, Oxford, Bodleian Library, MS Rawl. D. 252, fol.104v.

celestial power or demons. A wax lamina of Saturn (*lamina Saturni*) is recommended for freeing captives, a goal suitable to this planet.[37] But the devil is the dominant power in another wax lamina experiment, this time to catch a thief (Figure 30.4). This experiment must be performed within three days of the theft because if the thief has in the meantime confessed his crime or used his ill-gotten gains to give money to the poor or priests, or in any way for the love of God or the health of his soul, the art of magic will not prevail. The operator is told to get up early on the day of the Moon or Mercury and go to church and hear a mass. Afterwards, he inscribes in two places and colours on the lamina the names of four spirits ruled over by the kings of the south, east, west and north with their symbols and characters. The name "Sathan" (i.e. Satan) is placed in a central circle, which has an empty external band. A sixteenth-century copy of this figure indicates that this was where the user would write the names of the stolen goods. The scribe of this latter figure uses this band to express the idea that Satan was not summoned lightly: whatever appears in this circle ought to be feared.[38]

Independent circular magical figures

Medieval belief in the power of the word was reflected in the widespread use of textual amulets or *breve*, apotropaic texts copied onto flexible writing supports that were worn on the body for protection. Complex textual amulets sometimes included magic figures, seals, symbols and characters, copied alongside prayers, charms and devotional iconography. The most common graphic motifs were small, circular apotropaic figures copied in groups of between four and thirty figures (Figure 30.5). Since abstract diagrams are hard to interpret and their uses hard to remember, each figure had an outer band describing its properties, which also allowed the sets to be broken up and shared independently in the later Middle Ages. The large graphic element (*signum*) in the inner circle was usually inspired by the form of the Greek, Latin or Tau cross or had a resemblance to Solomonic seals, but could also include divine names, letters and formulas, and the Sator Arepo word square. These groups of circular figures appear to have been widely accepted as orthodox. They were collected by clerics, lay families and physicians and survive in various formats that were easy to carry or could be copied multiple times.

The primary function of these figures was protective, with each figure working against a particular physical or spiritual danger. These were orthodox figures, explicitly or implicitly evoking the cross and inscribed next to prayers, charms, religious iconography and professions of their angelic or divine provenance. The textual amulet was a pious object that could express its user's devotion: some figures were only supposed to work only if the bearer's faith were strong, although others claim to be effective even they had not confessed.[39] Why

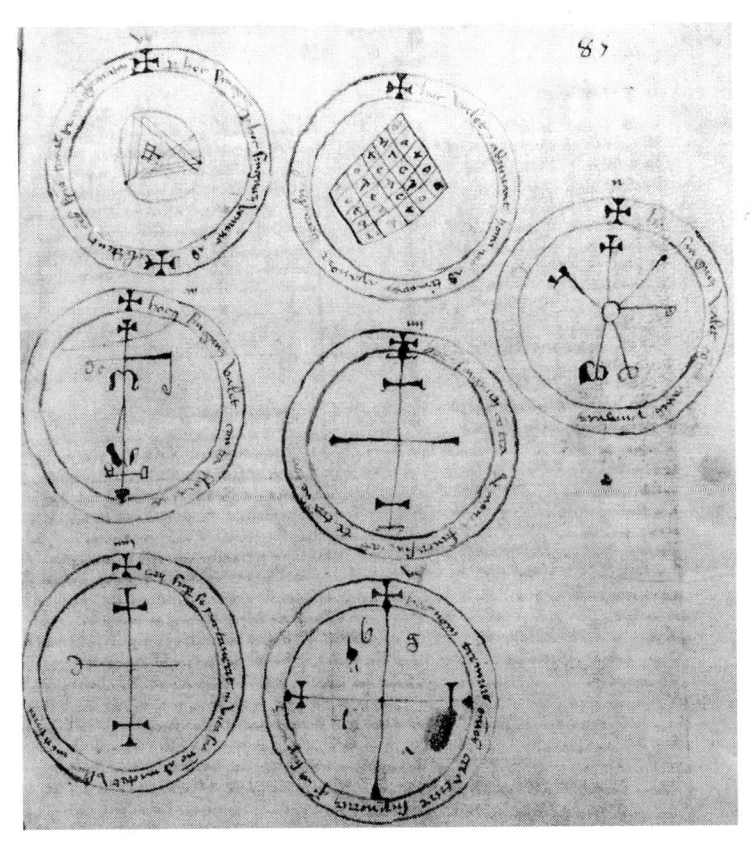

Figure 30.5 Seven circular magical figures, Paris, Bibliothèque nationale de France, MS lat. 3269, fol. 85r.

include graphic and often recognizably magical elements on a textual amulet? First, because their mystery evoked the sacred. The user is encouraged to view some of these figures as "the ineffable word of God", "the name of God by which all things were made", "the seal of King Solomon" or the special symbol (*signum*) of a particular saint.[40] The graphic form of these figures had other advantages, especially since the primary goal of textual amulets was to protect against the physical and spiritual blow of a sudden death. Figures could be activated by the gaze, a quicker stimulant of protection than the recitation of a charm or prayer and one that might be easier to locate quickly when it was needed.

The earliest surviving textual amulets with multiple figures date from the thirteenth century and are portable, densely written objects folded multiple times and intended to be carried on the body. The mid-thirteenth century Canterbury amulet (Canterbury Cathedral Library, Additional MS 23) has over 40 figures on one folded piece of parchment, including some magic seals without geometric enclosures and figures shaped like a lozenge and a mandorla.[41] The power of most of its figures was activated by the gaze and lasted only for a day. The figures that are interpretable (some have been partially erased by the practice of folding this amulet) offer protection against many natural disasters: sudden death, demons, flying insects, fire, flooding, storms, consumption (presumably by a wild animal) and thunder. One figure reveals the cross-fertilization of protective and ritual figures. It is a *Signum regis salomonis*, which not only protects against demons, but can also be used to make them compliant to the operator's wishes.

Although clearly multipurpose, textual amulets were also adapted to different users. The twelve figures on a textual amulet of ca. 1300 that belonged to a family in Aurillac reflect lay anxieties about human violence, illness, childbirth and resources.[42] Individual figures protect against enemies, gout, epilepsy, having your throat cut, fevers, demons, all perils, lightening, childbirth (this figure has the famous Sator Arepo word square) and illnesses of the eyes. Two figures offer more instrumental benefits: one gives its bearer eloquence (*bona eloquentia*), and another requests Jesus to give him his daily bread, presumably a reference to never going hungry. In contrast to this lay owned amulet clerical priorities focused more on harnessing of the power of spirits. Three of the seven numbered circular figures copied onto a spare leaf in an Italian preaching manual protect against physical dangers: flames, dogs and the loss of a member, but the remaining four are focused on power over others (Figure 30.6).[43] There are figures to make men fear the angel Barachiel (one of the seven Archangels in Eastern Orthodox tradition), to bring all spirits to obedience, to protect against demons and phantasms and to make all creatures tremble. The graphic form of these figures as well as their use represents cross-fertilization with the necromantic tradition of magic.[44]

Medieval magic figures were also disseminated by physicians to their patients. An amulet to protect against the plague in a late fifteenth-century English medical manuscript (Wellcome MS 404, f.32) has pleas for Christ to save its bearer inscribed in its inner circle and an outer inscription claiming that it was delivered into the hands of the Abbot of Corby by an angel on the order of Jesus Christ. In the centre of this figure are signs of the cross and abbreviated symbols of Christ's names. It is the only amulet in this physician's handbook, presumably because the plague required God's intervention more than other complaints. Another fifteenth-century English medical collection (San Marino, Huntington Library HM 64), that was owned by a physician interested in astrology and divination, has five numbered figures copied onto free spaces in the manuscript. These figures (called *signa*) are drawn in black and red and consist of cross shapes, letters and sacred names such as AGLA.

Figure 30.6 The figure of St Michael. Cambridge, University Library, Additional MS 3544, fol.93v.

Outer bands explain their use to protect against enemies (1) and sudden death (2), to aid in victory (3), and protect against fire and premature births (4) and demons (5).[45] In this case, the magic figures are not purely medical but have extended into other areas of potential interest to a physician's clients.[46]

In the later Middle Ages, the number and complexity of personal prophylactic objects increased: their ritual making became more complex, they combined different sources of power and they claimed to be effective for multiple uses.[47] An example of a circular amulet with these characteristics is the fourteenth-century figure on the flyleaf of British Library, Sloane MS 3556, which incorporates sacred formulas, crosses, pentacles, magical characters and names within its circular bands.[48] Although part of the ritual instructions for this figure is now missing, we can recover them from a sixteenth-century copy in a necromantic compilation, where it is titled as the figure (*figura*) or sphere (*spera*) of St Michael. The operator of the sphere of St Michael is instructed to purify his body and soul for eight days and then to inscribe the figure on gold or silver with dove's blood before sunrise on the day of the feast of the assumption of the Blessed Virgin Mary. The figure is then suffumigated with various spices and kept in a clean pyx when it is not being used.[49] When the bearer carries it faithfully (*fideliter*), the figure protects against dying in sin, poison, water, fire, and indeed, all infirmities of body and soul. Moreover, he will have an excellent fortune and gain the power to cast out demons from bodies, break chains and overcome all adversaries. Finally, as the effects of the figure are felt more fully, "you will turn your back on all evil" (*omne malum tergabis*). In this case, the figure clearly draws on the tradition of protective Christian amulets but it also incorporates the actions and habits of ritual magic: it will work only when the operator puts in spiritual effort, or at least uses the figure with appropriate respect, and it is intended to give him or her power over demons and the spiritual benefits of a pious life. From the fifteenth century onwards, small groups of circular amulets and larger multipurpose figures often found their way into necromantic compilations, where their protective value was especially valued for the risky work of summoning demons.[50]

Figures in ritual magic texts

In three important works of Christian ritual magic, the *Ars notoria*, the *Liber florum celestis doctrine* and the *Liber iuratus*, we can trace the construction, use and theorization of complex figures that draw on diverse Christian, Arabic and Jewish traditions. The *Ars notoria* was an influential and complex treatise written by a Christian in Northern Italy in the second half of the twelfth century that survives in various formats in more than fifty medieval manuscripts.[51] It claimed to miraculously endow the practitioner with knowledge of all the liberal arts, philosophy and theology, by means of angelic revelation and a divine infusion of wisdom. The practitioner of this art recited prayers while "inspecting" the *notae*, groups of figures that enclosed prayers (mainly consisting of *verba ignota*) and mysterious graphic motifs within geometrical armatures such as circles, triangles and rhomboids. The circle and other geometric forms evoked harmony and order, while incorporating motifs particular to the art being sought by the practitioner such as the parts of grammar or the zodiac signs. But the open-ended nature of the *notae* – their mixture of familiar and obscure elements and geometry broken up by sprouting characters – encouraged critics to read messages to demons into their inscrutability. The figures were accompanied by two main strategies to direct the reader towards a more orthodox interpretation. First, the text asserted a strong association between *figura* and *oratio*, which bound the spoken word and geometric forms closely together in the idea that "the figure is a certain sacramental and ineffable prayer that cannot be explained by human reason."[52] Second, drawings of miniature representational angels alongside the figures in many copies of this text directed the reader towards an interpretation of the *notae* as celestial or sacramental signs. Nevertheless, scribal creativity sometimes undermined these bids for orthodoxy, however, with stylized lions, oxen and dragons, swords, serpents and birds being drawn alongside the magical motifs and *verba ignota*.

In the early fourteenth century, a French Benedictine monk named John of Morigny wrote a book called the *Liber florum celestis doctrine* (The Flowers of Heavenly Teaching), a revision of the *Ars notoria* that tried to shift focus away from its unintelligibility and towards a less obscure ritual combination of Marian devotion and astrological ideas.[53] The *Liber florum* was a practical manual for achieving a visionary ascent to the presence of God and knowledge of all the arts and sciences. John's claims to have had revelatory experiences were viewed with suspicion and his work was burnt at the University of Paris in 1323. Nevertheless, his pragmatic approach to achieving a spiritual experience was attractive to many readers, and his text survives in three versions and more than twenty copies from across Europe.

John of Morigny's first attempt to rework the *Ars notoria* figures to fit his visionary approach was expressed in a text now known as the *Old Compilation Book of Figures* that survives in a single incomplete copy (Oxford, Bodleian, MS Liturg. 160). In its original version, the *Book of Figures* was supposed to present 91 figures to help the user obtain a visionary experience, including seven figures representing the Virgin, seven figures for the planets and twelve figures for the astrological houses. The astrological figures were not typical Christian choices to inspire a visionary ascent. Conscious of this issue, John followed the *Ars notoria* in placing emphasis on the link between the figure and prayer.[54] He instructs the user to visualize the figures in his or her mind with subtlety and passion, while petitioning God silently to grant them knowledge of one of the mechanical, virtutive and exceptive arts.[55] This knowledge was not supposed to be automatically produced by the ritual, but delivered by Christ and the Virgin, working through the angels.

Only two figures were copied into Oxford, Bodleian, MS Liturg. 160, small circular figures containing crosses, circles and a pentacle and groupings of letters that reference intercessionary pleas, the operator and his soul, and the property of the figure (i.e. its planetary body or the faculty it endows such as eloquence). Claire Fanger has noted that the first figure that opens the work (a circle bearing a tetragrammaton in Latin letters and other letters representing the mental faculties) is accompanied by visualizations involving the gate to Paradise being opened by an angel. The second figure, a pentacle with a complicated inscribed prayer, is said to be useful for recovery of visions lost due to disobedience.[56] Although each element in the two figures references a mainstream devotional technique, they are compressed together in an idiosyncratic way that accentuates their mystery. Tellingly, John reports the Virgin Mary cautioning him against his tendency to complexity, emphasizing that neither prayers, nor figures nor visualizations would have any effect without the operator's devotion of heart (I.iv.12.c); and in one place she accuses John of putting in his book "some nonsense about the angels which is not much use" (NC III.1.7.b).

Magical figures were, by definition, in some ways mysterious. So how they were interpreted was very difficult to control. John makes a determined effort to manage the inscrutability of his figures by explaining the letters and writings in the accompanying text, and by claiming that the cross was the central element in his figures and that all other shapes and representations were circumstantial.[57] But when he explains that the cross should be mentally supplied even when it is absent from a figure because it is the hidden source of their efficacy, his argument effectively reverts to the position of the *Ars notoria* and other texts that emphasize the mystery of figures and their workings.[58] John's figures also depended for their efficacy on celestial influences, an idea drawn from astrological image magic.[59] In particular, John noted that certain constellations and planetary conjunctions should be considered when making the figures because human reason was receptive to the influence of the heavenly bodies.[60] It is even possible that the idea of combining the power of the cross with celestial influences was drawn from Arabic magic. The author of the *Picatrix* praised the cross for being a universal figure (*figura universalis*) that stood for the latitude and longitude of all bodies, and claims that it was chosen by ancient wise men as the most useful receptacle of the powers of the planetary spirits.[61]

But the integration of astrological and Christian motifs and ideas was also typical of necromantic figures (such as the laminas considered above and the magic circles considered below) and this merging of genres made critics of the *Liber florum* uneasy. John himself admitted that circles and crosses were enough to identify his figures as composed "in the manner of necromantic figures" (*more figurarum nigromancie*).[62] When he rewrote his book he chose images of the Virgin Mary for his instrumental meditative figures. Though the new figures of the Virgin in many respects resemble the old, they are less complicated: the Virgin and child are set in a simple frame with four crosses drawn around it and mystery is now invested in the unusual attributes accompanying the Virgin rather than inscrutable graphic and letter combinations.

Control over the interpretation of mysterious figures was hindered by the creative choices of new users, but also by the fact that if they were considered powerful they might be detached from their original ritual contexts and adapted to new uses.[63] One of the most influential medieval magical figures was the *Sigillum Dei* (Seal of God), first described in the *Liber iuratus*, a work of ritual magic that circulated in two medieval versions.[64] The version of this text integrated within the *Summa sacre magice*, a compendium of magical texts written ca. 1346 by the Catalan or Valencian philosopher Beringarius Ganellus, describes how the seal can be used for six theurgical practices, including achieving the vision of God, redeeming the soul from purgatory and having power over all spirits.[65] In the truncated, "Northwestern" version of Honorius, represented by two Sloane manuscripts in the British Library, only the vision of God remains at the core of the ritual magic practices and the *Sigillum Dei* is given a prominent place at the beginning of the text.[66] In both Honorius texts, the seal is supposed to be worn by the operator when he conjures spirits. It forces the spirits to appear in an attractive and docile form and grant the operator his request.

Instructions for creating the *Sigillum Dei* describe in detail the sacred proportions of its geometrical figures, from the outer band containing the Great Schemhamphoras (the seventy-two letter name of God in the Jewish tradition) to an inner pentagram containing a Tau cross. The interlocking pattern of geometric shapes on this seal creates symmetrical bands on which magical words and letters are inscribed. This was a complex figure with challenging instructions, and surviving copies contain mistakes and deliberate simplifications as well as creative choices that reflect their makers' responses to the text.[67] When it became popular to transfer the seal onto three-dimensional objects, the potential challenges increased.

In ritual magic experiments, figures were frequently inscribed on rings and talismans to give the operator power when he was wearing them, and on mirrors to turn them into instruments in which visions would appear. The transfer from parchment figure to inscribed metal talismans in the sixteenth century in the case of the *Sigllum Dei* and the figure of St Michael reflects the value assigned to these figures, and their adaptation to new uses such as pendants or ritual concealments.[68] In fact, one of the original sources of inspiration for the *Sigillum Dei* may have been a circular gold or gilded silver mirror that is described in an experiment in the *Picatrix* to see spirits and other beings and make them obedient. This mirror has the same names of the seven planetary angels (Captiel, Satquiel, Samael, Raphael, Anael, Michael and Gabriel) as the Honorius *Sigillum Dei* and is also tempered with blood and suffumigated.[69]

The *Sigillum Dei* inscribed on a fifteenth-century or early sixteenth-century circular lead alloy disc that was concealed in a brick in Doornenburg Castle appears to have been simplified in order to make the work of cutting into the metal less onerous.[70] The most accurate

Figure 30.7 Matrix of a magic seal found in Devil's Dyke, Cambridgeshire. Oxford, Museum of the History of Science, inventory number 46378.

surviving *Sigillum Dei* in any media, however, is a sixteenth-century English matrix found at Devil's Dyke, Cambridgeshire (Figure 30.7).[71] The maker of this matrix paid close attention to the written instructions of the Honorius text, presumably in the expectation that his matrix would be used to produce many new metal copies. The matrix produces a seal in which syllables of the outer names are not only placed above the correct inner names (as in the Ganellus *Sigillum*) but also between the correct intersections and crosses, giving the seal a pleasing visual symmetry. The Devil's Dyke *Sigillum* is one of only four surviving seals that attempt the instructions' complex triple interlacing of an outer heptagon with an inner heptagram to give the compelling appearance of endless knots. In addition to the Devil's Dyke and Ganellus seals, the others are two idiosyncratic versions of the *Sigillum Dei* in the University of Pennsylvania, Schoenberg MS LJS 226 that combine curving ribbons with a flurry of crosses (f.4v) and new angel names (f.5).[72]

Magic circles

The iconic image of the medieval magician depicted a learned man standing in a magic circle outside of which demons were standing or swarming, sometimes seeming to be submissive, at others physically menacing.[73] Magic circles had become a significant instrument in Christian ritual magic by the late thirteenth century and were quickly disseminated into popular consciousness as a powerful image of the boundary between the human and spirit worlds and (depending on your viewpoint) human hubris or daring. This emblematic motif of medieval ritual magic was influenced by four traditions: circles in astral magic texts, the seals and pentacles of Solomonic magic, protective circular amulets and the thirteenth-century scholastic understanding of the cosmos.

The magic circles of Arabic astral magic texts demarcated a special space in which the magical practitioner performed his sacrifices to the planetary spirits and received the spirit delegated to speak to him in the smoke of the burnt sacrifice. In the *Picatrix*, four rituals to draw down the spirits of the Moon when it is in particular zodiac signs use magic circles as the locations for ritual animal sacrifices.[74] The practitioner stands or sits in the circle to invoke the spirits, and also places the sacrificial flesh, an image made from it, or the censer used to burn it in the centre of the figure. The circumferences of astral magic figures were diverse: drawn in the earth or demarcated by animals, branches, goose eggs, a trench filled with water, piles of straw or images shaped into creatures. But every demarcation of the figure had some connection to the sacrifice. For example, the ritual for speaking with Mercury when it is in Sagittarius in the *Astromagia* includes drawing a large angled figure on the ground in a remote mountain place and sitting within it. After the practitioner has prayed to Mercury, he is told to plant oak branches smeared with sacrificial blood in each internal angle of the figure. When one of these is burnt in a brazier in the middle of the figure, the spirit appointed by Mercury will come to speak to him.[75]

Astral magic texts contained prominent instructions for animal sacrifices in rituals to summon planetary spirits. Animal sacrifices were forbidden in the Christian religion and never associated with the cult of angels, so these planetary spirits were viewed by many Christian readers of astral magic texts — whether critics or practitioners — as malign or at best ambiguous. It did not help that Christian teaching tended towards a clear divide between good and bad spirits. When Christians came to write their own rituals to summon spirits, now often explicitly demons, they retained the link between magic circles and sacrifices, sometimes drawing the circle with the blood of a sacrificed animal or using a knife made from animal horn or constructing the circle out of animal skin.[76] But they also transformed the magic circle into a protective boundary between themselves and what they perceived to be a malefic spirit world.[77] In Christian ritual magic, spirits were usually compelled to remain outside the circle where the sacrifice was sometimes thrown to them. This cautionary approach is apparent even in a text like the *De secretis spirituum planetis* that has many features of astral magic and is concerned with summoning planetary angels rather than demons.[78] The operator of this text is told to draw a magic circle around the animal sacrificed to the planetary angel and its character, and to throw the sacrificial flesh outside the circle.[79] A composite magic circle accompanying the copy of this text in Wellcome MS 517 (Figures 30.8 and 30.9) illustrates the angel names and characters relevant to every operation.

Christian magic circles also drew their inspiration from contemporary cosmological, mathematical and astrological ideas. Magic texts offered glimpses of celestial structures, spirits and hierarchies to persuade the reader of the cosmological underpinnings of their operations. Some magic circles evoked a miniature cosmos with interior bands representing the heavens, characters evoking constellations (the *figurae stellarum*) and the names, seals and characters of celestial spirits. Other magic figures had a more terrestrial orientation, such as when they indicate the zonal areas that the planetary angels influenced or the demons of the four cardinal points.[80] The circle was not only a suitable representation of the concentric spheres of the cosmos but also shared with the Prime Mover the property of having no beginning and no end.[81] Reflecting this association with God, divine names were usually placed either in the centre of the circle or on the outer boundary between the human and spirit worlds where their protective power was most needed. Both celestial and divine names and symbols were intended to protect the practitioner within a ritually demarcated and empowered space.

The practitioner's protection from evil spirits was a high priority in necromantic experiments and it is therefore not surprising that some magic circles are filled with sacred names, petitions and symbols of the cross. Four magic circles in the fifteenth-century necromantic manual Munich, Bayerische Staatsbibliothek MS Clm 849 (henceforward Clm 849) fall into this category: a circle for having a response from spirits and three figures

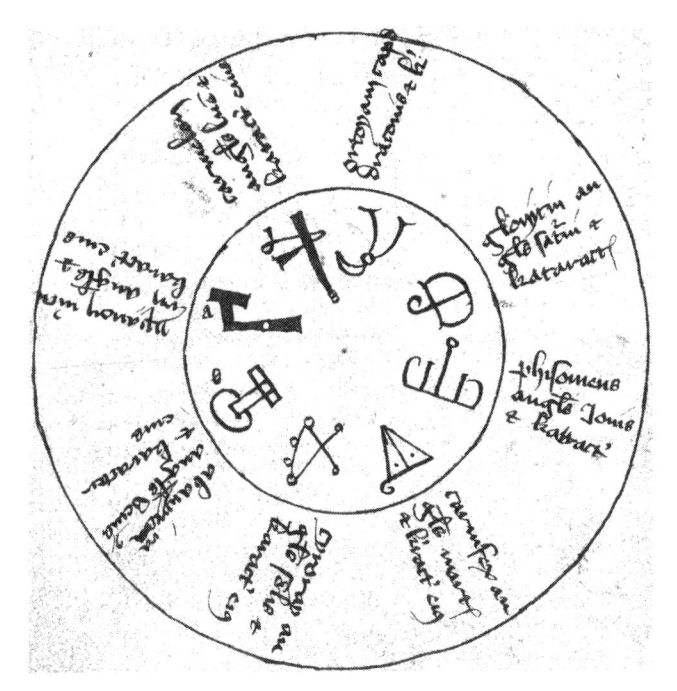

Figure 30.8 Composite magic circle with the names and characters of each planet, London, Wellcome Library, MS 517, fol. 234v.

for experiments to obtain information about a theft by gazing into a fingernail.[82] It seems likely that multiple orthodox motifs were chosen for operations to speak with spirits because this represented a particularly intense and dangerous kind of interaction with demons renowned for their skills at trickery and temptation. The sacred elements in the figures for the fingernail experiments were appropriate to the purity of the boy skryer on whom the success of these operations depended. Although there are some similarities between these figures and the circular protective figures discussed above, there are important differences in emphasis. The necromantic circles were intended to call down demons as well as protect from them; hence, their petitions focus on the power of God the Creator, while the circular amulets tend to appeal to Christ's mercy.

As John of Morigny noted regretfully, even figures with only circles and crosses were suggestive of demon conjuring to suspicious minds. The ways in which magic circles expressed one thing to their makers and another thing to their critics are unpacked in John Lydgate's representation of necromancy in his popular allegory of Christian life, the *Pylgremage of the Sowle* (1426).[83] The pilgrim protagonist of this narrative encounters a student of necromancy in a wood, standing in a magic circle, "within whiche (so god me save,) / I sawgh fful many a ffygure grave, / fful marvellous." According to Lydgate, the necromancer has a "cursyd ymagynacyoun" because he believes that he is God's messenger and able to command demons. He does not know what the magical characters drawn within the outer band of the circle mean, but he thinks that they make the spirits obey him. In contrast to this interpretation, the pilgrim interprets a "darkenesse hydde with-Inne" the characters as the marks of the devil that bind the necromancer to a treasonous allegiance with Satan and seal the fate of his soul.

447

Figure 30.9 The pilgrim and the student of necromancy from John Lydgate's *Pilgrimage of Man*. London, British Library, MS Cotton Tiberius AVII, fol. 44r.

Ritual magic texts were less concerned with the orthodoxy of magic circles, however, than with advising the practitioner on how to construct them and which spirits they were most suitable for. A chapter on magic circles (*De circulis*) attributed to Virgil divides them according to their use: identifying the spirits who are willing to descend (*circulus discretionis*), invoking spirits who can help and harm (*circulus invocationis*) and summoning spirits by the virtue of their superiors to help with the goal of the operation (*circulus provocationis*).[84] The cosmology implicit in these instructions relates more closely to the spirit hierarchies of astral magic than Christian demonology and this impression is reinforced by the fact that the text appears in a collection of works of image magic and astrology.

The adaptation of magic circles to different kinds of spirit was important in Christian ritual magic too, perhaps under the influence of magic texts like *De circulis*. The *Liber iuratus* recommends constructing different kinds of circles for the helpful spirits of the air and the malign spirits of earth. The malign spirits are summoned into a concave circular pit dug in the ground (called a *circulus in quo apparent spiritus*), while the practitioner stands in a separate circle, the "circle of invocation" (*circulus invocationis*) at a safe distance of nine feet to invoke them.[85] The magic circles of the *Liber iuratus* were taken up by Giorgio Anselmi, a professor of medicine at the Universities of Parma and Bologna, in his mid-fifteenth-century treatise on magic, the *Opus de magia disciplina*.[86] Anselmi's magic circles for evil demons include the same *circulus invocationis* divided in four and inscribed with the names Mesyas, Sother, Eloy, Sabbaoth for the practitioner, and, at nine paces away, a concave circle into which demons were summoned.

The *De circulis* proposes that circles have four general purposes: for self-defence, to accomplish the goal of the operation, to obtain love and to consult spirits.[87] The text notes that the practitioner (*artifex*) should usually have four companions, although one will suffice for the first or fourth goal.[88] The emphasis on love and speaking to spirits in this text is supported by the popularity of these types of experiments in necromantic manuals. The author of *De circulis* places the circle to provoke love (*circulus ad amorem*) in a separate category from others because it relies on sympathetic magic as well as conjuring spirits. The practitioner should take into this circle something from the object of desire (a man or woman) such as a piece of hair.[89]

The figures in two copies of a necromantic experiment to induce love illustrate the creativity of this element of the operation as well as the ways in which the techniques of sympathetic magic and conjuring spirits are combined in love magic.[90] The practitioner is instructed to draw the naked body of the woman he desires onto parchment made from the skin of a female dog in heat using blood from the heart of a dove. He then writes the names of six "hot" spirits, including Cupid and Satan, on different parts of the figure and his own name over her heart. Writing the demonic names on the image is a form of sympathetic magic intended to induce the spirits to enter the living body.[91] As each name is inscribed, the spirit is commanded to go to the woman and work on her body, heart and mind, until she is inflamed with a powerful love, desire and urgent restlessness.

If this first image is unsuccessful in provoking love, the operator is advised to construct a second figure: a magic circle drawn on the ground with a sword and inscribed with the names of different demons. These demons are then conjured to bring him the object of his desire. When she arrives, he touches her with the first image and by this physical action transfers the force of the image into her permanently so that she loves him for all eternity. The scribes of the two copies of this experiment chose to record different figures. In the Florence manuscript, a circular magic figure with the names of the six "hot" spirits is drawn quite informally at the bottom of a folio and has additional magical characters not mentioned in the text and (perhaps) the practitioner's own initials in the centre (Figure 30.10). By contrast, the scribe of the Munich copy recorded only the second magic circle as a large formal diagram, with the place of the operator (*magister*) marked clearly in the centre (Figure 30.11).

In general, there was a broad and diverse range of graphic symbols available to the authors and scribes of magic texts who could and did express their own interests, anxieties and proclivities in the choice of astral signs, Christian crosses or Solomonic pentacles. There were also iconographic changes over time, such as the dissemination of the graphic motifs of astral magic in the twelfth and thirteenth centuries, a later trend towards complex multipurpose objects and images, and sometimes, the replacement of obscure names with more acceptable crosses.[92] In the fifteenth century and into the early modern period, Solomonic influences, especially the use of pentacles, triangles and other bisecting lines, and the inscription of divine names, and Hebrew and pseudo-Hebrew lettering, began to dominate the iconography of figures in ritual magic texts.[93] This influence, an acknowledgement of Solomon's perceived power over demons in both magical and mainstream religious contexts, is also reflected in theoretical discussions of the use of figures.[94]

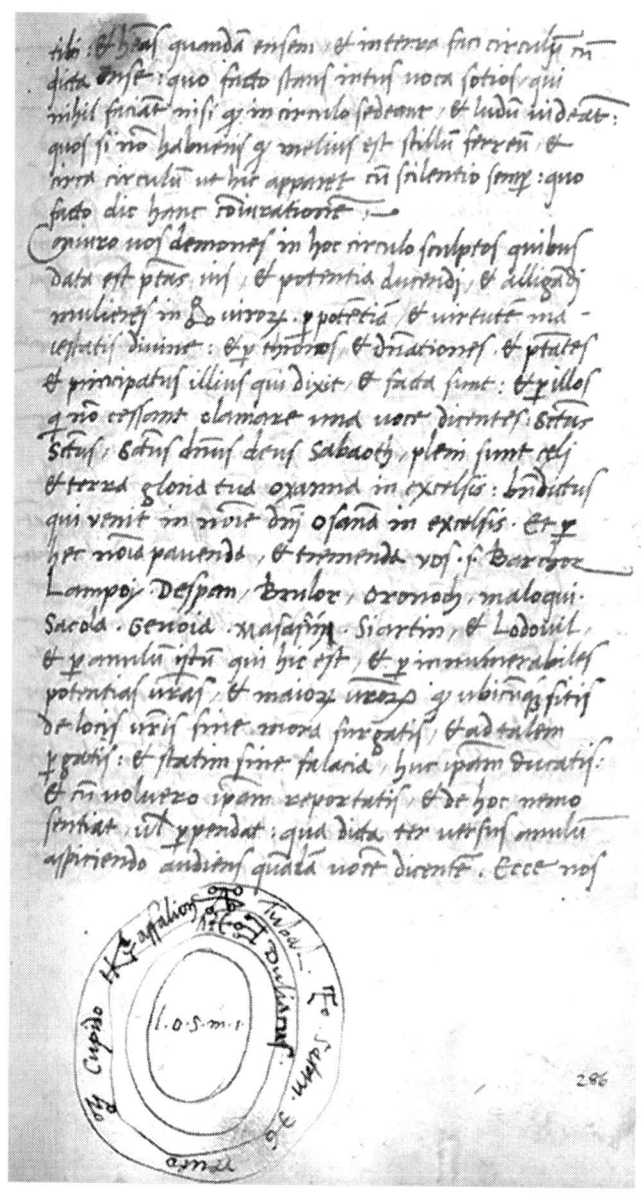

Figure 30.10 A magic circle from an experiment for love, Florence, Biblioteca Medicea Laurenziana, MS Plut. 18 sup. 38, fol. 286r.

Figure 30.11 A magic circle from an experiment for love. Munich, Bayerische Staatsbibliothek, MS Clm 849, fol. 10r.

In his *De occultis et manifestis*, the late fourteenth-century astrologer and physician Antonio da Montolmo used the typically Solomonic vocabulary of exorcism to describe the ritual inscription of the names of God on magic circles. Montolmo's category of figures includes both spatial and amuletic types, and he draws attention to the quintessentially Solomonic symbol of the pentacle, claiming that if this sign was inscribed with the name of God and carried with perfect devotion it would provide its bearer with perfect protection.[95] Giorgio Anselmi's chapter on magic circles in his fifteenth-century treatise on magic also emphasizes the use of pentacles, squares and triangles, magical characters and the inscription of divine names.

Future directions

Future work in this field will be able to add many more magical figures to those discussed, since every collection of ritual magic texts brings a subtly different set of visual elements into play with its cosmological ideas and ritual goals. In this context, it would be useful to develop a database of medieval magical figures and seals in order to track their use, selection and dissemination more precisely. A database of figures would allow further investigation into how these magical instruments draw together different iconographies – the sacred, the magical and the cosmological – and how their graphic elements relate to the text incorporated within or accompanying the figures. It would also be useful for identifying marks on objects and buildings that are likely to have had a ritual purpose rather than representing doodling, graffiti, decorative motifs, maker's marks, tally marks or any other kinds of visual communication. In spite of the variety of figures in surviving medieval manuscripts and the creativity of new scribal interpretations, there is a recognizable vocabulary of graphic elements across multiple magic texts that encouraged users' trust in their efficacy and critics' identification of them as deviant.

A final area of research that could be developed in this field relates to the cognitive science of looking, particularly in relation to diagrams. Like other diagram makers, the designers of medieval magical figures used strategies of visual language such as colour, shape, composition, framing, emphasis, vertical or horizontal orientation and placement on the page to engage their audience. These strategies provided information to the viewer and created perceptual points of attention like normative diagrams, but magical figures also signalled their occult power through the use of undecodable iconography, signs and patterns. Encountering and meditating on these, the viewer was not supposed to work towards an essential meaning but to be reassured by the power of a figure that evoked eternity, the cosmos, spirits and God.

Notes

1 This chapter is intended to be complementary to Alejandro García Avilés's chapter in this volume. Diagrams in the Medieval Kabbalah have received more attention than those in the Latin magical traditions. See Marla Segol's excellent book, *Word and Image in Medieval Kabbalah: The Texts, Commentaries, and Diagrams of the Sefer Yetsirah* (New York: Palgrave Macmillan, 2012).
2 Lee E. Brasseur, *Visualizing Technical Information: A Cultural Critique* (Amityville, NY: Baywood Publishing, 2003), 71.
3 Mary Carruthers, *The Book of Memory* (Cambridge: Cambridge University Press, 1992), 150 and 256.
4 H.A. Simon and J.H. Larkin, "Why a diagram is (Sometimes) worth ten thousand words," in *Models of Thought*, ed. H.A. Simon (New Haven, CT: Yale University Press, 1987), 413–37.
5 Al-Kindi, *De radiis*, ed. M.T. d'Alverny and F. Hudry, *Archives d'histoire doctrinale et littéraire du moyen Âge* 41 (1974): 250–52, ch. 7 (*De figuris*).
6 Nicolas Weill-Parot, *Les "images astrologiques" au Moyen Age et à la Renaissance: Spéculations intellectuelles et pratiques magiques (XIIe-XVe siècle)* (Paris: Honoré Champion, 2002).
7 Illustrations of the forms of the planets are outside the scope of this chapter. They are rare in Latin translations of Arabic magic texts, with some notable exceptions such as the forms of the planets in the copy of the *Picatrix* in Krakow, Biblioteka Jagiellonska, MS 793 and the illustrations in the *Libro de astromagia*.
8 Roger Bacon, *Opus tertium*, chapter 26 in *Opus tertium, Opus maius, Compendium philosophiae*, ed. J.S. Brewer (London, 1859) and *Opus maius*, part 4, in *Opus maius* I, ed. J.H. Bridges (Oxford, 1897), 374. Chinese ideograms had recently been brought to the attention of the West by William of Rubruck. For a further discussion of Roger Bacon's views, see Charles Burnett, "The Theory and Practice of

Powerful Words in Medieval Magical Texts," in *The Word in Medieval Logic, Theology and Psychology*, ed. Tetsuro Shimizu and Charles Burnett (Turnhout: Brepols, 2009), 215–31.

9 William of Auvergne, *De universo*, bk. 2, pt 3, ch. 22 in *Opera omnia*, 2 vols., vol. 1, ed. Franciscus Hotot (Paris: Andreas Pralard, 1674), 1059–61.

10 *Speculum astronomiae*, ch. 11, edited and translated by Paola Zambelli in Albertus Magnus, *The Speculum astronomiae and Its Enigma: Astrology, Theology, and Science in Albertus Magnus and His Contemporaries. A Critical Edition of the Speculum astronomiae* (Dordrecht: Kluwer, 1992), 240–47; On Thomas Aquinas's views, see Claire Fanger, "John the Monk's *Book of Visions* and its relation to the Ars notoria of Solomon" in *Conjuring Spirits: Texts and Traditions of Late Medieval Ritual Magic*, ed. Claire Fanger (University Park: Pennsylvania State University Press, 1994), 60–61. On the magic of images and idolatry, especially sculpted clay and wax figures, see Alejandro García Avilés's chapter in this volume.

11 Benoît Grévin and Julien Véronèse. "Les 'caractères' magiques au Moyen Âge (XIIe–XIVe siècle)," *Bibliothèque de l'École des Chartes* 162 (2004): 407–81. For examples of magical characters, see Figures 30.4, 30.6, 30.8, 30.9 and 30.11 in this chapter.

12 Some magic texts in circulation like the *De sigillis planetarum* were devoted specifically to seals and therefore provide good examples of this understudied visual motif. For examples of magic seals, see the interior graphic elements in Figure 30.5 in this chapter.

13 See Stephen Stallcup, The "Eye of Abraham" Charm for Thieves: Versions in Middle and Early Modern English," *Magic, Ritual, and Witchcraft* 10 (2015): 24–25.

14 My discussion here is based on the following Latin and vernacular copies, mainly in British manuscripts: Oxford, Bodleian Library [hereafter Bodleian], e Mus 219 (late thirteenth century); London, British Library [hereafter BL], MS Sloane 475 (fourteenth century); Munich, Bayerische Staatsbibliothek, Clm [hereafter Clm] MS 13057 (fifteenth century); London, Wellcome Library [hereafter Wellcome] MS 517 (fifteenth century, three versions of the experiment); BL Additional MS 34304; BL MS Sloane 2721 (fifteenth century) and BL Additional MS 34111 (1420–50). Stephen Stallcup edited the MS Add. 34111 copy and four later versions of the experiment in "The "Eye of Abraham" Charm for Thieves," 23–40.

15 Wellcome MS 517, fol. 124: "Et cum omnis oculum inspiceret si fur sit in domo videbis oculum eius destrum lacrimantem."

16 Wellcome MS 517, fols. 67, 81 and 124.

17 For Achar, see Flavius Josephus, *The Antiquities of the Jews*, Bk 5, ch. 1, 9–14, ed. G.P. Goold (Cambridge, MA: Harvard, 1934), 177–81.

18 Ancient lamellae were often placed in small metal tubular pendants hung from the neck, a practice that derived from Jewish and Egyptian traditions. Like some late medieval Christian laminas, *lamellae* from Jewish traditions place particular emphasis on the apotropaic power of angel names. Christian examples of *lamellae* appear as early as the second century CE: see Roy Kotansky, *Greek Magical Amulets: The Inscribed Gold, Silver, Copper, and Bronze Lamellae. Part I: Published Texts of Known Provenance* (Opladen: Westdeutscher Verlag, 1994). Amulets 35, 45, and 53 in the latter collection have invocations of Christ and allied powers.

19 For examples of these less common uses, see the instructions for a lead lamina to make all your enemies fear you (*Ut omnes inimici tui verebunt te*) in BL MS Sloane 475 (first quarter of the twelfth century), fol. 110v; a tin lamina to attract snakes (*Ut serpentes convenient in uno loco*) in BL MS Royal 12 B XXV (fourteenth century), fol. 65r and a lead lamina to keep bees from leaving (*Ne apes recedant de uase*) in Clm 7021 (first half of the fifteenth century), fol. 158. I am grateful to Karel Fraaije for the reference to the bee lamina.

20 BL Additional MS 15236 (4th quarter of the 13th or 1st quarter of the 14th century), fol. 31.

21 The five cross figure for making a lead lamina to heal wounds is unusual among the figures discussed in this chapter in being remarkably consistent across different manuscript copies, although there is some variation in the shape of the cross and not all experiments include the figure. The wound lamina figure is found in the following medieval manuscripts: Stockholm MS Co. Holm. x. 90, fols. 117–18; Bodleian, Laud misc. 553, fol. 56v; San Marino, Huntingdon Library HM 64, fol. 145; Durham Cosin V.III.10, fol. 30r; BL MS Sloane 1964, fol. 20; Bodleian, Additional. A. 106, fol. 149v; BL MS Sloane 2584, fol. 73 (with only four crosses); BL MS Sloane 3466, fol. 55 and Cambridge, Trinity College Library MS R.14.51 (921), fol. 29. A forthcoming article by Kathleen Walker-Meikle will provide a more extensive survey of Christian medical laminas in British manuscripts.

22 On this charm motif, see Peter Murray Jones and Lea T. Olsan, "Performative Rituals for Conception and Childbirth in England 900–1500," *Bulletin of the History of Medicine* 89 (2015): 415.
23 BL Sloane MS 475 (end of the eleventh or early twelfth century), at fols. 133v–34. For the barren tree instruction, see also Cambridge, Trinity College, MS O 1 58 and BL MS Additional 33996 (ca.1450).
24 BL Additional MS 15236 (4th quarter of the 13th or 1st quarter of the 14th century), fol. 31v.
25 Wellcome MS 517, fol. 67.
26 See, for example, the *Liber quindecim nominum* in Florence, Bibioteca Nazionale Centrale, II. iii. 214, fols. 41r–42v. This text describes how to make a silver lamina to provoke the love of a woman, a lead lamina to help a sick person, an iron lamina to ward off mice, a tin lamina to rid a beast of evil or a feverish patient of illness and a lamina of copper or wax for locating a fugitive slave.
27 The four laminas inscribed with figurative images are a tin lamina to draw clients to a physician, a silver lamina for increasing harvests and plants, a gold lamina for healing kidney stones (I v 30–32) and a silver lamina for increasing business (IV ix 44). The four laminas inscribed with magical characters are a red bronze lamina for making mice flee, a tin lamina for making flies go away, a lead lamina to create enmity and another lead lamina to curse a place so it is never populated (II ix, 2, 4, 6, 7).
28 *Picatrix: The Latin Version of the Ghayat Al-Hakim*, ed. David Pingree (London: Warburg Institute, 1986), II, v, 2.
29 *Picatrix*, ed. Pingree, II, ix, 2 and 4. Wellcome MS 517, fol. 235.
30 Edited by Jacques Sesiano in "Magic Squares for Daily Life," in *Studies in the History of the Exact Sciences in Honour of David Pingree*, ed. Charles Burnett, Jan Hogendijk, Kim Plofker and Michio Yano (Leiden: Brill, 2004), 716–26.
31 British Museum inventory number: OA.1361.b. Date: sixteenth to eighteenth century. Inscription: "Nihil deo impossibile quis sicut tu in fortibus O tetragrammaton qui aperuisti vulvam Rachelae concepit filiu[m]". On the image of Venus with eagle feet, see, *Picatrix*, II, x, 28 and 55 and the illustration in Krakow, Biblioteka Jagiellonska, MS 793, p. 382 where she also has the head of an eagle.
32 Rachel is first mentioned in Genesis, 29. The second but most beloved wife of Jacob, she had difficulty conceiving, but went on to have two sons, Joseph and Benjamin.
33 See Wellcome MS 517, fol. 224 and Clm MS 849, fol. 67v.
34 Of the many magical figures mentioned in this manuscript, only the following are illustrated: 1. A circular figure that is part of a conjuration to get spirits to depart peacefully (14v). 2. A square figure that is part of a skrying operation in a mirror or glass (23v). 3. Two circular figures that are part of an operation to constrain spirits (28v–29). 4. A square figure that is part of an operation to constrain spirits to do your will (46). 5. Two small circular figures that follow a prayer requesting God to protect the operator from all enemies visible and invisible, especially evil spirits and to give him power over them (fol. 51). 6. A square figure to be drawn with bat's blood on a window or in a circle as part of a conjuration for a horse (74v). 7. A drawing of a circle with an outer band that has not been filled in (fol. 79). 8 A small square figure filled with a grid and letters that should be drawn with bat's blood on a piece of vellum (*carta*) as part of an experiment for love (97v). 8. A square figure said to be a "Signa Salomonis" to protect against spirits (fol. 101). 9. A square figure in an experiment to identify a thief (104v).
35 Bodleian, Rawlinson MS D 252, fols. 36v, 46r, 52v–58r. Most of these references to laminas are not accompanied by images. An exception to this is a figure accompanying the Middle English experiment to invoke spirits on fol. 46 that describes a complex object consisting of a plate of lead or tin with its sides turned up. In each of its corners, further metal plates of silver, steel, brass and iron are placed. The object is inscribed with spirit names, obscure symbols and magical characters.
36 See for example, the prayer on fols. 46–47 which includes the commands "contestor per ista lamina" and "appareatis super ista lamina."
37 Bodleian, Rawlinson MS D 252, fols. 95–95v.
38 BL Sloane 3853, fol. 74. Another version of this square figure for binding a thief is found in the sixteenth-century necromantic manual, Cambridge University Library, MS Additional 3544, p. 44.
39 A figure in San Marino, Huntington Library HM 64, f.34, acts *Contra mortem subitam*. Its legend reads: "Qui hoc signum super se portat sine confessione non morietur." A figure in Canterbury Cathedral, Additional MS 23 will enable the operator to be saved wherever he is, but another offers its bearer protection from fire and water only if he or she has a strong belief in God.

40 See Canterbury Cathedral, Additional MS 23 for a figure with the "ineffabile nomen dei," a "figura sancto columchille" and a "signum regis salomonis," Paris, Bibliothèque nationale de France [hereafter BnF], MS lat. 3269 for a figure with the "Tetragrammaton," BL Harley Roll T. 11 for a figure "by which all things are made" and San Marino, Huntington Library, MS HM 64, for a "signum Sancti Michaelis."

41 This textual amulet has more than 20 magic figures (*figuras*) and seals (unenclosed graphic motifs) on its face and 25 figures on its dorse, including three that are unfinished. See Don C. Skemer, *Binding Words: Textual Amulets in the Middle Ages* (University Park: Pennsylvania State University Press, 2006), 199–212 and an edition of the texts in appendix 1.

42 See Alphonse Aymar, "Contribution à l'étude du folklore de la Haute-Auvergne. Le sachet accoucheur et ses mystères" in *Annales du Midi: revue archéologique, historique et philologique de la France méridionale*, 38 (1926): 273–347. The legends in the bands are transcribed on 347.

43 BnF lat. 3269 (end of the thirteenth century to early fourteenth century), fol. 85r. On fol. 84v and 85v are other charms and experiments against epilepsy, sword wounds and the bites of wild animals.

44 Figures 1 and 6 are similar to the circular figures in the necromantic compilation Bodleian, Rawlinson MS D 252 at fol. 51.

45 San Marino, Huntington Library HM 64 (with reference to the catalogue entry by C.W. Dutschke): fol. 17v, Contra inimicus [sic], 1, Si quis hoc signum super se portat nequid capi ab Inimicus [sic]; fol. 21v, Contra mortem subitam, 2, Qui hoc signum super se portat sine confessione non morietur; fol. 34, Pro victoria, 3, Hoc signum misit deus Regi Tedeon [?] qui cum isto pugnat victoriam habebit; fol. 34, Pro Igni, 4, Hoc signum crucis portans se non timebis ignem, [below the circle:] In quacumque domo ubi [the charm] fecerit vel ymago Virginis Dorothee eximie matris [sic] alme, Nullus abortivus infantis nascetur in illa ...; fol. 51, Contra Demones, 5, Signum sancti Michaelis quas omnes demones timent die qua videris demones non timebis.

46 See also the fifteenth-century medical manuscripts with magical figures: BL Royal MS 17 B XLVIII, BL Sloane MS 430 and BL Sloane MS 3556 discussed in Page, *Magic in Medieval Manuscripts*, 33–35.

47 E. Bozoky, "Private Reliquaries and Other Prophylactic Jewels," in *The Unorthodox Imagination in Late Medieval Britain*, ed. S. Page (Manchester: Manchester University Press), 115–30.

48 This figure is illustrated in Page, *Magic in Medieval Manuscripts*, 34.

49 BL Sloane MS 3556, fol. 1v, and Cambridge, University Library, Additional MS 3544, p. 93v–94v, ed. and trans. Francis Young, *The Cambridge Book of Magic. A Tudor Necromancer's Manual* (Cambridge: Texts in Early Modern Magic, 2015), 95–96. The Sloane MS text begins at the point where the materials to be suffumigated are described, then continues to the end of the instructions.

50 For a medieval example, see the group of nine small figures and one large multipurpose figure in BnF, ital. 1524 (1446), fols. 185–85v, ed. Florence Gal, Jean-Patrice Boudet and Laurence Moulinier-Brogi, *Vedrai Mirabilia: Un Libro Di Magia del Quattrocento* (Rome: Viella, 2017), 268–70 and plates IV–VI.

51 On the *Ars notoria*, see the edition by Julien Véronèse (Florence: Sismel Edizioni del Galluzzo, 2007) and his chapter on Solomonic magic in this volume.

52 *Ars notoria*, gloss on version B, ed. Véronèse, 142: "Figura vero est quedam sacramentalis et ineffabilis oratio que necquid per sensum humane rationis exponi."

53 On this text, see Nicholas Watson and Claire Fanger's edition of John of Morigny's *Liber florum celestis doctrine* (Toronto: Pontifical Institute of Medieval Studies, 2015) and Claire Fanger, *Rewriting Magic: An Exegesis of the Visionary Autobiography of a Fourteenth-Century French Monk* (University Park: Pennsylvania State University Press, 2015).

54 *The Old Compilation Book of Figures*, III. 10, ed. Fanger and Watson, *Liber florum* 372.

55 *Book of Figures*, III. 18. d, ed. Fanger and Watson, *Liber florum*, 3778–82.

56 Fanger, *Rewriting Magic*, 95–98.

57 The circular figures in Bodleian MS Liturg. 160, fol. 1r and 66r do give the cross a central position and the representations of the Virgin in Salzburg, Studienbibliothek Salzburg, Cod. M I 24, Bologna, Biblioteca Comunale dell'Archiginnasio, MS A. 165 and MS Clm 28864 are surrounded by four crosses.

58 *Book of Figures*, III. 11, ed. Fanger and Watson, *Liber florum*, 372–73.

59 See Fanger, *Rewriting Magic*, 124–30 on John's knowledge of image magic texts and likely adaptation of their visual lexicons, notably in relation to the anthropoid planetary figures of the *Picatrix*.

60 *Book of Figures*, III. 12. d, ed. Fanger and Watson, *Liber florum*, 373.
61 *Picatrix*, III. V.
62 New Compilation Book of Figures III.i.1.c. See Claire Fanger, "*Libri Nigromantici*: The Good, the Bad, and the Ambiguous in John of Morigny's *Flowers of Heavenly Teaching*," *Magic, Ritual, and Witchcraft* 7 (2012): 173.
63 In some cases, this means that the rituals to use them and their goals are no longer discernable.
64 Kassel, Murhardsche- und Landesbibliothek, MS Astron. 4° 3 and BL Sloane 313. The seals are at fols. 104 and fol. 4, respectively.
65 *Summa sacre magice* IV.1.5 and IV.I.6. On Beringarius Ganellus, see Damaris Gehr's chapter in this volume and Jan Veenstra, "Honorius and the Sigil of God: The *Liber iuratus* in Berengario Ganell's *Summa sacre magice*." in *Invoking Angels: Theurgic Ideas and Practices from the Thirteenth to the Sixteenth Century*, ed. Claire Fanger (University Park: Pennsylvania State University Press, 2012), 151–91.
66 The copy of the *Liber iuratus* in BL Sloane MS 3854, which does not include a representation of the *Sigillum Dei*, was edited by Gösta Hedegård, *Liber iuratus Honorii: A Critical Edition of the Latin Version of the Sworn Book of Honorius* (Stockholm: Almquist & Wiksell, 2002).
67 Creative interpretations of the seal are particularly apparent in examples from early modern ritual magic texts. Seven examples from post 1500 manuscripts and printed books are discussed by László Sándor Chardonnens and Jan R. Veenstra in "Carved in Lead and Concealed in Stone: A Late Medieval Sigillum Dei at Doornenburg Castle," in *Magic, Ritual, and Witchcraft*, 9 (2014): 117–56.
68 The *Sigillum Doornenburgensis* is an example of ritual concealment. Two surviving examples of modern minted pendant versions of the *Sigillum Dei* both have a provenance of Rome, Italy. The example in Pitt Rivers Museum, Oxford, *Sigillum Dei* (inventory number: 1985.50.619) is a 52 mm diameter circular pendant made of gilt bronze metal. Chardonnens and Veenstra briefly discuss an identical pendant *Sigillum Dei* that was discovered in the basement of an eighteenth-century house in Rome.
69 *Picatrix*, ed. Pingree, IV.vii. 23.
70 This seal is the subject of Chardonnens and Veenstra's article and called by them the *Sigillum Doornenburgensis*. It has a diameter of ca. 75 mm and was carved on a circular metal disc alloy containing a high proportion of lead.
71 Oxford Museum of the History of Science (inventory number: 463781), diameter of 53 mm. Devil's Dyke is an unusual landscape feature suitable for ritual placement: a linear earthen barrier probably constructed for defensive purposes in the Anglo-Saxon period.
72 The two seals are drawn on three leaves cut out of an earlier manuscript that have four large full page diagrams: a horoscopic figure relating to the angles of houses (f.3v), a cosmological diagram that indicates planetary rulerships over zodiac signs and months (f.4) and the two *Sigillum Dei* figures (f.4v and f.5). The leaves have been dated 1410 based on a note in the manuscript.
73 On this iconography, see Alejandro García Avilés's chapter in this volume. One of the few sustained discussions of magic circles in ritual magic texts is Richard Kieckhefer's *Forbidden Rites: A Necromancer's Manual of the Fifteenth Century* (University Park: Pennsylvania State University Press, 1997), 170–76, which focuses particularly on their different forms and protective function.
74 *Picatrix*, ed. Pingree, IV.ii and note also III.ix.16 in which seven sacrificial goats are placed in a circle.
75 *Astromagia* VI.2, chapter 9, ed. Alfonso d'Agostino (Naples: Liguori, 1992), 282. A space is left for the figure in the manuscript. On this work of astral magic, see Alejandro García Avilés's chapter in this volume.
76 See MS Florence, Biblioteca Laurentiana, P. 89, sup. Cod. 38, fols. 256v–60, Clm 849, fols. 8 and 107v–8 and Florence, Bibioteca Nazionale Centrale, II. iii. 214, fol. 79. A necromancer and his assistant who were caught in 1323 confessed to preparing a ritual to summon the demon Berich using a circle made from cat's skin: *Les grandes chroniques de France*, ed. Jules Marie Édouard Viard (Paris: Société de l'histoire de France, 1920), vol. 5, 269–72.
77 The protective magic circle is a topos of exempla stories as early as the thirteenth century: see Catherine Rider, *Magic and Religion in Medieval England* (London: Reaktion Books, 2012), 121–26.
78 The *De secretis spirituum planetis* survives in MS Wellcome 517, fols. 133–35v and Cambridge, UL, MS Dd. Xi. 45, fols. 134v–39.
79 The sacrificial meat is also thrown out of the circle in the "Experimentum verum et probatum ad amorem" ed. and trans. Juris Lidaka, in Fanger, ed., *Conjuring Spirits*, 60–61.

80 For a complex zonal circle to summon the spirits of the air, see the copy of the *Liber iuratus* in BL Sloane 3854 at fol. 133v.
81 Antonio da Montolmo, *De occultis et manifestis*, ch. 6, ed. Nicolas Weil-Parot [with collab. Julien Véronèse], in Fanger, ed., *Conjuring Spirits* (1994), 282–85.
82 Each experiment has a figure attached to it: 38 (fol. 99v), 39 (fol. 103), 40 (fol. 105v). The only other circular figure with orthodox elements in this manuscript (experiment 16, fols. 35v–36) is intended to be written on vellum and placed under the head while sleeping.
83 The *Pylgremage of the Sowle*, lines 18471–924. Lydgate's work is a translation (with some significant changes) of Guillaume de Deguilleville's fourteenth-century Old French *La Pèlerinage de l'Âme*.
84 BnF MS lat. 17,178, fol. 33: "Circulorum triplex est ordo: est enim circulus discretionis, circulus invocationis, circulus provocationis. Circulus discretionis sit autem nominibus descendere volentibus, ut sunt nomina principium. Circulus invocationis sit ut spiritus invocati qui iuvare possunt et nocere. Circulus provocationis sit ad provocandu spiritus in virtute superiorum, ut compellantur ad aliquid operandum."
85 BL Sloane MS 3854, fol. 137.
86 Florence, Biblioteca Medicea Laurenziana, MS Plut. 44, cod. 35 (1501–10), fols. 58r–60v. This sixteenth-century manuscript is the only surviving copy of this text and has three spaces where the figures for the chapter on magic circles were intended to be drawn.
87 BnF MS lat. 17,178, fol. 33: "Superius dictum est de circulis in speciali nunc dicendum est de eis in generali. Quattuor enim sunt circuli in generali necessarii. Primus ad defensionem propriam. Secundus ad impetrandum sibi vel alius. Tertius ad amorem obtinendum. Quartus ad consulendum."
88 BnF MS lat. 17,178, fol. 33: "In unoquoque istorum circulorum generalium sunt necessarie quattuor persone cum artifice, praeter in primo in quo sufficit una tamen eandem rem postulantes, In quarte tamen etiam potest una vel quattuor cum artifice, et sunt isti circuli totales."
89 BnF MS lat. 17,178, fol. 33: "Item est circulus ad amorem qui est circulus per se. Nec sequitur ordinem aliorum circulorum, sed sit per hunc modum: fiunt duo circuli ut dictum est in principio operis, tamen habeat aliquid artifex in circulo amoris de illa vel de illo pro quo intrat, ut crinem vel aliquid tale: et semper secum etc. Et semper invocationes faciendo dicat ut superius dictum."
90 Clm 849, fols. 8r–11v, ed. Kieckhefer, *Forbidden Rites*, 199–203 and Florence, Biblioteca Laurentiana, MS Plut. 89, sup. Cod. 38, fols. 284v–287.
91 This point is explicitly made in the *Picatrix*, book 1, ch. 5, 40, ed. Pingree, p. 24: "verba in ymaginibus sunt quemadmodum spiritus in corpore moventes spiritus et potencias versus illud opus."
92 In addition to John of Morigny's revision of the *Ars notoria*, see also the alterations to the figure in BL Sloane MS 513, fol. 199v.
93 Hebrew lettering is found in late medieval necromantic manuals, independent figures and ritual magic texts like John of Morigny's *Liber florum*.
94 On the "author-magician", see the chapter on Cecco d'Ascoli and Antonio da Montolmo in this volume.
95 Antonio da Montolmo, *De occultis et manifestis*, ed. Weill-Parot, 284–85.

PART V

ANTI-MAGICAL DISCOURSE IN THE LATER MIDDLE AGES

31

SCHOLASTICISM AND HIGH MEDIEVAL OPPOSITION TO MAGIC

David J. Collins

This chapter on the scholastic approach to magic is shaped by five propositions about the intellectual history of the High Middle Ages, particularly as it may pertain to magic. First, any evaluation of scholasticism is enriched by attention to the social context within which its particular methods and conclusions emerged. Second, scholastic conclusions on matters of philosophical and theological importance have, as a rule, more in continuity with their antecedents than in discontinuity. That is to say, scholastic thinkers can be counted on to have drawn heavily from and developed squarely upon earlier medieval thought, rather than to have rejected it. Third, scholastic opinions against magic, or any other topic for that matter, are often best understood in conjunction with the ideas and practices, often also magical, that scholastics were correspondingly promoting. Fourth, while today's historical scholarship should certainly rise to the challenge of identifying general trends among scholastic thinkers, unanimity in opinion or approach was not a defining characteristic of scholastic thought, including on magic, in affirmation or condemnation. Given the research tendencies of the last hundred years, it is incumbent on researchers to seek out and highlight scholastic heterogeneity vis-à-vis magic. And finally, a scholastic approach to magic, to the extent that one, or several, can be identified, warrants evaluation on its own merits and comprehensively, not merely, or even primarily, in anticipation of late medieval developments. Late scholastic writings on witchcraft and demonology have often been made into a lens through which the thirteenth-century scholastic writings on magic have been viewed, with results that can be quite distorted. This chapter will consequently focus on early and high scholasticism, that is, the twelfth to fourteenth century.

Evaluating scholastic approaches towards magic following these principles will constitute the substance of this chapter. Cautions and encouragements for ongoing research will flow naturally from this investigation. These goals will be pursued through several steps: first, after a sketch of scholasticism traditionally and narrowly understood as a development in the history of ideas with implications for the evaluation of magic, I will consider the milieus that fostered these intellectual developments, including not only centres of learning, but of patronage as well.[1] Second, I will consider a sampling of thirteenth-century thinkers, scholastics, who approached the challenge of understanding and evaluating magic. And third, I will evaluate the high medieval development of demonology with its implications, on the one side, for determining how magic worked, and on the other side, for social order and religious conformity.

Scholasticism and its context

Scholasticism is the form of philosophical inquiry characteristic to Western higher learning from the eleventh to the sixteenth century. Its principal characteristic is a confidence in dialectical reasoning (logic) as the foremost mode for interpreting texts, ascertaining truth and adjudicating conflicting opinions. The appeal of logic developed hand in hand with an exuberance for the thought of Aristotle as well as for the commentary and critique on Aristotle made in Muslim and Jewish centres of learning in the Mediterranean world. Scholasticism came to shape all disciplines of knowledge, including both theology and the study of the natural world. Method is more characteristic of it than content, and what we call scholasticism included a wide range of opinions on specific questions and inspired many schools of thoughts. Its pre-eminence was sharply challenged by Renaissance humanists and sixteenth-century Reformers who objected in various ways and for various reasons to the centrality of dialectical analysis and the Aristotelian shaping of Christian theology. Extensive reflection on natural philosophy and metaphysics made Aristotelianism significant for learned Western understandings of magic.[2]

In studying high medieval, Western Christian reflections on magic, the writings of Muslim and Jewish thinkers that entered the West along with those of Aristotle were also highly significant. There are two reasons for this: First, although Aristotle's writings on divination, magic and necromancy are limited, he did provide a metaphysics, a physics and a cosmology, on which later thinkers could and did base their own ideas about magic. Second, some later Mediterranean thinkers freely revised or rejected Aristotle's thinking on crucial natural philosophical questions to make the miraculous, the wondrous and the magical either more possible or less. In the course of appropriating these later writings on Aristotle, the Western Christian philosophers were challenged to take these amendments into account, or reject them. Such, for example, was the revision by Avicenna (980–1037), a Persian philosopher less enamoured of Aristotle than many of his contemporaries and widely read by thirteenth-century Western philosophers, of a principle of Aristotelian physics that material objects can effect change or motion in other objects only through material contact. Avicenna, in contrast, developed a notion of psychic effects on material objects that then supported forms of divination and prophesy. In the West, the thirteenth-century scholastic Albert the Great (1200–80) rejected Avicenna's argument on strictly Aristotelian grounds, thus attempting to return the conversation to more strictly Aristotelian terms. Albert's student Thomas Aquinas (1225–74), in contrast, decided to follow and revise Avicenna's proposal by positing the existence of intermediate objects to bridge the psychic and the material.

The reasons for the new exuberance for Aristotle beginning in the twelfth century are complex, and not entirely agreed upon today. Much of it had to do with the rediscovery of his writings on logic, which appealed to the growing number of scholars in the Christian West and their burgeoning schools. The importation and translation of works on logic were followed, most importantly for purposes of this chapter, by Aristotle's writings on natural philosophical topics. With them came the commentaries by such leading Mediterranean thinkers as Averroes (1126–98), Avicebron (1021–58), Avicenna and Maimonides (1138–1204). A third tier of writings brought into the Christian West in this time encompasses works on magic and related topics. Some of these had little or nothing to do with Aristotle but rode into the West on his coat-tails. The best known among those in this last category is the *Ghāyat al-Ḥakīm*, a work of astral magic written translated into Latin in the thirteenth century under the title the *Picatrix*.

The transmission of ideas and works from the Muslim Mediterranean world to the Christian European one required a significant mediating infrastructure. Two personalities who often are found collaborating in the workings of this infrastructure were princes and translators. The importance of the princely courts cannot be emphasized enough as they draw attention to the patronage that the intellectual revolution of the High Middle Ages was receiving from corners of medieval society not immediately associated with a culture of learning. Much interest in the intellectual revolution, including in magic, was generated in princely courts across Europe. They served as one port of entry for the ancient Greek and medieval Arabic and Hebrew writings. Two courts frequently mentioned in modern scholarship, often too hurriedly, are those of the emperor Frederick II (1194–1250) and of Alfonso X, called "the Wise," king of Castile (1221–84). Frederick brought leading astrologers to his court, most famously Michael Scot (1175–1232), and consulted them diligently before making any decision of weight. More detail circulates about the magical curiosity of the Castilian court under Alfonso, who sponsored the *Picatrix*'s translation from Arabic to Castilian and Latin. Research into other courtly milieus of the Central Middle Ages is patchy, Michael Ryan's study of the thirteenth-century Aragonese court being an especially helpful example.[3] The courtly milieu – or *demimonde*, as Edward Peters dubbed it – warrants further study for its fostering of magical practices and well as for its role in negotiating magic's condemnation.[4]

King Alfonso's engagement also draws attention to the network of translators and copyists which was central to the intellectual revolution of the High Middle Ages. The Iberian Peninsula emerged naturally and early as a centre for translation, given its multilingual, religiously and culturally diverse population. Archbishops of Toledo had sponsored translators – Mozarabs, Jewish rabbis and Cluniac monks among them – since the early twelfth century. Gerard of Cremona (1114–87) was the most famous of these Toledan translators. He translated Ptolemy's *Almagest* from Arabic to Latin with texts found in Toledo and compiled the "Toledan Tables," charts of celestial movements that were relied upon for astronomical and astrological purposes throughout the later Middle Ages, with the help of Arabic mathematics. Several Aristotelian treatises that undergirded magical texts, either Muslim or later Christian, were also first translated into Latin in Toledo, *On generation and corruption* and the *Meteorology* among them. Alfonso founded a centre of translation for his masters of the Mediterranean languages, the Escuela de Traductores de Toledo, which continued even more systematically to produce Latin and Castilian translations not only of diverse ancient philosophical texts but also of magic and esotericism such as works associated with the Jewish Kabbalah; the *Lapidario*, a work of mineralogy and geomancy; and Avicenna's medical *Book of Healing*. Frederick II's astrologer Michael Scot, who spend time with the translators in Toledo, produced Latin versions of several Arabic astronomical works as well as Averroes's commentaries on Aristotle's natural philosophy. Translating efforts can be found well beyond Toledo as well; these were an absolutely necessary precondition for scholastic engagement with magic.[5]

The Latin-language fruits of translation must themselves also be considered part of the infrastructure that made a scholastic approach to magic possible. While there is no overarching study of manuscript production and dissemination as pertains to texts of magic, divination and necromancy, partial studies have demonstrated how much light such research can shed on questions related to belief in and the practice of magic in the later Middle Ages. Monographic studies customarily serve not only as expositions of specific sorts of magic but also as bibliographic resources for important texts and manuscripts on these magic types; a classic of the genre is Thérèse Charmasson's 1980 study of geomancy with its extensive bibliography of these divinatory works. More recently, Richard Kieckhefer has called for attentiveness to magic as it is found in actual manuscripts and provided a seminal example in his study of a fifteenth-century necromancer's manual. Another example can be pointed to in Benedek Láng's explanation for the place of magic in the intellectual life of Central Europe through close examination of texts entering and circulating with that region. Owen Davies isolated a genre of book, the grimoire, and traced its production and dissemination from the Middle Ages to the modern era. Sophie Page's innovative work on a collection of magic texts in a single monastic library in Britain charts yet another way of accessing and assessing sympathy towards magic in the Christian West's learned, religious mainstream. The common denominator to these scholars' efforts is the conviction that medieval attitudes towards magic can be discerned from the books that compiled diverse texts of magic and the library that compiled diverse books of magic. This would be nowhere truer than in the bookish world of scholastic philosophers, theologians, prelates and lawyers.[6]

The aforementioned researchers emphasized, each in his or her own way and appropriate to the specific topic at hand, that ideas and practices pertaining to magic and contained in these books were the object of suspicion and that participants were thus under some threat of punishment from authorities. By the same token, the production, dissemination and possession of these books demonstrate that in this very same society, with all its complexities, there was a positive disposition and legitimated curiosity towards the thinking behind and practice of magic. This positive disposition within high medieval society is further indicated by the very people producing and possessing this literature: clerics working on it discreetly alongside fulfilment of their more publicly reputable duties and monks in eminent cloisters. The point in highlighting this is not to deny the incipient and real hostilities towards the magical in the High Middle Ages, especially as it came to represent thought and practices judged irrational and superstitious, but rather to warn against an overenthusiastic examination of condemnations and punishments, whose records are, in this question as in others, generally more appealing for historical research than the silence of their absence.

Scholastics and magic

High medieval scholastics were renowned for creating conceptual categories and making distinctions. These characteristics are obvious in their writing about magic. William of Auvergne, scholastic, theologian and bishop of Paris (1180/90–1249), made a distinction, novel in his day and with implications for centuries to come, that identified some magic as "natural." Developed in *De fide et legibus* and *De universo*, his concept of natural magic rested on the presupposition that the natural world follows established laws. These laws are readily graspable by human reason, thus "apparent." There are also laws that are hidden, or "occult," and while rational, not as apprehensible through the ordinary means of observation and reflection. Those who could manipulate natural objects according to these occult laws were practising natural magic. The concept of natural magic fits a middle category of engagement with the created world between demonic magic and experimental science (such as it existed in his day). William's new category of "natural magic" presupposed, affirmed and sharpened the notion of a demonic magic. In short, we see here an example of simultaneous scholastic condemnation and legitimation of "magic": William's distinction condemns certain kinds of magic as demonic and thus to be avoided in theory and practice, and affirms another kind of magic, "natural," as an appropriate form of investigation into and engagement with the created world.[7]

Another thirteenth-century figure famous for the distinctions he drew between the scientific and the demonic is Roger Bacon (1214–92). An English Franciscan, Bacon was drawn to Paris and became immersed in the high medieval appropriation of the new thought coming from the Islamic and Jewish Mediterranean world. In a systematic proposal for revising the West's educational program that he tendered to the Pope in 1262, he advocated for the incorporation of "experimental science" (*scientia experimentalis*) into the medieval university curriculum. By experimental science Bacon meant a testing of conclusions made with the other sciences through the human senses. His ruminations had positive implications especially for the practice of alchemy, a way of investigating material substances that was invigorated in the Christian West, again, through the introduction of texts of Arab and Persian origin. Bacon seems to have been drawn to alchemy by a text wrongly ascribed to Aristotle and circulating in thirteenth-century Europe, the *Secret of Secrets*. Other specifically alchemical texts that influenced Bacon and other scholastics were ascribed to Jābir ibn Hayyān (Latinized as Geber). Alchemy, though not welcomed into the medieval university curriculum, did attract the interest of many scholastics. Among the problems it posed Christian thinkers was its appeal to spirits, interpreted by many as demons. Working with a notion similar to William's natural magic, Bacon argued against the prevailing notion that alchemy succeeded only with demonic assistance. He outlined, rather, natural forces, latent in the objects, which the alchemist was striving to tap. Bacon's arguments attempted, analogously to William of Auvergne's, to remove alchemy from the shadow of the demonic.[8]

The study of celestial influences on the terrestrial world and human society posed similar challenges to scholastic thinkers. The study of the celestial bodies and their movements, the responsibility of mathematicians, was uncontroversial insofar as it was a study of God's Creation and the principal means for telling time and making calendrical calculations. The medieval Christian West had a more ambivalent stance regarding the study and exploitation of celestial influences: while certain kinds of influence on the natural world and human personality were so evident as to not inspire any philosophical or theological challenges, other aspects of what can be called astrology and astral magic contradicted Christian understandings of free will and conjured up the spectre of demonic interference. Albert the Great addressed this problem in his *Speculum astronomiae*. In the introduction, he drew the readers' attention to a vexing distinction between necromantic studies and astrological ones,

> For, since many of the previously mentioned books by pretending to be concerned with astrology disguise necromancy, they cause noble books written on the same [subject (astrology)] to be contaminated in the eyes of good men, and render them offensive and abominable.

Albert proceeded to differentiate two forms of wisdom (*sapientia*), legitimate in his eyes, that are given the name astronomy. The first accounts for the movement of celestial bodies and the relation of those movements to calculations of time through mathematics. The second is "the science of the stars," that is, the study of associations between celestial bodies and effects that they and their movements putatively have on the earthly world and human society and that reveal something about God, His nature, His providence, His designs in Creation. Albert asserted, as did most of his learned contemporaries, that this relationship between heavenly movements and earthly effects follows laws of nature and is rational. This wisdom is thus moral to the extent that it helps distinguish between right and wrong human action and rational to the extent that it reveals truth. It is further to be insulated from attempts to harness the powers of celestial bodies with "images, illusions and characters, rings and sigils," which practices, by Albert's lights, are demonically inspired and must be condemned.[9]

Albert's thinking on magic warrants extended consideration. He numbers among the most creative thinkers of his age as regards magic. His writings show more explicitly than those of many other scholastics a willingness to evaluate claims of magical power sympathetically before isolating what in them deserved condemnation. His commentary on the story of the magi in the Gospel of Saint Matthew, as he paused to consider how they knew to follow that one particular star, exemplifies this philosophical seriousness: the event the star signalled was of cosmic significance, but that meaning could not have been self-evident simply because of the newness or brightness of the star. Otherwise, surely more than these few wise men from the East would have followed it to Bethlehem. And if the star's meaning was not self-evident, the interpretive skill might have come from any number of sources, some of which could have been dissolute. Such reflections place Albert in a tradition stretching back to the earliest generation of Christian theologian of using the gospel episode as an opportunity to address a number of epistemological problems, in particular how sources of knowledge could be distinguished as in themselves good or evil, and also the problem of astrological knowledge, its epistemological validity and morality. Unease, for example, can be discerned already in Justin Martyr's second-century *Dialogue with Trypho* in which the wise men's interpretation of the celestial sign is explained with references to prophesies in the Old Testament and episodes of divinely inspired heathen diviners.[10] Albert's exposition falls in line with the intervening generations of theologians who unanimously celebrated the magi's apprehension as also divinely inspired and the first fruits of divine revelation among the gentiles. Such expositions, repeated throughout late Antiquity and the early Middle Ages, preemptively contradicted any charge of untoward magical awareness of the Saviour's birth, even long after Christian theologians lost their non-Christian interlocutors. At the same time, Albert's commentary did take some idiosyncratic turns, most strikingly when he designated the object of a magus's expertise as both "rational" and "magical" (*scientiae magicae*). In a substantial excursus, he laid out an elaborate classification of practitioners of magic, praising the magi as true philosophers, and distinguishing them from others – those who cast spells, necromancers, augurers and diviners, among others – whose claims are irrational or demonically inspired.[11]

Albert's approach to the biblical wise men highlights several general characteristics of a scholastic approach to magic. Albert clearly falls, for example, into a well-established tradition in the Latin West that understood "the magical" to be a moral and theological problem on account of its demonic associations. At the same time, theory, practice and phenomena that were otherwise understood to be magical were finely strained for aspects that were rational and natural, and organized for purposes of analysis. In the commentary on the Nativity in Matthew, this schoolman's attempt to exclude demonic aid from the wise men's undertaking, to identify their interpretations of biblical revelation as "rational," and to distinguish from their ways of coming to knowledge any hint of demonic aid, Albert's commentary on Matthew 2 reflects a mode of biblical exegesis and an approach to astrology that can be considered "scholastic."

William, Bacon and Albert, each in his own way, provide examples to support a central point of this essay, outlined in the opening paragraph, that understanding the scholastic criticism of magic needs to always keep within the field of view the philosophical and theological principles that the scholastics were attempting to preserve or even argue for as rational and good. Thus, Albert's condemnation of necromancy was offered by way of preserving and encouraging a study of the celestial bodies and their influences on terrestrial world and human society. In descrying the demonic, William of Auvergne protected for appropriate study of occult powers in created objects, which he called natural magic and recognized as philosophical. And in underwriting experimental science, Roger Bacon charted a path by which forms of alchemy might be recognized as legitimately scientific without requiring recourse to demonic aid or intervention.

Scholastic developments in magic

Measuring scholasticism's effect on the larger history of theological and philosophical tendencies in Western Christianity requires an appreciation of what preceded it. For our purposes, Augustine of Hippo (354–430) may be taken as foundational for early Western Christian thinking on magic and the touchstone for scholastic thinkers as they developed ways of thinking about magic. Augustine's teaching on magic can be arguably distilled down to one insistently made point: magic qua magic is demonic. In the Late Imperial period in which Augustine was writing, this perspective emerged from general opposition to Roman polytheism, which was rejected tout court as diabolical and contradicted a classical notion of the *daemon* as morally neutral, even benign. Faced with magic and miracle as it appeared in Old and New Testaments, Augustine identified a category of wondrous event that caused awe due to human unfamiliarity with the ordered working of nature rather than to either divine intervention or demonic manipulation. Genuine miracles were few by Augustine's lights and ultimately derivative of the one genuine miracle, that of Creation itself, which preceded and simultaneously established the very laws of nature whose violations could only occur with particular divine dispensation. Magic, more a matter of illusion and deceit, was most evidently dangerous as a misconstrued alternative to prayer. Or, in other words, there was a general concern that for some the reliance on magic and its requisite communication with the demonic could replace adoration of God and the invocation of saints.[12]

No scholastic rejected Augustine. A precise investigation of any scholastic's novelty of thought must instead be measured according to degrees of dependence, on the one hand, and divergence, on the other. A look to Aquinas can be helpful in understanding the scholastic dependence on Augustine because he diverged so little from Augustine's conclusions on magic, but also ranks among the most avid Aristotelianizers of the thirteenth century. Like Augustine, Aquinas took as his starting point the presumption that all magic is diabolic and thus sinful. He developed ideas of the sorcerers' tacit and express pacts with demons that enabled their magical practices. Magic consists most generally of illusions worked by the demons on their human victims in consequence of their superior familiarity with the workings of nature.

At least at first glance, Aquinas distinguished himself from Augustine on the question of divination, that is, the discernment of hidden and future knowledge, for his willingness to consider kinds of divination used in carefully delineated ways as less than completely repugnant. This impression has more to do with the new knowledge that the appropriation of Aristotelianism was compelling the attention of scholastics than with any theological reversal on the part of the scholastics. The influence of celestial bodies and movements on human society was self-evident to any thirteenth-century thinker. The challenge was in assessing human engagement with these influences as genuine or fraudulent, moral or wicked. Among the concerns against judicial astronomy, as the study of celestial influences on human action was designated, was that it undermined Christianity's fundamental stance that humans be morally free and thus responsible for their actions. Other mantic arts – the acquisition of hidden knowledge by ritualistic readings of crystals, bodily characteristics (palmistry and phrenology), ripples in water, patterns in cast bones, sticks, stones, etc. – also lent themselves to easy demonic manipulation, however accurate the knowledge revealed through them might be.

The attention to demonic associations with the practice of magic that is characteristic of Aquinas, that finds resonance in all other scholastic thinkers and that develops directly from Augustine even in a distinctly scholastic way culminates in the scholastic concern against necromancy and sorcery, that is, the conjuring of demons and the effecting of real changes in the natural world that would be impossible for the sorcerer on his own. Aquinas was scarcely willing to entertain this very last possibility. Unlike some other scholastics, he rejected the use of amulets for example as a way to harness energies emanating from celestial bodies. What is to be condemned in such astral magic is not that it actually manipulates nature but that it creates a moment in which demons can work mischief with the collaboration – sometimes explicit, other times implicit – of the sorcerer.[13]

While Aquinas's view on magic is in so many respects emblematic of *the* scholastic approach, intriguing points of contrast are to be noted with Albert's more expansively accepting view. Although Albert was certainly more engaged in fundamental questions regarding the workings and practice of magic and more nuanced in his condemnations than his more famous student, Albert's later reputation as a sorcerer, already established in the later Middle Ages, rested more on misinterpretations of his own work, misascribed works and a celebrity he ultimately achieved in the popular imagination. He had, after all, called himself "experienced" in magic in the *De anima*. Late in the nineteenth century, investigators working on behalf of a petition for Albert's canonization still felt obliged to repudiate Albert's lingering reputation as a practitioner of illicit magic.[14]

Albert's engagement with the theme derived from two greater, principal interests: first, he was interested in natural philosophy, that is, rational reflection on motion and change in the physical world, as well as related fields (by medieval reckoning) such as medicine, physics and astronomy. He was of course also a theologian and held the Dominican's most prestigious chair of theology at Paris, which is where he began his lifelong mentorship of Thomas. His expertise in both natural philosophy and theology is important to keep in mind, as is the distinction between them since it was a hallmark of the scholastic structuring of knowledge, that is, of *scientia*. His natural philosophical interests required him to consider how magic worked within the framework of a created world that followed natural laws even to the extent that magical events could be worked and occult knowledge accessed with the help of demons. Albert's philosophical reflections on magical topics axiomatically excluded the appeal to supernatural causes. From this overarching intellectual framework emerged a scholastic tendency to distinguish between natural and other than natural ways of manipulating the material world and between licit and illicit purposes. Causes and purposes did not necessarily, univocally correlate; and how scholastics linked them, especially how they balanced philosophical and theological arguments in doing so (philosophical arguments, for example, could not appeal to sources of divine revelation, that is, the Bible), determines any scholastic approach to magic.

Second, Albert was at the forefront of the medieval West's reception of Aristotle and of his Arab and Jewish commentators. This engagement is already perceptible in his first written work, the *De natura boni* (1230s), and all the more in the works produced once he arrived in Paris, where the new Aristotelianism was becoming a significant point of concern for theologians and other churchmen. His engagement is important for two reasons: first, because the legitimacy of magical phenomenon was in large part a function of how it worked, and the dominant understanding of how the natural world worked was shifting in this period towards an Aristotelian model; second, as mentioned above, because although Aristotle's writings little addressed topics that explicitly or directly might be considered magic by thirteenth-century lights, his Arab and Jewish commentators did, and an important aspect of the high medieval reception of Aristotelianism was figuring out whether and how to sieve the Arab and Jewish accretions out of the Aristotle. Albert, with the encouragement of his Dominican superiors, set about the unprecedented task of paraphrasing all known works of Aristotle, and commenting on many as well. In consequence, he was drawn to address topics such as astrology, divination, alchemy, etc., fields that the Mediterranean commentators had addressed extensively even if Aristotle had not, and were of broader contemporary interest to medieval Christian society.

Lynn Thorndike was the first modern historian to analyse Albert's understanding of magic and noted that Albert accepted the mainstream position that magic is due to demons. Albert judged the use of magic virtues in created objects as apostate and included even simple operations such as invocation, conjuration and suffumigations as demonic. He also expressed concern that the harnessing of astrological forces, while in itself not necessarily evil, verged on idolatry. Albert, nonetheless, understood the marvels of magic, even at its most elaborate, to pale in comparison to genuine divine miracles. Indeed, most of what humans see as magic Albert judged to be demonically inspired misperceptions, illusions and phantasms, rather than real change in the created world. In this respect, Albert followed the precedents set by Augustine and Peter Lombard (1100–60), remodelling them with his Aristotelianized anthropology. Thus, in his commentary on *De somno et vigilia*, he explained the possibility of these demonically manipulated illusions with reference to cerebral manipulations. Such control over corporeal beings by spiritual ones was a novel concept, certainly by earlier medieval standards, but also by ancient ones. On this point, however, we see Albert drawing on other leading interpreters of Aristotle, specifically the Persians Avicenna and Algazal, and their teachings on fascination.[15]

Albert also distinguished himself from other medieval Christian thinkers in his greater willingness to allow magic its rationality, and for condemnation looking more to its use than its nature. This is, for example, key to his defence of the magi and of the contrast he draws between them and other practitioners. The magi were experts in the magical sciences. This expression warrants underscoring, as to call something *scientia* presumes the natural workings of the created universe. *Scientia* was not, could not be, deceptive or in itself evil. Knowledge could indeed be used by demonic forces, and an advantage of demons was their superior knowledge of the workings of the natural world. But those workings – however occult they and their laws might be – were of divine origin and so good.

Demons and the law

A scholastic concern for the demonic has been touched on in passing several times so far and must now be focused on directly. As with the broader theme of magic, so much of what the scholastics understood of the demonic is indeed better understood as a change in degree than in kind from their predecessors. Still, an Aristotelianizing demonology arguably counts as the most dramatic scholastic novelty on the question of magic. Considerable attention has been paid lately to identifying how theologians and prelates came to regard the practicing of diabolical magic as a kind of heresy for the first time in the High Middle Ages. The hereticizing of diabolical magic and the diabolization of witchcraft provided footing for the rise of the witch trials in the early modern period. That magic could be a form of heresy is less self-evident than at first might be imagined since heresy was understood by the medieval church to be a form of belief and magic was a practice from which theological doctrine could at best only be inferred. Furthermore, there was a presumption in the older canons that demons could not effect real changes in the natural world but only delude humans into believing something illusory was real. In his *Satan the Heretic*, the historian of medieval religion Alain Boureau began his explanation of the change with an examination of the papal bull *Super illius specula* (1326). Issued by the second Avignonese pope John XXII (r. 1316–34), *Super illius specula* excommunicated anyone who invoked demons for magical purposes and based its severe penalty on the premises that the practice of magic indicated ipso facto distorted Christian faith and that devils could cause real evils through their human subjects. By Boureau's reckoning on these points, *Super illius* contradicts the tenth-century ecclesiastical legislation *Episcopi*, which presumed the ultimately delusory nature of demonic magic. Boureau continues his argument with reference to a larger context of papal politics, mendicant rivalries and social apocalypticism to suggest that *Super illius* is thus emblematic of a distinctive, fourteenth-century groundwork for the witch hunts as they broke out in the fifteenth century.[16]

The ecclesiastical condemnation of and concern for the workings of the demonic in Christian society raise the spectre of another figure, infamous to the high and late medieval periods, namely, the inquisitor and his role in the scholastic condemnation of magic. Little effort needs to be expended demonstrating that the inquisitors belonged to the scholastic milieu. They were the efficient cause, as it were, in the new implementation of the late Roman imperial legal system, first studied with exuberance by the *quattuor doctores* at the University in Bologna in the twelfth century and gradually implemented beginning in ecclesiastical courts and then civil ones on the continent through the thirteenth century. Just as *Super illius* could be taken as belonging to the opening round in a legal battle against demonic magic, the high point was *Summis desiderantis affectibus*. Issued in 1484 at the request of the Dominican inquisitor Heinrich Kramer (1430–1505) and printed as a forward to the text in the earliest editions of the witch-hunting manual the *Malleus Maleficarum*, this papal bull authorized inquisitorial proceedings against witchcraft in Germany and is thus taken as providing key endorsement of the mass trials against witches that occurred across large portions of Latin Christendom from the early fifteenth century till the late eighteenth. It should be noted that the notorious witch-hunting manuals of Western history, such as the *Malleus*, did not begin appearing until the fifteenth century, and the major witch trials followed them chronologically. In contrast, the two most famous inquisitorial manuals produced in the period at the focus of this essay – *Practica Inquisitionis Heretice Pravitatis* by Bernard Gui (1261/62–1331) and the *Directorium inquisitorum* by Nicolas Eymerich (1320–99), the inquisitor general in Aragon – have little to say about demonic magic.[17]

In contrast to the trials against witches in the later period, there were few trials against sorcerers in the earlier one. The trial and execution at the stake of Cecco d'Ascoli (1257–1327) is frequently cited. Cecco d'Ascoli was a mathematician, whose study of Johannes de Sacrobosco's *De Sphaera* led him to a blend of necromancy and astrology that troubled ecclesiastical and academic authorities. Put on trial several times, he was several times punished with penances, but finally executed in 1327 following his condemnation by Florentine inquisitors. Extant sorcery trial records show an increasing indictment and conviction rate of learned magicians for their reputed demonic proclivities in the twelfth to fourteenth centuries. At the same time, the high drama of the Cecco d'Ascoli trial seems to be the exception rather than the rule. As Sophie Page points out in *Magic in the Cloister*, Berengario Ganell, Antonio da Montolmo and Giorgio Anselmi, whose writings on magic appear no less provocative than Cecco's, died natural deaths. And although his *Liber florum celestis doctrina*, a work on learning gained from angels (*ars notoria*), was ceremonially burned in Paris, John of Morigny himself died of natural causes.[18]

Conclusions and future directions

Each of the principles laid out in the opening paragraph of this chapter proposes, directly and indirectly, challenges for future research. Some of the most promising research into high medieval learned approaches to magic has simply to do with bringing the research up to the same level of sophistication as shapes our understanding of late medieval and early modern magic. Some has to do with taking the best current research into scholastic philosophy, especially as it currently takes into account other, earlier Mediterranean (Jewish and Islamic) appropriations of Aristotle as well as the broader institutional and social context of Latin Christendom's twelfth- to fourteenth-century "intellectual revolution." In short, magic itself and the scholastic approaches to it deserve a precision in their analysis similar to scholasticism's more mainstream theological and philosophical ideas; and these resulting, new appreciations need in turn to be put in the broader social contexts of intellectual life, Mediterranean and Western European.

Looking chronologically back to eras before the scholastic also helps sharpen the focus on magic scholasticism. Scholasticism's conservativism and diversity make a modern approach to scholastic attitudes towards magic at best oblique. Consequently, this chapter, while indeed attempting to outline kinds of opposition to kinds of magic by a range of philosophers and theologians who followed scholastic modes of inquiry, has favoured an investigation of the strategies underlying their pronouncements on the magical. Thus, the attention given to scholasticism's infrastructure, which included communities of thinkers and institutions of learning, as well as networks of patronage and other support enabled intellectual interests to be developed and followed. Critical editions of scholasticism's first tier of thinkers – William of Auvergne, Robert Bacon, Albert the Great and Thomas Aquinas, among them – exist, and scholars have been turning productively to these writings with the newest questions about magic that are currently intriguing us. Their ideas followed and diverged from, in careful measure, their antecedents within the Western philosophical and theological traditions as well as from one another. Western thinking about magic – in favour or opposed – developed slowly. How much Augustine would recognize of himself in Aquinas is too hypothetical a question to receive a sustained answer here. But even while caution must be exercised in the necessary historical challenge of assessing the responsibility of an earlier generation for developments fostered in later generation, at a very basic level the church fathers of late Antiquity, the high scholastics of the Middle Ages and the late scholastics of the early modern period share several basic premises: that the workings of nature follow laws, that these laws and the powers of created objects can be studied and manipulated for good and for ill, and that demons can interfere in humans' appropriate interactions with the created world.

To the extent that magic gave access to characteristics of created reality, it was worth serious reflection to the scholastics; to the extent it involved demons, it was abhorrent. There was a scholastic way of thinking about demons, and at the same time and increasing through the later Middle Ages there was a concern about demons' interference in Christian society. Scholastic condemnations of magic, as well as their endorsements of and investigations into it, were shaped accordingly. But the thought on magic of many lesser scholastics, whose importance in particular times and places and influence on larger numbers of students cannot be doubted, has yet to be investigated, if only because the writings are less accessible. All the more important, in the current moment it would seem, is investigation into those networks of patronage and other support that made those scholastic ruminations possible, the ecclesiastical and princely courts, as well as the communities of translators and copyists. In a sense, the current challenge is to examine the high medieval attitude towards and practice of magic complementarily through lenses both of a narrow field of view that magnify for the sake of revealing more precise topographies and of wide field of view for the sake of exposing the broader connections between scholastic approaches to magic and other ideas and other contexts.

Notes

1 There are certain risks in insisting on a "scholastic culture" that encompasses "scholastic ideas," among them that things not related to the ideas and of significance for many more dimensions of high medieval culture disappear into the scholastic juggernaut. Nonetheless, historians of Western learning are finding great profit in evaluating ideas in the cultural and institutional contexts in which they are nurtured. Among those of an earlier generation who set that stage for scholasticism are a teacher–student pair who have been influential in the English-speaking world but whose legacies could not be more different: R.W. Southern, who in works such as *The Making of the Middle Ages* and the never completed *Scholastic Humanism and the Unification of Europe* put the philosophical movement in a historical, institutional and literary context, extracting it from the disembodied exuberance of the historians of ideas and rooting the neo-Aristotelian thought and its thinkers in time, space and culture. The other is his student R.I. Moore, whose not uncontroverted thesis in *The Formation of a Persecuting Society* correlated the rise of a "persecuting society" – the developing interest in and resources for the exercise of social control by civil and ecclesiastical elites, the invention and identification of scapegoats and their sustained persecution through the exercise of intellectually legitimated state power – and the rise of scholasticism. R.I. Moore, *The Formation of a Persecuting Society: Power and Deviance in Western Europe, 950–1250* (Oxford: Basil Blackwell, 1987); R.W. Southern, *The Making of the Middle Ages* (New Haven: Yale University Press, 1959); and *Scholastic Humanism and the Unification of Europe*, 2 vols. (Oxford: Blackwell, 1995 and 2001). A more recent and highly successful explanation of scholasticism within its cultural and institutional contexts is to be found in Ian P. Wei, *Intellectual Culture in Medieval Paris: Theologians and the University, c.1100-1330* (Cambridge: Cambridge University Press, 2012).
2 Many works describe scholasticism as a mode of philosophical inquiry and an educational approach. The classic studies still serve well to introduce readers to it: Etienne Gilson, *History of Christian Philosophy in the Middle Ages* (New York: Random House, 1955); Martin Grabmann, *Die Geschichte der scholastischen Methode*, 2 vols. (Basel: B. Schwabe, 1961); John Marenbon, *Later Medieval Philosophy (1150–1350): An Introduction* (London: Routledge & K. Paul, 1987).
3 Michael A. Ryan, *A Kingdom of Stargazers: Astrology and Authority in the Late Medieval Crown of Aragon* (Ithaca: Cornell University Press, 2011).

4 Edward Peters, *The Magician, the Witch, and the Law* (Philadelphia: University of Pennsylvania Press, 1978).
5 Charles Burnett, "The Translating Activity in Medieval Spain," in *Handbuch der Orientalistik: The Legacy of Muslim Spain*, ed. S.K. Jayyusi (Leiden: Brill, 1992); "The Coherence of the Arabic-Latin Translation Program in Toledo in the Twelfth Century," *Science in Context* 14 (2001).
6 Thérèse Charmasson, *Recherches sur une technique divinatoire, la géomancie dans l'Occident médiéval*, Centre de recherches d'histoire et de philologie de la IVe Section de l'École pratique des hautes études (Genève: Droz, 1980); Richard Kieckhefer, *Forbidden Rites: A Necromancer's Manual of the Fifteenth Century* (University Park: Pennsylvania State University Press, 1998); Benedek Láng, *Unlocked Books: Manuscripts of Learned Magic in the Medieval Libraries of Central Europe*, Magic in History (University Park: Pennsylvania State University Press, 2008); Owen Davies, *Grimoires: A History of Magic Books* (New York: Oxfrod University Press, 2009), 6–92; Sophie Page, *Magic in the Cloister: Pious Motives, Illicit Interests, and Occult Approaches to the Medieval Universe* (University Park: Pennsylvania State University Press, 2013). Fourteenth- and fifteenth-century books and collections are receiving more attention at this point than earlier period. In part this is due to how much more material there is to work with. Transmission history from earlier centuries has concentrated on works of highest profile such as the *Picatrix*: David Edwin Pingree, ed. *Picatrix: the Latin Version of the Ghāyat al-Hakīm*, Studies of the Warburg Institute (London: Warburg Institute, 1986); *Picatrix: Un traité de magie médiéval*, ed. Béatrice Bakhouche, Frédéric Fauquier and Brigitte Pérez-Jean, Miroir du Moyen Âge (Turnhout: Brepols, 2003).
7 William's most recent full biography dates from 1880: Noël Valois, *Guillaume d'Auvergne, évêque de Paris (1228–1249) sa vie et ses ouvrages* (Dubuque, IA: W. C. Brown Reprint Library, 1963). Addressing William's developing ideas on magic and demons: Thomas B. de Mayo, *The Demonology of William of Auvergne: By Fire and Sword* (Lewiston, NY: The Edwin Mellen Press, 2007). *De legibus*, c XXIV of William of Auvergne, *Opera omnia* (Paris: Andraea Pralard, 1674; repr. Frankfurt am Main: Minerva, 1963), 69.
8 Roger Bacon, "Epistola de Secretis Operibus," in *Opera quaedam hactenus inedita*, edited by J. S. Brewer (London, 1859), 523. George Molland, "Roger Bacon as Magician," *Traditio* 30 (1974): 445–60; Graziella Federici Vescovini, *Le Moyen Âge magique: La magie entre religion et science aux xiiie et xive siècles*, ed. Marta Cristiani, et al., Études de philosophie médiévale (Paris: Librairie philosophique J. Vrin, 2011), 27–31, 37–41, 54–7, 144–55, 250–55, 307–14.
9 Albertus Magnus, "Speculum astronomiae," in *The "Speculum astronomiae" and Its Enigma*, ed. Paola Zambelli (Dordrecht, the Netherlands: Kluwer Academic Publishers, 1992), 209. The debate over ascription is outlined here: Jeremiah Hackett, "Albert the Great and the *Speculum astronomiae*: The State of the Research at the Beginning of the Twenty-First Century," in *A Companion to Albert the Great*, ed. Irven Michael Resnick (Leiden: Brill, 2012), 437–49.
10 Justin Martyr, *Dialogue with Trypho*, cc. 77–9. See Wilhelm August Schulze, "Zur Geschichte der Auslegung von Matth. 2, 1–12," *Theologische Zeitschrift* 31 (1975): 150.
11 Albertus Magnus, *Super Mattheum*, c.2, v.1. Colon. Ed. XXI.1, page 46, lines 21–61.
12 Augustine of Hippo, *The City of God*, book 5, chapters 1–11; *On Christian Doctrine*, book 2, chapters 20–9; and *On the Divination of Demons*. Kyle Fraser, "The Contested Boundaries of 'Magic' and 'Religion' in Late Pagan Monotheism," *Magic, Ritual, and Witchcraft* 4 (2009): 131–51.
13 Thomas Aquinas, ST Ia qq 51, 57, 58, 64, 86, 109–11, 114–17; Ia-IIae qq 9, 102; IIa-IIae qq 36, 43, 90, 92–6, 154, 167, 172, 178; IIIa qq 36, 43. SCG IIIa 84–88, 92, 103–06, 154. Super Sent. Ia 38; IIa 7,8, 15, 25; IIIa 35; IV 9. And the treatises *De iudiciis astrorum*, *De sortibus*, *De operationibus occultis naturae*, and *De malo*. Aquinas in the original Latin is available online here: www.corpusthomisticum.org/. English translations of the two Summas can be found here: *The Summa theologica*, 2nd rev. ed., 22 vols., ed. and trans. Fathers of the English Dominican Province (London: Burns, Oates & Washbourne, 1912–36; reprinted in 5 vols., Westminster, MD: Christian Classics, 1981). *On the Truth of the Catholic Faith (Summa Contra Gentiles)*, 5 vols., ed. and trans. Anton C. Pegis, James F. Anderson, Vernon J. Bourke and Charles J. O'Neil (New York: Doubleday, 1955–57; reprinted as *Summa contra gentiles*, Notre Dame, IN: University of Notre Dame Press, 1975). See also Thomas Linsenmann, *Die Magie bei Thomas von Aquin*. vol. 44, ed. Michael Schmaus, et al., Veröffentlichungen des Grabmann-Institutes zur Erforschung der mittelalterlichen Theologie und Philosophie (Berlin: Akademie Verlag, 2000), 329–42.
14 David J. Collins, "Albertus, *Magnus* or *Magus*? Magic, Natural Philosophy, and Religious Reform in the Late Middle Ages," *Renaissance Quarterly* 63 (2010): 1–44.

15 Lynn Thorndike, *A History of Magic and Experimental Science*, 8 vols. (New York, 1923–58), 2: 551–60; Alessandro Palazzo, "Albert the Great's Doctrine of Fascination in the Context of His Philosophical System," in *Via Alberti*, ed. Ludger Honnefelder, Hannes Möhle and Susana Bullido del Barrio (Münster: Aschendorff, 2009), 135–215.
16 *Satan the Heretic* was received with much acclaim, but was also criticized for possibly exaggerating the real effects and contribution of *Super illius*. Alexander IV's decretal *Accusatus de heresi*, after all, had drawn the connection between heresy and magic already three quarters of a century earlier; and the *Super illius*, as well as nearly all the Pope's theological consultors in its composition, was scarcely heard of again after its promulgation. Alain Boureau, *Satan the Heretic: The Birth of Demonology in the Medieval West*, trans. Teresa Lavender Fagan (Chicago: University of Chicago Press, 2006). See also Henry Ansgar Kelly, review of *Satan the Heretic: The Birth of Demonology in the Medieval West* by Alain Boureau, *History of Religions* 49 (2009): 88–92; and Alain Boureau, "Demons and the Christian Community," in *Cambridge History of Christianity: Christianity in Western Europe, c. 1100–c. 1500*, ed. Miri Rubin and Walter Simons (Cambridge: Cambridge University Press, 2009), 420–32.
17 For the text with commentary: Heinrich (Institoris) Kramer, *Malleus Maleficarum*, ed. Christopher S. Mackay (Cambridge: Cambridge University Press, 2006).
18 Page, *Magic in the Cloister*, 132.

32

PASTORAL LITERATURE AND PREACHING

Kathleen Kamerick

What did the medieval Christian Church teach the laity about magic? This simple question has no straightforward answer. The problem of laypeople's belief in and practice of magic was bound to the more fundamental issue of what the laity needed to know in order to be saved. Did magic threaten one's salvation? Medieval pastoral texts such as sermons, manuals for confessors and works aiming to teach laypeople how to live as good Christians often took up the problem of magic, but it was rarely a major concern. These *pastoralia* – including both texts used by priests in their work of the care of souls as well as the diverse works of religious instruction read by laypeople – multiplied in Europe from the thirteenth to early sixteenth centuries in both Latin and the vernacular languages. Their profusion and diversity offer a potentially rich source for examining complex and even conflicting views of magic, as well as clerical–lay interactions over a contested subject. This essay focuses primarily on the research on *pastoralia* known in thirteenth- to fifteenth-century England, which has formed the core of much of the research to date, with some attention to the early Middle Ages and to other geographic areas.[1]

The outline of *pastoralia*'s development in England has been clearly laid out. In the early thirteenth century, works like Richard of Wetheringsett's *Qui bene praesunt* (c. 1215–1220) helped to codify several topics that pastoral instruction should include, among them the Creed and Lord's Prayer, the seven sacraments, the theological and cardinal virtues and the seven major vices, and the Ten Commandments.[2] The influence of this work combined with the impetus of the 1215 Fourth Lateran Council to encourage a number of thirteenth-century synods in England to produce recommendations for pastoral instruction. Around 1239, Bishop Robert Grosseteste of Lincoln, for example, worked up a pastoral syllabus that commanded parish priests to preach the Ten Commandments. Several decades later in 1281, the Archbishop of Canterbury John Pecham presided over a council at Lambeth that elaborated the requirements for priests in the *Ignorantia Sacerdotum*, ordering them to preach at least four times a year in English on the creed, the Decalogue, the Articles of Faith, as well as the Works of Mercy and the Deadly Sins, the sacraments and more.[3] This syllabus formed the core of religious instruction into the sixteenth century. It became part of William of Pagula's popular *Oculus Sacerdotis* (c. 1320), for instance, and was translated into English in John Mirk's *Instructions for Parish Priests*. The Pecham statutes were reproduced several times in the early print era such as in the *Exornatorium Curatorum* (c. 1516) printed by Wynkyn de Worde.[4]

This impulse for religious instruction in late medieval England led to the translation of many works from French and Latin to English as well as the composition of new *pastoralia*, including sermons, treatises on the Commandments or other elements of faith, and manuals for the instruction of both priests and laity. The advent of print, and especially the productions of Wynkyn de Worde and Richard Pynson, helped to meet the laity's increasing demand for religious texts.[5] Although magic rarely figured as a major concern in these texts, the dangers posed by magical practices nevertheless appear regularly in pastoral works. The *pastoralia* authors offer definitions of magic, examine its relationship to the devil, explain Church Fathers' teachings about it, discuss which practices are magical and which are not, and above all instruct Christians how to behave in regards to magical and superstitious practices. This literature promises insight into the dynamic between laypeople and clergy by showing how the medieval Christian Church tried to convince lay parishioners about magic's dangers, and even responded to contemporary magical practices.

While this diverse literature thus seems likely to reward its mining for medieval teachings about magic, it also involves some potential difficulties. The first is simply to understand what the parish priest and his parishioners learnt from *pastoralia*. R. N. Swanson has observed that most medieval laypeople received no formal religious education nor attained any depth of doctrinal understanding. In contrast, G. W. Bernard's investigation of "lay knowledge" warns against dismissing the ability of even illiterates to understand complex ideas, while acknowledging the problem of knowing what the laity thought.[6] This divergence indicates that the question of audience is critical in assessing *pastoralia*. Once a source's teachings on magic are established, we must then ask who might have read or heard this instruction, and how they might have received it. Joseph Goering, for example, argues that *pastoralia's* first audience was comprised of students in the cathedral schools, not the parish priests whose interest in such texts or ability to discern them was minimal.[7] The medieval laity's commonest source for religious instruction was likely sermons; yet, the surviving sermon texts may not reflect actual preaching practices. So Alan Fletcher has emphasized sermons' ephemeral nature, and his study of extant codices of sermons illuminates the disparity between the preached and written word.[8]

The issue of audience becomes more complicated as the growth of English literacy led to the increased production of vernacular works of religious instruction that found homes in the libraries of families like the fifteenth-century Norfolk Pastons.[9] By the end of the Middle Ages, members of the upper classes might read French and English and a bit of Latin, while English reading ability alone was common among the middle-level groups of merchants, yeomen and artisans, and could extend even to servants.[10] Laypeople sometimes owned texts originally aimed at the lower clergy as, for example, Thomas Dautree of York who bequeathed the *Pupilla Oculi* and a book of vices and virtues to clergy in his 1437 will.[11] As Alexandra Barratt points out, any work of religious instruction's "intended audience" may not correlate with what is known about its "demonstrable readership" or ownership. Her work exemplifies the importance of studying the audience and ownership of texts, and how *pastoralia* moved between clergy and laity, in any investigation of the teachings expounded in these works.[12]

In the early Middle Ages, penitentials, sermons and other pastoral texts discussed a wide variety of magical practices and typically yoked them to paganism, as their clerical authors evinced most anxiety about lingering pagan beliefs and practices. The Christian clergy linked forbidden magic – conjuring, love spells, contraceptive magic and many other practices – to the threat of persistent paganism. In *The Rise of Magic in Early Medieval Europe*, Valerie Flint places the teachings of pastoral literature alongside legal, literary and scientific texts to create a richly drawn tapestry of early medieval views of and teachings about magic. Flint's influential and controversial work proposes that Christian clergy battled pagan magic with Christian magic like miracles or "magic made respectable", and that they also simultaneously condemned pagan magic and adapted parts of it for a Christianized magic that included dubious practices like lot casting and binding and loosing charms.[13]

Other scholars of the early Middle Ages have also traced this ambiguity in regards to magic, this reluctance on the part of early medieval clerics to engage in complete denunciation of all practices that hint of magic. Karen Jolly rejects the notion of Christian magic as illogical, however, in her study of Anglo-Saxon religious beliefs, *Popular Religion in Late Saxon England: Elf Charms in Context*. Jolly shows that Abbot Aelfric of Eynsham's (c. 955–1010) vernacular homilies addressing miracles and magic relied on Augustinian ideas to condemn all magic as demonic in origin, but left the status of what Jolly identifies as the "middle practices" more fluid. Certain types of healing – such as using Christian words and rituals along with herbs, or saying Christian prayers to bless fields – fell into this middle ground and found a place in Aelfric's cosmology. So pagan charms received outright condemnation, but Christian words and rituals used as healing remedies attained acceptance.[14]

Scrutinizing early medieval pastoral literature's overall value as a source for the history of popular belief in *Pagan Survivals: Superstitions and Popular Cultures in Early Medieval Pastoral Literature*, Bernadette Filotas excavates discussions of magic from the fourth to the tenth centuries, expanding beyond works like penitentials and sermons to include councils, bishops' capitularies, canons and more.[15] She points to several reasons why pastoral literature is limited as a guide to contemporary magical (and other) beliefs and practices: hostile to magic, its clerical authors selectively indicted certain groups such as women and peasants for its practice; the same magical activities appear in sources that span centuries and many regions; the Latin of these sources may render invisible a cultural diversity by lumping together performers and rituals that would have been understood distinctly in their own cultures. So while Filotas valuably maps what the sources say about diverse forms of both beneficent and destructive magic and their amazingly varied practitioners – weather magicians, soothsayers, diviners, healers, enchanters – she also establishes why only careful comparison of these sources and attentiveness to their contexts can link a particular kind of magic to a specific time and place.

The flourishing of *pastoralia* in the High and Late Middle Ages has provided abundant material for studies of religious practice and belief in which magic often plays a role. Historians have mined *pastoralia* both for testimony of clerical views of magic and also evidence of magical practices, but the conclusions drawn from this material about magic's place in medieval culture have shifted over the past several decades. In his extensive compendium titled *Witchcraft in Old and New England* (first issued in 1929, then reprinted in 1956), G. L. Kittredge, for example, cited warnings against magic, witchcraft, charms and more that were drawn from assorted *pastoralia* covering a wide chronological swath, including an Anglo-Saxon penitential, a thirteenth-century German sermon, and especially the fourteenth-century Robert Mannyng of Brunne's *Handlyng Synne*. These sources contribute to an overcharged picture of magic's ubiquity in medieval belief and practice, reinforcing an argument that drew also on laws, court cases and other materials.[16]

Surveying the genre of homiletic literature several decades later, the pioneering G. R. Owst asserted that fourteenth-century English sermons "systematically" indicted sorcery.[17] Owst based this claim on his analysis of several fourteenth-century works that touched on a wide variety of practices, including necromancy, divination, augury, witchcraft, belief in the three Sister Fates, lot casting, wearing characters or figures depicted on parchment, the cult of time and seasons, and more. While Owst focused on familiar works like Brunne's *Handlyng Synne*, the preacher's handbook *Fasciculus Morum*, the Benedictine Ranulph Higden's *Speculum Curatorum* and the Dominican John Bromyard's *Summa Predicantium*, he also cites others less well known, quoting extensively from some texts only available in manuscript. Owst says homiletic manuals were often directed "expressly for the instruction of the rude", but then asserts that his mainly Latin sources exhibit a sophisticated learning that lay audiences could not absorb, and that preachers in English say much less on the subject.[18]

Owst aimed to stimulate further research in the topic by pointing to how little was known of the teachings about medieval magic, and he underscored the value of studying *pastoralia* in his study of the fifteenth-century Latin manual for preachers, the Dominican Alexander Carpenter's *Destructorium viciorum*. While critiquing the work for dullness and lack of originality, Owst established its importance for providing a panoramic view of late medieval preaching topics and authorities which includes a survey of Christian theologians' condemnations of magic, divination and superstition, subsets of the deadly sin of pride. Carpenter's popular text shows magic to be just one of many concerns for preachers, a spiritual danger that must be addressed but does not eclipse others. Owst's perception of the significance of Carpenter's text is borne out by its presence in monastic libraries and clerical wills, and its multiple printings before and after 1500.[19]

More recent investigations of pastoral teachings have made use of these earlier studies but in seeking to understand more about the production and audience of *pastoralia* have reached somewhat different conclusions. Since *pastoralia* reflected contemporary intellectual developments in Christian theology and influences such as Arabic natural philosophy but could also repeat and recycle older views, sifting the texts for magical practices of any particular era or region requires a fine analytical filter. Sustained analyses of *pastoralia*'s teachings about magic also seek to understand how *pastoralia* negotiated the differences between theological condemnations and pastoral awareness of common practices.

One conclusion arising from placing *pastoralia* in a broader context is that magic was a recurrent but typically secondary concern for authors who repeated almost by rote the condemnations and concerns of past eras. Investigating beliefs about the supernatural evidenced in medieval English chronicles, Carl Watkins notes that the worries about necromancy, sorcery and divination in late twelfth- and thirteenth-century pastoral handbooks by authors like Robert of Flamborough and Thomas of Chobham were, in fact, repeating standard admonitions from patristic texts. Watkins finds far more urgent warnings in *exempla*, synodal statutes and historical texts about the appropriation of holy words and holy objects like the host for magical purposes.[20]

The diversity of medieval religious beliefs and the accompanying ambiguous status of certain potentially magical practices have also been emphasized by several scholars. Surveying religion in England from 1000 to 1500, Andrew Brown highlights the variety of practices and views that comprised medieval Christianity. He shows how ambiguity could temper the outright prohibition of all magic by citing *Dives and Pauper*, an early fifteenth-century commentary on the Ten Commandments, whose clerical author condemned written charms except for those using words of the *Pater Noster*, Creed or Scripture.[21] Eamon Duffy's groundbreaking work *The Stripping of the Altars: Traditional Religion in England 1400–1580* finds no clear line separating prayers from magic, and using the evidence of the laity's own prayer books shows how laypeople adapted seemingly magical incantations and charms to religious use. Duffy asserts that scholars must view pastoral manuals' discussions of these practices critically, and that past failure to do so has led historians astray. Pastoral texts diverge on certain key points; some works, for instance, permitted holy charms to be used by pious people but others did not. The fifteenth-century *Doctrinal of Sapyence*, for instance, arraigned the sinfulness of believing that carrying written prayers could provide protection from sudden death or illness. The *Doctrinal* linked these beliefs to simple people whose ignorance excused them, but Duffy argues forcefully against this claim, showing that such prayers or charms were common among the clergy and nobility along with simpler folk.[22]

While the medieval *pastoralia* overall treat magic sporadically and inconsistently, their discussions of magic took on more urgency in relation to certain topics or, as mentioned above, in relation to some groups of people. Catherine Rider, for instance, has shown that thirteenth- and fourteenth-century confession manuals and synodal statutes reflect an ongoing worry about both magically caused impotence and its magical cures. These discussions belonged to the larger investigation of the question of marriage dissolution. Could magically caused impotence be grounds for annulment? And could it be magically cured? Drawing on canon law and theology, several writers addressed the problem in their manuals for confessors. Their disparate opinions may be represented by William of Pagula who wrote in his influential *Oculus Sacerdotis* (*c*. 1320) that magically caused impotence cannot be permanent and John de Burgo who adopted the *Oculus Sacerdotis* in his shorter *Pupilla Oculi* (1384) but said impotence magic could indeed be a lasting condition.[23] Rider's work points to an enduring worry among medieval clerical authors about the ties between sexuality, magic and reproduction, but also provides a model for carefully weighing the evidence of *pastoralia* by showing that impotence magic received varied treatments and emphases. The issue of magically caused impotence also forecasts one obsession of sixteenth-century witchcraft persecutions, and an informative link between these and the medieval discussions Rider sets out can be found in an early sixteenth-century lecture on marriage by William Hay, who studied in Paris and then lectured in theology at Aberdeen for thirty years. Hay passes fluidly from magic to witchcraft in pondering "whether witchcraft should be counted as a form of impotence" and asserting that certain women are "addicted to witchcraft and magic." The devil blocks human sexual intercourse "either by preventing the rigidity in the male organ or by obstructing the female organ", using women who summon demons to achieve these ends. Hay's lecture demonstrates the increased tendency at the end of the Middle Ages to associate women with demonic activity and dangerous magic.[24]

In *Magic and Religion in Medieval England*, Rider offers the most thorough study to date of *pastoralia's* teachings about magic from the thirteenth to fifteenth centuries.[25] This work provides a detailed survey of the magical beliefs and practices discussed in this literature, including divination, charms, prophecies and dream interpretations, beliefs in creatures like fairies and otherworldly beings, astrological image magic and the ritual magic known as the *Ars Notoria*. Rider's methodology addresses the problem of using *pastoralia* to understand medieval magic because of their reliance on much older texts and their tenuous relationship to real magical practices. Close readings of these works, for instance, can reveal their selective use of older texts and the addition of new details that reflected contemporary concerns. In addition, she points out that these sermons and confessors' manuals and other works must be placed within a broader context that includes court records, medical texts and other materials in order to understand the significance of their teachings on magic. While few of the medieval authors of pastoral works considered magic to be a major threat to the spiritual well-being of Christians, Rider shows that they exhibited most apprehension about the many regions where the lack of clear boundaries allowed magic, science and religion to overlap with one another. Biblical precedent authorized dream divination and lot casting, for example, and wearing stones or herbs to cure ailments seemed to draw on natural powers.[26] So ambiguity continued to beset the *pastoralia* when writers tried to separate the illicit and magical from the legitimately religious.

This large-scale canvass of magic in medieval *pastoralia* has been usefully complemented by the studies of single texts which show in detail how magic was treated in relation to other potential spiritual dangers. Michael Haren's analysis of the fourteenth-century confessors' manual titled *Memoriale Presbiterorum*, for instance, indicates the author's almost dismissive attitude towards magic. Like Filotas, Haren finds peasants and women singled out for attention, as the author's interrogation of peasants highlights their tendency to believe in "auguries and the chattering of birds", and old women are also said to practise superstitions. Female penitents are questioned about sorcery, but attention to women's possible sexual misdeeds outstrips magical issues, as sorcery appears as one item in a litany of sins that also includes abortion, harlotry, child exposure, adultery and irreverence towards husbands.[27]

In the fifteenth century, pastoral concerns about magic increasingly extended to include the even broader and more nebulous category of superstition, which often involved divination, charms and healing spells.[28] Michael Bailey credits a new focus on pastoral theology at German universities for prompting the composition of numerous treatises that treated superstitions as potentially demonic.[29] The late medieval French clergy also evinced mounting concerns about superstitions in sermons and other writings, including those of the prolific University of Paris chancellor Jean Gerson (1363–1429) who accused great nobles along with ordinary people of conferring with sorcerers and engaging in superstitious activities like consulting fortune tellers or trusting to charms, which he both regarded as a moral danger and loosely tied to sorcery.[30] Yet, scholars have shown that although the French clergy often condemned superstitions as potentially demonic in origin, they also viewed many such practices as simple foolishness stemming from the credulity of women in particular. Their responses to superstition therefore ranged from "contemptuous tolerance to censorship", as Madeleine Jeay put it.[31] Looking for evidence that the scholarly critique of superstition received a pastoral application, Euan Cameron also asserts that no consensus existed among the late medieval Christian clergy on how to preach and teach laypeople about superstitious practices.[32]

The intersection of magic and superstition in *pastoralia* also becomes clear in commentaries on the Ten Commandments, the teaching of which was a fundamental part of pastoral instruction as defined by Archbishop Pecham's syllabus. Decalogue discussions in manuals for confessors often state how one might violate each commandment, and late medieval teachings on the First Commandment, as Edward Peters notes, linked superstitions and sorcery to idolatry, perhaps the gravest sin.[33] Yet, understanding better how laypeople might have received this teaching leads us back to certain methodological issues in using *pastoralia*, as a few examples can indicate.

Cautions about superstitions and condemnations of magic appear often in sermons that expound the Ten Commandments, but these sermons also place magical activities within a broad spectrum of many sinful behaviours. This setting must be taken into account if we hope to understand what medieval laypeople understood as well as what they were taught in regards to magic. So a fifteenth-century English sermon glosses the Latin *Non habebis deos alienos* [Exodus 20:3] by quoting God himself who commands Christians to have "right belief and steadfast hope and perfect love to God and to no other against God." One violates this decree by believing in witchcraft and various "arts of the devil", or by allowing worldly things to come before their service and love of God such as work or pleasures of the flesh. Loving anything more than God is idolatrous.[34] This treatment alludes to the demonic link, but also suggests that witchcraft and divination are no more troublesome than fondness for food or sex.

Decalogue commentaries are also common in late medieval prayer books. As Eamon Duffy's work indicates, prayer books offer a deep well of material for apprehending how laypeople understood their faith.[35] Primers, or Books of Hours, as well as other kinds of devotional books ranging from deluxe productions to self-made efforts belonged to people of many social levels. Their Decalogue commentaries are typically quite brief. An early sixteenth-century Flemish book, for example, contains a group of instructional texts – the *Speculum Conscientie* – that explain the Commandments, the Seven Mortal Sins, the Works of Mercy, the sacraments and more. Lavishly illuminated on fine parchment, this book offered its affluent and Latin-reading lay reader a wide variety of prayers and religious instruction, the basics of the faith that a layperson ought to know. Its Latin First Commandment annotation warns succinctly against idolatry, invoking demons, divining or observing superstitious rites or days.[36] This terseness also characterizes vernacular explanations, even in books that seem aimed at the clergy. So, for example, the fifteenth-century compendium London B. L. Royal MS 8 F VII explains that the First Commandment is broken by worshipping any god other than Jesus Christ or believing in witchcraft, charms, conjurations or consent to raise the devil. All who do are accursed "as though they acted against the faith of Christendom."[37]

These fleeting references likely formed the most common teachings on magic that many parish priests or laypeople encountered, but their brevity makes interpretation difficult. One scholar suggests that their conciseness was intentional – rather than explaining at length the rationale behind the prohibition, laypeople were bluntly told to believe what "Holy Church" taught.[38] Although we might suspect that this limited the message's effectiveness, another possibility for understanding these texts is to see them as prompts. A parish priest might use such a list – charms, witchcraft, enchantments, conjurations, raising the devil – as memos to guide him in lengthier teachings on their dangers. Overall, the short Decalogue glosses examined to date aim to correct the ill-advised person placing hope in dream interpretation or charms, rather than in the one Christian God. This emphasis on human error rather than demons distinguishes these commentaries from Ten Commandment treatments in confession treatises that stress the link between magical practices and demon worship.[39]

Overall, while scholars have uncovered many texts that condemn magic, the research on *pastoralia* to date shows the overall attack on magic to be erratic and uneven. Any magic involved with demons was condemned as a great spiritual danger, but other forms of magic could be treated more tolerantly or even neutrally. One sermon even explains how to use image magic to punish enemies (as the wax image melts, so the flesh of the enemy vanishes away), but only as a metaphor for how confession will work for the penitent.[40] Inconsistencies in magic's condemnation, disagreements about what constitutes magic and contrasting views of the laity's capability for religious discernment meant that few clergy or laypeople were likely to integrate a powerful condemnation of magic into their religious understanding.

New directions for research

The findings on *pastoralia*'s teachings about magic, along with some of the problems in understanding this material, suggest areas for future research. The first emerges from the fact that even though magic, along with superstition and witchcraft, appears frequently in these works, it typically occupies a minor space.[41] So understanding the possible impact of these comments on magic on their readers and auditors requires that these texts not be isolated from the lessons, prayers and other materials that provided their larger context. How did the other teachings the reader encountered in this book or sermon align with those on magic? What overall lessons did the clerical or lay reader likely grasp from this work? A corollary to this endeavour should be the examination of the existing manuscripts and early printed books for physical evidence, including marginalia and underlinings, that can point to the texts most read, even if it cannot show how a reader responded to or acted upon a text.[42]

An example of the importance of thematic context is found in a sermon for the Feast of Mary Magdalene (22 July), likely preached in 1414 at the Hospital of St. Mary Magdalene on Burton Stone Lane in York to an audience of lay men and women. The sermon writer urges his audience to follow the example of Mary Magdalene as the epitome of faithful belief. As the five wits are too "feeble" to lead one in matters of faith, laypeople must believe, like the Magdalene, what Christ or later the holy church teaches. Those men and women who seek to prove everything, rather than submitting in obedience, have "fouly errored in their faith". Somewhat unexpectedly, this sermon then thunders briefly against magic. Many have disobeyed the holy church by believing in forbidden things like "charms and incantations" or using conjurations to find stolen items, by divining the future or believing in dreams. Many men consider it lawful to consult the "sortes apostolorum" to answer their questions. But this is forbidden by canon law, which judges as cursed and untrue in the faith the person who trusts in such conjurations or dreams, or believes that a person can be changed by witchcraft or sorcery into the likeness of an unreasonable beast. Anyone who teaches, believes or holds such are cursed solemnly three times a year. Finally, every man and woman should beware of such people and should they know any, for the salvation of both their souls, must make that person leave these practices and do not doubt it is forbidden by holy church.[43] This outburst against magical practices is powerful, but occupies less than one page (of slightly more than seventeen) in the modern edition of the sermon, and overall supports the greater lesson of the need for obedience to the church and faith in its teachings.

We will also understand more about what *pastoralia* taught both clergy and laity by paying attention to a text's availability and likely audiences. Scholars of early printed books, for example, have provided some guides to sermons and other instructional texts that were printed several times before 1520. While repeated printings are no guarantee of actual readership, they point both to a perceived demand for these materials and a probable audience. New editions have made some of these works better known, but many books popular in the era before the Reformation remain unfamiliar today, available only in manuscript or early printed editions.[44] So Anne T. Thayer argues that the essence of what was considered worth preaching about in an ordinary parish can be better understood by examining popular model sermon collections, citing the *Sermones discipuli de tempore et de sanctis* by the German Dominican Johannes Herolt (d. 1468), printed in eighty-four editions (or about 49,000 copies).[45]

Thayer's work highlights several authors whose writings were widespread and speak about issues relating to magic. A couple of examples can underscore the value of tracking these often printed texts. The first is Hendrik Herp (or Herpf, or in Latin Harphius) (d. 1477), a member of the Franciscan Observants in the Cologne Province and the prolific author of several mystical works. Many of Herp's writings, like *The Mirror of Perfection*, had a wide readership among clergy and laity. His sermon collection *Sermones de tempore, de sanctis*, printed in five editions between 1450 and 1520, won him a place on the list of popular preachers of the late Middle Ages.[46] Another of his sermon collections, which has received less scholarly attention, is titled *Speculum Aureum Decem Preceptorum Dei*, a compendium of hundreds of sermons on the Ten Commandments which was also printed several times between 1472 and 1520.[47] The First Commandment provides the occasion for commentary on magic, with Sermons Seven and Eight explicitly warning against the magical arts. So Sermon Seven begins by explaining that the commandment *Non habebis deos alienos coram me*

> prohibits those things that divert the human mind from reverence to its creator, and thus forbids all impious pacts with demons, whether these are through the incantations of words, or through the inscriptions of characters or images, or through the offerings of sacrifices. In these three things consist all the arts of magic.[48]

Herp's lengthy First Commandment sermons warrant more investigation, probably less for their novelty than because of his influence as a widely read writer. He explains that he wrote these sermons for the instruction of confessors and preachers and it is likely that their multiple printings made his ideas familiar to clergy around northern Europe.[49]

Another well-known author was Guido de Monte Roche (*c.* 1333), whose handbook for parish priests, *Manipulus Curatorum*, exists today in over 250 manuscript copies, and was printed in 122 editions between 1468 and 1501, for a total of some 60,000 copies spreading from London to Rome to Barcelona to Vienna.[50] He interprets the First Commandment to prohibit "all idolatries, all heresies, and all kind of witchcraft or divination" but bestows the fiercest condemnation on anyone who participates in "any divinations or auguries" for that person "has violated the Christian faith and baptism, and has become a pagan and an apostate enemy of God, and has gravely incurred the wrath of God forever...." The author also addresses what is and is not superstitious, and then warns people to be wary of "conjurors who use and recite the name of God and the angels...."[51] Close analysis of these arguments and references in Herp's and Guido de Monte Roche's manuals would provide a deeper knowledge of how late medieval preachers handled the subject of magic's dangers.

Finally, while this essay has focused mostly on medieval England, both the fifteenth-century advent of print and the increase in vernacular works of religious instruction point to the need for crossing geographical boundaries in future research. An early printed sermon sourcebook written in Latin like Herp's *Speculum Aureum*, for example, had an international audience, its readers in England linked to those throughout Europe in a transnational group whose own writings may reflect Herp's influence. Also, while many of the English vernacular teachings about magic exist only in manuscripts and have yet to be collated, these warnings in sermons and Decalogue commentaries must be compared with similar works in French, Italian and other languages, if we are to develop a deeper understanding of what lay Christians were taught about magic in the Middle Ages.

Notes

1 Leonard E. Boyle, "The Fourth Lateran Council and Manuals of Popular Theology," in *The Popular Literature of Medieval England*, ed. Thomas J. Heffernan (Knoxville: The University of Tennessee Press, 1985), 30–43, describes as *pastoralia* the vast array of materials in Latin and the vernacular used in the *cura animarum*, and read by both clergy and laity.
2 Joseph Goering, "The Summa 'Qui bene presunt' and Its Author," in *Literature and Religion in the Later Middle Ages: Philological Studies in Honor of Siegfried Wenzel* (Binghamton, NY: Medieval and Renaissance Text and Studies, 1995), 143–59.
3 *Councils & Synods with Other Documents Relating to the English Church*, volume II: *1205–1313*. ed. F.M. Powicke and C.R. Cheney (Oxford: Clarendon Press, 1964), 900–5; Leonard E. Boyle, "The *Oculus Sacerdotis* and Some Other Works of William of Pagula," reprinted in *Pastoral Care, Clerical Education and Canon Law, 1200–1400* (London: Variorum Reprints, 1981), Essay IV.
4 Judith Shaw, "The Influence of Canonical and Episcopal Reform on Popular Books of Instruction," in *Popular Literature*, 44–60; Alexandra Barratt, "Works of Religious Instruction," in *Middle English Prose: A Critical Guide to Major Authors and Genres*, ed. A.S.G. Edwards (New Brunswick: Rutgers University Press, 1984), 413–32; Andrew Reeves, "Teaching the Creed and Articles of Faith in England: 1215–81," in *A Companion to Pastoral Care in the Late Middle Ages (1200–1500)*, ed. Ronald J. Stansbury (Leiden: Brill, 2010), 41–72; H. Leith Spencer *English Preaching in the Late Middle Ages* (Oxford: Clarendon Press, 1991), 201–5. *Exornatorium Curatorum, edited from Wynkyn de Worde's Text in Cambridge, Corpus Christi College Sp. 335.2*, ed. Niamh Pattwell (Heidelberg: Universitätsverlag Winter, 2013).
5 Vincent Gillespie, "Vernacular Books of Religion," in *Looking in Holy Books: Essays on Late Medieval Religious Writing in England* (Turnhout: Brepols, 2011), 145–73; Lotte Hellinga, *William Caxton and Early Printing in England* (London: The British Library, 2010), 156–70.
6 R.N. Swanson, *Church and Society in Late Medieval England* (Oxford: Blackwell, 1989), 276–79. G.W. Bernard, *The Late Medieval English Church: Vitality and Vulnerability before the Break with Rome* (New Haven and London: Yale University Press, 2012), 87–116.
7 Joseph Goering, *William de Montibus (c. 1140–1213): The Schools and the Literature of Pastoral Care* (Toronto: Pontifical Institute of Mediaeval Studies, 1992), 60–65.
8 Alan John Fletcher, *Late Medieval Popular Preaching in Britain and Ireland* (Turnhout: Brepols, 2009), 12–13; see also Augustine Thompson's comments on audience reception of sermons in "From Texts to Preaching: Retrieving the Medieval Sermon as an Event," in *Preacher, Sermon and Audience in the Middle Ages*, ed. Carolyn Muessig (Leiden: Brill, 2002), 13–37.
9 Paul Strohm, "Writing and Reading," in *A Social History of England 1200–1500*, ed. Rosemary Horrox and W. Mark Ormrod (Cambridge: Cambridge University Press, 2006), 454–72.
10 On literacy and education in medieval England, see Ralph Hanna, "Literacy, schooling, universities," in *The Cambridge Companion to Medieval English Culture*, ed. Andrew Galloway (Cambridge: Cambridge University Press, 2011), 172–94; Nicholas Orme, *Medieval Schools from Roman Britain to Renaissance England* (New Haven and London: Yale University Press, 2006); J.B. Trapp, "Literacy, Books and Readers," in *The Cambridge History of the Book in Britain*, vol. III *1400–1557*, ed. Lotte Hellinga and J.B. Trapp (Cambridge: Cambridge University Press, 1999), 31–43; Jo Ann Hoeppner Moran, *The Growth of English Schooling 1340–1548* (Princeton: Princeton University Press, 1985), 150–81.
11 Susan H. Cavanaugh, *A Study of Books Privately Owned in England 1300–1450* (Ph.D. dissertation, University of Pennsylvania, 1980), 231–32.
12 Alexandra Barratt, "Spiritual Writings and Religious Instruction," in *The Cambridge History of the Book in Britain 1100–1400*, ed. Nigel J. Morgan and Rodney M. Thomson (Cambridge: Cambridge University Press, 2008), 340–66.
13 Valerie I.J. Flint, *The Rise of Magic in Early Medieval Europe* (Princeton: Princeton University Press, 1991); on the idea of Christian magic, see especially chapter 9. See also her essay "A Magic Universe," in *A Social History of England 1200–1500*, ed. Rosemary Horrox and W. Mark Ormrod (Cambridge: Cambridge University Press, 2006), 340–55.
14 Karen Louise Jolly, *Popular Religion in Late Saxon England: Elf Charms in Context* (Chapel Hill and London: University of North Carolina Press, 1996).
15 Bernadette Filotas, *Pagan Survivals: Superstitions and Popular Cultures in Early Medieval Pastoral Literature* (Toronto: Pontifical Institute of Mediaeval Studies, 2005).

16 George Lyman Kittredge, *Witchcraft in Old and New England* (1929 by Harvard; reprint 1956 New York: Russell & Russell), see 29–30, 42, 44, 51, 164–5.
17 G.R. Owst, "*Sortilegium* in English Homiletic Literature of the Fourteenth Century," in *Studies Presented to Sir Hilary Jenkinson*, ed. J. Conway Davies (London: Oxford University Press, 1957), 272.
18 Owst, "*Sortilegium*," 272, 301.
19 G.R. Owst, *The Destructorium Viciorum of Alexander Carpenter: A Fifteenth-Century Sequel to Literature and Pulpit in Medieval England* (London: S. P. C. K., 1952). The *Incunabula Short Title Catalogue* lists four editions before 1500. For ownership, see Kathleen Kamerick, "Shaping Superstition in Late Medieval England," *Magic, Ritual, and Witchcraft* 3, no. 1 (2008): 29–53.
20 Carl Watkins, *History and the Supernatural in Medieval England* (Cambridge: Cambridge University Press, 2007), 131–33.
21 Andrew Brown, *Church and Society in England 1000–1500* (Gordonsville, VA: Palgrave Macmillan, 2003), 77.
22 Eamon Duffy, *The Stripping of the Altars: Traditional Religion in England 1400–1580* (New Haven: Yale University Press, 1992); see especially Chapter 8, 266–98.
23 Catherine Rider, *Magic and Impotence in the Middle Ages* (Oxford: Oxford University Press, 2006), 106–07.
24 *William Hay's Lecture on Marriage*, ed. and trans. John C. Barry (Edinburgh: The Stair Society, 1967), 121–29. See also Michael D. Bailey, "The Feminization of Magic and the Emerging Idea of the Female Witch in the Late Middle Ages," *Essays in Medieval Studies* 19 (2002): 120–34.
25 Catherine Rider, *Magic and Religion in Medieval England* (London: Reaktion Books, 2012).
26 Rider, *Magic and Religion*, 46–69.
27 Michael Haren, *Sin and Society in Fourteenth-Century England: A Study of the Memoriale Presbiterorum* (Oxford: Clarendon Press, 2000), 149–50, 184.
28 See the definition of superstition in Euan Cameron, *Enchanted Europe: Superstition, Reason, and Religion, 1250-1750* (Oxford: Oxford University Press, 2010), 5.
29 Michael D. Bailey, "Concern over Superstition in Late Medieval Europe," in *The Religion of Fools? Superstition Past and Present*, ed. S.A. Smith and Alan Knight (Oxford: Oxford Journals, 2008), 115–33.
30 D. Catherine Brown, *Pastor and Laity in the Theology of Jean Gerson* (Cambridge: Cambridge University Press, 1987), 158–60.
31 Madeleine Jeay, "The Savage Mind of Late Medieval Preachers," *Medieval Folklore* 2, (1992): 49–66; F. Bonney, "Autour de Jean Gerson: Opinions de théologiens sur les superstitions et la sorcellerie au début du XV siècle," *Le Moyen Age* 77, no. 1 (1971): 85–98.
32 Cameron, *Enchanted Europe*, 135–39.
33 Edward Peters, "The Medieval Church and State on Superstition, Magic and Witchcraft: from Augustine to the Sixteenth Century," in *Witchcraft and Magic in Europe: The Middle Ages*, ed. Bengt Ankarloo and Stuart Clark (Philadelphia: University of Pennsylvania Press, 2002), 229.
34 Manchester, John Rylands University Library, MS English 109, f. 123v. See Veronica O'Mara and Suzanne Paul, *A Repertorium of Middle English Prose Sermons*, Part 3, (Turnhout, Belgium: Brepols, 2007), 1610–12, where the sermon's prohibition on witchcraft is transcribed. The *Repertorium* lists a number of additional sermons that address magic or witchcraft.
35 See Duffy, *Stripping of the Altars*, chapter 8; and *Marking the Hours: English People and Their Prayers 1240–1570* (New Haven: Yale University Press, 2006).
36 Copenhagen, Det Kongelige Bibliothek, GKS 1605, f. 20r-v. The same text is in BL Additional MS 18852, A Book of Hours of the Use of Rome made for Joanna I of Castile, made in Bruges c. 1486–506. On the *Speculum conscientiae*, see Margot Schmidt, "Miroir" in *Dictionnaire de Spiritualité*, vol. 10, pt. 2 (Paris: Beauchesne, 1980), 1293.
37 BL Royal MS 8 F VII, ff. 43v–44r. For additional examples, see London B.L. Additional MS 10053, f. 105r, and Edinburgh University Library MS 93, f. 4v; quoted in Anthony Martin, "The Middle English Versions of *The Ten Commandments* with special reference to Rylands English MS 85," *Bulletin of the John Rylands University Library* 64, no. 1 (1981), 212.
38 See Spencer, *Preaching*, 214.
39 Rider, *Magic and Religion*, 135.
40 D.M. Grisdale, ed., *Three Middle English Sermons from the Worcester Chapter Manuscript F.10* (University of Leeds: Leeds School of English Language Texts and Monographs 5, 1939), 60.

41 See Peters' comments in "Medieval Church and State," 176–77, on the place of sorcery and witchcraft in the legal, theological and devotional literature of the late Middle Ages.
42 See an excellent example of this kind of analysis by Anne T. Thayer and Katharine J. Lualdi in their *Introduction* to *Handbook for Curates: A Late Medieval Manual on Pastoral Ministry* by Guido of Monte Rochen (Washington, DC: Catholic University of America Press, 2011), xxxi–xli.
43 *Four Middle English Sermons edited from British Library MS Harley 2268*, ed. Virginia O'Mara (Heidelberg: C. Winter, 2002), 112–13; for the place and date on which the sermon was given, see 163ff.
44 Michael Milway, "Forgotten Best-Sellers from the Dawn of the Reformation," in *Continuity and Change: The Harvest of Late Medieval and Reformation History*, ed. Robert J. Bast and Andrew C. Gow (Leiden: Brill, 2000), 113–42, argues for investigating these works and discusses how to identify them.
45 Anne T. Thayer, *Penitence, Preaching and the Coming of the Reformation* (Aldershot England; Burlington, Vermont: Ashgate, 2002), 7–8; 21–22.
46 On Herp's mystical works, see Bernard McGinn, *The Varieties of Vernacular Mysticism (1350–1550)* (New York: Crossroad, 2012), 130–36; for his sermon collections, see Thayer, *Penitence, Preaching and the Coming of the Reformation*, Table 2.1, 17–9.
47 Printings include: Peter Schöffer (Mainz) 1472 and 1474; Anton Koberger (Nuremberg) 1481; Johann Froben (Basil) 1496; Johannem Knoblock (Strasbourg) 1520. London B. L. MS Additional 63787, given in the late fifteenth century to the chapel of St. Stephen's in Westminster, is a very high-quality manuscript copied from the 1474 Schöffer edition.
48 Henricus de Herpf, *Speculum aureum decem praeceptorum Dei* (Nuremberg: Anton Koberger), 1481.
49 The incipit of *Speculum aureum* states "per modum sermonum ad instructionem tam confessorum quam predicatorum."
50 See Thayer and Lualdi, *Introduction* to *Handbook for Curates*, xiii; Milway, "Forgotten Best-Sellers," 117.
51 *Handbook for Curates*, 294–96.

33

SUPERSTITION AND SORCERY

Michael D. Bailey

In 1398, the Faculty of Theology of the University of Paris condemned 28 articles pertaining to "magic arts", "sorceries" and "similar superstitions". The theologians left no doubt about the threat they felt such "nefarious, pestiferous, and monstrous abomination" presented to Christian society. They also stressed, however, that

> it is not our intention in any way to disparage licit and true traditions, science, or arts, but we will try to uproot and extirpate, insofar as we are able, the insane and sacrilegious errors of the foolish and the deadly rites that harm, contaminate, and infect orthodox faith and Christian religion.[1]

This was a necessary qualification because, as threatening and harmful as superstitious rites were understood to be, they frequently bordered on practices that were legitimate, respectable and in some cases even revered. The boundaries between licit and illicit acts could be very difficult to discern, even for highly educated experts. Medieval authorities did not need to debate whether superstition ought to be condemned, because for them the term *superstitio* always denoted a condemnable error. The troubling issue was instead what sort of practices were to be understood as superstitious. This chapter will address this question, examining how the medieval church defined superstition, surveying the kinds of practices, both common and elite, that could fall within this broad category, and outlining how levels of concern heightened over time.

The category of superstition, as deployed by medieval churchmen, encompassed a vast array of practices, ranging from simple rites for healing and protection to complex rituals for divination or demonic invocation. It was a far broader term than witchcraft (*maleficium*), sorcery (*sortilegium*) or even "the magical arts" (*artes magicae*). Often when exploring the history of magic, modern scholars have preferred those other categories, and have generally tried to understand them in as clear and precise a manner as possible. It is fairly standard, for example, for scholars to avoid referring to any form of harmful magic (*maleficium*) in the Middle Ages as "witchcraft" until we reach the fifteenth century and begin to encounter accusations of "witches" (*malefici* or *maleficae*) operating in clearly diabolical, conspiratorial cults.[2] Medieval writers, however, frequently lumped practices together rather than splitting them apart, particularly when it came to issuing condemnations. As important as it is to recognize the distinctions that existed within the practices they catalogued, therefore, we must also note the commonalities and connections church authorities saw between those practices, in order to understand the dilemmas they encountered when trying to parse condemnable superstitions from "true traditions, sciences, or arts".

487

While medieval magic and witchcraft are much studied topics, far less work has been done on superstition per se, and most scholarship has been limited in some way. It is, after all, the very expansiveness of superstition as a category that makes it a daunting topic for research. A fundamental study remains Dieter Harmening's *Superstitio*, but he ends his work with the thirteenth-century scholastics.[3] His student Karin Baumann addressed the late medieval period, but only through German vernacular sources, while Maria Montesano drew only on works by observant Franciscans.[4] Bernadette Filotas restricted her important study to penitential sources from the early medieval era.[5] Patrick Hersperger approached the issue exclusively through canon law.[6] Emilie Lasson and Krzysztof Bracha both focused on single texts by major fifteenth-century authors (although Bracha's study in fact ranges widely across all of late medieval superstition).[7] Jean Verdon offered a complete survey of the entire medieval period, but only as an overview.[8] Euan Cameron did excellent work integrating clerical opposition to medieval superstition into a narrative that extended through the Reformation and into the Enlightenment, but ultimately concentrated more on those later periods.[9] My own work, focused on the fourteenth and fifteenth centuries, has been restricted mostly to northern Europe, and, while I have tried to integrate a range of sources, I have relied most heavily on specialized theological works.[10] These are also the sources on which I will mainly draw in this essay.

My late medieval leanings notwithstanding, Christian authorities had been concerned about superstition from the earliest days of the church. Patristic texts provided essential definitions and descriptions of superstition, as a category, that would be reiterated for the next thousand years. Ecclesiastical leaders also debated superstition and perceived superstitious practices at church councils, spoke against them in sermons and made them a major focus of penitential literature.[11] Early in the eleventh century, Burchard of Worms collected many earlier pronouncements about superstition in his monumental *Decretum*, particularly in book 19, known independently as *Corrector sive medicus*.[12] In the high medieval period, sources on superstition multiplied. It continued to be treated in sermons and pastoral literature, and it was taken up more systematically in canon law.[13] Scholastic theologians addressed the abstract category in their commentaries and *summae*, and inquisitors used it to label strange practices that they encountered as they began to patrol the countryside.[14]

Only in the late medieval period did numerous specialized treatises dealing predominantly or even exclusively with the topic of *superstitio* finally appear.[15] While the intensity of their focus was new, however, the ideas they expressed were not; nor were many of the practices they condemned. They offer both a window into late medieval anxieties and a reflection of earlier concerns. Also by the late medieval period, one can effectively approach superstition, or the world of common practices that authorities might fear were superstitious, through vernacular literature. Perhaps the most remarkable and extended work of this kind is the anonymous *Evangiles des quenouilles*, dating from the mid-fifteenth century, which depicts a group of spinsters relating various beliefs and practices known among women to a male scribe over the course of several winter evenings. The character of the scribe begins by noting how most men treat this "wisdom" with "derision and mockery".[16] In fact, many churchmen would no doubt have subjected what they would have taken to be these women's obvious superstitions to far harsher condemnations. While works like the *Evangiles* remind us how rich and varied medieval reactions could be, however, I limit myself here mainly to what I regard as the mainstream of authoritative discourse, inevitably clerical and Latin, that shaped the idea of superstition over the medieval centuries.

Definitions and frameworks

Remarkably, given that the scope of superstition could be so vast, medieval churchmen really had only a couple of definitions to which they continually returned when trying to comprehend the parameters of *superstitio*. The first was provided by Augustine in the second book of his *De doctrina Christiana*. He wrote that

> superstition is anything instituted by men having to do with crafting or worshipping idols, or worshipping a created thing or any part of a created thing as if it were God, or consultations and pacts concerning prognostications agreed and entered into with demons.

He immediately added: "such are the efforts of the magic arts, which the poets are more accustomed to mention than to teach", as well as "the books of soothsayers and augurs", before concluding that "to this category also belong all amulets and healing charms that medical science condemns".[17] More than eight centuries later, Thomas Aquinas crafted the only definition that ever competed with Augustine's, declaring that

> superstition is a vice opposed to religion by excess, not because it gives more worship to God than true religion, but because it gives worship either to that which it ought not, or in some manner which it ought not.[18]

Like Augustine, what Thomas mainly meant to imply was the fearful possibility of worship offered to demons.

Beyond these two somewhat abstract definitions, medieval churchmen had only a handful of authoritative frameworks to help them understand the range of practices that might become superstitious. As noted above, Augustine mentioned some categories of potentially superstitious practices when he defined superstition in *De doctrina Christiana*: the magic arts in their entirety, divination and augury, and healing charms, and he would later add erroneous forms of astrology as well as "utterly inane observances" like stepping on the threshold whenever one passed one's house or going back to bed if one sneezed while dressing in the morning.[19] Another important typology was Isidore of Seville's categorization of different kinds of magicians in his early seventh-century work *Etymologies*. These included *malefici*, who could "agitate the elements, disturb the minds of people, and kill by the force of their spells without any drinking of poison"; necromancers, who raised the dead to prophesy; augurs, who divined by the flights of birds; astrologers (*mathematici*), who observed the course of the stars; *sortilegi* (a word that would later come to mean sorcerers more generally), who cast lots (*sortes*); as well as those who crafted magical amulets; and enchanters (*incantatores*), "who accomplish their art with words".[20]

Centuries later, Thomas Aquinas would, in addition to defining superstition, establish an influential system for categorizing practices. He focused in particular on forms of divination, although his categories were often expanded by later writers to include other practices as well. He first posed the basic question whether different forms of divination should be distinguished at all, since he regarded them as grounded in essentially the same kind of error. He took most of his forms of divination from Isidore but added others, such as chiromancy (palm reading) and spatulamancy (divination by animals' shoulder blades), knowledge of which had returned to the medieval West via Arabic sources during the twelfth century.[21]

He partitioned these practices into three broad groups: divination that drew explicitly on demons such as was the case with necromancy; the passive observation of signs such as augury or astrology; and active forms of divination such as casting lots. Subsequently, he introduced further categories, addressing the legitimacy of divination performed by means of demons, by the stars and heavenly bodies, by dreams, by augury and observance of omens, and by lots.[22]

The most influential framework, however, was established by Aquinas's contemporary William of Auvergne, a theologian and later Bishop of Paris from 1228 until 1249. In chapter 23 of his work *De legibus*, he laid out ten categories of "idolatry" (*idolatria*), which many later writers employed as categories of superstition.[23] The first and most terrible form consisted of rites performed explicitly through demonic agency. Then came other varieties, almost any of which might also involve demons in some fashion. There were rites directed to the stars, sun or moon, including erroneous astrology (2). There were practices entailing the four elements such as geo-, aero-, hydro- and pyromancy (3). People might craft supposedly animated statues to consult or worship (4), or they could employ images such as circles, triangles or pentagons in dubious ways (5), which churchmen readily interpreted as forms of demonic invocation. Other rites involved the improper use of written characters or figures (6), or of spoken words or names (7). People often attached special significance or power to particular times (8) such as the widespread belief that the so-called Egyptian Days each month were particularly unlucky. Similarly, some people falsely ascribed ominous power to "beginnings" or "initial causes" (*res initiales*) of any sort (9): a voyage, a marriage or a military expedition might be destined to succeed or fail depending on the time or conditions under which it began. William's tenth category of error was that of "discovery" (*inventio*), which meant regarding various everyday occurrences as omens. Encountering certain animals might portend good or bad fortune, as could crossing paths with a monk, finding a horseshoe or discovering a coin on the ground.

As precise as these categories could be, they rarely appeal to modern scholars seeking to craft typologies of medieval practices. Above all they focus mainly on supposed sources of power – demons, the stars, the power of spoken words or written characters – rather than the potential ends to which that power could be used, whereas modern scholars tend to categorize practices in terms of healing spells, harmful sorcery, love magic and the like.[24] Modern scholars also tend to emphasize the basic distinction between common practices widespread throughout medieval society and more rarified elite practices that required some degree of Latin learning and typically involved more complex procedures, often recorded in instructive books or manuals. Such distinctions were not formally part of any medieval typology of magical or superstitious practices. For example, William's category of rites focusing on astral bodies included both learned astrology and simple spells uttered to the rising sun or the new moon. Medieval writers did recognize this basic distinction, however, at least in their rhetoric if not in their abstract theorizing. They were keen to assert that many superstitions were mainly, if not exclusively, the domain of common folk, foolish men and, especially, "uneducated little women" (*indoctae mulierculae*).[25]

Common superstitions

The rites and observances that can be classified as common superstitions were extremely diverse. Probably the most universal were healing practices, which is certainly not surprising. In an era before much effective medicine, vulnerability to illness and injury was obviously a tremendous concern. Some of the practices that writers condemned or simply called into question can appear quite sensible. In the early fifteenth century, for example, the anonymous English didactic work *Dives and pauper* described how wounds should be cleaned with "blac wolle and olee" (black wool and oil). It also noted, however, that people often employed spoken charms as they performed this action, arousing concern among churchmen.[26] A half-century later, the Munich court physician Johannes Hartlieb reported that many people believed cleaning wounds with holy water guaranteed that they would not become infected.[27] The value of washing a wound was not in question, but the assumption that holy water would automatically block any infection could be deemed superstitious, since it presumed that divine power could be constrained to operate in a set way.

Medieval people recognized the medicinal powers of many herbs, roots and other plants, and insofar as they relied solely on the natural properties of such items they were immune to charges of superstition. Common practice, however, was often to pick medicinal plants at certain times, such as on the feast of Saint John (Midsummer Day) or under a full moon, in order to augment their power, which gave church authorities pause.[28] Authorities also worried about the common practice of reciting certain words while gathering herbs, even if these were entirely Christian formulas. Most churchmen condemned any such recitation, except in the case of the Apostles' Creed or Lord's Prayer, which, following a precedent long set in canon law, they judged to be legitimate and beneficial.[29] Words themselves, especially prayers or liturgical phrases, were widely believed to have great curative power. Many laypeople believed that the words used to consecrate the host during a Mass possessed healing virtues, or they used charms invoking Christ's wounds to heal their own injuries.[30]

Many healing practices appear to have been general in their intended effect, but some applied only to specific ailments. The most common of such rites mentioned in treatises against superstition dealt with fever.[31] Thomas Ebendorfer, a theologian in Vienna, related that people often said prayers, particularly the Pater Noster, to relieve fever. This was fine in itself, but they then added superstitious components to the rite such as saying the prayer only at a particular time.[32] Rites to cure toothaches also appear to have been common. Ebendorfer also decried the improper use of prayers for this purpose, while Denys the Carthusian criticized people who rinsed their mouths with holy water to relieve their pain.[33] Other practices aimed to relieve backaches or cure eye afflictions.[34]

Along with healing, protection from harm in various ways was a major focus of potentially superstitious rites. Many people apparently believed that attending Mass would not only benefit them spiritually but could protect them from specific physical maladies such as by preventing blindness.[35] Others held that wearing an amulet containing Gospel verses would ward off most diseases, while amulets containing the names of the biblical Three Kings were thought to control epilepsy.[36] One detailed rite involved placing a pig's shoulder blade on an altar and reading passages from the four Gospels over it. Thus empowered, it could be fashioned into a cross that would provide protection from "perils at sea, and from corporeal enemies, such as thieves, and from all misfortunes".[37] Numerous rites claimed to provide protection against dangerous animals, most frequently wolves.[38] Others promised to defend against serpents or to ward off caterpillars, insects, locusts or mice.[39]

Churchmen also frequently lambasted superstitious rites intended to control the weather, particularly to protect crops in the fields. Peasants might erect crosses to ward off storms or employ the Eucharist or ring church bells to the same end.[40] People apparently also gathered special herbs on Saint John's Day and burned them in their fields, invoked Christ against coming storms or hurled stones into the air to quell tempests.[41] Other rites simply aimed to increase the general health and fertility of crops.[42] Again we see how many of these rites were rooted in clearly Christian practices. What worried churchmen was the tenuous boundary between legitimate devotional behaviour and erroneous superstition, which even they often had trouble demarcating precisely.

Beyond active rites intended to achieve some specific end, medieval people took numerous occurrences as signs or omens, to the consternation of clerical authorities. Animal omens in particular appear to have abounded. Crows landing on a roof, an owl flying over a house or a rooster crowing before dawn were all held to portend misfortune.[43] Likewise if a cat or hare crossed one's path, this forebode ill.[44] Curiously, encountering a wolf, serpent or toad could all be good signs.[45] Some felt that encountering a clergyman while on a journey was an ill-omen.[46] Many people believed the flight of birds could reveal a favourable route for a journey, predict the outcome of a coming battle or foretell an approaching storm.[47] Murderers could be identified because blood would flow from the corpse when they were brought into its presence.[48] Thieves would be unable to swallow blessed cheese.[49]

Interestingly, although false astrology was a long-standing category of superstition, sources rarely present examples of ordinary people observing astral signs. Churchmen constantly rebuked astral divination in general, but they typically presented detailed accounts only of elite practices. They also frequently criticized divination from dreams, pronounced against the use of *sortes* (which could mean either casting lots or almost any other form of active divination) and condemned common beliefs that particular days or times were either lucky or unlucky, especially belief in the supposedly ominous Egyptian Days.[50] Of course, since all our sources were written by members of a literate elite, the insight they offer into common rites and observances is inevitably imperfect.[51] The churchmen who engaged in combatting superstition had a strong interest in understanding the practices they believed to exist all around them, but they inevitably saw common practices from their own perspective, framed by categories inherited from a long tradition of Christian writing against superstition and shaped also by a range of elite practices employed by people very much like themselves. Those rites, too, were an important component of medieval superstition.

Elite superstitions

While in modern parlance superstition tends to imply a foolish, poorly thought out, and above all unscientific belief or practice, in medieval Europe many aspects of learned art (*scientia*) could warrant the label *superstitio* if pursued improperly. Learned astrology, for example, and related forms of astral magic were often sharply contested. The practice of astrology had an impressive intellectual pedigree stretching back into antiquity, and it was championed as a legitimate science by major medieval thinkers like Albertus Magnus and Roger Bacon.[52] Other authorities, however, harshly criticized what they perceived to be improper forms of this art. Augustine did not hesitate to label it a "pernicious superstition", and Isidore of Seville held that astrology was always "partly natural, partly superstitious".[53] Medieval authorities agreed that heavenly bodies projected powerful energies towards the earth. Charting the position of the stars and attempting to calculate their effects on earth was a worthy science, and certain legitimate predictions could be based on such calculations. Problems arose when predictions were made about matters over which authorities felt the stars exerted no natural influence, although the exact nature of that distinction was a source of debate.

The most common astrological prognostications in medieval Europe were natal horoscopes. Authorities agreed that the bodies of newborn infants were highly impressionable, and so the force of the stars at the moment of one's birth might impart enduring characteristics that could shape one's destiny. There were even debates about whether the stars operated on Christ's physical body in this way.[54] Any narrow prediction about specific events in a person's later life, however, ran headlong into the divine promise of human free will. Between these two agreed-upon limits, authorities struggled to locate an exact divide between legitimate science and condemned superstition. Another widespread form of astrological practice involved "interrogations", in which astrologers sought to predict specific events based on the positions of the stars. People might inquire about the likely outcome of a battle, a marriage or a mercantile voyage if it were undertaken under certain astral signs. Again, authorities became suspicious when they felt that these predictions extended beyond occurrences that the natural energy of the stars could directly influence. At worst, they feared that demons entered into these operations, deceiving the unwary with false signs or conspiring to bring about predicted outcomes by their own power.[55]

Astrology was closely connected to other learned arts in the Middle Ages, perhaps none more than medicine. The German theologian Nicholas of Jauer repeatedly compared legitimate astrologers to physicians in that both expertly observed certain signs to "diagnose" otherwise unobservable conditions, and both were able to make informed predictions about future developments without entering into illicit divination.[56] Johannes Hartlieb, a physician himself, noted that doctors frequently needed to observe the heavens in order to treat their patients, since different astral energies could promote either illness or health.[57] But physicians could also lapse into superstition. Jean Gerson chastised the entire medical faculty of the University of Paris for allowing superstitious practices to infect their art, particularly in terms of their use of amulets, written characters and crafted figures.[58] He subsequently wrote a tract against potential superstitions pertaining to an astrological amulet in the form of a lion crafted by the dean of the medical faculty in Montpellier, although he noted that such images could be used legitimately, as the physician Arnau de Vilanova had done to treat Pope Boniface VIII a century earlier.[59]

Most authorities accepted that certain materials, like gold, had a natural affinity with and could help focus the natural energy of particular heavenly bodies, but they feared that crafted images, especially those with any figures or writing engraved on them, served instead to communicate with demons. Similarly, they felt that certain terrestrial materials – herbs, minerals, or gems – might possess powerful natural properties but could also be used in various demonic rites. Johannes Hartlieb addressed such dangers when he discussed books that taught how to use herbs, stones and roots to summon demons.[60]

Complex rituals intended to summon demons did indeed exist in the Middle Ages. This learned art, known as necromancy, was passed on through magical texts known not just to practitioners but to opponents as well. In the fourteenth century, the Catalan inquisitor Nicolau Eymerich mentioned manuals such as the *Table of Solomon* and *Sworn Book of Honorius*, which he had confiscated from magicians, and in the fifteenth century, Johannes Hartlieb mentioned several magical tomes, including both a *Key of Solomon* and a *Figure of Solomon*, as well as *Picatrix*, a famous text of astral magic that had originated in the Muslim world and passed into Europe through Spain.[61] These texts described rites that, to critics, demonstrated blatant worship to demons. As the inquisitor Eymerich wrote:

> In the aforesaid and some other books ... it appears indeed that invokers of demons manifestly exhibit the honor of worship to the demons they invoke, especially by sacrificing to them, adoring them, offering up execrable prayers ... by genuflecting,

by prostrating themselves, by observing chastity out of reverence for the demon or by its instruction, by fasting or otherwise afflicting their flesh ... by lighting candles, by burning incense or spices or other aromatics, by sacrificing birds or other animals.[62]

Such notions, including animal sacrifice, were not far-fetched, because necromantic texts themselves called for the sometimes gruesome killing of animals in certain rites. One powerful love spell required that a sorcerer bite out the heart of a dove with his own teeth and then use the blood to draw a figure on parchment made from the flesh of a female cat that had been skinned while in heat.[63]

Where opponents saw supplication and worship, practitioners claimed that they commanded demons through their rituals, drawing on the natural power of the substances they employed or even on the power of Christ. Many pointed to the biblical example from the Book of Tobit, in which young Tobit burns the heart and liver of a fish to drive away demons. Opponents responded, however, that this act had been accomplished by divine power, not fishy innards.[64] Because most necromancers were clergymen of some level (given the necessity of Latin learning to practice their craft), they could easily think of themselves as performing practices akin to the Christian rite of exorcism when they commanded demons to do their bidding. This was a powerful argument, but no less an authority than Thomas Aquinas provided what became the standard counterpoint: that faithful Christians could expel demons and drive them away but never compel them to perform services. To gain service, necromancers had to offer some form of adoration to the demons they summoned, whether they intended to or not.[65] And worship given to that which it ought not be given was, again according to Aquinas, the very definition of superstition.

Shifting focus of concerns

From the time of the early church fathers, Christian authorities had held a dichotomous view of potential superstitions. On the one hand, they were silly errors held only by the foolish and uneducated. In terms of their consequences, superstitious rites were often described as empty, worthless and vain. The proper response on the part of any serious thinker was disdain, but nothing more. On the other hand, superstitious rites were also seen as a primary means by which demons caught foolish people in their snares. Augustine himself demonstrated the derision that characterized so many intellectuals' attitudes towards *superstitio* when he repeated a remark by the Roman rhetorician Cato. Many people took it as an omen if they found that mice had chewed on their shoes at night. This was ridiculous, Cato quipped, although it certainly would have been a sign worthy of remark if the shoes had chewed on the mice.[66] Augustine also declared, however, that "all superstitious arts", no matter whether they were merely foolish or actually harmful, were "constituted through a certain pestiferous association of human beings and demons, as if by a pact of faithless and deceitful friendship", and so they should be "utterly repudiated and shunned by a Christian".[67]

Throughout the Middle Ages, the degree of concern churchmen directed against superstition depended to some extent on the depth of their concern about active demonic menace in the world. In general terms, a trajectory well known from the history of medieval magic continues to apply: lesser concerns and a focus on penance rather than punishment in the early medieval period gave way in later centuries to terrible fears, culminating in the notion of diabolical, conspiratorial witchcraft and the first large-scale witch-hunts in

Western Europe. Even as late as the early eleventh century, a legal source like the *Decretum* of Burchard of Worms could treat superstition mainly in terms of foolish error. Whether he was discussing the use of amulets, other healing rites, or practices intended to arouse love, cause impotence and infertility or control the weather, he often specified that the real superstition was to believe that these vain and empty actions could produce any real effects. The penalties he prescribed were always penances, mostly in the form of fasting.[68] Thereafter, attitudes began to harden, however, as churchmen began to express darker concerns and demand more serious penalties in papal proclamations, inquisitorial manuals, pastoral treatises and ultimately texts directed specifically against superstition and witchcraft. That increasingly specialized literature may not have initially reflected more widespread attitudes. An examination of more quotidian pastoral texts has found that magic was rarely a matter of deep concern to lower level church authorities, and that penance rather than harsh punishment remained the norm even into the late medieval centuries.[69] Nevertheless, the attitudes of high-ranking churchmen were clearly changing, and that shift ultimately had tremendous consequences for people at all levels of European society.[70]

Much of this shift in attitude can be attributed to the growing seriousness with which authorities regarded superstitious practices among elites like themselves, such as astrology and necromancy, which becomes evident in the twelfth and thirteenth centuries and develops dramatically in the fourteenth century.[71] In the fifteenth century, they began to (partially) reorient their condemnations of supposedly superstitious rites, now highly diabolized because of the need to address the explicitly demonic invocations of necromancers, back toward more common practices and more ordinary people. The shift is patent in the career of Jean Gerson. The Paris theology faculty's condemnation of 28 articles of superstition and sorcery was produced under his direction in 1398 and addressed learned magical practices almost exclusively. The specific kinds of rites it mentioned all involved complex rituals and elaborate paraphernalia: binding demons into gems, rings or mirrors; burning incense in the course of an invocation; saying prayers, performing ablutions or even celebrating Mass as part of these rites; offering the blood of hoopoes or other animals; or baptizing images of wax, copper, lead or gold.[72] In his own writings, Gerson addressed such elaborate rituals, but he also gave considerable attention to common practices. In his first known sermon against superstition, delivered at the French court in 1391, he indicated that the court was becoming infected with the superstitious beliefs of the common society surrounding it.[73] Similarly, a decade later, in his tract *On Errors Concerning the Magic Art*, he chastised the Paris Faculty of Medicine for condoning common healing practices that he called "the pestiferous and stupid superstitions of magicians and old sorceresses".[74] While he wrote works on learned astrology and astral image magic, he also wrote tracts against common superstitious connected to the observance of special days or to hearing a Mass.[75]

Gerson's influence on later churchmen who condemned superstition was pervasive, at least across much of northern Europe.[76] Most fifteenth-century treatises against superstition reflect his mix of high and low, elite and common. Most also reflect his intensely diabolized concerns, even in cases of the most seemingly benign common practices. Gerson maintained, for example, that even passive observances such as the belief that certain days were unlucky, which most previous authorities had judged to be a foolish but basically harmless error, represented an opportunity for demons to undermine the true faith. In this case, demons sought to work harm on supposedly unlucky days so that those false beliefs would be perpetuated.[77] Also in terms of clerical perceptions about the gendered nature of superstition, Gerson was a major transitional figure. While authorities who wrote mainly against elite practices focused necessarily on educated men, when Gerson turned to common superstitions he also turned against women, writing repeatedly of "old sorceresses" or "uneducated little women".[78] He was, of course, far from the first churchman to associate superstitious error especially with women, whom medieval authorities almost universally considered more foolish and prone to demonic deception than men, but his writings reflect a notable sharpening of this rhetoric that continued into the fifteenth century and beyond.[79]

Future directions

We are well informed about official attitudes towards superstition, and we can chart changing levels of concern with some degree of certainty. Far less clear is the nature and scope of the actual practices that led to the condemnations by legal and intellectual authorities over many centuries. The categories of practice they record are often highly generic and drawn in large measure from the writings of earlier authorities. Medieval churchmen regarded superstition as rooted, ultimately, in the eternal and unwavering malice of demons, who sought always to lead faithful Christians into error. One expert has described their view of superstition as essentially "ahistorical", while another has commented on the intensely "literary-traditional character" of their writing, unconcerned to reflect accurately the real world of beliefs and practices that existed around them.[80] Even when sources present a putatively contemporary practice in some detail, there can be room for doubt. In 1423, for example, the Vienna theologian Nicholas of Dinkelsbühl described a vernacular incantation intended to increase wealth, which called on the new moon. An anonymous treatise from southern Germany composed at roughly the same time described almost exactly the same spell.[81] Was this, however, actually a common practice in this region to which both writers were witness, or did one simply read and copy from the other?

Still, most scholars working in this area think that there are ways to discern at least the basic shape of real practices even from the largely proscriptive literature that church authorities produced.[82] One fruitful approach would be to pay more attention to shorter, more practical pastoral treatments of various forms of superstition and use these to try to inform our reading of longer manuals and treatises, which tend to be more encyclopaedic and generic.[83] Another approach would be to pay more attention to those churchmen who tolerated or even supported practices that most of their colleagues considered superstitious. The Zurich clergyman Felix Hemmerli, for example, wrote a series of tracts in the mid-fifteenth century on various blessings, charms, exorcisms and adjurations that he considered to be valid and legitimate practices.[84] Such tolerance can be found even in famously intolerant works. Treatises on witchcraft, which begin to appear in the fifteenth century, often discuss means of protection against bewitchment. These generally include officially sanctioned practices such as prayer, pilgrimage and making the sign of the cross, but also encompass amulets, incantations and herbal remedies, all of which could be viewed as superstitious but which authorities could be more willing to tolerate when set against the far greater perceived evil of diabolical witchcraft.[85]

Scholars are also increasingly turning away from the proscriptive dictates of the church and focusing on texts used by practitioners themselves. This is obviously more easily done for elite, learned practices. As mentioned above, medieval necromancers recorded their rites in magical manuals, some of which enjoyed wide circulation despite their illicit status. Other texts recorded other kinds of spiritual, astral or natural magic deemed superstitious by authorities.[86] The so-called *Ars Notoria*, for example, consisted of rituals for conjuring angelic spirits. Its practitioners claimed these rites had been used by Solomon. Its detractors argued that it was just another thinly veiled form of demonic invocation.[87] Astrological and alchemical texts abound, and need more systematic study. Even some forms of common practices can be approached in this way. A surprising number of textual amulets survive from the Middle Ages – bits of paper covered with written formulas and then worn on one's person, usually to heal or protect from harm.[88]

Amulets represent not just textual evidence of common practices that were frequently labelled superstitious but also an aspect of material culture. The majority of physical items used in magical or superstitious rites that have survived from the Middle Ages are representative of elite forms of practice: rings, gems, mirrors or astrological images, often inscribed with symbols and writing. The herbs and roots that so many texts tell us were used in common rites have long since rotted into dust. Archeology might uncover other kinds of items, although scholars face enormous problems determining solely from archeological remains when or if common items might have been used for magical purposes.[89] Relatively little work has been done in any of these areas, however, and the possibilities of future discoveries or methodological innovations are great.

Most basically, our understanding of the vast array of practices that could be lumped together under the heading of superstition in the Middle Ages will grow the more we look to what are now the margins of the field, whether these be methodological (material culture rather than texts), chronological (prior to the fourteenth and fifteenth centuries and the much studied rise of witchcraft) or geographical (Central and Eastern Europe rather than the West). We will also benefit by looking away from the well-studied narrative of increasing concern and condemnation to focus more on evidence of scepticism or toleration whenever we can find it. Finally, while most detailed work will need to focus on specific areas of practice, we should remember that for many medieval thinkers, essential connections existed between what to us can appear highly disparate practices. Even if these connections exist only in terms of formulaic expressions of possible demonic entanglements, they are still an essential part of medieval understandings of the broad range of belief and behaviour that could be labelled as superstitious.

Notes

1 *Chartularium Universitatis Parisiensis*. 4 vols. ed. Heinrich Denifle (1891–99; reprint Brussels: Culture et Civilisation, 1964), 4:32–6; translation from Lynn Thorndike, *University Records and Life in the Middle Ages* (New York: Columbia University Press, 1944), 261–66.
2 See most recently Catherine Rider, *Magic and Religion in Medieval England* (London: Reaktion, 2012), 15–6.
3 Dieter Harmening, *Superstitio: Überlieferungs- und theoriegeschichtliche Untersuchungen zur kirchlich-theologischen Aberglaubensliteratur des Mittelalters* (Berlin: Erich Schmidt, 1979).
4 Karin Baumann, *Aberglaube für Laien: Zur Programmatik und Überlieferung mittelalterlicher Superstitionenkritik*, 2 vols. (Würzburg: Königshausen & Neumann, 1989); Marina Montesano, *"Supra acqua et supra ad vento": "Superstizioni"*, maleficia *e* incantamenta *nei predicatori Francescani osservanti (Italia, sec. XV)* (Rome: Istituto Storico Italiano, 1999).
5 Bernadette Filotas, *Pagan Survivals, Superstitions, and Popular Cultures* (Toronto: Pontifical Institute of Medieval Studies, 2005).
6 Patrick Hersperger, *Kirche, Magie und "Aberglaube":* Superstitio *in der Kanonistik des 12. und 13. Jahrhunderts* (Cologne: Böhlau, 2010).
7 Emilie Lasson, *Superstitions médiévales: Une analyse d'après l'exégèse du premier commandement d'Ulrich de Pottenstein* (Paris: Honoré Champion, 2010); Krzysztof Bracha, *Des Teufels Lug und Trug: Nikolaus Magni von Jauer, ein Reformtheologe des 15. Jahrhunderts gegen Aberglaube und Götzendienst*, trans. Peter Chmiel (Dettelbach: J. H. Röll, 2013).

8 Jean Verdon, *Les superstitions au Moyen Age* (Paris: Perrin, 2008).
9 Euan Cameron, *Enchanted Europe: Superstition, Reason, and Religion, 1250–1750* (Oxford: Oxford University Press, 2010).
10 Michael D. Bailey, *Fearful Spirits, Reasoned Follies: The Boundaries of Superstition in Late Medieval Europe* (Ithaca, NY: Cornell University Press, 2013).
11 As an example of early sermons, see those of Caesarius of Arles, *Sancti Caesarii Arelatensis sermones*, ed. Germain Morin, Corpus Christianorum Series Latina 103–4 (Turnhout: Brepols, 1953); on penitential literature, see *Medieval Handbooks of Penance*, ed. and trans. John T. McNeill and Helena M. Gamer (New York: Columbia University Press, 1938).
12 Substantial sections are in *Medieval Handbooks of Penance*, otherwise see Burchard of Worms, *Decretorum libri viginti*, ed. J.-P. Migne, Patrologia Latina 140 (Paris: Garnier, 1880), cols. 537–1058.
13 Rider, *Magic and Religion*, stresses the importance of pastoral manuals; on canon law, see Hersperger, *Kirche, Magie und "Aberglaube"*.
14 For a famous example, see Jean-Claude Schmitt, *The Holy Greyhound: Guinefort, Healer of Children since the Thirteenth Century*, trans. Martin Thom (Cambridge: Cambridge University Press, 1983).
15 Bailey, *Fearful Spirits*, 255–65.
16 *The Distaff Gospels: A First Modern English Edition of "Les Évangiles des Quenouilles"*, transl. Madeleine Jeay and Kathleen Garay (Peterborough, ON: Broadview Press, 2006), 65.
17 Augustine, *De doctrina Christiana* 2.20(30), ed. Joseph Martin, Corpus Christianorum Series Latina 32 (Turnhout: Brepols, 1962):

> Superstitiosum est, quicquid institutum est ab hominibus ad facienda et colenda idola pertinens uel ad colendam sicut deum creaturam partemue ullam creaturae uel ad consultationes et pacta quaedam significationum cum daemonibus placita atque foederata, qualia sunt molimina magicarum artium, quae quidem commemorare potius quam docere adsolent poetae. Ex quo genere sunt, sed quasi licentiore uanitate, haruspicum et augurum libri. Ad hoc genus pertinent omnes etiam ligaturae atque remedia, quae medicorum quoque disciplina condemnat.

18 Aquinas, *Summa theologiae* 2.2.92.1, in *Summa theologiae: Latin Text and English Translation*, vol. 40, *Superstition and Irreverence*, ed. and trans. Thomas Franklin O'Meara O.P. and Michael John Duffy O.P. (New York: Blackfriars, 1968): "Sic igitur superstitio est vitium religioni oppositum secundum excessum, non quia plus exhibeat in cultum divinum quam vera religio, sed quia exhibit cultum divinum vel cui non debet, vel eo modo quo non debet" (I have modified O'Meara's and Duffy's translation).
19 Augustine, *De doctrina Christiana* 2.20(31)-2.21(32): "His adiunguntur milia inanissimarum obseruationum…".
20 Isidore, *Etymologiarum sive originum libri XX* 8.9.9-30, 2 vols. ed. W.M. Lindsay (1911; reprint Oxford: Clarendon, 1971): "Magi sunt, qui vulgo malefici ob facinorum magnitudinem nuncupantur. Hi et elementa concutiunt, turbant mentes hominum, ac sine ullo veneni haustu violentia tantum carminus interimunt" (8.9.9) and "Incantatores dicti sunt, qui artem verbis peragunt" (8.9.15).
21 Charles Burnett, "The Earliest Chiromancy in the West", *Journal of the Warburg and Courtauld Institutes* 50 (1987): 189–95; Charles Burnett, "An Islamic Divinatory Technique in Medieval Spain", in *The Arab Influence in Medieval Europe*, ed. Dionisius A. Agius and Richard Hitchcock (Reading, UK: Ithaca Press, 1994), 100–35.
22 Aquinas, *Summa theologiae* 2.2.95.3-8.
23 William, *De legibus* 23, in *Opera omnia* (Venice, 1591). The categories are then discussed in subsequent chapters, *De legibus* 24–27.
24 See typologies in Richard Kieckhefer, *Magic in the Middle Ages* (Cambridge: Cambridge University Press, 1989), 56–94; Karen Jolly, "Medieval Magic: Definitions, Beliefs, Practices", in *Witchcraft and Magic in Europe: The Middle Ages*, ed. Bengt Ankarloo and Stuart Clark (Philadelphia: University of Pennsylvania Press, 2002), 27–71.
25 Here Jean Gerson, *De erroribus circa artem magicam*, in *Oeuvres complètes*, 10 vols., ed. P. Glorieux (Paris: Desclée, 1960–73), 10:83, but similar language is found in many late medieval treatises on magic and superstition. Works by Gerson will subsequently be cited OC (for *Oeuvres complètes*) followed by volume and page number.
26 Anonymous, *Dives and Pauper*, 3 vols., Early English Text Society 275, 280, 323, ed. Priscilla Heath Barnum (Oxford: Oxford University Press, 1976, 1980, 2004), 1:168.

27 Johannes Hartlieb, *Das Buch aller verbotenen Künste, des Aberglaubens und der Zauberei*, ed. and trans. Falk Eisermann and Eckhard Graf (Ahlerstedt: Param, 1989), 78–80. While I will continue to cite from this German edition, an English translation is now available in *Hazards of the Dark Arts: Advice for Medieval Princes on Witchcraft and Magic*, trans. Richard Kieckhefer (University Park: Pennsylvania State University Press, 2017), 21–92

28 E.g. Hartlieb, *Buch aller verbotenen Künste*, 80; Martin of Arles, *De superstitionibus* (Rome, 1559), fol. 7r.

29 E.g. *Dives and pauper*, 1:158; Martin of Arles, *De superstitionibus*, fols. 7v and 68v-69r; Denys the Carthusian, *Contra vicia superstitionum* (Cologne, 1533), 603.

30 Heinrich of Gorkum, *De superstitiosis quibusdam casibus* (Blaubeuren, ca. 1477), fol. 4v; Johannes of Wünschelburg, *De superstitionibus*, Wrocław, Biblioteka Uniwersytecka, MS 239 (I F 212), fol. 236r.

31 Johannes of Wünschelburg, *De superstitionibus*, fol. 232v; Martin of Arles, *De superstitionibus*, fols. 25v-26r; Nicholas of Jauer, *De superstitionibus*, Philadelphia, University of Pennsylvania, MS Codex 78, fol. 56v.

32 Thomas Ebendorfer, *De decem praeceptis*, in Anton E. Schönbach, "Zeugnisse zur deutschen Volkskunde des Mittelalters", *Zeitschrift des Vereins für Volkskunde* 12 (1902): 1–14, at 7.

33 Denys the Carthusian, *Contra vicia superstitionum*, 612; Ebendorfer, *De decem praeceptis*, 7.

34 Johannes of Wünschelburg, *De superstitionibus*, fol. 233r; anonymous, *De superstitionibus*, Erlangen, Universitätsbibliothek, MS 585, fol. 176r.

35 Jean Gerson, *Adversus superstitionem in audiendo missam*, OC 10:141.

36 Johannes of Wünschelburg, *De superstitionibus*, fol. 235r; on the Three Kings amulet, see Don C. Skemer, *Binding Words: Textual Amulets in the Middle Ages* (University Park: Pennsylvania State University Press, 2006), 64–65.

37 Heinrich of Gorkum, *De superstitiosis quibusdam casibus*, fol. 3r-v: "creditur quod huiusmodi scapulis acquiratur virtus talis quod cruces facte de craneis illarum scapularum habeant virtutem preseruandi homines a periculis maris et ab inimicis corporalibus scilicet raptoribus et ab omnibus infortuniis".

38 Anonymous, *De superstitionibus*, fol. 176r; Denys the Carthusian, *Contra vicia superstitionum*, 612; Johannes of Wünschelburg, *De superstitionibus*, fol. 232v; Martin of Arles, *De superstitionibus*, fol. 28r; Nicholas of Jauer, *De superstitionibus*, fol. 57r.

39 Anonymous, *De superstitionibus*, fol. 176r; Hartlieb, *Buch aller verbotenen Künste*, 76; Johannes of Wünschelburg, *De superstitionibus*, fols. 233r, 235v; Martin of Arles, *De superstitionibus*, fol. 28r.

40 Heinrich of Gorkum, *De superstitiosis quibusdam casibus*, fol. 4v; Johannes of Wünschelburg, *De superstitionibus*, fol. 232v; Nicholas of Jauer, *De superstitionibus*, fol. 57r; Johannes Nider, *Preceptorium divine legis* 1.11.34(pp) (Milan, 1489).

41 Martin of Arles, *De superstitionibus*, fols. 7v, 29v, 61v.

42 Denys the Carthusian, *Contra vicia superstitionum*, 610; Nicholas of Jauer, *De superstitionibus*, fol. 56v.

43 Gerson, *Contra superstitiosam dierum observantiam*, OC 10:118.

44 Ebendorfer, *De decem praeceptis*, 9; Hartlieb, *Buch aller verbotenen Künste*, 90; Martin of Arles, *De superstitionibus*, fol. 18r.

45 Hartlieb, *Buch aller verbotenen Künste*, 80; Ebendorfer, *De decem praeceptis*, 9; Johannes of Wünschelburg, *De superstitionibus*, fol. 238v.

46 Jakob of Paradise, *De potestate demonum*, Munich, Bayerische Staatsbibliothek, Clm 18378, fol. 261r; Ulrich of Pottenstein, *Dekalog-Auslegung: Das erste Gebot, Text und Quellen*. ed. Gabriele Baptist-Hlawatsch (Tübingen: Max Niemeyer, 1995), 108.

47 Heinrich of Gorkum, *De superstitiosis quibusdam casibus*, fol. 1r.

48 Henricus Institoris O.P. and Jacobus Sprenger O.P., *Malleus maleficarum* 1.2, 2 vols., ed. and trans. Christopher Mackay (Cambridge: Cambridge University Press, 2006), 1: 239.

49 Johannes Hartlieb, *Buch aller verbotenen Künste*, 66.

50 These matters appear in almost every text on superstition in this period.

51 On this problem, see Bailey, *Fearful Spirits*, 29–33; Rider, *Magic and Religion*, 21–23.

52 Lynn Thorndike, *A History of Magic and Experimental Science*, 8 vols. (New York: Columbia University Press, 1923–58), 2:577–92, 659–77.

53 Augustine, *De doctrina Christiana* 2.21(32): "Neque illi ab hoc genere perniciosae superstitionis segregandi sunt, qui genethliaci propter natalium dierum considerationes, nunc autem uulgo mathematici uocantur"; Isidore, *Etymologiae* 3.27.1: "Astrologia vero partim naturalis, partim superstitiosa est".

54 As articulated by the fifteenth-century Cardinal Pierre d'Ailly in his *Apologetica defensio astronomice veritatis*, in d'Ailly, *Imago mundi et varia eiusdem auctoris et Joannis Gerson opuscula* (Louvain, ca. 1483), fol. 140v.
55 E.g. Denys the Carthusian, *Contra vicia superstitionum*, 601, 614–15; Jakob of Paradise, *De potestate demonum*, fols. 263r–264v; Nicholas of Jauer, *De superstitionibus*, fol. 40r-v; Jean Gerson, *Trilogium astrologiae theologizatae*, OC 10:96.
56 Nicholas of Jauer, *De superstitionibus*, fols. 37r, 40r, 50r. Such comparisons went back at least to Augustine, *De civitate dei* 10.32.
57 Hartlieb, *Buch aller verbotenen Künste*, 88.
58 Gerson, *De erroribus circa artem magicam*, passim.
59 Gerson, *Contra superstitionum sculpturae leonis*, OC 10:131. On Arnau and Boniface, see Nicolas Weill-Parot, *Les "images astrologiques" au Moyen Age et à la Renaissance: Spéculations intellectuelles et pratiques magiques (XIIe-XVe siècle)* (Paris: Honoré Champion, 2002), 477–79; Heinrich Finke, *Aus den Tagen Bonifaz VIII: Funde und Forschungen* (Münster: Aschendorffschen Buchhandlung, 1902), 200–9.
60 Hartlieb, *Buch aller verbotenen Künste*, 38.
61 Nicolau Eymerich, *Directorium inquisitorum* 2.43.1, ed. F. Peña (Rome, 1587), 338; Hartlieb, *Buch aller verbotenen Künste*, 34, 48. For an example of such a text, see Richard Kieckhefer, *Forbidden Rites: A Necromancer's Manual of the Fifteenth Century* (University Park: Pennsylvania State University Press, 1998).
62 Eymerich, *Directorium inquisitorum* 2.43.2, p. 338:

> In praedictis et aliis nonnullis libris, et inquisitionibus apparet, quod quidam daemones inuocantes manifeste exhibent honorem latriae demonibus inuocatis, utpote eis sacrificando, adorando, orationes execrabiles effundendo, … genuaflectendo, prostrationes faciendo, castitatem pro daemonis reuerentia, vel monito obseruando, iciunando, vel carnem suam alias macerando, … luminaria accendendo, thurificando de ambra, ligno aloes, et similibu aromaticis subfumigando, aues, vel animalia alia immolando.

63 Kieckhefer, *Forbidden Rites*, 82.
64 Johannes of Frankfurt, *Quaestio utrum potestas cohercendi demones fieri possit per caracteres, figuras atque verborum prolationes*, in *Quellen und Untersuchungen zur Geschichte des Hexenwahns und der Hexenverfolgung im Mittelalter*. ed. Joseph Hansen (1901; reprint Hildesheim: Georg Olms, 1963), 72; Jakob of Paradise, *De potestate demonum*, fol. 270r; Nicholas of Jauer, *De superstitionibus*, fol. 42v.
65 Aquinas, *Summa theologiae* 2.2.90.2, *Summa theologiae: Latin Text and English Translation, Religion and Worship*. vol. 39. ed. and transl. Kevin D. O'Rourke O.P. (New York: Blackfriars, 1964), 238–40.
66 Augustine, *De doctrina Christiana* 2.20(31).
67 Augustine, *De doctrina Christiana* 2.23(36): "Omnes igitur artes huiusmodi uel nugatoriae uel noxiae superstitionis ex quadam pestifera societate hominum et daemonum quasi pacta infidelis et dolosae amicitiae constituta sunt repudianda et fugienda christiano".
68 McNeill and Gamer, *Medieval Handbooks of Penance*, 321–45.
69 Rider, *Magic and Religion*, esp. chaps. 6–7.
70 For a different perspective, see Peter A. Morton, "Superstition, Witchcraft, and the First Commandment in the Late Middle Ages," *Magic, Ritual, and Witchcraft* 13 (2018): 40–70.
71 Bailey, *Fearful Spirits*, esp. chap. 2.
72 Articles 4, 10, 12, 20, 21.
73 Gerson, sermon "Regnum", OC 7.2:1000–01.
74 Gerson, *De erroribus circa artem magicam*, OC 10:77: "Incidit ut conquererer de superstitionibus pestiferis magicorum et stultitiis vetularum sortilegarum quae per quosdam ritus maledictos mederi patientibus pollicentur".
75 In Gerson, *Contra superstitiosam dierum observantiam*, *De observatione dierum quantum ad opera*, and *Adversus superstitionem in audiendo missam*, OC 10:116–21, 128–30, 141–43.
76 Bailey, *Fearful Spirits*, 144–45, 188–89; Bracha, *Teufels Lug und Trug*, 50–2.
77 Gerson, *Contra superstitiosam dierum observantiam*, OC 10:119.
78 "Vielles sorcières" in the sermon "Regnum" (OC 7.2:1001), "vetulae sortilegae" and "indoctae mulierculae" in *De erroribus circa artem magicam* (OC 10:77, 83), and "vetulae sortilegae, gallice vieilles sorcières" in *Contra superstitiosam dierum observantiam* (OC 10:120).
79 Bailey, *Fearful Spirits*, 185–88.
80 Baumann, *Aberglaube für Laien*, 1:274; Harmening, *Superstitio*, 72.

81 Nicholas of Dinkelsbühl, *De preceptis decalogi* (Strasbourg, 1516), fol. 29v: "Bis got, wilkum newer mon, holder her, mach mir myns geltes mer" (see also Baumann, *Aberglaube für Laien*, 2:544); anonymous, *De superstitionibus*, Munich, Bayerische Staatsbibliothek, Clm 4727, fol. 49r: "Pis got, wilkom ain newer man, holder herr, mach mir meins guets mer".
82 Bailey, *Fearful Spirits*, 28–33.
83 See Bailey, *Fearful Spirits*; and more programmatically Rider, *Magic and Religion*.
84 Collected in Hemmerli, *Varie oblectationis opuscula et tractatus* (Strasbourg, 1497 or later).
85 Bailey, *Fearful Spirits*, chap. 5.
86 Kieckhefer, *Forbidden Rites*; Benedek Láng, *Unlocked Books: Manuscripts of Learned Magic in the Medieval Libraries of Central Europe* (University Park: Pennsylvania State University Press, 2008); Frank Klassen, *The Transformations of Magic: Illicit Learned Magic in the Later Middle Ages and Renaissance* (University Park: Pennsylvania State University Press, 2013); Sophie Page, *Magic in the Cloister: Pious Motives, Illicit Interests, and Occult Approaches to the Medieval Universe* (University Park: Pennsylvania State University Press, 2013); Claire Fanger, *Rewriting Magic: An Exegesis of the Visionary Autobiography of a Fourteenth-Century French Monk* (University Park: Pennsylvania State University Press, 2015).
87 Julien Véronèse, *L'Ars notoria au Moyen Age: Introduction et édition critique* (Florence: Sismel Edizioni del Galluzzo: 2007); see also *Invoking Angels: Theurgic Ideas and Practices, Thirteenth to Sixteenth Centuries*, ed. Claire Fanger (University Park: Pennsylvania State University Press, 2012).
88 Skemer, *Binding Words*.
89 For a later period, see Brian Hoggard, "The Archeology of Counter-Witchcraft and Popular Magic", in *Beyond the Witch Trials: Witchcraft and Magic in Enlightenment Europe*, ed. Owen Davies and Willem de Blécourt (Manchester: Manchester University Press, 2004), 167–86.

34

WITCHCRAFT

Martine Ostorero

Despite their apparent similarity, the historiography of magic does not always intersect with the historiography of witch-hunting. The former focuses mainly on practices and rituals that were recorded by a relatively large literary production in the last centuries of the Middle Ages. The methods of production, sources of inspiration, circulation and reception of magical knowledge, along with its socio-economic impact, have been the subject of renewed attention in recent decades. Supported by these developments, critical editions of magical texts (in a broad sense) are being produced more and more frequently. Conversely, historians of witchcraft concentrate on its repression, which intensified only at the very end of the Middle Ages, in particular the fifteenth to seventeenth centuries. This is dependent on the sources available, that is to say – taking those which are most significant – an abundance of juridical material, a multitude of procedural manuals, doctrinal tracts or pamphlets against so-called male and female witches, as well as various official condemnations stemming from secular or ecclesiastical authorities. Most of these documents were produced by those who took part in the repression of witchcraft, and a very small proportion by possible male and female witches themselves. Due to the disparity between documentary sources relating to magic and witchcraft trials, a dialogue between the two fields is not always guaranteed, although it would lead to each increasing its respective knowledge base and both being better able to explore the continuities and points of difference between magic and witchcraft.

Furthermore, the distinction made by scholars between magic, sorcery and witchcraft has contributed to the creation of categories that are not always those employed by medieval writers.[1] The term "magic" groups together the practices of natural, ritual and demonic magic without differentiation, although medieval clerics attempted to distinguish them to establish a conceptual and normative framework. Medieval thinkers did not have a coherent category of sorcery (in the sense of maleficent magic), and the term can only be understood in opposition to witchcraft (or conspiratorial witchcraft), which did not develop until the fifteenth century. Likewise, people in the Middle Ages probably did not separate learned magicians and illiterate witches to the same extent as current historians. This is evident in the example of the injunction of 1430 by Amadeus VIII Duke of Savoy to simultaneously pursue "heretics, sorcerers, astrologers, soothsayers, the invokers of demons, immolators and other superstitious people" (*heretici, sortilegi, mathematici, divini, demonum invocatores, immolatores et hujusmodi supersticiosi*).[2] A later example is an engraving of Pieter Bruegel the Elder from c.1564 (*Saint James at the Sorcerer's Den*) which shows the coexistence of learned magicians, like Hermogenes, and witches, flying to the Sabbat riding on broomsticks, goats or monstrous creatures. Magic circles and hands of glory went hand in hand with cauldrons, cats and toads, the common thread being explained by the caption: these are *diabolica prestigii*, misleading and diabolical illusions that are shared by both magicians and witches. This engraving would serve as a reference model for images depicting witchcraft that were produced later, starting from Flanders.[3]

Finally, the richness of the lexical registers of magic and witchcraft in the Middle Ages, both in Latin and vernacular languages, is such that it makes reduction into the distinct categories of "magic" and "witchcraft" problematic, if not inadequate. This is even more the case when particular words undergo semantic mutations over the passage of time such as *nigromanticus* or *sortilegus*. This is not the place to elaborate on this, but it is necessary to bear in mind how important it is to pay attention to vocabulary and its pitfalls.[4]

The connections and continuities between the domains of magic and witchcraft are important. Hostility towards learned magic mutated into a distorted view of witchcraft over the course of the fifteenth century. Moreover, magical practices, whether sorceries (*sortilegium*) or evil practices (*maleficium*), were, for the most part, absorbed into the mythology of demonic witchcraft and of the Sabbat that developed at the beginning of the fifteenth century. We can also see that trials for witchcraft were frequently initiated by rumours or witness depositions that reported "traditional" practices of sorcery such as an illness produced by a powder or an ointment, the casting of an evil spell, etc. Over the course of the inquisitorial judicial procedure, these preliminary denunciations were integrated into the mythology of the Sabbat, which transformed them during the course of the interrogations. For example, the accused was brought to confess that an ointment was composed in part of the corpses of small children, and that it was made collectively on the Sabbat by a sect subject to the instructions of the devil. In 1437, the trial brought against Joubert de Bavière in Briançon transformed the necromancer into an expert on the Sabbat.[5]

Written sources also demonstrate this continuity between sorcery and witchcraft. For example, around 1430, the chronicler of Lucerne Hans Fründ juxtaposed witches and magicians (*hexssen und zuºbrern*), grouped together in Latin under the category of *sortilegi*, whose misdeeds he classifies as heresy.[6] The Dominican Jean Nider created an inventory of the different perpetrators of sins and mentions a necromancer in possession of "forbidden books" who later repented and became a monk, as well as infanticidal and cannibalistic witches; the powerful sorcerer Scaedeli who caused miscarriages; and a woman who practised bewitchments using images made of lead and who knew how to cast evil spells, all in the same chapter of his *Formicarius* (Part V, chapter 3).[7] Later, the *Flagellum maleficorum* of Pierre Mamoris (before 1462) also reflected this conception: the "Sabbat" (this tract is one of the first occurrences of the term) is included in the midst of an enumeration of various evil spells (*variorum maleficorum inducta narratio*). This also includes cases of divination, acts of prestidigitation and healing practices, as well as evil spells in the strict sense.[8] These attempts at categorization by medieval writers aimed above all to differentiate between legal and illegal practices, whether they were linked to the magical arts, witchcraft or superstitions. The use of demons drew a dividing line that was supported by the majority of clerics.

The heresy of magic and witchcraft

At the end of the Middle Ages, both ecclesiastical and secular authorities began to pay closer attention to magic, sorcery and witchcraft, to condemn them in the most severe terms and to further incriminate those who made use of them.

The problem of the categorization of the alleged crimes committed by male and female witches was an issue of the highest importance. It was also a potential source of tension between ecclesiastical and secular authorities. Did these evil spells legally qualify as heresy, apostasy and idolatry (through the worship of demons), superstitions, crimes (*maleficium* in the primary sense), treason to God or man or even homicide? The varied and multiple responses to this question depended on the type of tribunal to which a case of magic was brought, the procedure followed, and the way in which the crime was sentenced.

The assimilation of ritual magic and witchcraft with heresy is a strong tendency that can be observed over the course of the fourteenth and fifteenth centuries. Pope John XXII (1316–44) was particularly troubled by this issue, and began to connect the two, although without making a definitive ruling on this issue. The bull *Super illius specula* was the result of an extensive consultation of experts in around 1320, but probably remained unpublished at the time, even though mandates with similar contents had been sent by the pontifical court; for example, one was sent by Cardinal Guillaume de Peyre Godin to inquisitors in the south of France in 1320.[9] Nevertheless, inquisitors in the field, such as Bernard Gui and later Nicolas Eymerich, pleaded in favour of hunting magicians and sorcerers through the inquisition, and endeavoured to incriminate them by associating their crimes with heresy.[10] It is to Nicolas Eymerich that we owe the first attestation of *Super illius specula*, which he includes in his *Directorium inquisitorum* (completed around October 1376 in Avignon).[11] The mandate corresponds precisely with his views and particularly legitimises his actions, since almost fifty of the cases he took on in response to denunciations concerned magic and divination.[12]

In France and in the Papal States, in the first third of the fourteenth century, a significant number of cases of a political nature involved accusations of demonic magic, demon worship and heresy. This is the case with the lawsuits brought against the Templars (1307–14), the enquiry taken against bishop Guichard of Troyes (1307–14) and the accusations against Enguerrand de Marigny (1314) and Mahaut d'Artois (1316), led by Philippe the Fair and his jurists.[13] Some years later, Pope John XXII used similar accusations to bring his enemies into line such as the Visconti or the "rebels" of the March of Ancona who were accused of idolatry and heresy.[14] During the 1330s, the Avignonese papacy, particularly Benedict XII (1334–42) and then Gregory XI (1371–78), began to pay more attention to sorcerers, necromancers and the invokers of demons, whether they were clerics in the south of France or practitioners of magic who worked in a courtly environment. Nevertheless, until the turn of the fourteenth and fifteenth centuries, the main target of theologians and inquisitors was the ritual and learned magic of invokers of demons, rather than popular sorcery.[15] These developments significantly prepared the ground for witch-hunts.

In 1398, not long after France withdrew its obedience to the papacy, the theology faculty of the University of Paris produced a broad condemnation of ritual magic. Without actually qualifying it as heresy, it denounced the "errors" of magicians as unspeakable abominations. This condemnation took place in a context where cases of magic were disrupting the courts of France and Burgundy: the "madness" of King Charles VI jeopardized the French monarchy and brought about significant political tensions in which magic played a dominant role. Both the use of magic and its repression were at the core of the expression of power. In particular, they played a part in the definition of royal power and majesty (*majestas*), particularly as *lèse-majesté* had been equated with heresy since the decretal *Vergentis in senium* (1199).[16] In 1409, while still in the midst of the schism, Pope Alexander V gave a mandate to the Franciscan inquisitor Ponce Feugeyron to pursue sorcerers, soothsayers, the invokers of demons, enchanters, conjurers and superstitious diviners because they used forbidden and criminal (*nefarius*) arts, corrupting the populace and creating new sects.[17]

At the end of the Middle Ages, the field of heresy had increased considerably, and with it the capabilities of the inquisition. Heresy could include necromancy, the magical arts and witchcraft, as well as idolatry (i.e. demon worship), sexual deviance, rebellion and even *lèse-majesté*, which were all deemed attacks on and offences against God, nature and ecclesiastical authority.[18] Heresy was not only an issue of deviant religious beliefs or heterodox theological positions, but it integrated acts that were likely to cause damage to local communities, or even to harm the whole of Christian society. In this respect, the struggle against heresy engaged the secular authorities at every level (fiefdoms, towns, states) and in fact took on a political dimension.[19]

The assimilation of magical arts and the practices of witchcraft with heresy was largely due to the fact that people believed the efficacy of magical practices was linked to the intervention of demons. The practitioner was supposed to have made a sacrifice to the demons, or a pact with them that sealed his apostasy through the renunciation of his faith in God. Now, demon worship was the strongest form of rebellion against God, comparable with divine *lèse-majesté*, as well as reinforcing the heretical character of the crime. This was a theoretical and doctrinal position that had concrete consequences in judicial practice, reinforcing the actions of ecclesiastical tribunals and the use of the extraordinary inquisitorial procedural method. However, this extension of the notion of heresy, while it can be found in the discourse of particular theologians, judges or inquisitors, was never received nor applied universally. It is therefore always necessary to note other methods of supressing witchcraft and pockets of resistance to or scepticism about the pursuit of the fight against witchcraft.

A major shift in the fifteenth century

While it was frequently accepted up to around 1400 that certain individuals could produce evil spells with the help of demons, the first decades of the fifteenth century saw a more terrifying idea emerge: that there were men and women who formed a clandestine sect whose members renounced their faith and swore loyalty to the devil or demons through a pact. When called by the devil or demons, they would gather in remote places, most often by flying through the air. They would worship the devil, pervert Christian rites and sacraments, and perform evil practices against men, beasts and crops on his orders, aiming to destroy them or make them perish. They were suspected of engaging in sexual acts with demons. They killed small children and then ate their flesh, or used it to make harmful ointments or potions. Their existence constituted a major threat to society. It therefore seemed necessary to inform the authorities and the populace of this, and to prepare to fight against this new danger.

By creating what is commonly called the Witches' Sabbat, the Christian West began to believe that witches flew on broomsticks, ate children and worked secretly towards the destruction of Christian society under the aegis of the devil. This new belief constituted the base of doctrine on demonic witchcraft, which made the dramatic witch-hunts of the fifteenth to seventeenth centuries possible.

These new practices of witchcraft are characterized by four principal elements linked to evil acts: their collective dimension (secret sect or society), the absolute submission that connects the sorcerer to the devil (apostasy or demon worship), acts against nature such as cannibalism, infanticide and acts of sexual deviance, as well as, in most cases, the magical flight of witches through the air. This idea of the Sabbat was based on concepts that had undergone significant changes throughout the two previous centuries. Magic had been subject to a substantial process of demonization; the development of the persecution of heresy led to the creation of a polemical, stereotyped discourse that tended to render the heretic not only an underling of Satan but also a being who engaged in vile acts against nature, a sort of incarnation of absolute Evil.[20] Indeed, reflections on nature and the powers of demons underwent significant changes in the age of scholasticism, as Alain Boureau has demonstrated.[21] This scholastic demonology amply nourished tracts on witchcraft between the fifteenth and seventeenth centuries.

Jean-Patrice Boudet has, for his part, succinctly demonstrated four primary metamorphoses in the transformation of accusations of magic towards demonic witchcraft and the Sabbat: shifts from the guardian angel to a private demon; from homage (individual) to the Sabbat (collective); from magician to witch; and from denunciations made by neighbours to accusations pursued by the State.[22] The changes that took place during this period led to a new take on older conceptions of magic and sorcery. Attention was shifted from the individual who operated alone to secret sects or societies who produced evil potions together or collectively brought about storms. The protagonists were no longer mostly men, but now mostly women: the witch embodied the figure of the woman who had submitted to the devil to wreak havoc on the earth. Magical flight, which is to our eyes undoubtedly the most implausible element of the Sabbat, became the emblem of the new conception of witchcraft. The reality of nocturnal flight was promoted in order to make people believe in the possibility of secret gatherings between witches as well as to justify the witch-hunts.

These transformations also affected demonological concepts: while the magician invoked demons and compelled them to help him, profiting from demonic power, witches at the Sabbat irrevocably submitted themselves to demons that compelled them to harm society as a whole, animals and the produce of the land. The devil, Prince of Evil, directed the meetings of the sect and ruled in evil majesty over the witches. The fight therefore engaged not only the forces of the Church but also those of the State. Devils and demons also acquired corporeality and were incarnated, under the form of assumed bodies, by the side of the witches, even engaging in sexual intercourse. Finally, the realism of the Sabbat and demonic witchcraft, which met with its most ardent defenders in the middle of the fifteenth century, strongly undermined the formerly prevailing notion that demons were the masters of illusions and trickery. Witches were brought to justice because they were *really* trying to bring harm to others as the result of an alliance *really* sealed with demons. Actively looking for the mark of the devil on the body of the accused during judicial procedures is a pertinent example of this.[23]

Informing, describing the Sabbat and denouncing the gravity of crimes of witches (1420–40)

During the 1430s and 1440s, numerous texts describe and define precisely what is known as "*Sabbat*".[24] This idea was established over the course of two decades, in a territory centred on the Western Alps and the region of Lyon. Regions such as the Pyrenees and Italy also experienced similar changes in conceptions of witchcraft over the course of the first half of the fifteenth century. This belief spread quickly through other regions of Western Europe to take its place on the landscape of thought for many centuries, all the while undergoing changes from one region to another, sometimes of a significant nature.

These texts came from clerics, theologians, inquisitors or magistrates who were personally convinced of the reality of the Sabbat and sects of devil worshippers; in fact, they contributed to the creation and defence of this reality. They effectively tried to go against a more sceptical current of thinking which called into question the reality of the acts committed by witches and argued that witches were mostly victims of deceptions or illusions by demons (in the tradition of the canon *Episcopi*), even suffering from madness or melancholy. In contrast to this sceptical position, the "fanatics" of the Sabbat advocated the necessity for repression; and while they constituted a quantitative minority in the first half of the fifteenth century, their influence grew more and more in particular places or states (the Western Alps, western Switzerland, Savoy, Burgundy, as well as the north and the south of France) and in particular cultural settings (the Dominican or Franciscan inquisition, as well as the Council of Basel).

Six main texts, of various natures, bear witness to the emergence of this idea. The chronicler of Lucerne Hans Fründ reported on the first witch-hunt undertaken in Valais from 1428.[25] According to Fründ, Valais saw more than two hundred pyres lit over the course of a year and a half. A newly appeared sect of male and female witches made up of 700 individuals met in secret "schools" to meet the "evil spirit." This sect prepared to overturn Christian society in order to impose its own power, to elect a "king" and create special courts. The chronicler could not be more precise: in his eyes, witchcraft constituted a danger of the first order. Even if he was sometimes prone to exaggeration, a great witch-hunt was in fact conducted in Valais at least between 1428 and 1436.[26] Jean Nider, an observant Dominican and professor of theology at the University of Vienna, discussed the issue of witchcraft in his *Formicarius* (c.1436–38), a pastoral work. His analysis was based on information that he had received regarding witchcraft trials that took place in the Diocese of Lausanne and in Simmental.[27]

On the other side of the Alps, in the Dauphiné, Claude Tholosan, the principal judge (*judex major*) in the service of the King of France, composed a juridical treatise, the *Ut magorum et maleficiorum errores* (*So that the Errors of Magicians and Sorcerers...*), in which he demonstrated the gravity of the crimes of witches. At around the same time, the *Errores gazariorum* (*Errors of the Gazarii*), an anonymous pamphlet composed between 1436 and 1438 in the Aosta Valley, offered a systematic description of the ritual of the Sabbat, based on juridical activities. The enigmatic treatise on the *Vauderye de Lyonois* notes the difficulty experienced by the Dominicans of Lyon in instituting witch-hunting in this region of the Kingdom of France at the same time. These three texts, contemporary with each other and of a similar nature, offer a very systematic description of the Sabbat ritual as part of brief treatises whose primary objective is to denounce the evil spells of witches. By highlighting the dangerous nature of witches' crimes, these writers supported the condemnation of the rites and practices they described.

Finally, in *Le Champion des Dames* (*The Champion of Women*), a lengthy poem composed between 1440 and 1442, Martin Le Franc, a secretary of the antipope Felix V (the Duke of Savoy Amadeus VIII), offered one of the first descriptions of the Sabbat in a literary work, associating it primarily with women.[28] Le Franc, also provost of Lausanne, was aware of the persecutions in the Dauphiné, particularly in Vallouise (formerly *Valpute*), as well as in Piedmont (*mons d'Esture*, probably Stura di Demonte).[29] His poem, which took the form of a dialogue, offers a clear insight into the varied beliefs and mentalities about witchcraft that existed during this period.

Three of these texts are particularly helpful for understanding the changes that were then underway and the beginnings of repression. The treatise of Claude Tholosan, a doctor of law, is the fruit of his reflection after ten years of legal practice. Indeed, he had conducted about a hundred witchcraft trials, mostly in the Upper Dauphiné area, and mostly against women.[30] According to Tholosan, those accused belonged to a demonic sect with precise rituals and practices. He described the ceremony of apostasy and homage to the devil, followed by an orgiastic and cannibalistic banquet. He detailed the composition and effects of various evil spells; for example, sorcerers were capable of making men mad and preventing women from becoming pregnant.[31] Although he considered nocturnal flight a diabolical illusion, the Sabbat and the collection of activities of the sect are presented as real events and perceived as crimes of a grave nature, allowing him to justify repressive action against the witches. He also developed a precise legal discussion that aimed to assimilate the crime of witchcraft with the crime of homicide and above all with the crimes of divine and human *lèse-majesté*. This permitted him to justify the primacy of the justice of the Prince over the justice of the Church, and not to allow the courts of the Inquisition to act in their own right against the perpetrators of evil acts.[32] In fact, the secular powers in the Dauphiné appeared at the forefront of the fight against witches. Consequently, the role of Claude Tholosan was understood as a champion of princely absolutism.[33] In contrast to the *Errores gazariorum* and the *Vauderye de Lyonois*, Tholosan's work was not widely known outside the registers of the Dauphiné's treasury (*Quintus liber fachureriorum*), for which he was responsible. Nevertheless, the scale and precocity of the witch-hunts undertaken between 1424 and 1445 in the Dauphiné made considerable waves in the surrounding communities and contributed to the circulation of the idea of the Sabbat.

Close to the vision of demonic witchcraft transmitted by judge Tholosan is the *Errores gazariorum seu illorum qui scopam vel baculum equitare probantur* (*Errors of the Gazarii*), completed c. 1436–38[34] from which we learn how the devil attracted new followers to his sect and obliged them to pay him homage by kissing his posterior. All members of the sect celebrated the arrival of a new follower by eating various dishes, especially roasted or boiled children. The witches also made powders and ointments which, with the help of the devil, allowed them to kill men and animals or to destroy harvests. The author of the text, who remains anonymous, relied on the trials that took place in the Aosta Valley, in the duchy of Savoy; he makes reference to the trial of Jeannette Cauda, burnt at Chambave on 11 August 1428. Hunts for demonic witchcraft began in this region as early as 1428: noteworthy witch-hunts were undertaken in the years 1430, 1440 and 1460, mainly by Franciscan inquisitors, connected to the bishop's fiscal procurators (*procurator fiscalis*, the official who represented and defended a lord's interests).[35] It is likely that the author of this treaty was Ponce Feugeyron (or one of his acquaintances) because, armed with a papal mandate to act against sorcerers and invokers of demons, he was present in the Aosta Valley between 1434 and 1439, precisely when the *Errores gazariorum* was completed.[36] A manuscript of this pamphlet against sorcerers was circulated in the Diocese of Lausanne and was supplemented with information from lawsuits in the Vevey region.[37] Two manuscripts of the *Errores* are also preserved in collections of texts that are connected to the Council of Basel: it is worth noting this as we know that the council was an ideal environment for the circulation of texts on the Sabbat.[38] A third, later, manuscript was copied between 1451 and 1457 by the jurist Mathias Widmann von Kemnath (d. 1476), the court chaplain and astrologer of Prince Palatine Frederick I the Victorious (Friedrich I., der Siegreiche, 1425–76).[39] The treatise from the Aosta Valley also circulated in the Germanic world and was translated into German by Widmann, who included it in his *Chronik Friedrich (I.) des Siegreichen* (c. 1475).

The *Errores gazariorum* has many traits in common with a short tract usually referred to by its French name, the *Vauderye de Lyonois en brief*.[40] Composed in Latin by an unknown author at an unknown date, this text seeks to describe in great detail the organization and criminal practices of a diabolical sect referred to by the generic name "vaudois" (*valdesia*).

The apostate members of the sect, described in French as "faicturiers" and "faicturières," were supposed to gather at night in the "synagogue," also called a "faict" or "martinet" around a devil who exhibited all the attributes of monstrosity and abomination. They paid homage to him, desecrated Christian rites and indulged in feasting and sexual orgies. The unveiling of this secret society was announced with horror, but not given a theoretical emphasis. The tract described the enormity (*enormia*) of the crime of demonic witchcraft to better encourage its repression. The evocation of the crimes imputed to this sect was effectively correlated with specific judicial activity in the region of Lyon. Recent research, based on documentary discoveries, has made it possible to connect this text to the Dominican inquisition of Lyon and to postulate a date of completion at the very end of the 1430s. In fact, it is over the course of this decade that the prior of Lyon, Thomas Girbelli, and the inquisitor of the same convent, Jean Tacot, attempted to prosecute witches in the region of Lyon. However, they met with strong resistance on the part of the archbishop and the consular authorities of Lyon who hindered their aspirations towards repression. The tract *Vauderye de Lyonois* was written by the Dominicans of Lyon in order to solicit the political and financial support of the King of France and the pope. The recently discovered supplement to the treatise expresses this clearly (BnF, Collection Moreau n° 779). However, Girbelli and Tacot's efforts were unsuccessful, and the history of the Vauderie of Lyon was principally one of the failures of witch-hunting in this region of the Kingdom of France. In spite of this, the tract, now preserved in three manuscripts, enjoyed a circulation overseen by the network of the observant Dominicans: towards Burgundy in one direction, where the affair of the Vauderie of Arras (c.1460) gave its name to the tract, and in the other towards the town of Trier around 1470, at the door of the Empire, on the eve of the great witch-hunts.

In conclusion, therefore, these six initial documents offer a relatively similar idea of the Sabbat, which Richard Kieckhefer describes as the "Lausanne paradigm".[41] Other evidence demonstrates variations that refer to a different cultural universe, marked by the classical literary tradition of the vampire witch (*strix*, *strega*) and regional folklore. This is the case with sources from the Italian Peninsula, particularly the Umbrian paradigm, as the sermons of Bernardino of Siena particularly demonstrate (1427 and 1443). The observant Franciscan denounced the old soothsayers who were believed to go "running with Herodias" (*in curso cum Herodia*) and to transform themselves into cats or vampires (*strix, lamia*) to suck the blood of children. The witches described by the Italian authors (influenced by sporadic trials in the area) represent a combination of infanticidal vampire witches and the "Good Women" who flew with Dame Abonde or the goddess Diana.[42] They did not go to the "synagogue" often referenced in the Alps, but took part in a "game" (*ludus*) of Diana. There was little space for the devil; his role was solely to trick them. Finally, evil spells were perceived principally as the work of women, particularly those of a mature age. This alternative mythology of witchcraft tended to also circulate around the Alps and to meld sometimes with that of the Sabbat. However, some regions, such as the Germanic territories, showed themselves to be relatively unreceptive to either of the two conceptions and limited themselves to representations of the witch as a caster of evil spells.

The beginning of the witch-hunts

In the territory that covers the Western Alps, from the Dauphiné to the Leventina, passing through Savoy, Piedmont, the Barony of Vaud, Fribourg, Valais, the Bernese Oberland, Lucerne and the Aosta Valley, there are signs of an intense repression of witchcraft from the

1420s onwards. Based on a belief in the Witches' Sabbat, this took place in both ecclesiastical tribunals and secular courts.[43] The tracking down of "sects" of witches also developed during the same period in the Pyrenees. It intensified in the 1430s and was particularly well documented in the Dauphiné and in the most northerly part of the State of Savoy (Tarentaise, the Aosta Valley, Vaud, Savoyard Valais, Bresse and Bugey). From the 1440s, repression also touched the Burgundian States, the eastern parts of the Kingdom of France and the Empire. Various studies have reported on this in recent years, and a significant body of judicial material has now been edited, translated into French and commented upon.[44]

In the dioceses of Lausanne, Sion and Geneva, Dominican inquisitors and both episcopal and secular judges instigated trials according to the extraordinary inquisitorial procedure, that is to say by making use of denunciations and public rumours (*fama*) in order to arrest suspects, holding secret enquiries and using torture. Historians have at their disposal a register which was put together in the nineteenth century, which collects together nearly thirty lawsuits brought between 1438 and 1538 in the Diocese of Lausanne and the Bas-Valais.[45] The proceedings, which are particularly comprehensive, allow an examination of all the procedural phrases, and precisely record the interrogations of the accused. One of the specificities of trials in these regions in the fifteenth century consists of their very detailed descriptions of the Witches' Sabbat, called a "synagogue", which include clandestine meetings with the demon, banquets, anthropophagy of children, nocturnal flight on sticks or broomsticks and the preparation of evil ointments.

It is not that these regions were particularly populated by male and female witches, as contemporary accounts would have us believe, but rather that the authorities, the clerics and the elites were greatly convinced of the existence of these sects of devil worshipers, who were attempting to harm Christian society through every possible means. Armed with this conviction, the authorities initiated real witch-hunts and involved the local populations in the mechanisms of repression through encouraging denunciations.

In episcopal Valais, the Diet and the local assemblies introduced an edict in 1428 which condemned severely the meetings of witches and casters of spells. Initially, these secular political elites were in charge of the exercise of repression against witches: they almost did away with the inquisitors and episcopal justice.[46] However, as time went on, the bishop-princes of Sion acted both as inquisitors and as lords with *merum et mixtum imperium* (pure and mixed power – the highest kind of jurisdiction and competence in medieval Roman law), and investigated witchcraft cases fully. Frequent conflicts of jurisdiction therefore arose between the bishop-princes or their bailiffs and the mayors or the local communities, each claiming jurisdiction over the proceedings and the right to confiscate the goods of the accused. Trials for witchcraft played a major role in the competition for political and juridical power, even without the consideration of financial interests. After an initial, crucial, witch-hunt between 1428 and 1436, repression continued into the second half of the fifteenth century; roughly fifty cases are now known. Among them was the case of Françoise Bonvin, a rich widow accused of witchcraft and condemned to be burnt in 1467, after she had been denounced by three "witches". Unusually, she benefitted from a defence lawyer, who gathered 67 witnesses to establish the innocence and respectability of his client. The witnesses' stories portray a certain scepticism towards the development of the mythology of the Sabbat propagated by local authorities.[47]

The fight against demonic witchcraft was unleashed in a similar fashion in a large part of the States of Savoy from the 1430s, and was particularly well documented in the northern half of this area.[48] Franciscan or Dominican inquisitors, depending on the territories in question, were actively engaged in the pursuit of sorcerers, and worked closely with local church officials and judges. The impetus behind this repression came largely from the Duke of Savoy Amadeus VIII. It is to him that we owe the Statutes of Savoy of 1430, a significant legislative undertaking that attempted to reorganize and reform his vast state.[49] The first article of this ordinance targeted sorcerers, magicians and the invokers of demons. Amadeus VIII described the crimes of witchcraft and magic as heresy, which in fact fell under the jurisdiction of the ecclesiastical authorities. However, he believed that these crimes were so serious that they necessitated the involvement of all possible authorities. It is for this reason that he ordered all the judges and officials of his duchy, whether under the authority of the Church or the Prince, to take the lead in pursuing heresy and witchcraft, and to collaborate with the papal inquisition, to which he granted financial, material and institutional support.

The issues were at once political, juridical and financial. By positioning himself as a defender of human and divine majesty, wronged by the misdeeds of witches, Amadeus VIII defined the crime of demonic witchcraft as heresy against the state.[50] He was the first great secular prince to express it in these terms. Amadeus VIII's conviction of the evil practices of witches helped to light the pyres; his acceptance of the papal tiara on 17 December 1439 allowed him to further embody the defence of orthodoxy in his States. Witch-hunting can therefore be seen as a method of legitimizing the sovereignty of the duke-pope. Amadeus created a network of inquisitors, such as the Franciscans Ponce Feugeyron and Bérard Trémey, or the Dominicans Ulric de Torrenté and Pierre d'Aulnay, to continue the religious and ecclesiastical reform of his duchy. The inquisitor, who became an inescapable figure in the religious landscape of the 1430s, also embodied a particular idea of spiritual purification in the Savoyard state, under the aegis of its prince.

Far from the Alps in Catalonia, the community of Àneu (in the region of Pallars on the border with Foix and the valley of Aran) passed one of the first laws against demonic witches as early as 1424. Due to the "enormity" of the crimes committed "against God and the valley," the Statutes proscribed capital punishment by fire against those convicted of "going at night with the witches with the Goat of Biterne (presumably a demonic being), recognising him as lord and renouncing God, killing newborns and causing illnesses or using poison".[51] Although the effects of this ordinance are difficult to measure in the absence of surviving juridical material, documentary traces confirm the existence of a juridical repression from the 1420s onwards. It was conducted primarily by secular courts, and notably stimulated by the intensive activity of Dominican preachers (Vincent Ferrier, Pere Cerdà). The Catalan inquisition sometimes intervened in the proceedings to advise caution and moderation, a mark of its scepticism towards the collective dimension of the crime of witchcraft and towards the Sabbat. This repression, occurring at the same time as the first documented persecutions in the Alpine area, whether in Dauphiné (1424–45), Valais (1428–36) or the Savoy states, made Catalonia one of the cradles of witch-hunting in Europe.

The witch-hunt that reached Levantina in 1457–59 was the expression of a desire for local autonomy and occurred amidst a wealth of tensions between the people of the Canton of Uri and the Duke of Milan for control of the region.[52] The town of Lucerne also witnessed a significant repression, which targeted a clear majority of women (91% of those recorded between 1398 and 1551), as in the Dauphiné. In an urban context marked by significant reforms and an increased social control, the secular authorities and courts took over the pursuit of the crime of diabolical witchcraft.[53]

From the middle of the fifteenth century, the repression of demonic witchcraft spread towards the north of France, via Franche-Comté and Burgundy. The Vauderie d'Arras was the first large witch-hunt that took place in France in the Burgundian state, beginning in 1459. Those who were first accused were mostly condemned to the stake (a dozen), before the intervention of royal advisors who put an end to the hunt and rehabilitated the "vaudois" ("Waldensians") of Arras. While the procedural documents have vanished (they were destroyed after the ceremony of rehabilitation in 1491), the chronicle of Jacques Du Clercq allows us to reconstruct many of the events. As Franck Mercier has demonstrated, the Vauderie of Arras was the scene of competition between two sovereignties: the well-established Kingdom of France, and the Burgundian state that failed in the end to establish its longevity.[54] A legal brief produced on the occasion of the Vauderie of Arras, the *Recollectio... Valdensium ydolatrarum*, aimed to legitimate the persecutions of the "vaudois-witches" of Arras. Its anonymous author, perhaps Jacques du Bois, one of the judges of Arras, may have based it on one of the first tracts on demonology to address the issue of the Witches' Sabbat, the *Flagellum hereticorum fascinariorum (Scourge of Heretical Enchanters*, 1458) by Nicolas Jacquier. Indeed, it follows the broad strokes of Jacquier's discussion, particularly regarding the flight of witches during the Sabbat, while demonstrating the necessity for using the death penalty for demonic witches.

As we have seen, the secular authorities were aware of the changes underway in conceptions of witchcraft. They were also active in the repression of witchcraft, insofar as the crime pertained to damages to people or property, as opposed to cases with a particular "flavour of heresy." These crimes were concrete acts that directly infringed on the social order, for which the secular authorities were responsible. For the lay authorities, the pursuit of witches was also a way to assert their power in matters of high justice and to affirm their sovereignty, or indeed their majesty. The repression of witchcraft was not only the consequence of a religious and moral control exercised over populations who had been barely or badly Christianized, and who had retained their heterodox beliefs and practices. It was also a means by which a state, through its political and judicial apparatus, affirmed its authority in the defence of the public interest, and in the interest of social cohesion, and Christian orthodoxy.[55] The repression of witchcraft therefore had a significant political dimension in the context of the "super christianization of temporal power".[56] Compared to the ecclesiastical courts (including those of the inquisition), local and municipal secular tribunals dealt with the lion's share of witchcraft cases, since they were responsible for the majority of those condemned to death.[57] However, the situation differed significantly from one region or state to another, because the danger of the crime was perceived differently in different locations. The weapon of judicial repression did not have the same importance and the same stakes for different secular powers.

At the point at which witchcraft was reformulated as heresy, the secular princes tried to keep control of the repression of the crime and to actively take part in this campaign of repression. This initiative contributed to the legitimation and affirmation of their sovereign power. This is precisely what the judge Claude Tholosan managed to achieve to the advantage of the Dauphin of the King of France. According to Tholosan, acts of witchcraft were comparable to crimes of *lèse-majesté*, because they attacked sovereignty. Heresy had been linked to *lèse-majesté*, since the end of the twelfth century, under the pontificate of Innocent III (*Vergentis in senium*, 1199), which can be viewed, as Jacques Chiffoleau suggests, as the birth of a "heresy of the state".[58]

The papacy took a long time to react to witchcraft. The bulls enacted against demonic sorcery were usually rather sober and cautious, with the exception of Alexander V's bull in 1409, and in contrast to the proactive attitude of John XXII in the previous century. One does not find any allusions to the Sabbat, or aerial flights of witches, or to the dominant figure of the devil, in the bulls of Eugenius IV (1437/1445), Nicholas V (1451), Calixtus III (1457), Pius II (1459) or Innocent VIII (1484). However, Nicholas V did authorize the pursuit of magic that did not explicitly savour of heresy, and this consequently marks an expansion of the inquisitors' field of action of against witchcraft and magical practices. In papal bulls, the offence tends to be referred to as divine *lèse-majesté*, or a great scandal.[59]

Understanding, persuading and justification: treatises on demonology (1450–80)

From the 1440s, texts on witchcraft were not content solely to describe the Sabbat and the atrocities committed by witches, but rather they aimed above all to understand the reality of the evil spells and the interactions between demons and witches, and their consequences. Their objective was to determine the culpability of the presumed sorcerers and to confer an acceptable doctrinal framework on the tribunals, both in terms of law and theology. Autonomous tracts on demonology took off from the middle of the fifteenth century. Theorists of witchcraft or "demonologists" were mostly theologians or inquisitors, but also jurists or physicians. These were intellectuals who were trying to insert the new belief in the Sabbat into the traditional framework of Christian demonology, understood as knowledge which aimed to define the existence and the nature of demons and their powers of action on the world and on men. In order to achieve this, they had to redefine witchcraft through new questions brought on by the idea of the Sabbat. Their writings represent both syntheses and breaks with the past; they collated knowledge on the devil, magic and witchcraft, even possession, and compared it to the confessions of witches.[60]

Almost thirty texts were produced before the *Malleus Maleficarum* (Hammer of Witches) by Henrich Kramer/Institoris (1486). The *Malleus*'s fame, which owes much to the dawn of printing, has somewhat overshadowed these earlier texts, which are very interesting but still not well known. The discussion and reflections which Kramer proposed were already present in the works that preceded it. These works often bore the title of "hammer" (*malleus*) or "whip" (*flagellum*) of witches, revealing the aim of the author, or else bore the more sober titles of "tract", "brief work" (*opusculum*), "sermon" or "question", which bear witness to the intellectual operation that governed their writing.

On the whole, these texts tend to evaluate the possibility and consequently the reality of Witches' Sabbats and the acts of their protagonists. Their authors deploy arguments that seem rational: they employ the tools of scholastic reasoning and logic; they base their arguments on the texts of the Bible, the Church Fathers, Augustine, Gregory the Great and theologians (principally Thomas Aquinas) and even on hagiographical texts and *exempla*. These practical tracts are the fruit of late scholasticism, decidedly hybrid and sometimes distorted in the sense that they wanted to make the reader adopt certain points of view. However, they did not always emanate from deranged and perverse individuals, as one might be inclined to assume. Demonology must be understood as a true science: demonologists endeavoured to describe the place and functions of demons in the natural world. It is also a literature in which scholars can find the questions and divergences of demonologists.

Contradictory positions were defended; for example, it was possible for one author to assert that the devil really took witches to the Sabbat, while another defended the idea that the demon made them believe that they were going to the Sabbat in their dreams. Everything depended on the belief and the position of the author. There was also a certain amount of scepticism about the reality of the evil deeds and the Sabbats, especially in the initial stages of the discussion when there was a reaction against some of the more fanatical positions.

These texts on witchcraft were often produced as a result of trials, and aimed either to incite witch-hunting and to create a normative framework for it, or to justify an episode of repression. For many authors, the test of the reality of witchcraft resided in the confessions of the accused, often obtained under torture or the threat of torture. Thus, the texts and the trial proceedings were often aligned with each other.

Three tracts are particularly revealing about how the doctrine of witchcraft was elaborated: the *Tractatus contra invocatores demonum* (*Treatise Against Demon Invokers*) of Jean Vinet, (c. 1450–52) the *Flagellum hereticorum fascinariorum* (*Scourge of Heretical Enchanters*) of Nicolas Jacquier (1458) and the *Flagellum maleficorum* (*Scourge of Those Who Commit Evil Deeds*) of Pierre Mamoris (after 1462).[61] These three texts were among the first to discuss the issue of the Witches' Sabbat as part of a reflection on Christian demonology. All three works are by French authors: the Dominican Jean Vinet studied theology at Paris, where he taught the *Sentences* of Peter Lombard, before being named inquisitor of Carcassonne. Nicolas Jacquier, also a Dominican inquisitor, was attached to the convent at Dijon, then the convent at Lille, while carrying out numerous journeys to the east and north of France, principally between Lyon and the state of Burgundy. Pierre Mamoris, a secular clerk originally from Limoges, was a canon at Saintes and a professor of theology at the University of Poitiers.

Jean Vinet discussed the magical powers that humans could obtain by allying themselves with demons. Following the thought of Thomas Aquinas about the demonic pact, he believed that the efficacy of the magical arts was related to an alliance made with demons, which he forcefully condemned. The inquisitor of Carcassonne believed that the Witches' Sabbat was in fact possible: demons could meet human beings and unite with them (sexually and through a covenant), they could transport people from one place to another (the flight to the Sabbat) and they could help witches to perpetrate evil deeds. Vinet does not present himself as a fierce defender of the fight against witches, but he tries to define the boundary between the possible and the impossible, and between the acceptable and the unacceptable.

Vinet's contemporary Nicolas Jacquier went much further. Convinced of the reality of the Sabbat, he virulently denounced the danger of what he called "new sects of heretical witches" in his *Flagellum hereticorum fascinariorum* (1458). In Jacquier's eyes, the Witches' Sabbat was an anti-church, to which participants adhered voluntarily and consciously. It was a "cult" of demons, including ritual sacrifices which he believed embodied all the horror of the crimes of witches. The Burgundian inquisitor continually highlighted the corporeality of demons, who were perceptible to human senses; he recalled the real and corporeal presence of the demon at the Sabbat as a leitmotiv, also drawing support from Thomas Aquinas. His argument about sensory perception helped him to convince his detractors. Starting from the physical experience that man has with demonic corporeality, the latter becomes undeniable: the devil really and physically manifests himself, because the human being can, through using his or her external senses, touch him, hear him, see him and even smell his most fetid odour. The sexual union between a devil and a human, male or female, is manifest proof for him; it is for this reason, he explains, that the participants in the Sabbat return from the synagogue saying that they have been completely "exhausted by the extreme violence of pleasure" they had with demons.[62] Nicolas Jacquier is undoubtedly the fifteenth-century demonologist who tried most diligently to demonstrate what we can call "diabolic realism", that is to say the premise of the reality not only of the devil and demons but also of physical interactions between humans and demons. In fact, the "synagogue of the devil," which aimed to destroy Christianity, constituted a danger of the first order. With this in mind, Jacquier attempted to demonstrate that witches were not only heretics, but also "the worst heretics," expressing it in this form in order to justify the force of repression that needed to be taken against them. The inquisitor advocated a tightening of the judicial procedures against witches, in order to deny them any possibility of grace or salvation – they must be condemned to death on the first indictment (instead of after relapsing, as was more usual with inquisitorial trials). The *Flagellum*, a genuine plea for capital punishment, aimed to make witch-hunting both possible and effective.

The third tract in this group adopts another perspective that renders its author, Pierre Mamoris, more sympathetic. His *Flagellum maleficorum* (ca. 1462) offers a wide panorama of the misdeeds and magical practices attested in Poitou and the kingdom of Bourges in the middle of the fifteenth century, and which, according to him, had been multiplying since the Hundred Years' War. Recalling the statements of his contemporaries and his own personal experience, the author conducts a kind of ethnographic collecting of data at the beginning of his tract. As he states, he wants to "discover the truth" and above all, to persuade himself. Did magical arts derive their power from nature or from demons? Was the Sabbat real, or was it demonic trickery? In order to answer these questions, he compares and contrasts doctrine and knowledge. He seeks to adopt a position and does not hesitate to express his doubts. In fact, he modifies his point of view between the beginning and the end of his treatise, finally telling his readers that he had been convinced by the gravity of witches' evil actions, when he heard about a case, the indictment of Guillaume Adeline, which was a cause celebre at the time.[63]

Underneath an apparent, often misleading, uniformity, the fifteenth-century tracts on demonology diverge from each other due to their authors' positions, their intellectual points of reference and the context in which they were written. Each work is unique, even if the majority share the same obsession with demons. The authors of the tracts adopt significant differences in tone and method, which it is necessary to note. Christian demonology therefore opened a new range of possibilities for the Sabbat which the theologians of the fifteenth century explored in depth. The fact that the Sabbat could be understood intellectually either as a reality or as the result of an illusion or demonic deception lent them a considerable amount of freedom. Since both one thing and its opposite were often possible and conceivable, for example nocturnal flight, the Sabbat became an issue of belief, on which the theologians expressed their opinions. Moreover, the issues relating to demons had very broad implications, whether social, political, economic or cultural, because they were associated with the repression of witches. Linked to the new belief in the Sabbat, learned demonology had social repercussions of the first order in the fifteenth century.

The ambivalence of witchcraft

Witch-hunting was in part the result of an attitude towards magic that became more and more restrictive. Did it therefore also include a campaign against necromancers, learned magicians and even astrologers? It is not necessary to go this far, even if the breadth of the repression did succeed in drawing in some of these figures. In reality, witch-hunting, through the game of denunciations and rumours that were enough to open an inquisitorial procedure, was greatly nourished by the resentments, jealousies and interpersonal conflicts that simmered in the heart of families and local communities. It must be said that few true magicians and witches were sent to the pyre, although an infinite number of suspects or so-called witches were burnt, which allowed individuals to find a perpetrator of and an explanation for the misfortunes they were suffering. These victims of bad fortune created new victims.

Finally, it is important to remember that the practices of magic and witchcraft were not seen uniquely as damaging or harmful to others; they were not entirely reduced to *maleficium*. Medieval detractors of the magical arts and witchcraft have a tendency to highlight only the harmful and monstrous side of these practices, and consequently their illicit characteristics. In addition, the trial sources highlight all the evils for which the accused were held responsible (causing death and illness, destroying harvests, etc.). However, we must not forget the profoundly ambivalent nature of magic and witchcraft: the population turned often enough to magicians, soothsayers and sorcerers to be healed from an illness, to discover the future, to find something that had been lost or stolen, to ensure a good harvest, to find love or peace or even to benefit from a particular protection for a particular time (during birth, travel, etc.). Turning to magic was the result of individual needs, and expressed a desire to take control of one's life, regardless of social status and degree of Christianization. We know that many magicians and sorcerers were active at the court of King Charles VI of France, who suffered from epilepsy, to find a cure for his illness. Another example, among many, is that of Jeanne de Caboreto (Aosta Valley), who tried in vain to save a newborn that was close to death. She was accused in 1449 of being a witch, and of having wanted to kill the child.[64] This is a typical context for an accusation of witchcraft: when an attempt at healing failed, or magical protection proved ineffective. There is also the case of the last witch to have been executed at Geneva in 1652, a washerwoman known for her white soup with invigorating properties. When she refused to care for a desperate woman, she was accused by this woman of "brewing evil".[65]

Future directions

Largely arising out of the thinking of clerics and amplified during the course of inquisitorial proceedings, the ideas linked to witchcraft were subject to significant chronological and geographical variation. The "Sabbat" was not a universal concept, and was sometimes referred to by other names, such as the "Game of Diana" linked to the bloodsucking witches in Italy, or the "Goat of Biterne" mentioned in the area around the Pyrenees. Following Richard Kieckhefer, it is worth paying considerable attention to these different paradigms or mythologies of witchcraft as well as their dissemination and reception, whether geographical, cultural or sociopolitical. In addition, centres of resistance or scepticism towards belief in the Sabbat and demonic witchcraft would be worth examining, investigating their causes and motives. Why were certain regions better able to resist, or even remain impermeable to the attraction of, the most radical conceptions or forms of the Sabbat? Was it due to the regions' political, religious, social, cultural or even economic circumstances? Only a detailed analysis of local contexts and the forces at play within them can provide an answer.

As underlined at the beginning of the chapter, the dialogue between historians of magic and specialists in the repression of witchcraft should also be intensified. It would be better to equip all scholars with the necessary tools to examine the concept of the magical arts used by diverse medieval people (theologians, jurists, judges, defendants, etc.), and get beyond scholarly preoccupations with the opposition between popular and learned magic, which is not always functional in the existing documents. The impact of the condemnations of ritual magic in the fourteenth and fifteenth centuries on the paranoia that developed during the witch-hunt also needs to be assessed.

An enquiry into the extreme lexical diversity of witchcraft and magic must also be undertaken, paying attention to particular periods and locations, and particularly noting semantic developments and shifts. The following episode is revealing of the interest of this line of questioning. In 1524, the peasants of the town of Dommartin (Switzerland, Vaud) were accused of witchcraft: they were said to have been to the "synagogue" of the devil and to have killed beasts and men using an evil ointment. The peasants accused of witchcraft called themselves "astrologers" (*vocabantur adstrologoz*).[66] This kind of example draws attention to the moving boundary between witchcraft, demonology, magic and astrology, as well as their definitions and interpretations by different sections of society.

With regard to documentation, historians of witchcraft at the end of the Middle Ages owe much to Joseph Hansen's anthology of 1901, entitled *Quellen und Untersuchungen zur Geschichte des Hexenwahns und der Hexenverfolgungen im Mittelalter*. This work remains an essential base for scientific research. However, it is now necessary to develop the study of the manuscripts and texts which he used, to deepen knowledge of their authors and the context they were writing in, and to encourage the publication of complete critical editions. Hansen's anthology only included a few extracts of the tracts, which has had a detrimental impact on the understanding of the whole texts and gave a biased impression of their contents. Throughout the last century, other documents surfaced to complete the corpus, particularly those of Italian provenance.[67] It would also be worth renewing and enriching the available judicial documentation with critical editions of trials for witchcraft, paired, if possible, with translations to facilitate a broader public readership.[68] Considerable efforts have been made in recent decades, but there still is an abundance of judicial material. Furthermore, contextual documentation such as accounts, in so far as they have been preserved, should definitely be taken into account: it offers valuable insights into the material framework of the witch-hunts and can compensate for the absence of precise evidence about interrogation procedures or judicial sentences, in order to measure the extent of repression at a local level. By making use of sources that need to be looked at afresh and better contextualized, new research could also be further enriched by new avenues of enquiry and gain in precision.

Finally, the tools of the Digital Humanities can also offer new approaches to these texts and data. Digital editions of the sources for witchcraft would particularly favour the interrogation of vast corpuses, lexicological inquiry and textual comparisons. Moreover, the creation of interactive maps and databases identifying the documentary traces of witchcraft would allow us to better comprehend the scale of witch-hunting in diverse areas and over time.

Notes

1 Cf. especially Michael D. Bailey, *Fearful Spirits, Reasoned Follies: The Boundaries of Superstition in Late Medieval Europe* (Ithaca, NY: Cornell University Press, 2013); Michael D. Bailey, "From Sorcery to Witchcraft: Clerical Conceptions of Magic in the Later Middle Ages," *Speculum. A Journal of Medieval Studies* 76/4 (October 2001): 960–90; Michael D. Bailey, "Witchcraft, Superstition, and

Astrology in the Late Middle Ages," in *Chasses aux sorcières et démonologie. Entre discours et pratiques*, ed. Martine Ostorero, Georg Modestin and Kathrin Utz Tremp (Florence: Sismel Edizioni del Galluzzo, 2010), 349–66; Richard Kieckhefer, "Witchcraft, Necromancy, and Sorcery as Heresy," in *Chasses aux sorcières*, ed. Ostorero, Modestin and Utz Tremp, 133–53.

2   Martine Ostorero, "Amédée VIII et la répression de la sorcellerie démoniaque: une hérésie d'Etat," in *La Loi du Prince: les* Statuta Sabaudiae *d'Amédée VIII (1430)*, ed. Franco Morenzoni, in press.

3   Renilde Verwoort, *Bruegel's Witches: Witchcraft in the Low Countries between 1450 and 1700* (Bruges: Van de Wiele Publishing, 2015).

4   Jean-Patrice Boudet, *Entre science et "nigromance": Astrologie, divination et magie dans l'Occident médiéval (XIIe-XVe siècle)* (Paris: Publications de la Sorbonne, 2006), 90–98, 432–46; Marina Montesano, "Le rôle de la culture classique dans la définition des *maleficia*: une démonologie alternative?" in *Penser avec les démons: Démonologues et démonologies (XIIIe-XVIIe siècles)*, ed. Julien Véronèse and Martine Ostorero (Florence: Sismel Edizioni del Galluzzo, 2015), 277–92.

5   Joseph Hansen, *Quellen und Untersuchungen zur Geschichte des Hexenwahns und der Hexenverfolgung im Mittelalter* (Hildesheim: G. Olms, 2003), 539–44.

6   *L'imaginaire du sabbat: Edition critique des textes les plus anciens (1430c.–1440c)*, ed. Martine Ostorero, Agostino Paravicini Bagliani, Kathrin Utz Tremp and Catherine Chène (Lausanne: Cahiers lausannois d'histoire médiévale, 1999), 30.

7   *L'imaginaire du sabbat*, 144–61.

8   Martine Ostorero, *Le diable au sabbat. Littérature démonologique et sorcellerie (1440-1460)* (Florence: Sismel Edizioni del Galluzzo, 2011), 503–58.

9   Alain Boureau, *Le pape et les sorciers. Une consultation de Jean XXII sur la magie en 1320 (Manuscrit B.A.V Borghese 348)* (Rome: Ecole française de Rome, 2004), xvi–lii; Alain Boureau, *Satan hérétique. Naissance de la démonologie dans l'Occident médiéval (1280-1330)* (Paris: Odile Jacob, 2004), 7–91; Anneliese Maier, "Eine Verfügung Johanns XXII. über die Zuständigkeit der Inquisition für Zaubereiprozesse", *Archivum fratrum praedicatorum* 22 (1952): 226–27; Isabel Iribarren, "From Black Magic to Heresy: A Doctrinal Leap in the Pontificate of John XXII," *Church History* 76 (2007): 32–60.

10 Bernard Gui, *Manuel de l'inquisiteur*, ed. and trans. Guillaume Mollat (Paris: Les Belles Lettres, 2006); Nicolau Eymerich, Francisco Peña, *Le manuel des inquisiteurs*, intr., trans. and notes by Louis Sala-Molins (Paris: Albin Michel, 2001).

11 Julien Véronèse, "Le *Contra astrologos imperitos atque nigromanticos* (1395–96) de Nicolas Eymerich (O.P.): Contexte de rédaction, classification des arts magiques et divinatoires, édition critique partielle," in *Chasses aux sorcières*, ed. Ostorero, Modestin and Utz Tremp, 271–329; Julien Véronèse, "Nigromancie et hérésie: le *De jurisdictione inquisitorum in et contra christianos demones invocantes* (1359) de Nicolas Eymerich (O.P.)," in *Penser avec les démons*, 5–56; Cl. Heimann, *Nicolaus Eymerich (vor 1320–1399): Praedicator Veridicus, Inquisitor Intrepidus, Doctor Egregius: Leben und Werk eines Inquisitors* (Münster: Aschendorff, 2001); Cl. Heimann, "*Quis proprie hereticus est?*: Nicolaus Eymerichs Häresiebegriff und dessen Anwendung auf die Juden," in *Praedicatores, Inquisitores, I: The Dominicans and the Medieval Inquisition* (Roma: Istituto storico domenicano, 2004), 596–624; G. Macy, "Nicolas Eymeric and the Condemnation of Orthodoxy," in *The Devil, Heresy, and Witchcraft in the Middle Ages: Essays in Honor of Jeffrey B. Russell*, ed. Alberto Ferreiro (Leiden: Brill" 1998), 369–81.

12 Johannes Vincke, *Zur Vorgeschichte der Spanischen Inquisition. Die Inquisition in Aragon, Katalonien, Mallorca und Valencia während des 13. und 14. Jahrhunderts* (Bonn: Hanstein, 1941), 162–82; Boudet, *Entre science et "nigromance"*, 456–58, 484–87.

13 Norman Cohn, *Europe's Inner Demons: The Demonization of Christians in Medieval Christendom* (Chicago, IL: University of Chicago Press, 1975); James Given, "Chasing Phantoms: Philip IV and the Fantastic," in *Heresy and the Persecuting Society in the Middle Ages: Essays on the Work of R.I. Moore*. ed. Michael Frassetto (Leiden: Brill, 2006), 271–89; Julien Théry, "A Heresy of State: Philip the Fair, the Trial of the 'Perfidious Templars', and the Pontificalization of the French Monarchy," *Journal of Medieval Religious Cultures* 39/2 (2013): 117–48; Alain Provost, *Domus diaboli: un évêque en procès au temps de Philippe le Bel* (Paris: Belin, 2010).

14 Sylvain Parent, *Dans les abysses de l'infidélité. Les procès contre les ennemis de l'Église en Italie au temps de Jean XXII (1316–1334)* (Rome: École française de Rome, 2014).

15 Boudet, *Entre science et "nigromance"*, 459.

16 Jean-Patrice Boudet, "Les condamnations de la magie à Paris en 1398," *Revue Mabillon*, Nouvelle série 12 (t. 73) (2001): 121–57; Jean-Patrice Boudet, Jacques Chiffoleau, "Magie et construction de

la souveraineté sous le règne de Charles VI," in *De Frédéric II à Rodolphe II. Astrologie, divination et magie dans les cours (XIIIe-XVIIe siècle)*, ed. Jean-Patrice Boudet, Agostino Paravicini Bagliani and Martine Ostorero (Florence: Sismel Edizioni del Galluzzo, 2017), 157-239; Jacques Chiffoleau, "Note sur la bulle *Vergentis in senium*, la lutte contre les hérétiques du Midi, et la construction des majestés temporelles," in *Innocent III et le Midi* (Toulouse: Privat, 2015), 89–144 (Cahiers de Fanjeaux 50).

17 Martine Ostorero, "Itinéraire d'un inquisiteur gâté: Ponce Feugeyron, les juifs et le sabbat des sorciers," *Médiévales* 43 (2002): 103–18.

18 Jacques Chiffoleau, "Le crime de majesté, la politique et l'extraordinaire; note sur les collections érudites de procès de lèse-majesté du XVIIe siècle et leurs exemples médiévaux," in *Les procès politiques (XIVe-XVIIe siècle)*, ed. Yves-Marie Bercé (Rome: Ecole française de Rome, 2007), 577–662; Jacques Chiffoleau, "Avouer l'inavouable: l'émergence de la procédure inquisitoire à la fin du Moyen Âge," in *L'aveu. Histoire, sociologie, philosophie*, ed. Renaud Dulong (Paris: PUF, 2001), 57–98.

19 Kathrin Utz Tremp, *Von der Häresie zur Hexerei. "Wirkliche" und imaginäre Sekten im Spätmittelalter* (Hannover: Hahnsche Buchh., 2008); Richard Kieckhefer, "Witchcraft, Necromancy, and Sorcery as Heresy"; Jacques Chiffoleau, "L'hérésie de Jeanne. Note sur les qualifications dans le procès de Rouen," in *Jeanne d'Arc. Histoire et mythes*, ed. Jean-Patrice Boudet, Xavier Hélary (Paris: Presses universitaires de Rennes, 2014), 28–39; Alexander Patschovsky, "Heresy and Society: On the Political Function of Heresy in the Medieval World," in *Texts and the Repression of Medieval Heresy*, ed. Caterina Bruschi and Peter Biller (Woodbridge: York Medieval Press, 2003), 23–41.

20 Cohn, *Europe's Inner Demons*; Brian P. Levack, *The Witch-Hunt in Early Modern Europe* (London and New York: Longman, 1987); Michael D. Bailey, "The Medieval Concept of the Witches' Sabbath," *Exemplaria: A Journal of Theory in Medieval and Renaissance Studies*, 8 (1996): 419–39. The usefulness of the cumulative concept of the Sabbath is discussed especially by Richard Kieckhefer, "Witchcraft, Necromancy, and Sorcery as Heresy" and Richard Kieckhefer, "Mythologies of Witchcraft in the Fifteenth Century," *Magic, Ritual and Witchcraft* 1 (Summer 2006): 79–107; Utz Tremp, *Von der Häresie zur Hexerei*, 26–47.

21 Boureau, *Satan hérétique*.

22 Boudet, *Entre science et "nigromance"*, 468–508.

23 Martine Ostorero, "Les marques du diable sur le corps des sorcières (XIVe-XVIIe siècles), *Micrologus* XIII (2005): 359–88.

24 Editions, French translations and commentaries in *L'imaginaire du sabbat*; Franck Mercier and Martine Ostorero, *L'énigme de la Vauderie de Lyon. Enquête sur l'essor des chasses aux sorcières entre France et Empire (1430–1480)* (Florence: Sismel Edizioni del Galluzzo, 2015); Hansen, *Quellen und Untersuchungen*. Some English translation (from the extracts of Hansen, *Quellen*) in *The Witchcraft Sourcebook*, ed. Brian P. Levack (New York: Routledge, 2004) and in *Witch Beliefs and Witch Trials in the Middle Ages: Documents and Readings*, ed. P.G. Maxwell-Stuart (London: Continuum, 2011).

25 *L'imaginaire du sabbat*, 23–98. Another manuscript of this report (Strasbourg, Bibliothèque nationale et universitaire, 2.935), very close to the first, has been edited by G. Modestin, ""Von den hexen, so in Wallis verbrant wurdent". Eine wieder entdeckte Handschrift mit dem Bericht des Chronisten Hans Fründ über eine Hexenverfolgung im Wallis (1428)," *Vallesia* 60 (2005): 399–409.

26 Chantal Ammann-Doubliez, "La première chasse aux sorciers en Valais," in *L'imaginaire du sabbat*, 63–98; Chantal Ammann-Doubliez, "Les chasses aux sorciers vues sous un angle politique: pouvoirs et persécutions dans le diocèse de Sion au XVe siècle," in *Chasses aux sorcières*, ed. Ostorero, Modestin and Utz Tremp, 5–13.

27 Catherine Chène, dans *L'imaginaire du sabbat*, 99–265; Michael D. Bailey, *Battling Demons: Witchcraft, Heresy and Reform in the Late Middle Ages* (University Park: Pennsylvania University Press, 2003); Werner Tschacher, *Der Formicarius des Johann Nider von 1437/1438. Studien zu den Anfängen der europäischen Hexenverfolgungen im Spätmittelalter* (Aachen: Shaker, 2000).

28 *L'imaginaire du sabbat*, 439–508. Martin Le Franc, *Le Champion des Dames*, vol. IV, ed. Robert Deschaux (Paris: Honoré Champion, 1999), 113–46.

29 Luca Patria *"Sicut canis reddiens ad vomitum*. Lo spaesamento dei valdesi nel balivato sabaudo della diocesi di Torino fra tre e quattrocento", in *Valdesi medievali*. ed. Marina Benedetti (Torino: Claudiana, 2009), 152 and note 78.

30 *L'imaginaire du sabbat*, 355–438. On Tholosan and the witch-hunts in Dauphiné, see Pierrette Paravy, *De la chrétienté romaine à la Réforme en Dauphiné* (Rome: Ecole française de Rome, 1993), 771–905.

31 *L'imaginaire du sabbat*, 362–73.

32 *L'imaginaire du sabbat*, 379–415 et 420–31.
33 Mercier and Ostorero, *L'énigme de la Vauderie de Lyon*, 305–42.
34 *L'imaginaire du sabbat*, 267–337.
35 Cf. Silvia Bertolin and Ezio E. Gerbore, *La stregoneria nella Valle d'Aosta medievale* (Quart: Musemeci Editore, 2003); Silvia Bertolin, *Processi per fede e sortilegi nella valle d'Aosta del Quattrocento* (Aosta: Académie Saint-Anselme d'Aoste, 2012).
36 Martine Ostorero, "Itinéraire d'un inquisiteur gâté", 103–18; Thomas Bardelle, *Juden in einem Transit- und Brückenland: Studien zur Geschichte der Juden in Savoyen-Piemont bis zum Ende der Herrschaft Amadeus VIII* (Hannover: Hahnsche Buchh., 1998), 284–96.
37 *L'imaginaire du sabbat*, 269–75, 280–83 et 339–53.
38 Michael D. Bailey and Edward Peters, "A Sabbat of Demonologists," *The Historian* 65 (2003): 1375–95; Stephan Sudmann, "Hexen – Ketzer – Kirchenreform. Debatten des Basler Konzils im Vergleich," in *Chasses aux sorcières*, ed. Ostorero, Modestin and Utz Tremp, 169–97.
39 BAV, Pal. lat. 1381, f. 190r–192r; cf. Martine Ostorero, "Un manuscrit palatin des *Errores gazariorum*," in *Inquisition et sorcellerie en Suisse romande. Le registre Ac 29 des Archives cantonales vaudoises (1438–1528)*, ed. Martine Ostorero and Kathrin Utz Tremp, with Georg Modestin (Lausanne: Cahiers lausannois d'histoire médiévale, 2007), 493–504.
40 Mercier and Ostorero, *L'énigme de la Vauderie de Lyon*; Franck Mercier, "La vauderie de Lyon a-t-elle eu lieu? Un essai de recontextualisation (Lyon, vers 1430–1440?)" in *Chasses aux sorcières*, ed. Ostorero, Modestin and Utz Tremp, 27–44.
41 Richard Kieckhefer, "The First Wave of Trials for Diabolical Witchcraft," in *The Oxford Handbook of Witchcraft in Early Modern Europe and Colonial America*, ed. Brian P. Levack (Oxford: Oxford University Press, 2013), 159–78; Kieckhefer, "Mythologies of Witchcraft in the Fifteenth Century".
42 Marina Montesano, *"Supra acqua et supra ad vento". Superstizioni, maleficia e incantamenta nei predicatori francescani osservanti (Italia, sec. XV)* (Roma: Istituto storico italiano per il medio evo, 1999); Marina Montesano, "Le rôle de la culture classique dans la définition des maleficia. Une démonologie alternative?" in *Penser avec les démons*, 277–92; Franco Mormando, *The Preacher's Demons. Bernardino of Siena and the Social Underworld of Early Renaissance Italy* (Chicago, IL: University of Chicago Press, 1999).
43 Chantal Ammann-Doubliez, "La première chasse aux sorciers en Valais (1428–1436?)," in *L'imaginaire du sabbat*, 63–98; Bertolin and Gerbore, *La stregoneria*, 19–21; Félicien Gamba, "La sorcière de Saint-Vincent. Un procès d'hérésie et de sorcellerie au XVe siècle," *Bulletin de la Société académique, religieuse et scientifique du duché d'Aoste* 41 (1964): 283–311; Ferdinando Gabotto, *Roghi e vendette. Contribuito alla dissidenza religiosa in Piemonte prima della Riforma* (Pinerolo, 1898); Massimo Centini, *Streghe, roghi e diavoli: i processi di stregoneria in Piemonte*, (L'arciere, 1995); Paravy, *De la chrétienté romaine*, 771–905; Bernard Andenmatten and Kathrin Utz Tremp, "De l'hérésie à la sorcellerie: l'inquisiteur Ulric de Torrenté OP (vers 1420–1445) et l'affermissement de l'inquisition en Suisse romande, *Revue d'Histoire ecclésiastique suisse* 86 (1992): 69–119; Utz Tremp, *Von der Häresie zur Hexerei*, 441–623; Louis Binz, "Les débuts de la chasse aux sorcières dans le diocèse de Genève", *Bibliothèque d'Humanisme et Renaissance* 59/3 (1997): 561–81; Kathrin Utz Tremp, "Die frühesten Hexenprozesse im Alpenraum (1424–1429)," in *History of Witchcraft*, ed. Johannes Dillinger, Routledge, in press; Arno Borst, "Anfänge des Hexenwahns in den Alpen," in Arno Borst, *Barbaren, Ketzer und Artisten. Welten des Mittelalters* (München; Zürich: R. Piper, 1988), 262–86; Andreas Blauert, *Frühe Hexenverfolgungen: Ketzer-, Zauberei- und Hexenprozesse des 15. Jahrhunderts* (Hamburg: Junius, 1989).
44 In addition to the references cited in notes 43, 45 and 51–53, cf. mainly Sandrine Strobino, *Françoise sauvée des flammes? Une Valaisanne accusée de sorcellerie au XVe siècle* (Lausanne: Cahiers lausannois d'histoire médiévale, Lausanne, 1996); Sophie Simon, *"Si je le veux, il mourra!". Maléfices et sorcellerie dans la campagne genevoise (1497–1530)* (Lausanne: Cahiers lausannois d'histoire médiévale, 2007); Carine Dunand, *Des montagnards endiablés. Chasse aux sorciers dans la vallée de Chamonix (1448–1462)* (Lausanne: Cahiers lausannois d'histoire médiévale, 2009); Bertolin, *Processi per fede e sortilegi*; Utz Tremp, *Von der Häresie zur Hexerei*, 427–623; Ursula Gießmann, *Der letzte Gegenpapst: Felix V. Studien zu Herrschaftspraxis und Legitimationsstrategien (1434–1451)* (Köln, Weimar, Wien: Böhlau, 2014), 49–51.
45 This register is conserved at the Archives cantonales vaudoises, under the shelf mark Ac 29. *L'imaginaire du sabbat*, 339–53; Pierre-Han Choffat, *La Sorcellerie comme exutoire. Tensions et conflits locaux: Dommartin 1524–1528* (Lausanne: Cahiers lausannois d'histoire médiévale, 1989); Martine Ostorero, *"Folâtrer avec les démons." Sabbat et chasse aux sorciers à Vevey (1448)* (Lausanne: Cahiers

lausannois d'histoire médiévale, 2008); Eva Maier, *Trente ans avec le diable. Une nouvelle chasse aux sorciers sur la Riviera lémanique (1477–1484)* (Lausanne: Cahiers lausannois d'histoire médiévale, 1996); Laurence Pfister, *L'enfer sur terre. Sorcellerie à Dommartin (1498)* (Lausanne: Cahiers lausannois d'histoire médiévale, 1997); Georg Modestin, *Le diable chez l'évêque. Chasse aux sorciers dans le diocèse de Lausanne (vers 1460)* (Lausanne: Cahiers lausannois d'histoire médiévale, 1999); *Inquisition et sorcellerie en Suisse romande.*

46 Chantal Ammann-Doubliez, "Les chasses aux sorciers vues sous un angle politique," 5–13.
47 Strobino, *Françoise sauvée des flammes.*
48 See above, notes 43–44.
49 Ostorero, "Amédée VIII et la répression de la sorcellerie démoniaque: une hérésie d'Etat".
50 On the concept of Heresy of State, see Chiffoleau, "L'hérésie de Jeanne", 17 and note 13; Jacques Chiffoleau, "Sur le crime de majesté médiéval," in *Genèse de l'État moderne en Méditerranée* (Rome, Ecole française de Rome, 1993), 207–11; Théry, "A Heresy of State"; Mercier and Ostorero, *L'énigme de la Vauderie de Lyon*, 322–25.
51 Pau Castell i Granados, "Sortilegas, divinatrices et fetilleres. Les origines de la sorcellerie en Catalogne," *Cahiers de Recherches Médiévales et Humanistes* 22 (2011): 217–41; Pau Castell i Granados, *Orígens i evolució de la cacera de bruixes a Catalunya (segles XV–XVI)* (Unpublished Ph.D., Barcelona, 2013); Pau Castell i Granados, "'Wine vat witches suffocate children'. The Mythical Components of the Iberian Witch," in *eHumanista: Journal of Iberian Studies* 26 (2014), www.ehumanista.ucsb.edu.
52 Niklaus Schatzmann, *Verdorrende Bäume und Brote wie Kuhfladen. Hexenprozesse in der Leventina 1431–1459 und die Anfänge der Hexenverfolgung auf der Alpensüdseite* (Zürich: Chronos 2003), 283–97.
53 Laura Stokes, *Demons of Urban Reform. Early European Witch Trials and Criminal Justice, 1430–1530* (Basingstoke: Palgrave Macmillan, 2011).
54 Franck Mercier, *La Vauderie d'Arras. Une chasse aux sorcières à l'Automne du Moyen Age* (Rennes: Presses universitaires de Rennes, 2006).
55 Cf. especially Rita Voltmer,"Die politischen Funktionen der frühneuzeitlichen Hexenverfolgungen: Machtdemonstration, Kontrolle und Herrschaftsverdichtung im Rhein-Maas-Raum," in *Chasses aux sorcières.* ed. Ostorero, Modestin and Utz Tremp, 89–115; Rita Voltmer, *Hexenverfolgung und Herrschaftspraxis* (Trier: Spee, 2005); Brian P. Levack, "State Building and Witch-Hunting in Early Modern Europe," in *Witchcraft in Early Modern Europe*, ed. Jonathan Barry, Marianne Hester and Gareth Roberts (Cambridge: Cambridge University Press, 1996), 96–115.
56 Boudet, *Entre science et "nigromance"*, 503, 508; Jacques Krynen, *L'empire du roi. Idées et croyances politiques en France, XIIIe-XVe siècles* (Paris: Gallimard, 1993), 342.
57 Richard Kieckhefer, *European Witch Trials: Their Foundations in Popular and Learned Culture, 1300–1500* (London: Routledge and Kegan Paul, 1976); Boudet, *Entre science et "nigromance"*, 498–501.
58 Cf. Chiffoleau, "L'hérésie de Jeanne," sp. 17–18, note 13; Jacques Chiffoleau, *La Religion flamboyante. France (1320-1520)* (Paris: Seuil, 2011), 59–61.
59 Martine Ostorero, "Des papes face à la sorcellerie démoniaque (première moitié du xve s.): une dilatation du champ de l'hérésie?" in *Aux marges de l'hérésie au Moyen Âge*, ed. Franck Mercier and Isabelle Rosé (Rennes: Presses universitaires de Rennes, 2017), 153–84; Hansen, *Quellen*, 16–24.
60 Stuart Clark, *Thinking with Demons. The Idea of Witchcraft in Early Modern Europe* (Oxford: Clarendon Press, 1997); Walter Stephens, *Demon Lovers. Witchcraft, Sex and the Crisis of Belief* (Chicago, IL: University of Chicago Press, 2002); Ostorero, *Le diable au sabbat.*
61 For a detailed analysis of these three texts, see Ostorero, *Le diable au sabbat.* Extracts in Hansen, *Quellen*, 124–212.
62 Ostorero, *Le diable au sabbat*, 387–400; Stephens, *Demon Lovers*, 13–26; Matthew Champion, "Crushing the Canon: Nicolas Jacquier's Response to the Canon *Episcopi* in the *Flagellum haereticorum fascinariorum*," *Magic, Ritual and Witchcraft* 6/2 (Winter 2011): 183–211; Matthew Champion, "Scourging the Temple of God: Towards an Understanding of Nicolas Jacquier's *Flagellum haereticorum fascinariorum* (1458)," *Parergon* 28/1 (2011): 1–24.
63 Martine Ostorero, "Un prédicateur au cachot. Guillaume Adeline et le sabbat", *Médiévales* 44 (2003): 73–96.
64 Ed. Bertolin, *Processi per fede e sortilegi*, 117–73.
65 Michel Porret, *L'ombre du Diable: Michée Chauderon, dernière sorcière exécutée à Genève (1652)* (Chêne-Bourg: Georg, 2009).
66 Choffat, *La Sorcellerie comme exutoire*, 59.

67 Cf. for example Montesano, *"Supra acqua et supra ad vento"*; Mormando, *Preacher's Demons*; Fabio Troncarelli and Maria Paola Saci, "Il *De potestate spirituum* di Guglielmo Becchi," in *Stregoneria e streghe nell'Europa moderna. Convegno internazionale di studi*, (Pisa, 24–26 marzo 1994), ed. Giovanna Bosco and Patrizia Castelli (Pisa, 1996), 87–98; Fabio Troncarelli, *Le streghe. Tra superstizione e realtà, storie segrete e documenti inediti di un fenomeno tra i più inquietanti della società europea* (Roma, 1983).

68 Examples of english translations: See note 24 and the new serie directed by Richard Kieckhefer and Claire Fanger, *The Magic in History Sourcebooks series* (University Park, PA: The Pennsylvania State University Press): *Hazards of the Dark Arts. Advice for Medieval Princes on Witchcraft and Magic*, Translated by Richard Kieckhefer (2017) and *The Arras Witch Treatises. Johannes Tinctor's Invectives contre la secte de vauderie and the Recollectio casus, status et condicionis Valdensium ydolatrarum by the Anonymous of Arras (1460)*, Edited and translated by Andrew Colin Gow, Robert B. Desjardins, and François V. Pageau (2016).

35

EPILOGUE

Cosmology and magic – The angel of Mars in the *Libro de astromagia**

Alejandro García Avilés

The image on the front cover of this book comes from an acephalous manuscript known as *Libro de astromagia* (ca. 1280–84) ascribed to the court of Alfonso X the Wise of Castile (1252–84).[1] The angel of Mars stands in the centre of a sphere containing several images of Mars to be engraved for the fabrication of talismans, following different sources – especially the *Picatrix*, as declared in the text itself[2] – but without any mention of the function of the planetary angel.[3] This angel holds the sphere's rim with both hands as though to set it spinning. In other cosmological images of the time,[4] as well as some cosmological and eschatological images of the early Middle Ages,[5] angels appear around the celestial spheres or holding them. However, the angel of Mars in the *Libro de astromagia* actually seems to give movement to his planetary sphere. This image of an angel moving a planetary sphere is exceptional in the context of medieval iconography, but it has deep roots in contemporary ideas.

Although it is difficult to find philosophical speculation in Alfonso's work, there is in his courtly circle a precious witness to the polemics which this image derives from. John Gilles of Zamora was a Franciscan friar educated in Paris who would became the tutor of Alfonso's son, the forthcoming king Sancho IV. In his *Natural History*, an unfinished encyclopaedic work of a conservative character, Gilles introduces the problem of the motion of the planets and discusses the theories of Aristotle (which he dismisses), Averroes and Algazel, among others. In this work, he speaks about "what philosophers call immaterial [literally 'nude'] intelligences … and in the Scriptures spirits close to Our Lord, that is, angels".[6] This expression – "nude" or "separate" intelligences – points to a polemic current in the 1270s, when Gilles was studying in Paris and soon before Alfonso's *Libro de astromagia* was written and illustrated.[7] The problem of angels as the movers of the planets lay at the heart of a heated controversy in Paris at that time which set theologians against one another, with some of them attempting to reconcile Aristotelian physics with Christian teachings.

The debate about whether angels were the *motores spherae* was at stake in 1271, when the Superior of the Dominicans, John of Vercelli, sought the opinions of the most notable theologians of the order – Albertus Magnus, Thomas Aquinas and Robert Kilwardby – on forty-three questions, the first five of which concerned the causes of the movement of the

---

* This chapter was written in the course of Projects19905/GERM/15 (Fundación Séneca) and HAR2015-65105-P (MINECO) and has benefited from a MINECO travel grant (PRX17/00242). I'm grateful to Gerhard Wolf for the facilities I enjoyed during my stay as his guest in the Kunsthistorisches Institut in Florence.

heavens.[8] The evidence provided by these questions and their answers clearly shows the unease caused by the new Aristotelian-inspired angel lore, which had led some theologians to identify the separate intelligences with the angels of the Christian heavenly hierarchy. While his master Albert the Great refuses this identification – as does Kilwardby[9] – Aquinas states:

> However, in some works translated from the Arabic, the separate substances which we call angels are called 'intelligences,' and perhaps for this reason, that such substances are always actually understanding. But in works translated from the Greek, they are called 'intellects' or 'minds.'[10]

As many as twenty-six among the articles in the well-known Condemnations of 1277 by the Bishop of Paris, Étienne Tempier, are "Mistakes about the intelligences or angels".[11] The text of one of these articles in the Parisian Condemnation of 1277 specifies that the angel cannot produce immediate effects, like the movement of a *mobile*, but needs the mediation of a celestial sphere to give movement.[12]

Aristotle had suggested that the celestial movers were intellectual forces, separate from matter.[13] In his utopian political tract, *The Ideal City*, the tenth-century Muslim philosopher Alfarabi adapted this theory of "immaterial intelligences", but he argued that each immaterial intelligence should be associated with a single sphere (not a single movement).[14] Shortly afterwards, Alfarabi's idea was discussed by Avicenna in his *Metaphysics*,[15] in a section on the number of intelligences responsible for moving the spheres. Avicenna's discussion centred upon the two theories outlined, correctly attributing to Aristotle the one which ascribed every movement – not each sphere – to a separate intelligence, and contrasting it with Alfarabi's proposal, which, it seems, he preferred in the final analysis.[16] This idea became commonplace in the Islamic world:[17] for example, Algazel remarked in his summary of Avicenna's philosophy that "the souls <of the spheres> and the intelligences... are known as celestial spiritual angels".[18] It was through translations of Arabic works that Christian scholars – and also Jewish ones like Maimonides[19] – absorbed Aristotle's doctrine of celestial motors. The Aristotelian origin of the entire theory was never in doubt, and even such a confirmed Platonist as St Bonaventure was able to state confidently that Aristotle was correct when he said angels moved the heavenly spheres.[20] Thomas Aquinas definitely attributed to Avicenna the paternity of the idea that each separate substance corresponds to a planet.[21]

However, the idea was not an entirely new one. Ever since Classical times, theories attributed to "the most famous among the Babylonians" had identified the spirits that governed the seven planetary spheres as angels and archangels.[22] In Hellenism, plausibly under Iranian influence, the motion of the supralunar world was attributed to angels. Angels also seem ultimately to preside over the movement of the stars in Judeo-Christian apocalyptic texts.[23] Nicomachus of Gerasa knew the identification of planets with angels, who in his time were often identified with daemons.[24] Origen, who was familiar with Nicomachus, explains how planetary angels are intermediaries between God and men.[25] In the generation after Origen, two of Plotinus' students, Amelius and Porphyry, associate daemons with heavenly bodies. Much later, the identification of the cosmic intelligences as angels is said to have been introduced by John of Damascus.[26] Authors like Theodore of Mopsuestia, and following him Cosmas Indicopleustes, described angels as movers of the celestial bodies.[27] Even St Augustine admitted he was unsure whether or not to ascribe the sun, the moon and other heavenly bodies to the realm of the angelic, but John Philoponus rejected any notion that the celestial spheres were set in motion by angels[28] and ridiculed the idea of the "followers of Theodore," asking whether the angels are pushing the planets, pulling them or carrying them on their shoulders.[29]

EPILOGUE

The involvement of angels in the movement of the spheres was an issue which does not appear to have preoccupied very many early scholastic thinkers;[30] however, Dominicus Gundissalinus, probably alluding to Avicenna and Algazel, used the term "angels" for the intelligences that move the spheres.[31] By the mid-thirteenth century, the idea was familiar to Michael Scot, who linked each planet with the name of its guiding angel,[32] and we find spirits ruling over each of the revolving spheres of the planets in the *Liber de essentia spirituum*, a work known in the thirteenth century. For example, those of Mercury and the Moon are described as "the turners of the sphere of Mercury" and "the rotators of the orb of the Moon".[33] By the end of the thirteenth century, the theory that the planetary spheres were moved by angels had become part of the common intellectual property of the late Middle Ages. As Dante wrote succinctly in his *Convivio*: "the movers of the heavens are substances independent of matter, that is, they are Intelligences, popularly known as Angels".[34]

The Alfonsine miniatures in the *Libro de astromagia* are the clearest visual renderings of this theory. However, it was not the first time that a similar idea had found visual expression, as we learn from some Byzantine manuscripts illustrating Book IX of *Christian Topography* which are copies of late antique exemplars, where angels appear as movers of the celestial spheres, although in a very different visual rendering: the circle of stars contains twelve compartments, each holding one angel (in the Sinai manuscript) or two (in the Vatican manuscript).[35] Summarizing *Christian Topography*, Photius points out among Kosmas's views that: "all the stars, with the help of the angels, are kept in motion".[36] Some other manuscripts associate angels with the planetary spheres, as in the fifteenth-century Coëtivy Book of Hours,[37] but there are only a few examples where the angels are seen explicitly as celestial movers. In a diagram of the spheres in several manuscripts of the fourteenth-century *Breviari d'amor* by Matfré Ermengaud, one angel on each side seems to give movement to the spheres of the planets.[38] More explicitly, in another image usual in some manuscripts of this work, an angel stands on either side of the sphere of the universe, each turning a handle to rotate it on its axis.[39] A similar image including two angels rotating the *axis mundi* can be found in a mid-fourteenth-century manuscript of Bartholomeus Anglicus, *De proprietatibus rerum* (see Figure 35.1).[40]

The theory of angels as motors of the planets would survive for centuries.[41] It appears, for example, in the *Book of Angels* preserved in a fifteenth-century manuscript,[42] with images illustrating more or less related theories. Angels are shown moving the sphere of the entire universe in a fifteenth-century woodcut where, in a variant on the iconography associated with the Wheel of Fortune, an angel uses a handle to make the world spin on its axis, while the planets cling to its surface.[43] A somewhat related image appears on a contemporary Flemish tapestry now in the Museo de Santa Cruz at Toledo (Spain).[44] It differs, however, in one striking respect: the angel that turns the handle does not move a globe, but an astrolabe.

In the Italian Renaissance, the idea of angels as motors of the heavenly spheres received full credit. For example, Ludovico Lazzarelli declared that "each star has its own proper mover", which was illustrated by an angel holding the world,[45] and when at the beginning of the sixteenth century the Christian cabalist Johannes Reuchlin wrote his *De arte cabbalistica* he explained that

> The philosophers, and first among them the peripatetics, proved this, since every celestial sphere has besides its own essential form an intelligence next to it that moves it in orbit. That intelligence is called an angel because it has been sent for this duty. It has will and understanding, and in them fulfils the order of the Creator, like a power medium between God and nature.[46]

Figure 35.1 Angels rotating the universe from a French translation of Bartholomeus Anglicus, Bibliothèque Sainte-Geneviève, Paris, MS 1029, f. 108.

At about the same time, Raphael's drawings for the Chigi Chapel in Santa Maria del Popolo (Rome) were being transferred into mosaics (see Figure 35.2).[47]

This is perhaps the most familiar image associating the angels and the planets: the dome Raphael designed for Agostino Chigi in the Roman church of Santa Maria del Popolo, which – probably by means of Dante's *Convivium*[48] – reveals how medieval ideas, thought to be grounded in Aristotelian physics, were slotted into the framework of Christian cosmology. In the centre of this scheme is God, characterized with a theatrical gesture as the Aristotelian "Prime Mover", to whose will the planet-guiding angels bend themselves, directing the planets according to divine instruction. This is shown, for example, by the angel in charge of Mars, who we can see in Figure 35.3 in Pietro Facchetti's sixteenth-century painting after Raphael's drawing.[49]

Figure 35.2 The creation of the universe, dome of the Chigi Chapel, Santa Maria del Popolo (Rome).

Figure 35.3 Pietro Facchetti (after Raphael's drawings for the Chigi Capel), the angel of Mars guiding his planet. Museo Nacional del Prado.

In sum, the images of Alfonso X's *Libro de astromagia* representing the angel of Mars revolving the sphere of his planet are rooted in ancient thought through Arabic intermediaries. A main principle of Aristotle's *Physics* was that any movement has its mover. The movement *par excellence* was imprinted to the universe by the Prime Mover in the moment of Creation, and in the Middle Ages the Prime Mover would be identified as God. This can be seen in visual terms, for example, in a thirteenth-century manuscript of Aristotle's *Physics* with comments by Averroes,[50] where God gives movement to the sphere of the World illustrating the incipit "Omne quod movetur ab alio movetur".[51] Even more visually explicit is the opening miniature of an *Aristoteles latinus* now in Seville, where God imprints its first movement to the universe.[52]

The relationship between planets and angels has its roots in Antiquity, but the attribution of an angelic mover for each planetary sphere was specified by Arabic authors, notably Alfarabi and Avicenna. In a moment when the discussion on the celestial movers was at his height after the Parisian Condemnations of 1277, Alfonso X, following his Arabic sources, advocated in visual terms the idea that each planetary sphere is moved by its angel. The images in the *Libro de astromagia* are exceptional: although several medieval images seem to relate angels to the movements of the cosmos, there is no other visual rendering of the idea of angels as movers of the planetary spheres as explicit as this one until the sixteenth century, when we find a decoration showing an angel guiding each planet after designs by Raphael. In the dome covering the Capella Chigi in Santa Maria del Popolo, God appears theatrically as the First Mover surrounded by angels, and forming a ring below, the planets and the sphere of the fixed stars, each guided by an angel. In the case of Mars, following the Roman iconography of the god, he appears as a warrior, and the angel holds his hand, guiding his movements. While Raphael's iconography at the Chigi Chapel has been usually interpreted as a mere echo of Dante's cosmology, the medieval prehistory of the subject seems to be far more complex.

Notes

1 Rome, Vatican Library, MS Reg.Lat.1283ª, fol. 27r (see also 28v and 29v for other images of the angel of Mars moving its planetary sphere). Alfonso X, *Astromagia*, ed. and italian translation Alfonso d'Agostino (Naples: Liguori, 1992), 242. D'Agostino reproduces his edition as part of the commentary volume to the unreliable facsimile of this manuscript: *Tratado de astrología y magia*, ed. Carlos Alvar (Valencia: Grial, 2000). Alejandro García Avilés, "Two Astromagical Manuscripts of Alfonso X", *Journal of the Warburg and Courtauld Institutes* 59 (1996): 14–23; Alejandro García Avilés, "Imágenes mágicas: la obra astromágica de Alfonso X y su difusión en la Europa bajomedieval", in *Alfonso X: aportaciones de un rey castellano a la construcción de Europa*, ed. Miguel Rodríguez Llopis (Murcia: Editora Regional, 1997), 135–72. From a paleographical point of view, see Laura Fernández Fernández, *Arte y ciencia en el scriptorium de Alfonso X el Sabio*, El Puerto de Santa María (Cádiz) and Sevilla: Cátedra Alfonso X el Sabio and Universidad de Sevilla, 2013, pp. 293-319. It is surprising that there is no mention of this manuscript in Ana González Sánchez, *Alfonso X el mago*, (Madrid: Universidad Autónoma de Madrid, 2015), in spite of the title of one of the chapters, "Los libros de astromagia alfonsíes" (pp. 123–180), and that of the doctoral dissertation this book reproduces: *Tradición y fortuna de los libros de astromagia del scriptorium alfonsí*, (Madrid: Universidad Autónoma de Madrid, 2011). On Alfonso X and magic see Daniel Gregorio, *Alphonse X et la magie* (Valenciennes: Presses universitaires de Valenciennes, 2012).

2 *Picatrix*, II. 10, ed. David Pingree (London: Warburg Institute, 1986), 64ff.

EPILOGUE

3   This corresponds to an acephalous chapter, but soon after we can find a brief summary of the contents in the lost introduction: "We have told about the properties and the natures of Mars…" ("Dicho avemos las propiedades e las naturas de Mars…") (fol. 27r; *Astromagia*, ed. D'Agostino, 244); hence, probably it never was any mention to the function of the angel of Mars.

4   For example in a manuscript of Sacrobosco, *De sphaera*: Milan, Ambrosiana, A 183 inf, fol. 2r (thirteenth century (2nd half)–beginning of the fourteenth century); see Donatella Cantele, "Il sistema illustrativo del *De Sphaera* di Johannes de Sacrobosco", *Rivista di Storia della miniatura* 13 (2009): 97–107.

5   See Bianca Kühnel, *The End of Time in the Order of Things* (Regensburg: Schnell & Steiner, 2003), 368ff.

6   Johannis Aegidii Zamorensis, *Historia naturalis*, ed. and Spanish trans. Avelino Domínguez García and Luis García Ballester (Valladolid: Junta de Castilla y León, 1994), 1291–97, here 1292.

7   On the datation of this manuscript in 1282–84, see García Avilés, "Two astromagical manuscripts of Alfonso X".

8   Marie-Dominique Chenu, "Les reponses de S. Thomas et de Kilwardby a la consultation de Jean de Verceil (1271)", in *Mélanges Mandonnet. Etudes d'histoire litteraire et litteraire du Moyen-Âge*, vol. I (Paris: Vrin 1930), 191–222; Pierre Duhem, *Le système du monde: Histoire des doctrines cosmologiques de Platon à Copernic* <1913–1959>, vol. 6 (Paris: Hermann, 1954; rep. 1973), 29–59; James Weisheipl, "The Celestial Movers in Medieval Physics", in *The Dignity of Science. Studies in the Philosophy of Science Presented to W. H. Kane*, ed. J. A. Weisheipl (Washington: Catholic University of America, 1961), 150–90 (and in *The Thomist*, XXIV, 1961), now in James Weisheipl, *Nature and Motion in the Middle Ages*, (Washington, DC: Catholic University of America Press, 1985), 143–77. See also Paola Zambelli, "Le stelle 'sorde e mute' ed i loro 'motori' alle origini della scienza moderna?: un case-study storiografico," in *Historia philosophiae medii aevi*, ed. Burkhard Mojsisch and Olaf Pluta (Amsterdam and Philadelphia B. R. Grüner, 1991), 1099–117; Edward Grant, *Planets, Stars and Orbs. The Medieval Cosmos 1200–1687* (Cambridge: Cambridge University Press, 1994), 523ff.; Edward Grant, "Celestial Motions in the Late Middle Ages," *Early Science and Medicine* 2 (1997): 129–48.

9   Albert the Great, *In II Sent.*, dist. 3, a. 3 *Opera omnia*, 27: *Commentarii in II Sententiarum*, ed. Auguste Borgnet (Paris: Louis Vivès, 1894), 64–6: "Utrum nos vocemus angelos substantias illas separatas quas philosophi intelligentias vocant, ut quidam contentiose defendere praesumunt". In favour of this identity Albert cites Avicenna, Algazel and Maimonides, but his own response is negative. In his *Problemata determinata* Albert says: "Non est dubium quod corpora caelestia non movent angeli" (Albertus Magnus, *Problemata determinata XLIII*, ed. James Weisheipl, in *Opera omnia*, XVII/1, (Münster: Aschendorff, 1975), 48); see also Paola Zambelli, *The* Speculum astronomiae *and Its Enigma: Astrology, Theology and Science in Albertus Magnus and His Contemporaries* (Dordrecht, Boston, and London: Kluwer, 1992).

10 "In quibusdam tamen libris de arabico translatis, substantiae separatae quas angelos dicimus, Intelligentiae vocantur; forte propter hoc, quod huiusmodi substantiae semper actu intelligunt. In libris tamen de graeco translatis, dicuntur Intellectus seu Mentes." Thomas Aquinas, *Summa Theologiae* I 79, 10, resp, (Rome: Commisio Leonina, 1889), translation by the Dominican Fathers of the English-Speaking Province, newadvent.org/summa/1079.htm#article10. See also Thomas Litt, *Les corps célestes dans l'univers de Thomas d'Aquin* (Louvain: Publications universitaires, 1963), 99–108; Tiziana Suarez-Nani, *Les anges et la philosophie. Subjectivité et fonction cosmologique des substances séparées à la fin du XIIIe siècle* (Paris: J. Vrin, 2002), 103–42.

11 This is the count of the *Collectio errorum*: see Henryk Anzulewicz, "Eine weitere Überlieferung der 'Collectio errorum in Anglia et Parisius condemnatorum' im Ms. lat. fol. 456 der Staatsbibliothek Preußischer Kulturbesitz zu Berlin", *Franziskanische Studien* 47 (1992): 375–99 (387–88); *La condamnation parisienne de 1277*, ed. and French trans. David Piché with Claude Lafleur (Paris: Vrin, 1999), 297–99.

12 "Quod angelus non potest in actus oppositos immediate, set in actus mediatos, et hoc mediante alio, ut orbe." Art. 75 (59), *La condamnation parisienne de 1277*, 102; Roland Hisette, *Enquête sur les 219 article condamnés à Paris le 7 mars 1277* (Louvain-Paris: Publications universitaires-Vander-Oyez, 1977), 114; see also Carlos Steel, "Siger of Brabant versus Thomas Aquinas on the Possibility of Knowing the Separate Substances," in *Nach der Verurteilung von 1277: Philosophie und Theologie an der Universität von Paris im letzten Viertel des 13. Jahrhunderts*, ed. Jan A. Aertsen et al. (Berlin: Walter de Gruyter, 2001), 211–31.

13 *Metaphysics*, XII, 8; see Harry A. Wolfson, "The Plurality of Immovable Movers in Aristotle and Averroes", *Harvard Studies in Classical Philology* 63 (1958): 233–53 (now in Harry A. Wolfson, *Studies in the History of Philosophy and Religion* (Cambridge, MA: Harvard University Press, 1973), 1–21); Harry A. Wolfson, "The Problem of the Soul of the Spheres from the Byzantine Commentaries on Aristotle through the Arabs and St Thomas to Kepler," *Dumbarton Oaks Papers* 16 (1962): 67–93 (now in Wolfson, *Studies*, 22–59).

14 *Al-Farabi on the perfect state*, ed. and trans. Richard Walzern (Oxford: Clarendon Press, 1985), ch. XV. See Herbert A. Davidson, *Alfarabi, Avicenna, and Averroes on Intellect. Their Cosmologies, Theories of the Active Intellect and Theories of Human Intellect* (Oxford: Oxford University Press, 1992).

15 *Metaph.*, IX, 3 (*Liber de philosophia prima, sive scientia divina*, vol. 2, ed. Simone Van Riet (Louvain-Leiden: Peeters-Brill, 1980). See also Amos Bertolacci, *The reception of Aristotle's* Metaphysics *in Avicenna's* Kitab al-Sifa*: A Milestone of Western Metaphysical Thought* (Leiden: Brill, 2006), 467.

16 *Metaph.*, IX, 4.

17 On a late Islamic figurative tradition of the angels of the planets, see the work of Anna Caiozzo, specially her article "Les rituels théophaniques imagés et pratiques magiques: les anges planétaires dans le manuscrit persan 174 de Paris", *Studia Iranica* 29 (2000): 111–40.

18 Al-Ghazali, *Maqasid al-Falasifa*, quoted in Davidson, *Alfarabi, Avicenna, and Averroes on Intellect*, 134. See also Al-Ghazali, *The Niche for Lights* (*Mishkat al-Anwar*), trans. William H. T. Gairdner (London: Royal Asiatic Society, 1924), 170: "the mover of every several Heaven is another being, called an Angel". See Karl Allgaier, "Engel und Intelligenzen – Zur arabisch-lateinischen Proklos-Rezeption," in *Orientalische Kultur Und Europäisches Mittelalter*, ed. Albert Zimmermann et al. (Berlin: Walter De Gruyter, 2013), 172.

19 Moses Maimonides, *The Guide of the Perplexed*, trans. and intro. Shlomo Pines, (Chicago, IL: University of Chicago Press, 1963), I.49 (Pines 108), where the angels are described as "intellects separate from matter", and II.4 (Pines 258), II.6 (Pines 262), II.10 (Pines 273) and II.12 (Pines 280), where they are identified with the separate intellects.

20 *Collationes in Hexaemeron*, 5.26, trad. Jose de Vinck (Paterson: St Anthony Guild, 1970, 88–89). See David Keck, *Angels and Angelology in the Middle Ages* (New York and Oxford: Oxford University Press, 1998), 82. On Bonaventure's angelology, see Barbara Faes de Mottoni, *San Bonaventura e la scala di Giacobbe. Letture di angelologia* (Naples: Bibliopolis,1995); David Keck, *The Angelology of Saint Bonaventure and the Harvest of Medieval Angelology*, unpublished Ph.D. dissertation (Harvard University, 1992); David Keck, "Bonaventure's Angelology," in *A Companion to Bonaventure*, ed. Jared Goff (Leiden: Brill, 2014), 289–332.

21 *De substantiis separatis*, 2–10: "Aristotle attempts to find out the number of these <separate substances> on the basis of the number of motions of the heavenly bodies. But one of his followers, namely Avicenna assigns the number of these substances not according to the number of motions but rather according to the number of the planets and the other higher bodies, namely, the sphere of the fixed stars and the sphere without stars" trans. Francis J. Lescoe, *Thomas Aquinas, Treatise on Separate Substances* (West Hartford CN: Saint Joseph College, 1959). See James D. Collins, *The Thomistic Philosophy of the Angels* (Washington, DC: The Catholic University of America Press, 1947); Jean-Marie Vernier, *Les anges chez saint Thomas d"Aquin: Fondements historiques et principes philosophiques* (Paris: Nouvelles Éditions Latines, 1986); Tiziana Suarez-Nani, *Les anges et la philosophie*; Tiziana Suarez-Nani, *Connaissance et langage des anges selon Thomas d'Aquin et Gilles de Rome* (Paris: Vrin, 2002); Serge-Thomas Bonino, "Aristotelianism and Angelology According to Aquinas," in *Aristotle in Aquinas's Theology*, ed. Gilles Emery and Matthew Levering (Oxford: Oxford University Press, 2015), 29–47.

22 Franz Cumont, "Les anges du paganisme," *Revue de l'histoire des religions* 163, no. 4 (1915): 159–82. On planetary angels in late antiquity, see *Les Mages Hellenisés*, ed. Joseph Bidez and Franz Cumont (Paris: Les Belles Lettres, repr., 1973 [1938]), II, 271–75, 283–84; Hans G. Gundel, *Weltbild und Astrologie in den griechischen Zauberpapyri* (Munich: Beck 1968), 41–43; Alexander Toepel, "Planetary Demons in Early Jewish Literature", *Journal for the Study of the Pseudepigrapha* 14 (2005): 231–38.

23 *Asc. Is.* iv, 18; *II Henoch*, x, 8, cited in Jean Daniélou, *Théologie du Judéo-Christianisme* (Tournai: Desclée, 1958), 142. 1 Enoch 80.1 states that "all stars have their angelic guides": see Maxwell J. Davidson, *Angels at Qumran: A Comparative Study of 1 Enoch 1–36, 72–108 and Sectarians Writings from Qumran* (Sheffield: JSOT Press, 1992), 93. For a more general, but still useful account, see Harold B. Kuhn, "The Angelology of the Non-Canonical Jewish Apocalypses," *Journal of Biblical Literature*

67 (1948): 217–32. See also Martha Himmelfarb, *Ascent to Heaven in Jewish and Christian Apocalypses* (New York-Oxford: Oxford University Press, 1992).

24 *Apud* <Pseudo->Iamblichus, *Theologumena Arithmeticae*, 57.6–9, ed. Vittorio de Falco (Leipzig: Teubner, 1922); trans. Robin Waterfield, *The Theology of Arithmetic* (Grand Rapids, MI: Phanes Press, 1988), 88.

25 Origen, *Contra Celsus*, trans. M. Borret (Paris: Éditions du Cerf, 1967), 257; Origen, *Homily on Jeremiah*, 12.4. See A. Scott, *Origen and the Life of the Stars*, vol. 60 (Oxford: Oxford University Press, 1991), n. 42.

26 As quoted by Albertus Magnus (see Zambelli, *The Speculum astronomiae and Its Enigma*, 92 and 179 n. 46).

27 Theodore Mopsuesteni, *In Epistolas Beati Pauli Commentarii*, 270–71; cited by Harry A. Wolfson, "The Problem of the Soul," 70; now 26.

28 Augustine, *Enchiridion*, 58; John Philoponus, *De opificio mundi*, vi, 2. "Philoponus thought it utterly absurd of Theodore <of Mopsuestia> to suppose that the sun, moon and stars move because they are propelled by angels." Henry Chadwick, "Philoponus the Christian Theologian," in *Philoponus and the Rejection of Aristotelian Science*, ed. Richard Sorajbi (London: Duckworth, 1987), 41–56, here 51; see also Philoponus, *De opificio mundi*, 1, 12. See also Richard C. Dales, "The De-animation of the Heavens in the Middle Ages," *Journal of the History of Ideas* 41 (1980): 533.

29 John Philoponus, *De opificio mundi*, 1.12; also Narsai, *Homilies on Creation*, 2.372–421 and *passim*, ed. Phillippe Gignoux (Patrologia Orientalis 34, fasc. 3–4) (Paris: 1968). See Adam H. Becker, *Fear of God and the Beginning of Wisdom: The School of Nisibis and the Development of Scholastic Culture in Late Antique Mesopotamia* (Philadelphia: University of Pennsylvania Press, 2006), 122.

30 See Marcia L. Colish, "Early Scholastic Angelology," *Recherches de theologie ancienne et medievale* 62 (1995): 80–109. I'm grateful to Alberto Ara for sending me the concluding chapter of his unpublished dissertation: *Angeli e sostanze separate: l'idea di "Materia spiritualis" tra il secolo XII e il secolo XIII: ricognizione storico-testuale - Valutazione teoretica* (Firenze: Facoltà Teologica dell'Italia Centrale, 2005), 707–33.

31 Dominicus Gundissalinus, *De processione mundi*, trans. *The Procession of the World*, trans. John A. Laumakis, (Milwaukee: Marquette University Press, 2002), 73; cfr. the translation provided by Jean Jolivet, "The Arabic Inheritance," in *A History of Twelfth-Century Western Philosophy*, ed. Peter Dronke (Cambridge: Cambridge University Press 1988), 139.

32 Michael Scot, *Liber introductorius*, Munich, Staatsbibliothek, CLM 10268, fol. 95r; cited in Morpurgo, "Note in margine a un poemetto astrologico presente nei codici del *Liber particularis* di Michele Scoto," *Pluteus* 2, no. 12 (1984): 8. Some of the names used by Scot are also found in the *De secretis angelorum* copied in Florence: Biblioteca Nazionale, MS II.III.214; see David Pingree, "Learned Magic in the Time of Frederick II", *Micrologus* 2 (1994): 47 (now reprinted in *Transactions of the American Philosophical Society*, 104.3 (2014): 477–94).

33 Sophie Page, "Image-Magic Texts and a Platonic Cosmology at St Augustine's, Canterbury, in the Late Middle Ages," in *Magic and the Classical Tradition*, ed. Charles Burnett and W. F. Ryan (London: Warburg Institute, 2005), 82.

34 Dante, *Convivium*, II, iv.2, trans. Christopher Ryan, *The Banquet* (Saratoga: ANMA 1989), 49. See Maria Luisa Ardizzone, *Reading as the Angels Read: Speculation and Politics in Dante's "Banquet"* (Toronto: University of Toronto Press, 2016), 119 ff.; Stephen Bemrose, *Dante's Angelic Intelligences. Their Importance in the Cosmos and in Pre-Christian Religion*, Rome 1983, and the review-article by Zygmunt G. Baranski, "Dante tra dei pagani e angeli cristiani," *Filologia e critica* 9 (1984): 293–30. On angels and the planets in the *Divina Commedia*, see Alison Cornish, *Reading Dante's Stars* (New Haven: Yale University Press, 2000), 119–41. See also Graziella Federici Vescovini, "Dante et l'astronomie de son temps," in Ut philosophia poesis: *Questions philosophiques dans l'oeuvre de Dante, Pétrarque et Boccace*, ed. Joël Biard and Fosca Mariani Zin (Paris: Vrin, 2008), 129–50.

35 Rome, Vatican Library, MS Graec. 699 fol. 115v (Cosimo Stornajolo, *Le miniature della Topografia cristiana di Cosma Indicopleuste: codice vaticano greco 699* (Milan: U. Hoepli, 1908), 48–49, fig. 56; colour illustration in Marco Bussagli, "Cielo," in *Enciclopedia dell' Arte Medievale*, IV (Roma: Istituto dell'Enciclopedia italiana, 1993), 739–48, here 743); Mount Sinai, Monastery of Saint Catherine, cod. 1186, f. 181v (Kurt Weitzmann and George Galavaris, *The Monastery of Saint Catherine at Mount Sinai. The Illuminated Greek Manuscripts. I: From the Ninth to the Eleventh Century* (Princeton: Princeton University Press, 1991), 62, fig. 179; Maja Kominko, *The World of Kosmas. Illustrated Byzantine Codices of the Christian Topography* (Cambridge: Cambridge University Press, 2013), 210–13. See Cosmas Indicopleustès, *Topographie chrétienne*, vol. 1, ed. Wanda Wolska-Conus (Paris: Editions du Cerf, 1968), 400–03.

36 Photius, *Bibliotheka*, 36, trans. Nigel G. Wilson (Bristol: Bristol Classical Press, 1994).
37 Dublin, Chester Beatty Library, W.82, 151r (Paris, ca. 1443).
38 Katja Laske-Fix, *Der Bildzyklus des Breviari d'amor* (Munich and Zurich: Schnell und Steiner, 1973), fig. 28 (Escorial, S. I, n° 3 f. 51v). See also Joëlle Ducos, "La cosmologie dans le Breviari d'Amor de Matfre Ermengaud," in *La voix occitane*, ed. Guy Latry (Pessac: Presses universitaires de Bordeaux, 2009), 491–508.
39 Laske-Fix, *Der Bildzyklus*, fig. 10; see an extended comment on the corresponding miniatures in Escorial, S. I, n° 3 f. 35r and Madrid, Biblioteca Nacional, Res. 203 f. 24v in Carlos Miranda García, *Iconografía del* Breviari d'amor *(Escorial, ms. S. I. n° 3; Madrid, Biblioteca Nacional, ms. res. 203)*, unpublished Ph.D. dissertation (Madrid: Universidad Complutense, 1994), 309.
40 Paris, Bibl. Sainte-Geneviève, ms. 1029, f. 108.
41 See Mary S. Kelly, *Celestial motors: 1543–1632*, unpublished Ph.D. dissertation (University of Oklahoma, 1964).
42 Juris G. Lidaka, "*The Book of Angels, Rings, Characters and Images of the Planets* Attributed to Osbern Bokenham," in *Conjuring Spirits: Texts and Traditions of Medieval Ritual Magic*, ed. Claire Fanger (University Park: Pennsylvania State University Press, 1998), 32–75. See also Sophie Page, *Magic in the Cloister. Pious Motives, Illicit Interests, and Occult Approaches to the Medieval Universe* (University Park: Pennsylvania State University Press, 2013), 189, n. 26; Richard Kieckhefer, "Angel Magic and the Cult of Angels in the Later Middle Ages," in *Contesting Orthodoxy in Medieval and Early Modern Europe: Heresy, Magic and Witchcraft*, ed. Louise Nyholm Kallestrup and Raisa Maria Toivo (London: Palgrave Macmillan, 2017), 71–110.
43 Marco Bussagli, *Storia degli angeli. Racconto di immagini e di idee* (Milan: Rusconi, 1991), 216.
44 See Jean-Michel Massing, "The Movement of the Universe" in *Circa 1492: Art in the Age of Exploration*, ed. Jay A. Levenson (New Haven and Washington: Yale University Press and National Gallery of Art, 1991), 214–15.
45 Rome, Vatican Library, Biblioteca Urb. Lat. 716 (second half of the fifteenth century), fols. 7v and 10v; see *A Critical Edition of* De gentilium deorum imaginibus *by Ludovico Lazzarelli*, ed. and trans. William J. O'Neal (Lewiston: Edwin Mellen, 1997) 18–19; Maria Paola Saci, "Le miniature in alcuni codici di Ludovico Lazzarelli", *Rivista di storia della miniatura* 3 (1998): 115–30.
46 Johannes Reuchlin, *De arte cabbalistica libri tres*, Hagenau 1517, lib. III, fol. 76v–77r, reprinted with an English translation by Martin and Sarah Goodman, introd. by G. Lloyd-Jones (New York: Abaris, 1983) (repr. with an introduction by Moshe Idel, London: Bison, 1993), 347. On Reuchlin about angels, see Pierre Béhar, *Les langues occultes de la Renaissance* (Paris: Desjonquères, 1996), 40–45.
47 John Shearman, "The Chigi Chapel in S. Maria del Popolo", *Journal of the Warburg and Courtauld Institutes*, XXIV, 1961, 129–60; Kathleen Weill-Garris Brandt, "Cosmological Patterns in Raphael's Chigi Chapel in S. Maria del Popolo," in *Raffaello a Roma* (Rome: Edizioni dell'elefante, 1986), 127–58; Nicole Riegel, "Die Chigi-Kapelle in Santa Maria del Popolo. Eine kritische Revision", *Marburger Jahrbuch für Kunstwissenschaft* 30 (2003): 93–130; Florian Métral, "Au commencement était la fin. Retour sur la chapelle Chigi de Santa Maria del Popolo à Rome", *Studiolo* 12 (2015): 154–83.
48 The historiography on the subject is here indebted to Lewis Gruner, *The Mosaics of the Cupola in the "Capella Chigiana", Sta. Maria del Popolo, Rome, designed by Raffaelle Sanzio d"Urbino,* (London: Paul & Dominic Colnaghi, 1850), ii.
49 *Rafael en España (*Madrid, Museo del Prado, 1985), 150–53.
50 Paris, Bibliothèque Mazarine, 3469, fol. 273r (Paris, ca. 1280–85). See Hanna Wimmer, "Natura, God and Aristotle: Illustrating Concepts of Nature in Paris, bibliotèque Mazarine 3469," in *Art & Nature. Studies in Medieval Art and Architecture*, ed. Laura Cleaver, Kathryn Gerry and Jim Harris (London: Courtauld Institute, 2009), 8–21, here 8, fig. 2.
51 See James A. Weisheipl, "The Principle *Omne quod movetur ab alio movetur* in Medieval Physics", *Isis* 56 (1965): 26–45.
52 Seville, Biblioteca Capitular y Colombina, 56-1-27, fol. 1r. See Alejandro García Avilés and Antonia Martínez Ruipérez and, "Imaginando la naturaleza en la cultura visual del siglo XIII" in *Medieval Studies in Honor of Peter Linehan*, ed. Francisco J. Hernández, Rocío Sánchez Ameijeiras and Emma Falque (Florence: Sismel Edizioni del Galluzzo, 2018), 243–274.

FURTHER READING

This bibliography is a selective list of key studies which have influenced the field of medieval magic, as well as editions of important primary sources. For bibliography specific to individual chapters and references to unpublished sources, see the footnotes for each chapter.

Editions of primary texts

Alfonso X, *Lapidario, Libro de las formas y las imágenes que son en los cielos*, ed. Pedro Sánchez-Prieto (Madrid: Fundación José Antonio de Castro, 2014).

Alfonso X, *Astromagia*, ed. Alfonso D'Agostino (Naples: Liguori, 1992).

Al-Kindī, *De radiis*, ed. Marie-Thérèse d'Alverny and Francoise Hudry, *Archives d'histoire doctrinale et littéraire du moyen âge* 41 (1974): 139–260.

Antonio da Montolmo, "Antonio Da Montolmo's *De Occultis Et Manifestis* or *Liber Intelligentiarum*: An Annotated Critical Edition with English Translation and Introduction," ed. Nicolas Weill-Parot, in *Invoking Angels*, ed. Claire Fanger (University Park: Pennsylvania State University Press, 2012), 219–93.

Arnau de Vilanova, *Epistola de reprobacione nigromantice ficcionis, Arnaldi de Villanova Opera Medica Omnia (AVOMO)*, VII.1 (Barcelona: Universitat, 2005).

Bernard, Katy, *Compter, dire et figurer: édition et commentaire de textes divinatoires et magiques en occitan médiéval* (Bordeaux: Université Michel de Montaigne, 2007).

Boureau, Alain, *Le pape et les sorciers. Une consultation de Jean XXII sur la magie en 1320* (Rome: Ecole française de Rome, 2004).

Chaucer, Geoffrey, *The Riverside Chaucer*, ed. Larry D. Benson, 3rd edn. (Oxford: Oxford University Press, 1987).

Delatte, Louis (ed.), *Textes latins et vieux français relatifs aux Cyranides* (Liège-Paris: Université de Liège, 1942).

Delaurenti, Béatrice (ed.), "Pietro d'Abano et les incantations: présentation, édition et traduction de la *differentia 156* du *Conciliator*", in *Médecine, astrologie et magie entre Moyen Âge et Renaissance*, ed. Jean-Patrice Boudet et al. (Florence: Sismel Edizioni del Galluzzo, 2012), 39–105.

Delaurenti, Béatrice (ed.), "Variations sur le pouvoir des incantations: le traité *Ex Conciliatore in medicinis dictus Petrus de Albano* de Pierre Franchon de Zélande", *Archives d'histoire doctrinale et littéraire du Moyen Âge* 74 (2007): 173–235.

Draelants, Isabelle (ed.), *Le Liber de virtutibus herbarum, lapidum et animalium (Liber aggregationis), Un texte à succès attribué à Albert le Grand*, Micrologus Library 22, (Florence: Sismel Edizioni del Galluzzo, 2007).

Gal, F., J.-P. Boudet, and L. Moulinier (eds), *Vedrai mirabilia. Uno libro de magia dell' Quatrocentto* (Rome: Viella, 2017).

Hansen, Bert, *Nicole Oresme and The Marvels of Nature: A Study of His De Causis Mirabilium with Critical Edition, Translation, and Commentary* (Toronto: Pontifical Institute of Mediaeval Studies, 1985).

Hermes Trismegistus, *Astrologia et divinatoria*, ed. G. Bos, C. Burnett, T. Charmasson, P. Kunitzsch, F. Lelli and P. Lucentini, *Hermes Latinus*, vol. 4, part 4 (Turnhout: Brepols, 2001).

Hedegård, Gösta (ed.), *Liber iuratus Honorii: Critical Edition of the Latin Version of the Sworn Book of Honorius* (Stockholm: Almqvist & Wiksell, 2002).

L'imaginaire du sabbat. Edition critique des textes les plus anciens (1430c.–1440c.), ed. Martine Ostorero, Agostino Paravicini Bagliani, Kathrin Utz Tremp and Catherine Chène (Lausanne: Cahiers Lausannois d'Histoire Médiévale, 1999).

John of Morigny, *John of Morigny: 'Liber florum celestis doctrine', or 'Book of the Flowers of Heavenly Teaching': The New Compilation, with Independent Portions of the Old Compilation. An Edition and Commentary*, ed. Claire Fanger and Nicholas Watson (Toronto: Pontifical Institute of Mediaeval Studies, 2015).

Kieckhefer, Richard, *Forbidden Rites. A Necromancer's Manual of the Fifteenth Century* (Stroud: Sutton, 1997).

Kramer, Heinrich (Institoris), and Sprenger, Jakob, *Malleus Maleficarum*, ed. Christopher S. Mackay (Cambridge: Cambridge University Press, 2006).

Kyeser, Conrad, *Bellifortis*, 2 vols., ed. Götz Quarg (Düsseldorf: Verlag des Vereins Deutscher Ingenieurie, 1967).

Malory, Sir Thomas, *Le Morte Darthur*, 2 vols., ed. P.J.C. Field (Cambridge: D. S. Brewer, 2013).

Picatrix: The Latin Version of the Ghāyat al-Ḥakīm, ed. David Pingree (London: Warburg Institute, 1986).

Sannino, Antonella, *Il* De mirabilibus mundi *tra tradizione magica e filosofia naturale*, Microlous Library 41 (Florence: Sismel Edizioni del Galluzzo, 2011).

Sir Gawain and the Green Knight, in *The Poems of the Pearl Manuscript: "Pearl", "Cleanness", "Patience", "Sir Gawain and the Green Knight"*, ed. Malcolm Andrew and Ronald Waldron, 5th edn. (Exeter: Exeter University Press, 2007).

Véronèse, Julien, *L'Almandal et l'Almadel latins au Moyen Âge. Introduction et éditions critiques* (Florence: Sismel Edizioni del Galluzzo, 2012).

Véronèse, Julien, *L'Ars notoria au Moyen Âge. Introduction et édition critique* (Florence: Sismel Edizioni del Galluzzo, 2007).

Torrella, Jerome (Hieronymus Torrella), *Opus praeclarum de imaginibus astrologicis*, ed. Nicolas Weill-Parot (Florence: Sismel Edizioni del Galluzzo, 2008).

Wilcox, Judith, and John M. Riddle, "Qusta ibn Luqa's Physical Ligatures and the Recognition of the Placebo Effect," in *Medieval Encounters: Jewish, Christian and Muslim Culture in Confluence and Dialogue* 1 (1995): 1–48.

William of Palerne: An Alliterative Romance, ed. G.H.V. Bunt (Groningen: Bouma's Boekhuis, 1985).

Ywain and Gawain, Sir Percyvell of Gales, The Anturs of Arther, ed. Maldwyn Mills (London: Dent, 1992).

Zambelli, Paola, *The Speculum Astronomiae and Its Enigma: Astrology, Theology and Science in Albertus Magnus and His Contemporaries* (Dordrecht, Boston, and London: Kluwer Academic Publishers, 1992).

Secondary works

Bailey, Michael D., *Fearful Spirits, Reasoned Follies: The Boundaries of Superstition in Late Medieval Europe* (Ithaca, NY: Cornell University Press, 2013).

Bailey, Michael D., "The Feminization of Magic and the Emerging Idea of the Female Witch,", *Essays in Medieval Studies* 19 (2002): 120–134.

Bailey, Michael D., "From Sorcery to Witchcraft: Clerical Conceptions of Magic in the Later Middle Ages," *Speculum* 76 (2001): 960–90.

Boudet, Jean-Patrice, *Entre Science et Nigromance: Astrologie, divination et magie dans l'Occident médiéval* (Paris: Publications de la Sorbonne, 2006).

Boudet, Jean-Patrice, and Julien Véronèse, "Le secret dans la magie rituelle médiévale," *Micrologus* 14 (2006): 101–50.

Boudet, Jean-Patrice, "Les condamnations de la magie à Paris en 1398,", *Revue Mabillon* 12 (2001): 121–57.

FURTHER READING

Boudet, Jean-Patrice, Anna Caiozzo, and Nicolas Weill-Parot (eds.), *Images et magie. Picatrix entre Orient et Occident* (Paris: Honoré Champion, 2011).

Boudet, Jean-Patrice, Franck Collard, and Nicolas Weill-Parot (eds), *Médecine, astrologie et magic entre Moyen Âge et Renaissance: autour de Pietro d'Abano* (Florence: Sismel Edizioni del Galluzzo, 2013).

Boureau, Alain, *Satan hérétique. Histoire de la démonologie (1280–1330)* (Paris: Odile Jacob, 2004).

Bozoky, Edina, *Charmes et prières apotropaïques*, Typologie des sources du Moyen Âge occidental 86 (Turnhout: Brepols, 2003).

Bracha, Krzysztof, "Magic und Aberglaubenskritik in den Predigten des Spätmittelalters in Polen," in *Religion und Magie in Ostmitteleuropa (Spielräume theologischer Normierungsprozesse in Spätmittelalter und Frühe Neuzeit)*, ed. Thomas Wünsch (Berlin: LIT Verlag, 2006), 197–215.

Bremmer, J.N., and J.R. Veenstra (eds), *The Metamorphosis of Magic from Late Antiquity to the Early Modern Period* (Leuven: Peeters, 2002).

Breuer, Heidi, *Crafting the Witch: Gendering Magic in Medieval and Early Modern England* (New York: Routledge, 2009).

Burnett, Charles, *Magic and Divination in the Middle Ages: Texts and Techniques in the Islamic and Christian Worlds* (Aldershot: Ashgate, 1996).

Burnett, Charles, and W.F. Ryan (eds), *Magic and Classical Tradition* (London: Warburg Institute, 2006).

Cameron, Euan, *Enchanted Europe: Superstition, Reason, and Religion, 1250–1750* (Oxford: Oxford University Press, 2010).

Cohn, Norman, *Europe's Inner Demons: the Demonisation of Christians in Medieval Christendom*, 3rd edn. (London: Pimlico, 1993).

Collins, David J. (ed.), *The Cambridge History of Magic and Witchcraft in the West: From Antiquity to the Present* (Cambridge: Cambridge University Press, 2015).

Cooper, Helen, *The English Romance in Time: Transforming Motifs from Geoffrey of Monmouth to the Death of Shakespeare* (Oxford: Oxford University Press, 2004).

Csapodi, Csaba, and Klára Csapodiné Gárdonyi (eds), *Bibliotheca Corviniana: The Library of King Matthias Corvinus of Hungary* (Budapest: Helikon, 1990).

Dasen, Véronique, and Jean-Michel Spieser (eds), *Les savoirs magiques et leur transmission de l'Antiquité à la Renaissance* (Florence: Sismel Edizioni del Galluzzo, 2014).

Daston, Lorraine, and Katherine Park, *Wonders and the Order of Nature, 1150–1750* (New York: Zone Books, 1998).

Davies, Owen (ed.), *The Oxford Illustrated History of Witchcraft and Magic* (Oxford: Oxford University Press, 2017).

Delaurenti, Béatrice, *La puissance des mots, virtus verborum: débats doctrinaux sur le pouvoir des incantations au Moyen Âge* (Paris: Cerf, 2007).

Doggett, Laine E. *Love Cures: Healing and Love Magic in Old French Romance* (University Park: Pennsylvania State University Press, 2009).

Eamon, William, *Science and the Secrets of Nature: Books of Secrets in Medieval and Early Modern Culture* (Princeton: Princeton University Press, 1994).

Evans, Joan, *Magical Jewels of the Middle Ages and the Renaissance, Particularly in England* (Oxford: Clarendon Press, 1922).

Fanger, Claire, *Rewriting Magic. An Exegesis of the Visionary Autobiography of a Fourteenth-Century French Monk* (University Park: Pennsylvania State University Press, 2015).

Fanger, Claire (ed.), *Invoking Angels: Theurgic Ideas and Practices, Thirteenth to Sixteenth Centuries* (University Park: Pennsylvania State University Press, 2013).

Fanger, Claire (ed.), *Conjuring Spirits: Texts and Traditions of Medieval Ritual Magic* (University Park, Pennsylvania: Pennsylvania State University Press, 1998).

Flint, Valerie I.J. *The Rise of Magic in Early Medieval Europe* (Oxford: Clarendon Press, 1991).

García Avilés, Alejandro, "The Philosopher and the Magician: On Some Medieval Allegories of Magic," in *L'allegorie dans l'art du moyen age*, ed. Christian Heck (Turnhout: Brepols, 2011), 241–52.

García Avilés, Alejandro, "La cultura visual de la magia en la época de Alfonso X," *Alcanate: revista de estudios alfonsíes* 5, (2006–2007), 49–88.

Gilchrist, Roberta, "Magic for the Dead? The Archaeology of Magic in Later Medieval Burials," *Medieval Archaeology* 52 (2008): 119–59.

Giralt, Sebastià, "The Manuscript of a Medieval Necromancer: Magic in Occitan and Latin in ms. Vaticano, BAV, Barb. lat. 3589," *Revue d'Histoire des Textes*, n. s. 9 (2014): 221–72.

Grévin, Benoît, and Julien Véronèse, "Les 'caractères' magiques au Moyen Âge (XIIe-XIVe siècle)," *Bibliothèque de l'École des chartes* 162 (2004): 305–79.

Hanegraaff, Wouter, *Esotericism and the Academy: Rejected Knowledge in Western Culture* (Cambridge: Cambridge University Press, 2012).

Hansmann, Liselotte, and Lenz Kriss-Rettenbeck, *Amulett und Talisman: Erscheinungsform und Geschichte* (Munich: Callwey, 1966).

Harmening, Dieter, *Superstitio: Überlieferungs- und theoriegeschichtliche Untersuchungen zur kirchlich-theologischen Aberglaubensliteratur des Mittlealters* (Berlin: Erich Schmidt Verlag, 1979).

Heng, Geraldine, *Empire of Magic: Medieval Romance and the Politics of Cultural Fantasy* (New York: Columbia University Press, 2003).

Jolly, Karen, *Popular Religion in Late Saxon England. Elf Charms in Context* (Chapel Hill, NC: University of North Carolina, 1996).

Jolly, Karen, Catharina Raudvere, and Edward Peters, *Witchcraft and Magic in Europe: The Middle Ages* (London: Athlone, 2002).

Kieckhefer, Richard, "The Specific Rationality of Medieval Magic", *American Historical Review* 99 (1994): 813–36.

Kieckhefer, Richard, "The Holy and the Unholy: Sainthood, Witchcraft, and Magic in Late Medieval Europe", *Journal of Medieval and Renaissance Studies* 24 (1994): 355–85 reprinted in *Christendom and Its Discontents: Exclusion, Persecution, and Rebellion, 1000–1500*, ed. S. L. Waugh and P. Diehl (Cambridge: Cambridge University Press, 1996), 310–337.

Kieckhefer, Richard, *Magic in the Middle Ages* (Cambridge: Cambridge University Press, 1989).

Kieckhefer, Richard, *European Witch Trials: Their Foundations in Popular and Learned Culture, 1300–1500* (University of California Press, 1976).

Klaassen, Frank, *The Transformations of Magic: Illicit Learned Magic in the Later Middle Ages and Renaissance* (University Park: Pennsylvania State University Press, 2013).

Klaassen, Frank, "Learning and Masculinity in Manuscripts of Ritual Magic of the Later Middle Ages and Renaissance", *Sixteenth-Century Journal* 38/1 (2007): 49–76.

Láng, Benedek. *Unlocked Books: Manuscripts of Learned Magic in the Medieval Libraries of Central Europe* (University Park: Pennsylvania State University Press, 2008).

Linsenmann, Thomas, *Die Magie bei Thomas von Aquin* (Berlin: Akademie Verlag, 2000).

Lucentini, Paolo, and Vittoria Perrone Compagni, *I testi e I codici di Ermete nel Medioevo* (Florence: Edizioni Polistampa, 2001).

Lucentini, Paolo, Ilaria Parri, and Vittoria Perrone Compagni, *Hermetism from Late Antiquity to Humanism* (Turnhout: Brepols, 2003).

Marrone, Steven P., *A History of Science, Magic and Belief from Medieval to Early Modern Europe* (New York: Palgrave Macmillan, 2015).

Marrone, Steven P., "Magic and the Physical World in Thirteenth-Century Scholasticism," *Early Science and Medicine* 14 (2009): 158–85.

Meaney, Audrey L., "Women, Witchcraft and Magic in Anglo-Saxon England," in *Superstition and Popular Medicine in Anglo-Saxon England*, ed. D.G. Scragg (Manchester: Manchester Centre for Anglo-Saxon Studies, 1989), 9–40.

Meaney, Audrey L., *Anglo-Saxon Amulets and Curing Stones* (Oxford: British Archaeological Report 96, 1981).

Merrifield, Ralph, *The Archaeology of Ritual and Magic* (London: Batsford, 1987).

FURTHER READING

Mitchell, Stephen A., *Witchcraft and Magic in the Nordic Middle Ages* (Philadelphia: University of Pennsylvania Press, 2011).

Mitchell, Stephen A., Neil Price, Ronald Hutton, Diane Purkiss, Kimberly Patton, Catharina Raudvere, Carlo Severi, Miranda Aldhouse-Green, Sarah Semple, Aleks Pluskowski, Martin Carver, and Carlo Ginzburg, "Witchcraft and Deep Time – a Debate at Harvard," *Antiquity* 84 (2010): 864–79.

Montesano, Marina, *"Supra acqua et supra ad vento". Superstizioni, maleficia e incantamenta nei predicatori francescani osservanti (Italia, sec. XV)* (Roma: Istituto storico italiano per il medio evo, 1999).

Olsan, Lea T., "The Corpus of Charms in the Middle English Leechcraft Remedy Books," in *Charms, Charmers and Charming: International Research on Verbal Magic*, ed. Jonathan Roper (New York: Palgrave, 2009).

Ostorero, Martine, *Le diable au Sabbat: Littérature démonologique et sorcellerie (1440–1460)* (Florence: Sismel Edizioni del Galluzzo, 2011).

Ostorero, Martine, Agostino Paravicini Bagliani, and Kathrin Utz Tremp, *L'imaginaire du Sabbat: édition critique des textes les plus anciens (1430c.–1440c.)* (Lausanne: Université de Lausanne, 1999).

Page, Sophie, *Magic in the Cloister: Pious Motives, Illicit Interests, and Occult Approaches to the Medieval Universe* (University Park: Pennsylvania State University Press, 2013).

Peters, Edward, *The Magician, the Witch, and the Law*, Middle Ages Series (Philadelphia: University of Pennsylvania Press, 1978).

Pingree, David, "Learned Magic in the Time of Frederick II," *Micrologus* 2 (1994): 39–56.

Pingree, David, "The Diffusion of Arabic Magical Texts in Western Europe," in *La diffusione delle scienze islamische nel medio evo Europeo* (Roma: Accademia dei Lincei, 1987), 57–102.

Rider, Catherine, *Magic and Religion in Medieval England* (London: Reaktion Books, 2012).

Rider, Catherine, *Magic and Impotence in the Middle Ages* (Oxford: Oxford University Press, 2006).

Rollo, David, *Glamorous Sorcery. Magic and Literacy in the High Middle Ages* (Minneapolis and London: University of Minnesota Press, 2000).

Rosińska, Grażyna (ed.), *Scientific Writings and Astronomical Tables in Cracow: A Census of Manuscript Sources (XIVth–XVIth Centuries)* (Wrocław: Zakład Narodowy Imienia Ossolińskich, 1984).

Ryan, William Francis, *The Bathouse at Midnight: A Historical Survey of Magic and Divination in Russia* (Stroud: Sutton, 1999).

Saunders, Corinne, *Magic and the Supernatural in Medieval English Romance* (Cambridge: D. S. Brewer, 2010).

Skemer, Don C., *Binding Words: Textual Amulets in the Middle Ages* (University Park: Pennsylvania State University Press, 2006).

Sweeney, Michelle, *Magic in Medieval Romance from Chrétien de Troyes to Geoffrey Chaucer* (Dublin: Four Courts Press, 2000).

Thorndike, Lynn, *A History of Magic and Experimental Science*, 8 vols. (New York: Columbia University Press, 1923–58).

Utz Tremp, Kathrin, *Von der Häeresie zur Hexerei: "Wirkliche" und imaginäre Sekten im Spätmittelalter* (Hannover: Hahnsche Buchh., 2008).

van der Lugt, Maaike, "The Liber vaccae in the Medieval West or the Dangers and Attractions of Natural Magic," *Traditio* 64 (2009): 229–77.

Veenstra, Jan R., *Magic and Divination in the Courts of Burgundy and France: Text and Context of Laurens Pignon's "Contre les devineurs" (1411)* (Leiden: Brill, 1998).

Vescovini, G. Federici, *Medioevo magico: la magia tra religione e scienza nei secoli XIII e XIV* (Turin: UTET, 2008).

Weill-Parot, Nicolas, "Astrology, astral influences, and occult properties in the thirteenth and fourteenth centuries," *Traditio* 65 (2010): 201–30.

Weill-Parot, Nicolas, *Les "images astrologiques" au Moyen Âge et à la Renaissance* (Paris: Honoré Champion, 2002).

Zathey, Jerzy, "Per la storia dell'ambiente magico-astrologico a Cracovia nel Quattrocento," in *Magia, astrologia e religione nel Rinascimento: convegno polacco-italiano, Varsavia, 25–27 settembre 1972*, ed. Lech Szczucki (Wrocław: Zakład Narodowy im. Ossolińskich, 1974), 99–109.

INDEX

Note: Italic page numbers denote figures and page numbers followed by "n" denote endnotes.

Abbreviation of the Introduction to Astrology (Abu Ma'shar) 72
Abraham Ibn Ezra 90, 94, 181
"Abraham's Eye" charm 433–5
Abulafia, Abraham 94, 246
accusations of magic 349–51, 404, 504, 506
"addressative" magic 21, 230, 231
Aelfric of Eynsham 477
Aenigma de lapide (Enigma on the Stone) 118
Agrippa, Henry Cornelius 164, 180, 181, 201, 204, 221, 245–7, 264, 302, 320
Aided Conchobuir (The Violent Death of Conchobor) 128
Albert the Great *see* Albertus Magnus
Albertus Magnus 40, 45n27, 114, 118, 154, 158, 162, 171–3, 179–81, 187, 225, 239, 255–62, 268, 271–3, 293, 320–1, 340, 360, 462, 465–9, 471, 523–4
alchemical mass 116, 118
Alchemical Mass (Melchior) 113
alchemy 72, 290–1; Arabic works of 78; Bacon on 465; and Hermetic text of natural magic 158; as magic 20; medicinal 277; and Nordic Middle Ages 138
Ældre Borgarthings Christenret 139
Alemanno, Yohanan 87, 91, 94
Al-Filaha al-Nabatiyya (The Nabatean agriculture) (Ibn Wahshiyya) 75
Alfonsi, Petrus 74, 176, 408–9
Alfonso X, king of Castile and León 77, 91, 99, 178–9, 258, 293, 333–6, 402, 412–14, 416, 463, 523–8; French reception of works of 103; miniatures 525; scriptorium 101
Almagest (Ptolemy) 113, 463
Altrom tigi dá medar (The Fosterage of the House of Two Vessels) 130

Amadeus VIII, Duke of Savoy 502, 511
ambiguity: and the history of thought 32–4; magic and 32–4
ampullae 390–2
Anglicus, Bartholomeus 171, 410, 525, *526*
Anglicus, Gilbertus 306, 307
Anglo-Saxon medicine: magic in 300–1; overview 300
animal parts, in magic and ritual 162, 301, 389
"animal spirits" 269
Anne Pedersdotter (Wiers-Jenssen) 22
Anselmi, Giorgio 231, 257, 449, 451, 471
Anselm of Besate 89
Antipalus Maleficiorum 40, 188, 238
The Antiquities of the Jews (Josephus) 435
Antonio da Montolmo 225–35, 337, 451, 471; as author-magician 229–33; sources and meaning of magic 233–5
Aphorisms (Urso of Salerno) 87, 303
Apollonius of Tyana 76–8, 163, 179
Aquinas, Thomas 27, 29, 30–2, 41, 50, 62, 65, 174, 231, 255–7, 259–61, 270, 272, 291, 293, 296, 320–1, 346, 372, 433, 462, 467–8, 471, 489–90, 494, 514, 523, 524
Arabic magic 78; astrological talismans and 433; books 78–81; divisions of magic 72–5; magic as culmination of human knowledge 71–2; natural magic and 291–2; search for Arabic texts 75–8
Arabic texts 71–3, 75–8, 82, 84n28, 158, 205, 244, 302, 416, 432
archaeology: craft and technology 392–5; and materiality 388–90; and magic 383–98
The Archaeology of Ritual and Magic (Merrifield) 384
Arderne, John 305, 306

INDEX

Aristotelian physics 19, 169, 462, 523, 526
Aristotle 73, 77–8, 153, 157, 162, 169, 173, 186n67, 187, 234, 290, 314, 321, 323, 378–9, 462–3, 465, 469, 471, 523, 524, 528
Arnold of Villanova 269, 276, 493
ars magica 26, 49–51, 175, 178, 224n60, 234
Ars notoria 2, 27, 30–1, 32, 41, 45, 61, 64, 87, 115, 118, 175, 188–94, 196, 201, 203, 209n1, 212–14, 216–18, 220, 221, 296, 322, 339, 379, 433, 442, 443, 479, 496
Art de caractas (*Art of characters*) 105
Art de ymages (*Art of images*) 105
Artes liberales 408
artes magicae 26, 175, 487
The Ascent of Isaiah 217
asceticism 52, 348
"Asperges me" 372–3, *373*
aspergillum 372
Asprem, Egil 35n3, 60
astral magic 45n25, 86, 87, 91, 93, 99–101, 104, 176, 177, 187, 189, 195, 201, 202, 254, 255, 258, 264, 273, 276, 277, 282n91, 332, 334, 337, 409; texts 436, 445, 446
astrological images: development of 264; history of concept 254–8
Astrologumena Judaica (Leicht) 94
astrology: alchemy and 82, 120, 234, 239, 290–1, 301, 305, 469; astral magic and 86, 99, 276, 465; astronomy and 75, 78, 99, 108, 113, 120, 241, 255, 288; false 492; as a form of magic 20; Hugo of Santalla on 75, 76; Jewish 90, 94; in Krakow 113; learned 490, 492, 495; medical 103–4; natural 109; natural magic and 100, 117, 120, 264; non-determinist 108; as part of the mechanical sciences 177; passive observation of signs 490; Ptolemy on 255, 259, 277, 334, 463
Astronomical Tables (al-Khwārizmī) 72
astronomy 120, 172, 176; and Alfonso X 78; Alfonsine Castilian texts on 108; astrology and 75, 108, 113, 120, 241, 255, 288, 289; judicial 468; the liberal art 217, 241; practical 289; semi-sacral view of 221; theoretical 289
Ata gibor l'olam adonai 88
Augustine of Hippo, Saint 1, 27–30, 62, 170, 406, 467
Avicenna 159, 162, 166n41, 173, 174, 180, 256, 269, 270, 277–8, 320–1, 377, 462–3, 469, 524–5, 528

Bacon, Roger 27, 118, 161, 172, 180, 187, 188, 239, 259, 291, 293, 294–5, 297, 303, 377, 378, 415, 420, 433, 465, 467, 492
Bailey, Michael D. 7, 343, 344, 346, 351, 355, 480
de Bar, Jean 338, 339
Bald's Leechbook 300, 396
Ballenus, Hermes 357
Belenus, Hermes 153, 154, 156
baptism 51, 53–5, 65, 91, 96, 386, 195, 386, 483
Baumann, Karin 7, 488
Beatrice of Planissoles 92
Beckford, James A. 37
Bellicorum instrumentorum liber (Fontana) 336
Bellifortis (Kyeser) 114–15, 336, 339
Berger, Anna Maria Busse 375
Bernard, G. W. 476
Bernard of Clairvaux 15, 16
Bever, Edward 366, 367
Beves of Hampton 358, 359, 361, 362
Bhagavad Gita 52
Bible 123, 128, 218, 269–70, 513; Old Testament 88, 128; New Testament 88, 128
Biblioteca Jagiellonska 119
Bibliotheca Apostolica Vaticana 229, 230
"black magic" 202, 356
Bohemus, Henricus 115
Bonfini, Antonio 113
Bonvin, Françoise 510
Book of Abramelin 87, 94
Book of Astromagic (Alfonso X) *see Libro de Astromagia*
Book of Cleopatra 162, 303
Book of Creation 94
Book of Healing (Avicenna) *see* Avicenna
Book of Images (Thābit ibn Qurra) 293, 294
The Book of Medical Experiences 95
Book of Nabatean agriculture 334
The Book of Physical Virtues, Diseases and Treatments or Liber Medicinalis 157
Book of Prayers 214, 216, 217, 221, 222, 222n7
Book of Raziel see Liber Razielis
Book of Secrets (*Sefer ha-Razim*) (Rebiger and Schäfer) 87, 95
The Book of Segulot 95
Book of Stones (*De Lapidis*) 388, 414
Book of the Cow see *Liber Vaccae*
Book of the Garment (Wandrey) 87, 95
Book of the Marvels of the World see *De mirabilibus mundi*
Book of the Moon 87
Book of the Responding Entity 94
Book of the Upright (Wandrey) 88, 95

INDEX

The Book of Women's Love (Carmen Caballero-Navas) 95
Book on Talismans (*Liber prestigiorum Thebidis*) 71, 74, 75, 77
books of experiments (*libri experimentorum*) 294–5, 297
Boudet, Jean-Patrice 7, 102, 107, 195, 205, 206, 343, 344, 348, 350, 351, 506
Boureau, Alain 7, 296, 346, 470, 506
Bozoky, Edina 376
Bracha, Krzysztof 112, 488
Braekman, W.L. 304
Breuer, Heidi 346, 356
Brévart, Francis 301
Brewster, David 312
British Iron Age 394
Broedel, Hans-Peter 344
Bromyard, John 478
Brown, Andrew 478
Brzezinska, Anna 351
Buddhism 52
Burchard of Worms 376, 377, 488, 495
de Burgo, John 479
Burnett, Charles 2, 176–7, 181, 205, 372
Butler, Elizabeth 204, 205

de Caboreto, Jeanne 516
Cameron, Euan 390, 480, 488
Canon episcopi 139, 345, 420
Canon medicine (*Canon of medicine*) (Avicenna) 256
Canterbury Tales, the Parson's Tale (Chaucer) 357
Cantigas de Santa Maria (Alfonso X) 402, 412, 413
Capella, Martianus 378
Carpenter, Alexander 478
Castile 99–103
Catalan, magic in 103–4
Cauda, Jeannette 508
"celestial harmony" 269, 270, 273
Celestina (de Rojas) 346–7, 349
Celtic lands: divine magic 130–1; historical magical practices in Wales and Ireland 124–6; literary druids 127–30; literary magic in medieval Irish literature 126–7; magic in medieval Welsh literature 131–2
"Celtic magic" 125
Centiloquium (Ptolemy) 72, 75, 113, 259, 277, 417
Central and Eastern Europe: alchemical mass 116; astrology in Krakow 113; *Bellifortis* (Kyeser) 114–15; considerations on territorial and periodization issues 112; court of Matthias Corvinus 113–14; dissemination of manuscripts 117–18; Henry the Bohemian 115; highlights of the region 112–13; library of King Wenceslas IV 114; MS BJ 793 and the *Picatrix* 116–17; Nicholas of Montpellier 115–16; prayer book of King Wladislas and crystallomancy 115
Cesta spravedlivá (*The Rightful Way*) 118
de Chabannes, Adémar 416
Charles-Edwards, Thomas 128
Charles VI, King of France 336, 338, 504, 516
Charles VII, King of France 338
Charles VIII, King of France 275
Charmasson, Thérèse 464
charms 6, 8, 48, 87, 95, 120, 124–5, 132, 137–146, 162, 175, 299–308, 358, 362, 372–4, 376, 384, 386, 389–90, 395–6, 432–6, 439–40, 477–82, 489, 491, 496
Chaucer 124, 356–8, 367
Chiffoleau, Jacques 512
childbirth 304–8, 347, 389–90, 395, 435–6, 440
Chrétien de Troyes 356, 358–9
Christian Topography 525
Chronicon (de Chabannes) 416
Cibiniensis, Nicolaus Melchior 116
Cifuentes, Lluís 108
City of God (Augustine) 406, 416
Clavicula Salomonis 87, 104, 107, 188, 189, 193, 194, 195, 202–3, 234, 249, 336, 339
Le Clerc, Daniel 299
The Cloud of Unknowing 15, 19
Cobham, Eleanor 340, 351
Coeur, Jacques 338
A Cognitive Theory of Magic (Sørenson) 366
Cohn, Norman 7, 206
coins (in magic) 264, 296, 318, 365, 385, 390–2, 395–6, 490
Combarieu, Jules 371
Comestor, Petrus 259, 273
Commentary (Urso of Salerno) 303
Compagni, Vittoria Perrone 78, 154–6, 181, 205, 259
Compendium de radiis 270
Compendium of sacred magic see *Summa sacre magice*
Conclusiones (della Mirandola) 276–7
Conclusiones sive Theses DCCCC 257, 276, 277
Conquest of Abundance (Feyerabend) 34
Constantine the African 75, 171, 172, 175, 302, 305, 306
Conversations with His Nephew (Adelard of Bath) 378
Convivium (Dante) 526
Cooper, Helen 356
"cordial medicines" 269, 274, 281n71
Corrector sive medicus (Burchard of Worms) 488

INDEX

Cosmas Indicopleustes 524
Council of Pisa 92
courtly magic 331–2; in thirteenth century 332–6
craft and technology 392–5
Crafting the Witch (Breuer) 356
Crombie, Alistair 295
Cronaca fiorentina (di Coppo Stefani) 228

d'Abano, Pietro 174, 181, 256, 257, 259, 270–2, 277, 304, 336
Daniel of Morley 79, 155, 177, 178, 288
Daremberg, Charles 299
d'Artois, Mahaut 504
d'Ascoli, Cecco 225–35, 371, 471; and astrological nigromancy 225–8; sources and meaning of magic 233–5; tragic death and possible reasons 228–9
Daston, Lorraine 291
Data Neiringet (Aristotle) 77
Dau Gymro yn Taring (*Two Welshmen Tarrying*) 126
Davies, Owen 205, 464
d'Avray, D. L. 4, 57–60, 63, 65, 66
Day of Wrath 22
De anima (Avicenna) 270, 277, 329n43
De arte cabbalistica (Reuchlin) 525
De circulis 448–9
De civitate Dei (Saint Augustine) *see City of God*
De coniunctionibus maioribus (Albumasar) 113
Decretum (Gratian) 7, 175, 179, 306, 345, 420
De divisione philosophiae (Gundisalvi) 77, 176
De doctrina Christiana (Augustine) 28, 175, 406, 489
Dee, John 125, 164, 238
De erroribus philosophorum 269
De esse et essentiis (Aquinas) 260, 272
De essentiis (*On the essences*) (Hermann of Carinthia) 76–7
De fide et legibus (William of Auvergne) 464
De generatione et corruptione 171
De imaginibus diei et noctis 157, 163
De imaginibus septem planetarum (*The talismans of the seven planets*) 75, 157
De iudiciis nativitatum liber praeclarissimus (*Illustrious Book on the Judgments of Nativities*) (da Pizzano) 229
Delaurenti, Béatrice 376
De legibus (William of Auvergne) 79, 90, 188, 263, 464, 490
della Mirandola, Pico 88, 94, 257, 259, 276
Della Porta, Giambattista 264, 291, 296
De magia naturali (d'Étaples) 276
De mineralibus (Albertus Magnus) 171–3, 256

De mirabilibus mundi 87, 153–63, 173, 268, 271–2, 275–7, 320
demonic forces 412–14; and law 470–1
"demonic magic" 138, 202
demonization of magic 296
demonology, treatises on 513–15
De natura boni 469
De natura rerum (Thomas of Cantimpré) 171
De occultis et manifestis (da Montolmo) 205, 234, 337, 451
De officiis spirituum 188, 189, 191, 202
De ortu scientiarum (*On the rise of the sciences*) 72, 74, 77, 177
De physicis ligaturis (Qusta ibn Luca) 75, 171, 172, 304, 340
De principiis astrologie (*The principles of astrology*) 225
De proprietatibus rerum (Bartholomeus Anglicus) 171, 410, 525
De quatuor confectionibus (*The book on the four confections*) 73, 77, 78
De radiis stellarum (al-Kindî) 45n24, 269–70, 303, 410, 432–3
De rerum naturis (Hrabanus Maurus) 410
De secretis naturae (Apollonius) 76, 77, 163
De secretis spirituum planetis 446
De sigillis Salomonis 188
De somno et vigilia 469
De Sphaera (de Sacrobosco) 113, 471
Destructorium viciorum (Carpenter) 478
d'Étaples, Jacques Lefèvre 276
Determinationes magistrales (Garsia) 257
De universo (William of Auvergne) 79, 157, 178, 315, 318, 464
De viginti quattour horis 156–7, 163
devil-worshipping sect 3
De viribus cordis et medicinis cordialibus (Avicenna) 269, 277
De virtute universali 172
De virtutibus lapidum 172
De vita coelitus comparanda (Ficino) 257, 260, 262, 264, 416
De vita libri tres (*Three Books of Life*) (Ficino) 114, 257, 277
diabolica carmina 376
Dialogue with Trypho (Martyr) 466
Dillmann, François-Xavier 137
Directorium Inquisitorum (Eymerich) 245, 337, 470, 504
Disciplina clericalis (Alfonsi) 176, 408
Disputationes adversus astrologiam divinatricem (Mirandola) 259

INDEX

The Distaff Gospels 388, 488
divine magic 130–1
divisions of magic 72–5
Doctrinal of Sapyence 479
doctrine of *proprietas* 379
Doggett, Laine E. 346, 366
Don Quixote 87
Dorothea von Montau 17
Dreyer, Carl 22
Du Clercq, Jacques 512
Duffy, Eamon 95, 478–9, 481
Durandus, William 374
Durkheim, Emily 66
The Dybbuk 17

Eamon, William 291
Ebendorfer, Thomas 491
Eckhart, Meister 15–16
Egils saga Skalla-Grímssonar 141
Elements (Euclid) 72
elite superstition 492–4
Elizabeth I, Queen 125
Elucidarius magicæ (d'Abano) 271
Elucidation of Marvelous Things (*Lucidarius de rebus mirabilibus*): goals of 277; "imaginative spirits" 277; overview 268; "Summary on the Properties of the Heart" 269
Emerald Tablet 76
Entzauberung der Welt 59
Episcopi (Canon) 139, 345, 420
Erghome, John 204
Eriksson, Magnus 139
Ermengaud, Matfré 525
Errores gazariorum (*Errors of the Gazarii*) 507–8
Errores philosophorum 79
esotericism 29–31, 264; contemporary 43; western 43
Ethics (Aristotle) 234
Ett Forn-Svenskt Legendarium 141
Etymologies (Isidore of Seville) 171, 175, 489
Euclid 72
Evangiles des quenouilles see The Distaff Gospels
Evans-Pritchard, Edward 53, 63
Exornatorium Curatorum 475
Experimenta 104, 114, 116, 117, 158, 159, 176–9, 191, 192, 195, 272, 312, 326, 336
experimental science 175, 291, 295, 464, 465, 467
Experimenta Salomonis 106
Experimentum verissimum Salomonis 192
Eymerich, Nicolas 245, 337, 470, 493, 504

Falk, Ann-Britt 143
Fanger, Claire 4, 10, 57, 59, 62, 64–6, 348, 443
fantasy 355–6
Fasciculus Morum 414, 478
Feast of Mary Magdalene 482
female witch 344–7, 502, 503, 507, 510
"feminization" of witchcraft 350
Feugeyron, Ponce 504, 508, 511
Fevers 301, 304–6, 390, 440, 491
Feyerabend, Paul 34
Ficino, Marsilio 3, 113, 114, 175, 179, 181, 201, 221, 256–60, 262, 264, 276, 277, 378, 416
Fielding, Henry 374
Figures, magical 432–51; "Abraham's Eye" 434–5; in ritual magic texts 442–5; independent circular magical figures 438–42; laminas 435–8; magic circles 445–51; overview 432–3
Filotas, Bernadette 477, 480, 488
First Commandment 480, 481, 483
Flagellum hereticorum fascinariorum (*Scourge of Heretical Enchanters*) (Jacquier) 512, 514
Flagellum maleficorum (*Scourge of Those Who Commit Evil Deeds*) (Mamoris) 503, 514, 515
Fletcher, Alan 476
Flint, Valerie 48, 50, 51, 54, 58, 287, 355, 476–7
Flores super opera artis magice (*An anthology on the operation of the magical art*) 73
Flos naturarum (*The flower of natural things*) 75
Flowers of Heavenly Teaching (John of Morigny) see John of Morigny
Fontana, Giovanni 336
Forbuis Dromma Damghaire 129–30
Foucault, Michel 27, 39, 40, 44, 59, 64
Four Branches of the Mabinogi 124, 131
"four-handed translation" technique 91
Fournier, Jacques 92
de Fournival, Richard 6
The Four Rings of Solomon 31
Le Franc, Martin 507
de France, Marie 356, 359
di Francesco, Matteuccia 351, 352
Francho, Petrus *see* Peter of Zealand
Franklin's Tale (Chaucer) 357, 367
Frazer, James G. 17
Frederick I the Victorious 508
Frederick II 91, 177, 332–3, 463
Freind, John 299
Freud, Sigmund 18
From Hermes to Jabir (Pingree) 153, 158
Fründ, Lucerne Hans 503, 507

INDEX

Gabrovsky, Alexander 356
Gaddesden, John 306
Ganellus, Beringarius 40, 65, 237–50, 251n30, 252n40, 252n50, 337, 444, 445, 471; biographical information on 237–8; definition and treatment of magic 239–41; magical rituals, their ends and their relation to religious worship 241–4; sources of the *Summa* 244–7; subsequent reputation of 238–9
Garsia, Pedro 257
Gayad Alhaqim 101
gender and magic 343–51
gendering of magical practices 347–9
Geoffrey of Monmouth 87, 125
geomantia 26
Gerard of Cremona 77, 463
Gerson, Jean 420, 480, 493, 495–6
Gikatilla, Joseph 94
Giles of Rome 269
Gilles, John 523
Giszowiec, Petrus 116
Glosa super ymagines duodecim signorum Hermetis (Antonio) 229, 230
Gloss to *Aphorism* (Urso of Salerno) 303
Goal of the Wise see *Picatrix*
Godwin, Joscelyn 377–8
Goering, Joseph 476
Golden Rod (Hermes) 77
Gordon, Stephen 396
Gospel of Nicodemus 87
Grandes Chroniques de France 212, 215, 219, 221
Gratian 7, 175, 179, 306, 345, 372
Grecus, Thoz 77–9, 177, 246, 247
Greek culture 193, 287
de Grocheio, Johannes 378
Grosseteste, Robert 289–90, 295, 475
Gui, Bernard 7, 414, 470, 504
Guide for the Perplexed (Maimonides) 90
Gundisalvi, Dominicus 77, 78, 176–8, 288, 525

Hacking, Ian 66
Halevi, Judah 90
Handlyng Synne (Robert Mannyng of Brunne) 145, 477–8
Harari, Yuval 95
Haren, Michael 480
Harmening, Dieter 375, 488
Harpestreng, Henrik 145
Hartlieb, Johannes 491, 493
Hasidei Ashkenaz writings 93, 95
Havelok the Dane 126

Hay, William 479
Hebrew magic, Latin condemnations 89–90; future directions 93–6; magical texts and sharing of specialized traditions 86–9; overview 85–6; role of personal contact in Jewish-Christian exchanges 90–3; specialized and common traditions 90–3
Hekhalot mystical tradition 93, 95
Heng, Geraldine 356
Henry the Bohemian 113, 115, 339
Henry VI 338
heresy 7–8, 51, 53, 78, 92, 125, 179, 204, 207, 215, 276, 278, 338, 344, 350, 383, 414, 470, 503–5, 511–13
Hermann of Carinthia 76, 79
Hermes Trismegistus 76, 78, 156, 187, 229, 357, 416–17
Hermetic magic 6, 45n25, 87, 94, 105, 117–18, 153–64, 173–5, 202, 230, 234, 245, 247, 256
Herodotus 404
Herolt, Johannes 482
Herp, Hendrik 483
Hersperger, Patrick 7, 488
Hexaemeron 171
Higden, Ranulph 478
Historia de preliis Alexandri Magni 141
Historia regum Britannie 125
Historia scholastica (Comestor) 273
History of Magic and Experimental Science (Thorndike) 229, 259
History of the Crusades (William of Tyre) 415
History of the Kings of Britain (Geoffrey of Monmouth) 87, 125
Holy Roman Empire 101
Homilies (Nazianzenus) 406, *407*
Homo conditus 145
Horden, Peregrine 299
Hortus deliciarum 408
House of Fame (Chaucer) 357
Hugues Géraud of Cahors 91, 336
human knowledge, magic as culmination of 71–2
Hundred Aphorisms 87
Hungary 9, 112, 113, 119
Hutton, Ronald 127, 128, 133
Hygromantia Salomonis 193

Ibn Ezra, Abraham 90, 94, 181
Iceland 126, 136, 140, 142
The Ideal City (Aristotle) 524

543

INDEX

idolatry 28, 30, 90, 178, 188, 244, 249, 319, 403, 406–8, 414, 416–18, 433, 469, 480, 481, 490, 504, 505
Ignorantia Sacerdotum 475
illusion, Augustine on 312–14
illusion, medieval theories of 314–25
image magic 2, 29–31, 99, 102–5, 108, 109, 217, 357, 397, 414–18, 443, 448, 479, 481, 495
imaginative spirits (*spiritus imaginarii*) 269, 271, 273, 277
imago astronomica 337
impotence: caused by *maleficium* 306; and magic 306–7, 347, 479
independent circular magical figures 438–42
indirect delusions or tricks 325
infant corpses 389
Innocent VIII 257, 513
Instructions for Parish Priests (Mirk) 475
intellectual history 174, 355–6, 368
Ireland, historical magical practices in 124–6, 132
Irish magic 123–4
Isidore of Seville 19, 88, 171, 175, 179, 259, 325, 373, 377, 489, 492
Islam 99, 119
Ivarrondo, Alfonso 260

Jacquart, Danielle 305
Jacques III, King of Mallorca 337
Jacquier, Nicolas 512, 514–15
James, William 16
Jeay, Madeleine 480
Jesus Christ 76, 116, 372, 404–6, 440, 481
Jewish astrology 94
Jewish magic 85, 88–91, 93–6, 119, 145, 196, 333
Jewish Magic and Superstition: A Study in Folk Religion (Trachtenberg) 93
Jews 77, 78, 79, 85, 86–93, 95, 96, 99, 101, 244, 246, 404
Joan I of Navarre 91
Johannes Lasnioro (John of Laz) 118
John of Burgundy 338
John of Dacia 409
John of Morigny 22, 27, 31–3, 62, 64, 89, 113, 115, 191, 194, 201, 212–22, 339, 442–4, 447; composition of the *Liber florum* and 213–15; reception and use of the *Liber florum* 219–21; shape of the *Liber florum* and how it worked 216–19
John of Rupescissa 118, 277
John of Seville 74, 77–9, 87, 155, 157
Jolly, Karen 477
Jones, Peter Murray 5, 8
Jones, William R. 339
Josephus, Flavius 435
Jung, Carl Gustav 116

The Kabbalistic Library of Pico della Mirandola 95
Kabbalistic writings 94
Kamerick, Kathleen 7, 346
Kampfbegriffe 34
Kelleher, Richard 390
Key of Semiphoras (*Clau del Semiforas*) 104
Key of Solomon see Clavicula de Salomó, Clavicula di Salomone, Clavicula Salomonis
Kieckhefer, Richard 1, 4, 48, 50, 51, 54, 57–60, 64, 86, 108, 124, 192, 201, 205, 206, 208, 302, 336, 347, 348, 350, 355, 375, 385, 464, 509, 516
Kilwardby, Robert 523, 524
al-Kindî 65, 75, 77, 79, 154, 159, 175, 245, 246, 248, 269–73, 277, 278, 289, 303, 410, 432
Kitâb al-Nawâmîs (*Book of Laws*) 75, 153, 271
Kittredge, G. L. 206, 477
Klaassen, Frank 109, 276, 348, 366–7, 378
Konung Alexander 141
Kramer, Heinrich 324, 344, 470, 513
Kristeller, Paul Oskar 237
Kuzari (Halevi) 90
Kyeser, Conrad 113–15, 336, 339
Kyranides 117, 154, 157, 161–3, 171, 173, 340

Lacnunga 390
Ladurie, Emmanuel Le Roy 350
laminas 432, 433, 435–8
La musique et la magie 371
Láng, Benedek 112, 339, 464
Lapidario (Alfonso X) 100, 101, 334
lapis philosophorum 116
Lasson, Emilie 488
Latini, Brunetto 410–12, *411*
"Lausanne paradigm" 509
The Laws of Plato 158
Lazzarelli, Ludovico 525
Lebor Gabála Érenn (*The Book of the Taking of Ireland*) 130
Le Champion des Dames (*The Champion of Women*) 507
Leechbook III 300
Legenda aurea 141
Leicht, Reimund 82, 87, 94, 102
Le Morte Darthur (Malory) 358, 361, 364
Les Deux Amants (de France) 359
Letters on Demonology and Witchcraft (Scott) 312

INDEX

Levi, Eliphas 204
Levy-Strauss, Claude 174
Liber aggregationis 171–2, 320, 327n15, 340, 360, 361
Liberal Arts 113, 403, 408–12
Liber Aneguemis (*Nemith* or *Neumich*) see *Liber vaccae*
Liber Aneguemis minor see *Liber vaccae*
Liber Conplido (Abenragel) 101
Liber consecrationis (Scot) 332
Liber consecrationum 189, 191, 194, 202–3, 207
Liber de essentia spirituum 525
Liber de quattuor confectionibus ad omnia genera animalium capienda 154, 157
Liber de septem figuris septem planetarum (*The Book of the Seven Figures of the Seven Planets*) 436
Liber de sex rerum principiis 78
Liber experimentorum 104, 107, 109
Liber florum (John of Morigny) 22, 27, 31–2, 64, 212, 222, 442–3, 471; composition of 213–15; reception and use of 219–21; shape of 216–19
Liber Horoscopus 87
Liber imaginum Lunae 156, 157
Liber Intelligentiarum (Montolmo) 27
Liber introductorius (Frederick II and Scot) 40, 332–3
Liber iuratus 22, 27, 50, 61, 63, 89, 96, 203, 238, 239, 243, 247, 248, 249, 253n78, 402, 412, 442, 444, 448–9, 493
Liber orationum planetarum 104, 106, 155
Liber planetarum ex scientia Abel (*The book of planets from the knowledge of Abel*) 75, 155
Liber prestigiorum (Adelard) 77
Liber quorundam sapientum 105
Liber Razielis 87–8, 91, 94, 95, 101–5, 108, 109, 187–9, 193–6, 237, 335–6, 348
Liber regimentis (*Book of the Government*) 271
Liber Samayn 187, 189, 193
Liber Semamphoras 188, 245, 247
Liber Semiphoras 104, 248
Liber similitudinum (*Llibre de la semblança de tots els hòmens*) 104
Liber tegumenti (*Book of the Covering*) 271
Liber vaccae (*Book of the Cow*) 78, 87, 153–4, 158–61, 163, 271
Liber viginti quatuor philosophorum 78
Liber visionum (John of Morigny) 113, 115, 339
Libre del rey Peyre de Aragon (*Book of King Peter of Aragon*) 105–6
Libre de puritats (*Book of secrets*) 105, 106, 107, 109
Libre de ydeis (*Book of images*) 105, 107, 109

Libri naturales 409
Libri runarum 118
Libro Conplido (Abenragel) 103, 109
Libro de astromagia (Alfonso X) 78, 101–3, 334, 413, 414, 416, 523–8
Libro de las formas 101, 103
Libro de las formas e imágenes 108
Libro de las formas e ymagenes 334, 336
Libro de las formas y las imágenes (*Book of forms and images*) 78, 101
Lilium medicinae (Bernard of Gordon) 174
Livre des secrez de nature 103
Lombard, Peter 48, 306, 408, 469, 514
Longinus charm 372
Louis the Great, King of Hungary and Poland 112
Louis XI, King of France 338
Lucentini, Paolo 157, 181
Lucidarium artis nigromanticæ (d'Abano) 271
Lucidator dubitabilium astronomiæ (d'Abano) 272
Luhmann, Niklas 59
Luhrmann, Tanya 366
Lull, Raymond 87, 118
Lydgate, John 447, *448*

McCutcheon, Russel T. 38
Macer Floridus (Odo of Meung) 87
McGee, Timothy 371–2
McVaugh, Michael 8, 279n12, 306
magic: ambiguity and the history of thought 32–4; in Anglo-Saxon medicine 300–1; Augustine on 28–9, 312–14; in Catalan 103–4; clarifying terminology 37–9; common tradition of 86; condemnations of 89–90; craft and technology 392–5; as culmination of human knowledge 71–2; and the dead 395–6; defining 15–23; as discursive concept 39–43; divisions of 72–5; and gender 343–51; heresy of 503–5; as higher knowledge 29–30; and impotence 306–7; and materiality 388–90; and medicine 299–308; in medieval Christian Scandinavia 137–44; in medieval Welsh literature 131–2; as mistake in thinking 28–9; natural see natural magic; and natural philosophy 287–97; and performance 390–2; and political affairs 336–9; recent developments in history of 6–9; sacramental 31–2; sciences of 287–8; specialized traditions of 86; Thomas Aquinas on 30–1; western 187; as wrong religion 30–1
magical figures 255, 432, 433, 435, 438–42, *439*, 443, 444, 452

545

INDEX

magic circles 22, 49, 402, 412, *413*, 432, 436, 445–51, *447*, *450*, *451*, 502
Magic in History series 1
Magisterium divinale et sapientiale (William of Auvergne) 409
Magisterium eumantice artis 237, 238, 251n19
Malleus Maleficarum (Kramer and Sprenger) 320, 323–5, 344–6, 419, 470, 513
Mamoris, Pierre 503, 514, 515
Manfred, King of Sicily–Cecco 227
Manipulus Curatorum (de Monte Roche) 483
Marbode of Rennes 87, 171, 388
de Marigny, Enguerrand 504
Martini, Raymond 90
Martyr, Justin 466
marvels 153–64, 275, 291, 312, 315, 317, 320, 321, 358, 384, 388, 469
Mary, Virgin 32, 115, 220, 407, 435, 442–4
Marzio, Galeotto 113, 114, 262
material culture 9, 138, 143, 365, 383, 388, 390, 397, 402, 418, 497
materiality 384; and orality 301–2; and magic 388–90
materia medica 301, 389
Mathers, Gregory 204
Matthews, Thomas 406
Matthias, King of Hungary 113
Maurus, Hrabanus 410
Mauss, Marcel 24n13, 174
Meaney, Audrey L. 384, 399n30, 400n71
medicine 292, 358–61; Anglo-Saxon 300–1; cordial 269, 274; early theories and scholastic debates 302–4; and magic 299–308; medical conditions and complaints 304–6; and natural magic 358–61
Medieval Song in Romance Languages 375–6
Melchior, Nicolaus 113, 116, 118
Memoriale Presbiterorum (Haren) 480
Mercier, Franck 512
Merrifield, Ralph 384, 385, 387, 399n19
Mesca Ulad 128–9
Metaphysics (Avicenna) 524
Meteora (Aristotle) 321, 323
Meteorology (Gerard of Cremona) 463
Michael of Tarazona 75
Mignon, Pierre 338
Mirk, John 475
The Mirror of Perfection 483
Mitchell, Stephen A. 351
Mithridates, Flavius 88, 94, 95
Modlitewnik Władysława (Wladislas) 115

de Monte Roche, Guido 483
Montesano, Maria 488
Munich 157, 446, *451*
music 371–9; and archaeology 383–98
"musica practica" 374–7, 379
musica speculativa 374, 377–9
Muslims 79, 99, 105, 154, 301, 359, 462, 463, 493
mysticism 15–16, 19–21, 34, 60, 222

Naaman, Rabbi 89
Nabataean Agriculture 297
Nasci, Salamies 92
National University of Ireland, Maynooth 123
natura rerum literature 170–2
natural causation 28, 62, 295–6
Natural History (Gilles) 523
Natural History (*Naturalis historia*) (Pliny the Elder) 161, 171, 394
natural magic 2, 9, 19, 20, 23, 50, 54, 57, 60, 74, 78, 100, 114, 116–18, 120, 138, 144, 154, 157, 163, 170, 172, 174–6, 178, 179, 205, 252n41, 264, 274, 288, 291–2, 295–297, 314–15, 320, 358–62, 365, 388, 403, 464, 467
natural philosophy and magic 169, 174, 178, 287–97
natural properties: Arabic thought and 173–4; Hellenistic thought and 173–4; Hermetic thought and 173–4; medieval understanding and vocabulary of natural magic 174–6
Nazianzenus, Gregory 406
necromancy *see* nigromancy
Necromantia 71, 72, 74, 107, 202, 339
necromantic texts 203–6, 208, 494
Newman, William R. 290
Nicholas of Jauer 493
Nicholas of Montpellier 115–16
Nicholas V 513
Nicolaus Olah, Archbishop of Esztergom 116
Nicomachus of Gerasa 524
Nider, Jean 503, 507
nigromancy (*nigromantia*) 26, 27, 29, 31, 71, 72, 74, 174, 176–9, 201–6, 274–5, 361–5
non-magical religion 52, 63
Nordic magic 137, 140, 143–4
Nuova Cronaca (Villani) 228

objective magic 175
Occitan texts by and for magicians 104–7
"occult" 2, 6, 7, 19, 48, 49, 60, 99, 117, 127, 174, 181, 231, 276, 291, 295, 464
Oculus Sacerdotis (William of Pagula) 475, 479

546

INDEX

Odo of Meung 87
Odyssey (Homer) 129
Oidheadh Chloinne Tuireann (*The Tragic Deaths of the Children of Tuireann*) 133
Old Compilation Book of Figures 443; *see also* John of Morigny
Old English Herbarium 300
de Olkusz, Martin Bylica 114
Olsan, Lea T. 5, 8, 10n5, 306, 311n52, 365, 372
On Errors Concerning the Magic Art (Gerson) 495
"On Evil Spirits" 274
On generation and corruption (Gerard of Cremona) 463
On Incantations, Adjurations, and Suspension around the Neck (or *On Physical Ligatures*) 302
On Occult Properties (Ibn al-Jazzar) 87
On sorcery (*De sortilegiis*) 89
On Talismans 71, 74, 77
On the Division of Philosophy (Gundissalinus) 288
"On the Hunting of Truth" 273
On the Prolongation of Life and Retardation of Death (*libellus de prolongatione vitæ et retardatione mortis*) 268
On the Secrets of Nature 76
On the soul (Aristotle) 234
On the Stations for the Cult of Venus 87
On the Twelve Images 87, 91
"On the Wars and Future Acts of Men, and on their Present and Future Mores" 275
On the Wonders of the World 297
Opus de magia disciplina (Anselmi) 449
Opus imaginum 117, 255
Opus maius (Bacon) 27, 293, 433
Opus praeclarum de imaginibus astrologicis (Torrella) 254, 258–62
Opus Tertium (Bacon) 187, 378
orality 26, 301–2, 372
Oresme, Nicole 304, 320, 321–3, 376
Orthodox Christianity 112, 119
Otto, Bernd-Christian 4, 57, 59, 60–4
Owst, G. R. 8. 477–8
Oxford 79, 219, *405*, 436, *438*, 443, *445*, 456n68
Oxford English Dictionary 50, 52

Page, Sophie 45, 53, 162, 196, 276, 365, 464, 471
Pagel, Julius 299
Pannonius, Janus 114
Pantegni (Constantine the African) 306
Park, Katharine 291
pastoral literature 351, 475–83, 488
Pater Noster 55, 220, 300, 372, 478, 491
Pecham, John 475

Pedeir Keinc y Mabinogi (*The Four Branches of the Mabinogi*) 131
Pennsylvania State University Press 1
peperit charm 435
performance and magic 326, 299, 300, 307, 311n52, 390–2
Perrers, Alice 351, 352
Peter IV, King of Aragon 92
Peter of Zealand: on al-Kindî 269; on astrology 273; background 268; on *De radiis* and *Picatrix* 270; medical training 269; "nigromancy" 274–5; on witchcraft 271
Peters, Edward 206, 355, 463, 480
Peuerbach, Georgius 114
de Peyre Godin, Cardinal Guillaume 504
Philip the Good 338
Philoponus, John 524
Physics (Aristotle) 19, 169, 462, 523, 526, 528
Picatrix 21–2, 29–30, 62, 72, 78, 87, 91, 101–4, 106, 108, 113, 116–18, 154, 155, 158, 160, 161, 176, 178, 205, 230, 258, 270, 271, 276, 293, 334, 335, 340, 436, 443–5, 462, 463, 493, 523
Pike, Kenneth L. 38
pilgrim badges 301, 386–7, 390
Pingree, David 2, 79, 112, 153, 154, 156, 158, 180, 181, 192, 205, 255, 412
Pius II 513
de Pizan, Thomas 337, 338
Plato 75, 153, 271–3, 277, 408
Platonic magic 158
Platonic philosophy 113
Policraticus (John of Salisbury) 322, 377
Pope Alexander V 504
Pope Boniface VIII 256, 336, 493
Pope Calixtus III, 513
Pope Eugenius IV, 513
Pope Gregory XI, 504
Popes Gregory XII, 92
Pope John XXII 91, 229, 336, 337, 414, 470, 504, 513
Pope John XXIII 7
Practica (treatises on learned medicine) 305–8
Practica Inquisitionis Heretice Pravitatis (Gui) 470
practical astronomy 289
Practica nigromancie 202
Prayer Book of King Wladislas (Henry the Bohemian) 339
preaching 351, 440, 475–83
pre-Christian Nordic magic 136, 137
Principe, Lawrence M. 290, 295, 297

Processus de lapide philosophorum (*On the Philosopher's Stone*) 118
Processus sub forma missae (*Process in the Form of the Mass*) (Melchior) 116
property, in medieval *natura rerum* literature 170–2
Psalter of Eadwine 372
Ptolemy 72, 77, 113, 118, 227, 234, 253n78, 255, 277, 334, 417, 463
Pugio fidei (Martini) 90
Pupilla Oculi (de Burgo) 479
Pylgremage of the Sowle (Lydgate) 447
Pynson, Richard 476

Quadripartitum (Ptolemy) 113, 234, 334
Qui bene praesunt (Richard of Wetheringsett) 475
Qusta ibn Luqa 75, 153, 162, 171, 172, 302–4

Rabbinic literature 89, 90
Randles, Sarah 388
Rationale divinorum officiorum 374
Raudvere, Catharina 137
Recommendatio astronomiae 155, 165n20, 239
Regiomontanus, Johannes 114
religion, magic as wrong 30–1
religious magic 52, 58
Renaissance 79, 87, 101, 113, 125, 164, 170, 174, 181, 196, 201, 205–8, 221, 257, 259, 264, 287, 293, 296, 297, 320, 331, 339, 356, 365, 377, 378, 462, 525
reproduction and magic 347
Reuchlin, Johannes 525
Reynys, Robert 50, 52, 58, 304
Richard of Wetheringsett 475
Rider, Catherine 5, 48, 306, 308, 479–80
Rigaud, Eudes 48, 51
ritual deposition 143, 385–8, 392, 394
Robert Mannyng of Brunne 477–8
Robert of Flamborough 478
Roig, Jaime 92
de Rojas, Fernando 346–7
Rollo, David 331
romance and natural magic 358–61
romance language(s): Castile 99–103; circulation, persecution and survival of Romance language magic books 107–9; courtier's manual from Milan 107; French reception of Alfonsine works 103; future directions 109–10; learned magic in the vernacular 99–103; magic in Catalan 103–4; Occitan texts by and for magicians 104–7

romance language magic books 104, 107–9
Roman d'Alexandre 331
Roman de Troie (de Sainte-Maure) 331
Roper, Lyndal 365
Rosa Anglica (Gaddesden) 306
Rota Pythagorae 117

Sabbath, witches *see* Witches' sabbat
sacramental magic 31–2
de Sacrobosco, Johannes 113, 225, 226–228, 234, 471
Saint Peter 405, 406
de Sainte-Maure, Benoît 331
Salverte, Eusèbe 312
Samuel of Granada 92
Sannino, Antonella 297
San Vincenzo Maggiore 392–4, *393*
Satan the Heretic (Boureau) 470
Scandinavia 4, 136–45, 385, 395: "magic" in medieval Christian Scandinavia 137–44, Schäfer, Peter 95
Schäufelein, Hans 402
scholasticism: context 462–4; demons and the law 470–1; and magic 461–72, Schwartz, Dov 93
science: experimental 291; of images 292–4; medical 292; of properties 170, 174, 176–9
Scientific Revolution 295, 297
Scot, Michael 40, 155, 177, 178, 188, 332–3, 463, 525
Scott, Sir Walter 312
Secret of Secrets (Bacon) 87, 465
Secretum de sigillo Leonis 117
Secretum secretorum 112, 117, 187
Seelentrost 141
Sefer Yetsirah 88
Sentences (Lombard) 48, 306, 514
Sermones discipuli de tempore et de sanctis (Herolt) 482
Seven Deadly Sins 7, 357
sex and magic 107, 156, 162, 202, 303, 339, 343–49
Short Art (Lull) 87
Siælinna thrøst 141
Siete Partidas 100
Sigillum Dei (Seal of God) 444–5
Sigismund, Holy Roman Emperor and Hungarian king 115
signa 433, 440
Signum regis salomonis 440
SISMEL's *Micrologus Library* series 1
Skemer, Don C. 8

INDEX

Skírnismál 140
Smith, Jonathan Z. 26, 33, 62
sociocultural lexicography 51
Solomonic ritual magic 78, 175, 192; historiographical advances and future fields of research 192–6; problems of defining a corpus of 187–92
Solomonic tradition 6, 78, 99, 102, 109, 175, 187–200, 202–3, 205, 232–4, 245–9, 255, 277, 339, 371, 433, 439, 445, 449–51
Sørenson, Jesper 366
sortilegium 26, 27, 52, 141, 487, 503
Soziale Systeme 59
Speculum astronomiae 27, 40, 41, 74, 79, 157, 174–6, 181, 187–9, 202, 204, 230, 231, 234, 255–7, 261, 270, 272–3, 289, 337, 433, 465, 289, 293
Speculum Aureum Decem Preceptorum Dei 483
Speculum Curatorum (Higden) 478
Sprenger, Jacob 324, 344
Stallcup, Stephen 96
Standley, Eleanor R. 386, 395
Stausberg, Michael 61
Stephens, Walter 345
stereotypes and magic 7, 344–7
The Stripping of the Altars: Traditional Religion in England 1400–1580 (Duffy) 478–9
Sudhoff, Karl 299
Suffumigationes 157
Suggett, Richard 126
Summa for Confessors (Thomas of Chobham) 306
Summa Contra Gentiles (Aquinas) 320, 257, 259
Summa Predicantium (Bromyard) 478
"Summary on the Properties of the Heart" 269
Summa sacre magice (Ganellus) 40, 191, 237–50, 337, 444
Summa sacre magice (Montolmo) 27
Summa Theologica (Aquinas) 30, 41, 50, 270, 272, 346
Summis desiderantis affectibus 470
Super illius specula 229, 337, 470, 504
Superstitio (Harmening) 375, 488
superstition 3, 5, 7, 8, 27–31, 53, 58, 119, 139, 141, 170, 174, 179, 221, 260, 332, 344. 346, 365, 402, 406, 418, 478, 480, 482, 487–97, 503, 504
Suso, Henry 378
Swanson, R. N. 476
Swedish Older Law of Västergötland (*Äldre Västgötalagen*) 139
Sweeney, Michelle 355

Sword of Moses 95
Sworn Book of Honorius see Liber Iuratus
symbolic manipulation 17–19, 21–3, 60, 61, 65

Table of Solomon 80, 493
Tabulae Alphonsi (Johannes de Sacrobosco) 113
tabule magicales 246
Taussig, Michael 66
Techel/Azareus Complex 87, 96
Ten Commandments 7, 245, 475, 478, 480, 483
Teresa of Ávila 15, 16
Thabit ibn Qurra 71, 72, 74, 75, 79, 158, 178, 255, 293, 294, 337
Theatrum chemicum 268
Theodore of Mopsuestia 524
Theorica artium magicarum (*The theory of the magic arts*) 75, 175, 270, 432
Thesaurus Linguae Latinae 50
Thesaurus spirituum 202–3, 207
Thibaut de Sézanne 89
Tholosan, Claude 507–8, 512
Thomas, Keith 50–4, 206
Thomas of Cantimpré 87, 171
Thomas of Chobham 306, 478
Thorndike, Lynn 175, 192, 201, 204, 229, 259, 296, 469
Tomlinson, Gary 378
Torrella, Jerome 231, 254, 255, 258–62
Trachtenberg, Joshua 93
Tractado de la divinança (Lope de Barrientos) 103
Tractate Hekhalot (Klaus Herrmann) 95
Tractatus contra invocatores demonum (*Treatise Against Demon Invokers*) (Vinet) 514
translatio nigromantiae 331
translatio studii 331
Tratado de aojamiento o fascinación (Enrique de Villena) 101
Tremp, Kathrin Utz 8, 350
Tres boni fratres 304–5
Trésor (Latini) 410–12, *411*
Trismegistus, Hermes *see* Hermes Trismegistus
Trithemius, Johannes 40, 188, 189, 238, 276

universal virtue 173, 180
University of Krakow 113
University of Lausanne 8, 343
University of Paris 212, 215, 443, 480, 487, 493, 504
Urso of Salerno 303
Use of the Psalms (Bill Rebiger) 87, 95
Uses of the Torah 88

INDEX

Vauderye de Lyonois en brief 508–9
Véronèse, Julien 205, 348
Vikings 136, 144
de Vilanova, Arnau *see* Arnold of Villanova
Villani, Giovanni 228
Vinculum Salomonis 189, 191, 192, 194, 196, 202, 207
Vinet, Jean 514
Visconti, Filippo Maria 339
visual culture of magic: demonic forces 412–14; idolatry 406–8; Jesus Christ 404–6; Liberal Arts 408–12; magicians as wise men 402–4; magic of images 414–18
"vital spirits" 269
Vitéz, Johannes 113, 114
von Kemnath, Mathias Widmann 508

Waite, Arthur Edward 204
Wales: historical magical practices in 123–6
Walker, D. P. 205, 378
Warburg Institute 82
Watkins, Carl 478
Watson, Nicholas 348
Weber, Max 51, 66
Weill-Parot, Nicolas 21, 181, 205, 294
Wenceslas IV, "King of the Romans" and King of Bohemia 113–14, 339

Wene ngua 54
Wiers-Jenssen, Hans 22
William of Auvergne 2, 65, 79, 82, 90, 155, 157, 162, 175, 178, 179, 181, 188–91, 263, 289, 291, 296, 303, 314–25, 374, 402, 409, 416, 433, 464–5, 467, 471, 490; natural magic 314–15
William of Palerne 362–4, 367, 475
William of Tyre 415
witchcraft 271, 502–17; ambivalence of 515–16; "feminization" of 350; heresy of 503–5
witches, crimes of 506–9, 514
Witches' Sabbat 3, 23, 271, 343, 349, 505–10, 512–14
Witchhunts 3, 22, 315, 323, 470, 494, 502, 504–15, 517
Wladislas, King of Hungary and Bohemia 116
Woodville, Elizabeth 351
de Worde, Wynkyn 475–6
Wyclif, John 275–6

Yates, Frances 201, 205, 378
Ymagines duodecim signorum Hermetis 230
Ywain and Gawain 358, 360

Zambelli, Paola 181, 205
Zell, Michael 350, 351

Printed in Great Britain
by Amazon